Gathering to Save a Nation

CIVIL WAR AMERICA

Gary W. Gallagher, Peter S. Carmichael, Caroline E. Janney, and Aaron Sheehan-Dean, *editors*

This landmark series interprets broadly the history and culture of the Civil War era through the long nineteenth century and beyond. Drawing on diverse approaches and methods, the series publishes historical works that explore all aspects of the war, biographies of leading commanders, and tactical and campaign studies, along with select editions of primary sources. Together, these books shed new light on an era that remains central to our understanding of American and world history.

STEPHEN D. ENGLE

Gathering to Save a Nation

Lincoln and the Union's War Governors

The University of North Carolina Press *Chapel Hill*

© 2016 The University of North Carolina Press
All rights reserved
Set in Arno Pro by Westchester Publishing Services
Manufactured in the United States of America

The paper in this book meets the guidelines for permanence
and durability of the Committee on Production Guidelines for
Book Longevity of the Council on Library Resources.

The University of North Carolina Press has been a member of the
Green Press Initiative since 2003.

Library of Congress Cataloging-in-Publication Data
Names: Engle, Stephen Douglas, author.
Title: Gathering to save a nation : Lincoln and the Union's war governors /
    Stephen D. Engle.
Other titles: Civil War America (Series)
Description: Chapel Hill : University of North Carolina Press, [2016] |
    Series: Civil War America
Identifiers: LCCN 2015044922 | ISBN 9781469629339 (cloth : alk. paper) |
    ISBN 9781469629346 (ebook)
Subjects: LCSH: Lincoln, Abraham, 1809–1865—Relations with governors. |
    Governors—United States—Powers and duties. | Federal government—
    United States—History—18th century. | United States—History—Civil War,
    1861–1865—Recruiting, enlistment, etc. | United States—States—Politics and
    government. | United States—Politics and government—1861–1865.
Classification: LCC E459 .E54 2016 | DDC 973.7092–dc23 LC record
    available at http://lccn.loc.gov/2015044922

Jacket illustrations: Inauguration of Abraham Lincoln at the U.S. Capitol, 1861 (courtesy of
the Library of Congress, LC-DIG-ppmsca-53445); inset of Abraham Lincoln from 1864
portrait (courtesy of the Library of Congress, LC-DIG-ppmsca-19190).

An earlier version of Chapter 10 was published as "It's Time for the States to Speak to the
Federal Government: The Altoona Conference and Emancipation" in *Civil War History* 58:4
(December 2012). © 2012 by The Kent State University Press. Reprinted with permission.

For Stephanie, Claire, and Taylor

Contents

INTRODUCTION 1

CHAPTER ONE
It Is Your Business to Rise Up and Preserve the Union 8

CHAPTER TWO
If Blood Must Flow 32

CHAPTER THREE
I Don't Believe There Is Any North 54

CHAPTER FOUR
The Grandest Spectacle of the Century 78

CHAPTER FIVE
Doing the Very Best We Can 100

CHAPTER SIX
This Fearful Awakening 119

CHAPTER SEVEN
Crossing the Alps 142

CHAPTER EIGHT
Does the Governor Say He Will Come for Us? 165

CHAPTER NINE
The Duty of the Governors to Save the Country's Cause 189

CHAPTER TEN
They Are a Body of Wise and Patriotic Men 214

CHAPTER ELEVEN
Sinking in Despair 239

CHAPTER TWELVE
There Can Be No Difference of Purpose 263

CHAPTER THIRTEEN
Is It Well or Ill with Us? 289

CHAPTER FOURTEEN
Just Such Affliction 313

CHAPTER FIFTEEN
A Tub Thrown to the Whale 336

CHAPTER SIXTEEN
The Rebellion Still Refuses to Give Us Either Peace or Rest 358

CHAPTER SEVENTEEN
I Claim Not to Have Controlled Events 381

CHAPTER EIGHTEEN
Revolutions Never Go Backward 404

CHAPTER NINETEEN
The People Are Conscious of the Power 428

CHAPTER TWENTY
It Is Worth While to Live in These Days 451

EPILOGUE
Majestic Parts of That Magnificent Whole 475

Acknowledgments 483

Appendix. List of Governors 487

Notes 491

Bibliography 623

Index 693

Gathering to Save a Nation

Introduction

The American Civil War was as much a story of cooperation as it was of conflict. For all we know about why Southerners left the United States, historians still grapple over how and why Northerners restored them to the Union. Secession provided Unionists with an alarming example of just how fragile the federal system was in the mid-nineteenth century. Withdrawal in any form appeared destructive, almost madness, and it inspired loyal political leaders to demonstrate that states had more rights in the Union than outside of it. This revelation motivated loyal state leaders to unite in hopes of vindicating democracy. The ensuing war caused by the Southern departure, ironically, forged a powerful federal-state alliance that produced a Northern army powerful enough to defeat Confederates. Scholars seeking to uncover the Union's formula for victory have therefore expanded their investigations to include the character of governments (Northern and Southern) as contributing factors.

Northerners witnessed a surge of governmental activism at both the state and national levels that sustained mobilization throughout the war. The Union's defense in 1861 revealed intense nationalist feelings, but marshalling the resources necessary required an extraordinary coordination between the federal government and the states. Yet before Northern soldiers organized and marched off to war, the mobilization of men and matériel necessary to fight the war rested on the partnership between Abraham Lincoln and loyal state governors. It was this alliance that established and shaped the ways the Union applied its military power against the Confederacy in pursuit of victory. Only by examining this crucial partnership can we begin to understand how it contributed to the "new nation" Lincoln referred to at Gettysburg. In short, this work explores how Lincoln dealt with the "war governors," and they with him.

For all that has appeared in print on Lincoln and the Civil War in the 150 years since the conflict, only William Best Hesseltine's classic, *Lincoln and the War Governors*, serves as the seminal work on this important relationship. Characteristic of its time in contributing to the Lincoln idolatry, Hesseltine portrayed Lincoln as a master manipulator of political opinion and of conflicts with governors over mobilization. He argued that the president was the key figure who brought Northern governors into tow, doing what was needed despite them. "The victory of nationalism over localism, of centralization over states' rights," Hesseltine maintained, "was, in the last analysis, a victory of keener intellect over men of lesser minds." Consequently, "the history of the Civil War merges into the biography of the man in the White House."[1] That much is true.

Yet, in as much as scholars credit Lincoln for engineering Union victory, he also benefitted from the governors' collective efforts in aiding him. Hardly did the president regard his loyal chief executives as men of "lesser minds," or dismiss them as insignificant spectators watching the war unfold from the state capitals. Quite the contrary, loyal governors (whether Republican or Democrat) demonstrated considerable influence by collaborating with the president, partnering with him to mobilize for war, and, at times, pushing him toward greater national efforts. Governors experienced the same expansive powers that Lincoln enjoyed during the war. Given the federal structure of antebellum mobilization that leaned on state militias, governors held extraordinary power in wartime. The partnership between Lincoln and the governors came most dramatically in the area of national mobilization. Lincoln understood their importance far better than Hesseltine allowed. The president was neither in conflict with his loyal governors, nor did he see them as rival executives. Yes, they had disagreements, but Lincoln was not trying to overpower them politically, ruin their prestige, or dominate their affairs. Rather, he included them as essential and representative parts of the whole, which was essential to the Union's preservation and thus reinforced the federal-state partnership necessary to vindicate democracy. Without the willingness of loyal governors who agreed independently to uphold the Union, marshal their states' resources, and cooperate in establishing a national army, Lincoln would have been hard pressed to preserve the Union. William C. Harris takes this view in his volume *Lincoln and the Union Governors*, which provides a point of departure for challenging Hesseltine's thesis. In short, Harris argues that Lincoln recognized and respected the governors' political and constitutional authority and worked with them to maintain a unified war effort. He emphasizes their contributions and stresses that Lincoln relied upon these governors to win the war and preserve the Union.[2]

Northerners who remained in the Union clung to the notion that the bond between the nation and the states would have to be strengthened to achieve military victory. On a practical level, this took shape as Unionists mobilized for war. Through their cooperative spirit and willingness to coordinate military operations, loyal governors exercised important powers, and citizens looked to them for leadership. Governors' partnerships with Lincoln offer impressive examples of federal-state and state-federal cooperation that not only resulted in a Union victory, but also registered a triumph for the federal Union. Antebellum governance had been legislatively centered and regionally driven as a consequence of a decentralized political system. Both Lincoln and Jefferson Davis unavoidably fought the Civil War by summoning their states to action within, at first, a vastly decentralized federal system. As much as many Northerners accepted and even supported states' rights, however, they rejected the presumption of states' sovereignty over national sovereignty. The war presented them with the opportunity to emphasize the mutual respect and kinship among states that obliged all citizens to preserve the Union—even a union that contained slavery. In raising Northern armies, governors functioned as agents of a national coalition that stressed governmental activism and emphasized the United States as single nation. As such, preserving the Union gave the appearance of nationalism and required governors to play a crucial role in the war effort. By answering Lincoln's April 1861 call to arms, Northerners chose to emphasize the same rights Southerners did in leaving the Union, only they used them to cooperate with Lincoln. In doing so, they placed nation above state and relied on the Union's strengths to support a national authority. That strength sprang from the alliance between Lincoln and the governors, and it reinforced the federal Union's resiliency.[3]

Yet, fighting for the Union did not mean that Northerners lessened their commitment to local governance. On the contrary, the struggle between eastern conservatism and western liberalism kept popular sovereignty alive and pitted agrarian and industrial interests against one another. Supporting the national government and vindicating democracy, many Northerners believed, would preserve state and local autonomy. Lincoln understood the fusion of state politics and nationalist ideology and that state regiments organized by governors comprised his armies. Union governance derived from the mutually dependent relationship between national and state leaders who navigated the political shoals of mobilization, emancipation, and conscription. When Lincoln expanded his war aims and his national power to assist governors in maintaining support for the war, it tested popular sovereignty's limits. Secretary of the Navy Gideon Welles had predicted as much.

"The government will, doubtless, be stronger after the conflict is over, than it ever has been," he confided to his wife, "and there will be less liberty perhaps with greater security."[4] Even so, state executives clung to a wide range of powers and displayed skill in bringing together political worlds that prior to the war had existed independently of each another. Mobilizing and sustaining a volunteer spirit forced them, despite harbored jealousies and competing ambitions, to reach across state lines as well as cooperate with the national government. Governors worried as much about the expansion of national power as they did about the conduct of war, restoring Southern states to the Union, and freedom for slaves after the conflict. Unity was important for Northerners to achieve victory, yet they debated the nature of the Union they were preserving.

Governors were party spokesmen and policy formulators, yet in times of peace, they served as civic figureheads. Legislatures held nearly all administrative authority and delegated to governors limited powers suitable for the times. They had two primary functions as assigned by their state constitutions, executive and administrative. As the chief executive, governors supervised appointed and elected officials in the execution of state laws. Typically, state constitutions relegated them to be commanders in chief of the state militia, granted them the power to convene the legislature, create and submit budgets, fill vacancies in state offices, and some appointive powers. Administratively, however, constitutions limited their powers, often qualifying governors' veto power and restricting their oversight of elective officers. Before the war, the governors' cabinets were small and included a lieutenant governor, secretary of state, treasurer, auditor of public accounts, superintendent of schools, and, in some states, an attorney general. In many states, these positions were elective rather than appointive, thus minimizing control over these offices. With the assistance of an executive secretary and one or two clerks, governors supervised correspondence that attended to legal matters associated with state government, including institutions for the deaf and the insane, prisons, public schools, public works, and the Office of the Adjutant General. Chief executives gave an annual address surveying the state's government and recommended changes to improve their citizens' economic and social conditions.

The exigencies of war turned governors into powerful politicians, and voters closely monitored their performance not only in attending to soldier welfare, but also in maintaining a balance between local and national priorities. Governors relied on financiers and merchants to advise them in mobilizing the resources to raise and maintain armies and worked with legislators to accommodate the changes wrought by war. They made use of advances in weaponry, refrigeration, camp accouterments, medicine, and relied on agents to procure items essential to soldiering. Because governors assumed such vast power so quickly, citizens kept them accountable for their decisions. Because most gubernatorial terms were short, war governance was all the more answerable to the electorate. New Englanders went to the polls annually to elect governors, while California, Illinois, Iowa, Kansas, Michigan, Minnesota, New York, Ohio, West Virginia, and Wisconsin voters went to the polls biennially. Maryland, New Jersey, and Pennsylvania held elections every three years, while Delaware, Indiana, Kentucky, Missouri, and Oregon allowed their governors four-year terms. Most important, however, was that their authority as commanders in chief allowed them to issue executive orders and take emergency actions. Still, their formal powers did not equip them with the tools for leadership, and governors often relied on local, political, and financial advisors better suited to offer assistance.

Many chief executives came into office having won popularity and credibility because of their practical business experience, legal acumen, or previous political service. They had been farmers, merchants, journalists, lawyers, doctors, and bankers. Some were lifelong Democrats, some had been Whigs, while others rode the tide of a political movement over Kansas statehood that formed the Republican Party. They helped engineer victories that tied them across state lines and established a sectional identity composed of a vast new political assemblage dedicated to preserving the Union. With the war's outbreak they forged a stronger relationship between the government and its citizens by infusing a patriotic spirit among locals that tied them to a national cause. Along the way, governors politicized the regiments that went off to war to mobilize voters and maintain alliances at home. Thus, most of the Northern states remained strongly Republican throughout the war. The most prominent Republican governors included John A. Andrew (Massachusetts), Austin Blair (Michigan), William A. Buckingham (Connecticut), Andrew Curtin (Pennsylvania), Samuel Kirkwood (Iowa), Edwin D. Morgan (New York), Oliver P. Morton (Indiana), Israel Washburn Jr. (Maine), and Richard Yates (Illinois).[5]

The task of preserving the Union also fell on loyal Democratic governors, who while championing their party's causes, including states' rights and slavery, nonetheless supported the Union war effort. Notable Democrats (as well as those who joined the Union ticket in 1864) included

Thomas Bramlette (Kentucky), John Brough (Ohio), William Burton (Delaware), John Downey (California), Joel Parker (New Jersey), Horatio Seymour (New York), David Tod (Ohio), and John Whiteaker (Oregon). The choice to remain loyal and direct their states' resources to support Lincoln at first revealed the complex interplay of loyalty and locality. The war forced these political leaders to choose between their states' economic ties to vast Northern wage-based markets and their conservatism, which associated them with small government and hostility toward fugitive slaves. Those states that elected Democratic governors and legislatures in 1862 did so because of Union military defeat and the increasing radicalization of an administration that employed confiscation, emancipation, and conscription to win the war. In 1863–64, however, the military situation turned in the Union's favor, and Republicans regained much of the political ground they had lost.

Still, governors suffered intractable state legislators who fought them over appropriations, military arrests, and expansive national government. Such hostility often led to tension, as governors struggled to meet their national obligations to win the war while maintaining popular support at home. Despite governors' party affiliations, citizens counted on them to direct an expanding administrative structure to preserve the Union while implementing policies beneficial to the state. In short, they served as the Union's mainsprings of nationalism, but represented vast and diverse constituencies that left them unprotected by Washington bureaucracy.

Lincoln understood this direct accountability. He began the struggle aiming only to bring the old Union back together, fully aware of state integrity. As the conflict wore on, however, he far surpassed his opposite in making a federal system work—persuading, cajoling, relying on governors, encouraging their best efforts, and, through them, securing most of the support necessary from the state legislators who passed the various enabling bills. Yet the president brought unique strengths to the work of politicking with these men—unusual humility (studied, purposeful) and a quality that Harriet Beecher Stowe once described as "peculiar." "It is not aggressive so much as passive," she argued, "and among passive things it is like the strength not so much of a stone buttress, as of a wire cable. It is strength swaying to every influence, yielding on this side and on that to popular needs, yet tenaciously and inflexibly bound to carry its great end."[6] In short, Lincoln needed the loyal governors to preserve the Union. Through the political tug-of-war between federal and state executives, Union leadership found and justified a way to preserve the Union while accepting emancipation as a necessary part of the war effort. Consequently, the Union ultimately prevailed because loyal governors stood by Lincoln's war aims and encouraged him to undertake measures necessary to win, even at the risk to state authority and the alienation of its citizens.[7]

Questions that animate this study consider how and why the nature of the war—first defeating a rebellion and then liberating slaves—defined, limited, and intensified the partnership between governors and Lincoln. The Lincoln-governor alliance remained a powerful force during the war, and this work explores the ways in which military events influenced politics and civilian society, as well as the dual national and state allegiances that Americans in and out of uniform held during the mid-nineteenth century. Before the outbreak of hostilities, chief executives worked independently in responding to secession and the Confederacy's formation. Prewar cooperation among the governors carried into the mobilization that followed the firing on Fort Sumter, and it laid a foundation of cooperation that strengthened as the conflict expanded. The experience of war gave birth to a new understanding of the United States by 1865, one that governors and Lincoln designed. Still, as much as they worked toward a more perfect Union, it did not survive the peace they achieved.

Yet, for such an enormous subject, we know so little about it. The void is so impressive that it calls for an integrated approach in extracting from the governors' considerable perspective how this relationship prevailed during the conflict. While I have consulted the voluminous secondary literature about the war for contextualizing nation/state and civil/military affairs, I have remained close to the governors throughout the conflict. I have relied primarily on firsthand letters, diaries, government documents, and newspapers in telling their story. The net result is a book that focuses on a collection of leaders who helped Lincoln gather the resources to save a nation.[8]

CHAPTER ONE

It Is Your Business to Rise Up and Preserve the Union

Abraham Lincoln's departure from Springfield on 11 February 1861 was an inauspicious beginning for a president-elect. A cold rain fell from the early morning skies over the capital city. Illinois's favorite son stood on the Great Western Railroad platform about to board the two-car private train that would carry him to the nation's capital. There he would assume the presidency of a vast republic. "Perhaps they expected him to assume the air and tone of the president elect of thirty millions," wrote an observer, "and so awe them into forgetfulness of their old familiar intercourse with him as a citizen."[1] Even if Illinoisans did not remember any American president-elect asking people to pray, Lincoln would make the request. Just the week before, the United States had ideologically and geographically divided. Citizens of six slave states had removed themselves from the republic and, on 6 February, created a Confederacy. Shocked by the Southern departure, Northerners had trouble understanding how any state or citizen could survive outside the federal Union. "The vast majority of Americans cannot realize the idea that the Southerners really do not like the Union," wrote British correspondent Edward Dicey. "To themselves," he argued, "the Union appears so natural, so liberal, and so good a government, that it is impossible that anybody who has lived beneath its rule should leave it willingly." Yet, in Northern eyes, secession was "an unaccountable and inexplicable act of madness."[2]

Political compromise in previous decades confirmed that states had ample sovereignty. It remained to be seen if Southerners would enjoy this same autonomy in their new confederation. Northerners, however, had yet to test such sovereignty. Nevertheless, Lincoln removed his hat, paused a few seconds, and began to speak. "I now leave, not knowing when, or whether ever, I may return," he told the crowd, "with a task before me greater than that which rested upon Washington." Lincoln prayed, "Without the assistance of that Divine Being, who ever attended him, I cannot succeed." "With that assistance I cannot fail," he implored. "To His care commending you, as I hope in your prayers you will commend me," he concluded, "I bid you an affectionate farewell." Lincoln departed the quiet prairie city that had given him comfort and a homespun character. The echo from the crowd, "we will pray for you," lingered with him for miles.³ Lincoln's journey to the White House began.

Long Road to Washington

Lincoln meant for his journey to Washington to strengthen his ties to Northerners. He believed the South's secession was only a temporary expression, and so he refused to respond to it before he departed from Springfield. He did not, however, discourage the efforts of governors already working behind the scenes to mobilize. The president-elect wanted to see the people and they him. Among those who joined Lincoln was the newly elected Republican governor of Illinois, Richard Yates. The Yateses and Lincolns shared a past in Illinois. Lincoln had been a regular patron at the Yates's Springfield store. Illinoisans knew Dick Yates because he and Lincoln had both served in the state legislature as Whigs from the same district, but at different times. Yet they were unlike. At six feet four inches, Lincoln towered over most people of his time, making him seem gangly and awkward, while his ill-arranged dress and "shocking bad hat" made him appear folksy. His grizzled look mirrored the hardships he had endured in his life and reflected his republican virtues of civility, honesty, self-discipline, and forward thinking. Even if he appeared unsophisticated, Lincoln was perceptive, ambitious, and had a gift for managing people.⁴

Yates also had some distinguishing features. His winning ways and skilled oratory won him wide acclaim as "one of the ablest, if not the ablest and most impressive speakers in the country." John Hay characterized him as someone who stole hearts "by his frank blue eyes and sunshiny smile, as by the truth and eloquence of his fervid orations," something he honed at a young age. Yates credited his political aspirations to the distinguished Kentuckian Henry Clay, whose sparkling oratory convinced him to walk twelve miles to hear the great conciliator.⁵ "Wise in counsel, eloquent in the forum, warmly attached to his country," remarked the editor of the *Illinois State Journal*, Yates "has now the respect of the State, the confidence of his party and the love of his friends."⁶ Yates had campaigned unsuccessfully for a senatorial seat in the 1850s, and opponents labeled him an abolitionist. Lincoln urged him to run again, and in 1860 he won the Republican ticket for governor. Publicly, he supported Lincoln for the presidency, but privately he considered him inferior to Edward Bates of Missouri. He once jokingly said of

Lincoln that "we know he does not look very handsome," and "some of the papers say he is positively ugly." "Well," he continued, "if all the ugly men in the United States vote for him, he will surely be elected."[7]

Lincoln and Yates had become close friends over the years, and the president-elect was known to enjoy a good joke at his own expense. After his election, Lincoln used the Illinois Statehouse as his headquarters, and Yates took advantage of the president-elect's proximity to discuss secession, war, and cabinet appointments. It was in these days that Yates tried to enlist Lincoln's counsel about the January address he had prepared for the legislature. In it, he argued that the striking feature of the nation's political Union was that it could not be "dissolved by one State, nor by the people of one State or of a dozen States." He asserted that "This government was designed to be perpetual," and could be "dissolved only by revolution."[8]

The presidential train left Springfield and steamed 200 miles east across the midwestern prairie before it rolled into Indianapolis. Indiana's new Republican governor, Oliver P. Morton, welcomed Lincoln. Despite Lincoln's wish to minimize ceremonies, Morton arranged a king's reception. He tried to goad Lincoln into responding to the national crisis, but the president-elect declined. Instead, he told the Indianans that to save the Union, he needed "the hearts of a people like yours." "It is your business," he told them, "to rise up and preserve the Union and liberty for yourselves and not for me."[9] These simple words captured his journey's meaning—the Union's fate belonged to the people. Afterward, Lincoln and Morton rode together to the Bates House, where they found a crowd demanding a speech. "I feel for Mr. Lincoln," noted Calvin Fletcher, a wealthy and influential associate of Morton's, "he assumes a fearful responsibility."[10] The following morning Lincoln and Morton shared breakfast at the governor's mansion and returned to the hotel. Around noon the governor escorted Lincoln back to the station, where he boarded the train to Cincinnati. Yates returned to Springfield with friend Orville Browning, who remarked that he had had enough of the "grandstanding."[11]

Lincoln's visit pleased Morton. After all, Indiana was the anchor of the midwestern states that bordered the great Ohio River, which separated Northerners and Southerners. In Morton's mind, the key border state was Kentucky, and he wanted to know Lincoln's plans for keeping the state in the Union. Convinced that war was unavoidable, Morton had not waited on officials in Washington for direction, nor from lame-duck President James Buchanan. In fact, the approach of a showdown highlighted the governor's most distinguishing feature as a political figure: he was tenaciously protective of his citizens and his party. The Republican Party originated in the West, not the East, and political leaders wanted to steer the party toward industrial and agricultural connections that centered it on markets more than moral reform.[12]

Morton wanted to be a soldier, but the governorship suited him better. A *Chicago Tribune* editorial noted at his inaugural that he was "one of the most intellectual men of the state," who possessed a "large Websterian head and noble forehead," and "upon the stump or at the bar few men [were] his equals."[13] "Strong, earnest, logical," the thirty-eight-year-old "natural chieftain" had all the markings of an urbane man, yet he came from humble beginnings.[14] Reared by "old-fashioned Scottish Presbyterian aunts," the young Morton rejected his conservative upbringing and became an independent thinker.[15] After graduating from Miami Ohio University, he decided on a career in law, and soon his legal reputation reached far beyond Indiana, and he impressed his colleagues by his capacity to hold court on the political issues of the day. He entered the political arena when the Republican Party was in its infancy and assumed prominence in the new party. Expecting war and aware of the state's horrendous financial condition, Morton had wired the War Department in January about weapons and had petitioned the legislature for the authority to collect and distribute weapons at his discretion. Some Indiana legislators, suspicious of the new Republican chieftain, reluctantly agreed. The previous November Morton had declared that if South Carolina left the Union it would be "at the point of a bayonet." "If it was worth a bloody struggle to establish this Nation," he declared, "it is worth one to preserve it."[16]

Having deposited Lincoln into the hands of Ohio and Kentucky loyalists in Cincinnati, Morton returned to Indianapolis. On his train ride home he may have reflected on the letter he had written to Lincoln weeks before about Pennsylvania Republicans and the compromise measures before Congress. Morton believed these Republicans might compromise the integrity and future of the Republican Party by choosing to cooperate with secessionists over slavery. "The Union feeling is very strong—it is *stronger than any party*," he warned Lincoln, counseling him that, for all the intensity at the moment, time would wear out the revolution.[17]

Ohioans and Kentuckians, especially Ohio governor William Dennison, also worried about potential war that February. The Republican governor sent a legislative delegation to Cincinnati to meet Lincoln and escort him to

Columbus the following day. The president-elect made his way to Dennison's executive chambers, and from there the governor accompanied him to the legislative hall, where Lincoln addressed the assemblymen. Lincoln and Dennison retired to the executive mansion, and Dennison told Lincoln the discouraging news from his agents in Kentucky and about the suspect loyalties of Kentucky's Democratic governor Beriah Magoffin. Magoffin had called the Kentucky legislature into special session in January to consider Kentucky's future relations with the Union. He hoped legislators would follow his lead in calling for a convention. In the meantime, Magoffin warned Lincoln that Kentucky would "never stand by with arms folded while those States are struggling for their constitutional rights and resisting oppression, or being subjugated to an antislavery government."[18]

Lincoln was content to gather information and survey affairs as he rode the rails to Washington. After a reception at Deshler Hall, the president-elect and his wife took refuge in Dennison's home. The day was exhausting, but Lincoln's spirits brightened by the evening reception. He took time to greet the daughter of William T. Coggeshall, one-time editor of the *Ohio State Journal* and Dennison's current secretary. The child's face reddened as she asked: "Mr. President, what shall you do when you get to Washington?" Placing his hand on top of her head, Lincoln remarked: "What shall I do? Ask God. He knows best. But you, little one, can say when you grow up, that Abraham Lincoln bent half way to meet you."[19] A night telegram from Ohio senator Salmon P. Chase affirming Congress's approval of the Electoral College returns relieved Lincoln. Equally comforting was the news that Washington was calm, despite rumors that Southerners would use the approval as justification to seize the White House.[20]

At the age of forty-five, Dennison was governor of the nation's third largest state. A Miami University graduate of 1835, he spent several years studying law and accepted an appointment to the bar five years later, setting up his practice in Columbus. He supported Whig political doctrines that stressed an American economy of federal tariffs, national banks, and federally funded internal improvements. His legal acumen groomed him for politics, and in 1848 he won a seat in the Ohio Senate. As a legislator he fought to extend U.S. mail contracts and stage transport, while opposing Texas annexation and slavery's expansion. He also campaigned to remove Ohio's "Black Laws," and saw them through to repeal in 1849. The following year, he left public life and returned to legal practice. He became an authority in railroad finance and eventually accepted the presidency of both the Exchange Bank in Columbus and the Columbus and Xenia Railroad. Both positions allowed him to exercise his Whig principles, and in 1856 he seized the opportunity to work in the state to secure the nomination of Republican John Frémont. Ohioans elected Dennison a Republican governor in 1859.[21]

After a few days of traveling through small towns and cold weather, on 18 February, Lincoln's train steamed into Buffalo, where Governor Edwin D. Morgan's staff greeted him. That afternoon Lincoln's train arrived in Albany, where he delivered a brief speech to the throngs braving the cold. The 360-mile rail journey from Buffalo to Albany traced the Erie Canal, the nation's single greatest interregional market highway. The canal's success improved northern transportation and accounted for a surge in western population as well as increased markets in New York City. Lincoln's party then wound its way to the capital and passed under a banner stretching across a street that read: "Welcome to the Capital of the Empire State—No More Compromises." New York senator William Seward, soon to be secretary of state, had written to Morgan days before that he felt that displaying the American flag in these times was "more effective than the most eloquent speech."[22]

Lincoln met Morgan and other state officials in the executive chambers. Once inside, he turned to Morgan and asked, "do you think we can make these people hear us?" Morgan nodded approvingly and waved his hat back and forth to silence the crowd. "If you have found your fellow citizens in larger numbers elsewhere," Morgan declared, "you have not found, and I think, will not find, warmer hearts or a people more faithful to the Union, the constitution and the laws than you will meet in this time-honored city."[23] Morgan arranged to spend a private moment with the president-elect in his chambers, and that evening he hosted a small private dinner. Perhaps it was during this interlude that Morgan discussed a letter he had received from Worthington Snethen, a loyal Baltimore resident, warning of the unfriendly reception Lincoln would face in Baltimore. Seward also had advised Morgan that Maryland governor Thomas Hicks and the nation's highest-ranking commander, General Winfield Scott, shared apprehensions of a "revolutionary movement" in Maryland. Seward thought it wise to have a force of five thousand to ten thousand men in readiness within twenty-four hours' notice in case of a plot. Snethen, however, warned against any military mobilization, arguing that federal forces in Washington would agitate loyal Southerners. Snethen had given Lincoln cause for concern about Hicks declaring weeks before that, although the Union sentiment in Maryland was "overbearing all resistance," Hicks was "following, not leading, that sentiment."[24]

The following morning, Morgan accompanied Lincoln's party south along the Hudson to New York City, where it arrived at 3:00 P.M. to Mayor Fernando Wood's reception. A Democratic opportunist, Wood brazenly advocated New York City's secession to preserve the business relationship between New York's cotton merchants and southern planters. Illinoisan John Pope was part of the entourage that accompanied Lincoln from Springfield and remembered the long ride through the city streets. "Crowds of people," he recalled, "who lined the sidewalks and occupied every window and doorway which opened on the street, crowded and jammed together so it seemed that many of them must be trampled to death." "The ride down the city through these crowds of excited and anxious people was not encouraging," wrote Pope, "and seemed a chilly welcome of the President of the United States to the metropolis of the country."[25]

Walt Whitman later recalled that mild February day when he sat atop a covered carriage and gazed at the crowd of a quarter of a million people. Only the visit by Edward VII, Prince of Wales, the year before had drawn larger numbers, noted the editor for *Harper's Weekly*. The city's residents greeted the president-elect during the hour it took the procession to make its way to the Astor House Hotel. Lincoln thanked the crowd from the hotel balcony and retired to the quiet of his room. The following morning, he shared breakfast with Norman B. Judd, his chief advisor; Thurlow Weed, editor of the *Albany Evening Journal*; James W. Webb, also a prominent New York journalist, and Rhode Island's Republican governor William Sprague.[26]

The self-proclaimed "boy-governor," Sprague was wealthy, handsome, and exuded an air of confidence beyond his years. Sprague was thirteen when his father died, forcing him and his brother Amasa into the family cotton-mill business. During those years, the aspiring soldier enlisted in the Providence Marine Artillery Company. When his uncle died, he inherited the family business and became an accomplished businessman. By 1860, Sprague was a household name, and Rhode Island voters nominated him for governor on a ticket that fused Democrats, conservative Republicans, and conditional Unionists. By using his personal fortune to campaign, Sprague had broken the power of the opposition Radical candidate, Seth Padelford. Overshadowed by the small circle of companions he dined with on that cold February morning, Sprague nonetheless impressed Lincoln.[27]

The president-elect spent the afternoon receiving guests, and that evening he attended the reception at the Astor House. Morgan decided to "slip into a chair next to Lincoln's right at dinner," and continue his earlier conversations.²⁸ Tall and dignified looking, Morgan was hard to miss. He had a schoolmaster's confidence and flare for business. The onetime grocer moved from Massachusetts to New York and entered a mercantile career of high finance that brought him into prominent political circles. He had many talents, wrote a friend to Lincoln, and was "inflexibly honest," someone who had rare administrative abilities, "a rock-like solidity," and unimpeachable character that inspired confidence.²⁹ Morgan made the most of his time with Lincoln. Times were pressing, and Morgan needed financial relief for his mercantile and banker colleagues who had invested heavily in Southern goods. New York financiers had floated millions in loans to banks in the states forming the Confederacy. Amid the financial panic on Wall Street, financiers looked to the governor for relief. Approaching his second term, Morgan looked to the federal government to aid him in preserving financial stability.³⁰

Prominent in the Republican Party and well connected in financial circles, Morgan may have thought himself qualified for a cabinet position. Governing the Union's largest and wealthiest state, however, allowed him considerable influence in shaping national affairs. He was a seasoned politician, who, as the Republican Party's national chairman in 1856 and 1860, played a role in Lincoln's rise to prominence. By 1861, his eleven-year political career had served him well. So popular was Morgan that New Yorkers had reelected him by an overwhelming majority the year before. He had made great strides in pulling the state out of deep fiscal problems in his first term and relaxed after the legislature adjourned. Secession prompted Morgan to prepare for war, while his "recalcitrant" legislature prescribed a normal "peacetime program."³¹ He upheld two fundamental points about the nation's most pressing crisis over slavery: he thought it unlawful to interfere with state institutions, but argued that Congress had the right to legislate slavery out of the territories.³²

A thirty-four-gun salute signaled Lincoln's arrival in Trenton, New Jersey, where Republican governor Charles S. Olden and Attorney General William Dayton welcomed him. After a short carriage ride to the capitol, the president-elect addressed New Jersey legislators. Obstreperous Democrats, unreceptive to Lincoln, held a majority and shamelessly resolved that when they saw him, "they will have seen the ugliest man in the country." Recognizing Lincoln's height, members resolved to "always have a democratic member that shall exceed the President-elect by two and a half inches in height."³³ New Jersey was a bitterly divided state politically, and Olden sought to "heal the breach" by inviting Lincoln to the capital. Without delving into slavery and states' rights, Lincoln requested legislators to assist him in "piloting the ship of State through this voyage, surrounded by perils as it is." "For if it should suffer attack now," he declared, "there will be no pilot ever needed for another voyage."[34]

Later that afternoon Lincoln left the Jersey shore and arrived at Kensington Station in Philadelphia on his way to Harrisburg. Snethen's earlier suggestions of an unfriendly Baltimore reception for Lincoln turned out to be disconcerting. Scottish-born Allen Pinkerton, who ran a Chicago-based detective agency, had uncovered an elaborate assassination plot and explained these developments to Norman Judd. He advised Lincoln to cancel further appearances and steam to Washington secretly that evening. Equally alarming were the rumors that secessionists were plotting to murder Hicks to throw Maryland into the hands of disunionists. "The pressure there upon Hicks is fearful," Alexander McClure, Pennsylvania journalist and political ally, warned Lincoln weeks before. "If he should be compelled to yield you could never get to Washington except within a circle of bayonets."[35]

The news did not deter Lincoln, who decided to make his scheduled appearances. After a flag-raising ceremony at Independence Hall on the morning of 22 February, Lincoln's train left for the Pennsylvania capital. He arrived in Harrisburg four hours later, where Republican governor Andrew Curtin greeted him. By this time, Confederates had inaugurated Jefferson Davis provisional president, and news from the South worsened. Curtin reassured Lincoln that Pennsylvanians had prepared for war should peace discussions fail.[36]

Lincoln addressed the legislature later that day and spent the balance of his time in private at the Jones House hotel. He dined that evening with Curtin when close associates produced further evidence that an attempt would be made on Lincoln's life should he proceed as planned. Lincoln should return to Philadelphia, they urged, and from there he would leave for Washington. After dinner, Curtin and Ward Hill Lamon, a close friend of Lincoln's, who single-handedly served as his bodyguard, prepared to leave. Before going, Curtin pulled Lamon aside and asked if he was armed. Lamon confidently pulled open his coat and displayed a "small arsenal of deadly weapons, showing he was literally armed to the teeth."[37] Lamon then whisked Lincoln outside, and off they traveled to the outskirts of the city to board a special train bound for Philadelphia. There they would meet the late night train that would transport him to Washington. Illinois senator

Elihu Washburne met Lincoln at the station at six o'clock the next morning. Lincoln took up residence at Willard's Hotel, where he met Seward and, according to the *New York Times*, achieved the *"coup d'état."*[38]

Lincoln delivered more than one hundred speeches along the extraordinary journey. Its pageantry and extravagance rivaled the ascension of European kings, and yet he arrived in the capital city in darkness and without fanfare. He tried to impress the people even by the nature of the "prudent caution" in his words that he needed time to consider the best approach to the national crisis confronting him. He confessed that he had not developed any mature judgment about his reactions to the Confederacy's formation. He chose to be brief and self-deprecating, which endeared him to the people gathered at every stop. As the weary president-elect made speech after speech during the weeklong journey from Springfield, he reduced his whistle-stop performances to a few well-rehearsed phrases that revealed his characteristic caution, pragmatism, and humility. "It is with your aid, as the people," he declared at Poughkeepsie, New York, "that I think we shall be able to preserve—not the country, for the country will preserve itself, (cheers), but the institutions of the country—(great cheering)." One New Yorker got close enough to shake hands with Lincoln, commenting to the president-elect, "I hope you will take [care] of us," to which Lincoln fittingly responded, "But, you must take care of me."[39]

Southerners had taken much from Lincoln and the Union. Secession and the Confederacy's formation had altered the republic. His goal as president, however, had changed. His task was not only to lead the nation, but also to save it from itself. The Union was dissolving, and Lincoln rode the rails to Washington, passing tens of thousands of Northerners from whom much would be expected in the coming months, and even years. Many of the faces he had seen along his journey would soon be called forth to save the Union. Yet, it was not clear whether Lincoln was more impressed by his constituents or whether they were more impressed him. The times were impressive enough.[40]

Peace Conference

Washingtonians were not to be outdone by the brilliant ceremonies in honor of Lincoln during his journey that preceded his arrival. It would be a formidable effort, however, to improve the city's appearance, which, according to John Hay, resembled a "wilderness of a town."[41] Despite housing more than 60,000 inhabitants, the capital boasted few public buildings. One visitor observed that "the place seemed like a large village, with its preponderance of plain, low brick or wooden structures, wide, mostly unpaved streets, small shops, general lack of business activity, and a distinctly Southern air of indolence and sloth." The city's hotels were spacious, but were "poorly kept," and according to this correspondent, the city "could not boast a single decent restaurant, but had no end of bar rooms." To further diminish the capital's appeal was that there were neither omnibuses nor streetcars, and the shabby public carriages, with their ragged black drivers, were disgusting. Nonetheless, wrote one political correspondent, it was the "most important place in the Union." Someone even managed to place the American flag atop the partially constructed Washington Monument that towered some 228 feet above the Washington skyline, mirroring the unfinished work of solidifying the Union of states itself.[42]

In the initial days of his reception, Lincoln made time to confer with the Maryland governor. An Eastern Shore Maryland slave owner, Hicks was the most important of all the loyal governors. His state surrounded the nation's capital, and Baltimore was one of the most prominent railroad and harbor cities on the East Coast. These geographically distinguishing features, however, were beset by the complications of an intensely divided population. Maryland contained a free black population almost equal to its slave population, which helped explain its move toward universal emancipation in the previous decades. Hicks was ten years' Lincoln's senior and a seasoned politician. The Dorchester County native had worked the docks and the mercantile business before becoming sheriff. His long political life began as a Democrat in the 1830s, when he served as a Maryland Senate elector. He later served on the Governor's Council, until assuming the position of Register of Wills for Dorchester County, which he held until he became governor. He abandoned the Democratic Party for the Whigs and then switched to the Know-Nothing Party before joining the Republican Party in 1860.[43]

Elected governor in 1858, Hicks declared that Maryland was "devoted to the Union and all of the states," had "never listened to the suggestions of disunion from Southern states," and conversely "refused to join with the misguided people of the Northern states in their assaults on slavery."[44] John Brown's raid at Harpers Ferry in 1859 had so alarmed Marylanders, that Hicks sought a legislative appropriation of $70,000 to strengthen county militias and prevent further hostilities. The following year he refused to send a delegation to a Southern convention to consider resolutions aimed at adopting some "concerted action," in case of further Northern aggression. The assembly itself adopted the position that "should the hour ever arrive when the Union must be dissolved, Maryland will cast her lot with her sister states of the South and abide their fortune to the fullest extent."[45] Hicks had supported Tennessee Constitutional Union candidate John C. Bell in the recent election, and his loss discouraged Hicks and his supporters.[46]

In these critical months Hicks fell under the spell of John Pendleton Kennedy, Maryland's most famous literary son. Known for his 1832 classic of Virginia plantation life, *Swallow Barn; or a Sojourn in the Old Dominion*, Kennedy had recently written a critique of the sectional debate entitled *The Border States: Their Power and Duty in the Present Disorder of the Country*. Hicks read this work and it shaped his attitude about the crisis. He refused to allow secessionists or abolitionists to bully him and balked at summoning a special session of the General Assembly. He hoped to neutralize the approaching danger. Former Illinois newspaper editor Josiah M. Lucas had moved to Washington years before and became Hicks's close friend. Lucas was so concerned over events that he wrote Lincoln of Hicks's situation before the new president departed Springfield. "I know that he is undergoing a terrible pressure," Lucas confided to the president, "and it is even probable that the speaker of the House of Delegates and the president of the Senate will call the legislature together—if so, one of their first acts will be to pass an act putting the routes of travel under martial law."[47] During the secession winter, Hicks remained committed to the Union. "I have felt it necessary to hold the Executive rein with a firm hand," he wrote to William L. Wilcox, boasting that he was proud to preside over his loyal Marylanders, "standing firmly by the Union ready to face the disunionists, if they dare to lay violent hands upon that sacred legacy of our Patriot Fathers."[48] Marylanders' devotion to the Union and the Constitution was "unalterable," he replied to the Alabama commissioners hoping to lure him into the Confederacy. "If there *must* be secession or desertion from this Union," he maintained, "the people of Maryland think that those alone who refuse to comply with its duties should be deprived of its benefits."[49]

Loyalists stood by Hicks, and with good reason. His "firm and manly resistance of the efforts which have been made to swerve you from the path of duty which you had wisely resolved to follow" had impressed Curtin.[50] "I am a native of Maryland," Hicks responded to Curtin, "the owner of a number of slaves, and my feelings and sympathies are naturally with the South; but above and beyond all these, I am for the Union, and forgetting all but honor, am ready to sacrifice life and fortune to save and perpetuate the Union of the States formed by our Fathers under the Providence of God."[51] The editor of *Harper's Weekly* confirmed this sentiment. "We know of no man who occupies a more prominent position at the present time than the Governor of the State of Maryland," the editor declared.[52]

Hicks held up to the pressure, and his resistance to convening the legislature impressed his border state colleagues. Olden, for example, "implored" Hicks not to "yield to the demands of the 'secessionists.'" He declared that Lincoln's peaceful inauguration depended on his loyalty. Even Iowa's Republican governor Samuel J. Kirkwood, a Maryland native, interrupted plowing his fields to thank the governor for the "patriotic and manly stand you have taken against disunion and treason."[53] Before Lincoln left Springfield, Hicks had encouraged the border state governors of Virginia, Tennessee, Kentucky, and Missouri to work together to maintain the balance of power between North and South until Congress reached a compromise. He wrote to John J. Crittenden, Kentucky's Unionist senator and encouraged him to lead the forces toward compromise. Crittenden took the lead that December by bringing forth a series of conciliatory resolutions that fell into the hands of a committee of thirteen congressmen who, while inspired to save the Union, failed to agree on how they would work slavery into that Union. Congress's paralysis thus placed the Union's fate in the hands of the states.[54]

Virginia congressmen spearheaded the idea of a national conference and called on twenty-one states to dispatch delegates to the nation's capital to participate in a "Peace Conference." Morgan praised the idea, arguing that all efforts at peace be tried, yet others refused, desiring to wait until after Lincoln's inauguration. Maine governor Israel Washburn and Ohio's Dennison, however, opposed it and urged Yates to refuse the meeting because of Virginia's involvement. They feared such a meeting would undermine the Republican Party. Yates's close association with Lincoln convinced them that the president-elect was counseling his old colleague, and they wanted Lincoln's reaction. Washburn was also concerned about Seward's influence upon Lincoln, writing to his colleague Republican senator William Pitt Fessenden that having read the dispatches from his Washington friends he had a "[most] gloomy foreboding," about affairs. "If Mr. Seward has declared in substance, that the Union even for slavery is paramount to an organization where life & soul is liberty & justice & the constitution as it was made, there is henceforth—what but demoralization & defeat?"[55] "But," he concluded,

"I will not, cannot harbor the fear. I will wait for proof."[56] To New York congressman Charles Sedgwick, the governor was more emphatic. "The only fault in Seward's speech," he argued, "is that only wise men understand it—fools read 'compromise.'"[57]

Morton shared Washburn's concerns, but he considered it better to accept the invitation and act as a "powerful restraint upon any disposition" desiring "to compromise the integrity and future of the Republican party."[58] He believed it far better to take hold of the conference and "control it, than to stand by and suffer the consequences of its action when we have had no share in moulding [sic] it."[59] As for Lincoln's counsel, Yates found the president-elect uncomfortable with the peace proposition, and Lincoln advised the governor not "to take any action." In his words, he would "rather be hung by the neck till he was dead on the steps of the Capitol, before he would buy or beg a peaceful inauguration."[60] This masterful silence was not weakness on Lincoln's part. Quite the contrary, it was power, and Lincoln exercised a cautious pragmatism until Chief Justice Roger B. Taney had sworn him into office as president.[61]

The Peace Conference presented problems for national governance. In previous decades much of the nation's political course had relied on legislatively centered decisions. For governors, whose power suffered from constitutional limits, the appointment of delegates to a national conference to save the Union carried special importance, especially since some legislatures were not in session. These were unchartered waters, and governors weighed the alternatives carefully, recognizing the problems of acting independently. Yates consulted prominent state Republicans before deciding how to proceed. Charles Robinson, governor of the newly admitted state of Kansas, had no choice but to appoint delegates without the state legislature. He tapped close friend George W. Deitzler and counseled him that "the true policy for every good citizen to pursue is to set his face like flint against secession, to call it by its name, treason." The Ohio General Assembly allowed Dennison to appoint representatives, but required that the Senate confirm them. Morton bulldozed his way into appointing delegates and requested each delegate to draft an agreement that would promise their opposition to any new guarantee of slavery.[62] Curtin also appointed a radically minded Pennsylvania delegation, but was legislatively censored for choosing a partisan course."[63] New England governors fell into line behind Massachusetts governor John Andrew and supported the conference. New Jersey, Delaware, and Iowa either sent commissioners or drew on their congressional delegations to attend. Bullied by a Democratic Senate, Olden offered a conciliatory response in his address to assemblymen that New Jersey would make the reasonable concessions to save the Union.

Some 3,000 miles west, Democratic governor John W. Downey was heading off secession and a rumored Pacific Republic movement among his Californians. John Whiteaker, Oregon's proslavery governor, wanted to keep his newly admitted state neutral, but he did little to deter secessionism. The Democrat saw no need to attend the conference and instead worked to maintain peace among his divided population, which was connected to the Union only by a 2,700-mile-long trail dubbed the "Overland Trail." Besides, the conference might well be over before any West Coast delegates reached Washington. Alexander Randall, Wisconsin's Republican governor, reluctantly allowed legislators to decide, but they could not agree on whom to send, so they sent no one. Republican Alexander Ramsey balked at the thought of sending Minnesota delegates to the conference. Austin Blair, Michigan's Radical Republican governor, agreed with his assemblymen that he would not entertain any concession to traitors.[64]

Congress gave little attention to the conference regarded as the "last hope of the country," but it had served two purposes for Republicans and governors.[65] It centered the political debate in Washington on peace rather than on war, thus allowing Lincoln a quiet transition to the capital city. More important, it previewed the political cooperation among Northern states. Governors worked independently from one other, but shared a common goal of assisting the national administration. As party leaders, deciding on representation at the conference was an important exercise for governors. When, for example, the convention delegates had agreed on a series of compromises, Michigan's Radical Republican senator Zachariah Chandler looked to Blair for support. He feared these men might compromise Republican principles and wrote the governor, seeking send some "*stiff-backed men*" to counter those of weaker political constitutions, meaning those representing the manufacturing states. "Without a little blood-letting," Chandler chided, "this Union will not be worth a rush."[66] Still, no Michiganders came forth. In line with Blair's radicalism, Andrew, however, had reversed his position on the conference's merits and dispatched seven commissioners to Washington. He came to believe that its failure would provide the nation with no other alternative than war. To drive the point home, he wrote to Sumner that "if *these* seven men come home and report in Faneuil Hall that New England must stand ALONE—we can stand there."[67]

Hicks's encouragement of the Peace Conference cost him dearly. Anti-Lincoln Marylanders denounced him. Lincoln, however, admired the governor's determination to keep "the state out of the hands of a faction of scoundrels who are striving to make Maryland a cat's paw for the seizure of the seat of Government," as acknowledged by one proslavery Unionist, "and of course the battle ground of the civil war that must ensue."[68] Lincoln polled 2,204 Maryland votes out of 92,441, and preserving the Union was no easy course. Hicks understood his state's complex interplay of locality and loyalty. It did not help matters that Lincoln denied Marylanders the opportunity to see him as he passed through to Washington.[69]

Inauguration

"The golden days have fallen upon the capital," wrote Hay, signaling the arrival of the inauguration day.[70] New York political correspondent Henry Villard had finally arrived in Washington. He had traveled with Lincoln's train, but only as far as New York City, where, after ten days of the "wearisome sameness of the performances," he abandoned the "traveling show." A German native, Villard first met Lincoln years before, during the Lincoln-Douglas debates, which he covered for the New York press. When Lincoln became president, Villard held a fair degree of journalistic fame, and the *New York Herald* assigned him the task of covering Lincoln in Springfield. Now in Washington, amid the chaos of nearly 25,000 people hoping to catch a glimpse of the new president, Villard reacquainted himself with Lincoln. Shaking his hand after the ceremony, Villard remarked to Lincoln about having to ward off the crowd around Willard's Hotel "hovering about." "Yes," replied Lincoln, "it was bad enough in Springfield," but that was "child's play compared with this tussle here." "I am fair game for everybody of that hungry lot."[71]

Lincoln grew wise to the reporters and politicians seeking to undo his presidency before it began. The Washington spotlight would expose his weaknesses as well as highlight his strengths. His unusual appearance and his knack for relying on backcountry metaphors to answer important questions would be fodder for critics looking to undermine his modest public reputation made famous by his "House Divided" speech and his address at the Cooper Union Institute. Except for these addresses, many Southerners hoped the painfully awkward-looking president would prove as deficient in diplomacy as in appearance. It was an unforgiving public eye that fell upon him.

"I pity Mr. Lincoln," wrote Massachusetts attorney Andrew J. Clough, who traveled to Washington for the inaugural. "He has got a hard place and much difficulty to contend with."[72]

Lincoln arrived to preserve the Union in one of United States' most Southern cities. Washingtonians had long lived with Southern institutions. Even with its shabby appearance, there was a gentility surrounding the nation's capital. Large farms were home to prosperous families, and Washingtonians catered to wealthy political leaders. The city's identity reflected the national political culture. Northerners and Southerners worked to protect their special interests, yet they seldom socialized together. In fact, they remained resolute in their refusal to cross the proverbial cultural divide, particularly when it came to slavery. Yet, as the second session of the 36th Congress unfolded that winter, the political gulf between North and South widened, as congressmen gazed across the chamber's vacant seats once occupied by Southerners. It was the hope of those members present to restore secessionists peacefully before others left. Writing from his Washington hotel, Thurlow Weed was hopeful of such a prospect, and concluded to Morgan that "all looks like a pacific Inauguration."[73]

Lincoln's inaugural address served notice to those who prejudged him as a simple man from a simple state that his determination had brought him to Washington. He had maintained at least one definite belief throughout his political life—that the Union was perpetual, that it was "much older than the Constitution," and that it had matured as a theoretical and practical idea of government over the ages. For Lincoln, the Constitution's most important point was that it was intended to "form a more perfect Union." No state, upon its mere motion, could lawfully get out of the Union, and undertaking such a course would in fact prove insurrectionary or revolutionary. Seventy-two years had passed since the inauguration of the nation's first president, Lincoln concluded, and since that time the Union had remained "unbroken." To the extent of his ability, he would use the constitutional powers at his disposal to ensure that the "laws of the Union be faithfully executed in all States." Lincoln believed that the federal Union, "the bond of all things," had yet to be dissolved, but the Southerners' departure weakened the Union.[74]

The federal Union, Lincoln believed, drew its power from self-governance, aged and cured by previous generations. Political tradition dictated that Americans settled controversies by majority rule. Having chosen secession over submission, Confederates had established a ruinous precedent that undermined federalism. Lincoln's journey from Springfield gave him a glimpse of the Northerners who constituted the majority and on whom he would reply to vindicate democracy. His transition from private to public life, assuming his place over more than thirty million citizens, made him the leader in this crusade. "We will pray for you," reporters noted, was the most popular phrase offered the new president along his journey to Washington, and it represented a pledge of alliance.[75]

Lincoln, in fact, became their servant as well as their leader—a testament to his capacity to listen as well as guide the people. He was aware that much of the nation's political history had been one of conflict between the states and the national government. Secession was the antithesis of union, and Americans witnessed the republican powers moving in reverse. It provided Northerners the opportunity to rely more significantly than ever before on cooperative state power as the political agency for survival. Most Northerners agreed that secession was incompatible with the Union, and that only by working through state-federal and federal-state initiatives without undermining local self-governance, could they preserve the Union. Lincoln's arrival in Washington as the leader of a fairly new Republican Party governing a divided republic challenged political leaders to write a new history of federalism, one that featured collaboration instead of conflict.[76]

Some governors attended Lincoln's inaugural ceremony, but most read his address as it came over the wires. Republican governors used it to foster the cooperative spirit among their constituents to highlight the Union's indestructibility. Democratic governors used it as provocation for war and justification for marshaling resources to protect themselves against the Republicans' designs to contain slavery. Lincoln explained that the paramount issue was that no state, on its own motion, could rightfully leave the Union, and by doing seceding, the Confederate states had weakened the United States. Still, in its eloquence and powerful prose, Lincoln's inaugural address presented no solution to the crisis. "No man ever occupied the Presidential Chair in the midst of more trying responsibilities than does Mr. Lincoln," remarked the editor of the *Burlington Daily Hawk-Eye*.[77]

Rising Up

Governors had been preparing secretly for what many believed was an unavoidable military crisis, and Lincoln understood their defensive measures. War preparation expanded the chief executives' powers, allowing them to play leading, rather than secondary, roles in state and national affairs, and Lincoln leaned on them. Governors assessed their neglected arsenals and militias, and worked to transform them into resources on which Lincoln could rely. Weed understood the governors' importance and encouraged the state executives to advise Lincoln quietly in charting his course. "With wisdom and prudence," he counseled Lincoln, "we can unite the North by upholding the supremacy of the Constitution and laws," and "your Administration will have its foundation upon a rock."[78]

It was Weed's belief that the states formed the political rock necessary to support Lincoln, and governors would buoy Northern confidence. A meeting, he believed, might unify the peoples' sentiments on the national crisis, and would display Northern unanimity as a powerful warning to other Southern states considering secession. The Albany journalist had encouraged Morgan to gather the governors in New York City, which he did the day following South Carolina's secession from the Union. Invitations went out to Washburn, Andrew, Curtin, and Dennison, and the five governors met privately at the home of one of Morgan's relatives. The meeting highlighted those issues that might strengthen the Northern states as defenders of the Constitution "when (if ever) the unfortunate conflict shall come." The governors believed the repeal of their states' personal liberty laws might possibly avert a war, or at least the secession of additional states. Such a gesture might also provide economic relief as sectional events unfolded. New Yorkers and Bostonians in particular were beginning to fall on hard times. Morgan favored these personal liberty repeals. He expressed this sentiment to Vermont's Republican governor Erastus Fairbanks because he wanted the states to remove any laws he believed were "in conflict with the constitution."[79]

Newly elected governor Washburn was in New York City on his way to Augusta when he stopped off to attend the conference. He knew then that a "crisis confronted them and that more would be required from them than the regular duties of governor in ordinary times."[80] Illinois's outspoken Republican senator Lyman Trumbull told Lincoln about the meeting and that the governors agreed to maintain the Constitution and enforce the laws "at all hazards" and that they would recommend these sentiments to their legislatures. But to Weed, Lincoln wrote privately that "should the convocation of governors . . . seem desirous to know my views on the present aspect of things, tell them you judge from my speeches that I will be inflexible on the territorial question," and "that I probably think all opposition, real and apparent, to the fugitive slave [clause] of the constitution ought to be withdrawn."[81]

Andrew was reluctant to repeal Massachusetts's personal liberty laws, but following Rhode Island's and New Hampshire's repeal measures, he acquiesced. He refused, however, to retreat from his war preparations. Alarmed by information of an attack on Washington before Lincoln's inauguration, he secretly dispatched agents carrying letters to Washburn, Fairbanks, and New Hampshire's lame-duck Republican governor Ichabod Goodwin, advising them to be on alert. Like the minutemen decades before him, Andrew readied his militia and urged these state executives to make similar preparations to send troops to the nation's capital. Neither Sprague nor Connecticut's Republican governor William A. Buckingham appeared overly disturbed by Andrew's news, but acceded to his wishes. Their collective responses calmed Andrew, and when inauguration day passed quietly, he maintained his readiness to respond to the call for men.[82]

Of all the sitting governors, Goodwin was among the eldest at sixty-five years old and had cultivated an impressive business and political career. The Maine native moved to Portsmouth, New Hampshire, at a young age and engaged in the shipping business as a clerk for Samuel Lord, which allowed the eager apprentice to acquire a keen business sense. He embraced the bustling political culture of the 1830s and the emerging Whig Party, which he joined, and represented in the state legislature for several terms over the next two decades. He joined the Republican Party in the late 1850s and won the governorship in 1859 and again in 1860 when his popularity and moderate views carried his unopposed renomination. In January, however, Goodwin lost renomination to Nathaniel Springer Berry, a Republican more suited to the party's rising abolitionism in New Hampshire.[83]

From his winter travels to Washington, Andrew concluded that it was imperative for New England to cooperate publicly with the national government. After all, secessionists had not masked their intentions in leaving the Union, he argued, why should New Englanders mask theirs in supporting the Union. Upon returning to Boston, he resumed his correspondence with Senator Sumner and Congressman Charles Francis Adams Sr., who monitored the daily events around Capitol Hill. Although Adams assured Andrew that Washington would not be taken before Lincoln's inaugural, he advised him to undertake measures to counteract any movements that followed Lincoln's inaugural. "The proceedings," advised Adams, "should emanate spontaneously from the States, and not be traced to suggestions from this quarter."[84] Adams warned Andrew to be careful not to create a misapprehension among the loyal people of Maryland and Virginia of designs to strike.[85]

The significance in these weeks rested in what the governors accomplished. In striking a cooperative chord in mobilizing for war, governors took heed to the words that it was the business of the people to rise up and preserve the Union. Andrew took the lead in directing the governors' energies to inventory arms and militia. Many Northern governors saw in the crisis the necessity of partnering with the national government to preserve the Union. They regarded Kentucky as the most important border state, and Dennison quietly secured the services of the state's loyalists. West of the Appalachians, governors paid close attention to the Ohio and Mississippi rivers, as they served as the region's principal economic highways. Randall, Kirkwood, and Ramsey shared a mutual concern over hostile Indians. Yates also worried about the great "Father of Waters," a common interest among westerners, and vowed to protect it from "foreign hands."[86]

Rivers did not concern Andrew as much as a revolution in Republican power, or worse, a compromise resulting from the Peace Conference. Sumner had peppered him with letters from Washington that reflected the gloomy prospects of averting war. In his conversations with Edwin M. Stanton, Buchanan's attorney general, Stanton insisted that "everything was as bad as it could be" and that Virginia, Kentucky, and Maryland would secede. Distressed, Sumner agreed with Stanton's view that they were "in the midst of a revolution," and advised Andrew to steer clear of these political machinations.[87] Most pressing for Andrew, however, was that the outbreak of hostilities would force him to call upon his militiamen for defense. Most of these soldiers were Democrats, who might resist a Republican governor.[88]

Personal liberty laws, hijacked rivers, and fears of political revolution were legitimate concerns for governors moving to protect their states. Blair, however, feared the effect of hostilities on the Great Lakes and its seaways. Because it was almost surrounded by water, Michigan's vulnerability to disruptions on the coast troubled him. The tall lanky politician with a powerful speaking voice had recently denounced secession in his annual address and recommended enlarging the state militia and securing the Michigan coastline. Like many governors, Blair had an empty treasury and a scattered, ill-equipped militia, but he took great pride in marshaling for war, especially if it were to lead to slavery's abolition. Blair was born in 1818 to New England abolitionists who migrated to upstate New York and settled in Tompkins

County. Educated at Cazenovia Seminary and at Hamilton and Union colleges, Blair studied law. In 1841 he ventured to Jackson, Michigan, where he opened a legal practice. Politics drew him into the Whig Party, and voters elected him to the legislature in 1844, where he quickly won acclaim for his opposition to slavery. By 1848 his liberal ideas placed him in the Free-Soil Party, and six years later he helped found Michigan's Republican Party. Chandler defeated him for Congress in 1857, but he remained popular politically. He allowed his name to go forward in the 1860 gubernatorial campaign, which he won. He assumed his position in early January 1861, fully aware of the challenges confronting the republic. "If Lincoln don't take the reins vigorously in his [two] hands and smite these villains 'like a thugh [sic],'" he fumed to Chandler, "then the caucus is not worth [running] any longer."[89] He used his address to the legislature to convince members that "secession is revolution, and revolution in the overt act is treason, and must be treated as such," and anyone who thought otherwise had "read history to no purpose."[90]

Delayed by the Pony Express's long journey, news of the Confederacy's formation and Lincoln's inauguration reached Sacramento weeks later than in the east. California governor Downey called on Albert Sidney Johnston, a native Kentuckian and professional army man, to secure the California's forces against Indian depredations and secessionists plotting to establish a Pacific republic. Yet in early March Johnston relinquished his command to Brigadier General Edwin V. Sumner and headed east. Downey understood California's Southern ties, feared local uprisings, and aligned himself with the Union. "The people of California desire no change in our form of Government," he declared in his message to the legislature. "They desire no dismemberment that would weaken us as a powerful people."[91] The governor had personal reasons to remain in the Union. He had followed the Gold Rush to the golden state in 1849 and prospected for a time until opening a drugstore in Los Angeles. He quickly turned a considerable profit into land investment and at one point owned over 75,000 acres in southern California. He was a Douglas Democrat, and Californians elected him lieutenant governor in 1859, but, after five days in office, Governor Milton S. Latham accepted the congressional vacancy in the United States Senate. Downey assumed his place at the helm of the Union's most rapidly expanding state. At the young age of thirty-two, this short, hazel-eyed, and auburn-haired Irish-Catholic became the first foreign-born governor in the United States just ten years after arriving penniless in America.[92]

Mapped to heighten his visibility, Lincoln's journey from Springfield to Washington inspired loyalty, and Northern governors understood its significance. Dennison had mentioned to Norman Judd months before that uniting the Northern reaction to secession might "prepare the public mind" for any position Lincoln might be "called upon to take in assuming the reins of the government." It might be wise, Judd suggested, to line up the "official head of the Republican Party in the respective states" to help shape public sentiment to prepare them for whatever actions he might need to take in the coming months, including going to war. "A matured Northern public opinion seems to me of inestimable value if we are to have trying times when you shall be called upon to act." He added, "the Southern States are evidently acting in concert so far as their executives speak for the States. Why should not the same thing occur in the Republican States?"[93]

More than any governor, Andrew wanted to be in the vanguard of preserving the Union. He won his position in the 1860 election hoping to inspire loyalty to the Union. The Maine native and Bowdoin graduate was a political maverick with an acid tongue, whose self-assuredness sparked heated debate with his rivals. As a student he had adopted abolition and temperance, founded the Peace Society, and honed his literary skills under the tutelage of gifted tutor Henry Wadsworth Longfellow. He eventually took up the study and practice of law and settled in Boston. Within a few years he developed a prominent legal reputation and contributed funds to John Brown's defense. Shortly after his election, Andrew presented the assembly chairman with a musket used at the Battle of Lexington in 1775, and as he was handing the weapon over, he raised the old relic and kissed it. Henry Lee, among Andrew's most trusted staff members, witnessed the scene, recalling that spectators "felt cold chills run over" them. Andrew's zeal, wrote Lee, "inspired and kindled the people," and they elected him chair of the Massachusetts delegation that had nominated Lincoln.[94] "We claim you, Mr. Lincoln, as coming from Massachusetts," remarked Andrew at the time, "because of all the old Lincoln names are from Plymouth Colony."[95]

During the secession winter, Andrew assured Lincoln of his support. "If at any time, I can serve the cause by any word of mine, I am at your service," he wrote Lincoln, "I have nothing to ask for myself nor for any selfish end," and "I may sometimes venture to speak freely," only for the sake of preserving the Union.[96] "With all that can be said for our wealth and refinement and the solid structure of our society here," he told Lincoln, "the heart and hope and enterprize [sic] of the West are most needful for the country; and I trust that, while you will be comprehensive in your statesmanship, you will be seen always characteristically a Western man." Andrew advised that "Every good man of intelligence always does well, when he 'acts himself,'" and "we fail, when we try to please others and meet their wishes instead of following out our own best judgment." He closed by saying, "For one, I was never sorry for doing what my own judgment clearly dictated, and I always am sorry when I do not."[97] He declared "We will stand by you as we would, if you had been born and reared on Bunker Hill . . . we will be faithful to your administration and maintain your cause against all comers, so long as your plume shall lead the army in the way where points its immortal ideas and its unconquerable faith."[98]

Governing a dissolving nation forced Lincoln and his loyal governors into a partnership that changed federal-state and state-federal relations. Within weeks governors quietly prepared for war, journeyed with Lincoln, and gave shape to a cooperative framework to preserve the Union. Esprit de corps, more than any formal policies, engendered a mobilization that tied Northerners to the cause and their government. Although the Republican victory transferred federal power from Southern to Northern political leaders, the party was little more than a loose political organization marred by factions and divided by geography and ideology. Governors became architects in executing the Republican plan no matter how fractured Lincoln's cabinet. Believing it was their duty to preserve the Union, governors took the lead in rallying their citizens to the national cause. Indeed, as Andrew wrote to Charles Sumner's brother George, "We must *use* power, when we have it."[99] The time had come to see if Lincoln and the loyal governors could sustain federalism's founding architects as they governed a dissolving nation.

CHAPTER TWO

If Blood Must Flow

"The great event upon which rested the fears of nearly all the old women in the country—the inauguration of Abraham Lincoln, of Illinois, as President of the United States is concluded," remarked one Washington correspondent, "and the federal Capital is as peaceful as a country church-yard on Sunday."[1] The moment's tranquility, however, belied the storm ahead. Baltimorean George Whitmarsh noted in his diary that day that "the countrys [sic] prospects are darker this day than when the crisis first began."[2] When Lincoln retired in the late evening after the day's festive events, "the old problems were in new hands."[3] The morning following his inauguration, Lincoln found on his desk Major Robert Anderson's telegram that described his garrison's nearly exhausted supplies in Fort Sumter. The Kentucky-born West Pointer warned Lincoln of a showdown in Charleston harbor. This news, although not unexpected, made for anxious days.

The telegraph sped the news throughout the North. New York governor Edwin Morgan couched his anxiety with reassuring words to Lincoln expressing endorsement of the president's inauguration speech. "None can say, truthfully," he stated, "they do not understand its meaning." He continued, "Kind in spirit, firm in purpose, national to the highest degree, the points are well made and the call is fairly stated and most honorably met." He closed, "It cannot fail to command the confidence of the North and the respect of the South." Morgan confessed that he had tried for years to bring the government back to the principles of the Founding Fathers. The crisis in Charleston provided Lincoln and the governors the opportunity to partner in saving the Union.[4]

Morgan's gesture gratified Lincoln, but the feeling was short-lived. In the days and weeks ahead, events moved with a dizzying swiftness that forced Lincoln into a blur of cabinet meetings, conferences with Secretary of War Simon Cameron, and debates with congressional delegations over whether to supply the fort in Charleston harbor. Governors meanwhile prepared for the unavoidable conflict by arranging with bankers, merchants, and congressmen to finance armies, raise volunteers, and secure Northern borders when the hour arrived. Chief among their goals was cultivating support for the administration, and they used their influence with the president in dispensing federal patronage among their states.[5]

Anxious Days

Although a revolutionary undercurrent was bringing North and South to a great struggle, William Babcock Weeden, a Brown College graduate and soon to be officer in the Rhode Island Light Artillery, wrote that "events for the next six weeks wore the appearance of extraordinary calm upon the surface."[6] With congressmen having departed the nation's capital, it was the now "the dead season in Washington," as Charles Francis Adams described the remaining winter weeks.[7] Antebellum governance had been legislatively oriented, but preparations for armed conflict turned governors into military leaders. It allowed them the basis for framing a stronger alliance that dwarfed anything imaginable in peacetime. State executives became commanders in chief in national crises, and they harnessed the state's resources that supported the national administration. Lincoln understood the need to lean on the governors and expected cooperation from them in preserving the Union.[8]

Governors understood these expectations, but the inadequacy of their states' militias troubled them. Prior to the war, militias had fallen into serious decay, and their preparedness varied greatly among the states. Most militias were composed of undisciplined soldiers wholly unprepared for national defense. Indeed, many of their duties included maintaining public order and marching around parade grounds, but seldom, if ever, had they functioned collectively in military operations. The lack of trained officers, including those with combat experience, further weakened confidence that these units could be relied upon for any serious duty. Yet, constitutionally, these militias were the states' only defense. Indiana governor Oliver P. Morton knew his treasury was bankrupt, but it stunned him to learn that his state arsenal contained only 104 muskets of the nearly 600 to which his state was entitled. His militia existed on paper, but many of this organization's officers sympathized with the rebellion. Massachusetts governor John Andrew also worried about New England's empty state arsenals. The region's self-appointed procurement agent, he had a distinct advantage, as the regional prominence, material wealth, and political prestige of his state gave him importance. He took the lead in preparing New Englanders for war, telling the citizens they needed to "get accustomed to the smell of gunpowder." Convinced war was certain, he procured necessary supplies and even mapped out the route to Washington should his troops be called on to protect the capital.⁹

New England governors acknowledged Andrew's leadership. Maine governor Israel Washburn remarked that "wherever Massachusetts led," the commonwealth of Maine would follow—it would have to. Without sizeable reservoirs of men or resources, Maine was hard pressed to contribute substantially to a war effort. Still, the state's bustling factories, vast stretches of timber, and hardy workers and sailors compensated for this deficiency. The oldest and most prominent of six brothers, Washburn had been a founding member of the Republican Party in Maine and had spent the last ten years in Congress. He was reluctant to leave Washington to become the state's twenty-ninth governor, but Republicans were grateful to have him in Augusta. Still, with war imminent, serving as governor would be another matter altogether. It brought him into contact with Cameron, a man he loathed as "a politician of the lower law school of tactics & practices, whose disciples hold that the administration is chiefly desirable for its benefits to those who participate in it." Washburn had written Lincoln in January that "it would be difficult to make it understood how any one could be ignorant of this reputation, or doubt its essential justice."¹⁰

Connecticut's William Buckingham, Vermont's Erastus Fairbanks, and Rhode Island's William Sprague also recognized Andrew's importance, but looked for guidance from their legislatures, congressional delegations, and one another. Shrewd businessman that he was, Fairbanks enlisted the advice of Buckingham and Morgan to marshal men. Though Fairbanks was approaching seventy years of age, the dignified-looking politician had experience in running the gubernatorial office. He had done it once before in 1852–53, and understood how to manage the office—cautiously, prudently, and diplomatically. He was a staunch Congregationalist, served on many boards, and gave liberally of his personal wealth to the church. Buckingham was cut from the same cloth. Cautious by nature, the onetime farmer turned successful businessman avoided impulsive decisions. He was a "practical temperance man," whose "moral strength" played out as a teacher of Sunday school for nearly forty years. At fifty-seven years old, the short, robust, white-haired Connecticut native appeared as "a bluff-hearty English country squire," who had finally acquired aristocratic notoriety. His success in managing a dry goods store honed his business skills and earned him a profit, which he invested in the Hayward Rubber Company in Colchester. By 1858 Connecticut voters elected Buckingham governor over Gideon Welles. He won reelection in 1859 and 1860, and helped Lincoln garner the votes needed to win.[11]

As the winter days lingered, Andrew grew jittery. He enlisted Morgan to join him in offering military support to U.S. Commanding General Winfield Scott, who convinced Lincoln that supplying Fort Sumter would take months and that it was best to have Anderson withdraw. In a preemptive move, Andrew queried the commander as to how Massachusettsans could assist in upholding the laws and the integrity of the country. Scott, however, believed that such a display of forces would alarm Southerners, especially those still in the Union. Any public demonstration of mobilization, he argued, would confirm for Confederates what they wanted to believe about the newly elected administration and would work against the new president.[12]

Despite their shared market connections with Southerners, midwesterners took a decidedly opposite view, hoping that a war might finally subdue the decades-long slave power in Congress. Western governors led public opinion and urged vigorous war aims in their messages to state legislators. Iowans read about the events unfolding in the East, but none more closely than Samuel Kirkwood, Iowa's new Republican governor. The state executive had resisted convening his legislature until after Lincoln's inauguration. He warned Lincoln that pulling U.S. troops from the western forts would weaken his ability to prevent Indian depredations, and that while Iowans were willing to defend themselves, he needed arms. Kirkwood was an interesting blend of rugged Scotch-Irish physical features and a calm, inner disposition. Iowa's leading congressman Josiah Bushnell Grinnell characterized the old "Plow Handle" as someone who possessed a "temperament seeking ease rather than the theatre of adventure."[13] The governor hailed from Harford County, Maryland, but followed his father and brother to Ohio. As a young man, he took up the study and practice of law before moving to Iowa in 1855, where he settled into farming near Iowa City. The Kansas-Nebraska Act drove him into the Republican Party, and he was twice elected a state senator. James W. Grimes, the "Father of Republicanism in Iowa," groomed him for the governorship. Campaigning in his large slouch hat, farmer coat, and vest endeared him to the voters, who made him their governor in 1859. Up for reelection in the fall of 1861, Kirkwood set his sights not on his campaign, but rather on the crisis at hand. "It appears," he surmised to Grimes, "as if our Southern friends are determined on the destruction of our Government unless they can change its whole basis, and make it a government for the growth and spread of slavery."[14] He had visited Lincoln in

Springfield to learn if he could be depended upon to meet the coming difficulties. Lincoln convinced him that he would not compromise and would use all his powers to save the Union. The short conversation impressed Kirkwood so much that he recalled years later that Lincoln "was the right man in the right place, and the longer he lived the stronger that conviction grew."[15]

The inaugural feeling soon wore off, and the letters and telegrams arriving in the executive mansions pressing for action signaled a decisive change across the North. This presented difficulties for governors, who wanted to satisfy constituents calling on them to act, but who needed to take their cue from Lincoln. Preempting the president would make matters worse. Yet, governors feared the loss of time would add to the nation's unpreparedness once a war started. The "nation's sword had grown rusty and its purse empty," as Northerners and Southerners battled peacefully over slavery, tariffs, national banks, and states' rights. The "spring" of national government had been weakened but not broken, and governors stood by Lincoln in restoring federal prominence.[16]

Congress adjourned in early March, and for the next few weeks Lincoln buried himself in his executive duties. As compromise and conciliation faded, a showdown materialized in Charleston harbor. Governors informed Lincoln of their preparedness, and it buoyed his decision to provision Anderson's garrison. Newly appointed Treasury Secretary Salmon P. Chase agreed with the governors preparing for confrontation and wrote to Lincoln in these waning March days that if war was to be the consequence of an "attempt to provision Fort Sumter," then, he perceived it best to commence in consequence of military resistance to the administration's efforts to sustain federal troops stationed under governmental authority.[17]

Governors also gave Lincoln encouraging signs from the ballot box. Of all the Northern states, only the New England states held annual state elections, but not at the same time. New Hampshire voters went to the polls in March and elected Nathaniel Springer Berry, who although having been out of politics for nearly a decade, had made his antisecessionists views well known. "Natt" Berry was a veteran in state politics, having served the public for over twenty years prior to 1860. He lacked formal education and began a career as a tanner, but had entered the political arena inspired by the Jacksonian Democrats. By 1840 the Maine native was swept up in Free-Soil ideology and cut away his Democratic roots. In 1846 and in 1850 he ran unsuccessfully for governor, but by 1861 voters had come to his support. At sixty-five years old, the short, rectangular-faced governor "was a broad-minded man," wrote one observer, who was needed to steer citizens through the approaching war. Connecticut and Rhode Island held elections in early April, and voters reelected Buckingham and Sprague by large margins. Overly dramatized by the *New York Herald* as "a question of the life or the death to the Union," these elections indicated that New Englanders were mounting a counterrevolution to the Confederacy's formation. More important, Lincoln needed Berry, Buckingham, and Sprague to mobilize their states' industrial resources should war erupt.[18]

To capitalize on New England's victories, Pennsylvania governor Andrew Curtin, Washburn, Illinois governor Richard Yates, Morton, and Ohio governor William Dennison traveled to Washington to press Lincoln about Sumter. Having read the national newspapers bemoaning the lack of any national policy, these Republican governors insisted the president stand firm on his decision to supply Anderson. Fearing that Confederates would take the undefended capital, and surmising that Pennsylvanians were closest to Washington, Lincoln told Curtin to have his in-session legislature supply the state militia. "I think the necessity of being *ready* increases," wrote Lincoln on 8 April, "Look to it."[19] Curtin pressed his legislature to modify the militia laws and allow him the authority to distribute arms as he saw fit. Dennison, likewise, appreciated Lincoln's desire to maintain his course. "I pray you," he wrote "to direct all the energies of Govt. to the maintenance of all its rights *where* those rights have been assailed." "If blood must flow," he declared to Lincoln, "better for it to flow at Charleston than at Washington."[20]

Blood was about to flow. The *New York Herald* predicted the month before that if the Southern storm of secession had "*produced* a new nation, northern clouds were gathering to *save* an old one." The editor observed, "Growing blacker, and moving forward in dense masses charged with electricity," the showdown only "needs a word or a blow from one man to produce a collision and make the theory of the irrepressible conflict a fearful reality."[21] The blow came in the darkness of 12 April in Charleston Harbor, when the guns under Confederate General Pierre Gustav Toutant Beauregard's command commenced a thirty-four-hour bombardment, forcing Fort Sumter's surrender. Two days later, Anderson's humiliated garrison boarded transports and headed north, watching in the distance as jubilant Southerners hoisted the Palmetto flag above the fort. As Lincoln had told New Jersey legislators on his inaugural tour, the time had come to "put the foot down firmly."[22]

Call to Arms

For weeks, political leaders in Washington had devoted themselves to constitutional and peaceful means of compromise. Now it was Lincoln's goal to preserve the solemn oath registered in heaven to preserve, protect, and defend the government by force. Whatever "mystic chords of memory" that stretched across the North, swelling the "chorus of the Union," were sung by those states left to preserve it. The fall of Sumter inspired patriotism and, according to one observer, cast the Confederacy's formation as "a crime against Christianity, against patriotism, against humanity, against civilization, against progress, against personal and political honor."[23]

Lincoln's cabinet supported his decision to call up what the sixty-six-year-old Militia Act allowed—75,000 volunteer militiamen for ninety days. Paying them was another matter, and so was calling Congress into special session to do it, a move Lincoln feared might cause more problems. Lincoln moved swiftly but judiciously in justifying his call to arms in response to the attack on Sumter. He did so in part because he recognized that restoring the Union would require detaching some of its parts from the Confederacy. He also worried over whether governors of the slave states still in the Union would comply with his call. Nonetheless, just sixty-three days after leaving Springfield, Lincoln requested volunteers to come forth to defend the republic and its isolated and vulnerable capital. Buckingham was in Norwich at the time and wired a cable to Cameron advising that his legislature was about to convene in a few days and that he would direct them to cooperate with the president. To Lincoln he wired an equally encouraging note. Connecticut citizens "are loyal to the national union . . . they appreciate the efforts you are making to hold and possess the property of the United States," he declared, "and will be happy to render any service in their power to enable you to enforce the laws."[24] Many governors likewise assured Lincoln they would support him no matter the cost.

Southern war preparations had not surprised Buckingham. Several business acquaintances had been tracking the Southerners' demand for heavy quantities of gunpowder from Connecticut's Hazard Powder Company throughout the winter. Several friends had been securing vast amounts of raw cotton while it was in supply, while others had been selling large numbers of Colt army pistols. In January he had ordered the inspection and arming of militia units, but because the legislature controlled funding the militia, Buckingham had also to rely on citizen-inspired preparations. He secured a $50,000 personal loan to fund the regiment he pledged to the Union. To expedite the procurement of arms and payment of soldiers, the governor used his personal funds and his credit in financial circles to borrow thousands of dollars.[25]

Curtin was in Washington on patronage matters when Lincoln's call went over the wires, and he rushed to the White House to confer with the president and Scott over Washington's safety. Despite Scott's assurances to the contrary, Curtin maintained that it was a matter of time before the Confederates attempted to take the capital, and he offered five companies to assist those units forming in Washington. Sitting across from his old political adversary Cameron, Curtin held more power at the moment. Chief executive of the Union's second largest state, he was not about to be eclipsed by Cameron. Indeed, the governor would rather Lincoln pass over Pennsylvania entirely than to knight "Corruption Cameron" a cabinet minister. The son of Scot-Irish immigrants, Curtin was one of seven children. His father had been a successful iron manufacturer in Bellefonte for nearly forty years by the time Curtin was ready to attend Dickinson College, where he graduated with a law degree in 1837. That same year he entered the legal profession as a criminal lawyer and quickly earned a reputation as a gifted orator and skillful practitioner. He first entered public office serving on Governor James Pollock's staff as Secretary of the Commonwealth. A devoted Whig, Curtin was twice a presidential elector in 1848 and 1852, and his ambition led him to vie for a senatorial seat in 1854, where he ran unsuccessfully against Cameron. By 1860 he converted his Whig ideology, joined the Republican Party, and ran a successful campaign for the governorship against Democrat Henry D. Foster. His political appeal extended far beyond the courtroom and into the farms, factories, and bustling shops of Pennsylvania. Still, he never got over his loss to Cameron, whose recent cabinet appointment opened old wounds. At the moment, however, Lincoln needed Curtin more than Curtin needed Lincoln, and it gave the governor importance over Cameron.[26]

Minnesota governor Alexander Ramsey was also in Washington on patronage matters when Anderson surrendered, and, in the company of Minnesota senator Morton Wilkinson, he proceeded to Cameron's office to offer a regiment of Minnesota volunteers. There, he "found the Secretary with his hat on and papers in his hand, about to leave his office." Ramsey said, "As Governor of Minnesota," I wish to "tender a thousand men to defend the government."[27] Cameron was on his way to see Lincoln, and so he asked the governor to put his pledge in writing. Ramsey complied, but stipulated that because Minnesota's legislature was not in session, he would need the federal government to assume the burden of expenses. Cameron agreed and Ramsey wired his adjutant general to call for one infantry regiment for three months.[28]

A political veteran, the Minnesota governor knew his way around Washington. The eldest child of a Pennsylvania blacksmith, Ramsey had been orphaned at a young age, taught himself to read, and had at one time apprenticed to be a carpenter. His attendance at Lafayette College inspired him to study law, and, in 1839, he was admitted to the Pennsylvania bar. By the 1840s, his association with the Whig Party lured him to politics, and he served in the twenty-eighth and twenty-ninth Congresses, where he acquainted himself with the nation's most influential political leaders. He embraced the antislavery cause and had been among those who encouraged his Pennsylvania colleague David Wilmot to offer his legendary proviso calling for no further expansion of slavery in the territories. President Zachary Taylor appointed him Minnesota's territorial governor in 1849, and, after statehood, he joined the Republican Party. By 1860 had won the governorship.[29]

Lincoln accepted Ramsey's offer even though Minnesotans were among the North's most remotely located citizens, and the state was wholly unprepared to deliver them. The war might be over by the time they could be mustered into service and transported to Washington. No matter, Ramsey's offer bestowed on his volunteers the distinction of being Lincoln's first formally accepted unit into the new Union army. Lincoln's call for troops required only about half of the remaining Union states to send just one regiment. The lion's share of responsibility fell on New York, Pennsylvania, and Ohio. Throughout the next few days governors directed statehouse stenographers to wire the call to city officials; encouraged merchants, pastors, and shopkeepers to post patriotic notices; and enlisted scores of journalists to sound the call to arms in every hamlet. They wired federal congressmen to come home from Washington to confer over mobilizing the volunteers. Some governors were unaware of just how much executive power their constitutions allowed them in wartime, and they worried over the cost of summoning special legislative sessions. Western governors believed added sessions would burden citizens already suffering from the winter's economic hardships.

Such unsettling times spelled disaster for border state governors remaining in the Union. Virginia's secession two days after Lincoln's call for volunteers alarmed Maryland and Delaware residents, and Democrats encouraged governors Thomas Hicks and William Burton to join them. The Old Dominion's departure encouraged secessionist movements in Kentucky and Missouri, and Democrats pressed governors Beriah Magoffin and Claiborne Jackson to convene their legislatures and vote on the issue. Most state constitutions placed the power to convene the legislature in the governors' hands, but war declarations gave chief executives unprecedented power and responsibility as party leaders and militia commanders in mobilizing their states' men and resources. As much as Northerners looked to Lincoln for direction, they relied on governors to execute his war aims. This was especially important for border state governors, whose constituents pressed them to either respond to Lincoln's call or leave the Union. Even if they agreed to send troops, these Democratic governors feared their legislatures would oppose them. Thus, border state governors became the caretakers of what one journalist called "the garden of the continent," and whoever reaped the largest harvest of men and resources would prevail.[30]

The North was a giant with vast resources, but having relied over the decades on obedience to the laws to preserve order left citizens defenseless. Its national armories and arsenals were virtually empty, its regular army was scattered on frontier and seaboard stations, and state militias were untrained and unequipped. Despite this decayed military spirit, however, volunteers came forward, and national and state leaders were compelled to extract war materials from the private economy and channel them to the men. Cameron's requisition for six Indiana regiments stifled Morton's enthusiasm, who responded that he had 10,000 men in Indianapolis expecting to be mustered into service. The governor was so eager to be first in the fight that he interrupted Lew Wallace's address to a Clinton County Circuit Court jury with a telegram demanding he come to lead volunteers. Dennison boasted that Ohio would furnish the largest number of volunteers, and he walked the streets of Columbus with his adjutant general, personally delivering Lincoln's call to several of his volunteer company commanders. Yates convened his legislature and declared to his assemblymen that "the blood of twenty millions of freemen boils, with cauldron heat, to replace our national flag upon the very walls whence it was insulted and by traitor hands pulled down." Illinois residents, he boldly touted, would "wade through seas of blood before they will see a single star or a solitary stripe erased from the glorious flag of our Union."[31] The administration's firmness delighted Illinois resident Harvey Hogg, who informed Yates that he had "three thousand picked men . . . for the occasion," to go forth.[32]

Northern volunteers flocked to the ranks, but Lincoln's call, which had prompted Virginia's departure, had thrown Kentuckians and Missourians into bedlam. Missourians possessed a volatile past, and secessionists were secretly mobilizing to sever their state's Union ties. Cameron hoped to entice loyalists to support the cause before governors convened their legislatures. He tapped incoming Governor Claiborne Jackson for four regiments, but the states' rights advocate refused. To Lincoln, Jackson declared that "not one man will the State of Missouri furnish to carry on any such unholy crusade." A Kentucky native, who migrated west and who had served in the Black Hawk and Mexican wars, Jackson had also served the state in politics for the Democratic Party. He called his legislature into session, but until representatives met, he hoped to maintain neutrality.[33]

Lincoln was alarmed, though hardly surprised, by the negative dispatch he received from his native Kentucky. Having lost Virginia, and aware that Jackson was preparing to seize the St. Louis arsenal, he needed encouraging news. Aware of Beriah Magoffin's pro-Southern views, Dennison, Morton, and Yates had worked secretly to appease the Democratic governor, hoping he would use his power to keep Kentucky in the Union. Dennison had sent Thomas M. Key, a Kentucky Democrat living in Cincinnati, to confer with Magoffin. Key reported that the conversation was "satisfactory" and that the governor's policy was "friendly and prudent." Magoffin's short telegram to Lincoln, however, told a different story. "I say emphatically," he declared, "Kentucky will furnish no troops for the wicked purpose of subduing her sister Southern states."[34]

Whether or not Magoffin embraced neutrality honestly, his note to Lincoln branded him a traitor in Northern eyes. "It is evident," remarked one Iowa editor, "that Kentucky is trying to 'play possum' towards the Government and the North."[35] Kentuckian Jeremiah T. Boyle used the *Louisville Daily Journal* to goad Magoffin publicly into revealing his true course. "The final destiny of Kentucky and of the people of the State," he declared, "are more to be influenced by you in your official position than by any other citizen in it."[36] Cameron's lack of guidance in Kentucky concerned Curtin, and he dispatched Philadelphian Edward C. Biddle to Columbus to assist Dennison in negotiating with Magoffin. The Pennsylvania governor advised Dennison, Morton, and Biddle to meet and determine the best course for the Midwest. Meanwhile, Kentucky's legislature approved Magoffin's neutrality, and the governor mobilized and armed the state militia. His refusal to support Lincoln tarred him with the prosecessionist brush. "Gov.

Magoffin is not only a traitor," proclaimed an Illinois editor, "but he is also a consummate ass."[37]

Lincoln's call for volunteers further weakened the Union by driving more states, including Tennessee, into the Confederacy, but governors kept Maryland, Kentucky, and Missouri in the balance. Having served as little more than figureheads for decades, chief executives were about to change the federalist paradigm by partnering with Lincoln and exercising unprecedented power. Like Southerners, Northerners had been left alone in matters of economic, social, and political culture, and the interplay of locality and loyalty was more often driven by market relations than political devotion. Infused by the Republican Party's insistence on limiting slavery's expansion and by a belief that the Union must be preserved, governors now had the opportunity to demonstrate the constructive use of state power as well as that of an industrial economy. The call for volunteers came from Washington, but recruiting stations sprang up in local communities, and men were mustered into service through the states under the governors' supervision.

Governors endorsed Lincoln's course, but hesitated to undermine local governance in complying with national demands. The war gave rise to a political culture of negotiation among civil, military, and political leaders in deciding the division of power and authority not only within states, but also in determining state-federal relations. The national government had a wider presence in the North than in the South, and mobilizing the army created a mutually dependent relationship in which governors became political conduits between nation and state. Now the incalculable strength of more than twenty million citizens had awakened to combat the attempt to live outside the republic. "Never was there a greater delusion," boasted the editor of the *Illinois State Journal*, "than the common belief in the South that it would be impossible to rouse a sweeping war spirit in the free States."[38]

Rousing the loyal states' populace was not without notable impediments, despite popular enthusiasm. Several states were at a disadvantage in supporting the Union. Distance from Washington, the agrarian nature of their citizens, and the inadequacy of their laws to organize for war contributed to limitations. Iowa's situation, while somewhat extreme, typified the problems. Except for a few poorly armed and ill-equipped companies, the state had no military organization. The state constitution had few statutes that provided instructions about raising manpower and war materials, and no one in the capital city knew how many men comprised a regiment. Thus,

Kirkwood traveled to Davenport for the answer. The law mentioned divisions, brigades, regiments, and battalions, but none had ever existed. If they were necessary, the constitution made the governor commander of the army, navy, and militia of the state. Still, he had no troops he could command. More important, Kirkwood's lack of any military experience was typical of Northern governors. Chief executives had devoted themselves to state and local economic, educational, and political affairs; to preserving the rights of the individual in the face of government interference; and to preserving life itself. War was an altogether different proposition that centralized and redirected gubernatorial attention away from these concerns. When Lincoln's telegram reached Kirkwood, it had come over the wires at Davenport. From there state congressman William Vandever galloped on horseback with the telegram to Iowa City, where he found the governor on his farm, in his "overalls and stoga boots, looking after his stock." Kirkwood read the dispatch, looked at the legislator, and asked: "Why the President wants a *whole regiment of men!* Do you suppose, Mr. Vandever, I can raise that many?" Although the very means of how Kirkwood received the call was not typical of most governors, it revealed the realities of the nation's unpreparedness.[39]

Securing the Capital

The proximity of the nation's capital to the border between the Union and the Confederacy made it vulnerable to enemy capture, especially after Virginia's departure from the Union. Governors understood this weakness and had charted a course to land troops in Washington. More prepared for war than Kirkwood's Iowans, Andrew, Curtin, and Morgan forged ahead in preparing to defend Washington. Andrew had been actively rehearsing his part. "The sooner *we* get into working order & are under full sail," he counseled Lincoln, the more influence Republicans and the national government could exert in discouraging further secession and bringing an end to hostilities.[40]

The idea of saving Washington with Massachusetts men inspired Andrew. The day after receiving his requisition for two regiments, he had nearly 4,000 men in Boston ready to march, with hundreds pouring into the city daily. The governor practically exhausted himself in mobilizing volunteers and arranging transport and employed the services of wealthy Boston financier and confidant John Murray Forbes to procure military supplies.

Forbes was a Massachusetts railroad magnate, merchant, and radical abolitionist who had supplied New England antislavery forces in Kansas years before. He was instrumental in helping Andrew to assemble the men and send them to Washington. "As if by magic," wrote Massachusetts Adjutant General William Schouler, "the entire character of the State was changed: from a peaceful, industrious community, it became a camp of armed men; and the hum of labor gave place to the notes of fife and drum." He remarked, "It is impossible to overstate the excitement which pervaded the entire community through this eventful week."[41] One fifteen-year-old lad petitioned Andrew to allow him into the army despite his age. "I think that I am old enough to whip a Secessionist," the boy argued.[42]

Curtin also worked to put Pennsylvania troops in Washington, but it was their journey that worried him. Maryland hung in the balance during these days, and Northern soldiers would have to pass through Baltimore, a pro-Southern city with an agitated populace. On the morning of 18 April, the governor dispatched from Camp Curtin five companies numbering less than 500 men armed only with sabers. These Pennsylvanians suffered the taunts and bricks of hostile Baltimore crowds as they marched nearly two miles to exchange trains, but they made the journey safely and encamped that evening in the vacant chambers of the House of Representatives. As much as he wanted his soldiers in the nation's capital, Curtin vowed never to let another Pennsylvanian leave the state unarmed. Nonetheless, their passage and the hostile reception from residents inspired Baltimore's Mayor George Brown to wire Lincoln that if more troops were to pass through the city, they would have to "fight their way at every step," and that "the responsibility for the bloodshed will not rest upon me."[43]

No governor worried more than Hicks over the capital's security, and he had conferred with Lincoln days before the Pennsylvanians passed through his state. Lincoln assured him that Maryland volunteers were to be used only to defend the state and Washington. This was an important distinction for Hicks, especially since Democrats were pressing him to call the legislature into session to vote on secession. Hicks's belief that members would vote to sever ties with the Union convinced him to exercise his constitutional prerogative to refuse to convene legislators. He was torn between his responsibility to the national government and the pressure from Marylanders who wanted him to use those same troops against the Union. To keep the peace, he petitioned Cameron and Lincoln for weapons to arm loyal Marylanders. In the weeks since the Confederacy's formation, Hicks had endured considerable opposition to his loyal stance, including death threats. His refusal to assemble the legislature further enflamed already hostile Southern rights advocates. So overwhelmed was Hicks that he complained to Baltimore resident James L. Dorsey that it was "almost enough to perplex a saint," as "civil, military and personal duties come thick & fast, and nothing frets me more than the continued calls for letters to the present National Executive."[44]

Hicks was aware that discontented Marylanders would make it difficult for additional Union troops to pass through their state, even more so now as the Pennsylvania companies had upstaged them. The previous day, under pressure from Baltimore authorities, it appeared Hicks had buckled. He wired Lincoln an ambiguous note warning him not to send troops to assist him in keeping peace, or so Lincoln thought. What the governor meant was for Lincoln to avoid sending through Baltimore any more Northern troops bound for Washington. It was an unfortunate misunderstanding.[45]

Unaware of the trouble awaiting them in Baltimore were the men of the 6th Volunteer Infantry assembled in Boston and eager to sail for the capital. Before debarking on their journey, Andrew took a moment to acknowledge this historic occasion while presenting the soldiers with their regimental colors. "Yesterday you were citizens," Andrew declared, "to-day you are heroes," defenders of the "American Confederate Union," and while "we live that, that Union shall last."[46] Hardly had the volunteers jumped off the train in Baltimore on 19 April, when rowdies, surprised to see another, larger contingent of soldiers, began taunting them. The men made their way down the same street as the Pennsylvanians had the day before, when a politically charged mob attacked them, prompting the soldiers to fire in defense into the hostile crowd. The riot left four soldiers and twelve civilians dead, and shocked Hicks, as neither Lincoln nor Cameron had wired him of the timing of the regiment's passage. Hicks believed Lincoln had dismissed his warning about sending more troops to Baltimore. Yet, the governor had left out the critical word "through" in his message, and in reiterating his point, fired off another cable that read "send no troops *through* here." To calm the people and counter the hysteria, Hicks and Brown held a meeting later that day in Monument Square. Baltimoreans gathered to hear his call for an end to hostilities and lawlessness. "I bow in submission to the people," he declared, hoping to persuade them to return to civility and peace. "I am a Marylander, and I love my State, and I love the Union, but I will suffer my right arm to be torn from my body before I will raise it to strike a sister State."[47]

The Baltimore affair embarrassed the Lincoln administration and damaged Hicks's credibility in maintaining a neutral position, especially since he had issued a proclamation assuring his citizens that no troops would pass through Baltimore. The governor had warned Lincoln about sending troops through a besieged Baltimore, but the president refused to back down. He made it clear that the troops coming through the state were coming to do the work for the nation, and that if the rowdies in Baltimore were kept under control all would be fine. At days' end, however, Hicks grew alarmed for his citizens. He reluctantly agreed with the city's police chief that, given the civil unrest, it might be prudent to destroy the railroad bridges coming into the city to block the further passage of Union troops. Some defiant Marylanders got carried away and also cut the telegraph wires, which resulted in depriving Washington of wire service. Hicks absconded to Annapolis in the night, but not before detailing a committee to inform Lincoln of his decision.[48]

The president was emphatic in his response to the committee carrying the information about bridge destruction. Washington must be defended, Lincoln argued, Northern troops must come through Maryland. "Keep your rowdies in Baltimore," Lincoln declared, "and there will be no bloodshed." "Go home and tell your people that if they will not attack us, we will not attack them; but if they do attack us, we will return it, and that severely."[49] Like the firing on Fort Sumter, the Baltimore riot was a battle cry, this time with Northern casualties. Marylanders had attacked Massachusetts troops, and the consequences intensified the anger among not only Marylanders, but also among Northerners as they learned of the tragedy. Indeed, "a storm of indignation is sweeping over these Northern States," wrote Henry Gilmore to his father Joseph A. Gilmore, future New Hampshire governor, "and the feeling will be intensified a hundred fold when the sad news from Baltimore reaches the homes of our soldiers."[50] Northern journalists fanned the flames of retaliation. "If they kill our dog," declared the *Philadelphia Inquirer*, "it is only fair that their cat should suffer a similar fate."[51]

Andrew was working late at night when a telegraphic message confirmed that his Massachusetts soldiers had made it to Washington. The news that four soldiers had been killed while passing through Baltimore, however, stunned him. Having days before celebrated the soldiers' heroism in coming forward for the cause, he could not have imagined them falling on Maryland soil. The soldiers' deaths affected Andrew deeply and enflamed an already acrimonious New England populace, adding additional impulse to volunteering. Andrew attended to the details of returning the fallen soldiers to Boston, ensuring that they be shown great care in being preserved in ice and "tenderly sent forward by express to me."⁵² Still, he pressed on in assembling more units for Washington. He placed his war department in charge of managing Boston harbor traffic and the Springfield Arsenal. He charged former governor George S. Boutwell with designing a plan for the city's defense. Andrew knew his states' resources well and harnessed them effectively to support Lincoln. Whatever war materials his New England neighbors lacked, he loaned them, and for what Massachusetts lacked, he made arrangements to purchase from Europe. "The secret of it all," wrote Henry Gilmore to his father, "is that Gov. Andrew began his preparations for the sad alternative of civil war months ago."⁵³ Boutwell prophetically wrote to Cameron on Andrew's behalf that "the whole North is wild and determined in its enthusiasm." For he feared, "Should not the Government make another requisition, they will be needed."⁵⁴

New England governors followed Andrew's lead in depositing their soldiers in Washington. Sprague worked to place his Rhode Island regiment in Washington, called his legislature into session, urged a modernization of the state's militia laws, and authorized the state treasurer to acquire a loan of $500,000. In the meantime, he cabled fellow Rhode Islander Ambrose Burnside, already in Providence organizing the 1st Rhode Island, to take command. To ensure the men were properly equipped, supplied, and that transport was provided for their travel, Sprague drew on his personal fortune to procure these war materials. Hardly were Northern regiments better outfitted early in the war than those from Rhode Island and Massachusetts.⁵⁵

West of the Appalachians, governors concerned themselves more with being cut off from the capital than with transporting soldiers east for its safety. Saving Washington was paramount, they believed, but they needed to protect local citizens and resources from enemy depredations. Without direction from Washington because of severed communications, Yates refused to wait on War Department directives for securing rivers, arsenals, and his borders. Illinois was vulnerable to hostile invaders, and time was against them. The governor worried for his Missouri and Kentucky borders, where he understood secessionist companies to be forming. Because secessionists controlled Missouri's State Militia and police, Yates suggested that Lincoln withdraw guns from the St. Louis arsenal and halt the shipment of $200,000 about to be deposited in the subtreasury in that city. He encouraged Lincoln to consider raising a small army of about 20,000 troops to be concentrated in St. Louis or that region to keep Missouri in the Union. Yates also advised that troops be sent to Cairo, the small town on the Illinois-Kentucky border at the confluence of the Ohio and Cumberland Rivers. Cairo, he argued, was the "most important and commanding point of the West."[56] Never above expressing his candid opinions, Yates believed Cameron's usefulness in these early days came from his willingness to take advice rather than give it.

Rivers, Regions, and Responding to the Call

Dennison also worried about rivers, but not the Mississippi. Ohio River traffic caused him uneasiness, and he needed some heavy guns to defend Ohio's Gibraltar—Cincinnati. Like Morton and Yates, Dennison came under scrutiny by the state's sizable Democratic population that opposed Lincoln's actions. His public acknowledgment that Southern "fire-eaters" were to blame for the war made him the target of public recrimination. Dennison worked doggedly in the weeks following the fall of Sumter, but opponents condemned his mobilization efforts. Many critics charged that he had had enough trouble handling the governorship in peace time, and with nine months to go in his term, they expected nothing stellar in his performance. His chief assistant, Henry B. Carrington, Ohio's adjutant general, shouldered more than his share of wartime responsibilities. Worse, Dennison locked horns with Clement L. Vallandigham, the state's most outspoken loyal oppositionist. Even though he was opposed to slavery, Vallandigham was an ardent states' rights advocate who believed the national government had no authority to interfere with domestic institutions in the state. The rise of the Republican Party in Ohio, and its recent political success, gave him much to oppose.[57]

Local problems loomed larger than national ones for governors in the early weeks of the war, especially in the North's most remote states. Hostile Indians, not rivers, concerned governors west of the Mississippi, especially in Iowa and Kansas. The departure of military-age males from Iowa's small border communities alarmed citizens who believed their absence would embolden Indians to plunder their communities. In the northwestern part of the new state, Indians had harassed the citizens for years, and Kirkwood needed to safeguard the region. However, when volunteers came forward, Kirkwood was forced to decline their service for the army for lack of weapons. "Men are here with offers of their companies," he wrote one captain, "and almost quarrel with me because I can't receive them." He, nonetheless, encouraged his Iowans. "I have strong hope," he wrote Jesse Evans of Bedford, Iowa, that "Missouri will have too much sense to attack us." "Exposed as she is on three sides, to Illinois, Iowa & Kansas," he added, "a border war on her part will be madness but it is well to be prepared."[58] Meanwhile, Kirkwood moved "heaven & earth" to supply his soldiers and citizens. "If no arrangement has yet been made for arms for this state," he demanded to Cameron, "do, for God's sake, send us some."[59] To help matters along, Kirkwood gave liberally of his own funds to ensure that the soldiers had proper shoes, blankets, and food.[60]

Scarred by the frontier violence for years, Kansas Republican governor Charles Robinson shared Kirkwood's concerns, but not over hostile Indians. Robinson feared secessionist Missourians crossing over into Kansas and plundering border towns. George Deitzler, a farmer and onetime Kansas congressman, encouraged the governor to pledge publicly his loyalty to the Union to avoid suspicion. "Old Abe has decided 'to put his foot down firmly' against the Confederated government," Deitzler charged, and he "must be sustained." "Why not telegraph the President that Kansas will furnish 1000 or more troops if required," he advised Robinson, "secession flags are being raised all over Missouri," and "we must be ready for war."[61] Robinson worried that Kansans, many of whom had endured starvation from the harsh winter, would fall prey to Missouri guerrillas. He wired Cameron that Kansans were anxious to defend themselves, but they were isolated, entirely unarmed, and too poor to buy arms necessary for defense. Even if the state had the money, he argued, the arms would have to be transported through Missouri, which would be an "utter impossibility," since secessionists from that state were plotting to seize the 5,000 stand of arms stored in Fort Leavenworth, located near the Missouri border. If Cameron were willing to transfer these arms to the state of Kansas, Robinson pledged that he would be responsible to see that they be used only in local and national defense. "Without them," he warned, "we are a naked prey to any body of traitors who may choose to plunder us."[62]

Kansans were among the Union's most vulnerable loyalists, and Robinson needed to secure his home front more than defend Washington. The state had entered the Union with a bloodstained past centered upon slavery, and Robinson hoped the war to preserve the Union would settle disputes over the institution. He used his address to the legislature to proclaim his position, arguing that if it were true that slavery required the destruction of the Union, then it was time to ask if the Union's existence required slavery's destruction. To frontier Kansans and Missourians these sounded like fighting words, and they would remember them at the polls in April when deciding the state's senatorial race between Robinson and the popular but unscrupulous James H. Lane.[63]

Robinson was uniquely suited to govern Kansas through the Civil War. Born in Worcester County, Massachusetts, in 1818, he attended Amherst Academy and Berkshire Medical School. The California gold rush lured him to the West Coast in 1849, where he passed through Kansas territory. He supported California's admission into the Union as a free state, and defended squatters' rights, which eventually got him shot and jailed. While imprisoned, however, Californians elected him to the new state legislature, which forced his release. After two years, the doctor returned to Massachusetts. Inspired by the Kansas-Nebraska Act that opened the Kansas territory to slavery, Robinson led the New England Emigrant Aid Company's first colony to Kansas, hoping not only to spread free-soil ideology, but also to settle the territory by investing in and selling real estate. He arrived in Lawrence and made the city the location for his free-soil and investment headquarters. In December 1855 Robinson helped negotiate a peace settlement that ended the Wakarusa war between proslavery settlers and free-soil advocates around Lawrence. Proslavery supporters, recognized by Pierce's administration, arrested Robinson in May 1856 for his leadership in what they considered a treasonous and illegal government. He spent the next four months in confinement, safe from the brutality that became known as "Bleeding Kansas." Soon after John Brown departed the state, Robinson assumed newfound popularity, joined the Republican Party, and was elected the first state governor, taking office in 1861. "Charles Robinson assumes his official robes," remarked the *Lawrence Republican*, "with more prestige than [any] Governor ever had since the days when Isaiah sang his paean over young Hezekiah's accession.... May he be unto us all as a pillar of fire by night, and as a pillar of cloud by day."[64]

In April 1861, Robinson's decision not to convene the legislature appeared engineered to advance his political fortunes. It was no secret that he had traveled to the nation's capital the previous December to gain support from Chase, Seward, and Cameron for an appointment as Commissioner of Indian Affairs. Illinois senator Trumbull, however, understood Robinson's Machiavellian course and revealed his designs to the president. Lincoln appointed Indiana's William P. Dole for the post of Indian Commissioner, and Robinson threw himself into his executive duties. He sought to control April's senatorial election by supporting Thomas Ewing Jr. and Frederick Stanton. Yet, voters had elected James Lane and Samuel C. Pomeroy to the Senate, and Robinson had difficulty stirring support for Lincoln's call while keeping Lane from terrorizing Kansans sympathetic to slavery. The Kansas senator was, as one contemporary wrote, "hot-headed, rash, regardless of consequences, but not wanting in bravery," a man who looked and acted like the devil himself. Robinson's supporters so despised Lane that when he was elected senator, George W. Brown, editor of the *Kansas State Journal*, lowered the American flag above his building to half-mast.[65] Yet as much trouble as Lane would cause the chief executive, the war caused him more. "The day of compromises has past," Robinson wrote his wife, "thank heaven." "The struggle will be terrible," he predicted, "but the [result] will be peace & the downfall of slavery."[66]

Unlike Kirkwood and Robinson, whose states were vulnerable to border ruffians and Indian uprisings and who lacked the constitutional directives to expedite mobilization, other governors had an easier time. Older and more established, Vermont had a storied military tradition, and Fairbanks capitalized on it. The governor was at his St. Johnsbury home when Lincoln's call reached him. In the next days he called up ten militia companies, convened a special legislative session, and traveled to Montpelier to direct legislators looking for action. In the meantime, he dispatched procurement agents to Boston and Springfield. Soon military supplies were making their way to Rutland, where the troops were assembling. In pointing to tradition, Fairbanks declared that "we shall discredit our past history should we in this crisis, suffer Vermont to be behind her sister States in her patriotic sacrifices for the preservation of the Union and the Constitution."[67] Members of the General Assembly responded to Fairbanks's charge by appropriating $1 million for war expenses, and by investing in him broad powers to conduct affairs on behalf of the state to raise men and munitions.

Vermonters shared a proud military heritage that harkened back to the American Revolution, and they quickly proved to be a model in mobilizing for war. In every hamlet, citizens honored the Union, raised flags in the village squares, and encouraged a patriotic war spirit in their shops and through their hometown papers. The Town Hall in Burlington, the state's largest city, overflowed with more than a thousand citizens promoting volunteering. Vermont bankers added to the legislative appropriation by placing thousands of dollars at the governor's disposal. Students from Middlebury College and the University of Vermont formed military companies, and railroad companies offered free passage to the troops through the state. Wealthy citizens pledged private funds to equip the men, while town councils voted generous sums to assist the families left behind. George G. Benedict, president of the Vermont & Boston Telegraph Company at the time and eventual member of the 12th Vermont, recalled that "the State was in a blaze of patriotic feeling which melted all barriers of party, sect, or station." As Vermonters assumed their place in the new army, in the cap of every soldier was an evergreen sprig, the emblem worn by the Green Mountain Boys who had fought in previous wars.[68] "Vermont forever," boasted Henry Stevens to Fairbanks, "I am today prouder than ever to write G. M. B. [Green Mountain Boy] after my name, seeing the noble stand that little Vermont has taken in this great struggle."[69]

CHAPTER THREE

I Don't Believe There Is Any North

Lincoln was eager to have soldiers in Washington, and therefore the news from the statehouses encouraged him. Governors labored long hours scurrying, cajoling, and assembling the parts to produce a war engine, and their spirited dispatches indicated a Northern rousing. State capitals became bustling military hubs, and executive chambers became command stations. Assured for days by the state executives that soldiers would be forthcoming, Lincoln could hardly stand the wait. He grew anxious when he learned on 21 April that Marylanders had cut the telegraph wires north of Baltimore, thus severing Washington communications. The silence paralyzed the administration.[1]

For decades the national government had wrestled with the physical and political expansion of the United States. Consequently, much of the nation's federal history in this period had been one of conflict and compromise. The onset of war, however, brought federal governance into a cooperative phase in which nation and state would need to craft a partnership to mobilize and sustain efforts to achieve military success. Lincoln needed reassurance quickly, but the work of preserving the Union rested with glory-seeking volunteers who offered their service to the state militias. Many volunteers thought of themselves as the Union's representative parts, even if they shared different views on what precisely the Union meant. The circumstances that compelled them to fight for cause and country would take on greater significance as war endured. Still, it remained to be seen how the national government's call to arms would materialize. New York governor Edwin Morgan shared Lincoln's concern and allowed to Secretary of War Simon Cameron that he too was "painfully anxious to get news."[2] "There is a painful solicitation felt in every mind," he observed to Lincoln. "The People of the State of New York and of the entire North are deeply moved by events of the last eight days," he confirmed, "and will not easily be led from their belief that an active and a most vigorous war should be immediately made upon those who have deliberately undertaken to destroy the National Govt. For one, I can now perceive no course for the country but to rise as one man to crush out the treason."[3]

Morgan's communications went unread for nearly a week, but the maddening circumstance did not slacken his preparations. He secured $3 million from his legislature, disbursed agents to procure war materials, and secured funds from New York City's wealthiest financiers. The governor accepted more than his 30,000-volunteer quota, thinking he would need them. He did this for two reasons: financially he could afford them and politically he could not turn them away. In the silence of those days, Lincoln took "extralegal" measures to get the troops to the nation's capital by placing $2 million at Morgan's disposal. The governor tapped his cousin George D. Morgan to oversee the purchase of supplies and sent to Europe and Canada for arms. He also enlisted New York native Major General John E. Wool's services in procuring and distributing arms and supplies to Northern governors requesting assistance. Almost overnight, New York City became the Union's quartermaster depot as agents from several states scavenged for war materials. "It is impossible to describe the excited state of the people of the North," observed Wool, "New York City is ready to furnish 50,000 men for the defense of the Union and its preservation."[4]

Without cables from the administration the days seemed endless. "No intelligence from Washington," as one citizen described to Pennsylvania governor Curtin, meant "the suspense is awful!"[5] The call for volunteers and the wait for men unnerved the administration. Sent on Massachusetts governor Andrew's behalf, former governor George Boutwell picked up on the dispiritedness when he arrived in the capital city. "You may easily understand," he wired Andrew, that "the mighty public sentiment of the free States is not fully appreciated here."[6] The crisis's magnitude had not yet been equaled by the Northern reaction, and Washington's hollowness told the story of the Union's unpreparedness. So discouraged was Lincoln that he remarked in the presence of his private secretary, John Hay, "Why don't they come! Why don't they come!"[7]

Governors Respond

Lincoln understood that the Northern army would take shape one company at a time, but he could only imagine how hostility toward secession would materialize. Northerners had few deeply rooted distinguishing features that defined them beyond their opposition to slavery's expansion. Not until the mid-1850s when the Republican Party emerged over the Kansas crisis did Northerners share a singularly defining conviction. Out of the free-soil attitude of the 1840s that promoted pursing wealth freely came an increasing conviction among Northerners to contain slavery. The expansion west that produced the Compromise of 1850 set the republic on a collision course over whether or not slavery should carry into those new territories. When he was a congressman, Maine governor Israel Washburn predicted that the 1854 Kansas-Nebraska Bill, which permitted slavery's expansion, would produce a "North," and it did. Although few Northerners shared pro-black sentiments, the governor was confident the Northern populace's martial spirit would flow forth to crush the Confederacy. Raising a volunteer army represented the most striking expression of that sentiment.[8]

In these early weeks a Northern leviathan emerged. Its embryonic form began with volunteers, who enlisted in towns such as Bangor, Maine. Retired police officer Captain Levi Emerson drummed up loggers and policemen, and pledged the company's loyalty to the cause. Such volunteering snowballed into something more substantial than anyone imagined. The response of the states "proves that the nation was not dead, but sleeping," wrote John Hay. "The Governor of Rhode Island," he acknowledged, "elected by Democratic votes, clothed with the mortal power of his position and the material power of five millions of inherited wealth, whose villages dot the Mosahssuck river for miles, who pays his servants salaries that would buy Florida, telegraphs to the War Department, that a regiment is ready at once, and that he will leave his spinning-wheels and lead them to the field in person."[9]

The Northern uprising, noted one Rhode Islander, instilled in citizens a sense of purpose, a "belief in the indissoluble substance of the Union," and a belief in the necessity of "sacrificing life and property."[10] A conviction arose that Northerners would have to accomplish in war what they had failed to procure through peace. What was at stake was the survival of popular self-government that guaranteed and perpetuated individual freedoms, and a belief that the federal Union worked. The outpouring of support for these ideals was unprecedented. The *Wisconsin State Journal* acknowledged this sentiment, declaring that the Northern populaces' loyalty was thoroughly aroused, and the president should have called one hundred thousand more men. "The excitement is at fever heat," claimed the editor, "and the trouble is not to find recruits, but to decide who shall be compelled to remain at home."[11] Andrew rejoiced to Foxboro, Massachusetts, resident Francis Wright that it was time to awaken the giant of Northern patriotism. "Inspire your brothers, your fathers, your husbands with a spirit of self-sacrifice," he declared, "cheer the firesides of the families of those who have marched to war. Let there be no family circle in which a place is vacant, that shall want your sympathy and not receive it."[12]

The isolation from Washington following Lincoln's call did not paralyze governors. Connecticut governor William Buckingham was in Norwich when he learned the capital had been cut off. Fearing Confederates would attack the city, he dispatched his son-in-law, William A. Aiken, to the War Department with a note pledging Connecticut's support. Aiken arrived in Washington at night on 24 April and made his way to Scott's headquarters to hand "Old Fuss and Feathers" Buckingham's letter. The weather-beaten commander opened the letter, gazed at it, and then sprung from his chair. "Sir, you are the first man I have seen with a written dispatch for three days," he declared. "I have sent men out every day to get intelligence of the northern troops," yet "not one of them has returned." Then, glaring at Aiken, he asked "where are the troops?"[13] The following morning, Aiken rode to the White House and met with Lincoln. He found him seated near an open window peering through a large telescope across the river at Arlington Heights. Aiken approached him and presented the governor's letter expressing Connecticut's military support. Although Lincoln greeted him cordially, Aiken recalled the president "seemed depressed beyond measure," questioning "slowly and with a measured emphasis, 'What *is* the North about? *Do* they know our condition?'" "No," answered Aiken, "they certainly did not know when I left."[14]

Southerners knew what the war was about, and the bloodshed on Maryland soil prompted at least one native to attach meaning to their revolution. The Baltimore riot had inspired James Ryder Randall, a young Louisiana professor whose family resided in Baltimore, to compose some patriotic stanzas to memorialize his native state. Randall had followed the events of recent weeks in the New Orleans newspapers and saw that one of his closest friends and college roommates had been killed in the riot. Angered by the death, Randall composed a poem entitled "Maryland, My Maryland" and allowed it to be published in the local press. Within a few days, Baltimore's Southern press picked up the poem and celebrated its stanzas. Locals eventually set the lines to the music of the German Christmas carol "Tannenbaum, O Tannenbaum." Within weeks, Marylanders sympathetic to the Confederacy were singing "Maryland, My Maryland," which became an ominous overture for their governor, who was hoping to subdue them. Given the bloody affair in Baltimore and Maryland's association with slavery, many Northerners approved the designs to subdue the traitors. Ohioan J. Henry

Jordan, for example, shared with Curtin his views about the current state of affairs in Maryland. "The only way *Md.* Can be *kept* in the Union," he declared, "is by *Military force.*"¹⁵

Maryland, My Maryland

Northerners voiced outrage over the Baltimore riot, but none more than Benjamin F. Butler, a crass, self-absorbed political general, who had practiced law in Massachusetts and served in the state congress. Butler served as brigadier general of the Massachusetts militia just before the war, and his military rank and arrogance made him appear more important than he was. His least endearing quality at the time was the fact that he had been the Breckinridge Democrat candidate against Andrew in the recent gubernatorial election. Hicks's loyalty aside, it was unclear whether Maryland would remain in the Union, and Andrew needed to ensure safe passage for the rest of his Massachusetts boys. Cameron's dilatoriness so frustrated him that he appointed a commission to press his concerns on Lincoln, and he dispatched eminent Boston physician Dr. Samuel Gridley Howe to accompany Butler and survey the sanitary conditions of the Massachusetts camps. Butler won Lincoln's approval to eliminate the bottleneck troop passage at Baltimore and seized Maryland's capital city Annapolis on 25 April. From there he would transport Northern troops by rail to Washington and sidestep future Baltimore hysteria. Before landing his troops, however, Butler met privately with Hicks to discuss occupation terms for the capital city. Hicks reported that slaves and free blacks were intending to revolt in Annapolis and that residents were fleeing their homes. Butler allayed Hicks's fear that Northern forces would interfere with the laws of the state, but indicated that some retribution from military occupation could be expected. It would take days, but soon volunteers poured into Annapolis and into the nation's capital.¹⁶

Soon the stream of Northern volunteers materialized in Washington. Men from every walk of life, eager to enlist, received their regimental flags and now camped north of the Potomac River, in the House Chambers, and around the Washington Monument. In sending off the boys of the 1st Vermont Regiment, Governor Erastus Fairbanks took great pride in presenting the colors to Colonel John W. Phelps, a tall, strapping Vermonter and West Point graduate. "In your hands, supported by these troops," he challenged Phelps, "I feel this flag will never be dishonored, nor the State of Vermont disgraced." Pointing to the single star on the Vermont state flag, the governor handed him the national flag and added, "I charge you to remember that this flag represents but one star in that other flag, which I now present, bearing the national emblem, the stars and stripped [sic]."[17] Colonel Phelps accepted the flags and remarked that his men would defend the Constitution and the laws of the Union, in ways that would "meet the approval of the freemen in Vermont."[18] That day, noted the editor of the *Burlington Daily Free Press*, Vermont and the Union were one, and while Vermont was only a small state, "she has a name to be proud of in the history of her country," which "reaches back to the very birth of her existence."[19]

Significance of effort rather than state size bespoke the consolidation of volunteers into a national army. Before long, there were more troops in Washington than Lincoln could count, wrote John Ward of New York's 12th. So crowded were the streets and shops that one correspondent noted that residents needed a "password and countersigns now to cross its porch, and to gain admittance." Such a vast troop assemblage, however, caused debate among cabinet authorities and high-ranking commanders over whether to allow these regiments to retain their state identities or to accept new national designations. Governors favored state designations and pressed the War Department to allow regiments to carry state flags. If not handled judiciously, such decisions might give the impression that the national government had centralized too much too soon. It was Treasury Secretary Chase who spearheaded the idea of allowing regiments to retain state flags, arguing that he "would rather have no regiments raised in Ohio than that they should not be known as Ohio regiments."[20]

The response to Lincoln's call formed what Andrew described as an "American Confederate Union," and soon the army began to materialize as Lincoln hoped. Some governors either accompanied the men or followed days behind. Buckingham was among those chief executives whose close association with the soldiers early on earned him favor among his constituents at home and in the press. Referring to Connecticut's famed Revolutionary governor, Jonathan Trumbull, a *Hartford Evening Press* correspondent observed that "the spirit of Trumbull lives on in our Chief Magistrate [Buckingham]."[21] Like many governors, Buckingham had previously found himself hamstrung by constitutional limitations, jealous legislators, and a spirited but reckless press.[22]

Northern legislatures quickly came to appreciate that war allowed governors expansive powers to coincide with their new responsibilities. The arrival of regiments in Washington was the result of governors exercising cooperative mobilization in reaching across state lines to support the cause. The emerging ties between soldiers and governors established a personal kinship between citizen and political leader. Soon Washingtonians came to know the names of the loyal governors through their identification with various camps—"Camp Andrew," "Camp Morgan," and "Camp Sprague"— that dotted the city's landscape. However decentralized the federal system was in previous decades, the presence of state volunteers in the nation's capital was emblematic of an emerging state-driven national culture. Indeed, soldiers found themselves called by co-existing loyalties to nation and state that were drawn together in the Union to hold in place the experiment of self-government. It was neither an abolitionist's war, nor a Republican's war, but rather the patriot's war, whose chief goal was, in the words of Walt Whitman, "to stick together."[23] It was not a question of being an Ohioan or an American—people could be both, though one or the other loyalty might, at different times, be more important. Naturally, these loyalties would ebb and flow with the war's military, political, and social circumstances.

Marylanders were especially alarmed. Union control of the state was vital for Lincoln's limited war goals. Military occupation had political and strategic implications, and although Butler's occupation of Annapolis relieved Hicks, he recognized that the war's civil and political nature would require negotiations beyond his control. He cautioned Marylanders who opposed him to consider their allegiances, and Butler's arrival aided him. Far more serious for Hicks, however, was Maryland's role in determining how other border states might act. He was opposed to Maryland being an instrument for coercing his sister slave states to remain in the Union, yet he was no longer in a position of influence with them. In the end, the governor "deemed it best to bend a little to the storm," and called the legislature into session on 26 April.[24] Delegates assembled at Frederick, forty miles west of Baltimore, and voted against secession. Lincoln appreciated the governor's delay in convening the general assembly, despite death threats and rebukes against the chief executive. Hicks was firmly loyal and understood that whatever power he had as governor highlighted the degree to which he would have to bend in favor of the Union without breaking local governance.[25]

Civil war had come to Maryland, and Hicks walked a narrow line in steering his citizens through the war's early months. The Union army's presence in Maryland caused apprehension among slave owners, and Butler assured Hicks that his command would not interfere with the state laws. Within the next several weeks, however, Virginians crossed into Maryland

and seized cattle, grain, and canal boats, and threatened residents. Hicks complained to Virginia governor John Letcher that these unprovoked hostilities would incite bloodshed along the border towns, and he demanded that he subdue them. He also protested to Butler that the presence of black servants accompanying his army violated Maryland state law. "You can readily see that their presence here will be provocative of disorder and ill feeling," wrote Hicks, and, "I am sure you desire nothing of the kind. And I must urge you to send them back, and to permit no more to come here."[26] Maryland provided Lincoln's administration with valuable experience not only in handling border state loyalties, but also in establishing military occupation of Southern slave soil. Union occupation zones became a lure for free blacks and a menace to slave holders, and Hicks would have his hands full with prickly domestic issues. "The mere presence of these negroes in our state," Hicks warned Butler, "is a violation of our statutes ... and the General government ought not tolerate a violation of our laws by permitting them to accompany its troops."[27]

Governors across the North confronted an array of problems associated with mobilization. Supervising the volunteers pouring into capital cities as well as searching for competent officers was chief among them. Cameron neglected to compensate for the surplus of volunteers who arrived in state capitals, and governors pressed Cameron to accept additional regiments, or they would be forced to turn thousands away. Northerners were eager to fight for the cause. Washburn wrote to Vice-President Hamlin, "the ardor is irrepressible." The governor urged his Maine colleague to influence Lincoln and Cameron to accept more regiments. Hamlin acknowledged that the "whole country was wild with excitement," but he urged Washburn to make certain that the soldiers be "well uniformed and equipt [sic]," before they departed Maine.[28]

Several governors had problems turning volunteers away. One Iowa company threatened to mob their "great, good Governor Kirkwood," unless he accepted them on the spot.[29] As a compromise, he decided to arm Iowans to protect their communities against invasion. Similarly, Governor Charles Olden carped that New Jersey was miserably deficient in military preparations, and he hoped to convince Cameron to allow him additional men to protect the coast. "The spirit and enthusiasm of our people are excited to the highest pitch," he warned, "and the consequences here of disbanding these men would be extremely injurious."[30] Governor Richard Yates of Illinois wired Cameron that turning away volunteers would demoralize the national spirit. Andrew agreed and requested he be allowed to muster in the "Irish, Germans, and other tough men." William Dennison of Ohio apologized for being unable to repress the "ardor of the people," admitting that he could hardly stop short of twenty regiments. In the same vein, he boasted that the display of patriotism might serve as a useful message to Southerners that Northerners were just as eager to fight for the Union as Southerners were to rally to the Confederacy.[31]

Governors believed that accepting surplus regiments would enlarge the army and frighten Southerners into thinking that they had indeed awakened a Northern giant. They had no way of knowing how many citizens would respond to Lincoln's call. Notices blanketed nearly every city corner and every town. Communication interruptions with Washington in the week after the call caused governors to accept all the arriving volunteers, especially since many of them had traveled great distances and had endured significant hardships to enlist. Dennison used his state's divided political population and close proximity to the Southern states as an excuse for assuming extraordinary responsibilities in the absence of any directives. Several governors solved surplus dilemmas by securing funds from their legislatures to keep men in reserve units. It was a move that, while costly, proved to be politically and militarily astute. The call to arms generated a remarkable force of participatory citizenry, and governors refused to stifle the patriotism. Politics aside, Indiana's Morton accepted most of the 10,000 men he had in camps in Indianapolis based on the need for local defense along the Ohio River. He convened the legislature and declared that "upon the preservation of this government depends our prosperity and greatness as a nation, our liberty and happiness as individuals."[32]

Mobilization pulled Northerners away from their local communities and into national affairs. Governors of states skirting the Confederacy had a twofold obligation: sending troops to Lincoln and protecting border communities. Morton wanted to cooperate with Magoffin in protecting river towns, but he privately despised the Kentucky governor, offering to "furnish the rope to hang him."[33] Kentuckian William Nelson, a hard-bitten army commander, was in Louisville at the time and remarked to officer John B. S. Todd that "the people have absolutely gone mad" in Kentucky. "Gov. Magoffin is here doing all he can to encourage secession, damn him," he remarked.[34] These sentiments did little to counter the preconceived opinions that Magoffin supported the Confederacy and was stalling until he could gather enough arms to secede. Cameron tried to manage Kentucky affairs, but the demands of procuring and distributing arms overwhelmed him. Disparity existed between Washington and the state capitals, and the interruption of the mail and telegraph compounded the problems in these early weeks. Morton worked to stall Kentucky's departure from the Union, but Cameron responded that Indiana had exceeded its quota of men and weapons. The Indiana chief executive fired off a communiqué, placed it in the hands of John D. Howland, and instructed him to deliver it to Cameron. Indiana would "expend her best blood and treasure without limit for the successful prosecution of this war," Morton declared, and all he asked in return was that the state "be provided for by the General Government to the extent of its capacity."[35]

Like Kentucky, the slave state of Delaware remained in the Union, but its citizens were deeply divided, and its governor's loyalties were suspect. Democrat William Burton had no state militia through which he could accept and offer volunteers to Lincoln, and the state constitution lacked provisions to establish one. James A. Bayard and William G. Whiteley, Delaware senators with Southern sympathies, advised him to ignore Lincoln's call. They petitioned him to convene the legislature to determine the state's loyalties or to at least present a peaceable solution to the conflict. Volunteer companies had formed in the state, and Burton had commissioned their officers, but he had no power to order them into service. He made West Point graduate and Wilmington businessman Henry Du Pont a brigadier general to command the states' forces, and ordered the new commander to disarm the local militias in Delaware's southern counties. Given the Southern proclivities of some of the state's prominent businessmen, Du Pont's appointment encouraged Lincoln. Still, the editor of the *Newark Daily Mercury* declared that the "Union men in Delaware," including the governor, "were in a bad fix."[36] "We are betwixt as it were," wrote one Delawarean to the *New York Times*, "two raging seas, and the wave of National troubles tosses us like an empty bark upon the billows."[37] Burton struggled to raise his quota of 2,000 Delawareans and drew on Pennsylvanians and Marylanders to fill the ranks, despite Curtin's and Hicks's protests. Because Burton had not responded to Lincoln's call, Cameron authorized Brigadier General Robert Patterson to enlist these troops. To save money, Burton refused to call a special legislative session, and thus had little financial incentive to entice men to the ranks.[38]

A physician-turned-politician and a devout Episcopalian, the seventy-two-year-old Burton was elected governor in 1858. He walked with a cane, and he looked weak and sickly. The diminutive governor, however, had served in the state militia, and at one point was the sheriff of tumultuous Kent County. In 1848 his sympathy for Southern rights pulled him to the Democratic Party. In 1854 he ran unsuccessfully for the gubernatorial seat against American Party candidate Peter F. Causey. Recently elected by just 204 votes, Burton feared the complexity of governing Delaware's politically divided constituents. As governor of a slave state with less than 2,000 slaves, Burton's party clung to the states' rights doctrine. He sympathized with secessionists and considered a special convention to determine the state's course. Georgia's representatives invited him to join the Confederacy. Burton, however, agreed with his legislators, who responded that "as Delaware was the first to adopt, so will she be the last to abandon the Federal Constitution."[39] Still, in some localities, such as Sussex County, Delawareans met to emphasize that, while they clung to the Union, they denounced abolition. Republican editor and prominent German-American Henry Eckel observed to Lincoln that Delawareans were "peculiarly Situated here."[40] Indeed, the DuPont Company, located in Wilmington on Brandywine Creek, was the nation's chief supplier of gunpowder to the U.S. military.[41]

Burton and his legislators understood that while many residents possessed Southern social and political sympathies, the economic and constitutional ties to the Union would steer their loyalties in wartime. The governor's own daughter, Rhoda Wootten, for example, articulated this sentiment in a letter to her mother. "While we love the South and appreciate the gross injustice that she has suffered," she maintained, "we still prefer the Union, *as it is* to the Reign of Anarchy and ruin that must follow this bloody contest."[42] Had Maryland seceded, however, Burton might have buckled under the pressure, and Republicans worried that he might stockpile weapons and distribute them among his supporters. Delaware's free-soil sentiment and proximity to Philadelphia did not deter Burton from remaining a Democrat, and that worried Lincoln. To add to these fears were rumors the governor had encouraged legislators to hold a convention to consider the propriety of a secession ordinance. True or not, Eckel informed Lincoln that Delaware could be made Republican by the proper management of political appointments, which he argued, would "prove that we are classed with the North."[43] Although loyal Delawareans pressed Burton to convene the general assembly so they could pledge Union support, Seaford resident William Ross advised Burton against committing Delaware to support the "Black Republican war policy." "Kentucky has taken a noble stand," he fumed, "let Delaware profit by her example, I would die a thousand deaths rather than make war upon our brethren in Virginia."⁴⁴ The excitement and suspense surrounding Delaware's fate was insufferable for Wilmington native Anna M. Ferris, who penned in her diary that "the feeling of shame, indignation, & dread," was "indescribable," in these early weeks.⁴⁵

Despite the problems of volunteer surpluses and the uncertain direction of border state governors, most state executives ran their states with skill and direction in these early weeks of mobilization. Working without federal congressmen, and with little direction from Cameron, their efforts encouraged Lincoln that the partnership between nation and state was establishing a national existence. This partnership also pulled political and military leaders together to summon war resources. Governor Morgan and Major General Wool proved to be organizational models in accumulating and distributing New York's vast military resources, including supplying requisitions to other governors. Morgan worked the banks for funds, while Wool pressed mobilization forward and supervised the distribution of munitions to the states. Andrew obtained Cameron's approval to double production at the Springfield arsenal, while Yates secured authorization to seize the St. Louis arsenal. Across the vast stretches of the North, governors were giving shape to the Union war effort in ways that pulled them into the national scene.⁴⁶

There Is a North

Even if Washington appeared a "capital without a country," the beacon of Northern hopes shone brighter by late April, as the soldiers began to arrive. In weeks, governors pulled together an administrative structure that produced a national military coalition that displayed the Union's sovereignty, and yet reflected local pride. "I am happy," Andrew reassured Cameron, "that I find the amplest proof of warm devotion to the Country's Cause on every hand to day."⁴⁷ A powerful Republican Party had risen in recent years, and now the army of that party was beginning to materialize. Indeed, Washington was "rapidly becoming a northern city," wrote a Connecticut correspondent.⁴⁸ In spectacular fashion, the 7th New York and the 8th Massachusetts arrived, followed by two colorful Rhode Island regiments marching behind the youthful Governor Sprague on horseback. John Hay remarked that Sprague, obviously "very proud" of his family's "wealth and social standing," was, even in a uniform, still "a small insignificant youth who bought his place."⁴⁹

Soldiers arriving in Washington restored Lincoln's faith that there was a North. "The President and cabinet are gaining confidence," wrote a reassured Boutwell to Andrew.[50] A correspondent to the *Hartford Evening Press* commented on the troops' arrival and the confidence of the locals, arguing that these were "decidedly the finest body of men I have ever seen together—robust and hearty, all of them, with 'do or die' countenances."[51] Washingtonians took comfort in seeing thousands of soldiers hovering around campfires that lit up the night sky over Capitol Hill. During the day, soldiers drilling and marching in an array of bright and ornamental regimental colors gave the city a majestic appearance. "The Federal Capital at the present moment," wrote William O. Stoddard, Lincoln's third secretary, "offers a strange anomaly of an American city crowded with soldiers." "It is indeed a strange picture," he observed, "we are yet in the land which has, for half a century, been preeminently the 'land of peace,' and nevertheless two regiments, the *elite* of New-York and Massachusetts, occupy our beautiful Capitol, another watches over the safety of the General Post Office, Sprague's Rhode Islanders throng the echoing corridors of the Patent Office, and over twelve hundred 'Bay men' look out from behind the stately granite columns of the Treasury."[52] Jim Lane offered the services of his small sixty-man Frontier Guard to protect Lincoln, and for nearly a month this Kansas quasi-military force lodged his unit in the White House. One day, when John Hay entered the room, he noticed the Kansan peering through the glass and caught him remarking under his breath, "we have to whip these scoundrels like hell. They did a good thing stoning our men at Baltimore and shooting away the flag at Sumter." "It has set the great North howling for blood," he fumed, "and they'll have it."[53]

As a city that had witnessed federalism's shared governance, much of its political history had been a saga of conflict and compromise. The war, however, turned the political weathervane toward cooperation between nation and state. Washington became one grand military community, and Northerners urged national officials to keep the road to the capital clear. "For God's sake and our country's," wrote New York lawyer and West Point graduate John H. Martindale to Montgomery Blair, Lincoln's Postmaster General, "let us take hold of the military spirit of our people and direct it aright now, when we can."[54] Blair understood this military spirit, but, without volunteers, Washington was helpless to manufacture it. This placed the burden of responsibility on the governors, who helped construct a state-driven national army. "I am satisfied," he encouraged a frustrated Andrew, "that the people after all, will take care of the Government, and that we must look to them to do it, and I wish you to understand the truth in order that you may see that the responsibility rests upon your own people and that you must make at home, the necessary preparation and organization to carry on this war successfully."[55] Andrew echoed this sentiment, urging Blair to encourage Cameron and Lincoln to accept more men. "We are enlisted for the War," he wrote.[56]

May was a month of howling, confusion, and delay. Cameron recognized that the national government was unprepared to enlist thousands of soldiers, yet his primary focus was to protect the capital and raise and equip a national army to fight in Virginia. Thus, he relied on governors to mobilize, outfit, and transport their regiments, while he struggled to supply them once they arrived in Washington. After visiting Washington, John Tucker, Curtin's aide, alluded to the distress among Pennsylvanians enduring hardships in Washington. Listening to the complaints about the suffering and almost starvation, Tucker urged Cameron to remedy these problems before the conditions demoralized the men. Coordination for feeding the soldiers was so deficient, he complained, that Ohio troops coming through Philadelphia were forced to beg for food on the streets. "Unless there is some more regard for our patriotic soldiers," he argued, "I fear our great movement will be demoralized."[57]

The response to Lincoln's call far exceeded the government's ability to provide for the volunteers that came forward. The lack of adequate food, pay, and supplies forced Cameron to refuse to accept more than the prescribed regimental quotas. Yet, the steady stream coming forth complicated mobilization. Many governors reasoned that turning away soldiers carried greater political implications back home than accepting them without provisions. Governor Olden dispatched Colonel John G. Stevens to relate personally to Cameron the problems that persisted in maintaining the proper public sentiment in New Jersey. Like Cameron, governors operated in a makeshift atmosphere to accommodate the national mobilization, and they shared Olden's problems of having to collect taxes and borrow and spend money at immense levels. Olden was tenacious and displayed bipartisanship in mobilizing. Within days he raised $500,000 and pulled resources together to equip and transport the Jersey Blues, clad in their dark blue frock coats, to the front. He also petitioned the legislature to provide for the families the soldiers left behind.[58]

The North was a giant in size and resources, but harnessing these strengths remained in bureaucratic hands, some of which were unsuited to the task. Cameron stood within this group: administrative competence, strategic foresight, and tactful diplomacy were not among the secretary's strong suits. His weaknesses forced governors to compensate for the War Department's deficiencies. This was especially true for governors beyond the Appalachians, who urged Cameron to appoint military commanders knowledgeable of these states and their terrains. After all, governors bore the brunt of disaffected constituencies, and those chief executives up for re-election could not afford the political fallout emanating from mismanagement. Kirkwood spoke for border state governors when he professed to his legislature that he had two principle objects constantly in view, "the protection of our State against invasion and the prompt supply to the General Government of any further aid it may require." These objectives were difficult enough, but he also surmised that turning men away from the ranks would weaken Republicans in the state elections.[59]

In the absence of sound administrative directives, Dennison, Morton, and Yates shared the lead in establishing an organizational framework for working in concert to protect midwesterners. Not only were geography and rivers a vital concern for governors, but lack of financial resources, constitutional limitations, sizeable disloyal populations, and proximity to slave states also presented them with difficulties. Dennison's secretary Coggeshall worked closely with Dennison in these days, and noted the governor's cooperative efforts to relieve western Virginians. "His Conviction is Clear," remarked Coggeshall, "in plain defiance of public Misrepresentation, that just now he is *the* man to be Gov. of Ohio. His Confidence is firm that among the people his honor is undoubted."[60] When Virginia seceded, western Virginians maneuvered to pull themselves out of the Confederacy. Dennison encouraged separation from their Tidewater brethren, especially since Jackson and Magoffin had rejected Lincoln's call. Unionists in these border states feared for their safety. Worse, Cincinnati, one of the state's largest and wealthiest cities, was under the rule of a secessionist mayor, George Hatch. With a population of more than 160,000, Cincinnati might be good for 10,000 loyal volunteers, but Dennison feared losing the city if he sent them to Washington. "The lion in us is thoroughly roused," he told Cameron, pressing him to accept the twenty regiments he assembled for Ohio's defense. Cameron rejected the governor's rationale, but Dennison obtained legislative support, and retained several of the regiments for local defense.[61]

The Ties that Bind Kentucky

Although they maintained differing political views on slavery, residents of Ohio, Illinois, Indiana, western Virginia, and Kentucky shared an economic and cultural connection as the Ohio River joined them in a socioeconomic border state heartland west of the Appalachian Mountains. Residents— North and South—owed their livelihood to the rivers that carried market goods downstream, emptying into the Ohio River. The war threatened the economic bonds that had tied them together for decades, and steamers carrying soldiers now patrolled what was once an economic highway. In late April the residents of Kentucky's Carroll and Trimble Counties crossed the Ohio and met with Indianans from Madison and pledged mutual defense of the region in favor of the Union. Dennison, Morton, and Yates worked to protect river traffic, suggesting to Lincoln that trade be cut off with states rejecting his call. At one point, Morton wired Yates to stop a flat boat bound for Vicksburg, Mississippi, carrying bacon for Southern troops at Cairo, Illinois.[62]

Governors used regional connections to solve wartime crises. Morton remarked in his legislative address that heartland citizens were bound by the "dearest ties of blood and institutions," and that the citizens of the seceding states were "our brothers and fellow-countrymen."[63] Yates echoed these sentiments. "We draw the sword then, not in a spirit of indignation and revenge," he proclaimed to his assemblymen, "but clearly and unmistakably in self-defense, and in the protection of our own rights, our liberty, and security for our property."[64] "It is said," he declared, that "'when Greek meets Greek, then comes the tug of war.' ... When American shall meet American—when the fiery impetuous valor of the South shall come in contact with the cool determined bravery of the North," he boasted, "then blood shall flow to the horses' bridles."[65] Chicagoan John Wentworth agreed, writing to the governor that "tens of thousands of men here ... are *burning with impatient anxiety to punish the black hearted traitors* who have so grossly & causedly insulted our country & its glorious flag."[66] Fortunately for Yates, these inspiring impulses moved Springfield and Chicago bankers as well as legislators to advance him funds to defray war expenses until Treasury Secretary Chase could settle up.[67]

Kentucky's governor had not drawn the sword, but his stance of neutrality did not sit well north of the Ohio River. To maintain loyal ties, Dennison,

Morton, and Magoffin agreed to meet 30 April at Cincinnati's Spencer House and mediate a peace. Days prior to the meeting, the *Louisville Daily Journal* published a report that revealed Magoffin's intentions to supply troops to the Confederate war effort. This report, combined with his last minute decision to send Colonel Thomas P. Crittenden to the meeting in his place, appeared to confirm Magoffin's Confederate sympathies. His failure to attend the meeting forecast an ominous Kentucky future. Dennison feared events might be moving ahead of him, and he invited several governors to a conference in Cleveland to prepare for Kentucky's presumed secession. On 3 May, Dennison, Morton, Curtin, Randall, and Blair met with the personal agents of Morgan and Yates. Dennison also invited George B. McClellan, who had just the week before accepted command of his Ohio troops. McClellan sketched out to Dennison, General Scott, and Cameron his plans for the entire western front. He emphasized the importance of arming the western states, and had sent Pinkerton agents and staff members into Kentucky and western Virginia to gather intelligence. His reports justified their fears. Dennison provided intercepted dispatches as evidence that Magoffin was shipping weapons south. The governor wanted the war over quickly and advocated aggressive tactics.[68]

Governors at the Cleveland assemblage condemned the president's slowness in responding to pleas for weapons, and they urged a vigorous war. They feared Seward's conservative influence on Lincoln and used the results of their meeting as a counterweight. Members agreed to send personal agents to influence Lincoln. John Bigelow, New York lawyer and Morgan confidant who attended the meeting, recalled that Dennison wanted to march into Kentucky and Virginia and prohibit river traffic trade with secession states. The governors tapped Randall to draft their demands and wire them to Lincoln. Clevelanders serenaded the group outside the Angier House Hotel, and governors seized the occasion to do some grandstanding. Confident they had established a war plan for the West, Randall proclaimed to the crowd that there "was but one course to pursue," and that meant transporting an army down the Mississippi, and to "blaze a broad track through the whole South, from Montgomery to Charleston." "Charleston," he declared, "should be razed, till not one stone is left upon another, till there is no place left for the owl to hoot nor the bittern to mourn." Blair echoed his sentiment. "In the name of Michigan," he declared, "I promise to stand by you shoulder to shoulder, and to march beside you of Ohio, and beside them of Pennsylvania, and beside brave old Massachusetts—who has tenderly taken to her bosom her beloved dead."⁶⁹ News of the meeting spread in the press, and the governors' actions encouraged Northerners demanding the same aggressive spirit in Washington. The editor of the *Bangor Daily Whig and Courier* declared that it was time the loyal governors "act[ed] as a unit," and they did.⁷⁰

Lincoln received the Cleveland designees on the morning of 7 May, the day after the Kentucky General Assembly opened its special session. Among them were Dennison's agents and attorneys Joseph Swan, Noah H. Swayne, and Randall's operative, Thomas Hood. They emphasized to Lincoln the governors' desire to crush the rebellion quickly. Randall did not accompany the delegates to Washington, but returned to Madison and composed the group's "official" letter to Lincoln. That the governors convened should have impressed the president that a decided opinion existed among them. Lincoln, they believed, should adopt a more definite course in regard to these states. They appreciated the president's difficulties, but Washington was now safe, they argued, and it was time to turn national attention to the West. Rather than wait for the enemy to show up across the rivers, Randall reasoned, why not fortify the region to prevent it. "It was a matter of absolute necessity," wrote Randall, "not only for the Northern border states but for all the Northwestern States, to be able to control the business and commerce of the Ohio River and the Upper Mississippi in order to reach a vital part of this rebellion." There was a spirit evoked by the war that was driving them to action, he argued, and if the government would not permit this action, the states would act for themselves. Unless the national government harnessed and directed this action, Randall feared the Union's greatest strength would "prove our most dangerous weakness." In order for the national government to "retain the confidence of the people," he declared, it must "show some confidence in the people."⁷¹

Count Adam Gurowski, a State Department translator, was privy to the conversations spinning through the Lincoln administration about the governors' meeting. Their leadership impressed him. He remarked in his diary that the governors' meeting was "a bitter criticism of the slow, forbearing policy of the administration." "As it stands now," he wrote, "the administration, being the focus of activity, is tepid, if not cold and slow; the circumference, that is, the people, the States, are full of ire and of activity."⁷² Governors were the key players in Gurowski's circumference, and they used the popular ardor to apply pressure on Lincoln to move decisively against the Confederates. To emphasize the importance of Randall's report, Curtin wired

Lincoln and urged him to be decisive in handling the border states and to adopt aggressive war aims. "In my judgment," he continued, "the immediate suppression of treason and rebellion, by armed force, will alone satisfy the loyal and true men of this country, vindicate the integrity and honor of the Government and restore peace to our people."[73]

The war was a month old and already governors were trying to direct it. Given their labors in raising soldiers, they believed themselves entitled to decide how they should be used. Amassing an enormous Union army and sending it forth quickly, they believed, would end the war as abruptly as it began. Both the Cincinnati and the Cleveland conferences demonstrated that governors were managing a two-fold war, and that some were better at handling it than others. One war required governors to serve the national government's interests, the other kept their attention on defense of rivers, rails, arsenals, ruffians, and obstreperous legislatures. As much as governors sought federal directives in managing both wars, they often requested their state legislatures to provide for Washington's unresponsiveness.[74]

By chance, the governors' meeting coincided with Lincoln's call for an additional 42,000 men to be raised for three-year service or the duration of the war. Cameron urged governors to induce the thousands of men oversubscribing the state quotas to join the military for three-year's service. These volunteers, however, would muster into the volunteer army, but would be under the command of federal officers. Lincoln's decision allowed Cameron some breathing room in accepting more men, but it drew fire from governors worried over the potential problems. Governors pointed out that the federal Militia Acts of 1792 and 1795 allowed volunteers to serve only three months and only under governor-commissioned officers from the rank of colonel on down. This new call created confusion and required Cameron and the governors to solve these problems. The secretary, however, failed to designate state quotas, and consequently thousands more Northerners flocked to mustering stations. When Cameron finally assigned the quotas for the individual states, governors were already inundated with men drilling and training. Nonetheless, several governors brazenly urged a vigorous war. "We wish to go *onward*," Andrew chided a cabinet member, "not *stand still*."[75] He wanted to capitalize on the massive outpouring of patriotism, believing it would shorten the war. The additional troops, Lincoln hoped, would relieve the governors, and he assumed Congress would appropriate the necessary funds for the emerging national army when it convened in special session in July.[76]

War from the Statehouse

During these transformative weeks governors had no way of managing the tidal wave of men coming forth. There was a matter of pride at stake and governors wanted to acknowledge such patriotism. State pride inspired Sprague to offer his leadership to the Rhode Island volunteer ranks. The state constitution made him the militia's commander, and Rhode Islanders were averse to his acceptance of a rank below brigadier general. If the brash young Cranston native could not wear the stars of the brigadier in the field, he would not fight. "Were it otherwise," he acknowledged, "I would freely shoulder a musket as wear a sword." Sprague allowed that "I think the cause might be strengthened and our enemies somewhat depressed by such an appointment."[77]

Northern mobilization revealed a vastly larger republic than its political leaders imagined. Governors were hard-pressed to refuse volunteers, even while complaining they had not sufficient arms and camp equipage. They pressed Cameron to take the men, believing the awakened Northern military giant might sway the political atmosphere in border states and deter Confederates from going on the offensive. Such increases would provide for local defense and foster goodwill at home, while allowing the North to amass an army that was proportional to the cause. This revealed poor discretion on the governors' part, but it nonetheless publicly drove home the point that Washington was not prepared to create the vast army the people wanted them to establish. The fact that the army would swell beyond the national government's ability to arm the men, governors argued, was a good sign, and they were doing all they could to retain the men coming forward.[78]

Governors of the wealthier and more industrial states led the way in establishing a national financial apparatus on which Lincoln could rely. Morgan coordinated his efforts with those of New York City's Union Defense Committee, an emergency relief organization headed by New York Democrat John A. Dix. This committee collected and distributed money to aid the state's mobilization. Morgan organized a system that allowed New York manufacturers to bid for contracts, recognizing that many states would look to them for supplies. Cities such as Boston and New York City became distribution centers where governors accumulated and arranged for the shipping of military goods to Northern states. As the weeks passed, western governors such as Randall, Ramsey, and Kirkwood sent agents to the eastern cities to procure contracts for tents, rubber blankets, shoes, arms, and a mountain of other materials. Their local economies were not advanced enough for governors to keep war business local. Yet other governors, such as Yates and Morton, strove to keep business closer to home, emphasizing the need to keep state contracts for goods within the state to boost the economy and reduce the chances of corruption and fraud. Chicago, Cincinnati, Boston, and New York emerged as economic centers in supplying the armies' needs. Within weeks governors had worked so diligently that the editor of *Harper's Weekly* declared that with such support and resources it would be entirely Lincoln's fault if the war "was not brought to a speedy close."[79]

When they were not responding to soldiers and civilians, governors busied themselves by establishing the bureaucracy to open additional recruiting stations, and appointed recruiting agents, medical examiners and surgeons, chaplains, and quartermasters. In supervising the enlistment, governors were sensitive to their ethnic populations. Andrew's influential Irish population, for example, demanded that he remain cognizant of their needs in commissioning officers. Yates, Morton, Dennison, and Randall likewise responded to their German populations. In addition to ethnic considerations, governors in New Jersey, Delaware, Ohio, New York, and the West, for example, also worried over their sizeable Democratic minorities, hoping they would surrender partisan politics in favor of preserving the Union. Some governors moved "too heedlessly and hastily," but they moved "with unflinching resolution," no doubt pushed by a populace that came to believe "the Administration was underestimating the task ahead."[80] In the rush to appoint so many people in so little time, governors made unpopular appointments and their critics attacked them. Morton's opponents, for example, charged that he had simply appointed too many lawyers "who spent their time in the taverns talking politics," and was "willing to strengthen himself by uniting the debris of the Democratic Party to his fortunes."[81] Governors had to be evenhanded in enlisting troops from several political districts, and in the case of New York, Morgan had to be careful not to oversubscribe New Yorkers living in the city. Yates faced critics who accused him of enlisting too few regiments from Chicago. To pacify his German constituents, he accepted Frederick Hecker's German Regiment.[82]

The cachet of the governors raised the eyebrows of congressmen and senators, who traditionally had been the spokesmen for the states, and who had enjoyed considerable patronage powers in Washington. Governors had typically been political outsiders, relegated to managing state affairs, but the war brought them to Washington and into federal prominence. In seeking to advance their interests with Lincoln, they worked with congressmen more familiar with his ways. Those representatives from the East, each powerful enough in his own right, included Pennsylvanian Thaddeus Stevens, William Pitt Fessenden of Maine, Delawarean James A. Bayard, Charles Sumner of Massachusetts. Those from the West included Michigan's Zachariah Chandler, Illinoisans Lyman Trumbull and Elihu Washburne, Henry Rice of Minnesota, Missouri's Frank Blair, Oregon's Benjamin Stark and James Nesmith, George Julian of Indiana, Wisconsin's Timothy Howe, Iowan James Grimes, Ohioan Benjamin Wade, and Kansan Jim Lane.

Whatever glory that might have awaited them in Washington power circles, governors remained attentive to local affairs. Even in Vermont, where war fever ran high, there was much to remedy. The state's Adjutant General Henry H. Baxter carped that Fairbanks's agents were favoring Irishmen, which offended non-Irish Americans, who were eager to enlist. Another Vermonter groused that the surgeons Fairbanks had appointed to one regiment were habitually drunk and needed replacing. One Vermont sheriff requested Fairbanks's permission to remove secession flags from his town. Yet, for all the problems that resulted from the hasty mobilization, Fairbanks's critics could not deny that he strove to maintain harmony. A correspondent from the 2nd Vermont acknowledged the governor's hard work, citing the fact that his "activity and vigilance would do credit to a man in the prime of life, and which would elicit special commendation from every press in the State, were he a young man, has been giving his undivided attention to the outfit of the Second Regiment." He continued, "the people of Vermont will probably never know the extent of the pecuniary and other sacrifice which has been suffered and borne by Governor Fairbanks in the great cause in which we are all engaged." He pointed out that "It is not unknown that the great Fairbanks Scale Company of which the Governor is the senior partner, has branch houses in all the principal cities in the South," and "while there are honorable exceptions, it is not to be supposed that 'confiscation,' has left the Governor of the Green Mountain state unscathed."[83]

In the early weeks of mobilization it was important that governors maintained a favorable balance between national and state affairs, even while they attended to local issues. Pressure and accountability to make the proper appointments and to contain abuses inherent in mobilizing and standardizing the vast populations into an army became the governors' primary concern. Their offices became central lines of authority between Washington and the citizens. Southern Illinoisans, for example, urged Yates to defend their homeland or, if nothing else, supply them with weapons for local defense. Illinoisans across the Mississippi from St. Louis inundated the governor with more alarming reports. As much as he feared for Washington, Yates feared the uprising that might occur among his civilian constituents if he failed to supply them with arms to defend the state's borders. He wired General Wool that he hoped no further requisitions would be made on him. "We are so situated," he argued, "that it may become absolutely necessary to use every musket in our possession for our own defense."[84] "[A]s the War Dogs is about to be turned louse [sic] against our government," wrote Joshua League to Yates, "we the citizens of Perry County that is not inlisted [sic] in the war service at present is desirious [sic] of having the privalige [sic] of protecting our own homes and fire sides and to repell [sic] any invasion or of violence that dare disturb or invad [sic] our homes."[85] "In this bedlam," Yates complained, "we *must* find somebody who can organize regiments."[86] When Ulysses S. Grant arrived in Springfield, Yates found his man, and, slowly but surely, the commander restored order.[87]

The governors' political influence allowed them newfound prerogatives, including the justification to rebuke the administration over procedure. Morgan complained to Lincoln when the president authorized New York's Union Defense Committee to forward fourteen regiments to Washington without the governor's approval. Committee leaders were at odds with Albany's State Military Board, and Morgan worked with both groups in raising troops and in establishing himself as the state's commander in chief. He permitted the committee to raise independent regiments, but decreed that he would decide how they would be used in furnishing the state's quota. When members bypassed his orders and appealed to federal authorities to accept their regiments, Lincoln agreed. Morgan favored expediting troops to Washington, but not at the risk of violating the state constitution. Forwarding troops in this manner, he complained to Lincoln, "quite independent and irrespective of authority from the Executive of New York cannot fail to result in confusion and serious disaster." He added, "I may not possess authority to control men from New York, who volunteer into the service of the National Government direct, but I certainly ought to possess authority over the Military Regiments of the State."[88]

Critics howled over Morgan's procedural adherence. Lincoln explained that because the committee had just the week before informed him there were fourteen regiments in New York City besides the regiments Morgan was raising, something must be done with them because the committee could no longer safely keep them in the city. To avoid confrontation with Morgan's regiments, the president authorized the committee to forward them. He explained his reason for accepting the regiments from the Defense Committee and that he was not aware that Morgan had not approved of the Committee's decision to forward troops. Lincoln reassured Morgan that his acceptance of the men was in no way intended to suggest the governor was failing "in activity or in any duty." "On the contrary," he wrote, "I acknowledge you have done, and are doing nobly; and for which I tender you my sincere thanks."[89]

Undertaking the creation of a military force equal to the task of saving a vast decentralized federal system intensified the link between local communities and their leaders. Mobilization established an unprecedented connection between the home front and the war effort, though it did not translate into nationalism. Much had been done quickly to deposit thousands of soldiers in Washington, and as much as these units reflected the tremendous disparity among the North's local communities, it was evident a national state was emerging. Loyal citizens looked to the Union as the crucial guarantor of popular participation in government (and of democracy's survival in the Western world) and the opportunity to rise economically. Together, Lincoln and his governors groped their way toward establishing an administrative foundation upon which Northerners could rely to achieve their military goals. The war was taking on extraordinary shape, and governors were finding their place in preserving the Union.[90]

CHAPTER FOUR

The Grandest Spectacle of the Century

By early May, McClellan's orders placing him in command of the newly formed Department of the Ohio caught up with him in Cincinnati. To West Point–educated Irvin McDowell, Lincoln gave the Department of Northeastern Virginia. The force collecting in the border states alarmed residents, especially slave owners. General Butler's occupation of Annapolis and Maryland's vote against secession held the state in the Union, but Virginians and Tennesseans declared their support of the Confederacy. Missouri and Kentucky were teetering, and Lincoln turned his attention to these slave states, and the nation's most important rivers. The president needed to forestall secession in these states, curtail the activities of Magoffin and Jackson, and allow loyal governors time to deposit troops in Washington and Cincinnati.[1]

Border State Governors

Kentucky remained quiet, but hostilities erupted in St. Louis after Colonel Nathaniel Lyon uncovered information that Jackson planned to seize the state arsenal. On 10 May, his 6,000 soldiers surrounded the southern camp and forced Confederate commander Daniel Frost to surrender. In marching his troops through the streets, reminiscent of Baltimore, rioting broke out, and shots were fired. By day's end the violence left nearly thirty people dead. Fearing something like this would occur in St. Louis, Yates arranged with Lyon and loyal Missourian Francis P. "Frank" Blair Jr. to smuggle 20,000 muskets and 110,000 cartridges out of the arsenal.[2]

The Camp Jackson violence alarmed bordering governors that Missouri's conflict would spill into their states. Yates urged Lincoln to order General William Harney to return to St. Louis to preserve peace. Lincoln balanced Yates's concerns with Morton's Kentucky worries. The Indiana governor wired Robert Anderson in Cincinnati that despite Kentucky's legislative decision to adopt a Proclamation of Neutrality and Magoffin's promulgation that forbade any movement upon Kentucky soil, the Union commander should supply loyal Kentuckians with arms. Indeed, the "State of Magoffindom," as the *Cincinnati Gazette* dubbed Kentucky, was trying to remain in a "state of betweenity, like Mahomet's coffin."[3] Without loyal governors in Kentucky and Missouri, Lincoln relied on personal associates, such as Missourian Frank Blair and his older brother Montgomery. To help their cause, loyal Missourians enlisted James E. Yeatman, a St. Louis businessman, and Hamilton Rowan Gamble, a Missouri attorney and political leader already in Washington seeking assistance. In the meantime, Lincoln hoped loyal Missourians would produce a chief executive to keep the state in the Union.[4]

Closer to Washington, Butler's occupation went a long way toward establishing a more permanent military rule in Maryland. General Scott, however, found Baltimore's seizure alarming, and remarked that it was a "Godsend that it was without conflict of arms."[5] Butler's move so concerned Scott that he replaced him with Major General George Cadwallader, and ordered Butler to Fort Monroe to command and launch reconnaissance forays into Virginia. Butler's actions turned Lincoln's attention away from the bloodshed in St. Louis and Kentucky neutrality and toward military occupation and fugitive slaves who came inside Federal lines. The commander had a simple and but legal solution, declaring that property was property, whether it was picks, shovels, or slaves. He feared his army's presence might spark a slave rebellion, but maintained that once property came into his lines, there it remained. As much as Lincoln remained committed to extending civil guarantees to loyal Southerners, including slave owners, he accepted Butler's contraband policy. It placed Hicks between civil and military authorities seeking justice.[6]

Western Virginians also turned Lincoln away from Missouri and Maryland by rejecting secession and severing ties with the Tidewater and Piedmont elites. Meeting in Wheeling in mid-May, the delegates from the mountainous region hoped to attract more counties to join them in their pursuit of statehood. Even the *Providence Daily Journal* noted the separatist movement months before, observing that "the citizens of Western Virginia are thinking of having a little secession of their own." "They are strongly attached to the Union," and "do not like the treatment they have received from the slaveholders in the eastern part of the state; [and] they think that the present state constitution makes an unjust discrimination against them, and they detest the secession talk."[7] One resident wrote the *Baltimore American* editor that western Virginia "clings to the Union with a death-like grasp that ought to teach our Eastern Virginia brethren that they shall not (ordinance or no ordinance) attach us to King Cotton."[8] Western state leaders, including

John S. Carlisle, Francis S. Pierpont, Archibald W. Campbell, and Waitman T. Willey appealed to Yates, Andrew, Dennison, and Curtin for assistance. They needed Union soldiers to patrol the Ohio River and reconnoiter the western Virginian counties to encourage loyalists and dissuade guerrillas. Mountaineers' rejection of secession made it worse for themselves by desiring to establish a Union state. "Fathers are against sons" and "brothers are against brothers," wrote a concerned citizen from Petersham. "We have force enough in our own section," he allowed, "but we have no authority to act under."[9]

The war pulled border state citizens in opposite directions, and governors recognized the political consequences resulting from divided loyalties. Cooperating with the national government to raise an army to be used against their neighbors created anxiety among the mountaineers. The quest to become the thirty-fifth state added an extraordinary circumstance to their plight and had far-reaching political and constitutional implications. "The reorganization of the Government of Virginia in the west is the great movement of the day," wrote Attorney General Edward Bates to Gamble, "the 'spinal cord' of nationality—at once 'an example & fit instrument' for the restoration of all insurgent states."[10] Colonel Benjamin F. Kelly's arrival lifted part of that weight as he occupied Grafton in order to secure the Baltimore and Ohio Railroad where it junctioned with the Northwestern Virginia Railroad just below the Pennsylvania state line. The swift Federal operations secured the Ohio River and allowed governors time to encourage the new-state initiative.[11]

By the end of May, McDowell had moved his Federal troops south of the Potomac River and occupied Alexandria. The Ohio commander had been employed recently in the Adjutant General's Office and was Cameron's favorite to lead the command. Dennison, however, distrusted the appointment because McDowell lacked significant field command. He had more confidence in McClellan, whose repeated slights against Cameron highlighted the War Department's maddeningly slow work. One correspondent, however, blamed Scott, contending the commander did not intend to "hazard any aggressive movement" until he was thoroughly prepared.[12] Dennison, however, claimed great pride in knowing his department had the nation's finest commander at the helm. He had lobbied for McClellan's appointment because he feared the secessionists west of the Appalachian Mountains more than the Confederates across the Potomac River. Lincoln's concern over Kentucky confirmed this view. To add credence to their Cincinnati and Cleveland meetings, Dennison, Morton, Yates, and McClellan held a third conference in late May, this time in Indianapolis. They outlined a military plan for the western theater that justified increasing McClellan's army and argued that they could raise additional volunteers to supply McClellan with a sufficient force. If the Union expected to occupy Kentucky, loyalists would need to seize Louisville, Covington, Newport, and Columbus, as well as the railroads leading south. Yates was to deliver this "memorial" to Lincoln in person, but was to keep McClellan's name out of the conversation because the plan significantly revised Scott's overall plan for the war.[13]

The Indianapolis conference was timely. Cameron's recent call for more regiments had encouraged the governors assembling the volunteers. His recent circular stating that some regiments may not be called "before frost," however, surprised them. Cameron argued the new volunteers needed time to acquire discipline, obedience, and tactical instructions. He was admirably worried for the untested volunteers, but his reasoning did little to assuage governors working to get troops to the front. Many Northerners and journalists pressed political leaders to end the war quickly, and congressmen who remained in Washington had made this point known to Lincoln. Sumner wrote to Massachusetts governor Andrew that Lincoln and Cameron were under considerable pressure to take "active aggressive measures" and that soon there was sure to be a "collision."[14] Andrew welcomed the news. Sitting at Harvard's commencement with General Scott, waiting to receive their honorary Doctor of Law degrees, the governor scribbled some notes on his Psalm 78 sheet music in preparation for his acceptance speech. "Gen Scott," he boasted to the crowd, "You have given him a degree in the North," yet, "he will presently take several degrees in the South—where as a Doctor of the Laws, he will teach rebels obedience."[15]

Because it was out of the range of the Eastern press, few reporters took notice of Federal troops landing at Fort Leavenworth, a small frontier military outpost on the Missouri River north of Kansas City. This news relieved Kansas governor Charles Robinson, who feared invasion from border ruffians. "Missouri must be taught a lesson," he confided to his wife, "& I should be glad of an opportunity to give it."[16] More satisfying to Robinson was Lincoln's decision to relieve Harney and appoint Lyon commander of the Department of the West. His appointment also placed Missouri under McClellan's jurisdiction as a new member of the Department of the Ohio. The War Department moved the headquarters of the Department of the West to Fort Leavenworth, and Robinson assumed greater influence in shaping military affairs west of the Mississippi River.[17]

By June, governors and military commanders had pulled Northerners together without losing the border states. Missouri's secessionist governor was in flight, and St. Louis was in Union hands. Western Virginians were moving closer to statehood, but differences over slavery and fear of retribution plagued political discussions. Maryland had come under firm military rule, while Kentucky remained neutral. The governors had thus far organized war machinery and pressed the administration to move aggressively in the border states to prevent Confederate occupation. "The great mass of our citizens regard the present rebellion as the greatest crime ever committed against human authority," Connecticut governor William Buckingham wrote to New York City attorney Hiram Walbridge, "and feel the importance of suppressing it at the earliest moment."[18]

New England governors faced no border ruffians and worried little over runaway slaves or hostile Indians. Instead they grappled with businessmen and the War Department to procure supplies and supervised transport to Washington. Governor Washburn characterized this extraordinary undertaking to a British officer in requesting arms for his Maine volunteers. "The grandest spectacle of the Century is now being exhibited in America," he declared, "the strength of the Government, & the capacity of the people for governing, will be demonstrated not less by the events of this time than they were by those of the Revolutionary epoch." He argued that "The hundreds of millions that the rebellion will make us pay will be the best investment the country has made since the beginning. . . . It will be known, thank God, that *we are a nation*; a nation to be respected by all others, as well as by our own people."[19]

Politics of Mobilization

Governors were doing all they could to earn their citizens' and soldiers' respect. The War Department's lack of direction forced them to dispense patronage among the officers and shape the military one regiment at a time. It also made them responsible for recruiting soldiers, appointing officers, and managing expanding mobilization efforts. The more volunteers they mustered into service, the more responsibility they assumed in managing military details. So blatant were some governors in arranging affairs that Bates reprimanded Cameron for allowing such abuses of authority. "A loose idea seems to prevail in some quarters," lectured Bates, "that the Governors of the States have the right to control the organization of the troops from their respective States, even after they are received into the service of the United States." He advocated that the War Department retain these powers, arguing that if one governor was allowed to assume such power, "a combination of Governors might utterly disorganize an army in the face of the enemy it was called out to meet, or disband it entirely."[20]

Conceding even the most liberal constitutional powers to the states, Bates argued that once the troops were mustered into the Federal army, they must surrender their state ties. "That the Governors of the loyal States have, both personally and officially, rendered most valuable and effective service to the National Government in its efforts to suppress the present insurrection is well known," he reasoned, "but these labors are in aid of the Government and with its approbation. They are performed, not because it is a legal duty imposed by Congress, or, in many instances, even by their respective States, but under the impulse of a generous humanity and patriotism."[21]

Governors understood their labors were in aid of Lincoln's administration precisely because the central government could do little without them. Yet there were complex notions of loyalty that intertwined nation and state. Although Northerners were quick to speak of the political ties that bound them, the war presented a rapid pace for integrating military policies and increasing governmental cohesiveness among the loyal states that would eventually become the Union's crowning achievement. The Constitution shaped Lincoln's course and provided a framework on which the national government could wage war. The president's power as commander in chief justified much of his executive authority. But waging war resided in the human and patriotic impulse that Bates described. Northerners provided that impulse, and governors managed and directed the transformation of this federal-state enterprise. Before the war, the national government's preoccupation with expansion had resulted in mainly distributive policies regarding economic and political development that were conducive to local political economies. The war forced governors to reverse this trend. In other words, it was time to use state and local resources not only to advance state-federal relations, but also to strengthen the national government. State executives assumed far greater responsibilities in assisting an underdeveloped national government. Governors were the principal agents in redefining state-federal relations, and they were dependent on one another in supporting a national army. Even as they constituted parts of the whole, they took great care in communicating to soldiers how important the national war was in preserving democracy. "You go not to uphold the hands of Abraham

Lincoln," Governor Randall told the 2nd Wisconsin, "but of the President of the United States, not to fight for one for one section, or one State, but for the rights and liberties of the people of all sections and all the States."[22]

Mobilization required that governors extend the federal bridge to Washington. Yet, for all of their efforts in assembling, supplying, transporting, and providing pay, governors would have been appalled had they visited their troops in Washington that summer. In Washington on business, Andrew's liaison Forbes wired the governor about camp conditions and reported that, while Massachusettans were in good order, the conditions of other camps and men made him fear "a *big scare* at Washington one of these days."[23] Massachusetts senator Henry Wilson confirmed Forbes's assessment to Andrew, writing that the number of firearm injuries convinced him the soldiers should be deprived of weapons until they had been properly instructed in handling loaded revolvers. Alarmed by the shortage of qualified officers, Andrew enlisted the advice of Peleg Chandler, close friend and confidential aide, who steered him to Boston's blue-blooded families for possible candidates. Dennison's agent Richard M. Corwine wrote from Willard's Hotel that the Ohioans of the 1st and 2nd regiments were "very badly off," and in a "most deplorable" condition. Soldiers were in rags, he wrote, "mortified," and "broken in spirit," and had become the subject of jokes from citizens who referred to them as the "pauper" regiments. The governor assumed that once the men arrived in Washington the War Department would provide suitable clothes and camp equipage. When that did not happen, soldiers complained to families at home, and soon this resulted in rampant rumors that Dennison had not provided for his men.[24]

Leadership made a difference in combat, and governors sought professionally trained or experienced officers. Illinois governor Yates was fortunate early on that John Pope, a West Point graduate, was an Illinois resident, and he called on him to lead the state's forces assembling in Springfield. With the governor's endorsement, the president appointed Pope brigadier general in June and assigned him to Springfield. Pope had accompanied Lincoln's inaugural train to Washington, where he came to know Yates. Washburn had a similar experience in finding a professional commander for his Maine soldiers and appointed Oliver Otis Howard, a Maine native, who was teaching mathematics at the U.S. Military Academy. On meeting Howard in the Augusta statehouse, Washburn directed him to his regiment outside on the lawn, remarking that "you must hasten and help us to get it into shape." "I think, governor," said Congressman James G. Blaine grinning, and relieving

Howard, "you will have to let the colonel choose his adjutant and organize his staff himself." "Well, well; all right," remarked Washburn.[25]

Ironically, one of the nation's most learned military professionals, Henry W. Halleck, was in California when his appointment to major general arrived. He suspended his business and legal practice and returned to the military initially as commander of the California militia. Halleck was needed in the East, but delays in his orders kept him in San Francisco for months after Lincoln's call. It was just as well that he remained in California throughout the critical summer months; in fact, Halleck's military experience helped keep California in the Union. Governor Downey had presided over two stormy legislative sessions that indicated he supported compromise with the Southern Confederacy. California legislators were so concerned that they passed a resolution to uphold the Union and forced Downey to pledge his loyalty to the Lincoln administration. In the coming weeks, the governor traveled to Los Angeles and his estate-home in San Bernardino to reassure southern Californians that he would quell any attempt to sever the state's connection with the Union. Despite his Southern proclivities, Downey's sentiments went a long way in placing him in the Union fold. Halleck's short-lived tenure in the California state militia was nothing short of good fortune for Lincoln and loyal Californians.[26]

Constitutional authority in establishing a national volunteer army allowed governors to appoint officers below the rank of brigadier general. By attaching state-controlled militias to the emerging federal organization, it was natural that authorities would run into conflicts. When, for example, Governor Morgan appointed John Dix and James S. Wadsworth major generals of the New York volunteers, Cameron told him the president "reserved to himself" such appointments, and suspended their rank until Lincoln had approved their commissions and the senate confirmed them. Morgan responded that if governors could not appoint general officers, as he argued the federal Constitution and his New York constitution allowed, he had to limit camps of instruction for newly recruited troops to units no larger than a regiment, and use his influence in proper channels.[27]

Differences over mobilization and officer appointments forced Lincoln to provide more direction to the War Department. The president viewed the governors as partners in managing mobilization and recognized that not only were civil-military relations at work but also, more significantly, nation and state relations were at work. Building a national army required a foundation that respected local and state governance, and Lincoln chose his words carefully in corresponding with the governors. It was his responsibility to inspire governors to cooperate with him, even when they disagreed with his policies. In this, Lincoln became adept in dealing with the varied personalities of the Union's state executives. On paper, the president held state-federal relations together, but expanding the military establishment required skill in managing a vast mobilization within the decentralized political system. Cameron had allowed governors free rein in sending regiments forward largely because he did not know how many would come forth and because they were better suited to handle mustering volunteers into service. He reported to Lincoln in early July that the generous outpouring of volunteers embarrassed him. In just under three months, more than 200 regiments came forward for a call of 75,000 men. The enormous outpouring, governors believed, would deter secession in the border states and inspire confidence to advance the soldiers South quickly and decisively to suppress the rebellion.[28]

Governors welcomed what they considered an embarrassment of riches. They found ways to place as many men as possible into the ranks, and their efforts endeared them to the soldiers. Yates's visit to Washington that June delighted Illinois soldiers. "The praise of Illinois is on every lip," the governor acknowledged to Andrew McFarland of the 14th Illinois, "and I hesitate not now as her Governor to make proclamation in advance that when the day of battle comes glory will settle on all her banners." He encouraged McFarland, "This war will 'cost blood and treasure,' but it will be of incalculable benefit to this country and the world. The vindication of such a government as ours is cheap at any cost. It must be vindicated at the hazard even of national bankruptcy and the loss of thousands of valuable lives. As a historic fact it will be worth all it will cost though the rivers run with blood."[29]

Blood flowed in the mountains of western Virginia that summer. McClellan's victory at Philippi encouraged loyal residents meeting in Wheeling, and they named Francis Pierpont provisional governor of the newly emerging state. Pierpont had appealed to Lincoln to prevent the "evil-minded persons" who had banded together in military organizations from overthrowing the government and making war on the loyal people. As the Virginia separatists' leader, he called on the president to aid him in suppressing the violence in the mountains. Lincoln appreciated their secession from Virginia, but it added another wrinkle to his problems—the Constitution prohibited such action. Working through the details required time and calculation, neither of which mountaineers could afford. Lincoln supported the loyalists, but Pierpont was left to raise men and safeguard loyal citizens. Secessionists had warned the governor that if he remained at his home in Fairmont, he would either be arrested, or his home burned. Unionist Arthur I. Boreman lamented to Pierpont that "if these incarnate devils get their hands on a Union man they carry him off to Charleston and force him into the army."[30]

At forty-seven years old, Pierpont was prepared to assume the part as the provisional governor. Born in Marion County near Morgantown (West) Virginia, he had the benefit of a liberal education at Allegheny College and on graduation taught school for a time in Virginia and Mississippi, while studying law. In 1841 he was admitted to the bar, and he eventually landed a job as attorney for the Baltimore and Ohio Railroad. The conservative antislavery Whig impulses pulled him into politics, and he stumped his region for the Harrison-Tyler ticket in 1840, for Henry Clay in 1844, and Zachary Taylor in 1848. During the 1850s his sectional pride grew more pronounced as he viewed eastern taxes of the state burdensome to the small farmers, miners, and mountaineers of the western counties. Pierpont viewed the war as the opportunity to sever the political interests of the western region from those of the eastern tidewater elite. So important to Lincoln was Pierpont's leadership in the border region that even the *New Hampshire Patriot and State Gazette* acknowledged that in "his hands the cause of the Union is safe."[31]

When Pierpont accepted western Virginia's provisional governorship, Federal forces had expanded Union control deeper into Missouri. Lyon seized the state capital at Jefferson City and forced Jackson into the southwestern portion of the state. Concerned for Missourians, Lincoln nonetheless feared for Kansans. To protect loyalists, he appointed Lane a brigadier general, and despite Robinson's objections, authorized him to raise two regiments. Lane's brief stint guarding the White House impressed Lincoln, who thought it wiser to have Lane in Kansas, remarking to Cameron that "we need the services of such a man out there at once."[32] By summer Cameron created a new military district called the Western Department, which put Illinois and the states west of the Mississippi River under its domain. St. Louis served as headquarters. In just under three months, he reported that the Union army had amassed over 230,000 troops and had distributed them among thirteen military departments, costing the government an estimated $185 million. All of this had been done without Congress. Lincoln had exhausted all peaceful solutions and he had no alternative. "What they cannot take by an election," Lincoln argued, "neither can they take by a war."[33]

The conflict that had broken the bond between North and South was from Lincoln's vantage point, "a People's contest" putting border state residents especially at risk. John Carlisle represented those loyal western Virginians trying to establish a new state. He complained to Lincoln in early July that unless the mountaineers, "lying out without even a blanket, destitute of tents and camp equipage, destitute of arms and ammunition, for weeks and weeks," were supplied immediately, "we shall have to give up the contest."[34]

Congress Convenes

Congress's assemblage in the summer gave legislators a renewed purpose and bolstered the administration's confidence in what it had accomplished. The nation's capital, however, was different. Gone were slavery's ardent defenders who had held the republic hostage to the institution. Republicans dominated the legislature that gathered beneath the unfinished Capitol dome, overlaid by citizens-turned-soldiers encamped on Capitol Hill. Washington, however, had little to offer its defenders. "We yankees don't think much of either Washington city or the country about," wrote an unimpressed Massachusetts soldier, "I wouldn't give twenty-five cents for anything I've seen here yet."[35] Indeed, Leander Harris of the 4th New Hampshire wrote to his wife that "the principal productions of the place are soldiers, niggers, whores, and bad whiskey."[36]

The sleepy Southern city on the Potomac River displayed its newfound military significance. "The city presents a very war like appearance at present," wrote Pennsylvanian Joseph Schnell stationed near Georgetown, "the secessionists have to keep quiet or they will get a dose of powder and lead which they have been aching for for some time."[37] Never before in the history of the United States had more been done in such little time and without Congress. In the eighty days since the president's call for volunteers, governors had engineered a state-driven mobilization that produced a vast army. More than that, however, was their insistence that Lincoln use these volunteers to prosecute the war vigorously. Morgan wanted Congress to give the war some form by suppressing "the madmen" bent on destroying the country. It was fitting that, across from the military encampments on Capitol Hill, a crowd packed into the Smithsonian Institution to hear Pennsylvania journalist, former Democrat, and clerk in the House of Representatives John W. Forney give an impassioned eulogy for the late Stephen A. Douglas.

The Illinois Democrat had been a respected politician whose political career represented an era of compromise between North and South. Indeed, it was his Nebraska bill that resulted in the 1854 Kansas-Nebraska Act, which prompted the Republican Party's formation and the "madmen" who opposed them.[38]

Vice-president Hamlin called the Senate to order that 4 July, and his gavel's rap opened a new era. Now the fire-eaters were abolitionists and radicals seething for a vigorous war against secessionists. Congress followed Lincoln's lead by repaying the states and articulating a cohesive system for sustaining the war effort. Without Southerners in attendance, Northern Democratic congressmen, distrustful of Lincoln's ability, scrutinized the president's every move to ensure they were in harmony with their constituents. Sumner, Trumbull, Chandler, Benjamin Wade, and a host of other congressmen armed with journalistic support found fault with the commander in chief's handling of the war. Chandler of Michigan was loudest and articulated the views of his radical governor. Disgusted by Lincoln's conciliatory approach to the war thus far, the elder senator wired Lincoln before leaving Michigan. "You can not [sic] comprehend the state of feeling here," he declared, "our people are deeply almost frightfully, in earnest." He closed emphatically, "Pardon me when I say the People of Michigan think the time has arrived to commence hanging & so think I."[39]

Yet the energy of mobilization appeared to stall once soldiers arrived in Washington. Displaying their preparedness to the president seemed more important to commanders than charging down to Richmond. Two days after giving his "State of the Union" address Lincoln and Governor Sprague visited the 2nd Rhode Island "Flying artillery" encamped on Monument grounds. Brilliantly outfitted by the Sprague family, these farm boys and town folk had traveled to war in the "lap of luxury, with prepaid passage as a whole regiment on steamship and train," and "uniformed at state cost, and armed with weapons manufactured at the company owned by their commanding officer," and made a fine impression on the commander in chief.[40] "The display was a very handsome one," noted the *Washington Daily National Intelligencer*, "the patriotism of the little State of Rhode Island was the theme of every tongue."[41] In Washington circles, "Camp Sprague" took on a nomenclature depicting mobilization's glamorous side. Sprague impressed Lincoln by what he had accomplished in such little time. Riding around on his white horse, the "boy governor" cut a dashing figure. Horatio N. Taft, a Patent Office examiner in Washington, remarked the ladies "all want to see

Gov. Sprague."[42] No matter the impressions Sprague made on Washingtonians, the governor took great care of his soldiers.

Cameron could not boast of having made the same impression. His report to Congress embarrassed the president, and it was clear that governors had eclipsed the secretary by attending to the emerging army. Many governors sought to extend state benefits to the families soldiers left behind. Randall was especially devoted to the care of his Wisconsinites. He petitioned Cameron to approve his idea for circulating among the governors a note that emphasized increasing state benefits to these families. Citizens made significant sacrifices in volunteering to put down the rebellion, and the governor encouraged states to attend to their welfare during and after the conflict. "Each State," he argued, "has a rich reversionary interest in the citizen soldiers who represent it, and each State owes to itself and to every soldier an obligation to take care of that interest."[43] As much as Cameron wished to nationalize the armies, governors reminded soldiers that they represented states and local communities. Morgan was especially sensitive to state involvement in maintaining soldier welfare. The governor had placed more than 50,000 New Yorkers in the field, and he understood the "humane and enlightened spirit" that prompted Randall's letter. He agreed to cooperate "in any measure which will most effectually serve to secure the objects sought to be obtained."[44] As Morgan explained to his father, "you may well imagine, that 53 Regiments in the field, upon duty are quite enough for one State or *one Governor to look after* requiring as they do, something every day, and almost every hour."[45] By mid-July, governors had routinely bypassed Cameron and communicated directly with their congressmen or departmental commanders in attending to military details. Cameron himself was the cause of much blame as his orders and circulars were confusing, lacking in clarity, and often contradictory. He embarrassed the War Department by handing out commissions and contracts as political favors and by allowing independent commands. Although he cited lack of volunteering and patronage pressure as justification for accepting these commands, such units hampered governors attempting to rally the men to state ranks.[46]

Bull Run and the Business of War

Despite the past months' chaos, Federal troops pushed deeper into Virginia, much to the approval of an impatient press. Other than marching south and defeating the Confederates, there was little objective. Cameron found time to visit McDowell on 20 July at his Manassas, Virginia, headquarters to gain a verbal report on the preparations for the impending battle and perhaps to see his brother Colonel James Cameron of the 79th New York Infantry. McDowell convinced him that his battle preparations were sound, though he was worried about engaging the enemy with amateur soldiers. The commander had deployed his 35,000 men along a small meandering creek called Bull Run.[47]

Lincoln's cabinet spent the next day in the War Department's telegraph room awaiting word. Michigan governor Blair had just returned from the front, where he visited the Michigan soldiers and encouraged them. He had written his wife Louise his impressions of Washington and that he was awaiting news from the front. "The appearance of decay is everywhere in this southern country," he related, and while the National Hotel was something to boast about, it was nonetheless "low mean [and] dirty . . . and on the pattern of everything in Niggerdom."[48] When news from the front finally arrived, it revealed that the Confederates had stunned McDowell's Federals in an all-day battle characterized by unprecedented confusion. Thurlow Weed was in Washington at the time and was standing on the sidewalk in front of Willard's late at night when Colonel Burnside of the 1st Rhode Island Volunteers galloped down Pennsylvania Avenue, wearing the look that Weed "had dreaded."[49] It was a stark contrast to the vibrant pomp and circumstance in which Burnside had led his troops through Washington days before. Sprague had been with him that day and fell into the line of retreat. Indeed, he had had his horse shot out from underneath him. The Federal display overwhelmed Horace Greeley, who used his *New York Tribune* to criticize commanders for the humiliating defeat. Just the week before, his paper had led the vanguard "Forward to Richmond," and now he lamented "God forgive our rulers that this is so," he disclaimed, "but it is true, and cannot be disguised."[50]

The battle's results and the army's condition could not be concealed. Hastily appointed commanders, amateur soldiers, lack of discipline, and battlefield mismanagement all contributed to the humiliating debacle. Worse yet were the soldiers' stories and journalistic descriptions that confirmed initial reactions. Thomas Worthington of the 46th Ohio was typical in his assessment, writing to Dennison that the defeat was a "horrible dishonor," and that the capital seemed paralyzed by the result. The Ohioan complained that "the drunkenness of the troops had been continuous with little or nothing done to prevent it" and added that "hundreds had lain out on the side walks every night" and "that one fourth of the 10,000 who came into the city the previous day were drunk by sunset, that the volunteers would be the government if at least 60,000 regulars were not enlisted within a year."[51]

"Retreat to Washington," wrote the *New York Times*, was obvious on the soldier's faces who paraded looks of despair in the streets that came from having been so thoroughly unprepared.[52] In one day of fighting the Union army suffered nearly 3,000 casualties of those killed, wounded, and missing in action. The Northern populace had the battle it long desired, but not the result. The "forward to Richmond" chant no longer claimed newspaper mastheads. The war's tide changed that day. Mobilization had been an exercise in assembling Northern manpower that had woven the states together. The Battle of Bull Run tested not only the army's combat skill but also the war machinery's capacity to adapt to the expanding conflict. Distinguished landscaper Frederick Law Olmsted, who interrupted his work on New York's Central Park to serve as secretary of the Sanitary Commission, complained to Burton that more care needed to be given to the condition of men entering the military. Had better men mustered into service, he argued to the Delaware governor, "the result of the late disastrous battle at Bull's Run, would have been wholly different."[53]

Reports assigning blame for defeat spread like wildfire between Washington and the state capitals. "As in April," wrote former Massachusetts governor and Washington liaison Boutwell to Andrew, "so now we must rely upon your energy and forethought to supply the manifest deficiencies in the conduct of affairs at Washington."[54] Angered by the rout, Massachusetts native Charles P. Bowditch protested to his father that the North "seems in a torpor from which nothing can wake them except some terrible disaster ten times as severe as that which we have received. The country must be aroused to the sense of its dangers. . . . I hope as soon as you come back and see how torpid we are here that you will go and see Gov. Andrew, and Edwd. Everett . . . and make them get up a meeting in Faneuil Hall where patriotic addresses shall be made to rouse the people from their stupor."[55] Having read about Vermont's casualties, Governor Fairbanks found some consolation when he learned of a young Vermont seminary student's heroics. Rejected for service as solider, John C. Thayer became a cook instead. While the battle raged, he was left behind in camp until the impulse to join in the fight overcame him, and he grabbed the rifle from a disabled soldier and took off for the field. When the Federals retreated, Thayer was near a hospital that was overrun by Confederate cavalrymen, who charged toward them and, coming on Thayer, demanded his surrender. The young student managed to get off a shot killing the Confederate soldier and made off with his sword, sash, and other trophies. He reported this episode to Fairbanks, who rewarded his bravery by appointing him regimental chaplain.[56]

The humiliation of retreat, loss of soldier morale, and the need to attend to casualties forced governors to restore confidence among the soldiers rather than engage in the public condemnation. Because they appointed the lower-grade officers directing troops, chief executives needed to stand behind their choices, but changes were in order. Randall was in New York procuring supplies at the time and departed for the battlefield. On reaching Washington, he rode out to his units' camps, where he found the demoralized soldiers of the 2nd Wisconsin. He consoled the men and personally attended to them, hoping to lift their "drooping hearts." He assured them "the State had not forgotten them" and that "their welfare should be attended to, and the evils they had labored under remedied."[57] "Their [Wisconsin dignitaries] coming [to Washington] broke upon the monotony of our camp life with most blessed relief, and even a healing influence seemed to breathed upon our sick," wrote one soldier, "words cannot describe how we were thrilled and made glad by the presence and speeches of those Wisconsin men, who came and spoke and shook us by the hand for the loved ones we have left behind in our perilous march."[58]

There was criticism to go around and the press reported much of it. Yet it all came back to the commander in chief. Demoralized by the defeat, Lincoln found solace in the support of the governors, who refrained from attacking him. Rather than surrender to public recrimination for the loss, governors understood that such attacks would undermine the administration's credibility and the public's confidence in managing the war. There was no time to analyze the blame. Soldiers needed to know the cause on which they embarked would be more efficiently guided by their civilian leaders. This required a new military plan, new commanders, and better-trained soldiers. To provide this new leadership, Lincoln called on McClellan to replace McDowell, and the commander rode into the nation's capital on 26 July. The young, professionally trained commander, just thirty-five-years-old with a blue-blooded pedigree, had been victorious in the mountains. The battle of Rich Mountain, fought ten days before Bull Run, bolstered the confidence of the pro-Union legislators in Wheeling and encouraged governors of his fitness for command. McClellan's departure forced Lincoln to reorganize departmental commands. He replaced McClellan with Brigadier General William Rosecrans and ordered Brigadier General John C. Frémont to St. Louis to command the Western Department.[59]

Of all the commanders Lincoln could have chosen to bring him victory, McClellan looked and acted the part of a leader. Spoiled, arrogant, and ambitious, and yet entirely capable of winning the hearts of soldiers, McClellan was an eclectic mixture of outward military bearing and inward insecurity. Among the governors, only Dennison had any idea about the man. McClellan's usefulness was a matter of timing, for Lincoln needed his talents immediately. "Better one week of McClellan," Stoddard observed, "than a whole year of the red-tape officials who preceded him."[60] The commander's arrival even excited Governor Blair, who was in Washington visiting his Michigan soldiers. He seized the moment during a regimental serenade in Washington to place an encouraging spin on future military prospects. "[A]lthough our forces were checked, not defeated, at the late battle," he declared, "they will soon be prepared for a renewal of the fight, in defence [sic] of all that is dear to American freeman—the preservation of the Constitution and liberty." He proclaimed, "We now have a young man, a soldier of the West, General McClellan under whose lead our army cannot fail of victory."[61]

The commander's arrival signaled a departure from slovenly army ways. The drunken and disorderly soldiers who thronged the streets, noted an observer, "disappeared as if by magic" and "have withdrawn their dashing uniforms and military swagger from the halls and bar-rooms of Willard's, Brown's, and the National."[62] To save the nation, McClellan told Lincoln, would require 273,000 men in the Army of the Potomac and 20,000 to defend Washington. The commander surrounded himself with like-minded men to fill his officer's commissions. Inspired by the youthful change, Sprague petitioned McClellan for a place in his new command, but the general passed him over for professionals, among them Burnside, who accepted a brigadier general's commission in the volunteer army. The Battle of Bull Run's result had awakened the Northern populace to the grim realities of fighting a war over an expansive front, and it inspired volunteers to come forward. The combination of three-months' men and three-years' men had produced an army of more than 300,000 soldiers by the time of the battle. Yet nearly one-third of those men were due to muster out before Congress adjourned in early August. After the debacle of the battle, Lincoln petitioned Congress to expand the army by at least 400,000, and Congress granted his request by authorizing 500,000 men for three-year terms. All of this meant nothing, however, if the men could not be supplied, transported, properly drilled, and competently led.[63]

The army's expansion further burdened governors struggling through a national mobilization and resulted in hastily and impartially recruited regiments. Governor-appointed officers established a hybrid national army composed of men who carried regimental flags into battle bearing the name of their respective states. Lincoln's authority to appoint majors and brigadier generals made the newly emerging volunteer army have two heads. When governors placed whole divisions in the field, they thought they were entitled to have some say as to who should command them and bypassed Lincoln's authority. Bull Run changed Lincoln's attitude about accepting governors' recommendations. Shortly after the battle, the president instructed John Hay to seek from congressional representatives recommendations for general officers. Although governors believed themselves better suited to make recommendations, they conceded.[64]

To assist governors, the War Department established a military review board to evaluate officer fitness. Cameron supervised the board and weeded out incompetents. Yet, in many cases, soldiers weeded out undesirables and bunglers by complaining to their governors and congressmen, or simply by shaming them into resignation. Governors welcomed the national assistance and scoured their states for graduates of military schools and retired militiamen. Yates, Morgan, Washburn, and Andrew were aware of the incompetence and inefficiency. They attempted to have regular officers assigned to their regiments, but they were scarce. Andrew scoured Massachusetts to find competent officer material and complained a week after Bull Run that soldiers had elected officers against his wishes. To senators Sumner and Wilson he lodged his complaint against such elections. "Can it be intended by Congress," he wrote, "that the volunteers in the field should fill vacancies by election?" If this were true, he added, then "where is to be the source of discipline, when every candidate is seeking personal favor of the men."[65] About to dispatch five Ohio regiments to Frémont's command in St. Louis, Dennison followed suit by writing to Cameron that he wanted "energetic men, graduates of West Point." "The country demands educated military men at the head of regiments," he argued, "and I fully concur."[66] As much as they wanted to accommodate soldiers' democratic tendencies, governors feared that political favoritism would cost regiments on the battlefield.

Volunteering continued after Bull Run, and it pressured Cameron to continue to accept independent commands. Tired of working against the

War Department in accepting these units, Morton requested Cameron to accept regiments "only through me." Worse yet, ninety-day enlistees were returning home, in many cases without pay. Some governors pressed their congressional delegations to make arrangements to secure the men's pay, but only after they had returned home. No doubt Cameron's responsibility, paying the men often fell to governors in these months, who secured the funds to maintain favorable soldier morale.[67]

Governors exercised discretion in their officer appointments, especially those in states with sizeable Democratic and ethnic populations. Regiments were colorful but complex combinations of farmers, urban workers, immigrants, and professionals that transformed political, social, and cultural communities into military kinships. Finding suitable officers to accommodate the political and ethnic constituencies involved leaning on community leaders and those with military experience. Governors searched for officers in the larger towns and cities where political and economic power was concentrated and the propensity for education existed. They listened to townspeople and local politicians to be careful not to put their sons, brothers, and fathers in the hands of imbeciles and inexperienced glory seekers. New Jersey's Olden, for example, was among those governors whose deeply divided citizenry challenged his appointments. Publicly, he was loyal to the core, but he shied away from speaking when it came to slavery and abolition. He played commonsense politics and came under the critical journalistic microscope. Although well known in financial circles, the Republican native's political past had been undistinguished, and he won the governorship by a slight margin in 1859. When the war erupted, he preferred conciliation to armed conflict and thus searching for competent and politically suitable commanders was difficult. Morton of Indiana, however, was overwhelmingly popular and made appointments independently. Buckingham, Morgan, and Fairbanks drew on the advice of self-appointed committees, which appeared more democratic. Still, the task of selecting officers proved daunting. After following a regiment through the streets of Boston, Andrew wrote to a young officer, "Let each one think that the regiment depends on him," he counseled, "as much as if he was the only officer in it." He observed, "A man must *see* a thing in his mind before he can *do* it with his hand." Unless the officer had seen every step of the process, "he has not seen it at all."[68]

To meet the army's increased size, governors labored long hours interviewing chaplains, surgeons, and commissary agents. Stirred by the recent Virginia defeat, one Ohio physician wrote to Dennison that he "resolved to lend a helping hand" in determining the fitness of surgeons to serve in the army.[69] The outpouring required the appointment of hundreds of lieutenants and captains and tens of majors and colonels, and governors made mistakes. When a young Massachusetts colonel marched his men draped in wool overcoats through Boston and Washington in the summer heat, soldiers complained to the governor. Andrew responded that the colonel's "*overcoat* march in Boston nearly drove me mad, and its repetition in Washington is too much even for a fool to do, or a saint to bear." He confessed to his friend Charles Sumner, "I made an inexcusable blunder in appointing him [the officer]."[70] When governors erred, the War Department was close behind with examining boards to make changes.[71]

Raising a strong volunteer Federal army challenged governors seeking their constituents' confidence. Inexperience, delay, and confusion handicapped their efforts early on and resulted in frustration. The Union's loss at Bull Run resulted in a more expansive Northern mobilization, especially since Lincoln needed more troops to secure the border states. Cameron accepted all the regiments governors could forward, and state executives worked with commanders to manage local affairs. Occupation of hostile localities more than mobilization exposed the complexities of waging a national war against Southern sympathizers while protecting Southern Unionists. Border state governors navigated the political shoals of state and local governance through civil and military waters. In Missouri, for example, Governor Gamble worked with Frémont to restore peace, and the commander bypassed civil procedures to do it. Missourians were joining ranks for both sides, and Cameron allowed Frémont a liberal rein to call on western governors for troops. Still, when troops arrived in St. Louis they lacked sufficient arms, equipment, and training. Worse yet was their unpreparedness for engaging in the frontier warfare associated with settling the states west of the Mississippi.[72]

Gamble labored to support Frémont that summer, but Missouri's unsettled circumstances unnerved him. The Missouri State Convention that met in March had followed Gamble's lead by rejecting secession. Delegates promoted themselves as potential mediators at a national meeting to consider constitutional amendments to settle the slavery issue. Before they adjourned, members selected a small committee to monitor events and approved a measure to reconvene delegates in an emergency. Thinking he had smothered secession, Gamble traveled to Washington to see his brother-in-law Edward Bates. He left thinking he might retire "'to spend his last days in the quietude of his home, undisturbed by the rude tumults of the world.'"[73] The Camp Jackson violence had panicked Missouri delegates, and they reconvened the legislature after Governor Jackson departed Jefferson City. Gamble recommended the delegates expel Jackson and secessionist legislators and devise procedures to hold elections for their offices in November. For his leadership, loyal delegates had rewarded Gamble by appointing him the state's provisional governor until elections could be held in November.[74]

Gamble was a logical choice to lead Missouri through the political whirlwind. A Virginia native, he attended Hampden-Sydney College and later studied law, eventually gaining an appointment to Virginia's superior court. Shortly after he moved to St. Louis, his older brother Archibald Gamble, who clerked in the St. Louis circuit court, offered him employment. He renewed his legal practice in St. Louis and traveled the Missouri frontier as a prosecuting attorney the same year its residents applied for statehood. Politics drew him into leadership, and he served the Whig Party as state representative. Within two decades, the Missouri lawyer had scaled the ranks of the St. Louis elite in political and legal circles and ran successfully for a post on the Missouri Supreme Court. He remained on the bench until 1854 and was one of the dissenting votes in the *Dred Scott* case. In that year, failing health forced him to retire, and five years later he traveled to Pennsylvania. The outbreak of hostilities inspired him to return to Missouri and help keep the state in the Union. His kinship with Bates convinced loyal Missourians that Gamble would have influence in Washington.[75]

By early August, border state governors had adjusted to the demands of a more formally organized mobilization. They navigated civil-military channels conducive to managing a conciliatory policy directed by national troops within their borders. Lincoln too adapted and emerged as a strong commander in chief, directing military movements in the several theaters of war. He ordered a joint movement in the West to seize Memphis and East Tennessee, which meant moving though neutral Kentucky. Without a loyal Kentucky governor, the president threaded military operations through his confidantes, including Morton, Dennison, and Yates. He advised Frémont to forge ahead in organizing western troops in Missouri and wired Gamble a short communiqué supporting the governor's promise to protect loyal Missourians. Wartime adjustments required policies that established important connections between disparate political and military cultures. In three months the cooperation between nation and state gave the appearance of solidarity.[76]

Two weeks after Bull Run Congress adjourned, and war management fell back to loyal governors and commanders. Amid those summer weeks, the Congress had authorized raising 500,000 three-year soldiers, approved a $250 million loan in bonds and notes, increased the tariff, passed an income tax, and levied a direct tax of $20 million on the states and territories. Most important for governors, however, the president signed the "indemnification act," which required the national government to reimburse the states for "enrolling, subsisting, clothing, supplying, arming, equipping, paying, and transporting its troops."[77] The rapid expansion exposed the federal system's weaknesses, and Cameron had fumbled through these months. Thomas Scott's appointment to assist him helped alleviate these deficiencies. A man with remarkable business and managerial sense, Scott came to Washington in April to head the War Department's telegraph and railroad operations. His work as vice president of the mammoth Pennsylvania Railroad made him especially suited to the task. Because railroad and telegraph companies were privately owned, it forced the government to rely on them, and thus brought private, state, and national entities together. Scott's duties had expanded during the summer, and he had grown into the job, giving some much-needed definition to the War Department. He instituted a set of procedures that restructured not only private-public transactions, but also nation-state transactions, including reimbursement to states, which had amassed significant debt.[78]

Within four months, a Northern leviathan emerged from thousands of local communities populated by citizens eager to vindicate democracy and preserve the Union. The time had come to teach Southern fire-eaters that "there is a *North*," wrote an inspired Michigan soldier to Blair, "which has equal rights and a voice." He declared, "The arrogance of the South has become intolerable," and he expected governors to take necessary steps to prosecute the war vigorously.[79] Thus far, governors had taken several steps to not only prosecute the war, but also to stay in line with Lincoln's limited war aims to achieve the ultimate objective of preserving the Union. They used their legislative messages and their private and public correspondence with officers, congressmen, soldiers, and civilians to explain the war as a contest to rescue the Union from dissolution. To invest citizens in the war and shape public sentiment, chief executives emphasized duty, citizenship, and obligation to the cause. When they could, governors lectured citizens on the Constitution, political systems, and the republic's great clashes between nation and state, as well as on the theory and practice of self-government.

CHAPTER FIVE

Doing the Very Best We Can

For Americans accustomed to legislative directives, White House–statehouse directives appeared unnatural. So much power concentrated in so few executives was undemocratic, especially as none could foresee how the war would develop. Within months, however, the arrangement produced a war machine that cemented a federal-state alliance. Many Northerners came to rely on these executives to help them cope with the war's exigencies. Lack of pay, equipment, and supplies, and a relentless press that criticized the administration's unpreparedness countered the earlier enthusiasm. Governors balanced national and local responsibilities, and citizens depended on them for aid in adjusting to war.

Seasonal changes, news from the front, and criticism over army administration tested governors' capacity to maintain popular support for preserving the Union. When rumors reached Cameron that Confederates were planning an attack on Washington, he queried governors about sending regiments forward. They responded that the harvest season, coupled with the extended enlistment period from three-months to three years, kept some Northerners at home. Even soldiers due to muster out were unenthusiastic about reenlisting. Public recrimination against the administration for having mismanaged the war deterred potential volunteers. Despite raising bounties and promising competent officers, governors found it difficult to overcome these obstacles. In Connecticut, for example, Buckingham saw the need to stifle disloyal sentiments by issuing a proclamation that outlined the dangers from "unauthorized speech and reckless conduct," such as public displays of peace flags.[1] While the Constitution guaranteed "liberty of speech and of the press," it also held "the person and the press responsible for the evils which result from the liberty." Buckingham called on law officers to be "diligent and fearless in arresting . . . those who are guilty of sedition and treason, and of those who are embraced in combinations to obstruct the execution of the laws."[2]

Warring

Governors expected that public enthusiasm would wane after the Bull Run defeat, and they combated naysayer rhetoric, even supporting the government's arrest of dissidents. Buckingham, for example, applauded the arrest of outspoken peace advocate Ellis B. Schnabel for "making treasonable harangues at peace meetings," in Morris, Connecticut. The governor confided to Secretary of the Navy Gideon Welles that Schnabel's arrest was "the best news I have heard to-day. I trust and know it will have a just affect upon traitors here."[3] Phineas T. Barnum, the great impresario of his day, wrote to Lincoln that Schnabel's arrest was so effective in rendering "secessionists *so scarce*, I cannot find one for exhibition in my museum."[4] To appease citizens angered by such arrests, Buckingham sought incentives for enlistees to re-enlist for three years and personally offered $2,500 to fund the soldiers' expenses.[5]

Governors understood the link between home front and battlefront, and many of them frequented the ranks to reinforce that connection. Their arrival in camp carrying packages and newspapers represented home. Emphasis on local community, whether through speeches or correspondence with the soldiers, was part of the nationalizing experience. Fighting to preserve the Union was as much a fight to maintain home and community, and it gave new meaning to the cause. Governors reminded soldiers that their presence in the ranks represented democratic ideals, and that they were representative parts of the whole. When the troops of the 1st Connecticut Infantry returned to New Haven in late July, Buckingham welcomed them. He marched at the head of these tattered men, many outfitted in captured Confederate clothes or pants made from blankets. He made it known that even while these men looked disheveled, they had nonetheless signed up for another three years. As a testament to their Yankee resolve, these short-term veterans presented quite a spectacle in New Haven and stoked the fires of enthusiasm.[6]

The outpouring of troops in the weeks after Bull Run quickly waned. Governors were eager to restore popular confidence in the war effort, but the chronic lack of pay worked against them. Morgan wired Cameron in mid-August that nonpayment of the regiments recently returned from service discouraged citizens. Some soldiers loafed in New York City waiting for pay. Worse yet was that agricultural labor at that time of the year commanded higher wages than soldiering. Governor Andrew agreed that the harvest and the recent repulses negatively impacted volunteering, but more critical was that Massachusetts had yet to draw on the National Treasury for the cost of raising volunteers. Congress had legalized, adopted, and directed the war's prosecution and volunteer enlistment, yet representatives failed to formalize a blueprint for state-federal relations. It fell to the governors, however, to preserve popular support that produced volunteers for the ranks. Andrew considered it prudent for Cameron to adopt a more efficient course in coordinating mobilization through federal and state agents to avoid further embarrassment. Although he perceived a revived spirit among his Massachusettans, his state had not been paid for the last several months. If Cameron needed governors to hasten troops forward to fend off an attack on the capital, Andrew needed money, precise orders, and a plan for the coming months.[7]

To compensate for the slow enrollment, Cameron accepted independent units for temporary service. He sought the governors' responses over whether accepting such units would impede the organization of the volunteer forces now being enrolled for three years. Many responded that accepting independent units would embarrass them. Blair was so incensed that he wished to say a few words that were "not appropriate for the telegraph." He appealed to Cameron not to accept independent regiments from any state as they introduced "confusion and discord into all our affairs."[8]

By mid-August border state governors found compensating for sluggish volunteering even more problematic. Confederate President Jefferson Davis approved raising Confederate troops in Missouri, Kentucky, Maryland, and Delaware. The Union's disastrous showing at the Battle of Wilson's Creek, fought 10 August just southwest of Springfield, Missouri, encouraged Davis's efforts. Generals Sterling Price and Benjamin McCulloch won a strategic victory for the Southern cause and prepared to lure Missourians into the Confederacy. Iowa governor Kirkwood was in Washington in the days following the battle, and when news surfaced that his Iowa boys had performed well at the Missouri battle, "every man who saw me had to shake hands with me." He boasted to his Iowa colleagues, "Placing my hat at an angle of 45 degree, I stalked through the [capitol] building as though I owned it—and they let me."[9] Nevertheless, a second Union defeat, resulting in some 1,300 casualties, distressed Gamble. Secessionists joined the Confederate ranks, and Frémont called on the War Department for more troops. Known for his western expeditions, before the war that earned him the nickname the "Pathfinder," Frémont was just the commander to transform northwestern farm boys into soldiers. Fearing that soldiers' terms were about to expire, he wired governors for additional regiments. Randall responded that he could send a crack German regiment, but Wisconsin farmers were harvesting their crops. Yates had warned Frémont about the vast departmental responsibilities, and Missouri's problems appeared insurmountable. The commander was reluctant to move until reinforcements arrived. Gamble strengthened his efforts by harnessing resources to protect loyal Missourians. He created a state militia, called for 42,000 men for six-month enlistments, and asked Lincoln to cover the expense. Despite their opposing views on slavery, Gamble's ability to work with Frémont hinged on their willingness to agree that keeping Missouri in the Union was more important than protecting slavery.[10]

Frémont and Gamble sustained the Union's hold on Missouri, yet supplying the troops remained challenging. Congress had allowed the president to accept independent regiments when governors were unable to meet their quotas. However well intended, this practice worked against governors because commanders could raise units from several states, thus reducing the number of potential state volunteers. Many governors, including Morgan, complained that crossovers in authority hindered state recruiting and clarified to Cameron that mustering men into the ranks belonged to the governors. Dennison was more emphatic. "It is not possible," he protested, "to pursue any system in organizing troops in Ohio so long as you authorize the raising of any outside of the discretion and immediate direction of the Governor." He fumed, "I pray you to issue no more such."[11] Pennsylvania governor Curtin also complained and demanded the War Department eliminate such practices. Lincoln settled the confusion by ordering all independent commands to report to state governors, who would reorganize them and prepare them for service.[12]

Even as the government accepted regiments into service, quartermasters could not supply them adequately. Governors therefore increased their assistance to the soldiers. When Indiana governor Morton learned that his soldiers in western Virginia needed overcoats, he supervised the acquisition and distribution of some 8,000 overcoats. He hired purchasing agents, armed them with state funds, and sent them scouring for supplies. Like many governors, Morton sent financial agents into the ranks to act as depositors for the soldiers who wanted to deposit their pay into their local banks. So efficient was Morton that soldiers relied on him for supplies. When members of the 12th Indiana refused to depart Indianapolis until they had rifled muskets to replace the old smooth-bores, the colonel had Morton lecture them. He "regretted it as much as they [did] that they could not be furnished the best arms in the service," but if they waited, he argued, another "Bull Run defeat might be the result."[13] The men gave him "three hearty cheers" and marched off to war.[14]

Cameron's mismanagement made McClellan's appointment as commander of the Army of the Potomac timely. Governors welcomed anyone who brought a professional military bearing to manpower flow and appointment of qualified officers. Secretary of the Navy Welles witnessed these changes in Washington, writing to his wife that since he left Hartford six months before, events were "extraordinary ... much like a dream." He admitted, "As a people we are undergoing a transformation," and the result he predicted would be a "modified government of a different nationality in some respects from that we have known."[15]

No better transformative evidence existed than in Missouri, Kentucky, and Maryland, where governors worked with commanders to solve problems. Governor Gamble, Generals Frémont and Pope cooperated to maintain peace among the divided Missourians, but commanders tried to stifle disloyal activities by imposing military justice. The governor complained to Lincoln that the departure of loyal volunteers from northern Missouri would weaken Pope's strategy. To protect loyalists in southwestern Missouri, Frémont declared martial law. Such approaches, while militarily prudent, created hostility toward Gamble's administration. The fallout from Missouri's military rule alarmed nearby governors, whose citizens feared ruffians seeking revenge. "In my judgment," Kirkwood argued, "the Union men there [Northern Missouri] should be armed and organized and backed by a strong armed and organized force in Iowa." If Union troops could form and make a stand along the Missouri-Iowa border, he argued, it would drive out border ruffians, who he believed "ought to be hung."[16]

Kentuckians were in no better condition. The legislature had pledged its support to the Union during the weeks of secession, but the governor's refusal to provide troops for Lincoln's call had cast him a traitor. Magoffin's neutral stance provoked Union legislators, who in June's special elections seized an overwhelming majority. Yet, the governor's determination to keep Kentucky neutral was no surprise. Magoffin was an agrarian Democrat and a devoted native. Upon graduation from college he moved to Jackson, Mississippi, to embark on a legal career, but ill health forced him to return to Kentucky. He married into a political family and joined the Democratic

Party. In 1859 he ran successfully for governor and followed secession closely. In January 1861 he convened the Kentucky General Assembly and requested legislators to call for a sovereignty convention, but representatives balked. In early August state election returns boasted a two-thirds Unionist majority in both houses, and Magoffin was a governor without a state. The governor corresponded little with Lincoln over the summer and proclaimed neutrality to disguise his Confederate sympathies. Without the governor's cooperation, Lincoln relied on Kentuckians Joshua Speed and William Nelson. Convinced there was sizable Union support in the state, these loyalists encouraged the recruitment of companies in defiance of Magoffin's neutrality. When the governor demanded that Lincoln remove the loyal force, the president refused. He argued that he was responding to "the urgent solicitation of many Kentuckians, and in accordance with what I believed, and still believe, to be the wish of a majority of all the Union-loving people of Kentucky."[17] Yates, Morton, and Dennison offered Lincoln assistance. "We can easily secure means of transportation that will be ready for use at a moment's notice," they agreed, to keep Kentucky in the Union and safeguard Illinois, Indiana, and Ohio from disaster.[18]

The Politics of Expansion

Recruiting moved slowly in early September, yet the Union army expanded across the several-hundred-mile border between North and South. Morgan had promised to steer 100,000 New Yorkers into the ranks by December to accommodate the army's increasing demands. When he could, he organized complete regiments rather than allowing partial regiments to offer their services, and offered agents two-dollar premiums if they enlisted thirty-two volunteers. Across rural New York, the governor established regimental camps so farmers could be quartered near their homes. Andrew also promised additional regiments, but a jurisdictional dispute over command distracted him. In August Cameron had authorized Brigadier General Thomas W. Sherman to recruit 12,000 men in New England for an undisclosed campaign and had sent circulars to the governors to supply the men. General Butler, however, had also been scheming, and he sought permission to raise 5,000 New England recruits, mainly Democrats, for a Gulf Coast expedition. He argued that his plan was important politically and militarily, because it appealed to the region's loyal opposition. Lincoln consented, provided the commander gained the New England governors' approval. General Sherman, however, had already pressed Andrew for troops for his expected Southern campaign, and when Butler came to Boston calling for troops under Lincoln's authorization, the governor protested. Responsible for the irregularities, Lincoln wrote to Andrew, seeking his support of the plan. Andrew consented, but demanded that Sherman recruit his force before Butler, and Lincoln honored his request. To hasten recruiting and strip Andrew of appointing officers, Butler traveled to Washington, secured Cameron's appointment in the hastily created Department of New England, returned to his Boston headquarters, and authorized a half-month's advance pay to his recruits.[19]

Butler's actions caused friction between Washington and Boston. When Andrew learned that the commander had granted bounties and commissions to some of the "Hunker Democrats" in the state, he overruled him. To defend his case, Butler appeared at the Capitol, but Andrew refused to receive him and, in fact, also denied him a room in the statehouse to conduct business. The governor complained that Butler's men had been raised in violation of the law, the War Department orders, and against his authority. "I mean to do, just what I have from the first persistently done," Andrew responded, "and that is, too hold with an iron hand and unswerving purpose all the powers which, by the laws pertain to me officially."[20] Furious, Butler wired Cameron that Andrew's "doctrine of secession did not seem to me any more sound uttered by a Governor north of Mason and Dixon's line than if proclaimed by Governor Magoffin south." He challenged Cameron, arguing that "now becomes a question of the utmost moment to the United States." He asked, "Will you recruit your own men under your own authority, or will you allow the authority to be wrested from you by the states?"[21] For the next few months, the civil-military squabble deteriorated into a series of insulting exchanges between Andrew and Butler that failed to settle the affair.

Had matters of a more serious nature not directed Lincoln away from the Andrew-Butler squabble, he might have given it more attention. After all, the administration had muddied the civil-military waters, and the president's silence infuriated Andrew, who believed Lincoln had abandoned him. But at the moment, Gamble needed Lincoln to weigh in on Frémont's actions in Missouri. On 30 August, the commander declared martial law throughout the state, and authorized the confiscation of all property and the emancipation of slaves. The news shocked slaveholding Unionists whom Lincoln had lured into believing his war aims did not include abolishing slavery. Gamble had reassured planters that he would reward their loyalty by protecting their slaves, and Frémont's proclamation undermined all he had accomplished that summer. Declaring martial law was risky, but Pope had been fueling Frémont's fire. The commander argued that the war in Missouri could "only be ended by making all engaged in it suffer for every act of hostility committed."[22] His order not only exceeded his authority, but also jeopardized the work of loyal Kentuckians, Marylanders, and western Virginians. Joshua Speed, Lincoln's Kentucky friend, was in Cincinnati preparing to meet with Yates and Morton on Kentucky matters and wrote Lincoln that Frémont's proclamation would hurt Kentucky loyalists. "Our Constitution & laws both prohibit the emancipation of slaves among us— even in small numbers," he advised Lincoln, "[i]f a military commander can turn them loose by the thousand by mere proclamation," it would prove disastrous.[23]

Lincoln favored working within the Constitution, especially when it involved slavery, and he asked Frémont to rescind his orders. Yet circumstances in St. Louis were far different from those in Washington, and Frémont refused to back down from his proclamation unless Lincoln ordered him to do so. Retracting his orders would undermine his credibility, especially since Radical Republicans applauded his vigor. "This is as much a movement in the war as a battle," he argued.[24] The president wanted to avoid associating emancipation with the preservation of the Union, but Frémont had forced his hand, and Lincoln ordered the commander to rescind his proclamation. A retraction, however, carried broader implications and wider repercussions than undermining loyal Union efforts in Missouri. Lincoln had drawn fire for his conciliatory handling of the border states. "Our President has broken his own neck if he has not destroyed his country," wrote Chicago journalist Horace White to Lincoln's colleague David Davis. "The public rage here, caused by his order countermanding Frémont's Proclamation is *fearful*, and my own indignation, I confess, is too deep for words."[25] To lessen the injury to his ego, Frémont demanded that Lincoln deny Gamble authorization in raising future troops. Gamble left for Washington the day before Frémont issued his proclamation, and the commander thought the governor was plotting to undermine him. Nevertheless, Gamble cooperated with Frémont, assembled ten regiments, and asked Lincoln to "allow them to come forward."[26]

Gamble had reason to discredit the commander, but he needed permission to raise a state militia to shield his administration from the fallout.

Soon relations worsened between Frémont and Gamble, and neither man trusted each other. Gamble used his private meeting with the president to convince him that Frémont's course would prove fatal for Missouri's loyalists, and Lincoln sent Gamble back to St. Louis armed with a letter to Frémont. The governor returned, delivered Lincoln's letter, and waited while Frémont read it. The two men exchanged complaints about each other's mishandling of appointments and the overall dissatisfaction of civil-military relations in the past month. It was a cordial meeting, but failed to undo their mutual animosity. Indeed, just the opposite. Frémont and Gamble expected the other to fail and ruin affairs in Missouri. The commander's aggressive tactics in Missouri had far-reaching implications. Lincoln was unwilling to expand his war aims early on, especially since he had yet to be victorious on the battlefield. Yet some journalists supported Frémont's proclamation, believing it reflected the attitude of many Northerners. Gamble believed otherwise. Seizing property and confiscating and liberating slaves was one thing, but occupying the soil of loyal Missouri slave owners would incite them to oppose Lincoln. Northern citizens, after all, were volunteering to preserve the Union, not emancipate slaves. "If Frémont has done nothing else," wrote Lincoln's secretary, "he has divided the North, as by sabre cut, *permanently*, into the new shape of 'conservatives' and 'radicals,' and the two factions, seeking for the most part the same ends but by different means, will be developed into regular form before the adjourning of this Congress."[27]

The politics of Frémont's command also affected civil-military governance in Kansas. Writing from Topeka, Governor Robinson assured Frémont that although secessionists were threatening Kansans, he was doing all he could to safeguard the state from border ruffians. Provided Cameron returned the government stores to Fort Leavenworth and removed Lane's brigade from the region, all would be well. Robinson needed relief, and he petitioned Cameron to allow Charles R. Jennison to organize a regiment of home guards to patrol the Kansas-Missouri border. The governor needed the reckless Lane out of command, and out of the state. "Missouri must be taught a lesson," he declared to his wife Sara, "& I should be glad of an opportunity to give it."[28] Similar to the Andrew-Butler and the Gamble-Frémont confrontations, Robinson contended with Lane.[29]

Amid worsening civil-military relations, military events took a decisive turn. On 3 September, Confederates stole into Kentucky and seized Hickman and Columbus on the Mississippi River. It was as bold a move as Frémont's proclamation. Governors expected that war would soon come to

Kentucky. Armed with information from his scouts, Morton wired General Scott the week before that an invasion was eminent. "At the risk of being considered troublesome," Morton wrote, "I will say the conspiracy to precipitate Kentucky into revolution is complete." He warned, "The blow may be struck at any moment." He admonished Scott, "If we lose Kentucky now, God help us."[30] Perhaps it was during this telegraphic exchange while Lincoln was in the War Department that Lincoln jokingly commented that he would like to give the Indiana governor a lesson in geography. "Morton is a good fellow," he remarked, "but at times he is the skeerdest man I know of."[31] "Skeered" or not, wrote one Indiana woman, Morton "is thoroughly alive to the interests and necessities of our Government."[32] If Lincoln needed Kentucky on his side, he could thank Morton for assistance.

Cameron directed midwestern governors to hasten soldiers to Cairo, Illinois, where Ulysses S. Grant was organizing a command. This directive reduced the number of troops pledged to St. Louis, Cincinnati, and Washington, but Cameron could not avoid it. Kentucky became the focal point for the moment, and Morton became its self-appointed "guardian spirit," a gesture that loyal Kentuckians long remembered.[33] When asked by an Indianan why she was so anxious to meet Morton that fall, a Kentucky woman responded "because he is *our* Governor as well as yours, and has been ever since the beginning of the rebellion."[34]

The war that had rankled Marylanders, Missourians, and western Virginians had now come to Kentuckians. Geographically positioned in the western heartland, citizens had been of two minds, one that favored slavery and the other that favored free labor. Residents were torn between market allegiances formed over the years and a political culture that was no longer able to settle disputes by compromise. Had Frémont been in Kentucky, Unionists feared they might have already lost the state, but thanks to the Confederate invasion there was hope. Grant's proclamation to Paducah Kentuckians was more conciliatory than Frémont's policy. The commander asserted that the "strong arm of the Government" had arrived, but with a conciliatory greeting. "I have come among you not as an enemy, but as your friend and fellow-citizen," he declared. "Not to injure or annoy you, but to respect the rights and to defend and enforce the rights of all loyal citizens."[35]

Lincoln had allowed Kentuckians neutrality during the summer, much to the chagrin of western governors. Still, he endorsed the recruiting of Kentucky Unionists. Loyalists established camps in Cincinnati and, with the aid of Morton and Dennison, smuggled arms into the hands of volunteers assembling under Union General William "Bull" Nelson at Camp Dick Robinson near Frankfort. Paducah was located at the confluence of the Tennessee and Ohio Rivers, and Grant, recognizing its strategic importance, seized the small river hamlet on 6 September. Using Cairo as a base, he placed Brigadier General Charles F. Smith in command of western Kentucky, and loyal Kentuckians welcomed Union forces. To anchor eastern Kentucky, Lincoln sent Brigadier General George H. Thomas. Kentucky legislators had tolerated the secessionists' divisive rhetoric, and when they convened 2 September, members pressed Magoffin to remove Confederate troops from the state. Magoffin vetoed such measures and argued that the resolution did not include federal troops. Kentucky legislators overrode the veto and claimed victory. The president authorized Kentucky native Robert Anderson, who had been readying his men across the river for weeks, to cross into Louisville and establish headquarters.[36]

Anderson's new assignment redirected the attention of midwestern governors toward Kentucky. Since the hostilities erupted, they had raised and sent troops to Washington, Cincinnati, and St. Louis. Now they directed troops to Louisville. As the war expanded, it made sense that Cameron relied on states east of the Appalachian Mountains to send troops to Washington, and on those states west of the mountains to forward troops to the heartland. Proximity, cost, and military necessity, however, determined these distributions as the war unfolded. Confederate General Leonidas Polk's occupation of Columbus, Kentucky in early September voided the state's neutrality and forced Unionists to respond. Lincoln now contended with three military fronts. Governors raised troops to outfit the emerging national armies that stretched across over 1,300 miles of the border between North and South.[37]

Governors understood Kentucky's importance to the Union, but Gamble refused to allow loyal Missourians to suffer while Lincoln focused on Kentucky. He asked Bates to call on Lincoln for supplies to arm men holding onto Missouri. "In Common justice, send the arms at once," Gamble warned, arguing that in lieu of that, "I shall conclude that Mo is to be abandoned to devastation and ruin."[38] Bates later attempted to rationalize Lincoln's attitude toward Missouri to Gamble. "The President, poor man, is in great distress at the way things are going, without (as he supposes) power to change the current," he allowed, "he is an intelligent and virtuous man but . . . he has no will, nobody afraid of him."[39] To buoy his confidence that he was handling Missouri affairs better than Frémont, Gamble's nephew praised him for his patience. "You acted the patriot and the statesman throughout," he acknowledged, "under his [Frémont's] rule we have already lost the Indian and other Territories, most of Missouri and if he is retained in the command of the west, we will lose Missouri and Illinois."[40]

The civil-military stress in Missouri had repercussions for neighboring states. "If he [Frémont] were the veriest fool that ever wore a sword," Gamble wrote to Lincoln, "I would be perfectly satisfied that he should have all the glory of the achievement if the enemy should be driven from the state."[41] To Montgomery Blair, however, the governor explained more pressing matters. The state was bankrupt, its bonds would sell not on the market, and he had financially overextended himself. Lincoln had promised funds, but none had arrived. The financial matters alone worried Gamble, but with the legislature set to convene in early October and the state election just weeks away, he was unsure of Missouri's future. Adding to Gamble's troubles was Frémont's disregard for Lincoln, and the fact that the commander had ordered thousands of his original emancipation decrees be distributed throughout Missouri, and that he had arrested Frank Blair for conspiring against him. Lincoln had dispatched Cameron and Nicolay to St. Louis, and Nicolay reported that the "universal opinion" was that Frémont had "utterly failed, *and that he ought to be removed*—that any change will be for the better."[42] Lincoln replaced the commander a week later with Brigadier General David Hunter. Governors wanting to bend the war toward a more radical and abolitionist arc disapproved of Frémont's removal. Expecting rancor from New England governors, Lincoln sent Blair to Boston to soften the blow with Andrew before the official announcement.[43]

Lincoln's removal of Frémont temporarily smothered the civil-military flames in Missouri, but it ignited fires elsewhere. After Congress adjourned, Lane returned to Kansas with a brigadier general's commission, expecting to suppress Missouri insurrectionists. He supported Frémont's proclamation and had raised an independent force to control local matters. Robinson had tried to dissolve Lane's unit by denying him weapons, but Lane requested that Lincoln establish a new military department and appoint him commander. He had also written to Union General Samuel Sturgis in early October that the confiscation of slaves and other property useful to the army "should follow treason as the thunder peals follows the lightening flash." He exclaimed, "I had a man cowardly shot in the woods by the very man, I have no-doubt, whose property you are so anxious to protect."[44] Gamble understood Robinson's predicament, and he used what influence he had with Lincoln in support of the Kansas governor. "Allow me to say to you that the friends of the Union in Missouri and particularly those upon its Western frontier," Gamble wired Lincoln, "will look with horror upon that man when clothed with military authority," adding that "he is himself utterly lawless, suited only to lead a force of robbers."[45] Lincoln refused to consider Lane's plan and remained committed to Robinson's more cautious approach to keeping the peace in Kansas.[46]

Before the Frémont hysteria carried into Kentucky, governors needed to solidify Union control over the state. Lincoln agreed. "To lose Kentucky," he declared to Orville H. Browning, who filled Stephen A. Douglas's Senate seat after his death, "is nearly the same as to lose the whole game." He asserted that with "Kentucky gone, we can not hold Missouri, nor as I think, Maryland."[47] The president was especially grateful to Morton, who assisted Kentucky loyalists. A *Louisville Daily Journal* reporter noted that Morton had been "Kentucky's guardian spirit from the very commencement of the dangers that darkly threaten[ed] her existence."[48] "There is no man in the nation to whom Kentucky owes a larger debt of gratitude than to Morton," wrote the editor of the *Lexington Observer*.[49]

As much as governors waded through the politics of civil-military command in Missouri, Kansas, and Kentucky, the approaching autumn signaled another wrinkle. The changing climate would hinder northwestern governors' contributions to the war effort. The winter snows and frozen waterways typically closed river, rail, and lake traffic and isolated Minnesota, Wisconsin, and Michigan. Ramsey warned Cameron that navigation on the Mississippi River would close in two months. With his treasury emptied, he sent the bills detailing the costs thus far in the war, but it took months for reimbursement. This circumstance hampered his ability to pay bills owed by the state to local, regional, and eastern banks. Morgan was aware of such financial hardships and had advised Cameron that his agents had exhausted their influence in Europe. The governor had shouldered much of the war's financial responsibility, and he needed relief. Montgomery C. Meigs, quartermaster general, was aware of this circumstance. "No nation probably ever so quickly and so thoroughly organized and equipped so large an army," he wrote to Morgan, "and so nearly paid its way as we have done."[50]

To aid them in solving civil-military crises, regimental deficiencies, and financial shortages, governors often visited Washington. They used these occasions to visit the ranks and frequently invited Lincoln along. The president enjoyed socializing with the soldiers, and governors benefited from the confidential exchanges during the carriage rides. "He, more clearly than any man about him, has comprehended the nature and the magnitude of the rebellion," observed a correspondent to the *Chicago Tribune*, yet Lincoln "is neither omnipotent nor omnipresent" and relied on those around him to carry out the acts he directed.[51] Curtin was in Washington in September, and he and Lincoln delivered regimental colors to several Pennsylvania units. Curtin used such moments to reinforce to the soldiers that their representation in arms was symbolic of Pennsylvania's place in the Union. "I place in your hands the honor of your State," the governor said, as Lincoln looked on, "thousands of your fellow-citizens at home look to you to vindicate the honor of your great State.... They look to you ... to vindicate the great government to sustain legitimate power and to crush out rebellion."[52]

Fall Elections

As autumn approached, the war advanced politically. Northern voters in nine states went to the polls. California, Maine, and Vermont opened the electoral season in early September, followed in October by Massachusetts and midwesterners in Iowa, Minnesota, and Ohio. Wisconsin and Maryland held November elections. Though last in election timetables, Maryland was first on Lincoln's mind. Maryland voters would replace Hicks, and the election would require military supervision. New Englanders went to the polls yearly to elect their governors. Thus, Andrew and Washburn campaigned for reelection amid their other duties and won wide appeal among voters. Republicans nominated Washburn without opposition, and voters reelected the executive by a large majority. "Next to Vermont," wrote the editor of the *Chicago Tribune*, "Maine has each year led off in the progressive demonstrations of the time, and again in 1861 she has set the nail that shall be driven in the coffin of Northern toryism."[53] Andrew also ran unopposed and won the Massachusetts election by an overwhelming majority. His election emboldened him to consider pushing black enlistments on Cameron.[54]

Vermonters could be harsh on state administrators, and, despite New England's political tradition of entitling governors to successive terms, Erastus Fairbanks decided not to seek a third term. For a governor who never drew his salary from the treasury, and whose business firms in the South had lost thousands of dollars, Fairbanks had suffered under close public scrutiny. His son Franklin noticed this criticism. "It must be exceedingly annoying to you," he wrote, "to listen to such remarks & insinuations, & you have our warm sympathy, & earnest desire that you may soon be relieved from this state of trial & anxiety." He further encouraged him, "I sincerely hope that you will not be effected by the taunts & jeers of the ungrateful portion of the state but will stand *firm* to your rights."[55] Republicans looked to conservative Frederick Holbrook. The youngest of ten children, Holbrook received an education at the Berkshire Gymnasium. His peers recognized his intellectual and leadership abilities and named him captain to a small military company, which forever won him the characterization as "Captain" Holbrook. The death of his father and a reversal of the family fortune forced him to return home and engage in agriculture. He devoted his life to agrarian pursuits and won wide acclaim for publishing articles in the finest agricultural journals. He helped found the Vermont State Agricultural Society and served as president, which gave him exposure in political circles. His victory over Democrat Andrew Tracy by more than 27,000 votes began an election season of favor and fortune for Republicans.[56]

Iowans went to the polls in early October. As much as Kirkwood wanted outsiders to believe there was one party for the Union, he could not escape the political divisiveness that characterized the state's political culture. Despite opposition from the southern counties and a slate of four candidates for opponents, Kirkwood won nomination on the first ballot. "You have doubtless heard," wrote longtime friend William B. Allison after the convention, "that the rubicon is passed," yet "it is useless to disguise or deny the fact [that] there was a most bitter and determined opposition in the Convention to your re-nomination."[57] Despite personal attacks, Kirkwood was undeterred. The state's most pressing problem was not his; it stemmed from Iowans' failure to provide enough funds to supply the soldiers. Not as endearing as he might have been under the circumstances, the governor nonetheless blamed his enemies for the state's shortcomings. He was reelected easily and continued his work for the Union.[58]

Kirkwood's naysayers were incomparable to the Democratic opposition in Ohio. Then again, Dennison was no Kirkwood. His flair for pomposity, his "aloofness" from the press, and his occasional "confrontational attitude" with political and military leaders undermined the population's confidence in him. Party leaders held a Union convention and nominated David Tod, a Democrat turned Unionist, who won Ohio's two-year gubernatorial term by more than 55,000 votes. An Ohio native, Tod was the son of a prominent Youngstown judge and followed him into the profession, eventually proving to be a successful lawyer. His legal interest grew into politics, and Ohio Democrats elected him to the Ohio Senate in 1838. He earned a reputation for his proslavery views and supported legislation to enforce the return of runaways. He twice ran unsuccessfully for state governor in the 1840s and turned to business where he became involved with the coal and iron industries of the Mahoning Valley. By 1860 he returned to politics and presided over the Democratic National Convention in Baltimore in 1860, where he helped to secure Douglas's nomination as a presidential candidate. When the war broke out he joined the newly formed Union Party. Coggeshall noted in his diary that Tod was a "good Union man," though with a "'powerful mean' political record."[59] Nevertheless, Ohioans believed he could handle the war's demands.[60]

War beyond Washington

It was difficult for national authorities to imagine the war beyond Washington. It was harder yet for them to fathom the conflict beyond the Appalachians, so governors helped them. For months Dennison, Yates, and Morton had uncovered secessionist plots in Missouri, Kentucky, and western Virginia. Morton shared his information with Lincoln to keep the president attuned to the western war. "It will be a sad day to you and to the Nation when Kentucky drifts into revolution," he wrote Lincoln, "the misfortune at Bull's run [sic] would be a mere trifle compared with it." He demanded "vigor sagacity and preparation."[61] Lincoln appreciated the governor's apprehension, but he needed Morton to understand the war in Washington. "I write this letter," Lincoln began, "because I wish you to believe of us (as we certainly believe of you) that we are doing the very best we can." Lincoln wired, "While I write this, I am, if not in *range,* at least in *hearing* of cannon-shot, from an army of enemies more than a hundred thousand strong." Yet at Louisville, "there is not a single hostile armed soldier within forty miles, nor any force known to be moving upon it from any distance."[62]

Morton had little patience for Lincoln's excuses and even less for Cameron's bungling practices. "Our border," he declared, "has been in a state of feverish anxiety and alarm, and I am constantly in receipt of letters, messages and committees asking for guns and that preparations should be made for their defense." He wrote, "The question was asked every day, what have you heard from Washington? What is the Government doing or what does it promise to do for us?" Given Cameron's lack of attention to the war beyond the Appalachians, Morton told Indianans they must rely on their home resources for defense. "In this contest," he urged, "the Government is compelled to lean upon the States for its Armies; and in my opinion the hands of the men who labor without ceasing to sustain the Government should be held up and not depressed by indifference to their recommendations or demands."[63]

Greatness could be expected of McClellan, but by October complaints surfaced criticizing the army's inactivity. "The public spirit is beginning to quail under the depressing influence of our prolonged inaction," wrote Bates, summarizing the mood in Washington. "We absolutely need some dashing expeditions," he wrote in his diary, "some victories, great or small, to stimulate the zeal of the country, and, as I think, to keep up the credit of the Government."[64] It was a mystery to Count Adam Gurowski why McClellan kept his headquarters in Washington "among the flunkeys, wiseacres, and spit-lickers."[65] Delawarean James R. Latimer agreed, complaining to a friend in October that "the whole proceedings at Washington (military) is a mystery to me," and that he could not understand how, "with an overwhelming force, McClellan seems to be satisfied to rest secure in his inactivity, while Kentucky and Missouri are in the agonies of death."[66]

Lincoln hoped to deliver loyal Kentuckians from secessionist marauders by replacing Anderson with Brigadier General William T. Sherman, a hard-bitten West Pointer. Sherman recognized he would have to "move heaven and earth to get the arms, clothing, and money" necessary to safeguard the state, and that "the power which controls the Ohio and Mississippi will ultimately control this continent." Shortly after arriving, he complained to Dennison about the difficulties in organizing his expeditions and that he feared he had not enough men to be successful.[67] To better comprehend the western war, Cameron toured the Midwest in October, and he stopped off in Louisville on his return from St. Louis. There he met Sherman, who declared that his vast 300-mile line would require more than 200,000 troops. "Great God," the secretary remarked, "where are they to come from?"[68] In Cameron's mind, governors had committed themselves to meeting the War Department's quotas to supply eastern and western armies, as well as the units forming in New England, but equipping these men stalled their efforts. Sherman's "gloomy" assessment was shocking and convinced Cameron that the commander's responsibilities had overwhelmed him. In the frenzy of Frémont's proclamation, the saving grace for Lincoln was that Sherman returned runaway slaves found in Union camps.[69]

The war behind the front lines also moved Lincoln to expand his suspension of the writ of habeas corpus between Washington and Maine. He feared disloyalty to his war aims, and the directive applied only to military personnel. He directed Secretary of State Seward to confer with governors of the Atlantic Coast states and those bordering the Great Lakes to safeguard the port cities in case Europeans entered the war. Maine exceeded all other states in shipbuilding, furnishing some "two-fifths of the sailing tonnage of the entire merchant-service." Washburn responded with an impressively detailed report outlining a plan of defensive fortifications on the Maine Coast and suggested that Portland be designated the Union's principle naval depot. Lincoln thought the report insightful and sent it to the Engineer and Ordnance bureaus for examination.[70]

For all the warring in the West, the politics of expansion, and election excitement, the most alarming news that fall came from Leesburg, Virginia, where on 21 October, the Confederates defeated the Federals at Ball's Bluff on the Potomac River. News of the defeat sped through the press, adding renewed fire to the smoldering demoralization among Northerners. Andrew was so inflamed that he wrote to the *Boston Journal*, hinting that it was Butler whose careless attention to detail in arming the men caused them defeat at Ball's Bluff. Yet critics also charged that Andrew allowed inferior arms to go forward, and the tensions between Bostonians and the governor soured into a series of back-and-forth exchanges. Yet not all Washingtonians lost hope. "Strange as it may seem at first thought," wrote Stoddard, "the battle of Leesburg has done the whole army a good service . . . . [it] has furnished our camp fires with a theme for conversation, which is having a decided effect upon the *morale* of the army."[71]

Amid Lincoln's handling of Frémont's proclamation, the Ball's Bluff fiasco heightened Northern bitterness toward an administration that appeared to be paralyzed by conciliatory policies to keep border states in the Union. Military reversals also inspired congressional Radicals to establish a committee to examine the commanders' conduct when they convened in December. Nevertheless, the battle proved to be a weathervane pointing the direction for governors to press the administration for a more vigorous war against slavery. "O God," Andrew fumed to a friend, "for a Cameronian battle-cry; for a grand, inspiring, electric shout, coming from the high priests themselves, from the very Jerusalem of our cause!" He added, "I wait to hear it, and believe it will yet burst forth, and ring in all our ears," but "this people must be *welded* together with the fire itself, both of the spirit and the flesh."[72]

In addition to suffering battlefield losses, governors had yet to be reimbursed for their war debts by the Treasury, and creditors were calling in loans. Many chief executives had overextended their states, and the rewards they believed would be won on the battlefield had not materialized. Lincoln and the governors had united Northerners in preserving the Union and had fortified state and national loyalties. Yet, the president's retraction of Frémont's proclamation, his conciliatory policy toward border states, and the Treasury's unsettled claims aggravated Republicans and stifled Northern enthusiasm. Governors had assembled a giant army, yet Lincoln refused to use it to prosecute the war vigorously. They had rushed soldiers forward only to have them sit idle in camps, often grousing about their dissatisfaction in letters home. Governors were responsible for thousands of soldiers, and they wanted some say in how they should be used. Sending citizen-soldiers off to war generated local pride and established a kinship between governors and their constituents. Far from home, men needed governors behind them, responding to their requests, bringing replacements forward, and providing for their families. Governors visited the soldiers, and their presence in camp reminded them their state and country needed them in the cause. It remained to be seen what these men could achieve, but governors demonstrated they would do all in their power to advance their success.[73]

CHAPTER SIX

This Fearful Awakening

Three thousand miles separated Washington from Sacramento and Salem, and the deeply held convictions of North and South had conflicted Pacific Coast residents for months. Californians and Oregonians expectantly awaited news from the East. Many citizens had protested Lincoln's election, but presidential electors cast their votes in his favor, and much depended on his administration's direction. When the California State Legislature adjourned in May, members had resolved that they would stand with the Union. Until the September elections, however, Democrats controlled political patronage, the state's treasury, and the militia. California Republicans, however, looked to change that and had sent delegations to Springfield and Washington to shore up appointments.

Leland Stanford was among the political leaders who campaigned to win loyalists to the Republican Party at the September polls. He promoted protection of local interests and strove to keep the Union from further disruption, while advancing the nation's economy with the national government's aid. In his camp was longtime Lincoln friend Edward D. Baker, who had worked to keep the state in the Union. Baker's unsuccessful attempt to win a senate seat, however, forced him to move to Oregon, where Republicans convinced him to run for office. In 1860 the Oregon legislature elected him the state's first Republican senator and looked to him for reassurances that loyalists would prevail in supporting Lincoln. Three days after the battle of Ball's Bluff, however, unpleasant news arrived in the Sacramento Capitol. On the afternoon of 24 October, far removed from the conflict, Californians celebrated the completion of the transcontinental telegraph, a forty-four-hour magnetic connection that replaced the ten-day news delay between the Northern states and California. It was a magnificent achievement that reflected the bond between the Atlantic and Pacific Coast states, yet the room grew silent when the dispatch came over the wires. "Colonel [Edward] Baker was killed in Battle on the 21st, while in the act of cheering on his command," read the dispatch. Horace Carpentier, president of the Overland Telegraph Company, was saddened by the news. Just seven months before, Baker sat across from Lincoln in the carriage that traveled up Pennsylvania

Avenue to his inaugural. Still, knowing Californians were devoted to the Union reassured Lincoln, and he relied on his Pacific Coast governors to make good on their pledge to support him.[1]

Californians and Oregonians

Californians elected Leland Stanford their eighth governor on 4 September. He succeeded the outspoken Irishman John Downey. That day he sent a message to Lincoln characterizing his election as a "triumph and overwhelming victory in favor of the Union and the National Administration."[2] Stanford became California's Republican Party instrument, having campaigned that summer on a platform that supported Lincoln and the Union's preservation. Californians owed much of their state's recent progress to Republicans' expansive notions and the positive use of governmental power in promoting national development. Stanford capitalized on his business success to advance his political interests. A native New Yorker, he had worked for his father until the age of seventeen, when he entered Ithaca's Clinton Institute. He studied law at Cazenovia Seminary, passed the New York bar in 1848, and shortly after moved to Port Washington, Wisconsin, to embark on his legal career. It was in Port Washington that he found a passion for politics, public speaking, and journalism. He served briefly as district attorney of Washington County and also founded a newspaper in the city. In 1852, a fire destroyed his law office, and the young penniless lawyer headed to the California gold mines and panned the mines of the Sierra Nevada. To subsidize his mining exploits, Stanford joined his brothers in keeping a general store until 1856, when he moved to San Francisco. There he pursued mercantile and political interests and helped organize the state's Republican Party. He kept a hand in mining and soon became the principal stockholder in the Amador Quartz Mine, which allowed him to co-fund the Central Pacific Railroad with Collis P. Huntington, Mark Hopkins, and Charles Crocker. He was well known for his business associations, and the railroad made him president in 1861.[3]

The governor's financial prominence allowed him to remain president of the Central Pacific Railroad; he was personally responsible for its funding. Despite the military crisis, Lincoln had not lost interest in connecting the nation's coastlines by rail. Visionary that he was, Stanford urged Republicans to align with the antislavery cause and depart from the state's political past of avoiding the issue. "Patriots of the Atlantic States," read a

California dispatch, "your brothers of the Pacific shore meet you with these glad tidings, and wish you God speed in the sacred cause of the Union."[4]

Loyal Californians were grateful to previous governor Downey for keeping the state in the Union. He ensured that gold continued to travel east, especially as the Union war effort relied on it. Just the year before, the *Los Angeles Star* reported that more than $40 million worth of gold headed back East. Downey had initially opposed Lincoln's policies, but he had remained loyal, adhered to the Constitution, and fortified the borders and principal cities. He subdued Californians bent on forming a Pacific Republic with Oregon and surrounding territories, and, although the California press praised his efforts, they criticized his military appointments and his allowing weapons to be shipped to the lower counties, where they fell into secessionists' hands.

Brigadier General Edwin V. Sumner's arrival changed California's political fortunes. A career officer, Sumner assembled the frontier forces to safeguard San Francisco and concentrated Federals to secure the state's Union ties and protection from hostile Indians. After Bull Run, Pony Express riders arrived in Sacramento with notes from Lincoln ordering Downey to raise 6,000 volunteers and five companies of cavalry to guard the Overland Mail Route to Salt Lake City. Yet Downey waited until after Californians went to the polls in September before calling on men to serve. By this time, Lincoln called Sumner to serve in the East and sent General George Wright from Oregon to replace him. Downey welcomed the change, convinced that his record in "quieting Indian disturbances" would serve Californians well. Nevertheless, Downey's popularity waned in the summer, and critics accused him of disloyalty because he opposed the use of federal power in subduing Southerners rather than defending the capital. This "anti-coercion" policy, combined with his outspokenness against Lincoln personally, identified him as a Confederate sympathizer.[5]

Oregon's governor, "Honest John" Whiteaker, had similar problems. Voters had gone for Lincoln the year before, but secessionist sympathies had surfaced in the southern portion of the new state, where they expected the governor to support their actions. Oregonians were farmers, miners, and merchants who had migrated west from Missouri or Kentucky in the decade prior to the war. They carried with them cultural ties and hardened political views endorsing slavery and states' rights that resulted in Democratic majorities in the legislature. Though they supported the Union and desired statehood, Oregonians nonetheless supported the traditions of limited government, and even those who were antislavery were hardly abolitionists. They feared blacks would undermine the value of white labor in the region, and thus sympathized with the South's desire to defend its domestic institutions.[6]

Amid the crisis over Kansas statehood in the years before the Civil War, Oregonians plunged into the same process and in 1858 elected sixty-one-year-old Whiteaker their first state governor. Congress delayed admitting the new state until February 1859, when Whiteaker took office. A native Indianan and a self-educated farmer, carpenter, and cabinetmaker who moved from job to job, Whiteaker succumbed to the California Gold Rush in 1849. He profited enough to return to Indiana to retrieve his wife and headed back to Eugene City, where he bought a farm. He became active in local politics, serving first as a county probate judge and then as territorial legislator before running successfully on the Democratic ticket for governor. He spent his first term settling disputed land claims and persuading residents to live off the Oregonian economy, often promoting the vast resources of the state. Citizens respected his message and rewarded him with the nickname "Old Soap, Socks, and Pickles."[7]

Although he supported land laws against the speculators and urged that Salem remain the capital, his ardently proslavery views alienated many of his followers. Lincoln and Cameron bypassed him in raising Union troops and relied instead on more devoted loyalists, such as Democrat Benjamin F. Harding, speaker of the Oregon House of Representatives, for support. Thus, Whiteaker's governorship came under scrutiny by Oregonians wanting to remain loyal. Not galvanized by the war, he had sent his vague, uninspiring address to the legislature from his Lane County farm in late May. He also prohibited Union flags and Union meetings, condemning them as "inflammatory" and counterproductive to reunion. While he admitted these meetings had merit, he proclaimed, "we should deceive ourselves, and mistake for Union meetings those which are held for the purpose of manufacturing partisan sentiment."[8] Statements such as these drew spirited responses in the press. One editor characterized Whiteaker's rise to power as if he "had been elevated from his natural dunghill to a high position by political demagogues." The editor went on to say that he was "the biggest ass in the state" and as "rotten a traitor as Jeff Davis."[9]

"Old Whit" had initially favored neutrality when the war broke out and had discouraged recruiting volunteers for the Union. He eventually responded to General Wright's call for a regiment to help stabilize affairs in California and to help safeguard Oregonians from Indian attacks. He also appointed Benjamin Stark, a controversial, politically ambitious, and outspoken pro-slavery Democrat, to succeed the fallen Baker in the Senate. This act drew condemnation from the Oregon press, which attacked him for insulting the people. A correspondent to the *St. Louis Daily Missouri Republican* remarked that Whiteaker had taken advantage of "the decree of God, which left the seat of Baker vacant," and "dared to pollute it by forcing into its occupancy a semi-secessionist."[10] By the fall, the regular army departed the state and left Oregonians to protect the Northwest frontier. Whiteaker came under fire for failing to support the troops adequately and for allowing them to leave without protest. "Gov. Whiteaker is too busy fiddling for Jeff. Davis, or too much afraid of correspondence with a Republican administration," decried the *Oregon Statesman*, "to demand any protection from the United States. . . . He perhaps thinks it better that 'Oregonians' . . . should be massacred rather than seek the polluting protection of 'Lincoln's black republican army.'" In a war that demanded unceasing loyalty to the Union cause, Whiteaker's appeal would be short lived with his constituency and with Lincoln.[11]

Command Changes

Despite their sizable pro-Southern populations and different party affiliations, Stanford and Whiteaker kept California and Oregon in the Union. Lincoln could do little for these westerners, especially now that the war had expanded into the border states. By early November the army's leadership took a significant turn as Lincoln accepted Scott's resignation and appointed McClellan commander of all U.S. forces. Border state governors especially welcomed the change because McClellan was a conservative Democrat determined to keep slavery out of the war. Missouri governor Gamble secured modification of the state's militia laws and won legislators' approval to negotiate with national authorities in governing state affairs. The governor arrived in Washington in early November hoping to convince the president he needed federal cooperation. Lincoln requested Gamble compose a memorandum for circulation among the high-ranking civil and military authorities, including McClellan. The memorandum argued that Missourians would likely volunteer for the state militia if they could be assured of remaining in the state. Gamble, however, needed federal funds to pay those troops. The issue of command, however, seemed unavoidably cumbersome. Gamble reasoned that the departmental commander, or a subordinate, be placed in charge of the militia to secure state-federal cooperation. His plan convinced McClellan and won Lincoln's approval. With these assurances, Gamble returned to St. Louis having claimed a small but important victory for loyal Missourians.[12]

To accommodate the Union's expanding military responsibility, McClellan reorganized the western departments. He eliminated the Department of the West and created a new Department of Kansas with headquarters at Fort Leavenworth, where he sent Hunter. He added a new Department of Missouri with headquarters in St. Louis, where he ordered Halleck. Missouri's new commander had a long list of military accomplishments, and Gamble felt he could benefit from a West Pointer in Missouri. Yet Halleck's endorsements failed to identify his antiforeign sentiments and disdain for politicians. Gamble was aware, however, that Halleck had been McClellan's rival for Scott's position. Thus, McClellan wanted Halleck far from Washington. At the time, it was unimportant that Halleck's new department stretched east into Kentucky and Tennessee, making him responsible for the region west of the Cumberland River. Restructuring the western command prompted the reorganization of the Department of the Ohio, which, besides Ohio, placed Indiana, Michigan, Tennessee, and Kentucky east of the Cumberland River under its domain. Having decided that Sherman was unfit to command in Kentucky, McClellan replaced him with prewar friend Brigadier General Don Carlos Buell, a commander whose flamboyant name belied a rough-hewn military discipline.[13]

At the time few political leaders in Washington considered these military changes dramatic. As Lincoln saw it, at the helm of the government's armies was a triumvirate of professionally trained commanders. The cumulative experience of McClellan, Halleck, and Buell was impressive, yet they believed themselves better suited than politicians to run the war. As conservative Democrats, they tolerated civil authorities more than they appreciated them. The Union's most important commands now rested in the hands of commanders who understood they were fighting a limited war for limited goals. The problem was that all three commanders were fighting border war politics as well as Confederate enemies. In giving Buell his new command, McClellan penned carefully worded instructions that it was "absolutely necessary that we shall hold all the State of Kentucky; not only that, but that the majority of its inhabitants shall be warmly in favor of our cause." It was possible, he wrote, "that the conduct of our political affairs in Kentucky" was "more important than that of our military operations." To accomplish the administration's goals, he reminded Buell that he was fighting only to preserve the Union.[14]

Governors accepted the command changes. In fact, they lauded them. Commanders who could restore order within the border states, improve mobilization, and establish confidence in the ranks were acceptable. In recent weeks soldiers tired of sitting in camp found governors useful as outlets to express their views over these changes. Ohioan Simeon Nash, for example, wrote to Dennison that he feared the new commanders were "too frightened and lacked audacity in their movements." Lincoln "did not want war in earnest," he argued, and Ohioans were "losing confidence in Lincoln's administration."[15] Governors meanwhile continued to organize and deliver regiment after regiment. From Vermont to Iowa, they supplied the armies and commissioned officers to command them. Besides infantry regiments, governors were now assembling additional cavalry, artillery, and medical units. After the lull in volunteering during the harvest season, recruiting increased, and the army grew. Dennison reported that recruiting was "doing nobly." So encouraged was Morgan that he sought permission to raise another twenty-five regiments, bringing New York's total to 125,000 men. Governors tried to find places for all volunteers and provided inspiring words when sending off new regiments. In seeing the men of the 5th New Hampshire off from Concord, Berry had no doubt the men "would give a good account of themselves." He was so enthused that he accompanied them to Washington.[16]

Of all the problems confronting the governors, keeping the soldiers paid was the most troublesome. Many governors had overcommitted themselves and their legislatures financially to keep pace in paying volunteers. Governor Olden complained that while New Jersey had supplied its share of troops, the national government had not supplied its share of the financial burden. "To complete what has been done," he complained, "the State has advanced over $700,000, and has received from the U.S. Treasury $74,000."[17] Olden instructed his attorney general, Frederick T. Frelinghuysen, to provide Chase with state expenditures to show that many of the loans to the state were temporary. "Our political position is somewhat different from that of other northern States," he argued, "if not hampered, we have the ability to do much for the nation in this crisis, our people make good soldiers, a liberal bounty is voted, our most worthy and patriotic Governor is a business man of no ordinary character—And if we can have a settlement with the Government, we can continue to send forward our troops."[18] With winter approaching, Olden appealed to wealthy New Jerseyans to aid him in procuring India Rubber blankets for the troops.[19]

Financial problems reflected the slow transition to a national mobilization. The centralization of procurement took time and coordination. For months governors had been the principal agents for the soldiers and used personal connections to secure war materials. Their authority coincided with republican traditions of American political development that kept decision making closer to home and privileged the party in power. Governors sought to localize the purchase of materials. This would bolster the local economy and improve their political currency among the citizens. As the war expanded and more volunteers came forward, governors reached into other state economies for camp equipage, weapons, and specialty items. This practice made it difficult to standardize uniforms and weapons and worked against nationalizing efforts within the Union commands. State agents working against each other to provide the best supplies for their troops drove up the prices and pressed the economy to increase supply to meet demand. The expanding army, however, exhausted state funds and contributed to the breakdown of the traditional state-oriented procurement. Moving away from these traditions forced governors to rely on federal funds, which made them dependent on federal control.

By the fall the War Department transferred procurement to the U.S. military quartermaster. Looking to standardize military equipment and reduce fraud, the transfer of power forced governors to relinquish their control. Several governors, including Yates, Washburn, and Morton, initially resisted the transfer of authority, arguing that quartermasters worked too slowly and inefficiently. They allowed state officials to continue to buy war materials. As the armies took on a national shape, so too did the military economy become more centralized and nationalized. The shift in authority from the states to the national government appeared yet another challenge to waging war within a federal structure that allowed governors economic and political influence. Governors found themselves displaced by the encroaching, yet undefined, national authority of bureaucratic professionals. Still, as U.S. officials arrived in state capitals, governors cooperated with military officials to ensure that their troops were well supplied and that their local economies benefitted by the new arrangement. They continued to travel to the camps and supply the men, attend to the welfare of soldiers' families, influence Union war aims, and work to keep their party in power.[20]

Governors also experienced newfound power by furloughing soldiers home to vote. As the war unfolded, state legislatures worked to devise constitutional mechanisms to enfranchise soldiers who were away from the states since most states required the voter to be present at the polls. Prior to the war, only Pennsylvania allowed for absentee voting to enfranchise the soldiers. As it existed, the system favored Republican governors, who pulled strings with the War Department to ensure that soldiers in the field, many believed to be Republican, could get home to exercise their franchise. The state elections in the fall, however, came off with minimal furlough activity, but legislators were keen to revise their constitutions when they convened the following year to provide for absentee voting to enfranchise soldiers in the field. In the first week of November, Minnesotans, Wisconsinites, and Marylanders went to the polls to elect governors, and Republicans and Unionists carried the day. Ramsey's popularity easily won him renomination, but Minnesota's Democrats complained the governor seemed more concerned in jockeying for a Senate seat than caring for the soldiers. Congressman William Windom believed that Ramsey's "neglect" of the soldiers would prove fatal at the polls. Oppositionist newspapers printed soldiers' letters criticizing his military appointments. So concerned was the governor that he traveled to Washington and visited his soldiers encamped near the Potomac to placate them. Despite the negative attacks, voters preferred him to Edward O. Hamblin. Neighboring Wisconsinites, however, were not so pleased with their governor's war record. Critics charged Randall with patronage abuse, fiscal mismanagement, and blamed him for the statewide banking crisis. Worse yet was the governor's failure to exact from the national government the funds it owed the state legislature to cover expenses for the troops, including their pay. Although he worked to pull the state out of financial chaos, he strained relations with Cameron and lost his constituents' confidence. Worn down by a mountain of criticism, Randall decided against seeking a third term, and Lincoln rewarded him by appointing him minister to Rome. Republicans nominated Louis Powell Harvey, Randall's competent secretary of state, and devised a platform to help bring financial security to the state. He defeated Democrat Benjamin Ferguson by more than 8,000 votes.[21]

Harvey provided a refreshing change to Wisconsin politics. Self-taught as an adolescent and later educated at Western Reserve College, the New Englander embarked on a teaching career. He moved to Southport (Kenosha) Wisconsin in 1840, where he established an academy and also became a newspaper editor. He moved to Clinton in 1847 and joined the local Whig Party. He was active in the Congregational Church, and parishioners believed he possessed a good "Christian" character, which included abstinence from alcohol. Six years later, he won a seat in the State Senate, and Republicans reelected him in 1857. Wisconsin's seventh governor continued Randall's policies in caring for the Wisconsin soldiers and their families.[22]

Marylanders also went to the polls, but under military supervision. Voters elected Unionist candidate Augustus Williamson Bradford governor by a large margin over Peace Democrat Benjamin C. Howard. To guarantee victory, Maryland's Union soldiers had been furloughed for thirty days to vote, and General Dix had ordered the U.S. marshals and the provost marshals to "satisfy themselves as to the qualifications of the voters," and to arrest dis-loyalists "to prevent the pollution of the ballot boxes by their votes."[23] Sitting Governor Hicks had warned the administration of the growing dis-Unionist sentiment. Given the election provisions, the vote transpired relatively peacefully, although there were some arrests of disloyalists. As a Unionist "with a will," declared the *Louisville Daily Journal*, Bradford's "ascension to power puts an end to vacillation and tremor in the Department of his State toward the Nation."[24]

A Maryland native, Bradford embarked on a legal career in Baltimore until politics attracted his attention in the 1830s. He embraced the Whig Party, and because he was a slave owner, Marylanders judged his political experience worthy of their confidence. "His integrity is without the shadow of a stain," remarked a newspaper correspondent, "and his patriotic devotion to the Union and the Constitution is unquestionable."[25] Hicks considered Bradford's victory vindication of his own course, provided Lincoln could trust him. Unlike Hicks, who sold his slaves at the beginning of the war, Lincoln was suspicious of the incoming executive, whose son had enlisted in the Confederate cavalry. The national government had used force in deciding the election, and Bradford knew it. George Vickers, a prominent Chestertown lawyer, wrote to Bradford weeks before the election that Union soldiers were to be used at the polls, and Bradford protested to Lincoln that military supervision was justly obnoxious to the public sentiment. Lincoln, however, defended his decision and cited his course in Missouri as evidence of its justification. "In this struggle for the nation's life," he wrote, "I can not so confidently rely on those whose elections may have depended upon disloyal votes. Such men, when elected, may prove true; but such votes are given them in the expectation that they will prove false."[26]

Although not voting for a governor, western Virginians had placed their faith in delegates they sent to Wheeling to adopt a constitution for a new state named Kanawha. On 24 October citizens from thirty-nine counties approved an ordinance favoring statehood. Whether or not voting verbally at polls supervised by Union soldiers affected the result, the victory margin favored the pro-Union state. In separating from Virginia, mountaineers were charting a course that demonstrated secession's irony. That citizens chose to remain in the Union by having to create a new state was not lost on Lincoln and Northerners fighting a war against secession. Yet the president gave little attention to the separatist movement. Governors and Cameron, however, closely monitored events in the loyal counties. The secretary urged Pierpont, the mountaineer political leader, to select someone whose discretion and intelligence was equal to this important movement and who could speak for the governor in Washington.[27]

The election season's end and the stalled military campaigns allowed governors and departmental commanders relief in working through civil-military problems. That voters endorsed Lincoln's war policies by keeping Republicans and Unionists in office was an encouraging sign. Still, Northerners were adjusting to the war and to the expanding national government, even while they remained cautious of federal mandates. Many governors had empty treasuries, increasing numbers of refugees, ill-equipped offices to collect taxes, and political offices left vacant by officials unwilling to pledge their loyalty to state and national governments. To make matters worse, mutinous troops complained to governors that they had been unpaid, had no arms or clothes, and that hospitals overflowed with sick. When Halleck arrived in St. Louis, he wired McClellan that affairs were in "complete chaos."[28] Yet, in working through his problems, he, like McClellan and Buell, wielded a firm administrative hand that offended governors accustomed to having their way in civil-military affairs. Yates, for example, took offense when Halleck countermanded one of his orders, and the governor complained to Washington. Lincoln, however, supported the commander's attempts to wrest troops away from state governance and toward military governance. Professional commanders wished to nationalize the army, meaning to replace state loyalties with an allegiance to federal commanders, but with no victories to justify their actions, such confrontations caused friction between Lincoln and the governors.[29]

Events in the border states that summer and fall stirred Lincoln's desire to take a first step in developing a blueprint for emancipation. The presence of slaves in Washington added to the president's hatred of the institution, a feeling shared by some Northern soldiers who made Washington their military home. Stationed in Maryland, Calvin Burbank of the 2nd New Hampshire regiment was shocked by the institution and how it had undermined the local economy. "We at the North do not know or realize, nor can we," wrote Burbank to his cousin, "Till seen with our own eyes the absolute degradation of everything connected with it. Shame on the man who shall uphold it."[30] Lincoln understood that keeping slaves out of the war would prove valuable in maintaining border state loyalties. So he chose to buy their freedom with conciliation and goodwill rather than seize it with bayonets. He hoped slave owners were willing to sell their slaves and chose Delaware as a test case for compensation. The state contained fewer than 1,800 slaves, a number made all the more stark in comparison with the state's 18,000 free blacks. Contemplating compensated emancipation in Delaware, however, required negotiation with a Democratic governor. Burton had been forwarding troops to the Union armies, but this had not come without complaint. Citing a lack of state militia and constitutional impediments to establish one, Burton appeared to be more trouble than his troops were worth. The embarrassing recalcitrance by Democratic Senators James Bayard and Willard Saulsbury convinced Lincoln they could not be trusted. He summoned Dover attorney and Delaware senator George P. Fisher to Washington to react to an idea that authorized the national government to compensate the state of Delaware in bonds provided the state would abolish slavery through compensation of slave owners. Fisher agreed to support the president's bill, but recommended the number be increased from $300 to $500 a slave. Lincoln agreed, penned a draft for Delaware legislators to consider, handed it to Fisher, and sent the senator back to Dover.[31]

Lincoln's compensated emancipation would be the subject of much debate in the coming months. Radicals pressed him to get the war moving to undermine the Confederate war effort by emancipating their slaves. The armies of McClellan, Buell, and Halleck were not moving. Although Northern troops were holding ground in the border states, they had not moved the military border. To allow Halleck military leverage in Missouri, Lincoln allowed the commander to suspend the writ of habeas corpus within his military department. Meanwhile, he queried McClellan just "how *long*" before the Army of the Potomac moved.[32]

The army's immobility that autumn allowed governors the opportunity to visit their troops. Andrew left behind his long days at the statehouse and journeyed to Washington for business and to investigate regimental complaints. Soldiers had battered him with letters reporting drunkenness, lack of overcoats and pay, and low morale festering from idleness. Privy to cabinet administrative gossip, Gurowski reported the mood in Washington to the chief executive. The Polish count believed Andrew was the darling of Northern governors and frequently corresponded with him over war aims. The governor "acts promptly, decisively; feels and speaks ardently," he penned in his diary. Hardworking, jovial, blissfully unaware of giving offense, and painfully blunt, Andrew to Gurowski personified the "genuine American people." In assessing the administration's handling of the war, Gurowski told Andrew that "slowly but uninteruptedly [sic] we are [Drifting] to anarchy."[33] He confided that "The Cabinet is savage [against] McClellan for having allowed to close to the Potomac." He added that "Scott stirs up the fire" and "tries hard to oust out McClellan whom he hates and put in Halleck, whom he considers to be *all together* his own, Scott's man." He predicted that "Undoubtedly we shall have a battle soon . . . what results no body [sic] knows. But I have *strong reasons* to suppose that if we win victory, Seward & Scott are ready to proffer to the rebels terms of pacification. I am positive about the reasons which make me say this, but I recommend *my name to your absolute discretion*."[34] Such sentiments unnerved Andrew, and when he arrived in Washington, the soldiers confirmed the gloom. "There is a feeling of depression gaining upon the army," he wrote to a friend, "they justly complain of treachery, corruption, political fanaticism, and fatuity in the conduct of our affairs." He added, "The President is, tis said, dissatisfied . . . the Cabinet are not a band of Brothers," and yet he allowed that there was no cause for alarm as these problems would soon blow away.[35]

The silence along the Potomac that fall annoyed Lincoln. The president needed swifter movement. Congressmen were arriving in Washington and expected to see evidence of success. Representatives would demand reasonable justification for his management of the war and his expenditures since their last assemblage. In the days before Congress convened, political leaders milled in and around Willard's Hotel discussing the war, the commanders leading the armies, and Lincoln's war aims. Indeed, six months had passed and there was little the government's armies could boast.[36]

Congressional Fallout

The reconvening of the Thirty-seventh Congress drew throngs of journalists to the capital city to record the daily sessions. On a "cool, cloudy, and a trifle wintry" 3 December, a clerk read Lincoln's "state of the Union."[37] More a chronicle of events since July than his usual elegantly worded documents, Lincoln's address acknowledged that the nation was facing "unprecedented political troubles." While it gratified the president to know the peoples' patriotism had proven "equal to the occasion," he failed to connect these results with the labors performed in getting these men in the field, equipped, armed, and paid. In what he had earlier declared was a "People's Contest," Lincoln had conspicuously failed to mention the governors.[38]

Congressional leaders brought Lincoln's management under a political microscope. "The people of the nation," professed one correspondent, "never before in its history turned so intent an eye upon their national Legislature."[39] In a war being fought on such a grand scale, it was paramount that a system of checks and balances be established to make those in office accountable to the people. The nation's chief executive, its congressmen, and commanders, as well as its governors had partnered to create a Northern force capable of saving the Union. Even the capital city had been transformed. The "Washington of to-day [1861]," acknowledged one reporter, "is totally different from the Washington of 1860."[40] Within a week, House and Senate members, determined to bring more accountability, formed a Joint Committee on the Conduct of the War. Known as the War Committee, this group was branded by critics as the self-appointed "Jacobin Club" or "smelling committee," whose responsibilities included investigating the Union's handling of military affairs.[41]

Outspoken abolitionist and stubbornly combative Ohioan Benjamin Wade chaired the committee. Other members included Zachariah Chandler of Michigan, Indianan George Julian, John Covode of Pennsylvania, and Daniel Gooch of Massachusetts. The odd men out were Democrats Andrew Johnson of Tennessee and Moses Fowler Odell of New York. It did not matter that the members lacked military knowledge. They compensated for this deficiency by endorsing emancipation and a vigorous prosecution of the war, hoping one would lead to the other. Committee members met secretly in the basement of the capitol, which did not bode well for their reputation for undermining commanders and political leaders. Already some of the congressmen had been critical of McClellan and Lincoln, while lauding the work of Frémont in Missouri. Indeed, some praised Butler. "I have carefully watched the progress of events and must confess that I begin to despair of ever putting down this rebellion through the instrumentality of this administration," Wade wrote to Chandler in October, "they are blundering, cowardly, and inefficient."[42]

Governors welcomed the War Committee if for no other reason than it would look into the ineptness of Cameron's office. Lincoln, it appeared, had lost touch with his war secretary. The recent acrimony against Cameron came from his insistence in a November report to Lincoln to arm the slaves. The secretary had solicited the counsel of several colleagues, including Edwin M. Stanton, the War Department's legal advisor, before presenting it to the president. Reporters publicized the report before Cameron sent it to Lincoln. The president was not prepared to acquiesce on this point, and he demanded that Cameron remove the language. Cameron initially refused, but Lincoln finally convinced him to replace the language dealing with arming the slaves. He requested Montgomery Blair to wire postmasters, ordering them to stop transmission of Cameron's initial report. Lincoln approved a new, less-controversial paragraph, and sent it forth. The fiasco, however, gave the appearance that Lincoln and Cameron were divided on the issue. "What does Mr. Cameron want to make a stir about the slaves for?" wrote John Call Dalton Jr., a New York physician serving in South Carolina, to his brother. "It's perfectly ridiculous to talk about 'arming' them. You might just as well pitch the muskets into the Potomac for any good they would do."[43]

Cameron's untimely report, his difference of opinion, and his earlier support of Frémont's proclamation, as well as his irresponsibility in dealing in war contracts, led Lincoln to dismiss him. The president waited, however, until the opportunity presented itself to lessen the blow to Cameron. Rumor of his removal was hardly news to Cameron. His close associates had alerted him weeks before that the axe was about to fall on him. Lincoln had taken great pains not to drag slavery into the war, yet hiding his true convictions about the institution made for interesting Washington gossip. Given the War Committee's Radical composition, Lincoln would need to find a judicious replacement, and he waited until the rumors faded to shake up his cabinet.[44]

The Joint Committee provided governors with an important outlet for their complaints against the administration and the War Department. Having political connections with the committee suited Governors Morton, Dennison, Blair, Morgan, and Curtin, even more so because they agreed with its Radical views. Committee members favored Republican commanders and were eager to turn the war into something more than the Union's preservation. Some representatives believed that the only way to preserve the Union was to abolish slavery or at least to use the slaves against the enemy. Many governors agreed. In the Joint Committee governors found allies to support commanders who shared their antislavery views. Yet, the Union's three principle commanders were Democrats, opposed to expanding the war beyond Lincoln's limited aims.[45]

Winter's advance brought a slowdown to overland operations, and military officials turned their attention to coastal fortifications. River traffic on the upper Mississippi ceased that time of year, forcing Ramsey and Randall to struggle with manpower needs. The Union's interior waterways, port cities, and coastlines concerned Lincoln, and in mid-December he sent Congress copies of correspondence between himself and Washburn on the subject of fortifications of the seacoast and Great Lakes. Olden reminded Lincoln of the "exposed and defenseless condition" of the Delaware River and Philadelphia. The governor asserted that the recent complications with Great Britain had worried him because Forts Delaware and Mifflin were ill equipped. Because of the vulnerability of the Du Pont powder mills, he urged Lincoln to secure those forts.[46]

Governors used the absence of military campaigns to shore up their regional defenses. They worked with commanders to patrol rivers and made use of naval advances. Yet the Union's presence in Maryland, Kentucky, Virginia, and Missouri presented more prickly issues as slaves showed up in camps. Halleck, for example, was bent on keeping slaves out of his camps. He justified his exclusion order by arguing that slaves passing through his camps were giving information to the enemy. Gamble supported the commander, but because Congress was in session, representatives debated over what to do with runaway slaves. By late December Halleck declared martial law in his department, citing the need to strike at Confederate support among civilians. He enlisted Lincoln's advice before making the declaration, which endeared him to the administration and won him praise from Gamble.[47]

Civil-Military Diplomacy

Runaway slaves were not Halleck's only problem. The conduct of Union commanders outside his jurisdiction, namely Lane in Kansas, had done irreparable damage to his department. "It will take 20,000 men to counteract" Lane's effect in the state, declared Halleck. He complained about the "injudicious orders of the War Department and jealousies of the Governors of States."[48] It did not surprise Halleck that the governors exercised significant power over the troops. What surprised him was the power they held over commanders. Lane proved to be the exception. Governor Robinson had been at "swords' points" with the commander for months and had repeatedly warned the administration of Lane's destructive ways. He had alluded to these problems earlier, warning Frémont that what Kansans "have to fear, and do fear, is that Lane's brigade will get up a war by going over the [Missouri] line, committing depredations, and then returning into our State." The governor urged, "If you will remove the supplies at Fort Scott to the interior, and relieve us of the Lane brigade, I will guarantee Kansas from invasion from Missouri."[49] Robinson wanted Lincoln to investigate Kansas affairs, appoint an impartial commission, and if Lane's charges against him were false, he wanted the commander removed. Lane had spearheaded an effort to use the Republican Party to call for an election to oust Robinson. The problem for Halleck and Robinson was that Lincoln supported Lane and gave him command of Kansas against Robinson's objections. As problems mounted in Kansas and Missouri, the governor became disillusioned over the national government's lack of commitment to the trans-Mississippi war.[50]

The longer the war stood still, the more complicated federal-state cooperation became. Elihu Washburne was in St. Louis on a congressional directive to investigate government contracts, and his assessment revealed serious problems. He wired Lincoln that "to add to the miserable condition of things in this State, the enclosed slip will show you what is going on in Kanzas [sic] between Jim Lane and Robinson."[51] He concluded, "God only knows what is to be the outcome of matters in this State ... the robberies, the frauds, the peculations in the govt. which have already come to our knowledge, are absolutely frightful."[52] Amid these problems came the scandalous Kansas election in which Republican George A. Crawford ran unopposed and won. Robinson refuted the contest, remained in office, and sought to remove Lane. The Kansas Supreme Court interceded to determine the election's constitutionality, and Thomas Ewing Jr. entered the Lane-Robinson feud. As much as he wanted to see Robinson out of office, however, the outspoken Unionist lawyer-turned judge ruled in *Crawford v. Robinson* that the governor was entitled to serve in the state's executive office until the election the following year.[53]

Nothing else compared to the Robinson-Lane feud, but for commanders to have to handle the jealousies of governors was not uncommon. Buell fell into poor relations with midwestern governors Dennison, Morton, and Yates. He and Halleck initially found little use for them. Buell complained to McClellan that these "officious" governors were causing him problems. Dennison, he complained, "evidently looks upon all Ohio troops as his army." Buell was told "He requires morning reports from them, and their quartermasters to forward their returns to him."[54] Yet he boasted to McClellan that he would end this business. A career army man, Buell was unsuited to the volunteer and state-oriented nature of the Civil War and followed McClellan's lead in professionalizing his army. Within a month into his command he complained that he still "suffered annoyance" from officious governors, who sent their staff officers to look after their troops.[55] In time Buell thought he could correct these problems, but the harder he worked to eliminate the "ill-judged interference of State authorities," the more they worked to maintain their connection to the troops.[56]

Given the shoddy manner in which the War Department had handled their volunteers up to this point, governors typically refused to allow anyone to sever their ties to the men. They held currency in shaping war policy because they organized the manpower and served as the chief instruments of their state's political party. They also used their connections with members of the War Committee to their advantage. In early December Andrew again came to Washington to instruct the administration on the war's proper conduct with regard to fugitive slaves. When a Massachusetts officer reported that soldiers had returned fugitive slaves to their masters, Andrew wrote to Cameron in disbelief. Believing that his men opposed the institution of slavery, he could not imagine they engaged in such practices. "Massachusetts does not send her citizens forth," he wired the secretary, "to become the hunters of men or to engage in the seizure and return to captivity of persons claimed to be fugitive slaves." He demanded that Cameron "secure the soldiers of this Commonwealth from being participators in such dirty and despotic work."[57]

When word reached General Charles P. Stone, the brigade commander, that Andrew had instructed Cameron to desist from such acts, he acknowledged that Andrew was the chief magistrate of the state to which those troops belonged. Still, he argued that such distinction did not give Andrew the right "to assume control of the interior discipline of the regiment, nor does it give him authority to command the punishment of a meritorious officer for any offense, either real or imaginary." He boldly declared, "I am not aware that there are here Michigan, New York, Pennsylvania, Minnesota or Massachusetts troops," but what he did know was that "there are here U.S. troops collected from all those States," and that it was his job to teach them their duty.[58] Stone forwarded Andrew's letter to McClellan, characterizing it as "dangerous interference." McClellan responded to the governor that when accepted into the Federal army, volunteers were completely removed from the authority of the governors, which he argued was for the soldiers' benefit.[59]

Had the Andrew-Stone dispute remained a minor civil-military disagreement, it might have had a short life. Andrew, however, used the affair to push for the expansion of Union war aims, sent the entire correspondence to Massachusetts senator Charles Sumner, and encouraged him to address the matter on Capitol Hill. Andrew knew Sumner's feelings on the issue and that the senator had denounced Halleck, Buell, and McClellan for keeping slaves out of Union lines. When Congress convened he would use a larger stage to expose the issue and the commanding generals who endorsed such a policy. Meanwhile, Andrew responded to McClellan, lecturing him on the role of governors. As much as commanders attempted to nationalize the army, governors reminded them that soldiers carried regimental flags into combat bearing state colors and representing state sovereignty. Andrew had sufficiently antagonized McClellan, which resulted in a series of insulting exchanges.[60]

Gamble shared Andrew's frustration with Lincoln's war aims, but for different reasons. He worried that Congress, behind the lead of Sumner, would wage war on slavery, thus undermining his work among Unionists. "I look with deep anxiety to the action of Congress," he wrote colleague David Pitman. "If the abolitionists shall be able to carry through the two houses their scheme for turning the present war into one against slavery as an institution," he fumed, "the question will be one of the greatest magnitude to the country whether the President will have the firmness to breast the current." He charged that "If he should yield to the malignant influence of those black hearted and insane abolitionists, I have no longer a hope for the restoration of peace and order."[61]

Lincoln meanwhile rose above such problems in hopes of remaining cordial with the governors. Often these problems arose from personal as well as professional differences. The daily correspondence with governors required as much tact on Lincoln's part as it did the governors'. He accommodated them when he could, even in small ways, believing that it benefited him with the Northern populace. Cameron sent the governors a circular encouraging the appointment of foreign officers to regimental commands, arguing that many candidates possessed military education and experience. Randall responded by pointing out to the secretary that in selecting officers for appointment, particularly foreign officers, his experience in appointing such officers of alleged skill and ability had not been encouraging enough to "repeat the experiment."[62]

By the close of 1861 the governors had been instrumental in placing a national army in the field. The realization that the war was not a glorious venture, however, had diminished their grand illusions. Beyond delivering patriotic oratory designed to promote volunteerism, governors now responded to soldiers' complaints. Still, there remained the prickly issues of command appointments, promotions, wartime contracts, and slaves in Union camps as armies penetrated deeper into the Confederacy. Changing wartime policies brought changing roles for the governors. Governors not only conducted an overwhelming daily correspondence that grew with each passing week, but also traveled their states and steamed to Washington and New York to conduct procurement business. On one of his trips to Washington, Morgan took time out to visit the New York regiments across the Potomac River to deliver packages and personal letters. Morgan was not alone that December, as several governors inspected camps and hospitals, reassuring their soldiers that they were not forgotten. Washburn worried about his Maine boys, camped around Washington, suffering from lack of adequate camp equipage. "I really wish you could find time some Saturday," he urged his colleague Fessenden, "to take an [airing] (& you ought to for your own sake) & visit the camps, and that you would then give me the witness of your eyes & ears & nose."[63] Private William Wells of the 3rd Vermont Cavalry wrote his parents from Burlington before departing for Washington that Governor Holbrook was "a *bully* man for us" and was going to accompany the men to the front, declaring that "unless we get some good quarters we shall return to Vt."[64] Learning of widespread sickness in the camps around Alexandria, the governor dispatched Edward E. Phelps, a prominent Vermont surgeon, to attend to the boys suffering from disease and appointed the well-connected and financially astute Frank Howe as military agent for Vermont in New York City.[65]

Much had changed since Fort Sumter, and Northerners waged war on a scale that reflected those changes. "The conspiracy against the Government," reported Cameron, "extended over an area of 733,144 square miles ... stripped us of arms and munitions, and scattered our Navy to the most distant quarters of the globe." Consequently, the effort to restore the Union, in his calculation, had already become "the most gigantic endeavor in the history of civil war."[66] By the eve of the New Year, the Union army had exceeded the requested 500,000 men, and Congress provided some $500 million for its expansion. What Cameron and Lincoln were most inspired by was the strength of the Union's institutions. Stanton acknowledged that without "conscriptions, levies, drafts, or other extraordinary expedients," the Northern states had raised a greater force than that gathered by Napoleon. Massachusetts alone provided such evidence, remarked Cameron, acknowledging that one-sixth of its entire population was already in the field. In the face of violence Maryland and Missouri Unionists had prevailed thanks to Hicks and Gamble. Loyalists in Kentucky and western Virginia had also wrested the political culture from secessionists. In the midst of all these accomplishments, however, disloyal Kentuckians created a "Provisional Government of Kentucky" at Russellville in November and made George W. Johnson, a boyish-looking lawyer and wealthy planter, the provisional governor, leaving Magoffin "out in the cold." Meanwhile, Kentucky legislators took a recess, "determined to keep watch on Magoffin for the remainder of his term," and contemplated their next move.[67]

The congressional session that winter focused on military operations, and Lincoln and his commanders felt added pressure to meet the expectations of those creating the armies and navies. Months before, the cause had aroused the "national heart," and now it was time to arouse the fighting spirit among the commanders. Bringing the nation's railroads, telegraphs, finances, and a grand volunteer army under national control exercised nationalistic impulses. Political leaders could not afford for the Northern war effort to suffer because of reluctant commanders, misguided cabinet officers, frustrating civil-military affairs, and a conciliatory, limited war policy. The last several months had been an education, and congressmen carped about accountability and changes in war aims. It was time to take the war to Southerners, Radicals argued, not Southern soil. When Sumner rose on the Senate floor on 18 December, he voiced a desire to change the military's war aims, arguing that the administration should no longer require commanders to return fugitive slaves to their masters. The senator chafed under the influence that border states held over the president, and the revocation of Frémont's proclamation especially disappointed him. Andrew's views on the matter fueled his fire. "The Governor of my State has charged me with a communication to the Secretary of War on this subject," he proclaimed, "complaining of this outrage, treating it as an indignity to the men, and as an act unworthy of our national flag." He declared, "I agree with the Governor of Massachusetts, and when I call attention to this abuse now, I make myself his representative, as also the representative of my own opinions."[68] To Andrew, the senator wrote that he hoped Andrew's message would keep Massachusetts ahead, "where she always has been, in the ideas of our movement." He wrote, "Let the doctrine of Emancipation be proclaimed as an essential and happy agency in subduing a wicked rebellion. In this way you will help a majority of the Cabinet, whose opinions on this subject are fixed, and precede the President himself by a few weeks."[69]

By forming a Confederacy, firing on Fort Sumter, and defeating Federals in battle, Southerners had awakened a patriotic spirit among the Union states. Northerners had displayed a cooperativeness unlike anything in national history, but they had little to boast for their efforts. Few citizens, North or South, recognized just how powerful the federal government could be, given its political compromises of the past. A fair degree of ignorance about the nature of the Union's political culture pervaded local communities, and governors played a role in educating the citizenry about national ideals and individual liberties. "In truth," wrote one well-placed observer, "it is more than likely that we sorely needed this fearful awakening, that the best part of our political system should not become irretrievably paralyzed and corrupted."[70] Even as the war's centralizing tendencies forced them to give up their procurement authority, governors understood the extraordinary relationship the war had forged between nation and state. "President Lincoln's war proclamation came upon us like a bugle blast in the night," wrote the *New York Herald*, "in that defenceless [sic] condition, resulting from a long reign of peace, under which we were becoming rusty and luxurious, we were suddenly called to the sternest realities of a tremendous armed insurrection."[71]

Governors had grown with the war; they understood firsthand the costs and sacrifice and became aware of the dangers of popular disillusionment. By December's end, Lincoln had taken the war to a new level by personally directing military operations. In the dead of winter, he was about to throw a log on the fire. McClellan was sick with typhoid, and somebody needed to get the armies moving before Radical congressmen expanded the Union's war aims. On New Years' Eve, the president wired a short communiqué that spoke volumes. "General McClellan is sick," he wrote Halleck, "Are General Buell and yourself in concert?" Acting in concert was a departure from the "formless" conflict that had spread across the nation. Coordinating military operations east and west of the Appalachians became far more cumbersome than Cameron imagined. McClellan, Halleck, and Buell clung to Lincoln's limited war aims, but governors feared military inaction and public criticism would undermine volunteering. As Lincoln's secretary Stoddard prophesied, "already we can see the indications of trouble to come."[72]

CHAPTER SEVEN

Crossing the Alps

By the New Year, Lincoln's conciliatory policy and stubborn military commanders disgusted abolitionist governors. State assemblymen who convened for their legislative sessions, however, had other reasons to be indignant. Much had happened since representatives last gathered, and governors exercised unprecedented power. Democratic legislators denounced centralized governance in federal and state executives. They defended personal liberty laws, condemned the suspension of the writ of habeas corpus, and together with Republicans, worked to assist invalid soldiers, aid families, protect borders and coastlines, and maintain vibrant local economies. Party leaders prepared for the coming elections and organized to determine candidates. As the sessions unfolded, Democrats challenged federal initiatives they believed Republicans used to change the Union. In the dead of winter, as soldiers hovered around campfires awaiting orders, political leaders were waging war.

The Politics of War

State capitals had changed since congressmen last convened. Arriving in Des Moines, representatives found the small hamlet had transformed into a vast military station. The war was nine months old, and hundreds of soldiers had passed through on their way to the front. Most had never seen the capital or the governor. Kirkwood connected with the Iowa farm boys, visited the camps, talked with the men, and assured them he would attend to their welfare. He also followed soldiers through correspondence. His nephew Samuel Kirkwood Clark joined the cavalry early in the war, and his recent promotion to lieutenant prompted the governor to advise him. "You must not allow yourself to become proud and overbearing," he instructed, "in short, you must use your influence to see that 'the right' is done at all times and under all circumstances."[1]

Kirkwood's advice mirrored his attitude about Union war aims, which was embedded in his address to the Iowa legislature. Northerners had avoided war until Sumter, he argued, but, compelled to engage, they should wage such a war that ensured Southerners would never again attempt secession. A conservative frontiersman, Kirkwood nonetheless supported waging a harsh war against Confederates. He was hesitant to take a bold stand against slavery, fearing it would turn away potential volunteers. "I will not be misunderstood," he declared, "this war is waged by our Government for the preservation of the Union, and not for the extinction of Slavery, unless the preservation of one shall require the extinction of the other."[2] He acknowledged that the war would be long and that Iowans would face unprecedented burdens requiring dedication and sacrifice. His chief concern was getting derelict tax-paying Iowans to support the war effort. George B. Corkhill interrupted his studies at Harvard Law School to enlist in the army and by the New Year was in Washington working as a commissary agent. Frustrated by the war's slow progress, the young officer found Kirkwood's message resonant. "Would to God," he wrote Kirkwood, "the administration was thoroughly imbued with your views, and *would act on them*."[3]

In Lansing, Blair's address to Michigan legislators carried a more Radical message. The governor urged the Union armies to carry forth with a courage like that which accompanied Napoleon across the Alps, dragging his cannon through the snow to "meet the power of the enemy." Declared the clerk who read the governor's message, "To treat the enemy gently is to excite derision, to protect his slave property, is to help him to butcher our people." Thus, consequently, "he must be met with an activity and a purpose equal to his own."[4] The education in mobilization was over, and Blair wanted Lincoln to strike at rebel property and liberate slaves. "The people are right but very many of the politicians are woefully wrong," wrote Blair to Kalamazoo resident Charles May.[5]

Blair's Radicalism had deep roots. He was raised by abolitionist parents and classically educated at Cazenovia Seminary and Hamilton and Union Colleges. He trained in law then moved to Jackson, Michigan, where he tried his hand in politics. In his first term as a Whig representative, he favored revisions to the state constitution that would strike the word "white" as it applied to electors. Even abolitionists were taken aback by his views, which cost him reelection. Blair, however, persevered and eventually won over the electorate and the gubernatorial office in 1860. Lincoln's victory disappointed him, and when the war broke out, he joined his Radical governors in pressing for a harsh war that liberated slaves. Meanwhile, he rolled up his sleeves and put men in the field even at personal expense. Like Iowa, Michigan comprised mainly hardscrabble, modest, but persistent farmers, who translated the war into a broader contest between bondage and pursing wealth freely. Although most residents were not pro-black, they resented slavery's oppression as it undermined the free laborer seeking economic independence. Citizens were "filled with the spirit of liberty, and love for free institutions" and sought to protect their agrarian lifestyle.[6] Standing in the way of that new Union, Blair believed, were conservative commanders and the president.[7]

Maryland residents shared the agrarian traditions of Northerners, but slavery connected them with Southern customs. Citizens remained divided over the conflict, and Governor Bradford continued Hicks's commitment to leave the institution undisturbed. Yet he argued that the one source stronger than the desire to found a separate government was the source that opposed it. He looked to his assemblymen to aid his course, but legislators who stood by the Union also stood by states' rights and slavery. Still, among the first acts of the new legislature was the appropriation of $7,000 to Andrew for the distribution to the family members of the 6th Massachusetts soldiers killed the previous April. In the same session, however, legislators also approved an amendment that forbade amending the federal Constitution to allow Congress the authority to interfere with slavery. Legislators imposed the death penalty for any person found guilty of treason against the state. Such legislation benefited Bradford in governing the state, but concerned colleagues about his Union loyalties should war aims change.[8]

There was little military action in December and January, yet disease permeated Union camps. Governors had difficulty accepting why the ranks were shrinking in a war no one was fighting. Waiting for months, Northerners grew impatient. "Old John Brown," declared the *Chicago Tribune* editor, "with sixteen men and an *idea*, struck more terror into Virginia than does the great Army of the Potomac, destitute of that '*idea*.'"[9] Editorials such as these gave Northerners the impression that national administrators and generals suffered from paralysis. Congressmen, meanwhile, concerned themselves with wider efforts to sustain and adjust to the army's needs. Governors, however, focused on maintaining the manpower flow, troop morale, and home front enthusiasm. They pressed Lincoln to promote a more vigorous war for fear of losing Northern enthusiasm. With McClellan sick and Wade's impatient War Committee anxious to expand war aims, Lincoln acted his part as commander in chief.[10]

The president expected that two professionally trained veterans would coordinate military operations in the West. Prodding Buell to move into

East Tennessee to protect loyalists made perfect political sense, Lincoln thought. Buell, however, argued that it was not good military strategy, especially in the winter, when the army would be forced to extend its supply line into hostile countryside. Halleck agreed. "I am satisfied," he wrote, "the authorities at Washington do not appreciate the difficulties with which I have to contend here." He argued that "The operations of Lane, Jennison, and others have so enraged the people of Missouri, that it is estimated that there is a majority of 80,000 against the Government." He declared, "I am in the condition of a carpenter who is required to build a bridge with a dull ax, a broken saw, and rotten timber."[11] Halleck's list of problems further demoralized the president, who wrote on the back of a dispatch before sending it to McClellan, "It is exceedingly discouraging. . . . As everywhere else, nothing can be done."[12]

Buell and McClellan recognized the civilian arm of authority that governed the armies, yet they failed to fully appreciate the iron fist that came with it. Wade's committee, along with Radical governors, demanded that commanders get the war moving, and Lincoln pressed commanders. "Delay is ruining us," Lincoln wired Buell, "and it is indispensable for me to have something definite."[13] Attorney General Bates advised Lincoln "to command the commanders" to achieve his goals. If the president did so, Bates proposed that "the affairs of the war and the aspect of the whole country, will be quickly and greatly changed for the better."[14] Lincoln never shirked from assuming responsibility for Union war aims, which he believed were in tune with most Northerners. One Ohio sergeant was so impressed by the president that he likened him to a "second Christ" and "Solomon's peer in wisdom."[15] Still, Lincoln was out of answers and without disciples. On 10 January, hoping for some good news, the president walked to Meigs's office and sunk himself in a chair. "General, what shall I do?" he asked. "The people are impatient," he remarked, "Chase has no money and he tells me he can raise no more; the General of the Army has typhoid fever. The bottom is out of the tub. What shall I do?"[16]

The war looked no better from the Northern statehouses than it did from Washington. Affairs "look gloomy enough here," wrote Yates to Lyman Trumbull, the U.S. senator from Illinois. "Secessionism holds its head up around here," he lamented.[17] Andrew too read letter after letter complaining of hardships. Horace Binney Sargent, a frustrated officer stationed at Annapolis, aired his frustration to the governor. "This policy of striking soft in battle seems to me a monstrous policy," he declared. "History is full of lessons," he proclaimed, "we are attempting to conquer the rebellious states and forget the *end* & the *means* of conquest." He maintained, "the thing we seek," was not to avenge or insult Southerners, but "*permanent* dominion; & what instance is there of a permanent dominion without changing, revolutionizing, absorbing, the institutions, life, and manners of the conquered peoples?" He ended by saying, "*This army must not come back . . .* settlement—migration must put the seal on battle, or we gain nothing."[18]

Timing worked in Lincoln's favor that January when Cassius M. Clay resigned his post as minister to Russia. Lincoln used the opportunity to offer Cameron the post, and appointed Edwin McMasters Stanton the new war secretary. The transition produced little fanfare, but Stanton would soon rule "like a czar."[19] When the news became public, Morton wired Cameron a consoling note. "It is a leading feature in the policy of the opponents of the war," he confided, "to charge corruption against every man engaged in its prosecution and to break down the war by breaking down the confidence of the people in those who are carrying it on."[20]

Stanton's War

Stanton was no Cameron. He came to the War Department understanding the conflict, and Cameron left befuddled by it. His name seemed overblown, and though standing only five feet eight inches, he carried an air of entitlement. No one exercised power over him, and he ignored those who disagreed with him. Noah Brooks, journalist and editor, characterized him as a " 'Bull-head,' " meaning "opinionated, implacable, intent, and not easily turned from any purpose."[21] A *Chicago Tribune* reporter dubbed him the "Bull Dog."[22] Alexander McClure remarked that he was capable of the "grandest and the meanest of actions of any great man."[23] Even his critics, however, could not deny that Stanton was a shrewd lawyer who had practiced before the Supreme Court. President James Buchanan appointed him attorney general in 1860, and it was Stanton who guided Buchanan's course through secession. He had opposed Lincoln in 1860 and reluctantly agreed to serve under Cameron. Stanton was a conservative Democrat who spared no feelings and who injured people by verbal abusing them with his blunt, overbearing manner. But he was the man for the job or, as John Hay put it, "a very good pattern for a Secretary of War." No longer would the War Department remain passive against arrogant commanders. Among his first acts was to organize a secret service to ferret out contract fraud both civil and military. "You have a Herculean work before you," wrote Joseph Medill of the *Chicago Tribune*, and "the country looks to you with longing heart to infuse vigor, system, honesty and *fight* into the service," he concluded.[24] Stanton gave the War Department a new identity and another leader in shaping war policy. He could ill afford to risk Lincoln's favor with Northern governors, because he needed these political leaders more then they needed him. Governors stirred the popular acceptance and commitment to the war, and they paid attention to military efficiency and civilian morale. Andrew was glad to see Lincoln recognizing Stanton's "high ability" and "patriotic services." He remarked, "Of one thing we may, I think be sure, that the slip-shod and [inconclusive] manner in which the department has been conducted will cease."[25]

Governors welcomed Stanton. His arrival coincided with a shift in federal power that brought supplying and paying volunteer regiments under national control. They believed Stanton would be more effective than Cameron, especially when it came to soldier pay. "The truth is that Congress is so busy discussing the eternal nigger question that they fail to make appropriations, and the financial departments are dead broke," Halleck complained, and that "we have more difficulties to conquer with our own men than with the enemy."[26] To assess civil-military affairs beyond the Appalachian Mountains, Stanton sent Scott to examine the military departments. Pacific coast citizens, however, were not included in the tour. Although the California press reported that record winter floods had forced the legislature's adjournment for a few days, Governor Stanford reported that he had assembled some 6,000 volunteers, who soon hoped to report that "they had done something for their country."[27] The new governor appreciated Downey's and Wright's attention to detail, which made his transition easier, and he promised the same cooperative spirit in the Department of the Pacific. Oregonians, however, suffered through the winter, combating Indian depredations on the northeastern frontier. These hostilities hindered Whiteaker's efforts, and by the New Year, the governor had mustered only a few infantry and cavalry companies, and most of those units Wright needed in his department.[28]

Even with Stanton's arrival the national government could not keep pace in supplying the armies and failed to settle ongoing civil-military disputes. The Andrew-Butler quarrel, which embarrassed the administration in the fall, worsened when the War Department delayed Butler's expedition to Ship Island. The commander traveled to Washington to enlist help in getting around Andrew. The governor argued that the new regiments had been collected illegally and in contempt of the War Department, and he refused to commission officers. He expected Lincoln to terminate the expedition, but he refused. "I will be greatly obliged," he wrote Andrew, "if you will arrange somehow with General Butler to officer his two unofficered regiments."[29] Andrew responded that there were names on Butler's list that, in good conscience, he could not appoint. He claimed that Butler's whole operation was ill conceived and that his recruitment of troops in Massachusetts was illegal. Not wanting to appear insubordinate, Andrew allowed to Lincoln that as much as he wanted to comply, he needed to be cautious. When Sumner informed him that Stanton was willing to entertain the governor's "programme [sic]," Andrew responded that "the President has my programme" and demanded that his letters "should be directly, and not indirectly, answered by the President or Department."[30] "*I am right*," he declared to Frank Howe, "I know I am."[31]

Had Cameron still been in office Andrew might have pushed the secretary into a corner. Yet Stanton found the correspondence fatiguing. To strengthen his case, Butler traveled to Washington and called on fellow Democrat Stanton. The commander also outlined a proposal for creating a Department of the Gulf, which he argued would require about 15,000 troops, the number of troops in his New England command. Whether he had information about the Navy's plan to move against New Orleans was unknown. Yet Butler impressed Stanton enough that the secretary rescinded Butler's orders to Virginia, ordered him to the Gulf Coast, and called on congressional Radicals and Gustavus Fox to persuade McClellan of the plan's merits. Butler's plans moved forward, and the dispute with Andrew seemingly ended when Lincoln abolished the Department of New England. Andrew accepted Butler's men as part of the state's volunteers.[32]

The Andrew-Butler controversy highlighted the frustrations of waging a state-oriented national war. Andrew was persuasive, but military realities trumped constitutional prerogative. As much as the conflict was a "citizens' war," the civil-military management impaired federal-state supervision, even while Lincoln and the governors sought to accomplish the same goal. Frank Howe wrote to Andrew that, "while Butler's paid men here have and are working their hardest," the "tide had set the other way ... the feelings of all those in the cabinet are with you."[33] He told the governor, "Mr. Lincoln told me he would like to see you," and advised him to come to Washington as he had "learned [of] some wrinkles here, which will help matters," and that he would wait until he arrived to converse on matters.[34]

McClellan believed himself above such civil-military squabbles. His splendid sense of public relations had lulled Lincoln into believing that his authority had not exceeded his ability. In recent months, however, he failed to appreciate the politics that characterized the national war. His concerns highlighted a more fundamental conflict between civilians, who were raising volunteer armies, and the commanders who were directing them. The general in chief pointed out military reasons for his delay, including complaints that governors passed over qualified candidates for command and appointed men out of political or personal considerations. To remedy this problem, he suggested asking Congress for a law regulating the promotion and supply of vacancies in the volunteer regiments, but Stanton never gave it much attention.[35]

In McClellan's incapacitated state, Lincoln's cabinet and Radical congressmen pressed the president to take the army away from the commander. It was true the conservative triumvirate of McClellan, Halleck, and Buell was far different from Frémont, Butler, and Hunter. As meddlesome as governors had been in military affairs, they argued that a vigorously prosecuted war would end the fighting sooner and thus allow their soldiers to return to their homes. Such a strategy, they maintained, would antagonize Missourians, Kentuckians, and Marylanders, but it might end the conflict quickly. Amassing large armies and strategically placing them along the borders, governors believed, was sure to deter Confederates from carrying on the war. As Kirkwood and Blair had acknowledged in their addresses, governors sought to capitalize on the Union's strength to overwhelm Confederates before the war expanded. Superior Northern leadership, they maintained, was important in sustaining popular will.

If, as Southern critics charged, Northern abolitionists had provoked the war, Radical governors such as Andrew, Yates, Morton, Blair, and Washburn demanded abolishing slavery to help end the war. Other governors, such as Tod, Harvey, Bradford, and Burton, appeared content to avoid the issue. At the moment, however, vigorous war meant getting the armies moving and ending conciliatory policies. The more McClellan and his appointees complained and dawdled, the more they drew suspicion to themselves that they were avoiding fighting the war until their armies were fully prepared. They sought to wage the limited war that Lincoln desired. McClellan, Halleck, and Buell attempted to nationalize and stabilize their commands, and the winter slowdown afforded them time to undertake these changes. That Congress convened during this lull pitted spirited political war aims against the army's lackluster military movements.[36]

The war's political nature forced governors to consider not only their constituents' abolitionist impulses, but also their pluralistic composition. Although most immigrants had not voted for Lincoln in 1860, many nonetheless enlisted in his war. Yet these volunteers added ethnic solidarity to regimental organization. Immigrant enlistees sought to preserve the Union while advancing their own status by displaying devotion to democracy. For some, fighting for the Union provided them the opportunity to earn respectability among Americans. Governors recognized these desires and, when they could, allowed Germans to fight with Germans, or Irishmen to fight alongside Irishmen. The war provided ethnic groups an opportunity to unite in solidarity to defend the Union they cherished. Governors often provided the War Department with suitable candidates for command and worked together with officials to arrange suitable officers for these regiments. Buckingham's 9th Connecticut Irish Regiment, for example, and Andrew's Irish regiments, as well as the German regiments of Yates, Tod, Morton, Morgan, reflected this solidarity.[37]

The question of abolition and ethnic considerations heightened gubernatorial sensibilities but were not more important than keeping peace between warring factions. The Robinson-Lane rivalry typified the recriminatory actions between proslavery and antislavery forces that unsettled the state of Kansas. Lane's men stole slaves; robbed civilians; and burned barns, grain, and forage, and this eroded Robinson's hold on the populace. Since the war began, this feud had drawn significant public attention. John Hay wrote that "no good thing will come out of Kansas until Jim Lane has retired to private life and the cormorants that surround him see no prospect for plunder in his train."[38] Into this acrimonious environment arrived General David Hunter, commander of the Department of Kansas. Complaining the command was too insignificant for an officer of his rank, Hunter was furious when he learned that Lane had won Lincoln's approval for a Texas expedition that would strip Kansas of troops. He sought an explanation from McClellan, who responded that Lane's command was under Hunter's supervision and the commander could suspend the operation. Halleck and Hunter tried to reduce the Kansas-Missouri war, but militant free-state guerrilla Jayhawkers plundered the western Missouri border along the Missouri River, destroying Union sentiment. Resolute abolitionists clad in U.S. uniforms, Generals Lane and Jennison claimed to be carrying out federal orders in terrorizing slave owners and disloyalists, which undermined the efforts of Robinson and Gamble. Halleck wired Hunter that the only way to keep the peace between Kansans and Missourians was to keep them apart, acknowledging that "we have numerous old grudges to settle."[39]

The Kansas-Missouri war spread north to Iowa. Alarming field reports forced Kirkwood to call on Halleck for protection. Colonel Henry. C. Nutt wired the governor that thirty "rank" secessionist families had crossed into the southwestern portion of the state and brought more than 100 horses, hoping to sell them to Confederate agents. Nutt feared that Jayhawkers would soon hunt these families down, and he wired Kirkwood to send federal forces to Fort Leavenworth. Kirkwood wanted to avoid making his state an "asylum for rebels and traitors," and urged Halleck's protection. The governor decided against calling out any state troops to avoid escalating the hatred among Iowans. Meanwhile, he wired Secretary of State Seward that while secession sentiments pervaded in the region, the safety of all citizens required the prompt arrest of the rebels who had fled from Missouri into Iowa. If not, he warned Seward, Jayhawkers would take matters into their own hands, and a small border war would ensue.[40]

The scattered operations in the western states convinced Halleck that the war had been "conducted upon what may be called pepper-box strategy—scattering our troops so as to render them inferior in numbers in any place where they can meet the enemy."[41] Increasingly problematic was the continued lack of pay for soldiers, which promoted desertion and discouraged enlistment. "I assure you," wrote Captain Algernon S. Baxter, assistant quartermaster from Cairo, to Captain Lewis B. Parsons of the St. Louis Quartermaster Office, "I had rather be in the bottom of the Mississippi than work night and day as I do without being sustained by Government." He lamented, "To tell you the truth, we are on our last legs."[42]

Western Strategy and Idling Politics

By late January, Halleck alluded to General Pope that the new "*furore*, 'On to Richmond!' is abating," and this reprieve would give him time to organize forces for the new campaign in the West. He ordered General Grant to call on western governors for additional troops. The irascible West Pointer could not be bothered by events far away from his department. He approved of Grant's amphibious expedition up the Tennessee River, while he kept his eye east of the Mississippi. He pinpointed the Confederate's weakness where the Cumberland and Tennessee Rivers emptied into the Ohio River. Penetration of the Southern heartland along the rivers required cooperation between himself and Buell. He also needed to trust Grant with amphibious expeditions in what could become a sizable campaign. The recent Union victory at the tiny Kentucky crossroads near the town of Mill Springs on 19 January gave Northerners something to applaud, but it hardly overshadowed McClellan's maddening inactivity.[43]

Military success in the West could not advance the Union war effort unless armies occupied the soil they won in battle. Occupation required an increase in the army, allowing it to stretch over hundreds of miles. If Union commands were successful in moving the war's border deeper into the Confederacy, it would strain the current arrangement between nation and state in supplying those armies. In recent months, the transfer of power from state to national authorities represented a departure from the traditional federal arrangement and left governors somewhat powerless in providing for their men. Stanton assumed the helm at a time when supplying the ranks fell exclusively to Meigs's quartermasters. Yet commanders communicated their needs to governors, who had busied themselves during the winter attending to invalid soldiers returning home and in revitalizing local economies. New York attorney Dexter Hawkins, for example, encouraged Washburn to detail someone to New York City, where many of Maine's invalid soldiers had been forced to remain for want of clothes, food, pay, and the very basic necessities of life. Already acting in such capacity for other New England states was Frank Howe, upon whom Washburn also came to rely for such services. This new arrangement frustrated some governors, even as they consented to it. In this transition, Tod, for example, requested Stanton to clarify where the governor's authority ended and where national authority began. "I feel myself so much embarrassed," he wired Stanton, "for the want of well defined rule or order, in the administration of my military duties, that I am constrained to call your attention to the matter."[44]

By January's end Lincoln had lost his patience with commanders determined to wait out the winter before campaigning. He issued President's Special War Order No. 1, which called the Army of the Potomac into an expedition for the immediate object of "seizing and occupying a point upon the Rail Road South Westward of what is known of Manassas Junction," and set the departure date for 22 February.[45] He took possession of railroads and telegraphs, and sent Scott on an information-gathering trip through the Midwest to ascertain the viability of sending a portion of McClellan's army to the West to break through Confederate General Albert Sidney Johnston's defensive line stretching from the Appalachians to the Mississippi. Scott met with governors, conferred with Buell and Halleck, and sent word back to Washington that affirmed the Confederate weakness. At the moment, a quick victory looked more promising in Tennessee than in Virginia, and Lincoln's optimism grew with each western wire that came into the War Department.[46]

Scott was in Louisville on 6 February, conferring with Buell, when news came over the wires announcing that Flag Officer Andrew Foote had captured Fort Henry on the Tennessee River. This enabled Grant to land his 15,000 troops on the east bank of the river. Finally, Halleck could claim a victory and laud himself the architect of the operation that bagged a flooded river fort. That something had been accomplished under such disorganized circumstances delighted Halleck, who declared that the Union flag would "never be removed" from Tennessee. He suggested to McClellan that an entire overhaul of the western departments would bring about more success and suggested that he should be given command. He failed to acknowledge that it was Morton who supplied Foote the gunpowder that allowed his fleet to bombard the fort. To follow up his success, Grant marched on to Fort Donelson, some twelve miles to the east on the Cumberland River. He allowed Brigadier. General John A. McClernand the vanguard, but his soldiers had been taken from Hunter's Kansas Department, which left Robinson and Kirkwood without defense against border ruffians. Confederates evacuated Bowling Green, Kentucky, and Buell's army marched almost unopposed to the Tennessee line. These advances forced Johnston to decide between defending Fort Donelson, or evacuating the river fort, retreating south, and reassembling his small Confederate army. The latter decision meant giving up Nashville and middle Tennessee's resources, so Johnston pressed his luck and sent roughly half his men to Donelson and sent the rest of his army south.[47]

The Brunt of Battle

In the week between the fall of Fort Henry and the attack on Fort Donelson twelve miles away, midwestern governors were thrown into a panic. Buell and Halleck moved the war deeper into enemy territory, and they were demanding more men and more celerity in getting them forward. In three brutally frigid days along the Cumberland River bank, Grant's men fought and won the battle of Fort Donelson that opened middle Tennessee to Union advances. It was a legitimate Union victory on secessionist soil, but it brought the war's incalculable destruction home to Northerners. McClellan was with Curtin that morning when the news came over the wires in his private room. The commander apologized for reading the dispatch in front of the governor, "which he did with a strong but suppressed emotion," and then rushed to the War Department. Some 300 spectators were assembled outside Stanton's office, and McClellan bypassed them in a "breathless haste," and announced the news. Just a month into office, the normally composed cabinet member threw up his hat and proposed three cheers for the Union's first legitimate victory.[48]

News of the Union victory spread like wildfire. On the morning of the seventeenth, Iowan Frank W. Palmer, printer of the court, burst into the Iowa House of Representatives, sprinted to the desk of the House Speaker, and whispered the great news. Leaping from his chair, the Iowa politician shouted that Grant had captured Fort Donelson, and the news echoed through the halls of the old capitol building, causing a rousing cheer. Even better news was that Halleck had singled out the soldiers of the 2nd Iowa for having "proved themselves the bravest of the brave," and that they "had the honor of heading the column which entered Fort Donelson."[49]

Scott was in Louisville when news of the battle appeared over the wires, and from there Stanton ordered him to Illinois, Iowa, Wisconsin, and Minnesota to confer with those governors preparing to send relief expeditions to Donelson. By this time, Stanton had tallied the governors' reports indicating there was a force large enough, he believed, to win the war. Besides, the war beyond the Appalachian Mountains looked promising. Eastern governors applauded the efforts of their western colleagues. To Yates, Washburn sent a personal note of congratulations. "Maine assures Illinois that she rejoices in her glory," he declared.[50] "It is a cheering thought," Yates responded, "that the glory of one is the glory of the other." Between the "denizens of the prairie" and the dwellers of the "pine covered hills," he wrote, "there is a holy bond of 'Union.'"[51] Kirkwood likewise responded with thanks and an acknowledgment that "their well-earned fame is very dear to our people."[52]

Northern newspapers credited Stanton for the victories, but the war secretary shunned the accolades. That credit, he argued, went to the "gallant officers and soldiers that fought the battles," and while admitting that he had heard of "military combinations and organizing victory" (no doubt referring to McClellan), the only way to win battles was by the same manner in which they had been won in the days of Joshua, "by boldly pursuing and striking the foe."⁵³ For Tennesseans, the only fate worse than having surrendered at Forts Henry and Donelson was the humiliation of the Union occupation and Nashville's surrender the following week. Tennesseans could hardly imagine having given up so much in so few weeks. Stanton explained to *New York Tribune* journalist Charles Dana that the true character of the war was best characterized by Grant's message to Buckner: "I propose to move immediately on your works." Stanton believed that Federals could sweep through Kentucky and Tennessee and that the North had the resources to effectively end the war in that region. "We have had no war," Stanton declared to Dana, "we have not even been playing war."⁵⁴

With Nashville under Union control, Buell issued orders that outlined the limited war conduct he desired to maintain while occupying the Southern city. Peaceable citizens were not to be molested, private homes were not to be invaded, and private property was not to be confiscated. The Union victories moved a war that had been frozen for months, and Halleck urged Stanton to let him concentrate his efforts on the western war and to give him overall command. Stanton agreed, writing to Scott that Halleck's activity had "made a very strong impression upon the public mind," and led him to "think that the western operations may very wisely be placed under his command."⁵⁵

With middle Tennessee occupied, Lincoln tested the waters of reconciliation. Northern soldiers occupying the region were under strict orders to respect civil guarantees of Republican government in the hopes of luring Southerners back to the Union. Scott had traveled with Buell's army and felt the "pulse of the Nashville people," which convinced him that Lincoln's administration would be able to reconstruct the "rebel states, as fast as the army may take military possession of them." He contended, "The reorganisation [*sic*] of these rebel states is a matter of great importance and should receive serious consideration & prompt action."⁵⁶ That same day, Stanton notified Senator Andrew Johnson that Lincoln had appointed Johnson military governor of Tennessee. With the bold stroke of a pen, the president swung his reconstruction plan into motion, and Johnson was his man.⁵⁷

Meanwhile, newspapers printed casualty lists, which tempered the governors' enthusiasm. Many chief executives hastened to Fort Donelson to relieve the privations of the wounded soldiers. Kirkwood was so overwhelmed by the reports that he secured legislative support to send a commission to care for the wounded Iowans. Having been responsible for organizing thousands of citizen-soldiers, it was fitting that they attend to them after large-scale battles. The war was no longer a series of maps, telegrams, and supplies. Combat realities signaled an important shift in gubernatorial responsibilities from mobilization to relief. The celebratory call to arms had passed. Now came the pacing of halls, the sleepless nights awaiting news from the front, and the gathering of medical supplies. One Illinoisan wrote that Yates's office was never without a package marked "Sufferings of troops."[58]

Yates's dedication represented the link between local and national institutions and the guardianship governors assumed over the volunteers. Soldiers viewed governors as representatives who shared their values, rather than political leaders who mediated national affairs. Governors reciprocated these sentiments, often reminding soldiers they were fighting as members of states within a federal army. At one point Yates allegedly remarked to his son after the war that he felt like he "had fathered those boys," claiming that each of them "was my boy," and the men reciprocated the feeling by calling him "The Soldier's Friend."[59] Seeing the boys of the 11th Illinois off from Camp Butler in early February, Yates made known his profound affection for them. "I feel it in my heart to say," he declared, "that wherever you go, the eyes and thoughts and hearts of the Governor and State officers will follow you."[60] With thousands of Illinois troops engaged in the fight at Fort Donelson, Yates set out for Cairo to lend his personal supervision of soldier relief. He was the first man off his chartered hospital boat. Two soldiers ran to the plank and handed the governor a wounded soldier. "He was just one mass of blood and gore," Yates recalled. As he turned and carried the soldier back up the plank, Yates had just reached the deck of the steamboat when the boy soldier opened his eyes. The boy struggled to speak and, only after a "convulsive coughing" spell, was able to whisper, "Oh, who are you?" "Oh, my boy," said Yates, "I am the governor of Illinois." Managing one last breath, the boy said, "Tell my mother," and then he expired.[61]

Morton sought neither the fame nor glory of Yates. Instead, he steamed to Fort Donelson with an expedition of physicians and nurses. His determination impressed the editor of the *Indianapolis Daily Journal*, who declared that he was "ever alive to the interests and wants of the soldiers."[62] The Indiana chief executive recognized the need for soldier relief and established the Indiana Sanitary Commission in February, employing agents in Washington, Louisville, Nashville, Memphis, and Cairo. These agents rented houses and procured sanitary supplies for the more than 60,000 soldiers in the field and transported them to other agents in other cities. Agents facilitated furloughs, arranged troop transportation home, visited the hospitals, and distributed payments to soldiers and their families. The governor took pride in supervising the labors of attending to the Indianans he sent to the field.[63]

Despite the governors' efforts in attending to the soldiers, Halleck continued to wrestle soldiers from state control. This caused some grumbling on the part of the troops and governors, Halleck admitted to Stanton, but he was satisfied that it was the only way to get these forces promptly into the field. As much as Gamble wanted loyal Missourians near their homes, the truth was it was harder to discipline them. Complaints from Halleck and Buell as well as the Butler-Andrew feud caused Stanton to issue General Orders No. 18, reminding commanders that governors were the legal authorities for raising volunteer regiments and commissioning their officers and that no independent organizations would be recognized. Conversely, Stanton reiterated to governors that all requisitions should be channeled through quartermasters. Yet quartermasters moved slower than governors. Morgan, for example, proved to be a master in mobilizing, transporting, and supplying his New Yorkers. At McClellan's urgent request, he marshaled thirteen regiments, and in less than a week he moved 8,000 men from New York to Washington, a feat yet unsurpassed in the war.[64]

Halleck's and Buell's occupations of Missouri and Tennessee aided civil governance. At Gamble's request, the commander ordered that in all future Missouri elections, voters, including licensed attorneys, counselors, and proctors, would be required to take a loyalty oath. The commanders' orders were similar in dictating the conduct for their armies in these politically divided regions. The orders instructed soldiers to provide evidence by their noble and lawful actions that they came "merely to crush out rebellion and to restore the peace and the benefits of the Constitution and the Union of which they have been deprived by selfish and unprincipled leaders." Halleck declared, "By our acts we will undeceive them." He proclaimed, "In restoring to them the glorious flag of the Union, we will assure them that they shall enjoy under its folds the same protection of life and property as in former days."[65] Even after learning that some forty-two officers had been poisoned by provisions left behind in Mud Town, Arkansas, Halleck refused to retaliate by adopting the same "barbarous mode of warfare."[66]

Lincoln believed his limited war aims would reduce civilian resistance against his armies. It was a noble gesture to conciliate Southerners, but Buell's and Halleck's rigid adherence to his rules eroded the loyalty in the ranks and did little to stifle guerrilla depredations. Hostilities in Kansas escalated beyond Robinson's civil control and prompted Hunter to declare martial law. Desperados and Jayhawkers compromised the Union cause in the border counties of Kansas and Missouri, and Robinson was caught between Hunter and Lane. Lincoln finally decreed that Lane would report to Hunter.[67]

By early March, journalists covering the western departments applauded Halleck's exploits. The commander had managed operations on both sides of the Mississippi River while maintaining justice among disloyal Missourians and assisting Hunter against treasonous Kansans. Lincoln recognized his efforts and, on 10 March, relieved McClellan of overall command, placed him at the helm of the Army of the Potomac, and combined all the departments that stretched west of the Appalachian Mountains to Kansas. He gave this new Department of the Mississippi to Halleck. To spare Halleck the unpleasant task of relieving Hunter, Lincoln sent Hunter south to command the newly merged departments of the South and Florida. Between the Department of the Potomac and Halleck's new department, Lincoln created the Mountain Department and pulled Frémont from the shelf to command it. With few slaves in the region to liberate, the Old Pathfinder could cause little damage. Besides, he was a favorite among the Radicals. His appointment would also help quiet members of Wade's Joint Committee and perhaps curry favor among the Germans during an election year. The most important appointment, however, was the president's selection of Johnson who was responsible for restoring civil government to loyal Tennesseans.[68]

Just twenty-two square feet of railroad connected the Memphis and Charleston and the Mobile and Ohio railroad lines at Corinth, Mississippi, but Halleck wanted his name on it. The commander ordered Pope to besiege New Madrid, Missouri, and dispatched Curtis and Sigel (both Union Generals) to the small mountains of northwest Arkansas near Fayetteville at a place called Pea Ridge to keep the Confederates from concentrating in Mississippi. Having shelved Grant for petty misconduct, Halleck dispatched General Charles F. Smith to move up the Tennessee River. After a long winter that cast shadows of military inertia and frustration over the administration, in addition to the victories at Forts Henry and Donelson, and the capture of Nashville, these three Union movements were about to help Lincoln put the bottom back in the tub. McClellan, however, had not been a part of them, a fact the administration and the observant press continually noted. "The upshot" of the recent directive, Bates wrote, was that it relieved

McClellan from the post of general-in-chief and hereinafter required all commanding generals to report directly to the War Department.[69] Lincoln, meanwhile, consulted his cabinet over compensated emancipation, the return of fugitive slaves, and abolishing slavery in Washington. Stanton won wide acclaim for his energy and forthrightness and, according to Lincoln's secretary Stoddard, had won "to a most remarkable degree, the confidence of the whole people." He remarked, "They believe him to be in earnest, *terribly* in earnest, and that he will be the strong right hand of the President."[70]

Union victories and political changes in February and March were the most decisive yet of the war because they brought more territory and more slaves under Union control and complicated Lincoln's efforts to keep emancipation out of the war. These changes helped crystalize the complications with Lincoln's conciliatory war aims. The credibility of those aims required positioning armies to implement them. The war in the West gave commanders, soldiers, and political leaders the opportunity to judge the merits of limited war in the occupied Confederacy. Union troops penetrating deeper south had far more influence in changing the war than politicians in Washington. Victories at Mill Spring, Forts Henry and Donelson, the capture of Nashville and New Madrid, and the most recent success at Pea Ridge, stirred confidence in the Northern populace.

The Tennessee victories made the silence along the Potomac even more maddening. Free time in camp afforded disgruntled soldiers time to correspond with governors and express their sentiments for expediting the war. Yet soldiers' frustrations about conciliation were not limited to McClellan's or Halleck's armies. Colonel Sargent wrote to Andrew from Beaufort, South Carolina, of dissatisfaction. "Vindicating the majesty of an insulted Government, by extirpating all *rebels*, & fumigating their nests with the brimstone of unmitigated Hell," declared Sargent, "I conceive to be the holy purpose of our further efforts, . . . [& I hope] I shall have a chance to do something . . . in 'the Great Fumigation,'" before the rebellion has ended.[71] Sargent's tone was not lost on the governor, but he tried in vain to inspire Lincoln's administration to follow the lead of the Joint Committee regarding the conduct of the war. His correspondence with soldiers and citizens had grown substantially over the months. He even received a letter from a Lawrence, Kansas, resident, who pleaded for the governor to "do something to make this proslavery administration change its policy." He declared, "Delaware, Maryland, Kentucky, & Missouri have more influence at Washington than

Massachusetts, New York, Pennsylvania, and Ohio, but it is time that the loyal states speak out."[72]

Governors tried to force Lincoln's hand early on. Conciliation, they complained, might win over some Southerners, but at the cost of eroding Northern goodwill and thus reducing the volunteer spirit. Such policies, they argued, emboldened Southern enemies. Halleck's new appointment came with assurances that he could succeed in the West by balancing military and political objectives. He restored Grant to command and ordered Sherman to land his division at a tiny insignificant dock called "Pittsburg Landing" on the western bank of the Tennessee River. Armies were on the move, and soldiers held out hope that western victories would change the political climate in Washington. Major Joseph Warren Keifer of the 3rd Ohio encamped in Nashville reported to his wife that, for the first time in months, the political horizon had brightened, and he predicted that "the whole character of the war will be changed."[73]

The war was about to change, but not for the better. McClellan's departure from Washington and assignment to the Virginia Peninsula relieved governors. In his absence, Lincoln appointed New Yorker James S. Wadsworth, military governor for the District of Columbia. By this time, Butler had landed his Federal forces at Ship Island, Mississippi, where he assumed command of the Union expedition to secure the Gulf Coast. Meanwhile, Confederate Stonewall Jackson slipped into the Shenandoah Valley and opened his offensive near Winchester, Virginia, at the battle of Kernstown. He was to keep Washington defenses from reinforcing McClellan. Federals managed to win the hard-fought contest, but even in victory Lincoln decided to keep a sizable force nearer the nation's capital. All of this activity suggested that Union armies were on the eve of perhaps closing in on a much-expected victory. So confident was mountaineer political leader Pierpont about McClellan's prospect of victory that he wired Lincoln and suggested that the "certainty of the rebellion being shortly put down in the State, I deem it important that I should issue a circular letter to the people ... calling upon them to co-operate with me in restoring the government of the State." Lincoln responded that while things were improving, he advised Pierpont to "make haste slowly," and to "draw up your proclamation carefully."[74] Lincoln, however, was careful to avoid being overconfident.

Before state assemblymen adjourned that spring, legislators responded to the escalating war by approving policies designed to guard state sovereignty and keep Union war aims limited and within the bounds of the Constitution. Several governors had taken advantage of wartime liberties to patronize political leaders, and legislators established measures that made governors accountable for the expansion of their authority. Illinois legislators especially scrutinized Yates's conduct. Representatives targeted his questionable appointments and alleged fraud in financial contracts. Some Democrats were so outraged that they sought to limit the chief executive's term to two years. Backed into a political corner, Yates launched a counterattack against his adversaries. He characterized them as conspirators and used the press to accuse them of collusion with the Knights of the Golden Circle, a group of disloyalists pledged to overtake the state. When the national government denied Yates his due share to reimburse the state's wartime contracts, he claimed that state authorities had exceeded their authority and sought permission to arrest suspected secessionists. The governor concluded that any Illinoisan who disagreed with his or Lincoln's policies was guilty of treason, and he looked for Lincoln's support. Yet Lincoln refused to save him, at least not in March. So disheartened was Yates that he wrote Trumbull that he could forgive Lincoln for his "personal neglect" and his "habitual disregard of all my requests," provided he acted more decisively. "I have lost (I know not how) all the influence I ever had with Mr. Lincoln," he confided in Trumbull, "I do congratulate myself that I have done much in getting up our great Illinois army but I have had no credit for it from Mr. Lincoln."[75] The demoralized governor decided to enter the ranks, and he dispatched circulars to gather officers' reaction to the idea. "Would that I could have a place in the field," he expressed to Trumbull, "I believe the Illinois Army would shout throughout all its regiments if I could."[76] When the circular caught up with the army, one soldier replied that "there was enough Drunken Major Generals in the Army now" and that commissioning the governor would only add to their problems.[77]

The change of seasons brought adjournment to many Northern legislatures, and the press shifted its attention back to the national administration. Trumbull reported to Yates that Lincoln was "waking up to the fact that we are in a critical condition, [and] that the responsibility is upon *him*. I think he has resolved hereafter not to content himself with throwing all army movements on the Generals commanding, on the ground that he is no military man."[78] Lincoln was no military man, but he shouldered the war's burdens, met critics head on, and exercised a visible hand in directing the military. The recent battle of Hampton Roads, fought off the Virginia Coast 8–9 March, convinced him to safeguard Northern ports and waterways.

Orders went out to Governors Morgan, Andrew, Curtin, Olden, Burton, and Washburn to construct timber rafts and place batteries at port cities. The Union's early success on the waterways was not lost on Washington and not on the governors of states with coastal cities. Curtin, Burton, and Olden met in Philadelphia to confer over the Delaware River defenses. Andrew had already scouted possibilities for purchasing additional ships at Liverpool and wired Lincoln, introducing him to agents recommended for negotiations over seas. Meanwhile, he called on congressional colleagues to dredge up some plans from the War Department's engineer, who had been working on plans for Maine's seacoast.[79]

Stanton had something to do with waking Lincoln up to military realities. Directing the war over the telegraph required hours of deciphering numerous telegrams from commanders and governors struggling to lead the war in fields that stretched some 3,000 miles. As determined as Stanton was about directing military affairs, he nonetheless allowed governors and commanders to settle regional and civil-military issues. They, better than he, understood the war on the ground. Halleck and Morton, for example, experienced civil-military friction during the Donelson campaign, but Stanton remained a bystander. The haughty commander viewed Morton as meddlesome and attempted to minimize his influence over the troops. Morton's soldiers, however, remained devoted to him, as they would to most governors. When Halleck blocked the governor's attempt to supply his Indianans near New Madrid, Missouri, with clothing, Morton went around him. Perhaps slighted by the soldiers' loyalty to their governors, Halleck came to appreciate the crucial role they played in aiding the soldiers, if for no other reason than to strengthen his command.[80]

By early April, Stanton believed the Union war had outgrown the state-oriented approach to mobilization. The Union's more than 700,000 soldiers appeared sufficient to win the war, and Stanton halted recruiting. He issued a short one-line telegram to every loyal governor on 3 April that read: "Volunteer recruiting will cease from this date."[81] This was a temporary shutdown, as he explained to the Senate Military Committee, he ordered superintendents to disband their staffs, sell the property, and ordered officers to join their regiments in the field. Just two days after McClellan moved up the Virginia Peninsula, governors were left alone to replenish the ranks. Frustrated by the chaos of raising men, Stanton needed time to evaluate the most effective means of replenishing the existing ranks before adding new regiments. Although the press howled over this shutdown, Stanton remarked to Charles Dana that he was not "in the smallest degree dismayed or disheartened, by any setbacks." On the contrary, "by God's blessing," he confided, "we shall prevail," and he felt "a deep *earnest* growing up around me." He remarked, "We have no jokes or trivialities, but all with whom I act show that they are now in dead earnest." All he needed was "reasonable time and patience."[82]

Stanton had reason to be encouraged. Federal armies won victories in the West, Lincoln had confidence in McClellan's plan, and on paper numbers in the ranks were high. Besides, given the sluggish and poorly managed mobilization thus far, the secretary planned to overhaul the recruiting process. Nonetheless, he remarked to Halleck that the order was "for the purpose of compelling returns from the respective governors."[83] Ironically, before Congress adjourned, it granted Lincoln the power to call for 500,000 troops, and it appeared the national government would assume recruiting for the new levies, an idea McClellan hoped to infuse into the national culture. Stanton refused the idea, and instead ordered commanders to call on governors for recruits. Just weeks before Lincoln had concluded that "the great rebellion has passed the climax of its energy and power, and is visibly on the wane."[84]

Beyond regimental mobilization, state auditors pored over annual reports, and it was clear that many states were in dire financial stress. Governors had desperately pulled together resources to pay for the war at the expense of other commitments. The war came on quickly, and governors expanded their cabinets to meet their vast responsibilities. Many capital cities were in remote areas like Hartford, Montpelier, Augusta, Concord, Harrisburg, Lansing, and St. Paul, which required shuttling between the statehouses and larger water-born cities where governors often conducted business. They channeled relief efforts through private and volunteer agencies to maintain popular support for the war. Buckingham served as president of the Connecticut Chaplains' Aid Association and directed members to supply Connecticut regiments with chapel tents, libraries, and local newspapers. Olden spent the winter focused almost exclusively on soldier and family welfare and keeping citizens employed. To remind him of their Republican loyalties, soldiers from the 3rd New Jersey regiment sent Olden captured Confederate flags to hang in the executive mansion. The Jersey Blues were proud to fight for Olden, who, according to the *Newark Daily Mercury*, was "an Executive who, fully comprehending his duty to the nation and his fellow citizens, has discharged with unsparing energy and self-sacrifice, all the responsibilities of his position."[85]

By the spring, the great irony thus far in the war was that death, desertion, and sickness reduced the armies more rapidly than governors could recruit for them. Stanton's shutdown encouraged many prospective volunteers to remain at home and plant their crops. Yet, when commanders wired in their requests to replenish the ranks, pulling citizens away from their farms worked against governors, especially those seeking reelection. As much as military news dominated the national headlines, editors connected news from the front to the war's political course, and governors were sensitive to local affairs, including supporting farmers needing to recover winter losses by remaining at home.[86]

Locally, the political weathervane told the story of the war. New Hampshire voters went to the polls annually in early March, and this year, they reelected Berry. His victory signaled that while most citizens were satisfied with his war management, Democrats made significant gains. Despite some initial disenchantment among soldiers, Berry's honesty amid wartime profiteering and corruption, as well as his bipartisan patronage impressed voters. Although a Republican, Berry became what the *Nashua Telegraph* described as the "Governor of the loyal people of all parties."[87] Yet New Hampshire was not without its critics of Lincoln's administration, evidenced by the sizable Democratic gains. Berry expressed to his Republican friend George G. Fogg, whom Lincoln had appointed minister to Switzerland in 1861, that New Hampshire oppositionists were doing all they could to undermine the credibility of the national government's handling of the war. "But my old friend, *cheer up.* 'There is [sic] better days coming,'" he wrote encouragingly, "before your eyes shall see this *scrawl* you will have heard of the glorious victories at Port Royal, Hilton Head, at Roanoke Island, at Mill Springs, through Kentucky, Missouri, at Fort Henry, Fort Donelson, Nashville." He boasted, "That the glorious old Flag now waives [sic] at some point or points in about all the seceded States, and my firm conviction is that before you will read this letter the rebellion will be bleeding at every [home], if not lifeless and powerless at the feet of the constitution and the Union." He argued, "When honest old Abe, (I view him a god send to America) was inducted into the Presidential chair, Rebellion was arrogant in the South, and taunting Lincoln, and the government as being powerless and at their disposal." But, he declared, "a miracle has been wrought in the loyal States."[88]

CHAPTER EIGHT

Does the Governor Say He Will Come for Us?

Taunting the national government as powerless had some foundation. That an army of roughly 16,000 soldiers was in place to defend 31 million Americans when the Civil War erupted was something of an anomaly—so vast a country defended by so tiny an army reflected Republican attitudes toward national defense. More extraordinary was the miracle that had been performed in swiftly mobilizing thousands of Northerners into an army. Confederates had awakened a Northern giant that showed signs of asserting its power that spring, and governors were anxious to get the war moving and remained attentive to their soldiers. McClellan's mammoth Army of the Potomac sailed for Fort Monroe in mid-March and, on arrival, commenced its march up the Virginia Peninsula. Pressured to strengthen Frémont's Mountain Department and worried over Washington's safety, Lincoln pulled German-born Louis Blenker's division from McClellan's army and assigned it to Frémont. The German's reassignment unnerved McClellan and rightfully so. Northern attention was on his Grand Army as it embarked on what many hoped would prove the deathblow to the Confederacy. Governors welcomed this offensive, but it remained to be seen if it would change the war's direction. In the meantime, they remained near stenographers who transmitted frontline news.[1]

The political mud deepened by the day. Lincoln summoned Governors Curtin, Morton, Tod, and Washburn to Washington to discuss their state militias and to share his thoughts on emancipation. Reluctant to adopt radical measures against slavery, the president encouraged congressional measures to abolish the institution in the District of Columbia and prohibit the return of fugitive slaves within the ranks. Many governors welcomed these changes as a sign the administration was moving closer to expanding Union war aims. Governors closer to Washington expectedly howled at the decision, especially Bradford and Burton. But Lincoln was undeterred. The Emancipation Proclamation was surely "incubating in his portfolio," and "was gathering vital force in the minds of the cabinet for its final exposition," wrote one contemporary.[2]

April elections in Rhode Island and Connecticut confirmed New England's approval of Republican war aims and carried forward the fall's electoral momentum. Voters reelected Sprague and Buckingham, both of whom endorsed Lincoln's policies. Sprague ran unopposed on the Union Party ticket and received nearly every vote cast. Buckingham benefitted from Democratic Party divisions and ran as the nominee of both the Republican and Union parties. The *Hartford Evening Press* endorsed both governors and declared that since the eruption of the war the year before, Buckingham had "shown himself a true patriot and Christian gentleman." "We cannot afford to part with him in this crisis," the editor declared.[3] Like Sprague's Rhode Islanders, Connecticutans elected Buckingham to "proclaim unmistakably their abhorrence of the slaveholders' rebellion, and their determination to stand by the Stars and Stripes."[4]

The Bitterness of Shiloh

Yet the war was about to experience its greatest contest yet. For two days, from 6–7 April, more than 65,000 Union and Confederate soldiers fought the battle of Shiloh, just up the bank from Pittsburg Landing on the Tennessee River in Tennessee. The combined Union armies of Grant and Buell suffered more than 13,000 casualties. "If the reports which we publish this morning approach the truth," wrote the *Indianapolis Daily Journal*, then "the greatest battle of the last half century, in any part of the world, has been fought."[5] Although the Union won the contest, something convinced Halleck to come to Pittsburg Landing. If there had been a surprise along the Tennessee, the departmental commander would need to minimize the fallout, reprimand those at fault, and take charge of the offensive to Corinth. At the time, Halleck's only relief was Pope's victory in taking Island No. 10. Public and journalistic acrimony accompanied the praise for the Union victory, but Halleck's arrival brought relief to Northerners seeking answers. "This great man is now in command at Pittsburg Landing," proclaimed the *Louisville Daily Journal*, "the question now is, whether the last rebel gun will be fired east or west of the Alleghanies."[6] Halleck believed himself the great man in command, but he was a thousand miles from the Virginia Peninsula, where Lincoln needed McClellan to be a great man. Having come through hell at Shiloh, Alexander Varian of the 1st Ohio agreed, writing to his sister that he hoped McClellan would do as well as they had at Shiloh, arguing that it was time "the 'flower of the Army' did *something*."[7]

New England's political victories reflected confidence in Lincoln's war management. The success at Shiloh, however, came at significant cost, and the flood of battlefield information revealed its horrific details. Iowan William R. Stimson survived the battle and assured his family that his unit made the Confederates "bleed for every inch they got."[8] Governors hurried to Pittsburg Landing to survey the damage and relieve the suffering. Having been to Fort Donelson, Yates knew what to expect, but nothing prepared him for the scene at Pittsburg Landing. He charted several steamers, assembled over 100 doctors and nurses, gathered 3,000 Enfields, procured ice and fruit, and steamed for the battlefield. The governor arrived a week after the battle and witnessed devastation beyond anything he had imagined. He spent several days riding from camp to camp, attending the soldiers. "The Illinois soldiers had heard of the coming and mission of the Governor," wrote one soldier, "and wherever he was recognized cheers went up for 'Dick Yates,' the soldier's friend."[9] Troops adored Yates and they found comfort in his attention to their welfare. "Does the Governor say he will come for us?" inquired a young Illinoisan shortly before he died, because "Dick Yates never broke his word to a soldier." He arranged to transfer wounded soldiers to state hospitals and funded their transport.[10]

Morton also rushed to the battlefield. The governor had previously sent agents to Halleck's headquarters to secure the relocation of ailing soldiers to Indiana hospitals. In the meantime, he chartered steamers and assembled a medical expedition of more than sixty physicians and over 300 nurses to accompany him. Like Yates, he spent days visiting the soldiers and securing their transport home. On the return trip, just as the steamer was about to debark, a Kentucky officer, who was in charge of several wounded men, sought out the boat captain and pressed him to take his wounded aboard. "But my orders, sir," replied the captain "allow me to take only Indiana troops." "But damn it, sir," retorted the officer, "isn't Morton Governor of Kentucky? If he can care for our state he certainly will protect you in caring for our soldiers."[11]

When news of Shiloh reached Madison, Governor Harvey organized a relief expedition and recruited the Commissary General Colonel Edward R. Wadsworth, the Wisconsin Surgeon General Erastus B. Wolcott, and Milwaukeean General Edward H. Brodhead to accompany him. The group departed three days after the battle and streamed south to Pittsburg Landing, where they found over 200 wounded Wisconsin soldiers suffering from want of medical attention. The governor's presence among the men stirred him emotionally. He was so moved by the scene that he penned his wife a short note of his experience "Yesterday was the day of my life," he wrote, "thank God for the impulse that brought me here." He added that "I am well, and have done more good by coming than I can tell you." He singled out the men of the 16th Wisconsin who had been in the thick of the fighting on the morning of the 6th and suffered enormous casualties. "[W]hen I think of the splendid material enlisted in that regiment, equal to the best Wisconsin has sent to the field, and what they might have done for their country, and what fame they would have won for themselves and their State," he expressed, "I can but feel indignant."[12]

Harvey's crew spent several days at Pittsburg Landing before returning to Madison. They stopped downstream at Savannah on 19 April, and that night, while Harvey was standing on board the steamer *Dunleith* awaiting the approaching steamer *Minnehaha*, he lost his footing and plunged between the two steamers into the Tennessee River. Reuben Wilson, an accompanying doctor, bent down and extended his cane to the governor, but Harvey grabbed it with such force that it jerked out of Wilson's hand. John G. Clark, another physician, jumped overboard, managed to hold on to the wheel of the steamer, and reached out for Harvey, hoping to clasp his hand, but the swift current swept the governor away underneath a nearby flatboat. The party labored throughout the night to rescue Harvey, but the incessant rain and swift swollen river worked against them. The governor's body was discovered days later along the riverbank. The news of Harvey's death hit Madison like a bombshell as Lt. Governor Edward Salomon was sworn into office. Wisconsinites mourned the loss of "the soldier's governor," who in such a short time had managed to claim federal funds owed Wisconsin during Randall's tenure, arranged for the state to keep a share of its direct tax, and had already taken several trips for soldier relief. The new governor was a German revolutionary who fled to the United States to escape persecution. Although a successful Milwaukee lawyer and lifelong Democrat, Salomon was better known for tending bar. He supported the Union war effort, however, and Republicans had chosen him as lieutenant governor to draw Germans into the Republican Party.[13]

Shiloh changed the war on many fronts. Western campaigns began to make national headlines, but editors also brought the war home in the form of casualty lists. In taking New Madrid, Missouri, Pope added to Halleck's fortunes, and Yates capitalized on the victory and pressed Lincoln to have Pope transferred to the regular army, urging his promotion to major general "as a token of gratitude to Illinois."[14] Lincoln appreciated the general's "splendid achievements," but he wanted the governor to know "that Major Generalships in the Regular Army, are not as plenty as blackberries."[15] Yates understood this fact, but two weeks after the fighting on what one Indiana soldier called the "Waterloo field of the American Continent," western armies appeared to be winning Lincoln's war. Union forces began their bombardment of New Orleans, an important city left undefended when Confederate General Johnston withdrew forces from the Gulf Coast to reinforce armies in the heartland, and, by 25 April, Federal vessels landed at the city wharfs and began the land offensive to overtake the city, which surrendered the following day.[16]

Halleck claimed credit for the western victories and took charge of command problems. Grant sunk into the background and suffered journalistic criticism for being surprised at Shiloh. Meanwhile, McClellan sat on the Virginia Peninsula complaining about troops taken from his command. McClellan believed he had no friends in Washington and feared Lincoln would relieve him any day. Halleck also demanded more reinforcements but, unlike McClellan, had something to show for his efforts. Halleck supposed he was on the verge of fighting what would be the grandest battle of the war and could not understand Stanton's cessation of recruiting. Traveling with Halleck, Scott wrote Stanton that overwhelming sickness and other disabilities within the western armies had reduced the ranks, and that if something was not done soon, "our army of the West will dwindle so rapidly that it will not be possible to occupy positions and make advance movements with rapidity and reasonable certainty of success." With the "sickly season" now approaching, he argued, "I do hope that the numbers *now in the field* will be fully maintained until the rebellion is crushed."[17]

Iron Fist in a Velvet Glove

Western victories gave congressional Radicals the war they desired, and they increased Stanton's drive to crush the Confederates quickly. Yet the administration appeared to be gripped by McClellan's campaign. His army, perhaps more than any, provided the populace with a military barometer upon which it gauged Union hopes. The president's limited war policies for armies occupying Confederate soil, however, dissipated the momentum gained on the battlefield. "The sooner our govt gets over the idea that we are *fighting friends*, the sooner this war will come to an end," wrote frustrated Wisconsinite Lucius Fairchild to his father from Falmouth. "I tell you the people of the South are terribly in earnest & nothing but the strong arm of power will ever bring them back to us."[18]

Several governors were pressing Lincoln to use the strong arm of national power, and there was evidence that many Northerners wanted the same. Whatever the Federals had won at Shiloh paled in comparison to the laments heaped upon McClellan for not doing what western commanders had done. Even General Hunter had won acclaim with Northerners wanting to expand the war by ordering the emancipation of slaves in Florida, Georgia, and South Carolina and authorized the arming of blacks in those states. Radical governors considered the gesture a victory toward prosecuting the war more vigorously, but Lincoln rescinded the orders. The war was moving, except onto the Confederate capital's doorstep. Thus, the momentum gained could not be lost on dillydallying and maneuvering. "I think we are after the rebels with sharpsticks," boasted an encouraged Washburn to Fessenden.[19]

Washburn wanted Lincoln to use his stick on McClellan. By early May the president had grown impatient with the commander and sailed for Hampton Roads for a conference. Lincoln's meeting with McClellan was a disappointment. Yet he departed the peninsula energized by seeing the men in the field. A week later, however, "Stonewall" Jackson launched a countermove in the Shenandoah Valley, while Halleck crept to Corinth. The commander feared another surprise attack and went into a siege mentality. Like McClellan, he complained that interdepartmental politics plagued his command. Despite their importance, by mid-May both McClellan's and Halleck's campaigns took a backseat to Jackson's blitzkrieg maneuvers in the valley. The Confederate commander concealed his movements so effectively that he confused Banks, slipped across the Massanutten Mountains, and headed north toward Front Royal. The Confederate advance alarmed Northerners. Alexander McClure shared the alarm, writing from Chambersburg to Curtin that Pennsylvanians in the region were "anxious about the safety of the border because of the retreat of Banks."[20]

More than any Confederate movement thus far in the war, Jackson's Valley Campaign gripped Washington with panic and set in motion a series of events that ironically helped change Union war aims. Governors had clamored for an aggressive war from the beginning, and they had done all in their power to accommodate the war effort. As much as soldiers and the administration appreciated those efforts, their advice in connecting replacement capacity with war aims had gone unheeded. The Confederate advance heightened reliance on federal-state war management. On 19 May Stanton called on the governors for new regiments and used the enemy advance as justification. He sent circulars to all the governors inquiring as to how soon they could raise and organize six or more infantry regiments. Given that Stanton had stopped recruiting the month before, these wires surprised governors and journalists covering the war. Several editors alleged the administration had not been truthful regarding military affairs in the valley. To Andrew, Sprague, and Curtin the news was more alarming. "Send all the troops forward that you can immediately," read a wire. "Banks is completely routed," and the enemy was advancing upon Harpers Ferry.[21]

By day's end, however, the Union commander had recovered and arrived near the Potomac. Nonetheless, governors started recruiting for new regiments. Their announcements set off an editorial frenzy that chastised the War Department for misguiding the public about the war's progress. The collective response from the governors was a resounding doubt that so many volunteers could be raised and forwarded so quickly. With two major Federal offensives underway, valuable time had been lost since recruiting ceased, and the new directives appeared unreasonable. A call "so sudden and unforewarned finds me without materials for an intelligent reply," wrote Andrew, "our young men are all preoccupied by other views."[22] The governor seized the opportunity the enemy advance had given him to lecture Stanton about war aims. If a "real call" for additional regiments were ordered, Andrew believed he could raise the levies in forty days. "If our people feel that they are going into the South to help fight rebels, who will kill and destroy them by all means known to savages as well as civilized man, will deceive them by fraudulent flags of truce and lying pretenses..., will use their negro slaves against them." The governor believed Lincoln's call on the people would be "heavy on their patriotism." He added "But if the President will sustain General [David] Hunter, recognize all men, even black men, as legally capable of that loyalty the blacks are waiting to manifest, and let them fight, with God and human nature on their side, the roads will swarm if need be, with multitudes whom New England would pour out to obey your call."[23]

Promising a harsher war that included confiscation, emancipation, and black enlistment might incentivize volunteering, but it might not. Departing from conciliation and limited war aims would wreck havoc on Southerners, but it could possibly unhinge Northerners as well. Boston mayor Joseph T. Wightman wrote to Lincoln and repudiated Andrew's claim.

Andrew might represent some Bostonians in mingling emancipation with preservation of the Union, he argued, but that idea, Wightman wrote Lincoln, "is viewed with the strongest feelings of disapprobation," and they applauded his resisting such measures and retaining McClellan. "I am confident," he added, "that if this subject was introduced, in conformity with the views of Governor Andrews, it would produce a serious if not an irreparable injury to the cause of enlistment."[24] The unpopularity resided not only at home, but also with his troops. Corporal John W. Chase of the 1st Massachusetts Light Artillery wrote his brother from Virginia that the "nigger talk of John A Andrews [sic] & Co is not relished very well out here." Declared Chase, "If he [Andrew] wants to enlist niggers, he had better let the white men come home. God knows it is bad enough to be a Soldier without mixing ourselves up with niggers, and if Mass has no white men she had better let the States that have send the troops wanted."[25]

There was no denying that emancipation of Confederate slaves and enlistment of blacks would complicate Union volunteering. Race relations had not progressed far enough to persuade Northerners that the war advanced an emancipationist attitude even while they fought to preserve the Union. Only battlefield losses could move them to accept such extraordinary measures and, tragically, that would take time. Yet knowing this did not deter Andrew from trying. The governor viewed the war as the opportunity to unshackle the democratic republic from the institution that had caused the conflict. Besides, emancipation would weaken the Confederate war effort, and enlisting blacks in the military would demonstrate the administration's desire to establish a new Union. Truth be told, since the conflict began, the governor believed Lincoln's perception of Southern Unionism misguided and faulted the president for relying on conciliation to win back Southerners.

Lincoln had already considered departing from his limited war because he understood that his current course was eroding the popular support necessary to replenish the ranks. Military setbacks weighed heavily on the president, but as much as he needed to win on the battlefield, he needed to carry public opinion at home. Governors kept him apprised of manpower problems. If part of the Confederacy's strategy was to undermine the Northern will to fight, Andrew refused to wait for another Union loss to bring Lincoln or Northerners to accept his views. He took bold steps in arguing that black enlistment and emancipation would bring troops forward for a shorter war. These measures would deprive the enemy of its most valuable resource and give the war a spark of idealism. The army needed men, and he wanted to convince them that enlistment terms could only be shortened by waging all-out war. If citizens desired a shorter war, they would have to tolerate changes in the composition of the Union army and its objectives. Washburn supported Andrew. "The govt. says in affect that it needs the men & must have them, & have them they shall," he argued, but "what's the use to send more soldiers to loaf near Manassas or contract fatal diseases at Yorktown." Now there was one "full chorus," demanding to know "why it is that we are to send our noble, ingenious, industrious young men, the strength, hope & ornament of the State, or be cut down by thousands by the [deadly] malaria of a southern summer when the govt could use in their stead, [negroes] acclimated, loyal, & willing."[26] Washburn had confided to Hamlin that the people of Maine were "faithful, confiding, [and] patriotic," and that they "*do* believe in the President," that they "trust, honor, & love him," but he acknowledged they are "confident that the time has come when they should be terribly in earnest in carrying on this war."[27]

Obliging Stanton's Call

Many governors had grown frustrated by discouraging official reports, soldier's letters, and newspaper articles describing the bloodbath at Shiloh; the delay on the Virginia Peninsula; and the justification for keeping slavery out of the war. State legislatures had adjourned without making appropriations for additional regiments, and governors were out of incentives. Andrew resorted to theatrics and assembled the Massachusetts militia on Boston Common, where he posted a startling proclamation. "The wiley and barbarous horde of traitors to the People, to the Government, to our Country and to Liberty," it read, "menace again the national capital. They have attacked and routed Major General Banks, and are advancing on Harper's [sic] Ferry and are marching on Washington."[28] Governors responded likewise by attempting to shock the people to the cause, hoping the perceived panic in the Shenandoah Valley would inspire volunteers. Yet at the height of planting season, it would take months to organize new regiments. New York's Morgan pointed out the additional costs of raising the men and needed to know precisely how these men would be used, especially since he had no funds for additional volunteers. Struggling to procure state hospital accommodations, Olden replied that he could have three New Jersey regiments ready in ninety days. Newly elected Pierpont of the proposed state of

West Virginia responded that having "discouraged all idea of further volunteering among the people, they have engaged in other pursuits for the season."[29]

Other governors struggled as well. Kirkwood and Ramsey complained that meeting Halleck's requests would unduly tax Iowans and Minnesotans during the planting season. Holbrook had no militia to draw from, and the 8th Vermont had departed only a few months earlier. Under the circumstances, the governor argued that his tiny state was mainly agricultural and most of his young men had made seasonal arrangements. The *Providence Daily Journal* reported that New England farmers were reluctant to enlist because the summer harvest was a particularly good one and they were anxious to make the most of it. Berry enlarged state bounties to fifty dollars to inspire volunteering, but he wired Stanton that even this inducement would do little. Burton struggled with an unruly Democratic population that threatened violence to intimidate Unionists from volunteering. Wilmington native and close reader of the national press Anna M. Ferris noted in her diary that the sudden call for troops appeared to cause "more alarm" than was necessary. "The Governors of the States," she wrote, "are calling on the militia, fresh troops are called for to protect the Capitol & the scenes of last spring are reenacted." Although the defeat of Banks was "unexpected & disastrous enough," she concluded, "the alarm it created seems very disproportionate to the cause."[30]

A week after Stanton's circular, Lincoln returned to Washington from Aquia Creek. He spent 24 May in the War Department positioning his commanders like chess pieces. He ordered Frémont's army to the valley, suspended McDowell's movement set to join McClellan, and directed them both to cut off Jackson's retreat. To protect Harpers Ferry he dispatched General Rufus Saxton. Responding to Morgan's query about whether militia regiments would be accepted, Stanton replied the same day that three-month militiamen would be received in addition to volunteers for the war. Washburn pressed Stanton to take his three-month men "in lieu of drafting" until he could provide his quota of three-year recruits, which would "be most expeditious." Stanton allowed it and made allowances for other governors. For someone who had spent the last four months overruling governors, these allowances gave the impression that he was desperate.[31]

Governors used whatever means necessary to raise Stanton's new regiments, including advance pay and special allowances for families. Confiscation, emancipation, and black enlistments remained in suspension. Jackson's defeat of Banks at the battle of Winchester on 25 May shocked Stanton into wiring governors again. He demanded they forward all three-year men, militia, and three-month, men reasoning they would serve less time because the war would be won in a year. Banks's army retreated to Harpers Ferry, and the administration feared the Confederates would soon be at the gateway of the valley. If they crossed the Potomac, they could threaten Washington. Meanwhile, Stanton ordered all mustering officers to assist governors in enlisting and transporting men to the front. The *Hartford Daily Times* editor remarked that the Confederate victory had "frightened the Secretary of War to a remarkable degree."[32] Whether alarmed, frustrated, or both, Lincoln recognized what McClellan could not. "I think the time is near," he wrote McClellan, "when you must either attack Richmond or give up the job and come to the defence [sic] of Washington."[33]

The timing of Jackson's victory and Halleck's impending battle near Corinth unnerved Lincoln and Stanton. Halleck's dispatches forewarned of a contest larger than Shiloh, and governors traveling with the western army called on Washington to allow them to bring forward more soldiers. For all the governors' meddling ways, Halleck was able to use them to influence Lincoln. "The enemy are in great force at Corinth," Morton wired Lincoln, "and have recently received reinforcements." He warned, "It is fearful to contemplate the consequences of a defeat at Corinth."[34] Morton traveled with Sherman's division along the advance and rode with the commander during the day. Indiana soldiers appreciated his accompanying them. "[H]e seems to think a good deal of his pets [soldiers]," wrote James C. Vanderbilt to his mother, "and his pets think a good deal of him."[35] For a desk executive, he won acclaim for remaining calm under fire. Oblivious to dangers around him while accompanying the men digging entrenchments, Morton was nearly killed at one point when the Confederates shelled the men of the 9th Indiana and the 6th Kentucky. Colonel Walter C. Whitaker of the 6th Kentucky reported that when a shell fell and exploded "but a few feet from Governor Morton," he "stood like a veteran."[36]

As Lincoln and Stanton saw it, Halleck's imminent battle paled in comparison to the calamity about to occur near Washington. Without giving offense, Lincoln needed Halleck to understand that the war closer to Washington was more important than in front of Corinth. "I mean to cast no blame when I tell you each of our commanders along our line from Richmond to Corinth supposes himself to be confronted by numbers superior to his own." He wrote, "Under this pressure we thinned the line on the upper Potomac until yesterday it was broken, at heavy loss to us, and Gen. Banks put in great peril, out of which he is not yet extricated, and may be actually captured."[37]

On 26 May, the day after Stanton wired governors, Banks retreated across the Potomac and saved his army. The withdrawal relieved Lincoln, and he ordered Stanton to instruct governors to discharge whatever three-months men that had come forward and fill up the three-years regiments as rapidly as possible. On paper, Lincoln's instructions appeared uncomplicated. Yet public condemnation escalated. Northerners viewed the administration's impulsive reaction to Banks's defeat as poor war management. Anna Ferris detected the change in Wilmington, noting in her diary that "the public excitement is rapidly subsiding & the panic is dying out—as it was caused very much by the official orders to the Governors by the War Department," all of which, she concluded, simply "greatly impairs our confidence," in those running the war.[38] She surmised that many Northerners were losing confidence in the War Department. Yet the alarm also had also proven useful. The wires that Sunday evening helped provoke what the *Providence Daily Journal* declared was "another grand uprising of the north," which would counter the impression among Southerners and Europeans that the Union had exhausted its military strength.[39]

Governors questioned Stanton's abrupt directive to bring troops forward as much as they had questioned his cessation of recruiting. They welcomed national assistance to spur volunteering, but not in this manner. Once Lincoln's call for troops went public, it was hard to turn citizens away. Despite the initial forecast that governors would have trouble raising volunteers because of the summer harvest, Andrew had roughly 2,500 men on Boston Common, Morgan had some 10,000 in New York City, and Tod reported that hundreds had flocked to Columbus. The sudden change embarrassed them, and governors pressed the secretary to accept the men for short-term enlistments. Andrew called on Massachusetts congressman Samuel Hooper to derive some clarity from Lincoln as to the unexpected counterorder. Hooper replied that although there had been consultation with Stanton, the president had made the order. Stanton, however, became the scapegoat. When staff members counseled Andrew to publicly blame Stanton for the turnaround, Andrew leaped from his chair, his arms in the air, and exclaimed, "No, sir! If the people of Massachusetts don't know John A. Andrew well enough without rushing into print with a 'card' to explain his acts every time that somebody is frightened, then let him be misrepresented and misunderstood till the end of time!" He declared, "I will have nothing printed on the subject."[40]

Criticism mounted over the administration's change of directives, but Stanton was unaffected. He answered only to Lincoln. "I am not disturbed by the howling of those who are at your heels and mine," he wrote Andrew.[41] Still, Northerners had given much to the administration, and governors expected much in return, precisely because they were answerable to constituents at home, not Lincoln. The recent turn of events indicated that the military rewards had not equaled the North's sacrifices. Governors needed reassurance that national administrators were not frittering away the state-oriented war and eroding Northern confidence by their mismanagement. Lincoln was hard pressed to continue to justify to governors his limited war aims and his command of the armies. Andrew was not alone in castigating Lincoln for his overindulgence of conservative commanders. Sumner laid the blame for the recent scare on McClellan and revealed to Andrew the high gossip among his Washington colleagues. "The whole trouble is perfectly traceable to McClellan," he complained to Andrew, "who took away to Yorktown an amount of troops beyond what he was authorized to & *was to leave Washington defenseless.*" To appease the governor, Sumner admitted that Stanton informed him that a decree of Emancipation would be issued within two months. "I say nothing of the time, but I know that it must come," he confided. "Chase with whom I dined alone this evening, agrees with me that the war can be ended only through Emancipation."[42] Andrew agreed.

Stanton's conflicting directives revealed much about the reasons for the lack of success in eastern campaigns. Under the circumstances, governors enlisted the volunteers who had come forward and pressed Stanton to make use of them. Stanton convinced Lincoln to appease the governors by accepting and paying the militiamen and moving on. Lincoln agreed, and Stanton canceled the previous order and accepted the volunteers in good faith. Governors believed the men could be produced, but argued that inducements such as partial bounties up front might help encourage volunteering for longer periods, as would pledging to care for the welfare of their families. "Say to the boys one and all," wrote Kirkwood to Colonel Addison H. Saunders, "I am delighted with them," and "expect to hear from them in the next battle." Reading the governor's letter aloud comforted the soldiers.[43]

The call for new levies could not have been more timely. Disease and sickness had depleted Halleck's army, but, by the end of May, they finally reached Corinth, Mississippi. The soldiers, however, discovered a few raggedly residents, some skeletal-looking dogs, and the railroad junction, but no Confederate army. Confederate General Beauregard had given the Union's most learned and methodical military officer the slip by a ruse and escaped in the night on rail cars to Tupelo, Mississippi. Having "worked like galley slaves before Corinth," wrote a New York correspondent, the capture seemed hollow and added to the dissatisfaction that with such an enormous army so little had been accomplished.[44] Nevertheless, Halleck claimed the victory, and although soldiers appreciated his military genius, dubbing him "Old Brains," the commander had been outwitted.[45]

Stanton restored the volunteer recruiting service on 6 June, and governors welcomed the change. Still, they worried over scores of soldiers that had been absent from their regiments; a fact Stanton called a "serious evil." Three days later, he queried them about the state of enlistments and when they would be ready to march to Annapolis. Wisconsin's Salomon responded that problems were still emanating from the order shutting down recruiting, and Michigan's Blair wired that while he would raise a regiment, it was "the worst season of the year to recruit," and the drain on manpower in Michigan had been considerable.[46] Morgan suggested that regimental vacancies be retained as an incentive and reward for persons sent to recruit for them, and that arrangements should be made for immediate payment of expenses. Morton had graver concerns. He was willing to send as many troops as he could, but worried that events in Kentucky threatened Indiana river towns. Andrew and Tod, however, had no problem raising and forwarding troops, but were impatient over the administration's reluctance to abandon conciliation. Sumner admitted to Andrew that his previous call for "firing into the magazine," meaning using slaves to fight against the Confederates, was entirely appropriate and that he regretted the Lincoln's refusal to adopt the governor's course. *"That would have been Statesmanship,"* he declared to Andrew, "Alas! We have not had any such thing."[47]

Dangerous Combinations

Stanton used Jackson's exploits to press the governors for men, yet Halleck also needed soldiers. His army was occupying vast expanses of the Southern heartland, and he had divided his command into thirds, sending Sherman to Memphis, Buell toward East Tennessee, while the remainder of the army remained in northwestern Mississippi. To be conducted successfully, all of these commands needed additional troops, especially as the summer heat and disease had reduced the ranks. Failure to capture Beauregard frustrated soldiers, and the war had turned them into occupiers of people and repairers of bridges and railroads. Sitting idle in camp had demoralizing consequences. The presence of Union soldiers in the heart of the western Confederacy invited recrimination on them by inhospitable Southerners. The only bright spot was the Union's hold on the Mississippi River from Memphis to Vicksburg, Mississippi.[48]

Halleck's hollow victory prompted McClellan to suggest again that he be reinforced with men from West, but Stanton refused. The commander did not need more men, Lincoln believed, he needed to be more effective with the soldiers he had. Jackson had embarrassed the Union command and prevented Lincoln from reinforcing McClellan. More important, he demonstrated to Washington just how much could be achieved with so little. However short-lived the Confederate success was, it inspired the War Department to ignite national recruiting again. Yet in the words of Buckingham, governors needed justification to "show our citizens that a necessity exists for such service."[49] Connecticut's Buckingham understood that he and his Radical colleagues were ahead of the administration and the people when it came to war aims. Confiscation and emancipation would complicate the work of Northern armies, but he reasoned that the Union's best hope of success would be to embrace these changes even if Northerners walked backward toward accepting them.[50]

Governors had expected more aggressive measures from the administration and from McClellan. They understood that the longer the war lasted the more motivated enemies at home were in undermining the war effort. Morton, for example, wired Lincoln that secret political organizations were operating in Indiana that sought to embarrass all efforts to recruit men, to embitter public sentiment and manufacture public opinion against the collection of taxes, and foster distrust toward the government. These enemies were doing "incalculable injury to the Union cause," by making "invidious, malignant, and vituperative attacks upon Union men." He had been aware of these attacks for weeks, and he needed to break up these "unlawful and dangerous combinations" to avoid continued interference.[51]

Gamble also had problems raising volunteers. Conditions were so desperate in Missouri that he petitioned Lincoln to prohibit Missouri troops from entering Kansas to curb retaliation against Jayhawkers. He hoped that Robinson would reciprocate the gesture. When Halleck departed St. Louis and joined the army at Pittsburg Landing it complicated the governor's hold on the state. Halleck left Brigadier General John Schofield in command of the state militia forces, which, based on an earlier arrangement, were supposed to cooperate with Federal forces. A West Pointer, Schofield had impressed Halleck with his extreme measures against guerrillas. More aggravating was that neither governors nor commanders had any real influence in ceasing intrastate invasions beyond the Mississippi, a fact that worsened when it involved liberating slaves. Gamble attempted to pacify Missouri slave owners by allowing them to take their slaves south to Texas or Arkansas, but Halleck stopped the practice, arguing that parties going south would carry vital information to the enemy. To gain support for his efforts, he convened the state legislature. Mounting war debt, guerilla attacks, loyalty oaths, restructuring congressional districts, and postponing elections until voter determinations were made were all issues needing attention. Moreover, he worried that unless a Union man continued as governor, Missouri's star might drop out of the Union. "You know that I have staked my all upon the maintenance of the authority of the Federal Government within the State of Missouri," Gamble explained to Lincoln, "and the quiet submission of the State to the laws of the Union."[52] He reasoned, "I think I have a right to expect that you will not allow me to be embarrassed in my endeavours [sic] to accomplish this result, by any hindrance which you can remove."[53]

Things were no better in Kansas. "The State was born in commotion," wrote a Missouri editor, "and has been rocked with excitement from the very start," having given "the Administration at Washington almost as much trouble as if she belonged among the seceded States."[54] When Stanton transferred Hunter, he replaced him with Brigadier General James G. Blunt, a Maine abolitionist, whose lack of any substantial military experience and questionable virtues suited Lane fine. Robinson, however, considered Blunt's appointment an insult to Kansas troops. Meanwhile, Halleck had ordered the Federal troops in Kansas south to support his small armies in Arkansas. The Robinson-Lane feud escalated when Lane's supporters Mark W. Delahay, William Weer, and Sidney Clarke charged the governor with war-bond fraud and influenced legislators to bring impeachment proceedings against him. One Kansas editor likened the acrimonious feud to a "Kilkenny cat fight, credible to neither, and one which is observed with disgust by the whole people of the State."[55] Amid this crisis, Lane wired Chase to withhold federal funds due Kansas until impeachment could be resolved, but this hurt citizens. To plead his case, Robinson left for Washington. After a week, he left confident that he had explained matters sufficiently to Chase and Lincoln. On his return trip, however, he contracted smallpox and spent several weeks in a Buffalo hospital, which delayed his return to Kansas until late May. By the time he arrived in Topeka, legislators had voted to remove him from office. Wilson Shannon, a former territorial governor in Kansas, came to the governor's defense, arguing that the charges had not proven complicity against Robinson, and the jury exonerated him.[56]

By the war's second summer, governors contended with several hindrances to volunteering. Seasonal harvest, home-front opposition, lack of pay, uninspired war aims, mounting casualty lists, and journalistic reminders of gruesome combat all combined to impede their efforts. To encourage enlistment, Lincoln had Congress authorize a $2 premium to each accepted recruit who volunteered for three years and advance pay for these enlistees for their first month of service. Yet the War Department had been administering two armies—a large volunteer force and a small regular force—and the cessation of recruiting and its renewal so abruptly destroyed administrative efficiency. The recent confusion over three-months and three-years men further unraveled the process.[57]

Citizens at home seldom missed an opportunity to remind governors they were managing two war fronts—national and local. The pressing need for troops and political dissension at home fostered a gloomy atmosphere and forecast challenges ahead. Still, there was reason to believe the Union sentiment that New England voters expressed in the spring elections was still alive. Far removed from the eastern theaters, loyal Oregonians had established a Union Party and nominated Republican Addison Crandall Gibbs, who in the recent June election polled more than 67 percent of the Oregon vote. Attracting Republicans and Douglas Democrats, Gibbs was nothing like "Old Whit," and his support for the Union was never in question. Although he lacked the flare of his predecessor, was more reserved, and shunned the spotlight, Gibbs was just what Oregonians needed to expand Union support. He had labored behind the scenes to establish Lincoln's credibility. "[T]here is no such a thing as Politics now," wrote one colleague, "the word is *Union*, and nothing else."[58] At thirty-seven years old, the quiet, unassuming New York native had previously taught school and studied law. He was admitted to the bar in 1849 and decided to head west. Gibbs settled first in California and the following year moved north to southern Oregon, eventually settling in Gardiner on the Umpqua River, where he assumed a position in the Customs Office. So impressed by his legal and business skills were Oregonians that they elected him to the territorial legislature in 1850. He moved to Portland in 1858 where, as a Douglas Democrat, he served in the legislature. Nonetheless, Gibbs was aware of Oregonians' divisiveness and worked behind the scenes to promote the Union. He opposed slavery, and, shortly after the attack on Fort Sumter, he declared to a group at Fort Dalles on the Columbia River, at the end of the Oregon Trail, that "he was in favor of the Union with but one if, and that if it hung every traitor north and south."[59]

Gibbs's Radicalism and recent victory found favor with eastern governors trying to convince Lincoln that employing every available measure to shorten the war might attract more volunteers. At the moment, however, it appeared that governors were using more vigorous measures to raise soldiers than commanders were using in waging war. It was not that the armies lacked the fighting spirit, but rather that they were governed by policies that shackled this spirit. Halleck's success in the West put a new face on the war, yet Confederate resistance remained strong against Lincoln's conciliatory policies. The Union losses during the Seven Days' Battles (25 June to 1 July) ended the North's momentum and diminished Northern morale. McClellan's push on Richmond stalled, and newly appointed Confederate General Robert E. Lee seized the initiative and counterattacked the Union army, dislodging it from around the Confederate capital. To relieve the pressure from McClellan's front, Lincoln established a new army called the Army of Virginia, detached Pope from Halleck's command to lead it, and directed the commander toward Manassas to pressure Richmond from the north. Pleading to Stanton, McClellan closed a late June telegram, "for the sake of the country secure unity of action & bring the best men forward." He wired, "Had I (20,000) twenty thousand or even (10,000) ten thousand fresh troops to use tomorrow, I could take Richmond."[60]

Even in defeat McClellan advanced the Union war effort. The Seven Days' contest was significant in that it pushed political and military leaders toward a harsher war that included emancipation. Lincoln and Congress both reacted to these battles with renewed attention to emancipation. In recent months governors had lobbied to use runaway slaves in the Union army, enlist black troops, and emancipate slaves. Passing through Washington on his return from McClellan's Virginia headquarters, Pierpont hoped to confer with Lincoln about employing slaves in the Union armies. Unable to meet with the president, Pierpont put his thoughts in writing. He wanted Lincoln to know that, while at the front, he "saw his men there in the hot sun throwing up breast works and making ditches—The water is bad—The men become overheated—drink the bad water and get sick."[61] He suggested gathering up the slaves from Alexandria, Norfolk, and on the Peninsula belonging to rebels, and use them to do the work of the soldiers in front of Richmond, which would free up the soldiers for fighting. Lincoln was sympathetic, but the timing was not suitable to use slaves or free blacks in the Union armies. The president had another idea that might prevent such radical measures. He discussed with Seward an idea to "endeavor to rouse the popular feeling and raise troops to reinforce the Army." The president's limited aims were not the problem, Seward maintained, but rather the problem was the apparent lack of Northern patriotism. He told a New York delegation of Congressional Republicans that "they could serve their country better in this crisis by going home to encourage the formation of regiments than by remaining in their seats till [sic] the adjournment."[62]

By the summer of 1862 saving the Union was losing its appeal in attracting volunteers. Governors tried to counter Northern apathy, but neither Jackson's exploits nor Southern reluctance to embrace Lincoln's conciliation could induce Northerners to come forward quickly enough to reverse Union losses. Governors hesitated to blame citizens for the lack of volunteering and instead acknowledged their sacrifices as evidence of Republican virtue. In the state-oriented national war they applauded soldiers, but stressed that unless citizens sustained the armies, their slain countrymen will have died in vain. "To hold back *now* in giving the support which, *more than ever before* is required," Sprague argued, "would be to add to a lack of patriotism."[63] However divided Northerners were about Lincoln's handling of the war thus far, most governors maintained that only by employing all measures would the national government be in a position to end the conflict.

Astor House Ruse

By the summer Union casualty lists were mounting and publicly daunting. Governor Holbrook spent days noting the telegraphic dispatches from McClellan's front on the Peninsula. He was aghast to learn of the tragedy of his 5th Vermont boys, who held the rear guard at Savage's Station, and who reportedly suffered the highest loss of life by a Vermont regiment in the entire war. As McClellan's and Halleck's diseased and wounded men swelled the hospitals and camps, Confederate guerrillas disrupted Union lines. Lincoln was despondent. The dark days of late June had robbed him of his "courage and faith" regarding the military prospects looming for his armies in Virginia. Calling for additional men at a time when his credibility seemed at risk with the Northern populace might cause alarm. As much as Lincoln understood that his armies needed troops, he understood the timing was wrong to ask for volunteers. Such a call would draw attention to the reality that casualties were higher than anticipated and that the men who were expected to come forward had not materialized.[64]

Lincoln related his view of the current military situation to Seward on 28 June. He argued that no matter whether he transferred existing troops or armies from East to West or West to East, the Confederates would send a force where the bulk of the Union armies were not. Soldiers were occupying too much Southern soil for the size of the North's armies. "What should be done," he instructed, "is to hold what we have in the West, open the Mississippi, and take Chattanooga & East Tennessee, without more—a reasonable force should, in every event, be kept about Washington for it's [sic] protection."[65] There was no alternative, Lincoln concluded, the country needed to "give us a hundred thousand new troops in the shortest possible time." He impressed upon Seward that "I expect to maintain this contest until successful, or till I die, or am conquered, or my term expires, or Congress or the country forsakes me."[66]

Congressmen shared the president's despondency. "This is a dark hour," Sumner wrote to Andrew, "the future is murky. Nobody can see day light on any vista in any direction. Stanton says today that 'Washington is in as much danger as Richmond.'"[67] Accompanied by Chase, the senator rode to the Soldiers Home to visit Lincoln. In relating the carriage conversation to Andrew, Sumner reported that Chase "thinks that we must meet some great calamity before a proper policy can be adopted." Sumner conveyed, "This is hard, very hard."[68] Andrew agreed. Something dramatic, like the firing on Fort Sumter had the previous year, would have to awaken the volunteer spirit. The sense of urgency, Northern morale, and popular commitment had waned, and governors were handicapped by a national administration that appeared paralyzed. Andrew aired his acrimony toward the administration at a small celebration at Abington. "If there is any mistake it is not in the conscience and heart of this people," Andrew declared to the crowd, "they are ready to go faster than their leaders will lead."[69]

Seward carried Lincoln's letter with him to New York City, where he arranged to meet with Thurlow Weed, Morgan, Curtin, and Olden about engineering a call for troops. He arrived at the Astor House on 29 June and met with the mayors of Philadelphia and New York City, as well as members of New York's Union Defense Committee. Seward shared with members the telegrams attesting to the dire military situation and advised them of Lincoln's plan to call for more troops to aid McClellan, as well as maintain Union strongholds in northern Alabama, Tennessee, Kentucky, and Missouri. Lincoln's desire, Seward told them, was to have governors petition him to raise more men. Placing the call in the hands of the governors would save the administration embarrassment. Curtin agreed. Besides the "material aid," he argued, the president and the Union needed "the moral reinforcement that would come from an expression of confidence on the part of the governors of the loyal states."[70] It was more judicious and more effective to have governors spearhead the call, especially if it coincided with a more vigorous prosecution of the war, something Curtin was confident most governors could agree on. Seward requested that Curtin put his idea in writing and wired it to the president. Lincoln approved Curtin's plan and allowed him to communicate his desires to all governors. Seward thought it wise to have Morgan act as his intermediary. Andrew was on his way to a Fourth of July celebration in Windham, Maine, when he received Morgan's telegram asking him to sign a memorial to Lincoln asking for men. He refused, citing suspicion of a trick "emanating from Seward's friends" to "disarm the radical Republicans," but Stanton refused to issue the call without Andrew's consent.[71]

The approving telegrams wired in were encouraging signs, and they reflected the partnership Lincoln had forged with his governors. Curtin was so encouraged that he enlisted the counsel of Tod and Andrew about assembling the governors in the coming months for a conference, perhaps at Altoona, to discuss and unite behind a more vigorous prosecution of the war. Seward "brightened at the thought," and, with the consent of his colleagues, Curtin wired the proposal to Lincoln, who approved, hinting that he had decided to announce an Emancipation Proclamation. Curtin assured him the Altoona gathering would endorse such a proclamation. All seemed on course, until Morgan balked at the idea unless he, and other governors, could secure from the $100 federal bounty an advance of $25 for the soldiers. Andrew had worked for weeks to get advance bounties for his Massachusetts volunteers, but Stanton refused. He even leaned on Massachusetts senator Henry Wilson, who chaired the Senate Military Committee, to secure congressional approval for advance bounties, which he did on 21 June.

Thus, Andrew had already gained federal approval and replied to Morgan's communiqué that "if $25 bounty in hand were authorized, it would bring many recruits whose duties at home now delay or prevent them."[72] To induce the governors to accept Lincoln's clever coup, Seward had previously wired Stanton asking him how much money he could offer them for collecting, organizing, and drilling volunteers. Stanton replied that the Adjutant General had $9 million he could lay at their disposal, and there was an officer in every state to pay expenses.[73]

On Morgan's request, Seward sent another communiqué late on the night of the 30th asking Stanton to authorize the bounty, which Seward argued was illegal, but necessary. Under the circumstances, Stanton agreed. Feeling confident they had reached an agreement, and one that called for 200,000 troops, or whatever the president desired, Seward and Morgan wired the Northern governors for their reaction, and seventeen replied favorably. Andrew still held out for a more radical measure to coincide with providing more troops, such as freeing and arming the slaves of the Confederacy. Sprague was in Washington at the time, and Kirkwood could not be reached. Burton wrote Curtin a note shortly afterward that he "cordially" joined the gubernatorial chorus requesting the president to call out as many troops as "will be sufficient to crush this rebellion," and Curtin wanted to be sure his Delaware neighbor was not left out. He sent Burton's note with his own endorsement that it was important Burton's name be appended to the call, "as he represents a Border State, and the sentiment of his communication is admirable."[74]

Lost in the master narrative of the Civil War, the significance that governors had spoken with one voice was not lost on Lincoln. Their cooperation placed in his hands a cleverly engineered request to ask them for additional troops to swiftly crush the rebellion. The ruse had been effected—as it appeared that "public enthusiasm was ahead of, not behind, federal needs."[75] Before Lincoln went public with this call, he arranged to send Seward to Cleveland to meet with Tod, Morton, Blair, Salomon, and John B. Temple, president of the Military Board of Kentucky, to explain the call's rationale. Andrew's refusal to sign the petition, however, stalled the initiative, and Lincoln sent Seward to Boston instead. Stanton delayed issuing the call until Andrew was on board. To Cleveland he sent telegraph operator Anson Stager and Assistant U.S. Adjutant General Catharinus P. Buckingham, who, after meeting at the Angier House, concluded that "all feel right and will do their duty."[76] Andrew returned to Boston and found there a "breezy discussion" over his initial refusal to sign the memorial. To clarify his position, he returned a letter to Francis P. Blair Sr., who had inquired if Stanton had omitted Andrew's name. "After all the efforts that I have unceasingly made to have some of those in power treat this as a *war* and not as a *picnic*, or a *caucus*, to accept troops, to raise troops, even to accept from Massachusetts," he explained, "I am glad [not] to have suffered the final humiliation of having my name printed to a document dictated at Washington, but apparently emanating from the governors—merely to save appearances."[77] Lincoln's failure to allow black enlistments or to emancipate slaves as a precondition for the enlistment of these new regiments infuriated Andrew. "I believe we are doomed unless we will awake to reason," he allowed to Blair, "but I am a follower, not a leader."[78] Even the Polish count in Stanton's office, who kept Andrew abreast of Washington's inside affairs, penned in his diary that "it was a poor trick to gather by telegraph the signatures of the governors for an offer of troops to the President."[79]

Andrew consented on 2 July, but Stanton allegedly backdated the exchange between the governor and the president to save face. Armed with the Astor House request and browbeaten by Stanton, Lincoln decided to call out 300,000 men for three years "to bring this unnecessary and injurious civil war to a speedy and satisfactory conclusion." Quotas were forthcoming for the new regiments. Morgan thought it was a misprint as he read it in the newspaper and wrote to Lincoln asking him if the call was for 300,000 or 200,000. Lincoln responded that he "thought safest to mark high enough," which prompted his decision.[80] Two days later, however, feeling he might have injured the governors, Lincoln justified his call by writing privately to every governor that he "should not want the half of 300,000 new troops if I could have them now." Lincoln argued, "If I had 50,000 additional troops here now, I believe I could substantially close the war in two weeks." He added, "If I get 50,000 new men in a month I shall have lost 20,000 old ones during the same month," and the "quicker you send the fewer you will have to send."[81]

Lincoln used the governors' petition to spur McClellan. "The Governors of eighteen States," he declared, "offer me a new levy of 300,000 men, which I accept."[82] Yet McClellan's trifling complaints had lost him much credibility in Washington. His efforts on the peninsula had gained little and had cost the nation much. The Northern populace turned away from the battlefield and looked to governors to engineer a renewed war spirit and stiffen public morale. "Close your manufactories [*sic*] and workshops," declared Buckingham, "turn aside from your farms and your business, leave for a while your families and your homes, meet face to face the enemies of your liberties!"[83] Serving his fifth term as governor, Buckingham was known as the "captain general." Soldiers of the 1st Connecticut Heavy Artillery could testify why. As they were about to embark on McClellan's grand campaign, Buckingham spent time in their Alexandria camp. Before the unit's departure he took supply requests and assured the men that he would see they had everything they needed. "Well, boys," asked Buckingham, "is there anything else I can do for you?" remembered one observer.[84] "If you can hurry up the paymaster we shall be obliged to you," said one soldier, "for it is a long time since we have seen him." The governor responded, "Certainly, I'll see what I can do about it," and, before he departed, he wrote a personal check and had it drawn for the amount owed to the soldiers.[85]

CHAPTER NINE

The Duty of the Governors to Save the Country's Cause

In the wake of the Seven Days' Battle, the crisis of manpower and deteriorating morale grew into a miserable Northern cloud that hung over eastern state capitals as well as Washington. It was an unshakeable despair that many Northerners experienced. Still, the "backstage maneuvering" of inducing governors to call for additional men without alarming Northerners had worked. Lincoln, however, could not convince McClellan that it was impossible to reinforce him. If the commander was not strong enough to face the enemy, he needed to fall back and wait. "We still have strength enough in the country," the president closed his message, "and will bring it out."[1] Lincoln's patience with McClellan had worn thin, as had the patience of even McClellan's supporters.

Because the Virginia battle had sapped Northern optimism, tapping further into the Union's strength, the need to adopt a more revolutionary attitude toward the means to achieve the Union's goal was heightened. This would involve striking at slavery in the Confederacy. That some 700,000 Northerners had come forward in the previous year reflected the popularity of the Union's cause. Calling for 300,000 additional men sent a different message. According to the press, it appeared that the administration was losing the war and its leadership was in disarray. "There is a feeling of gloom" in Washington, wrote a colleague to Andrew, arguing that governors should not give another man until there were changes in "this corrupt & cowardly cabinet."[2] Charles Gibson to Gamble that "The Secretary of War this morning said in my presence that we had met with a 'very serious disaster.' There has been desperate fighting at Richmond for a week past the result of all which is that McClellan no longer holds his former position . . . that he has retired with great loss—that he is scared & in short that Richmond is *not* to be taken at present."[3]

Gurowski's blistering depiction of the administration fueled Andrew's acrimony. The Polish assistant complained to Andrew that it was hard to witness the "noblest cause & the noblest people going to pieces."[4] He added, "The fashion here is now to ascribe all the evils to the Congress, to accuse the people at large of slowness in sacrificing itself to the cause." True or not, Gurowski's assessment riled an already agitated Andrew. Seward and Blair, Gurowski argued, had "frightened poor Lincoln out his senses; by assuring him that any large proclamation of emancipation will *occasion* in the North serious riots & counter-revolutions in favor of slavery. *I am positive about the above*. For all these evils I see no cure." He fumed, "The vitality of the people may gain new success, but all this will come to naught in the hands of the administration.... Oh for a man! For a man! Not for the 300,000."[5]

Lincoln's New Call

New Jersey governor Olden was in search of such a man and threw an iron on Lincoln's fire on 3 July. He urged the president to decide which theater was the most important and concentrate the existing regiments against the enemy. McClellan might be better reinforced by men in the field, he advised Lincoln, even at the risk of abandoning certain points. If the president wanted men immediately, Olden advised calling them for shorter enlistment terms and providing for their families in advance. More men would come forward for shorter enlistments and advance bounties. Thinking of the political elections ahead, Olden also insisted that Lincoln allow him to appoint a general to command the new troops. "This is no matter of foolish State pride with me but to my mind it has political bearings of importance in this State," he informed the president, "there is a loyal Douglass Democrat among us—a gentleman of influence who graduated at West Point in the class with Genl. McCall who I should like to state would be recommended to command the Brigade." Lincoln would later approve of Olden's request.[6]

Lincoln considered concentrating combat-tested soldiers on a single front and called on Halleck to send McClellan troops. He even allowed Sprague to travel to Corinth to convince the commander of the idea. "Nothing can save us," the governor wrote, "but the immediate transfer of Halleck and 50000. men."[7] Sprague was so impressed with Halleck's military skill that he felt only Halleck's army could unravel McClellan's predicament. Still, he considered Halleck selfish and more interested in concentrating power around himself, which, he argued, was "one great source of our ruin."[8] Halleck protested against surrendering what had cost his army so much blood and treasure and was "worth three Richmonds."[9] To send troops east would undermine all the commander had gained and, more important, would fail to provide an occupational hold on the Southern people. Besides, if Lincoln reduced Halleck's army, it would diminish the East Tennessee campaign so desperate to Lincoln. Dennison advised Lincoln that he might get more midwestern volunteers if he could assure them they would defend the West rather than tell them they were to go on the James River at this season and to fight with McClellan against the best portion of the Confederate army. The soldiers' mood had turned sour, and letters home provided evidence of the discontent. William Caldwell of the 70th Ohio boiled over to his father from Moscow, Tennessee, that it was "high time that a new policy was inaugurated." He insisted, "Let the President stand out from the people, let him take a step in advance. He should lead public opinion, not follow it."[10]

Positioned between the civil and military contours of war, the governors encouraged Lincoln to bring out the North's strength. With the Union's largest army stalled at the gates of Richmond, Confederate resistance against the massive army was impressive. The war was moving into a contest of not only commanders and battlefields, but also popular will. Wanting to avoid the embarrassment of not meeting his quota, Buckingham wired Stanton that he was doing all in his power to organize new regiments. The governor recognized the limitations in having to organize regiments quickly throughout the state, and allowed Connecticutans to share in the executive decisions to avoid his being accused of playing favorites. He delegated important power to local war committees and allowed them free reign in recruiting, planning rallies, establishing bounties, and calculating their share of the quota, and even accepted their recommendations for field officers. Buckingham exercised a visible hand in allowing the interdependence between local self-rule and national unity to produce the new regiments. Like several governors, he also promoted the arrest of military dissidents, who undermined regimental cohesion.[11]

As much as Congress and governors were pushing him to embrace a more vigorous war, Lincoln exercised patience. The president knew that most of the white population would accept emancipation only as a means to smite the Confederates—and thus moved carefully. He had grown with the war in the last several months, and the call for more men provided him the opportunity to see if Northerners would renew their commitment to the cause. In the midst of military setbacks, the administration searched for ways to make the war more meaningful at the local level and stiffen Northern morale. Governors considered this paramount in sustaining the armies and maintaining an effective federal-state partnership. After all, governors believed they understood their states, their people, and their unique circumstances better than the president. "Think of this new call," proclaimed Washburn to Fessenden, "for the life blood of Maine, made necessary by the wretched policy of playing war."[12] He fumed to Seward, "The hard common sense of the people is coming to this, that unless there is a thorough change in the manner of carrying on the war, the Adm. is ruined."[13]

Lincoln listened to governors pulling the war's ox cart. Neither McClellan nor Buell were pulling the war forward, in fact, they were slowing it down. Yet Lincoln had grown frustrated by the futility of conciliation, so had the press and the soldiers. "The universal demand is for greater vigor and a more unsparing policy in dealing with the rebellion," declared the *Newark Daily Mercury*, "The nation wants no more of the rose-water, kid glove policy."[14] By July governors exercised their influence in pressing a change in Union war aims. The disparity among state populations, however, complicated incentives for volunteerism. Unlike the more prosperous eastern populations, western agrarians were hard pressed to leave home and hearth for the ranks. The offer of nine months' steady work at good wages from September to May might lure farm-laborers into the army, but only if they feared being drafted. Morton understood this feature of Indiana's population and argued that draft threats might induce military-age males into the military. This would allow governors national leverage in generating recruitment, despite its overbearing appearance. "If Congress shall adjourn without doing this," he argued, "you will doubtless have to call them together for the purpose." He closed his telegram: "We send you this as the result of our conclusions from what we know of the condition of the Northwest."[15] Morgan agreed writing Lincoln that "Congress should not adjourn without providing by law, if it has the power to do it, for filling up the volunteer regiments in the field and those now organizing by a draft."[16]

Citizen morale had waned in recent months, and Yates blamed Lincoln. Andrew had laid the groundwork for a changed military policy in late May by connecting manpower needs with new directives. The time had come for Yates to stand on his stump in Springfield. On the morning of 11 July, the Ohio governor came into his office "looking weighed down by the discouragements of the situation," as his secretary John Moses recalled. He "sat at his desk some time, reflecting," and then "seized his pen and began to write furiously, pausing occasionally to think."[17] He completed his draft, gave it to Moses, and instructed him to copy the dispatch and wire it to Washington,

New York, Philadelphia, and all the large cities. Moses noticed the letter was addressed to Lincoln and, before leaving the room, queried Yates if he had consulted with colleagues about it contents. "No, sir," he answered, "I have consulted no one," but "let me ask you, do you think what I have recommended is right?" Moses agreed that it was right, but cautioned that it might be "a doubtful policy at this time." Yates sounded off, "If it is right, I will risk the policy and take the consequences. We have been beating about the bushes long enough." And with that Yates ordered Moses to send the dispatch. His message rang loud and clear as it came over the wires. "The crisis of the war and our national existence is upon us," he told Lincoln, "the time has come for the adoption of more decisive measures. Greater animus and earnestness must be infused into our military movements; blows must be struck at the vital points of the Rebellion." He went on to add that the government "should employ every available means compatible with the rules of warfare to subdue the traitors; summon to the standard of the republic all men willing to fight for the Union." Generals, he maintained, should not be permitted "to fritter away the sinews of our brave men in guarding the property of traitors and in driving back into their hands loyal blacks who offer us their labor & seek shelter with the federal flag." He informed Lincoln that the mild and conciliatory means had failed to reduce traitors to obedience. In fact, he argued, Confederates had been defiant against the Union's conservative policies and had employed every possible means to wage war. "Mr. Lincoln," Yates declared, "the crisis demands greater efforts and sterner measures. Proclaim anew the good old motto of the republic—liberty and union now and forever one & inseparable and accept the services of all loyal men."[18]

Yates's letter revealed the disparity between Lincoln's amiable conciliatory goals and the war's destructive realities. That summer letters poured into state capitals and urged governors to fix the administration's problems and suppress nefarious disloyal groups. Soldiers and civilians educated governors about the hardships and frustrations of waging a limited war against the Confederates. This shared experience moved one Connecticutan to observe that governors "understood one another, and were well agreed as to what ought to be done, and might be done, and it was no small part of their work to induce the general government to adopt certain measures, as well as pledge their States to help carry out those measures."[19]

Like Andrew, Yates had stifled his abolitionism for months in his correspondence with Lincoln. But his recent epistle represented an emerging viewpoint among many governors. The time had come to accept emancipation as a necessary war measure to defeat the Confederacy. Taking slaves punished slaveholders, and Yates was pushing the president to accept this reality. If Lincoln wanted more men to shorten the war, governors argued, the administration would have to broaden its targets. No longer should soldiers safeguard rebel cabbage patches as had Buell's army when marching to Chattanooga. Soldiers should not stand guard over runaway slaves or return them to their owners. Congress had outlawed this practice in March. Soldiers should not be deprived of living off the countryside. Without naming Buell, Yates drew attention to his campaign. The back-and-forth communications between midwestern governors and their soldiers told the story of his command's discontent. Halleck had even come around to expanding war aims. When McClellan complained that he could not purchase milk from the Confederates for the wounded soldiers, Halleck told him it was time for Union soldiers to take their cows and milk them. However hospitable Lincoln was in justifying his war aims, governors viewed themselves as a team of companions with popular credibility to provide direction to the national government. Even the *Illinois State Journal* acknowledged that "Mr. Lincoln cannot disregard," Yates's letter.[20] If some Northerners objected to his lecturing the president, as did the *St. Louis Daily Missouri Republican*, the *Chicago Times*, and the *Illinois State Register*, many agreed with his sentiments. "Well done, Governor Yates," declared the *Chicago Tribune*, "you lead the van."[21]

Governors believed that Lincoln's policies had failed to appease traitors, and several, including Andrew, Sprague, Blair, and Salomon, had suggested arming slaves and free blacks to help compensate for sluggish volunteering. They criticized the administration's failure to embrace black soldiers as a viable alternative. Although Yates's legislature had voted to exclude blacks from its borders, other governors had no such barrier. Blair endorsed using slaves as soldiers and relied on Chandler's influence in Washington to bring about the change. "McClellan will not make Negroes to dig ditches, cut down timber & do hard work," Chandler fumed, "but will force my brave boys to do this menial work & die in doing it rather than take Negro Slaves belonging to rebels & who only ask freedom in return." He fumed, "40,000 brave men have been sacrificed in this Negrophoby [and] I will no longer keep quiet."[22]

Lincoln was despondent about McClellan's advance on Richmond and needed to inspire the commander. He visited the commander at Harrison's

Landing, and when Lincoln arrived, McClellan handed him a letter expressing his views about the war's progress and emancipation of slaves. The "Harrison's Landing Letter" convinced Lincoln that walking backward toward the enemy, as McClellan had done, was no longer practical. He decided to withdraw the Army of the Potomac from the Peninsula and return it to Washington. So bad was the fallout that Tod offered Stanton some advice. "For God's sake," he wired, "stop the wrangling between the friends of McClellan and yourself in Congress. . . . I ask this as the friend of both."[23]

Lincoln returned to Washington determined to make some changes. Morgan's suggestion of a state draft had some merit, and so did Yates's letter. "'Dick, hold still and see the salvation of God,'" was Lincoln's initial reply to Yates, mimicking the words of Moses to the Israelites at the Red Sea. "The people *in the long run are* wiser than the politicians," he said, "and I believe they are awake and are on the right side which is our side *and* the Lords [sic] side."[24] Recalling McClellan from the peninsula was just the beginning. The president's ideas on confiscation and emancipation had been incubating for some time, yet he feared he might win a policy and lose an army. Andrew worried about winning the army, but would risk the policy to end the war sooner. He had leaned on Senator Wilson to establish congressional policies that would advance the war in ways the War Department could not. Wilson devised procedures for a national draft that governors could use to their benefit. He drafted policies that allowed the president to call up state militias into national service for no more than nine months and stipulated that the national government could intervene in the process to make all necessary regulations. During these intense days, Lincoln took the occasion of a carriage ride to the funeral of Stanton's infant son to confide his feelings to Welles and Seward that the time had come to free the slaves, or else "be ourselves subdued."[25]

Changing War Aims

By the summer of 1862 the experience of war had proven that winning the conflict required utilizing all the Union's resources. Neither McClellan nor Buell displayed enthusiasm for prosecuting a vigorous war, and Lincoln needed a change. He summoned Pope east to take command of a new army and worked with congressmen to effect national policies that would bring men forth. Several governors delighted in these changes as well as in the president's appointment of Halleck as general in chief. Before the commander departed for Washington, however, Lincoln ordered him to check the "stampede" in Kentucky caused by John Hunt Morgan's raid. With Halleck at the helm in Washington, McClellan and Buell would feel the pressure of the war's changing nature. Lincoln was moving toward the Radicals' course, which slightly lessened their criticism of him. Buckingham wired Lincoln and Stanton some words of encouragement to attest to the societal linkage. "We were never more engaged in raising troops," he exclaimed, "the excitement is great, the spirit determined."[26]

Yates's letter permeated the press, and telegrams from around the country poured into Springfield. Henry County lawyer Levi North's response typified the favorable sentiment. "I heartily approve of your views," he wrote, "we have wasted men and money enough in strategy, and intrenching [sic] swamps." He added, "Heretofore I have felt that we were only making 'pleasant acquaintants' and playing war down South," and "rest assured that no act of your very active and useful career as Governor of Illinois has struck the popular judgments with more favor."[27] To soften the blow due to expected congressional changes, Lincoln summoned border state senators and congressmen to the White House and appealed to them to support compensated emancipation before Congress adjourned. The president signed a congressional bill that outlawed slavery in U.S. territories. Still, compensated emancipation drew opposition. Delaware's congressional triumvirate of George P. Fisher, Willard Saulsbury, and James A. Bayard opposed Lincoln and made hard work for Burton in recruiting for a war that was embracing radical changes. It was not so much that Delaware slaves were contributing to the enemy war effort as it was a matter of racial inferiority in keeping them in their place. When the time came to abolish the institution within their borders, Delawareans would "do so in their own way."[28]

As much as many Northerners opposed turning the war into a crusade to liberate slaves, the tumultuous summer atmosphere heightened their expectations for a change in the means to win the war by pursuing emancipation. Governors were aware of this opposition, but they became increasingly sensitive to confiscation and emancipation as a condition for victory. Emancipation was becoming more widely appreciated as a necessary means to achieve victory—and a good thing to have in place going forward because it would remove the internal friction that had brought secession and war. Robert Cameron, a farmer from Riceford, Minnesota, presented his views to Ramsey as plainly as possible. "The almost universal feeling of the farmers of this part of the state," he protested, "is, that they will not enlist nor advise any one else to enlist; unless the administration will immediately assume an active anti-slavery policy for conducting the war, enlist blacks as well as whites, and remove from command those two *arch traitors* McClellan and Halleck." In fact he considered it the duty of the governors "to not only request but demand of the administration the removal of all commanding officers who like McClellan & Halleck have shown themselves to be either traitors or sympathizers with treason by being more careful of the property of traitors than of themselves [and] of their soldiers."[29] Ramsey had received numerous letters attesting to the same sentiment, and he used a visit to survey hospital conditions to ascertain the views of the soldiers. Eli Southworth, for example, wrote to his mother that he was glad the governor paid a visit to the camps, as Ramsey solicited and listened to their opinions about politics.[30]

The key in sustaining home front to battlefront connections lay in the governors' abilities to maintain popular support for the war. They raised soldiers' bounties and aid for their families; they talked politics in the camps, used the press as their mouthpieces, and relied on state and volunteer agencies to produce relief that made volunteering hospitable. Yet the fact remained that unless citizens believed the national administration was in tune with their sacrifices, they would not come forward. Northerners wanted a shortened war, but were divided over how it could be achieved. Andrew stressed that unless the army confiscated slaves and received black volunteers, replenishing armies would be difficult. The armies could persist no longer in keeping slaves out of their path. Commanders should have the power to confiscate all property deemed usable to their armies. "The success of Armies depends so much upon the proper management of the Generals who command them," Sprague counseled Lincoln, "that I venture to suggest that they be held well in hand, and to a strict responsibility for results." Referring to either McClellan or Halleck, he added, "I beg that he should be only entrusted with the command of the army, without directly or indirectly interfearing [sic] with the policy of the Government." He cautioned Lincoln, "Men cannot do both well . . . hold I pray you, the members of your Cabinet, to a strict subordination to their respective duties."[31]

Sprague returned to Providence from his western tour and perceived his citizens' demoralization. "The people are depressed," he told Lincoln, and "the real cause is in the 'Fire in your rear' which I named to you, and until the country can see this forever extinguished they will continue to work with half hearted energy, which is the forrunner [sic] of unsuccess."[32] McClellan's defeat, however, had not demoralized all New Englanders. Buckingham and Holbrook reported that McClellan's Virginia repulses had inspired some Connecticutans and Vermonters to join the ranks. Buoyed by his nomination for a second term, Holbrook echoed this sentiment, wiring Stanton there was "much enthusiasm" in Vermont about furnishing its quota.[33] In the weeks to come the 9th Vermont rolled into New York City and marched down Broadway to thousands of cheering onlookers. The unit was the first to come forward following Lincoln's call. Stanton was so impressed that he wired Holbrook congratulations over the new regiment, remarking that Vermont's "response to that call was worth 20,000 men to the cause." The *Chicago Tribune* picked up their story and ran it to inspire midwesterners.[34]

These hopeful expectations soon waned, however, as communiqués revealed Northern apathy. Stanton was, as one Illinois journalist put it, "the 'best abused' man in the nation," but had decided to play the hand governors offered him. He decided to wage harsh war at home and use the weight of the national government to aid governors who had appealed for help. He blazed a trail to Capitol Hill and urged congressmen to act on pending legislation to expand the power of the national government. This new legislation highlighted an important departure in the democratic republic's military tradition. Previously, citizens had considered conscription distasteful and undemocratic, but Lincoln understood that expanding Union war aims was useless without the armies to carry out his objectives. Governors presented a strong case that unless the administration's objectives changed, the armies would remain deficient.[35]

This departure took the form of the Militia Act, and Lincoln signed the bill on 17 July. It made no reference to drafting, but instead was a broad document to be invoked when the president felt it appropriate to call additional men into service. It was intended to assist governors by keeping the recruiting system within state power, and by inspiring volunteers to come forward before being coerced by draft. Lincoln reserved the right to call into service all able-bodied militia men (including blacks) between the ages of eighteen and forty-five for no more than nine months (three times the previous limit), to assign quotas to states, to make all necessary rules and regulations, and to enforce them. Governors, however, were to administer the enrollment of men. Equally important was the Second Confiscation Act, approved the same day, which authorized Union armies to seize property (including slaves) of persons in rebellion against the United States. The act also provided the basis for accepting slaves into the Union armies. The hard war the governors, the Northern populace, and Congress wanted to wage, however, would be hard to wage from Washington. Unless commanders accepted these policies, and had the manpower to enforce them as they moved deeper into the Confederate heartland, such changes were little more than words on paper.[36]

Conscription and confiscation, two new preconditions for military success, changed the manner in which armies were to be drawn and used. Lincoln later explained to Henry J. Raymond, editor of the *New York Times*, that "things had gone from bad to worse, until I felt we had reached the end of our rope on the operations we had been pursuing." He confided, "We had just about played out our last card, and must change our tactics or lose the game."[37] Lincoln had already consented to emancipate slaves to win the war; he needed to put it in writing. Confiscating Confederate slaves was risky, but he believed there was no other way to inspire volunteers to come forward. Northern citizens wanted a shorter conflict, which meant accepting conscription, confiscation, and eventually emancipation as the administration's attempt to win them over. Those who opposed his policies, he hoped, could be induced into volunteering for fear of being drafted. In either case, it was clear that one resolution fed the other in raising men. For those traitors at home, who threatened violence against such propositions, Yates offered a solution. Any turncoat who dared to tear down the flag of the United States, either symbolically or literally, he told constituents to "shoot him down as you would a dog and I will pardon you the offense."[38]

The Second Confiscation Act sparked debate on Capitol Hill between Radicals and conservatives over the use of blacks in the army, but it brought new life to the governors' task of raising men. It went into effect sixty days after it was enacted. Still, Northerners interpreted it as a sign that representatives in Washington had come to their senses. The "Curtain had fallen," remarked the *Hartford Evening Press*, "the North now *feels*, what it has only coldly known before, that little less than annihilation of traitors and their possessions will restore peace."[39] "There appears to be a new life in the army since the government has decided to use the black folks to help put down the rebellion," wrote Captain William B. Britton of the 8th Wisconsin. "The men are anxious to have them to do their work for them and if need be to shoulder the musket," he added.[40] Andrew's friends had peppered him for weeks over administrative machinations. "The conciliatory policy has ruined us," argued Henry Ingersoll Bowditch. Lincoln had been told repeatedly about these policy shortcomings and about McClellan's unbending ways in conducting his brand of warfare. "Let the people of the North be told now that they stand before the world *whipped*," he declared, "and the only thing remaining to restore themselves to respectability and honor is *to win the game* at all hazards—vindicate the freeman over slave [and their *white* slave men] and leave every thing else to be settled after the victory shall be won."[41]

The somber mood in Washington was not lost on Lincoln. On 22 July he called a cabinet meeting to discuss arming blacks and emancipating Confederate slaves, hopeful that Pope would pull off the victory that McClellan could not. With Halleck at the helm, great things might be achieved. With these expectations Lincoln read a draft of his Emancipation Proclamation before the assembled members, which designated 1 January 1863 as the day the proclamation would become effective. Seward feared foreign repercussions and worried over Northern despondency, and he convinced the president to wait for a victory before making the announcement.[42]

As despondent as Lincoln may have been in those days, he never lost his confidence in the people, even if he feared the people had lost their confidence in him. "Whether retiring from July heats at the 'Soldier's Home,'" wrote his secretary, "or holding long conferences in the old room looking out on the Potomac, or listening to the 'click' in the telegraph room at the War Office," Lincoln still wore the "same firm yet thoughtful face," and pondered "his orders and proclamations with the same sound common sense and coolness, as if McClellan's dispatches came from the other side of Richmond." He posited, "This is why the mutual understanding between him and the people is so perfect."[43] Stoddard argued that Lincoln's problem was never the people, but rather his commanders.

Into this maelstrom came Halleck, who arrived in Washington on 23 July. Ironically, in the time between when he left St. Louis and when he arrived in the nation's capital, the war had changed. Having weathered Missouri's political problems and egos, the nation's capital was a wonderful reprieve. He found his calling strategizing behind a desk, pushing paper, smoking cigars, and issuing orders from his new headquarters. Still, the mood in the ranks had deteriorated beyond even Halleck's magic touch. Discouraged New Yorker Corporal Almon Graham penned in his diary near Culpepper, Virginia, that everywhere the news was discouraging and that "matters seem to be changing from bad to worse, Gen. Halleck is to be commander-in-chief." Wrote Graham, "The question is no longer 'how we can save the union,'" but "what can we do for the nigger."[44]

Declining manpower did not translate into declining state power. In fact, it brought federal-state relations closer to solving national objectives and highlighted the states' willingness to sacrifice for the national cause. Governors had helped engineer Lincoln's July call, and, despite their difficulties, they had made progress in raising volunteers. They used Congress's new legislation to stiffen the popular will and hoped it would bear fruit. Each state, however, produced a different crop, and the uniqueness of the effort told the story of a Union fighting a national war with local communities. Border states were especially vulnerable to federal changes. In Baltimore, Bradford assembled some of Maryland's most prominent citizens to discuss inducements for raising Maryland's quota of 4,000 men. Bradford used this support to stir the morale among his loyalists. "Men of Maryland I look to you with confidence," he began, "to be among the foremost in responding to this call." He continued, "There are reasons why you should be . . . you are, as it were, the natural bodyguard of the Capital of the Nation."[45] By late July the governor had much to encourage him. At a Union meeting in Baltimore's Monument Square he boasted to the crowd that Maryland had come to the rescue once and he was confident it would again. He told citizens that a municipal legislature had already pledged liberal sums for bounties to be paid for the volunteers.[46]

Still, there was the devilish problem of runaway slaves. Bradford's attempt to have the national government enforce the Fugitive Slave Law proved futile. As the summer fields lay barren and uncultivated, it reminded slave owners of the war's effects on its citizens. John H. Bayne, an influential Unionist, was so discouraged he wrote Bradford that slaves were passing out of Maryland, through the District, and into Alexandria, Virginia. He demanded the governor stop this practice. Bradford had no answer for Bayne and had no authority to protect Maryland slaves or slave owners, and had no money to raise units to hunt down runaways. Having lost his slaves in the war, the governor commiserated that such losses were "one of the casualties of *war*, one of the direct and anticipated fruits of this atrocious rebellion, got up under the pretense of establishing a better security for his very species of property." He hoped that despite such losses, however, Marylanders could remain loyal and rise above seeking retribution or alternatives such as siding with the secessionists.[47] In responding to Montgomery Blair, Bradford answered that "to get the land out of the hands of the Secessionists . . . I can find no other solution than to get the Secessionists out of the land."[48]

By the end of July, Lincoln was desperate to turn the Union's military fortunes around to diffuse the public acrimony against him. Conciliation had run its course, Congress had given him newfound power with the Militia Act, and, on 28 July, he wired the governors seeking progress reports in recruiting. He sent Nicolay to Indianapolis to ascertain from Morton and other governors the extent of their home-front problems. The president was interested in the movements in Tennessee and Kentucky because he had reports suggesting Confederates were planning to invade Kentucky to influence August elections. Within a few days of his arrival, Nicolay concurred. Tod warned that Confederates had purportedly planned a raid on Frankfort when the Kentucky legislature opened in a week.[49]

Governors reported that restoring the existing ranks was going slowly, but that recruiting for shorter terms and new regiments was progressing satisfactorily. Naturally, the nine-month term was a more popular term than the three-year term. Morgan was confident about the "motion of things" in New York, but reminded Lincoln that recruiting for existing regiments had not been under governors' control for some time and was causing serious delays. Olden reported the spirit of New Jerseyans was improving, but advised Stanton that soldiers should be paid the advance bounty at the time of enlistment rather than when the company mustered into service. Morton quipped that Indiana would be the first state to furnish its quota, but indicated the difficulty in recruiting for old regiments while new ones were forming. "The two systems come into conflict and mutually defeat each other," he concluded. It was best to wait a few weeks, he advised, and then recruit for the old regiments.[50] Blair wired from Detroit that there was little he could do to recruit for old regiments until the new ones were filled. Nonetheless, the governor had reason to be encouraged. Letters from citizens such as Henry Waldron indicated that the feeling among residents was good and that although the obstacles were many, "there is a determination to overcome them at every sacrifice."[51]

West of the Mississippi, chief executives tried in vain to bring peace to the guerrilla-ridden regions. General Schofield's 17,000 troops, many of whom were stationed along the Arkansas border, were insufficient to counter roving Confederates. To meet the emergency, Schofield called on Gamble's 3,000 state militiamen to join his army, but many of the men refused to leave the state, so Gamble sought permission to keep the men in Missouri by requesting permission to raise an enrolled Missouri militia, whose operations would be carried out within Missouri's borders. Attuned to the local crisis,

Halleck granted the request, and, within a week, more than 20,000 loyal Missourians came forward to enlist. It was a unique arrangement, as the militiamen were to be paid by the state, but supplied and transported by the War Department.[52]

The Want of the Hour

Meanwhile, Pope departed Washington to join the Army of Virginia, and Lincoln ordered McClellan's army to Washington. Yet raising additional troops remained the "want of the hour," as the *Hartford Evening Press* put it.[53] Lincoln understood this and on 4 August invoked the Militia Act. Governors knew that this reality would be forthcoming, but had not anticipated it so soon, and not without warning. Only one month after his call for 300,000 men, the new call to furnish an additional 300,000 militiamen for nine months made it appear as though 600,000 troops were needed. According to the recent law, Lincoln could not force citizens into the U.S. Army, but he could draft members of state militias for nine months to make up quota deficiencies. According to Stanton's General Orders No. 94, governors had until 15 August to supply their quotas from Lincoln's July and August call. The problem was that the July directive called for three-year men and the August directive called for nine-month men. Yet, the August call was in actuality designed to spur on volunteers to fill the July call. To further complicate matters, Stanton decreed that four nine-month volunteers equaled one three-year recruit. Finally, governors had national assistance in pulling Northerners into compliance, but the combined calls set in motion a confusing array of problems. Worse yet was that they had a mere two weeks to comply.[54]

Stanton's call, accompanied by threat of a draft, was a milestone in the Northern war effort. The *Harper's Weekly* editor hailed it as a turning point in the war, a victory of the Union's superiority. The North could satisfy several more drafts, he argued, and while "the work has to get done," he was confident Northerners "can and will do it." Indeed, he noted, Northern capacity was greater than the work ahead. The citizens were "only just waking to the fact that this is a death-struggle for them as well as for the rebels."[55] Lincoln's new call for men inspired James S. Gibbons, a New York abolitionist, to compose a patriotic recruiting song entitled, "We are Coming, Father Abraham, Three Hundred Thousand More."[56] As Julia Ward Howe had done months before by refashioning "Old John Brown" into "The Battle

Hymn of The Republic," so too did Gibbons inspire a new spirit of kinship between soldiers and Lincoln.[57] Across the North, governors issued stirring proclamations. A lumberman from Flint, Michigan, Henry Howland Crapo, was so inspired that he wrote his son William in Massachusetts that he would sell his entire business so that his workers would go fight. "Our country *must be saved*,—our government *must be preserved*, let the sacrifice be what it may. I do not know how you feel in New England," he wrote, "but here the spirit of '76 is springing up, & by those who can not fight, money will be furnished like water."[58]

By August, encouraging signs also came with complaints. Those communities that had given the most volunteers protested that the War Department should credit their quota. In the first call, the North's largest cities—New York, Philadelphia, and Boston—furnished more than their share of volunteers. Stanton had already concluded as much and adjusted quotas for accountability. Still, neither Stanton nor governors had an answer for a Chicago widow and mother lamenting her losses by the "curse of the present rebellion," and having "suffered greatly from being left helpless & alone by the death of my dear & loved husband." She protested conscription because it included married men. "Great-God," she wailed, "spare the noble women of our loved land the dread misery of their husbands & fathers being dragged by conscription from their thresholds & they left to toil & suffer on in misery & alone."[59]

As enthusiastic as governors were to have national assistance, it remained to be seen how citizens would react. There was great promise to be gained from the change in recruiting, governors believed, but they also knew that some citizens would resist the new directive. A variety of problems would accompany Lincoln's call. Raising funds to accommodate the army's expansion forced governors to borrow large sums of money, or use personal funds, to carry through the enrollment, as well as sustain those families left without incomes. Morgan, for example, secured credit from New York bankers. He foresaw the war would be longer than Lincoln expected, and insisted on three-year enlistments, which deviated from Stanton's directives. Over the longer period, Morgan believed, this would establish a more judicious apportionment of volunteers, in that one three-year soldier equaled four nine-month men. While many New Yorkers were in favor of the Militia Bill and supported Morgan's execution of it, many governors feared it would buckle federalized recruiting. Businessmen, manufacturers, and religious zealots all applied for exemptions. At one point the president of Yale University wrote Buckingham to remind him that all faculty, as well as Connecticut residents attending college, were exempt from the draft, and expected the governor to honor the century's-old statute.[60]

Whatever military momentum Federal armies had achieved in the spring had dissipated by the summer. Pope's army meandered in northern Virginia, while Buell inched his way to Chattanooga, expecting to reach the city before Braxton Bragg did. The Union's problems, however, had not lulled Confederates to sleep, yet many Northerners had also come around to fully appreciate the military ebb and flow. "The Government is evidently waking up to a juster appreciation" of the war, editorialized the *Burlington Daily Free Press*, "the feeling has been very general that the chief officers of the Government were lagging behind the sentiment of the people, and endangering the success of the national cause by lukewarmness, or excessive tenderness for the feeling of the rebels."[61] Indeed, Lieutenant Samuel Fiske of the 14th Connecticut Volunteers wrote his brother Asa, a chaplain with the 4th Minnesota, that he hoped the administration was "beginning to come up a little to the demands of the people that this war be carried on in earnest."[62]

Allowing governors the power to draft gave the appearance that Lincoln had "come up" to Northerners' demands. The draft indicated to Confederates that Northerners were earnest in carrying on the war, and it dispelled the delusion they would tire from fatigue. "They will learn that we are not behind them in determination," wrote the *Harper's Weekly* editor, "and are far ahead of them in men, money, and resources."[63] Conscription had given governors the iron fist necessary to incentivize enlistment. Some citizens, however, believed that had Lincoln waged a vigorous war since the conflict began, a draft would be unnecessary. New Yorker James Alexander Hamilton, who sat on New York's National War Committee, aired his disappointment to Lincoln and Morgan over the progress of the war and the administration's lack of vigor. "The people of the loyal States," he wrote the president, "have through all the accustomed channels expressed their most unequivocal conviction that the war must be conducted with a vigor and sternness which has no other limit than that which may be demanded by the laws of war; that all the rights of property of rebels of every kind, slaves included, shall be destroyed." He encouraged Morgan to use his gubernatorial position to lead the administration and suggested that loyal governors meet in Washington to press Lincoln to vigorously prosecute the war by carrying out the recent Confiscation Act.[64]

The draft was a suitable measure to assist governors with recruiting, and while many communities were pressed to fill the July call and struggled during harvest without laborers and farmers, some citizens supported the measure Daniel Horn of the 78th Ohio, for example, wrote his wife shortly after the call that "he was glad for it," and that "maybe they will catch some of the men that helped to bring the war about, especially some of the nigger croakers and abolitionists."[65] Still, governors' had difficulty in remaining sensitive to soldiers pressing for a more vigorous war so they could get home sooner, and civilians fearing a draft would cost their communities further hardship. Equally troublesome was Union leadership unwilling to wage an expanded war. Buell's lethargy had so infuriated Morton that he lobbied for a brigadier generalship to gain command of Kentucky's military affairs. "Gov. Morton is one of our best Governors," wrote Lincoln to Stanton, "but I do not think he would be the best Military commander."[66] Morton was popular, but Lincoln needed him right where he was.

As much as they wanted to avoid the unpleasant business of managing enrollment, governors nonetheless instructed county sheriffs to enroll all able-bodied male citizens between the ages of eighteen and forty-five. They appointed commissioners, examined surgeons for each county, and relied on citizens and social organizations to assist. Some states lacked provisions for such an undertaking and called on Stanton for guidance. In Maine, Washburn queried whether "a few smart drummer boys under eighteen" could be enlisted with parent's consent.[67] From Leavenworth, General Lane boasted that "recruiting opens up beautifully" and that even without Stanton's authorization, reported that Kansas was "good for four regiments of whites and two of blacks."[68] In response to Lincoln's July call, but in defiance of his refusal to accept black soldiers, Lane organized escaped slaves into the 1st Kansas Colored Volunteers. Stanton, Lincoln, and Halleck all objected, but momentum to support his regiment was building.[69]

The draft and black enlistment complicated the coming elections. Several governorships were about to turnover, and political leaders needed to maintain their party's hold on the state. Delaware was one of five Union states in which governors served a four-year term, and Burton's tenure was ending. Although he resisted Lincoln's expansion of war aims and opposed abolition, the Democratic Unionist nonetheless supported the war despite a legislature comprised of conservatives sympathetic with the South. When hostilities erupted, the governor's appointment of Henry du Pont to lead the state militia also preserved the Du Pont powder mills, which furnished

Union armies with gunpowder. Burton looked to fraternal organizations to assist in recruiting, while his congressmen looked to extend the draft date until 15 September. Distrustful of Burton, some members such as Unionist George Fisher urged Lincoln to deny the governor power over the state's draft machinery. He explained that the draft would result in pulling Unionists into the ranks and away from the polls, reducing Lincoln's support. He asked Lincoln to allow troops to remain until after the 4 November election so they could vote. Burton was on the way out of office, and his role in the draft could significantly affect the coming election and alter the Union majority. Lincoln responded that postponing the draft was not an option, and neither was minimizing the governor's power. He assured Fisher that Stanton would check any wrongdoing by Burton, but that it would not be "justified to thus snub the Governor who is apparently doing right."[70]

The Mechanics of Drafting

Enrollment proved challenging. Determining exemptions and credits for furnishing troops under the previous call, as well as securing pay, supplies, substitutes, bounties, and equipment, plagued the governors' efforts. Many chief executives found solutions on a case-by-case basis without consulting the War Department. Curtin, for example, granted informal exemptions to mill workers, railroad employees, physicians, some clergy, and conscientious objectors. Because the Pennsylvania Railroad employed hundreds of men who were forced to enroll, the railroad's owners donated $50,000 to the state for volunteer bonuses for men not employed by the railroad. Ohioans demurred to serving under officers they had not selected, and they criticized Tod for not suppressing malcontents who publicly opposed the war. One such Ohioan was Copperhead Edson B. Olds, who, it was alleged, had advised Democrats "not to volunteer" and to resist the draft, "even to the shedding of blood."[71] Tod wrote Seward about this "shrewd, cunning man" who caused trouble and urged the secretary to have him arrested. Seward acquiesced and imprisoned Olds, which drew fire from Ohioans crying that such an arrest was "a flagrant, usurpation of the sovereignty of the States, and a violation of his constitutional rights."[72]

Andrew reasoned that Massachusetts, unlike Tod and Curtin's agrarian states, was among the wealthier and more industrial states, and that conscription would weaken its industrial labor supply. Many of his citizens were financially suited to pay for substitutes from other states, and he supported sending agents from as far away as California and Europe to fill Massachusetts's regiments. Yet Andrew touched a political nerve when he advised Lincoln that harsher means on Southerners rather than threatening Northerners with conscription would end the war sooner. "The iron is hot," declared Andrew, "strike quick." He added, "Our people want nothing to spur them but assurance from Washington that the enemy shall be conquered and right vindicated at all hazards by all means."[73]

Andrew's thoughts on emancipation had been simmering for months, and, the slower the war's progress, the more rapidly his views matured. Gurowski nurtured this progression. He corresponded with the governor frequently that August, arguing that the real evil behind the current war "formula" was Seward, Blair, and Weed. Andrew invited Gurowski to suggest any practical measures "besides that of trying to enlighten the public mind," and the count responded with a solution. "What the Senate could not do," he counseled Andrew, "the *United Governors* may do, if they have the moral courage to shake at the formula." He advised, "The governors may Declare, united or separately, to Mr. Lincoln that the country is in danger, that there is no time to stand upon formulas, that if Mr. Lincoln does not see the imminent danger, the people & the governors see it." He reasoned, "it is the Duty of the Governors to save the Country's cause in spite of the faults & predilections of the president & that therefore the governors implore & if necessary Declare that the President *must* change his adviser, or that the governors will be obliged to authoritatively & emphatically warn the American people & appeal to it." He closed, "The governors ought by every step & in every occasion publicly & deliberately show their Distrust in Seward & their *absolute, absolute, absolute confidence in Stanton*."[74]

The words "moral courage" raised the governor's hackles. He capitalized on an opportunity to preach the "gospel of liberty" to his fellow Massachusetts men. On a mid-August afternoon Andrew addressed several thousand worshippers at a Methodist camp meeting on Martha's Vineyard. In what he later considered his greatest speech, Andrew took his emancipation rhetoric to new heights. "I have never believed it to be possible [he said, in speaking of slavery] that this controversy should end, and peace resume her sway," Andrew argued, "until that dreadful iniquity has been trodden beneath our feet." He continued, "The day our government turned its back on the proclamation of General Hunter the blessing of God has been withdrawn from our arms." He declared, "I know not what record of sin awaits me in the other world but this I know, that I never was mean enough to despise any man because he was ignorant, or because he was poor, or because he was black." Andrew held the crowd spellbound, and when he was finished, they were ready for emancipation. The speech was so impressive that several newspapers picked up its contents and ran it days later. Still, many Northerners were not ready to embrace the black man—slave or free.[75]

Whether or not Northerners supported the abolitionists' drive to emancipate Confederate slaves, conscripting men would advance their cause. Failure to raise troops, Andrew believed, would force citizens to accept emancipation and black enlistments as a compromise. The War Department's regulations stipulated that "all able-bodied male citizens of the respective states" were to be enrolled in the militia of the United States. The question for the *Liberator* was whether "colored men are citizens of Massachusetts, which no one, I presume, will have the hardihood to deny, inasmuch as they are tax payers, voters, jurors, and eligible to office, and there is no inequality founded upon distinction of races known to our laws."[76] To press his views on Lincoln, Andrew called on Edward Kinsley to carry a message to the White House. Kinsley agreed, departed for Washington, and initially called on Senator Sumner. After explaining Andrew's views, the senator encouraged him on to Lincoln. That evening he met Lincoln and repeated the conversation he had with Sumner and Andrew. Encouraged by the conversation, Lincoln replied, "when we have the Governor of Massachusetts to send us troops in the way he has, and when we have him to utter such prayers for us, I have no doubt that we shall succeed."[77]

Once enrollment began, problems abounded. Yates was inspecting the camps in Chicago when he acknowledged to Lincoln that large numbers of citizens were leaving the city to escape the draft, and he asked for authority to declare martial law again. Stanton attempted to rectify escaping the draft by issuing General Orders No. 104, which prohibited citizens liable for draft from leaving the state. Salomon of Wisconsin telegraphed that the "spirit of volunteering to avoid draft" was very active, and that the harvest also delayed the process. He informed Stanton that those counties that had already oversubscribed should be credited, and that to cut off volunteering by 15 August as prescribed would "check the spirit among the loyal people of this State, who are thoroughly aroused to the determination to fill all by volunteering." He requested, "Do not put a damper upon the present enthusiasm of our people.... I must have the authority asked for."[78] Pennsylvanians had also come forth, and Curtin wired Lincoln that 13,000 volunteers would leave as soon as transportation allowed. The governor had returned from

Pittsburgh, where he gave a speech criticizing the administration for just now recognizing that "we are actually engaged in war."[79] Holbrook also admitted that drafting would not be necessary in Vermont, as he could not keep pace with enlistments. The problem, however, was that Green Mountain men were still in Vermont and not in the armies in Virginia.[80]

Nonetheless, governors complained they could not meet their quotas by mid-August and that raising new regiments might alleviate sluggish volunteering. Weed wrote Stanton that Morgan could organize his whole quota earlier if allowed new regiments. As the *New York Times* acknowledged, however, Stanton wanted the draft to commence if for no other purpose than to demonstrate that "the Government has power to compel its citizens to its support."[81] Conscription would equalize military burdens and rectify the political inequity represented in the ranks. Illinoisan Joab Powell, who lost two sons killed at Fort Donelson, understood this concept. He expressed to Yates that "the drafting system may bear down on a few persons that are loyal, but a very large majority of those now subject to the draft are disloyal and will remain until [*sic*] there is some means used to break their backs take a son or Brother Cousin or nephew put him in the army and you find there is a growing interest amongst his friend for the welfare of our Country." In short, he argued that the time had come to put these slackers in the army and make them know their place, and they would soon come to respect and fear the power of the government.[82]

In Kansas, Robinson used the enrollment to compel Lane to comply with his civil directives. He demanded that Stanton clarify Lane's authority in raising unauthorized black regiments. Stanton regretted the lack of harmony between military and civil officials, believing that all men should be united in their efforts against the enemy. As Robinson saw it, Lane *was* the enemy, and he needed Stanton to come to his defense. Knowing his term was about to end, the embittered governor ignored Lane's military commissions and cited the Kansas constitution as justification for his course. Stanton responded, however, that if Robinson failed to commission Lane's appointments, the War Department would stamp them. The governor lashed out that while the secretary may "have the power to override the constitution and the laws," he had not "the power to make the present Governor of Kansas dishonor his state." Stanton commissioned Lane's officers, and relations deteriorated between Robinson and the Lincoln administration.[83]

Civil-military affairs were no better in Kentucky. Buell's failure to catch Bragg at Chattanooga that summer allowed Confederate General Kirby

Smith to steal into Kentucky when voters were heading to the polls to determine Magoffin's successor. Political leaders had engineered Magoffin's exit from office by striking an agreement that allowed sixty-two-year-old James F. Robinson to replace him. On 18 August, Robinson succeeded Magoffin. A native Kentuckian and lifelong Democrat, Robinson came late to the Whig Party in 1851, when he was elected to the Kentucky Senate. He studied law and was admitted to the bar, embarking on his legal practice in Georgetown, Kentucky. The day he entered his executive office scores of letters detailing the magnitude of Kentucky's problems lay on his desk. "We think our troops are defending the wrong border," complained Robert D. Murray, arguing that Kentuckians would rather die "defending our homes, than to have them desolated by the enemy."[84] Robinson urged Lincoln to avoid leaving Kentucky defenseless. Still, Kentuckians, like Kansans, were harassed by a war that was greater in the state than outside it.[85]

Within a matter of weeks the disparity between governors enrolling volunteers and national authorities providing pay and supplies revealed regional weaknesses. To compensate for shortages, governors finessed enrollment to suit local needs. Several governors, such as Morton, Curtin, Andrew, and Morgan, secured funds to supply the men's bounties and advance pay. This put men in the ranks more quickly, but with inferior arms. Kirkwood stressed "every nerve" to meet the exigencies of war, but agents informed him that secret societies had formed in southern Iowa to prevent the draft and the collection of taxes. Yates argued he had 50,000 volunteers ready to take the field, but waited on pay and equipment, and accused Lincoln of delaying his efforts. By late August, governors had battered the War Department with hundreds of wires revealing their problems. While some chief executives boasted success, thanks in large measure to wealthy urban associations that raised plentiful bounties, others complained of having to use liberal exemptions for railroad workers, millworkers, physicians, clergymen, sons of widows, lunatics, criminals, and drunkards. So chaotic was the enrollment that Stanton informed governors that he would "endeavor to accommodate to meet necessities in particular cases so far as may be consistent with the service and natural exigencies."[86]

The timing of enrollment coincided with the political canvass that summer, and governors worried it would work against them. Many believed Republicans would outnumber Democrats in volunteering, and when they departed the state it would weaken the political culture. Several governors counseled Stanton to postpone the draft until after the coming election.

Morton ignored the date and wired Stanton he was postponing Indiana's draft. Stanton replied that because Indiana had responded so "promptly and liberally to the call" he would afford Morton time to get things right. As more governors wrote in, Stanton lifted the draft date and encouraged governors to resort to such measures "as soon as possible."[87]

Governors employed incentives, appealed to local pride, and used their own funds to assist families, all to avoid the shame of the draft. Kirkwood called a special session of the Iowa General Assembly to appropriate welfare relief and to provide him funds to purchase and distribute weapons among loyal citizens to safeguard their localities. He used the press to appeal to Iowans for supplies to assist the soldiers. Andrew hoped the administration would embrace black regiments and emancipation. Lane's actions had already demonstrated that fugitive slaves were willing to enlist, but Andrew held out for emancipation to undermine the Confederate war effort. "Unless a new life is breathed into the govt at Washington, our efforts will be in vain," he concluded to Gurowski.[88] Several governors rallied behind black enlistment. Wisconsin's blacks encouraged Salomon to press Lincoln to accept their enlistment. Cornelius Butler of Kenosha had written Salomon to "lay before your excellency the hope and desire of the colored men of this State to do something to aid the government at this time." Salomon forwarded these sentiments to Stanton, asking if he might encourage such expressions, but neither Lincoln nor Stanton were willing to receive them. When learning of the president's attitude, one resident expressed to Salomon that a "great many [residents] express the hope that the Govs of the North will refuse to send [any] troops unless they receive all *Black* as well as *White* & Force the Pres. to receive them or resign."[89]

Still, most conservatives were not ready to acquiesce that the war was being fought to free slaves and were hesitant to enlist blacks. When journalists made it appear that Connecticut blacks were eager to fight and that whites were willing to allow this, Buckingham was not convinced. "It seems to me that the time may yet come when a regiment of colored men may be profitably employed," he responded to an outspoken Connecticutan, "but now, if a company of that class should be introduced into a regiment, or a regiment into a brigade, . . . *it would create so much unpleasant feeling and irritation that more evil than good would result*."[90]

In the midst of changing war aims, another drama unfolded in the Northwest, and it directed the attention of northwestern governors away from draft concerns and to the home front. In mid-August some 500 Sioux Indians went on the warpath as a consequence of starvation and governmental frauds perpetrated by Indian agents. The first wave of attacks came on the morning of the 18th, as a band of Dakota braves swooped down along the Minnesota River in Redwood County and slaughtered a group of traders. The massacre widened to surrounding areas, and by evening a desperate call went out from Fort Ridgely for help. Fearing depredations would spread, citizens fled to the Minnesota River fort for safety. Ramsey looked to longtime friend Henry H. Sibley for relief. He called out the militias of the affected counties and placed them under Sibley's command. In the following weeks a full-scale war erupted, as Sibley's 1,600 mounted men sought out the perpetrators. Ramsey expected assistance from Stanton, but convened the assembly in case no governmental funds were forthcoming. When he learned that Stanton had no funds to combat Indians, he allowed commanders to take provisions from private citizens. In the meantime, Ramsey convinced Halleck that he needed more time to meet his quota.[91]

The Indian uprising spread panic to northwestern Wisconsin, and citizens appealed to Salomon for protection. The governor wired Stanton for ammunition to supply citizens in those regions, but Stanton replied that he needed "satisfactory evidence" that a military necessity existed. "As Executive of the State," Salomon declared, "you must allow me to be the judge of the necessity for ammunition," adding that "your delays are cruel."[92] He made it clear that if the state was willing to allow national authorities control in these matters, they had better be prepared to act responsibly, or he would. There was a general fear that the Sioux uprising might escalate into an all-out Indian war in the Northwest. Kirkwood wired Stanton that the Yankton Indians on Iowa's western border had joined forces with the Sioux and threatened the entire frontier. "Something must be done at once," he demanded.[93] As the summer continued, the expansion of military fronts reminded governors of their responsibility for local defense.

CHAPTER TEN

They Are a Body of Wise and Patriotic Men

Stanton's response to the Sioux uprising reflected the disparity between waging a national war and maintaining peace on the home front. Northerners had come to accept a war that had enjoined thousands of local communities in a common cause despite the distance between, say, the Minnesota frontier and Washington. Civilians watched soldiers leave for a war they followed through letters, newspapers, official decrees, and self-sacrifice. Eighty-seven-year-old New Yorker Montgomery Stevens was among those followers who had grown tired of Lincoln's limited war. Older than the Union, and "having some considerable knowledge of political matters," Stevens predicted "slavery would destroy this Union." He stated, "That irrepressible conflict I then foresaw is now upon us," and he urged the secretary to wage war in earnest. "Fight we must," he declared, "for fight us they will."[1] Governors appreciated such sentiments and adjusted to the world the war made.

By September, however, the Union's performance had not equaled Northern sacrifices, and another adjustment appeared necessary. Although Lincoln had come to accept emancipation as a war measure, his failure to act publicly on this belief inspired Radical governors to spearhead a move. In the coming weeks Lee and Bragg's invasions of Maryland and Kentucky weighed on their sensibilities. Governors prodded members of Lincoln's administration to accept their influence in managing a war they believed was in tune with the people. Yet many Northerners who had cared little for the slave accepted the reality that emancipation could bring victory in wake of demoralizing summer defeats and shorten enlistment terms. Citizens were conservative on racial matters and permitted Lincoln's emancipation as a condition of victory more than as a moral reform. Governors, however, welcomed congressional changes that summer, but feared losing momentum due to presidential paralysis. Andrew mapped out a new promised land despite the attitude of his conservative Bostonians. "Perhaps we are doing as well as other States," he lashed out at the administration, "but it nearly drives me *mad* when I see the American armies running before a generation of scoundrels, and American liberty almost prostrate before a power which challenges government itself, outrages humanity, and defies God." He declared, "God only knows whether the President will ever burst his bonds of Border-Stateism and McClellan, but the people somehow are blessed with an instinct of faith, before which, I believe, mountains themselves will move."[2]

Andrew wanted to move mountains, but he yielded to Sprague's suggestion that New England governors meet to discuss war policies. "If the Govt. stir the enemy one half as much as they do the people, or exhaust them in that proposition," Sprague wrote Andrew, "I will find no fault."[3] He declared, "I am heartily sick and tired of any double policy," to a war meeting crowd assembled in Newport. "No white gloved handling will do this," he proclaimed, we must "strike him [the enemy] in his vital parts."[4] Sprague wanted to stir the governors and wrote to his New England colleagues about a meeting to discuss influencing the administration. Washburn needed little priming. "It is time for the States to speak to the federal govt.," he wrote Andrew, "if the latter will do what should have been done months ago, we will have nothing but victories; remove incompetent, and [unfaithful] Generals & emancipate & employ the slaves." He asked, "Does any man suppose we can ever live with the South & slavery, after all that has happened? The President should be [awoke at last]."[5]

Providence

Andrew requested that Sprague have Brown University president Reverend Barnas Sears invite the New England governors to summer commencement. This would avoid attracting public attention and allow them to discuss freely their thoughts on war aims. On 3 September, Andrew, Sprague, Washburn, Buckingham, and New York National War Committee members Charles Gould, Prosper M. Wetmore, and Nehemiah Knight converged on Providence. Washburn broke away from campaigning for Abner Coburn and attended the conference, but Holbrook needed to shore up his reelection and was unable to attend. Nonetheless, the governors wanted to make Lincoln aware of their impatience over his delay in emancipating slaves, which, they believed, would reduce enlistment periods and inspire volunteerism.[6]

At the commencement dinner that evening Sprague gave the opening address, offering generalizations about the Union's uninspiring military fortunes. Washburn followed with a short speech that blamed slavery and the federal government for prolonging the conflict. "Whenever in the history of the world were men of the north inferior to men of the south," he declared, "whenever were the forces of intelligence inferior to the power of ignorance, or the power of industry subordinate to that of idleness—whenever was liberty subordinate to slavery—No, sirs it cannot be, it must not be, it shall not be." Referring to the administration's reluctance to emancipate slaves, he argued, "we must have a policy and know what we are about."[7] The governor had recently forwarded a letter to Lincoln from a Maine surgeon in McClellan's army that argued if the administration did not abandon conciliation there would be a revolt. "It occurred to me," he wired Lincoln, "that the observations of an officer so near to Genl. McClellan, & so intimate with him ... would possibly throw some light upon a question most interesting to the loyal people of the United States."[8]

Buckingham arrived after dinner, as did the members of the New York War Committee. They met in the City Hotel and discussed enlistment of slaves and free blacks, and the draft. The late debacle in Virginia underscored their intentions to stir up Lincoln's paralyzed administration. "I should be rejoiced," declared the editor of the *Bangor Daily Whig and Courier*, "to be able to chronicle the fact that the loyal Governors of the FREE STATES had held a high Parliament, and respectfully advised that the efforts of the country should have a new and decisive direction—and that the Border States should no longer *hold the Free North in*, while the rebels are almost throttling the nation in its very capital."[9] It appeared that the governors' intentions to change the war resonated with the people, and in their address to Lincoln they argued for a change in generals and in the cabinet. The delegation tapped Hamilton and fellow New Yorkers John Austin Stevens, Jr., John E. Williams, and Nehemiah Knight to travel to Washington and present the Providence sentiments to Lincoln. The group initially met Treasury Secretary Chase, who counseled Hamilton to tread lightly with the president. Undeterred, the New Yorkers exercised little diplomacy. Williams was so blunt in demanding McClellan and Seward's removal that Lincoln abruptly ended the meeting.[10]

Hamilton returned the following day and argued that "in the opinion of some of the Governors of loyal States, the public mind was desponding, and dissatisfied with the Administration in consequence of the reverses to which our armies had been subjected."[11] In an attempt to convince Lincoln that Seward was paralyzing the administration, Hamilton cited a letter from the secretary that was unfavorable to the president. Lincoln leaped up, pointed at the men, and responded "you, gentlemen, to hang Mr. Seward, would destroy this Government." Hamilton responded that he was merely performing his duty in relating the situation's gravity. The meeting disbanded, and Lincoln had the governors' views whether he liked how he got them or not.[12]

Governors returned to their statehouses and awaited reports of the meeting. Andrew arrived back in Boston, where he received Curtin's invitation to a governor's conference at Altoona. He also found a letter from Gurowski, who relayed the mood in Washington. "If the people will be saved," he challenged Andrew, "it will not be by Lincoln, Seward or MacClellan."[13] Andrew accepted Curtin's invitation and responded to Gurowski. "Besides doing my proper work," he stated, "I am sadly but firmly trying to help organize some movement, if possible to save the Prest from the infamy of ruining his country."[14] It was serendipitous that Gould wrote to Andrew the same day, demanding that "the loyal governors to meet in council and point out the remedy," resulting from the "stupendous blunder" committed at Washington. Gould believed thousands of Northerners had "turned their minds to the same point."[15]

In early September the *Chicago Tribune* published the proceedings of a Union meeting in that city recommending a meeting of the loyal governors to aid "the president to devise plans that may be effective in rescuing the Union from its great peril." "The governors of the loyal States know the sentiments of the people better than the president, as they reside among and mingle with them," noted the editor, "they are a body of wise and patriotic men," and "might be able to point out the radical defects in the present mode of conducting the war, and to propose some plan giving reasonable promise of success." If Lincoln trusted the people, as he made clear on many occasions, then it was time to allow them a stratagem to offer their opinions. Governors served this purpose, as they would be a "body of counselors [sic] speaking for the people of their respective States," and whose advice Lincoln respects. "We think it is the duty of the State executives to hold such a convocation immediately," the editor urged.[16] The sentiment for a governors' meeting was gaining momentum.

The Providence meeting stirred New England governors. Berry had previously wired Lincoln that despite the "clandestine appliances of prominent Secessionists here," New Hampshire's "hardy and noble sons are determined to bear their full share in the perils and sacrifices necessary for its preservation."[17] Yet, the army's use of Northern soldiers to protect rebel property confounded him. "*Confidentially* we beg leave to Say," he began, that our reading, thinking, intelligent, patriotic young men are inquiring with commendable Solicitude into the propriety of wasting their strength and energy daily and nightly watchings [*sic*] of Rebel estates and other property, or in keeping accurate and detailed accounts of all such property as is of absolute necessity for their comfort and convenience while prosecuting the war, or in building corduroy roads and bridges in Chickahominy Swamps—digging trenches, piling fortifications and the like, while they believe, strong and willing hands wait only to be invited to this laborious Service, that they too may show their appreciation of the glorious boon of freedom.[18]

As Washburn's gubernatorial tenure ended that September, his tone with Hamlin, Fessenden, and Charles Sedgwick intensified. To Sedgwick, he wrote that he was ashamed of him for saying that McClellan was incompetent, for "he is a man of real power." After all, Washburn argued, the commander kept 200,000 troops idle in camp for six months despite daily entreaties from the president to move forward, remained on the peninsula while the army withered away, and retained his command. McClellan was "*no* common man," he maintained, quite the contrary, he was "*a man of remarkable power.*"[19] Consoling Fessenden over his son's recent battlefield death, the seasoned politician aired his frustration over the administration's handling of the war. "What are we coming to," he wrote, "I confess the future is to me shaded with the gloomiest hues. . . . The President seems to have no firmness, the cabinet is broken into miserable factions. I have faith in Stanton, but in no other member, unless it be Chase for times like these." He despaired, "We must have a new, distinct, earnest policy, or the country is ruined, & I do not believe such a policy possible with the present cabinet. A war cabinet united in policy & purpose will give us the right commanders." Curtin's governors' conference might provide a solution.[20]

Lincoln also searched for solutions. The press reported that Union casualties at the Second Battle of Bull Run exceeded 10,000, and that Confederates were poised to raid the Northern states. Lincoln had nowhere to turn for commanders to head off Lee's forces heading north. Pope had lost the confidence of the soldiers and of his superiors. Despite his reservations about bringing McClellan back, the president thought more of the morale of the men than his own misgivings and presumed political fallout. On 2 September he restored "Little Mac" to command his old army in what must have been an episode of supreme irony. The change inspired Salomon to write Yates about the proposed meeting of governors. Although not offended by McClellan's reinstatement, he nonetheless agreed he would attend the meeting. The return of the commander, however, pushed Robinson over the edge. "I cannot write about the war," he declared to his wife, "[Granny] Lincoln has that coward McClellan in command again."[21]

The War on Many Fronts

On 4 September Lee's army began crossing the Potomac River near Leesburg, Virginia, while Jackson's men established a base at Frederick, Maryland. The Maryland Campaign threw border state residents into a panic. Bradford called on Stanton to assist him in preparing for the draft. Resistance was mounting, and he had already arrested several antagonists, but Stanton had no men. Reading the reports in the Michigan papers and conferring with Michigan governor Blair about army movements in Maryland, Chandler grew despondent over the Union's fate. The senator supported Blair's Radicalism and leaned on him to bring about changes, thinking he could inspire an undertaking by the governors. He wrote his Illinois colleague Trumbull that he feared "nothing will now save us but *a demand* of the loyal governors, *backed by a threat*—that a change in policy & men shall *instantly* be made."[22]

Lee's Army of Northern Virginia inched closer to Pennsylvania with McClellan's army in pursuit, and Andrew sent freight cars loaded with medical supplies to Baltimore. Pennsylvania's state officials removed the state treasury from Harrisburg and transported deposits to New York. Curtin's intelligence led him to believe that Philadelphia was the Confederates' target, and he wired McClellan. "No doubt appears to exist as to the intention of the enemy to invade our state," he warned the commander.[23] Two days later, however, he wired McClellan that his intelligence reported the Confederates were amassed near Frederick, with not less than 120,000 men, and were preparing to give battle. Whether rightfully panicked or not, Curtin's alarm annoyed Welles. "Our Pennsylvania friends have been exceedingly alarmed, more than they should have been," he confided to his wife, "Gov. Curtin is a very exciteable [sic] man, and not capable of looking at things deliberately."[24]

The enemy in the East was not Lincoln's only concern. West of the Mississippi River the Sioux uprising had intensified, and Ramsey needed more time to meet his quota. Minnesota residents, he argued, would not enlist when Indians threatened their homes. Besides, there was hardly anyone to draft. Stanton denied his request, and Ramsey appealed to Lincoln. "The Indian outbreak has come upon us suddenly," he declared, "half the population of the State are fugitives."[25] Lincoln had sent Nicolay to St. Paul in July to investigate the state of affairs, and his report confirmed the desperation. "The Indian war grows more extensive," he wrote, and "the settlers of the whole border are in panic and flight, leaving their harvest to waste in the field, as I myself have seen even in the neighborhoods where there is no danger."[26] Lincoln sympathized with Ramsey, and in explaining that he could not extend the draft date, he understood that "necessity knows no law" and the governor should "attend to the Indians."[27] To assist Ramsey, he created a new Military Department of the Northwest comprising Minnesota, Wisconsin, Iowa, and the Dakota territories. He made St. Paul the headquarters and banished the defeated Pope to the new command.[28]

Meanwhile, Confederate General Bragg entered Kentucky and headed north to Louisville. Morton suspected secret societies were about to launch guerrilla raids on his Indiana river towns and he summoned able-bodied men to organize for defense. What added to the alarm was the confusion stemming from the reorganization of the Department of the Ohio, which left Louisville abandoned. Morton sent an expedition into Kentucky to protect the city. He consulted with Robinson, and they secured additional batteries from Halleck. To hasten the men forward, Morton borrowed money to pay the bounties. It was during these frenzied days that he allegedly walked into an Indianapolis bank, asked for $30,000, and, finding a market basket, placed the rolled up greenbacks inside, and walked back to his office. All told, the governor borrowed $500,000 in just a few days to pay the men. Still, Buell's pursuit of Bragg through Kentucky did not bode well for the administration or for Northern morale. Buell appeared to be more popular with Confederates than with his own soldiers, many of whom wrote to their governors. By mid-September Bragg's invasion forced Union General Wright to suspend business in Cincinnati, declare martial law, and order troops from Louisville to Cincinnati, despite the objections of General Jeremiah T. Boyle and Robinson. The Kentucky governor protested to Halleck against the movement of troops to Cincinnati. "If Louisville is taken," he declared, "the State is gone."[29]

There was little uplifting news in September, and Northern morale deteriorated. Two major Confederate offensives had gained national press, and the administration struggled to combat them. It was during these dark days that Illinois resident Portia Gage, abolitionist and women's rights activist, sent a letter to all loyal governors, entitled "An Appeal to the Governors of the Free States." Her intention was to reinforce the sentiment of Horace Greeley's *New York Tribune* article that appeared 20 August, entitled "The Prayer of Twenty Millions," which urged the president to liberate slaves. Although Lincoln had decided to depart from his limited war approach, many Northerners had seen few signs of his new war aims. Gage appealed to the governors to take action to end slavery. "You as Governors of Sovereign States," she argued, "have a right (and we *beseech* you to *enforce* it) to demand of the President when he calls for men to tell you what he wants of them.... We feel that it is your *duty* to demand of him to tell you in plain words which he intends shall live," slavery or freedom. She urged the governors "acting of one accord" to refuse to furnish men "to restore the Union *as it was*."[30]

William Gannaway Brownlow, popularly known as "Parson" Brownlow from his days as a circuit-riding Tennessee preacher, who had endured Confederate imprisonment, voiced almost the same opinion in calling on the Northern governors. Widely known for his recently published book explaining the rise and fall of secession, Brownlow gained notoriety during a summer tour of the Northern states. Northern newspapers printed his 7 September "Address to the Governors of the Loyal States," beseeching them to convene. Brownlow called upon governors, as representatives of the people, to "address yourselves in unmistakable terms, to the civil and military authorities of the United States."[31] He urged them to call on Lincoln and press him to place commanders in the armies who would not "study how to kill off leading rebels without hurting them," but who would use "every possible way to crush out this infernal rebellion."[32]

Although the president had decided to end conciliation (influenced in large measure by the Seven Days' Battles), shelve the generals in favor of it, and emancipate rebel slaves, Northerners had apparently not seen evidence of these designs. Governors decided to engineer some public directives to make Lincoln aware of their frustration. As popular demand for more aggressive generals, harsher enforcement of confiscation, and a more strident movement for emancipation fell away from Lincoln's paralyzed administration, citizens looked to governors to close the ranks and help expand the war. Governor Blair and Senator Chandler represented this despondency, having already registered their views arguing that confiscation should be enforced by commanders, slaves should be used for menial service, and soldiers no longer used to protect citizens. "*Com* pell [*sic*] your Generals to obey the Laws & the Country will Call blessed," Chandler wrote Lincoln. "You can form no conception of the public sentiment in the North West," he argued, "I was called radical in Washington, but I find myself so far behind the people that I am almost ashamed of my laggardness."[33]

The *New York Times* captured the popular sentiment, arguing that it was "utterly useless to disguise the fact, and worse than futile to deny it, that a profound and most anxious apprehension had . . . seized the public mind." The editor contended, "The reverses which have befallen our arms . . . the bold formidable invasion by the rebels of the loyal States, and the apparent paralysis of the Executive Department carried distrust and dismay to the popular heart, and demanded the prompt action of the State authorities to reassure the public mind, by showing a second line of defense against the advancing enemy."[34] In Northern eyes, the Maryland and Kentucky invasions obscured Union gains in Missouri, most of Tennessee, western Virginia, much of southern Louisiana, and northern Arkansas and Mississippi. To many citizens, it looked as though Southerners were looking to preempt Lincoln's call for troops.

The president was under political pressure from Congress and his cabinet to raise troops, even more so as the call for volunteers was slow and several governors responded that they could not meet their quotas, draft or no draft. By September, whether it was through eliminating commanders who promoted conciliation, emancipating slaves, or threatening to draft military-age males, Lincoln needed to replenish the ranks. Several governors had pressed him to accept black volunteers. Blair declared at a Detroit political gathering that he was "utterly unable to see why it is not proper to use a rebel's sacred nigger . . . . I am entirely unable to see, too why Sambo shouldn't be permitted to carry a musket."[35] When rumors spread that Sprague was raising a regiment of black soldiers, Sergeant Charles E. Perkins of the 2nd Rhode Island queried his sister from Virginia over public reaction. "Is thare [*sic*] not white men enough to put this rebellion [*sic*] down," he asked, "or has our government got to call on the niger to fight?" He maintained, "If thare [*sic*] hant [*sic*] white men enough out North to put this thing down, I think the best thing [is] that few we have got out here had better come home and let the trouble drop."[36]

Governors responded to the growing popular sentiment that demanded a meeting. Curtin had mentioned the idea of a governor's meeting in late June while meeting with Seward in New York. The secretary mentioned the idea to Lincoln, who approved. Curtin wired Andrew that, in the "present emergency," the loyal governors should meet "to take measures for the more active support of the government." Andrew agreed, and the invitations went out for a 24 September gathering to assess whether governors were united in this venture. Curtin chose Altoona as the meeting place because of its accessibility by rail, and because its seclusion would allow the governors privacy. Mobilization had melded governors into a partnership with Lincoln, but giving the war definite aim required decisive action. If handled judiciously, this influence could restore the people's faith that federalism was alive insofar as the government could take direction from the states without undermining the Union's credibility. "Unless all State lines are to be blotted out, and all local authority merged in the central sovereignty of the Federal Government," noted an insightful *New York Times* editor, "it would seem to be eminently proper that the States, should by separate action if need be, reinforce the General Government, and give it the aid of their counsel, their courage and strength."[37] Their influence might demonstrate that states had more power in the Union than outside of it. Anton B. Schaeffer, a frustrated Missouri private who had been inspired by Yates's July letter, favored such a gathering. "Could not the governors of the loyal states act in common on the President an [sic] the means to influence the fire," he queried "to drive his generals to a speedy termination of the war, for everybody is anxious to go home, the patriotism of last years has disappeared." Schaeffer felt assured that "A convention of all the governors of the northern States will affect this when they ask the President to resign his office, if they don't want to see them calling their Volunteers back to their resp. States, or require him to put other generals; who know how to make war."[38]

As governors prepared to travel to Altoona, McClellan's army marched to catch Lee near the town of Sharpsburg north of the Potomac River. The meeting gave these "feeble patriots" a "backbone," as Iowa congressman Josiah Bushnell Grinnell later put it, and it was "a reassuring voice to soldiers tired of the camp and fearful of the 'Fire in the rear.'"[39] Morgan was on his way out of office and decided against attending the meeting, but he responded to Curtin that he was "for continuing this war to the end without qualification or condition."[40] He asserted that "If the interests of the Country can be promoted by the consultation suggested, I shall then be happy to co-operate with the Governors of Loyal States."[41] Curtin regretted Morgan's absence and responded that "in the existing state of the country I cannot refuse to meet my brothers in conference, as their wisdom may suggest something useful which has not occurred to me."[42] Like Morgan, Gamble had exigencies in Missouri that prevented his attendance. In fact, his brother-in-law discouraged from attending, saying the meeting had revolutionary intentions. He advised that, given the current tide swelling against Gamble in Washington, it would be better to remain in Missouri.[43]

Acting of One Accord

Rumors of the governors' meeting spread through the press. Some Democratic newspapers characterized it as a treasonous cabal, hoping to play on the fears of disillusioned Northerners, who winced at anything resembling states' rights. "We trust the Altoona Convention will not be held," advised the *Louisville Daily Journal*, but if it was held, the editor hoped that Lincoln would have national troops on hand to arrest the conspirators, should they talk of treason.[44] Illinois journalist Logan Uriah Reavis bought into this contrived rhetoric, protesting to Yates that as "wise and patriotic as the loyal governors may be," the meeting constituted an "arrogation of power that is unprecedented in any age or nation, and unfit for American sanction." He feared the governors might overplay their hand and cautioned Yates against dictating policy to Lincoln. Governors were "men of great ability" he argued, and well suited to their roles, but Lincoln was superior in ability. "I know of no governor in any state who I believe equal in ability to Mr. Lincoln," he warned Yates, "besides he has in his councils as great men as the Republic can produce. With this combination of talent and experience," he assured him, "I feel that our cause is doing the best it can under the circumstances."[45]

More sensible papers printed what was common knowledge. Northerners, especially Radical Republicans, were angry, and Andrew and Curtin called the meeting to give a paralyzed administration some direction. The slumbering Northern body politic believed that Lincoln's deficiencies were the politicians around him, and that governors spoke for the people. They, rather than cabinet members, were well suited to strike a balance between popular thought and national action. "I do not venture to suggest what your action in the meeting you are about to hold at Altoona should be," confided John Pope to Yates, "I only express to you my firm conviction that unless the present system with its leaders be swept away & the Administration relieved from the Pretorian control which has dominated over it, our Government is not worth a days' purchase."[46] Blair wrote, "The gloom that overspread the loyal states on account of these disasters and the movement of Gen. Lee's

Army north for the invasion of the border states occasioned very great depression in the public mind," and "it was necessary to relieve this situation promptly and nothing could accomplish this so effectively as the energetic action of the War Governors unless it should be a victory of the National Arms."[47]

Northerners identified their governors as their spokesmen. Representative of this public acrimony was Mrs. [W. M.] Tracy Cutler of Dwight, Illinois, who, upon learning of the Altoona meeting, wrote Yates that it was her "earnest prayer" the governor would "use all due effort to change the policy of the administration" and that she spoke "the sentiments of a multitude of good and true people." She advised, "Urge the removal of all proslavery generals at least from the western department." She wrote, "Speak sharp words to the President against such traitors as Buell."[48]

Despite whatever views citizens aired to their governors, or what newspapers reported, the fact was governors organized to discuss state drafts, war aims, emancipation, and conservative commanders. When Tod received his invitation, he wired Stanton, asking him if he had any suggestions. Stanton replied that he had no suggestions but hoped "its counsels may be wise and productive of good."[49] That governors initiated such a meeting impressed Stanton, but he was not surprised. Curtin and Andrew informed Lincoln of the meeting and that only "good" was to come of it. The president confided in them his decision to announce the Emancipation Proclamation and "asked if they wished him to defer its issuance until they had requested him to act," as they had before in June when calling for troops. The governors responded that "he should by all means bring it out first and they would follow it with a strong address of commendation."[50] Such support buoyed Lincoln's confidence. Buckingham recalled the feeling during these days. "The governors of the loyal states were a harmonious family of officials then," he observed, "one common and great cause making us brothers in feeling."[51]

It was not unfathomable to imagine that Lincoln was apprehensive over the meeting, given the depressing news of late. At the very least, Lincoln the politician understood that he could not afford to dismiss the governors' opinions. After all, it was an election year, and running the risk of alienating the state leaders of his party might prove disastrous. They believed that emancipation would save them from resorting to more desperate means. Lincoln was eager for anything positive on the military front. On 16 September he wired Curtin "What do you hear from Gen. McClellan's army?"[52] Curtin responded that Pennsylvanians were responding to his call, and though it was not definite, his telegraph operator at Hagerstown reported that a battle was "progressing near the Potomac, between Sharpsburg and Williamsport."[53] Lincoln wrote back the following morning that McClellan "was up with the engulf at Sharpsburg, and was waiting for heavy fog to rise."[54]

On 17 September the titanic contest near Antietam Creek changed the Union's course. Although Northern casualties tolled more than 12,400, Lincoln at least had something on the scale of Shiloh that he could claim was victory and could thus act publicly on what he had been thinking for months. McClellan claimed victory and took pleasure in writing to his wife three days afterward of his accomplishment. "I feel some little pride," he remarked, "in having with a beaten and demoralized army defeated Lee so utterly, & saved the North so completely." Alluding to the governors' meeting, the commander concluded that an initial step was already taking shape. "An opportunity has presented itself through the Governors of some of the states to enable me to take my stand," he wrote, and "I have insisted that Stanton shall be removed & that Halleck shall give way to me as Comdr in Chief."[55]

Like Shiloh, Antietam changed the war in incalculable ways. "I have just passed over a part of the field," wrote Connecticut Lieutenant Fiske, who wrote to the *Springfield Republican* in the guise of Dunn Browne, "and yet I have encountered nearly a thousand dead bodies of rebels lying still unburied in groves and corn-fields, on hill sides and in trenches."[56] Arriving at the battlefield soon after the guns silenced, Curtin carried the wounded to ambulances and impressed at least one unsuspecting soldier. Desperately in love with a young Ohio soldier, Catharine E. Davidson had disguised herself as a soldier and joined the same unit to be with her companion. She was wounded in the arm, and Curtin carried her to an ambulance. Thinking she might not survive her wounds, she gave Curtin her ring as a thank-you for his kindness. Curtin placed the ring on his finger as a token of remembrance and continued his work among the wounded. Davidson survived the amputation and a year later showed up at the Continental Hotel in Philadelphia, where Curtin was speaking. She introduced herself and identified the ring to Curtin, who, after listening to her, filled out an order to provide her with an artificial arm.[57]

Five days after Antietam reddened the Maryland landscape, Lincoln issued the preliminary Emancipation Proclamation, which gave Confederate slave owners 100 days to emancipate their slaves. Refusal to comply would result in Lincoln declaring them free. The *Hartford Evening Press* hailed it "the most important document in the history of our government since its constitutional establishment; it is a landmark in the progress of freedom and civilization everywhere."⁵⁸ Finally, Radical governors had what they wanted. Quietly rejoicing, Andrew remarked to his military secretary that although the proclamation was "a poor *document*, it was a mighty *act*; slow, somewhat halting, wrong in its delay till January, but grand and sublime after all." He wrote, " 'Prophets and kings' have waited for this day, but died without the sight." He declared, "Our Republicans must make it their business to sustain this act of Lincoln, and we will drive the conservatism of a proslavery Hunkerism and the reactionaries of despotism into the very caves and holes of the earth."⁵⁹

In the highly charged September days the governors' meeting was the most promising politically engineered design to move the administration in line with the people it represented. If Lincoln had decided to embrace more aggressive and expansive war measures, citizens had yet to see them. The editor of the *St. Louis Daily Missouri Republican* asserted that Lincoln needed to issue his proclamation to avoid being publicly embarrassed by the governors meeting, and to avoid political fallout from the New York Republican Convention that opened the same week. "There seems to be a strange coincidence in the time of these conventions and the publication of the proclamation," wrote the editor.⁶⁰ It was a striking coincidence, noted the editor, made more coincidental given the president's recent remarks to a visiting delegation of Chicago clergymen, that he had no power to emancipate slaves. "What *good* would a proclamation of emancipation from me do, especially as we are now situated," he argued to the ministers, "I do not want to issue a document that the whole world will see must necessarily be inoperative, like the Pope's bull against the comet!"⁶¹ It was not so much if Lincoln's words would or would not free the slaves, but rather if would he listen to people tired of fighting a limited war simply to placate border state representatives.⁶²

The Confederate army in the East was in retreat as governors made their way to Altoona. They headquartered their meeting at the Logan House Hotel, once a famous hostelry transformed into one of the country's most modern hotels of the day. That morning J. Edgar Thompson of the Pennsylvania Railroad had arranged for the dignitaries to tour Horseshoe Curve, a famous railroad curve through Kittanning Gap a few miles away. The tourists returned around noon and found the remaining guests gathered in the ladies' parlor. Here, for the first time in the republic's history, were governors in a stand of federal solidarity. The hour and the men attracted attention. A *New York Herald* correspondent commented on the memorable meeting and on the group's physical appearance. Andrew was abolitionism's conscience, yet for all of his influence and powerful intellect, his stubby features were disappointing, especially when contrasted with Sprague and Salomon, who possessed the youth and attractiveness the press had attributed to them. With their broad shoulders, elegant dress, and fine manners, Bradford and Tod were the most distinguished looking. Washburn looked like a diminutive but proper scholar-politician, which contrasted with Berry's overgrown farmer-like features. Curtin and Yates were radiant and showy in dress, but their manners were quite different, as Curtin appeared more sincere than Yates. Pierpont and Kirkwood were carelessly dressed, unpolished in manners, and the least impressive.[63]

At one o'clock Curtin appeared in the lobby and directed the governors to the east parlor, where they took their seats around an oversized walnut table. He invited all others to leave and closed the door. Curtin called the meeting to order, introduced the guests, and explained the rationale for their presence. He brought his statehouse stenographer with the government cipher, hoping to send a wire to Lincoln that evening. For the next several hours these political leaders discussed the current of war. The meeting recessed at 3:00 P.M., reconvened an hour later, and remained in session until late into the evening. Curtin was so encouraged by the day's proceedings that he commented to his telegraph operator that he might be sending a communication to Lincoln by day's end. When the governors returned from their hour-long recess, however, the war against McClellan opened. Andrew launched into a defense of Lincoln's Emancipation Proclamation and attacked McClellan, demanding that the "traitor" be terminated as commander. Sprague agreed, arguing that Antietam had been a Confederate victory. Curtin defended McClellan for not only winning the decisive battle, but also for saving Pennsylvania, and asked who would replace him. "Frémont" would replace the commander, Andrew replied. At that point, Tod questioned anyone who would attempt to remove McClellan, given his popularity with the soldiers. Curtin looked for support from Bradford, who acknowledged that while "there was a blemish in McClellan's character," the timing was all wrong for removal. For the next several hours the governors debated, with Yates, Andrew, and Sprague opposing Curtin, Bradford, and Tod. Olden was absent from the meeting, so McClellan got no support from his native state of New Jersey.[64]

The discussion went on until about 8:00 P.M., when the governors recessed a second time. They reconvened an hour later, when Andrew presented a resolution that endorsed Lincoln's Emancipation Proclamation and "reaffirmed radical principles," including significant command changes. So animated was the governor that a correspondent for a Washington-based paper peering through the hotel windows commented on his physical gestures during the meeting. The governors continued their earlier discussions over Northern desires for a shorter war, and, lacking any hope for a renewed sense of purpose, decided Lincoln's proclamation might provide the spark, but only if commanders embraced it. Therefore, McClellan and Buell would have to be replaced.[65]

The governors worked late into the night and drew crowds of Altoonans and reporters to the parlor. Just fifteen years old, John Markley had been sent to Altoona that day for an old egg stove and, on reaching the town, inquired what the attraction was at the hotel. Learning that the Union governors were in conference, he worked his way to the window. He had "a desire to see what a Governor looked like" and managed to peer through the window at the "sober and intelligent lot of men."[66] Newspaper correspondents remained glued to the doors, listening intently. Their peering through the keyhole and parlor windows added drama to the closed meeting. By midnight the governors' emerging decisions were wired to those governors not in attendance, and the proxies of Holbrook, Gamble, and Robinson (KS) came over the wires, confirming their agreement with Lincoln's proclamation and the governors' course to press for a more vigorous war. As the clock moved toward 3:00 a.m., the meeting waned. Governors agreed to support Lincoln's proclamation and urged him to organize 100,000 reserves for emergencies like the one in Maryland. They also requested that Lincoln establish an ambulance corps to relieve Halleck of caring for the wounded. By night's end the meeting adjourned, and reporters swarmed the executives leaving the parlor. One correspondent stopped Andrew and queried whether the meeting had been satisfactory. Fatigued, Andrew shrugged and replied "I suppose some may think so" and retired to his room.[67]

Members elected Bradford to draft the resolutions into an address to be wired to Lincoln and those governors not present. Although some governors had expressed their dissatisfaction with members of Lincoln's cabinet, it was decided to leave that matter out. Governors who signed the address in Altoona included Curtin, Andrew, Yates, Washburn, Salomon, Kirkwood, Morton (Rose), Sprague, Pierpont, Tod, and Berry. Blair arrived from

Detroit in the early morning in time to affix his signature to the "Address." Buckingham, Fairbanks, Robinson (KS), Ramsey, and Whiteaker wired their approval. Olden, Morgan, Burton, Gamble, Bradford, and Robinson (KY) declined to sign the Altoona manifesto. It was ironic that Bradford, who framed the address, wavered over whether slavery had anything to do with the war. He thought the meeting "serviceable," and he was with them "in heart and soul," but he was a poor man, and signing the address might ruin him. "It was not that I questioned the propriety of striking an *effectual* blow at the rebellion, by means of slavery, [or] that I doubted the policy of that act," he later wrote Montgomery Blair, "on the contrary could the President by proclamation or otherwise effectively emancipate every slave in the South and thereby subtract from the power of the rebellion four millions of its inhabitants. I should rejoice to see it done and as a necessary means of shortening the war," but he worried over the constitutional implications.[68] The governors pledged their support of Lincoln and declared that "the decision of the President to strike at the root of the rebellion will lend new vigor to the efforts and new life and hope to the hearts of the people."[69] Lincoln accepted the telegraphic address and responded to Andrew: "The Emancipation Proclamation has been promulgated. Come to Washington for further conference."[70]

Editor of the Springfield, Massachusetts, *Republican*, Josiah G. Holland, reported after the war that Lincoln admitted he hardly took notice of the Altoona meeting. "The fact is," Holland remembered Lincoln saying, "I never thought of the meeting of the governors at Altoona, and I can hardly remember that I knew anything about it."[71] Holland's recollection contradicted the record and obscured Altoona's significance. Lincoln was aware of the meeting, had been in contact with at least two governors, and understood its political significance. In a postwar interview with historian Rufus Wilson, Curtin described that "there was a full and complete agreement between the President and the gentlemen who took part in the Altoona conference." He maintained that "Andrew and I went to see the President," and "he told us that he was preparing a proclamation that would emancipate slaves, and asked us if it would not be advisable for him to wait until we had requested him to act before issuing it. We told him by all means he should issue it first and we would at once follow it up with a strong address of commendation and support. As a result of our interview with the President it was agreed that the course which Governor Andrew and I proposed should be followed." Curtin acknowledged that governors "feared that the bold stand would cost us one election, but subsequent events showed that we struck while the iron was hot and had touched the popular chord."[72]

If Lincoln was "reluctant to be out in front of public opinion," many governors had no problem leading the charge, even at the risk of their political futures.[73] Despite their individuality as state leaders, most governors shared the same party affiliation, and by mid-September they had one common goal—supply manpower to end the war quickly and remove obstacles, including slavery, to achieve that goal. They were not meeting to embarrass the government nor Lincoln, but rather to add credibility to the national government's handling of the war. Coincidence or not, some governors, such as Andrew and Curtin, concluded in the summer that the only way to end the war sooner was to emancipate Confederate slaves, but only Lincoln had the power to do so. Numerous papers published the address as evidence that governors had significant influence in restoring confidence among national leaders, and reassured soldiers that political leaders were strengthening the army. Even the obscure Amherst, New Hampshire, paper *The Farmer's Cabinet* published the governors' address to Lincoln. Nearly two years later, Kentucky congressman Robert Mallory challenged George Boutwell on the House floor regarding Altoona's significance and its connection to the conduct of the war. Under the editorial guise "A Historical Enigma," the *Washington Daily National Intelligencer* ran the conversation between Mallory and Boutwell to assert the governors' importance. Mallory contended that the war had been changed by the Emancipation Proclamation, which he added was the result of the "'pressure' of certain Republican Governors, assembled in convention at Altoona, in Pennsylvania, which, in connection with other influences tending to the same end, had caused the President to abandon his original policy in this matter."[74] Boutwell denied the relevance of the Altoona meeting, arguing that Antietam was the singular contingency prompting the proclamation. If that were the case, the editor rebutted, why had the president argued against the proclamation to "the Chicago memorialists," shortly before the meeting?[75]

Whatever influence governors had on Lincoln's decision to announce his Emancipation Proclamation came from their decision to meet in Altoona, not the actual conference. James G. Randall argued decades ago that the significance of the governors' influence was that such a meeting was called at all, not in what was discussed, because the battle of Antietam had "stolen their thunder" and provided the victory Lincoln needed to announce his preliminary proclamation. Blair observed at the time that the real significance of the governors' gathering was the effect their unanimity in favor of Emancipation had on the country, a sentiment Alexander McClure confirmed years later in a conversation he reputedly had with Confederate vice-president Alexander Stephens. It was Curtin, Stephens argued, who "delivered the most destructive blow to the South in 1862," when Southerners "believed that the North was on the point of surrendering the conflict." It was "the Altoona Conference of Northern Governors," the former vice-president declared, that was the turning point. "But for that conference," he went on, "the North would have been demoralized by the emancipation proclamation and the failures of the Union army, and that peace would have come on some compromise and honorable basis."[76]

Still, the press and its sensational portrayal of the meeting played a role in how the conference was remembered. According to the *New Hampshire Patriot and State Gazette*, it would "go down in history as a conclave convoked by uneasy ambitious, disloyal demagogues, for the consummation of some foul conspiracy against a country which their reckless and mercenary projects had already brought to the very brink of ruin."[77] Many correspondents, including a reporter from the *Chicago Tribune*, argued that the governors were simply trying to hold up the president's hands "until final victory crowns the arms of the republic."[78] Yet the editor of the *Weekly Wisconsin Patriot* declared from Madison that the meeting would "stink in the nostrils of the people for ages."[79] A correspondent to the *New York World* perhaps best summarized the damage done by the press about the conference. "However questionable the policy of their meeting may have been," he wrote, "vastly more harm has been done by the lying and sensational reports concerning their action than could have been done by the meeting itself."[80] Indeed, when Berry read the *New York Herald's* report, he rebuffed the wild accusations days later by writing a letter to the editor, arguing that "the implications contained in the correspondence from Altoona are without foundation." He declared, "The meeting was characterized by the most kindly harmony of sentiment and unanimity of action in support of the Government in a most vigorous prosecution of the war for the suppression of the Rebellion."[81]

Governors Go to Washington

The governors arrived in Washington on 26 September, and their presence there was more impressive than it was in Altoona. Lincoln greeted the governors around noon. Despite reports about the governors' secret intentions, the meeting was a symbolic cooperative gesture between the nation and the states. From the governors Lincoln needed men and continued support, and from the president the governors needed change to inspire men to come forward and a continued recognition that Lincoln's national war was state-driven. Governors understood the war at the local level: they saw the men off, exchanged correspondence, walked through the camps, and attended to their welfare. In an election year, it remained to be seen if these changes would result in Republican victories.[82]

Lincoln accepted the Altoona address, thanked the governors, and acknowledged that their support had assured him of his decision to issue his proclamation. He related the origins of the document. "There is a little history connected with that Proclamation," the president told the governors. "I wrote it last spring and folded it up and placed it in my drawer." He said, "It was written and lying there when Mr. Greely [sic] made that strong demand for a proclamation of emancipation, to which I replied. I suppose you all have seen both papers." He explained that, one day after a cabinet meeting, he pulled the document from his drawer, read it to his colleagues, and asked for their reaction. Chase immediately approved, and, in the silence that followed, Seward spoke up, remarking "I don't think it would be wise to issue that proclamation now. In the face of the bad fortune we have had in the field it will sound like a Spanish pronunciamento. I would advise you to wait until we have some military success." Lincoln confessed, "I put it back in the drawer and it staid there until after the battle of Antietam."[83]

The three-hour conversation then turned to a series of specific requests, which Lincoln promised he would consider. Having traveled from Iowa, Kirkwood was not about to leave without commenting that McClellan was not popular among Iowans, and that he was unfit to command an army. "Although his men were well equipped, well disciplined, and fought as bravely as men ever fought," he said, hunching forward, "they were constantly being defeated."[84] Lincoln tried to spin a joke out of the remark. "You Iowa people then judge generals as you do lawyers," he smiled, "by their success in trying cases." Kirkwood responded, "Yes, something like that; the lawyer who is always losing his cases, especially when he was right and had justice on his side don't get much practice in Iowa." Lincoln kept up his good humor, such that Kirkwood pressed his luck. "Mr. President," he said, "our Iowa people fear and I fear the Administration is afraid to remove Gen. McClellan." Lincoln's temper changed, and Kirkwood changed his tone.

Understand me, we fear that the strong efforts made by Gen. McClellan and his toadies in the army to attach his soldiers to him personally and their efforts and the efforts of a certain class of politicians outside the army to cause his soldiers to believe that the severe criticisms to which the General has been subjected are intended to apply to them (the soldiers) as well as to him (their commander) have so prejudiced his soldiers' minds as to make it unsafe to remove him for fear his removal might cause insubordination, perhaps mutiny; that is what I meant when I spoke of your being afraid to remove him.[85]

Lincoln listened intently and then slowly, but "with emphasis," responded, "Gov. Kirkwood, if I believed our cause would be benefitted by removing Gen. McClellan to-morrow, I would remove him to-morrow," but "I do not so believe to-day, but if the time shall come when I shall so believe," he ended, "I will remove him promptly, and not till then."[86]

Kirkwood fired another shot across Lincoln's bow. "I should be glad, Mr. President, to be able to tell the people of Iowa that you believe in the loyalty and patriotism of George B. McClellan," he added. Removing his feet from atop the desk, Lincoln sprang to his feet, straightened up "two inches taller than usual," and snapped back, "Loyal! George B. McClellan is as loyal as any one of you." He then paused and captured his composure. "I'll tell you gentlemen," he confided, "Gen. McClellan is an exceedingly well-informed General, and is very careful, in fact, too careful, and the great trouble with him is that when he wins a victory he doesn't know what to do with it." Blair then played his hand. "Why not *try* another man, Mr. Lincoln," he suggested. Lincoln responded, "Ah; but I might lose an army by that."[87] This "unhorsed" Blair and diffused the tension of the moment, but Blair, Kirkwood, and others were not convinced. Still, the group talked for nearly three hours, "running over a great many topics, in which the greatest harmony prevailed."[88]

Lincoln had been uncertain about the impact of emancipating slaves, but the governors' arrival in Washington reassured him that it was the right thing to do. Confiscation, state drafts, excessive bounties, what more was there to expand the war to entice Northerners to volunteer? From Hartford, Buckingham wrote Lincoln the same day congratulating him on emancipation. "Have we not too long deluded ourselves with the idea that mild and conciliatory measures would influence them to return to their allegiance," he queried, adding, "I trust we shall press with increased energy and power every war measure, as the most economical, humane, and Christian policy which can be adopted to save our national Union."[89]

So it was that Lincoln yielded to the war's exigencies. "Next to the Proclamation of Emancipation," remarked Philadelphia journalist John Russell Young, the Altoona conference was "the most decisive civil event of the war," as it "roused the latent fires of the Union."[90] It was a "weathervane" that calibrated the Radical Republican's long-term political goals, yet its immediate impact was questionable.[91] That no formal proceedings were kept at Altoona added to its mystery, which the Democratic press used to incite an already swelling peace movement. According to one contemporary, the conference was "the best political means attainable for carrying the loyal state organizations through the powerful undercurrents of this trying navigation," in meeting their obligations to the Union.[92] It reinforced the national government both militarily and politically, and the Republican press considered it a rather innocuous event. "Mr. Lincoln and the Governors in Perfect Accord," ran the *New York Tribune* 29 September headline certifying Northern solidarity.[93]

The governors remained in Washington for several days and held separate interviews with Lincoln. Given West Virginia's tenuous statehood, Pierpont asserted his place at Altoona. His emerging state had committed thousands of loyalists to the Union ranks, but citizens had not settled the question of slavery. Congress had not acted, and opponents protested against abolitionist interference with state institutions. Pierpont asked Lincoln if he was "satisfied that all the members of his cabinet were the best men he could select, and if he had assurances that the union sentiment of the country fully approved of them."[94] Lincoln discussed the merits of his political team and, after a short pause, related a humorous story to Pierpont, and requested that he not to repeat it, and sent him on his way.[95]

Chase took advantage of the governors' visit to Washington. He left a card at the National Hotel desk to see Berry, went to see Kirkwood, and later called on Salomon, Andrew, Bradford, Sprague, Tod, Blair, Yates, and Pierpont at Willard's. Yates and McClernand accepted his dinner invitation, and the commander "made a very favorable impression" on Chase by outlining his plan for opening the Mississippi River. He was so taken with the commander's idea that he promised him an interview with the president. When Stanton got wind of the meeting, he asked Lincoln what he thought of his Illinois commander. Lincoln replied that although brave and capable, McClernand was "too desirous to be independent of everybody else," and left it at that.⁹⁶ Nonetheless, Lincoln invited McClernand to accompany him to Antietam, and along the way the commander did some campaigning of his own.⁹⁷

Yates visited Stanton to gain support for the western war. When he arrived at the War Department he witnessed the secretary dismiss Kirkwood "as if he were the subordinate officer of a country militia company."⁹⁸ Yates took offense and commented to John Moses that "it would be just as well for the Secretary not to attempt any kind of 'foolishness' with him." Turning toward Yates, Stanton remarked, "well, there is another one of them gone; I was in hopes I had gotten rid of you d—d Governors-what do you want, Yates?" Yates replied, "By G—d, sir, I want, in the first place, to be treated like a gentleman." "I would like to have you understand, Stanton," Yates responded, "that I am the Governor of the great State of Illinois, and as such am entitled to be respected." "I'd like to know what would become of you, or this war," he scolded the secretary, "but for the support of the loyal Governors of the free States." "I did not come here to beg for anything," he stated, "but to inform you, as the head of the War Office of the Government, what are the just demands of the State of Illinois, which I am here to see respected." The atmosphere was tense, but Stanton cowered, apologized, and explained there had been "an unusual amount of friction in his office that morning," and asked the governor to "overlook his abruptness and apparent want of courtesy." The two men calmed down, and by the end of their meeting, departed on friendly terms. Yates never again trusted Stanton.⁹⁹

Although Lincoln's Emancipation Proclamation had not fully satisfied the Radical governors, many figured the proclamation would prove the death knell of the Confederacy. Sprague wrote Lincoln that his "Proclamation changes somewhat the policy of the war," but without soldiers to liberate slaves it was nothing more than a political gesture. The governor pressed Lincoln about enlisting black soldiers, arguing that it would not only add manpower to the armies, but also reinforce the North's commitment to ending the war at all costs. He maintained "this would kill the prejudice, and confine public opinion to but one issue, and compell [sic] all to unite."¹⁰⁰ Although he did not care to be authorized to raise the first regiment, he advised Lincoln to give Andrew the authority. Lincoln refused.¹⁰¹

In the flurry of dispatches related to Lee's Maryland invasion, the Emancipation Proclamation, and the governors' conference, Lincoln had little time to celebrate Republican victories in September's elections. Given the demoralizing summer losses and threat of conscription, successes in Vermont, Maine, and California strengthened Republican management of the war. Holbrook easily defeated Peace Democrat Benjamin Smalley, and Republicans retained a majority in the legislature. In Maine, Republican Abner Coburn won the governorship over Democrat Bion Bradbury, and his party also carried the legislature. A Maine native, the fifty-nine-year-old Coburn had been trained to take over the family farm and surveying business. He attended the common schools and worked alongside his father learning the cattle business. After a few years he joined his father and brother Philander in the firm of Eleazar Coburn & Sons. When his father died, he and his brother inherited the business, renamed it A & P Coburn Surveyors, and made a career of buying, surveying, and timbering Maine's vast forests. The brothers became the largest landowners in Maine, and Coburn eventually became the president of the Maine Central Railroad. By the 1830s, he joined the Whig Party and served as a state representative. He joined Washburn in founding Maine's Republican Party in 1854 and had served on the councils of the previous two governors Hannibal Hamlin and Joseph Williams.[102]

Stanford rallied California Republicans to support Lincoln's expanding war policy, and in their recent election, they won 94 of the 120 seats in the legislature. As the war deepened the cleavage among Radicals, moderates, and conservatives, Stanford stood with the administration. From Sacramento, he wired a 7 September cable to Lincoln that read: "Our general election was held yesterday. The result is a triumph and overwhelming victory in favor of the Union and the National Administration."[103] The governor also noted the Emancipation Proclamation's significance and remarked to the legislature that it would be "memorable as the commencement of a new era in human progress."[104]

As much as governors believed they had an accurate read on their constituents, no one could have predicted what lay ahead. If conscription and emancipation removed obstacles to the Radical Republican path to war, it nonetheless strengthened antiblack and antifederal expansion Democrats clinging to a conservative course. The division among governors at Altoona gave the opposition conspiratorial leverage. Critics vehemently resisted conscription and the proclamation, and some governors had difficulty convincing legislators that it was an appropriate war measure, and thus had trouble soliciting funds to support bounties. Bradford's refusal to sign the Altoona Address encouraged Maryland and New Jersey Democrats to stand firm against expanding Union war aims. Conditions were such in Missouri that Gamble requested federal funds to defend against guerrillas retaliating against

Lincoln's proclamation. The governor was desperate, and while he did not embrace Lincoln's new pronouncement, he recognized the utility of its objective, and counseled his constituents to support his cause.[105]

As much as governors believed conscription and emancipation would fill the armies, it came at significant cost. Changing the means to hasten the war's conclusion, they believed, would increase opposition seeking to undermine their efforts. Congressional and state election setbacks in the fall underscored the degree to which Democrats could assail Republicans for moving too quickly on emancipation. Yet it did not deter them. To stifle opposition, Lincoln suspended the writ of habeas corpus throughout the country two days after announcing his preliminary proclamation. Lee's departure from Maryland brightened Northern skies, but Bragg's army threatened the Kentucky capital. Morton had gone to Louisville the week before, listened to the soldiers' complaints against Buell, and demanded his removal. He included in his attacks the "foul-mouthed bully" Nelson, whose disparaging remarks toward Indianans led to his death in late September. Indiana Colonel Jefferson C. Davis gunned down Nelson in Louisville's Galt House Hotel. Morton was present at the killing, and news blazed through the press. Days later, Morton left for Washington to urge Lincoln to remove Buell, which he did. Robinson, however, needed Buell in command because he believed the commander's removal would "operate most disastrously upon the Union cause in KY." He wrote, "I assure you Mr. President that it is the universal opinion of every Gentleman of loyalty & intelligence here that the displacement of Genl Buell from his present command will do more injury to the military operations in Kentucky than any movement that could be made."[106] Robinson got his wish, and Lincoln reinstated Buell.[107]

CHAPTER ELEVEN

Sinking in Despair

On the morning of 1 October, Lincoln left Washington for Antietam. It had been nearly two weeks since the battle that inspired his decision to make the Emancipation Proclamation, and it was time he witnessed the sacrifice that justified his pronouncement. Initial response to emancipation discouraged him, and he was not surprised by the war he provoked at home. Still, he believed that once the public clamor against him waned, citizens would see the proclamation's crippling effects on the Confederacy. Governors had convinced him that they had no choice. Lincoln spent the next few days walking among the camps and makeshift hospitals. A Maine chaplain remarked that "it did us all good," to "look into his [Lincoln's] honest face as he rode in front of every regiment of the corps separately, uncovering his head at every regimental flag."[1] He probably missed what was left of the 7th Maine, a unit for which Washburn held special affection. So pathetically "reduced and shattered" was the regiment that McClellan ordered the remaining sixty-five soldiers home, writing to Washburn "that it might be recruited and reorganized under your personal supervision."[2] Still, no matter how many men came forward, they could not account for the thousands lost at Antietam.

Northerners expected better news from the West. Confederate Generals Earl Van Dorn and Sterling Price had pinned down General William S. Rosecrans's Union army in Arkansas, preventing him from sending reinforcements to Buell. The battle that never commenced at Corinth in May when Beauregard slipped away from Halleck now bloodied the tiny Mississippi hamlet in a two-day fight that took place 3–4 October. Although Federals won the engagement, the Confederates slipped away. Bragg's invasion of Kentucky, meanwhile, had thrown the entire Midwest into a panic, and the fall elections were pulling men home to vote. The invasion so outraged one Kentucky chaplain, he wrote to Robinson that he was inspired to "buckle on a 'revolver,' shoulder a double barreled shot gun, & go with other native Kentuckians in pursuit of the robber."[3]

The Confederate invasion prevented Morton from attending Altoona, and the governor blamed Buell. Indignant, he traveled to Washington to have the commander removed. When he arrived at Brown's Hotel, he fired off a letter to Lincoln that if the army did not make great progress within the next sixty days the cause would be nearly lost. He highlighted the problems with relying on paper money, the dangers of foreign intervention to assist the Confederates, and command problems, which came from having a leader whose heart was not in the cause. Union armies would never succeed, he argued, until Lincoln placed the leadership in the hands of men who were in earnest of prosecuting the war. What Morton failed to say to Lincoln he worked into an impromptu speech in front of the Metropolitan Hotel to more than a thousand congregants. "We were suffering from many evils," he declared, "one of which was that all our generals had parties. McClellan, Frémont, Pope, Buell, all had their parties."[4]

Governors awaited favorable news from the front that October, but when reports arrived they were good, not great. Colonel Thomas Allen informed Yates, "'we have met the enemy,' whipped them, but they are not ours!"[5] The battle along Doctor's Creek near Perryville, Kentucky, fought 8 October, ended in Union victory. Yet even with fewer troops engaged, Buell's army suffered more casualties than Bragg, who stole away southeast. Thus the Union had effectively gained nothing more than it already controlled, and it allowed the enemy to escape. The news of Perryville failed to bolster Union hopes. In fact, it added to the hostility already swirling about the maddeningly slow Buell. Mounting casualties and failure to pursue to the enemy in Maryland, and now in Kentucky, weighed heavily on governors looking to inspire volunteers.[6]

Swords at the Ballot Box

The battleground moved to the ballot box in October. Another wave of state elections was about to break, and the results could change the war. Northerners boasted about progress, but they complained that it came at great sacrifice. They had not forgotten the summer's failed military campaigns, and Lincoln's proclamation had led to more Northern acrimony. The suspension of the writ of habeas corpus did not help public acceptance. Political opponents attacked Lincoln as a dictator and despot, a man who trampled the Constitution. The longer the war, the greater the popular dissent, and governors used what influence they had to shore up support. Stanton dispatched provost-marshals to the states, and governors used them to arrest draft resisters and citizens who discouraged enlistment, engaged in treasonable acts, or intimidated voters. Voters were encouraged to separate devotion to the cause from devotion to its leaders. The call for men during summer harvest was fraught with bureaucratic disaster. The defeat at Bull Run as well as the stalemates at Antietam and Perryville left little hope for Northerners that thought Republicans could bring an end to the conflict. The "mighty act" of emancipation left the old Union behind, and forced citizens to consider the implications of black migration. Blair made his views clear to legislators who were considering a constitutional amendment that would enfranchise blacks. The time had come, he argued "when the colored men of America should be allowed to assume their rightful position as citizens of the Republic, *upon an equality in all respects with their white brethren*, and especially that Michigan ought no longer to permit in her constitution a word which creates an unjust distinction between her citizens."[7]

Some governors shared Blair's Radical views, but others, such as Yates, had problems reconciling their proequality views with unreceptive legislatures. Illinois assemblymen, for example, passed laws forbidding blacks from entering the state, and the army's collection of refugee slaves at Cairo violated the state's "Negro Exclusion" law. "The colorphobia of all the West is intense," wrote a Chicago correspondent, "you have no idea of the strength and meanness of the prejudice against the unfortunate negro in two-thirds of the State."[8] On the election eve Yates had reason to be concerned. Robert Smith, an Alton, Illinois, Republican running for office, complained that a "great *fuss* is being made by Ultra Southern Sympathisers [*sic*], on account of *Negroes* coming into our State." "Cannot you get the President or Sec of War to *publish*, that there is no intention to send them," he urged. "I am a Candidate for Congress, and do not want votes made against me, on the Negro question."[9] When Dix considered shipping 2,000 refugees from Fortress Monroe to Northern cities to relieve their suffering, Andrew and Sprague initially approved, but asked Stanton to sideline the idea. Andrew presided over the Educational Commission for Freedmen, a Boston missionary group that sent agents into the South to help former slaves transition out of bondage, but sending them north before elections might prove costly. Besides, he was aware of the divided attitudes over black migration. Other New England governors feared their importation because they felt could not make the transition to the New England climate. They also feared these freedmen would remain jobless because they lacked skills. "Now what is the government to do with the contraband elephant," scoffed one New York paper, "the Western States won't have them, the Middle

States don't want them, and now even Gov. Andrew promptly declares that they shan't set foot upon the soil of the old Bay State."[10] Andrew understood that as much as abolition was alive in New England, many citizens would not abandon their conservatism. One Windsor, Vermont, father wrote to his sons in the army that as far as he was concerned the blacks were "just about as much consequence as so many rattlesnakes," concluding that "the less we have to do with them the better we be off."[11]

Into this backdrop came the fall elections. Voters in New Hampshire, Rhode Island, and Connecticut had elected Republicans and Unionists earlier in the year before congressional changes and emancipation. In June, Oregonians had also elected a Republican-Unionist governor. In September, Maine, Vermont, and California voters favored the change in Union policies, but had not the advantage of passing judgment on emancipation. Thus, going into the fall canvass, Northerners had a question to answer: Had the president gone too far, or had he failed to go far enough in winning the war? Voters in Ohio, Indiana, and Pennsylvania cast their ballots in October, while the remaining Northern states held November elections. Several states held gubernatorial elections in the fall, including Delaware, Kansas, New York, New Jersey, Michigan, and Massachusetts. Still, much damage could be done by obstreperous legislatures voted in by these elections, and it was clear that both parties had been taken to extremes. For the Republicans, the Chandler-Wade-Sumner Radical cabal hoping to oust Buell and McClellan, arm black troops, and emancipate slaves battled the administrative conservative Seward-Blair-Bates triumvirate that drew fire by advocating gradual emancipation for a lenient reconstruction of the South. The Democrats had also lodged themselves into two camps. Those who favored an end to the war by negotiation without shredding the Constitution or emancipating slaves combated opponents proposing to end the war by fighting it, and who escaped suspicion by claiming to be loyal. Still, no matter the party, the issues were clear enough for even common folk to cast a ballot that gave them some sense they could change the war by voting. Some states had recently established mechanisms for soldiers to vote in the field.[12]

October's election results reflected Northern opposition to expanding federal aims and foretold significant changes. It presumed that the Altoona governors were ahead of their constituents, which was an odd position, given that many were elected annually. Democrats polled large majorities in the midwestern states, despite the governors' efforts in getting some troops furloughed home to vote. In Ohio, they took all state offices up for election and fourteen of the nineteen congressional seats. Indianans also elected congressional senators, including the seat left vacant by the expulsion of Jesse D. Bright, whom Morton replaced with Joseph Wright in January. When it was over, Indiana had gone to the Democrats. Morton's friend Calvin Fletcher penned the results in his diary, adding, "May God save my dear country."[13]

Whatever the president gained by emancipating rebel slaves, he lost by disaffecting Northern conservatives, who not only disagreed with him over emancipation, but also the suspension of the writ. Others opposed him for his retention of conservative commanders bent on waging their own war. Morton, Tod, Yates, and Blair received complaints from disgruntled soldiers and army correspondents arguing that Buell and McClellan had been the cause of recent political losses. These governors pursued their removal before the November elections and made plans for Washington. "In the Northwest distrust and despair are seizing upon the hearts of the people," Morton declared.[14] Given draft concerns, Morton was angry that he was forced to raise more men to fight under such imbecilic military commanders. "It is my solemn conviction," he wrote to Lincoln, "that we will never succeed until the leadership of our armies is placed in the hands of men who are greatly in earnest and who are profoundly convinced of the justice of our cause."[15] Tod wrote Stanton, "With one voice, so far as it has reached me, the army from Ohio demand the removal of General Buell."[16] Stanton responded that he had urged his removal for two months, "had it done once, when it was revoked by the President."[17]

The signs pointing Lincoln toward dismissing Buell and McClellan were clear. Horace White, Lincoln's close associate and chairman of the Illinois Republican Party State Central Committee, warned that "*if* we are beaten [politically] in this State two weeks hence," he declared, "it will be because McClellan & Buell *won't fight*."[18] Lincoln relieved Buell 24 October and replaced him with General William S. Rosecrans, who had recently won the battles of Corinth and Iuka. Yates and Morton were so relieved that they wired the president that Buell's dismissal rendered their trip unnecessary. To minimize the political fallout and retain a portion of the conservative vote, Lincoln left McClellan in command. Buell's dismissal and the governors' reaction provided McClellan a clue that he might be next if he refused to pursue the enemy, and two days later he crossed his army over the Potomac into Virginia.[19]

Electoral losses in October were not unexpected, but they worried Lincoln. Democrats had proven more effective in appealing to conservatives than the president imagined. Still, there was hope, as Pennsylvanians had gone Republican, and the prospects for victory looked promising for November's canvass. If soldiers were allowed to vote in the field, Republicans might have significant gains. Yates reported, however, that Illinois's returns were worse than those in Ohio and Indiana. Trumbull was so downcast he wrote Chandler that he feared a "humiliating compromise" was on the horizon. The result especially discouraged Yates, because he had aspirations of filling Douglas's old Senate seat, but needed a Republican majority in the legislature to carry him. Illinois Democrats, however, pulled off a grand sweep at the polls and sent a message to Lincoln that they now controlled the power of the purse and the power to override his patronage. "If *Politicians* desire a prolongation of this war, they can have it for a time," wrote a frustrated Chicagoan, "but I tell you Governor Yates, *the People*, are daily, & hourly arming themselves with a weapon which will one day fall with destructive force upon the heads of all intriguing, dishonest & deceptive Politicians—that weapon, is *intelligence*."[20]

Missourians had postponed their summer elections until November, when delegates arranged for soldiers to vote. Still, voters went to the polls under guard and elected a majority of emancipationist representatives, including Frank Blair. Even though Missouri was exempt from the Emancipation Proclamation, Gamble's lack of enthusiasm for it, and his hesitancy to wage harsh war at home, cost his party. Led by abolitionist Charles D. Drake, antislavery Radicals demanded immediate emancipation, and they needed Gamble to support their charge. Conservatives used Gamble to move toward gradual emancipation. Still, the election results gratified Lincoln, and Gamble, despite his enemies, managed to negotiate the difficult shoals of Missouri's political-military waters to maintain Republican support.[21]

Delawareans also went to the polls under supervision. Peace rallies led to several military arrests that summer, and Congressman Sidney George Fisher feared that with so many Republican voters away in the field, Democrats might disrupt the polls. He appealed to federal authorities to oversee the election by placing more than 1,000 troops at the polls. William Cannon, the Unconditional Unionist candidate for governor, knew the election would be close. Republican delegates unified themselves with war Democrats, changed their party name to the Union Party, and emphasized cause over leaders. Fisher requested that Stanton, Seward, and Weed pressure Lincoln for assistance. "We are in imminent danger of losing every thing here," he implored Weed, and he pleaded to meet with Lincoln and the governor in Washington.[22] On election day, Federal troops supervised one of the closest elections in Delaware history up to that point. Fisher's premonitions came true, as he lost his seat to Democrat William Temple. Although Delawareans assumed that Democrats would take the state legislature, voters surprised Cannon by electing him governor. With Cannon polling just over 100 more votes than Democratic candidate Samuel Jefferson, the press alleged that the Sussex County native stole the election under armed guard. Cannon was a judicious choice for governor. A self-made farmer and businessman, the enterprising Delawarean expanded his interests to include banking, and eventually he became director of the Delaware Railroad. As a Democrat, he served in the Delaware Assembly for two terms, first in 1845 and again in 1847, but delegates snubbed him three times when he attempted to secure the gubernatorial nomination. When the war broke out, Cannon supported the Union's war aims, and when he was mentioned as a possible candidate for governor, he left the Democrats and switched parties. After election, he faced a Democratic assembly that despised him for bolting the party and supporting Lincoln's abolitionist war. Still, one resident assigned reasons for his fitness for the office, saying he was "*an unconditional, sound, thorough Union man.*"[23]

Far to the west, Kansans also went to the polls in November amid the escalating Robinson-Lane feud. Lane led Republicans in supporting Leavenworth merchant Thomas Carney for governor. Having combated Lane long enough, Robinson lost his enthusiasm for the fight and stopped supporting Lincoln. Lane's enemies staged a Union Party convention and nominated Democrat William R. Wagstaff for governor. Still, they were no match for Lane's Republicanism, which produced Carney's victory, as well as the victory of Republican congressman A. Carter Wilder. In reporting the election returns, the *Emporia News* editor noted that Kansans "don't take any half-way does," in supporting emancipation, "they go the whole hog."[24] At thirty-five years old, Kansas's second governor had a pedigree much like many of his fellow citizens, but he was no political charlatan. The native Ohioan worked in the mercantile business and eventually became a partner in one of the country's most lucrative dry-goods businesses. In 1857 he ventured to Leavenworth and became among the state's wealthiest citizens, using his personal fortune to assume the payment of the state debt to eastern banks. Kansans never forgot his generosity. "No man in Kansas is better qualified" for the governorship than Carney, declared the *Leavenworth Daily Times*, whose "integrity and strict honesty" would prove "a guarantee against any repetition of the disgraceful occurrences which have marked the action of our State Executive so far."[25] Carney's governorship came under Lane's watchful eye, and under the command of General Samuel R. Curtis, who in September took over the newly created Department of Missouri, which included Kansas, Missouri, Arkansas, and the Indian Territory.[26]

New York voters were no less conflicted than Kansans, Delawareans, or Missourians, and the election results were mortifying. The Republican press declared that to lose the state was just as disastrous as was New Orleans falling under Union occupation. Morgan had decided he would not seek reelection, and it was just as well, since his moderate views and failure to appear at Altoona made him the "subject of barroom attacks" in certain New York boroughs. In fact, he looked forward to returning to business and was confident that Republicans would win the contest, confessing to Welles that James Wadsworth would win easily. Having canvassed the state, Senator Preston King confirmed Morgan's prediction. "We think there can be no reasonable doubt of Wadsworth's election," he assured Morgan, concluding that "the election of Seymour would be a great public calamity."[27] Yet New Yorkers did turn to hard-bitten states'-rights Constitutional Democrat Horatio Seymour for governor. Seymour laid the war's responsibility on the North and the Republican Party's fanatical leaders. "The country is to be brought back to the principles established by the founders," he told a Utica crowd.[28] Since the death of Stephen A. Douglas, it appeared that no Northern Democrat had assumed the mantle of the anti-Republican masses more than Seymour. Even popular congressman Roscoe Conkling, who had supported Lincoln, lost his seat. Seymour assumed the governorship of the largest and wealthiest state. Eager to exercise his new position, he promised to combat Lincoln's arbitrary arrests, "even if the streets be made to run red with blood."[29]

The conservative resurgence was genuine, and Sumner was inconsolable, writing to Lincoln that the political result was "worse for our country than the bloodiest disaster on any field of battle."[30] Well-known New York City socialite Maria Lydig Daly concurred, remarking in her diary that there "has never been so great a revolution of public feeling." She declared, "Everything two years ago was carried by the Republicans, but now radicals have ruined themselves and abolitionism."[31] Unsurprisingly, discouragement swept through the ranks. Walter Stone Poor of the 10th New York wrote that

Seymour's victory should be considered a turning point in the war. "I hope the government will receive it here for what it is," he declared, "a terribly earnest warning that there must be no trifling, no more delay, that politics must no longer control promotion, that treason cannot shield itself under the very shadow of the capitol, that imbecile generals must be laid aside."[32] Aware of the political fallout, Weed dashed off to Albany to steer Seymour toward more patriotic tendencies. A native of western New York, the fifty-two-year-old Seymour looked every bit the rabidly conservative lawyer politician that he was when his portrait appeared on the cover of *Harper's Weekly*. Admitted to the bar in 1832, Seymour began his political career as William L. Marcy's chief political lieutenant, and his service in the legislature made him a leader in the Democratic Party. He had previously served as governor and had clung to conservative values, expecting to keep government small, civil liberties untouched, Americans free from arbitrary arrests, and slaves where they were. He carried these views forth, but now faced a Republican-controlled legislature.[33]

Neighboring New Jerseyans also found fault with the Republican Party's handling of the war and made a dramatic change, but more in personalities than in politics. Voters elected Democrats to four out of five of the state's House seats, and Joel Parker, a Douglas Democrat, to the executive mansion, in a landslide victory. Parker won over Republicans and War Democrats by supporting a military end to the conflict and stifling party factionalism. He defeated Marcus L. Ward by the largest margin in state history up to that time. Discovering that "oil and water could be mixed very easily," the sarcastic *Newark Daily Mercury* claimed that his victory, though discouraging to the Republicans, was nonetheless a triumph for the "Union supporting wing of the party."[34] The affable, robust, and outspoken native was everything Olden was not. Parker developed into a remarkable stump speaker. When he was a young lawyer, peers had regarded him as a kind, genial, sociable man, and, as he matured, he possessed command of the courtroom as a brilliant prosecutor. He first entered politics in 1847 as a candidate to the House of Assembly, where he introduced personal and property tax reform and suffrage reform. When the war broke out Olden made Parker a major general of the state militia. He criticized Lincoln's administration as the war dragged on and, by the summer of 1862, targeted the president's suspension of the writ of habeas corpus as unconstitutional. A "strict constructionist," the new governor desired to restrict the national and the state governments to their "respective constitutional spheres."[35]

In other states, Republican and Unionist voters unified to reelect incumbent governors. Blair's participation at Altoona and his support of emancipation and black equality drew criticism from conservatives. Yet he remained the darling of the Michigan Radicals. Voters elected him for another two-year term over Byron G. Stout. Chandler also retained his seat. The Republican Unionist ticket kept "the true faith," according to the *New York Daily Tribune*, and gave Republicans their largest victories of any Northern state. "We saved the state," wrote state assemblyman Henry H. Crapo to his son William, "to stand by the side of Massachusetts. I am indeed proud to think that both my native & adoptive states are true to the cause of free institutions, & our government."[36] Massachusetts voters also kept the Radical faith, although Republicans split over Lincoln's emancipation and Sumner's reelection. Radicals remained steadfast behind Andrew, but conservatives fashioned themselves into the People's Party and nominated Charles Devens. The governor's opposition came chiefly from critics who believed he harassed Lincoln into the announcing the Emancipation Proclamation. Andrew took little part in the campaign, contending that if his record would not reelect him, he preferred to be defeated. "The meeting [at Altoona]," he declared, "was one which, whether as citizens or magistrates, we had a right to hold."[37] Whatever his faults, it was hard to deny the governor's impressive record, and he won by more than 25,000 votes, although he lost in Boston.[38]

Marching On

Democratic victories gained Northerners' attention, but they by no means spelled disaster for the Union. Republicans, in some cases, adjusted electoral procedures to allow soldiers to vote, which helped maintain their control in Congress. Even in states where Democrats won the governorship, it did not portend that they would not support the Union in subduing the military conflict. "The victory of the Democratic party doesn't mean that the North is opposed to the war, or sympathizes with the rebellion," wrote Lieutenant Samuel Fiske to the *Springfield Republican* from Fredericksburg, "but it does mean that the nation is disgusted with the mode in which the war has been carried on."[39] The fall elections reflected national disagreement over conscription, emancipation, and the suspension of habeas corpus, yet governors remained committed to the men. First and foremost, soldiers needed to be assured that their governors agreed with the policies they were enforcing in the field. Campaigning in Mississippi, Captain William B. Britton of the 8th Wisconsin wanted his governor to embrace Lincoln's emancipation, arguing that "every man in my company would vote for a man that would use his influence in congress to have the war carried on to the satisfaction of the large majority of the people of the north—that is, no compromise—war for the Union—war to the end." His regiment's motto was " 'Leave nothing and take everything.' "[40]

Sidetracked by the elections, governors struggled to meet their quotas, labored over enrollment, and combated draft opposition. Enrolling military-age males during elections turned violent and forced provost marshals to arrest and detain rebellious citizens until after elections. Andrew reported that while 15,000 men had come forward to volunteer, he was still several thousand short. Consequently he would have to draft, which fell chiefly on Boston, a city he declared was "more slack" in its enlistments than any other section of the state. He kept some troops on alert to counter potential riots resulting from delays in bounties and advance pay. Tod petitioned Stanton about offering bounties and advance pay after the original 15 September draft date, but Stanton refused. Without any "well-defined authority," the governor exempted all state and county officers as well as citizens of "religious denominations whose creed forbids taking up arms," for payment of $200. He used the funds for soldier relief and for hiring substitutes, and reported that Ohio's draft progressed "harmoniously." Curtin, however, had warned the War Department that refusing the advance pay and bounties would cause disaffection. Formidable resistance had formed in Pennsylvania, and "we must treat the draft delicately in this State," he admonished Stanton. Resistance in Schuylkill County, a western mining community, forced Curtin to ask for a suspension, but the secretary refused. Curtin was ill at the time and relied on Alexander McClure to appeal to Lincoln. To avoid civil-military collision, Lincoln suggested the governor should work with the draft commissioner to adjust the quotas, allowing him to exempt the miners before the troops strong-armed workers into compliance.[41]

For those states that had not met their quotas, Stanton threatened to send in energetic provost marshals. In Wisconsin, Indiana, and Maryland, where there was dangerous opposition, he authorized the governors to use troops. When more than 1,000 armed men attacked the draft commissioner in Ozaukee County, Wisconsin, Salomon ordered out eight companies and subdued the uprising. To make an example of the affair, the governor arrested 150 protestors. The prisoners later appealed and won a ruling from the state supreme court that Lincoln had no power to suspend the writ of habeas corpus in Wisconsin, and the case turned into a legal tug-of-war between civil and military authorities that lasted for weeks. In this politically charged environment, the draft continued, but conditions deteriorated. Determined to deter other such scenes, Salomon issued a proclamation to his fellow Milwaukeeans that it was his duty to "execute this draft," and that he would not "shrink from the responsibilities which the laws impose upon me." He warned, "If bloodshed should occur, the responsibility must fall upon the heads of those who resist the laws."[42]

Despite the delays in raising men and bounties, Union armies moved further south. Lincoln endorsed an expedition to Vicksburg, and Stanton asked western governors for regiments. Yates responded that he would "strain every nerve to let the largest number possible of Illinoisans participate in the proposed glorious expedition."[43] The governor had played a role in getting McClernand an independent command, thinking it might diffuse Democratic opposition, but the commander would be operating in the same region where Grant was already organizing a campaign. Nonetheless, he headed back to Illinois, but stopped off at Indianapolis to discuss his plans with Morton, who endorsed the idea. The governor believed that after a fatiguing summer campaign that wasted valuable men and Northern patience, such a campaign would cultivate administrative and political support among disgruntled citizens. Besides, rumors were afoot that midwesterners were considering "a Northwestern Confederacy—as a preparatory step to annexation with the South," he told Lincoln, and that recent political rhetoric encouraged westerners to believe that they had "no interests or sympathies in common with the people of the Northern and Eastern states."[44] Lincoln understood Morton's concerns, but when McClernand steamed into Springfield in late October and prepared for his campaign, it caused evils of a different sort.[45]

Lincoln's problems were just beginning that fall. As much as governors supported emancipation and conscription, they needed Lincoln to understand the gravity of home-front reactions to these new directions. Curtin recovered from his illness and traveled to Washington in early November to confer with Lincoln over election results and Stanton's maddening response to the Schuylkill episode. They might also have discussed McClellan's future, since the meeting coincided with Lincoln's decision to remove the commander. On 7 November the president removed McClellan and placed Burnside at the helm of the battered Army of the Potomac. McClellan's dismissal overshadowed the appointment of Banks in New Orleans to command the Department of the Gulf. Clearly, opening the Mississippi River was the commander in chief's main design, and the crass and ungovernable Butler would no longer do.[46]

It was no secret that McClellan had not lived up to expectations. Governors welcomed the removal of the inert mass called McClellan and believed they had something to do with his dismissal. Sprague telegraphed Lincoln, "Manhood and I thank you Sir for changing the Commanding General Army Potomac."[47] Buckingham ordered a salute of 100 guns at Hartford on the occasion of McClellan's departure. On the eve of an offensive campaign, however, confidence, organization, and eye for detail departed with the commander. If his dismissal solved one problem, it created others, and Lincoln's cabinet members aired their views about his decisions. The state of military affairs disgusted Halleck. He had enough of the shameful prodding of generals, the loathsome political posturing, and the constant hand-holding of Burnside. He confided to Gamble that "there is an immobility here that exceeds all that any man can conceive of." He added, "It requires the lever of Archimedes to move this inert mass."[48] By mid-November Burnside had presented a plan of attack to Lincoln and headed for Fredericksburg, where Lee's army was concentrating along the Rappahannock River, just 50 miles north of Richmond. For all that had gone wrong, brighter days were expected. Sprague wired a congratulatory note to Burnside to boost his confidence and perhaps ingratiate himself into the command McClellan had denied him. "Your well known energy, skill, and patriotism, will, I feel sure, restore confidence to a disheartened people," Sprague wrote.[49] Although Kirkwood confessed to a friend that he "felt discouraged" as a result of the Democratic victories in the Northern elections, he was encouraged by the appointment of Burnside. "All we need is to have fighting Generals," he confided to Iowa congressman William B. Allison, "men who will allow our people to strike and we are safe."[50]

To compound manpower problems, Indian troubles remained a drain on western governors, and, pressed by concerns closer to Washington, Stanton was unreceptive. Years of injustice and exploitation exploded on the frontier, and governors in these regions managed two wars. Farther to the west, similar hostilities plagued newly elected Oregon governor Addison Gibbs, who had settled into his gubernatorial duties in early September. He struggled to maintain peace between overzealous transient miners seeking new mines, desperate farmers hoping to recover their losses from the previous year's ruins, and a weakened Nez Perce tribe that was on the warpath resulting from encroachments on their reservation. These heightened tensions, combined with safeguarding the Oregon Trail, confounded the new Republican governor. Governor Whiteaker, a Democrat, had not helped his successor. His farewell address, described by the correspondent to the *Portland Daily Times* as a "low, dirty, boiled down, double distilled, secession effort," offended incoming representatives.[51] Nonetheless, Gibbs wired Lincoln a copy of his inaugural address to the legislature with a note of confidence. "Continued reverses east and our indians [sic] may cause us trouble here, *when* we begin to collect taxes," he argued, "but I think we can preserve the peace."[52] Gibbs was a refreshing change for Oregonian Unionists and for Lincoln, yet white Oregonians and settlers in the nearby territory, and not the Indians, required the governor's attention. Citizens seeking new mining opportunities had exploited the Indians. In retaliation, Indian Agent John W. Anderson wrote that a portion of the Nez Perce tribe were disaffected toward the whites, and he feared they would retaliate on the settlers on their lands. In the meantime, Gibbs worked with General Wright to keep military units nearby the reservation to maintain peace, while allowing enterprising miners to continue to work the mines unobstructed. In reality, only the approaching winter helped Gibbs pacify civil discontent.[53]

In the upper Northwest the struggle between residents and the Dakota Indians spread, and governors grew frustrated by the administration's neglect. After using Minnesota troops for weeks in retaliation against the Indians, Ramsey appealed to Lincoln. "This is not our war," he declared, "it is a National War." He expected the president to treat it as such by sending troops.[54] When Pope arrived, he fell into the Dakota maelstrom and concluded the situation was beyond anything he imagined. "There will be no peace in this region," he wrote, until the "maniacs" and "wild beasts" had been killed or driven out.[55] Within six weeks, Sibley's expedition captured several hundred Sioux to stand trial for murder and rape. Anxious to commute executions, Ramsey insisted his white population could no longer tolerate their presence and that those convicted "assassins" would have to be executed and the others driven out of the state. He wired Lincoln that every Sioux Indian condemned by the military court would be executed. "It would be wrong upon principle and policy to refuse this," he argued.[56] Lincoln reviewed the broader issues. He dispatched his assistant secretary of the Interior John P. Usher to Minnesota to join Nicolay in surveying the state of affairs. Ramsey, however, wired Lincoln that "nothing but the Speedy execution of the tried and convicted Sioux Indians will save us here from Scenes of outrage."[57] Lincoln turned to Judge Advocate General Holt for advice, and together they worked through the list of more than 300 condemned Sioux warriors, whittling it down to thirty-nine Indians sentenced to be executed on 26 December.[58]

Throughout the fall, post-election analysis, Indian problems, and state drafts consumed national attention. Despite Stanton and Halleck's best intentions, the press located the blame in Washington, suggesting that administrative inertia had prolonged the war. Political leaders had frittered away the nation's resources, and the desire to distribute the burden of soldiering by conscripting men seemed ill timed. Perhaps the Mississippi River campaign could reinvigorate enlistments and capitalize on Lincoln's emancipation. Lincoln hoped for the same in the East. In late November he made a trip to Aquia Creek to confer with Burnside, who impressed the president with his plan to launch a frontal assault against Fredericksburg, where the Confederates had dug in. Stanton remained in Washington, preparing his report to Congress, and requested governors to provide him the numbers of volunteers mustered since July. In compiling their reports, governors reflected on the changes in recent months and issued proclamations to highlight the soldiers' sacrifices and to comfort citizens disillusioned by the war.[59]

Andrew shared his citizens' despondency. He was a dedicated reformer who advocated for the downtrodden, broken, and exploited classes. In his early days as a Boston lawyer, he visited prisons and freely advised inmates. He was devoted abolitionist, who had raised funds for John Brown's defense. The war gave him the opportunity to carry the Union's moral cause into the ranks. When he visited the soldiers, he reminded them of the war's true purpose—to advance free-soil principles and vindicate democracy. He had written Sumner that fall to enlist his support in suggesting to Stanton the idea of establishing a War Department bureau to handle the freed slaves who had been laboring for the Union army without pay. Stanton, however, paid it little attention, and the constant struggle to get the administration to embrace his Radicalism fatigued him. In the meantime, Andrew accepted an invitation to share his Thanksgiving meal with the family of Lewis Hayden, a former slave of Kentuckian Henry Clay, who had financed his own escape and ended up in Boston, where he ran a used clothing store and became an abolitionist. His Beacon Hill home had been a stop on the Underground Railroad. When the war broke out, Hayden found employment as a messenger in the Massachusetts Statehouse thanks to Andrew. It was during this dinner that Hayden and Andrew reputedly discussed influencing Lincoln to accept blacks into the military. Still, both gentlemen could be thankful they were not in Burnside's army assembling pontoons to cross the icy cold Rappahannock River to launch his offensive. "It looks very dark now as the old saying is," wrote Franklin J. Candee of the 2nd Connecticut from his Virginia camp, "*it is always darkest before its day* and I don't see how it can get any darker."[60]

December Blundering

As the Thirty-seventh Congress opened its lame-duck session on 1 December, Stoddard wrote from Washington that "winter is at last upon us in bitter earnest." He observed that "The suffering in the army must have been great for the past ten days," as the cold air chilled him to bone walking to Capitol Hill to hear Lincoln's address.[61] Yet there were graver concerns for the president. Negative reactions to his proclamation and his suspension of the writ of habeas corpus, as well as public acrimony over depleted army ranks, mounting casualties, and Indian problems all weighed heavily on his mind. Most worrisome was a demoralized army near Fredericksburg. Upon giving his "State of the Union" address to Secretary Nicolay, Lincoln was hopeful the year would end with military victory. He focused attention on foreign affairs, finances, the transcontinental railroad, agriculture, Indian affairs, and compensated emancipation. In his final paragraphs, he urged Congress to unite behind him in rising to the occasion, to "think and act anew" by casting off the "dogmas of the quiet past," which he argued were "inadequate to the stormy present." He argued, "Fellow-citizens, *we* cannot escape history," and in "*giving* freedom to the slave, we *assure* freedom to the *free*—honorable alike in what we give, and what we preserve." He challenged citizens, "We shall nobly save, or meanly lose the last best, hope of earth."[62]

Governors read Lincoln's eloquent address, but they scrutinized Stanton's report. Both documents revealed that saving the republic was more challenging than establishing one. Lincoln's calls for additional volunteers in July and August had produced just over 500,000 new volunteers. Most of these men were three-year enlistees, some of these originally drafted, and the remaining 86,000 to 87,000 men were nine-month militia drafted. Some states had filled their quotas without resorting to a draft. Still, the call for men, Stanton noted, afforded occasions for disloyal persons to work against the draft. Stanton understood that in some states these treasonous civilians had been and would continue to be successful in discouraging enlistments. As he reflected on the year's problems, what complicated the draft for governors, Stanton added, was that it played into the Confederate strategy to "divide and distract the people of the North."[63]

By the end of the first week in December, Federals fought and won the Battle of Prairie Grove, some twelve miles southwest of Fayetteville, Arkansas. Although minor in comparison to the battles of late, it was an important victory for Lincoln and Gamble. It afforded the Union army the upper hand in northwest Arkansas and allowed the governor to keep his Missouri militiamen close to home. He wired Lincoln that it was better to keep the northern counties quiet, and Lincoln requested Curtis to confer with the governor as to the viability of the two commands in the state. Curtis was quick to exercise great caution and courtesy toward state troops. "I, and all good Union men," he wired, "dread the least conflict of sovereignties," and "wherever a community can maintain the peace with civil laws and the Enrolled Militia," he declared, "I shall gladly relinquish military authority."[64]

As winter approached, it pleased Lincoln that the Mississippi River was gradually falling into Union hands. Still, he could not shake his focus on the army nearest Washington. He had taken McClellan from these soldiers and suffered for days awaiting news from Burnside's army near Fredericksburg. Governors combed the morning reports and the daily newspapers for news from the eastern front. Morton's friend Fletcher read in the Indianapolis papers that Burnside had crossed the Rappahannock, and the men worried about the army's prospects. "We are interested in its result," he wrote in his diary, "but dare not promise much as we have been so often disappointed."[65]

Fletcher's belief was well placed, given the casualty toll in the last six months, but it was about to get worse. On a foggy 11 December, the Army of the Potomac began crossing the Rappahannock River to Fredericksburg, and by midmorning the Union artillery had positioned itself to open fire on the city. Lincoln had gone for an afternoon carriage and on returning heard the news that Burnside had crossed the river. He hurried to the War Department to examine the wires. For the rest of the evening and into the following days the wires described a crushing Union defeat. Burnside's army retreated across the river humiliated, broken, and demoralized. Peering through his eyeglasses from atop Stafford Heights across the river, the disaster was more stunning than even he imagined. Death notices, wounded notices, and missing-in-action notices, more than 12,000 total, told the tale as reports trickled into the War Department and newspaper offices. The

Bangor Daily Whig and Courier published a Christmas Day list of fifty wounded that read "leg amputated . . . lost his sight . . . both arms amputated," and two days later more of the same for the 208 listed as wounded.⁶⁶ The loss at Fredericksburg completely unsettled Lincoln, and Burnside shrank into despondency. Many of the newly mustered recruits, dubbed by veterans the "two hundred dollar men" (yet ironically they had yet to receive pay), received their first baptism by fire.⁶⁷ Governors were aghast at the horrific reports and newspaper accounts of the gruesome aftermath. "Thank God it is no worse," wrote the correspondent to the *Chicago Tribune*.⁶⁸ Colonel Aaron Stevens of the 13th New Hampshire reported his regiment's performance to Berry. "After what your Excellency has read and heard concerning the battle of Fredericksburg," he confessed, "I need not say to you that the fierceness of the fight during that long, bloody and disastrous day exceeds any description of which my pen is capable."⁶⁹

Washburn had traveled to Virginia to visit his Maine boys and, looking for answers to explain the debacle, wrote the vice president. "Hannibal," he queried, "what does it mean?"⁷⁰ "The logic of all this war & [history]," he answered, "is, that blundering is to continue until we will cease the greatest blundering—that of thinking that the Union is to be saved on the foundation of the continuation of slavery—the practice of rank injustice." He queried the vice president, "Why have our rulers so little regard for the true & brave white men of the North? Will they continue to sacrifice them? Why will they refuse to save whites by employing black men?" Washburn acknowledged that even in this recent defeat, Lincoln "had faith & sense enough to know that any backing down is death."⁷¹ Writing to his sister Nettie from Nashville, even Ohioan Alexander Varian agreed. "If *the party spirit in the North could be stopped*," he declared, "the war would be carried differently." He warned, "This same party spirit will be the ruination of the government I am afraid. *The North is divided against itself*, while the South is *as one man*."⁷²

Curtin interrupted his medical treatment and hastened to Fredericksburg. He arrived the day after the battle, and after an emotional afternoon attending to the wounded soldiers, he headed to Willard's Hotel in Washington where he found a message waiting for him. Lincoln needed to see him at the White House. Curtin arrived after midnight, wet, crestfallen, and disheveled. "Well, Governor, so you have been down to the battlefield," rolled off the president's lips as he lay in bed. "Battlefield," remarked the weary chief executive, "Slaughter-pen! It was a terrible slaughter, Mr. Lincoln."

The look of despair on the president's face spoke volumes as he rolled back the covers, slipped out of bed, and began his characteristic hand wringing and murmuring aloud. "What has God put me in this place for," he exhaled.[73] Watching the chief executive pace around the room, Curtin was thinking just the opposite—why had God strewn his Pennsylvanians across the battlefield. Still, he could see the pain on Lincoln's face. "I would give all I possess to know how to rescue you from this terrible war," uttered Curtin.[74]

The "long waves of wounded," wrote Noah Brooks, came into Washington, "creeping, shuffling, limping, and hobbling along, full 1,500 strong, so faint and longing for rest; so weary, oh so weary, that the heart bleeds at the pitiful sight."[75] Buckingham received damning reports highlighting the wretched conditions of his Connecticutans who had gone into battle without knapsacks, overcoats, blankets, shoes, and several months' pay. "Private letters, going into every home in the North," griped the *Hartford Evening Press*, "tell the sad story of bad food, scant clothing, no shelter, and little care of the sick."[76] The governor enlisted agents, procured medical supplies and provisions, and accepted the services of surgeons, who volunteered to head to the Virginia front the same day the battle ended. He used his personal agent John Almy to ensure that those invalids, who needed to be brought back north, were transported to New York where they could be hospitalized. Almy established an organization called the "Sons of Connecticut" to assist him in this work. Witnessing the troops coming into Washington, Delaware senator James H. Bayard reported to his son Thomas, "the army must be awfully demoralized."[77]

On 17 December another bombshell hit Washington. Rumors leaked that thirty-two Republican senators had concluded to shake the up administration. The group cited Seward's harmful influence on Lincoln as the cause. The news blindsided Lincoln, but not the secretary of state. The New Yorker understood opponents in Congress would be calling for his dismissal after the recent defeat, and he tried to upstage them by resigning. On learning of the caucus, Lincoln remarked that "I have been more distressed" by this meeting "than by any event in my life."[78] The Republican Party was still new, and its leading senators and governors believed that one of their chief responsibilities was to help the guide the president. That Lincoln's cabinet members shared little affinity for one another was hardly a secret; neither was it a secret that Lincoln's favorite was Seward. Governors understood these divisions and, at times, exploited them to their advantage. Seward's resignation seemed like a play for attention, for he was known for stealing thunder or holding court in cabinet meetings. Nine senators visited Lincoln on the evening of 18 December, advised him that thirty-one senators consented to make the call, and complained that he had not consulted his cabinet enough. Even when the cabinet did meet, Seward monopolized the deliberations. Meanwhile, gossip spread throughout the otherwise cold and dreary city. Stoddard wrote that the rumors in the capital indicated that "some demand one head, and some another, until it would seem that if all are to be satisfied, the Cabinet and the Army will be like the Roman Emperor's garden."[79]

Lincoln set out to diffuse this ministerial crisis on the night of 19 December and convened the cabinet and the senatorial committee together at the White House, but had shrewdly invited them independently. The political leaders met together like schoolyard bullies, and after several hours it became obvious that nothing was to be accomplished. In the end, Lincoln made it clear that although he sought the advice of the assembled men, he was not obliged to accept it. The president understood that his cabinet members would disagree, they always had. Indeed, hearing such dissimilar views had made him a more formidable chief executive. Treasury Secretary Chase resigned shortly after the meeting, which gave the president the opportunity he needed to appease both factions. Thus, within three days, the high Republican command had played their hand with the president, and he had dispensed with their facade, rejected their resignations, and sent them back to their respective offices. Whatever faults they brought with them to Washington, Lincoln decided not to choose new horses midstream. "They may be pulling in seven different directions, to the great detriment and peril of the country," concluded a *Chicago Tribune* correspondent, "but when assembled as a Cabinet, with the President's eyes and ears attending them, they may be—are—as consonant as David's harp of solemn sound."[80]

Winter Miseries

The seemingly clever political machinations in Washington obscured the moment's more important issues. The Army of the Potomac needed attention, comfort, and encouragement. Although the soldiers had fought gallantly, little consolation could be found in what they accomplished. Lincoln summoned Burnside to Washington to discuss the recent battle and to strategize his army's next move. After all, there was a war to fight, wounded to attend to, and commanders in the West eager to bring down Vicksburg.

Even the reluctant Rosecrans, who had pressed the War Department for men, horses, and better officers, had stirred up a fuss at Murfreesboro along the Stones River and, by 31 December, had pinned down Bragg. Yet the commander failed to seize the offensive, and Bragg stole the initiative and drove the Federals to the banks of the Stones River. In the coming days, it would get worse.[81]

Military campaigns aside, the undeniable fact about the Civil War was that reconstruction of the Union had begun far away from the Confederate guns that opened on Fort Sumter. That Union soldiers occupied Southern communities complicated local governance and established the conditions for a new Union. Western Virginians had changed the Union's contours by separating from Virginia. Despite constitutional limitations, the mountaineers' separatist movement amounted to secession from the Confederacy. Yet slaves had also complicated the war by showing up in Union camps, even more so with the pronouncement of the coming Emancipation Proclamation. One Anne Arundel County slave owner wrote Bradford, requesting him to issue a proclamation stating that the president's proclamation did not apply to Maryland slaves. The governor hesitated to put anything in a formal memorandum and instead responded with a message to be posted in his county that the proclamation only applied to the rebellious states. A slave owner himself, Bradford realized the institution was dying out in Maryland, but he refused to draw attention to the proclamation's failure to free Maryland slaves. The governor, however, used the opportunity to stake his claim by replacing the recently deceased Maryland senator James Alfred Pearce, a conservative slaveholder, with the ever-loyal Hicks, who placed himself in Maryland's emerging pro-emancipation corner. Privately, however, Bradford confessed to Montgomery Blair that he never doubted "that one consequence of this war will be substantially to put an end to that institution," and he wished Maryland slave owners would understand this fact.[82]

By the end of the year whether or not the militia draft proved a failure was not as significant as the relationship it had forged between Lincoln, Stanton, and the governors in transforming a state-oriented volunteer force into a national army. Working through military and political problems forged a stronger bond between the nation and the states, even while leaders remained sensitive to their regional and local problems. The burden of preserving the Union at times committed governors to unpopular ideas. Yet several executives proved more effective than others in raising the levies, in part because of their personal competence and devotion to local constituents.

Morton had drawn national praise for attending to soldier welfare. "The peculiar and constant attention to the troops his state has sent out so promptly," reported the *New York Tribune*, "is the prominent feature of Governor Morton's most admirable administration."[83] Holbrook was also noted for his devotion to the soldiers, especially those of the 9th Vermont. Upon learning of members being captured at Harpers Ferry and sent to Chicago to await parole, he worked with Vermont's senators to get them home.[84]

It was during these winter days that western Virginian governor Francis Pierpont, political leader, paid attention to General Banks's movements. Learning that Lincoln had transferred the commander from Virginia to New Orleans, he decided to travel to Washington to confer with the president. Pierpont's brother had written the governor weeks before, alerting him to the problems of local defense in the mountaineer region. He forwarded these concerns to Lincoln, voiced his protest against Banks's reassignment, and shared his opinion on the conduct of the war. Lincoln agreed with the governor's views on concentrating Union forces on Richmond. "I believe if I were going to give my opinion on the mode for the speedy termination of this war," Lincoln responded, "I don't know in what particular I should differ from your views."[85] But New Orleans was important for reasons beyond military significance. "If an intelligent angel from heaven, would drop down in one corner of this room and sit there for two weeks hearing all that is said to me," he told Pierpont, "I think he would come to the conclusion that this war was being prosecuted to obtain cotton from the South for the Northern cotton mills!" He added, "So, Gen. Banks has to go to Louisiana to get the cotton." He stressed, "I am so dependent on New England and those using cotton, for money, men and supplies that I cannot do as I wish under the circumstances."[86]

The year came to a close, but even with New Orleans, Nashville, and several hundred Confederate square miles under Union occupation, Lincoln's memo to Burnside told the story. "I have good reason for saying," wrote Lincoln, "you must not make a general movement of the army without letting me know."[87] Burnside was a general without an army, at least in spirit. Lincoln knew this, and so did the governors. Having observed the machinations of the cabinet and senators, Halleck believed the nation was drifting toward ruin, remarking that "there is not a single great and patriotic statesman to be found in the cabinet or in the halls of congress," and only God, apparently, could save the Union.[88] Andrew agreed. Writing to Sumner on Christmas Day, he alluded to the squabbling, arguing that a government should do more and debate less.[89]

Many Northerners agreed. Letters from demoralized soldiers and citizens poured into the statehouses, testifying to their hardships. Calvin Fletcher despaired over national affairs and braced himself to hear of the loss of his son Stephen Keyes Fletcher, who was fighting in Kentucky. "This is a sad eve," he entered into his diary on a snowy December 29, "our news is to the effect that our army seems demoralized & have lost their spirit—All looks gloomy."[90] Morton had no explanation for Fletcher. Despondent Northerners believed themselves at the bottom of the Union well, and, as for the "Seymourites," Andrew argued, who were carping about the Emancipation Proclamation, "we ought to be preparing the proof" that no matter "how much the critics may blow and fume about it, the house *will go up*."[91]

Yet for all of the military suffering, there was evidence soldiers had not died in vain, and that the preservation of a new Union was progressing in the Blue Ridge Mountains. The *Hartford Evening Press* acknowledged that the new state's prospects marked an era "in the progress of the great revolution the nation is now undergoing."[92] Having gained congressional approval, Pierpont expected Lincoln's signature on the bill creating West Virginia any day. When none came, the provisional chief executive fretted over a possible veto, and he wired Lincoln that such rejection would be "disastrous to the Union cause in Western Virginia." A week later he wired Lincoln a final telegram asking him to read carefully the letter sent by Archibald W. Campbell, which Pierpont endorsed. "The union men of West Va were not originally for the Union because of the new state," he wrote, "but the sentiment for the two have become identified," and "if one is stricken down I dont [sic] know what is become of the other."[93] Loyal mountaineers had invested much in statehood, and it came at great sacrifice. Theirs was more than a political venture; it was a means to break the shackles from the eastern, slaveholding, tidewater elite. Northerners were fighting to prove that secession could not undo the Union, and yet against all odds, these Blue Ridge zealots had seceded from the Confederacy. Lincoln understood their risks, in fact he applauded them. As he ended his duties that New Year's Eve, he pored over depressing military telegrams. If Northern armies had failed to give him the victories he needed, the time had come to admit West Virginia as the Union's thirty-fifth state and to send a resounding message to Confederates that their dominion was shrinking.[94]

Exceptional times required exceptional measures, and Lincoln confessed, shortly before his death, that it was Pierpont's final telegram that moved him to sign the bill. In preparing his memorandum, he made a marginal note in which he concluded that "the admission of the new state, turns that much slave soil to free; and thus, is certain, and irrevocable encroachment upon the cause of the rebellion."[95] Unprecedented in their time, Lincoln's decisions to admit West Virginia, emancipate slaves, and draft citizens had changed the Union. By year's end in 1862, the war that had begun in April 1861 had given birth to a new state, brought freedom to Confederate slaves, and inspired a resolve among Northerners to vindicate democracy by sharing its responsibilities via state conscription. Writing to Montgomery Blair, Thomas Hicks confided that he had "great faith in the honesty, Patriotism, and determination of the President to do right."[96]

CHAPTER TWELVE

There Can Be No Difference of Purpose

New Year's Day dawned in Washington like any other mid-Atlantic winter morning—indistinguishable, clear, but cold. By evening, however, the fog, rain, and mud returned, and so had the Union's humiliation over Fredericksburg. Encamped at Fairfax Station, New Yorker Almon Graham's diary entry reflected the sentiment. "Surely as a nation," he wrote, "we are little nearer peace than we were a year ago."[1] A Massachusetts officer agreed, and wrote to Andrew that the "news of the fearfull [sic] and apparently *worse* than unnecessary slaughter at Fredericksburg has just come to our sad hearts and I am so sick. I do not wish to live to see my country once so great and glorious . . . vanquished in such a disgracefull [sic] rebelion [sic]."[2] Burnside's admission that he had lost faith in the administration and in himself worsened the disgrace. He admitted to Halleck that he "ought to retire to private life." Lincoln, however, refused to accept the commander's resignation. With Halleck's blessing, he authorized Burnside to organize a second offensive on Fredericksburg.[3]

Despite the debacle, Andrew celebrated the New Year and the Emancipation Proclamation with a 100-gun salute on Boston Common to mark the new era. Thousands of Delawareans came to Dover Green to hear William Cannon's inaugural speech, hopeful that his words could unite the divided citizenry to support Lincoln's war aims. Hostility to his election lingered, and it was rumored the governor might be prevented from giving his address to the assembly, as Democrats refused him the use of the facilities. In Augusta, Maine, crowds braved the inclement weather to hear the message of their new chief executive Abner Coburn, who did not disappoint them. "I can see no line of patriotism or of safety, except in a cordial, unreserved support of the policy enunciated by the President," he argued. "To resist, or combine against it, is to run all the hazards of anarchy," he warned.[4]

A Changed War

On 1 January 1863, Lincoln proclaimed that, as a necessary war measure for suppressing the rebellion, slaves in the Confederate states were officially free. When the prescribed hour arrived that afternoon, Lincoln affixed his signature to the emancipation document before him. The news delighted the governor who had volunteered the first regiment to preserve the Union. "To-day, the sun in his course shines upon no American bondsman," Ramsey declared in his final address to the Minnesota legislature. "By the Proclamation of the President, the shackles have fallen from the limbs of *nearly* every slave."[5] The editor of the *Burlington Daily Free Press* noted that "Throughout the civilized world, this act of the President will be noticed, and for ages to come, the finger of history will point to it as one of unsurpassed consequence in the progress of human affairs."[6] Yet the proclamation did not apply to slaves in the Union, and it could only be as effective as the armies that enforced it moving through the South. Even the editor of the *Oregon Statesman* declared that the proclamation "falls dead at its utterance, only as it is, and shall be, enforced at the point of a bayonet."[7] But many of the soldiers carrying the bayonets were against the proclamation, as were many Democrats in the state legislatures. Indiana assemblymen, for example, declared that Lincoln's proclamation was unconstitutional and would cause the Union incalculable injury by dividing friends and uniting enemies. They argued that it would lead to the state being overrun by a degraded black population. One Indiana soldier wrote Morton that there were "butternuts in our camp who are opposed to the war and the presidents proclimation [sic]" but that there were a few soldiers who were "in favor of this war exterminating slavery."[8] Morton interpreted these sentiments as antiadministration and disloyal, and used his influence with Stanton to have officers expressing such views dismissed from service.[9]

Lincoln's proclamation crystallized divisions within political parties, and, although the measure garnered support from soldiers, it also drew criticism. "I scarcely know what to think of the *President's late "Emancipation Proclamation,"* wrote Alexander Varian to his sister. "Regarding it strictly as a War measure it may do, but it seems to me that if they would let the niggers alone & go to *hanging every traitor* they catch the war would be the sooner over."[10] Aetna Pettis, a Michigan soldier, wrote to his wife that he would just as soon stay home and take care of his family rather than "fighting to free Nigers [sic]."[11] Even New York soldier George A. Mitchell surmised to his parents that "the emancipation proclamation of 'Honest Abe' has created more dissatisfaction and more 'croaking' than the affair at Fredericksburgh [sic] did."[12]

As much as governors stood behind emancipation, they were hard pressed to convince opponents that it was as a tool to end the war quicker and thus attract volunteers to shorter enlistments. They understood that most citizens did not support it as a stand-alone reason to shed huge amounts of blood, and thus they followed Lincoln's lead in presenting it strictly as a military measure to help save the Union. If it had become a war for emancipation (and black enlistment) in the eyes of many Northern citizens, it was because military necessity demanded it. Yates's pro-emancipation address to the legislature prodded representatives to relax Illinois's immigration laws prohibiting blacks from the state. He contended that blacks were no menace to citizens and in fact could be used to fill the ranks. Besides, the war would not end until slavery was removed from the South, and Northerners would have to accept that fact. "My trust is in God," wrote one Illinoisan to Yates, "but I must confess that I see but little of his work." He warned, "I am afraid the Democrats will make an onslaught on you this winter.... If they do[,] veto in Gods name any action they may take, and the loyal people will back you up."[13] True to form, Democrats assailed Yates, and a mean-spirited "nincompoop from Peoria," wrote a Springfield journalist, cleverly but maliciously proposed that Yates's recommendation be referred to a "committee of three American citizens of African descent."[14] In addition to limiting the publication of Yates's address, by the end of the first week in session Copperhead legislators had "not uttered one loyal word," fumed the *Chicago Tribune's* correspondent, but had "belched treason, day and night."[15] Brigadier General William Ward Orme, a former Illinois lawyer, wrote Supreme Court judge David Davis that he had recently visited Yates, who he declared was "very much dispirited." He observed, "I think from all I saw & heard that this State is *on the verge* of revolution," and that the "slightest spark applied to the magazine of public feeling of the State will cause an explosion."[16]

Despite emancipation's unpopularity, many Northerners hailed it a success and considered it a milestone in securing the Union's perpetuity. Blair's rousing address to legislators underscored emancipation's significance, and he argued that the time had come to hammer confiscation, emancipation, and Republican doctrines into the Confederate coffin. More pressing, however, was the legislature's duty to follow the soldiers in the field and the hospital and to "make its active sympathy and aid manifest in all their trials and sufferings."[17] He added, "It is in the hospital that the soldier needs sympathy and help.... He who is bravest in the active duties of the field, grows a child when languishing of disease in the hospital."[18] In Wheeling, western Virginians were marking another milestone as they celebrated Lincoln's signature on the resolution for statehood. "The wildest enthusiasm prevails," wrote Pierpont's wife Julia, "the people are running to & fro, each one anxious to bear the Glad Tidings of this great Joy." The jubilant wire read, "God bless you, you have signed the *Bill*." She added, "In the name of the loyal Ladies of West Va, we thanks [sic] you, for our blessed *New Year's Gift*. You have saved us from contempt and disgrace."[19]

Even while governors explained political priorities and soldier welfare to legislators, a patient Rosecrans sat with some 45,000 freezing troops west of the Stones River near Murfreesboro. The commander was hoping to claim victory in Tennessee, secure the Nashville and Chattanooga Railroad, and liberate slaves. By 3 January, the arrival of reinforcements provided Rosecrans the confidence he needed to continue the fight at Stones River, and Bragg's army withdrew to Tullahoma. Old Rosy claimed victory, but the human cost (more than 13,200 soldiers killed, wounded, or missing) was so devastating that the commander refused to pursue Bragg. For a president who had freed millions of slaves, it was an inauspicious beginning to the New Year. Still, the victory lessoned the disgrace of Fredericksburg and provided editors with something positive to print. Governors too needed encouraging news from the field to counter the damaging recriminations from the loss on the Rappahannock.[20]

The gruesome reports and casualty lists from Murfreesboro aided dissidents opposing the war. Morton discussed with Calvin Fletcher evidence of a plot to take Indiana out of the Union and join the slave states in establishing a new empire. Some legislators feared that Democrats would elect secessionist senators and propose treasonous legislation, so they encouraged state assemblymen to return home to prevent a quorum in the legislature. Morton's secretary confirmed the mood to John Nicolay. "We are upon the eve of civil war in Indiana," he warned, "and you need not be surprised to hear of a collision here at any time."[21] Fletcher supported the governor's idea to form armed societies in every county to combat the local opposition and offered him $100 to help him do so. In the larger Northern cities, and in even in Oregon, where Gibbs needed to squelch the Democrats' peace movements, similar clubs already existed, and Morton now wanted to encourage them in Indiana to sniff out secession sympathizers. Conditions were so bad that the legislature refused to hear his annual message, and even when he sent it in written form, legislators refused to receive it. "We can easily dispose of him when the time comes," the rumors allowed, "it will be an irrepressible assassination—that is all."[22] Morton informed Stanton that legislators were plotting to pass a joint resolution that would acknowledge the Southern Confederacy and urge the northwestern states to dissolve all constitutional relations with the New England states. "The same thing is on foot in Illinois," he warned.[23]

Indiana and Illinois Republicans believed there was some merit to the notion that New Englanders were getting rich from the heavy railroad tolls paid by westerners. Opening the Mississippi River, they believed, held wide currency in the Midwest if for no other reason than to ease the financial load of heavy shipping costs east. Their legislatures were so occupied by an increasing dependency on New Englanders for trade that some members resolved to send an emissary to England and Canada to pursue more direct trade routes. The rumors of his assemblymen alarmed Yates, and he wrote to Morton that "the legislature here is a wild, rampant, revolutionary body— will attempt to legislate all power out of my hands."[24] In case the opposition turned violent, Yates needed to know if he could count on his Indiana colleague.[25]

With many state legislatures in session, governors looked to secure funds for the soldiers, their families, and for local defense. Lincoln's administration remained focused on the enemy at the front, and as much as governors tried to assist in forwarding men to the ranks, they spent much of their time combating the enemy in the rear. Campaigns were under way on western waters as the Union Navy continued its stranglehold on Confederate shipping. McClernand steamed down the Mississippi with the new Army of the Mississippi, and a river squadron under David Dixon Porter was on its way south to the mouth of the Arkansas River. The operation resulted in the capture of Fort Hindman, some fifty miles upstream from the confluence of the rivers, and McClernand assumed this might divert Confederates away from Vicksburg and give Grant an advantage. His unauthorized venture, however, ultimately did little to assist Grant, who ordered the commander to join him.[26]

The end of January brought more political challenges to the administration as new governors came into office. On a cold 20 January, thousands of New Jerseyans journeyed to Trenton over frozen roads to hear their new governor's inaugural message. Joel Parker encouraged legislators to remain steadfast in preserving the Union as it was. He criticized the president for expanding the war's purpose, for authorizing arbitrary arrests, and for emancipating slaves. The new governor implored Lincoln to exercise the same self-restraint he was asking of his citizens in returning to a strict adherence to the Constitution. Democrats came into the new session and initiated antiwar and antiblack resolutions so outrageous that they embarrassed even the party's radicals. Newspapers printed these resolutions, which found their way into the New Jersey ranks. Soldiers responded by signing formal protests against these resolutions and in support of a vigorous prosecution of the war, and sent them to Parker. Still, for all the inauguration pageantry, the governor could not escape the criticism leveled at him for playing what one observer called, "follow the leader" behind Seymour. "Gov. Parker gives ten words to Southern rebels, and then ten paragraphs to the evils of subduing them," commented the *Chicago Tribune*.[27]

When the Kansas legislature opened in Topeka, Robinson "surrendered his office" to Thomas Carney, who capitalized on the relative calm that allowed him to continue his predecessor's legislative and executive initiatives. Gone were the days of constitutional struggles and power plays over politics, but the Civil War remained. Like their neighbors, Missourians had not enjoyed peace since the war opened. Gamble struggled to maintain his political grip on the crisis as well as keep the peace between the slave owners and slaves. To help stabilize affairs, he had requested that Lincoln have Curtis suspend the assessment system of taxing disloyalists because it produced great distress. When Missouri congressmen visited the president and pressed him to discontinue the assessments, Lincoln wired Curtis to ascertain the problems. "I am having a good deal of trouble with Missouri matters," he argued.[28] The president had grown wise to residents who criticized the governor's loyalty. It was apparent that fraud had been perpetrated in collecting assessments, but Lincoln hardly blamed Gamble for a "system that was liable to such abuses." Instead, he decided that Curtis and Gamble should cooperate. He advised them that "acting together, you could double your stock of pertinent information."[29] Curtis agreed not to interfere with Gamble's operations so long as the governor ensured that civil authority would be restored under his governance with the Enrolled Militia. Circumstances, however, were beyond cooperation.[30]

Raising Black Troops

As state legislatures debated Lincoln's new policies, federal congressmen sought approval for authorizing the War Department to raise black troops. It was a controversial, though necessary, move, which produced legal complications and racial tension. The military and political reverses weighed heavily on soldiers and civilians, and the frustration transformed Northern thinking about enlisting black troops even while it triggered fear among the populace. New Yorker Hervey Howe wrote his brother from Fredericksburg and explained that, while "many among us are bitter against it," calling it a "disgrace to the Nation and to the soldiers already in the field to have the blacks brought in with them," he acknowledged that "others think it is right the blacks should be made to fight for the slaves since this war has assumed such an abolition character."[31] Edwin O. Wentworth of the 37th Massachusetts regiment wrote to his brother from camp near Falmouth, Virginia, that he feared the "army of negroes" would "amount to nothing, for white men will not fight beside them; and even if they would, not enough can be raised to do any good." From what he had read about soldiers embracing emancipation, and about their willingness to die "if thereby the nigger can be freed," was a "d—ed lie."[32]

Enlisting blacks as Union soldiers was not an easy undertaking, but some governors had already proposed such ideas to their legislatures. The need for more soldiers and laborers, as well as the reports that contraband blacks had proven effective in minor combat, made it clear that arming blacks had become a wartime reality. Several commanders had experimented with using black soldiers. Thomas Wentworth Higginson, a Massachusetts colonel, was tapped to command the 1st South Carolina Volunteer Infantry made up of contraband slaves, and in January he had led his men on a successful raid in South Carolina. That same month, the War Department accepted Lane's 1st Kansas Colored Volunteers into federal service. As some Northerners interpreted the changed conflict, it was now a white man's war to free Confederate slaves, and it made sense that blacks should also shoulder a musket. Pressed for men, and burdened by draft resistance, governors were under pressure to fill quotas, and these experiences helped convince Lincoln to consider Andrew's proposal to raise an all-black regiment. Many New Englanders praised Lincoln's emancipation, suspension of habeas corpus, and black enlistment. Buckingham forwarded a copy of the Connecticut Assembly's resolutions that acknowledged their unshaken "confidence in the patriotism and integrity of the president."[33]

Yet, as much as these sentiments gratified Lincoln, the Democratic upsurge in the fall elections left some governors with unreceptive legislatures, especially now that federal congressmen were considering black enlistment. Legislators opposed to emancipation and conscription increased their hostility toward governors who supported black troops. Democratic legislators attempted to withhold funds, investigated executive financial transactions, retaliated against the suppression of civil liberties, proposed resolutions to withdraw the Emancipation Proclamation, and delayed legislative action regarding military matters. The Illinois legislature, for example, passed a resolution to allow Yates $50,000 to use at his discretion, but Democrat Alexander Starne, the state treasurer, refused to release the funds. Indiana assemblymen reached new heights in recalcitrance. Democrats conspired to establish a military board in the state to wrest executive power from Morton, who knew that even if he vetoed the measure, legislators would override him. Instead, he broke up the legislature before it could vote on the bill. He transported Republican assemblymen out of the city to prevent a quorum. One Indianapolis editor remarked that the legislature "died without making a will. Its effects were in a strong box and there was no key left to unlock it."[34] Indiana Sargent James Thomas was so exasperated by reading about the obstreperous legislators in the press that he wrote Morton, demanding he "hang the last one of them or Send them to the army & we will do the work for them."[35]

Cannon faced similar problems as the Delaware General Assembly accused him of having been elected "by federal bayonets, not by the will of the people" and rejected many of his resolutions, including an appropriation of $25,000 for welfare relief. Two of his enemies in Congress, Willard Saulsbury and James A. Bayard, had already made national headlines for assailing Lincoln, declaring the president a "weak and imbecile man," who was a "tyrant" and "a man perfectly regardless of every Constitutional right of the people."[36] Worse yet were the allegations that dissidents working out of Wilmington had engaged in illicit trade with Confederates. Cannon's enemies boasted that although more than 5,000 Delawareans served in the military, "not one dollar of money has the State of Delaware contributed to carry on this war."[37]

Morton and Cannon's troubles paled in comparison to the problems Tod endured. Although the Ohio legislature and the Democratic press condemned the Union's new war aims, Congressman Clement Laird Vallandigham, the vociferous Copperhead, had opposed the war from the start. He hoped to win the gubernatorial seat in 1863 and dethrone the Republicans, and used his departure from Congress to voice his hostility to the Lincoln administration. "Vallandigham," remarked Lyman Trumbull, "was the incarnation of Copperheadism," who, in his farewell speech of 14 January entitled "The Constitution-Peace-Reunion," had stretched the limits of dissent, as he "discharged all the pro-slavery virus that he had been collecting from his boyhood days."[38] On that day, Trumbull remembered that it took him two hours to prove: "(1) That the Southern Confederacy never could be conquered; (2) that the Union could never be restored by war; (3) that it could be restored by peace; (4) that whatever else might happen, African slavery would be 'fifty-fold stronger' at the end of the war than it had at the beginning."[39]

Critical editors and obstinate legislators who contested governors found little favor with the soldiers, who read of their traitorous conduct in the newspapers. Soon entire regiments rallied behind their governors in protesting these actions. The soldiers of the 14th Connecticut, for example, endorsed Buckingham's leadership and the current war aims, and resolved to fight the "fire in the rear."[40] George Pratt Scudder of the 45th Pennsylvania complained that the "olive branch of peace extended by political scoundrels and rascals are doing more injury to our cause—Prolonging the war—More than all the defeats and disasters that has happened to our Armies and Navies."[41] Illinois officers drafted resolutions to Yates, and to their hometown newspapers, declaring that they were "in favor of a vigorous prosecution of the war, and that we will uphold our President and our Governor in all their efforts to crush the rebellion and restore the Union."[42] To counter Democratic opposition, Morton engineered a scheme to procure support from his soldiers by requesting public resolutions endorsing his course. Indiana officers of some twenty-two regiments encamped nearby in Ambrose also adopted resolutions urging their representatives to prosecute the war and sustain the governor's efforts.[43]

Lincoln was aware of the hostility against the governors and feared enemies at home as much as he feared those at the front. Governors tried to reclaim some semblance of political decorum amid stormy legislative sessions that schemed to upend Lincoln's new war aims. These legislative machinations weighed heavily on Lincoln. Burnside was preparing another offensive with an army reeling from defeat, and he needed reassurances. By 21 January, rain poured over the Army of the Potomac as it tried to position pontoons across the Rappahannock River to withstand nearly 120,000 soldiers. The following day, "the bottom dropped out of the roads," as one Vermonter put it, and the entire Federal army was stuck in the Virginia mud. Vulnerable to a Confederate attack, the commander turned back and aborted what disgracefully became known as the "Mud March."[44] Burnside's march was a disaster, and soldiers complained to governors. Coburn's incoming correspondence from Maine soldiers told the story. There were reports of wounded soldiers with undressed wounds suffering on board transports for more than twenty hours in the driving rains without shelter, comfort, or food. Coburn asked the legislature for permission to have John W. Hathaway permanently stationed in Washington to look after the soldiers. The campaign thoroughly demoralized soldiers and undermined the commander's credibility with Lincoln. The president replaced him with West Point graduate General Joseph Hooker, a hard-bitten, combat-experienced commander not above self-advancement, who, because of a journalistic misprint, earned the nickname "Fighting Joe Hooker." Lincoln's appointment elated Andrew, who wrote the new commander a congratulatory letter. "Tell the boys," he declared, "that *all* have a country; *all* will hereafter have a history." He then advised the Massachusetts-born commander to have officers "read at the head of every regiment," which would inculcate the president's message into the ranks.[45]

January closed, and governors struggled to console citizens suffering from the hardships of losing family members to a war the Union was not winning. The winter weather made their sacrifice more aggravating. Northern disenchantment cost Lincoln allies who initially had been swayed by his executive abilities. Some conservatives demanded the Emancipation Proclamation be rescinded. His decision to allow Buckingham and Sprague to enlist black volunteers helped relieve those fearing conscription, but the units never materialized. Andrew, however, proceeded with great care in organizing such a regiment. He was anxious to see it succeed to demonstrate the "desirability of the innovation which he had so earnestly advocated," and to undermine the "prejudice and disparagement, even in those circles where it would have been least looked for."[46] Yet the governor had not enough military-age blacks in Massachusetts to form a complete regiment, and he appealed to Stanton for authorization to recruit them from outside the state. Stanton initially refused, but Andrew persevered. He asked John Murray Forbes to assist him. Forbes's prominence in the highbrow financial community made him sensitive to the governor's intentions. He pressed Stanton and Lincoln to accept Andrew's proposal and enlisted the support of Sumner, Chandler, and Grimes. Andrew also called on George Luther Stearns, noted Massachusetts abolitionist and one of the chief financiers of the Emigrant Aid Company, to hire agents and employ prominent blacks to assist him in recruiting.[47]

By the time Stanton came around to the idea, Andrew had two young candidates in mind for officering his newly designated 54th Massachusetts: Robert Gould Shaw, a Harvard-educated captain in the 2nd Massachusetts, and fellow Harvard graduate Norwood Penrose Hallowell, also a captain in the 20th Massachusetts. Andrew had great expectations for the command, which he considered to be "the most important corps to be organized during the whole war" and "a model for all future Colored Regiments."[48] He understood Stanton's concerns that by permitting him to bid for Southern blacks it would allow Northern whites to remain unconscripted. Border state governors complained that they could not handle the increasing numbers of slaves coming into Federal lines offering to fight. Such was the administrative pressure that in the coming months the War Department established a Bureau of Colored Troops and sent Northern agents into Southern areas under Union occupation to handle matters of personnel, pay, and recruitment. The bureau also searched for competent white officers. Yet the responsibility for recruiting black troops in the North fell almost exclusively to governors and state authorities, who relied on Federal agents in the occupied South to assist them. Consequently, the declining number of white volunteers and the increasing needs of the Union army forced governors to take advantage of using former slaves to help meet manpower quotas. Still, only in a few states, such as those in New England, did raising black regiments affect quotas.[49]

The threat of a draft convinced some soldiers that they could live with the change of fighting alongside black troops. Iowan Isaac Marsh had come to terms with the proposition. "You may be astonished to hear me say," he wrote his wife, "that the arming of the negroes is just what we want it meets with nearly universal approbation in the army.... I dont [sic] care if they are one 2 mile thick in every Battel [sic] they will stop Bullets as well as white people."[50] John Beatty of the 2nd Minnesota had been opposed to arming free blacks, but changed his mind, concluding that if "slavery [was] the cornerstone of the Confederacy," then it was time to "tear up the cornerstone," in any way possible, and allow blacks to shoulder a musket.[51]

Not all governors shared Andrew's enthusiasm in raising black regiments. New York's Horatio Seymour vehemently opposed enlisting black soldiers, and Lincoln was not about to challenge the governor, despite numerous pleas requesting federal authorization to do so. Some midwestern governors beset with recalcitrant legislatures were slow to embrace the idea.

Iowa's Kirkwood had gone back and forth on the proposition. He confessed to Halleck at one point that "when this war is over & we have summed up the entire loss it has imposed on the country I shall have no regrets if it is found that a part of the dead are *niggers* and that *all* are not white men."[52] By the New Year, the governor resisted requesting permission to raise a black regiment in Iowa because "he feared that no sooner would a negro be enlisted than he would be claimed as a slave." Still, he supported black enlistments, believing that the war would eventually extend freedom to thousands who have been slaves, while saving the lives "'of our own dear friends who have gone and who must yet go to the field.'"[53]

Enlisting blacks in the Union army expectedly came with complaints and confusion from border state governors. Bradford had received complaints over the illegal recruitment of Maryland slaves into the Union army. Much of his correspondence concerned Marylanders who harbored runaway slaves in violation of state law. When G. Fred Maddox, St. Mary's County state attorney, expressed to Bradford his dissatisfaction over the problems resulting from Lincoln's proclamation, he questioned the governor as to whether he would protect the people, should the county sheriff attempt to return a slave to its owner. "We are excluded," from the proclamation he complained, "and worst served—worst served, because the proclamation bears upon its face protection to us, and comes into our midst in Peace and cheats us of our property."[54] Bradford replied that the circumstances requiring Maddox to write his letter represented the nation's extraordinary circumstances. "A single word explains this change of circumstance," wrote Bradford, "We are in a state of War."[55] Thus, he argued, it was no time to trifle over the normal functions of law that complicated public procedures that stood in the way of preserving the Union. Indeed, at a January banquet welcoming General Robert C. Schenk to command, the governor clarified his views. "The loyal men of Maryland have but one purpose and one hope—but one ambition and one thought," he declared, "and that is—the *Union*, its restoration, its preservation, its perpetuity."[56]

Division at Home and in the Ranks

Lincoln shared Bradford's thoughts in saving the Union, but at the moment he had accomplished more on paper than in the field to do it. Grant's unsuccessful attempts to get past Vicksburg disappointed him, and he grew frustrated with Rosecrans for not pursuing Bragg. Northern discontent had made its way into daily editorials, onto governors' desks, and had stirred a fuss on Capitol Hill. "The truth is," observed Stoddard, "there is at this present [moment] but one great danger; only one thing which can possibly stand between us and ultimate success and safety, and that is *division among ourselves*."[57] As the winter weeks progressed, it was difficult to sustain home front morale, especially as secret societies advocating peace and encouraging desertion had gained momentum. Soldiers were aware of the low morale and sent home encouraging words that emphasized saving the Union over supporting its leaders. Writing to his wife from Louisiana, New Yorker John B. Burrud spoke for many soldiers who considered the struggle more important than the Revolutionary War, arguing that "if we fail to sustain the Union we bid goodbye to free government."[58]

Of all the governors, none believed he was more menaced by home front dissension than Indiana's Morton. The governor was so distressed that he requested that Lincoln meet him at Harrisburg to discuss his evidence. Whether or not Lincoln was convinced of the plot, he could not leave Washington without drawing suspicion about his trip. Lincoln was wise to suspect Morton's dramatic depiction of the West, but the election results and raids into Kentucky gave his story some credibility. Indianans were inundated with newspaper reports by Democratic editors detailing the plans supporting the Northwest Confederacy. They implicated Seymour and prominent Pennsylvania Democrats as accomplices, and with good reason. Seymour's January message spoke to their desires. The plot was to join the midwestern and northwestern states, leaving the slave states independent, which would allow them to propose a reconstruction plan to Confederate leaders without the New England states. The abuse New Englanders would suffer was well deserved. As the logic went, they had brought on the war by a financial crusade against slavery and now Northerners suffered because of the heavy tariffs levied for the benefit of New England companies. Such a separation would free the Northwest from the exorbitant freights charged by eastern railroad companies connecting the West with eastern cities. "They are using every means in their power," Morton warned Lincoln, "to corrupt and debauch the public mind." Only conquest of the Mississippi River, combined with a vast distribution of documents and literature to combat the misunderstandings of the people in the region, would combat "these impending evils."[59]

Yates also served a discontented populace. He knew there would be consequences from emancipation and black enlistments. Talk of insubordination became so alarming in the 109th Illinois stationed at Holly Springs that Grant was forced to disband the regiment. Yates was so concerned he wrote Chase that he was sitting on a stack of Copperhead problems. He also wired Lincoln to expect a visit from Colonel Robert Kirkham of the 56th Illinois, whom Yates wrote "knows what is going on here."[60] The governor summoned General John Palmer to Springfield in February to protect the citizens from "the great danger" expected from the Knights of the Golden Circle and showed him scores of letters as evidence. "I found the governor thoroughly alarmed on account of these letters," Palmer recalled, "and assigned to me the duty of going to Washington and consulting the president and secretary of war as to the propriety of raising a number of regiments for service in the State of Illinois."[61]

As in Maryland, emancipation did not affect Kentucky slaves, but dissension in the state escalated, and Robinson feared it would "fire the whole South."[62] Halleck made the president aware of the rumors that indicated if Lincoln issued his proclamation, the Kentucky legislature would "legislate the state out of the Union," and worse, the governor's message would "favor such action."[63] Robinson denounced the proclamation in his message to the legislature, and Kentucky Unionists warned him that such pronouncements would ruin Kentucky and drive the state further into rebellion. They counseled him to "do better," which he consented to do. By early February, the governor's actions convinced Lincoln to raise 20,000 Kentuckians for twelve months to safeguard the state, but the president reserved the right to use them outside of Kentucky if he deemed it necessary.[64]

Missouri slaves were also untouched by Lincoln's proclamation, but the political fallout complicated what was already an antagonistic relationship between civil and military leaders. Mired in a struggle with Curtis to keep the state in the Union, Gamble needed Lincoln to support his plan to safeguard northern Missouri. The governor's enemies, however, had so disparaged his reputation and cast him as a proslavery man that Lincoln waivered. Curtis wired Senator Wilson, chairman of the Senate Military Committee, protesting Gamble's authority, and argued that his militia should be under the control of the United States. "Governor Gamble is a pro-slavery Union man," he asserted, "and he is so fearful of abolition haste he may be and is deceived in some instances," by Missourians professing loyalty to the Union but who, in actuality, were rebels.[65] Gamble's son-in-law, Charles Gibson, countered such accusations by confiding to Lincoln that "there is a growing discontent ... that deserves your most serious consideration," which he attributed to the "maladministration of federal affairs in that State."⁶⁶

For all the bleak news that winter, midwestern governors delighted in reports that Colonel Charles Ellet Jr. managed to steam the Union ram *Queen of the West* past the batteries at Vicksburg. Grant's men had dug away at the Louisiana soil across from the city for weeks, and Ellet's success gave them hope they too might steam past the Mississippi Gibraltar. The only telling sign that war was about to break open anew in mid-February, however, was Congress's approval of not only using blacks to fight, but also its consent to establish a national conscription act to stimulate volunteerism. The idea of national conscription to assist governors with meeting their quotas had been swirling around Washington that winter. Tod advised Stanton that if the administration needed more men, then Congress should arrange a "uniform system of drafting." "With this," he argued, "Ohio will, in my opinion, respond to any further calls made upon her, but without it it would be possible to raise any considerable number."⁶⁷

Governors understood that their willingness to accept conscription the previous summer would likely give way to a national conscription effort. To shorten the war, Lincoln needed means and authority to stretch the long arm of War Department into the states and extract the men to do it. Besides, the reports from the War Department told the story. According to Stanton's assistant, more than 100,000 soldiers were absent from the army, and their influence had become "every day more injurious, not only reducing the forces in the field and exciting discontent throughout the country, but tending greatly to bring into contempt the authority of the Government." Desertion was no longer regarded as a "crime among the class of men who are guilty of it," wrote Buckingham, "but has come to be considered as only an expert method of obtaining bounties and hiring substitutes."⁶⁸ Rosecrans was especially worried over desertion, and urged Ramsey to treat these rascals as criminals. The time had come to bring the system of raising volunteers under national government. In the same way they had endorsed confiscation, state conscription, emancipation, and black enlistment, governors believed the benefits would outweigh the problems. If it brought on resistance and animosity at home, soldiers relied on governors' to stifle such opposition. As winter wound down, military campaigns got underway, and if the Union was worth fighting for, then all military-age males should shoulder the burden of the freedom that came with it.⁶⁹

Congressmen recognized the need to enact conscription laws before the session closed. Massachusetts Senator Wilson led the way in gathering congressional support for a conscription act. The first national Enrollment Act made liable all male citizens between the ages of twenty and forty-five, and exempted those who were physically and mentally unfit for service, had been convicted of a felony, or who had special circumstances related to dependents. The act empowered the president to set draft quotas apportioned along congressional districts within states, based on need and accounting for those troops already in the service, but did not offer occupational deferments. Exemptions could be obtained when draftees hired a substitute, or purchased his way out of the draft for $300. The act helped move public resistance to raising black regiments to a more acceptable position, as Northern whites concluded it would now save them from conscription. New York journalist Charles G. Halpine of Hunter's staff serving in South Carolina was so inspired that he composed "Sambo's Right to Be Kilt," a satirical poem on the usefulness of the very race Northerners had considered degraded. Finally, the Union had found a place to assimilate blacks into white culture—the battlefield.[70]

National Conscription

"Stormy March has come at last," wrote Edwin O. Wentworth from Falmouth, Virginia, to his wife, "with howling winds and raging blast."[71] Two days later Lincoln signed the National Conscription Act, and Congress adjourned, having completed a remarkable legislative session. The inhospitable winter weather had disappeared, and all seemed tranquil in Washington. The Virginia front was quiet as well. "I have no news to write," confessed a private in the 11th Massachusetts, "every thing is quiet—no signs of movement." He acknowledged, "The President is now responsible for the suppression of the rebellion, but the people in the loyal States have got to stand by *him*, and the acts of Congress."[72] Yet the calm belied the storm ahead. News made its way through the wires, and citizens awakened to conscription's realities. Devised the previous year to boost volunteering, state conscription had been modestly successful. Yet on the heels of emancipation and black enlistment, national conscription made the Northern war effort appear weak and implied that governors had failed to maintain the volunteer spirit. Many Southerners interpreted it as a sign that Northerners refused to volunteer in protest of Lincoln's emancipation and of the kind of federal supremacy that was the very reason they had seceded.

Lincoln placed conscription in the hands of the Office of the Provost Marshal General, commanded by James B. Fry, a West Point disciplinarian. Governors had worked with provost marshals the previous year in managing state enrollment and welcomed the War Department's assistance in federalizing conscription. Even as volunteers trickled forward, expanding the manpower source was necessary to carry on the war and the occupation of conquered Southern soil. The new act placed conscription in federal hands and assigned provost marshals to congressional districts within the states. They were authorized to offer draftees the same bounty as volunteers (except those who paid $300 commutation or provided a substitute) and, if necessary, to establish quotas. Lincoln reserved the right to invoke the act only when governors determined that state recruiting efforts had failed, but, in the meantime, Fry's office assigned quotas to districts. Assessing quotas highlighted the conflict's political nature. Democrats had not been as enthused about joining the ranks as Republicans had. The recent election had given the Democratic Party a boost in several states where the protests were the loudest, only to be combated by Republicans claiming exemptions for large numbers of men already in the field. Seymour declared that quotas were biased, the Conscription Act was vague, and that Lincoln's usurpation of state power was unconstitutional. The governor worked with national authorities to ensure New York was not oversubscribed.[73]

Lincoln allowed soldiers away from the ranks until 1 April to return, and he warned those "evil-disposed and disloyal persons," who had encouraged desertion, to desist.[74] Governors supported these new measures, but there were loopholes, which produced ill will. Morton targeted the commutation section, which allowed every man who could "beg or borrow" $300 the chance to relieve himself from the draft. "I can assure you," he complained to Lincoln, "that this feature in the Bill is creating much excitement and ill feeling towards the Government among the poorer classes," which may lead to a "popular storm" of protest. He allowed that movements were underway to raise money to purchase the exemption of Democrats.[75]

Congressional adjournment did not end the flurry of political debate. The spring elections drew considerable national attention, especially since the Union's war aims had changed in the last several months. In Rhode Island, Sprague sought a U.S. Senate seat. His courtship of Kate Chase, the daughter of Treasury Secretary Chase, and his flagging manufacturing business may have inspired the change. Perhaps he thought he might be able to exert more influence in Washington as a senator in getting permits to transport Southern cotton to Rhode Island and in pressing Lincoln to allow black enlistment. Thus, when Senator James F. Simmons resigned the previous August, it opened Sprague's way to Washington. Legislators elected Lieutenant Governor Samuel G. Arnold to fill his vacancy until March. When Sprague vacated the governorship, it fell to William Cole Cozzens, who was the presiding officer in the Rhode Island Senate. A Newport resident, Cozzens was a career mercantilist, devout Episcopalian, and seasoned legislator, who held the gubernatorial seat until the April elections.[76]

New Hampshire voters were the first to express their approval or displeasure with the new war aims. Emancipation advanced the war in the South, they believed, yet conscription advanced a war in the North. While these aims were intended to be mutually beneficial, voters decided their merits at the polls. The editor of the *New Hampshire Statesman* picked up on the election's significance, professing that while New Hampshire was "not a great State," its voice in the coming election "will be more significant than that of New-York in quiet times—more significant than that of New-York last November." If the Democrats won the race, noted the editor, "it will be regarded as cumulative evidence that the North is not merely willing, but desirous that the War be ended by an inglorious surrender to blood-thirsty conspirators and red-handed rebels."[77] Given the dismal outcome the previous fall, Republicans hoped voters would favor these new federal directions. New Hampshire residents had not known the depressed economic conditions, heavy taxes, and arbitrary actions by the federal government experienced by other states. Joseph Albee Gilmore, a prominent businessman and railroad executive, won the Republican nomination for governor and expected to carry the party's counterattack against outspoken Democrats, who protested Lincoln's expansion of the war. The Union's dismal showing at Fredericksburg, where nearly half of New Hampshire's enlisted men fought, helped the Democrats. Ira Eastman, a superior court judge from Gilmanton, won the Democratic nomination, and a nasty race ensued. "The party against you is unscrupulous and may be ferocious," Baron Stow warned Gilmore.[78] Apprehensive about the outcome, Republicans tapped Gilmore's brother-in-law, William E. Chandler, a crafty, bespectacled lawyer and the House Speaker, to engineer a split in the opposition by enticing Colonel Walter Harriman of the 11th New Hampshire to run as a "War"

Democrat. When New Hampshirites went to the polls in March, Chandler's scheme worked only well enough to get the race thrown into the Republican legislature to decide the result when it reconvened in June. Thus, for nearly three months, New Hampshire hung in the balance.[79]

Connecticut Republicans renominated Buckingham in a "poorly attended" Union convention held a few weeks before the April election, and they prepared for a close race.[80] Democrats clung to the coattails of Vallandigham's antiadministration peace offerings, nominated Thomas H. Seymour, and engaged in a recriminatory campaign against Buckingham's blind allegiance to Lincoln. Fearing a loss at the polls, Buckingham relied on agents to poll the troops who could be sent home to vote for the Republican ticket, and, under the guise of duty, Stanton allowed them home. Soldiers in the field overwhelmingly endorsed Buckingham, and many signed resolutions urging their home-front voters to favor the governor, who ultimately won the contest. "Governor Buckingham has filled the office of the Executive of the State," declared the soldiers of the 1st Connecticut Artillery, "to the entire satisfaction of the soldiers whom Connecticut has sent to fight the battles of freedom, and they prefer him."[81] Lieutenant Henry Perkins Goddard wrote his hometown paper, the *Norwich Bulletin*, that the soldiers of the 14th Connecticut knew that Buckingham "has shed tears of sympathy for their misfortunes and has done his best to alleviate them." He described that "The Fourteenth Regiment is composed mainly of men who can read and think for themselves, and though there is some difference of political opinion ... two thirds of our two hundred and twenty-five men for duty would, if they had the power, cast their votes for William A. Buckingham."[82]

In Minnesota, Governor Ramsey's recent selection to Congress to fill the seat of Senator Henry Rice and the resignation of Lieutenant Governor Donnelly, who was also elected to Congress, allowed Henry A. Swift, sitting president pro tempore of the Minnesota Senate, to become Minnesota's third governor. But, because Ramsey did not relinquish the executive office until July, the unelected Swift had little authority. Before leaving office, Ramsey oversaw the reimbursement of Minnesotans whose homes had been destroyed by Indians, the transport of convicts to prisons in Iowa, and the banishment of the Sioux Indians.[83] In the meantime, he secured the best arms for troops fighting with Rosecrans's army. Swift had an interesting path to power. He left Ohio in 1853, having graduated Western Reserve College with distinction, tutored briefly on a Mississippi plantation, and, after being admitted to the bar, ventured west to Minnesota, where he practiced law.

His political aspirations grew with a trip to Washington in the winter of 1857–58, when he gained experience in acquiring land grants for railroads and in assisting his political colleagues in their push for Minnesota statehood. At forty years old, the diffident Ohio native devoted his attention to soldier welfare.[84]

As the spring election season opened, Grant had made progress in getting to Vicksburg, and governors had encouraging signs from the front to sway the electorate. Grant ordered General Banks up the Mississippi River from New Orleans toward Port Hudson, which forced the Confederates to decide whether to hold the southern or northern end of the river. The commander's alleged drinking, however, prompted Lincoln and Stanton to send Charles Dana, managing editor of the *New York Tribune*, to serve as the paper's correspondent covering Grant's command, which allowed them to watch the general. Winter weather was giving way to spring, and the Confederates would soon be on the move elsewhere. Grant, however, had no intention of giving up on Vicksburg. He needed his circumstances to change or to change them himself.[85]

Meanwhile, Lincoln sent Burnside to Ohio to replace General Wright and to assist Tod in stifling political enemies. For over a year Tod had combated fiery editorials in the press written by Democrats discouraging enlistments, and he used his power to have journalistic traitors arrested. The previous summer, he facilitated the arrest of Democratic Congressman Edson B. Olds, a peace advocate, who had discouraged enlistments. During his four-month incarceration at Fort Lafayette in New York, Olds brought kidnapping charges against the governor. In the spring, authorities arrested the governor, but Tod's lawyers argued successfully that he was absolved from legal action while in office. Olds harassed the governor for the remainder of the war. The case was among the most celebrated in Ohio's political history and indicative of the degree to which Democrats would go to assail the chief executive.[86]

Governors tried in vain to keep the Northern populace focused on the Union cause more than on Union leaders, but emancipation and conscription worked against them. Even with the threat of the draft, governors struggled to fill up existing units or raise new regiments while thousands of soldiers were away on leave. As chief executives saw it, the real crisis now was that once soldiers went on leave, they faced formidable opposition at home to returning to battle. Evidence of disloyalty was convincing, and Kirkwood had written to Senator Grimes two months before that it could not be ignored. Iowa's Knights of the Golden Circle presented him a "very unfortunate condition of affairs," he informed Stanton.[87] The group's object was to embarrass the administration by encouraging desertions, protecting deserters from arrest, and preparing the public mind for armed resistance to conscription. Change would come in the fall elections, Kirkwood warned, unless he could maintain order. Desperate to maintain peace, Kirkwood armed companies in each of the southern counties and advised Gamble to do the same, "if for no other reason, on the ground of 'a proper comity to this State, which is not willing to have its peace endangered by vagabonds, robbers and murderers from Missouri.'"[88] By the end of March, letters from Iowa's border residents pleading for protection moved him to request Stanton to have federal marshals "hunt up" all the men who were known to be engaged in treasonous activities. When rumors surfaced that Lincoln offered Kirkwood an ambassadorship to Denmark, residents beseeched the governor to remain in office, at least until the fall election. He understood his role in igniting the revolution that emancipation and conscription had ignited. "I supported the administration in conducting the war, before it struck at slavery," Kirkwood declared. "I support it now when it strikes at slavery and I shall continue to support it if it ceases to strike at slavery."[89]

Stanton worried over western dissension, especially since state legislatures fanned oppositionists' fires. The War Department's acceptance of black regiments into federal service coincided with threats of national conscription, and the secretary sought to ease pressure among the states by expanding the use of contraband slaves. Lincoln, meanwhile, expected good news from the front, but he would have settled for good news from the rear, especially in New York. Thurlow Weed had emphasized the significance of Seymour's election to Lincoln in December when in Washington. "Governor Seymour has greater power just now for good than any other man in the country," Lincoln remarked. "He can wheel the Democratic Party into line, put down the rebellion, and preserve the government."[90] Lincoln understood this power, but despite everything Congress and the governors had done in advancing a more vigorous war on paper, much had gone wrong on the battlefield, and Seymour used it to his advantage. He denounced the War Department's meddling in state affairs, the administration's abuse of civil liberties, the suspension of habeas corpus, and its defiance of local self-government. Most important he claimed that Lincoln lost the western states when he abandoned conciliation. The Union, Seymour believed, resided not in the New England states that embraced the expansion of federal power, but in the central and western states with the greatest population and resources that resisted it. The governor "imagined himself to be not a mere citizen of the United States, but a kind of subordinate sovereign—governor of New York State—bound to work out a policy differing from the then policy of the Union."[91]

So important was the governor's message that distinguished New York lawyer John V. L. Pruyn invited Seymour and other close friends to his Albany home to review the contents before he delivered it. Upon delivery, his words stirred state legislators and political leaders around the country. Naval Secretary Welles recorded in his diary that it was sad to witness "the spirit of party overpowering patriotism" in New York. The "jesuitical and heartless insincerity of Seymour," he noted, "is devoid of true patriotism, weak in statesmanship, and a discredit to the position he occupies. Unhallowed partisan and personal aspirations are moving springs with him."[92] Even Lord Lyons, British Minister to the United States, remarked to British Foreign Secretary Earl Russell that Seymour's address had pronounced at "great length and in severe terms a condemnation of the arbitrary arrests, the proclamation of martial law, and other proceedings of the Federal Executive Government," which in Seymour's view were as much a violation of the Constitution as the rebellion itself.[93] So impressed were Indiana's Democratic assemblymen that they approved a resolution in praise of Seymour's denunciations.[94]

Seymour's address provoked a storm of protest against him both in the ranks and in the legislature. Cavalryman Morris E. Fitch, for example, wrote his brother that he did not want to "be led by such vile hypocrites as Horatio Seymour or any of his followers," who had told his New Yorkers that if there was a draft, to resist it. Although he wished that all "niggers, nigger drivers and rebel owners was drove into the sea where the Devil drove the hogs," Fitch urged his family to understand that the true design of the Emancipation Proclamation was to weaken the Confederacy.[95] The Republican legislature agreed, and took the wind from Seymour's sails. He suffered his first setback in March, when representatives locked horns over replacing Republican senator Preston King. Weed labored to secure Morgan's election as senator, arguing he had been a model governor in working with his legislature, and in meeting the needs of the War Department with great efficiency. His commission as a major general was a compliment to the more than 150,000 soldiers he placed in the field, though he never accepted any payment. As he had been in the dark days when Washington had been cut off from the North, Morgan had again become the man of the hour. He was "gifted by nature with a fine physical organization—a quick, active intellect, and [possessed] a long and intimate familiarity with men and affairs," boasted Weed's *Albany Evening Journal*.[96] Still popular among New Yorkers, Morgan found the possibility of extending his political arm to Capitol Hill excited him, and he allowed Weed to campaign for him.[97]

As much as Morgan's senatorial bid encouraged Lincoln, Weed's retirement from the *Albany Evening Journal* gave the president "a good deal of uneasiness."[98] He needed to reach out and cultivate the new governor's support. After all, even Seymour's adversaries described him "as a gentleman of commanding talents, high culture," a political leader of "bland and winning manners, admired social and domestic life."[99] Hoping the governor would not bring New York into conflict with the national government, Lincoln extended his hand to Seymour. It was time Lincoln accepted defeat in New York. "Dear Sir," the president began his confidential letter of 23 March, "you and I are substantially strangers; and I write this chiefly that we may become better acquainted." He wrote, "I, for the time being, am at the head of a nation which is in great peril; and you are at the head of the greatest State of that nation." He added, "As to maintaining the nation's life, and integrity, I assume, and believe, there can be no difference of *purpose* between you and me. If we should differ as to the *means*, it is important that such differences should be as small as possible—that it should not be enhanced by unjust suspicions on one side or the other." He concluded by appealing to Seymour's patriotism and cooperation, and invited Seymour to air his views.[100]

Silence was power, and Seymour waited a few weeks as he calculated his response. Schooled in the "politics of the Albany Regency—Van Buren and Marcy," the governor "preferred to talk than write letters," as conversations were "off the record." For important matters Seymour entrusted his younger brother John to act as his liaison in Washington. In fact, John had already reported on his interview with Lincoln in which the president stated that "he had the same stake in the life of the country as the governor—that, if the Union were broken up, there would be no 'next President' of the United States."[101] More important, he related that Lincoln believed that there were but three possible courses currently: fight until Confederate leaders were overthrown, demand a cease-fire and permit a division of the Union, or negotiate for compromise. To relieve the president, Seymour replied that his brother had no presidential aspirations because it was too much trouble.

Lincoln could attest to the trouble, yet at the moment he needed to disarm the governor by enlisting his support.[102]

Across much of the North, the end of March looked nothing like spring, as the cold weather lingered well into April. It had been a depressing winter, but the seasonal change brought with it the adjournment of many state legislatures and a welcome reprieve for some governors. The divisive issues of emancipation, black enlistments, and national conscription had invigorated the political scene on the state level. It revealed the extremes to which oppositionists would go to oppose these new conditions and the governors. In Illinois, the Democrats forced Yates's hand by adjourning in mid-February and postponing reconvening until June 2, so that peace delegates could travel to Capitol Hill and consult about a possible truce. Yates informed Lincoln of this turn of events and wired Stanton that he needed some units to remain at home to return deserters and to protect civilians against vigilantes opposing the draft.[103]

The situation was no better in New Jersey, where Republicans fired cannons in celebration of the Democratic legislators' departure from Trenton. Before they adjourned, congressmen passed a series of "Peace Resolutions" in protest of sacrificing their citizens to free slaves. They demanded that Parker act on their behalf in sending these resolutions to Congress. Although many soldiers believed that such Copperheadism did represent the majority of New Jerseyans, they were nonetheless embarrassed and ashamed by political representatives who engaged in such treasonous acts. "Language fails me," wrote one lieutenant, "in expressing my hate and disgust for these vile, sneaking, croaking copperhead traitors."[104] Despite such mean-spirited posturing, Parker supporters prevailed in keeping their governor sufficiently funded and armed to conduct efforts to sustain Lincoln and never really impeded his progress in restoring the Union.[105]

Antiwar dissidents gained considerable momentum, and this aroused pro-Union and pro-war citizens to come forth and privately fund the war effort. In fact, the Copperhead movement sparked an even greater movement of loyal organizations to combat their negative influence. Union Leagues had established a bipartisan patriotism that was emerging throughout the North, and governors drew on the clubs' resources to make up for the inadequacies of their state treasuries. Andrew encouraged membership in the Union Club of Boston, which was modeled after the clubs in New York City and Philadelphia and headed by Samuel Gray Ward, close associate Ralph Waldo Emerson, and Forbes. Curtin used Philadelphia's membership to help his course in Pennsylvania. Soldiers in the field appreciated these patriotic associations. Encamped near Harpers Ferry, Robert Kirkwood of the 1st Maryland wrote his mother that "all appear to be in the best of spirits, the union feeling is stronger everyday those great union associations and speeches at the North and in the Border states has produced a good affect among the troops here [and] I hope the same will exist through out [sic] the Loyal states in order to swamp the copper heads who are trying to prolong the war by spreading their secession poison throughout the country."[106]

Californians and Oregonians were no different than other Northerners in protesting emancipation, conscription, black enlistment, and the suspension of the writ of habeas corpus. California's Stanford had made great strides in acknowledging the significance of emancipation on the Confederacy, calling it a "great Moral Declaration." Having stated four years before that he preferred "the white man to the Negro as an inhabitant of our country," the governor's attitude change reflected the times.[107] Wright had arrested recalcitrant citizens who encouraged desertion or engaged in other treasonous activities and hoped to discourage dissenter groups such as the Knights of the Golden Circle. He called upon Stanford and Oregon's Gibbs to arm with federal weapons loyal militia groups, which were used as a kind of military police. He understood the paramount importance of using governors' power and authority in policing the population and supplied them with arms to do so. When Stanton disapproved of his course and suspended weapon shipments, Stanford wired a copy of a Senate resolution requesting the national government supply the governor with arms. Stanton responded that a 15,000 stand "of the best Springfield muskets" were on their way, and that he could send 15,000 more as well as five complete batteries.

Meanwhile, Pacific Coast governors continued to safeguard Union possessions. They organized coastal patrols, constructed forts to allow the army to protect the mining regions, suppressed Confederate-supported uprisings in southern California, and combated Indian uprisings. Stanford called on frontier citizens to raise companies for protection, and Gibbs relied on the 1st Oregon Cavalry to assist in the construction of forts to protect against Indians. Yet when soldiers abandoned Fort Hoskins near Corvallis, one resident protested to Gibbs. "Here are 2,500 of the worst Indians on the coast," he wrote, "Indians who have been engaged in war; who have destroyed settlements, burned infants, carried off women captive, surrounded and nearly captured companies of U.S. troops ... who have been led to believe the

Government has failed." With these atrocities in view and the abandonment of soldiers, miners expecting to return to the mines were turned away. Gibbs ordered a small detachment to man the fort until a company of volunteers could be dispatched to protect the residents. To add to West Coast concerns, Californians eager to participate in the conflict had been lured by Boston agents offering sizeable bounties and enlisted in Massachusetts regiments for service. Andrew endorsed the practice, but Stanford considered it officious and self-serving.[108] The war at home was spreading.

CHAPTER THIRTEEN

Is It Well or Ill with Us?

Connecticut voters traveled to the polls in early April and reelected Buckingham by a 3,000-vote majority over Seymour. In the face of changing war aims, the governor relied on patronage, troop furloughs, and Union leagues to secure his election. Democratic gains, however, made for a stormy legislative session when representatives gathered in May. Buckingham's victory confirmed that most residents endorsed ending the war on the battlefield rather than in peace talks. Welles sent the governor a congratulatory note, but acknowledged the misfortune that the opposition "secured so large a vote for a candidate whose avowed sympathies are with traitors, and whose platform is devoid of honest patriotism."[1] Buckingham agreed, wiring Stanton that "the copperheads have sunk into their hides & hiding places & I only hope that whenever they make their appearance again they will receive the indignation & contempt which treason merits."[2] The Connecticut result buoyed New Englanders and gave evidence of political fortunes to come. "The great 'tidal wave' sweeps on," declared the *Providence Daily Journal*, "New England stands with unbroken ranks for the government and the war."[3]

Rhode Islanders held elections the same week, following a muddled political campaign. To replace Sprague, Republicans settled on James Y. Smith of Providence. Smith had been Sprague's party rival in 1861, but now drew on the governor's popular support to succeed him. The Democrats' canvass came to an unfortunate end, as the *New York Times* remarked, "they can't find one of their own party who wants [the] office."[4] According to the editor, it was rumored that Cozzen refused to be nominated by the Democrats "because he has too much loyalty to be a candidate of a party [that] regards the war as 'dishonorable,' and declares that our brave soldiers who laid down their lives in the battles of the Union were 'sacrificed to the fanaticism of New-England.'" The correspondent remarked that such was the fate of the New England Copperheads, and that "when bad men combine, good men must unite."[5] Thus, loyal Rhode Islanders responded by forming Union leagues to support the government's vigorous prosecution of the war. There were no major battles to sway public opinion away from the Republicans, and they carried nearly every county in the state. Smith won the April election by more than 2,700 votes. The Connecticut native had many attributes. He had excelled in business at a young age and moved to Providence, where he used his talents to secure prominence as a lumberman. He invested in the manufacture of cotton in Williamantic, Connecticut, and Woonsocket, Rhode Island, and quickly amassed a small fortune that enabled him to retire from the lumber business and concentrate on his manufacturing interests. Smith was a shrewd businessman in the state's budding cotton manufacturing industry, and his work ethic made him successful. He was at one time a conservative Democrat, but Rhode Islanders elected him mayor of Providence without a party affiliation. His victory, on the heels of Buckingham's election, prompted the *Chicago Tribune* to declare that the "splendor of the late triumphs of the Union cause in the North, goes far toward wiping out the stain of last year's defeats."[6]

Andrew was also up for reelection, but not until the fall, and it did not deter him from advancing his views about black enlistments. He began his April correspondence to Stanton by encouraging the secretary to see affairs his way. Spring had arrived in Boston, and the governor's windblown strolls to the office signaled that it was time to expand the manpower source for the military campaigns that would soon follow. He requested that Stanton consider organizing black troops in North Carolina and pressed him to dispatch the emerging all-black 54th regiment south to encourage blacks there to join the Union regiments. "When our regiment gets there," he argued, "it will be the nest egg of a brigade," as he believed the work was "already ripe."[7] The governor wanted to bring his proposition to "the public mind," hoping that its success would stifle criticism. "Unless we do it in Massachusetts," he wrote, "it cannot be expected elsewhere, while if we do it others will ultimately and indeed soon follow." In the meantime, he wanted Stanton to send the 54th regiment to South Carolina, where, under General Hunter, black troops would be appreciated and allowed a place in active war.[8]

Before the spring campaigns opened, several governors traveled to Washington to confer with Lincoln about additional black regiments, home-front dissension, and soldier welfare. Many believed that convalescing soldiers would be better cared for closer to home and that such arrangements would encourage volunteering. Wisconsin governor Salomon arrived to discuss the establishment of a general hospital at Milwaukee to care for soldiers of the Northwest. Passing through New York City, the governor might have made time to hear Indiana governor Morton's rousing speech at the Maison Dorée Hotel. Morton was also on his way to Washington, and Mayor Opdyke invited the governor to give a public address. Given his concerns that a Northwest Confederacy movement was purportedly underway, Morton used the occasion to emphasize the country's reliance on the Mississippi River for trade and that Union campaigns should secure dominance in this region.[9]

Enemies and Politics in the Rear

Despite New England's political victories, Northerners appeared to be risking their own cause. Dissension had escalated into violence, desertion was rampant, and secret societies kept governors focused on local rather than national affairs. Chief executives appealed to the War Department to keep troops at home to safeguard communities, return deserters, and stifle enrollment hostilities. When Burnside sent Illinois troops guarding prisoners to Kentucky, it left the governor nearly defenseless, and Yates complained to Stanton. From Harrisburg, Curtin reported that dissident Pennsylvanians had joined secret anticonscription leagues and pledged to resist the draft. Some of these groups met at taverns, schoolhouses, and in barns, and were instigated by the *Reading Eagle*, a German newspaper "bitterly hostile to the administration."[10] The winter had taken its toll on the governor, and his debilitating health and the hostility toward him for supporting Lincoln's new war aims discouraged him. The governor decided he would not serve another term and wired Lincoln that he would entertain any offer for a federal position, perhaps as a foreign minister. Lincoln wired back that if Curtin desired to go abroad he could do so with a first-class appointment.[11]

To assist midwestern governors in stifling disloyalty, Burnside issued General Order No. 38 in his newly assigned Department of the Ohio. This order authorized the military arrest of anyone engaged in treasonous activities or in sympathy with the enemy, and ordered the death penalty for anyone found guilty of assisting Confederates. It also provided for the deportation of Southern sympathizers to enemy lines. Burnside would have extended his military arm into Indiana, but Morton feared it was more like an iron fist and resisted the idea, even though many Radical Republicans would have welcomed the heavy-handed approach.[12]

For all the backstage maneuvering in managing enrollment and stifling opposition, western governors were delighted to read about the Union's progress on the Mississippi that spring. For months, Confederates and swampy terrain stymied Grant's campaign to take Vicksburg, but failure hardened the commander's resolve. The night passage by the Mississippi river city by

Acting Rear Admiral David D. Porter's flotilla on 16 April was the key to Grant's buildup of forces for his ambitious overland offensive, and the commander expected to ferry troops across the mile-wide expanse at Bruinsburg. From there troops would move northeast toward Jackson, the Mississippi state capital, and then west to Vicksburg. Grant's ambitious scheme worried Lincoln, but he feared General Hooker faced greater challenges in Virginia. The president visited the commander at Falmouth on the Rappahannock River and reminded him that Lee's army, not the Confederate capital, was his target. After several days of inspections, Lincoln returned to Washington, encouraged by his visit. In the meantime, West Virginia voters had ratified their state constitution, which included a provision for the gradual emancipation of slaves, and Lincoln signed the congressional act that admitted the new state to the Union, effective 20 June. Pierpont had done his duty in shepherding legislators through the process, but he would not be a candidate for the gubernatorial post for the new state. Instead, he supported Arthur I. Boreman, a Wood County Whig, for that post.[13]

By the end of April, enrollment management and soldier welfare consumed governors' days, but Hooker's overconfidence and soldiers' lack of morale facing impending battle troubled them. Given the Fredericksburg debacle, several governors traveled to Virginia to encourage their troops. Reports from the field agitated Coburn, and he toured the Maine camps, yet his presence did little to relieve their anxieties about the imminent battle. Charles Mattocks of the 17th Maine remarked in his diary that the "Gov. is not much of a speechmaker any way, but seems to be a jolly old soul."[14] John Haley was less charitable. "Governor Coburn is, without exception, the most wretched speechmaker that ever burnished the cushion of the governor's chair," he declared. "What sin have we committed," he confided, "that we should be so punished, and on the eve of battle, too?"[15] Having undertaken his new role, Governor Parker was eager to review his Jersey Blues at the front. Colonel Robert McAllister wrote that the boys welcomed the governor "handsomely," and impressed him that they could "march well, drill well, show off well" and were eager to prove their mettle. Parker made a speech before departing and convinced the soldiers that he would "be all right on the war question."[16] Germans of the 11th Corps were especially pleased to see Curtin. Colonel Alwin von Matzdorff of the 75th Pennsylvania recalled the governor's gesture of stopping by his tent to share some wine. These Germans were more impressed, however, by the arrival of Salomon, a German native, who had traveled from Madison to ensure that his Wisconsin soldiers were well equipped on the eve of battle. The governor's heritage found wide acceptance among those who could openly converse in their native language, and who "decorated the camp with boughs and festoons." "In my whole life," remarked the German chief executive, "I have never before been so proud of my German descent as I am now in the camp of the Twenty-sixth Regiment."[17]

Governors departed the front, knowing it would not be long before news of the impending battle came over the wires. Curtin returned to Harrisburg and pestered Lincoln with telegrams about the 4,000 Confederate cavalrymen near Morgantown heading for Pennsylvania. Lincoln reassured the governor that Pennsylvanians should not expect an invasion and that he saw no good reason to trouble the people unnecessarily by calling out the militia. Chief executives followed military operations closely that spring, and by 30 April, they learned that Grant had transported his army across the Mississippi and headed for the state capital at Jackson. Stanton kept a close watch on Grant's movements through his private correspondence with Dana, the New York journalist, who reported that McClernand was conniving to get Grant out of command. Yates had been instrumental in McClernand's gaining command, and the correspondence between Yates and McClernand confirmed Dana's assessment. "Time is passing," McClernand wrote Yates, hoping for a change, "& the Republic is dying of *inertia*."[18] He declared, "If, as you & other loyal governors recommended, the government would give me an independent command, I could do something for the Country." He wrote, "Come down and see us. Bring Gov. Morton & Kirkwood if you can—at all events, come yourself."[19] Although McClernand believed he could do something with an independent command, Lincoln and Stanton had grown tired of his machinations.

At the Front

It took little prodding to get governors to travel to the front, so Yates accepted McClernand's invitation, and, with Elihu B. Washburne, he debarked for Smith's plantation near Columbus, Mississippi. The governor's arrival in late April was a welcome scene. "The soldier boys think there is no one to excel 'Uncle Dick Yates,'" remarked Albert O. Marshall of the 33rd Illinois. "They do not stop for any ceremony, but at once cry out 'Hurrah for Dick

Yates,'" he declared, "all who can near him shake hands with him." He boasted, "Every Illinois boy knows him by sight," and "it is plain that Governor Yates is popular with the soldier boys."[20]

Beneath the shady Oaks at Magnolia Church, Yates and Washburne attended to the wounded troops and arranged to send the most serious medical cases back to Illinois. During the battle of Port Gibson fought on 1 May, Yates expanded his war experience by accompanying Grant to the front. Both men came under enemy fire, and Yates appeared to "bob and weave" in the saddle. Amused, Grant remarked, "Governor, it's too late to dodge after the ball has passed."[21] Yates survived, and sent a dispatch to Springfield describing the victory and that the Illinois troops displayed the "greatest gallantry." On his return trip to Springfield, Yates suffered a bout with dysentery that detained him in Memphis for several days. As much as he wanted to break bread with the troops, living the soldier life took its toll on the governor. Nonetheless, Yates wanted to be with them when they opened the Mississippi River.[22]

Grant's achievements encouraged Lincoln as well as the governors supplying the commander troops, but reports from the Rappahannock countered their feelings. In the first week of May, Hooker and Lee's armies bloodied the Wilderness Woods near Chancellorsville, and on 6 May, the Union commander withdrew his army north of the river. It was a painful message "Fighting Joe" wired to Lincoln, reporting his loss. Noah Brooks was conversing with physician Anson Henry, an Illinois friend staying at the White House, when Lincoln entered the room carrying a field telegram. After closing the door, a "ghost-like" president approached the men, looking as careworn as ever. "Had a thunderbolt fallen upon the President," remarked Brooks, "he could not have been more overwhelmed."[23] Lincoln's face, "usually sallow, was ashen in hue" and his whole body seemed broken as he gave Brooks the telegram.[24] As Brooks read the news of Hooker's withdrawal from the south side of the Rappahannock, the president's appearance "was piteous." Walking back and forth in the room with his hands clutched behind him, he could only find the utterances, "My God! My God! What will the country say! What will the country say!"[25]

It was an inglorious retreat as the wagon trains and ambulance boats, heavy-laden with wounded soldiers, sloshed their way to safety. Lincoln left the same day for Hooker's headquarters. Stanton, however, reported the unpleasant news to the governors and found the casualty figures estimating upward of 17,000 staggering. "This is the darkest day of the whole war," he remarked, "It seems as if the bottom had fallen out."[26] It was the height of despair in Washington, and the wires to governors, who were laboring to counter political dissent and legislative recalcitrance, failed to relieve them. Governors had struggled to foster an atmosphere conducive to sustaining the armies, and many citizens looked to them to carry the president through the downward spiral. They understood these military ebbs and flows and resisted piling on the acrimony. Instead, they needed honest answers. On the day after the battle, Lincoln searched for a response to a telling communiqué from Morton. "Is it well or ill with us?" read the short note that came from Indianapolis.[27] Andrew was also deeply concerned but managed to mask his emotions. "May I ask if the storm and rise of the Rappahannock determined Hooker's recrossing?" he queried Stanton.[28]

Stanton's masterful spin put a positive twist on the disaster. He reported that while Hooker failed, there was "no serious disaster to the organization and efficiency of the army." Hooker would "speedily resume offensive operations," he declared.[29] Lincoln's tone to the commander, however, spoke volumes. "My Dear Sir," he began, "the recent movement of your army is ended without effecting its object," and an "early movement would ... help to supersede the bad moral effect of the recent one, which is said to be considerably injurious."[30] Governors cared less for the army's organization and efficiency than they did for its morale and battlefield success. Army correspondents revealed that the result was more injurious than Stanton admitted. Their reports were shocking and prompted several governors to travel to Virginia. Blair surprised the boys of the First Division of the Fifth Corps, arriving in camp days after the battle. Lieutenant John Bancroft of the 4th Michigan was pleased to hear from the governor that citizens at home prayed for them and counted on them to bring victory. Curtin returned to the camps, listened to the soldiers and commanders, and concluded that Hooker's leadership was sorely lacking. Passing through Washington on his return to Harrisburg, he came upon the demoralized men of the 148th Pennsylvania. Curtin knew many of these men, as they were drawn from his home county. "Vain indeed were his efforts to cancel his sad emotions," recalled Captain Robert H. Forster, who reported that Curtin's voice cracked and quivered while speaking, so that "few that heard his touching and pathetic words will ever forget it."[31]

Governors were hard pressed to turn their attention away from the news at Chancellorsville and Vicksburg that first week in May. Yet when military authorities barged into Clement Vallandigham's Ohio home and dragged him to headquarters, it made national headlines. Burnside ordered the former congressman's arrest after a treasonous speech, and days later he was tried and convicted under military tribunal for violating General Order No. 38. In the coming weeks, Lincoln would order the irascible Ohioan sent behind Confederate lines to Wilmington, North Carolina, and he would not be allowed to return to the Union. In the meantime, the arrest touched off protests across the North as outraged citizens denounced the administration for overpowering the citizenry. Yet many soldiers applauded his incarceration. "No news has reached the army of late that has caused so much shouting and cheering," Ephraim Holloway wrote his wife, "as did the news of the arrest of that arch traitor Valandigham [sic]. We hope they will hang him."[32]

Nonetheless, the Ohioan's arrest on the heels of Hooker's defeat hampered governors seeking to proceed peacefully with enrollment. Commissioners had made progress in the last few months, but the figures were confusing, and governors feared recent events would weaken their efforts. When Provost Marshal Fry's office completed its review, the assessment revealed that eleven states were delinquent by roughly 87,000 soldiers, but the remaining states had excesses of more than 100,000 soldiers. Thus, under Lincoln's 1862 calls the armies on paper were oversubscribed by 13,000 men. This gave the appearance that conscription had proven successful. Yet it also revealed that several states were carrying more than their share of the war's burden, while others were significantly delinquent. Publicizing this information would cause a "bad feeling," and Fry warned Stanton to call for a draft only in the deficient states, and to do it quietly, communicating through provost marshals. Given the draft's explosive nature, Fry hoped to avoid further fallout. Stanton, however, refused the advice, and wired the governors their excesses and deficiencies.[33]

His circulars touched off a firestorm of protest, prompting a barrage of exchanges between governors and the War Department over assessments. Iowa, for example, had met its quota, but Kirkwood believed enrolling men along political districts would cause problems, and he urged Fry to equalize assessments among counties and townships. Indiana had also exceeded its quota, and, knowing his state was exempt, Morton recommended that conscription be made immediately and that it be large enough to concentrate on opening the Mississippi River. Holbrook was surprised that Vermont was found deficient and maintained that his figures confirmed the state had fulfilled its quota. Buckingham owned up to his shortage, but the Connecticut press had given his residents the impression the state had filled its quota. It would take some time to dispel this error in order that a draft be conducted, but Buckingham anticipated no problems. If there was to be resistance to the draft, he argued, "it might as well be here as anywhere."[34] Massachusetts was also deficient, but the organization of black regiments encouraged Andrew. Hunter wired the governor from Hilton Head that he was satisfied "with the results of the organization of negro regiments," and with a "few more regiments of intelligent colored men from the North," he could make "extensive excursions upon the mainland."[35]

To assist with the organization of black regiments, governors worked with Major Charles W. Foster, who administrated the Bureau of Colored Troops (BCT), and who relied on Southern agents to supply former slaves for Northern units. Having raised more than 2,400 soldiers for the First Brigade of the New York State Colored Volunteers, Major Henry M. Herman petitioned Stanton to have the national government recognize them. The Association for Promoting Colored Volunteers strengthened Herman's efforts by petitioning Lincoln to accept them, but the president could not accept the regiment until New York governor Seymour recognized it as a state unit. However, Seymour was opposed to the national government's recruitment of blacks. In protest, prominent New Yorkers, including Horace Greeley, William Cullen Bryant, and Mayor George Opdyke, sent a delegation to Washington to enlist Lincoln's favor in using New York blacks. The delegation reported that some 3,000 blacks had already consented to enlist, and that perhaps as many 10,000 could be ready in two months.[36]

By the time Stanton issued his quota circulars, Grant was driving the Confederates out of Jackson, Mississippi, and toward Vicksburg to lay siege to the city. The advance resulted in the battle of Champion's Hill. Banks, meanwhile, made his way to Port Hudson, Louisiana, above Baton Rouge and, on 18 May, defeated Johnston's Confederates at the battle of Big Black River. As successful as these ventures were, they came at a heavy price. Commanders flooded governors with requests for medical supplies, personnel, and additional troops to sustain the Union grip on these important river cities, and this placed an unprecedented burden on the chief executives. Salomon pulled together an expedition, departed Madison, and headed south with the intention of transferring soldiers to Northern hospitals. The expedition stopped briefly at St. Louis, where the governor found the Western

Sanitary Commission with an Iowa delegation, including Kirkwood. When the boat arrived at Chickasaw Bayou, the governors visited the troops. To buoy their spirits, Kirkwood told his Iowans that "all the prettiest and best Iowa girls were going to wait for husbands until they got home."[37] Kirkwood took special interest in his troops, scouring the Mississippi countryside for them, and they appreciated his attention to their welfare. The governor requested that Stanton transport the most seriously wounded Iowans to the Keokuk Hospital. Wherever he went, his Iowans cheered him. His visit generated so much applause that the Confederates fired a few volleys into the Iowa camps to subdue them. One soldier recalled that, given the dust on the road, had he met the governor anywhere on the march, "I might possibly have asked him what *train* he belonged to, very innocently, mistaking him for a teamster."[38]

As much as Gamble wanted to assist Grant and travel to Mississippi to see his soldiers, he had no Missourians to send, and spent more time in Washington than in the field with his troops. The governor was stymied by his personal war with Curtis and personally conferred with Lincoln to have the commander removed. Curtis's abolitionist ways were undercutting civil governance, and Gamble urged Lincoln to replace the commander. Lincoln finally relieved Curtis and appointed John Schofield in his place. Gamble welcomed the change and placed the enrolled militia and provisional regiments under his command. With Curtis gone, Gamble could take gradual emancipation to the state convention. Still, the change did little to quell the acrimony between Missouri's political factions. Critics complained that Gamble was proslavery and that Schofield was too conservative, and their protests to Lincoln caused the president to snap. "It is very painful to me," he wired, "that you in Missouri can not, or will not settle your factional quarrel among yourselves."[39] He continued, "I have been tormented with it beyond endurance for months, by both sides," and "neither side pays the least respect to my appeals to your reason." Lincoln stood firm, and Schofield remained.[40] The president did not relieve Curtis because of any conviction that he had done anything wrong, but because the commander represented one faction among the Union men and Gamble represented the other. Since he could not relieve Gamble, he relieved Curtis. In giving Schofield the command, he offered his advice. "If both factions, or neither, shall abuse you, you will probably, be about right," Lincoln wrote, "beware of being assailed by one and praised by the other."[41]

Politics of Conscription

As much as governors favored black enlistments and conscription, nationalizing the army came at considerable cost. Copperheads had grown more aggressive in their efforts against federal expansion, and it complicated the civil-military management of the war. Having won the Union's most important governorship, New York's Seymour was their idol. The conservative intellectual gave states' rights advocates respectable leadership. In crossing swords with the president, he opposed emancipation, conscription, and Vallandigham's arrest. Yet Seymour met with New York's provost marshal, Colonel Robert Nugent, and convinced him that he would throw no obstacles in the way of the national authorities carrying out the enrollment. The governor had pledged as much some weeks before in a letter to Lincoln. "For the preservation of the Union," he wrote Lincoln, "I am ready to make every sacrifice."[42] Although he made it clear that New Yorkers had oversubscribed to the president's 1862 calls, Nugent apprised Stanton that a large number of these men deserted before the regiments left the state or before they mustered into the U.S. service. He trusted that Stanton and Seymour could come to a speedy and amicable agreement on the precise number to be credited to New York.[43]

Even while agreeing to preserve the Union, Seymour wanted to change Lincoln's course. Vallandigham's arrest, he believed, gave him justification. He wrote to Ohio congressman George H. Pendleton that he had waited until the case went public before he denounced the act as "cowardly, brutal, and infamous." He wrote, "Unless the case shall assume some new aspect, I shall take an early public occasion to express my views upon the subject."[44] The opportunity presented itself on 16 May, when the outspoken railroad executive Erastus Corning headed a formal public meeting in Albany to protest Lincoln's action. Although unable to attend, Seymour made his views known in a letter to the group that the arrest dishonored the Union and that it will "not merely be a step towards revolution—it is revolution; it will not only lead to military despotism, it establishes military despotism."[45] Seymour used the occasion to provide a different path toward defeat of the rebellion. His letter circulated through the Northern press, which enflamed the oppositionist fires against Lincoln. New Yorker John Mullaly argued that Seymour understood the "spirit of the people of the Empire State," and that his citizens would stand by him "with guns and bayonets in their hands, at all hazards."⁴⁶ It was hard to believe, however, that Seymour had employed any less objectionable language in this letter than had Vallandigham himself.

Seymour's criticism of Lincoln was harsh, but Major Alexander S. Diven, acting assistant in the Provost Marshals Office, assured Fry that despite the condemnation, Seymour had privately agreed to cooperate in raising the soldiers, just not black New Yorkers. The governor understood there would be a fuss over conscription's constitutionality, but thought it would be for the courts to decide. Still, Seymour wanted Diven to personally relate to Lincoln "that he was exceedingly tenacious in relation to the question of arbitrary arrests."⁴⁷ Lincoln responded to the Albany meeting and Seymour's letter after receiving their formal resolutions. In a carefully worded rejoinder to Corning, which he also sent to the *New York Tribune*, the president acknowledged the divisiveness of his actions, but argued that he was guarding the public safety. The Ohioan's actions necessitated the suspension of the writ of habeas corpus. Now a senator, Morgan applauded Lincoln's manifesto, praising it as "timely, wise, one of your best State Papers and was really necessary under the drift which affairs have taken."⁴⁸

Lincoln had taken a bold stand, and, now more than ever, he tried to make people realize that emancipation, conscription, and black enlistment, all exceptional measures, were worth their sacrifices. He depended on governors to assist him in fighting back the tidal wave of opposition forming across the North. Seymour spent his first months in office questioning the validity of these measures and assailing Lincoln for transforming the Union. The governor had risen to prominence on the war's failures, and his success was a reminder that Lincoln had lost much in preserving the Union. His public condemnation of Lincoln infuriated Radical governors who had risked everything to overcome the Union's limitations in winning the war on the battlefield. Andrew had taken a bold stand in demonstrating that the rewards of preserving equality were worth fighting for in the field and at home. It was fitting that Seymour's manifesto aired about the time that Andrew was in Readville attending the sendoff ceremony for the 54th Massachusetts. The all-black regiment was evidence that a new Union was emerging—one that brought honor and respect upon those who carried the cause of equality into combat. One observer recalled that it was "one of the most memorable scenes of Andrew's governorship,—a scene in which every detail that struck the eye, every act that was done, was significant."⁴⁹ Even as he handed over the silk "emblematic banner," Andrew confessed that he was unprepared to present such a banner, "for we are fighting now a battle, not merely for country, not merely for humanity, not merely for civilization, but for the religion of our Lord itself."[50]

Although Seymour and Andrew represented polar ends of the Union's preservation, neither had a magic a formula for raising men. Managing the national enrollment stalled the enlistment of new soldiers at time when they were most needed in the field. The reports of Chancellorsville stunted volunteering, and the Army of the Potomac suffered the humiliation of allowing Lee the opportunity to launch a new Northern invasion. Grant's army, meanwhile, expanded its penetration of the Confederate heartland, and the commander needed troops to maintain his offensive. Raising volunteers under the new arrangement nationalized the war effort in the field, yet its benefits were slow to catch on at home. Stories circulated that, once mustered into service, soldiers contended with delinquent pay, low morale, and discord over regimental consolidation. Commanders adjusted to the new army, and welcomed additional troops, but some officers resisted new regiments at the expense of filling up old ones. Bearing down on Vicksburg, Sherman wired Stanton that consolidation would dismiss many valuable officers when the military needs them and would "create a good deal of unpleasant feeling in the Army." Besides, he argued, "the veteran regiments are worth more to the Government to-day, even when simmered down to not more than 300 well disciplined, able-bodied men, than any new and green regiments of 1,000 men each that the Government can procure."[51]

As much as governors followed their soldiers, they also paid close attention to draft preparations. The partisan press publicized enrollment transgressions and sensationalized conscription's injustice, often inciting hostility toward commissioners. On the afternoon of 18 May, an Irishman armed with a spade and accompanied by several irate women waving stones broke into the Milwaukee Provost Marshal's Office and attacked one of the enrolling officers. Within days it became apparent that antidraft Milwaukeeans would cause Salomon considerable difficulty. "From the time the enrolling officers entered upon their duties in that place until now," wrote Captain James M. Tillapaugh of the Provost Marshal's Office, "they have been assailed in the most violent manner by the Germans and the Irish."[52] Pennsylvanians also opposed the draft. Reports arrived from Lancaster, Bedford, and Chambersburg that detailed the trouble of arresting citizens resisting enrollment. Curtin petitioned Stanton to allow him to raise 50,000 militiamen for sixty days to safeguard enrollment officers, but the secretary refused.

The governor worried over another Northern invasion and bypassed the secretary and wired Lincoln for assistance.[53]

Enrollment opposition was the least of Arthur I. Boreman's worries. West Virginia's Republican candidate for governor had run unopposed, and voters elected him on 28 May. Still, it was a humbling circumstance to be inaugurated governor of the guerrilla-infested and poverty-ridden Mountaineer State. The statehouse was a modest, unassuming three-story building known as the Linsly Institute in Wheeling on the Ohio River and it mirrored the state's helplessness. The Union that West Virginians entered had changed since the process of statehood began. Citizens now resisted the dispiritedness caused by the Union's dismal military forecast. The atmosphere turned to apprehension, animosity, and hostility among citizens. Boreman was aware of this threatening atmosphere, writing to Pierpont months before that he was "more fearful . . . for the future of West Virginia than ever heretofore."[54] In his departing speech, Pierpont declared to the gallery that Boreman was worthy of the peoples' confidence, that "he is in this cause as steel." When he closed, Boreman gave the state's first inaugural address.[55] "This State is the child of the rebellion," he declared, "yet its peace and prosperity depended on the permanence of the American Union."[56] A small chorus of young women broke into "E Pluribus Unum," after his speech, a small band played the Star Spangled Banner, and the celebration of West Virginia ended. The timing of West Virginia's admission into the Union could not have been under more trying circumstances in the nation's history. Still, the governor's rise to political prominence mirrored the citizens' quest for statehood. The rugged Pennsylvania native had moved to Virginia at a young age, worked in the mercantile business, studied law, and established a practice in Parkersburg. He was a member of the Whig Party, served as a delegate from Wood County from 1855 to 1861, and had been a member of the Constitutional Union Party. Now the state's chief executive with few resources, the governor resorted to local defense.[57]

Maintaining local defense and safeguarding enrollment officers forced some chief executives to exert more control. The suspension of habeas corpus brought out guardian impulses among some governors seeking to use the national government in expansive, but productive, ways. If all Burnside had been guilty of by arresting Vallandigham was embarrassing the administration, Lincoln saw him through the ordeal. The general kept his command, but the rancor against the president intensified. Morton protested to Lincoln that it had turned "mere clamor and general opposition" to the administration "into bitter hostility to the Government and the War." The Indiana Legislature had failed to make appropriations to carry on state government, and Democratic Party leaders used Lincoln's suspension of the writ against the governor. Morton objected to temporary departmental commanders, some of whom were poor politicians and unsuited to qualify the political consequences of their action. Morton acknowledged that Burnside's order had been issued without Lincoln's knowledge, yet he told the president, "your subsequent silence gives it your ratification before the public." If the midwestern states were to be treated as insurrectionist and governed by military power, "let it be done by the highest authority and invested with some dignity." Morton argued that the preservation of the peace and loyalty of the northwestern states should be handled by state authorities, to be aided and supported by federal power only when necessary. Lincoln took Morton's sentiments under consideration. He wanted to continue their "good understanding" of one another and to leave state affairs in the hands of governors.[58]

Morton's frustration reflected the problems governors faced in proceeding with enrollment while avoiding assaults on individual liberties. Such difficulties played into the hands of oppositionists seeking to exploit these challenges. Democrats cited such tyranny as the motivation for avoiding the draft and deserting. The resentment and skepticism would gain momentum, governors argued, until Union armies claimed a major victory that could justify such measures. In the meantime, those legislatures having Democratic majorities caused governors problems. Indiana legislators abandoned Morton, and Democrats threatened to buy exemptions to remain at home, forcing Republicans to enlist and therefore taking them out of participation in the fall election. The Democratic press flooded readers with reports detailing home-front violence resulting from the draft and arbitrary arrests. Peace advocates and Lincoln supporters clashed, while civil and military authorities tried to sustain the flow of manpower. Although Ohio had supplied men in excess of its quotas, desertion, sickness, and campaigning had depleted the ranks, and a draft provoked armed resistance. In Holmes County, dissidents mobbed the jail and liberated citizens arrested for treasonous activities. Burnside dispatched soldiers to suppress the vigilantes, and Governor Tod approved these actions and told his citizens that the commander was authorized to "show them no quarter whatever." It was a sad affair, symbolic of the war's local nature.[59]

Lincoln was sensitive to governors' concerns about local dissension. To preserve peace in the regions affected by civil hostility and to keep

Confederate raiders out, he created a new department called the Department of Susquehanna, comprising eastern Ohio, western Pennsylvania, and West Virginia. He placed New York native and West Point graduate Major General Darius Nash Couch in command of 30,000 troops to protect the region. Stanton tapped Seymour for the bulk of the troops, and the governor promised to consolidate the thousands of enlisted volunteers into regiments and dispatch them to Philadelphia immediately.[60]

Northern Invasion

As the war's third summer approached, governors tracked Union advances in the West, hoping for a miracle victory. They desperately needed military success to convince Northerners that their sacrifices were not in vain. The Mississippi campaign gave them something to celebrate. A glimmer of good news came on 8 June, when Banks invaded Port Hudson. Combined with Grant's siege of Vicksburg, this good fortune helped restore midwestern governors' faith that there was something positive to report. The following week, however, Lee's Confederates were on the move north again. The advance alarmed Marylanders, Pennsylvanians, and New Jerseyites, who petitioned their governors to arrange local defense. Convinced the enemy had made its way into Pennsylvania, Curtin secured Stanton's permission to call out the militia, and the governor made an emotional appeal to all citizens. Bradford and Parker echoed these sentiments. "When our own territory is threatened by an invader," charged Bradford, "let it never be said that we lacked the spirit to meet the emergency, or looked to others to provide for our defense."[61] The threat of war on Union soil heightened the cooperative spirit among these governors, who turned their attention away from suppressing local dissidents and on defending their states.

Confederates also pressed north down the Shenandoah Valley. The campaign brought on the two-day battle of Winchester on the 14–15 June, which resulted in the Union defeat of General Robert Milroy's forces, and the loss of some 4,000 Union soldiers. Buckingham was especially distraught by the news, as he learned the 18th Connecticut had been badly cut up. He dispatched Henry B. Norton, a Norwich businessman, to attend to the wounded and supervise getting them home. Eastern governors, many of whom had quota deficiencies, were reeling from Lee's invasion and forced Stanton to allow them short-term volunteers. On 15 June, Lincoln called forth 100,000 men into the service of the militia from Maryland, Pennsylvania, Ohio, and West

Virginia to serve for six months. Stanton explained the justification for the call by wiring governors that enemy forces were moving forward to invade Maryland and Pennsylvania. The eastern front seemed to be caving northward, and Curtin feared it was about to envelope Harrisburg. Residents desperate to leave the Pennsylvania capital crowded into omnibuses and carriages and thronged the railroad platforms to escape. Curtin supervised his staff while they packed up the state archives and valuable state papers to relocate them to safety. Politics aside, Seymour responded that he had ordered his New York troops to Philadelphia and to Harrisburg. Their arrival in the Pennsylvania capital relieved Curtin.[62]

The nation's eyes followed Lee's army as it pushed north toward the Maryland and Pennsylvania borders. Parker steered New Jerseyites away from debating the Vallandigham case and into the ranks to save their sister states. Boreman's West Virginians hunkered down for another series of blitzkrieg attacks as the armies passed through their region, denying many communities statehood celebrations. Bradford had difficulty meeting Lincoln's call and rightfully so. The governor was weighed down by enrollment, panic, and runaway slaves. He forwarded cases to Lincoln that involved owners seeking the governor's assistance in reclaiming runaways who had absconded to Washington. The governor was especially sensitive to this issue because he had received complaints from local sheriffs under pressure from citizens to have their slaves returned. The recent turn of events, he argued, further aggravated his ability to solve these local governance issues.[63]

Lee's offensive inspired a resurgence of public displays of patriotism that reawakened Northerners to use the advantage of their superior numbers against the enemy, but manufacturing manpower results took time, even among Pennsylvanians. Although Curtin raised the patriotic feeling among the populace, scandal had rocked the state government, political and military authorities argued over priorities, and political conventions opened across many states, directing interests toward politics. The early summer witnessed the opening of political canvasses, and several governorships were on the ballot, though none more important than Ohio's. While most governors boasted of volunteers streaming forward, Tod worried about the opposition at home. That Ohio Democrats expected to nominate Vallandigham attracted national attention. Confederates had no use for the firebrand, and sent him to Windsor, Canada, where he opened his campaign for the office of the chief executive. At the convention's opening, delegates sent twenty-one Democrats to Washington and demanded Lincoln allow the Copperhead to return to Ohio. Tod wired a short note to Lincoln and urged him to "treat the Vallandigham Committee about to call upon you with the contempt they richly merit."⁶⁴ Copperheads there had risen to new heights in underhandedness, and it had affected soldiers' attitudes. Lucius Wood wrote his brother that he "would rather shoot one northern copperhead than 2 rebels in arms."⁶⁵ Lincoln was undeterred by the threat, but given the Republicans' success in the spring elections, he did not fear Vallandigham, and eventually allowed his return.⁶⁶

The Union Party convention in Columbus had no such chaos, yet despite campaigning rigorously, Tod lost renomination to John Brough, a railroad executive. The governor apologized to Lincoln that supporters attributed his defeat to the president's war measures. "Do not for a moment believe it," the defeated governor wired Lincoln, "personal considerations alone was the cause of my defeat."⁶⁷ Former governor Dennison wrote to Lincoln that his administration should regard Brough's nomination as approval of the most vigorous policy for prosecuting the war. Tod rose above the political muck and continued to support Lincoln. He even raised Ohio's first black regiment, which he boasted to Lincoln was progressing. Undeterred by criticism, the governor was gratified by those who endorsed his decision to raise such a regiment. "He [the colored soldier] has proved himself to be a good soldier," he wrote Stanton, "put him then upon an equality so far as dollars and cents are concerned."⁶⁸ Giles Waldo Shurtleff, whom Tod tapped to command the regiment, noted a significant change in Tod's attitude since his election two years before. "The governor seems a different man from Governor Tod of last year," he wrote. "His interest is enlisted in behalf of the blacks and he is thoroughly in earnest in his efforts to support the administration in all its measures."⁶⁹

Yates was locked in a nasty battle with Illinois Copperheads and wired Stanton that under the circumstances he could not pull volunteers forward. "None but Union men would volunteer, and, since the revocation of the order for the suppression of the *Times* [Chicago], the excitement is intense." The Democratic convention for the Northwest was about to convene, and Yates feared it would generate opposition, if not revolution, against the government. "Under these circumstances," he wrote, "I do not feel at liberty to promise you troops from Illinois."⁷⁰

Kirkwood had not returned from Vicksburg when Lincoln's call came over the wires, and his secretary responded that three to four six-month regiments could be raised in twenty days. Throughout the next few days, governors wired in their assurances that they would meet Lincoln's call, but it would take time. Holbrook reported that he could raise a few regiments, but it would take a month, and, to encourage enlistment, he advised a shorter term, and that the term be credited to their quota toward the draft. Vermonters were not panicked by the Confederate surge north, but they were not immune from internal dissension caused by conscription. Tensions flared in Rutland, and Governor Holbrook feared it would spread to other towns. Some Irish laborers in the marble quarries had raised nearly 1,000 strong, and the more hostile members violently attacked the enrolling officer, sheriff, and accompanying surgeon. General Thomas G. Pitcher appealed to Holbrook, and the governor forwarded his request for assistance to subdue them to Stanton. Stanton considered declaring martial law to subdue such occurrences, but Halleck was hesitant to extend the iron fist of the War Department, believing civil authorities could handle Vermont's affairs. Halleck concluded that as much as possible, governors should handle these matters without the aid of the military. The recent experience in Ohio convinced him that such moves would prove injurious, as citizens would take offense at the assumption of law by the military and governors would suffer the consequences of civil unrest. After all, even national conscription relied on localized state and voluntary efforts for its successful execution.[71]

That Lee's invasion moved more swiftly than the Northern response was no surprise. Had the commander read the Northern papers, he would have been encouraged by stories that described enrollment problems, Copperhead resistance, and scheming Democrats at Northern conventions. Many governors endured significant unrest when they most needed to support the war effort. Morton safeguarded his Indianans by raising local forces in local communities, and he called on the War Department for 25,000 arms and twelve pieces of field artillery to equip these forces. Without legislative assistance, the governor established a Bureau of Finance, raised private funds, and relied on Stanton to support his operations. He appointed William H. Terrell as his financial secretary to oversee the funds. Yet he had no money to disperse to destitute families, pay surgeons he sent to care for the wounded, or to pay the interest on the state debt. Morton suffered from the debilitating effects of the state's financial crisis, which the Democrats used to shame him into calling a special session of the legislature. After weeks of recriminatory editorials by the opposition press, Morton secretly left for Washington.[72]

For the first time in the war, Morton needed Lincoln more than Lincoln needed the governor. When it came to his soldiers, the governor took no shame in steaming to Washington and calling on the president for assistance. After Morton explained his circumstances, Lincoln remarked that he knew of no law that would allow him to give Morton the money and instead sent him to Stanton. When the governor related his troubles to Stanton and explained that Lincoln found no law to help, the secretary rumbled 'By God, I will find a law," and he did.[73] On 18 June, Stanton had Lincoln authorize $250,000 to be advanced to Morton to pay off the interest, which would negate calling a special legislative session. The governor was to conduct the military operations within the state as he saw fit. "If the cause fails we shall both be covered with prosecutions," Morton replied, to which Stanton remarked, "if the cause fails, I do not wish to live."[74] Morton was grateful for Stanton's support, and before he departed Washington, he left Stanton a letter. "I could not leave the city without again expressing to you my appreciation and gratitude for the service you have done my state," he acknowledged. "Heaven has endowed you with a soul and ability," wrote Morton, "to comprehend the times and grapple with the questions presented."[75] The governor departed Washington for New York, where he met with fellow Indianan James F. D. Lanier, now a prominent banker. Morton secured the funds to pay the state interest, but John C. Walker, agent of the State, and Morton's bitter opponent, refused to provide Lanier with the books of his office in order to determine the stockholder of the state stocks. Morton's problems were only getting worse. In the face of such hardships, which the press publicized, William Taylor Stott, a soldier in the 18th Indiana, remarked in his diary that "Gov. Morton is running the machine on his own responsibility."[76]

Illinois legislators were no kinder to Yates. For months Democrats rejected the belief that reestablishing the Union could be achieved by continued fighting and emancipating slaves. They protested Yates's blind allegiance to Lincoln and berated his inattention to black migration into southern Illinois. The disaffection over Lincoln's expanded war aims forced representatives into a political war to curtail the governor's power. They embarrassed the chief executive by introducing proposals to reduce his term, investigating his military appointments and financial transactions, and by gerrymandering the state's political districts to their favor. The events of May and early June, namely the arrest of Vallandigham and the military suppression of Illinois newspapers, confirmed that Radical Republicans endorsed harsh military rule not only at the front but also in the rear. Yates feared the Democratic Convention of the Northwest, scheduled to open in mid-June, would undermine raising volunteers in the politically charged atmosphere. When legislators returned to Springfield in June expecting to reconvene, Democrats intended to seize the reins of Illinois. Therefore, after a brief recess that commenced in mid-February and lasted until spring, Yates resorted to extreme measures. On 10 June, he used an obscure constitutional technicality that adjourned the legislature until "the Saturday next preceding the first Monday in January 1865," because "the past history of the present assembly," he argued, presented "no reasonable hope of beneficial results to the citizens of the State or the army in the field."[77]

It was as if the governor had altered the setting sun. With an "iron will worthy of Cromwell himself," noted an impressed midwestern correspondent, and a "nerve like that of Andrew Jackson," Yates prorogued the legislature. "I sent my polite note to them," he later recalled in Cromwellian fashion, "telling them in the language of the soldiers to the rebels, to 'skedaddle.'"[78] As much as Lincoln argued that extreme times required extreme measures, so too had Yates come to believe this, and turned his Union Leaguers into peace-keeping forces within the state. In later years, Yates likened himself to the "Commander-in-Chief of the army and navy of Illinois," and recalled that the enemy, whom he dubbed the disloyal legislators, "had taken possession and fortified themselves in the State House at Springfield," and "resolved to usurp the powers of their commander-in-chief, and to run the government upon the style and manner of the rebel states."[79] Pressed from the rear, the governor "sent out a party of reconnoisance [sic]; called my staff," and "resolved to attack the enemy in his stronghold, and put them to rout or die in the last ditch." He continued, "I then went to work and prepared a deadly missive, which Ike Cook called a 'perouge' and as soon as it was finished I went and fired it into the ranks of the enemy, and such a grand 'skedallel' [sic] you have not seen since the evacuation of Atlanta."[80]

Yates's extraordinary move led to mayhem, and involved the Illinois Supreme Court, which agreed with the chief executive's decision. The Democratic press, however, assailed him. The opposition was so great that thousands of detractors attended what the press characterized as "the most tremendous gathering of the people ever witnessed in Illinois" at the Springfield fairgrounds to protest his actions.[81] Alfred Churchill of Rome, Illinois, advised Yates to nominate Lincoln for president and Horatio Seymour for vice president to settle the political waters. "By doing so you establish a party which will rule in any event, war or peace, union or disunion," he sarcastically reasoned, and "without such a course you are whipped, for the volunteers *will vote the next Presidential election* with whom you, on a clean party ticket, stand not Governor."[82] The *Burlington Daily Hawk-eye*, however, reported that while the "virtuous Copperheads will howl over this check mate.... Other people will rejoice that an assemblage like that is at last deprived of all power to do evil."[83] Yates's extreme measures spoke volumes to his gubernatorial power. Senator Isaac Funk of McLean County declared that "hell itself could not spew out a more traitorous crew than some of the men that disgrace this legislature, this State, and this country."[84]

Although Lincoln had removed Curtis, Gamble had it no better in Missouri. Amid enrolling Missourians, he convened the state's Constitutional Convention to revise the constitution to include gradual emancipation. Although the governor was not the proslavery advocate many of his critics claimed he was, Gamble's message, nonetheless, explained that he yielded to free-soilism and to those Missourians who believed the state's deteriorating economy would profit from free labor. He chaired the Committee on Emancipation, hoping to encourage conservatives and Radicals to work together. He argued that the only way to maintain the Union was to cleanse Missouri "of the institution which forms the bond of cement among the rebellious States."[85] In this charged atmosphere, the former Missouri Supreme Court justice, who had dissented in the famous Dred Scott case, steered members toward an acceptance of a constitutional provision that provided for gradual emancipation. The article allowed slave owners time to find laborers to maintain their operations. In his final proceeding, Gamble warned Missouri legislators of the dangers to come. "We must have no such Utopian notions," he argued, "as that by breaking off his shackles the slave becomes an angel—becomes at once an intelligent man, capable of sustaining himself under all the trials of life." He warned, "Do not fall into such a notion as that," concluding that "everybody who has ever seen five negroes together knows better than that."[86]

With his work done, Gamble resigned. Whether Missourians agreed with his tactics, his attitude, or his racial beliefs, few loyalists had done more to keep Missouri out of the Confederacy. In his departing words, the aged frontier lawyer could look back on his short but stormy reign as governor with a sense of accomplishment. His physical appearance at the convention told the story of the last two years as his careworn body, wrinkled face, and thinning gray hair reflected the unforgiving nature of his office. He was among Lincoln's most important governors and was credited with standing by the Union and Lincoln even when it was unpopular. "When I was chosen to the office," he addressed his colleagues, "the only question which engaged our attention was, whether the *status* of Missouri as a State in the Union could be preserved; whether our rights as citizens of the United States could be protected against those who sought to bind us to the Confederacy of the revolted States." He closed, "I regard such questions as settled, and that there is no further demand upon me to continue the sacrifice of my own tastes and interests."[87] No matter how Missourians greeted Gamble's resignation, Lincoln worried over the state's fate without him. In the time he had left, the governor pledged to cooperate with Schofield, including the raising of the few free blacks for the U.S. Colored Regiments. Loyalists feared that, without Gamble, the state would succumb to tyranny, and friends convinced him to rescind his resignation. By the convention's end, he had.[88]

By late June Grant was pounding away on the western front at Vicksburg and found it necessary to relieve McClernand from command. Yates protested his removal. He suggested to Lincoln that, with some western troops, McClernand might be sent to Pennsylvania, which was sure to "inspire great hope and confidence in the Northwest, and perhaps throughout the country."[89] As much as Yates remained loyal to McClernand, Grant was not about to be deterred from his assault. His only relief came from Tennessee, where Rosecrans's timely decision to pin down Bragg's Confederates at Tullahoma gave Davis pause for concern. Now there were several military fronts actively under way and not enough men to meet the demands of the sieges in Louisiana and Mississippi, the advance in Tennessee, and Lee's invasion into Pennsylvania.[90]

For governors who combated state legislators and unruly draft resistors, Governor Jubal Early swung their attention to Gettysburg, Pennsylvania, on 26 June, when his Confederates rolled into town. The Northern invasion was hardly a surprise. Curtin passed along information detailing enemy operations to Stanton and, in the meantime, challenged citizens to come forward to repel the advance. About the speech Curtin gave in Harrisburg, one witness remarked that Curtin flatly challenged his constituents, saying that any man who would not enlist for the six months "was a coward, or words to that effect."[91] The news was demoralizing, especially in Washington. Lincoln wore a dispirited look. Gurowski often met the president during these days and noted that he looked "exhausted, care-worn, spiritless, extinct." He observed, "Lincoln's looks are those of a man whose nights are sleepless and whose days are comfortless."[92] In contemplating his command change, Lincoln ignored the clamoring for McClellan. Instead, he relieved Hooker and replaced him with George Gordon Meade, a tall, confident, combat-tested Pennsylvanian who had won the affection of the soldiers. Halleck was glad to be done with the haughty, backbiting Hooker, who shifted the blame for his faults to everyone but himself. Meade's appointment, however, did little to calm the fears of Pennsylvanians and their neighbors. "The people of New Jersey," wrote Parker, "are apprehensive that the invasion of the enemy may extend to her soil."[93] To repel the invasion and remove the apathy among his citizens, he wired Lincoln that New Jerseyites wanted McClellan at the helm of the army. Lincoln stood by his decision. "I beg you to be assured," wrote Lincoln, "that no one out of my position can know so well as if he were in it, the difficulties and involvements of replacing Gen. McClellan in command—and this aside from any imputations upon him."[94] Parker conferred with Curtin and called out volunteers to join the state militia and help defend her sister state. When two Jersey Blue regiments about to be discharged from the service offered to assist Curtin, it allowed Parker a defense along the Susquehanna River. As the days passed and relief came, Curtin breathed a little easier and wrote Parker a note of thanks for his "promptness" in responding to Curtin's call for assistance.[95]

Although hardly newsworthy, given the military events of late June, Lincoln won a small victory in New England. The New Hampshire legislature finally settled on Joseph Gilmore as their new governor by a vote of 192 to 133. Ironically, he had polled 2,500 fewer votes than Eastman. The result of the several-week-long political saga relieved the president because it reflected the growing political support for Republicans despite military setbacks and the rise of Copperheadism. A Vermont native, the fifty-two-year-old Gilmore was one of fourteen children who had grown up fatherless. He attended the common schools run by the Baptists, and as a teenager went to Boston, where he clerked in a mercantile store. Several years later he moved to Concord, New Hampshire, and continued his mercantile interests. He became so successful that he invested in local railroads and, by 1848, became superintendent of construction for the Concord and Claremont line. His business interests lured him to the Whig Party, and, by the late 1850s, he had switched to the Republican Party. In 1859 voters elected him to the state Senate. Yet, with all of his favorable qualities, the thirty-seventh governor had developed a weakness for drink, was self-absorbed, and some of his worst enemies were family members. Having made his way in life by his wits, he was dubbed by some residents "that rascal Gilmore." His first order of business was to meet Lincoln's call, continue enrollment, and prepare relief expeditions for Vermonters about to fall in Pennsylvania.[96]

CHAPTER FOURTEEN

Just Such Affliction

When Calvin Fletcher opened his Indiana newspaper to the news that Lee had invaded Pennsylvania, it moved him to note a foreboding prediction in his diary. "I feel our federal government needs just such affliction to mak [sic] us harmonious & united," he inscribed, "that invasion alone will make the free states including Mo. Ky. West Va. Part of Tenn. & Md sensible of the value of peace & the union & sensible of the great wrong of secession."[1] Fletcher's entry spoke volumes. Governors had worked feverishly to provide Lincoln the armies he needed to end the war, but their best efforts and expansive war measures were not enough to convince Northerners they were winning the war. Lee hoped that his campaign would demoralize the populace into forcing Lincoln to negotiate peace. News of the Southern attack spun through the press, and the time had come to awaken the Northern giant—again.[2]

As July opened, eastern governors stayed close to their stenographers. Curtin bunkered in Harrisburg, as did Bradford in Annapolis. Lincoln remained in the telegraph room, pouring over field dispatches. It was "an anxious day" in Washington as Chase described it.[3] Telegrams reported that General John Buford's Federal cavalry had discovered Confederates near the small town of Gettysburg, and that fighting had broken out between the small units. The discovery touched off an epic battle that lasted three days. Here was the great Union stand, the "just affliction" on Northern soil that Fletcher hoped would unite the people and inspire them to come forward. The national government had expanded it powers over the military, and governors feared another Union defeat might inspire a resurgence of states' rights that could prove destructive behind the lines and at the coming elections.[4]

Gettysburg and Its Aftermath

By the evening of 3 July, more than 165,000 Northerners and Southerners had fought one another in repeated bloody assaults. One correspondent traveling with the Army of the Potomac sat down to describe the contest.

"The sun of Austerlitz," he opened his lengthy report, "is not more memorable than that which is just flinging its dying rays over the field of this ... successful battle."[5] For three days the wires reported the horrific contest, but, standing on the battlefield, it was not possible to look across the landscape and see anything but death and destruction. As much as General Meade was positioned to pursue a retreating Lee, he admitted that his first week in command was perhaps the army's most ominous. Soldiers had saved the Union against invasion, but the hard fighting renewed his respect for the enemy, the same enemy that had thrashed the Union at Chancellorsville and Fredericksburg.[6]

Lincoln was disappointed with the overall outcome of Gettysburg, especially because Lee got away. Still, he claimed in a press release that the victory "was such as to cover that Army with the highest honor, to promise a great success to the cause of the Union, and to claim the condolence of all for the many gallant fallen."[7] Governors with troops at Gettysburg drew little encouragement from the victory—casualty figures disheartened them more. Some chief executives rushed to the battlefield to supervise getting the most serious cases sent home. Curtin was among the first governors to arrive, and he found hundreds of bloated and bloodstained bodies strewn across the battlefield. He spent days in the makeshift hospitals. "He was around to see the boys and give the boys a chance to see him," wrote Charles Merrick to his wife. He is "social and makes himself quite popular by his ease and freedom with the boys, and the sympathy he manifests for the wounded."[8] To honor the fallen soldiers, Curtin appointed David Wills, a local banker, to oversee the details of establishing a cemetery. So overwhelming was the undertaking that Wills designated a suitable place where the battle occurred to establish a common burial ground.

New to his office, Gilmore was detained by political affairs, but he sent forward physicians and nurses for his wounded New Hampshirites. Until he could leave for the front, Parker sent agents to supervise the relocation of dead New Jerseyites to burial grounds "with appropriate ceremonies." As the gruesome details poured into the War Department and Northern statehouses, they reported thousands of casualties, totaling roughly 23,000 killed, missing, and wounded. The numbers were staggering, and governors were hard pressed to translate this human sacrifice into something worthy of their efforts. News from the West, however, assuaged their reservations about what lay ahead. Grant had forced the surrender of Vicksburg on 4 July, resulting in the capture of nearly 30,000 Confederate soldiers. To add to his army's good fortune, Banks ended his siege of Port Hudson further downstream and forced the Confederates to surrender four days later.⁹

The victories at Gettysburg, Vicksburg, and Port Hudson gave Northerners much-needed encouragement. These successes rejuvenated the populace in time to rekindle a patriotic spirit in celebration of national independence. Noah Brooks remarked from Washington that "the 'old-fashioned Fourth of July' appears to be the order of the day with our people here, who believe that the dawning of a national existence should always be commemorated although the national life may be threatened."¹⁰ Similar scenes played out in many state capitals, where governors rejoiced in their residents' commitment to preserving national goals. Cannon was especially elated, given the closeness of Lee's invasion to Delaware. "The defence [sic] of your soil," he proclaimed to Delawareans, "lies in keeping open the door of communication, through which re-inforcements can be forwarded." He continued, "The true military line of this State is the bank of the Susquehanna," and "the most effective way to prevent the spoliation of your house is to keep the enemy outside of it."¹¹

Lee's army withdrew through Maryland and crossed the Potomac back into Virginia. The Union victory changed the tide of the war in the East, and, combined with Vicksburg's surrender, it gave the president hope that the fall elections would also turn in his favor. The Union's success bolstered Northern optimism, and governors increased their attention to soldier relief to maintain positive attitudes in the ranks. Yet Confederate invasions had not ended. On 8 July, Confederate General John Hunt Morgan's foray into Kentucky spilled into Indiana and eventually Ohio. With roughly 2,400 cavalrymen, he hoped to divert Burnside's Army of the Ohio from aiding Rosecrans's army in middle Tennessee, and expected to awaken Confederate sympathies among Kentuckians and midwesterners tired of the war. The raid proved more of a nuisance than an invasion, but it distracted Stanton from his objective of forwarding troops to the Union armies in Tennessee and Mississippi. It also panicked residents along the northern banks of Ohio, and forced governors to call on militias to defend their soil. Morton, however, lacked the funds to pay the soldiers.¹²

By the second week in July, another war erupted behind Union lines. After months of enrollment, the draft commenced in many states, and it touched off violent protests. Despite the recent victories, governors needed coercive measures to continue the flow of manpower, but the autocratic national stimulus did not make their jobs easier. There was confusion over quotas, credits, exemptions, commutations, and substitutions. Whatever its merits, conscription gave the impression of being oppressive and odious, and favorable to the wealthy classes. More than that, it made the Union appear weak, uninspired to carry on the war, and played into the hands of Copperheads. In celebrating Vicksburg's capture, Yates attempted to combat such attitudes in a Chicago speech by highlighting all the government had accomplished thus far in the war. The new measures of emancipation and conscription would ultimately bring victory, he argued, especially since "we now see the beginning of the end."[13]

For such a loyal city, New York became the nations' battleground over conscription. Seymour, reveling in the resurgence of states'-rights thinking, felt he held the upper hand against Lincoln's policies. Recent victories, however, had stolen his thunder. In a July Fourth celebration speech at the Academy of Music, the governor denied the administration any credit for these victories and attacked Lincoln's despotism. Yet the governor's blistering epistle fanned oppositionists' flames to such a degree that it put him at odds with members of his own constituency. James Gordon Bennett, whose *New York Herald* had celebrated the Republican defeat the previous year, vilified Seymour's speech as an attempt to distort the battles' significance before the fall elections. "In the midst of ... the greatest victory of the war just electrifying the country," Bennett observed, "these political trimmers spent the precious hours of our national anniversary in talking about the arrest of Vallandigham and the suppression of a few tuppenny papers, and the awful despotism which these actions of the administration had imposed upon the country. We are sick to nausea of such silly, brainless prattle."[14]

Fearing he had gone too far and that Democratic reporters had exaggerated his comments, Seymour sent staff member John Dash Van Buren to Washington with personal assurances to Lincoln and Stanton. All was well between Seymour and the president, Van Buren confided, and he urged Lincoln to "pay no attention to newspaper statements as to the Governor's unfriendliness."[15] Still, the governor was aware of Fry's decision to put the draft in motion, but he was unaware of the precise date that officials had determined to draw names. The recent battle forced the governor to empty New York City of soldiers, and Seymour had sent Adjutant General John T. Sprague to Washington to petition Lincoln to postpone drawing of names until the troops returned. Having sent Sprague on his way and expecting a postponement, Seymour traveled to New Brunswick, New Jersey, to inspect harbor defenses and visit relatives. Fry, however, forbade Sprague to communicate with Lincoln, and the message was never delivered. Thus, it was by chance that Seymour was out of the city when the draft commenced on Saturday, 11 July. The following day, New Yorkers opened their papers and examined the names of drafted and exempted residents in the city wards. By the afternoon, mobs had formed and began rioting in the streets. These protests touched off a massive weeklong violent campaign as ruffians and thugs destroyed much of Manhattan's Upper East Side, which forced Mayor Opdyke to call on state and federal troops for assistance.[16]

Seymour had just stepped out of his carriage at the Old Bridge Station in New Jersey when a national guardsman handed him the mayor's telegram. New York City was in a state of emergency, prompting his immediate return. He arrived in the city at noon the following day, assessed police reports, issued a proclamation against violence, and promised to suppress the vigilantes. He then set out on foot for City Hall, where he gathered more intelligence. There he addressed the crowd, acknowledging them with the words "My Friends," a salutation for which the pro-Lincoln press ridiculed him. He spent the rest of the day canvassing the city and making additional speeches in an attempt to calm his constituents. By the days' end, troops had arrived.[17]

For all he had done to encourage opposition to Lincoln, Seymour worked hard to bring the riots to a close, and chose a conciliatory course in handling New Yorkers. Yet residents whipped themselves into rage over the draft in hopes that Seymour would seize the revolutionary moment to force Lincoln to his knees and to buckle to postponement. Radicals alleged that Seymour had "purposely denuded the city of militia so as to give an opportunity for the riot," which was "perfectly consistent with his character; by no means disloyal, but showing gentleness where vigor and determination were requisite; censuring unlawful deeds, but haggling over constitutional rights at a most inopportune time."[18] It seemed a fitting gesture for a governor "to extinguish the flames he has contributed to kindle," noted a perceptive Welles in his diary, as the riots were simply the "fruit of the seed sown by the Seymours and others."[19]

Whatever Lincoln believed about Seymour's role in provoking the riot, he nonetheless agreed to adjust the quotas in some districts and allow the reenrollment in others. Yet he refused to suspend the draft. In response, Seymour set out on a month-long course to filibuster Lincoln, which bought some political time for the governor to suppress the uprising. Meanwhile, Assistant Provost Marshal Nugent wrote to Seymour and Opdyke that, given the circumstances, Fry approved of temporarily suspending the draft in New York City and Brooklyn. The governor and mayor pressed him to make it public, and the papers ran the story, which restored peace to the city. Two days later, Seymour wired New York railroad magnate Samuel Sloan that he had dispatched his adjutant-general to Washington and secured the suspension of the draft until New York furnished its quota. The *New York Times* printed the letter, giving the appearance the government had "yielded" to Seymour. The publication heightened the problems for provost marshals executing the draft. "If New York is exempt," wrote Provost Marshal Diven, "of course other States will claim as much."[20] "The whole Country is observing with interest the course of the Administration in dealing with the New York Conscription," wrote Philadelphian Robert A. Maxwell to Lincoln. "If not proceeded," he warned, "the Union goes up in a blaze of State Rights."[21] New York attorney and abolitionist John Jay, grandson of the nation's first chief justice, confided to Stanton that indeed these were litigious times. "I am convinced," he wrote, "that the Secession leaders of the North have for two years hoped for an opportunity of resisting the National authority under colors on pretense of State authority."[22] Playing his partisan hand, Seymour sent Samuel J. Tilden, New York Democrat and prominent attorney, to Washington to communicate the governor's views on state matters and to stall Lincoln's decision.[23]

Stanton fumed at the dispatches coming over the wires. The secretary had corresponded about the riots with New York attorney James T. Brady, who feared further collision between state and federal authorities. Stanton held firm and replied that if Lincoln was forced to negotiate with state executives over the execution of a congressional act, then the problem that the rebellion desired to solve was determined. "Seymour," he maintained, "stands to-day [sic] on the platform of Slidell, Davis, and Benjamin; and if he is to be judged whether the Conscription Act is constitutional and may be enforced or resisted as he or other state authorities may decide, then the rebellion is consummated, and the national government abolished."[24] Annoyed more than alarmed, Halleck declared that the riots were Seymour's fault, and that he hated to take men away from pursuing Lee and transport them to New York City to suppress the unnecessary rioting. "He acts a man stark mad," Halleck exclaimed. Given the governor's "conduct," Halleck questioned whether or not Seymour had "inherited his father's insanity," as this was "the most charitable view" he could fathom as a consequence of recent events.[25]

The New York riots attracted national attention. "Every loyal citizen in the country," declared *Harper's Weekly*, "is profoundly interested in the conduct of the Governor of New York in a crisis so important as this."[26] Hundreds of miles away, Colonel Edward J. Wood of the 48th Indiana wrote his wife from Vicksburg that Seymour's actions were "a base concession to a traitorous, inhuman, fiendish mob, with whom reason was but as idle wind, and fair words but gave them time to prepare for worse acts of diabolism." He added, "Grape and canister were the only arguments such fellows could appreciate."[27] Yates reportedly remarked that had he been governor of New York, he would have told rioters that every house in the city "would be laid in ashes and the streets run with blood before the legally constituted authority should have yielded to the mob."[28] Such talk incited a would-be assassin to fire a shot at Yates through his office window while he washed up after working late.[29]

The draft's execution and the New York riots touched off similar outbreaks in Boston, Hartford, Detroit, Troy, Rutland, Wooster, Pottsville, and other Northern cities. Armed with paving stones, bricks, clubs, and old muskets, antidraft mobs targeted enrollment officers, policemen, and political officials, and ransacked offices and stores, and liberated criminals from jails. Andrew was at Harvard College taking part in commencement exercises when news of troubles in Boston reached him, prompting his return to the capitol building. Concerned for the harbor, he ordered soldiers to safeguard the city armory and ordered artillery units to Cooper Street in its defense. The arrival of 300 soldiers on the evening of 14 July helped strengthen his efforts in aiding the police and the militia in securing the armory. When rioters finally burst through the doors of the building that evening, the soldiers inside fired a canon, killing several Bostonians, which sent a message to the public that Andrew would not tolerate such nonsense.[30]

War on the Home Front

The charged atmosphere ignited by the draft did not surprise governors, but they monitored federal reaction. "The enforcement of the draft throughout the country," wrote Kirkwood to Stanton, "depends upon its enforcement in New York City."[31] John S. Newberry wired Stanton from Detroit's Provost Marshal's office that it would be "the height of folly" to "attempt the enforcement of the draft without a strong military force to protect the office and papers."[32] Blair cut short his relief expedition in Pennsylvania and returned to the city to discourage mobs and safeguard the Dearborn arsenal. New Jerseyites were no less agitated, but Parker was confident that volunteers had oversubscribed the state quota. As much as he appreciated federal assistance, the governor confessed to Lincoln that he failed to understand the language of the congressional measure. Besides, given its questionable constitutionality, and the violence it provoked among New Yorkers, he feared the same in New Jersey. When Stanton informed Parker that New Jersey was behind in meeting its quota by 12,000 troops, Lincoln relieved the governor by saying if he could get 8,000 men, New Jersey would not endure a draft. In the end, Parker met his quota and avoided the draft that summer.[33]

Western governors also met draft resistance. As they had the previous autumn, Milwaukeeans vehemently protested the draft's execution. General Pope expected violence, and he understood from Wisconsin governor Salomon that the men assigned to protect against the mobs could not be trusted. Pope asked for 700 troops to be assigned to Minnesota, Wisconsin, and Iowa for the purpose of protecting enrollment officers. For a city of roughly 65,000 residents, of which some two-thirds were foreign-born, the provost marshal reported that it would be "recklessness and foolhardiness to attempt a draft in this city without protection."[34] Minnesotans were less agitated, but were no better prepared to meet their draft quota. Governor Swift argued that the state's rural and scattered inhabitants were in no condition to leave their homes, and that residents in the frontier counties had fallen prey to Indian outrages. Minnesotans lived in fear of pillage, and Swift requested that Stanton delay the draft until Indian troubles subsided. The War Department rejected the request, as there were no legal provisions for postponement.[35]

For all the protests against the draft, however, governors enjoyed some benefits from the fear of its execution. It strengthened confidence among the soldiers that the power of the government was distributing the war's burden among all able-bodied, military-age males. Henry T. Young of the 7th Wisconsin informed his wife that the New York riot was a good thing "for it has taught the disloyal portion of the citizens of the North that we have a Govt. that is able and will enforce the laws."[36] Although imperfect, the draft provided Lincoln and governors a more nationalistically oriented mechanism to replenish the ranks. Fry reported that while there was nominal resistance in the New England states, other states presented more serious problems. Except for New Hampshire, New Englanders filled their quotas, though drafting was less than hospitable, as township officials pressed governors to relieve them from the corruption of bounty jumpers. In Rhode Island, however, Governor Smith reported that the draft was "progressing favorably and that the people received it cheerfully, many of our first men desiring to enter into the service of their country, now called upon, looking upon substitution or commutation as almost dishonorable."[37]

As the summer weather heated up, the draft kept governors busy with bureaucracy, but it was by no means the only issue fueling civil unrest. Although geographically isolated from Confederate invasions, Oregonians and Californians shared the problems associated with discontent. By the summer of 1863, migration west persisted as miners, merchants, and entrepreneurs advanced frontier settlements. Lincoln supported the westward expansion, provided it remained under Republican control. Governors Gibbs and Stanford helped foster Unionism and had established formidable political bases, but emancipation, conscription, and black enlistment increased anti-Republican sentiment. By August, they worried the influx of trans-Mississippi residents, thousands of whom were pro-Southern and desiring to escape the guerrilla war, would strengthen the antiwar Democrats. They also worried that lucrative mining had attracted reckless miners, who held no regard for Indians. Many of these glory seekers threatened to incite Indian uprisings against the Union and seize abandoned forts for their protection. Stanton responded by reorganizing the military districts. Yet governors could not raise sufficient forces to combat the Indians, protect the Oregon Trail, and maintain peace among the miners. Gibbs's chief objective was to construct frontier forts at Boise and Klamath to protect residents against the Snake Indians and secessionists coming into the Willamette Valley. He managed to enlist only one company, however, as Oregonians were more interested in mining for gold than hunting down Indians. Gibbs had warned against perceived secret Copperhead threats, but Wright refused to release federal arms to the state militia.[38]

In California, Stanford had problems in his last months, not with the draft, black troops, or Confederate invasion, but with disputes over safeguarding San Francisco. He was also in a showdown between the miners and federal authorities over the New Almaden Quicksilver Mine, which he feared would backfire against Republicans in the September election. The San Francisco press urged Stanford to protect the city against Confederate cruiser bombardments, and the governor secured Stanton's support to fund the construction of batteries. More important than coastal protection was the security of the New Almaden Mine. The Supreme Court had given the federal government legal ownership in March, but miners protested the decision, fearing the government would seize all the mines on public land. To settle matters, Lincoln sent Leonard Swett to California, who arrived in July armed with a military writ to use Wright's forces to take possession of New Almaden. Miners, however, refused to relinquish control, and tensions escalated among California's anti-administration groups. Frederick Low, who was serving as the collector of the Port of San Francisco and campaigning for the governorship at the time, feared Lincoln's seizure of the quicksilver mine would be disastrous. "The secessionists," he wrote Chase, "will seize upon it as a pretext for a general uprising I fear."[39] He urged the secretary to have Lincoln call off Wright's troops. With political campaigns under way in California, and the popular Democrat Downey seeking a return to the governorship, Stanford worried that Republicans would suffer at the polls unless military authorities backed down. Given the hostile circumstances, Wright assured the miners that he would take no further action, and withdrew. Stanford's explosive controversy ended, and the governor claimed a minor, but timely, victory.[40]

Civil unrest, whether among miners, Indians, or disgruntled Democrats, turned governors away from soldier relief following Gettysburg and Vicksburg. While many chief executives combatted Copperheads, border state governors struggled to settle factional quarrels. Gamble led a successful political campaign to end slavery in Missouri by 1870, and he assumed the ordinance would placate loyal slave owners. His advocacy, however, placed him in a dispute among Missouri Unionists. Despite his best efforts, the governor was sore at Lincoln for having characterized him as the leader of a faction in a letter to Schofield. Had the *St. Louis Missouri Democrat* not published the letter, Gamble would never have known Lincoln had made these comments. Yet the governor refused to allow the opportunity to pass without writing to Lincoln that his letter had insulted him. "If making to you the proper representation of facts constituted me the head of a faction," declared Gamble, "then I have been such," but only because "I was performing a simple duty to you," as president."[41] Gamble's tone angered Lincoln, but the president replied calmly that any perceived slight was unintentional and invited the governor to Washington to smooth things over. Gamble had gone to Philadelphia with his wife on a medical visit and from there steamed on to Washington and met with Lincoln. It was an abbreviated meeting, cut short by an interruption, which infuriated Gamble, who believed that the president had planned the interruption. To add injury to his bruised ego, on his return trip the governor had his right elbow smashed by a bridge trestle, and it landed him in the hospital. Until his return, his lieutenant governor, Willard P. Hall, handled state and military affairs.[42]

Kansans were equally embroiled in factional and personal quarrels, and Governor Carney had made several earlier trips to Washington to gain Lincoln's support. General Blunt had caused more problems than he solved, the governor argued, and Stanton's refusal to authorize a regiment of home guards for local defense infuriated him. Desperate, he called on State Senator William H. M. Fishback to support a legislative petition for congressional funds, but General Lane rejected the idea. Fishback eventually won the assistance of Senator Pomeroy, who shepherded the idea through the War Department, but Stanton placed Blunt in charge of the commissions. Carney had aspirations for the Senate and believed that Blunt, swayed by Lane, would use his patronage against the governor. Thus, Carney traveled to Washington to confer with Lincoln. He spent several weeks in the nation's capital, but never met with the president. Instead, he penned a letter from his hotel the day he departed for Topeka. The governor demanded Blunt's removal, asked for authorization to commission officers in Kansas, and insisted that military authorities be ordered to respect civil law. Lincoln agreed and told Stanton to honor the governor's request. Carney, however, had no knowledge of this because he left Washington before seeing Lincoln, and, in fact, fired off another letter from Pittsburgh claiming that "Kansas has never yet been treated as other loyal States are treated."[43] The governor returned to Topeka, where he found Lincoln's letter explaining that whatever appointments he had been denied was the result of arrangements before Carney became governor. As far as eliminating Blunt from Kansas, "the thing should not be hastily done," argued Lincoln, for he was in the midst of a campaign in the southern portion of the state. The president assured Carney that he would "take care that he [Blunt] shall not any more, take persons charged with civil crimes, out of the custody of the courts and turn them over to mobs to be hanged."[44]

Kansans and Missourians epitomized the intractable political struggle among Unionists vying for power. Yet the enemy in the front reclaimed national news when Federal troops captured General Morgan at Buffington Island, ending his ten-day-long blitzkrieg through Indiana and Ohio. Tod's call for men had brought forth thousands of men expecting to be formed into companies, but Morgan's capture forced the governor to send them home. The editor of the *Ohio State Journal* criticized Tod for his misguided call, and opponents castigated the governor by dubbing his unwarranted panic "Tod's Elephant." The abrupt release angered Ohioans, who were more incensed when they learned that Morgan had cost the state $600,000 in damages. It did not help that the governor agreed to pay volunteers for an invasion that ended before the units were formed. The raid had also cost Morton, who returned to Indianapolis, having deposited Stanton's loan money in New York. Now the governor needed to use a significant portion of the money to pay for those expenses. Despite the lack of funds, Ohioans and Indianans worked together to consolidate public defense against Morgan's raiders, much like Pennsylvanians, New Jerseyites, and New Yorkers had to combat Lee. The public sentiment impressed Morton, and he issued a proclamation thanking his Indianans for the "alacrity with which they had responded to his call," and concluded that Morgan's "wonderful uprising would exert a marked influence throughout the country."[45]

Summer Woes

The war was far from over in the East. By mid-July, Lee had escaped back into Virginia, much to Lincoln's disappointment. As much as Richmond had been the administration's objective the year before, Southern armies were now Lincoln's target. The president's displeasure traveled by gossip to the army and prompted Meade to resign, but Lincoln refused to accept his resignation. He could not condemn a commander whom he had just two weeks before placed in command. Besides, he had no one to replace him. Lee's army ventured south, and fighting in the Lower Shenandoah Valley escalated. Meade crossed the Potomac on 19 July and headed toward Harpers Ferry, but proved no better suited to pin down Lee than had his predecessors. By the end of July, John Singleton Mosby, the dashing "Gray Ghost," emerged as the Virginia counterweight to Morgan's Ohio escapades and disrupted Meade's army as it inched further south. Rosecrans, meanwhile, had been successful in keeping Confederates in the West from reinforcing either Lee or Johnston by moving toward Chattanooga. In South Carolina, Federal operations were moving toward an investment of Charleston Harbor, and while the assault on Fort Wagner resulted in Union disaster, it demonstrated the mettle of those black soldiers who fought, especially those in the 54th Massachusetts. By August, several Union black regiments had been mustered into service. "It is undoubtedly desirable," explained

Buckingham to Connecticut resident Ebenezer D. Bassett, "that the government should be able to avail itself of the services of all its able bodied men."[46] Seymour, however, remained committed to keeping New York regiments all white.[47]

The summer's military successes renewed Northerners' confidence they could repel Confederate invasions, and it boosted morale among the soldiers, especially those in the West. Despite sluggish volunteering, draft problems, and civil unrest, there was evidence that Northern sacrifice had contributed to military gain. Citizens had grown accustomed to war and were settling into the reality that ending the conflict could only be accomplished on the battlefield. In his report to Seward, General Meigs remarked, "the whole Nation is becoming familiar with arms."[48] Ohio cavalryman William Curry confirmed such sentiments by writing to his wife that he was "glad to hear of the Union people getting waked up [,] for it is time."[49] Part of the Union's awakening came from the realization that the nation and the states could quarrel and still cooperate in the cause. In addition to Lincoln's quarrels with Gamble and Carney, Seymour's machinations epitomized this obstructionist cooperation. In early August he demanded that Lincoln suspend the draft in New York, at least until he could verify its discriminatory character. The governor argued that, given the vast quota discrepancies and that conscription had come upon the nation at a time of great peril, citizens were left unprepared for such a call. New York had oversubscribed by some 42,000 troops, he argued, and quotas assigned were disproportionate and discriminated against Democratic districts. Many Republicans had already enlisted, and it was no surprise that the draft fell indiscriminately on Democrats. Given Seymour's recalcitrance, Major Frederick Townsend, acting provost marshal in Albany, had no confidence that state authorities would assist with the draft, and he wired Fry that the governor was "a dangerous man with a mind congenitally predisposed to lunacy, and always directed by the absorbing impulse of inordinate ambition."[50]

Townsend had an accurate read on Seymour, and Lincoln held firm to a draft in New York. Quota discrepancies aside, Seymour then turned the issue on the act's unconstitutionality. "In the minds of the American people," he contended, "this Government and our people have more to fear from acquiescence in the disorganizing teachings that war suspends their legal rights or destroys their legal remedy than they have to fear from resistance to the doctrine that measures can be enforced without regard to the decisions of judicial tribunals."[51] Seymour was confident that his figures and his reasoning would convince the administration to suspend the draft in New York, but Stanton refused. To reinforce the government's stance, Stanton sent General Dix to replace General Wool, and the new commander informed Seymour the draft would proceed, with or without state assistance. For all of the governor's filibustering, to save face, he wrote Tilden that "it will do no good, except making up a record." He concluded, "I look for nothing but hostility, but I shall do my duty, and demand my rights, and let consequences take care of themselves."[52] The draft progressed in New York's western cities, and Lincoln finally responded to Seymour's letter. Despite whatever disparities existed in the quota numbers, he argued, the Union was facing an enemy who drove every able-bodied man he could reach into the ranks, "very much as a butcher drives bullocks into a slaughter pen." He argued, "My purpose is to be in my action just and constitutional, and yet practical, in performing the important duty with which I am charged."[53] The president was prepared to use military force in New York if resistance got out of hand. Seymour fell into line.[54]

August's summer heat raised the mercury in Washington, and residents and soldiers suffered mercilessly. To get away from the fatiguing communication over quota discrepancies, Lincoln spent many of those close humid nights at the Soldiers' Home. "The cares and responsibilities of his office are obviously telling upon the health of the President," wrote a Washington correspondent, "he looks thin and feeble, and his eyes have lost their humorous expression. His friends entertain much solicitude about his health and have endeavored to persuade him to leave the capitol to recuperate, but so far the pilot sticks to his helm, and does not seem disposed to leave it so long as he has strength to hold."[55] Gilmore's contacts relayed Lincoln's condition to the governor, and he invited him to the White Mountains for a visit. Besides, wrote Gilmore, "your presence here would do us good."[56] Although he needed a reprieve after sparring with Seymour, Carney, and Gamble, Lincoln declined the invitation. He stayed in Washington, pacing the floor of the War Department's telegraph office, hoping for some favorable news.[57]

Gilmore's invitation was but a glimmer of relief in an otherwise gloomy home front forecast. Copperheads were on the move in Illinois, and Yates wired Lincoln that they would resist a draft should one commence. Large mobs also had formed in Iowa, most alarmingly in Keokuk County along the Mississippi, and Kirkwood secured additional troops from Stanton. In West Virginia, Boreman had become so despondent over guerrillas that he gave up on national assistance and resorted to local defense. With fall elections approaching, governors could ill-afford to alienate citizens, even while the national armies needed men. Yet, thus far in the war, nothing on the home front compared to William Clarke Quantrill's raid on Lawrence in the early morning darkness of 21 August. The Confederate guerrilla's band of irregulars destroyed the small Kansas town and massacred 150 unsuspecting civilians. The unprecedented raid shocked Northerners. Like John Brown four years before, Carney inspired loyal Kansans to bring the bushwhackers to justice. "Disaster has again fallen upon our State," Carney wired Schofield, "Lawrence is in ashes."[58] Within days, fighting spread to Missouri, as angry Kansans swept across the border in search of Quantrill's men. Carney relied on Ewing's federal forces to retaliate, but the commander lacked the federal resources to protect citizens. Fearful of another strike, the governor ordered Kansans in the border counties to leave. Lane blamed Schofield and Carney for the massacre, and demanded a retaliatory invasion into Missouri. Schofield arrived in Leavenworth and hoped to calm Carney, but the governor was beyond compromise. In the meantime, Lane whipped Radical Kansans into a fury and demanded they assemble at Paola to organize against Missourians. Carney initially refused to prevent this movement, hoping it would backfire against Lane, but when Schofield pressed him, the governor called Kansans to his aid. In the end, Lane's "venegeance-bent" Paola movement fizzled out, and Carney convinced Stanton to supply the militia and bring the state under control. In the week following the Lawrence massacre, Ewing received orders to banish roughly 20,000 Missourians along the Kansas border, and he assigned the unscrupulous Jayhawker, Charles "Doc" Jennison, to undertake the mission.[59]

Autumn Campaigns

In the midst of the Quantrill hysteria, state campaigns got underway. Republicans hoped to capitalize on the summer's military victories and Lincoln's moderation in preventing Radicals from leading the party. Union leagues sprang up to combat the Copperheads, and because they supported the administration, their members gave Republicans a boost at the polls. At stake was the continuation or rejection of Lincoln's policies, and local politics hinged on the means of ending the war. Lincoln's suspension of the writ of habeas corpus, arbitrary arrests, and conscription weighed heavily on civilians, and in some states, conventions placed nominees on the ballot that indicated another Democratic sweep of power. Yet extremists undermined their own campaigns and discredited the party. Most important to the Union cause, however, was that one-third of the Union's states would be electing new governors, and Republicans needed to remain in office to continue the federal-state partnership in meeting the war's demands. Governors feared that conscription would interfere with the elections, and they worked with military commanders to furlough troops home to ensure Republican victory.[60]

New Englanders had gone to the polls in the spring and kept Republicans in the New Hampshire, Rhode Island, and Connecticut statehouses. Still, there were important gubernatorial contests in Maine and Vermont in September and in Massachusetts in November. In the summer convention in Maine, Washburn helped establish a base of support between Republicans and War Democrats, resulting in a Union Party that nominated Samuel Cony for governor. Although a one-time Democrat, Cony supported the Union, and campaigned against Democrat Bion Bradbury, who condemned Lincoln's strong national control and civil rights violations. Vermont Republicans unanimously nominated John Gregory Smith and supported the administration's war aims. Democrats nominated Timothy P. Redfield and launched a fanatical campaign to end civil liberty abuses. Massachusetts Republicans had no reason to look beyond Andrew and renominated him for governor, despite his having been ridiculed for not bringing forth the "swarms" that he promised. Democrats chose Henry W. Paine, whose vehement condemnation of Lincoln's policies pushed the antiwar rhetoric to new heights, and undid their campaign before it got started.[61]

Kentuckians spent the prior months canvassing gubernatorial nominees, and voters journeyed to the polls in early August. The summer's battlefield victories had come at an opportune time, though Robinson chose not to seek reelection and instead supported Union Democrat and ex-military man Thomas E. Bramlette for the governorship. Amid Kentucky's political atmosphere, the issue of use of black troops edged its way into the contest between Bramlette and conservative Democrat and former Kentucky governor Charles A. Wickliffe. Bramlette highlighted the issue during his campaign, vowing to "sweep away emancipation, confiscation [and] negro regiments."[62] To secure Bramlette's victory, Burnside declared martial law, arrested opponents, and had the troops furloughed home. With these efforts, Bramlette defeated Wickliffe by a margin of more than 50,000 votes. The new governor was well suited to the office. Educated in the common schools, the Kentucky native eventually read law, was admitted to the bar, and moved to Louisville to set up his practice. Impressed by his legal insight, voters elected him to the General Assembly. He was soon after appointed state attorney, and eventually elected a district judge, a position he held until outbreak of the Civil War. He resigned to accept a colonelcy to command the 3rd Kentucky Infantry, but in 1862 Lincoln appointed him U.S. district attorney for Kentucky. Since his nomination for governor in May 1863, however, the war had changed, and his governorship would be fraught with protecting slavery, while succumbing to black enlistment. His troubles began with Burnside's recent order to General Boyle to carry out the impressment of thousands of slaves to work the roads and railroads, and to pay the slave owners for their services.[63]

The national press highlighted Bramlette's victory as a counterweight to Morgan's raid. Northerners hoped the victory might influence voters in Pennsylvania, Ohio, Iowa, Minnesota, Wisconsin, and even in California, where governorships were turning over. Pennsylvania Democrats were no match for Curtin's war record, and neither was their candidate, George W. Woodward. On his way to visit the Army of the Potomac in late August, Curtin visited Lincoln and discussed the upcoming election, draft quotas, and his desire to have troops furloughed home. Stanton, however, balked. McClure alluded to the rejection weeks before in a letter to Eli Slifer, secretary of the Commonwealth. "The Governor will fail at Washington I fear," he wrote, "[Stanton] is so bitterly against him that he will interfere against any movement the Governor may desire." He asserted that Stanton "seems to be actuated all the time by the impression that Gov. Curtin is only seeking popularity in all these efforts; and he does not particularly desire him to be popular."[64] Stanton was angry over Curtin's earlier visit to secure payment for the outstanding federal vouchers that were owed Pennsylvania. But the governor stood his ground. The elections were coming, and he needed to pay off debts and secure passage home for his Pennsylvanians. Still, he contemplated retirement. Failing health, a fatiguing schedule, and pressure from his wife convinced him to consider traveling abroad to improve his health. Lincoln sensed the governor's exhaustion and offered him a diplomatic position. When rumors surfaced, Pennsylvanians urged Curtin to decline the president's offer. Party loyalty and public encouragement convinced him to remain in the race for a second term, but failing health prevented him from countering the opposition's smear tactics.

Whatever his faults, the governor remained widely popular. Soldiers adored the chief executive. "We all love Andy Curtin," wrote a soldier convalescing in a Harrisburg Hospital.[65]

Tod of Ohio was also popular with Republicans and considered a second term, but stepped aside when Republicans and War Democrats united and nominated John Brough. Having stumped the state in favor of Lincoln's war policies, Brough made significant progress among the Unionists. "Either slavery must be torn out root and branch," he declared to a Cleveland audience in July, "or our Government will exist no longer."[66] Peace Democrats turned to Vallandigham, and the contest turned visceral. Cavalryman Clemens Clendenen was so outraged he wrote to his family that Vallandigham was "nothing more nor les [sic] than a trible [sic] tongued hydra headed cloven footed, heaven forsaken, hell begotten pucilanimas curse."[67] Still, Tod called on Morton and Yates to assist him in canvassing the state for the Union Party, and relied on Lincoln Leagues to garner support for Brough.[68]

Iowa's "old plough handle" Kirkwood could have easily won reelection over Democrat James M. Tuttle, partly because his state did not endure a draft that summer and partly because soldiers respected him. Having suffered the debilitating effects of traveling back and forth across the state, however, the governor decided against another term. Republicans nominated William M. Stone, an abolitionist and a popular choice among the soldiers, as his successor. To Jed Lake, Kirkwood expressed his relief in being out of office. "I am the tiredst [sic] man in Iowa," he confessed.[69] Kirkwood's commitment to soldier welfare was impressive, and his efforts endeared him to even his enemies. As he told it, fighting for the Union had given new meaning to Iowa citizenship. "When this war began," he declared on the campaign trail, "Iowa had no history. People in the East knew there was such a State west of the Mississippi, but they supposed it was inhabited by a few white persons and a good many Indians, and that the balance of the population was composed of wolves."[70] He boasted, "*Iowa has a name now*, and it will be a shame . . . if the soldiers who are in front of the enemy cannot be assured that their wives and children and loved ones at home can be protected from traitors in the rear."[71]

Minnesotans had also made history in the war, and their governors endured significant home-front hostility. Swift succeeded Ramsey in July when his term expired, and, sensing the state's changing political climate, the interim executive stepped aside, which allowed Republicans to nominate Stephen Miller, a recently promoted brigadier general with an outstanding service record. Still, he would have to win over Henry T. Wells, a popular Democrat from Minneapolis. Wisconsin's governor shared Swift's unusual path to the statehouse, having stepped into the governorship by virtue of Harvey's death the year before. Salomon's experience in fighting the Sioux and quelling the draft riots convinced the Prussian-born governor that he could do the job another term, and so he sought the nomination. Republicans, however, felt no obligation to Salomon and, given the split in the Democratic Party, bypassed him for James T. Lewis, who, like Cony and Brough, helped form a Union Party coalition with War Democrats. The departure of Unionists left the Democrats in the hands of peace radicals, who nominated Henry L. Palmer, who ran such a debasing campaign against Lincoln that several party leaders denounced him.[72]

The summer's political conventions opened during major military campaigns, the draft, and Copperheads seeking to topple their parties. Yet New York City's draft violence and the brutality of Quantrill's raid worked against political leaders seeking to end the war through peace negotiations. Seymour hoped to extend the Democratic sweep of the political culture a year more. "If the conservative men in the central parts of the Union will act in concert," he declared, "they can control the policy of the government."[73] Such rhetoric helped torpedo Republican opposition, and, when the September elections came off in Vermont, California, and Maine, voters kept Unionist candidates in power. Smith took the gubernatorial seat in Vermont by a landslide and Unionist Republican Low soundly defeated Downey by more than 20,000 votes. In Maine, Cony polled 17,000 votes more than Bradbury in the largest voter turnout in a decade. Unlike their Republican colleagues elected in the spring, Republicans and War Democrats had united in the belief that the only way to end the war was by fighting. These victories were encouraging signs to an electorate about to vote in October and November that the Union tide was shifting away from wooing Southerners and toward subjugating them.

The September governors were an eclectic group. Smith was a native of St. Albans and had a blue-blooded pedigree that stretched back nearly two centuries. After graduating from the University of Vermont, he studied law at Yale University. He returned to Vermont to practice law, but his father's death in 1858 made him the president of the Vermont Central Railroad. His first experience in politics came in 1858, when Vermonters elected him to the state legislature on the Republican ticket. He eventually rose to become the House speaker in 1861 and 1862. By 1863, he was poised to become the chief executive. Low was also a New England native, but instead of pursuing law and politics, he chose business. At fifteen, he ventured to Boston and apprenticed in the prominent East Indian mercantile business owned by Charles Russell and Russell Sturgis. At the young age of twenty-one he followed the Gold Rush in 1849, settling first in San Francisco, where he went into the mercantile business with his brother Charles, under the name of the Low Brothers and Company. Low rose to prominence during California's political infancy, joined the Republican Party, and was elected to Congress shortly after the Civil War broke out. An error in California's political apportionment denied him his seat until Congress reviewed the case and eventually permitted him his term. Chase had recently appointed him collector for the Port of San Francisco, and he was instrumental in resolving the New Almaden Mine quarrel. His election made him California's first chief executive to serve a four-year term. Cony was a distinguished lawyer who studied at Brown University and later followed his father into politics. The Maine native served as a state representative, land agent, probate judge, and, from 1850 until 1855, as state treasurer. By the time of the Civil War, he had joined the Republican Party and was serving in the state legislature. Cony had impressed Coburn and Washburn, who campaigned vigorously to get him in office. When victory came, Washburn reported to Lincoln that Cony's election "was won upon the question of the square & unqualified support of your Administration & its policy."[74]

Newspapers reporting these political victories reflected the growing acceptance among Northerners that sustaining the administration meant using unrelenting force. Indeed, it was as the *Indianapolis Daily Journal* editorialized, "the heel of the man has 'bruised the head of the serpent,' down East terribly."[75] For all the complaining Democrats did over black enlistments and how emancipation and conscription violated the constitution, Republicans recognized that such stratagems weakened the Confederacy. Despite Copperhead resistance, New Englanders and Californians objected less to the national government's expansive measures, deemed necessary to bring about victory, than they did their constitutional underpinnings. Part of this acceptance had to do with their proximity to the conflict, and part of it had to do with the acceptance that reconstruction of the Union went forward with the war. Whether Northerners fully appreciated it at the time, the fact was that the war set in motion a transformative relationship between national and state governments as a means to bring about military victory.

Few citizens could better understand the politics of reconstruction than Marylanders, Missourians, and Kentuckians, who were exempt from emancipation, but whose slave and free populations were recruited for black regiments. Bramlette's recent victory did not end the quarrels with Stanton over black recruitment, but elections in Maryland and Missouri could produce victories for emancipationists, provided black enlistment was handled judiciously. Stanton authorized enlisting Maryland's blacks into federal service to be credited to the state quota in July, and appointed abolitionist Colonel William Birney to organize the regiment under Schenck's supervision. Although the order was well intentioned, citizens decried that recruiting runaway slaves, or those taken by the military, would result in labor shortages and weaken the state's economy. Bradford agreed that enlisting slaves without the consent of the owner violated state law, but he prodded citizens to prepare for the inevitable end of the institution. "It sometimes really almost seems that there is a determination somewhere to get up if possible something of a civil war in Maryland," he told Montgomery Blair, "just as we are about to subdue it everywhere else."[76] He supported the conservative wing of Unionists, who favored emancipation, but not without some regard to slaveholder's constitutional rights and financial concerns. The times were changing, and he knew it. To support his cause in the coming election, Bradford advised using the military to subject all military-age male citizens to an oath pledging their loyalty to the Union and to "forever oppose secession, rebellion, and the disintegration of the Federal Union."[77] He traveled to Washington and conferred with Lincoln and Stanton, hoping they would hold off on raising a black regiment in the state at least until after the election. Recruiting would continue, they argued, but they assured Bradford that the War Department had not authorized anyone to enlist slaves. Yet the governor left Washington unconvinced that anything would be done to prevent it. He complained to Blair that if the national government was not authorizing it, "then why, in God's name, permit it?"[78]

The summer heat dissipated with the arrival of autumn, and so had Missourians' patience over Governor Gamble and General Schofield's conservative approach to emancipation. Radicals demanded the commander's resignation, the termination of Gamble's provisional government, and the appointment of a seventy-man committee to appeal to Lincoln to relieve their grudges. B. Gratz Brown wrote Lincoln that Schofield was not to be trusted to carry out federal instructions "for his sympathy is all with the Gamble Dynasty *if not worse*."[79] While Gamble was convalescing in

Pennsylvania, Schofield had reluctantly begun the work of enrolling blacks to fight, and placed it in the hands of unenthused provost marshals, which slowed the process. Even still, loyal slave owners flooded the governor's office with complaints of runaway slaves, and by the time the governor returned to Missouri, the delegation had departed for Washington to influence Lincoln to limit his power.[80]

Black recruitment consumed significant attention among border state governors, but the issue of equal pay for these soldiers came under Massachusetts governor Andrew's care. The governor arrived in Washington in mid-September to fulfill a promise he had made to Colonel Shaw before his death at Fort Wagner—to secure equal pay for the men of the 54th and 55th Massachusetts regiments. Stanton and Andrew had sparred over equal pay, and recent discussions had soured Andrew against the administration. Like all governors, the war forced Andrew to cooperate with the national government out of necessity without any defined procedure, and Stanton's "eccentricities of judgment and temper fell heavily," on chief executives seeking justice for their constituents. Consequently, he returned to Boston determined to gain the support of representatives to sponsor legislation in December when Congress convened.[81]

The problems associated with factional quarrels, black enlistment, and equal pay left the front pages of national newspapers on 19 September. On that day, the armies of Rosecrans and Bragg met southeast of Chattanooga along opposite sides of Chickamauga Creek and engaged in a two-day battle resulting in Union defeat. As the Federals retreated to Chattanooga, field reports estimating casualties arrived in the War Department. Of the nearly 60,000 Union soldiers engaged, more than 16,000 were listed as casualties. Equally disheartening for Northerners was the feeling that the administration had bungled, and that costs far exceeded gains. The result overwhelmed the president. He considered removing Rosecrans, who he claimed was "confused and stunned like a duck hit on the head," but in the end, retained him. Once again, governors accumulated medical stores and rushed agents to the field. The battlefield's location and the coming elections, however, prevented most governors from traveling to the front.[82]

Lincoln had done all he could to secure victory at the October and November polls. He had worked with governors to lessen the blow of the draft, suspended the writ of habeas corpus to combat Copperheads, lined up military supervision at the polls, and furloughed troops home to vote. The recent battle, however, sent pro-administration editors into a tailspin, while oppositionist editors emphasized Lincoln's heavy handedness in abusing civil liberties. They stressed the importance of the elections and argued that furloughing soldiers home would weaken the Union's grip on the enemy in Virginia and Tennessee. Worse yet, Democrats had made a fuss over monies owed the state from the national government for expenses incurred by summer invasions, and this would hurt Republican candidates. Having returned from western Pennsylvania where he was campaigning, Curtin informed Lincoln that failure to pay the expenses owed the state was doing him "great injury" and might affect the outcome of the election in his state. "It is hard that I should suffer personally, but for the Governm't [*sic*] it is suicide," he told the president.[83]

Lincoln spent 30 September entertaining Missouri's "Jacobin Delegation," known as Lane's "little army."[84] The president listened patiently and allowed them due time to make their case. After the Missourians left, Lincoln entertained Carney and some prominent Kansans, who argued that Schofield was satisfactory to them. There were no easy solutions for Missourians or Kansans, and Lincoln waited before responding. The president appreciated that Gamble's problems were bigger than the office he occupied. The governor had come under fire for not only dragging his feet in recruiting black soldiers, but also for allowing flagrant abuses to be committed by civilians marauding the countryside, as well as quarreling with commanders. Lincoln too could be accused of as much.[85]

CHAPTER FIFTEEN

A Tub Thrown to the Whale

Gamble's return to Springfield was anything but cordial, but he expected to finish what he started by keeping loyalists in power until the war ended. Jo Shelby's Confederate cavalry invasion, however, added to his problems. When his raiders crossed into Missouri in early October, it threw residents into a panic and alarmed bordering Iowans and Illinoisans, who looked to Yates and Kirkwood for protection. The president, meanwhile, was sequestered by a week of interviews about Missouri affairs. When he had time, Lincoln responded to the Missouri delegation's "address" and provided his justification for keeping Schofield and the Enrolled Militia, and in supporting those, who only by law, could vote in Missouri. Although critics, such as Joseph Medill, the *Chicago Tribune's* sardonic editor, told Lincoln that he was being "woefully deceived," the president stood his ground. "I hold whoever commands in Missouri or elsewhere," he stated, "responsible to me, and not to either radicals or conservatives."[1] Besides, Gamble needed Lincoln's support to counter Shelby's raid.[2]

Quarrels between Radicals and conservatives in the border states did not deter Stanton from advancing the national front by ordering black enlistments. Governors welcomed the initiative but it complicated relations among slave owners, civil authorities, and military commanders. Bradford had discussed with Stanton the problems resulting from slave enlistments without owner consent. The secretary had agreed that Maryland's free blacks could enlist, that slaves could enlist with owner consent, and that if slave owners wanted to enlist their slaves they would be compensated. On receiving the note, Lincoln responded that while he did not object to the first two proposals, compensation troubled him, and he invited the governor to the White House to "fix up definitely in writing" the terms.[3] Until he could clarify the misunderstanding, Lincoln directed Stanton to suspend recruiting of Maryland blacks to defuse protest on the eve of the elections. Bradford arrived in early October, conferred with the president, and both men agreed that enlisting free blacks should continue. Only loyal slave owners, however, could offer their slaves for military service, and file deeds of manumission in return for compensation. When Bradford returned to Annapolis, he wired

Lincoln that the thirty-day time period they agreed on to allow for the enlistment of slaves offered by their owners was "entirely too short."[4] To ease the tension, Lincoln allowed him sixty days for the first enlistments and ordered General Schenck to restrain overzealous recruiters.[5]

Recruiting and Campaigning

Besides supervising black enlistments that fall, Stanton and Fry engaged in the unpopular duties of returning deserters, denying bounty requests, and carrying out national conscription. They represented the national government's long arm and kept stenographers busy administrating enrollment matters. Occasionally, Stanton reported good news to Lincoln, such as Kirkwood's telegram that Iowa had met its quota. Other governors were not as fortunate, and Stanton wired those with shortages, such as Salomon, Gilmore, and Buckingham, to prepare their citizens. Fry projected additional quotas for future calls in Illinois, Massachusetts, Pennsylvania, and Delaware. With a draft looming, Reverend John A. Hawley wrote to Salomon to gain his cooperation in allowing Wisconsin blacks to enlist in Illinois regiments. Yates supported the idea, arguing to the Prussian governor that enlisting blacks would not only diminish the need of white men to fight but would also "help to draw those of the South to our standard & diminish resources of enemy & bring out the manhood of the Negro & do justice to his race."[6]

The timing of the draft and the fall elections produced Northern apprehension, and governors worked to focus voters on the national cause. Many chief executives used the opportunity to advance bounty inducements to avoid conscription, and to petition legislatures to revise state constitutions to allow soldiers to vote in the field. Smith pressed Stanton to authorize bounties for new recruits and to allow states to expand programs for soldier welfare. With his legislature in session, the governor urged representatives to consider an act permitting Vermont soldiers to vote in the field. He also authorized towns to raise bounty funds and to provide those funds for the care of Vermont's wounded soldiers. He enlisted Senator Foote's influence to have the soldiers of the 9th Vermont that were suffering at Yorktown to be relocated to a more hospitable climate or furloughed home. Whether it involved bounties, furloughs, or recruiting for regiments, Fry was always mindful to emphasize to governors that "nothing can now be better for the public interests, than for the State and General Government to work harmoniously together in devoting this most favorable recruiting season to raising men."⁷

The national press scrutinized the political campaigns that October, and Lincoln hoped for a reversal of the 1862 returns. Adding to September's success, victories in Ohio, Pennsylvania, Iowa, and Indiana might win back control of the House of Representatives and determine the course of the next year's presidential election. Indeed, Lincoln found time to ponder a late September wire from Gibbs. The governor advised the president that to continue the political harmony between Republicans and War Democrats in the 1864 campaign, party managers might consider that the name Republican be changed to Union. Although supportive of Lincoln's war aims, Gibbs himself had been an old Douglas Democrat, and he confessed that he saw "more Jacksonian democracy in the measures of your Administration, than can be found among all your opponents [sic]." Therefore, he concluded, "I am decidedly of the opinion that the next National convention should be called as a Union convention."⁸

Gibbs's forecast was prophetic, but the road to an 1864 victory started with the 1863 elections. What Calvin Fletcher judged as perhaps the "most important day in America," 13 October, came off in favor of the Republicans, and early wires related local victories.⁹ Senator Grimes of Iowa wired Lincoln that Republicans had swept the state, boasting that "we could not have asked for more."¹⁰ From Ohio came additional good news. "God be praised," wrote Governor Tod, "our majority on the home vote cannot be less than 30,000."¹¹ Curtin also had reason to be pleased. "Pennsylvania stands by you," came the news from James M. Scovel from Pittsburgh, "keeping step with Maine & California to the music of the Union."¹² Pennsylvanians re-elected Curtin by more than 15,000 votes, and Republicans carried the legislature. Stanton had mixed feelings about the victory, because he had been bullied into allowing troops home to vote to retain his nemesis. One paper even reported that Stanton boasted to a crowd "I elected Gov. Curtin; for I sent him 15,000 more votes than he had majority."¹³ Even Morton, who was with Chase celebrating at the Burnet House, had something to boast, as Indiana returns showed "an enormous union gain keeping pace with that in Ohio."¹⁴

The election results encouraged Lincoln. Republicans received the electorate's confidence for successfully handling the war effort and moving toward victory. Some governors used the president's influence in state victories, and Lincoln appreciated their collective role in advancing his war aims.

After all, the victories at Gettysburg and Vicksburg gave the Northern populace something to celebrate. Defeat robbed Democrats, who claimed the war was a failure, and it smothered their fire. Soldiers' letters to governors confirmed that fighting the war to victory was their sole objective, and that Republicans, with or without Lincoln, were determined to achieve this objective. Despite the Union's divided political culture, Northerners had come together, nation and state, to see the war through to victory. By canvassing for weeks, pressing Stanton for troop furloughs home to vote, and by initiating legislation to allow soldiers to vote in the field, governors helped close the ranks behind Republican goals. Morton had especially distinguished himself, and the *New York Times* lionized the governor for his efforts. His "pre-eminent devotion to the cause, and his signal executive ability," the editor argued, had been the difference between what Indiana had done for the war, and what New York had done in the war under Seymour's leadership.[15]

The victories ushered in new governors in the middle of war. Iowans had a new chief executive, but they could thank Kirkwood for securing weapons to arm county militias, canvassing vigorously, and for stifling Copperheads. Stone amassed a large victory over Tuttle. The new governor shared Kirkwood's endearing features and had impressed his comrades as a first-rate soldier and officer. Taylor Pierce of the 22nd Iowa Volunteers remarked to his wife when he heard Iowans were considering nominating Stone that he was the right choice, and while he did not want to lose him from the ranks, Pierce "would like to see him at the head of affairs of the State for he would give the copperheads hell."[16] A New York native, Stone worked at an early age as a hired farmhand and occasionally as a team driver on the Ohio Canal. In his spare time he studied law and, within a few years, was admitted to the bar. He initially practiced in Ohio before moving to Iowa. He arrived in Knoxville in 1854 and eventually bought the local newspaper, the *Knoxville Journal*. His legal and journalistic interests turned him toward politics, and he joined the newly formed Republican Party. When the Civil War broke out, he joined the 3rd Iowa and fought at Shiloh, where he was wounded and taken prisoner. Exchanged months later, his military exploits had so impressed Republicans that delegates tapped him to replace Kirkwood.[17]

Ohioans had also elected a new governor, but there was more to cheer about because the campaign generated record voter turnout and resulted in Vallandigham's defeat. Writing from a Cincinnati hospital, Lucius Wood confirmed Brough's popularity among the soldiers. "[M]ay my right arm fall powerless by my side," he wrote, "ere I give my suffrage to one [Vallandigham] who can not sympathize with those who are striving to maintain the honor of our nation."[18] Tod shared this opinion. "God be praised," he wired Lincoln.[19] Despite being slighted in his bid for renomination, the governor had arranged to furlough soldiers home to vote, and called on Yates and Morton to campaign. As it turned out, Brough did not need the soldiers. The Union Democrat defeated Vallandigham by more than 100,000 votes. For all the rhetoric Ohioans tolerated from Vallandigham, the soldiers wanted a part in his demise. On his deathbed, one Ohio soldier uttered his last wish to his regimental chaplain to tell his brother, who was a Vallandigham man, "to vote for John Brough & the Union ticket." Lincoln was delighted that Ohio voters agreed with his course, or at least pleased they voted against Vallandigham's. "Glory to God in the highest," Lincoln remarked, "Ohio has saved the nation."[20] Brough joined Cony, Low, Smith, and Stone as the Union's new governors, although he had little of the dash or pedigree of his colleagues. Born the son of a tavern keeper and orphaned at the age of eleven, he apprenticed as a reporter while attending high school and college in Marietta, Ohio. The tide of Jacksonian Democracy swept him into the Democratic Party, and he embarked on a political career while studying law. He clerked in the Ohio Senate and served as legislative correspondent. His political views over slavery hardened, and he attacked abolitionism and promoted the return of fugitive slaves to their masters. Voters elected him to the Ohio General Assembly, where he served as chairman of the Committee on Banking and Currency and as State Auditor. When the Whigs seized state power in 1844, it drove Brough back to journalism, and eventually he and his brother purchased the *Cincinnati Advertiser* and renamed it the *Enquirer*. When the war came, he was practicing law and managing the Madison and Indiana Railroad. Considered the "best known man in Ohio," Brough looked to be the right man at the right time for Ohio's seemingly divided political culture, despite his half-hearted support for Lincoln early in the war.[21]

The day following the elections Lincoln consolidated the Departments of the Ohio, the Cumberland, and the Tennessee into the Military Division of the Mississippi, and placed Grant in command. These arrangements placed Sherman in command of the Department of the Tennessee, and left Burnside in command of the Department of the Ohio, but replaced Rosecrans, who had lost his soldiers' confidence. Stanton allowed Grant the courtesy of naming Rosecrans's replacement, and he chose the doggedly persistent Thomas and ordered him to hold Chattanooga at all costs.[22]

October Call for Men

By October, the problems with national conscription convinced Lincoln and the governors that despite distributing the war's burden along political districts, it had failed to produce men. The president abandoned his vision for a national army under congressional control, and he now relied on governors to intensify their enlistment efforts. War-weariness and Copperheads had impeded federal-state efforts, and governors relied on national coercion as much as they could in providing men for the armies. On 17 October Lincoln issued a call for 300,000 more three-year volunteers, and assigned 5 January as the day of the draft. The federal-state alliance established programs to decrease the number of drafted men by seeking to enroll blacks, foreigners, and members of the Invalid Corps, as well as border state slaves. The Union had expanded its control of Southern soil, and Lincoln needed additional men to advance the military fronts as well as maintain a stronghold on occupied areas. Yet states were nearly drained, and, with the economy paying higher wages to laborers than to soldiers, the prospects of raising more men proved daunting for governors. Even worse was that, despite their best efforts, draft corruption abounded.[23]

Lincoln's new push for men came at a time when the economic hardships of the war's first two years had given way to mild prosperity among Northerners, and the pull to the army had lost its allure. Parker urged New Jerseyites to come forward before matters degenerated into desperate measures at home. Seymour weighed in on citizens' sensibilities and their commitment to upholding the Constitution. Still, as much as he opposed the draft, he opposed black enlistment even more. Some governors arranged more lucrative inducements to bring men forward. Andrew convened a special legislative session and secured to a state bounty of $325 over what the national government was offering. He pressed Stanton to accept state recruitment of black soldiers, but the secretary refused. To offset labor shortages, the governor encouraged Massachusetts industrialists to hire black laborers to work in the factories or mills, but many were unreceptive to the idea. Having aggravated Stanton, Forbes, Andrew's liaison in Washington, urged Andrew to stay out of the conversation for a while to allow Congress to take up the matter. Massachusetts "is looked upon as entirely monomaniac upon the 'everlasting Nigger,'" he wrote Andrew.[24] The editor of the *Cincinnati Daily Enquirer* agreed. Thanks to Andrew, Massachusetts was the "bellwether [sic] in the Republican flock." He declared, "She leads and all the

Republicans in other States follow," and "is now after a perfect equality of the negro soldier with the white."²⁵ Bradford struggled to follow Andrew's lead in Maryland and dreaded a draft, but worse, he feared repercussions over reports that black troops were recruiting in St. Mary's County, which caused problems of a different nature. When Lincoln learned of these activities, he advised General Schenck to remove the black regiment. "It seems to me," he wrote the commander, "we could send white men to recruit better than to send negroes, and thus inaugurate [sic] homicides on punctillio."²⁶ The change relieved the governor.

October's Republican victories helped restore national confidence in the party's war management, especially since Chickamauga had dampened the enthusiasm of summer victories. Political leaders and supportive editors translated hostility toward emancipation and conscription into opposition to Union victory. Lincoln's call for more soldiers gave antiwar and antiadministration critics the opportunity to turn their opposition more radical and racial. As November elections neared, the discord among political, civil, and military officials had grown acrimonious. Lincoln learned that Tennessee oppositionist Emerson Etheridge, clerk of the U.S. House of Representatives, was planning to refuse credentials by some Republican congressmen in attempt to guarantee a conservative majority in electing a House speaker the following month. James R. Hood, postmaster at Chattanooga, Tennessee, who revealed this scheme to Lincoln, advised him to obtain corrected certificates from the governors as a way to foil the plot. Given the rumors swirling about political fraud and military interference at the polls, the president needed the governors' assurance that those members elected to Congress were legitimately elected and would not be challenged once they arrived to claim their seat. In this way, Hood was sure Lincoln could dissolve the "quasi-revolutionary act." Quietly, the president worked with governors to prepare official documents certifying their representatives' elections.²⁷

Early November brought confirmation that, despite the antiadministration critics, the Northern political culture was embracing Lincoln's expanded war. The year's political victories thus far reflected the president's faith in the governors' ability not only to raise men for the armies, but also to steer their constituents behind him. Emancipation, conscription, and black enlistments had been blunt instruments, but Lincoln used them to aid governors, not to eclipse them in managing state affairs. The pressure to expand federal power to assist the states had transformed federal-state relations, and, whether they agreed with all of them or not, governors accepted the changes necessitated by war. Providing men for vast armies challenged their cooperation and increased reliance on mutually beneficial policies and practices to achieve success. National conscription intensified federal-state cooperation and taught civil and military leaders that the federal government should do more to aid states.

By the fall of 1863 the president-governor alliance had gained legitimacy in surmounting wartime obstacles. Governors, however, worried that increasing casualty rates, rampant desertions, and ill treatment of Union prisoners might negatively influence the November outcome. In addition, military supervision at the polls had garnered national attention, and no one more than Bradford worried over its explosive nature. Conservatives and Radicals were locked in a bitter power struggle, and the governor feared that military supervision at the Maryland polls would provoke violence. Conservatives pressed Bradford into protesting its unconstitutionality to the president, and the governor believed he had convinced Lincoln to not use the military. Such supervision, he argued, "would justly be obnoxious to the public sentiment of the State."[28] Lincoln appreciated Bradford's concerns, but replied that it was imperative to have only loyalists vote, and that under Schenck's supervision, the army would remain at the polls. He argued that maintaining peace did not constitute "just cause of offence to Maryland," and reminded the governor that General Dix had secured his election in 1861.[29] Lincoln's concerns were valid, but Bradford believed Lincoln and Schenck had undermined his credibility and insulted Marylanders. Bradford fumed over Lincoln's stubbornness and, insulted by the characterization of his election, responded that his victory of more than 15,000 voters could scarcely be the result of military supervision at the polls.[30]

Changing Political Tide

Despite the bristling Northern atmosphere and the clatter over the November elections, voters came and went quietly from the polls. In those states where military supervision was necessary, Republicans and Unionists prevailed. Marylanders were not electing a governor, and even with the perceived troubles at the polls, Union candidates professing to end slavery carried the day. Still, irregularities and misconduct caused Bradford to complain to Lincoln. Missouri Unionists also took advantage of federal bayonets and turned out in large numbers to support Radicals. To avoid embarrassment in Delaware, Cannon secured authorization to furlough soldiers home to vote. Many Democrats boycotted the polls because the governor had secured them with Schenck's federal troops, who administered loyalty oaths. Oppositionists meeting in New Castle days before the election declared that Cannon had subverted the state laws by strong-arming the electorate. To protest his actions, Democrats stayed away from the polls. When the legislature convened in January, members castigated the governor for his use of the military and denounced his acts as unconstitutional. Parker, however, could not claim victory for his New Jersey Unionists. The old War Democrat, however, was careful not to interfere at the polls to avoid drawing more criticism. New Jersey voters believed the contest turned more on expansive national power than summer military victories, and Democrats railed against the unconstitutionality of emancipation, conscription, and arbitrary arrests. In the end, they kept a slight hold on the legislature, but recognized their diminishing influence in a political culture that embraced the war's nationalizing tendencies.[31]

In New York, voters who supported Seymour were "attempting to carry water on both shoulders; opposing the administration yet sustaining its principal undertaking; in favor of ending the war, yet claiming that they were for its vigorous prosecution."[32] The outspoken governor had not made their job any easier. In just a few months, the chief executive had generated a list of enemies that far exceeded his friends. His opposition to the draft, abusive denunciations of the administration, and his howling against an expansive national government cost his party dearly. "We at the National Capital are waiting with feverish interest for the returns" from the New York elections, wrote Stoddard. "It is not enough that all the rest are right," he concluded, "if New-York is wrong."[33] Many Northerners considered the New York contest a precursor to the 1864 presidential election, and they waited to see if voters would sustain the Democrats or support the Unionists. Seymour's veto of the Soldier's Voting Bill that would have allowed troops to vote in the field forced Stanton to furlough thousands of soldiers home. Beyond Seymour's battle with Lincoln over quotas, his opponents criticized him for forcing Lincoln to pull troops from the Pennsylvania battlefield to assist with New York City's riots and allowing Lee to retreat south. To strengthen their canvass, Unionists imported Yates, Curtin, and Andrew, among other prominent Republicans, to stump the state. Senator Morgan wrote John Forney that New York's election could not be overestimated. "Our defeat here," he told the journalist and secretary of the U.S. Senate, "would be more disastrous to the country than the loss of a battle."[34] When it was over, New York Unionists regained what they had lost in 1862, and the state landed safely in the hands of those who questioned more than endorsed their governor's administration. "New-York stands purged," declared the *New York Times*, "there is not a trace left of the dishonor Horatio Seymour has put upon her."[35]

Despite the national attention drawn to New York and the federal influences in Delaware, Missouri, and Maryland, voters in Massachusetts calmly kept Andrew and the Republicans in power without Stanton's backing. They were the lone New Englanders traveling to the polls that fall, and voters prided themselves on advancing the war by ballots as well as by bayonets. Andrew's reelection was never in question, but it was nonetheless more gratifying that he won more than twice the votes as distinguished Cambridge lawyer Henry Paine. Democrats mounted a spirited campaign by arguing that Lincoln's sole purpose in the war was neither the Union's preservation nor the Constitution's restoration, but emancipation. They used his arbitrary arrests, encroachment on states' rights, and the governor's Radicalism to sway the electorate, but their expectations exceeded Paine's popularity. Andrew's victory solidified New England's support of Lincoln's war aims and confirmed the president's popularity in leading the Radical vanguard to end slavery and advance equality for black soldiers.[36]

Minnesota's election also passed off quietly, and Republicans gave German native Stephen Miller a narrow victory over Wells. The result revealed that Minnesotans were not as flush with confidence about the Union's triumph as New Englanders. Still, they needed federal support in fighting the Sioux. Miller was a timely choice for the governorship as he brought military and business experience to the office. An aspiring entrepreneur, the Pennsylvania native moved to Minnesota in 1858, opened a mercantile store in St. Cloud, and he joined the Republican Party. When the war broke out, he enlisted in the 1st Minnesota, served in the Army of the Potomac, and fought admirably, earning a promotion to colonel of the 7th Minnesota. He fought against the Sioux in 1862 and commanded the District of Minnesota in the summer of 1863, rising to the rank of brigadier general. Unlike in Minnesota, Wisconsin Republicans put Lewis in office by a large margin. Currently the secretary of state and widely popular, Lewis was the fourth governor to serve during the Civil War. The New York native grew up near Rochester, and read law and taught school before embarking on a legal and political career. He arrived in Wisconsin in the 1840s, and initially served as district attorney and probate judge before voters elected him to the Wisconsin's Constitutional Convention and State Assembly. He was practicing law when the war erupted, and his considerable political experience as well as his popularity helped build a coalition between Republicans and War Democrats.[37]

Whether Northerners credited Lincoln with engineering political victories, or recognized Stanton for furloughing soldiers home, governors used emancipation, positive use of national power, and black enlistment to convince voters that these would shorten the war. Republicans had connected emancipation to the Union's preservation to combat Democratic opposition and discrimination against blacks. Governors campaigned not only to advance the national cause, but also to keep their citizens and soldiers cognizant of their political power at home. If voters went to the polls with Lincoln's reelection on their minds, it was because governors had connected the ballot box to the battlefield. Governors forged relationships with soldiers through recruiting, and they were attentive to the political significance in maintaining that bond. Parker spoke for many governors when he urged Lincoln in early November to place recruiting in the hands of the state authorities, arguing that the men could be raised much sooner. To support his case he enclosed copies of letters from the assistant provost marshal of New Jersey and the New Jersey adjutant general.[38]

Governors rallied voters to the polls, calmed their fears about military interference, and explained the justification for supporting the Union. True, many Northerners were satisfied with Lincoln, as they were with their Republican and Unionist governors. Yet the constant need to replenish the armies had taken its toll on military-age males. To be sure, as one Connecticut officer put it, "Father Abraham isn't over modest in his calls upon us," quipping that "the play naturally gets deeper and deeper, and the small stakes put up at first do not long answer to keep up the excitement of the game."[39] Although the Northern press briefly distracted the populace with election news, headlines soon returned to the military front. Meade had pushed across the Rappahannock and forced Lee to withdraw to the Rapidan without much fighting. As promising as that was, Lincoln was more encouraged that Sherman's four divisions remained on the Tennessee River near Chattanooga, and that Burnside had laid siege to Knoxville.

As the autumn temperatures cooled down, the war heated up, and governors scurried to avoid a January draft. They used the political victories to reinvigorate the populace to come forward, but overcoming the shortcomings of national conscription forced them to expand their efforts. Thus, they continued to rely on provost marshals and extravagant bounties. Curtin agreed with Parker about conscription's failure, and he suggested to Lincoln that experience demonstrated the men had been more readily raised through state management than through national agency. The bureaucracy alone was maddening. He outlined for Lincoln's approval a plan that returned recruiting authority to the governors. He also proposed that regiments be consolidated, state bounties be used to coerce enlistments, and that veterans be sent home to recruit. Aware of conscription's deficiencies, Stanton and Fry had already concluded as much, and allowed governors the lead in restoring the ranks.[40]

By the fall of 1863, the war had ebbed and flowed on many fronts. Before the winter ice formed on Lake Erie, rumors surfaced that an expedition was underway to liberate Confederate prisoners on Johnson's Island, Lake Erie. The Northern press caught wind of the plot and sensationalized its significance. British Minister Lord Lyons informed Stanton that, according to the governor-general of Canada, a plot of hostile persons to the United States had found an asylum in Canada and planned to seize the steamboats on Lake Erie and overtake Johnson's Island. Canadian authorities reported on the raid, and Stanton had no reason to doubt this news. He requested that Curtin, Tod, Blair, Morton, and Seymour, as well as the military commanders of those departments prepare units for defense. Although the rumors alarmed Dix, Tod wired that, with the force now at Johnson's Island and Buffalo, "we have nothing to fear." Within a few weeks, however, the plot never materialized.[41]

Northern optimism continued that fall as congressmen prepared to return to Washington. There was reason to be hopeful about success from Grant's Tennessee offensive about to break open at Chattanooga. The president expected the commander to redeem the Union's loss at Chickamauga, and governors had worked to replenish the armies to do it. He could ill-afford another loss, and the campaign weighed on him as he traveled to Pennsylvania. Working with Gettysburg agent David Wills, Curtin secured the president's attendance at the ceremony dedicating a national cemetery on 19 November. The governor had gained support among his colleagues for plans to purchase the battlegrounds and consecrate a national cemetery. Ward Lamon served as master of ceremonies and emphasized the role of states by inviting the governors to attend the service. Some chief executives cited political and conscription duties as too pressing to attend, but they sent representatives. Seymour arrived in the New York train station, where he met several governors heading to the ceremony. When they arrived in Harrisburg, they boarded a special "Governors' Train," and steamed on to Gettysburg. When Brough arrived, Seymour queried the burly executive about Vallandigham. The Ohioan replied that "Ambrose Burnside's prisoner of state was then 'in Canada.'"[42] When the governors arrived at Harrisburg, Curtin accompanied them to Gettysburg. Ramsey had been detained and arrived late, as did Morton, whose arrival had been trumpeted by the New York press.[43]

Whatever public accolades Lincoln drew for traveling to Gettysburg paled in comparison to the somberness of his journey. As he got closer to the town he must have noticed the windows of the homes draped in black cloth and the stacks of coffins at the train station when he arrived. He could not shake the troubles he left in Washington. Governors, however, were less distressed now that elections had passed and the political horizon for Lincoln's reelection looked favorable. The president could find consolation that recent victories had validated his handling of the war and that Union soldiers at Gettysburg had not died in vain. Whatever his shortcomings in managing the war, the armies endured and the people supported them. Although small in comparison to the number engaged in the July battle, some 40,000 citizens gathered at the sacred grounds. For all the formality associated with the president's visit, his presence was more symbolic than what he said. He came not as a Republican, not as an Illinoisan, and not to give a grand speech to be remembered by the ages. It was not intended to be his day, but a day to honor the slain. Hardly were there words to merit the occasion of consecrating the deaths of so many for such a noble cause.[44]

For all its perfection in prose, it was Lincoln's attendance as well as his short speech that made a lasting impression on the attendees. More would be made of his few words than probably anything else he said as president—just not at that time. At its conclusion, Tod was standing near Lincoln when he congratulated Edward Everett, the nation's famed scholar and orator, on his speech, comprising more than 13,000 eloquently spoken words. "Mr. President," replied Everett, "your short address will be remembered and quoted when I am gone and my oration long forgotten."[45] The editor of *Harper's Weekly* agreed. "The words of the President were from the heart to the heart," he observed, "they can not be read, even without kindling emotion." He concluded, "It was as simple and felicitous and earnest a word as was ever spoken."[46] Even a simple Maryland farmer, a severe critic of Lincoln who stood at the foot of the platform, was reduced to tears. "I will never say another word against Mr. Lincoln as long as I live," he commented to a bystander.[47]

There was nobility in fighting to preserve the Union, and reporters understood the day was about the men whose graves lined the meadows, not Lincoln's words that seemingly converted the war into a revolutionary struggle to destroy slavery. Indeed, it would be hard to imagine that audience members, citizens at home, and soldiers in the ranks accepted the Gettysburg Address as more than political oratory as they listened or read it in the press. To be sure, broad concepts about equality and freedom were intertwined with preservation of the Union, which soldiers believed they were making greater by their suffering. Yet, military contingency had grafted emancipation and black enlistment as necessary instruments to help relieve that suffering in preserving of the Union. Governors had witnessed countless numbers of corpses passing through the train stations and the wharves. Many had attended small ceremonies in the field after battle. Thus, it was proper, observed a Northern correspondent, that governors be present at Gettysburg "to pay the tribute of respect and gratitude to" the dead.[48] After the president's address, the governors briefly conferred with Lincoln, and before departing, they gave short addresses to their soldiers drawn up for review. A stranger to the ranks, Seymour's words resonated more with the press than it did with the soldiers. The artillerists of the 5th New York, however, marched to Seymour's temporary headquarters, and the governor appeared, presented the men with a silk regimental flag, and spoke a few words.[49]

Lincoln contracted a mild case of smallpox after his trip, and spent the next few weeks semi-quarantined in the White House. While convalescing, the president had the benefit of reading Northerners' reactions to his Gettysburg address. He caught a mild reprieve weeks later, when Schenck resigned his commission to take his seat in Congress, and Maryland loyalists rejoiced. The melancholy at Gettysburg accompanied governors back to their state capitols, where they learned that Grant had gone on the offensive at Chattanooga. On 23 November, the battle to dislodge the Confederates from the Tennessee River city opened, and in two days, Grant had beaten Bragg and sent his army back across Chickamauga Creek.[50]

The fighting at Chattanooga rivaled any battle thus far in the war, but the Union's 5,800 casualties were minimal when compared to the numbers engaged. As November closed, so did a chapter in the history of the western war. Grant went into winter quarters and considered his next move. He could thank Stanton for providing extra troops to take and hold both Chattanooga and Knoxville. Within a few weeks Longstreet gave up Knoxville, and the Federals moved in. The Union's control of Tennessee delighted governors struggling to keep pace with desertion, sickness, and loss. Many chief executives had dispatched relief expeditions to Chattanooga, and some made the effort to venture south to assess their soldiers. For all his efforts, Grant received a simple message from Lincoln that read "well done."[51] Indeed, two words never spoke louder than this "voice" of the Union.

Wartime Realities

Accompanying the Union's military success was the arrival of Northern congressmen to Washington to open the war's third winter session. To the nation's capital came political leaders that made up the Thirty-eighth Congress, some of whom witnessed workers placing the crowning section, "Statue of Freedom," on the Capitol Dome.[52] The session opened on a "glorious" 7 December "with a sunlight as brilliant as June; the air clear, bracing, full of electricity and life, yet cold enough to make the blazing logs in the fireplace yonder decidedly disagreeable."[53] Congressmen moved beyond battles, strategies, and war aims, indeed there was no looming battle nearby nor threatening cabinet resignations. Their conversations centered on occupation and reconstruction, as well as on budgeting for the national government's expansion. Members aligned themselves behind two factions: the Radicals, whose hatred of slavery had driven them to revolution and made black equality a war aim, and the conservatives, whose aversion to expansive wartime measures had compelled them to rally in defense of the Constitution and states rights.

Yet, despite these divisions, the year's events brought Lincoln and governors closer together in recognizing the benefits of their mutual objectives. The North's political culture grafted powers conducive to war business on to governors who saw themselves as agents of an increasingly active national authority. Military success, occupation, and reconstruction had closed the ranks between the Republicans and War Democrats, and resulted in the election of a new slate of governors and legislatures that came to the war at the high tide of this new national-state alliance. Gibbs had indicated as much to Lincoln months before. "Let no man talk of a Republican victory," declared the *New York Times*, "thousands of war Democrats labored for it with as great zeal as any. It is no partyism, it is patriotism that has so gloriously carried the day."[54]

The Unionist coalition reflected the North's political reconstruction, shaped by the continued adjustment to wartime needs. As the war endured, state and national leaders cooperated in maintaining national armies while managing political, economic, and social affairs at home. Lincoln and the governors had learned from mobilizing, warring, and nationalizing themselves into a more centralized war machine. Evidence that Northerners approved of this new arrangement started with the Republicans' success at the spring electoral and carried through November. It was time to exercise full advantage of the partnership that prevailed between Lincoln and his governors. Chief executives reassured the president even in his darkest hours that they stood behind the Emancipation Proclamation, enlistment of black soldiers, conscription, the suspension of habeas corpus, and the repeated calls for men. They had become agents of federal power, but not at the expense of losing prestige or political sovereignty over state affairs. Even while disagreeing with them, Lincoln demonstrated that he could listen to the governors. He understood their significance in the national contest and leaned on them to sustain his military and political course. "He executes the will of the people," sermonized Reverend Henry Fowler to his Auburn, New York, congregation. "His wisdom consists in carrying out the good sense of the nation."[55] Prominent New England abolitionist Wendell Phillips agreed. In a December speech at the Cooper Institute, he argued that Lincoln grew with the war "because we watered him," and that he advanced "because the nation pushed him on."[56] Many governors grew as well, especially those who had been in office when the Union's war aims expanded. And, as one group of governors that had grown with him prepared to exit their offices, a new collection prepared to arrive. Out went some old stalwarts and friends, including Tod, Stanford, Kirkwood, Holbrook, and Robinson (KY), as well as some not-so-collegial chief executives, including Swift, Salomon, Robinson (KS), Burton, Coburn, Berry, and Cozzens, all who had helped bring about the success of 1863.

Lincoln had given reconstruction of the occupied states considerable thought during the autumn, and the result was his Proclamation of Amnesty and Reconstruction, which articulated his plans. Dennison remarked that it "was the right word at the right time."[57] A clerk read Lincoln's annual address to federal Congressmen, and apparently the almighty was at work in improving national affairs. The president had discussed his message weeks before with Chandler, who advised him about its charge. Lincoln wanted to highlight the recent elections without appearing too brash. "I hope to 'stand firm' enough to not go backward," he stated, "and yet not go forward fast enough to wreck the country's cause."[58] That was classic Lincoln—desiring to stay in tune with the people, even while advancing his course. "The President has often been accused of tardily following the people instead of leading public opinion," noted the editor for *Harper's Weekly*, "but it is his great merit that he early saw this to be a war in which the people must save themselves." He added, "If they were unequal to the task, a popular government was a failure, and therefore he has sought only to be the executive magistrate of their will, which he has divined with more sagacity than any public figure in our history."[59] A week later, Lincoln sent Congress his plan to assist freedmen in the Southern states by organizing a Federal Bureau of Emancipation, which expanded the federal government in unprecedented ways. As Noah Brooks observed, Lincoln's message had "pleased the radicals and satisfied the conservatives by plainly projecting a plan of reconstruction, which is just alike to popular rights, to the cause of liberty and to the loyal people of all sections of the Union."[60]

Given the Union army's expansive Southern occupation, it seemed inevitable that such an idea would surface. Many governors understood that reconstruction of the Union—North and South—commenced with the outbreak of war. Although untouched from campaigning and away from the battlefield, governors witnessed the war's imprint on Northern society at home. The government grew, and the economy had generated prosperity, yet it did little to lessen the losses and hardships at home. Governors especially felt these losses in the winter, when statehouses became the gathering place for orphans, widows, and destitute citizens milling around in search of provisions. Several governors journeyed to the front to share their holidays with the soldiers, hoping to buoy their spirits. Others remained close to their offices to care for locals seeking assistance. Curtin long remembered his Thanksgiving Day that year. Stepping from his office at the capitol one afternoon, "two ragged" orphans confronted him, and "appealed to him for alms." They pleaded their sad cases of dead fathers, disabled mothers, and their lives having been reduced to begging for food in the streets. Overcome with grief, Curtin extended to them what funds he could, and continued home. Later that day while dining with his family, he could not shake the image of those poor children and at one point exploded: "Great God! Is it possible that the people of Pennsylvania can feast this day, while the children of her soldiers who have fallen in this war beg bread from door to door?" He pledged that day to have the state take care of Pennsylvania's orphans.[61]

States had significantly expanded relief efforts during the war, and they coincided with a national administration that brought communication, rail transport, relief associations, and a regulated currency under a more centralized governance structure. If the republic grew more quickly over space than over time during the antebellum decades, the Civil War reversed that trend. The titanic changes in industry alone accelerated and modernized the patterns of daily life. Northerners came to depend on the expansive economy and encroaching government to accommodate their lives. The war inaugurated the shift of Americans from a vast unorganized republican society into a well-organized industrial Union that benefitted from the mutual dependency between nation and state. If there were tendencies that encouraged the establishment of a more national culture before the war, the republic had slowly groped its way toward accepting them. The conflict, however, accelerated these tendencies.

The war had been an incalculable undertaking. It detached thousands of Northerners from home and the individualism they had known for decades, and knitted them into the largest, most nationalized undertaking the republic had ever known. From the scattered hamlets of the North came volunteers who understood that the Union's significance was measured by their dependency not only on those fighting in different theaters, but also on those citizens behind the lines maintaining the armies. Compiling data for a new book entitled *Six Months in the Federal States* published in 1863, British journalist Edward Dicey reflected on the North's wartime transformation. "The one clearest result of this war," he argued, "has been to bring the people of the [northern] States together—to give them common recollections, common interests, and common dangers." He concluded, "This, in itself, must lead to a more real Union." The time had come to repatriate the occupied Southerners back into a Union that had been transformed, and it seemed only fitting that the process commence while the troops could supervise its execution. Whatever the South's future held, Lincoln remained committed to allowing states back into their proper relationship with the federal government. Yet the Union of 1861, which they left, had fundamentally changed by 1863, and, according to Dicey, the difficulties of "restoring the *status quo* in the insurgent States will convince the popular mind of the necessity of a more united and centralized Government."[62] The editor of *Harper's Weekly* agreed, remarking that the work before Congress in reconstructing the republic would "take rank in history, and if it be well done, will elevate the frame of the body to a level with that of the most distinguished legislative assemblies of the past."⁶³

Like the new statue placed on the Capitol that December, the republic had crowning achievements, but there was work to be done. In the days while Lincoln regained his strength, among his first orders of business was to respond to Curtin's late November letter protesting another useless draft. The governor reiterated his plans to raise troops through state authorities, especially during the winter. Lincoln forwarded the letter to the War Department for a quick response. When he recovered, Lincoln tackled the lingering problems in Missouri by dismissing Schofield, who had interfered with the legislature and who allegedly sympathized with pro-Confederate marauders. He replaced him with Rosecrans, thinking the Ohioan might be more amenable to Radicals. It remained to be seen, however, if Gamble could survive Schofield's departure and the increasingly Radical climate.⁶⁴

Evidence that Northern reconstruction advanced with the war could be found in the acknowledgment that going backward was no longer viable if politically aligned with the administration. Emancipation and conscription changed the political and social landscape. Governors pursued every avenue to meet Lincoln's call, and even those who opposed the president found it difficult to combat the shortage of manpower while refusing black enlistments. Leaders of New York's Union League, including Alex Van Rensselaer, George Bliss, and Le Grand B. Cannon, petitioned Seymour to allow New York's black soldiers to enlist, or at least not obstruct their efforts. The governor replied that the matter rested with the War Department. Thinking they had won his endorsement, these members appealed to Stanton, asking for authorization to raise a black regiment. Stanton initially rejected their appeal, perhaps thinking he might injure the feelings of Seymour. When relating the story to Morgan, however, he queried him: "[D]o you think I am going to make a fool of myself?"⁶⁵ When Morgan replied that his refusal would "discourage five hundred of New York's leading and politically active citizens," the secretary reconsidered his answer and gave his permission to raise one infantry regiment. Finally, the standoff was over, and New York blacks would enter the military, carrying the state colors. The news delighted New Yorker Hervey L. Howe, who having witnessed their service in South Carolina, expressed to his brother his favorable attitude toward their acceptance. "[W]e have a great many Colored soldiers here who are doing every thing could be asked of Soldiers," he noted, "experience has prooved [*sic*] that Colored men, and evin [*sic*] freed slaves can do good service in any place, although many [whites] are prejudice against color they like to see them doing the work."[66]

By the end of 1863, governmental expansion and centralized mobilization could hardly go unnoticed. Stanton's annual report to Lincoln read like an almanac of economic, social, and political change. It no longer mattered whether change came from national, state, or local communities, so long as the cumulative result pushed the North closer to victory. However much the push-pull between the nation and the states had abused political sensitivities among Northerners, the governors had assisted Lincoln in producing military results beneficial to the Union. In his chronicle of battles, prisoners of war, fallout from national conscription, and evils of desertion, Stanton indicated that the bustling economy had caught up to, and surpassed, the demands the war placed on it. Even resistance to black enlistment was fading as a result of the gallant performances of black soldiers on the battlefield. Indeed, he argued, the time had come to correct the disparity in pay. Andrew had won a small victory. The fortunes of war, however, that had fundamentally changed the population waging it, also brought thousands of invalids home or into Northern hospitals. As much as the government sought to relieve the suffering of the growing number of ex-slaves, so too would it need to provide relief for those injured in combat.[67]

Although Federal forces were firmly planted in nearly every Confederate state, and Southern repatriation slowly cast off the yoke of its leaders, it remained to be seen how much longer Northerners could endure the war. The populace had grown accustomed to expansive governance, yet local communities served as the spring to the fountain of armies. Although the draft had stimulated modest volunteerism, the coercive aspects of conscription had failed to produce the manpower necessary for the armies. Even as they protested the draft, Seymour and Parker never ceased to raise volunteers. Unenthused by the practical application of enrollment in New Hampshire's First Congressional District, Gilmore nonetheless worked within the system to make necessary changes. Governor Bramlette also needed more competent officers to handle the "evils" that recruiting camps along the Kentucky-Tennessee border had produced. He suggested some remedies to Lincoln, advising him that "a little kindly aid—a tub thrown to the whale—will greatly promote the success of the Union men of Kentucky."[68]

Lincoln would have his armies, but winter exacerbated Northern war-weariness. Morton provided the best summation of the Union's recruiting problems. "The men know that after field operations shall have opened in the spring they cannot be spared," he reasoned, "and are becoming satisfied they will not be furloughed this winter," and he feared that the opportunity of re-enlisting the army would be lost. Most perceptively, he wrote that the "commanding officers in the field have had armies furnished to them and know but little of the difficulties in creating them."[69] Morton had witnessed mobilization, nationalization of the armies, and the expansion of the government. Few political figures understood better than Morton the sacrifices of war and the labors involved in attending to soldier and civilian relief. In recent months he had received hundreds of letters from civilians detailing these privations. Mary Sherman of Moors Hill had written to him detailing the realities of women in Dearborn County. "Mr. Morton [sic]," she began, "i take my pen in hand to in form [sic] you how us poor Soldiers wifes [sic] are treated Some times we have Some thing to eat and Some times we don't and there a[r]nt But four Soldiers wifes in Moors Hill[.]" "[A]ll of our Children are naked for Clothing," she sorrowfully acknowledged, "and they pretend to do [illegible] things and Don't Do any thing and there is a man in this town that Says let the Soldiers wifes [sic] go to the poor house where they Belong and i want you to raly [sic] up the loyal men if we have got any Among us."[70]

When their legislatures were not in session, governors used the capitol buildings as depots for storing aid to be dispensed to citizens and soldiers. December was an especially busy month, as citizens flocked to the statehouses in search of relief. Buckingham used his office to store vegetables, bandages, medical supplies, and care packages of all kinds, and allowed the New Haven Soldier's Aid Society to use the rooms to coordinate shipping goods to the soldiers. Organizations such as these coordinated their efforts with the Sanitary Commission and other privately run organizations. Yates also used his offices for storage of provisions. As casualties mounted, so did citizens' relief efforts and the demands to the governors protesting their hospitalization in the camps. Among his last formal acts of the year was to send destitute Sarah Mason a consoling letter and twenty dollars out of his own pocket to help her make it through the winter.[71]

Gamble had not the good fortune in providing for his soldiers or using Missouri's capitol for such relief. The legislature had extended its spring session throughout the summer and fall, and the stress of fighting with the

Radicals exhausted him. Lincoln's removal of Schofield did little to close the ranks among Radical and conservative Unionists. The war in Missouri was beyond Lincoln's influence, and Gamble lacked the physical constitution to endure the constant harassment. The only good news was that he had used state troops to drive Shelby's Confederates from the state. Still, the legislature worked against him, forcing him to veto several measures he thought dangerous to state administration. Worse yet for the governor was that he had slipped on the icy steps leading up to the Executive Mansion and broke the same arm he had injured months before while returning from Washington. Recovery from his previous elbow injury had been slow, and, at sixty-five years of age, a break to the same elbow forced him into a prolonged recuperation. His health deteriorated as he spent December bedridden, though he managed to dictate orders to commanders and clerks. Reading the morning newspapers did little to soothe his mind. The Springfield papers printed the violent speeches against him delivered at a recent meeting of the Union League.[72]

During Gamble's convalescence, Willard Preble Hall assumed his executive duties. A Virginia native, Hall attended Yale College, and, on graduation in 1839, he ventured to Missouri with his father and studied law under the tutelage of his brother Judge William A. Hall. The family settled in north central Missouri, and Hall served as circuit attorney and eventually as a state representative. The Mexican War interrupted his political aspirations, and he joined the 1st Missouri Cavalry. He returned to Missouri after the war, and Democrats elected him to Congress, where he served from 1847 to 1853. He was a member of the Constitutional Convention that kept Missouri in the Union, and voters rewarded him by electing him lieutenant governor. Hall was a talented lawyer and experienced politician, but he was no match for Radicals, who welcomed the change in leadership. Almost as if they had willed Gamble's physical deterioration, the governor never recuperated.[73]

CHAPTER SIXTEEN

The Rebellion Still Refuses to Give Us Either Peace or Rest

New Year's Day in the nation's capital was "foggy and cloudy," wrote Stoddard, and a "cold, bracing wind came from the northwest, changing the air, freezing the mud, and letting the bright winter sunlight in on us again."[1] The past weeks had days with temperatures that dipped well below anything in recent memory. Nonetheless, Washingtonians ushered in the New Year with great cheer. Lincoln's anecdotal secretary wrote that the "hospitable houses all over the city, in greater numbers than ever before, were thrown open to the merry crowd of 'callers' and the day passed off in fine style." He added, "All men seemed full of hope."[2] The editor of *Harper's Weekly* agreed, noting that "a year never opened more full of promise for the country and the cause" than New Year's 1864. "No man who truly comprehended the magnitude of our war, or has thoughtfully studied its development," he wrote, "could have expected that we should stand at this time with so firm a hold upon the future as we have."[3]

Snowstorms blanketed much of the northern landscape, and Minnesotans, Iowans, Wisconsinites, and Michiganders suffered from an intense storm that passed through the region, derailing several trains. Many stations throughout the Midwest shut down, and thousands of cattle and hogs froze to death in cars stalled on the tracks. One Illinois farmer complained of having lost over 1,000 sheep to the freezing temperatures, and newspapers reported the considerable losses in the ranks because of exposure. At Camp Morton some guards had frozen to death standing their posts during the night. Many residents could not recall a colder period in their lives, and they exchanged their wagons for sleighs as wintry conditions turned their roads to paths.[4]

New Year at the Statehouse

Getting to the capitols in the Northern states was no easy task, but despite the storms across the Midwest and New England, New Year's celebrations came off undeterred. Cony's inauguration was a "brilliant and successful affair," wrote a Maine journalist, and the citizens appeared rejuvenated by the

Unionism that prevailed since his September victory.[5] There was renewed hope for the success of the spring and summer military campaigns, but citizens would be content with victories away from the battlefield. Cony's election the previous year represented the fusion of Republicans and War Democrats into the Union Party, and the new coalition permeated state legislatures. The new alliance added a patriotic endorsement to the cause by shifting its focus away from the slave and conscription, and toward freedmen and the Southern states. The editor of *Harper's Weekly* argued that it was time to do away with the designations Republicans and Democrats, that they were "wholly out of date," and that congressman should be reclassified as "A" for pro-administration and "O" for opposition.[6] States' rights was a product of a perpetual Union, he argued. The logic of the times had brought Northerners to understand that war had reconstructed their social and political institutions. The only hope of preserving the fruits of that reconstruction was in maintaining the cooperation between nation and state to settle the question that now confronted them.[7]

For weeks Lincoln and Congress worked to map out the means to restore the constitutional relations between Northern and Southern states. Lincoln tightened his grip over reconstruction, yet his lenient course became more unpopular in Washington. Military success in the West and the previous year's political endorsement had encouraged him to reinaugurate loyal state governments in the South. Yet, as much attention as congressmen had placed on reconstructing Southerners, Union armies would first have to defeat the Confederates. Inspired by a sense of optimism, governors continued their efforts to close out the war for the administration, but their problems remained unchanged. Although the summer of 1863 had brought the Union much-needed success, those victories depleted the armies and disillusioned citizens. Governors channeled private aid, public funds, and their personal finances to suffering families and requested state bounties for the enlarging armies. Soldiers understood that they were fighting for Lincoln, but they valued governors who attended to their problems in the ranks and at home. Curtin highlighted this connection in his second inaugural address by reminding legislators that the horrible sacrifice of war had not broken the spirit of Pennsylvanians, and that he was merely governing citizens who must continue to subordinate all things to the "preservation of our national life." If critics could charge him with any crime, it was that he followed Lincoln's lead in preserving the Union, even when it meant an end to slavery.[8]

As governors worked to develop humanitarian aid they also sought to restore their dominance over recruiting. Andrew supported Curtin's proposal to return recruiting to state authorities. Indeed, he never surrendered it. As much as governors needed the threat of a federal draft to boost volunteerism, they had reluctantly allowed Fry's provost marshals to intervene. At best it created a chaotic bureaucracy no one could have predicted. The draft represented expansive government for citizens unaccustomed to federal power, but the presence of agents seemed unnatural and provoking. Fry was smart enough to place his chief marshals overseeing the draft in state capitals to work closely with state executives. Consequently, governors exerted their influence in the administration of the process by recommending clerks, surgeons, and other functionaries, who facilitated the draft. Andrew understood better than Stanton the demands in raising Massachusettsans for the Union armies and protecting them at home. He believed governors and veteran soldiers were the most effective recruiting agents. Chief executives worked with legislators to balance these responsibilities and devised the means to postpone and modify the draft to suit the needs of their citizenry. Andrew and his legislative colleagues prepared for the journey ahead, and, when they adjourned from their first day's business, they walked to the Old South Church, where visiting Amherst College President Reverend William A. Stearns gave a sermon. After acknowledging that it would require "hard blows" to conquer the Southern people, Stearns encouraged the leaders to look to the omnipotent forces that would assist them in their travails. "If a sparrow cannot fall without His notice," he proclaimed, "a government cannot rise without His aid."[9]

Miles to the south in Annapolis there were no sparrow references in Bradford's message to the legislature. His words signaled an end to New Year's celebrations and a return to wartime realities under a Unionist legislature. In their recent elections Marylanders had departed from tradition and embarked on the long road to abolish slavery in their state, a fact Bradford argued would make citizens more prosperous. Desperate times required desperate measures, and governors understood this wartime reality. Brough in Ohio presented perhaps the best summation of why extreme measures were needed. "As we have not provoked this war, but sought rather to avoid it," his inaugural address read, "we are not responsible for its consequences."[10] Michigan's Blair proclaimed the same message to his assemblymen in Lansing. "The period is itself revolutionary and altogether extraordinary," he argued, "the rebellion still refuses to give us either peace or rest; and no human forecast seems sufficient to provide for all the exigencies of a single year."[11] The chief executive had impressed at least one convalescing soldier in Lansing who appreciated Blair's dedication to the cause and his soldiers. "I feel gratified," the soldier wrote to the governor, "for the unwearied energy, ability, and single-mindedness of purpose evinced in the discharge of the Honorable though difficult duties."[12]

The revolution to which Brough and Blair alluded required unconditional support of the administration. It also required that governors take more strident measures to combat home-front dissidents determined to undermine national objectives. Given the recent groundswell of Unionism that carried through the elections, governors could not afford any reverses. Disaffection would weaken the good work they accomplished in bringing forth what volunteers they had in the last few months. In his course to preserve peace behind the lines, Brough relied on the military. He left a note at the Neil House for the German-born General Samuel Heintzelman, who had arrived in Columbus to take command of the Northern Department consisting of the states of Ohio, Michigan, Wisconsin, Illinois, and Indiana. He told the commander that secret organizations had undermined recruiting by slandering emancipation and conscription and by preying on workers concerned they would lose jobs to freedmen coming into the state. Clandestine groups such as the Knights of the Golden Circle and Sons of Liberty had subverted the population, and Brough needed Heintzelman to stifle them. In just a short time, the commander came to believe the enemy behind the lines was undercutting Northern morale, and turned what he initially thought to be a docile tour of duty into a war on dissidents.[13]

With conscription proven a failure, the lure of sizable bounties was the only coercive measure governors had left to meet the president's October call. Congress had provided for bounties for volunteers until 5 January, after which time drafting would resume in those states that had not met their quotas. This encouraged citizens to volunteer, and Lincoln recommended to Congress that it extend the bounties until 1 March. Stanton consented and wired the president that governors preferred raising volunteers by bounty rather than by draft. Veterans, they argued, who had become inured to service, constituted a cheaper force even when paid a bounty than raw recruits or drafted men who were not paid a bounty. Still, some governors, such as Brough, believed bounties had a corrupting influence because the financial inequities between districts favored certain localities over others. Some local communities, the governor argued, had bankrupted themselves to avoid the draft, and weakened the government's credibility among the people. Yet, given the government's weak financial condition and the cessation of recruiting, there were no viable alternatives. Stanton's December report revealed that, with the threat of conscription, the governors managed to enlist more than 420,000 soldiers in response to the 1862 calls. Between January and June 1863, however, that number had significantly decreased, and since the 30 June 1863 call, fewer than 17,000 volunteers had come forward. Thus, by the beginning of 1864, the Union armies were lacking the manpower to replenish the ranks. Such deficits, when combined with the nearly 250,000 absent from duty, caused Lincoln and Stanton apprehension.[14]

Indiana was having an easier time, despite conspirator plots to undermine recruiting. Morton boasted that recruiting for the old regiments was going so well that he questioned "must it stop to-day?"[15] Andrew complimented Stanton and Lincoln on their recruiting letter as "eminently right" and stated that recruiting was "going on bravely in Massachusetts."[16] Smith wired in that Vermonters had filled the state quota to the tune of a 270-man surplus. Thanks to the extension, Curtin responded that recruiting was "going on handsomely now."[17] The new date for bounties, however, caused Gilmore's New Hampshirites problems, as the towns had already advanced the funds for bounties on the assumption the amount would be promptly refunded. After exerting themselves, he wired Stanton, it "looks to them like bad faith on the part of the Government and is causing a clamor that I am unable to meet." He informed Stanton, "You have no idea of the trouble this is creating, and the copperheads are jubilant." Stanton responded that he would make good on their commitments.[18]

Bramlette, however, had no good news. A mysterious wire suggested Lincoln had ordered the removal of soldiers from Kentucky to Knoxville, and the governor protested this would leave Kentuckians defenseless. The telegram surprised Lincoln, and he responded that nothing was known in Washington of the order. If such movement had been an ordered, Lincoln replied, it presumably came from Grant, who would not leave Kentucky to ruin. Still, the miscommunication aggravated Bramlette. The men recently raised in Kentucky had come from exposed border counties that had already filled their quota of men, and only upon *"faith"* that these new recruits would be used to defend Kentucky did they come forward. After complaining of being abandoned, the governor changed his tune and assured Lincoln that Kentuckians could go it alone without military assistance, if only to assert his place in state politics. "We are in and of the Union and will live and die there," he closed. "Rebel outrages cannot drive us, nor federal injustice divert us from the true line of patriotism. The Government is ours ... [and] death only can deprive us of it."¹⁹ Lincoln's tone had not changed when he responded a week later that, despite whatever the governor might think, it was his presidential discretion to give direction to Grant, which he argued, was "neither cruelty, bad faith or dishonor."²⁰ Bramlette, however, interpreted Lincoln's stance as justification to use his discretion to deny officers coming into Kentucky the ability to recruit for black regiments.²¹

Governors found the bounties an effective inducement for raising men. Still, confusion over enrollment figures and bounty discrepancies prevailed, and so did concern over the coming spring campaigns. No one better than Morton understood these problems, and he feared Southerners were coming forward in greater numbers than Northerners. To combat this increasing enemy force, Morton insisted the administration call for all the men required to bring the war to a speedy close. He argued that winter weather left agricultural laborers unemployed, and they would more eagerly enlist now rather than after farming operations were resumed in the spring. Besides, he argued, the larger the force, the quicker the success and the end of the immense drain upon the Treasury, which had become "the terror of all intelligent minds." Morton sought to capitalize on the administration's popularity, and he worried that if the war dragged on, oppositionists might undermine Lincoln's candidacy for reelection.²²

The president was popular, and the war's continuation could weaken his support, but national attention remained on Congress. At the moment it appeared that the military measures the Union employed to occupy and reconstruct Confederate states might return civil governance to political leaders, who, once the war ended, could leave slavery untouched. Consequently, as a precondition for readmission into the Union, congressional leaders needed to abolish slavery in the United States. Senate Radicals had taken the lead in this venture and in mid-January presented a joint resolution to abolish the institution by constitutional amendment. Such discussion moved Attorney General Bates to write in his diary that "Cicero was right when he said that 'in every Civil war, Success is dangerous, because it is sure to beget arrogance and a disregard of the *laws of the Government*'—(i.e., the Constitution) [.]"²³

In the dead of winter, congressional abolitionists waged war, but it was hardly a surprise to governors, some of whom had sought the measure since the war's inception. Chief executives scrutinized legislative headlines that featured abolition and Lincoln's proclamation of amnesty and reconstruction for Southerners. The president's course encouraged many governors. Yet Republicans and Democrats carped about his 10 percent plan, which allowed Southerners to take an oath, hold elections, and establish state government. Seymour attacked Lincoln by arguing that under his plan the power of 16,533,383 Northerners in New York, Pennsylvania, Illinois, Indiana, Massachusetts, Missouri, Kentucky, and Wisconsin would cast the same number of electoral votes as the nearly 70,000 so-called reconstructed Southerners. The president could control a minority population, extend citizens suffrage, and use them to strengthen Congress to support his course. "Fourteen hundred men in Florida," Seymour argued, "would balance in the Senate of the United States the power of New York." So long as the troops remained in these nine states, Lincoln would control political machinery that established a system of Southern "rotten boroughs" that would govern the nation.[24] According to the *New York Times*, Seymour's "churlish, cold, narrow, malignant, [and] soulless" annual message was "enough to make every citizen of this State hang his head for shame."[25] Fortunately for Lincoln, the legislature to which he delivered his message had a Unionist majority, and representatives diverted their attention to more important matters. They prepared the constitutional conditions that would allow New York soldiers to vote in the field. As Seymour's radicalism amplified, many New Yorkers "renounced him and abjured him," noted a New York editor, "but the man is unchanged."[26]

Tired of the New Jersey Copperheads' political shenanigans, Parker lessened his opposition to Lincoln. He declared to his legislators that however unconstitutional Lincoln's policies, the only way to end the conflict was by forcing the Confederates to surrender. It was time to get behind those managing the war, or at least get out of their way. "There has not been a day since the inauguration of Governor Parker," remarked a Camden editor, "that he has not devoted his entire energies and official position to aid the Government in putting down the Rebellion."[27] The governor endorsed absentee voting, but he also supported his legislature's opposition to black recruitment in New Jersey. In the meantime, he protected the state's railroad monopoly in the face of federal interference by arguing that state authorities deserved to handle fraudulent monopolies. Although he fulfilled his responsibility in meeting manpower needs, congressional Radicals viewed New Jerseyitess as "uncooperative, if not hostile to the Union cause."[28]

Border state legislators, especially those in Missouri and Maryland, were locked in heated debate over abolition and black enlistment, even as their chief executives walked backward to embrace both measures. Lincoln hoped Rosecrans's appointment would mollify Missouri Radicals, but the commander needed Gamble's veteran influence. The ailing governor summoned only enough energy to dictate a brief message to the legislature. His bout with pneumonia overcame him, and, on 31 January, Missouri's war governor died. Despite the recriminatory attitude oppositionists heaped upon him for his pro-administration views and conservative politics, Missourians were distraught over his death. Legislators honored him for a month by wearing black crepe armbands, and it seemed as though even his enemies were genuinely affected by his loss. Gamble's death was a "calamity," wrote Bates, "for he stood, like a lighthouse on a rock in the edge of a stormy sea, not only to give warning of the danger, but to resist its violence."[29]

Like Missourians, Marylanders struggled to adjust to black enlistment, despite showing signs of embracing abolition. Legislators complained to Lincoln that the reduction of slave labor due to these enlistments resulted in the loss of labor to till the soil. Union officers had aggressively recruited for the ranks, and representatives wanted the president to right these wrongs. For Marylanders, the war brought significant hardships, broken families, and ruined homesteads. In the coming weeks, Bradford's appeals for troops persuaded the Maryland legislature to allow him to pay a $300 bounty over the national bounty to any Marylander, except slaves, who enlisted before March. To each slave owner, the legislature approved a $100 bounty, in addition to the national bounty of $300.[30]

Copperheads, Conspiracies, and Slaves

February opened as brutally cold across the North as January had. The draft deadline passed quietly, and, instead of imposing a draft, Lincoln ordered another call for men to serve three years or the duration of the war. This time he needed 500,000 men and set 10 March as the draft date. Having already consented to bring Grant east to command all the armies, he hoped this change might inspire volunteering, especially among easterners. Indeed, he had nothing left in his arsenal, and there were widespread expectations for victory with one more military season of campaigning. Yet the War Department still found problems beyond their control. Stanton dropped the controversial commutation feature, but prices for substitutes escalated out of control. Cannon called for a special session of the Delaware legislature to address bounty problems. Buckingham found it difficult to find trustworthy agents to recruit his black regiments, which resulted in many citizens being "defrauded of their state bounty." Wanting to relieve the sick and wounded Connecticut soldiers, he ordered the state treasurer to credit his salary for the last eighteen months to the State Fund.[31] The stream of volunteers that had come forth in recent months had stalled, and, like many chief executives, Andrew found himself with a task likened to that of a man with a "jug of molasses to empty." Not only was he pushing the administration to credit states for citizens who enlisted in the Navy, but he also resorted to importing mercenaries. Stanton was concerned about rushing non-English-speaking immigrants to the front, but Andrew spared no efforts to have the Europeans put under the command of officers who shared the same tongue. For all his efforts in meeting state quotas, Andrew came under attack and later legislative review for what appeared to tarnish the state's patriotic reputation by circumventing quotas.[32]

To compensate for sluggish volunteering, Stanton had Congress authorize the recruitment of border state slaves, including those of loyal masters. The summer before, Union commanders in Kentucky had advised against enrolling free blacks, arguing that for the few hundred blacks they might enroll, they would lose thousands of whites who refused to serve with them. Bramlette agreed, and won a six-month reprieve. This new directive appeared to contradict the arrangement, and the secretary had allowed recruiting in Kentucky. When Bramlette discovered the War Department had approved a recruiting post in Paducah for such purposes, he convinced commanders to suspend their actions until he could obtain some clarification from Lincoln. As much as slavery appeared to be dying in the state, some Kentuckians were not prepared for abolition. In the meantime, Bramlette wrote Lincoln a spirited letter that emphasized Kentuckians' adherence to a strict set of constitutional principles, arguing that "nothing beyond the *militia*" may be called out or drafted for military service.[33] In the rebellious states, he argued, the national government could affect such an order, but not in the states still legally in the Union. "Kentucky is the friend not the belligerent [sic] of the Government," he claimed, and those officers detailed to Kentucky to organize slaves "have no law to warrant their action, and no competent authority to shield them from the penalties of our violated laws." The governor had faith that Stanton would do right in dealing "justly and wisely with my people upon this delicate subject," and urged Lincoln to "remove this evil, and correct this wrong, and thus save me the necessity which my Executive duty imposes of arraying the civil powers of the State against these persons."[34] As much as Bramlette believed he had convinced Lincoln and Stanton to suspend recruiting, they were immovable over the enrollment of border state slaves, and whatever evil existed, they argued, had cost the government nothing, even if Kentuckians voted against Lincoln in the fall.[35]

Lincoln was keenly aware of the dissatisfaction among Missourians, Marylanders, and Kentuckians over black enrollment, but a glimmer of hope came from Des Moines in the form of a short telegram. "There will be no draft in Iowa," Stone assured Lincoln. "You shall have our quota without it," he wrote.[36] "We are coming, Father Abraham," was his message, "with 500,000 more."[37] Similarly, in Illinois, Yates wanted to send more troops to Lincoln, but the opposition was unbearable, so he concentrated on soldier welfare during the harsh winter. Like Yates, many governors worked around the inconveniences placed on them by uncooperative Copperhead legislatures, and raised personal and private funds to assist soldiers' families in desperate straits, including funds to educate their orphans. Yates even secured from Lincoln a government lot in Springfield for the construction of a "Soldier's Home."[38]

For all of their perceived idolatry of Lincoln, many soldiers considered their governors their chief advocates. Chief executives expanded their efforts during the winter to relieve the deprivations of camp. They also celebrated those veterans who returned home to recruit. Smith applauded the return of veterans of the 5th Vermont, who received furloughs to Burlington to recruit. He arranged a grand reception for their arrival and spent several days celebrating their accomplishments. On that cold February day when they left to rejoin their comrades at the front, Smith presented them with a new stand of colors and promised to visit them at the front. By the end of the month, the governor kept his promise, and, with several distinguished Vermonters, he ventured to Virginia. In fact, the governor, along with Vermont congressman Frederick E. Woodbridge and Senator George Edmunds, accompanied the soldiers on the march from Brandy Station to Madison Court House. Charles Dubois of the 3rd Vermont appreciated their visit and in particular their willingness to live the Spartan soldier life. When he awoke one morning, the governor found himself "wading arround [sic] in three inches of snow," which according to Dubois, "must have felt he was not so very far away from home."[39]

Governors who visited the ranks that winter were easy targets—both good and bad—for the press. Yates did not disappoint reporters eager to humiliate him. The typical travel associates of the "Glorious Dick Yates" were "'bottle holders'" and "private correspondents, paid to glorify the Governor and advance his political career."[40] Many Democratic journalists shamed him as self-serving and as overindulging with his soldiers. As much as soldiers loved him, they came to see another side of their beloved governor, whose weakness for drink frequently overcame him. In late February he traveled to Chicago to welcome home the 39th Illinois, known as the "Yates Phalanx," and whether drunk or not, he gave perhaps his most electrifying address. At one point, he declared that he favored sending two peace commissioners to Richmond to meet with the high command. Walking across the stage where one of two 600-pounder solid shot from Morris Island were posted, he said, "I would name this (placing his foot on one of the shot) for one of them and I would name that (pointing to the conical shot) as the other."[41]

Yates's references to cannon fire reminded Chicagoans that peace was still far off. Among the larger offensive undertakings in the winter of 1864 was Sherman's campaign to destroy the railroads in Mississippi. After leaving Vicksburg with 26,000 men, the commander headed for Meridian and, within two weeks, had captured the city. Sherman had help, as the Union hoped to draw Confederates out of Mississippi and Georgia by launching a Florida expedition that landed General Truman Seymour's men at Jacksonville and directed them west toward the state capital in Tallahassee. As campaigning got underway, governors devoted their efforts to complying with Lincoln's call. Up for reelection in the coming weeks, Gilmore was relieved when the War Department determined that New Hampshire had met its quota. Morton expected to meet his target, but had relied on veteran units to recruit for their ranks, and wired Stanton for an extension of leave for the 35th Indiana (Irish) home from Chattanooga to continue. As much as he wanted to aid the governor, the secretary noted that extending time for one unit deprived another of its leave, and that it might endanger the "whole organization of the Army." He explained, "Nothing is so disorganizing as the changes of regulations in special cases, and there is nothing so embarrassing in the administration of this Department."[42] Morton acquiesced and put the regiment in motion the following day.[43]

Andrew had also embarked on a new campaign that February, but it never got under sail. As much as the governor advocated for racial equality in the ranks, at the moment he needed recruits. When he came into possession of information that former slaves and free blacks who desired to head north from Washington had been not been allowed to leave, he sent Oliver C. Gibbs to meet with Lincoln, ascertain the reason they were denied, and to present the governor's protest. Massachusettsans had expended considerable energies and contributed large resources to the war effort, Andrew argued, and the state needed all the laborers it could get because of the sacrifices of men enlisting in the military and now the navy. "How long then can we continue to furnish soldiers," he maintained, "help clothe the army, fabricate ships, machinery and munitions for war, subscribe to the National Loans, and furnish internal revenue if persons desiring to make their way hither are forbidden to come?"[44] As noble as the governor's words appeared, his motives failed to impress the president, who knew that Andrew was luring Virginia's black troops to fill Massachusetts quotas, and that he was willing to pay $300 in bounties. The president responded that Andrew was entitled to believe that "all the colored people South of Washington were struggling to get to Massachusetts" and that citizens were "anxious to receive them," but the governor had been misinformed. "You are engaged in trying to raise colored troops for the U. S. and wish to take recruits from Virginia, through Washington, to Massachusetts for that object," he argued, "and the loyal Governor of Virginia, also trying to raise troops for us, objects to your taking his material away." The president reminded Andrew that what he did for one governor, he must do for another. Lincoln ended by saying if it were true that "Massachusetts wishes to afford a permanent home within her borders, for all, or even a large number of colored persons who will come to her, I shall be only too glad to know it." He closed, "It would give relief in a very difficult point," referring to the emancipated slaves of the Confederacy.[45] A week later, however, Lincoln allowed them to pass to Andrew's promised land.[46]

By mid-February, Unionist majorities took steps in their legislatures to insure Lincoln's renomination. Union Leagues and other Republican organizations from Maine to California were looking to Lincoln, rather than switch to Treasury Secretary Chase or General Frémont, to finish the war. For all the rhetoric that credited Lincoln with having engineered the Union's success, governors had quietly worked to support him. Many Northerners assumed that Lincoln's reelection was a foregone conclusion. Low bragged to the president that California legislators had adopted patriotic resolutions expressing loyalty to the president. His letter encouraged Lincoln, who remarked to Noah Brooks that of all the conciliatory resolutions he "thought them the best he had received."[47] The Republican National Committee met in Washington and endorsed Lincoln by a majority vote. Indiana assemblymen were so exuberant that they sent their endorsement by unanimously electing Lincoln men to the June convention. Still, as much as Indianans endorsed Lincoln, many concurred with Calvin Fletcher, who confided to his diary that he was not the best man, but rather "to save collission [sic] of friends of the Union & encourage the rebels," they would support him.[48] Many Indianans idolized Morton and thought him worthy of the presidency, and their support moved delegates to nominate him for a fifth term.[49]

Lincoln's opponents criticized Republicans for courting state legislatures to steer the public's confidence toward the president's corner by announcing their support of him. It did not help him that Radicals, including Andrew, Yates, Morton, Carney, and Boreman, entertained hopes of other presidential candidates carrying their states in the fall. Given their political prestige, governors welded significant influence in the emerging Unionist political culture. Congressional Radicals hoped to counter Lincoln's popularity by mounting a public offensive to promote Chase as the alternative candidate. The cabal called for an anonymous attack on Lincoln and his supporters for their disgraceful display of inducing state legislatures to support Lincoln's candidacy for reelection. Mainstream Republicans foiled the plan, which led to the publication of a letter authored by Radical Republican Kansas senator Samuel Pomeroy, who championed Chase for president as Lincoln's intellectual superior. Pomeroy argued that Chase was the only man to lead the Union to victory, and linked Carney to the effort. The affair embarrassed Chase, who offered to resign. He eventually withdrew his name for consideration and soon found his office was the target of investigation for alleged abuses.[50]

As the political drama swirled around Washington, state legislators caucused for congressmen and gubernatorial candidates for the upcoming elections. Northerners expected that the next few months would determine the fate of the Union, and they believed the path to victory began in the legislative halls. As the congressional session unfolded, Lincoln approved Congress's decision to provide $300 compensation to loyal slave owners whose slaves enlisted in the Union army and freedom to those slaves on mustering out of service. The same act also increased bounties, redefined draft quotas and credits, stiffened the penalties for draft resistance, subjected blacks to the draft, and provided that those who opposed bearing arms for religious reasons should be assigned noncombatant tasks. It gave the president the authority to call more men if he desired. The cumulative impact of congressional help afforded governors some much-needed relief.[51]

As Northern legislatures worked to adjust to wartime needs, Copperheads worked to repudiate them. In Columbus, Ohio, General Heintzelman had just retired for the night on 2 March, when a courier awakened him with a pressing telegram from Halleck. It reported that Copperheads were on the warpath in the small Illinois town of Paris. The commander headed to Illinois, but stopped in Indianapolis and met Morton the following day. The governor's informants reported that the incident was not urgent, but Heintzelman continued to the Illinois border town to placate Yates. By the time he arrived, Union soldiers had diffused the situation with only one casualty, and Heintzelman found the town of Paris "perfectly quiet." When he returned to Indianapolis, however, Morton presented him with information that a much larger Copperhead plot had emerged in the Midwest, and that vigilantes planned to murder political leaders, including governors. Morton's evidence appeared to be credible. To avenge his political loss, Vallandigham encouraged secret organizations to menace loyal citizens. Recently elected supreme commander of the Copperhead organization known as the Sons of Liberty, the Ohioan pledged to unite members across Ohio, Illinois, Indiana, Kentucky, and Missouri, and even in New York, Pennsylvania, Delaware, and Maryland. These "Dark Lantern" groups had recruited members during the winter and had secretly stored arms for uprisings in the spring. The Copperhead frenzy even swept Brough into a state of alarm, as his spies fed him information confirming the presence of large numbers of secret treasonable societies in Ohio. These spies informed Brough that Copperhead membership exceeded 100,000, and that they had plans to destroy arsenals, railroads, telegraph wires, and raid prison camps, posing a credible threat.[52]

Governors were aware that these secret societies strove to undermine their efforts in fulfilling Lincoln's call before spring campaigns opened. As much as armies might close the war, local defense kept the peace, and governors remained attentive to these concerns. Still, it was expected that supplying armies would win the war quicker, and this undercut home-front dissension. The hopes for an early defeat appeared justified. Sherman was making his way to Vicksburg from his southern expedition when Lincoln approved of Congress's revival of the grade of lieutenant general and made it known that he intended to give it to Grant. The commander's success had eclipsed all others, convincing the president that Grant could force

Confederate surrender. True to form, Yates rode on the coattails of the commander's promotion and bragged to John How of St. Louis that it was "a proud reflection for me that I had the honor of Commissioning as Colonel the man who in less than three years time by his brilliant military achievements has achieved a name honored throughout the world, and of whom it may be truly said he is 'The hero who never lost a battle.'"[53]

Grant's Army

Lincoln named Grant the nation's highest ranking military officer and summoned him to Washington to accept command of all the armies. "I cannot withhold my congratulations upon your new military programme announced in our Morning papers," Dennison professed to Lincoln. "It seems to me you have placed Grant, Halleck, Sherman & McPherson exactly where they should be."[54] As the bleak winter began to give way to spring, the war had taken some significant turns. Lincoln applauded Marylanders' move to abolish slavery, especially since it came from the voters. He wrote to Maryland congressman John A. Creswell that he wished success to emancipation in Maryland, but thought it better to come from the ballot box rather than the presidency. The president's call for more troops and Grant's appointment to command the Union armies gave the impression that war was about to be waged in earnest. Yet Washingtonians hardly noticed the instrument of earnest war when it appeared in the capital city. There was no crowd, no parade, and, in fact, no one recognized the commander when he arrived at Willard's Hotel on the afternoon of 8 March, until the clerk recognized his signature in the guest register.[55]

Lincoln and Grant had never met, though it mattered little at the time. They had nothing in common but their homespun features and their desire to end the war. So it seemed better that their relationship had been forged out of military necessity rather than politics. Grant's new title merited the nation's approval of his military accomplishments. The onetime leather store clerk was now in command of over a half million men spread out over seventeen military departments, all being fed by governors who championed his new assignment. If it were "God's will," as Lincoln remarked, handing Grant the commission, the country trusted and sustained him, and the Union's governors stood by him.[56]

That same day Chase withdrew from the presidential race, and Lincoln had one thing left to do to secure his own reelection. As Grant headed into the Virginia landscape to meet his chief subordinate Meade, the president gave General Franz Sigel a command worthy of his political prominence. Against his better judgment and Halleck's wishes, Lincoln assigned Sigel to the Department of West Virginia. The president's gesture went a long way toward soothing the injured feelings among the Germans supporting Frémont as the next president. They appreciated the president's restoration of the symbol of their ethnic pride. "I am very glad you gave Sigel the Dept. of West-Virginia," wrote German-American leader Carl Schurz to Lincoln, "it was a very judicious measure in every respect."[57] It was, for among Lincoln's many virtues was an intrusive desire and capacity to exploit his position to win, whether on the battlefield or in politics. Grant shared the same virtue, and before departing Washington he interrupted a cabinet meeting to tell Lincoln he was heading for Nashville. There he would meet up with Sherman, his new commander of the West. "The hopes, fears and prayers of a whole nation go with him to his arduous work," remarked Stoddard. "Truly a vast responsibility is on his shoulders—greater by far than any one man would willingly *assume*."[58]

Although there was "little fuss made over his [Grant's] visit" to Washington, the shakeup in command left Halleck without a job. Lincoln made him chief of staff, a fitting title for someone who assumed the hollow duties of pushing paper.[59] "Old Brains" found the role of being a subordinate humbling, but he supported Grant, though now he walked a step behind. Governors welcomed the change, especially Curtin, Morton, Yates, and Andrew, who had grown frustrated with Halleck's lack of appreciation for their efforts. When Grant named Sherman supreme commander of the West, the commander's old position went to General James B. McPherson. The command changes also initiated the Red River Campaign, commanded by General Andrew J. Smith, who directed his gunboats along the river to Alexandria, Louisiana. The war was opening anew, and Lincoln had taken on a more determined persona.[60]

Thus far it had been a triumphant winter, but spring brought a dampened spirit that cast a shadow of uneasiness. Winter conditions exacerbated the already deteriorating circumstances in Kansas, and Carney's supporters had schemed to seize power from Lane. Senator Pomeroy confided to Carney that his candidacy would be welcomed in the U.S. Senate. He encouraged the governor to arrange it in the legislature to be elected and replace Lane. Such collusion was typical of Kansas politics, and by February legislators had conferred the Senate seat on the governor. Carney's detractors assailed him and declared his election illegal. Having been informed of these machinations, Lincoln took issue with Carney's self-serving ambitions and rewarded Lane by appointing Curtis to command the department. He gave the commander latitude in dispensing national patronage in the state until Congress adjourned and Lane could return to Kansas and work for Lincoln's nomination. Carney's actions enraged opponents, who shamed him for engineering his election the year before the seat became vacant. They convinced the legislature to declare his victory illegitimate. Although Carney had considerable support among Kansans, he traveled to Washington to confer with Pomeroy and Radical Republicans Wade, Chandler, and John Sherman about his candidacy. The governor needed to authenticate their alleged support, which had influenced him to seek such a golden political fleece. In the end, Carney learned that he had suffered the same fate as Chase. Pomeroy had deceived him, Lincoln knew it, and the governor returned to Topeka humiliated.[61]

Cracks in the Union coalition also appeared in Kentucky, where relations between Lincoln and Bramlette deteriorated over slave enrollment. Despite the efforts of Lincoln and Robinson to keep Kentucky in the Union thus far in the war, its leaders had given signs that Kentuckians were unwilling to throw off their Southern shackles. They were unreceptive to arming military-aged slaves to fight, and the legislature had, just weeks before, endorsed this attitude by prohibiting such action. Lincoln refused to back down, however, and provost marshals prepared to enroll Kentucky slaves. Having just entered his duties as chief executive months before, Bramlette needed time to "unify the sentiment of the people in harmony with the legitimate measures of the Administration for the suppression of the rebellion," and registered another complaint to the president. "Can there be any good resulting from the enrollment and draft of slaves in Kentucky?" he closed.[62] Lincoln pondered the governor's letter, but Bramlette did himself no favors by attending a reception at Lexington honoring Frank Wolford, the flamboyant colonel of the 1st Kentucky Union Cavalry. Unionists invited Bramlette to join the dignitaries seated on the platform as a show of support, and the governor sat silent while Wolford denounced the president over slave enrollment. The governor's lack of dissent insulted Major William H. Sidell, acting provost marshal, who interpreted his silence as an endorsement of Wolford's speech. The Lexington affair drew national press, and correspondents made it appear that Lincoln and the governor were heading toward a showdown over slave enlistments. Bramlette wired William C. Goodloe, recently resigned from General Green C. Smith's staff as assistant adjutant general that "if the President does not, upon my demand, stop the negro Enrollment, I will."[63] To press his point at the White House, he called on his close friend Robert J. Breckinridge, a prominent Kentucky slave owner, Presbyterian minister, and Lincoln advisor. In the meantime, the governor warned Federal commander General Stephen Burbridge that he would execute Kentucky laws when it came to forcibly abducting slaves into the military without the owner's consent, and would "use every means to remove the occasion of such persons who claim to act under federal authority."[64]

Lincoln dismissed Wolford from the ranks, which led to the deterioration of Kentucky's civil-military relations as well as those between Lincoln and Bramlette. Unionist John A. Jacobs was so concerned about the confrontation he wrote Lincoln that enrolling Kentucky slaves was "distasteful and obnoxious" to loyal Kentuckians, and that there was "no small danger of its producing an outbreak of a portion of our loyal people." He "dreadfully fear[ed] a conflict between the Federal and State authorities." He suggested that if slave owners, whether loyal or not, were paid $300 for each slave recruited it would "quiet opposition."[65] Given the problems in Maryland, it was understood, in so far as the *Louisville Daily Journal* saw it, that "the sooner Kentucky recognizes that God is against slavery, and directing the agencies of war and the feelings of the world to destroy it, the better for her."[66]

Early Elections

While Kentucky faced an impending showdown, New Hampshirites went to the polls in the year's first election. It was an important contest for Lincoln's reelection because it was expected to be a close race. Its significance was not lost on Gilmore, Stanton, or the soldiers. Indeed, the overbearing governor, whose ailing health had limited him from stumping, wired Lincoln weeks before that it was imperative that some New Hampshire companies be furloughed home to vote to secure victory. Congressman Edward H. Rollins wired Lincoln that political affairs in the state had "assumed so serious and important an aspect" that he sought a personal interview with the president to strategize. Gilmore owed his election to the legislature because no candidates received a majority vote in the 1863 election. Once in office, he recommended a soldier's voting bill to the legislature, but the New

Hampshire Supreme Court struck it down as unconstitutional, and he had made little headway since. Lincoln needed Gilmore's legislative allies, the state's Lincoln Leagues, and leading Republicans to inspire New Hampshirites to vote for the Republican ticket. He also relied upon Stanton to furlough soldiers home, and the War Secretary complied. The prospect of another term animated Lincoln, and he enlisted the services of General Edward W. Hincks, an invalid Massachusetts officer, for assistance. "I want you to go to New Hampshire and take part in the campaign," Lincoln told Hincks, "I regard it as more important to carry this New Hampshire state election than to whip the enemy on any battlefield where he can be reached."[67] In the meantime, Stanton extended furloughs for the 6th New Hampshire.[68]

As "surprising to the victors as to the vanquished," Gilmore won reelection over Democrat Edward W. Harrington by more than 5,000 votes. Equally important was that New Hampshire voters also put a Unionist majority in the legislature. Gilmore had been successful the previous year in meeting Lincoln's calls, raising troop bounties, and arranging free transportation home for the soldiers. To carry the Republican ticket Gilmore believed he needed the soldiers. Besides the 6th New Hampshire, he also furloughed the soldiers of the 14th New Hampshire home in late February. When asked during one of his speeches why a New Hampshire cavalry unit was sent home, Gilmore reportedly responded: "I brought them home to vote for me!"[69] The governor was not ashamed to admit that victory at the polls was worth the risk in the field. Political victory, he argued, was just as important as military victory, yet it was largely due to Stanton. Although critics charged him with being self-serving and corrupt, his reputation would survive so long as he won. "State gone for the Union Ticket," wired New Hampshire House Speaker William Chandler and Congressman Rollins, "will that do, Mr. President."[70] Gilmore was in Boston when he heard of his victory, and he wired Stanton and Lincoln of the good news that the "Granite State has uttered her voice in favor of the war policy of the Government."[71]

New Hampshire's news gratified Lincoln, but the telegram from Maine congressman James G. Blaine was even more reassuring. "Both branches of the Maine legislature have this day adopted resolutions cordially recommending your renomination," wired the veteran senator on 3 March. "Every Union member voted in favor of them."[72] Meanwhile, Smith had arrived in Washington to confer with Lincoln about consolidating the 1st and 3rd Rhode Island cavalries, and perhaps lobby on Capitol Hill for a senatorship.

The chief executive refused to endorse the reelection of Senator Henry B. Anthony. Offended by the rejection and thinking he might seek the seat, Anthony launched an attack on the governor in the press. A talented and widely popular administrator, Smith, like his predecessor, Sprague, had spent his personal fortune assisting Rhode Islanders through the conflict. Anthony had used his family-owned paper, the *Providence Daily Journal,* as his mouthpiece to attack Smith for supporting Lincoln's radical war measures. In the end, the dispute between Smith and Anthony split the Republican Party for the April election, but Smith managed a slim reelection victory. The legislature, however, was firmly Union, and recommended Lincoln as its first choice for president.[73]

In winter, attention to the Union's coastlines and waterways garnered more attention because the inclement weather stalled land operations. Governors whose states were vulnerable to waterborne attacks shored up regional defenses despite limited federal assistance. Now governors feared the push for land troops would weaken those efforts. For two years New England governors had urged Lincoln to count Navy enlistments on state quotas, but the land war assumed more attention. In mid-March the administration finally acknowledged the shortage of sailors and the importance of the New England Coast, and made accommodations. According to Gustavus Fox, one-third of the sailors were about to be discharged, one-third of the Pacific Squadron was laid up for want of men, and the remaining squadron was lacking sufficient ships. Additionally, there were more than thirty-five vessels waiting on crews, and the Atlantic Squadron had been reduced and would be hard pressed to assist Grant, should he need naval assistance. The shortage convinced Lincoln to call out 200,000 men for the Navy and allow governors additional forces.

The winter had been unduly harsh on military operations, and governors struggled to maintain their commitment to the national forces while attending to local conditions. Pennsylvania soldiers had bemoaned the wretched conditions in their rendezvous camps across the state and demanded the governor's attention. "Scenes of tyranny & oppression," a soldier informed Curtin, "more compatable [sic] with the barbarous usages of savage nations, than consistent with the enlightened age in which we live," existed in the Philadelphia camp. This state of affairs forced Curtin's return from Cuba, where he had been recuperating.[74]

As spring arrived, Lincoln's war behind the lines had grown more intense. Having done all he could to keep Kentuckians in the Union, he was trying to bring Kentuckians into line with the recruitment of slaves, and thankfully so was Bramlette. For all his threats about opposing black enrollment, the governor had finally come around to the idea, though why was not clear. Perhaps he thought, as other governors did, that it was better to use slaves to fill the state quota than to resort to the draft. Bramlette had recently met with Reverend Robert J. Breckinridge, a mutual friend of Lincoln's; outspoken editor of the *Frankfort Commonwealth*, Albert G. Hodges; Louisville physician Theodore S. Bell; and General Burbridge, a Kentucky native in command of the District of Kentucky. Whatever the contents of the discussion, the meeting moved Bramlette to issue a proclamation advising Kentuckians to comply with the federal enrollment of blacks. Convinced of Bramlette's newfound attitude, Burbridge wired Lincoln that "Kentucky will do her duty to the Nation. There need be no fears about the enrollment in this State."[75] The governor came to believe that the war was ending slavery in his state, but many Kentuckians were reluctant to accept the changes that came with emancipation. Meanwhile, the governor set out for Washington, Burbridge set about recruiting blacks, and the impasse was over. Bramlette arrived at the White House with Hodges and former Senator Archibald Dixon and conferred with Lincoln. The governor admitted that if the draft were administered in Kentucky, it would not be opposed, but he needed quota adjustments. Lincoln sent Bramlette to the War Department and asked Stanton to adjust Kentucky quotas as a consequence of volunteers having gone into Confederate military. Lincoln further instructed that black enlistments be counted in compensating for the state's Union quota. Lincoln thought Bramlette's requests were reasonable and urged Stanton to give the governor a "full hearing" and to do the best he could to "effect these objects."[76] Lincoln thought the matter had been settled. Two days later, in asking for the release of a young imprisoned rebel Kentuckian, the governor expressed his confidence that even the small changes they had previously discussed in Washington would allow him to more liberally extend such requests. There was nothing in his letter that indicated he and Lincoln had not seen eye to eye while in Washington.[77]

By the end of March, it appeared that Bramlette had come around on black enlistment, but even still, it did not make things any easier for him. The national press reported black enrollment problems in all the border states. Even while moving toward the acceptance of abolition, Bradford continued to navigate the treacherous shoals between angry slave owners and federal officers accused of illegal recruitments. Conditions had deteriorated such that Bradford informed Lincoln of the problems in Prince George's County, in which black soldiers had taken possession of a jail and set twenty-one prisoners free. "The occurrence of so unprecedented an outrage within 18 miles of the National Capital," Bradford wrote, "ought not probably to pass unnoticed," especially as Maryland representatives on Capitol Hill were embattled in trying to abolish slavery.[78] General Lew Wallace, now in command of the Middle Department, called on Lincoln to bring together Bradford and Maryland congressman Henry Winter Davis to settle disputes before the state convention opened and repudiated their colleagues' good work.[79]

As spring elections unfolded and state legislatures chose their delegates to national conventions, it was important that governors encourage legislators to accept the reconstruction brought on by the war. Although largely untouched by the war, even Californians and Oregonians had come to terms with emancipation. Abolition and black enlistments had not really impacted Pacific Coast citizens, and so it was easy for voters to embrace both as preconditions for Union success. California Republicans boasted that they were ahead of the rest of the Union in endorsing the end of slavery, denouncing it as morally inhumane even if they remained racially biased. Even Gibbs fired off an inaugural dispatch in early March denouncing the institution. "Our telegraph is complete," read his wire from Portland greeting the President. "Let the Pacific railroad, with a branch to Oregon, soon follow. We want no Pacific republic. No compromise with rebels in arms. No more slavery."[80] This was just the news Lincoln needed from his West Coast governors—short, simple, but direct wires that spoke volumes. Although neither Gibbs nor Low had much to offer Lincoln in the way of troops, their moral support went a long way in confirming for the chief executive that they stood behind his presidency.

Still, away from the battlefield, all eyes were on New Hampshire. Even Gilmore could sense from his Concord correspondence that Lincoln's course on the political road ahead needed something to inspire the commander in chief. He sent the president a jug of Shaker maple syrup, which was supposed to be "all right." "May it serve to mitigate the bitterness and smooth the roughness of your official life," was his attached message.[81] Since his inauguration, Lincoln's official life had consisted of embittered days and what seemed like an endless night. As the spring rains arrived, the quiet military front was about to shed its winter seclusion. Grant returned to Washington after his brief trip west and observed the political heat emanating from

Capitol Hill, where Radicals urged General Meade's removal for not being aggressive enough. Yet, the new chief saw something in the Spanish-born commander and retained him. To avoid the political fuss, Grant traveled to Culpeper Court House, where he established his headquarters. Confident that Grant was poised to open the war against the enemy at the front, Lincoln despaired on learning the same week that Copperheads were equally poised to win the war behind the lines. Three hundred Copperheads descended on unsuspecting Federal soldiers home on furlough at Charleston, Illinois. Yates's war was far from over.[82]

CHAPTER SEVENTEEN

I Claim Not to Have Controlled Events

April brought a departure from the icy, congealed conditions in camps where soldiers suffered the long, dreary winter, and a return to the inclement and mud-laden spring. "Mud it was," concluded Stoddard, "that scared McClellan away from Manassas, crippled him on the Peninsula, delayed Burnside's pontoons, drove back one of Meade's advances, and did more than anything else to facilitate Lee's escape at Falling Water's, after the Gettysburg fight."[1] No significant fighting had occurred in recent months, except in Arkansas where the Confederates had stalled Banks on the Red River, and in Florida where they had rebuffed the Federal expedition against the capital. Grant, however, was accustomed to inhospitable weather, and prepared for his campaign against Lee. Other than that, skirmishing characterized the winter weeks as campaigns progressed slowly.[2]

Victories at Home

As the military fronts remained quiet, Northerners at home were moving the war to the ballot box. Not as momentous as battles, political victories were no less significant. To add to the good fortune in New Hampshire, news came from Connecticut. "Union State ticket elected," wired Buckingham. "Majority probably over 6,000."[3] He added, "In the opinion of many, our election in 1860 was the pivot on which events turned which led to the election of your Excellency to the Presidency and now if it shall lead to results none will feel worse than the copperhead sympathisers [sic] with traitors in Conn."[4] With no military victories yet to boast in the New Year, Stanton was grateful for Buckingham's reelection. "Accept for yourself and the patriotic people of your State," he wired, "my hearty congratulations for the great victory you have achieved in behalf of our country."[5] This was good news because it discouraged Confederates who hoped for some early Union reverses at the polls. More important, it revealed that the new party coalition of Republicans and War Democrats was on the rise, and that the Copperheadism of Origen S. Seymour, the nephew of New York's governor, was no match for Buckingham's war record. Accustomed to dissident chicanery, Andrew was unsurprised to learn while campaigning for Buckingham in Middletown, Connecticut, that some Copperheads had set fire to a barn belonging to a Union man in hopes of breaking up the meeting where he was speaking. Members of the audience managed to extinguish the fire, and the political rally continued. Yet, while New Englanders led by example at the polls, the *New York Times* hinted that more work was to be done across the North in making good on their quotas. Lincoln, nonetheless, welcomed the good news from Hartford.[6]

However much Lincoln's agents had influenced New England elections and worked state legislatures to advance their early support for his renomination, governors remained their states' party leaders and welded considerable power. The legislative upsurge committed delegates to Lincoln's candidacy months before the convention, and it drew criticism from the press, eager to see what Grant could do on the battlefield. Much had been made of Lincoln's ability to control events and shape the contours of the war, yet the president understood the conflict was larger than the presidency. The war had forced his hand in making decisions he believed rang true to the Union's spirit, but were no less unpopular. To the Kentuckians who had recently arrived to confer their enlisting slaves, Lincoln justified his position. "I am naturally anti-slavery," he reasoned to Kentucky journalist Hodges. "If slavery is not wrong, nothing is wrong. I can not remember when I did not so think, and feel."[7] He added, "And yet, I have never understood that the Presidency conferred upon me an unrestricted right to act officially upon this judgment and feeling."[8] Lincoln's understanding of executive power had grown significantly since he declared the conflict a "people's contest." He had power to emancipate slaves since the war opened, but refused to accept Frémont's proclamation in 1861 because he did not then think it a necessity. He rejected Cameron's idea of arming blacks to fight for the same reason. Even Hunter's attempted military emancipation he forbade, citing the same justification. Therefore, Lincoln believed his timing was better than Frémont's, Cameron's, and Hunter's when it came to expanding war aims. Yet citizens, including governors, had questioned the president's early prudence.[9]

That Lincoln waited for more than a year to wield a heavy hand against the Confederates gave rise to speculation that he could have ended the war sooner had he pursued a vigorous approach from the beginning. Governors complained that, in trying to win a Southern constituency he never had, Lincoln had prolonged the conflict. A vote against secession was not a vote for the Union, they argued, and not an endorsement of his presidency. Congressional Radicals and like-minded governors had prodded the president to accept an expansive war from the beginning, pointing to the necessity of ending the war quickly to avoid a long, drawn-out war that would exhaust the republic's resources and bleed the North of its loyal citizens. By 1864 Lincoln could argue that he had not pushed these sentiments on the people, but rather was reacting to pressure from them. Using this rationale, omnipotent forces had moved Lincoln to acknowledge his power. "I claim not to have controlled events," he reasoned, "but confess plainly that events have controlled me." At the end of three years, Lincoln refused to take credit for what he considered to be God's work; he was merely the instrument of preserving the Union.[10]

In this theological sense, Lincoln was a leader of mortals by allowing himself to enact God's plan, to be pulled along by the people, who recognized Lincoln as a leader, and elected him president. Indeed, Buckingham alluded to this fact in 1860 when Republicans nominated Lincoln. "That God may direct events so that you shall be the Chief Executive of this Nation and give you wisdom to discharge much high duties," wrote the governor, was the desire of many Northerners.[11] But there was more to Lincoln's genius than God's design. Whatever political acumen and leadership abilities he possessed, it was the president's ability to read people and his sense of timing in handling the delicate balance of issues and power that enhanced his credibility among governors. "He executes the will of the people," declared Reverend Henry Fowler from New York, and "his wisdom consists in carrying out the good sense of the nation."[12]

Senators followed Lincoln's lead, and by the end of the first week in April passed a joint resolution abolishing slavery in the United States by approving the Thirteenth Amendment. The war had revolutionized the times even in Delaware. Anna Ferris noted these changes in her diary. Englishman George Thomson, distinguished antislavery orator, had just arrived in Wilmington from Washington, where he had given a speech on the House floor in favor of abolition. "His appearance & reception amongst us is a significant sign of the revolution through which we are passing," Ferris observed. "When here 30 years ago he was threatened with martyrdom & driven from the country, for the expression of his Anti-Slavery views." She concluded, "Now he is received everywhere with acclamation, & has almost a national welcome." Ferris perceptively interpreted his reception as a sign of the "beginning of the end" of the institution.[13] The Delaware native had diagnosed the Northerners' dilemma. If it was necessary to emancipate Confederate slaves and enlist blacks in the Union military to win the war, then it was necessary to abolish the institution to advance a more perfect Union.

Northern armies were on the move, and governors, accustomed to the ebb and flow of military operations, prepared themselves for the telegraphic onslaught. Grant steered clear of Washington and accompanied the Army of the Potomac in the field. The commander had a clear mission when he took charge of all the Union armies—end the conflict by all means. "Wherever Lee goes," Grant told Meade, "there you will go also."[14] Indeed, Grant had decided the best way to get at Lee and keep him pinned down was to have Union armies hold Lee's reinforcements in check. In one of his prairie-like metaphors, Lincoln put Grant's strategy into western layman's terms. "Those not skinning," he reasoned, "can hold a leg."[15] Sherman's target was the Confederate army in Georgia, Banks would try to redeem himself by taking Mobile, Butler would head up the Virginia Peninsula and threaten the Confederate capitol, while Sigel headed south up the Shenandoah Valley to keep the Confederates from reinforcing Richmond. With governors and Stanton throwing their combined efforts behind the plan, it could not fail, despite the fact that three-year men were due to muster out.[16]

As much as governors kept an eye on the national armies that spring, they kept an even closer watch over the soldiers and local governance. Morton was disappointed to learn that Indiana cavalrymen, who rode their own horses into the ranks, had their horses transferred to other units. He argued to Stanton that these soldiers had been promised they could keep the horses they brought with them and that the orders to the contrary discouraged them. Stanton responded that once the horses became government property, the men had "no right to control the Government in their use." He was correct, but what appeared a simple matter gave offense to the governor. Stanton respected Morton, and he attempted to soothe the governor's feelings. "I have perfect confidence in your patriotic zeal and influence overcoming all personal considerations and dissatisfaction in this urgent hour," he wrote. "Come, gird yourself up, and once more to the field, old chief, with every horse and man!"[17] Stanton's reputation as the "bulldog" reflected his relentless enforcement of policy, and if it won him few friends it nonetheless established the contours of national authority in administering the war. Still, it was hard for governors to reconcile national military policy with local sentiment, especially when they appeared to be at odds. When Gilmore traveled to Washington in April to lobby for a Concord-based hospital, Stanton refused. On the heels of an important New Hampshire victory, the rejection annoyed the governor.[18]

By mid-April Lincoln had recovered from a recent sickness, and, to assuage tempers in Maryland, he traveled to Baltimore as Bradford's guest to attend the opening of the Maryland State Fair. His ulterior motive was to encourage state representatives to revise Maryland's constitution to do away with slavery. Nonetheless, Lincoln's attendance soothed the governor's wounded feelings over the enlistment of Maryland slaves. Still, it was odd to see Lincoln strolling through the grounds with the governor's wife Elizabeth on his arm. Bradford, however, took advantage of the president's visit to discuss the summer campaigns and the legislature's progress in abolishing slavery. The president's brief address gave him the opportunity to explain the significance of the change that war had wrought in three years. He used Maryland as the example to acknowledge how the "world moves." Looking out at the soldiers gathered, the president remarked that "three years ago, the same soldiers could not so much as pass through Baltimore." He acknowledged that "The change from then till now, is both great, and gratifying," but "the change within Baltimore is part only of a far wider change." He noted, "The people of Maryland have been doing something to define liberty," and this was evidence of that greater change.[19]

The war was moving, and, given the experience of the past three springs, governors prepared for summer campaigns that would bleed them of their soldiers. Even in victory came significant loss. Having witnessed war weariness among the populace, governors searched for ways to end the conflict quickly, before home-front dissidents overcame them. Several chief executives developed an idea and used the occasion of General Heintzelman's arrival in Indianapolis to proffer it. On 16 April, in Morton's chambers, the commander met with Morton, Yates, and Brough, where they laid out plans to combat the Order of the American Knights. Copperhead activities had spread into Canada, and reports indicated that some 3,000 members had schemed to raid the prison at Johnson's Island on Sandusky Bay in Lake Erie. Worse yet was the possibility of another Confederate cavalry strike into the Midwest that would alarm citizens just as Lincoln was contemplating another call for men and before the North's political conventions. Heintzelman was convinced, and they agreed to invite Blair, Stone, and Lewis to join them in Washington, where the entire group could relay their concerns to the president.[20]

The governors arrived in Washington days later, where they joined Curtin at the War Department and presented Stanton with an idea for men. Brough presented the governors' proposal to raise 85,000 militiamen for one hundred days by early May. This would free up veteran soldiers to support Grant's summer campaign by using the militia as a national guard to combat Copperheads in their states. It was an important move on their part, since the War Department's postponement of the 10 March draft. Ohio, Illinois, and Indiana would shoulder the lion's portion, raising 70,000 men, and Iowa and Wisconsin would make up the difference. No bounties would be paid to these men, and they were not to be credited to the draft quotas. Stanton wired Grant, who was impressed by the grand idea. Stanton arranged a meeting that same evening for the governors to discuss the idea with Lincoln and Halleck. "Old Brains" was so enthused that he wired Seymour to call on the New York militia to act in the city as short-term guards to relieve Dix, who had been asked to forward to Grant all force possible. Two days after the meeting Lincoln accepted the proposition and directed Stanton to carry it into execution by securing a $25 million congressional appropriation to pay for the additional forces. The governors returned home enthusiastic that they had moved the war closer to its ending.[21]

For a war the administration wanted Northerners to believe it was winning, the call for the short-term men appeared ambitious. Governors had taken a risk, but it was one they believed worth taking. Chief executives were attuned to home-front mutineers and had grown frustrated by their paralyzing influence. In an election year, governors could ill afford to wait until Copperheads undermined their efforts. Rather it was better to deter them by ensuring that while the armies drained the local communities of their military-age males they had force enough to repel uprisings. Instead of returning home, Blair and Lewis remained in Washington to visit their soldiers. They understood from Stanton that Meade's nearly 100,000-man army had crossed the Rapidan River, pushed into the Wilderness woods just west of Fredericksburg, and was pressing Lee's Confederates to battle. Military correspondents characterized the unfolding engagement as the beginning of the end, and they wanted to be nearby to assist. Commencing on 1 May, the two mammoth armies fought over the wooded landscape and across the sparsely open fields in a series of brutal struggles. By sunset on 6 May, another bloody battle ended in the Wilderness woods with little success to report. "The excitement of waiting for slow-coming dispatches from the battle," remarked Stoddard in Washington, "is not more exhausting or depressing."²² Lewis spent days visiting wounded Wisconsin soldiers in the hospitals and the regiments in the "Iron Brigade" before they crossed the Rapidan. He presented a new flag to the soldiers of the 5th Wisconsin and attended to the wounded. As details of the engagement unfolded, the governor ordered his Surgeon General Erastus B. Wolcott and members of the "Wisconsin Soldiers' Aid Society" residing in Washington to the front.²³

Buckingham was not among those governors Stanton relied on for short-term troops, but he shared the secretary's trepidation over the recent turn of events in Virginia. Thousands of his Connecticutans had fought in the Wilderness woods, and the wires pouring in from commands and agents seeking surgeons and medical supplies convinced him to race to the front. The chief executive had arrived shortly after giving his opening address to the legislature in New Haven. The governor declared that slavery was dead and that "the events of the past urge us to adopt some measure which shall terminate in favor of freedom that controversy which must ever exist so long as a part of the nation remains free and a part enslaved."²⁴ Parker also assembled a team of doctors and nurses and hastened to Virginia, where scores of his Jersey Blues had been among those units badly cut up. When he stopped in Washington, however, Stanton's urgent request for militia caught up with him and forced the governor to return to Trenton, but not before seeing some of his soldiers in hospitals in the city. Parker sent his team and hospital supplies on to Fredericksburg. The carnage of war had so moved Parker that in the weeks to come he would soften his opposition to using Southern blacks in his New Jersey regiments.²⁵

Of the Union soldiers engaged during the Union's Wilderness campaign, more than 17,500 were casualties, a staggering figure for the first week of May. Grant's foray had opened a campaign that would continue throughout the spring and summer. Lincoln received reports confirming the bloodbath at the Wilderness woods, and they discouraged him. It was an eerie circumstance. "The city is very quiet now," wrote a Pennsylvanian who was at Willard's Hotel. "Men talk in whisper, you will see a general expression of suspense on mens [sic] faces, a great struggle is just now going on, all eyes are turned toward it."²⁶ It was a sign of things to come. Andrew learned of the carnage from his colleague Henry Wilson, who assisted in attending to the wounded. "If that scene could have been presented to me before the war," he wrote, "anxious as I was for the preservation of the Union, I should have said: 'The cost is too great; erring sisters, go in peace.'"²⁷ The cost was going to be great, and as much as Lincoln publicly displayed confidence in

Grant, it did little for Northern morale. Stanton knew all too well the other side of war as he wired Brough, Morton, Yates, Stone, and Lewis that their 100-day men could not "be ready for the field too soon."[28]

Despair in the Ranks

Balancing home-front disaffection and battlefront defeat became more difficult for governors as the spring campaigns unfolded. Stanton had even called on Andrew to send a battalion of heavy artillery and all unattached companies employed in garrison duty. Already behind in his quota, and having raked the North and South for black troops, Andrew protested. He enlisted Sumner to plead his case that those troops were needed to remain. Already irritated over the pay discrepancy involving Samuel Harrison, black chaplain of the 54th Massachusetts, who refused to take any pay less than his white counterparts, Andrew wanted the issue placed before the president. The governor persisted and relied on Sumner to right this injustice by pressing him to see Lincoln. "For God's sake," he wrote, "how long is the injustice of the Government to be continued towards these men?"[29] William L. Mead of the 127th New York, agreed, writing from South Carolina that these soldiers had "done great service and ought to have justice done them."[30] In the weeks to come, Andrew would place the issue of equal pay before Lincoln and use Harrison as a test case.[31]

The president received Bates's decision that nothing prohibited black soldiers from receiving regular pay, but Lincoln lacked the constitutional means to effect the change. His rationale did not please Andrew. "For fear the uniform may dignify the enfranchised slave, or make the black man seem like a free citizen," wrote Andrew on the back of private letter, "the government means to disgrace and degrade him, so that he may always be in his own eyes, and in the eyes of all men, 'only a nigger.' "[32] Andrew called on congressmen to bring about equal pay for black soldiers. In the weeks of late spring he would expand his political arsenal to include prominent Boston lawyer and friend George S. Hale. Whatever his feelings for Lincoln or Stanton, Andrew had a higher calling. "I have been impelled by a duty I could not put aside," he confided to Sumner.[33] Andrew met with Forbes, his liaison in Washington, who wrote to New York congressman Sedgwick that Lincoln "naturally declines to interfere with Congress in debating the point."[34] Still, Andrew hammered away at pay equity, and soldiers appreciated his sentiments. Although it proved to be a struggle, Congress finally took up the issue and in June executed the measure of equal pay, retroactive to the first of the year, to begin 1 August. Charles W. Lenox wrote a war-weary Andrew the following day. "My only motive in writing this," he scribbled, "is that you may know that there is at least one member of the Fifty-fourth who knows that Mass [sic] has done more for his race, than all the States, and that your Excellency has done more than all Governors put together for their benefit."[35] The battle over equal pay had ended, but Andrew's vigor was waning as his health began to deteriorate.[36]

Meade resumed his course at the Virginia front, maneuvered to a place called Spotsylvania Court House, and renewed the fight with Lee for the next two weeks. Grant was committed to staying on Lee and not pulling back. He ordered Sherman to use his Federals to strike at the Confederate army in Georgia to help his cause in Virginia—thus commencing a several-month-long campaign through the Southeast. Butler and Sigel struggled to keep the Confederates pinned down on the Peninsula and in the Shenandoah Valley. In mid-May came the news that Grant's leg holders, Sigel and Butler, had failed. Suffering defeat at the battle of New Market on 15 May, the humiliated German tucked his tail and headed back down the valley to Harpers Ferry with the Confederates in pursuit. The German's battlefield ineptness was only surpassed by Butler's loss the following day at the battle of Drewry's Bluff, and Banks's failed campaign.[37]

Whether or not he was successful on the battlefield, the combined efforts of Grant's armies had added vigor to the war, but not without tremendous cost. Stanton painted a favorable picture to governors to soften the blow of what they would read in the official reports and newspapers. Grant knew it, Lincoln knew it, and the Northern people knew it—the Army of the Potomac had been defeated again. Still, Lincoln's confidence in Grant remained unshaken, but he knew that for Grant to be successful he would need more men. For that he needed governors to remain optimistic and energetic in sustaining the flow of manpower to the armies. Indeed, at one point during the fight on the third day, Grant allegedly remarked to Meade, "Well, Meade, if they are going to make a Kilkenny cat affair of this, our cat has got the longest tail."[38] Grant was correct, but the seesaw of forces to which he referred weighed heavily on the Northern populace.

Grant relied on the governors to feed the Union's armies and to help with morale. Cony had traveled to Washington to attend to his wounded Maine soldiers and obtained authority to ship many of them back home, where he arranged hospital accommodations. Bradford knew the armies were in need of troops, but before the draft should commence in Maryland, he wanted proper credit for the slaves mustered into service. The governor had called a special session of the legislature that convened in late April to take up the question of abolishing slavery in the state. He informed Fry that depletion of slaves had been so severe that much of the arable land in the agricultural counties had been left uncultivated. Thus, the slaves from those districts should be counted toward the state quota to avoid drafting in those districts, or, at the very least, there should be a postponement of the draft until the figures were in. Slave owners battered Bradford with complaints that Federal soldiers were forcing slaves into the ranks. Bradford passed these complaints along to Lincoln and the War Department. Given the allowances, Fry wrote, "Maryland has received 'liberal considerations,' and that Your Excellency's claim for 'simple justice' has been more than satisfied."[39]

Andrew also complained that an expectant draft would complicate his efforts in getting men off to war. Lincoln's recent call for sailors might offset discrepancies in his states' land forces. Yet, at the moment, the governor complained that more than sixty wounded soldiers passed through the surgeon's hand at Faneuil Hall daily, and the number was increasing. Without wanting to appear insubordinate, Andrew wanted Massachusetts to be left alone to raise their quota the best and most hospitable way possible. Seymour agreed, wiring Stanton that he was beset by draft problems in New York City. He complained that 8,000 to 10,000 men were on strike. New York journalist Thurlow Weed was so concerned that he wired Morgan to use his influence to stop the draft immediately. To add to the drama were the rumors announcing another call for men. Before Lincoln had consented, however, two New York newspapers scandalously issued a proclamation that Lincoln was about to issue a call, which caused a stir across the North and sent Wall Street spiraling in speculation. Irritated by the episode, Lincoln had the papers suppressed and purged his anger to Curtin, who was with Lincoln when he received the news. The governor understood that Lincoln fought the war on many fronts. Governors fought the same war, just on a smaller scale. They were in daily contact with the president, the War Department, provost marshals, soldiers, citizens, bankers, chaplains, and a host of other constituents. They too pored over a vast correspondence that joined them as companions in a common cause. Their collective efforts at the state level, whether successes or failures, had advanced the partnership with Lincoln seeking victory on the battlefield. By the spring, governors adhered to the national strategy even when it appeared there were insurmountable odds. As Grant's men fought Lee's army for every inch of Virginia soil, governors were doing all they could to influence their legislatures to line up for the president and the Union. As they saw it, the soldiers needed political reinforcement to confirm that their course, for which thousands had already sacrificed their lives, would preserve the Union.[40]

Northerners placed confidence in the governors by depending on them to manage their political and military fronts in the war. Their messages to the legislatures reaffirmed their prestige within political parties. Many governors urged Lincoln's renomination at the convention as the only means to end the war, and delegates across the North fell into line. In several states residents held town and county ballots that unified Republicans and Democrats for nomination. Although New Hampshire had already cast their lot with Lincoln, abolitionists in Massachusetts stalled Andrew's attempts to swing the pendulum behind Lincoln. Nonetheless, the legislature eventually supported Lincoln, as did Ohio and Pennsylvania. Seymour took no action to secure Lincoln's favor. Weed, Greeley, and Roscoe Conkling assumed the role of carrying the Lincoln torch in the New York legislature and in the Union State Convention when it met in late May.[41]

Knowledge that states were lining up for him comforted Lincoln, but enemy operations and civil-military discord in Missouri and Kansas threatened to undermine his support. "It appears to me," wrote Hall to Lincoln that "Military affairs west [of] the Mississippi river are getting very badly for us," and the governor pressed Lincoln to consolidate military departments under one command.[42] The division among commanders and departments had complicated matters for state authorities, and given the rather small number of Confederate troops and limited breathing room, a combined national and state force would certainly fare better. So bad were affairs in Kansas that the *Chicago Tribune* remarked, "the pot of politics is boiling most furiously in 'bleeding Kansas.'" Noted the editor, "All the witches Shakespeare marshaled under the leadership of Hecate could not have conjured a more delightful 'hell broth.'"[43] Carney arrived in Washington and, accompanied by Pomeroy, conferred with Lincoln about the violence in Kansas and about his election fiasco. Privy to recent political affairs in Kansas that made national headlines, Lincoln had little time to untangle the mess. In a rushed interview, he focused more on the rival factions at work than the Confederates, and pawned them off on Stanton, who was too busy to see them. Instead, the secretary wrote them a note. "I wish you and Lane would make a sincere effort to get out of the mood you are in," Stanton wrote. "[It] does neither of you any good—it gives you the means of tormenting my life out of me, and nothing else."[44]

Kansas politicians had tormented Lincoln and Stanton, yet Carney had done his duty to put Kansans in the ranks for the army. Now he offered 2,000 men to Stanton to be used for 100 days, like his midwestern colleagues, but wanted them to remain in Kansas. Times were challenging, and Kansans were nearly destitute. Army pay at least provided some financial assistance for impoverished families. Inhospitable weather and bushwhackers had destroyed many of their farms, and legislators lacked funds to assist families. Lincoln, however, had grown wise to the state's political leaders, who he believed worsened the plight of Kansans. "The merits of the Kansas people need not to be argued to me," he argued, "they are just as good as any other loyal and patriotic people," and "as such, to the best of my ability, I have always treated them, and intend to treat them." Yet, he argued, there was "not a more foolish or demoralizing way of conducting a political rivalry, than these fierce and bitter struggles for patronage."[45] As for the governor's troop demands, Lincoln concluded that he would neither accept nor reject it until he was ready. The president's attitude offended Carney, who responded that Kansas was in deep distress and needed the "fostering care of the Government," to protect the families who were finding it extremely difficult to continue to sacrifice their sons to fight for a cause they appeared to be losing at home. Nonetheless, Lincoln continued to support General Lane, who undermined Carney at every turn.[46]

Had political fortunes carried to the battlefield that spring it might have buoyed Northern confidence in Grant. The president needed an early blow against the Confederates to merit his renomination's support. Although Sigel failed at New Market, Stanton wired his gubernatorial confidants the "highly satisfactory" news of Sherman's movements in Georgia, Butler's attack at Fort Darling, and General Philip H. Sheridan's successful cavalry raids near Richmond. As the governors worked to bring volunteers forward, Stanton continued to portray things favorably. "Everything continues to look well," he wired Brough.[47] Lincoln also encouraged Morton, Yates, Stone, and Lewis to forward troops to meet the needs of Sherman's army bearing down on Atlanta, which he remarked "promises much good." He added, "Please put your best efforts into the work."[48] The arm of the Union military stretched further into Georgia and hundreds of miles away from its supply base at Louisville, which, ironically, required almost as many men to secure the rails northward as Sherman needed to fight the Confederates at the front.[49]

It had been days since Stanton had wired the midwestern governors, and Brough was concerned. He read something worrisome into Stanton's silence. The president was anxious over Grant's Virginia stalemate and Sherman's vulnerability in Georgia, a feeling that was all too common. The chief executive queried Stanton on May 24, hoping for some definite news about the military fronts. Stanton thought it better to allow Lincoln to respond, and the president confided that "we had nothing bad from any where." Quite the contrary, wrote the president, "I have just seen a dispatch of Grant ... which ends as follows: 'Every thing looks exceedingly favorable for us.'"[50]

Stanton reassured the governors that Grant was driving the Confederates back and that Union losses were inconsiderable. He sent personal congratulations to Brough for putting 32,000 Ohioans of the 100,000 pledged in the field. "This prompt and energetic action of yourself, your staff, and the loyal people of the State," Stanton wired, "exhibits an unmatched effort of devoted patriotism and stern determination to spare no sacrifice to maintain the National Government and overthrow the rebellion."[51] Brough's pluck in getting up the men pleased Ohio political leader and lifelong Democrat Andrew Evans of Brown County. He wrote to his son Sam, who was an officer in the 59th United States Colored Troops (USCT) that "'Old Brough' says now is the time and that 100 days will probably decide the fate of the Rebellion and that it is of the utmost importance that we have plenty of men to ensure a victory." Evans continued, "He says these 100 days men must be exempt from the present draft, which will draw on the copperheads, the more, & if they won't go, we will get their money, and 'if they won't fish he'll make them cut bait.' He's all right."[52]

As favorable as the military news appeared in the papers, Grant's persistence to remain in Lee's front still sent thousands of casualties to hospitals and to their graves. Governors had a difficult time reconciling so much loss with so little gain, especially since it looked as though the new commander cared little for the soldiers he left on the battlefield. Smith left Brattleboro accompanied by twenty surgeons and rushed to Virginia to care for his Vermonters. He had just visited the front in late February and found the men in fine spirits. By the time he returned to Fredericksburg, however, the carnage was more than he could have imagined. The city had become "one vast hospital." One New York surgeon remarked that he had been working day and night for nearly a week and could hardly hold a scalpel. As the ambulances came in by the hundreds, with men waiting for amputations, Smith wrote "it is a scene of horror such as I never saw."[53] Smith remained with the wounded men comforting them and arranging for them to be transported back to Vermont. He wrote a hasty wire to the editor of the *Burlington Daily Free Press* that read: "Have just returned from Fredericksburg and our wounded, securing for them all the care possible though suffering badly." He continued, "The First Brigade entered the field thirty-four hundred and ninety strong," but "up to last Saturday lost twenty-seven hundred and ninety."[54]

Key defeats forced Grant to lessen the role of some politically valuable commanders such as Sigel. The German's reassignment caused an uproar among German-Americans, who constituted a significant portion of the Northern population in some of the critical border states and states where Democrats had triumphed recently. Adding to the demoralized state of the Union high command was the news that Lee had forced Grant back across the North Anna River after several days of serious fighting. Yet the commander was determined to stay the course and would march and give battle repeatedly to keep the Confederate commander pinned down. Grant's tenacity was commendable, but he was in the thick of a campaign when several thousand veterans were mustering out after three years of service. Although numbering fewer than 10,000, these retiring veterans further burdened mustering officers. Indeed, three years before, mustering agents scurried to enlist the groundswell of oversubscribed regiments. Now it took such a force to muster them out. Governors were seemingly building a new army at the most critical time of the war, and new relations of trust and honor would have to be forged on the new battlefields of Virginia, Georgia, and elsewhere.[55]

Union Nominations

The Union war effort suffered another blow in late May when a small but rather exercised contingent of Radical Republicans, including many Germans, met in Cleveland to protest the president's candidacy in the coming election. The assembly nominated Frémont, a commander waiting in New York to be reassigned, and pledged him to more punitive war aims and reconstruction efforts. The commander's nomination was hardly a surprise, given that his conservative detractors were urging peace as the means to end the war. Democrats were planning to nominate McClellan, whose popularity had soared with every Union defeat. The Republican convention was scheduled to meet in Baltimore in the second week in June, and Lincoln needed something encouraging, especially since Northern delegates were making their way to Washington to confer with their congressional colleagues before heading to the convention city.[56]

News from the Virginia front did little to lift Lincoln's spirits. Reports from Grant's overland campaign revealed that the commander was losing his long drawn-out battle against the Confederates at Cold Harbor, a little obscure crossroads name for the local hotel, just ten miles northeast of Richmond. In one of the bloodiest days of the war (3 June), the Confederates slaughtered the Union men in the Union's frontal assaults, amounting to shear butchery and resulting in the loss of roughly 4,000 Federals—a figure hardly imaginable given the previous week's death toll. Thus far, Grant's war record in the East was hardly distinguishing. He had amassed an army of casualties, but had nothing to show for it except Lincoln's continued praise and support. Having fought against Lee since July, Meade was perceptive enough to observe to his wife that Grant had "had his eyes opened and is willing to admit now that Virginia and Lee's army is not Tennessee and Bragg's army." He concluded, "Whether the people will ever realize this fact remains to be seen."[57]

Governors held high expectations for Grant that June. They hoped to report great victories to their citizens to accompany political success. Gilmore had recently pulled off a historic political victory in New Hampshire, signaling perhaps the most extraordinary "manifestations of public opinion ever witnessed in the state," which he hoped to boast of at his inaugural.[58] Beneath Concord's overcast skies, the new governor rode into Concord to assume the reins of chief executive. Former governors Goodwin, Berry, and the visiting Andrew accompanied him to the capitol building in a barouche drawn by six horses. Although worn down by years of harsh weather and financial neglect, the New Hampshire Statehouse was at one time known for an elegance unsurpassed by any other building north of New York's City Hall. Its physical appearance in 1864 was symbolic in its representation of the state's commitment to the cause—fatigued, stressed, but still standing as a tiny pillar of commitment to the Union. Despite having few generals in the contest, Gilmore nonetheless had overseen thousands of New Hampshirites off to war and thousands more whose fellow countrymen at home followed them with great pride. "If New Hampshire has few generals," he quipped in his address to the legislature, "she has many heroes," and he went on to list their many accomplishments.⁵⁹ From the capitol lawn, the governor declared to the crowd that his New Hampshire men had "proved themselves firm as [the] granite of their native hills in resisting the shock of war; terrible as the lightning which plays about their summits."⁶⁰ Little did he know that hundreds of miles away, the "men of granite" in the 11th New Hampshire of the 9th Corps had prepared for battle and, on the evening of 2 June, had pinned their names to their uniforms so that they could be identified after what was surely to come.⁶¹

Governors found little to console them after Cold Harbor. They concluded that Lee's influence now was due more to his capacity to send Union casualties home than in refusing Grant's stubborn attacks at that front. Speaking at the Great Central Fair in Philadelphia's Logan Square, Cannon, along with Parker and Curtin, made their tasks clear to the Sanitary Commission audience. "No earthly cause has now such claims upon our energy, our patriotism and our benevolence," declared Cannon, "as that which seeks to comfort those who have been stricken in defense of our country."⁶² Far removed from the war, residents of Bangor, Maine, shared that sentiment. In the June heat, thousands of citizens had gathered to consecrate a fifty-eight-square-foot granite monument to the fallen soldiers. "Many an eye was wet in the vast assemblage," wrote a Bangor editor, "as they gazed upon those emblems of Liberty, which sons, husbands, and brothers laid down their lives to protect."⁶³ On that day, the war came home to Northerners as memorialized by Cony in his remarks. "These monuments," he observed solemnly, "thickly scattered over the State, in all time to come will be witnesses of the enormous sacrifices which Maine has made in the prosecution of this war for the preservation of the republic."⁶⁴

Reckless though it appeared, Grant's Cold Harbor attack was part of his grand scheme to stay on Lee, and Lincoln needed to publicly support the commander. It made political sense, because he needed the continued cooperation of governors in bringing men forward, even as legislators, journalists, and citizens complained of the losses. Nothing could be gained by criticizing his great commander, in fact, it would appear all too familiar. After all, how would it look if Lincoln found cause for concern about the commander whom he had just months before given command of all the Union soldiers, especially in an election year. Governors followed the same course and shied away from public condemnation. As the armies continued to face off against one another in Virginia, Georgia, and elsewhere, cabinet members, congressmen, and Washingtonians bore witness to the toll the war had taken on the president. Antiwar sentiment soared, while the morale of the troops and the civilians sank the hopes of a successful summer. Still, no one knew or could even predict at the time that Lee had won his last battle of the war. And yet for all his victories in the West, Grant had yet to win in Virginia. The jubilance that soared with Grant's arrival in the East had been soured by the filling of hospitals in and around Washington with wounded soldiers. Although there were mixed reactions to Grant within the army—among officers and men—many sang his praises. "It is wonderful how entirely the army confides in General Grant," remarked the correspondent to *Harper's Weekly*, "every soldier's tongue is full of his praises." Noted one wounded soldier, " 'He is one of us, this Unconditional Surrender General, and he will bring us through, God willing, just as surely as the sun shines.' "[65]

Lincoln caught a mild reprieve from military events on 7 June, when Republicans and War Democrats came together in Baltimore and nominated him as the National Union Party candidate. Given that none of the major political bosses endorsed Frémont, Radicals gave into the tide sweeping in Lincoln's favor. His nomination was proof that the unconditional Union sentiment had fused all factions into one party. Besides, Lincoln had by this time endorsed a constitutional amendment to abolish slavery, and this afforded Union Party leaders the ability to write abolition into the campaign platform. New York senator Morgan chaired the National Union Committee, which boasted of the Union's laurels and pledged to end the war on the battlefield. The veteran politician then handed the chair's gavel of the committee to former Ohio governor Dennison to carry on the proceedings. Stone represented Iowa at the convention and fought for the honor to be the one to shout Lincoln's name to the delegates, but managed only to second the nomination made by Illinoisan Burton C. Cook. Lincoln had shied away from making suggestions about the vice presidency and, much to his credit, abstained from helping frame the platform. He remained focused on the front, but ensured Seward was present to secure a course for his reelection in the fall. That Unionists nominated for vice president War Democrat Andrew Johnson, current governor of Reconstructed Tennessee who had endeared himself to Radicals, indicated that Lincoln's silence was motive enough for a change. Hamlin, however, was confident of being renominated, despite New England opposition. Sumner's hatred of William Pitt Fessenden, Maine's veteran senator, had grown so bitter in the recent congressional session that he wanted the senator out of the chamber. The senator plotted to have Hamlin removed from vice-presidential consideration so he could return to Maine and run against Fessenden in the senatorial contest. As news of the convention spread, several governors, including Andrew, Buckingham, Blair, Yates, and Stone accepted the predictable outcome. Privately, however, they had reservations.[66]

Days after the Union Convention, John Hunt Morgan raided Kentucky, hoping to cut Sherman's lifeline and perhaps foster membership in secret organizations. Bramlette reported that he had no troops to spare and that these kinds of raids and "internal trouble in Indiana and Illinois promised a warm summer's work," and he would need troops for self-protection. Morgan's raid alarmed Brough and Morton, both of whom resorted to local defense. Bramlette remained at Frankfort to defend the Kentucky Capitol and the state's archives from destruction. When the Confederates arrived along the Georgetown Pike, the chief executive went to the fort overlooking the city and entered the ranks as a "high private." The governor armed himself and prepared to fight alongside fifty citizens until reinforcements arrived to relieve the small band of defenders. "Right gallantly did he [Bramlette] and his comrades stand their ground and repulse the rebel charge," observed a correspondent to the *Frankfort Commonwealth*.[67] After two days (11–12 June) of fighting near Cynthiana, Kentucky, Burbridge's Union forces defeated Morgan, and the governor claimed peace in the state.

The Kentucky raid and Virginia's combat losses had not prevented Lincoln from being optimistic. Still, the summer curtain was about to go up on military campaigns. The president's endorsement of a constitutional amendment abolishing slavery would challenge governors seeking to reconcile this measure with the desire to conquer the Southern people. Disheartening news from the front might help swell Lincoln's opposition, and, as such, Democrats postponed their national convention from July until late August. Seymour was in favor of the move, much to the displeasure of the would-be candidate George B. McClellan. Attending a dedication ceremony at West Point to honor the Union's dead soldiers, Seymour had the chance to discuss the idea with McClellan. The commander confessed to his wife that he was not convinced by Seymour's reasoning to postpone the convention. Meanwhile, Grant moved out from Cold Harbor and began to reposition his massive army across the James River in a feat of military operations to move south of Richmond near Petersburg to begin his investment of the city.[68]

Lincoln's renomination encouraged dispirited governors facing enormous casualties, embittered antiwar dissidents, and a trickle of volunteers. Many chief executives stood by him, thinking he could bring them victory, others supported him, fearful that a change would weaken the Union. Voters needed to show confidence in their leaders and were willing to have Lincoln pull them along—so long as the journey ended in victory. Even in California, Low announced that "Mr. Lincoln was, and is, unquestionably the choice of the loyal masses."[69] Still, the euphoria of the Union Convention would pass, and events in the coming months would determine his future. The president recognized the significance of Northern support. The Union Party had decided that he at least was "not unworthy to remain" as president.[70] He compared the decision to the "story of an old Dutch farmer, who remarked to a companion once that 'it was not best to swap horses when crossing streams.'"[71] An unamused *Louisville Daily Journal* editor, however, remarked that Lincoln's metaphor reflected "Dutch obstinacy" and "blind pernacity," and "not a commendation of intelligent prudence." He continued, "It teaches under the garb of irony the folly of stubbornly holding on to the tail of the wrong horse," and the people had considered as much.[72]

Civil-Military Problems

Summer's arrival brought rumors of Vallandigham's reappearance in Ohio, which added to the already heightened fears of subversive activities in the midwestern states. Morton, Brough, and Yates headed the list of alarmed statesmen, and rightfully so. The gubernatorial triumvirate petitioned Lincoln, Stanton, as well as Heintzelman to have the Ohioan arrested again. But Lincoln and Stanton decided to leave the troublesome Copperhead alone. Perhaps by spewing his Radical jargon, they thought, the Ohioan might undermine his own following, and the Republicans could benefit at the polls.[73]

Governors meanwhile plodded through the civil-military problems associated with the enrollment of black soldiers. When Kentuckians failed to meet their quota with white volunteers, Burbridge began recruiting slaves. Bramlette reminded Stanton of their conversation when he was in Washington in March. The governor believed that he had convinced Lincoln to shelve slave enrollment, fearing that whites would stop volunteering if such enrollment preceded and arguing that he needed extra time. When provost marshals reported that most districts were deficient, Burbridge went about his business. Although the commander was sensitive to the delicate task of recruiting slaves and attempted to ensure that the laws were faithfully executed, abuses prevailed. Consequently, Bramlette arrested recruiting officers and expected Stanton to support him. The governor gave signs that he was cooperating with the military authorities in Kentucky, but the lack of white volunteers forced his hand, and he entrenched himself against Stanton. Although Unionists still supported the governor, he could not shake his critics or abandon his conservatism. Regardless of his loyalties, Bramlette governed a state that was plunging further into guerrilla warfare to combat the emerging status of blacks—free and slave.[74]

Kentucky problems aside, Lincoln had complications closer to home that June. Two days after formally accepting the nomination for the presidency, he conferred with Brough about Treasury Secretary Chase's recent resignation. The governor offered to intercede on the secretary's behalf, but Lincoln declined. "But this is the third time he [Chase] has thrown this [a resignation] at me," he scoffed at Brough, "and I do not think I am called on to continue to beg him to take it back, especially when the country would not go to destruction in consequence."[75] Wise to the larger political ripples, Brough reasoned with Lincoln. "This is not simply a personal matter," the governor stated, "the people will not understand it. They will insist that there is no longer harmony in the Councils of the nation, and that the retiracy [retirement?] of the Sec'y of the Treasury is a sure indication that the bottom is about to fall out. Therefore, to save the Country from this backset, if you will give me time, I think Ohio can close the breach and the world be none the wiser." Lincoln declined, however. "I know you doctored the matter up once," he acknowledged, "but on the whole, Brough, I reckon you had better let it alone this time."[76] Before he left, Brough asked Lincoln who he had settled on for Chase's replacement. Although he had someone in mind, Lincoln would not divulge his choice, thinking it better for Brough not to know. After all, Brough had "doctored it up" before conversing with Chase the month before and, together with some friends, talked him out of resigning. The old warhorse followed up a few weeks after the meeting with a letter to his colleague Brough. "Few things," he wrote, "in my public experience, have given me so much satisfaction, as your manifestations of sympathy and friendship." He acknowledged, "I have followed your counsel because I was sure it was the counsel of a patriot & a friend."[77] Brough was about to head for Stanton's office when Lincoln stopped him and urged him to keep the secret.[78]

Brough respected the president's confidence, and during his interview with Stanton that late afternoon he disclosed nothing. The following morning, the chief executive returned to the War Department and continued their discussion of military operations, manpower, and the current state of political affairs. When a messenger interrupted and delivered them each a note from Chase announcing his resignation, Stanton read his, placed the paper in his pocket, and slumped into his chair. Sensing his time had come to leave, Brough rose from his chair and stepped toward the door, until Stanton halted him. "For God's sake," he petitioned, "don't leave me yet."[79] Perhaps smirking, Brough responded, "I think you have quite as much as you can digest today." Startled, Stanton asked, "What do you refer to?" Brough came back, "I mean that little paper in your pocket." "What do you know of it?" Stanton asked. "Oh, I knew of it last night," he replied. "You did," said Stanton, "d—n you, and did not tell me of it? Is that being friendly?" Brough explained that he was sworn to secrecy, and when Stanton asked who would replace Chase, the governor responded it was Tod. "Then we are gone," Stanton gasped. Before he left, Brough gave Stanton a parting comforting assurance that Tod's appointment "*will never be accepted*." "Then," Stanton challenged Brough, "remember that I hold you personally responsible for the result."[80] The conversation was over, and Brough rode over to call upon Chase.[81]

To reward Ohioans for supporting him, Lincoln looked to one of their famous sons to replace Chase. He named Tod, a hard-money conservative opposed to Chase's proliferation of paper money to keep the economy steaming. Flattered by the offer, Tod, however, declined on account of failing health, surmising he would not make it through a Senate confirmation. After consoling Chase, the Ohio chief executive drove back to the White House to see Lincoln, who had second-guessed his decision, and later that evening received a note from Stanton who had learned of Tod's declination. "You may go where you please, Brough," the note read, "I am going to bed to sleep. *We are safe for another day*."[82] Brough returned to the White House the following day and was conversing with Lincoln over the appointment when a messenger entered the room and laid the note on the table with the name Fessenden on the upside. "There is your man," declared Brough confidently. Lincoln, however, contended that Maine's veteran senator would not accept the post. "The public will compel him to," Brough responded, and Lincoln accepted the governor's recommendation.[83] It might be the last time he offered Lincoln advice as governor. Weeks before, Brough had made it known that he would not seek reelection. His bulldog tenaciousness had endeared him to Lincoln, but it had cost him at home among his Ohio constituents. In the end, Lincoln turned to Fessenden, who, although unwilling, was more than qualified, having chaired the Senate Finance Committee. Given the recent snub by the Union Committee, which did not renominate Maine's Hamlin as vice president, it helped soothe injured feelings that the tiny New England state had not been left out in the cold.[84]

Washington's political machinations that spring accompanied the challenge to sustain the armies in the field. For all of their efforts, governors could not solve the problems produced by conscription, bounties, and mounting casualty lists. Although tens of thousands of veterans reenlisted, tens of thousands refused. Thus, the Union's superiority in numbers over the Confederacy was handicapped by an inability to deliver soldiers to the ranks. As battlefield reports poured into the statehouses, they withered the Northern spirit, and episodes of desperation appeared before governors. It was perhaps at this point in the war when Buckingham halted an executive meeting to see an "old and feeble woman dressed in simple mourning," who had been ushered into the room and allowed to explain the nature of her visit. Her only son, a private in the 14th Connecticut Infantry, had been killed in the recent action, she explained, leaving her with the grandson, and, as a remembrance of his duty, she wanted to pay for the cost of her son's rifle. "'John didn't have much to leave his boy besides a good name and a patriotic example,'" she spoke softly, "'but I want to get that rifle so that the boy can be reminded of his father while he is growing up.'" Moved by the woman's touching and fitting gesture, the governor refused her money, remarking that "he [the little boy] should have her son's rifle if he had to go in person to the regiment to get it." He then escorted her to the door, down the steps, and saw her off. "Gentleman," he said upon returning to his colleagues, "what are our labors and sacrifices compared to hers? The daily evidence I receive of the heroism of our Connecticut women, inspires me with confidence as nothing else could."[85]

Grant worked to earn Northern respect by defeating Lee, but his movements failed to reassure the people. Despite his urgency, it was the commander's perceived recklessness that drew spirited critiques from the press. The commander's ambitious strategy to exhaust the enemy at the front had emptied numerous regiments by sending thousands of casualties to the rear. Northerners were concerned that if he failed to bring Lee to surrender, they might lack the capacity to sustain his course much longer. Even the outgoing Chase penned in his diary in those early summer days the concern questioning "can we keep Grant & Sherman so furnished with men & means that they can inflict decisive blows on the rebellion?"[86] Only time would tell.

As June ended, members of the Thirty-eighth Congress prepared to close their legislative session and leave the capital city. The war appeared to move more swiftly in Washington than on the battlefield. Lincoln had achieved some success that kept his reelection hopes alive. Now came the time, according to one Indiana colonel, who wrote his wife from Huntsville, Alabama, the "iron must enter the soul of the North, as it has entered the South, before its wise purposes can be accomplished." Although he acknowledged that it had "given her sons to battle and poured her treasures into the Government chests," he declared, "the North has laid no sacrifices on the altar of Liberty commensurate with the magnitude of the interests [involved]."[87] Now was the truest test of the Union's endurance, even if it took all summer.

It was during these long days, heavy-laden with frustration, that Morton asked Fletcher to meet him at the Capitol. The chief executive appeared unusually downtrodden and exhausted. The "iron" had left his soul, and gone too was his fortitude. He confided that "pecuniary difficulties" in the coming "canvass for Governor would cost him largely & he could not bear the expense." Days before, Carrington had reported that some 30,000 Indianans had reputedly aligned with a secret Copperhead society and were scheming to take over the state government. Thinking he might save the state the humiliation, Morton decided to resign. His wife had already "given up her carriage & horses" he told Fletcher, and "his house was visited by soldiers & soldiers wives & childrin [sic] evry [sic] whom he could not turn off empty & c." The governor's decision impressed his friend, as did his charity. Fletcher, however, had no doubt it was the people's duty to raise the funds for Morton's campaign, and made it his purpose to keep him in office. Fletcher himself pledged a large sum to the campaign, concluding that Morton's services "cant be dispensed with."[88]

CHAPTER EIGHTEEN

Revolutions Never Go Backward

Traveling between Washington and Indianapolis, visiting Indiana camps along the way, Morton became depressed, reflecting the exasperation of carrying on a war from the rear without much progress at the front. Other than the long casualty lists and the endless bickering with opponents, Morton had little to show for his efforts. Reading the local newspapers, he, like many of his gubernatorial colleagues, concluded that Grant and Sherman's persistent attempt to pin down Lee and Johnston's armies would take all summer. This meant more casualties arriving in an already overflowing series of ill-equipped hospitals, which would undermine volunteering. The fall election would depend on how satisfied Northerners were with Lincoln and Grant's handling of the war. Congress adjourned in July, and Lincoln turned his attention away from politics to campaigns. The pressing concern for Washingtonians was Confederate General Jubal Early's advance down the valley from Winchester toward Harpers Ferry. Curtin, Bradford, and Parker feared the army would attack the Capitol. After New Market, Halleck reassigned Sigel to defend Harpers Ferry and placed David Hunter in charge of the Union's valley forces. Confederates wasted no time in pouncing on the German commander, driving him across the Potomac River and passing into Maryland.[1]

The Late National Humiliation

Early's crossing of the Potomac River squelched Independence Day celebrations. His approach threw Marylanders, Pennsylvanians, and Washingtonians into what Bates described as a "ludicrous terror." The *Washington Daily National Intelligencer* editor was more caustic, referring to the raid as the "late national humiliation." Stanton wired Seymour and Curtin for 24,000 militia and requested 4,000 men from Massachusetts to garrison fortifications around Washington. Cannon appealed to his Delawareans to provide mounted support for protection. A threatened capital city prompted Morton and Andrew to travel to Washington to confer over the 100-day men. Unable to make it to Washington, Brough wired in from the Continental

Hotel in Philadelphia that he had 10,000 men ready for this service, but feared he might have to turn them away unless the administration would accept them. Stanton responded that Seymour and Andrew were complying "handsomely" with their requisition for troops and wanted to avoid the shame of having "a State Executive disown the national service and require his troops to be sworn into the State service to repel and invasion."[2] To offset the deficiencies caused by sending troops to Washington, Seymour called upon New Yorkers to join the state militia.[3]

On 9 July, just a few miles southeast of Frederick, Maryland, along the Monocacy River, a small Federal army engaged Early's significantly larger force of Confederates. Although the one-day's fighting stalled the commander's advance, Early pressed on toward Washington. The panic forced Lincoln to return to the White House from the Soldiers' Home. Stanton called for added assistance, but Copperheads preoccupied western governors. Bramlette combated guerrilla problems and proposed to Stanton that he be allowed to organize a Kentucky state force similar to that in Missouri. Instead, Lincoln proclaimed martial law in Kentucky to help restore the peace and aid Burbridge in his hunt for guerrillas. Stanton was delighted by these measures, especially with state elections just weeks away.[4]

The Confederate raid into Maryland once again awakened Northerners to action, but governors had a difficult time channeling it into the ranks. Convincing men to volunteer for Grant's bludgeoned regiments in Virginia was difficult. They fared no better in recruiting for regiments in Georgia suffering the summer heat. Defending the nation's capital with short-term troops, however, would be easier, and governors demanded that their citizens rally to protect Washington. Cony proclaimed that the capital was in danger and that it was time to invite every Maine citizen to constitute himself a recruiting officer. "As the fathers of the Revolutionary days 'left the plow in the furrow,'" he argued, now it was time for their sons to "leave the grass in the swath, to repel the invasion of our soil."[5] Given the hostile attitude toward conscription, Cony needed such an invasion to coerce them into believing the government needed their services.[6]

Early, however, overplayed his hand in crossing into Maryland, as Federals turned his forces away and forced them to skirmish their way back toward Leesburg, where they crossed back into Virginia. Lincoln was furious that the commander escaped into the Shenandoah Valley. Early's raid, however, did bring some volunteers into recruiting stations, but once the scare had ended, Stanton ordered governors to turn them away. Lincoln was preparing a new call for twelve-month men and it would conflict with his effort to raise long-term volunteers. Yet some governors took advantage of these short-term enlistments. Cony needed soldiers for coastal defense, especially at Fort Popham on the mouth of the Kennebec River, where a small raiding party threatened its garrison. Stanton granted Cony's request, and the governor invited Lincoln to join the congressional delegation visiting the state to inspect Maine's fortifications, but the president declined.[7]

Three thousand miles west, Gibbs also worried about his Oregon coast, fearing Confederates might strike at the mouth of the Columbia River. Lincoln had sent General Irvin McDowell to manage affairs in the Department of the Pacific and to keep the peace among miners, Indians, and Californians. The governor also cooperated with General Benjamin Alvord in patrolling the Oregon Trail, and drew Oregon's Loyal Leagues to combat the few but vocal Copperheads protesting Lincoln's war polices. In writing to Yates, his longtime friend from his Illinois days, Oregonian Unionist David Newsom put western politics in perspective for the governor. "We of Oregon cannot fight for our good old Government," he acknowledged, "but we can speak & write, and send large contributions to the Sanitary & Christian Commission in the U.S. and thereby show our hearts are in the *right place*." He continued, "We have here some base Copperheads who hurrah for Jeff & his Bogus Confederacy," but "under the Loyal Leagues of Oregon, our state is safe, and she stands forth with her Loyal Sisters, in moral power & political Union." Confident in the Republican Party's success, Newsom assured Yates that Oregon was "safe for *Honest Abe*, at the ensuing election." He maintained, "We never can exist, as a happy nation—half free & half slave. Under our worthy President, we hope to reconstruct & mould [sic] a more perfect form of Government that shall *endure*."[8]

Many Northern governors had long concluded that the unnatural tie between slavery and freedom must end. Even Bradford, a slave owner himself, held conflicting views on the subject. Two years before he had freed Marylander Samuel Green, a black minister imprisoned in 1857 for possessing a copy of *Uncle Tom's Cabin* and for his alleged involvement with the Underground Railroad. The proximity of the governor's home to the enemy line did not help his circumstances. When Harry Gilmor's Confederate raiders crossed the Potomac and plundered Maryland just outside Baltimore, the commander also sent a small detail to destroy the governor's home. On the morning of 11 July, soldiers escorted Bradford's wife and family outside, where they watched Confederates ignite the fire. A Confederate officer read an order from General Bradley Johnson ordering the house to be razed in retaliation for the burning of Virginia governor John Letcher's home. Within minutes, the governor's residence was engulfed in flames, destroying all its valuables, including important state papers. The irony of losing his home to those supportive of slavery was not lost on the governor, who was left on his own to protect loyal Marylanders against marauders.[9]

By the end of the second week in July, governors expected Lincoln to call for additional troops, especially since it appeared as though more troops were leaving the ranks than entering them. The recent raid on Washington and the escalating number of soldiers away on leave left him no choice. He needed troops not only for the Georgia and Virginia theaters, but also to maintain Southern occupation and protect hundreds of miles of supply lines. Several governors were privy to the call, days before it went over the wires. They raised concerns about how the War Department would handle bounty jumpers, conscripts, and substitutes that were in line to replace thousands of veterans who did not reenlist. Soldiers regarded many of these newcomers with contempt, and governors sought to reduce the corruption that came with filling the previous year's call. Despite the call's unpopularity, Lincoln called for 500,000 volunteers on 18 July. He made a "bold stroke," said Noah Brooks, and took the people at their word "right in the face of a general election."[10]

Lincoln gave governors until 4 September to meet their quotas, but the longer commanders waited for men, the greater the risk to the army. Leaders complained that replacing men leaving the field when their enlistments ran out was too slow. Governors understood this, and dispatched medical inspectors and recruiting agents armed with bounty dollars to the camps to bolster reenlistment before soldiers mustered out. Troop needs stressed Sherman, who failed to understand the difficulties at home and unwisely antagonized those supplying the troops. Minnesota governor Miller supported Sherman, but not the commander's attitude about the draft, and not in the matter of state care for soldiers. The governor considered the draft "deeply humiliating" and in his message to the Minnesota legislature urged his assemblymen to attach stiff penalties to desertion. When Sherman refused a railroad pass for a state medical inspector, Miller took offense and explained that his efforts were designed to assist the commander by attending to soldier welfare. Sherman failed to see this, and the two men disputed over civil-military priorities.[11]

Falling behind in his quota, Cannon called Delaware legislators into special session to provide bounties to assist him. Thomas F. Bayard, supposed member of the Knights of the Golden Circle, however, worked against him in carrying on "this great John Brown raid—sometimes called in mockery, 'a war for the Union.'"[12] Bayard urged representative James M. Williams to use his influence to defeat Cannon's measure, arguing that what was once a "wise, simple, easy course of action marked out for us in this State at the very beginning of this dreadful war," had gone bust. "The insolence of this so-called 'Governor'," he fumed, "a wretch holding a place obtained by fraud, [preying] and military force," had presumed "to call upon the Legislative majority of State-Rights Peace Democrats to vote monies to be expended under *his* direction to raise troops, who are first, to be used to re-elect Lincoln, and then to spread new fury and devastation among Southern homes."[13] He protested, "For God's sake, let Delaware men consider that the negro substitutes they may furnish will be their guards at the polls—and their jailers in Bastiles [sic]." Bayard's advice was, "Do not give a dollar toward's [sic] Cannon's scheme."[14] Cannon, however, used his July message to convince representatives to accept black enlistments to overcome the state's 3,000-man shortfall. For all his efforts in complying with the national government, the governor's reputation suffered. "No one has contributed so much as he has done," declared the *House Journal*, "to the unjust and cruel oppression of the people of the State." Because Cannon appealed to federal power, critics charged that he had "caused a majority of the legal voters of this State to be deprived by military force of the enjoyment of their constitutional rights as electors ... has caused fathers and mothers, wives and children, relatives and friends, to shed tears of bitterness on account of the wrongs inflicted through his agency."[15] When the assembly adjourned on 12 August, Cannon had failed to convince legislators to accept black enlistment. The legislators continued to characterize blacks as "little elevated above savage tribes."[16]

Curtin and Bradford used the late emergency as justification to position short-term troops along the Pennsylvania-Maryland border to deter future invasions. Lincoln refused this deployment, and Curtin appealed to his legislature to provide for such a force, despite the expense. Stanton had allowed Cony to raise men for special service to fortify the Maine coast, but did not allow these men to count toward the recent call. Once the danger had passed, he ordered Cony to release them. Stanton left it up to the governor to decide whether to inform his constituents "that this pitiful favor" had been refused to them or to appeal to "their patriotism and paramount interest in the national existence to answer the President's call and afford him the means to put an end to the war that has cost them so much blood and so much treasure."[17] For the moment, it appeared that Lincoln's objectives remained in Virginia and on Lee's army. Governors continued to stoke the patriotic fires to meet Lincoln's call, but reports from the field countered enthusiasm. When Early's forces turned northward and pinned down the Federals that pursued him up the valley, it resulted in defeat at the battle of Kernstown on 24 July. The Federals under General George Crook retreated back through Winchester in disgrace. Inspired by the victory and hoping to draw forces back down the valley, Early dispatched John McCausland to cross the Potomac and enter Maryland. By late July, the cavalrymen entered Chambersburg, Pennsylvania, razed the town, and moved on to destroy other towns. Lincoln's decision disallowing a force on the Pennsylvania-Maryland border infuriated Curtin and Bradford.[18]

The governors' efforts were further weakened by a national drought brought on by the summer heat, which deepened the afflictions of many Northern communities forced to give up farmers for the draft. Union momentum had stalled, and it discouraged volunteering. The crisis especially plagued midwesterners, as Copperheads took advantage of conditions by encouraging military-age men to man their farms and fields instead of enlisting. Whether or not the disaffection was genuine was not as significant as the fuss opponents made over Republican leadership in the midwestern states. Rumors spread that conspirators plotted a counterrevolution for 20 July, in which armed uprisings were to commence in Indiana, Ohio, Missouri, and Illinois. Leaders had allegedly schemed to depose the current governors and replace them with provisional chief executives, who, with the aid of the Sons of Liberty, would make way for the new Northwestern Confederacy. Led by Indianans Harrison H. Dodd, William A. Bowles, Lambdin P. Milligan, and Andrew Humphreys, the plan included the release of Confederate prisoners at Rock Island, Cincinnati, Springfield, Chicago, and Indianapolis. They would arm these prisoners and send them to Indianapolis and Springfield to establish the beachheads of their new confederacy. Jefferson Davis was supposedly behind the plot, hatched in the spring, and had enlisted commissioners to visit Canada. There they met with Vallandigham, who assisted them in their efforts to negotiate for peace with Horace Greeley, who had boomeranged Lincoln into agreeing to the overture.[19]

Governors devoted much attention to such threats and worked with commanders and provost marshals to unmask the conspirators and minimize the declining morale in the local communities. They made use of spies to gather intelligence to diffuse the conspiracy before it got started. At one point, Morton stunned one of his many visitors by asking if he knew of such activities to overtake the administrations across the midwestern states. When the visitor denied having any knowledge of any such information, the governor pulled a series of letters from his desk drawer and read the report of a meeting at which this person had made a speech denouncing the governor. "The old man sank into a chair and became as pale as death," and left the room.[20] There was ample political currency to be made from the affair, and Morton's exposure of such conspirators helped Lincoln's campaign. It identified treason within the Democratic Party and went a long way to convince Northern voters that Lincoln's reelection would end such groups. To squelch his Illinois desperados, Yates requested that Stanton send him a district commander to handle these affairs and to keep soldiers home long enough to vote. Colonel Edward Prince offered the governor a solution for dealing with traitors. The commander implored Yates to "banish every man woman & child beyond the limits of the U.S. whose sympathies are not with the United States and whose influence may in any way endanger the peace and safety of the country."[21] Evidence from Morton and Yates disclosing the subversive activities influenced Stanton that there was something to the conspiracy. The secretary turned the matter over to Judge Advocate General Joseph Holt, a celebrated Kentucky lawyer. The investigation was a tall order, with leads that spread across hundreds of miles. Yet, given the coming election, revelations of such plots helped to secure Republican victories in national and state contests. Thus, to make an example of these secret operatives, Morton and Yates charged these societies with treason, urged the arrest of their members, and assisted in hunting them down.[22]

After all the kitchen gossip, barn meetings, and backwoods drilling, no insurrection came to pass on 20 July. In the meantime, Morton wanted Stanton to correct abuses caused by agents from eastern states who were enticing Kentucky and Tennessee blacks to travel back east and enlist as substitutes. Congressmen had recently repealed the commutation clause of the Conscription Act, and the governor sought redress. Attuned to such illegalities, John Murray Forbes encouraged Andrew not to "let the *sharks* go down into the rebel states—such men would discredit our whole plan."[23] Andrew, however, released agents to many Southern states, which drew spirited responses from commanders as well as other governors. Sherman aired his views to Massachusetts agent John A. Spooner in late July. Not only was the commander opposed to the law that allowed Spooner to be in the South, but he regarded these profiteering agents as "a nuisance." Besides, he argued, the "duty of citizens to fight for their country is too sacred ... to be peddled off by buying up the refuse of other States." This practice was "unjust to the Soldiers and Volunteers who are fighting," he added, because the "negro is in a transition state and is not the equal of the white man."[24] What made matters worse for Andrew was not only had his search for recruits outside the state spiraled out of control, but also recruitment for his black regiments had degenerated into an ugly hunt for former slaves. "The whole system is damnable," wrote close friend and former aide Albert G. Browne Jr., who was in Hilton Head, South Carolina, on assignment from the Treasury Department. "I can conceive nothing worse on the coast of Africa."[25] He went on, "These men have been hunted like wild beasts and ruthlessly dragged from their families." And, worse, they received only a portion of their promised money.[26]

The war moved slowly in the summer, and Northerners had difficulty in identifying if Union prospects were improving. Even when newspapers reported victory, casualty lists eclipsed the jubilation. Sherman and Grant's armies appeared the focus of the press, and Northerners paid close attention to their campaigns. Federals besieging Petersburg had tried everything to pry Lee from his lines, but they met with little success, and correspondents ensured that rank-and-file frustration made its way home. In the early morning hours of 30 July, an explosion along the Union siege lines at Petersburg failed to give Federals the advantage they expected. Instead, Confederates slaughtered over 4,000 Union soldiers. The Battle of the Crater, as it was aptly named, for the crater-sized hole it left in the earth, was one of the most appalling days of the entire conflict. "It was the saddest affair I have witnessed in this war," Grant wired Halleck shortly afterward.[27] Critics used the episode to undermine Grant's leadership and to spread destructive rumors about the hypocrisy of using blacks in the field. Part of the plan relied on using General Edward Ferrero's all-black division to lead the assault, but Meade replaced them, fearing that if the operation failed, Confederates would murder these troops, and the political fallout would benefit Democrats in November. Columnists turned their attacks on Andrew for befriending blacks and for obtaining equal pay for them. The previous month, Congress provided equal pay to black soldiers and remedial back pay for the months of inferior compensation. "Many of your beloved brethren in color,—I mean the niggers, for I believe you are half nigger your self[,]—have seriously died [at the Crater] before Petersburg," wrote a contemptuous Northerner to Andrew.[28]

News of the Crater hollowed out the Northern spirit. Althea Cooper's husband Corporal Abram Nash Cooper of the 90th Pennsylvania had been missing for weeks, prompting her to petition Curtin to ascertain his fate. "I have no means to support myself and child," she pleaded to Curtin, "and would earnestly pray your early attention."[29] Such deprivations weighed heavily on governors. Frustrated by his state's financial despondency and the lack of legislative support in recruiting, Gilmore waited for news from Virginia. His New Hampshire boys were in the thick of the fighting at Petersburg, and he needed some positive news to report to his constituents contemplating volunteering. The governor found some consolation when two captured Confederate flags arrived in Concord. "These trophies," wrote Colonel Aaron F. Stevens to Gilmore, "are entrusted to your care as mementoes of the gallantry of the young men who took them," as a memorial to their "gallantry and success."[30]

Pressing Demands of War

August did "not open cheerfully," Noah Brooks observed.[31] While Radicals and peace advocates spouted rhetoric about how to the end the war and handle Reconstruction, governors attended to the soldiers. The promise of the spring had dissipated, and from the state capitols, the war appeared to be far from over. There was nothing left in Lincoln's arsenal to end the war except to continue to replenish the armies without breaking Northern morale. Governors had instigated changing the Union's war aims precisely because they understood that the longer the conflict endured, the heavier the toll at home. Lincoln knew this, but by the summer, he seemed powerless. The war had become as much a contest to endure difficulties at home as it was to defeat the enemy on the battlefield. The home struggle belonged to governors, who continued to manage the states' pressing demands while fulfilling their national obligations and worrying over elections.

From the latest dispatches, the conflict was shaping up to be a series of Federal sieges, guerrilla raids, and Copperhead antics. Governors shared Welles's fears that the Petersburg failure and Chambersburg raid had emboldened Confederates to harass the Northern frontiers. The draft looming in early September coincided with elections in Vermont and Maine, and governors worried that raids would undercut volunteering and political support. Even when men did enlist, paymasters could not pay the volunteers until a company organization was complete. In August Brough urged Stanton to modify this order. "You want men," he stated. "We want to avoid troubles that look formidable in enforcing the draft." He advised that while it might be more labor to make some adjustments, the end would justify the means.[32] Stanton, however, denied Brough's request. Commanders appreciated Stanton's close adherence to regulations, but not at the expense of causing delays, and appreciated chief executives who found ways around Stanton. "Thank Heaven for Governors who have straight and unyielding spinal columns," remarked the editor of the *Iowa Daily State Register*.[33]

Seymour had considerable experience in getting around Stanton. He shared Brough's concern over the financial hardships that soldier pay produced. Besides complaining that quotas assigned to New York were much larger than those demanded from other Atlantic states, the governor argued that in some districts, such as Brooklyn, there were excessive numbers of women and aliens because they had been drawn there for work. He complained that the draft in New York City created a "terrible affliction," as a majority of inhabitants lived entirely on daily wages. These residents must receive wages "with regularity to enable them to give food, fuel, and shelter to the families." The soldiers' pay was not conducive to their lifestyles. Members of the New York County Union Central Committee, who went to Washington, reinforced the governor's sentiments. Despite their best efforts, however, Fry and Stanton failed to appease Seymour.[34]

That summer and fall elections that still hung in the balance inspired some guerrilla bands to become more active. Yet in Missouri and parts of Midwest, guerrilla warfare prevailed year-round. "This condition of things," Missouri governor Hall wrote Judge Advocate General Holt, "affords another of the ever-multiplying evidences of the utter demoralization of this rebellion and of those supporting and sympathizing with it."[35] Yates informed Stanton that serious disturbances had broken out in Fayette and Montgomery, and that unless the military authorities came to his aid, civil war would "soon be inaugurated in that State."[36] The chief executive urged Stanton to make Illinois a military district and to send troops to suppress the uprising. Yates, no doubt, believed that failure to control Illinois's military affairs would ruin his bid for the U.S. Senate. "Universal dissatisfaction exists," he wired Lincoln, "at the threatened draft, under these circumstances."[37] Morton's bid for reelection gave Indiana Copperheads a new lease on life. In a series of statewide debates against Democratic opponent Joseph E. McDonald, the governor became an open target for assailants. Morton worried about carrying Indiana for the Union ticket and emphasized to Lincoln that "the opposition intend to fight with a desperation and bitterness unparalleled in the history of political warfare."[38] Hiram S. Turnley, an Indiana politician who helped nominate Lincoln in 1860, echoed the sentiment, flatly warning Lincoln that if voters failed to elect Morton and carry the state for Lincoln in November, "it will be your fault, it can be looked upon in no other light."[39]

Lincoln understood the politics of war unraveling before him that summer, and he made some command changes to minimize the political fallout. To redeem the Federal advantage in the Shenandoah Valley, he turned to Sheridan and ordered him to protect the region and clear it of Confederate sympathizers. The Federals bought some time and good fortune when Admiral David Farragut forced the surrender of Fort Gaines in Mobile Bay, which helped Grant's campaign. The politics of Reconstruction, however, also needed Lincoln's visible hand. He had come under attack for his pocket veto of the Wade-Davis Bill, which outlined a Radical Reconstruction plan. Republican congressmen Richard Wade and Henry Winter Davis authored a manifesto that appeared in the papers and claimed that Lincoln's desire to handle Reconstruction solely from the White House blinded him from cooperating. Federals had humiliated themselves at Petersburg and by allowing Confederate raids in Pennsylvania and Maryland. Indications prevailed that Lincoln's nomination had been premature.[40]

Lincoln had already concluded that he needed to be more involved. He responded to former governor Randall, who encouraged him to take a vacation, that it would do him no good. His thoughts about the present times would follow him wherever he went. "I cannot but feel that the weal or woe of this great nation will be decided in the approaching canvas," he responded.[41] At the moment, the woe came not only from the front lines, but also from the rear. If states had to resort to a draft just before elections, it would not bode well for governors. Halleck informed Grant that "there was scarcely nothing coming in under the President's call," and he feared the commander would be asked to send troops from his front to enforce the draft. "I have not been a believer in most of the plots, secret societies, &c., of which so many pretended discoveries," he told Grant, "but the people in many parts of the North and West now talk openly and boldly of resisting the draft, and it is believed that the leaders of the peace branch of the Democratic Party are doing all in their power to bring about this result."[42] Grant, however, was undeterred. To help quiet the home front, the commander advised Lincoln to rely on governors for militia to prevent taking men from Virginia or Georgia during the height of their campaigns. Governors had proposed this in the spring, and while thousands of short-term men had come forward to protect the home front, Stanton turned them away. Nonetheless, chief executives could not keep pace with Grant and Sherman's dangerously ambitious offensives.[43]

By the third week of August, the political canvass had demoralized Lincoln. Perhaps persuaded by Weed's estrangement from him, the president discussed the New York election with Congressman Reuben Fenton, who was running against Seymour. Reared in a small town on the border of New York and Pennsylvania, Fenton was a founding member of the state's Republican Party, a seasoned political veteran, and a senior member of Congress. Although the New York Convention was two weeks away, Fenton was still the Union Party's frontrunner to oust Seymour in the North's most important race. "You will have a hard fight," confided Lincoln, but "I am very desirous that you should win the battle." He stated that "New York should be on our side by honest possession," but "[t]here is some trouble among our folks over there, which we must try and manage." The president encouraged Fenton to enlist the counsel and cooperation of the party leaders to fix matters in New York to secure victory in November. Many New Yorkers had decided Lincoln would lose the election based on the mood of their countrymen and the press that fed them. Horace Greeley, who prided himself on reflecting the Northern pulse, wrote to George Opdyke that Lincoln was already beaten. "He cannot be elected," wrote the *New York Tribune* editor on 18 August, "and we must have another ticket to save us from utter overthrow."[44] In the next days, Lincoln convened his cabinet and presented members with a memo they were to sign without reading. The "Blind Memorandum," as it was known, revealed that the president expected defeat in the coming election, and that, in such an event, it would be his duty to cooperate with the president-elect. For the moment, he put the document in his desk.[45]

Northern Political Weathervane

The war's weathervane twirled back and forth, and governors were caught in the political crosswinds. Some governors wired Stanton that war-weary Northerners were so desperate to escape the draft that they abandoned their homes and headed north or west. Lewis had problems resulting from citizens who left the state under the guise of "visiting," and unless something was done, he argued, many Wisconsin towns would be nearly devoid of a male population of military age. Citizens throughout the state inundated the governor with complaints, lamenting their various problems. "Are there no means for arresting this stampede from our State?" wrote Dr. Erastus B. Wolcott to Lewis. Worse yet, fumed Wolcott, "thousands of those shameless vagabonds are passing through our State from Minnesota, the number being swelled by at least as many more on their way through."[46] Wrote Edward N. Brodhead to Lewis, "Our State and the State of Minnesota are being depopulated of men liable to the draft," and that while leaving the state would surely kill the draft, what was worse was that these men would be back in time to vote.[47]

Lincoln's presidency suffered from draft inequities, desertions, guerrilla raids, but, most important, from the inability to overcome Northern exhaustion associated with casualties. He needed a victory that harpooned the Confederate war effort and gave evidence to citizens that the end was in sight. Meanwhile, party leaders prepared for the worst—defeat at the polls. As stenographers busied themselves transmitting cables between statehouses and the War Department over the draft, some twenty-five Radical Republicans assembled at the home of George Opdyke on 19 August to discuss future prospects. They needed to gauge the sentiment of the people over whether to call for a new convention in September "to concentrate the union strength on some candidate who commands the confidence of the country, even by a new nomination if necessary."[48] New York's journalistic intelligentsia, Horace Greeley, Theodore Tilton, and Parke Godwin, had grown frustrated, instigated the meeting, and invited Andrew to attend. The "national nervousness" over Lincoln's chances concerned the governor, who had kept in touch with the New Yorkers in previous months about the coming election. Indeed, just the week before, Andrew invited Seymour to discuss the political future and asked the New Yorker "whether we might not unite to strengthen the arms of our National power." Seymour agreed to the meeting, came to Boston, but after two hours the stalwart governors failed to unite on any point other than the fact that they both held strong convictions, and Seymour returned to Albany.[49]

The editors drafted a series of questions to governors soliciting their opinions on whether Lincoln would carry their states and if he should remain on the ticket. Members agreed to reconvene after the Democratic

Convention gathered in Chicago and nominated a candidate. On 31 August, the delegates chose McClellan over Thomas Seymour, former governor of Connecticut, and cousin to Horatio Seymour, the Convention's president and the governor of New York. There was some talk of a secret movement by Washington's leading Democrats to nominate Brough, though nothing came of it. The platform spoke to the president's usurpation and abuse of power and pledged constituents to uphold the Federal Union under the Constitution as it was. Still, it reflected the interests of the few rather than the many, as most Democrats supported ending the war on the battlefield, however unpopular they claimed Lincoln was. It was clear that supporters of both Seymours had wanted to use the New York governor against McClellan as a candidate, but he was not willing to be used as a political pawn. The New York chief executive "blows hot & cold," declared the *New York World* editor, and "professes not to be a candidate *& will be none if I can help it*."[50] Having lost on the first ballot to the Peace Democrats lining up behind McClellan, Seymour was disappointed. After all, he made it known at the convention that he was not "unwilling to be drafted as the compromise candidate" between the Peace and War factions.[51]

When the New York journalists met again on 30 August, they met at David Dudley Field's New York City home. Sumner could not attend this meeting, but made his thoughts known to Andrew, who did. Sumner believed the Republican Convention was premature, "ill-considered & unreasonable." He argued that, "The country needs a maturer birth," and saw "no way of meeting the difficulties from the candidacy of Mr. Lincoln, *unless he withdraws patriotically & kindly, so as to leave no breach in the party*."[52] Armed with these sentiments, members wired the governors the circular of questions and sent a delegation to Washington to request that Lincoln withdraw his candidacy. In responding to the missive, Cannon replied that Lincoln would carry Delaware. Although a month ago "Mr. Lincoln's re-election would have been an improbability—perhaps an impossibility," wrote Cannon, and that "even now, the true interests of the Country would be better served by an abler and more vigorous administration, guided by the counsels of wiser and better," but now "the dissatisfaction and the despondency ... have been changed into acquiescence."[53] He told Greeley, "The settled determination seems to be to accept Mr. Lincoln with all his faults, real or supposed."[54] Cannon's letter spoke to the party and the cause more than to Lincoln's fitness for the post, and he pledged to work for the success of both. Besides, he expected divisions among Democrats to work in his favor.[55]

Gilmore too believed in the cause, but recent events left him indignant. The legislature had failed to settle the state's military and financial affairs, and the recent call left him without means to assist the New Hampshire soldiers. Moreover, Lincoln's management had not impressed him. "He has disappointed the expectations of the people and has no hold on their affections," he argued. "We shall probably carry New Hampshire for the Union candidate, whoever he may be," he added, "but in my own opinion it would have been wisdom to have delayed our nomination and finally put some other man in the field." He remarked, "We could make a [better] fight on Johnson than we can on Lincoln, but Salmon P. Chase or Charles Francis Adams, John A. Dix, or even Daniel S. Dickinson would be better yet." He advised, "If Frémont and Lincoln could be induced to *withdraw* and a new candidate be put up I should most heartily endorse the movement." He declared, "We are contending on principles, and my objection to Abraham Lincoln is that he has not run the machine according to God's time-table as I try to run my railroads." He concluded, "We want a President who will sacrifice every-thing to permanent, glorious and regenerated Union."[56]

Blair had just returned to Michigan from the front, and he carried home the frustrations of his soldiers. Despite military setbacks, he responded that the Republican Party would carry Lincoln to victory. The governor was not a Lincoln man and "regretted his nomination at Baltimore," but he was "sure that any attempt now to substitute another candidate would result in disaster."[57] The governor was equally blunt about the election with his close friend Chandler. "Of course we shall forget all causes of discontent and shutting our eyes to all faults," he allowed. "Go in for Abraham with might & main."[58]

Pennsylvania governor Curtin was in Saratoga Springs convalescing when his letter arrived. Citing state problems as evidence of divisions caused by Lincoln's candidacy, he believed Lincoln would lose. The governor was physically worn down, and the struggle to stay on top of his gubernatorial responsibilities fatigued him. Just weeks before he had confided to Eli Slifer that "altho [sic] fighting hard [,] my heart is not on the office."[59] Cony of Maine wrote from Augusta that any change would acknowledge a "weakness not existing," that it was "ill advised," and would prove "fatal in its consequences."[60] Up for reelection in September, Smith replied from Brattleboro that "it would be extremely prejudicial to the Union cause to attempt" any change. Vermonters would stand by the president. Having polled some prominent Rhodes Islanders, Smith responded that, although he was on board with the current administration, some changes would have to be made in the provost marshal's policy and "proper manifestations of respect to state rights."⁶¹ Ohio's Brough responded that he not only "regarded the election of Lincoln as a *probability*," he was "satisfied that unity and co-operation in the Union element can easily make it a *certainty*."⁶²

Andrew was more acerbic. Lincoln's nomination had been a mistake in his view, but the timing for a change was wrong. In his view, Lincoln lacked the qualities of leadership that were "a gift of God and not a device of man." He remarked, "Without this, his other qualities, as an able and devoted magistrate and most estimable citizen, leave it necessary for us to make a certain allowance for a measure of success which, under the more magnetic influence of a positive man, of clear purpose and more prophetic nature would be surely ours." Nonetheless, he declared, "Massachusetts will vote for the Union Cause at all events, and will support Mr. Lincoln so long as he remains its candidate."⁶³

"In my judgment," Lewis declared from Madison, Wisconsin, voters would give Lincoln a large majority, and "the interests of the Union party, the honor of the Nation and the good of Mankind, demand that Mr Lincoln should be sustained and re-elected."⁶⁴ Stone had recently returned to Des Moines after visiting the troops in the western armies. Discussions with Iowa soldiers and prominent citizens convinced the governor that Lincoln would carry the state, not because of his popularity, but because the people were "fully impressed ... with the mighty issues at stake and the disastrous consequences which would inevitably result from in his defeat." He declared, "No well informed person thinks otherwise."⁶⁵ Boreman approved of Lincoln's candidacy, arguing that West Virginians would regard a change as "an evidence of the weakness of our cause," and would contribute to the defeat of any such replacement. It was time to support Lincoln as if he were the "strongest man in the party, (as I believe he is)."⁶⁶ Miller agreed, and argued that Minnesotans would consider that a change of men would be seen as a "confession of weakness, as would chill the Union masses, encourage the opposition, and result in disaster."⁶⁷ Although he could think of several persons more imminently qualified than Lincoln, Connecticut's Buckingham too allowed that it was "too late to talk about another candidate with hope of success for the Union cause."⁶⁸

Conspicuously absent in his reply was New Jersey's Parker, who had confided to John Danforth of Connecticut that he did not answer because the public sentiment had not fully developed to enable him to form a decided opinion. By July, however, he had, and he was in favor of McClellan, had "always considered him a patriot," and hoped he received the nomination. The press printed the correspondence that clearly identified Parker as a McClellan man and undermined the governor's credibility among Republicans and some soldiers. He favored the commander's conservatism and believed him to be the most fit and available candidate.[69]

The recent communications inspired Andrew to enlist Yates, Brough, Morton, and other western governors to meet in Washington to discuss the "present attitude of our public affairs with the President." Andrew argued, "It seems to me of the first importance that the President should be rescued from the influences which threaten him," and "I want the President to take hold of his occasion, and really lead, as he might, the country, by exhibiting, in the person of the man who wields its highest powers, a genuine representative of democratic instincts and principles."[70] Meanwhile, Andrew wrote Frank Howe of his plans to go to Washington, but he wanted a meeting with new the chairman of the Republican National Committee, Henry Raymond, and told this to Morgan when passing through New York. "We have concluded that instead of thinking it possible to get another candidate," he wrote Howe, "we must make Lincoln pull himself in the right direction, do it *now*, do it vigorously and put all nonsense, & all fears behind him."[71]

By the time Yates received his letter from New York he had finally come full circle on Lincoln, perhaps thinking he could ride his coattails to the Senate. In the previous year he had privately denounced him, but "publicly endorsed the Union."[72] By the spring of 1864, he had even endorsed Lincoln's Reconstruction policies. But the president's pocket veto of the Wade-Davis Bill in the summer prompted Yates to carp against him, and, thinking he was on the way out of office and needing to salvage his own political aspirations to be senator, he joined those who desired a substitution for the White House. Yet, when he received Greeley's letter, he informed the New Yorkers there was no other man but Lincoln. "The substitution of another man at this late day," he contended, "would be disastrous in the highest degree."[73] He concluded, "It is too late to change now. The masses of the Union Party and the Western Army would not fall into line." Citing a biblical reference, he reminded them of Lot's wife. "She looked back from behind him," he declared, "and she became a pillar of salt." He emphasized, "Be not afraid that Mr. Lincoln has required the abandonment of slavery as the basis of a proposition from the rebels." He declared, "'Revolutions never go backward.' Let our motto be that of Mr. Webster—a little changed, 'Not Liberty first and Union afterwards'—nor 'Union first and *Liberty* afterwards,' but 'Liberty and Union' now and forever, one and inseparable."74

Carney was the last to respond to the New Yorkers' query. The governor confessed that "the shock to Mr. Lincolns [*sic*] popularity, even in Kansas, within the last six months, has been severe." "Our people regard the cause above the man," he candidly remarked. "Were it not for this," he added, "loyal as they are, he could be beaten, if a candidate equally loyal were in the field." More important, Carney wanted the New York journalists to know that public opinion was against the president. Had it not been for the conviction of the people to rise to meet the duties of the hour to save the Union, he maintained, "Mr. Lincoln would be repudiated by a majority of the people of the West." Of all Northern governors, Carney was the lone soul who expressed that he would support a change.75

Greeley had his results, and it undermined any anti-Lincoln agenda. Governors were not only barometers of public opinion, but also engineers of it. They now had, at least in the view of party leaders, confirmation that the Union Party and ending the conflict by fighting were more appealing than Lincoln himself. Tilton wrote to Nicolay on 6 September before receiving all of the governors' responses, but days after Sherman captured Atlanta, that Lincoln would surely be reelected. "All divisions are going to be healed," he wrote, "I have never seen such a sudden lighting up of public mind as since the late victory at Atlanta."76 Nicolay's assessment that "encouraging news from all quarters" solidified his victory perhaps gave Lincoln confidence. "The Atlanta victory alone," Nicolay boasted, "ought to win the Presidential contest for us."77 Indeed, Taylor Pierce of the 22nd Iowa wrote to his wife that "as sure as the sun shines," the fall of Atlanta would soon be followed by the fall of Richmond and that the "Copperheads and McClelland will wilt in the November frost."78

That Greeley and his associates enlisted the governors' counsel was a testament to the chief executives' political significance. They had become instrumental in gauging and guiding their voters' sentiments. Governors corresponded daily with soldiers and civilians, came to know their politics as well as their attitudes about commanders, and they protected their interests. Governors helped counter the political barnburners, and stood by Lincoln even when they disagreed with him, or thought him less than qualified for the job. At the moment at least, they believed he stood for something—winning, and that required continued cooperation. Governors had insisted on a more vigorous war, and they now had it. If Andrew, Blair, Morton,

Yates, and other Radicals stood "aloof" when others rallied to Lincoln's side, it was not because they wanted to abandon him. Rather they had more pressing concerns—namely suppressing dissidents and preparing the way for absentee voting among soldiers.[79]

Atlanta

Summer's end brought closure to another harvest season. With it came the expectation that Northerners must unite behind Lincoln at the polls or appear weak before the Confederacy. Thus, when the opening days of September brought national news that Sherman had taken Atlanta, it was time for celebration. For a city that few Northerners could imagine was so eminently valuable to winning the conflict three years before, the victory changed the war's course. Unlike Shiloh, Antietam, or Gettysburg, taking Atlanta was akin to capturing New Orleans and Nashville because it was a strategically valuable city and fell under Lincoln's Reconstruction. The Union's success at Atlanta perhaps persuaded the governors in their responses to Tilton and company. More than any other victory of the war, it gave the Union what it needed politically more than militarily, and governors could now boast to their citizens to join the victorious regiments in Georgia. "How absolutely this success was," wrote one chronicler, "to turn the scale in Lincoln's favor one could at the moment only guess; still a victory so opportune must be made to serve the new movement to the utmost."[80] Charles Sedgwick confided to Forbes that Atlanta had turned the tide in Lincoln's favor. "No man ever was elected to an important office who will get so many unwilling & indifferent votes as L.," wrote the representative. "The *cause* takes the man along."[81]

Whether or not Lincoln's candidacy was seriously threatened, Sherman's victory and the governors' backing helped strengthen his candidacy. Andrew supposed the time had come to arouse the public in favor of Lincoln. He encouraged Forbes to visit Lincoln and to "have a frank talk, try to bring him out a little, by proposing to support and to 'put him through,' by encouragement and friendship."[82] Meanwhile, he encouraged the crowds in Boston's Faneuil Hall to celebrate recent victories, renew their confidence that it was still a people's contest, support Lincoln, and break their despondency (mirrored by Republican leaders) and join the "cannon fever."[83] To Yates, Brough, and Curtin, however, Andrew remarked that "the President should be rescued from the influences which threaten him." He noted, "I want the President now to take hold of this occasion and really lead, as he might, the country, by exhibiting in the person who wields its highest power, the genuine representative of democratic instincts and principles."[84] He confessed the same to Howe, that his purpose in visiting Washington was to stop the cabal against Lincoln and to "take hold, put Lincoln through, guard & protect him if we can, lash ourselves to the mast, & confront the gale."[85]

Even in victory, Atlanta meant casualties. Governors remained close by telegraph operators, who sat in rooms in the statehouses and transcribed news of the war from magnetic wires. The conflict was no longer a matter of putting regiments in the field. By the late summer, it was a matter of providing relief for the soldiers mustering out, returning home, or convalescing. Many soldiers could thank governors for initiating efforts for administering their care after leaving their units. The war had revolutionized the ways in which citizens lived, and the economic changes reflected America's entrepreneurial spirit. Andrew spoke to wartime advances in an address to the New England Agricultural Society in Springfield in early September. Boasting of New England's contributions to the nation in technology, industry, and agriculture, Andrew reassured his listeners that the region would come out of the war much stronger, more economically vital. The real contribution to the republic was not to be found in the fields, on the rivers, or in the mountains, he argued, but by greatness in "the highest development and cultivation of the faculties of *men*." He championed, "In a word," let "the production and diffusion of *Ideas*" be the beacon of their noble identity in the vast nation of men, farms, and machines.[86]

After Atlanta, the war settled into a back-and-forth struggle around Petersburg and in the Shenandoah Valley. Georgians evacuated their beloved city, and Sherman invested the Southern soil with Union troops. It was a testament to the changes Andrew highlighted in Boston that telegraph wires webbed throughout the Confederacy transmitted the war back to the War Department and to all the North's capital cities. Still, the victory in Atlanta and Admiral Farragut's capture of Mobile only partially eclipsed the complaints about the apportionment of men across political districts and the miscalculation of quota credits. Still, Stanton was delighted to hear that Smith had convinced Vermont legislators to establish a state militia and only needed arms from the federal government. Indeed, he applauded Smith's efforts and sent him the weapons. "Until the present rebellion," he wrote Smith, "I was of those who hoped there would be war no more and that

mankind had become wise enough under our Government to live at peace....
I am now in favor of arming every freeman."[87] Small local victory though it
was, it represented the influence that governors had acquired in managing
the national war.

Lincoln needed Atlanta now as much as he had needed Kentucky in 1861,
but he was still losing Kentucky in the current election. The excitement of
Sherman's victory overshadowed the September draft scheduled to commence, and Bramlette complained that Lincoln's suspension of habeas
corpus treated Kentucky as though it was a rebellious and conquered province. Military authorities had interfered with the August elections, he argued,
and had made outrageous assessments on the citizens. "The course pursued
by many of those intrusted [sic] with Federal authority in Kentucky," he
complained, "has made to your Administration and re-election thousands
of bitter and irreconcilable opponents, where a wise and just policy and action would more easily have made friends." He told Lincoln, "We are for
preserving the rights and liberties of our own race and upholding the character and dignity of our position." He added, "We are not willing to sacrifice
a single life or imperil the smallest right of free white men for the sake of the
negro."[88] The governor's attitude did not surprise Lincoln. Kentuckians
were less vital to the cause now that the war turned on victory in Georgia
and Virginia. That federal and state political leaders moved to embrace
abolishing slavery was a reality that came with defeating the Confederacy,
whether Kentuckians liked it or not. For all of the problems Missourians
had given Lincoln, even they had undertaken to break the shackles of the
institution under Gamble's tutelage. Bradford had also encouraged Marylanders who embraced abolition, even knowing it would cost him reelection.
Maryland's legislators voted to revise their constitution to end the peculiar
institution and laid their decision before the Maryland voters in the October
election. In a state that had been bitterly divided in 1861, abolition marked
a milestone in just how much the war had changed Marylanders.[89]

Stanton used Sherman's victory to spur volunteerism and asked Grant to
communicate his views to the chief executives. A telegram from the lieutenant general would spur volunteerism and justify the draft. "The worst difficulty," Stanton complained to Grant, "is likely to be in Ohio, Indiana, and
Illinois, from the desire of the candidates to retain their men until after the
election." He added, "We have not got a single regiment from Indiana," asserting that "Morton came here specially to have the draft postponed, but
was peremptorily refused." He concluded, "A special call from you would

aid the Department in overcoming the local inertia and personal interests that favor delay."[90]

Union advances also carried currency at the polls. Gubernatorial elections came off annually in September for Vermont and Maine, and Northerners believed these elections would forecast results in the following months, and they attracted considerable interest. Amassing a majority of more than 20,000 votes over Democrat Timothy P. Redfield, Vermont's Smith easily retained his seat. "Vermont has opened the ball," proclaimed the *Burlington Daily Free Press*, "and opened it handsomely for the Union, and for Abraham Lincoln."[91] So elated was Stanton about the victory that he wired Smith his personal congratulations. "*All Hail* to the *Green Mountain Boys*," he boomed, "they have smote the rebel sympathizers at home as their gallant brothers smite the foes of their Country on the field of battle."[92] Maine voters advanced the political front and kept Cony and the Unionists in power. The following day, the chief executive wired Stanton the good news of his victory over Democrat Judge Joseph Howard. "Maine gave you as good as a re-enforcement of 50,000 men yesterday," he boasted to Stanton, "hold your hand lightly for a time and we will attend to your demands."[93] But Stanton did not budge. "Having routed the enemies of the Union at the polls," he charged, "let the patriots of Maine hasten to bare their banner on to victory over the rebels in the field." He pressed, "I have to-day urgent appeals for immediate draft from Atlanta and Petersburg," declaring that, "it must go on without an hour's delay."[94] Noted one journalist, "We have opportunity . . . to say that with the soldiers, Governor Cony enjoys a popularity unknown to his predecessors."[95]

The excitement over the Union's recent military and political victories, however, failed to distract Stanton from executing the draft. The secretary hoped these combined successes would revive the patriotic spirit and induce volunteers to enlist. But governors convinced him to extend the date until 19 September, as the enrollment appeared unfair and fraught with weakness. Many chief executives agreed with Maine congressman James G. Blaine's assessment that the longer it lasted, the worse it would get. He wrote, "The dreaded draft is now going on all over the country," but "like the old ladies' tea party, 'It will be good to have it over with.'" Blaine concluded, "If it goes on in the slow process, it will about ruin us in the October elections of Pennsylvania and Ohio, whereas if the quick process were adopted, we should have fifteen or eighteen unembarrassed days for marshaling our political forces in those States and would close with a 'blaze of glory and a big victory,' settling conclusively the Presidential struggle."[96] Governors would have desired nothing less than a blaze of glory to close out the war, but citizens had grown immune to its effects. Yates responded to Stanton's circular that given the problems with Illinois's quotas and credits, he could not be responsible for the consequences when the draft commenced. "In my opinion," he wired Lincoln, "it will not only endanger the peace of the State, but will hopelessly defeat us in the coming election."[97] To relieve governors, Fry consented to reduce the quotas in some districts, but he warned them that the army was "jealously watching whether the draft will be suspended or enforced."[98]

By summer's end, the war broke open full-scale in the Shenandoah Valley. Sheridan's 40,000 Federals waged an all-out assault against Early's Confederates outside of Winchester, Virginia. The battle opened on 19 September, and by the day's end, the Union forces had forced the Confederates into retreat. Union casualties, however, totaled more than 4,000, and it appeared that little had been accomplished in the third battle of Winchester, when in fact it gave the Federals the upper hand in the Shenandoah Valley. Democrats, however, capitalized on the casualties in the press, and looked to Seymour to exploit the defeat by campaigning outside the state. Yet the governor devoted his energies to winning New York, and rightfully so. McClellan was a viable candidate, but Lincoln was implausibly popular. As the election approached, the president urged Stanton to allow his commanders to relax the rules preventing soldiers going home to vote. For all his passivity in engineering his renomination, the president invested considerable energy in promoting his reelection, especially among the soldiers. He even allowed the debunked Sigel a visit to Washington to plead his case for reinstatement, thinking it might soothe the German press before the election. Lincoln understood the stakes involved in his reelection, and he pressed Stanton to accommodate the governors. Like those of many states, Indiana's state constitution did not provide for voting in the field, and Morton worked to get soldiers home to vote to ensure a Republican victory. He urged the draft be delayed until after October, offered to pay for soldier transportation home, and sent agents to retrieve the sick and wounded. The governor also won approval to allow furloughed soldiers an extension until after the November election. Yet Sherman was equally determined to keep the men in the field and refused to release soldiers. In the face of such opposition, Morton reasoned to Stanton that "if it were possible that you could see and hear what we ... have seen and heard, no word from us would be needed."[99] Autumn had arrived in full force, and Lincoln worried about the coming elections. He needed to shed those who had become political thorns in his side, even if he liked them. To win in November, Lincoln thought, Cabinet member Montgomery Blair had become too much of a liability and had to go. The president accepted his postmaster general's resignation, and named former Ohio governor Dennison in his place. For all of his faults as governor, Dennison had more than compensated for his deficiencies by his loyalty to Lincoln, to the party, and to the cause. By all means, he was a judicious choice. Yet, there were other matters to be considered. Curtin, for example, had come to Washington to heal the rift with the president over accusations he was tampering with the soldier vote. The public knew that Curtin and Stanton were bitter antagonists, but the feud played out in the papers that fall when rumors surfaced the governor was "not behaving well, and that his action in the matter of soldier votes," might undermine Curtin's ability to carry the state, which reflected poorly on Lincoln. The president expected the governor to canvass the state to build his majority and to attend political meetings in Washington. Yet his health had deteriorated such that his physician ordered him to Saratoga Springs for a week's quiet.[100]

CHAPTER NINETEEN

The People Are Conscious of the Power

By October, General Sherman's and Sheridan's victories had placed Lincoln on firm political ground for reelection, but there was work to be done at the ballot box and in the field to secure his victory. Northerners were making their way to the polls in early October when Confederate General Sterling Price pushed across the Arkansas border into Missouri and launched a campaign to bring the region under Confederate control. General Rosecrans pressed Missouri governor Hall to call out the enrolled militia of the central and southeastern regions, and the fight for the trans-Mississippi reopened. For months Rosecrans believed that a conspiracy existed between Southern and Northern members of the Order of American Knights. The OAK had drawn its membership largely from disaffected Northerners who opposed the war. Its members had allegedly planned to raid Northern prisons and free Southerners, form a new army out of these prisoners, and use it against the Union. Price's raid confirmed what governors had been telling Secretary of War Stanton for months, and they believed it was part of a vast northwestern conspiracy about to break open.

Problems on the Borders

Rosecrans convinced midwestern governors that tens of thousands of conspirators had joined ranks to undermine the coming election. It was the last opportunity for subversives to sabotage Lincoln's reelection. The commander believed there was collusion between Price and the Copperheads, and he requested that Stanton terminate the draft. This sparked the president's attention, and he sent Nicolay to St. Louis to survey the situation. Scores of letters describing Missouri's guerrilla warfare littered Hall's desk, and he feared it would undermine the state legislature's good work. Violence threatened to spill into Kansas, and General Curtis ordered Governor Carney to call out the Kansas militia to prepare for the onslaught. The governor ordered businesses suspended, labor shut down, and citizens to arm themselves. "You will do so, as you have always promptly done when your soil has been invaded," he declared. "The call this time will come to you louder and stronger because you know the foe will seek to glut his vengeance upon you." He argued, "The work to be done now is to protect the State against marauder and murderer."[1] As had the thousands of midwesterners from Iowa, Indiana, Illinois, and Wisconsin answered the call for one-hundred-day men to aid in Sherman's campaign, so now did hundreds of Kansans come forth.[2]

Price's raid was not the Union's only challenge that fall. Sherman suffered Confederate attacks on his supply lines to loosen his clasp on Atlanta and prevent him from heading to Savannah. Except for guerrilla raids, Sheridan had secured the Shenandoah Valley from a Confederate advance. Governors turned their attention to local matters to shore up defense against guerrillas and to secure electoral conditions. Discouraged by bushwhackers and the lack of national assistance, Boreman used local citizens to defend against guerrillas in West Virginia, who roamed the hills, preying on mountaineers. To counter the notorious Brigadier General Alfred Eugene "Mudwall" Jackson, Boreman authorized citizens to take matters into their own hands. To restore some semblance of peace, he encouraged loyalists to seek out thieves and outlaws and to capture, punish, and even kill them. Accustomed to the uncivil wars that had raged in the hills of West Virginia and Kentucky for years, mountaineers believed that self-governance began with a rifle or a pistol.[3]

Worse than Southern guerillas for some governors, were the organized bands of Northern traitors. Yates, Brough, and Morton had worried for months over dissident criminals in their states. They had foiled several plots, but could not bring conspirators to justice. As elections neared, evidence of conspiracies resurfaced. In early October, 300 members of the Knights of the Golden Circle, aided by Kentuckians, rose up against the draft in Crawford and Orange Counties. Fry sent agents to authenticate Morton's belief that Copperhead Indianans posed a serious threat to his governance and conscription hostilities. Their reports confirmed the governor's concerns and helped convince military authorities to arrest Milligan, Dodd, Bowles, and their accomplices Horace Heffren, Andrew Humphreys, and Stephen Horsey, on conspiracy charges against the United States. The exposure of the Sons of Liberty justified the demand for troops to prevent armed insurrection. Whatever truth existed about the extent of the Copperhead intentions, Morton believed he was in danger of not being reelected. More than that, he feared Lincoln's loss would undermine the war effort.[4]

Despite the conspirators' defiance, governors used whatever means they could to maintain peace while inducing men to volunteer that fall. They secured additional bounty funds, extended draft dates, and requested that the War Department cancel the draft until after the October and November elections. They cited Sherman's advances as evidence that Northern armies were winning the war and that Northern occupation had undermined the Confederate war effort. Conscription had proven a failure, but they argued that confiscation and emancipation had wrought significant changes in Southern nationalism, especially in the border states. Marylanders were about to plow slavery under free soil. Emancipation had become a wartime necessity, and governors expected the measure to aid them in their recruitment efforts by convincing citizens that it would shorten the war. It was inevitable that such a movement would make its way into the Union's slave states as well. Lincoln approved of Maryland's abolition movement and communicated his sentiments to Henry W. Hoffman, lawyer and Baltimore Customs collector. "It needs not be a secret," wrote Lincoln, "that I wish success of the provision." He added, "I wish to see, in process of disappearing, that only thing which could ever could bring this nation to civil war," and "I shall be gratified exceedingly if the good people of the State shall, by their votes, ratify the new constitution."[5]

Lincoln suffered the challenges of succumbing to a war in earnest. Few would remember the war's fumbling opening months, the paralyzing effects of limited war, and the federal expansion in emancipating Confederate slaves and conscripting Northern males. The contest would be long remembered for how it ended, and how it defined the presidency and the republic. Lincoln had been the Union's visible hand in convincing Northerners that their sacrifice was worth the victory they hoped to gain. There was much at stake, not necessarily for him, but for those he had called and had sent to the battlefield to preserve the Union. October's results would provide an indication of how Northerners evaluated his presidency. Such victories would prove that voters embraced the Union of 1864 over the Union of 1861. Governors believed that soldiers might decide the results in several states, including Indiana, Ohio, and Pennsylvania. Determined to secure preservation of the new Union, Morton, Brough, and Yates believed October's results would influence voters the following month to support Lincoln. Morton needed Republicans to regain control of the legislature and went to Washington to urge Lincoln to suspend the draft, hoping to undercut the Copperheads. An Indiana political victory, he argued, would help Lincoln more than the soldiers would help Sherman's army. Lincoln refused, arguing that it would be "better that we both should be beaten than that the forces in front of the enemy should be weakened on account of the absence of these men."[6] The president, however, turned to Sherman for help, and the commander agreed to furlough Indiana soldiers home to vote. It was a critical election indeed. Even seventy-nine-year-old War of 1812 veteran Joseph Shaw, who was blind and feeble, wrote Lincoln that he had been hauled some four miles to Versailles, Indiana, to vote for Morton. He hoped to live long enough to vote for the Lincoln-Johnson ticket in November "to sustain the Union and the country."[7]

For all the national attention on the October elections, governors delivered the president wonderful news that autumn. Indianans reelected Morton by a sizeable majority; Pennsylvanians, with the aid of the soldier vote, gave Unionists the overall victory; and Ohio had also all gone for the Union Party. Their success contributed to significant gains in Congress and reversed the lingering misfortunes of two years before. An impressed *New York Times* editor attributed Morton's victory to his oratorical labors and his steadfast devotion despite a legislature that had abandoned him. "With a Legislature against him of the most factious and disloyal character," noted the editor, Morton "kept Indiana the very foremost of all the Western States."[8] The October election results encouraged Northerners about the favorable prospects of the national election in November. General Robert McAllister of New Jersey wrote his wife Ellen that "if New Jersey troops were alowed [sic] to vote, our little state would be all right for Lincoln."[9]

The October victories in Indiana, Ohio, and Pennsylvania turned the political weathervane in Lincoln's favor. Unionist Marylanders, however, had something greater than a political triumph to celebrate. Voters approved the abolition of slavery beginning on 1 November. Still, opponents accused Bradford of fraud and wanted the soldier's vote dismissed, but the governor refused. Loyalists welcomed the new constitution no matter how it became law and heaped considerable praise on the governor. Bradford had played a significant role in seeing the measure through its favorable course. Perhaps his resoluteness had to do with the realization that in the coming weeks he would not be reelected governor. He would spend the next year as a lame duck. The new state constitution that abolished slavery also mandated that in the November election Marylanders would be electing a new governor for a term to commence in January 1866. "Through night and storm," boasted Charles C. Fulton, editor of the *Baltimore American*, "this watchful pilot [Bradford] remained at his post; true to his instincts as a man of unflinching honor, of unbending rectitude, of unswerving patriotism." He remarked, "When Maryland receives the benefits which will be conferred upon her by the operation of the new Constitution, there will be no prouder name for her to cherish than that of its defender, Augustus W. Bradford."[10]

In the coming days, as Tidewater slaves assembled to witness the dawning of a new day, Maryland loyalists could not contain themselves. Some traveled to Washington, where they serenaded Lincoln on the White House lawn. He complimented them for making their soil free to 87,000 slaves. "I had rather have Maryland upon that issue," he remarked, "than have a State twice its size upon the Presidential issue; it cleans up a piece of ground."[11] Remarked General William C. Brown to Colonel Lockwood Doty of the New York Bureau of Military Statistics from Frederick, Maryland, "I would like to say many things about the change in 'Maryland.' Oh, what a glorious change.... These are glorious times to live."[12] Wrote the *Illinois State Journal*, "'My Maryland, My Maryland,' no longer. It is the Maryland of traitors no longer—but of loyal men."[13] The blessing of freedom, however, presented Bradford with new problems. Petitions citing the state's black codes, which bound black children to long terms of apprenticeship, poured into his office. Now he was responsible for suppressing violence, discrimination, and punitive measures against the freedmen. Until the legislature met, he worked with General Wallace to establish a set of transitional measures to bring freedmen under military protection and established the boundaries of freedom.[14]

Public attention turned away from elections when Jubal Early halted his retreat up the Shenandoah Valley near Cedar Creek and, on 19 October, attacked Sheridan's unsuspecting Federal army. Curtin suspected such a move and, two days before, telegraphed Lincoln that "the enemy has arranged for a raid into Pennsylvania" and that he was concerned that it would impact the election.[15] Lincoln responded that Sheridan's force had not been reduced and that there was not much danger of a raid into Pennsylvania. Curtin had heard this before. The daylong battle looked to be a Confederate rout in the morning, until Sheridan arrived on the scene from Winchester, rallied his men, and managed to counterattack, driving the Confederates back to Fisher's Hill. It was Sheridan's fortune to have fought the last major battle in the war's most storied valley, having galloped his way into victory and Civil War folklore. Yet, even in victory, and an important one for political as well as military reasons, the Union suffered more losses than Confederates.[16]

Had it not been for Sheridan's exploits in Virginia and Price's trans-Mississippi raid, perhaps more would have been made of the Confederate raid into Vermont. Part of the northwestern conspiracy, some two dozen cavalrymen crossed the Canadian border and ransacked the tiny New England railroad hamlet of St. Albans. The bushwhackers even visited the governor's residence under the guise of locals and walked the grounds and stables, staking out their designs to torch the mansion. Smith was attending a legislative session in Montpelier, and the only inhabitants at home were Smith's wife Anna Eliza and a few servants, who learned of the raids when a young servant girl from a neighboring home darted home to inform her. The governor's wife barricaded the doors and "took her stand in front of the house," when her brother-in-law, F. Stewart Stranahan, a member of General George Custer's staff home on sick leave, galloped up and informed her that the raiders had left. The governor was in conference with Adjutant General Peter T. Washburn and Assemblyman John W. Stewart when the news of the raid came over the wires. Worried for his wife, he set things in motion to apprehend the culprits, stopping all trains going in and out of the state. He then called on the men at the U.S. hospital at Montpelier, organized home guards and other veteran units in the area, and began a search for the raiders. "We have had (to use *Cousin Joe's* forcible expression) a 'Raid from hell,'" wrote Anna Smith to her husband. "For about half an hour yesterday afternoon," she confided, "I thought that we should be burnt up, and robbed." She declared, "How foolish and frantic our people have been not to heed your warning. I hope this affair will settle matters at once."[17]

Canadian authorities caught the St. Albans guerrillas, but the raid worried Joseph Hooker. Lincoln had reassigned the commander from Sherman's army and placed him in charge of the Northern Department, comprising the states of Michigan, Ohio, Indiana, and Illinois and headquartered in Cincinnati. He called on Stanton to allow Blair to raise a regiment of twelve-month men to report to his command in order to safeguard the Michigan-Canadian border before the Detroit River froze. Meanwhile, Smith dispatched his brother, Vermont assemblyman Worthington C. Smith, to Washington with a letter detailing his plans to secure Vermont's exposed frontier.[18]

With each new wave of guerrilla attacks, governors became more aggressive in combatting bushwhacker resistance. Missourians, however, found little relief. By the time Nicolay arrived in St. Louis, he discovered a battle was about to break open near Kansas City. It did not help Hall's administration that rumors circulated indicating that Rosecrans was about to be removed. By 23 October, the combined forces of Curtis and Blunt defeated Price and Jo Shelby's Confederates in the battle of Westport. The Union victory forced the Confederates to retreat toward Kansas and was a turning point in the trans-Mississippi war. In the coming days, the Federals regrouped and pursued the Confederates, and Hall encouraged Lincoln to keep Rosecrans in command. "He understands our affairs & our people," argued Hall, and "he knows the true cause of our troubles & is better able than almost any one else to correct it." Besides, he concluded, Rosecrans was a man of "undoubted talents," possessed a "sound heart," and would do "what is right." Amid these pressing affairs Nicolay was confident that Union men would cast their votes for Lincoln.[19]

Fall Elections

By November, all eyes were on the telegraphic dispatches and the newspapers reporting the waning days of the political canvass. Never before in American history were the cables linking towns and cities so important in relaying news between the White House and state capitals. The correspondence between soldiers and families revealed the importance of the coming election. "Our election is coming off soon," wrote John Gibbons of Madison, Wisconsin, to his son, who was soldiering a musket, "you must try and do what you can to elect 'old Abe,' he is our only hope to close this war as it should be closed."[20] From the smallest hamlets to the prominent urban cities, election chatter filled daily discussions. "It is impossible," wrote Wilmington resident Anna Ferris, "to pass anyone in the street & catch a word that is spoken, without finding that the one subject is agitated by all—. All that makes our country dear to us & is to make it great & glorious in the future is to be preserved or lost—."[21]

Since the war began, Republican governors and state representatives had worked to make allowances for absentee soldier voting, but as the war continued, it became necessary to accelerate military suffrage provisions. Following Iowa and Minnesota's 1862 provisions, several Northern states constructed legal means of extending the franchise so soldiers could vote in state and national elections. Pennsylvania already had absentee voting and, despite constitutional scrutiny to eliminate fraud, had used it in previous elections. Nearly all states followed suit and had by this time enacted provisions to enfranchise soldiers. These states included: Connecticut, Vermont, New Hampshire, Rhode Island, Kentucky, Maryland, New York, Wisconsin, Ohio, West Virginia, Michigan, Kansas, Maine, California, Missouri, and Illinois. Massachusetts, New Jersey, Delaware, Indiana, and Oregon refused to enact soldier voting laws. Despite constitutional impediments, judicial scrutiny, Democratic opposition, and invitations to fraud, Republican governors relied on the soldier votes, believing many soldiers to be Republican, which would ensure party victory. In the coming election, they projected the same.[22]

Governors stumped important cities on weeklong tours beginning in New York. Andrew practically exhausted himself, and at one point in Lockport, his nose bled, forcing him to return to Boston. For Morton's efforts, the *New York Times* paid a fitting tribute to his influence on New York voters. "All honor, we say, to Governor Morton," remarked the editor, "the competent contrast to Governor Seymour in the times that tried men's souls."[23] The New York governor, however, countered Unionists by spending nearly every day since mid-October canvassing the state, assailing their party and Fenton for his abolition record. So confident was the chief executive that Democrats would win in New York, he boasted to McClellan of the coming victory. "I have for many years canvassed this state and I have never seen so much spirit and enthusiasm in the Democratic party," he observed. "I may be mistaken, but I feel a great political revolution is going on."[24] A revolution was sweeping across New York, but Seymour and McClellan would soon be among the vanquished. The governor's bold assertions, however, mischaracterized the work he had done for the Union. There was some truth to the *St. Louis Daily Missouri Republican's* depiction that he was a man of "true grit." Publicly denounced by the abolitionists and the ultraradical press as the "villain's friend," and loathed by Republicans, Seymour pressed on. Still, whether feared, despised, or revered, noted the paper's editor, Seymour has "been behind our loyal Executive in furnishing and equipping soldiers, and in supporting the Government and [the] Union."[25]

There was something admirable, and yet contemptible, about Seymour's loyal opposition. He continued the flow of manpower to Union armies, yet he refused to accept the change Union war aims had wrought. The governor scoffed at the offer by New York's Union League Club to raise and fund a black regiment from the city. He argued that he lacked the authority to grant such a request and directed members to Stanton, who had apparently approved such regiments elsewhere in the state. Fighting for his political life,

Seymour overplayed his hand by disfranchising New York soldiers in the field and by using National Guards at the polls. Stanton assumed the governor would use Guard members to intimidate Union Party voters, and he countered his move. Seymour responded by issuing a proclamation that asserted the rights of military commanders to interfere with elections. As predicted, however, Union Party leaders pounced on these frauds to expose Seymour. General Dix was a native New Yorker, and his political aspirations concerned Stanton, who thought the governor might coerce the commander to cower in a face-off for power. When Grant offered Butler as a military mediator, the secretary acquiesced and sent Butler to New York City. Morgan urged Stanton to send 3,000 troops to New York to oversee the election, and the secretary obliged and placed the men under Butler's command. For all the rumors swirling about the city indicating there would be violence at the polls, Butler's presence challenged Seymour's power and stifled the supposed violence. Although these actions were an affront to his credibility as the supreme state authority, Seymour "did not resort to violence in protecting state rights," wrote one contemporary, yet "he was perilously near to that."[26] He issued circulars to the officers and surgeons of the New York regiments to carry out the Soldier Voting Act by issuing ballots to every unit. Yet the fraud in the ranks was so rampant that one unidentified soldier wrote Seymour that he deemed it his duty to relate that when a Republican appeared in camp to take the votes, he only took Lincoln votes and refused envelopes to Democrats. In the end, Seymour could not keep his political hold on the state and Butler, who reveled in the showdown with a political adversary, appeared to have saved the day in the city.[27]

Translating field victories into expectant political success, Lincoln and the governors monitored the telegraph machine throughout the days and nights, hoping for good news. Lincoln's close friend Noah Brooks visited the White House on the day of the presidential election. It was gloomy and rainy when he arrived. It was noon, and to his surprise he found the president alone and the marble halls nearly deserted. "As if by common consent," he remembered, "everybody had avoided the White House." Stanton's illness kept him home. Even filled with troops, Washington seemed vacant. It was a quiet day, noted Brooks, and Lincoln invited the journalist to spend the afternoon with him. The president "took no pains to conceal his anxious interest in the result of the election," recalled Brooks. "I am just enough of a politician to know that there was not much doubt about the result of the Baltimore convention," he said to Brooks, "but about this thing I am very far from being uncertain."²⁸ Forty-three months before, Lincoln waited anxiously hoping for the "North" to materialize along the Potomac. Its shape and size remained to be seen. Only the arrival of Northern regiments gave the president some sense of the Union identity, as thousands of soldiers flocked to the cause that belonged to the people. Lincoln's task was to engineer a victory that prevented the Union's dissolution. His future now belonged to the voters, who could change the war's course. The masthead of Washington's leading newspaper, the *Washington Daily National Intelligencer*, appeared larger than life as its words in bold read: "Day of Decision."²⁹

Later that chilly, rainy evening, Lincoln, Brooks, and John Hay walked to the War Department, where they met Stanton. Together they waited with great expectation for the day's results that would come over the wires. Governors paced the statehouse floors, eagerly awaiting the results from the cities, townships, and from the field. Although October's elections had provided indications of the political tide, a Union Party victory was not a foregone conclusion. Governors believed the soldier vote would be needed in several states. Yates requested that Lincoln allow several regiments to remain in the state long enough to vote. "It need not detain them longer than four days," he argued, "and the necessity for electing a loyal State senate is absolute, an increase of three members of Congress . . . depends on these regiments; and the Presidential and State tickets need that aid to guarantee success." He had advised, "Defeat in Illinois," would be "worse than defeat in the field."³⁰

Northern voters went to the polls on 8 November for a political contest whose significance was akin to the battle at Antietam. A Lincoln victory would forever alter the Union's landscape. Soldiers understood its meaning. "Today the great conflict is taking place between the opposing principles of our nations [*sic*] honor or disgrace," wrote New Yorker William L. Mead, stationed in Beaufort, South Carolina. "Now is the time for the people to judge the proper course to pursue—whether for *country* above *party* or party before country."³¹ Late in the evening Brooks noticed that Indiana returns arrived in Washington. "The first gun came from Indiana," he recalled.³² Morton felt singularly responsible for the result, and he reported from Indianapolis that Lincoln had carried 1,500 votes in the capital city. As the night wore on, more good news came from Baltimore and Boston. Like Lincoln, Andrew wanted to finish the war in office. His margin of victory trumped all governors by claiming more than a 76,000-vote majority for an unprecedented fifth term, just 2,000 shy of Lincoln's majority. The convalescing chief executive wired Frank Howe, "We have knocked down, and stamped out the last Copperhead ghost in Massachusetts."³³ To friend Francis P. Blair Sr., he breathed a sigh of relief, "A weight seems lifted from my heart."³⁴ Andrew looked to parlay his victory into a cabinet position. He was aware of the political shuffling underway in Washington and hoped the post of attorney general might come vacant. If peace was imminent, he surmised, the presidential cabinet, not the governorship, was the place to influence Reconstruction policies.³⁵

Union gains came in like a trickle of rain rather than a steady downpour. Curtin wired in that Pennsylvania had gone for Lincoln. Low sent warm "greetings" from San Francisco, boasting of a 20,000- to 30,000-vote majority. Despite his party's embarrassing resistance to embrace civil rights for California's minorities, the governor exhibited an impartial attitude by urging civil treatment of Indians and Chinese.³⁶ The greatest triumph, however, was over Seymour. The New York race was so close that some papers proclaimed a Democratic victory, hoping to forestall the embarrassment of losing, yet Northerners were aware of their schemes. "I had rather Lincoln should [lose] N.Y.," wrote Calvin Fletcher, "than that Seymour . . . should be elected."³⁷ Wrote New Yorker James. H. Purdy to his cousin, "The Copperheads here are completely dumbfounded at the magnitude of their defeat," and, apparently, "the Lord did not mean that such a party should rule this nation."³⁸ As the hours passed midnight, capitols wired in the news from Madison, Albany, Lansing, and Annapolis. By late night, a Northern gale that "proverbially accompanies the November election," had shut down western lines and cut off dispatches from Illinois, Iowa, and other states.³⁹ Eastern results, however, continued to pour in. News came over the wires from Concord that New Hampshirites had elected Lincoln. Neighboring Vermonters rewarded the administration for its attention to the St. Albans affair and for attending to the welfare of the soldiers. Even the restive Halleck commented on the victory over the opposition, remarking sarcastically that "the price of *copper* has fallen very much within the last few days."⁴⁰

In the coming days, wires from western cities revealed Lincoln's victory beyond the Appalachians. Only Kentucky went against the president, failing to reward him for his efforts in keeping the state in the Union. Bramlette had warned Lincoln that Stephen Burbridge had undermined the Union cause by ruthlessly enforcing martial law. The commander had pursed "a course calculated to exasperate and infuriate rather than pacify and conciliate," Bramlette complained.⁴¹ Editor Hodges of the *Frankfort Common-*

wealth concurred, had gone to Washington, and told Lincoln that Bramlette was cooperating with military authorities, but that Burbridge had not reciprocated the cooperation. Lincoln, however, had information that the commander's arrests were justified and implicated Bramlette in stirring up antiadministration malcontents. Elisha H. Ludington, an assistant inspector general, agreed, reporting to Stanton that undermanned Union forces compelled Kentuckians to exact reprisals on marauders. "Not a regiment raised in Kentucky," he argued, "ought to serve in the State." Although Bramlette preferred "union to rebellion," concluded the inspector, he "loves slavery also." Wrote Ludington, "He has slender capacity, great vanity, and greater ambition," and "he hopes to gratify his aspirations for election to U.S. Senate by yielding to the pressure bearing upon him from the slave interests in the State." He remarked, "The Governor's policy is simply self first, State second, Union last."[42]

Amid clandestine activities, insubordinate legislators, and a treasonous press, governors played an important role in producing the Union's winning ticket. "Today has been fought the great battle of the war," wrote Van Bennett of the 12th Wisconsin on Election Day. "The people have decided the fate of the nation."[43] Although it is debatable how much difference the soldiers' votes made in the results, governors engineered the means to enfranchise them, working with Lincoln and commanders. They were committed to the electoral process as a reflection of their devotion to their countrymen. As much as soldiers believed Lincoln was the Union's architect in steering their armies toward victory, they also believed governors were the engineers laboring to sustain him. Compared to state legislators, chief executives were more representative of the people, more in touch with their constituents, and more attentive to the soldiers.[44]

Changing the Political Guard

Significant change accompanied the November elections. Several governors ended their terms. Michigan's Blair had senatorial aspirations, but even after Chandler's victory in the Senate, he quietly stepped aside for Henry Howland Crapo to take the governorship. Crapo won the Republican nomination in the summer and outdistanced his Democratic opponent William M. Fenton by nearly 20,000 votes. He had written his son weeks before, "I can whip him [Fenton] any day—even on the stomp [*sic*]." He boasted, "I determine to make for myself a reputation throughout the state, which should command the respect & ensure the confidence of the intelligent & influential men of the party; and I feel now that I have succeeded."[45] And that he did. The fifty-year-old Massachusetts native was well groomed to assume Michigan's gubernatorial duties, though he came from humble beginnings. Reared on his father's Dartmouth, Massachusetts, farm, he lacked formal schooling, but studied independently and eventually became a teacher. In New Bedford he got involved in municipal administration as town clerk, treasurer, tax collector, and justice of the peace. Land investments lured him to Flint, Michigan, in 1856, and he continued his civic career, serving as the town's mayor. Best known for lumbering and milling, he grew his holdings into the state's largest by 1860. He served Genesee residents in the Michigan Senate in 1862. With Michigan in Crapo's competent hands, Blair faded into private life and worked to recover the financial losses he had endured as governor. Still, he had won the hearts and minds of his citizens and soldiers, who forever associated his leadership with contributing to the Union's success.[46]

Yates was constitutionally unable to run for another term and therefore helped campaign for General Richard Oglesby, who won the Republican nomination and the political victory. After seventeen years in politics, and despite a weakness for "wine and women," Yates believed Illinois legislators owed him a Senate seat. "You have grappled with the brood of Copperheads legitimate descendants of South Carolina Rattlesnakes, of Illinois," David Newsom told him, "and your course & cause being that of Loyalty, the strong arm of the brave & true Illinoisans has sustained you."[47] Yet the governor was not without his failings, and it was not so much his political liabilities that undermined his credibility, but rather his personal shortcomings. "Yates is very strong as governor," wrote Illinois Judge Joseph Gillespie to John M. Palmer, "but he has his drawbacks; wine and women [,] Dick is charged with having a weakness for." He argued, "Whether this charge is true or false, it tells."[48]

Carney shared Yates's quest to secure a seat on Capitol Hill, but he had Jayhawked his way to victory and watched his popularity wane. Once widely admired, Kansans disapproved of his self-serving ways. It did not help the governor that in the weeks before the election the Kansas press printed a letter he had written to Minnola resident Amos Hanna that criticized Lane. As Carney's star fell, Lane's soared, and it allowed him to persuade Republicans to nominate Samuel J. Crawford, a popular military commander. Crawford commanded the 2nd Kansas Colored Regiment, but recently had been brevetted a brigadier general for his bravery at the Battle of Mine

Creek. Nominated governor in September, Crawford took military leave in Kansas, and when Price's raid flared up, the commander reported to Curtis's staff for duty. At twenty-nine years of age, the young Kansan had little time to campaign for governor. Thanks to overzealous Kansas journalists, however, he pulled off a victory over the anti-Lane Republican-Union candidate Judge Solon O. Thacher by a vote of 13,387 to 8,448. It was a stunning success, given that Crawford had moved to Kansas only four years before. A native Indianan, he studied law at Cincinnati College and carried his legal career west to Garnett, Kansas. He participated in the Republican Party's organization, and voters rewarded him with a legislative seat the same year. In 1861 he resigned to become a captain in the 2nd Kansas Infantry and fought in many of the western battles. By 1863 he won promotion to colonel and assumed the command of the 2nd Kansas Cavalry. Still, opponents believed Crawford was Lane's candidate, and that he would no doubt "prostitute the Executive patronage to place him again in the U.S. Senate."[49]

Missourians also favored military experience and voted for Republican Thomas Clement Fletcher over Democrat Thomas L. Price. A brigadier general marching with Sherman's army to Savannah, Fletcher became Missouri's eighteenth governor by more than 40,000 votes. His victory encouraged Unionists that Missourians had finally embraced Lincoln's war aims. Fletcher's slave-owning parents hailed from Maryland and moved west in 1818, settling in the township of Herculaneum along the Mississippi River. He served as a clerk in the circuit court of Jefferson County and, before the war, had secured employment as a land agent for the Pacific Railroad, which landed him in St. Louis. When the Republican Party emerged in Missouri, Fletcher abandoned his proslavery roots, joined the movement, and served as a delegate to the party's national convention. When the war opened he volunteered in the St. Louis provost marshal's office, and, the following year, he recruited the 31st Missouri Volunteers and served as colonel. He fought in several western campaigns, was wounded and captured in December 1862, and sent to Libby Prison. Exchanged the following May, Fletcher returned to the field, but an illness forced him to return to Missouri in the late summer of 1864, until Rosecrans called on him to help stall Price's advance. Republican leaders exploited his popularity at the polls.[50]

Marylanders found little else to exploit with Bradford, and turned to native Virginian and former Know Nothing-turned-Unionist Thomas Swann to lead the state out of bondage. The former lawyer served as Baltimore's mayor before the war and had introduced notable civic changes. He abandoned the American Party for the Union Party, and in the summer delegates unanimously nominated him for governor. He defeated Chestertown attorney Democrat Ezekiel F. Chambers by more than 8,000 votes. To ensure Swann's victory, Bradford exercised the recently ratified state constitution, which allowed him to administer test oaths. Although opponents contested that these were not to take effect until the next year's election, Bradford nonetheless used them. Under the 1864 Maryland Constitution, the governor-elect could not take office until Bradford's three-year term expired in January 1866. It was an odd arrangement that left lame-duck Bradford in office for an entire year after the election.[51]

The moral effect of the election carried impressive implications. The busy political season gave way to a calming autumn that had borne success. Northerners had sustained the revolution to preserve the Union, both at the state and national levels. It was during this time that Lincoln summoned his cabinet members and revealed to them the contents of the envelope that contained the memorandum he had written and asked them to sign on 23 August. It pledged them to support the president-elect, and in their presence he read the despondent letter. With victory behind him and four more presidential years ahead, Lincoln needed to end conflict on the battlefield. Even Seymour conceded total victory to Republicans. "I am satisfied with the result of the election," the governor wrote to his sister afterward. "We had a large majority of the real voters of the State but it is better to give the Republicans the whole responsibility."[52]

By mid-November Lincoln wired governors, asking them to estimate the election results in their states in preparation for his address to Congress. Their returns were astounding. For all the negative press that disparaged the president's leadership, lamented Northern weariness, and emphasized a general displeasure with the war, voters confirmed that forcing Confederate surrender could not be accomplished without Lincoln. The commander in chief had finally produced a winning formula, even at significant cost. The Union Party prevailed, having given Republicans a sizeable majority in Congress. Even New Yorkers had gone for Lincoln. The greater triumph, however, belonged to Fenton, who defeated Seymour by 9,000 votes. Soldiers were made ecstatic by the news. They seldom if ever saw Seymour, and only in recent months did he appear at hospitals. "No sympathy, no care, no relief came to their bedside," wrote a correspondent to the *Buffalo Express*, until the governor needed their votes. One convalescing soldier at Stanton Hospital in Washington recalled that when agents arranged for travel home, they inquired for whom they would be voting. When this soldier responded that he would vote for Fenton, the agent replied, "Then I can do nothing for you." Had the soldier agreed he would vote for Seymour, however, the agent promised a furlough. "I will rot in the hospital first," was the soldier's reply.[53]

During Fenton's campaign he promised to align himself with Lincoln, the Union, and the soldiers, and his candidacy endeared him to the rank and file. "We now have a gov. that will stand by the Administration under all circumstances," declared General William C. Brown to a New York colonel. "Hurrah for the New York State. Hurrah for our Country."[54] The new governor basked in having trumped the nation's most prominent Democrat. The New York native attended the Pleasant Hill and Fredonia Academies and, on graduation, pursued the study of law, which carried him into business pursuits. By the early 1850s, he became involved in the Democratic Party, and won a seat in Congress. He voted against the Kansas-Nebraska Bill, and when the Republican Party emerged, he carried his antislavery views into the new organization. He was so popular that voters returned him to Congress in successive elections until his gubernatorial bid. Indeed, in painting his gubernatorial portrait, the artist observed that "this gentleman will not only prove to be 'the right man in the right place,' but that he will continue to rise in confidence and esteem of the people throughout the State and the nation."[55]

Although Northerners applauded the victory, some expressed disappointment. Besides Kentucky, the president lost in Delaware and New Jersey, though it came as no surprise. Weeks before the election, in perhaps the largest gathering of Delawareans in its history, some 5,000 Democrats had gathered in Dover to celebrate McClellan's candidacy and denounce Lincoln. Indeed, just ten days before the election, Cannon urged Stanton to guard the polls to keep the peace and furlough soldiers near Petersburg and in Baltimore home to vote. Stanton was out, so the governor left a note for him and called on Lew Wallace for military supervision to ensure a free and fair election. "Without the vote of our troops in the field," Cannon wrote, "it will be utterly impossible to carry our State, and the election of U.S. Senators, Representatives to Congress and Emancipation in Delaware, depends upon the result."[56] As free and fair as any wartime election could be in a bitterly divided state, Lincoln lost. On learning that her beloved Delaware had gone for McClellan, Ferris lamented the loss in her diary. "She [Delaware] is chained to Slavery & Democracy for a new term," she deplored. "In the midst of the general joy & triumph, we feel grieved & humiliated."[57] Unlike Cannon, Parker helped to ensure McClellan's victory in New Jersey by stumping the state and denounced Lincoln's abuse of civil liberties and usurpation of power. The governor was known for his strict adherence to states' rights, and, in the face of federal expansion, New Jerseyites could thank Parker for not yielding any "right of the State of New Jersey," and that no citizen during his administration had "been deprived of his liberty without due process of law."[58]

The elections' impact was a milestone in the contemporary political culture. Since New Englanders had gone to the state polls in the spring, governors had worked to ensure that soldiers could vote in the national election. "The circumstances under which it [the election] has taken place are of extraordinary character," wrote the editor of the *New Hampshire Statesman*.[59] *Harper's Weekly* editor George Curtis captured the moment's significance. "Votes are valuable," he argued, "when there are men behind them, as [Ralph Waldo] Emerson says of words." It remained to be seen if Union men would stand behind their popular political expression by coming forward. The war did not stop for the election, and governors continued to search for volunteers, safeguard home fronts, and attend to the welfare of the veterans and their families. Illinois's new governor, Oglesby, wired Lincoln words of congratulations with the sentiment of caution. "Allow me in common with the masses of the country who always speak from the heart," he wrote, "to congratulate you upon your Second great success—." Oglesby confessed that he desponded over rumors that Lincoln might not be a candidate and was "glad that again your wisdom exceeded all the wisdom of the scribes and Pharisees."[60] Having canvassed Illinois in the summer and fall, Oglesby was convinced that Lincoln was "still the Idol and the hope of the people," but these same people expressed that perhaps his chief fault "seems to have been a somewhat too much indulgence in clemency to Traitors and their confederates under your power." The war had spread beyond the battlefield, Oglesby advised, and the general consensus among the people was in favor of forcing "the rebels to submit humbly to the Laws without a single indulgence."[61]

Lincoln believed in the people and in their devotion to the Union, even when he doubted his candidacy. The war strengthened the Union even as it scarred the populace. Governors had exhausted neither Northern manpower, nor its resources, and, if necessary, could continue the fight indefinitely. If the election results were demoralizing to Southerners, Northerners saw it vindication of popular democracy. In trumpeting the late success, *Harper's Weekly* perceived that Lincoln's victory had affirmed what Northerners came to believe—"the people are conscious of the power and force of their own Government." Wrote Curtis, "No system in history was ever exposed to such a strain directly along the fibre as that which ours has endured in the war and the political campaign, and no other could possibly have endured it successfully."[62] Lincoln's victory resulted from the "general intelligence of the people," who believed in perpetual federal partnership between nation and state. Determination to secure that alliance brought citizens to accept that only a vigorous and unyielding war would end the conflict and deter future challenges. Federalism worked because national and state leaders cooperated to make it work.[63]

Reaping the Harvest

The triumphant election season inspired governors to use the opportunity of Thanksgiving Day to express appreciation and humiliation. Some chief executives traveled long distances to be among the soldiers in the field, while others arranged to ensure that soldiers shared a holiday feast. Gilmore sent Larkin Mason to Washington to supervise the distribution of over 15,000 pounds of turkey and chicken for the New Hampshire boys in the Army of the Potomac. "True it has cost lots of money," Mason wrote Gilmore, but "it will be as popular a move as you have ever made." He boasted, "Not a N.H. man in the field or in the hospital or on detailed service failed to be provided for from our preparations except the 8th and 14th Regts." At each camp the boys serenaded Mason, who responded that he was merely an agent of Gilmore, who "has always been the soldiers [*sic*] friend." Orchestrating a feast that fed more than 6,000 men, Gilmore's Thanksgiving gesture was long remembered among the New Hampshire troops.[64] Brough had similar thoughts about the festive day, not only for the soldiers, but also for their families at home. Soldier pay was notoriously behind, but Ohioans waited on bounties that never came that fall. These circumstances, combined with a shrinking local economy, resulted in hardships for many families suffering from want of relief. In the Cincinnati area alone some 4,000 families were on assistance. So wretched were conditions that Brough issued a circular in mid-November to the military committees of Ohio counties seeking relief funds for such families. He cited Thanksgiving as the suitable occasion to share wood, money, and food with the disheartened and less fortunate townspeople. "I do not ask *charity* for the families of these men,' he appealed. "I ask open manifestations of gratitude."[65]

Meanwhile, Sherman left Atlanta with his 65,000 soldiers and continued his conquest of Georgia by heading for Savannah. Confederate General John B. Hood hoped to counter his offensive, but decided it better to move his Army of Tennessee back into Tennessee to cut Union supply lines. Instead of drawing Sherman back through Georgia, this move pulled Union General Thomas's Army of the Cumberland northward toward Columbia. As the closing days of November turned cold and wintry, so too did these armies move closer to a grand battle just south of the Tennessee capital. Although Thomas was reluctant to give battle, his superiority of numbers prompted Lincoln to press him to attack. By 30 November, near the town of Franklin, some fifteen miles south of Nashville, soldiers engaged in another brutal conflict on the Tennessee soil. Of the roughly 25,000 Federals engaged, over 2,300 men were lost. Confederates suffered more than twice as many casualties, despite engaging roughly the same number of troops. The following morning Schofield and Thomas headed for Nashville, dug in around the city, and prepared to save the capital. Confederates swung around to Murfreesboro and probed for days, trying to draw out the Federals, until inclement weather and sheer exhaustion stalled operations.[66]

The din of battle crackled through the Tennessee woods that autumn while Northern representatives made their way to Washington to open the second session of the Thirty-eighth Congress. There were great expectations that this session would finish what congressmen had begun the previous winter. Lincoln's State of the Union, delivered on 6 December gave reason to be optimistic, as it spoke of improved foreign relations, increased federal expenditures, and tremendous growth. Yet the sixty-second paragraph moved his message away from railroads and public lands and focused on the conflict. "The war continues," Lincoln argued "all the important lines and positions . . . have been maintained, and our arms have steadily advanced," and while these were important, he declared that "important movements have also occurred during the year to the effect of moulding [*sic*] society for the durability of the Union."[67] For all the fighting and Reconstruction efforts, Maryland had proven to be the example of "complete success" thus far in the war, because slavery had been abolished. "Like another foul spirit, being driven out," Lincoln maintained, "it may seek to tear her, but it will woo her no more."[68] In the end, the popular verdict confirmed that Lincoln's message had the benefit of political security and military foresight. The "just cause" Northerners were fighting for had borne fruit in not only preserving the Union but also abolishing the institution Southerners hoped to avoid losing. Noah Brooks observed that even naysayers such as Thaddeus Stevens remarked that the message was "the wisest and best which the President ever sent to Congress, and leading men generally concur in the opinion of the critically wise Pennsylvanian."[69]

Governors read Lincoln's message as it came over the wires, but they paid closer attention to the correspondents' reports from Union armies in Tennessee and Georgia. Under administrative pressure to attack, Thomas did his part and threw his 50,000 Federals against Hood's 25,000 Confederates. In the showdown over Nashville both armies engaged with full force for two days from 15 to 16 December, and Thomas managed to break the Confederates, forcing them to withdraw. It was an impressive victory with comparatively few casualties, and dealt a considerable blow to Southerners hoping to hold onto what was left of the Confederate heartland. Hood's army crossed the Tennessee River and headed south. Awakened before midnight to the good news, Stanton wired back, "We will give you a hundred guns in the morning."[70] He wired a congratulatory communiqué to the governors to bolster their spirits, hopeful they could use the victory to induce volunteers to the ranks.[71]

Days after the Union triumph at Franklin, Lincoln called for another 300,000 volunteers within fifty days. Yet federal coercion produced more problems than it solved, and governors once again argued over credits and relied on state and local assistance. Conscription had lost its influence in encouraging men forward and revealed the limited nature of patriotism that severely plagued governors' efforts. In echoing Emerson's words, Curtis had identified the problems of standing behind the votes. To continue the war that Northern voters hoped to carry on, governors would have to rely more on the efficiency of soldiers in the ranks than the numeric superiority Grant and Sherman demanded. Governors worked with Fry to raise new regiments, but they were convinced that the reenlistment of veterans would prove more effective in the field. In short, the administrators and wagers of war had woven themselves into one national acceptance of what precisely would win the war.[72]

Sherman's exploits in Georgia helped crystalize these attitudes. In his campaign from Atlanta to Savannah, dubbed the "march to the sea," the commander scorched the countryside. Vengeful soldiers tired of the war determined to stamp out the rebellion by plundering the landscape to demoralize civilians. By the third week in December, Sherman's army reached Savannah, invested it, and offered it to Lincoln as a Christmas gift. Along the way, however, Sherman had driven slaves away from his ranks, and the political fallout was more daunting than even the commander had assumed. Arriving in Georgia's river city, Reuben Farnum, a Minnesota artillerist, had never been farther away from home and wrote to his family of Sherman's scorched earth policy. "I never saw such a destruction of property in my life," he reported. "I don't believe thare [sic] war left a nough [sic] to fead [sic] what cattles [sic] that ware left in the counttrey [sic]. I don't know what the wamon [sic] and children is going to eat but I don't know as I care."[73] Still, the commander needed to make use of the fugitive slaves.

Sherman's capture of Savannah, in Lincoln's words, brought "those who sat in darkness, to see a great light."[74] It was welcome news indeed, and it buoyed morale among Northerners facing the hardships of another daunting winter at war. On hearing the news, Smith wired his compliments from Montpelier. "Accept my congratulations at the splendid Christmas Gift from Maj Gen Sherman," he wrote. "The Nation will be pleased to share it with you."[75] Governors followed Sherman's army closely, and as much as they could, attended to the welfare of the soldiers. Coordinating relief efforts over several hundred miles, however, became costly. Too, it was more difficult and dangerous for political officials to travel into the Deep South. Governors increasingly relied on quartermasters, sanitary commissions, and local relief societies to channel additional aid to the men of Sherman's army. Still, soldiers looked to governors for support, especially with winter approaching. Letters poured into statehouses seeking humanitarian aid. From Augusta to Madison governors spent the Christmas season complying with Lincoln's call. The well of manpower, however, had frozen over and so had the hospitable mood of the election. Northerners prepared to endure another long and inhospitable winter that would aggravate suffering. Soldiers and their families struggled to meet the cruelties of war and increasingly turned to governors for assistance. Once again, the winter brought renewed attentiveness to relief, and governors assumed greater importance among their constituents, who had grown accustomed to assistance. "I have seen many sad sights in the hospitals and on the battlefields," wrote Connecticutan Robert R. Corson to Buckingham, having journeyed back to Hartford from Camp Parole in Annapolis where he observed the wretched conditions, "but there is nothing that makes my heart so sick as the story of these poor boys sufferings, from their own lips."[76]

Winter weather had fully enveloped the capital city, and Washington resumed its place as a hotbed of gossip, lobbying, and political intrigue. Whether in the nation's capital or in state capitals, legislative sessions turned on political power and reminded governors that they were party leaders. Lincoln benefited from their allegiance to cause and to comrade. When Gilmore discovered that Nehemiah G. Ordway had made some disparaging remarks about Amos Tuck, he wired Lincoln in Tuck's defense. Ordway had been a New Hampshire Republican state senator and postal agent, and was serving as the sergeant-at-arms for the House of Representatives. He had written Lincoln on several occasions during the war to report on the state's political-military matters. Tuck, too, was a loyal Republican, but Ordway had gossiped that he allegedly used his influence as a Boston naval agent to advance Chase's recent presidential candidacy. Gilmore dispelled such rumors to save Lincoln from the "pernicious influence" of those who would like nothing better than to see the Union dissolved or weakened by deceiving the president. It was supporters like Tuck, Gilmore argued, who supported Lincoln during the "darkest times of the last four years," and who had "been an unfaltering friend to yourself and to your administration, ready to defend both on all occasions."[77]

Yates was no stranger to lobbying, and the congressional session also brought him to Capitol Hill to campaign for a Senate seat. He spent much of his time conversing with colleagues about his fitness for the post. He bragged to Stephen S. Phelps that 95 percent of all Union members as well as "nearly all our soldiers in the field desire my election."[78] The governor had considerable support from the press, especially from Springfield's *Illinois State Journal*. Yet, he could not overcome the *Chicago Tribune's* opposition, as well as Democratic state papers that exposed his weakness for drinking. More important, however, was that his opposition worked in his favor by promoting only one candidate. Indeed, Republicans Logan, Palmer, and Washburne condemned Yates more than they campaigned for themselves, which in the end backfired. As the year ended, Yates's prospects appeared favorable.[79]

Few political leaders understood legislative pressures better than Stanton. After all, his appointment came during the winter of 1862, when congressmen pressed Lincoln to remove Cameron. While in Washington, representatives inundated the secretary with laborious rounds of interviews, correspondence, and frequent applications and inquiries. Governors routinely worked directly with Stanton, but failing that, went to Lincoln, or through congressmen. Managing the war through telegraphic dispatches expedited decisions and influence, and governors exploited such technology. Even draped with national power, Stanton could not shed his quick temper, shameful arrogance, and insufferable attention to rules. The secretary cared little for popularity. He lacked respect for most of his colleagues, thinking them intellectually inferior. Often they were. Governors knew Stanton to have an ugly, unpardonable side, often suffering outbursts on his visitors, but they seldom witnessed these tantrums. Yet the War Department's "bulldog" contributed significantly to the Union's success by bringing the nation's warring resources under his watchful eye. Indeed, his singular mission throughout the war was to nationalize and maintain the flow of manpower to the armies. He recognized early on that governors played an influential role in his efforts. Even if he initially failed to respect loyal chief executives, as he did West Pointers, he grew to respect them as partners in the enterprise. Gradually his aversion to their incessant ways dissipated, and he learned to rely on them for advice in military matters. He had concluded long before December that conscription was no longer useful, largely because governors convinced him of its waning influence. Bounties had corrupted the practice of raising volunteers, but governors had little else to induce men into the ranks. When Brough advised that raising new regiments might induce his Ohioans to enlist, Stanton allowed him to raise ten new regiments. When large numbers of Southern refugees, women, and children entirely destitute were coming into Indianapolis, Morton sought Stanton's assistance in obtaining federal relief. Stanton, however, could find nothing in the existing laws that provided such assistance, but pressed Congress to adopt appropriate legislation granting him authority to assist. Though these decisions by Stanton were minor, they demonstrated how he achieved federal-state cooperation.[80]

CHAPTER TWENTY

It Is Worth While to Live in These Days

New Year's Day fell on Sunday in 1865. Washington was blanketed by an inhospitable sleet and fog, and the gloomy weather belied the hopeful spirit of residents thronging the capital. Northerners had much to celebrate. "There are few faithful American citizens who can doubt that the new year will be a happy one," wrote *Harper's Weekly*. "This is the moment of the year, when men examine their moral, social, and financial accounts; when they form good resolutions."[1] Governors hoped such resolutions included joining the military. Although Union commanders had positioned their armies to end the conflict, there was much work to be done in replenishing the ranks. Inaugural messages, such as Fenton's, inspired citizens to come forward to aid the armies and end the conflict. Days later, however, he boarded a train and headed for Washington to convince the War Department to revise New York's excessive quota.[2]

In Indianapolis, black Indianans commemorated the Emancipation Proclamation's anniversary by celebrating in the streets. Many governors incorporated black freedom in their inaugurals, especially since they understood that the abolition amendment was before Congress. They hoped to persuade legislators to accept black freedom, and used Maryland and Missouri as examples to encourage similar movements in Kentucky and Delaware. Fletcher came into office when Radical Unionists demanded immediate emancipation in Missouri, and he pledged to see slavery abolished. "The only instance in the world's history of a rebellion against an existing Government in the name of and for the sake of Slavery," he argued, "has resulted in the enlargement of Liberty: and the retributive Nemesis has sent the system of Slavery crashing down to hopeless destruction in the conflagration of a civil strife lighted by its own hand."[3]

Yet many Northerners had not embraced all the war's changes, especially when it came to black equality. There was never broad support for what might be termed equal rights for freed people, even if the Constitution and self-government had implied it for decades. Even those governors who advanced the abolitionist front did so at great risk of alienating the electorate. That emancipation was a military necessity to win the war allowed governors the means to soften the blow for Northern conservatives and win themselves the gubernatorial office. Governors followed the same path that Lincoln charted early in the war by emphasizing to the citizenry that the Constitution implicitly maintained that all men were equal, and that even a political majority could not deny these principles. Owning a slave was fundamentally at odds with the notion of pursuing wealth freely that many Northerners, including conservatives, who respected the Constitution, subscribed too. Yet, they did so while maintaining antiblack feelings. One young New Hampshire soldier could not wait to get home, accompanied by his "first rate 'darkey,'" who would do all his chores. "Perhaps you *think* that you could never get over the feeling of disgust at the sight of a negro," he wrote his wife from Maryland, "but I *know* that you would." However, "Do not imagine," he confessed, "that I have become a 'nigger worshiper' or that I have been converted to any of the opinions of Wendall [*sic*] Phillips, in regard to 'negro equality,' for what I have learned, on the subject, by personal observation, goes directly against any such theory, and I never yet, begun to believe in the doctrine that 'all men are created equal,' but I do not believe, that because the negro is not equal to the white race, that he ought to be banished from the face of the earth."[4]

Stanton worried that such attitudes might pervade the army as it advanced deeper into the South. Union military success brought equally great responsibilities in caring for the freedmen. He especially fretted about Sherman, who disapproved of the army's use of blacks and preferred them in subordinate roles. The secretary had taken a reprieve from his office and, despite a serious illness, traveled to Georgia to settle the mingling issues of captured cotton, prisoner exchange, organization of black troops, and the seizure of Confederate property. Since the previous May, when Sherman left Tennessee, until December, when he reached Savannah, the commander's campaign had been a remarkable military achievement. It was a bold move that struck at civilian populations, and editors likened its significance to Napoleon's celebrated march from Warsaw to Moscow in 1812. The commander was anxious to press north through the Carolinas on his way to Virginia and expected to liberate thousands of slaves along the way. Stanton needed reassurance that he would handle free blacks according to government policies.[5]

Triumph over Obstacles

On a cold, serene 6 January morning, Morton stood before his assemblymen with a reinvigorated spirit buoyed by his reelection. Like Lincoln, he had weathered the political storm of 1864, though unlike Lincoln, the governor survived it alone, abandoned by a cantankerous legislature that had assailed his administration. Morton was among the few governors who remained in office throughout the war. The state constitution prohibited a chief executive to serve more than four years, but he came into office while serving as lieutenant governor, which permitted him a term of his own. Besides, few political leaders could counter his popularity. Forced to run Indiana's war machine practically single-handedly, Morton proved more than qualified to meet the challenges presented by his opposition. For all his faults, Morton "kept pace with the people" in moving them to support the Union. For the next hour his message described in detail all he had done without legislators and urged them that the time had come for them to meet the changes created by the war. "Whatever it may cost us to preserve the Union," he argued, "we may be assured it will cost us everything to lose it."[6] Simple in its summation, Morton's words represented the nature of the struggle to preserve the Union since the war's inception. The reward was equal to, if not greater than, the sacrifice. Governors translated the war into a contest to safeguard national sovereignty and vindicate democracy.

Yates also had Senate aspirations, and, by the first week in January, legislators voted in his favor over James C. Robinson. For all their efforts in exposing his personal failings, the anti-Yates men could not undermine the governor's popularity. The war governor gave his final message on 2 January, and it chronicled the details of a turbulent past year. Most significantly, however, was that he urged representatives to repeal Illinois's black laws. Black abolitionist and prominent Chicagoan John Jones had organized a movement to repeal the laws the previous year and had petitioned Yates to promote the passage through the legislature. In his parting words, Yates explained the rationale for their repeal. Slavery had been a "solar eclipse" upon the land, he argued, and the Emancipation Proclamation removed the "black wall." Legislators had the opportunity to remove the wall in Illinois by repealing the black laws. The reestablishment of a united government must commence over "the grave of treason," hallowed by those who died to make it so. Dubbed the "soldier's friend," Yates carried the tribute with great pride, and passed the torch to the new governor.[7]

Oglesby had also endeared himself to soldiers. A Kentucky native, he had been orphaned as a young boy and forced to live with an uncle in Decatur, Illinois. He fought in the Mexican War and afterward traveled to Louisville to study law and two years later ventured to California. He joined the Republican Party in the 1850s, and became so popular that in 1860 Illinoisans voted him into the state senate. In April 1861 he halted his political career to join the Union cause as colonel of the 8th Illinois. Serving under Grant, his hospitable demeanor won him favor with the troops and his superiors, and he soon became known as "Uncle Dick." He saw action in the western theater and by the spring of 1862 was promoted to brigadier general. He suffered severe wounds in his chest and back at the Battle of Corinth in October 1862, which hospitalized him for a period. He continued to serve throughout 1863 and 1864, but he resigned his commission in May to return to politics. "Eloquent, earnest, patriotic and brave," noted an Illinois editor, "there is no loyal man whose heart does not kindle with enthusiasm at the mention of the name of 'Dick Oglesby,' the hero of Corinth."[8]

Changing of the guard continued in Michigan, where Blair stepped aside for Crapo. The aging chief executive was as popular as Yates and Morton, and voters endorsed his radicalism and his attention to the soldiers. His last words to legislators urged them to care for the soldiers, especially those returning home and in need of convalescence. He had sent 90,000 volunteers to war and felt personally responsible for them. "Under the hard experiences of the past four years," he remarked, "the relations sustained by the State and National governments towards [sic] each other have come to be more clearly understood and more accurately defined." He continued, "We understand now the full meaning of that pernicious phrase 'sovereign States,' which had stealthily crept its way ... into the common language of the people." He added, "Under this teaching, the foundations of loyalty and fidelity to the National Government were sapped, and insensibly the false theory grew and extended itself, until, under the shadow of that Upas tree, the whole body of the rebellion found shelter." The war's exigencies, he maintained, necessitated the exercise of the utmost powers of sovereignty of both nation and state. Yet Northerners had acquiesced with great unanimity to the constitutional power conferred on the national government. In doing so, he argued, they confirmed that "there is, and can be, under the Constitution of the United States, only one paramount sovereign authority," which Blair argued was the federal government. The war helped strengthen the national government, and citizens rallied to its defense to ensure its preservation.[9]

New to the offices they assumed, incoming governors, as well as the veteran chief executives, continued the maintenance of nearly one million soldiers. The national government had expanded during the war to meet the army's needs, and governors helped engineer a state-oriented activism to assist what had become the nation's largest institution. But, by early 1865, governors faced the increasing burdens of relying on state assistance to assume the flow of casualties behind the lines. As much as Lincoln's December call signaled to the Confederate high command that he was digging deeper to end the conflict, governors were more inundated by the soldiers coming home than they were by volunteers coming forward. Although newspaper coverage of winter victories might spur volunteers forward, Democratic journalists also covered casualty rates and the destitution at home. Several governors addressed these needs to their legislatures, hoping to convince members to press on until surrender. Smith, for example, told Rhode Island assemblymen that "whatever difficulties there may be to overcome," he would work to resolve them, provided they work together until the end of the conflict.[10] Oglesby had not even been inaugurated when he received Schofield's request for new regiments to replenish those mustering out of the 23rd Army Corps.[11]

Most Northerners failed to recognize that Lincoln's call for additional troops was to compensate for the sizeable shortfall resulting from the previous July call. The deficiency attested to conscription's failure, but, besides bounties, it was the federal government's only resource to induce men to enlist. Many governors resented having to resort, once again, to account for their quotas, believing they had convinced Stanton of the draft's inefficiency. Lewis wired Stanton that drafting in Wisconsin was a failure and that a feeling was "gaining ground in the West, and particularly in this State, that the Western States have been called upon to furnish more than their due proportion of men."[12] The governor convinced Fry to investigate Wisconsin quota figures and correct any errors. Miller had similar problems and disputed Minnesota's figures. Minnesotans were busy protecting their frontier from Indian raids, he argued, and the demand for more men would "discourage the most loyal and active supporters of the Government amongst us."[13] He protested the legislature's pending provision that authorized men of means to procure substitutes from among those who may have been enrolled and liable to military duty. "I have not a doubt," he complained to Senator Ramsey, "that this is another attempt of eastern capital to fill the quota of the wealthy states from the North West."[14] He told Stanton that delays in pay had demoralized the soldiers and forced families to endure severe hardships. One Minnesota soldier had not been paid in eight months, he complained, arguing that "this is discreditable to our Gov't, inconvenient to the soldier and distressing to his family."[15]

Many adjutant generals agreed that the draft was a failure and proposed to Stanton that governors assume full responsibility for recruiting so that a "better class of men" could be obtained for the service. Yet Andrew's friends were lobbying for his selection to Lincoln's new cabinet, and they worried that drawing too much attention over formulas might jeopardize his candidacy. Andrew was wise to his own shortcomings, even if he saw them as virtues. "I think the truth is," he confessed to Weed, "I am too obstinate, and insusceptible to external influences by great men to be very acceptable in Washington." Besides, he believed the administration lacked "coherence, method, purpose and consistency,—not in the sense which impugns its patriotism or its philanthropies . . . but in a sense which affects its intelligent unity."[16] Andrew was among Sumner's chief rivals as New England's most-esteemed political leader, and the senator encouraged the governor to stay the course in Boston. Writing to a friend, Sumner advised that it was in Andrew's "best interest" to remain in Boston, where he was more effective and had developed a connection with the people, having just been reelected by a sizeable majority.[17]

As governors sparred with the War Department to avoid the 15 February draft, lame-duck congressmen argued over the Thirteenth Amendment. The debate appeared to turn the conflict into a struggle some Americans had perhaps perceived the war to be about in 1861. Even as the deliberations continued in Washington, Missourians convened in St. Louis and amended its state constitution to include slavery's abolition. Fletcher wired Stanton the good news, saying that he was writing from "free Missouri to a true friend" to "prove that by deeds, not words, we signalize our deliverance."[18] He also sent dispatches announcing the news to several governors, including Curtin. "To the Governor of Pennsylvania," read a wire, "Free Missouri greets her eldest sister." Curtin replied that Pennsylvanians welcomed "her disenthralled sister of Missouri, redeemed in the agony of the nation, and amid the throes of a wanton rebellion: Her offering to liberty comes baptized in her richest blood."[19] Although Fletcher rejoiced, he prepared for repercussions. He replaced Copperhead militia officers with radical men, which caused a stir within the state militia and touched off local wars. So concerned was Lincoln over the "irregular violence" that he wired General

Grenville Dodge to appeal to the people "to go to their homes and let one another alone."[20] It appeared to Lincoln that the Union troops were causing as much problem as the guerrillas, and he proposed removing them if necessary. Fletcher, however, protested the removal but continued to negotiate with Lincoln in returning Missourians to civil governance. It would take more time, he argued, but in two months, he would have his wish.[21] Kentucky's ongoing guerrilla warfare also worried Morton and Brough. Even on the way out of office Blair had his problems with guerrillas from Canada crossing into Michigan, and he needed assistance. Hooker took these matters seriously because he had confidential information that Confederate refugees might attack Cleveland or Detroit, "for purposes of plunder and incendiarism."[22] Hooker wrote Brough, "I need not tell you, Governor that if anything of this sort is attempted I intend that somebody shall be hurt before it is over, if I have to go to Canada to do it."[23]

With Sherman's worries behind him, Stanton departed Savannah and sailed to Wilmington, North Carolina, to congratulate Admiral David Porter on his capture of Fort Fisher, located on the Cape Fear River. Porter's gunboats forced the coastal stronghold to surrender after a three-day assault. Fort Fisher was known as the Southern Gibraltar, and the victory had strategic implications as the fort was the last major port open to the Confederacy and had provided refuge to blockade runners supplying the Army of Northern Virginia. Seizure of the port and release of the Union blockading fleet encouraged Stanton that the war would not last much longer. Sherman outlined to the secretary his plans to march through South Carolina, en route to Goldsborough, North Carolina. It was an ambitious campaign, and one that would require additional manpower. Stanton returned to Washington buoyed by the commander's expectations. He was eager to bring additional troops forward to sustain Sherman's campaign, as well as assist Grant's army at Petersburg.[24]

Stanton's journey to Georgia and North Carolina encouraged him that Confederate defeat was not far off. Union armies had positioned themselves to aid Grant's efforts in Virginia, and it was a matter of time before Lee's army succumbed to surrender. Back in Washington, the secretary turned to the politics of war. Fenton arrived to discuss New York quotas. Having reviewed the figures, the chief executive argued that New York had actually exceeded its quotas by more than 5,000 men. Fry concurred and admitted that careless mustering officers and ignorance of the law had caused the confusion. Informed of these new developments, Fenton returned to New

York believing he had convinced Lincoln that they were "more than half right," and thus the president called upon Stanton to work out a compromise. There was something about Fry's characterization of bungled management that worried Lincoln. To clarify precisely where formulas had gone awry, he appointed a board to examine proper quotas and credits and to settle all disputes. Given the difficulty of arriving at figures agreed upon by both Stanton and the governors, this became an enormous undertaking. Such problems convinced Lincoln to postpone the draft.[25]

Thirteenth Amendment

By January's end, Lincoln and Stanton had turned their attention away from the draft, quotas, and bounty corruption and directed their efforts to the Thirteenth Amendment. Lincoln worked for weeks to secure the votes for the amendment before the war ended, but encouraged Grant to press on. Still, he allowed Confederate commissioners the opportunity to discuss peace and permitted them to pass through Union lines at City Point. Meanwhile, he waited for the outcome on Capitol Hill. Although the Senate had passed the Thirteenth Amendment the previous spring with little fanfare, Lincoln asked the lame-duck House members to consider the amendment. On 31 January, before a packed gallery, representatives prevailed on the momentous issue of the nineteenth century. Indeed, a trail of people lined the corridors and lobbies stretching outside in anticipation of transmitting the news from the chambers like a grand tidal wave of information to the streets. "The scene in the House last evening . . . was entirely without precedent in all our national history," declared the Washington correspondent to the *Boston Daily Advertiser*. "I doubt if three thousand persons ever sat in a higher state of anxious suspense than those in that full chamber did during the call of the roll on the final vote."[26] When the Speaker announced the requisite two-thirds vote had been achieved, a more heroic exhibition could not have captured the celebration of that historic moment. Word immediately went out to Lincoln and the War Department, and telegraph operators furiously tapped the news through the wires across the North. Spirited newsboys carrying evening editions of papers dotted Washington's streets shouting "great Union victory—another great victory."[27] Carl Schurz, founding member of Wisconsin's Republican Party, witnessed the scene and reported the spectacle to his wife. "The galleries were crowded and even the floor of the house was filled with spectators," he noted, and when the word of the final vote was given and Speaker Schuyler Colfax called for adjournment, the House exploded with excitement. "The ladies waved their handkerchiefs," he observed, "the men threw their hats into the air, they embraced, they shook hands, and ten minutes passed before the hurrahing and the enthusiastic racket ceased." Schurz remarked, "I will tell you that in the moment when the enthusiasm broke forth in the house I did not join in the shouts. I believe I should have been unable to speak." The moment moved him to conclude: "It is worth while to live in these days." For Radical Republicans such as Schurz, who had labored "in the interest of great ideas" such as abolition, the amendment was the nation's reward.[28]

It was a victory like none other, yet the army was small, just a tiny cadre of political leaders. Casualties were not soldiers, but slave owners, who had become victims of their own revolution. Although the institution had been the cause for political antagonism and bloodshed over the last several decades, it took only 119 members of the House, armed with a singular purpose, to abolish slavery. As much as Union armies had changed the Southern landscape, Federal congressmen shaped the contours of its future. Lincoln shared the euphoria of the momentous day and reveled in submitting the Thirteenth Amendment to the states for ratification. However the war began, and for whatever purpose people believed they were fighting, slavery's abolition worked its way backward into the history of the war, becoming inseparably linked to Union war aims. The most divisive issue of the American people for over half a century had been slavery, argued Captain Henry Boyd of the 4th Vermont, sitting in camp near Petersburg, and some of the greatest minds could not solve it. It has been the "damning sin of our nation," he wrote, so much so that the federal government had "seen fit to change the constitution prohibiting human servitude ever again to stain our land."[29]

Wanting to sound the bells heard round the world signaling freedom for slaves, Andrew wired Lincoln and requested that he telegraph as soon as he affixed his signature to the amendment. "I desire to echo it immediately by a National Salute on Boston Common," he wrote, "with a chorus of all the Church bells of Massachusetts."[30] Eager to be the first state to ratify the amendment, Oglesby wired Lincoln that same evening that Illinois legislators had approved the amendment by a large majority even before the official copy reached Springfield. It was a stunning victory, made all the more relevant given that those same legislators had only days before repealed the state's black laws. "Illinois has repealed her black laws," noted *Harper's*

Weekly, "indeed she could hardly help wiping the stain from her face when her neighbor Missouri was lifting her whole body out of the slough."[31]

Sustained by his triumph, Lincoln arranged to join Seward at Hampton Roads, where he conferred with Confederate officials Alexander H. Stephens, John A. Campbell, and Robert Hunter. The conference lasted for four hours, yet Lincoln was unable to secure unconditional surrender of the Confederate forces. He even offered to compensate slave owners if Southern states ratified the Thirteenth Amendment, but the commissioners refused. That negotiations would end in failure hardly surprised Lincoln. He understood the determination of political leaders to carry on the war for their purposes. Lincoln was equally determined. The Confederacy would have to be forced into submission on the battlefield, and he was confident surrender was forthcoming. Sherman's army had trekked across the rivers and swamps of South Carolina, leaving destruction in its wake, and Grant continued his relentless assault against Lee. Lincoln and Seward left the conference concluding that the prospects of a reunified nation, tragically, would mean more casualties until leaders were convinced otherwise.[32]

Upon Lincoln's return, news greeted him that Northern legislatures had lined up behind the Thirteenth Amendment. After Illinois, several states, including Rhode Island, Michigan, Maryland, New York, Pennsylvania, West Virginia, Missouri, Maine, Kansas, and Massachusetts, immediately ratified the amendment. A week later, Ohio, Indiana, Minnesota, and Wisconsin representatives also endorsed the amendment. Other states, including Vermont, Connecticut, and New Hampshire, joined in the movement in the coming months. Delawareans and Kentuckians, however, rejected the amendment. Delaware governor Cannon prevailed on representatives to ratify the amendment, but the Democratic legislature refused. Copperhead members had been relentless in their opposition to the war, often to the governor's embarrassment. In his recent message, Cannon recommended that representatives provide bounties and land tracts to incentivize volunteering, but instead members offered greater inducements to citizens who secured substitutes. The *Delaware Republican* editor declared that such actions were shameful and "would disgrace the Hottentots."[33] Yet in the coming weeks Delaware's Unionism lost its chief advocate. Cannon succumbed to typhoid-pneumonia he contracted after helping to extinguish a fire and died on 1 March, at his Bridgeville residence. Lieutenant Governor Gove Saulsbury, a Kent County physician and prominent Democrat, who was then the presiding officer of the Senate, succeeded him. Cannon had cast aside his devotion to the Democratic Party when the war broke out and kept Delaware in the Union. He plunged himself into supporting the war and Lincoln's cause, but his opponents, including members of the Copperhead press, criticized him unmercifully. In many respects, he was likened to Hicks, Gamble, and Morton, who suffered similar abuse but who refused to waiver. In short, Delaware's Unionism died with Cannon.[34]

Kentuckians were just as antagonistic as Delawareans were toward the Thirteenth Amendment. Perhaps they believed Lincoln's protection of slavery in the Union states was their reward for remaining loyal. Yet, after four years of Kentucky's allegiance, Bramlette feared the amendment might force the state out of the Union. Kentucky legislators rejoiced in rejecting the amendment. The governor told representatives, however, that once enough states had ratified it Kentuckians would be forced to comply whether they liked it or not. More frustrating to Kentucky slave owners, however, was that slaves recruited into the Union military had brought on increased guerrilla warfare. "I suppose you are aware there is a big game between Bramlette and Burbridge," reported Shelbyville lawyer John B. Cochran to James Speed, Lincoln's new attorney general, and that "the guerrillas are devastating our state robbing and murdering everywhere."[35] Lincoln made Bramlette's life easier by removing Burbridge and replacing him with General John M. Palmer. The decision was intended to restore harmony between Lincoln and Kentuckians, but it would take time.[36]

New Jersey and Indiana were just as divided in deciding the color of their political stripes on the amendment. Parker had admirably navigated the treacherous political shoals of his divided state, yet he possessed a perplexing blend of Republican virtues and Democratic impulses. In his January message, he argued that while emancipation had many virtues, it should be left to the Southern people. The governor's desire to extend a conciliatory Reconstruction policy to Southerners cost him politically. When his name was suggested as a candidate to replace Senator John Ten Eyck, the governor had done little to improve his image by leading the charge to reject the Thirteenth Amendment. Still, because New Jersey was a state that had no slaves, it seemed unfathomable for voters not to abolish the institution, especially since they had sent New Jerseyites to fight a war that required emancipation to win. "It is humiliating to reflect," noted the editor of the *Trenton Daily State Gazette and Republican*, "that at a time when Missouri, Maryland, Kentucky, and West Virginia are striving to free themselves from the shackles of slavery the Governor of the *Free State* of New Jersey, should gravely put forth objections to the emancipation of the slaves, and recommend that it be left to the 'operation of the Divine Will,' without any effort on our part."[37] Only after its enactment did New Jersey ratify the amendment, as did California, Oregon, and Iowa.

There was no more humiliating relationship than that between Morton and Indiana legislators. Still, "only after long partisan debates and every parliamentary procrastination known to legislators" did Indiana ratify the Thirteenth Amendment.[38] It had been a long and acrimonious struggle to expand the administration's war aims, but ratification confirmed that Morton, like several Radical governors, understood the weapon of slavery could be used against the Confederacy. However much Morton had overstepped his bounds and antagonized conservatives in the past years, Lincoln and many Indianans would rather have Morton in their camp rather than outside of it. Indeed, George Julian, Radical Indiana senator, acknowledged that as much as he and Morton were enemies, the chief executive was a "sort of phenomenal figure in American politics during the war period, and played a very remarkable part in the affairs of Indiana." Julian described that "He was made for revolutionary times," and that when Indiana's history was written, "it might fitly contain a chapter on 'The Reign of Oliver P. Morton.'"[39]

For the moment it appeared as though the revolution had quieted down. By mid-February, Sherman's army crossed the Congaree River and caught its first glimpse of Columbia, South Carolina. His Federals swarmed the city to conquer the recalcitrant residents, and the commander accepted its surrender on 17 February. For days afterward, Union soldiers set Columbia ablaze, and destroyed whatever gave the city its economy. More than any other event in recent months, Sherman's capture of the South Carolina capital spurred recruiting for the governors—the end was in sight, and thus their time in the service would be short. Still, some complained over quotas and requested adjustments forcing Lincoln to acquiesce.[40]

In those joyous days accompanying Sherman's burning of Columbia, came sadness to Marylanders. Senator Hicks, a former governor as important to Maryland as Cannon was to Delaware, had died from paralysis. Having suffered a violent ankle sprain tripping on a carriage step, Hicks's condition worsened after a skin infection caused his right foot to be amputated. Although he had recently sold his farm to a Northern gentleman and had planned to retire, the sixty-six-year-old career politician died from apoplexy in Washington's Metropolitan Hotel. As dictated by tradition, congressmen gathered two days later in the Senate chambers to pay homage to the fallen Marylander. The former governor had commanded significant power in holding Maryland in the Union, and his death perhaps reminded Lincoln of those precious days when Maryland was more important than Kentucky. As much as he may have needed his native state in those critical days, he needed Maryland more. Indeed, when it appeared that representatives were about to abolish slavery months before, Hicks willingly conceded some $20,000 worth of his own slaves to help preserve the Union in Maryland. His death allowed the hard-bitten abolitionist John A. J. Creswell to ascend the ranks on Capitol Hill and work with Swann to transition Maryland through peace and liberation.[41]

Still, the war moved on, and border state governors combatted guerrilla warfare. Fletcher needed federal assistance to suppress bushwhackers in Missouri. Lincoln responded that the cure for these malcontents was within easy reach. He encouraged the governor to consider holding neighborhood meetings for the purpose of coming to peace. "At such meetings old friendships will cross the memory," he prophesied, "and honor and Christian Charity will come in to help."[42] Fletcher responded that Lincoln's policy would never work, because the war had wrought far too much collateral damage. "The State being infested with thousands of outlaws who are naturally and practically 'robbers' and 'cut-throats,'" he told Lincoln, "no good man desires to reach any understanding with them or to enter into any agreement to leave them alone."[43] Try as he might, Fletcher could not make Lincoln understand the war beyond the Mississippi River, few governors could. Even former army commander Crawford came to fully grasp the term "Jayhawking." Kansans struggled with a guerrilla warfare that had deteriorated conditions in the southwestern portion of the state. The governor traveled to Washington to convince Lincoln that affairs in Kansas were especially hostile and asked him to call off the draft. Sympathetic, Stanton allowed Crawford credit for an additional 3,000 men, and the governor wired his secretary in Topeka the good news.[44]

Californians and Oregonians read with great interest the military exploits of the eastern armies and the antics of border state guerrillas. Low and Gibbs had fought their personal wars much like Missourians, Kansans, and Minnesotans did against Indians, guerrillas, and marauders. Completely unprepared to safeguard the vast frontier and coast, both governors relied significantly upon the citizen-parties to assist them, especially in early spring, when Stanton removed General Alvord from command. His decision allowed General McDowell to centralize greater power in himself, but it lessened the number of units Low and Gibbs could rely on for protection. Gibbs protested Alvord's loss because the commander had brought order to Oregon. "The order," he supposed, "was probably procured through the influence of Senators [Benjamin F.] Harding and [James W.] Nesmith, neither of whom, in my judgment, ever intended to act with the Union Party."[45]

March arrived, and Northern attention turned to Washington and to Lincoln's second inaugural address. Ironically, just four years before, Lincoln came to the capital when the Union was dissolving and Northerners were apprehensive about its prospects. Their hopes, remarked *Harper's Weekly*, "wavered toward some deep resource of statesmanship, as yet unknown, which might master the storm and save the Republic." Northern expectations centered on Lincoln in large measure because his election had instigated secession, and his movement against the Confederacy would reflect the sentiments of the people. At the time, the national consciousness had found little expression of itself, wrote the editor, but now Lincoln had established a more perfect Union. Thousands of spectators arrived in Washington, anxious to hear his forecast for a reunified nation. Yet the late winter weather was anything but pleasant for the occasion. It was cold, windy, and muddy, left that way by a recent storm. News that eighteen states had ratified the Thirteenth Amendment and that Grant was about to end hostilities encouraged Lincoln as he drafted his second inaugural address.[46]

Glory of the Moment

The sun rose on the morning of 4 March, but it was hardly noticeable. It rained intermittently, and a steady wind blew that commenced an inhospitable day for Lincoln to deliver his second inaugural address. Still, the inclement weather did little to dampen the spirit of the capital city's finest moment. "As the hour of noon arrived," wrote Noah Brooks, "flocks of women streamed around the Capitol, in most wretched, wretched plight; crinoline was smashed, skirts bedaubed, and more antique, velvet, laces and such dry goods were streaked with mud from end to end."[47] Wrote Thomas Taylor of the 47th Ohio, who was passing through Washington, "A few minutes before the president appeared," the morning skies "cleared up and the sun shone out in its most glorious effulgence." Soon to become more than just the simple, unremarkable address that it was on paper, Lincoln's eloquent words did not disappoint the bedraggled Ohio soldier standing some thirty feet from the presidential scaffold.

> After the applause of the multitude was hushed, [Lincoln] arose, bowed—rather ungracefully and read his address. His countenance was radiant with hope, though furrowed with wrinkles sparkling with life full of freshness—beaming with humor and smiling with the greatest complacency as though he perfectly understood that every one in that vast assembly appreciated his efforts and meaning.... When he spoke of peace his upturned eyes, his depth of [tone] was of the heart ascending in [suppliant] words to the throne of the mighty Rulers of nations—He is not care worn, is not sad—his whole condition indicates a healthy cheerful state of mind and body and that he is full of compassion for the suffering necessarily incurred.[48]

"Simple and solemn" was how *Harper's Weekly* described Lincoln's address, concluding that the president "neither speculates, nor prophesizes, nor sentimentalizes," about the nation's struggle. "Four years have revealed to every mind the ghastly truth that the Government of the United States is struggling in a death-grapple with slavery," wrote the editor, "and as a new epoch of the Government opens in civil war, its Chief Magistrate states the vital point of the contest, and invokes God's blessing upon the effort of the country to finish its work in triumph."[49] Draped in his distinguished Supreme Court justice robes, Chase administered the oath, and the pomp and circumstance that dignified the occasion ended, to the approval of the attendees. Afterward the president shook hands with some 6,000 of the estimated 50,000 attendees, dined with his distinguished guests, and later attended the grand Inaugural Ball in the "Hall of Patents" and other adjacent buildings.[50]

Governors who were unable to travel to Washington read Lincoln's speech in the newspapers or over the wires as it tapped into the statehouses. Even if some governors thought him less popular in the 1864 campaign, they had not abandoned him. The Union was greater than the presidency and worth fighting for to preserve. Now, as the conflict neared its close, chief executives turned their attention to binding up the nation's wounds that Lincoln had alluded to in his address. It was just another fleeting moment engulfed by a war that had crippled the republic. Days later, Fletcher attempted Lincoln's conciliatory course of "malice toward none and charity for all" and issued a proclamation to his "fellow" Missourians. The time had

466 It Is Worth While to Live in These Days

come, he argued, to respect the supremacy of civil law and unite as members of one state and respect the Union authority. For all his good intentions, Fletcher's sentiments fell on deaf ears in Missouri.[51]

By mid-March Northerners read with great interest the news from the Virginia front, hopeful of Lee's surrender. Several governors, including Morton, had passed through Washington on their way to visit the troops. On one occasion Lincoln accompanied Morton in his presentation of a Confederate flag recently captured by Indiana soldiers at Fort Anderson, North Carolina. The governor met Lincoln at the National Hotel on the afternoon of 17 March, along with several Indiana officers for the ceremony. After exiting their carriage, Lincoln and Morton left the street and moments later appeared on the balcony of the hotel with the flag from the soldiers of the 140th Indiana. Morton spoke a few words to quiet the crowd and thanked his soldiers. "I have seen dark hours," he declared, "but my faith in the success of the cause has never been depressed."[52] Walt Whitman was standing below the balcony amidst the elm trees and noted that when Lincoln came forward, a hush came over the crowd. In his brief address the president was careful not to praise the Indianans above those men from other states, "remembering that all have done so well."[53] They had performed well, so well, in fact, that Lincoln took the opportunity to point out that the Confederacy must be at the bottom of their resources if they were considering employing slaves as soldiers. The question, he asked, was would those slaves fight for a people who had enslaved them against those who had liberated them.[54]

Despite rumors of a coming surrender and peace, the war had not stopped. Governors continued to deliver volunteers to satisfy their quotas, authorized arrests, and rounded up bounty jumpers. Fenton was doing all in his power to fulfill New York's quota and secured a suspension of the draft in New York City on 17 March to honor the anniversary of Saint Patrick and to avoid violence. Andrew pressed Lincoln to consider pardoning all persons under sentence for desertion or absence without leave, in which no aggravating circumstances appear and upon the recommendation of responsible parties. He argued this would be the "crowning act of kindness and would endear not only the Commander-in-Chief, but the Government itself, to the soldiers and their relatives, many of whom have been alienated by what seems to them the unjustifiable severity of the punishment of their father, brothers, and relatives." He continued, "I trust under such restrictions as many secure this kindness to the deserving you will frame and promulgate a general pardon and amnesty to all."[55]

The following week Lincoln set out for Grant's headquarters aboard the *River Queen* and arrived on the evening of 24 March. In the next few days he reviewed the camps and the soldiers and conferred with officers. Sherman arrived on the evening of 27 March, but conspicuously uninvited was "Old Brains." The two armies of the Potomac and the James were now positioned to close in on Lee, and Lincoln, Grant, and Sherman discussed a strategy for ending the conflict. When Sherman turned to the subject of peace and asked Lincoln what he had in mind, the president replied that he simply wanted to allow Confederates to go home so they could begin the process of returning to the Union. On 1 April, Lincoln sat aboard the *River Queen* in the spring air waiting for reports from the field. Lee abandoned his Petersburg lines and directed his dwindling army to Five Forks, a series of crossroads to the southwest. Meanwhile, the Confederate government hurriedly packed up its administrative documents and skedaddled south to Danville. Two days later General Godfrey Weitzel wired Stanton a short, but much anticipated telegram that read "I took Richmond at 8:15 A.M." The commander established headquarters in Davis's home.[56] Lincoln traveled to Richmond, where he encountered the war's wretched devastation, present everywhere in Richmond's burnt, desolate, and skeletal features. Lincoln was accompanied by a small military entourage, and it was fitting that, among the initial residents who recognized the president, no doubt by his legendary stovepipe hat, were a few black workers. Fatigue, fright, and destitution could hardly do justice to the scene that must have impressed him upon encountering the refugees. Such was the impression of Weitzel, who accompanied the president. When Weitzel asked what he should do in regard to the conquered people, "If I were in your place," Lincoln remarked consolingly, "I'd let 'em up easy, let 'em up easy."[57]

When Federal troops entered Richmond, Stanton conveyed the jubilant news to all the governors that the war was nearing its end. Andrew was among the first to respond about the forecast. "I give you joy on these triumphant victories," he wrote. "Our people, by common impulse, abandoned business to-day for thanksgiving and rejoicing."[58] Referencing that Weitzel's Division of the 25th Corps was reportedly the first to enter Richmond, Andrew remarked, "the colored man, received last, got in first and thus the Scripture is fulfilled."[59] Ironically, it was the "colored man" that would become the target of political focus, and it was imperative that the Republican Party finish the job. Andrew had alluded to this sentiment months before, when speaking to the New England Agricultural Society in Springfield. "The duty of suppressing the rebellion," he declared to his audience, "involves that of restoring and reconstructing order, society, civilization, where treason and slavery have subverted them."[60] Richmond's capitulation signaled more than just military success to Andrew, as it did for many governors. It was symbolic of slavery's demise, and the surrender of that class of people he believed had caused the war. He championed the revolution the war wrought and wanted capitulation to serve notice that the war had done more than defeated Confederates. It had ended slavery. Months before, a Virginia slave had sent the governor a gavel made from the whipping-post that stood in the rear of the Courthouse at Hampton. The message that accompanied the gavel told the story of those men and women whose backs had been lacerated by the whip. Moved by the gesture, Andrew presented the gavel to Lewis Hayden, his longtime capitol clerk, Boston abolitionist, and president of the Association of Free Colored Citizens of Massachusetts. "I know of no place more fitting for the preservation of these memorials of the barbarous institution that is now tottering to its rapidly approaching fall," wrote Andrew, "than the association of free colored citizens of Massachusetts over which you preside."[61]

That the Confederate capital surrendered was no surprise to Northerners who followed military events daily, and neither was the jubilation that followed. Startled just before midday by the "joyful clangor of the bells" in Wilmington, Anna Ferris noted in her diary that the fall of Richmond signaled that "through a Red Sea of blood, through a long struggle of suffering & agony, the promised land of peace & liberty is reached at last & at the end now that it is attained, seems worth the struggle, dreadful as it has been."[62] Still, there was work to be done, and New Englanders closely in tune with military events went to the polls in March and April in hopes of closing the war's final chapter by maintaining Republican majorities. News that Richmond had fallen helped decide these contests, and expected Unionist advantages resulted in light voter turnouts. New Hampshire voters expressed their approval of the war's direction by electing Republican Frederick Smyth. "Altogether, New Hampshire has done well," remarked the *New York Times*, "and nobly responds to the great military victories now being won almost daily in the heart of Jeff Davis' dominions."[63] The Candia, New Hampshire, native's banking and business experience in railroads had made him popular in Manchester over Democrat Edward W. Harrington, who had also run unsuccessfully against Gilmore the previous year. Having been Manchester's mayor throughout 1864, Smyth had made a name for himself, and, with the end of the war in sight, his business savvy was just what the state needed to restore financial stability and settle the financial claims against the federal government. On his way out of office, Gilmore spent the next few weeks pressing Stanton for the federal money owed New Hampshire and denying rumors that he had sold state bonds for his own personal use. Meanwhile, he traveled to New York to raise money to provide relief for the soldiers.[64]

Although there was reasonable doubt whether Unionists could carry all of Connecticut's congressional districts, the governorship was never in question. From Hartford came glad tidings. Voters reelected Buckingham by an 11,000-vote majority over Democrat Origen S. Seymour, signaling another victory. "Connecticut is all right," wrote N. B. Tower from Indiana to his cousin in Hartford. "Buckingham another term for governor."[65] Nehemiah D. Sperry, chairman of Connecticut's Union State Committee, wired a cable to the *New York Times* reporting the victory. "So New England will send none but Republicans to Congress next Winter," he declared. "Of twenty-one State Senators, we elect every man." He thought, "Glory enough for one day, three times three, for Grant and our crowning victory."[66] In Rhode Island, Republicans carried the day by more than 10,000 votes. It was a historic political moment, as voters reelected Smith in every district without opposition. His nearest opponent won only 100 votes. Rhode Island polled only about half the voters and also reelected Unionists to the federal Congress.[67] New England's political victories continued the avalanche of Unionism Grant and Sherman had won on the battlefield.

With surrender imminent, and Stanton in need of his attention, Lincoln departed for Washington on 8 April. The following day, Lee surrendered to Grant at the tiny Virginia crossroads known as Appomattox Courthouse nearly 100 miles west of Richmond. That evening, journalist Charles Dana, who had been traveling with Grant's army, sent Stanton a wire from Richmond that reflected the mood in the defeated capital. "The city is perfectly quiet," it read, "and there is more security for person and property than has existed here for many months."[68] Charles Francis Adams Jr., a colonel with the 5th Massachusetts Cavalry, a black regiment that entered Richmond, wrote to Andrew on his unit's conduct. How ironic it was, he noted, that a "regiment of black Cavalry from the State of

Massachusetts [could march] amid the wildest enthusiasm into the Capital of the State of Virginia."[69]

By the time Lincoln returned to Washington, the news of Lee's surrender had reached the nation's capital. The cannon boom signaling the Confederate surrender aroused Washingtonians and shattered the windows in the houses around Lafayette Square. Despite the rain and mud, hundreds of residents sloshed up Pennsylvania Avenue, the group increasing in size with every step until they reached the White House. The crowd demanded the president's appearance, and Lincoln finally appeared at the window, spoke a few words, and then instructed the band to commence playing "Dixie" and then "Yankee Doodle."[70] "Never, in the history of the National Metropolis," declared the *Washington Daily National Intelligencer*, "was such a scene of brilliancy, beauty, and general rejoicing witnessed here as that in which the whole population participated last evening."[71]

Great Men

Samuel Hawkins Byers, a young Iowa soldier recently discharged from Sherman's army, passed through Washington in the war's final days and witnessed the scene. As he walked through the city, his "mind crowded every moment with the thoughts of what had taken place here in the last four years." He recalled, "Soldiers I saw everywhere, with arms and without arms," and "negroes, now freedman, by the ten thousand fairly darkened the population." He acknowledged, "If I wanted to see great men, notorious men, men making history, all kinds of men, I had only to step into the corridors of the National." He observed, "Washington City . . . was a spectacle."[72]

Tucked away in the North's remote state capitals, governors also celebrated the news. Congratulatory telegrams flooded Stanton's stenographer. "Glory to God in the highest," wired Cony from Augusta. "Thanks be to God who giveth us the victory," wired Miller from St. Paul. Oglesby started for Washington to participate in the celebration. Stanton invited governors to a flag-raising ceremony in Fort Sumter on 14 April, and Smith embarked from St. Albans for the long journey, eager to pass through the nation's capital to see his Vermonters.[73] Stanton suspended recruiting across the North, but it would take months to reduce the armies. In one final visit to the front, Curtin headed to Virginia. From Albany came Fenton's cable on 11 April, asking the president to designate April 20th as a day of National Thanksgiving in a public proclamation. "The God of battles has blessed our arms and the cause of human freedom, under His approving smiles, and the patriotic and brave men in the field," proclaimed Brough.[74]

Governors set out on the business of demobilizing their regiments on what was an otherwise glorious Good Friday morning, 14 April, when Thomas Swann and Senator Creswell conferred with Lincoln over appointments. Shortly afterward came Yates and William Pitt Kellogg, seeking an appointment as the customs collector for the Port of New Orleans. Before they left, Lincoln invited them to join him that evening at the theater, but the gentlemen declined and retired to the Old National Hotel that afternoon. Lincoln went for a carriage ride with his wife and returned around six o'clock that evening. He found Oglesby and the Illinois State Adjutant Isham N. Haynie waiting on him outside the White House. Lincoln waved them inside and the Illinoisans retired to the president's room, where they had a long discussion. The president invited them to join him that evening at Ford's Theatre, but Oglesby and Haynie declined, citing fatigue from the long train ride.[75] After another appointment, Lincoln left for Ford's Theatre, accompanied by his wife; Clara Harris, daughter of New York senator Ira Harris; and her fiancé Major Henry R. Rathbone. That evening Northerners went to sleep with a "sense of peace & happiness long unknown," wrote Anna Ferris, believing a degree of calm had been restored to the republic.[76]

More than 600 miles to the west, a distraught messenger awakened Morton at about two o'clock in the morning. Sitting up in bed, the governor looked at the disheveled lad, took the telegram, and, without opening it, remarked solemnly "Lincoln is killed!"[77] Indeed, it was as the wire read. Shortly after ten o'clock, John Wilkes Booth had shot Lincoln during the third act of *Our American Cousin*. "A shock from Heaven, laying half the city in instant ruins," wrote the editor of the *Boston Daily Advertiser*, "would not have startled us as did the word that started out from Ford's Theatre half an hour ago that the President had been shot."[78] Yates had decided to go to the theater that evening after all and rushed to the National Hotel, where he awakened Kellogg. "Oh, Kellogg," he gasped, "the President has been shot."[79] Oglesby and Haynie hurried to the Petersen House, where they remained until morning—Oglesby stood at the head of the bed where Lincoln lay. As the rain poured that ominous morning, it was as if something had hindered the sun rising over the Maryland landscape. In the early morning, Yates and Kellogg stood across the street and watched the president's associates come and go. As dawn approached on 15 April, and the lamplights gave way to the emerging sunbeams, a "look of unspeakable peace came upon his worn features," and the president expired.⁸⁰ Indeed, for someone who often remarked "that it was wise to wait for the developments of the Providence," events had controlled Lincoln one last time.⁸¹

So quickly had the flags adorning the Northern cities with celebration over Sherman's victories turned black as the light came upon the next day to the announcement that Lincoln had died. "God save the Republic," wrote a grieving Boston editor.⁸² A deep gloom hung over Washington as well as the many cities and tiny hamlets scattered across the Northern landscape. Willard's and the Old National hotels had never been as quiet as they were when Brough and other governors poured into their parlors in the days following Lincoln's death. Window shades were pulled down in mourning, and the life that was the nation's capital was vacant. Indeed, the city's streets, like those across the North, were rolled up with silence. It was as if time stood still. "No living man ever dreamed that it was possible that the intense joy of the nation over the recent happy deliverance from war," remarked a dazed Noah Brooks, "could be or would be so soon turned to grief more intense and bitter than ever nation before had known."⁸³ The collective sounds of church bells that tolled in rhythm seemed to suggest a kind of emotional breathing as they cracked the silence of Northern streets. Never again would Willard's, Washington, or the Northern populace be the same. Not even the pen of Walt Whitman, America's most noble author, could describe the mingled feelings of that day, at least not yet. "Lincoln's death—black, black, black," was all he managed to jot down in his notebook, while walking along a Brooklyn street.⁸⁴

The visiting Illinoisans assembled in Yates's hotel room to work out the details for returning Lincoln to Springfield. They delegated Oglesby to call on the family to confer over the arrangements. Still, the mood could not be shaken. Civil War had ushered in unprecedented times, but Lincoln's assassination was the first in American history. As far away as California that fateful day the *San Francisco Daily Alta California* ran an article that likened the mood of the assassination to the loss of "a dead father, son or brother," who "lay in every house."⁸⁵ Lincoln's death brought people together, but it also reminded them of the bitter disputes that had divided them. Morton petitioned Indianans to close their businesses and join him the day following the assassination at the capitol square. Several legislators joined him, including Senator Thomas A. Hendricks, a notoriously anti-Lincoln Democrat, who ran against Morton in 1864. When the senator rose to speak, members rushed forward to hang the "American Tallyrand [sic]," and shouted "kill him! Hang him!"[86] Morton was forced to restrain crowd members personally. When the governor rose to speak, the crowd was electric with enthusiasm, but Morton spoke only a few words. George Washington had fathered the new nation, he declared to the largest crowd ever assembled in the capitol square, and Lincoln had saved it.[87]

As mourners gathered in Washington to attend the funeral on 19 April, church bells across the North rang in unison every hour. Andrew, Parker, Fenton, Brough, Buckingham, and Oglesby walked to the ceremony as plain, humble, and simple men enjoined with Lincoln by the struggle that had infused a spirit of nationalism. The casket was placed in the East Room, where only invited guests were allowed to view the remains. Thereafter, amidst the tolling bells, the hearse, draped in black and drawn by six gray horses, made its way up Pennsylvania Avenue. Thousands of onlookers lined the streets toward the Capitol, where Lincoln's remains lay in state for public review in the Rotunda.[88]

Of all the days Lincoln spent in office, few of them were in peace. It was a sad commentary on a republic that had saved itself only to bury the person responsible for its salvation. Brough directed the details for the journey back to Illinois, and Oglesby accompanied Lincoln's nine-car funeral train as it retraced its journey back through the Northern states. It would be hard to imagine larger crowds than those that came out to see the president in 1861 during his journey of triumph, but his sudden death at the hands of an assassin prompted crowds to gather in aggregates unsurpassed in American history. Lincoln "hated the arrogance of triumph," wrote Nicolay and Hay, and, ironically due to the president's misfortune, "the country lost sight of the vast national success" it had achieved. Lincoln himself would have been glad to know, acknowledged his secretaries, that "his passage to eternity would prevent too loud an exultation over the vanquished."[89] On the morning of 21 April, the funeral train steamed out of Washington, bound for Springfield. Nine days later, Morton and his colleague Fletcher met the party at the Indiana-Ohio state line. Traveling with other dignitaries, the gentlemen proceeded with the train to Indianapolis before heading out that evening for its final destination. When the funeral procession reached the Illinois state line, members placed Lincoln's casket in the hearse recently used to transport Missouri's deceased governor Gamble. From Chicago it departed toward the Illinois State Capitol, where it arrived on 3 May. For the first time in four years, Lincoln returned to his beloved Illinoisans.[90] "*Never was King or Emperor honored with such obsequies,*" noted an overwhelmed

Harper's Weekly editor, "as those with which our Republic has laid to rest its greatest hero."[91]

So began the incalculable legacy that was Abraham Lincoln. In his death was born a new life that eclipsed his imperfections and one that inseparably linked the Union's preservation with slavery's abolition. He began the war fully aware that he needed loyal governors to rally citizens, marshal resources, and support his political objectives, but not confident he was equal to the challenge. Ralph Waldo Emerson, New England's distinguished laureate, believed he was. Emerson had great respect for the president and on 19 April eulogized Lincoln before a Concord crowd. His address was entitled "The Greatness of a Plain American," and in meeting under the "calamity which darkens down over the minds of good men in civil society," he reminded mourners that Lincoln had "stood before us as a man of the people." Remarked Emerson, "This man grew according to need. His mind mastered the problem of the day; and as the problem grew, so did his comprehension of it." He continued, "Rarely was a man so fitted to the event" and "it cannot be said there is any exaggeration of his worth."[92]

Epilogue
Majestic Parts of That Magnificent Whole

For all the rhetoric mourning Lincoln's loss and acknowledging his greatness, Northerners had not forgotten their governors. The war had schooled citizens in governmental power and provided the impetus for state expansion in effecting social and political change. Governors had grown in prominence because they had been willing to accept the challenges necessary to preserve the Union. They managed the vast new organization that reflected a national community. Along the way they adapted to the political tug-of-war between civil and military authorities and between national and local interests that characterized the conflict. Even as soldiers entered the ranks through state regiments, the war had woven them together in a common cause that provided a sense of nationalism. Their experience engendered a more meaningful relationship between the citizen and the government, and, as much as they could, governors became conduits of information and communication. The ballot box made them accountable to the people in guiding them through the war's vicissitudes.

Departing the ranks of a vast national military institution had symbolic importance. It meant an end to the kinships that formed between comrades, a shared experience, and an awareness that they had participated in the government's greatest achievement. Soldiers had been part of an extraordinary organization whose size, strength, and power was unmatched in the republic's brief history. It also meant departing an organizing structure that had centralized federal power and governmental activism in the hands of national leaders. As centralized power accompanied them into the ranks, so too would diffused power accompany them home. War had placed great responsibility on the states, and governors had given shape to the mobilization of national forces. So too would they assist in the mass exodus from the military.

War Governors

In the weeks and months following Appomattox, some governors performed their last acts by attending the mustering out of regiments that slowly withdrew from the South. Although unconvinced that their work was complete, they nonetheless detailed agents to commence the army's demobilization, which provided a distraction from Lincoln's death. Even in surrender, the fear of more Confederate uprisings kept Stanton and the chief executives on alert. Still, new hospitals would have to be built, more relief agencies were needed, and retooling the soldiers to civilian life was necessary. Like the national government, state governments embarked on the establishment of the economic and social corridors attuned to peace. Addressing a crowd at Elgin, Yates emphasized the state's commitment to the orphans of deceased Illinois soldiers. "[T]he living are left with us," he declared, "the wounded and the disabled, the widow and the orphan, the sorrowing and the stricken, the needy and the destitute—and will we not honor the dead by comforting the living."[1] When the battle-scarred Pennsylvanians passed through Harrisburg's Camp Curtin before scattering to their homes, Curtin accepted the regimental flags one by one and deposited them in the state capitol to serve as wartime remembrances. "I receive these battered and war-torn flags to be preserved as part of your history in the archives of the State," he stated. "How can I express to you the full measure of your services to your country and your fellow citizens who have remained at home!" He declared, "You bring to us a government restored and saved."[2]

Smith was especially proud of his Vermont boys, who had endured significant losses during the war, and he traveled to Virginia to review them one last time. These were the faces of the soldiers he wanted to remember. In early June he walked the lines of the 1st Brigade at Bailey's Cross Roads. Standing in the hot sun with the few thousand soldiers who would return home to Vermont, the governor reveled in the moment. Although he missed the pomp and circumstance that had accompanied their march to war, he nonetheless had shared with them an experience few others could boast of in the brief history of their country. Smith's tribute to those soldiers was all the more remarkable in light of the fact that, of the 20,000 volunteers who had served their state, all who were left were those standing before the governor. Vermont adjutant general Peter T. Washburn recalled that the occasion "was one of deep interest," because before the governor stood "the scarred, sun-burned and war-worn veterans whom the State had sent into the field, entrusted with the maintenance of her honor, who met the enemy in many a fierce and sanguinary conflict, and some of them in every battle in which the Army of the Potomac had participated," and "whose names have been household words in Vermont for the last four years."[3] On that day, 660 soldiers of the original five Vermont regiments, still wearing the evergreen sprig in their caps, mustered out of service. It was the last time these men, whom their governor called the "Vermont brigade," would stand together on Confederate soil.[4]

However passionate Northerners were about the Union's indivisibility, the fighting had demonstrated that there was indeed a North, and its existence amplified federalism's resiliency. In the face of Southern dissolution and antagonism to the Republican Party, Northern mobilization had reflected the popular desire to save the Union. Governors had established a partnership with Lincoln that demonstrated the powerful bond between the nation and the states. The war had proven that the republic the Founding Fathers engineered decades before had matured into a more perfect Union of states. Bradford viewed the conflict as a "challenge to the American Republic, sent by the Almighty to tear away from us a black idol," which was a startling revelation, given that he had been a slave owner and that Maryland's constitution had limited his executive governance.[5] Even if they failed to articulate their role in federalist terms, governors' cooperative actions preserved the Union. The experience broadened and deepened the states' political cultures in their relations to the national government and their responsibilities to their soldiers and civilians. That thousands of Northerners had marched and fought their way across the Southern states provided them with a more profound nationalistic perspective. Andrew Hale Young, a New Hampshire soldier on his way home, remarked to his wife that while he dared not commit pen to paper to describe the awful tragedy, he was "not one of those who think the loss is irreparable." He proclaimed, "Our nation is too great and strong to be dependent upon any one man. Neither can any one man betray it."[6] Bramlette uttered similar sentiments to the throngs gathered in front of the Louisville court house in the days following Lincoln's assassination. "While we mourn the death of the Chief Executive of our nation," he declared, "we should remember that this great country of ours is not dependent upon the life of even our greatest man." He argued, "That life is in the heart of the nation, and you must destroy the people before you can destroy this firm Government of ours."[7]

Like Lincoln, governors grew with the war, and at times displayed self-discipline, steady purpose, and quiet assertiveness. Yet these chief executives became something more than the offices they held. They were more than figureheads; their names were associated with something remarkable. Working as independent parts of the whole, these chief executives had cooperated to restore federalism's credibility and preserve the Union. The centrality of their efforts remained vital to achieving military victory throughout the conflict. Along the way, they placed soldiers in the field who forged new loyalties between nation and state, and who demonstrated the bond that was the Union. Volunteers as diverse as the regimental flags that identified them carried into the ranks a loyalty to neighbor, community, and state along with the belief that the war was worth fighting to maintain popular self-government. And so, as soon as the guns silenced, citizens began to honor the governors and memorialize their efforts with celebrations, festivals, and statues. Connecticutans established "Buckingham Day" as a tribute to their war governor. When the soldiers came together each year to recollect the days of the war, they remembered their governors as companions in the cause, partners with Lincoln who contributed to the Union success. Governors had gone into the war with "distinct and righteous convictions," and supported Lincoln even when they disagreed with him.[8]

In his 3 May address to the legislature, Buckingham alluded to the distinctions between state and national governments. He argued that although states' rights and national sovereignty "were in inherent in, and essential to, our complex system of government," they should "act in harmony, in order to secure the highest benefit."[9] Governors were essential to this harmony. "It was the duty of these 'War Governors,' as they were called," wrote the *New York Times*, "to hold up the hands of the national Executive during a time of unprecedented trial." It was their task to rally the people, to guide and direct the unbridled enthusiasm of their fellow-citizens, and to provide the ways and means to maintain state troops in the field and to look after their welfare once they returned home. "They were raised up, as Lincoln was, for a special purpose," wrote the *Times*, and for all of their efforts, "we cannot afford to allow any slight to be cast upon the labors of those men upon whom Lincoln relied with composure during the darkest days of the Republic."[10]

The loyal governors were no more special than any of their predecessors, but because the times were exceptional, they too became exceptional leaders. This was not because they were more patriotic than anyone, or possessed the wisdom of the ages, but rather because they were committed to the cause, and formed an alliance with Lincoln and Stanton. They remained sagacious in their judgments, pesky advisors to the president, and were magnanimous enough to win the respect of their soldiers. One contemporary related a story Lincoln told that revealed how governors earned his respect. Acknowledging the many objections he received from Governor Curtin of Pennsylvania, who complained over the problems resulting in his state from the execution of the president's orders, Lincoln remarked that the governor's tone frequently worried Stanton, who thought that Curtin might not comply with War Department directives. Handing the dispatches over to Stanton on one occasion, Lincoln advised the secretary to "never mind these dispatches, they don't mean anything." In his metaphorical style, the president explained his reasoning. "Gov. Curtin is a like a boy I once saw at the launching of a ship," he explained. "When everything was ready they picked out this boy and set him on the ship to knock away the trigger and let her go. He had to do the job well, by a direct, vigorous blow, and then lie flat and keep still while the ship moved over him. The boy did everything right; but yelled as if he were being murdered from the time he got under the keel until he got out." Said Lincoln, "I thought the skin was all scraped off his back, but his hide was not touched. The master of the yard told me that this boy was always chosen for that job; that he had never been hurt, but that he always squealed in that way." Lincoln told Stanton, "That's just the way, that Gov. Andy Curtin does. He only wants to make you understand how hard his task is."[11]

The task of mobilizing for war and sustaining support for the effort was challenging. Lincoln had summoned Northerners to rise up in 1861, and they did. By leaving their farms, their towns, their harbors, as well as their civil communities, volunteers joined a new military community, which was governed by a disciplined regimen and a system of codes that defined the military. Governors functioned as guardians of their citizen-soldiers by attending to their welfare and by celebrating and reinforcing their civic duty to the national cause. They balanced the demands between the expanding national government and their state legislatures, who opposed them. Lincoln needed these chief executives more than they needed the president, and, by the end of the war, they established a more perfect Union. "Mighty changes are in the near future," Blair remarked at the end of the war. The "work of ages is being done in months now."[12] In his final address before the Massachusetts legislature in January 1866, Andrew perhaps best summarized the partnership between Lincoln and the war governors. "It seems to me," he argued, "that the stream of life through both State and Nation forms a double source," that was the "distinguishing element of its vital power."[13] And so it was that the loyal states that made up the Union between 1861 and 1865, led by their governors, had at last "found their true distinction, not as an independent governmental action, but in their becoming the majestic parts of that magnificent whole—the American Union."[14]

Americans entered peace with the expectation that a new republic had been born from the war. For many citizens, they entered reunification from the remains of causes that had divergent paths. In his address commemorating the flag-raising ceremony at Fort Sumter the day of Lincoln's assassination, Reverend Henry Ward Beecher spoke to these issues. He declared that "the South shall have just those rights that every Eastern, every Middle, every Western State has—no more, no less." He maintained, "We are not seeking our own aggrandizement by impoverishing the South. Its prosperity is an indispensable element of our own. We have shown by all that we have suffered in war how great is our estimate of the importance of the Southern States of this Union, and we will measure that estimate now in peace by still greater exertions for their rebuilding."[15]

The United States to which Southerners succumbed in 1865 had fundamentally changed from the one they departed four years earlier. The sectionalism and slavery that had characterized the old republic gave way to governmental power's expansive nature and the fear of its new responsibilities. In the postwar era, the struggle that characterized the republic's new political culture was between liberty and tyranny, and the forces of localism, conservatism, party politics, ethnic diversity, and a widespread belief in laissez-faire shrank state governments and diffused power to local municipalities. Industrialization's accelerated pace, the government's active intervention in the economy, and the explosion of charitable and service organizations associated with the war came under legislators' watchful eyes. The 1870s depression the growing number of Democratic majorities in state legislatures, and an increasing desire to return Northerners to peace though local control further undermined these political economic conditions.

After 1865, each passing year distanced the war governors from the cause that defined them. Only when they attended postwar soldiers' reunions or celebrations to honor the war's memory did they garner the esteem and respect they held between 1861 and 1865. In February 1888, New York City's Saturday Night Club honored those War Governors still alive by inviting them to the Hoffman House for dinner. Curtin, Blair, Berry, Fletcher, Kirkwood, Lewis, Salomon, Smith, and Sprague attended the event and drew high praise for their after-dinner comments. Curtin gave perhaps the most rousing speech of the evening by declaring that "the war had to come." He argued, "This great country, with its declaration of liberty to the whole world, could not allow it to remain only half free."[16] Although some of these governors went on to distinguished political careers in Congress, most returned to obscurity and faded into historical memory. Nearly thirty years after the war, on the occasion of Austin Blair's death, the *New York Times* wrote that his departure had removed the last of but two of the "famous 'war governors' of our time." Wrote the editor, "What a list of distinguished men is found in the 'war governors.'" Soon they would be "nothing more than a memory."[17]

Acknowledgments

This book originated out of a conversation I had with Hans Trefousse in an open-air café in Halle, Germany, in the summer of 1996. I was on a Fulbright, teaching at Martin Luther University, and Hans was traveling in Europe. He made time to give a lecture to my proseminar based on an essay he had written on Northern political culture during the Civil War for an edited volume entitled *On the Road to Total War: The American Civil War and the German Wars of Unification, 1861–1871*. Our luncheon led us to discuss wartime political culture and the struggle among Northern state leaders seeking to facilitate and maintain popular support for the war by changing the means of accomplishing victory. I was in search of another book project, and he encouraged me to tackle a comprehensive investigation of Northern mobilization with the aim of providing a broad analysis of nation-state relations. Hans was a remarkable scholar, wonderful friend, and a tremendous influence on my early years as I explored nineteenth-century German-American culture, and I promised to tackle this challenge. Still, I did not think twenty years would pass before I could bring something to see the light of day. Although Hans died in 2010, he would appreciate that I took his advice as well as the acknowledgment that I was the benefactor in our friendship.

Along the way to completing this book I have incurred debts too numerous to acknowledge, but the following pages highlight the most important ones. First and foremost I have to acknowledge that the best thing about Florida Atlantic University is the students, who remind me every day of just how lucky I am to be teaching them something about the past in hopes that they might find it useful in understanding the present. In these years I have called upon the university to support my research, and my colleagues did not disappoint me. I am thankful for the research fellowships the department, college, and university awarded me, as well as two sabbaticals—one I spent at the Huntington Library in California, and the other I utilized to write the manuscript's early portions. In between those sabbaticals I chaired the History Department and came to know my colleagues in special ways. I am thankful that Boyd Breslow, Heather Frazer, Patty Kollander, Eric Hanne, Sandy Norman, Ben Lowe, and Mark Rose saved me from myself on more than one occasion. Boyd has been especially patient with my intrusions upon his time, and our early morning conversations have benefitted me more than he knows. It was during my time as chair that I was fortunate to make the acquaintance of Hugh Ripley, who befriended our faculty and personally oversaw the acquisition of thousands of library books on the American Civil War. I also have had the pleasure of working with Zella Linn, the department's executive administrator. She managed my research accounts, assisted me with the Society of Civil War Historians membership, and provided the daily congeniality that made working with her an absolute delight.

There has been a brigade of archivists and librarians who made this work possible. Long before digitization, Dr. Darlene Parrish located every newspaper, every article, every obscure pamphlet and manuscript I requested through the university's interlibrary loan office. Thanks too go to the talented History Department work-study students, who assisted me while I was chair. Kate Dahlstrand distinguished herself in my classes so much so that I enlisted her technological and research acumen—and thankfully so. The research for this project required me to conduct research in twenty-four Northern states, and I am especially grateful to those institutions that awarded me fellowships, including the Gilder Lehrman Institute of American History, the Huntington Library and Botanical Gardens, the Filson Historical Society, Minnesota Historical Society, State Historical Society of Wisconsin, Bentley Historical Society, and the Indiana Historical Society.

The following repositories also deserve special thanks for assisting me with this project: Repositories of the West: California State Archives—Linda Johnson; Bancroft Library; Huntington Library and Botanical Gardens; Claremont Graduate School; Oregon Historical Society; Oregon State Archives; University of Oregon Libraries; Midwest Repositories: Kansas State Archives—Kim Baker; Kansas State Historical Society; University of Kansas Libraries; Iowa State Archives, and the State Historical Society—Sara Egge and Jeremy Pritchard; Kansas City Public Library—Georgia Murphy; Missouri State Archives, Missouri Historical Society—Dennis Norcott; State Historical Society of Wisconsin; Minnesota Historical Society/State Archives; Abraham Lincoln Presidential Library—Glenna Schroeder-Lein and Boyd Murphree; Chicago History Museum; Indiana Historical Society, Indiana State Archives Steve Towne for his encyclopedic knowledge of Indiana resources; Wabash College Library—Beth Swift and Geoffrey Lambert; Ohio State Archives and the Ohio Historical Society—Valerie Hudson; Western Reserve Historical Society; Kentucky State Archives—Amanda Hoover; the Filson Historical Society—Jim Holmberg; Kentucky Historical Society; Bentley Historical Library and the William L. Clements Library at the University of Michigan; Michigan State Archives; Michigan State University Library; Burton Historical Library—Jeffrey Powell and Barry Neal Johnson; Pennsylvania State Archives; Historical Society of Pennsylvania; United States Army Military History Institute; Dickinson College Library; New Jersey State Archives; New Jersey Historical Society—Monica Ward and Maureen O'Rourke; Historical Society of Princeton—Jeanette Cafaro; Bucknell University Library; Delaware Public Archives; Delaware Historical Society; University of Delaware Library; Maryland State Archives; Maryland Historical Society; University of Maryland Libraries—Elizabeth Novara; Virginia Historical Society; West Virginia State Archives—Joe Geiger; Gilder Lehrman Institute of American History; New York Historical Society; Syracuse University Library; New York Public Library; New York State Library—Christine Beauregard and Cindi Starke; University of Rochester Library; Buffalo and Erie County Historical Society—Richard Tripoli; Bowdoin College Library; Connecticut Historical Society—Cynthia Harbeson; Connecticut State Archives; Massachusetts Historical Society—Mary Fabiszewski; New Hampshire State Archives; New Hampshire Historical Society—Bill Copeley, Dartmouth University Libraries; Vermont Historical Society and State Archives—Kathy Waters; University of Vermont; Maine State Archives—Jeff Brown; University of Maine Library; Library of Congress—John Sellers and Bonnie Coles; and finally National Archives and Records Administration—Trevor Plante.

Over the years I have spent countless hours on the road researching these governors, and I spent some of those trips with David Coles, who still impresses me as the Civil War's most learned scholar. I am also grateful to Jim Marten, friend, colleague, and all-around good guy, who invited me to give the Frank Klement Lecture at Marquette University, where I first presented my ideas about Abraham Lincoln and the War Governors. I am thankful to Ruth Robbins and Mary McLaughlin who invited me to be a part of the Smithsonian Institution Associates Program, where I shared my thoughts on the governors even while lecturing on various Civil War topics to very learned Washington audiences. My work has led me to new acquaintances/friendships with several scholars and has rekindled old ones, including with Michael Burlingame, Walter Stahr, T. Michael Parrish, Richard Carwardine, John T. Hubbell, John Childrey, Vernon Burton, Elizabeth Leonard, Bill Blair, Brooks Simpson, Caroline Janney, and Matt Gallman. Additionally, Bill Marvel's generosity afforded me some much-needed New England research material. Gary W. Gallagher has been a great friend over the years, and I am grateful he read this work for the press and offered his invaluable insight. Truth be told, Gary's literary acumen and unselfishness has left an indelible mark on a generation of scholars. The anonymous reader also deserves thanks for challenging me to expand my conclusions, even while pressing me to shorten the manuscript. In the end, however, every author should have the chance to work with Mark Simpson-Vos, whose support, enthusiasm, and professionalism has been the kind authors expect, but do not always receive. Thanks too goes to Virginia Perrin, who copyedited the manuscript. I owe much to my mentors Jim Jones, Joe Richardson, Hans Trefousse, Larry Balsamo, and John Stealey III, who unknowingly molded me into the scholar they thought I could be. I am thankful to have been lucky enough to be a grad student of Jim Jones, and also to call him friend. Still, any shortcomings are my own.

Finally, I would like to thank my brother Prescott, whose unabashedly giving spirit never fail me. Our annual trips across the Potomac on the "Old Jube" are cherished memories. To my in-laws, Don and Gail, truly blessed people, who allowed me to become a part of Sulgrave Farm, I am deeply grateful. Thanks simply cannot do justice to my wife Stephanie, who is the love of my life, and the ideal academic partner. She reads insatiably, has extraordinary literary skill, can weigh in on any serious conversation, and thankfully, is a gentle critic. My children (Claire and Taylor), the joys of my life, were in middle school and high school when I started this project, but are now grown—a reminder that time does not stop even for those who record the past. Honestly, this book could have been finished years ago had I not taken the time to watch them on the soccer field, and the baseball diamond. I was blessed to have been in the middle of a whirlwind of activity during those years, especially during the summer when Engle Family Camp Woebegone was in session. Through it all, Stephanie kept me sane while I plugged along, simply watching the world around me evolve as I became what I studied. Indeed, I have walked backward into the modern world of PowerPoint, Skype, and I-technology. "I" still use chalk, and the oldest, most technologically challenged classrooms on campus. Surely my next move on campus will be to the "T" (Temporary) buildings, an affectionate name for those structures used during World War Two by soldiers who were in training. No matter, "I" shall prevail.

The one person who infused in me self-discipline and self-reliance long before I ever saw a college classroom was my father. If he never understood the academic life, he was proud nonetheless and made sure I knew it, reminding me that I was among the few people lucky enough to make a difference.

Steve Engle
Boca Raton, Florida

Appendix
List of Governors

Western States

CALIFORNIA

John Downey (1860–62) D
Leland Stanford (1862–63) R
Frederick Low (1863–67) R

ILLINOIS

Richard Yates (1861–65) R
Richard Oglesby (1865–69) R

INDIANA

Oliver P. Morton (1861–65) R

IOWA

Samuel Kirkwood (1860–64) R
William Stone (1864–68) R

KANSAS

Charles Robinson (1861–63) R
Thomas Carney (1863–65) R
Samuel J. Crawford (1865–) R

KENTUCKY

Beriah Magoffin (1859–62) D
James Robinson (1862–63) U
Thomas Bramlette (1863–67) U

MICHIGAN

Austin Blair (1861–65) R
Henry Crapo (1865–69) R

MINNESOTA

Alexander Ramsey (1860–63) R
Henry Swift (1863–64) R
Stephen Miller (1864–66) R

MISSOURI

Claiborne Jackson (1861) D
Hamilton Gamble (1861–64) U
Willard Hall (1864–65) U
Thomas Fletcher (1865–69) R

OHIO

William Dennison (1860–62) R
David Tod (1862–64) U
John Brough (1864–65) R

OREGON

John Whiteaker (1859–62) D
Addison Gibbs (1862–66) R

WISCONSIN

Alexander Randall (1858–62) R
Louis P. Harvey (1862) R
Edward Salomon (1862–64) R
James Lewis (1864–66) R

Eastern States

CONNECTICUT

William Buckingham (1858–66) R

DELAWARE

William Burton (1860–63) D
William Cannon (1863–65) U
Gove Saulsbury (1865–69) R

MAINE

Israel Washburn (1861–63) R
Abner Coburn (1863–64) R
Samuel Cony (1864–67) R

MARYLAND

Thomas Hicks (1858–62) American
Augustus Williamson Bradford (1862–66) U
Thomas Swann (1865–) R

MASSACHUSETTS

John Andrew (1861–66) R

NEW HAMPSHIRE

Nathaniel Berry (1861–63) R
Joseph Gilmore (1863–65) R
Frederick Smyth (1865–67) R

NEW JERSEY

Charles Olden (1860–63) R
Joel Parker (1863–66) D

NEW YORK

Edwin Morgan (1859–63) R
Horatio Seymour (1863–65) D
Reuben Fenton (1865–69) R

PENNSYLVANIA

Andrew Curtin (1861–67) R

RHODE ISLAND

William Sprague (1860–63) R
William Cozzens (1863) D
James Smith (1863–66) R

VERMONT

Erastus Fairbanks (1860–61) R
Frederick Holbrook (1861–63) R
John Smith (1863–65) R

WEST VIRGINIA

Arthur Boreman (1863–69) R

D: Democrsat; R: Republican; U: Unionist

Notes

List of Abbreviations

ARCHIVE ABBREVIATIONS

ALPL	Abraham Lincoln Presidential Library
BCL	Bowdoin College Library
BECHS	Buffalo and Erie County Historical Society
BHL	Bentley Historical Library
BL	Bancroft Library
BPL	Boston Public Library
BUL	Bucknell University Library
CaSA	California State Archives
CHM	Chicago History Museum
CGS	Claremont Graduate School
CtHS	Connecticut Historical Society
CtSA	Connecticut State Archives
CW	The collected Works of Abraham Lincoln
DC	Dartmouth College Library
DCL	Dickinson College Library
DHS	Delaware Historical Society
DPA	Delaware Public Archives
DPL	Detroit Public Library
FHS	Filson Historical Society
HoL	Houghton Library of Harvard
HL	Huntington Library
HSP	Historical Society of Princeton
IaSA	Iowa State Archives
IHS	Indiana Historical Society
ISA	Indiana State Archives
ISL	Indiana State Library
IUPUI	Indiana University-Purdue University Indianapolis
KCPL	Kansas City Public Library
KDLA	Kentucky Department of Libraries and Archives
KHS	Kentucky Historical Society
KSA	Kansas State Archives
KSHS	Kansas State Historical Society
LC	Library of Congress
LP	Lincoln Papers
MdHS	Maryland Historical Society
MdSA	Maryland State Archives
MeSA	Maine State Archives

MHS   Massachusetts Historical Society
MiSA   Michigan State Archives
MiSUA   Michigan State University Archives
MnHS   Minnesota Historical Society
MoHS   Missouri Historical Society
MSA   Massachusetts State Archives
NARA   National Archives and Records Administration
NHDRMA   New Hampshire Division of Records Management and Archives
NHHS   New Hampshire Historical Society
NJHS   New Jersey Historical Society
NYHS   New York Historical Society
NYSL   New York State Library
OHS   Ohio Historical Society
OhSA   Ohio State Archives
OrHS   Oregon Historical Society
PSA   Pennsylvania State Archives
RISA   Rhode Island State Archives
RUL   Rutgers University Libraries
SHSI   State Historical Society of Iowa
SHSW   State Historical Society of Wisconsin
SUL   Syracuse University Library
UDL   University of Delaware Library
UKL   University of Kansas Library
UML   University of Maryland Libraries
UMeL   University of Maine Library
UOL   University of Oregon Library
UR   University of Rochester Library
USAMHI   United States Army Military History Institute
UVAL   University of Virginia Library
UVL   University of Vermont Library
VHS   Vermont Historical Society
VSA   Vermont State Archives and Records Administration
VSAL   Virginia State Archives and Libraries
WLCL   William L. Clements Library
WRHS   Western Reserve Historical Society
WvDCH   West Virginia Division of Culture and History

NEWSPAPER ABBREVIATIONS

AA   *Albany Argus* (New York)
AEJ   *Albany Evening Journal* (New York)
AS   *American Standard* (Jersey City, New Jersey)
BA   *Baltimore American*
BC   *Baltimore Clipper*
BDA   *Boston Daily Advertiser*
BDFP   *Burlington Daily Free Press* (Vermont)
BDG   *Baltimore Daily Gazette*
BDHE   *Burlington Daily Hawk-eye* (Iowa)

BDJ	*Boston Daily Journal*
BDWC	*Bangor Daily Whig and Courier* (Maine)
BG	*Boston Globe*
BP	*Boston Post*
BS	*Baltimore Sun*
BWHE	*Burlington Weekly Hawk-eye*
CA	*Christian Advocate* (New York)
CC	*Cincinnati Commercial*
CCR	*Cass County Republican*
CDE	*Cincinnati Daily Enquirer*
CDG	*Cincinnati Daily Gazette*
ChAdv	*Christian Advocate*
ChiTi	*Chicago Times*
ChiTri	*Chicago Tribune*
CP	*Central Press* (Bellefonte, Pennsylvania)
DDA	*Detroit Daily Advertiser*
Del	*Delawarean* (Dover)
DFP	*Detroit Free Press*
DG	*Democratic Gazette* (Wilmington, Delaware)
DOS	*Daily Ohio Statesman* (Columbus)
DPU	*Daily Patriot and Union* (Harrisburg, Pennsylvania)
DR	*Delaware Republican* (Wilmington)
EN	*Emporia News* (Emporia, Kansas)
ET	*Evening Telegraph* (Harrisburg, Pennsylvania)
FC	*Frankfort Commonwealth*
FCab	*Farmer's Cabinet* (Amherst, New Hampshire)
FLIM	*Frank Leslie's Illustrated Magazine*
HC	*Hartford Courant*
HDT	*Hartford Daily Times*
HEP	*Hartford Evening Press*
HW	*Harper's Weekly*
IDSR	*Iowa Daily State Register*
InDJ	*Indianapolis Daily Journal*
InDSS	*Indianapolis Daily State Sentinel*
ISJ	*Illinois State Journal* (Springfield)
ISR	*Illinois State Register* (Springfield)
KJ	*Kennebec Journal* (Maine)
LAS	*Los Angeles Star*
Lbr	*Liberator* (Boston)
LDC	*Leavenworth Daily Conservative*
LDJ	*Louisville Daily Journal*
LDT	*Leavenworth Daily Times*
LI	*Lancaster Intelligencer* (Pennsylvania)
LR	*Lawrence Republican* (Kansas)
MD	*Missouri Democrat*
MF	*Maine Farmer*
MS	*Milwaukee Sentinel*

NA	*North American* (Boston)
NADL	*New Albany Daily Ledger*
NDM	*Newark Daily Mercury* (New Jersey)
NHP	*New Haven Palladium* (Connecticut)
NHPSG	*New Hampshire Patriot and State Gazette* (Concord)
NHS	*New-Hampshire Statesman* (Concord)
NLT	*New London Telegram* (Connecticut)
NT	*National Tribune* (Washington, D.C.)
NYE	*New York Evangelist*
NYH	*New York Herald*
NYI	*New York Independent*
NYJC	*New York Journal of Commerce*
NYOC	*New York Observer and Chronicle*
NYS	*New York Sun*
NYTi	*New York Times*
NYTri	*New York Tribune*
NYW	*New York World*
OA	*Oregon Argus* (Oregon City)
ODS	*Ohio Daily Statesman*
Or	*Oregonian* (Portland, Oregon)
OS	*Oregon Statesman* (Oregon City)
OSent	*Oregon Sentinel* (Jacksonville)
PDT	*Portland Daily Times* (Oregon)
PDJ	*Providence Daily Journal* (Rhode Island)
PhiBu	*Philadelphia Bulletin*
PhiIn	*Philadelphia Inquirer*
SDU	*Sacramento Daily Union*
SEP	*Saturday Evening Post*
SFDAC	*San Francisco Daily Alta California*
SFDEB	*San Francisco Daily Evening Bulletin*
SR	*State Republican* (Eugene, Oregon)
StAM	*St. Albans Messenger* (Vermont)
StCD	*St. Cloud Democrat* (Minnesota)
StLDMR	*St. Louis Daily Missouri Republican*
StLMD	*St. Louis Missouri Democrat*
StPDG	*St. Paul Daily Globe* (Minnesota)
StPDP	*St. Paul Daily Press* (Minnesota)
StPDPi	*St. Paul Daily Pioneer* (Minnesota)
TDSGR	*Trenton Daily State Gazette and Republican*
TDTA	*Trenton Daily True American*
ToTri	*Topeka Tribune*
VWSJ	*Vermont Watchman and State Journal*
WDI	*Wheeling Daily Intelligencer*
WDNI	*Washington Daily National Intelligencer*
WES	*Washington Evening Star*
WH	*Wellsburg Herald* (West Virginia)
WSJ	*Wisconsin State Journal* (Madison)
WWP	*Weekly Wisconsin Patriot*

Introduction

1. Hesseltine, *Lincoln and the War Governors*, 3–9, 390–93; Jeffreys-Jones and Collins, *The Growth of Federal Power in American History*, 36–50; McPherson and Cooper, *Writing the Civil War*, 3–5, 112–33.
2. Harris, *Lincoln and the Union Governors*, 1–3.
3. Benedict, "Abraham Lincoln and Federalism," 1–45; McPherson and Cooper, *Writing the Civil War*, 8–25, 112–34.
4. Gideon Welles to M. J. W. [Mary Jane Welles], 5 May 1861, Gideon Welles Papers, Library of Congress, Washington, D.C. (LC); Sribnick, *A Legacy of Innovation*, vi–vii, 1–21, 167–75; Brooks, *A Legacy of Leadership*, 2–8; Balogh, *A Government Out of Sight*, 285–303; Paludan, "Federalism in the Civil War Era," 27–39; Benedict, "Abraham Lincoln and Federalism," 1–45; Shannon, *The Organization and Administration of the Union Army, 1861–1865*, 1:15, 17; Basler, *The Collected Works of Abraham Lincoln*, 4:196, 269, 433–35, hereinafter cited as *CW*; Barney, *The Passage of the Republic*, 200–230; Lipson, *The American Governor from Figurehead to Leader*, 1–55; Jeffreys-Jones and Collins, *The Growth of Federal Power in American History*, 36–156; Neely, *Lincoln and the Triumph of the Nation*, 269–71; Gallman, *The North Fights the Civil War*; Bensel, *Yankee Leviathan*, 18–37, 64–85; Bright and Harding, *Statemaking and Social Movements*, 121–58; Parish, *The North and the Nation in the Era of the Civil War*, 92–112; Smith, *No Party Now*, 7–30; Gallagher, *The Union War*, 1–6; Elazar, *Cooperation and Conflict: Readings in American Federalism*, 83–128; Elazar, *The American Partnership*, 2–24; Parish, "A Talent for Survival: American Federalism in the Era of the Civil War," 178–92; Elazar, "Civil War and the Preservation of Federalism," 39–58.
5. Grant, *North over South*, 131–37; Fairlie, "The State Governor: I," 370–83.
6. Taken from the *Boston Watchman and Reflector*, as printed in the *BDFP*, 16 Jan. 1864; *BDHE*, 18 Jan. 1864.
7. *NYTi*, 2 Nov. 1877; Sribnick, *A Legacy of Innovation*, 1–21; Balogh, *A Government Out of Sight*, 285–308; Smith, *No Party Now*, 6–7.
8. McPherson and Cooper, *Writing the Civil War*, 112–33.

Chapter One

1. *NHS*, 16 Mar. 1861; *HW*, 9 Feb. 1861; *ISJ*, 11 Feb. 1861; *NYH*, 12 Feb. 1861.
2. Dicey, *Spectator of America*, 296.
3. Basler, *CW*, 4:190, 228–29; Holland, *Holland's Life of Abraham Lincoln*, 211; *WES*, 12 Feb. 1861; *ISJ*, 6, 12, 13 Feb. 1861; Baringer, *A House Dividing: Lincoln as President-Elect*, 265–67; Villard and Villard, *Lincoln on the Eve of 1861: A Journalist's Story by Henry Villard*, 75–79; Villard, *Memoirs*, 1:149; Holzer, *Lincoln: President-Elect*, 298–302; Smith, *No Party Now*, 30–31; Burlingame, *Lincoln's Journalist: John Hay's Anonymous Writings for the Press, 1860–1864*, 24.
4. *NYTi*, 18, 19 Feb. 1861; Holzer, *President-Elect*, 279–305; McClure, *Abraham Lincoln and Men of War-Times*, 80; Perret, *Lincoln's War*, 335; Lyman Trumbull to Lincoln, 2 Dec. 1860, Abraham Lincoln Papers, Library of Congress, Washington, D.C., from the online American Memory Collection, (hereafter, LP, LC). Memory.loc.gov/ammem/alhtml/malhome.html; Burlingame, *An Oral History of Abraham Lincoln*, 107–22; Weeden, *War Government*, 56; *NHS*, 16 Mar. 1861; Burton, *The Age of Lincoln*; Donald, *Lincoln*; Gideon Welles to E. T. W. [Edgar T. Welles], 16 Feb. 1861, Welles Papers, LC.
5. Krenkel, *Richard Yates: Civil War Governor*, 50–54, 164–65; Lusk, *Politics and Politicians*, 101; Cozzens and Girardi, *The Military Memoirs of General John Pope*, 4–5; *ISJ*, 14

Jan., 18, 23 Feb. 1861; 14 Jul. 1863; *NYTi*, 18 Feb. 1861, 28 Jul. 1884; Brooks, *Washington in Lincoln's Time*, 29; Burlingame, *Lincoln's Journalist*, 7; Yates Jr., "Richard Yates: War Governor of Illinois," 184; Kimball, "Richard Yates," 1–7, 82; Reavis, *The Life and Public Services of Richard Yates*, 10–12, 28.

6. *ISJ*, 14 Jan. 1861; Nortrup, "Richard Yates: A Personal Glimpse of the Illinois Soldier's Friend," 122.

7. Yates Jr., "Richard Yates," 197; Reavis, *Yates*, 15–18, 12–16; Kimball, "Richard Yates," 3–6, 82–83; Lusk, *Politics and Politicians*, 100–109; Krenkel, *Richard Yates*, 15, 22, 41–42, 50–52, 109, 116, 137–38; *ISJ*, 14 Jul. 1863; Sobel and Raimo, *Biographical Directory of the Governors of the United States, 1789–1978*, 1:374.

8. *Inaugural Address of Richard Yates, Governor of Illinois to the General Assembly, January 14, 1861*, 17; Nortrup, "Richard Yates," 165–72; Pease and Randall, *The Diary of Orville Hickman Browning*, 1:379–81, 394–95, 407; Hofer, "Development of the Peace Movement in Illinois during the Civil War," 114; *ISJ*, 9 Jun. 1860, 15 Jan. 1861; Lyman Trumbull to Yates, 19 Dec. 1860, Allen C. Fuller to Yates, 30 Dec. 1860, J. B. Turner to Yates, 1 Jan. 1860, Richard Yates Papers, ALPL; Baringer, *A House Dividing*, 265–68; Villard, *Memoirs*, 1:148; Bohn, "Richard Yates: An Appraisal of His Value as the Civil War Governor of Illinois," 17–37; Lincoln to Oglesby, 8 Sept. 1854, LP, LC.

9. Basler, *CW*, 4:193–95; *InDJ*, 12, 13 Feb. 1861; Sylvester, "Oliver P. Morton and Hoosier Politics during the Civil War," 72–73; Cottman, "Lincoln in Indianapolis," 2–11; Holzer, *President-Elect*, 307–10; Burlingame, *Lincoln's Journalist*, 25.

10. Thornbrough, Riker, and Corpuz, *The Diary of Calvin Fletcher*, 7:44; Cottman, "Lincoln in Indianapolis," 2–11; Holzer, *President-Elect*, 311–13; Burlingame, *Lincoln's Journalist*, 25; *InDJ*, 12, 13 Feb. 1861.

11. *WES*, 13 Feb. 1861; Basler, *CW*, 4:193–94; Baringer, *A House Dividing*, 269–72; Randall, *Lincoln the President*, 1:275; Pease and Randall, *Diary of Browning*, 1:454–55; Thornbrough, Riker, and Corpuz, *Diary of Calvin Fletcher*, 7:43–45; Cottman, "Lincoln in Indianapolis," 2–11; Holzer, *President-Elect*, 311–14; *InDJ*, 12, 13 Feb. 1861.

12. Foulke, *Life of Oliver P. Morton*, 1:66–67; Sylvester, "Morton," 74–77; *InDJ*, 23 Jan. 1861; *InDSS*, 23 Jan. 1861; Hesseltine, *Lincoln and the War Governors*, 35–42.

13. Foulke, *Morton*, 1:101; *NYTi*, 2 Nov. 1877.

14. Thornbrough, Riker, and Corpuz, *Diary of Calvin Fletcher*, 7:432–33; Weeden, *War Government*, 143; Sylvester, "Morton"; Thornburgh, "Oliver P. Morton: The Great War Governor," 66–91; *NYTi*, 2 Nov. 1877.

15. Weeden, *War Government*, 143; Thornburgh, "Oliver P. Morton," 66–91.

16. *InDJ*, 27 Nov. 1860, 23 Jan. 1861; Weeden, *War Government*, 136–43; French, *Life, Speeches, State Papers and Public Services of Governor Oliver P. Morton*, 136–39; Hesseltine, *Lincoln and the War Governors*, 42–43; Sylvester, "Morton," 66–76; *OR*, series 3, 1:41; *InDSS*, 23 Jan. 1861; Foulke, *Morton*, 1:38–39, 112; Thornbrough, *Diary of Calvin Fletcher*, 7:22.

17. Morton to Lincoln, 29 Jan. 1861 (italics in original), LP, LC; *NYTi*, 18, 19 Feb. 1861; Holzer, *President-Elect*, 312–17; *NYTi*, 2 Nov. 1877.

18. Speed, *The Union Cause in Kentucky, 1860–1865*, 26–35; Harris, *Lincoln and the Border States*, 24–26; Mulligan, "Lest the Rebels Come to Power: The Life of William Dennison," 133–36; Holzer, *President-Elect*, 317–21; *NYTri*, 14 Feb. 1861; Villard and Villard, *Lincoln on the Eve of 1861*, 81–83; Holland, *Lincoln*, 217; *NYTi*, 18 Feb. 1861.

19. Busbey, "Recollections of Abraham Lincoln and the Civil War," 282; Mulligan, "Dennison," 133–36; Holzer, *President-Elect*, 317–21; Baringer, *A House Dividing*, 275–77; Harris, *Lincoln and the Border States*, 25–26.

20. Baringer, *A House Dividing*, 275–77; Villard and Villard, *Lincoln on the Eve of 1861*, 81–83; *NYTri*, 14 Feb. 1861; *NYTi*, 18 Feb. 1861; Holzer, *President-Elect*, 317–21; Burlingame, *Lincoln's Journalist*, 28.

21. Mulligan, "Dennison," 145; Reid, *Ohio in the War*, 1:1017–19; *NYTi*, 16 Jun. 1882; Sobel and Raimo, *Directory of Governors*, 3:1208–9; Hesseltine, *Lincoln and the War Governors*, 39–40; *HW*, 28 Jan. 1865.

22. William Seward to Morgan, 14 Feb. 1861, Edwin Morgan Papers, NYSL; Morgan to Lincoln, 13 Feb. 1861, LP, LC; *NYTi*, 14, 15 Feb. 1861; *PhiIn*, 17, 18 Feb. 1861; *ChiTri*, 16 Feb. 1861; Holzer, *President-Elect*, 333–63.

23. *NYH*, 19 Feb 1861; *NYTi*, 19, 20 Feb. 1861; Rawley, *Edwin D. Morgan, 1811–1883: Merchant in Politics*, 128–29; Rawley, "Lincoln and Governor Morgan," 280–84. A portion of the quote taken from the *NYH* is also cited in Holzer, *President-Elect*, 349–50.

24. Worthington G. Snethen to Lincoln, 8 Jan., 15 Feb. 1861, LP, LC; Seward to Morgan, Private, 11 Feb. 1861, Morgan Papers, NYSL; *NYTi*, 15, 18, 19, 20 Feb. 1861; *PhiIn* 18, 19 Feb. 1861; Villard and Villard, *Lincoln on the Eve of 1861*, 90–92; Hicks to Scott, 11 Jan. 1861, Thomas Hicks Papers, MdHS; Hicks to Scott, 25 Jan. 1861, Governor's Letter Books, MdSA; *ChiTri*, 19 Feb. 1861; Erasamus D. Keyes to Morgan, 11 Feb. 1861, Lincoln to Morgan, 4 Feb. 1861, and Weed to Morgan, 11 Feb. 1861, Morgan Papers, NYSL; Nicklason, "The Secession Winter and the Committee of Five," 380–85; Rawley, *Morgan*, 128–29; Rawley, "Lincoln and Governor Morgan," 280–84; *NDM*, 19 Feb. 1861; Mitgang, *Abraham Lincoln*, 229–30; Holzer, *The State of the Union*, 5–11; Holzer, *President-Elect*, 325–53, 383; Burlingame, *Lincoln's Journalist*, 34–35; *WES*, 19 Feb. 1861; Delaware governor William Burton to Hicks, 8 Jan. 1861, Executive Papers, DPA.

25. Cozzens and Girardi, *Military Memoirs of Pope*, 179; Brummer, *Political History of New York State during the Period of the Civil War*, 123–24; *NYH*, 19, 20 Feb. 1861; Holzer, *President-Elect*, 352–57; Schutz and Trenerry, *Abandoned by Lincoln: A Military Biography of General John Pope*, 60; *NDM*, 19, 20 Feb. 1861; Rawley, "Lincoln and Morgan," 280–84; *NYTi*, 11 Dec. 1860, 18, 19 Feb. 1861.

26. Villard and Villard, *Lincoln on the Eve of 1861*, 95; *HW*, 2 Mar. 1861; *NYTi*, 18, 19, 20, 21 Feb. 1861; *BDA*, 20 Feb. 1861; Epstein, *Lincoln and Whitman: Parallel Lives in Civil War Washington*, 61; Holzer, *President-Elect*, 356–61; *NDM*, 20 Feb. 1861; Rawley, "Lincoln and Morgan," 280–84.

27. Stone, *Rhode Island in the Rebellion*, xvi–xix; Lamphier, *Kate Chase and William Sprague: Politics and Gender in a Civil War Marriage*, 27–40; Dennett, *Lincoln and the Civil War Diaries and Letters of John Hay*, 12; Carroll, *Rhode Island: Three Centuries of Democracy*, 2:596–97; *HW*, 5 Apr. 1862; Shoemaker, *The Last of the War Governors*, 7–11; Smith, *No Party Now*, 90.

28. Rawley, "Lincoln and Morgan," 280–84; *NYTi*, 18, 19, 20, Feb. 1861; *PhiIn*, 20, 21 Feb. 1861.

29. Frank P. Blair Sr. to Lincoln, 14 Jan. 1861, LP, LC; Villard and Villard, *Lincoln on the Eve of 1861*, 95; Villard, *Memoirs*, 1:151–52; Rawley, *Morgan*, 137–38; Weeden, *War Government*, 221–22; Hesseltine, *War Governors*, 30–31; Alexander, *A Political History of the State of New York*, 2:248; Baringer, *A House Dividing*, 282–85; Rawley, *Morgan*, 137–38; Rawley, "Lincoln and Morgan," 280–82.

30. Morgan to Lincoln, 20 Nov. 1860, 19, 30 Jan. 1861, Lincoln to Morgan, 4 Feb. 1861, LP, LC; Rawley, *Morgan*, 120–29; Rawley, "Lincoln and Morgan," 280–84; Heslin, "Peaceful Compromise in New York City, 1860–61," 349–62.

31. Rawley, *Morgan*, 120–24, 130; Rawley, "Lincoln and Morgan," 280–84; Heslin, "Peaceful Compromise," 349–62.

32. Rawley, *Morgan*, 96, 85–119, 123; Lincoln, *State of New York: Messages of the Governors*, 5:249–74; McClure, *Lincoln and Men of War-Times*, 40–41; Rawley, "Lincoln and Morgan," 272–300; *NYTri*, 22 May 1860.

33. Miers, *New Jersey and the Civil War*, 1–13; *NDM*, 22 Feb. 1861; *TDSGR*, 23 Feb. 1861; Platt, *Charles Perrin Smith: New Jersey Political Reminiscences, 1828–1882*, 114–15; *NYH*, 20, 21, 22 Feb. 1861; Holzer, *President-Elect*, 350–79.

34. Basler, *CW*, 4:236–37; *NYTri*, 22 Feb. 1861; *TDSGR*, 23 Feb. 1861; *NYTi*, 22 Feb. 1861; Cozzens and Girardi, *Military Memoirs of Pope*, 178–79; Olden to Lincoln, 1 Feb., Lincoln to Olden, 6 Feb. 1861, LP, LC; Miers, *New Jersey and the Civil War*, 1–13; Holzer, *President-Elect*, 371–74; Platt, *Perrin Smith*, 114–15; Address from Governors to Olden, Olden Family Papers, HSP; *NDM*, 22 Feb. 1861; Burlingame, *Lincoln's Journalist*, 39.

35. Alexander McClure to Lincoln, 15 Jan. 1861, LP, LC; *BDA*, 27 Feb., 12 Apr. 1861; *BA*, 14, 25 Feb. 1861; Burlingame, *Abraham Lincoln: A Life*, 2:32–34; Holzer, *President-Elect*, 375–77, 384–89; Baker, *The Politics of Continuity: Maryland Political Parties From 1858 to 1870*, 66–69; *BS*, 22 Feb. 1861; George, "Philadelphians Greet Their President Elect, 1861," 381–90; "The Diary of Sidney George Fisher, 1861," 70–75; Wainwright, *Philadelphia Perspective: The Diary of Sidney George Fisher*, 22–24.

36. Mansch, *Abraham Lincoln*, 179–80; Baringer, *A House Dividing*, 292–93; Basler, *CW*, 4:241–43; Donald, *Lincoln*, 277; *NYTi*, 23, 24, 25 Feb. 1861; McClure to Lincoln, 15 Jan. 1861, LP, LC; McClure, *Lincoln and Men of War-Times*, 50–51; Holzer, *President-Elect*, 375–77, 384–89; Nicklason, "Secession Winter," 380–85; *PhiIn*, 23, 25 Feb. 1861; Stashower, *The Hour of Peril*, 250–51.

37. McClure, *Lincoln and Men of War-Times*, 50–53; Holzer, *President-Elect*, 390–98; Schouler, *A History of Massachusetts in the Civil War*, 1:59–65; Cozzens, *Battles and Leaders of the Civil War*, 5:23; George Stearns to Hicks, 7 Feb., and Hicks to Scott, 9 Feb. 1861, Hicks Papers, MdHS; *PhiIn*, 23, 25 Feb. 1861; Burlingame, *Lincoln*, 2:36–38; *NYTi*, 23, 25 Feb. 1861; Taylor, *William Henry Seward*, 136–37.

38. *NYTi*, 23, 25, 26 Feb. 1861; *BA*, 25 Feb. 1861; Basler, *CW*, 4:243–46; Lamon, *The Life of Abraham Lincoln*, 522–26; Donald, *Lincoln*, 278; Holzer, *President-Elect*, 390–96; Stahr, *Seward: Lincoln's Indispensable Man*, 222; *WES*, 23 Feb. 1861; Harris, "Austin Blair of Michigan: A Political Biography," 101; Blair to Chandler, 27 Feb. 1861, Zachariah Chandler Papers, LC; George, "Philadelphians Greet Their President Elect," 381–90; *PhiIn*, 25 Feb. 1861.

39. *NYTi*, 21 Feb. 1861; Randall, *Lincoln*, 1:279; Holzer, *President-Elect*, 388–90; Cozzens and Girardi, *Military Memoirs of Pope*, 181–82.

40. Nevins, *The Emergence of Lincoln*, 451; Burlingame, *The Inner World of Abraham Lincoln*, 236–37; Carwardine, *Lincoln: A Life of Purpose and Power*, 4; Randall, *Lincoln*, 1:290–91.

41. Burlingame, *At Lincoln's Side*, 6; *WES*, 23 Feb. 1861.

42. *WES*, 2, 5, 19, 23 Feb. 1861; Villard, *Memoirs*, 1:154–55; Detzer, *Dissonance: The Turbulent Days Between Fort Sumter and Bull Run*, 3–7.

43. Clark, "Politics in Maryland during the Civil War," 36:240–49, 38:230–33; *BA*, 6, 9 Jan., 7, 9, 20, 21 Feb. 1861; *WES*, 8, 21 Feb. 1861; Lathrop, *The Life and Times of Samuel J. Kirkwood*, 109; Holzer, *President-Elect*, 419–25.

44. Radcliffe, *Governor Thomas H. Hicks of Maryland and the Civil War*, 14–15; A. R. Wright to Hicks, 21 Feb. 1861, Governor's Letter Books, MdSA; Hicks to Wright, 1 Mar. 1861, MdSA.

45. Radcliffe, *Hicks*, 16–17; Hicks to Magoffin, 10 Dec. 1860, Hicks Papers, MdHS.

46. Radcliffe, *Hicks*, 19–20.

47. Josiah M. Lucas to Lincoln, 10 Jan. 1861, LP, LC; Nesenhoener, "Maintaining the Center: John Pendleton Kennedy, the Border States, and the Secession Crisis," 413–26; Wells, "The Transformation of John Pendleton Kennedy," 291–308; *BA*, 7, 9, 14, 20, 21 Feb. 1861.

48. Hicks to William L. Wilcox, 24 Jan. 1861, Hicks Papers, MdHS; Mitchell, *Maryland Voices of the Civil War*, 19; Cozzens, *Battles and Leaders*, 5:22–31.

49. Hicks to Alabama Commissioners, 8 Jan. 1861, Governor's Letter Books, MdSA; Harris, *Lincoln and the Border States*, 28–29.

50. Curtin to Hicks, 15 Jan. 1861, Hicks to Curtin, 19 Jan. 1861, Governor's Letter Books, MdSA; Alexander McClure to Lincoln, 15 Jan. 1861, and Curtin to McClure, 2 Jan. 1861, LP, LC; Josiah M. Lucas to Hicks, 11 Jan. 1861, Payne to Hicks, 18 Jan. 1861, Hicks Papers, MdHS; Curtin to Hicks, 15 Jan. 1861, Governor's Letter Books, MdSA; *BA*, 7 Feb. 1861.

51. Hicks to Curtin, 19 Jan. 1861, Governor's Letter Books, MdSA.

52. *HW*, 16 Feb. 1861.

53. Radcliffe, *Hicks*, 29–43; Hicks to Wilcox, 24 Jan. 1861, Hicks Papers, MdHS; *BA*, 16 Jan. 1861; Curtin to Hicks, 15 Jan. 1861, and Hicks to Curtin, 19 Jan. 1861, Governor's Letter Books, MdSA; Lathrop, *Kirkwood*, 109; "Letters of a War Governor," 40; Alexander McClure to Lincoln, 15 Jan. 1861, and Curtin to McClure, 2 Jan. 1861, LP, LC.

54. "The Secession Movement in Kentucky," 262–65; Hicks to John Crittenden, 13 Dec. 1860, Hicks Papers, MdHS.

55. Washburn to Fessenden, 14 Jan. 1861, William Pitt Fessenden Papers, WRHS; Gunderson, "The Washington Peace Conference of 1861: Selection of Delegates," 347–48; Gunderson, *Old Gentleman's Convention*, 33–34; Dennison to Yates, 26 Jan. 1861, LP, LC; Dennison to Morgan, 26 Jan. 1861, and Weed to Morgan, 11, 28 Feb. 1861, Morgan Papers, NYSL; Washburn to John Andrew, 31 Jan. 1861, Andrew Papers, MHS; *NYTi*, 5, 25, 26 Feb., 5 Mar. 1861; Pearson, *The Life of John A. Andrew*, 1:159; Heslin, "Peaceful Compromise," 349–62; White, *The Life of Lyman Trumbull*, 110–12; McClintock, *Lincoln and the Decision for War*, 179–81; Lee, "The Corwin Amendment in the Secession Crisis," 1–26; Crofts, *Reluctant Confederates*, 138–39, 209–14; Marvel, *Mr. Lincoln Goes to War*, 11; Carroll, *Rhode Island*, 1:595–98; *WES*, 9, 16 Feb. 1861; John Wilson to Yates, 1 Jan. 1861, Yates Papers, ALPL; Rawley, "Lincoln and Morgan," 272–300; Mulligan, "Dennison," 133–35; Dennison to Andrew, 31 Jan. 1861, Washburn to Andrew, 1 Feb. 1861, Massachusetts Governors Papers, Executive Department Letters, Official Letters from Other States, 1861, MSA; Kelsey, "Maine's War Governor: Israel Washburn Jr. and the Race to Save the Union," 235–57; "Letters of a War Governor," 321–28, 372–78.

56. Washburn to Fessenden, 14 Jan. 1861, Fessenden Papers, WRHS.

57. Washburn to Charles Sedgwick, 22 Jan. 1861, Charles Sedgwick Papers, SUL; Cooper, *We Have the War Upon Us*, 171–83.

58. Gunderson, "Peace Conference," 348; Morton to Yates, 25 Jan. 1861, Morton to Lincoln, 29 Jan. 1861, LP, LC; Nation and Towne, *Indiana's War*, 41–42.

59. Morton to Lincoln, 29 Jan. 1861, LP, LC; Crofts, *Reluctant Confederates*, 209–14; Sylvester, "Morton," 67–70.

60. As cited in Burlingame, *Lincoln*.

61. Donald, *Lincoln*, 280–95.

62. Clark, *Samuel J. Kirkwood*, 174–75; Charles Robinson to Sara Robinson, 20 Oct. 1860, 11, 19 Jan. 1861, Charles and Sara T. D. Robinson Papers, KSHS; *BDA*, 27 Mar. 1861; Dennison to Yates, 26 Jan. 1861, LP, LC; Koerner to Trumbull, 19 Feb. 1861, Trumbull

Papers, LC; Wilson, *Governor Charles Robinson of Kansas*, 74; *ToTri*, 16, 23 Feb., 1 Jun. 1861; Lincoln, *Messages of the Governors*, 5:387–88; Charles W. Elliott to Fairbanks, 13 Feb. 1861, Erastus Fairbanks Papers, VSA; Morgan to Robinson, [10] Feb. 1861, Governor's Letter Books, Morgan Papers, NYSL; *LDT*, 30 Jan., 8 Feb. 1861; *Ohio House Journal*, 1861, Columbus, 1861, 102–12; *Ohio Senate Journal*, 1861, 57–59; Gunderson, "Peace Conference," 350–53; Gunderson, *Old Gentleman's Convention*, 35–37, 79–80; Stampp, "Letters from the Washington Peace Conference of 1861," 394–403; *Indiana House Journal*, 1861, 278; *Indiana Senate Journal*, 1861, 222; McClintock, *Lincoln and Decision for War*, 179–81; Crofts, *Reluctant Confederates*, 209–14; Smith, *Thomas Ewing Jr.*, 126; Sylvester, "Morton," 66–70.

63. Gunderson, "Peace Conference," 350–54; Davis, *Pennsylvania Politics, 1860–1883*, 164–68; Shankman, *The Pennsylvania Anti-war Movement, 1861–1865*, 46–60.

64. Randall to Doolittle, 17 Jan. 1861, James R. Doolittle Papers, SHSW; *WSJ*, 13, 14 Feb. 1861; Gunderson, "Peace Conference," 356–59; Quiner, *The Military History of Wisconsin*, 40; Current, *The History of Wisconsin*, 293–95; *New Jersey Senate Journal*, 1861, 81, 97–104, 108–21; *SFDAC*, 4, 7 Feb. 1861; *LAS*, 1 Jan., 16 Feb. 1861; *Annual Message of Governor John G. Downey to the Legislature of the State of California*, Jan. 7, 1861; Downey to Lincoln, 13 Dec. 1860, William H. Seward Papers, Special Collection, UR; Kennedy, *The Contest for California in 1861*, 76–82; Lathrop, *Kirkwood*, 109–11; Buckingham, *Buckingham*, 79; *MS*, 5 Feb. 1861; Harris, "Austin Blair," 50–51; Hesseltine, *Lincoln and the War Governors*, 126–31; Marszalek, *Commander of All Lincoln's Armies*, 103; Gunderson, *Old Gentleman's Convention*, 38–39; Johannsen, "John Whiteaker, Governor of Oregon," 80; McArthur, *The Enemy Never Came*, 26–28; Benedict, *Vermont in the Civil War*, 1:14–15; *Wisconsin Senate Journal*, 1861, 115–85; *Wisconsin Assembly Journal*, 1861, 183–92, 211, 220, 248–61, 269–99; *Minnesota House Journal*, Third Session, 1861, 166–77; *Minnesota Senate Journal*, 1861, 123–53; Haugland, "Alexander Ramsey and the Republican Party," 112–17; *DFP*, 6 Feb. 1861; Blair to Chandler, 27 Feb. 1861, Chandler Papers, LC; *Michigan House Journal*, 1861, 544, 690–92; *Michigan Senate Journal*, 1861, 197–200, 254–72; Schouler, *Massachusetts in the Civil War*, 1:28–29; Shafer, *Men of Granite: New Hampshire's Soldiers in the Civil War*, 17; Asa Fowler to Joseph A. Gilmore, 10 Feb. 1861, Joseph Gilmore Papers, NHHS; *NHPSG*, 6 Feb. 1861; Dell, *Lincoln and the War Democrats*, 34–35, 45; Hamrogue, "John A. Andrew," 70–78; Pearson, *Andrew*, 1:154; Francis W. Bird to Andrew, 31 Jan. 1861, and Charles Francis Adams to Andrew, 4 Jan. 1861 "private and confidential," 28, and 8 Feb. 1861, Andrew Papers, MHS; Nicklason, "Secession Winter," 380–82; Johannsen, "A Breckinridge Democrat on the Secession Crisis: Letters of Isaac I. Stevens," 283–310; Ford, "Sumner's Letters to Governor Andrew," 223–33.

65. *NHPSG*, 6 Feb. 1861; Gunderson, "Peace Conference," 356–59; Stampp, "Letters of the Washington Conference," 403; Weed to Morgan, 28 Feb. 1861, Morgan Papers, NYSL; McClintock, *Lincoln and Decision for War*, 181–86; Zacharias, "John L. Crittenden Crusades for the Union and Neutrality in Kentucky," 193–205; Harris, *Lincoln and the Border States*, 30–35.

66. Chandler to Blair, 11 Feb. 1861, Blair to Chandler, 27 Feb. 1861, Chandler Papers, LC; Harris, *Public Life of Zachariah Chandler*, 53–55; Hesseltine, *Lincoln and the War Governors*, 128; May, *Michigan and the Civil War Years*, 4–5; Fuller, *Messages of the Governors of Michigan*, 2:442; Gunderson, *Old Gentlemen's Convention*, 66–74; *DFP*, 3, 15, 17, 23 Feb. 1861; Harris, "Blair," 95–99; Fennimore, "Austin Blair: Civil War Governor, 1861–1862," 49:193–201; Moore, "The Days of Fife and Drum," 438–40; Green, *Freedom, Union, and Power*, 13–29; Chandler to Gen. George D. Hill, 11 Jan. 1861, George D. Hill Papers, BHL; David [Pratt] to Blair, 29 Dec. 1860, RG 44 Military Correspondence, War Matters, MiSA.

67. Ford, "Sumner's Letters," 223–33; Hamrogue, "Andrew," 74–78; Charles Francis Adams to Andrew, 8 Feb. 1861, Andrew Papers, MHS; Andrew to Charles Sumner, 30 Jan. 1861, Charles Sumner Papers, HoL; Palmer, *The Selected Letters of Charles Sumner*, 2:40–41, 43, 47–48, 55–58.

68. Mitchell, *Maryland Voices*, 23; Radcliffe, *Hicks*, 36–41, 48–49; *BS*, 28 Feb. 1861; Baringer, *A House Dividing*, 310–23; *BA*, 6, 7, 25 Feb., 2, 5, 9 Mar. 1861; Morton to Yates, 26 Jan. 1861, LP, LC.

69. Radcliffe, *Hicks*, 43–50; Manakee, *Maryland in the Civil War*, 24–29; Mitchell, *Maryland Voices*, 34–41.

70. Burlingame, *Lincoln's Journalist*, 48.

71. Baringer, *A House Dividing*, 302–3; Villard, *Memoirs*, 1:148–60; *HW*, 16 Mar. 1861; Burlingame, *Lincoln's Journalist*, 52–54; Marvel, *Mr. Lincoln Goes to War*, 10–15.

72. Andrew J. Clough to Wife, 2, 3 Mar. 1861, Andrew J. Clough Papers, Marvin and Sybil Weiner Spirit of America Collection, Florida Atlantic University, Boca Raton, Florida; Randall, *Lincoln*, 1:291–93; Rawley, *The Politics of Union*, 12; Holzer, *Lincoln at Cooper Union*; *NYTi*, 18 Feb. 1861.

73. Weed to Morgan, 4 Mar. 1861, Morgan Papers, NYSL; Furguson, *Freedom Rising*, 12–22; Baringer, *A House Dividing*, 297–315.

74. Basler, *CW*, 4:262–71; Randall, *Lincoln*, 1:300; Burlingame, *Lincoln*, 2:58–63; Holzer, *President-Elect*, 450–63; Burlingame, *Lincoln's Journalist*, 52–56; Weeden, *War Government*, 2–33; McClintock, *Lincoln and Decision for War*, 187–226; Adams, *Autobiography*, 97; *WES*, 4 Mar. 1861.

75. *NHS*, 16 Mar. 1861; Basler, *CW*, 4:262–71; Burlingame, *Lincoln*, 2:58–63; Holzer, *President-Elect*, 450–63.

76. Adams, *Autobiography*, 97–98; Ford, "Sumner's Letters," 223–33; Weeden, *War Government*, x–xi; Marvel, *Mr. Lincoln Goes to War*, 10–15; *WES*, 4 Mar. 1861.

77. *BDHE*, 6 Mar. 1861; Burlingame, *Lincoln*, 2:52–68; Donald, *Lincoln*, 282–87; Randall, *Lincoln*, 1:293–315; Basler, *CW*, 4:262–71; *ISJ*, 11 Mar. 1861.

78. Weed to Lincoln, 11 Dec. 1860, LP, LC; Cooper, *We Have War Upon Us*, 60–68; Basler, *CW*, 4:154; Hesseltine, *Lincoln and the War Governors*, 102; Rawley, *The Politics of Union*, 2; Paludan, *The Presidency of Abraham Lincoln*, 24–25; McClintock, *Lincoln and the Decision for War*, 187–225; Laas, *Wartime Washington*, 23–24.

79. Trumbull to Lincoln, 24 Dec. 1860, Trumbull Papers, LC; Lincoln to Trumbull, 21 Dec., Weed to Lincoln, 23 Dec. 1860, LP, LC; Cooper, *We Have War Upon Us*, 60–68; Rawley, *Morgan*, 121–27; Weed, *Memoir*, 2:310–11; Morgan to Fairbanks, 12 Jan. 1861, and Morgan to Washburn, 12 Dec. 1860, Morgan Papers, NYSL; Hesseltine, *Lincoln and the War Governors*, 102–3; Niven, *Connecticut for the Union*, 35–36.

80. Hunt, *Israel, Elihu and Cadwallader Washburn*, 83; Morgan to Washburn, 20 Dec. 1860, as cited in Hunt, *Washburn*, 83; Abbott, *Cotton and Capital*, 67–70.

81. Basler, *CW*, 4:154; Weed to Lincoln, 24 Dec. 1860, LP, LC; Weed, *Autobiography*, 2:310–11; Hunt, *Washburn*, 75, 83; Abbott, *Cotton and Capital*, 67–70; Hesseltine, *Lincoln and the War Governors*, 102–11.

82. Fairbanks to Andrew, 19 Jan. 1861, Andrew Papers, MHS; Benedict, *Vermont*, 1:4–7; Hesseltine, *Lincoln and the War Governors*, 112–13; Hamrogue, "Andrew," 49–50, 63–68; Benedict, *Vermont*, 1:4–5; Browne, *Sketch of the Official Life of John A. Andrew*, 28; Miller, "Brahmin Janissaries," 211; Schouler, *Massachusetts in the Civil War*, 1:16–17; Hesseltine, *Lincoln and the War Governors*, 109–14, 125; Pierce, *Memoirs and Letters of Charles Sumner*, 4:18–21; General Orders, 227, 17 Jan. 1861, Orderly Book of First Brigade, Third Regiment Artillery, CtHS;

Gideon Welles to Buckingham, 2 Feb. 1861, Welles Papers, LC; Andrew to Morgan, 31 Jan. 1861, Massachusetts Governors Papers, Executive Department Letters, MSA; Orr, "Cities at War," 33–34.

83. Sobel and Raimo, *Directory of Governors*, 1:962–63; Hesseltine, *Lincoln and the War Governors*, 23–24, 113; Shafer, *Men of Granite*, 28; *WES*, 10 Jan. 1861; *NHS*, 12 Jan., 9 Feb. 1861; Marvel, "Answering Lincoln's Call: The First New Hampshire Volunteers," 139–50; *A Memorial. Nathaniel Springer Berry of Bristol, New Hampshire*, 7–43; Renda, "Credit and Culpability," 8–11; *NHPSG*, 30 Jan., 13, 20 Feb. 1861; Renda, *Running on the Record*, 98–99.

84. Pearson, *Andrew*, 1:142–43; Andrew to Sumner, 5 Dec. 1860, 4, 15, 20, 28, 29, 30 Jan., 3, 6 Feb. 1861, Sumner Papers, HoL.

85. Pearson, *Andrew*, 1:142–43; Bowen, *Massachusetts in the War, 1861–1865*, 1:1–5; Henry Gilmore to Joseph Gilmore, 19 Apr. 1861, Gilmore Papers, NHHS; Nicklason, "Secession Winter," 380–81; Hesseltine, *Lincoln and the War Governors*, 113–14; *NYTi*, 7 Jan. 1861.

86. *NYTi*, 8 Jan. 1861; Morton S. Wilkinson and Henry M. Rice to Alexander Ramsey, in the Alexander Ramsey Papers, MnHS; Henry Rice to Ramsey, 2 Dec. 1860, 20 Jan. 1861; William Windom to Ramsey, 25 Dec. 1860, 18 Jan. 1861, and Morton Wilkinson to Ramsey, 11 Jan. 1861, Governor's Papers, MnHS; *ISJ*, 8, 11 Jan. 1861; Hesseltine, *Lincoln and the War Governors*, 119–21; Bensel, *Yankee Leviathan*, 5–24; Haugland, "Politics, Patronage, and Ramsey's Rise to Power," 324–28; Guentzel, "Alexander Ramsey," 333–60; *StPDP*, 23 Dec. 1860, 6, 10 Jan. 1861; Schmidt, "Dependence of the Lincoln Administration," 9; Charles Francis Adams to Andrew, 4 Jan., Fairbanks to Andrew, 19 Jan. 1861, Andrew Papers, MHS; Miller, "Brahmin Janissaries," 211–12; Browne, *Andrew*, 28; *HW*, 23 Feb. 1861; Hamrogue, "Andrew," 49–51.

87. Thomas and Hyman, *Stanton*, 111; Sumner to Andrew, 26, 28 Jan. 1861, Andrew Papers, MHS; Sumner to Andrew, 21, 23, 24, 26 Jan., 5, 6 Feb., Andrew to Sumner, 15, 20, 28, 29, 30, 31 Jan., 3, 6 Feb. 1861, Sumner Papers, HoL; Ford, "Sumner's Letters," 223–33; Andrew to Montgomery Blair, 23 Jan. 1861, Blair Family Papers, LC; Turner, "Secession Movement," 262–67.

88. Detzer, *Dissonance*, 83–88; Butler, *Autobiography and Personal Reminiscences of Major-General Benjamin F. Butler's Book*, 150–74; Butler, *Private and Official Correspondence*, 1:5–13; Trefousse, *Ben Butler*; Miller, "Brahmin Janissaries," 203–8; Hamrogue, "Andrew," 50–64.

89. Blair to Chandler, 27 Feb. 1861, Chandler Papers, LC; Fennimore, "Blair," 49:366–69; *NYTi*, 5 Jan. 1861, 7 Aug. 1894; Hesseltine, *Lincoln and the War Governors*, 115–16; Fennimore, "Blair," 49:193–201; Woodford, *Father Abraham's Children*, 19–20; Fuller, *Messages*, 94, 418–20; *DFP*, 4 Jan. 1861; Robertson, *Michigan in the War*, 10–13; Mitchell, "The Organizational Performance of Michigan's Adjutant General," 123–24; Moore, "Days of Fife and Drum," 437–40.

90. Fuller, *Messages*, 441; Schmidt, "Dependence of Lincoln Administration on Governors," 7; May, *Michigan and the Civil War*, 4.

91. *LAS*, 18 May, 15 Jun. 1861; Roland, *Albert Sidney Johnston*, 242–47; *OR*, series 1, 50:452–53, 456, 469; Warner, *Generals in Blue*, 489–90; Kibby, "Union Loyalty of California's Governors," 314–17.

92. Melendy and Gilbert, *The Governors of California*, 101–13; Kibby, "Union Loyalty of California's Governors," 314–19; Macleod, "John G. Downey as One of the Kings," 327–30; Roland, *Johnston*, 242–46; *LAS*, 22 Jun. 1861; *SFDAC*, 8 Jan. 1861; Matthews, *The Golden State in the Civil War*, 84–110; Robinson, *Los Angeles in Civil War Days, 1860–1865*, 33–34.

93. Norman Judd to Lincoln, 3 Dec. 1860, LP, LC.

94. Morse, *Memoir of Colonel Henry Lee*, 56–57; Basler, *CW*, 4:186; Andrew to Lincoln, 1 Feb. 1861, LP, LC; Hamrogue, "Andrew," 56–57; Andrew to Lee, 25 Jan. 1861, Lee Family Papers, MHS; Pearson, *Andrew*, 1:152–53; *NYTi*, 5 Jun. 1883; Nevins, *War Becomes Revolution*, 305–6; *The Nation*, 29 Jul. 1881, 77–78; Albert Browne to Charles Sumner, 19 Dec. 1860, Sumner Papers, HoL; Chandler, *Andrew*; Schouler, *Massachusetts in the Civil War*, 1:11–13; Clarke, *Memorial and Biographical Sketches*, 1–67; *The Ballad of the Blunder-buss*, 1–30.

95. Segal, *Conversations with Lincoln*, 30–32; Bowen, *Massachusetts in the War*, 1:1–3; Cleaveland and Packard, *History of Bowdoin College*, 496–97; Alumni Biographical Files, and Scrapbook, John Andrew, George J. Mitchell Department of Special Collections and Archives, BCL; Hesseltine, *Lincoln and the War Governors*, 20–21; Pearson, *Andrew*, 1:16; Schouler, *Massachusetts in the Civil War*, 1:11–13.

96. Andrew to Lincoln, 20 Jan. 1861, LP, LC; Pearson, *Andrew*, 1:242; Schouler, *Massachusetts in the Civil War*, 1:11–13; Andrew to Blair, 23 Jan., 2 Feb. 1861, Blair Family Papers, LC; Miller, "Brahmin Janissaries," 205–8; Egle, *Andrew Gregg Curtin*, 310; Hesseltine, *Lincoln and the War Governors*, 20–23; Hamrogue, "Andrew," 63–65.

97. Andrew to Lincoln, 20 Jan. 1861, LP, LC.

98. Ibid.; Bowen, *Massachusetts in the War*, 1:1–3; Hesseltine, *Lincoln and the War Governors*, 20–23; Pearson, *Andrew*, 1:242–45; Segal, *Conversations*, 30–32; *The Nation*, 29 Jul. 1881, 77–78; Nevins, *War Becomes Revolution*, 305–6; Schouler, *Massachusetts in the Civil War*, 1:11–13; Hamrogue, "Andrew," 50–56.

99. Andrew to Sumner, 11 Mar. 1861, Sumner Papers, HoL; Donald, *Charles Sumner and the Rights of Man*, 124; Bensel, *Yankee Leviathan*, 85–93.

Chapter Two

1. *LDJ*, 8 Mar. 1861; *HW*, 16 Mar. 1861.

2. George Whitmarsh Diary, 4 Mar. 1861, MdHS.

3. Meneely, *War Department*, 65; Perret, *Lincoln's War*, 3; McClintock, *Lincoln and the Decision for War*, 187–225; McPherson, *Tried By War*, 13; Marvel, *Mr. Lincoln Goes to War*, 14–15; *NYH*, 4 Mar. 1861.

4. Morgan to Lincoln, 5 Mar. 1861, LP, LC; Weed to Morgan, 4 Mar. 1861, Morgan Papers, NYSL; Basler, *CW*, 4:279; Burlingame, *With Lincoln in the White House*, 46–47; Basler, *CW*, 4:322; *NYTi*, 13 Apr. 1861; Miller, *President Lincoln*, 49; Pease and Randall, *Diary of Browning*, 1:476; Meneely, *War Department*, 65, 85; *OR*, series 3, 1:312; Leonard, *Lincoln's Forgotten Ally: Judge Advocate General Joseph Holt*, 128–29.

5. Folwell, *A History of Minnesota*, 2:67–68; McClintock, *Lincoln and the Decision for War*, 187–220; Shutes, *Lincoln and California*, 57–65; Edward Baker to Lincoln, 3 Apr. 1861, and Ira Rankin with endorsement of Leland Stanford to Lincoln, 3 Apr. 1861, LP, LC; *SDU*, 20, 24 Apr. 1861; *SFDAC*, 8 Dec. 1860, 11 Apr., 6 May 1861; *OR*, series 1, 50:470–71; *OS*, 22 Apr. 1861; Cyrus Aldrich to Ramsey, 23 Dec. 1860, Morton Wilkinson to Ramsey, 28 Jan., Stephen Miller to Ramsey, 26 Feb., Miller to Ramsey, 8, 27 Mar., 3 Apr. 1861, Ramsey Papers, MnHS. *StPDP*, 17 Mar. 1861; *WES*, 7 Mar. 1861; Haugland, "Politics, Patronage, and Ramsey's Rise to Power," 324–28; Haugland, "Alexander Ramsey and the Republican Party," 100–118.

6. Weeden, *War Government*, 52.

7. Adams, *Autobiography*, 103; Bullard, "When Lincoln Ruled Alone," 301–47.

8. Weeden, *War Government*, x–xiii; Wilson, *The Business of Civil War*, 7–9; Bensel, *Yankee Leviathan*, 64–137.

9. Pearson, *Andrew*, 1:142–43; Bowen, *Massachusetts in the War*, 1:1–5; *OR*, series 3, 1:36–37, 41, 54–55; *BDA*, 17 Apr. 1861; Schouler, *Massachusetts in the Civil War*, 1:34–37; Foulke, *Morton*, 1:112; Sylvester, "Morton," 66–77; *InDJ*, 15, 22 Apr. 1861; Parsons, "Indiana and the Call for Volunteers, April 1861," 2–9.

10. Washburn to Lincoln, 21 Jan., Fessenden to Lincoln, 20 Jan., Andrew to Lincoln, 20 Jan. 1861, LP, LC; Howard, *Autobiography of Oliver Otis Howard*, 1:114–15; Hesseltine, *Lincoln and the War Governors*, 80–81, 114; Hunt, *Washburn*, 7, 29–77; Schouler, *Massachusetts in the Civil War*, 1:16–17 *NYTi*, 7 Jan. 1861; *In Memoriam: Israel Washburn, Jr.*; Kelsey, "Maine's War Governor," 235–57; Hannibal Hamlin to Ellie Hamlin, 10 Jun., 13 Dec. 1860, Hannibal Hamlin Papers, Special Collections, Fogler Library, UMeL; Whalon, "Maine Republicans," 50–115, 140–43; Whalon, "Israel Washburn and the War Department," 79–85.

11. Buckingham to Lincoln, 25 May 1860, LP, LC; Fairbanks to Andrew, 7 Jan. 1861, Andrew Papers, MHS; Fairbanks to Morgan, 7 Jan. 1861, Morgan Papers, NYSL; Bowen, *Massachusetts in the War*, 1:1–5; Hesseltine, *Lincoln and the War Governors*, 113–14; *PhiIn*, 2 Apr. 1861; Benedict, *Vermont*, 1:4–7; Niven, *Connecticut for the Union*, 22–23, 33–35; Buckingham, *Life of Buckingham*, 31–76, 444–86; Porter, "Memoir of the Hon. William A. Buckingham," 9; *NYE*, 22 Feb. 1894; *NYTi*, 1 Apr. 1861, 5 Feb. 1875; *Dedication of the Statue of Governor Buckingham*, 3–23; Warshauer, *Connecticut in the American Civil War*, 49–51; Newell, "Erastus Fairbanks," 59–64; *BDFP*, 16, 18 Apr. 1861.

12. Bowen, *Massachusetts in the War*, 1:1–5; *OR*, series 3, 1:36–37, 41, 54–55; Gunderson, *Old Gentlemen's Convention*, 19–20; John Forbes to Andrew, 2 Feb. 1861; Scott to Morgan, 17 Jan., Morgan to Preston King, 26 Jan., Morgan to Scott, 15 Jan. 1861, Morgan Papers and Letter Books, NYSL; White, *Trumbull*, 120–21; T. S. Mather to Yates, "Confidential," 29 Jan. 1861, Yates Papers, ALPL; Hamrogue, "Andrew," 58–66.

13. Grinnell, *Men and Events of Forty Years*, 258–59; *NYTi*, 3 Sept. 1894; Lathrop, *Kirkwood*, 7–109; Foulke, *Morton*, 1:113–14; Weeden, *War Government*, 145; *OR*, series 3, 1:64; Thornbrough, *Indiana in the Civil War Era*, 102–3; *InDSS*, 6, 11, 15 Apr. 1861; *WSJ*, 30 Mar., 2 Apr. 1861; Current, *History of Wisconsin*, 293–96; Fish, "The Raising of the Wisconsin Volunteers, 1861," 259–66; Piston, "The 1st Iowa Volunteers," 6–7; Briggs, "The Enlistment of Iowa Troops during the Civil War," 323–43; Upham, "Arms and Equipment for the Iowa Troops in the Civil War," 3–52; "Letters of a War Governor," 2:372–78.

14. Clark, *Kirkwood*, 173–74; "Letters of a War Governor," 7:39–40; *NYTi*, 3 Sept. 1894; Lathrop, *Kirkwood*, 7–109; Egle, *Curtin*, 311; Hesseltine, *Lincoln and the War Governors*, 52, 118.

15. Lathrop, *Kirkwood*, 105–9; Briggs, "Enlistment of Iowa Troops," 323–43; "Letters of a War Governor," 7:34–38; Clark, *Kirkwood*, 86–143, 177–78; Byers, *Iowa in War Times*, 35; *NYTi*, 3 Sept. 1894; Rosenberg, "The Election of 1859 in Iowa," 1–22; Hesseltine, *Lincoln and the War Governors*, 52, 118; *ISJ*, 6 Feb. 1861.

16. Rawley, *The Politics of Union*, 4–16; Bensel, *Yankee Leviathan*, 94–154; McClintock, *Lincoln and the Decision for War*, 187–225; T. S. Mater to Yates, 29 Jan. 1861, Yates Papers, ALPL; Yates to Trumbull, 22 Jan. 1861, Trumbull Papers, LC; Foulke, *Morton*, 1:112–13; Sylvester, "Morton," 77–79; *InDJ*, 15, 22 Apr. 1861.

17. Niven, *Chase Papers*, 3:55; McPherson, *Tried by War*, 16–21; Marvel, *Mr. Lincoln Goes to War*, 19–22, 10–17; Hesseltine, *Lincoln and the War Governors*, 139–43; John A. Gilmer to Lincoln, "private and confidential," 29 Dec. 1860, LP, LC; *Congressional Globe*, 36th Con-

gress, 2nd session, 1285, 1403; Lee, "The Corwin Amendment," 1–26; Lincoln to Fairbanks, 16 Mar. 1861, Fairbanks Papers, VSA; *HW*, 9, 16 Mar. 1861; *BA*, 5 Mar. 1861; *NYTi*, 5 Mar. 1861.

18. *NYH*, 11, 12 Mar. 1861; *A Memorial, Nathaniel Berry*, 24–43; 2 Apr. 1861; *NHS*, 16 Mar. 1861; *NHPSG*, 13, 16 Mar. 1861; *NYTi*, 13, 14, 29, 30 Mar. 1861; Renda, "Credit and Culpability: New Hampshire Politics," 8–15; *ChAdv*, 17 May 1894; Sobel and Raimo, *Directory of Governors*, 3:963–64; Hesseltine, *Lincoln and the War Governors*, 113–14, 141–42; Shafer, *Men of Granite*, 28; Croffut and Morris, *Military and Civil History of Connecticut during the War*, 37; Buckingham, *Buckingham*, 91; Scott, "Press Opposition to Lincoln in New Hampshire," 326–41; Egle, *Curtin*, 311; Burlingame, *Lincoln*, 2:126.

19. Basler, *CW*, 4:324; Egle, *Curtin*, 41–42; McPherson, *Tried by War*, 21; *WDNI*, 11 Apr. 1861; Oyos, "The Mobilization of Ohio Militia in the Civil War," 158–60; *PDJ*, 12 Apr. 1861; *DFP*, 12 Apr. 1861.

20. Dennison to Lincoln, 10 Apr. 1861, LP, LC; *BS*, 9 Apr. 1861; *DFP*, 13 Apr. 1861.

21. *NYH*, 4 Mar. 1861.

22. Basler, *CW*, 4:236–37; Meneely, *War Department*, 100–101; Lincoln to Scott, 14 Apr. 1861, LP, LC; McClintock, *Lincoln and the Decision for War*, 226–50; Marvel, *Mr. Lincoln Goes to War*, 22–28; Cooper, *We Have War Upon Us*, 268–70.

23. Holland, *Lincoln*, 244–45; Basler, *CW*, 4:271; Paludan, *Presidency of Lincoln*, 60–65; Weeden, *War Government*, 62; Bullard, "When Lincoln Ruled Alone," 301–49.

24. Buckingham to Lincoln, 15 Apr. 1861, LP, LC; Burlingame, *Lincoln*, 2: 132–34; Perret, *Lincoln's War*, 31; McClintock, *Lincoln and the Decision for War*, 226–50; McPherson, *Tried by War*, 21–24; Bullard, "When Lincoln Ruled Alone," 301–49; *WES*, 18 Apr. 1861; *HEP*, 17, 20 Apr. 1861; Bancroft, *History of the Pacific States of North America*, 2:455.

25. *OR*, series 3, 1:66–68; Niven, *Connecticut for the Union*, 40–49; Croffut and Morris, *Connecticut during the War*, 58–71; Meneely, *War Department*, 100–102; *HEP*, 1 May 1861; Joseph B. Hall to *Bangor Daily Whig and Courier*, 18 Apr. 1861, Governor's Telegram Book, MeSA; Thomas Clark to Buckingham, 28 Apr., and J. H. Lester to Buckingham, 22 Apr., E. Jackson to Buckingham, 22 Apr., Vincent Putnam to Buckingham, 19 Apr. 1861, Governor's Correspondence, Connecticut State Archives, CtSA; Warshauer, *Connecticut in the Civil War*, 49–53; Gallman, *The North Fights the Civil War*, 22–61.

26. Egle, *Curtin*, 103, 215–23, 36–42, 103, 123; McClure, *Lincoln and Men of War-Times*, 82–84, 140; Weeden, *War Government*, 88–89; Bradley, *Cameron*, 168–73; Albright, "The Civil War Career of Andrew Gregg Curtin," 48:151–52, 47:323–42; "Governor Curtin: Phrenological Character Biography," *American Phrenological Journal* 38 (Oct. 1863): 112–13; Hesseltine, *Lincoln and the War Governors*, 31–32; Leach, *Reveille in Washington, 1860–1865*, 41; *OR*, series 3, 1:66–68; Curtin and Alexander McClure to Lincoln, 15 Apr. 1861, LP, LC; Mansch, *President-Elect*, 179; Detzer, *Dissonance*, 71–73.

27. Moe, *The Last Full Measure*, 8; Folwell, *Minnesota*, 2:76–77; *WDNI*, 17 Apr. 1861; Haugland, "Ramsey's Rise to Power," 324–28; Haugland, "Ramsey and the Republican Party," 114–16; *OR*, series 3, 1:67; "April 1861, Minnesota Goes to War," 212; Ramsey to Cameron, 14 Apr. 1861, Ramsey Papers, Ramsey Diary (Executive Journals), 3 Apr. 1861, MnHS; *StPDP*, 16, 17 Apr. 1861; Stephen Miller to Ramsey, 27 Mar. 1861, Ramsey Papers, MnHS; Ramsey Diary, 3–13 Apr. 1861, MnHS; Ramsey, "Minnesota and the War," 227–28.

28. Guentzel, "Ramsey," 349–65; Ramsey to Cameron, 14 Apr. 1861, Ramsey Papers, MnHS; *OR*, series 3, 1:67; Folwell, *History of Minnesota*, 2:76–81; *StPDP*, 16, 17 Apr. 1861; *WDNI*, 17 Apr. 1861; Haugland, "Ramsey's Rise to Power," 324–26; Ignatius Donnelly to

Kate Donnelly, 17 Apr. 1861, Ignatius Donnelly Papers, MnHS; Ramsey, "Minnesota and the War," 227–28.

29. Folwell, *History of Minnesota*, 2:61; Baker, *Lives of Governors of Minnesota*, 1; Hesseltine, *Lincoln and the War Governors*, 50–51; Haugland, "Ramsey and the Republican Party," 76–110.

30. *HW*, 20 Apr. 1861; Moe, *Last Full Measure*, 8; Folwell, *Minnesota*, 2:76–81; Harris, *Lincoln and the Border States*, 20–25, 119–27.

31. *OR*, series 3, 1:67–75; Mulligan, "Dennison," 145–46; Schaefer, "Governor William Dennison and Military Preparation in Ohio, 1861," 52–61; Eddy, *The Patriotism of Illinois*, 1:92; *ISJ*, 24 Apr. 1861; John Wilson to Yates, 1 Jan. 1861, Yates Papers, ALPL; Trumbull to Lincoln, 21 Apr. 1861, LP, LC; Guentzel, "Ramsey," 360–65; Hesseltine, *Lincoln and the War Governors*, 146–47; Thornbrough, *Indiana*, 103–5; Foulke, *Morton*, 1:116–17; Terrell, *Indiana in the War of the Rebellion*, 7; Sylvester, "Morton," 82–83; Wallace, *Autobiography*, 1:261–68; *InDJ*, 15 Apr. 1861; Parsons, "Indiana and the Call for Volunteers," 2–9.

32. Harvey Hogg to Yates, 13 Apr. 1861, Yates Papers, ALPL.

33. *OR*, series 3, 1:690, 1:81; Phillips, *Missouri's Confederate Governor: Claiborne Fox Jackson*, 245–50; Johnson and Buel, *Battles and Leaders*, 1:262–77; Avery and Shoemaker, *The Messages and Proclamations of the Governors of the State of Missouri*, 3:317–24, 328–42; Harris, *Lincoln and the Border States*, 119–27.

34. *OR*, series 3, 1:70–73; Dennison to Magoffin, 17 Apr. 1861, Thomas Key to Dennison, 20 Apr. 1861, Dennison to Lincoln, 16 Apr. 1861, Governors Papers and Correspondence, OHS; Chase to Dennison, 21 Apr., Curtin to Dennison, 25 Apr. 1861, Adjutant General, Correspondence to the Governor and Adjutant General of Ohio, Series 147, online collection OHS (hereafter Series 147, OHS); McClintock, *Lincoln and the Decision for War*, 226–50; McPherson, *Tried by War*, 32–34; Dues, "Governor Beriah Magoffin of Kentucky," 22–25; Turner, "Secession Movement," 265–69; Marvel, *Mr. Lincoln Goes to War*, 25–29, 188–90; John Clay to Cameron, 19 Apr. 1861, Simon Cameron Papers, LC; *ISJ*, 22 May 1861; Stampp, "Kentucky's Influence upon Indiana in the Crisis of 1861," 268–69; *InDJ*, 2 May 1861; *CDE*, 23, 28 Apr., 8 May 1861; Avery, *Messages*, 3:343–48; Porter, *Ohio Politics*, 74–77; Mulligan, "Dennison," 148–55; Hicks to Magoffin, 10 Dec., Hicks to John Crittenden, 13 Dec. 1860, Hicks Papers, MdHS; *LDJ*, 14, 18, 19 Jan., 26, 29 Apr. 1861; Harris, *Lincoln and the Border States*, 39, 80–85; Towne, *Surveillance and Spies*, 197–98.

35. *BDHE*, 28 May 1861.

36. *LDJ*, 19, 30 Apr. 1861.

37. *ISJ*, 22 May 1861; Dues, "Magoffin," 22–25; *InDJ*, 2 May 1861; Curtin to Dennison, 25 Apr., Chase to Dennison, 21 Apr. 1861, Series 147, OHS; Johnson and Buel, *Battles and Leaders*, 1:373–91; Turner, "Secession Movement," 267–68; Marvel, *Mr. Lincoln Goes to War*, 188–90; Stampp, "Kentucky's Influence," 268–70; Oyos, "Ohio Militia," 159–61; Harris, *Lincoln and the Border States*, 80–87.

38. *ISJ*, 20 Apr. 1861; Paludan, *Presidency of Lincoln*, 72; Hesseltine, *Lincoln and the War Governors*, 166; McClintock, *Lincoln and the Decision for War*, 226–50; *WES*, 13 Apr. 1861; *BDHE*, 17 Apr. 1861; Bensel, *Yankee Leviathan*, 94–103.

39. Lathrop, *Kirkwood*, 113–15; Hake, "The Political Firecracker: Samuel J. Kirkwood," 5–6; Hinckley, "Davenport in the Civil War," 401–3; Hesseltine, *Lincoln and the War Governors*, 146–47; Paludan, *Presidency of Lincoln*, 72; Thomas, *Abraham Lincoln: A Biography*, 258–59; Briggs, "Enlistment of Iowa Troops," 323–43; *BDHE*, 22, 27 Apr. 1861.

40. Andrew to Lincoln, 11 Mar. 1861, LP, LC; Bowen, *Massachusetts in the War*, 1:33–35.

41. Schouler, *Massachusetts in the Civil War*, 1:50; Pearson, *Andrew*, 1:210, 183, 179–81; Butler, *Butler's Book*, 174; Butler, *Correspondence*, 1:13–18; Hughes, *Letters and Recollections of John Murray Forbes*; Weeden, *War Government*, 69, 157; Abbott, *Cotton and Capital*, 66–69; Hesseltine, *Lincoln and the War Governors*, 148–51; Hamrogue, "Andrew," 58–66, 80–83; BDA, 17, 20 Apr. 1861.

42. SDU, 14 May 1861.

43. Brown to Lincoln, 18 Apr., Brown and Hicks to Lincoln, 18 Apr. 1861, LP, LC; Mitchell, *Maryland Voices*, 50; McClure, *Lincoln and Men of War-Times*, 65; Davis, *Pennsylvania Politics*, 188–89; Orr, "Cities at War," 76, 79; OR, series 3, 1:105; Morgan to Cameron, 19 Apr. 1861, Morgan Letter Books, NYSL; Mitchell, "The Whirlwind Now Gathering," 203–32; WDNI, 23 Apr. 1861; BA, 22, 23, 24 Apr. 1861; BDA, 22 Apr. 1861; Hicks to Lincoln, 22 Apr. 1861, Governor's Letter Books, MdSA; Albright, "Curtin," 48:153–55; Burlingame, *Lincoln*, 2:140–45; Harris, *Lincoln and the Border States*, 42–53; Detzer, *Dissonance*, 73–79.

44. Hicks to James L. Dorsey, 22 Mar. 1861, Hicks Papers, MdHS; Hicks to Cameron, 17, 20 Apr., Cameron to Hicks, 17 Apr., Hicks to Lincoln, 17 Apr. 1861, Governor's Letter Books, MdSA; BA, 13 Apr. 1861; Scott to Lincoln, 18 Apr. 1861, LP, LC; Burlingame, *Lincoln*, 2:143–45; Lockwood and Lockwood, *The Siege of Washington*, 107–54; Harris, *Lincoln and the Border States*, 42–53; Detzer, *Dissonance*, 75–79.

45. OR, series 1, 2:12–24, 577, 581–82, 587; Brown and Hicks to Lincoln, 18 Apr., Hicks to Lincoln, 22 Apr., Hicks to Cameron, 20 Apr. 1861, LP, LC; Radcliffe, *Hicks*, 50–56; Mitchell, *Maryland Voices*, 48–64; Donald, *Lincoln*, 297–98; Burlingame, *Lincoln*, 2:141–42; Cozzens, *Battles and Leaders*, 5:22–31; BS, 19, 20, 22 Apr. 1861; Harris, *Lincoln and the Border States*, 30–37; Detzer, *Dissonance*, 90–96.

46. Schouler, *Massachusetts in the Civil War*, 1:76; Hamrogue, "Andrew," 80–85; WES, 20 Apr. 1861; BDA, 19, 22 Apr. 1861; NYTi, 17, 18 Apr. 1861; Detzer, *Dissonance*, 90–110.

47. BS, 19, 20, 22, 23 Apr. 1861; *ChiTri*, 20 Apr. 1861; Radcliffe, *Hicks*, 48–55; OR, series 1, 2:12–21; Brown to Lincoln, 18 Apr. 1861, LP, LC, with Hicks's endorsement attached; Mitchell, *Maryland Voices*, 48–73; Burlingame, *Lincoln*, 2:141; Donald, *Lincoln*, 297–98; Cameron to Hicks, 18 Apr. 1861, Governor's Letter Books, MdSA; WDNI, 18, 23, Apr. 1861; Johnson and Buel, *Battles and Leaders*, 5:22–31; Mitchell, "Whirlwind Now Gathering," 203–32; Bullard, "When Lincoln Ruled Alone," 301–49; Seward to Hicks, 22 Apr. 1861, Governor's Letter Books, MdSA; Snyder, "'Making No Child's Play of the Matter,'" 304–31.

48. OR, series 1, 2:12–15; Detzer, *Dissonance*, 145–53; BS, 13 May 1861; McPherson, *Tried by War*, 24–28; WES, 20 Apr. 1861; Hicks to Cameron, 20 Apr. 1861, and to editor of the [Baltimore] *American*, 8 May 1861, Governor's Letter Books, MdSA; Mitchell, "Whirlwind Now Gathering," 203–32; Burlingame, *Lincoln*, 2:143–48; Bullard, "When Lincoln Ruled Alone," 301–49; Hamrogue, "Andrew," 58–62; Forbes to Andrew, 7 Feb. 1861, Andrew Papers, MHS; *PhiIn*, 22 Apr. 1861; BA, 22, 23, 24 Apr. 1861; WDNI, 23 Apr. 1861; James Dorsey to Levin Richardson, 19 Apr. 1861, Levin Richardson Papers, MdHS; Harris, *Lincoln and the Border States*, 43–50.

49. Basler, CW, 4:340–42; Mitchell, *Maryland Voices*, 48–73; Lincoln to Hicks, 20 Apr. 1861, Governor's Letter Books, MdSA.

50. Henry Gilmore to Joseph A. Gilmore, 19 Apr. 1861, Gilmore Papers, NHHS.

51. *PhiIn*, 26 Apr. 1861.

52. NDM, 22 Apr. 1861; *PhiIn*, 22 Apr. 1861; BDA, 20, 22, 23 Apr. 1861; BDWC, 23 Apr. 1861; Pearson, *Andrew*, 1:191; Hamrogue, "Andrew," 86; WDNI, 24 Apr. 1861.

53. Henry Gilmore to Joseph A. Gilmore, 19 Apr. 1861, Gilmore Papers, NHHS; Washburn to Andrew, 24 May 1861, Executive Correspondence, MeSA; Boutwell, *Reminiscences of Sixty Years*, 1:284–86; Weeden, *War Government*, 70; *OR*, series 3, 1:99.

54. *OR*, series 3, 1:78–79, 85–86, 99–100, 104, 120, 135; Boutwell to Andrew, 28 Apr., 2 May 1861, Andrew Papers, MHS; Boutwell, *Reminiscences of Sixty Years*, 1:284–92.

55. *PhiIn*, 26 Apr. 1861; Sprague to Lincoln, 11 Apr. 1861, LP, LC; *Acts and Resolves, Special Session of the Rhode Island Legislature, April, 1861*, 212–22; Spicer, *History of the Ninth and Tenth Regiments*, 24–25; Marvel, *Burnside*, 14; Schouler, *Massachusetts in the Civil War*, 1:133–36; Carroll, *Rhode Island*, 2:599; *WDNI*, 19, 23 Apr. 1861; Morgan to Cameron, 19 Apr. 1861, Morgan Letter Books, NYSL; *PDJ*, 15, 16, 19 Apr. 1861; Washburn to Curtin, 20 Apr., Washburn to Andrew, 21 Apr. 1861, Governor's Telegram Book, MeSA.

56. *OR*, series 3, 1:80–81; Randall, *Lincoln*, 1:356; A Unionist to Yates, 22 Apr., Patrick H. Lang to Yates, 28 May, Griffin Garland to Yates, 29 May 1861, Yates Papers, ALPL; Trumbull to Lincoln, 21 Apr., O. H. Browning to Lincoln, 18 Apr. 1861, LP, LC; Lathrop, *Kirkwood*, 119–21; Dell, *War Democrats*, 63; *ISJ*, 29 Apr. 1861; Egle, *Curtin*, 341–47.

57. *OR*, series 3, 1:101; Mulligan, "Dennison," 144–49; Wilson, *Business of the Civil War*, 11; *ISJ*, 24 May 1861; Oyos, "Ohio Militia," 158–63; Fisher, "Groping toward Victory," 26–44; Porter, *Ohio Politics*, 74–77.

58. Clark, *Kirkwood*, 183–85, 253–54; Kirkwood to Jesse Evans, 30 Apr. 1861, Kirkwood Military Letter Books, IaSA; Phillips, *Jackson*, 240–55; Briggs, "Enlistment of Iowa Troops," 323–43.

59. *OR*, series 3, 1:86–87, 89, 127–28; Cimbala and Miller, *Union Soldiers and the Northern Home Front*, 30–68.

60. Upham, "Arms and Equipment for the Iowa Troops," 8–12, 29–30; Clark, *Kirkwood*, 187–91; Piston, "The 1st Iowa Volunteers," 7–23.

61. George W. Deitzler to Robinson, 16 Apr., and Robinson to Sara, 19 Apr. 1861, Robinson Papers, KSHS.

62. *OR*, series 3, 1:112–13; Blackmar, *Robinson*; Cheatham, "Divided Loyalties in Civil War Kansas," 93–107; Robinson's Message to the Legislature, 26 Mar. 1861, *House Journal of the Legislative Assembly of the State of Kansas*, 33–43; *ToTri*, 23 Feb., 30 Mar. 1861; *LDT*, 23 Feb. 1861.

63. Castel, *Civil War Kansas*, 41; *Kansas Senate Journal*, 1861, 28; Robinson's Message, 43; *ToTri*, 23 Feb., 30 Mar. 1861; Blackmar, *Robinson*, 267–68; Cheatham, "Divided Loyalties in Kansas," 93–107; *LDT*, 8, 21 Feb. 1861; Gambone, "Samuel C. Pomeroy and the Senatorial Election of 1861," 15–31; Smith, *Ewing*, 122–24, 150–51.

64. Ponce, *Kansas's War: The Civil War in Documents*, 43; Castel, *Civil War Kansas*, 18–19, 26–46; *LDT*, 16 Nov. 1861; *ToTri*, 23, 30 Mar. 1861; Goodrich, *War to the Knife: Bleeding Kansas, 1854–1861*, 11–50; Blackmar, *Robinson*; *NYTi*, 18 Aug. 1894.

65. Castel, *Civil War Kansas*, 18–50; Goodrich, *War to the Knife*, 35–50; Wilson, *Robinson*, 74–76; *Kansas House Journal*, 1861, 228, and *Kansas Senate Journal*, 1861, 460, 494–509, 539; Blackmar, *Robinson*, 267–73; Benedict, *Jayhawkers*; Gambone, "Senatorial Election of 1861," 15–31; Robinson to Wife (Sara), 11 Jan. 1861, Robinson Papers, KSHS; Smith, *Ewing*, 122–24.

66. Robinson to Sara, 19 Apr. 1861, Robinson Papers, KSHS.

67. Miller, *States at War*, 1:575; *OR*, series 3, 1:86–87, 194–96; Benedict, *Vermont*, 1:15–25; Crockett, *Vermont: The Green Mountain State*, 3:502–9; Sherman, "St. Johnsbury Puts

the Civil War to Rest," 63–66; Briggs, "Enlistment of Iowa Troops," 323–48; Pollock, "The Iowa War Loan of 1861," 467–502; *BDFP*, 16, 18, 24, 25 Apr. 1861.

68. *OR*, series 3, 1:86–87, 194–96; Benedict, *Vermont*, 1:15–25; Crockett, *Vermont: The Green Mountain State*, 3:502–9; Sherman, "St. Johnsbury Puts the Civil War to Rest," 63–66; Briggs, "Enlistment of Iowa Troops," 323–48; Pollock, "The Iowa War Loan of 1861," 467–502; *BDFP*, 16, 18, 24, 25 Apr. 1861.

69. Henry Stevens to Fairbanks, 11 May 1861, Fairbanks Papers, VSA; Edward Kirkwood to Welles, 16 Apr. 1861, Welles Papers, LC.

Chapter Three

1. Burlingame, *Lincoln*, 2:140–47; Donald, *Lincoln*, 298–99; Mitchel, *The Vacant Chair: The Northern Soldier Leaves Home*, 154; Meneely, *War Department*, 101–3; *WDNI*, 19 Apr. 1861; *BDA*, 15 May 1861; *StLDMR*, 18 Apr. 1861; Benedict, *Vermont*, 1:15–25.

2. Morgan to Cameron, 22 Apr. 1861, Morgan Letter Books, NYSL; Balogh, *A Government Out of Sight*, 281–301.

3. Morgan to Lincoln, 21 Apr., George D. Morgan and Thurlow Weed to Lincoln, 21 Apr. 1861, Seward Papers, UR.

4. *OR*, series 3, 1:104–7, 136; Randall, *Lincoln*, 1:364; Meneely, *War Department*, 114–23; Niven, *Chase Papers*, 3:60–61; Rawley, *Morgan*, 142–60; Morgan to Rt. Hon. Viscount Palmerston, 23 Apr. 1861, Morgan to E. Head, 22 Apr. 1861, Cameron to Morgan, 20, 29 Apr., Chase to Dix, Blatchford, Opdyke, 29, 30 Apr. 1861, Morgan to George Morgan, 2, 27, 29 Apr., 3 May 1861; Ira Harris to Morgan, 29 Apr. 1861, King to Morgan, 25 Apr., Morgan to Weed, 25 Apr., Morgan to Cameron, 26 Apr. 1861, Morgan Papers and Letter Books, NYSL; Shannon, *Organization and Administration of the Union Army*, 1:61–62; Orr, "Cities at War," 91–92; Bullard, "When Lincoln Ruled Alone," 301–49; Bradley, *Cameron*, 196–97; Burlingame, *Lincoln*, 2:163; *ChiTri*, 30 Apr. 1861; Gideon Welles to M. J. W. [Mary Jane Welles, wife], 21 Apr. 1861, Welles Papers, LC; *HW*, 27 Apr. 1861.

5. *OR*, series 3, 1:104–7, 136.

6. Boutwell, *Reminiscences of Sixty Years*, 1:286; Weeden, *War Government*, 70; Andrew to Boutwell, 25 Apr. 1861, Massachusetts Governors, Letters Official, 1861, MSA; Hamrogue, "Andrew," 87; Miller, "Brahmin Janissaries," 205–7.

7. Nicolay and Hay, *Abraham Lincoln: A History*, 4:152; Tarbell, "Lincoln Gathering an Army," 325; Villard, *Memoirs*, 1:169–70; Burlingame, *Lincoln*, 2:146–47; Donald, *Lincoln*, 298–99; Miller, *President Lincoln*, 107.

8. Grant, *North over South*, 131–37; Speech in House of Representatives, 10 May 1854, *Congressional Globe*, 33rd Congress, 1st Session, appendix, 714–15; *In Memoriam, Israel Washburn*, 14–17; *BDWC*, 3 Jun. 1854.

9. Burlingame, *Lincoln's Journalist*, 57; Dimeglio, "Civil War Bangor," 8–11; *NDM*, 3 May 1861; Whalon, "Maine Republicans," 94–100; Gara, "Slavery and the Slave Power: A Crucial Distinction," 5–18.

10. Weeden, *War Government*, 64.

11. *WSJ*, 17, 20, 22 Apr. 1861; *OR*, series 3, 1:91; Fish, "The Raising of the Wisconsin Volunteers," 259–66.

12. Andrew to Mrs. Francis Wright, 19 Apr. 1861, Massachusetts Governors, Letters Official, 1861, MSA.

13. Niven, *Connecticut for the Union*, 52–53; Croffut and Morris, *Connecticut during the War*, 839–41; Buckingham to Cameron, 21 Apr. 1861, Record Group 107, Records of the

Secretary of War, Letters Received, "irregular series," National Archives and Records Administration, Washington, D. C. (NARA); William Aiken to Welles, 24 May 1861, Welles Papers, LC.

14. Niven, *Connecticut for the Union*, 52–53; Croffut and Morris, *Connecticut during the War*, 840–41; Buckingham to Cameron, 21 Apr. 1861, RG 107, Letters Received, "irregular series," NARA.

15. J. Henry Jordan to Curtin, 22 Apr. 1861, Executive Correspondence (Andrew Curtin), PSA; Manakee, *Maryland*, 44–46; Mitchell, *Maryland Voices*, 70, 85–86; *BS*, 29 Apr. 1861; Nesenhoener, "Maintaining the Center," 413–26; Bullard, "When Lincoln Ruled Alone," 301–49; *WDNI*, 23 Apr. 1861; Harris, *Lincoln and the Border States*, 42–79; Towers, "Strange Bedfellows," 7–36.

16. Butler, *Butler's Book*, 171–211; Nolan, *Benjamin Franklin Butler*, 68–88; Bowen, *Massachusetts in the War*, 1:21–24; Andrew to Cameron, 22 Apr. 1861, RG 107, Letters Received, "irregular series," NARA; Detzer, *Dissonance*, 83–88; Butler, *Correspondence*, 1:18–28; Andrew to Hamlin, 20 Apr., Andrew to Cameron, 20 Apr., Andrew to Washburn, 20 Apr. 1861, Massachusetts Governors, Letters Official, 1861, MSA; Schouler, *Massachusetts in the Civil War*, 1:118, 140–61; Hamrogue, "Andrew," 118–20; Andrew to Howe, 2 May, Howe to Andrew, 7 May, Hoar to Andrew, 7 May, Wilson to Andrew, 8 May 1861, Andrew Papers, MHS; *WES*, 23 Apr. 1861; *BS*, 29, 30 Apr. 1861; Butler to Hicks, 22 Apr., Hicks to Butler, 23 Apr. 1861, Governor's Letter Books, MdSA; Snyder, "Governor Hicks and the Secession Crisis Reconsidered," 304–31; Towers, "Strange Bedfellows," 7–30.

17. Benedict, *Vermont*, 1:32–33; *BDFP*, 19 Apr. 1861.

18. Benedict, *Vermont*, 1:33.

19. *BDFP*, 18, 19, 24 Apr. 1861.

20. Meneely, *War Department*, 120–25, 153–54; Nevins, *The Improvised War*, 168–69; John Ward to Charlie, 3 May 1861, John Ward Papers, LC; *WES*, 27 Apr. 1861.

21. *HEP*, 9 May 1861; Schouler, *Massachusetts in the Civil War*, 1:76–77.

22. Niven, *Connecticut for the Union*, 55; *Message of His Excellency William A. Buckingham . . . to the Legislature of the State*, 1 May 1861, 3–18; Welles to M. J. W., 5 May 1861, Welles Papers, LC.

23. Rawley, *The Politics of Union*, 19; Meneely, *War Department*, 114–23; Shannon, *Organization of the Union Army*, 1:53–58; Marvel, *Mr. Lincoln Goes to War*, 44–49.

24. Radcliffe, *Hicks*, 62–64; *BS*, 22 Apr. 1861; Mitchell, *Maryland Voices*, 65–80; Butler, *Butler's Book*, 195–205; Butler, *Correspondence*, 1:18–28; *WES*, 23 Apr. 1861; *BS*, 29, 30 Apr. 1861; *PhiIn*, 11, 22 May 1861; Harris, *Lincoln and the Border States*, 42–79; Snyder, "Governor Hicks and the Secession Crisis Reconsidered," 304–31.

25. Butler, *Butler's Book*, 200–11; *BS*, 22 Apr. 1861; Trefousse, *Ben Butler*, 17–60; Grimsley, *The Hard Hand of War: Union Military Policy toward Southern Civilians, 1861–1865*, 52; Mitchell, *Maryland Voices*, 65–75, 90–91; Radcliffe, *Hicks*, 62–69; *WES*, 29 Apr. 1861; Butler, *Correspondence*, 1:3–32; *BS*, 29, 30 Apr. 1861; Hicks Message to Legislature, 25 Apr. 1861, Governor's Letter Books, MdSA; *PhiIn*, 29 Apr., 17 May 1861; *Baltimore American*, 25, 29 Apr. 1861; Harris, *Lincoln and the Border States*, 42–79; Snyder, "Governor Hicks and the Secession Crisis Reconsidered," 304–31; Cannon, "Lincoln's Divided Backyard: Maryland in the Civil War Era," 3–5.

26. Hicks to Butler, 10 May, Butler to Hicks, 23 Apr., C.F. Neumen to Hicks, 25, 27 Apr., Hicks to Butler, 10 May, Hicks to John Letcher, 1 May, Hicks to Lincoln, 8 May, Cameron to Hicks, 10 May, and Thomas J. Jackson to John Letcher, 6 May 1861, Governor's Letter Books, MdSA. Hicks to Lincoln, 8 May 1861, LP, LC; Mitchell, *Mary-

land Voices, 90–93; Marvel, *Mr. Lincoln Goes to War*, 94–95; *WES*, 8 Jun. 1861; *BS*, 3, 13, 17, 19 May 1861; Snyder, "Governor Hicks and the Secession Crisis Reconsidered," 304–31.

27. Hicks to Butler, 10 May 1861, Governor's Letter Books, MdSA; *BS*, 1, 4 Jun. 1861; *PhiIn*, 22 May 1861.

28. Hamlin to Washburn, 23, 30 Apr., Cameron to Washburn, 26 Apr. 1861, Executive Correspondence, MeSA; Washburn to Hamlin, 24, 26, 27 Apr. 1861, Washburn to Cameron, [nd] May 1861, Governor's Telegram Books, MeSA; Washburn to Hamlin, 28 Apr. 1861, Israel Washburn Jr. Papers, LC; Washburn to Hamlin, 26, 30 Apr. 1861, Hamlin Papers, UMeL; Whalon, "Washburn and the War Department," 79–85; *BDWC*, 19, 22, 25, 26 Apr. 1861; *KJ*, 8, 22 March 1861; Andrew to Hamlin, 20 Apr. 1861, Massachusetts Governors, Letters Official, 1861, MSA; Kelsey, *Israel Washburn Jr., Maine's Little-Known Giant of the Civil War*, 112–25.

29. Byers, *With Fire and Sword*, 13; Briggs, "Enlistment of Iowa Troops," 323–48; Washburn to Yates, Curtin, and Dennison, [nd] 1861, Executive Correspondence, MeSA; Washburn to Fessenden, 13, 14 May 1861, Fessenden Papers, WRHS.

30. *OR*, series 3, 1:119, 134, 142–45; *NDM*, 17, 18, 19 Apr., 9 May 1861; Platt, *Perrin Smith*, 112–13; Foster, *New Jersey and Rebellion*, 1–38; *NYTi*, 19 Apr. 1861; Clark, *Kirkwood*, 187–91, 254–55; Shambaugh, *The Messages and Proclamations of the Governors of Iowa*, 2:277–78; Kirkwood to [Jesse Evans], 30 Apr. 1861, Military Letter Books, Samuel J. Kirkwood Papers, SHSI.

31. *OR*, series 3, 1:101–2, 105, 109, 111–13; Andrew to Cameron, 25 Apr. 1861, RG 107, Letters Received, irregular series, NARA; *SLDMR*, 25 Apr. 1861; Samito, *Becoming American Under Fire*, 28; Mowry, "A Statesman's Letters of the Civil War Period," 43–50.

32. Foulke, *Morton*, 1:118–21; *WDNI*, 2 May 1861; Sylvester, "Morton," 92–96; *OR*, series 3, 1:150–51; Albright, "Curtin," 48:154–56; Nevins, *Improvised War*, 173–416; Meneely, *War Department*, 144; *PhiIn*, 18, 21 May 1861.

33. Thornbrough, Riker, and Corpuz, *Diary of Fletcher*, 7:96–97.

34. Nelson to Todd, 18, 22 Apr. 1861, LP, LC; Johnson and Buel, *Battles and Leaders*, 1:373–93; Harris, *Lincoln and the Border States*, 80–87.

35. *OR*, series 3, 1:115–16, 125–26; Thornbrough, Riker, and Corpuz, *Diary of Fletcher*, 7:105–6; Foulke, *Morton*, 1:125; Benedict, *Vermont*, 1:23–37; Niven, *Connecticut for the Union*, 56–57; Croffut and Morris, *Connecticut during the War*, 73–74; Message of Buckingham, 1 May 1861, 11–12; *BDFP*, 24 Apr. 1861, Fairbanks, Message to Legislature, 23 Apr. 1861; Andrew to Fairbanks, 25 Apr. 1861, Massachusetts Governors, Letters Official, 1861, MSA.

36. *NDM*, 22 Apr., 4 May 1861; *BS*, 15 May 1861; *OR*, series 3, 1:114; Cowden, "Heaven Will Frown on Such a Cause as This," 74–76; *WDNI*, 29 Apr. 1861; *PhiIn*, 2 May 1861; *DR*, 25 Apr., 20 May 1861; *TDSGR*, 1, 6 May 1861; Spruance, *Delaware Stays in the Union*, 15–16; Munroe, *History of Delaware*, 134; *Dover Del*, 2 Jun. 1861; Hancock, "The Political History of Delaware during the Civil War, Part II: The Coming of the War," 7:240–59; Wilkinson, "The Brandywine Home Front during the Civil War, Part I: 1861," 9:270–72; Miller, *States at War*, 4:59–88.

37. *NYTi*, 12 May 1861.

38. Hancock, "Political History of Delaware, Part III," 7:358; Scharf, *History of Delaware, 1609–1888*, 1:367; *OR*, series 3, 1:110, 124–25; *WDNI*, 29 Apr. 1861; *DR*, 2 May 1861; Burton to Edward W. Gilpin, 23 Apr. 1861, Executive Papers, DPA; Harris, *Lincoln and the Border States*, 38–40.

39. Hancock, "Political History of Delaware, Part II," 7:224–25; *Journal of the Senate of the State of Delaware, 1861,* 151, 155–56; Munroe, *History of Delaware,* 132; Reed, "Lincoln's Compensated Emancipation Plan and Its Relation to Delaware," 36.

40. Henry Eckel to Lincoln, 9 Apr. 1861, LP, LC; *DR,* 2 May 1861; Reed, "Lincoln's Emancipation Plan," 36; Hicks to Burton, 2 Jan. 1861, Hicks Papers, MdHS.

41. Hicks to Burton, 2 Jan. 1861, Hicks Papers, MdHS; Wilkinson, "Brandywine Home Front," 9:266–72; Hancock, "Political History of Delaware, Part II," 7:224–43.

42. Hancock, "Political History of Delaware, Part II," 7:240–59; Burton to Edward Wootten, 24 May 1861, Burton-Wootten Papers, DPA.

43. Eckel to Lincoln, 9 Apr., Curtin to Lincoln, 30 Apr. 1861, LP, LC; *DR,* 2, 13 May 1861, 16 Oct. 1862; Cowden, *"Heaven Will Frown,"* 75–76; *PhiIn,* 25 Apr. 1861; Hancock, *Delaware during the Civil War,* 88–101.

44. William Ross to Burton, 22 May 1861, Burton-Wootten Papers, DPA.

45. Hancock, "Civil War Diaries of Anna M. Ferris," 229; Hancock, "Political History of Delaware, Part II," 7:248–59; Cowden, *"Heaven Will Frown,"* 75–77; *DR,* 2, 13 May 1861.

46. *OR,* series 3, 1:114–15; Nevins, *The Improvised War,* 88–89; *NHPSG,* 24 Apr., 1 May 1861; Cameron to Morgan, 29 Apr., Chase to Dix, Blatchford, Opdyke, 30 Apr. 1861, Morgan Papers, NYSL; Rawley, "Lincoln and Morgan," 282–87; Andrew to Cameron, 15 Apr. 1861, RG 107, Letters Received, "irregular series," NARA; Meneely, *War Department,* 116–22; Schouler, *Massachusetts in the Civil War,* 1:122–24, 130–31; Hamrogue, "Andrew," 92–102, 112–14; Andrew to Washburn, 22, 24 Apr., Andrew to Buckingham, 30 Apr. 1861; Andrew to Cameron, 18 Apr. 1861, Massachusetts Governors, Letters Official, 1861, MSA; *BDWC,* 30 Apr. 1861; Renda, "New Hampshire Politics," 11–16; *NHS,* 20 Apr. 1861; Andrew to Ichabod Goodwin, 24 Apr. 1861, Ichabod Goodwin Papers, NHHS; Cameron to William Pitt Fessenden, 27 Apr., Cameron to Washburn, 29 Apr. 1861, Washburn to Gideon Welles, 7 May 1861, Executive Correspondence, MeSA; Washburn to Hamlin, 5 May 1861, Washburn Papers, LC; *NYTi,* 24 Jul. 1861; Godwin to Andrew, 23 Apr. 1861, Massachusetts Governors Papers, Executive Department Letters, 1861, MSA.

47. Andrew to Cameron, 15, 18 Apr. 1861, RG 107, Letters Received, "irregular series," NARA; Parish, *The North and the Nation in the Era of the Civil War,* 92–93.

48. *HEP,* 8, 9 May 1861.

49. Dennett, *Diaries and Letters of Hay,* 12; Burlingame, *At Lincoln's Side: John Hay's Civil War Correspondence and Selected Writings,* 259; Cozzens, *Battles and Leaders,* 6:19–26; *WES,* 29 Apr. 1861.

50. Boutwell, *Reminiscences of Sixty Years,* 1:289–90.

51. *HEP,* 8 May 1861.

52. Burlingame, *Dispatches from Lincoln's White House,* 1, 144; Villard, *Memoirs,* 1:170; Furgurson, *Freedom Rising,* 80–83; Marvel, *Mr. Lincoln Goes to War,* 44–57; *WES,* 2 May 1861; *WDNI,* 3 May 1861.

53. Burlingame and Ettlinger, *Inside Lincoln's White House: The Complete Civil War Diary of John Hay,* 13; Furgurson, *Freedom Rising,* 80–85; Staudenraus, *Mr. Lincoln's Washington,* 25; Benedict, *Jayhawkers: The Civil War Brigade of James Henry Lane,* 27–30; Stephenson, *Political Career of General James H. Lane,* 105–6; *WES,* 27 Apr. 1861; *LDT,* 26 Apr. 1861; *NYTi,* 19 Apr. 1861.

54. *OR,* series 3, 1:110.

55. Blair to Andrew, 11 May 1861, Andrew Papers, MHS; Andrew to Quartermaster, 11 May 1861, Lee Family Papers, MHS.

56. Andrew to Montgomery Blair, 6 May 1861, Andrew Letterbook, MHS, and Andrew to Blair, 6 May 1861, Massachusetts Governors, Letters Official, MSA.

57. *OR*, series 3, 1:196–98; Shannon, *Organization of the Union Army*, 1:52–55.

58. John G. Nicolay to Olden, 10 May, Cameron to Olden, 21 May, Gideon Welles to Olden, 21, 25 May 1861, Olden Family Papers, HSP; *OR*, series 3, 1:187–88; Foster, *New Jersey and the Rebellion*, 1–38; *TDSGR*, 16, 17, 19, 22 Apr. 1861; Jackson, *New Jerseyans in the Civil War*, 39–44; Olden to Marcus Ward and Joseph Bradley, 3 May 1861, Marcus Ward Papers, NJHS; *DFP*, 1 Jun. 1861; Hesseltine, *Lincoln and the War Governors*, 158, 212; Platt, *Perrin Smith*, 112–14; Miers, *New Jersey and the Civil War*, 15–20; *WES*, 6 May 1861; Stellhorn and Birker, *The Governors of New Jersey, 1664–1974*, 129–31; *NDM*, 1, 4 May 1861.

59. *OR*, series 3, 1:186–87; Clark, *Kirkwood*, 191–94; W. H. Kinsman to Kirkwood, 29 May, James Grimes to Kirkwood, 17 Apr., J. Rolleshun to Kirkwood, 22 Apr., and George C. Herberling to Kirkwood, 24 Apr., and John C. Ellud to Kirkwood, 26 Apr., B. J. Allison to Kirkwood, 1 May 1861, Governor's Correspondence, ISA; Shannon, *Organization of the Union Army*, 1, 85–86; Byers, *Iowa in War Times*, 45; *WDNI*, 27 May 1861; Briggs, "Enlistment of the Iowa Troops," 323–48; *BDHE*, 31 May 1861.

60. William T. Coggeshall Diary, 4 Jun. 1861, ALPL; Towne, *Surveillance and Spies in the Civil War*, 16–21.

61. *OR*, series 3, 1:101; Oyos, "Ohio Militia," 165–74; Fisher, "Groping toward Victory," 26–27; Mulligan, "Dennison," 153–69; Chase to Dennison, 5, 9 May, James W. Ripley to Chase, 5 May, Cameron to Dennison, 9 May 1861, Series 147, OHS; *OR*, series 1, 52, part 2: 68–70; Hesseltine and Wolf, "The Cleveland Conference of 1861," 258–65; Reid, *Ohio in the War*, 1:39; Chase to Dennison, 30 Apr. 1861, Governor's Correspondence, OHS; J. Todd, J. W. Clark to Dennison, 16 Apr. 1861, R. Smith to Dennison, 25 Apr., J. K. Harnfeld to Dennison, 1 May 1861, Telegraphic Dispatches, series 145, OhSA; Sears, *The Civil War Papers of George B. McClellan: Selected Correspondence, 1860–1865*, 6–7; Abbott, *Ohio's War Governors*, 14–18; Thomas, "Campaigns of Generals McClellan and Rosecrans in Western Virginia, 1861–1862," 245–50; *NYTi*, 25 Apr., 14 May, 8 Jun. 1861; *PhiIn*, 24 Apr. 1861; Arthur I. Boreman to Lincoln, 18 Jun. 1861, Seward Papers, UR; Zimring, "'Secession in Favor of the Constitution': How West Virginia Justified Separate Statehood during the Civil War," 23–51.

62. Foulke, *Morton*, 1:124–25; Magoffin to Morton, 25 Apr., 1861, LP, LC; French, *Morton*, 194–96; Johnson and Buel, *Battles and Leaders*, 1:373–93; Hesseltine, *Lincoln and the War Governors*, 158–59; *WDNI*, 2 May 1861; Stampp, "Kentucky's Influence," 268–71; *InDJ*, 2, 3 May 1861; Thomas, "Campaigns of McClellan and Rosecrans," 245–50; Magoffin to Dennison, 25 Apr. 1861, Telegraphic Dispatches, series 145, OhSA; *LDJ*, 25 Apr., 3, 4 May 1861; *StLDMR*, 26 Apr. 1861; Engle, *Struggle for the Heartland*, 1–19; Hess, *The Civil War in the West*, 11.

63. Foulke, *Morton*, 1:119; Sylvester, "Morton," 100–14.

64. Message of Yates to Illinois General Assembly, 23 Apr. 1861, *Illinois Senate Journal*, 5–19; Kimball, "Yates," 16; Sylvester, "Morton," 100–14; *ChiTri*, 30 Apr. 1861.

65. Message of Yates to Illinois General Assembly, 23 Apr. 1861, *Illinois Senate Journal*, 5–19; *ISJ*, 1 May 1861; Kimball, "Yates," 28–29.

66. John Wentworth to Yates, 29 Apr. 1861, John Wentworth Papers, DC.

67. Kimball, "Yates," 31–33; *ChiTri*, 30 Apr. 1861.

68. Bigelow, *Retrospections of an Active Life*, 1:349–50; Curtin to Morgan, 29 Apr., Morgan to Dennison, 2 May, Chase to Dix, Blatchford, Opdyke, 30 Apr. 1861, Morgan Papers

and Letter Books, NYSL; Morgan to Dennison, 28, 29 Apr., 2 May 1861, Series 147, OHS; Crittenden to Dennison, 30 Apr., Dennison to Crittenden, 1 May 1861, Governor's Papers, OHS; Magoffin to Morton, 25 Apr. 1861, LP, LC; Magoffin to Dennison, 25, 26 Apr. 1861, Telegraphic Dispatches, series 145, OhSA; Coggeshall Diary, 2, 3, 4 May 1861, ALPL; Mulligan, "Dennison," 161–63, 196–200; Sears, *McClellan*, 68–69; *WSJ*, 9 May 1861; Foulke, *Morton*, 1:134–39; Dell, *War Democrats*, 89–90; Johnson and Buel, *Battles and Leaders*, 1:373–93; Dues, "Magoffin," 22–28; *InDJ*, 2, 3 May 1861; *LDJ*, 25 Apr., 2, 3 May 1861; *StLDMR*, 26 Apr. 1861; French, *Morton*, 193–98; Abbott, *Ohio's War Governors*, 14–19; Terrell, *Indiana in the War*, 7–9, 212, 215, 221–23; Weeden, *War Government*, 163; *OR*, series 3, 1:125–26; Harbison, "Lincoln and Indiana Republicans, 1861–1862," 283–84; *WDNI*, 9 May 1861; *ISJ*, 24 May 1861; *InDJ*, 2, 3 May 1861; *DFP*, 3, 9, 10, 17 May 1861.

69. *WSJ*, 9 May 1861; *DFP*, 10 May 1861; *LDJ*, 2, 3 May 1861; *PhiIn*, 8 May 1861; Quiner, *Military History of Wisconsin*, 64–66; Sears, *Papers of McClellan*, 10–19; Meneely, *War Department*, 177–79; Mulligan, "Dennison," 194–200; Hesseltine and Wolf, "Cleveland Conference," 260–65; Curtin to Dennison, 25 Apr., Crittenden to Dennison, 30 Apr., Morgan to Dennison, 29 Apr., 2 May 1861, Series 147, OHS; Morgan to John Dix, 7, 9 May 1861, Morgan Letter Books, NYSL; *OR*, series 3, 1:69, 95, 97–99, 167–70; Fennimore, "Blair," 49:213–14; Bigelow, *Retrospections*, 1:350–52; Randall to Lincoln, 6 May Dennison to Lincoln, 7 May 1861, LP, LC; Johnson and Buel, *Battles and Leaders*, 1:373–93; Turner, "Secession Movement," 268–71.

70. *BDWC*, 9 May 1861; *HEP*, 9, 15 May 1861; *WSJ*, 9 May 1861; *MS*, 9, 10 May 1861; *PhiIn*, 8 May 1861; *NYTi*, 16 May 1861.

71. *OR*, series 3, 1:167–70; Randall to Lincoln, 6, 10 May, and Dennison to Lincoln, 7 May, Charles A. Wickliffe to Lincoln, 28 May 1861, LP, LC; *NYTi*, 16 May 1861; Quiner, *History of Wisconsin*, 64; *WSJ*, 9, 10 May 1861.

72. Gurowski, *Diary* (4 Mar. 1861, to 12 Nov. 1862), 1:46; Hesseltine, *Lincoln and the War Governors*, 162.

73. Curtin to Lincoln, 10 May 1861, LP, LC.

74. McClellan to Dennison, 13 May 1861, McClellan Papers, LC, also in Sears, *Papers of McClellan*, 18–19; *OR*, series 3, 1:207–8; Nevins, *The Improvised War*, 173; Randall to Curtin, 29 May 1861, Executive Correspondence, PSA.

75. As quoted in Nevins, *The Improvised War*, 173; Meneely, *War Department*, 135–47; Millett and Maslowski, *For the Common Defense*, 163–65; Orr, "Cities at War," 105, 108–110; Schouler, *Massachusetts in the Civil War*, 1:167; *OR*, series 3, 1:213–14; *NYTri*, 16 May 1861; Pritchett, Katzman, and Dellon, "The Union Defense Committee of the City of New York during the Civil War," 142–60; Buckingham, *Buckingham*, 163–64; Weeden, *War Government*, 179–88; Egle, *Curtin*, 228–29; Washburn to Andrew and Morgan, 21 May, Cameron to Washburn, 26 Apr., Gideon Welles to Washburn, "confidential," 22 Apr., and see also Washburn to Lot Morrill, 10 May 1861, Executive Correspondence, MeSA; Washburn to Fessenden, 13, 14 May 1861, Fessenden Papers, WRHS.

76. *OR*, series 3, 1:131–35, 145–49; Shannon, *Organization of the Union Army*, 1:34–37; Nevins, *The Improvised War*, 173; Pearson, *Andrew*, 1:233–35; Andrew to Chase, 5 May, Andrew to Blair, 6 May, Andrew to Scott, 9 May, 1861, Massachusetts Governors, Letters Official, 1861, MSA.

77. *OR*, series 3, 1:193; Dennett, *Lincoln and the Civil War Diaries of John Hay*, 12; *DFP*, 5 May 1861; Hesseltine, *Lincoln and the War Governors*, 170–71; *WDNI*, 27 May 1861.

78. *OR*, series 3, 1:300–30; Nevins, *The Improvised War*, 171; James S. Negley to Curtin, 21 May 1861, Executive Correspondence, PSA.

79. *HW*, 4 May 1861; Williams, *Lincoln Finds a General: A Military Study of the Civil War*, 1:61–62; Nevins, *The Improvised War*, 88–89; *OR*, series 3, 1:130–31, 177; Morgan to Lincoln, 26 May 1861, LP, LC; Cameron to Morgan, 20, 29 Apr. 1861, Morgan Papers, NYSL; Pritchett, Katzman, and Dellon, "Union Defense Committee," 142–60; Wilson, *Business of the Civil War*, 12–20; Meneely, *War Department*, 136–39; Stevens, *Union Defense Committee of City of New York Minutes*; Barrows, *William M. Evarts*, 102–3; Rawley, *Morgan*, 151; Shannon, *Organization of the Union Army*, 1:52–58; Hamrogue, "Andrew," 100–106.

80. As quoted in Nevins, *The Improvised War*, 88, 173–77; Keller, *Chancellorsville and the Germans*, 30–32; Engle, "A Raised Consciousness: Franz Sigel and German Ethnic Identity in the Civil War," 1–18; Ural, *Civil War Citizens: Race, Ethnicity, and Identity in America's Bloodiest Conflict*, 11–55; Schouler, *Massachusetts in the Civil War*, 1:50–119; Burton, *Melting Pot Soldiers*, 126–34; *BDA*, 15, 31 May 1861; George D. Welles to Andrew, 3 May, Jun. 22, Ebenezer R. Hoar to Andrew, 7 May, Henry Wilson to Andrew, 8 May, [M. Beau] to Andrew, 11 May 1861, Andrew Papers, MHS; Samito, *Becoming American*, 28, 32.

81. As quoted in Foulke, *Morton*, 1:152; *InDJ*, 1 Jun. 1861; Terrell, *Indiana in the War*, 18–20; Thornbrough, *Indiana in the Civil War*, 163–69.

82. Foulke, *Morton*, 1:150–53; Quiner, *Military History of Wisconsin*, 51–54; Mulligan, "Dennison," 150–58; *ISJ*, 24, 28 May, 1 Jun. 1861; *ChiTri*, 24, 30 May 1861; *DFP*, 1 Jun. 1861; *StLDMR*, 3 Jun. 1861.

83. Wickman, *Letters to Vermont*, 1:65–70; Newell, "Fairbanks," 59–64; Fairbanks to E. P. Walton, 11 May, Peter S. Washburn to Fairbanks, 14 Jun., Washburn to Fairbanks, 14 Jun., Charles F. Storrs and others to Baxter, 11 May, Baxter to Fairbanks, 18 May, William T. George to Fairbanks, 30 May 1861, Fairbanks Papers, VSA.

84. *OR*, series 3, 1:145–48; Mulligan, "Dennison," 178–79; Reverend D. M. Lee to Yates, 2 May, A. Clybourn to Yates, 3 May 1861, Yates Papers, ALPL; Towne, *Surveillance and Spies*, 15–16.

85. Joshua League to Yates, 13 May 1861, Yates Papers, ALPL.

86. As quoted in Nevins, *The Improvised War*, 328; Meneely, *War Department*, 178.

87. Lewis, *Captain Sam Grant*, 400–427; Hesseltine, *Lincoln and the War Governors*, 173–74; Shannon, *Organization of the Union Army*, 1:88–90; Simpson, *Ulysses S. Grant: Triumph Over Adversity, 1822–1865*, 78–83; Yates, "Yates," 194; Kimball, "Yates," 39–40; Grant, *Personal Memoirs of U. S. Grant*, 1:230–35.

88. Morgan to Lincoln, 19 May, Morgan to Cameron, 15 May 1861, Morgan Papers, NYSL; Rawley, *Morgan*, 147; Morgan to Lincoln, 26 May 1861, Lincoln to Sprague, 10 May 1861, LP, LC; Meneely, *War Department*, 156–67; Weeden, *War Government*, 179–88; Perret, *Lincoln's War*, 42–43; Keneally, *American Scoundrel: The Life of the Notorious Civil War General Dan Sickles*, 218–23; *OR*, series 3, vol. 1, 178–79; Burlingame, *Lincoln*, 2:165–66; Shannon, *Organization of the Union Army*, 1:52–60; Messent and Courtney, *The Civil War Letters of Joseph Hopkins Twichell: A Chaplain's Story*, 18–26; Brummer, *Political History of New York*, 125–26.

89. Lincoln to Morgan, 20 May 1861, Morgan to Cameron, 15 May 1861, Morgan Papers, NYSL; Rawley, *Morgan*, 147–48; Weeden, *War Government*, 179–88; Pritchett, Katzman, and Dellon, "Union Defense Committee," 142–60; Basler, *CW*, 4:375–76, 382; *OR*, series 3, 1:206, 217; Meneely, *War Department*, 156–67; *NYTri*, 3 May 1861.

Chapter Four

1. Sears, *McClellan*, 72–74; *OR*, series 1:52, 137; Phillips, *Jackson*, 245–63; Avery and Shoemaker, *Messages*, 3:343–48, 373–89; *StLDMR*, 23 Apr., 6, 8, 12 May 1861.

2. *ChiTri*, 29 Apr. 1861; *BDHE*, 1 May 1861; *StLDMR*, 12 May 1861; Adams, *William S. Harney*, 161, 217–35; Parrish, *Blair*, 96–97; Williams, *The Wild Life of the Army*, 1; Phillips, *Jackson*, 250–57; Phillips, *Damned Yankee: The Life of General Nathaniel Lyon*, 175–214; Eddy, *Patriotism of Illinois*, 1:102–5; Johnson and Buel, *Battles and Leaders*, 1:262–77; *ToTri*, 18 May 1861; *LDT*, 18 Jun. 1861; Harris, *Lincoln and the Border States*, 126–37.

3. As cited in the *BDHE*, 24 May 1861, referring to the notion that Muhammad was suspended without supports from the ceiling of his tomb. Astor, *Rebels on the Border*, 61–63; *Report of the Adjutant General of the State of Kansas, 1861–1865*, 73; Orville H. Browning to Edwin D. Morgan, 11 May 1861, Morgan Papers, NYSL; Phillips, *Lyon*, 175–214; Phillips, *Jackson*, 250–60; Johnson and Buel, *Battles and Leaders*, 1:373–93; Cozzens, *Battles and Leaders*, 5:67–91; Turner, "Secession Movement," 270–72; *LDJ*, 21, 22, 24 May 1861; Wish, "Civil War Letters and Dispatches," 62–63.

4. *OR*, series 1, 3:374–76; Adams, *Harney*, 213–42; Parrish, *Blair*, 106–7; Cozzens, *Battles and Leaders*, 5:67–91; Harris, *Lincoln and the Border States*, 126–38; *OR*, series 1, 3:374–76; Gamble and Yeatman to Lincoln, 15 May 1861, LP, LC; Phillips, *Jackson*, 251–63; *ChiTri*, 5 Jun. 1861; Boman, *Lincoln and Citizens' Rights*, 21–24.

5. *OR*, series 1, 2:28–30; Butler, *Butler Book*, 237–40; Manakee, *Maryland*, 50; Marvel, *Mr. Lincoln Goes to War*, 67–68.

6. *OR*, series 1, 2:648–51; Butler, *Butler Book*, 237–77; Marvel, *Mr. Lincoln Goes to War*, 67–77; *DFP*, 19 May 1861; Witt, *Lincoln's Code*, 202–7.

7. *PDJ*, 3 Jan. 1861; *NYTi*, 8, 14, 15, 16, 17 May 1861; Moore, "Slavery as a Factor in the Formation of West Virginia," 68–75; Woodward, "Opinions of President Lincoln and His Cabinet on Statehood for Western Virginia, 1862–1863," 157–84; Ham, "The Mind of a Copperhead," 97–100; Pierpont, *Letter of Governor Pierpont to His Excellency the President and the Honorable Congress of the United States*, 5–7; Arthur I. Boreman to Lincoln, 18 Jun. 1861, Seward Papers, UR; Stealey, "West Virginia's Constitutional Critique of Virginia," 9–47; Stealey, *West Virginia's Civil War-Era Constitution*, 37–106; *HW*, 6 Jul. 1861; Zimring, "'Secession in Favor of the Constitution,'" 23–51.

8. *BA*, 7 Feb., 30 Apr. 1861.

9. *ChiTri*, 29 May 1861; Langford, "Constitutional Issues," 12–31; Moore, "Slavery as a Factor," 68–75; Woodward, "Opinions on Statehood for Western Virginia," 159–84; Ham, "Mind of a Copperhead," 97–100; Shaffer, "Lincoln and the 'Vast Question' of West Virginia," 86–100; Burlingame, *Lincoln*, 2:159–60; *StLDMR*, 15 May 1861; *HEP*, 15 May 1861; Boreman to Lincoln, 18 Jun. 1861, Seward Papers, UR; Stealey, "West Virginia's Constitutional Critique," 9–47; Stealey, *West Virginia's Civil War-Era Constitution*, 37–106; Zimring, "'Secession in Favor of the Constitution,'" 23–51; Curtin to Andrew, 26 Apr., Carlisle to Andrew, 28 Apr., 30 May, Campbell to Andrew, 18, 28 May, 1861, Massachusetts Governors Papers, Executive Department Letters, 1861, MSA.

10. Bates to Gamble, 16 Jul. 1861, Hamilton Gamble Papers, MoHS; Boreman to Lincoln, 18 Jun. 1861, Seward Papers, UR.

11. Lewis, *How West Virginia was Made*, 369–72; Ham, "The Mind of a Copperhead," 97–102; Smith, *The Borderland in the Civil War*, 185–220; Stealey, *West Virginia's Civil War-Era Constitution*, 37–106; Ambler, "The Formation of West Virginia: Debates and Proceedings," 171–79; Ambler, *Pierpont*, 81–101; Eicher, *Longest Night*, 72–75.

12. *NDM*, 25 May 1861; John Dix to Edwards Pierrepont, 17 Jul. 1861, John Dix Papers, SUL; Sears, *Papers of McClellan*, 18–19; *NDM*, 25 May 1861; Weeden, *War Government*, 87.

13. Sears, *McClellan*, 74; *OR*, series 1, 52:146–47, series 3, 1:158, 230; McClellan to Dennison, 25 May 1861; Sears, *Papers of McClellan*, 25; *StLDMR*, 24, 25 May 1861; *CDE*, 24 May 1861; Mulligan, "Dennison," 208–9; Report of Governors Meeting, 24 May 1861, series 147, OHS; Meneely, *War Department*, 182; McClellan to Lincoln, 30 May 1861, LP, LC; Harbison, "Lincoln and Indiana Republicans," 283–84; Foulke, *Morton*, 1:140–41; Harris, *Lincoln and the Border States*, 90–91.

14. Sumner to Andrew, 24 May 1861, Andrew Papers, MHS; Randall, *Lincoln*, 1:384; *OR*, series 3, 1:230–31; Meneely, *War Department*, 182.

15. *BDWC*, 22 Jul. 1861; Weeden, *War Government*, 93.

16. Robinson to Sara, 17, 30 June 1861, Robinson Papers, KSHS.

17. *OR*, series 1, 3:374–81, 384; Lincoln to Francis P. Blair, 18 May, and Samuel T. Glover to Lincoln, 24 May 1861, LP, LC; *ToTri*, 26 Apr., 25 May 1861.

18. William A. Buckingham to Hiram Walbridge, 6 Jun. 1861, as cited in *Correspondence Between His Excellency President Abraham Lincoln, and The Hon. Simon Cameron, Secretary of War*, 15.

19. Washburn to E. H. Morse, 8 Jun., Washburn to Lincoln, 28 Jun., Washburn to Cameron, 28 Jun., and Washburn to Andrew, 19 Jul. 1861, Executive Correspondence, MeSA; Washburn to Fessenden, 13, 14 May, 18, 21, 22, 29 Jun., 9 Jul. 1861, Fessenden Papers, WRHS; *ChiTri*, 25 Jun. 1861; *Correspondence Between Lincoln and Cameron*, 1–21.

20. *OR*, series 3, 2:149–52; *ChiTri*, 25 Jun. 1861. Edwin Bryant Quiner, who wrote *The Military History of Wisconsin*, also kept a scrapbook of newspaper articles in the *WSJ*, *MS*, and other local newspapers from regimental correspondents in Wisconsin units. This scrapbook is in the Wisconsin Historical Society in Madison, Wisconsin, and has been digitized in the "Wisconsin in the Civil War" Digital Collection, 1:14–114, hereafter cited as Quiner Scrapbook.

21. *OR*, series 3, 2:149–52.

22. Quiner Scrapbook, 1:82; Weeden, *War Government*, 189; Parish, *The North and the Nation in the Era of the Civil War*, 8–85; Folwell, *Minnesota*, 88–89; Jeffreys-Jones and Collins, *Growth of Federal Power*, 62–63.

23. Forbes to Andrew, 9 Jun. 1861, Andrew Papers, MHS; Pearson, *Andrew*, 1:218–19; John Forbes to Andrew, 2 May 1861, Lee Family Papers, MHS; *NYTi*, 10 May, 7, 8 Jul. 1861.

24. Jacob Ammen Diary, 22, 27 Jun., 25 Jul. 1861, Jacob Ammen Papers, ALPL; R. M. Corwine to Dennison, 2, 3, 4, 5, 6, 12, 22 Jun. 1861, George W. McCook to Dennison, to William T. Bascom, 24 Jun. 1861, series 147, OHS; Dennison to Chase, 10 Jun. 1861, Telegraphic Dispatches, series 144, OhSA; Chase to Dennison, 30 May 1861, Telegraphic Dispatches, series 145, OhSA; Meneely, *War Department*, 205; Fisher, "Groping toward Victory," 26–32, 42–44; *NDM*, 2 Sept. 1861; *NYTi*, 7 Jun. 1861; Macnamara, *The History of the Ninth Regiment Massachusetts Volunteer Infantry*, 22–25; Burton, *Melting Pot Soldiers*, 46–47, 72, 75, 112–28; Wilson to Andrew, 27 Jun., Andrew to Peleg Chandler, 29 Jun., Samuel Gridley Howe to Andrew, 9 May 1861, Andrew Papers, MHS; Miller, "Brahmin Janissaries," 214–15; Hamrogue, "Andrew," 89–121; *NDM*, 29, 31 Jul. 1861; *NHPSG*, 7 Aug. 1861.

25. Howard, *Autobiography*, 1:114–15; Cameron to Washburn, 22 May, Lot M. Morrill to Washburn, 27, Washburn to Hamlin, 27 May 1861, Executive Correspondence, MeSA; *BDWC*, 8 Jun. 1861; Executive Correspondence, MeSA; Jordan, *The Civil War Journals of John Mead Gould*, 17; Schutz and Trenerry, *Pope*, 62–63; Cozzens and Girardi, *Pope's Memoirs*, 4–5; Yates to Lincoln, 8 May, Yates to Chase, 8 May, Pope to Lincoln, 20 Apr. Trumbull to Lincoln, 9 May, 1861, LP, LC; Pope to Yates, 15 May, Pope to Trumbull 6 Jul., 1861, Richard Yates Papers, FHS; Leonard F. Ross to Yates, 7 Jun. 1861, Logan Uriah Reavis Papers, CHM; John Pope to Trumbull, 16 Jun. 1861, Trumbull Papers, LC.

26. *SDU*, 13, 14, 15, 18, 21, 22, 28 May 1861; *LAS*, 18 May, 15, 22 Jun. 1861; *ISJ*, 10 Jul. 1861; *OR*, series 3, 1:336–37; Marszalek, *Halleck*, 90–107; Prezelski, *Californio Lancers*, 19–25.

27. [Thomas Hambly] to Cameron, 31 May, Lincoln to Cameron, 14 May 1861, Simon Cameron Papers, LC; James Hamilton to Morgan, 15 May, Cameron to Morgan, 3 Jun, 18 Aug. 1861, Morgan Papers, Morgan to Lincoln, 19 May 1861, Morgan Letter Books, NYSL; *Annual Report of the Adjutant General of the State of New York, 1861*, 8–35; Rawley, "Lincoln and Morgan," 280–90; *OR*, series 3, 1:246–54, 1:290; Meneely, *War Department*, 150–55, 154–55; Beatie, *Army of the Potomac*, 2:226–27.

28. *OR*, series 3, 1:284, 301–21; Andrew to Lincoln, 27 Jun. 1861, LP, LC; Donald, *Lincoln*, 301; Seward, *Seward at Washington*, 590; Burlingame, *Dispatches from Lincoln's White House: The Anonymous Civil War Journalism of Presidential Secretary William O. Stoddard*, 14; Orr, "'All Manner of Schemes and Rascalities,'" in Slap, *This Distracted and Anarchical People: New Answers for Old Questions about the Civil War-Era North*, 81–103.

29. Yates to Andrew McFarland, 10 Jun. 1861, Reavis Papers, CHM.

30. Boreman to Pierpont, 26 Jul. 1861, Pierpont-Samuels Papers, West Virginia Division of Culture and History, Archives and History, Charleston, West Virginia (WvDCH); Boreman to Lincoln, 18 Jun. 1861, Seward Papers, UR; Pierpont to Lincoln, 29 Jun. 1861, Virginia Governor's Executive Letter books, Virginia State Archives and Libraries, Richmond, Virginia (VSAL); Pierpont to Lincoln, 21 Jun. 1861, LP, LC; *LDJ*, 3 Jun. 1861; *WDNI*, 26 Jun. 1861; Zimring, "'Secession in Favor of the Constitution,'" 23–51; *OR*, series 1, 2:713; Moore, *Rebellion Record*, 2:162–63; Langford, "Constitutional Issues," 12–31; Woodward, "Opinions of Lincoln," 157–84.

31. *NHPSG*, 3 Jul. 1861; *PhiIn*, 26 Jun. 1861; Ambler, *Pierpont*, 84–105; *WDNI*, 26 Jun. 1861; Pierpont to B. D. [McGinnis], 4 Jul., Pierpont to Edward Bates, 15 Jul., Pierpont to John Carlisle, 16 Jul. 1861, Governor's Executive Letter books, VSAL; Zimring, "'Secession in Favor of the Constitution,'" 23–51.

32. *OR*, series 3, 1:280; Niven, *Chase Papers*, 3:106–7; John [?] Bowen to Cameron, 5 Jul., C. Baldwin to Samuel Kirkwood, 29 Jun. 1861, RG 107, Letters Received, "irregular series," NARA; Benedict, *Lane*, 33; Blackmar, *Robinson*, 272–76; Sutherland, *A Savage Conflict*, 11–17; Castel, "Civil War Kansas and the Negro," 125–38; Johnson and Buel, *Battles and Leaders*, 1:262–77; *ToTri*, 11, 25 May 1861; *LDT*, 22 Jun., 4, 30 Jul., 4, 10 Aug. 1861; *StLDMR*, 28 Jun. 1861; Thomas Bowen to Kirkwood, 23, 26 May, W. R. Laughlin to Kirkwood, 24 May, Jesse Evans to Kirkwood, 27 May, A. W. Ballard to Kirkwood, 23 Jun. 1861, Governor's Correspondence, IaSA.

33. *OR*, series 3, 1:301–10, 311–21; series 1, 3:390, 468–69; Basler, *CW*, 4:414; Minor, "Lane and Lincoln," 186–94; Johnson and Buel, *Battles and Leaders*, 1:278–88, 373–93; *ISJ*, 17 Jul. 1861; *ChiTri*, 27 Jun. 1861; Donald, *Lincoln*, 299–304; Paludan, *Presidency of Lincoln*, 69–94; McDonald, *States' Rights and the Union*, 194–98.

34. *OR*, series 3, 1:323–24; Meneely, *War Department*, 179; W. W. Johnson to Dennison, 9 Jul. 1861, series 147, OHS.

35. J. H. Hendrick to Friend Uel Spencer, 10 Sept. 1861, Uel Spencer Papers, DC.
36. Leander Harris to Wife, 30 Sept. 1861, Leander Harris Papers, DC.
37. Joseph Schnell to Mother, 2 Jul. 1861, Joseph Schnell Papers, LC.
38. *WES*, 5, 6 Jul. 1861; *TDSGR*, 5 Dec. 1861; *StLDMR*, 7 Jun. 1861; Welles to E. T. W., 9 Jun. 1861, Welles Papers, LC; Morgan to Jasper Morgan, 4 Jul. 1861, Morgan Letter books, NYSL; Catton, *The Coming Fury*, 418; Miller, *Lincoln*, 152–54.
39. Chandler to Lincoln, 15 Jun. 1861, LP, LC; McClure, *Lincoln and Men of War-Times*, 62; Harris, *Chandler*, 57–58; Fennimore, "Blair," 49:200–207; Chandler to Wife, 16 Jul., Ben Wade to Chandler, 1 Oct. 1861, Chandler Papers, LC.
40. Young, *For Love and Liberty*, 284; *PhiIn*, 1 Jun. 1861; *LDJ*, 1 Jun. 1861; *WES*, 10 Jul. 1861; *WDNI*, 25 Jun. 1861.
41. *WDNI*, 25 Jun. 1861; *CDE*, 8 May 1861.
42. Horatio Nelson Taft Diary, 8 May 1861, LC.
43. *OR*, series 3, 1:327, 330–31; *WSJ*, 22 Jul. 1861; *MS*, 24 Apr., 15, 25 Jun. 1861; Quiner Scrapbook, 1:14–114.
44. *WSJ*, 22 Jul. 1861, reprint of Morgan to Randall, 13 Jul. 1861, Starkweather to Randall, 10 Jul. 1861; *OR*, series 3, 1:330–31.
45. Morgan to Jasper Morgan, 4 Jul. 1861, Morgan Letter books, NYSL; William Nelson to Morgan, 9 Jun. 1861, Morgan Papers, NYSL; Rawley, *Morgan*, 146, 161; Shannon, *Organization of the Union Army*, 1:115–16; *OR*, series 3, 1:273, 698.
46. Beatie, *Army of the Potomac*, 2:226–27; Martindale to Morgan, 20 Jun., King to Morgan, 6, 13, 25 Jul. 1861, Morgan Papers, NYSL; Morgan to Lincoln, 1 Jul., Morgan to Seward, 1 Jul., "confidential," Morgan to Preston King, 2 Jul. 1861, Morgan Letter books, NYSL; Morgan to Lincoln, 8 Jul. 1861, Abraham Lincoln Papers, HL; *OR*, series 3, 1:72, 178, 229, 299, 332, 344–45, 425–34; Meneely, *War Department*, 166–67, 210–11; Rawley, *Morgan*, 149–51.
47. Bradley, *Cameron*, 178; *NYTi*, 27 Jul. 1861; Bates, *Lincoln in the Telegraph Office*, 88–92; *Congressional Globe*, 37th Session, 1st session, 222–23; Davis, *Battle at Bull Run*, 35–158; Eicher, *Longest Night*, 81–101.
48. Blair to Louise, 20 Jul. 1861, Austin Blair Papers, Burton Historical Collection, DPL; *NYTi*, 31 Jul. 1861.
49. Weed, *Autobiography*, 2:344; Marvel, *Burnside*, 28–29; Morgan to Lincoln, 20 Jul. 1861, LP, LC; Davis, *Battle at Bull Run*, 35–240; Eicher, *Longest Night*, 81–101.
50. *NYTri*, 26 Jun., 16, 23 Jul. 1861; *NYTi*, 10 Feb. 1862; Marvel, *Burnside*, 24–29; *PhiIn*, 24 Jul. 1861; Field, *State of Rhode Island and Providence Plantations at the End of the Century*, 1:517; *WDNI*, 27 Jul. 1861; Woodbury, *The Second Rhode Island Regiment*, 34.
51. Thomas Worthington to Dennison, 22 Jul. 1861, series 147, OHS; Bates, *Lincoln in Telegraph Office*, 40–41, 88–94; *InDJ*, 23 Jul. 1861.
52. *NYTi*, 31 Jul. 1861; Rawley, *Morgan*, 161; Rawley, "Lincoln and Morgan," 288–89; Morgan to Lincoln, 20, 23 Jul. 1861, LP, LC; *WDNI*, 27 Jul. 1861; *PhiIn*, 26 Jul. 1861; Harris, "Blair," 120–21; *DFP*, 4 Aug. 1861.
53. Olmsted to Burton, 19 Aug. 1861, Executive Papers, DPA; Bucke, Harned, and Traubel, *Complete Writings of Walt Whitman*, 4:32–36; Catton, *Coming Fury*, 466; Niven, *Connecticut for the Union*, 130; Davis, *Bull Run*, 35–249.
54. As quoted in Hamrogue, "Andrew," 109–10.
55. "War Letters of Charles P. Bowditch," 415–16.
56. John C. Thayer to Fairbanks, 10 Aug. 1861, Fairbanks Papers, VSA; *StAM*, 1 Aug. 1861; Benedict, *Vermont*, 1:86.

57. Quiner, *Military History of Wisconsin*, 83, 211; *MS*, 30 Jul. 1861, 19 Aug. 1862; *WSJ*, 11, 24 Jul., 16 Aug. 1861; Meneely, *War Department*, 193; S. D. Bradford to Morgan, 23, 25 Jul. 1861, Morgan Papers, NYSL.

58. *MS*, 19 Aug. 1861; McClure to Eli Slifer, 23 Jul. 1861, Eli Slifer-Dill Papers, Special Collections, DCL.

59. Sears, *Papers of McClellan*, 70–71; *OR*, series 1, 2:752–58; Johnson and Buel, *Battles and Leaders*, 1:278–88; Thomas, "Campaigns of McClellan," 245–85.

60. Burlingame, *Stoddard*, 16–17.

61. *PhiIn*, 26 Jul. 1861.

62. Burlingame, *Stoddard*, 16–17; Charles Sedgwick to Dora, 1, 3 Aug. 1861, Sedgwick Papers, SUL.

63. *OR*, series 1, 5:6–7; Sears, *McClellan*, 95–120; Nevins, *The Improvised War*, 269–71; Marvel, *Burnside*, 31; White, *Emancipation, the Union Army, and the Reelection of Abraham Lincoln*, 168.

64. Beatie, *Army of the Potomac*, 2:226–31; King to Morgan, 25 Jul., 30 Aug., Cameron to Morgan, 18 Aug. 1861, Morgan Papers, NYSL; Morgan to King, 30 Jul. 1861, Morgan Letter books, NYSL; Williams, *Lincoln Finds a General*, 1:116–19, 400; Shannon, *Organization of the Union Army*, 46–50; Perret, *Lincoln's War*, 67–69; William "Bull" Nelson to Chase, 11, 16, 23, 26 Jul. 1861, Chase Papers, LC; Niven, *Connecticut for the Union*, 51; *HEP*, 31 Aug. 1861.

65. As quoted in Beatie, *Army of the Potomac*, 2:176–77, 189–225, 233; Meneely, *War Department*, 196; *BDA*, 24 Jul. 1861; George D. Wells to Andrew, 22 Jul. 1861, Andrew Papers, MHS; Sumner to Andrew, 9 Jul., 11 Aug. 1861, Sumner Papers, HoL; Benedict, *Vermont*, 1:88–90; Moe, *Last Full Measure*, 65–69; Upton, *The Military Policy of the United States*, 242–43; Washburn to Oliver O. Howard, 8, 23 Aug. 1861, Oliver O. Howard Papers, BCL; Miller, "Brahmin Janissaries," 215; Pearson, *Andrew*, 1:238; *OR*, series 3, 1:348–49, 352; 380–84; Williams, *Lincoln Finds a General*, 1:116–19; William Buckingham to Daniel Tyler, 12 Aug. 1861, James A. Howard Papers, CtHS.

66. *OR*, series 3, 2:380.

67. *OR*, series 3, 1:297, 350; Morton to Lincoln, 23 Jul. 1861, LP, LC; Coggeshall Diary, 27 Jul., 13 Sept., 25 Nov. 1861, ALPL; Weeden, *War Government*, 90–91; Egle, *Curtin*, 269–73; Nathaniel Berry to Dennison, 26 Jul., Edward Stine to C. P. Buckingham, 11, 22 Jul., Lorin Andrews to Dennison, 26 Jul. 1861, series 147, OHS; Dennison to Cameron, 2, 3 Aug., Dennison to Chase, 2 Aug. 1861, Telegraphic Dispatches, series 144, OhSA; Cameron to Dennison, 4 Aug. 1861, Telegraphic Dispatches, series 145, OhSA; Mulligan "Dennison," 171–76; Fisher, "Groping toward Victory," 26–35; *NHPSG*, 17, 24 Jul. 1861; Allison, "New Hampshire Contribution to Berdan's Volunteer Sharpshooters," 174–83; *NHS*, 8 Jun. 1861; Edmund Weston to Fairbanks, 2, 14 Aug. 1861, Fairbanks Papers, VSA.

68. Pearson, *Andrew*, 1:229–31; Niven, *Connecticut for the Union*, 278; Croffut and Morris, *Connecticut during the Civil War*, 75; Benedict, *Vermont*, 1:25–35; John Porter to Fairbanks, 4 May, Henry Brock to Fairbanks, 18 Jun. 1861, Fairbanks Papers, VHS; *BDFR*, 26 Jul. 1861; Weeden, *War Government*, 200; Butler, *Butler's Book*, 1:307; Dell, *War Democrats*, 93; Hamrogue, "Andrew," 121–26; *NHPSG*, 7 Aug. 1861; Gillette, *Jersey Blue: Civilian Politics in New Jersey, 1854–1865*, 60–61; Jackson, *New Jerseyans in the Civil War*, 29–40; Stellhorn and Birker, *Governors of New Jersey*, 129–31; *TDSGR*, 15 Mar., 4 Jun. 1861.

69. Dr. J. Morgan to AG. C. P. Buckingham, 25 Jul. 1861, series 147, OHS; *OR*, series 3, 1:350–66, 415; Nevins, *The Improvised War*, 277–81; Meneely, *War Department*, 195–96; William Duffield to Austin Blair, 23 Aug. 1861, Blair Papers, DPL.

70. Pearson, *Andrew*, 1:233–35; Nevins, *The Improvised War*, 278–79.

71. Shannon, *Organization of the Union Army*, 1:186–87; Ford, *Adams Letters*, 1:13.

72. *OR*, series 3, 1:377, 380; Parrish, *Blair*, 35–47; Johnson and Buel, *Battles and Leaders*, 1:278–88; Gibson to Gamble, 2 Aug. 1861, Gamble Papers, MoHS; Harris, *Lincoln and the Border States*, 126–50.

73. As quoted in Boman, *Gamble*, 108; Phillips, "Hamilton Rowan Gamble and the Provisional Government of Missouri," 1–6; *Journal of the Missouri State Convention, July 1861*, 34–40; *OR*, series 1, 3:412–29; Phillips, *Jackson*, 263–65; Johnson and Buel, *Battles and Leaders*, 1:262–77, 278–88; Rosin, "Hamilton Rowan Gamble," 145–99; Boman, *Lincoln and Citizens' Rights in Missouri*, 30–35; Harris, *Lincoln and the Border States*, 126–50.

74. James S. Rollins to Gamble, 17 Jul., Bates to Gamble, 2 Aug., Gibson to Gamble, 2 Aug. 1861, Gamble Papers, MoHS; Boman, *Gamble*, 104–15; Phillips, "Gamble and the Provisional Government of Missouri," 1–6; *Journal of the Missouri State Convention*, Jul. 1861, 9–12, 34–49, 69–73, 102, 109–11; *StLDMR*, 30 Jul., 2 Aug. 1861; Johnson and Buel, *Battles and Leaders*, 1:262–77; Siddali, *Missouri's War*, 191; Rosin, "Gamble," 129–99; Avery and Shoemaker, *Messages*, 3:405–14; Boman, *Lincoln and Citizens' Rights in Missouri*, 21–22; Harris, *Lincoln and the Border States*, 126–50; Neely, *Lincoln and the Triumph of the Nation*, 269–71.

75. Boman, *Gamble*, 4:115; Rosin, "Gamble," 1–129; Avery and Shoemaker, *Messages*, 3:405–10; *StLDMR*, 12 Mar. 1865; Hesseltine, *Lincoln and the War Governors*, 217; Harris, *Lincoln and the Border States*, 126–50.

76. Basler, *CW*, 4:457–58, 470–71; Gamble to Cameron, Cameron Papers, LC; *NYTri*, 6 Aug. 1861; Olden to Lincoln, 3 Aug. 1861, LP, LC; Olden to Lincoln, 3 Aug. 1861, Olden Papers, HSP; *OR*, series 3, 1:364–65, 385; *NDM*, 29 Jul. 1861; Johnson and Buel, *Battles and Leaders*, 1:373–93; Seward to Morgan, 3 Aug. 1861, Morgan Papers, NYSL; Morgan to Lincoln, 23 Jul. 1861, telegram and letter dated the same, LP, LC; *OR*, series 3, 1:364–71; Burlingame, *Lincoln*, 2:180–200; Gallman, *The North Fights the Civil War*, 2–62.

77. Wilson, *Business of the Civil War*, 10; Sinsi, *Sacred Debts: State Civil War Claims, 1861–1880*, 9–12.

78. Meneely, *War Department*, 126–31; Paludan, *Presidency of Lincoln*, 82–84; Churella, *The Pennsylvania Railroad: Building an Empire, 1846–1917*, 1:288–90; Lathrop, *Kirkwood*, 117–20; Briggs, "Enlistment of the Iowa Troops," 323–48; *BDHE*, 8, 27 Jul. 1861; Burlingame, *Stoddard*, 18–20; *OR*, series 3, 1:311–21, 364–71, 386–89, series 1, 3:413, 52:187; Clark, *Kirkwood*, 255; Shambaugh, *Messages*, 2:278; Angevine, *The Railroad and the State*, 131–64.

79. J. R. [White] to Blair, 1 Aug. 1861, RG 44, Records of the Executive Office, 1810–1910, MiSA; Henry Crapo to William Crapo, 25 Apr., 12 May 1861, Henry Howland Crapo Papers, BHL.

Chapter Five

1. Buckingham, *Buckingham*, 184–85; *ChiTri*, 26 Aug. 1861; *NHPSG*, 18 Sept. 1861; Talmadge, "A Peace Movement in Civil War Connecticut," 310–11; *OR*, series 3, 1:410–25; Hesseltine, *Lincoln and the War Governors*, 182–83.

2. Buckingham, *Buckingham*, 184–85; *NHPSG*, 18 Sept. 1861.

3. Buckingham to Welles, 30 Aug. 1861, Gideon Welles Papers, CtHS; *NYTi*, 1 Sept. 1861; *NHP*, 29 Aug. 1861; *OR*, series 2, 2:620.

4. Phineas T. Barnum to Lincoln, 30 Aug. 1861, LP, LC; *OR*, series 2, 2:620; Buckingham to Gideon Welles, 30 Aug. 1861, Welles Papers, CtHS; *NYTi*, 1 Sept. 1861; A. A. [Petagru] to Buckingham, 24 Aug. 1861, Governor's Correspondence, CtSA.

5. *BDWC*, 21 Oct. 1861; Joseph Sheldon to Buckingham, 1 Aug. 1861, Governor's Papers, CtSA; Warshauer, "Copperheads in Connecticut," in Slap, *This Distracted and Anarchical People: New Answers for Old Questions about the Civil War-Era North*, 60–80.

6. Niven, *Connecticut for the Union*, 61–64; Croffut and Morris, *Connecticut during the Civil War*, 102; Buckingham, *Buckingham*, 182–85; *HEP*, 26 Jun., 19, 31 Aug., 20 Sept. 1861; *BDWC*, 21 Oct. 1861; Henry Birge to Buckingham, 9 Sept., 28 Oct. 1861, Henry Birge Papers, CtHS; *HT*, 14 Oct. 1861.

7. *OR*, series 3, 1:415–16, 420, 443–44; Morgan to Cameron, 13 Aug. 1861, Cameron Papers, LC; Preston King to Morgan, 27 Aug. 1861, Marsena Patrick to Morgan, 14 Aug. 1861, Morgan Papers, NYSL; Meneely, *War Department*, 226; *NYH*, 1 Aug. 1861; Benedict, *Vermont*, 1:33–59; Citizens of Barre, Vt., to Fairbanks, 4 Sept. 1861, Fairbanks Papers, VHS; Cameron to Fairbanks, 15 Sept., E. H. Stroughton to Fairbanks, 16 Sep., William Skinner to Fairbanks, 16 Sept. 1861, Fairbanks Papers, VSA; Morgan to Seward, 7 Aug. 1861, LP, LC; *BDA*, 9 Aug. 1861; George Sturges to Dennison, 18 Aug., and L. M. Hubby to Dennison, 22 Aug. 1861, series 147, OHS; Frederick Law Olmsted to Curtin, 17 Aug. 1861, Executive Correspondence, PSA; Charles Sumner to Andrew, 11 Aug. 1861, Andrew Papers, MHS; Andrew to [?], 23 Aug. 1861, Massachusetts Governors, Letters Official, 1861, MSA.

8. *OR*, series 3, 1:425–34.

9. *BDHE*, 17 Sept. 1861; Clark, *Kirkwood*, 204–6; Lathrop, *Kirkwood*, 142; Phillips, *Lyon*, 214–64; Eicher, *The Longest Night*, 103–7.

10. Boman, *Gamble*, 11630; Parrish, *Blair*, 119; Phillips, *Lyon*, 214–64; Rosin, "Gamble," 210–15; Boman, *Lincoln and Citizens' Rights in Missouri*, 36–62; Gibson to Gamble, 19 Aug., J. O. Davis to Gamble, 22 Aug., John S. Phelps to Gamble, 8 Aug., Gibson to Gamble, 8 Aug., Gamble to Lincoln, 26 Aug., James Birch to Gamble, [august], 1861, Gamble Papers, MoHS; Nevins, *The Improvised War*, 319, 324–25; Isaac H. Sturgeon to Cameron, 25 Aug. 1861, "private," Cameron Papers, LC; Harris, *Lincoln and the Border States*, 145–58; Morton to Lincoln, 3 Aug., and Leslie Combs to Lincoln, 14 Aug. 1861, LP, LC; Johnson and Buel, *Battles and Leaders*, 1:278–97; *OR*, series 1, 3:412–13, 439–43, series 3, 1:350–461; Fremont to Cameron, 24 Aug. 1861, "unofficial," Cameron Papers, LC; Sutherland, *Savage Conflict*, 16–25; Pope to Yates, 16 Aug. 1861, Yates Papers, FHS; Bahde, "'Our Cause Is a Common One': Home Guards, Union Leagues, and Republican Citizenship in Illinois, 1861–1863," 78.

11. *OR*, series 3, 1:110, 124–26, 410–11, 447, 638, 784; Weeden, *War Government*, 196–98; P. Frazer Smith to Curtin, 20 Aug. 1861, Executive Correspondence, PSA; Hesseltine, *Lincoln and the War Governors*, 183–84; [?] H. Sturgeon to Cameron, 25 Aug. 1861, "private," Cameron Papers, LC; *DR*, 30 May 1861; Hamilton, *Reminiscences*, 498–99; Hamilton to Lincoln, 11 Aug. 1861, LP, LC; Mulligan, "Dennison," 174–75; Fisher, "Groping toward Victory," 26–35; Dennison to Cameron, 23 Aug. 1861, Telegraphic Dispatches, series 144, OhSA.

12. Curtin to Lincoln, 21 Aug., P. Frazer Smith to Curtin, 20 Aug. 1861, Executive Correspondence, PSA. Oddly, the president never received the letter because Cameron filed it away and admitted as much when Curtin sent a special courier with another message. Meneely, *War Department*, 211–12; *OR*, series 3, 1:439–41; Curtin to Cameron, 18 Sept. 1861, Curtin Letter Books, PSA; Nevins, *The Improvised War*, 235.

13. French, *Morton*, 202–4, 211–25; Foulke, *Morton*, 1:157–62; *InDJ*, 6 Sept. 1862.

14. French, *Morton*, 202–4, 211–25; Foulke, *Morton*, 2:157–62; James C. Vanderbilt to Mother, 2 Oct. 1861, James C. Vanderbilt Papers, ISA; Wilson, *Business of Civil War*, 22; Yates to John Wood, 5 Nov., Martin H. Cassell to Yates, 16 Nov. 1861, Yates Papers, ALPL.

15. Welles to M. J. W., 21 Aug. 1861, Welles Papers, LC; *OR*, series 3, 1:465; *OR*, series 1, 5:575; Sears, *Papers of McClellan*, 87–88; Wilson, *Business of Civil War*, 22; Yates to John Wood, 5 Nov., Martin H. Cassell to Yates, 16 Nov. 1861, Yates Papers, ALPL.

16. *OR*, series 3, 1:466–67, series 1, 3:412–19; Sutherland, *Savage Conflict*, 16–25; Jesse Evans to Kirkwood, 27 May, 18 Jun., Thomas M. Bowen to Kirkwood, 21 Jul., Cyrus Bussey to Kirkwood, 27 Jul., 6 Aug. 1861, Kirkwood Papers, SHSI; Robert N. Smith to Gamble, 13 Aug., Charles D. Drake to Gamble, 3 Aug., George Brown to Gamble, 10 Aug., Charles Gibson to Gamble, 8, 19 Aug., Gamble to Lincoln, 26 Aug. 1861, Gamble Papers, MoHS; Johnson and Buel, *Battles and Leaders*, 1:278–88; Boman, *Gamble*, 124–28; Schutz and Trenerry, *Pope*, 66–70; Boman, *Lincoln and Citizens' Rights in Missouri*, 36–62; Rosin, "Gamble," 210–20; Harris, *Lincoln and the Border States*, 80–107, 145–58.

17. Basler, *CW*, 4:497; Magoffin to Lincoln, 19 Aug., Joseph Holt to Lincoln, 2 Sept. 1861, LP, LC; Magoffin to Isham Harris, 12 Aug. 1861, Beriah Magoffin Papers, LC; *WDNI*, 7 Sept. 1861; *LDJ*, 5, 6 Sept. 1861; Harris, *Lincoln and the Border States*, 80–107; Dues, "Magoffin," 22–28.

18. George Prentice, T. S. Bell, and J. S. Speed to Yates, 30 Aug. 1861, Yates Papers, FHS; *InDJ*, 20 Sept. 1861; Harris, *Lincoln and the Border States*, 80–107.

19. Rawley, *Morgan*, 164–65; *OR*, series 3, 1:452–53, 465, series 1, 1:811–66, 51:491, 3, 1:423, 476–79, 811–66; series 1, 4:600; Shannon, *Organization of the Union Army*, 2:53; Cameron to Morgan, "confidential," 27 Aug. 1861, Cameron Papers, LC; Elbridge Smith to Fairbanks, 10 Sept. 1861, Fairbanks Papers, VSA; Butler, *Butler's Book*, 294–320; Schouler, *Massachusetts in the Civil War*, 1:226–27, 251–81; Cameron to Ichabod Goodwin, 27 Aug. 1861, "confidential," Ichabod Goodwin Papers, NHHS; Andrew, *Correspondence between Gov. Andrew and Maj. Gen. Butler*, 3–19; Hesseltine, *Lincoln and the War Governors*, 185–87; Andrew to [unidentified], 13 Aug. 1861, Andrew Papers, MHS; Thomas Scott to Washburn, 10 Aug., Cameron to Washburn, 27 Aug. 1861, "confidential," Executive Correspondence, MeSA; Washburn to Thomas Sherman, 9, 10 Sept. 1861, Governor's Telegram Books, MeSA; Pearson, *Andrew*, 1:283–311; Meneely, *War Department*, 211–18; Trefousse, *Butler*, 88–89; Butler, *Correspondence*, 1:254–300; Weeden, *War Government*, 197–201; Hamrogue, "Andrew," 121–26; *NHPSG*, 18 Sept., 9 Oct. 1861; *OR*, series 3, 1, 653–55; Buckingham to Lincoln, 11 Sept. 1861, LP, LC.

20. Meneely, *War Department*, 210–20; Butler, *Correspondence*, 1:254–63; Weeden, *War Government*, 197–204; Schouler, *Massachusetts in the Civil War*, 1:269–75; Hamrogue, "Andrew," 121–31; Andrew, *Correspondence between Andrew and Butler*, 20–86; Hesseltine, *Lincoln and the War Governors*, 186–91; Trefousse, *Butler*, 88–94; Butler, *Butler's Book*, 294–308; Pearson, *Andrew*, 1:233.

21. *OR*, series 3, 1:655; Hesseltine, *Lincoln and the War Governors*, 186–91; Trefousse, *Butler*, 88–94; Meneely, *War Department*, 210–20; Weeden, *War Government*, 197–204; Schouler, *Massachusetts in the Civil War*, 1:270–81; Sennott, *Sennott on Andrew and Butler*, 1–16.

22. *OR*, series 1, 3:456–57, 466–68, series 3, 1:498–502, 541, 551–52, 652–56, 811–98; Boman, *Lincoln and Citizens' Rights in Missouri*, 36–62; Harris, *Lincoln and the Border States*, 146–58; Johnson and Buel, *Battles and Leaders*, 1:278–88; Sutherland, *Savage Conflict*, 24–25; *LDJ*, 3 Sept. 1861: *ISJ*, 2, 3 Sept. 1861; Parrish, *Blair*, 121–22; Nevins, *Fremont*, 504–5; *StLDMR*, 3, 13 Sept. 1861; Boman, *Gamble*, 127–29; Meneely, *War Department*, 210–20; Trefousse, *Butler*, 88–94; Hesseltine, *Lincoln and the War Governors*, 186–91; Pearson, *Andrew*, 1:284–319; Morse, *Memoir of Lee*, 74–75; Hamrogue, "Andrew," 127–29; Andrew, *Correspondence between Andrew and Butler*, 33–86; Henry Lee to Wife, 2 Nov., Andrew to

Lee, 4 Nov., Andrew to Blair, 6 Nov. 1861, Lee Family Papers, MHS; Burlingame, *Lincoln*, 2:434–35; Schouler, *Massachusetts in the Civil War*, 1:200, 252, 280–82. Frank Howe to Andrew, 23 Jan. 1862, Andrew Papers, MHS; *WDNI*, 10 Sept. 1861; *BDA*, 7 Sept. 1861.

23. Speed to Lincoln, 1 Sept. 1861, LP, LC; Burlingame, *Lincoln*, 2:201–3.

24. *OR*, series 1, 3:477–78; *ISJ*, 2, 3 Sept. 1861; *StLDMR*, 3, 13, Sept. 1861; Harris, *Lincoln and the Border States*, 146–58; Parrish, *Blair*, 121–22; Nevins, *Fremont*, 504–5; Donald, *Lincoln*, 316–17; Johnson and Buel, *Battles and Leaders*, 1:278–88; *WDNI*, 23 Sept. 1861; Boman, *Lincoln and Citizens' Rights in Missouri*, 36–62; Yates to Fremont, 27 Aug. 1861, Reavis Papers, CHM; Burlingame, *Lincoln*, 2: 202–3.

25. Horace White to David Davis, 14 Sept. 1861, David Davis Papers, ALPL.

26. Fremont to Lincoln, 5 Sept. 1861, LP, LC; Fremont to Lincoln, 3 Sept. 1861, Seward Papers, UR; Fremont to Lincoln, 3 Sept. 1861, LP, LC; Boman, *Gamble*, 127–31; Johnson and Buel, *Battles and Leaders*, 1:278–88; Rosin, "Gamble," 210–25; Gamble to Charles Gibson, 20 Sept. 1861, Gamble Papers, MoHS; *PhiIn*, 12 Sept. 1861; *ISJ*, 3 Sept. 1861; *LDJ*, 22 Oct. 1861; Yates to Fremont, 27 Aug. 1861, Reavis Papers, CHM; Harris, *Lincoln and the Border States*, 146–58; *InDJ*, 20 Sept. 1861.

27. Burlingame, *Stoddard*, 33; Gamble to Charles Gibson, 20 Sept., Gamble to Lincoln, 13 Sept. 1861, LP, LC; *PhiIn*, 5 Sept. 1861; James [Matsons] to Gamble, 13 Sept., Gamble to Gibson, 19 Sept. 1861, Gamble Papers, MoHS; *OR*, series 1, 3:470; *NYTi*, 5 Sept. 1861; Boman, *Gamble*, 127–33; Johnson and Buel, *Battles and Leaders*, 1:278–88; Rosin, "Gamble," 210–20; Burlingame, *With Lincoln in the White House*, 56–57; Harris, *Lincoln and the Border States*, 146–58; Donald, *Lincoln*, 316–17; Isaac P. Christaney to Blair, 18 Oct. 1861, Blair Papers, DPL; *DFP*, 5 Oct. 1861; Hesseltine, *Lincoln and the War Governors*, 221, 230; Harris, "Blair," 122–24; Yates to Koerner, 23 Sept. 1861, Yates Papers, ALPL; *ISJ*, 14 Sept. 1861; Pearson, *Andrew*, 1:1–4; Schouler, *Massachusetts in the Civil War*, 234–35; Pierpont to Lincoln, 3, 12 Sept. 1861, LP, LC; 3 Sept. 1861, Cameron Papers, LC; Pierpont to Thomas Harrington, 16 Jul., Pierpont to Ralph Goorell, 16 Jul., Pierpont to John Zeigler, 23 Jul., Pierpont to Cameron, 27, 31 Jul., Pierpont to Cameron, 31 Jul., 1 Oct., Pierpont to Ward H. Lamon, 8 Aug., Pierpont to James B. Brown, 25 Aug., Pierpont to Chase, 25 Oct. 1861, Governor's Executive Letter Books, VSAL.

28. Robinson to Sara, 17 Jun., Robinson to Fremont, 1 Sept., E. S. Lowman to Robinson, 13 Aug. 1861, Robinson Papers, KSHS; *OR*, series 1, 3:405, 468–69; Mark Delahay to Lincoln, 25 Sept. 1861, LP, LC; Benedict, *Lane*, 56–59, 72–73; Blackmar, *Robinson*, 272–76; Sutherland, *Savage Conflict*, 16–25; *BDHE*, 24 Aug. 1861; *ToTri*, 17 Aug. 1861; *StLDMR*, 16 Oct. 1861.

29. Robinson to Sara 17 Jun., Robinson to Fremont, 1 Sept. 1861, Robinson Papers, KSHS; Cheatham, "Desperate Characters: The Development and Impact of the Confederate Guerrillas in Kansas," 144–61; *ToTri*, 17 Aug. 1861.

30. *OR*, series 1, 4:255–56; Foulke, *Morton*, 1:143–44; Joshua Speed to Lincoln, 1 Sept., Jeremiah T. Boyle, John J. Speed, and Joshua F. Speed to Lincoln, 2 Sept. 1861, LP, LC; Harbison, "Lincoln and Indiana Republicans," 286–87; Johnson and Buel, *Battles and Leaders*, 1:373–93; *InDJ*, 20 Sept. 1861; Coggeshall Diary, 30, 31 Aug. 1861, ALPL.

31. Wilson, *A Few Facts and Actors in the Tragedy of the Civil War in the United States*, 111.

32. *LDJ*, 22 Oct. 1861.

33. As quoted in French, *Morton*, 208; *OR*, series 1, 4:266, 275–77; French, *Morton*, 207–9; *InDJ*, 20 Sept. 1861.

34. French, *Morton*, 208–9; *OR*, series 2, 1:685, series 3, 1:480–82; Mitchell, *Maryland Voices*, 242–43.

35. *OR*, series 1, 52:189, series 3, 1:489.

36. *OR*, series 1, 3:479–503; Simpson, *Grant*, 92–93; Johnson and Buel, *Battles and Leaders*, 1:373–93; *WDNI*, 20 Sept. 1861; Magoffin's *Message to the General Assembly*, Sept, 2, 1861, in the *Journal of the House of Representatives of the Commonwealth of Kentucky*, 15–36; *LDJ*, 5, 6, 7, 11, 13 Sept. 1861.

37. Gamble to Bates, 17 Sept. 1861, LP, LC; Lincoln to Cameron, 20 Sept. 1861, Cameron Papers, LC; Magoffin's *Message to General Assembly*, 29.

38. Gamble to Bates, 17 Sept. 1861, LP, LC; Lincoln to Cameron, 20 Sept. 1861, Cameron Papers, LC; *LDJ*, 10 Sept. 1861.

39. Bates to Gamble, 27 Sept., 3 Oct. 1861, Gamble Papers, MoHS; Rosin, "Gamble," 219.

40. Gibson to Gamble, 27 Sept., John S. Phelps to Gamble, 3 Oct. 1861, Gamble Papers, MoHS. Gamble Papers, MoHS.

41. Gamble to Lincoln, 3 Oct. 1861, LP, LC.

42. Basler, *CW*, 4:549–50, 4:515; 4:531–32; Nicolay to Lincoln, 21 Oct., Gamble to Montgomery Blair, 5 Oct., Speed to Lincoln, 3, 7 Sept. 1861, and Green Adams and James Speed to Lincoln, 2 Sept., Jessie Fremont to Lincoln, 10 Sept. 1861, Lincoln to Jessie Fremont, 12 Sept., Jesse Fremont to Ward Lamon, 26 Oct. 1861, LP, LC; Bradley, *Cameron*, 191; *StLDMR*, 15, 19 Sept., 1, 9, 15 Oct. 1861; Burlingame, *With Lincoln in the White House*, 60; Rosin, "Gamble," 215–46; Avery and Shoemaker, *Messages*, 3:415–17; LP, LC; *InDJ*, 17 Oct. 1861; Parrish, *Blair*, 124–28; Burlingame, *Lincoln's Journalist*, 102; Barton Bates to Edward Bates, 10 Oct. 1861, Edward Bates Papers, MoHS; Siddali, *Missouri in Documents*, 107–8; Morton to Cameron, 11 Oct. 1861, Cameron Papers, LC.

43. Basler, *CW*, 4:550; Thomas, *Lincoln*, 278–79; Miller, *Lincoln's Abolitionist General: The Biography of David Hunter*, 72–79; Harbison, "Lincoln and the Indiana Republicans," 289–90; Donald, *Lincoln*, 316; Burlingame, *Lincoln*, 2:210–11.

44. *OR*, series 1, 3:516, 529–30; Benedict, *Lane*, 58–65; Blackmar, *Robinson*, 279–81; Sutherland, *Savage Conflict*, 16; *LDT*, 12 Sept. 1861; *StLDMR*, 16 Oct. 1861; Abraham Allen to Gamble, 13 Oct. 1861, Gamble Papers, MoHS; Robinson to Maj. Gen. James Blood, 24 Aug. 1861, Robinson Papers, KSHS.

45. Gamble to Lincoln, 18 Oct., Mark Delahay to Lincoln, 25 Sept. 1861, LP, LC; *StLDMR*, 13 Oct. 1861.

46. Mark Delahay to Lincoln, 25 Sept. 1861, LP, LC; *NYTi*, 18 Aug. 1894; Ponce, *Kansas's War*, 56–60.

47. Basler, *CW*, 4:531–32; *OR*, series 3, 1:499–515, series 1, 52:191; Yates to M.C. Hunter, 18 Jun. 1861, Yates Papers, ALPL.

48. As quoted in Foulke, *Morton*, 1:148; *WDNI*, 23, 24 Sept. 1861; *InDJ*, 20 Sept. 1861.

49. Foulke, *Morton*, 1:148.

50. *OR*, series 3, 1:559, 547; Seward to Morgan, 28 Sept., Richard Delafield to Morgan, 16 Aug., 5 Sept. 1861, Morgan Papers, NYSL; Weeden, *War Government*, 98–99; *NYTi*, 8 Oct. 1861; *ChiTri*, 11 Oct. 1861; Lincoln, *State of New York: Messages of the Governors*, 1862, 406–11; Rawley, *Morgan*, 152; Meneely, *War Department*, 207; Keller, *Chancellorsville and the Germans*, 30, 32; Burton, *Melting Pot Soldiers*; Guentzel, "Ramsey," 365–81; Ramsey to Ignatius Donnelly, 27 Sept. 1861, Governor's Papers, Ramsey Diary, (Executive Journals), 27 Sept. 1861, MnHS; *StPDPi*, 20 Aug. 1861; Bahde, " 'Our Cause Is a Common One,' " 66–78; Fairbanks to Cameron, 26 Sept. 1861, Fairbanks Papers, VHS; Knight, *No Braver Deeds*, 33; BDFP, 22 Oct., 6 Nov. 1861; R. H. Stuart to Fairbanks, 16 Sept., N. Lord, Jr. to Fairbanks, 19 Sept., Louis A. Derville to Fairbanks, 12 Sept. 1861, Fairbanks Papers, VSA.

51. *ChiTri*, 26 Aug. 1861; *OR*, series 3, 1:513–19, 526–62, Basler, *CW*, 4:533, 537–41; Yates to Lincoln, 28 Sept., Curtin to Cameron, 18 Sept. 1861, LP, LC; *InDJ*, 20 Sept. 1861.

52. *WDNI*, 12 Sept. 1861; *WES*, 10, 11 Sept. 1861; *New York Herald*, 11 Sept. 1861; Curtin to Lincoln, 10 Sept. 1861, LP, LC; Sears, *Papers of McClellan*, 98; McLaughlin, "'Dear Sister Jennie—Dear Brother Jacob,'" 120.

53. *ChiTri*, 10 Sept. 1861; Hunt, *Washburn*, 101–2; Hamlin to Washburn, 27 May, 17 Jun., 6 Sept., 14, 23 Oct., 21, 22 Nov., Washburn to Cameron, 8 Oct., Washburn to William Pitt Fessenden, 9 Oct., Washburn to Blaine, 15 Oct. 1861, Washburn to Meigs, 15 Oct., Washburn to Cameron, 15 Oct. 1861, Executive Correspondence, MeSA; *WDNI*, 15 Sept. 1861; *BDWC*, 19 Aug., 16 Sept. 1861; Sobel and Raimo, *Directory of Governors*, 2:612; Smith, *No Party Now*, 40–41; *NDM*, 9 Sept. 1861; *NYI*, 3 Oct. 1861, speech by Charles Sumner on Andrew's renomination.

54. Pearson, *Andrew*, 1:320; Morse, *Memoir of Lee*, 236–55; *NHPSG*, 13 Nov. 1861; Hesseltine, *Lincoln and the War Governors*, 227–28; Schouler, *Massachusetts in the Civil War*, 1:216, 249–51; Bowen, *Massachusetts in the War*, 1:33–35; Browne, *Andrew*, 40–51, 142–44; Hamrogue, "Andrew," 114–16, 136–40; *BDA*, 5 Sept., 28 Oct., 2, 6 Nov. 1861; *WDNI*, 3 Oct. 1861; Pierce, *Memoirs of Sumner*, 4:43; *OR*, series 3, 1:524; Seraile, "The Struggle to Raise Black Regiments in New York State, 1861–1864," 215–33; Woodward and Drum, *The Negro in Military Service of the United States, 1939–1886*, 2:813; Phisterer, *New York in the War of the Rebellion, 1861 to 1865*, 1:22.

55. Franklin Fairbanks to Father, 10, 18 Oct. 1861, Fairbanks Papers, VHS; Benedict, *Vermont*, 1:4; *BDWC*, 14 Sept. 1861; *BDFP*, 18, 22, 23 Oct. 1861.

56. *WDNI*, 14 Sept. 1861; *NHPSG*, 11 Sept. 1861; *BDWC*, 14 Sept. 1861; Benedict, *Vermont*, 1:4; *NYTi*, 17 Feb. 1895; Hesseltine, *Lincoln and the War Governors*, 222–28; Dell, *War Democrats*, 109–10; Moore, "Frederick Holbrook," 65–78; *BDFP*, 28 Aug., 18, 22, 23 Oct. 1861; *HEP*, 4 Sept. 1861; Sobel and Raimon, *Directory of the Governors*, 3:1580–81.

57. Clark, *Kirkwood*, 195–98; Lathrop, *Kirkwood*, 142–48; Byers, *Iowa in War Times*, 48–49; *WDNI*, 12 Oct. 1861; *BDHE*, 10, 16 Sept. 1861.

58. Lathrop, *Kirkwood*, 118–203; Byers, *Iowa in War Times*, 49–52; Clark, *Kirkwood*, 195–97; Fullbrook, "Relief Work in Iowa during the Civil War," 155–276; *BDHE*, 16 Sept., 23 Oct. 1861.

59. Coggeshall Diary, 5, 7 Sept. 1861, ALPL; Trester, "Tod," 107–22; Reid, *Ohio in the War*, 1:53–61; Wright, "Tod," 101–25; Thomas and Hyman, *Stanton*, 34–39; *Ohio State Journal*, 10, 11 Sept. 1861; Abbott, *Ohio's War Governors*, 22; Taylor, "The Supply for Tomorrow Must Not Fail," 10; James F. Noble to Dennison, 31 Aug. 1861, series 147, OHS; *NYTi*, 12, 19 Aug., 14 Nov. 1862; Dell, *Lincoln and the War Democrats*, 110–11; Cardinal, "The Ohio Democracy and the Crisis of Disunion, 1860–1861," 36–40; Fisher, "Groping toward Victory," 25–35; Porter, *Ohio Politics*, 77–91; Mulligan, "Dennison," 213–16, 238–40; John B. Carey to Doctor Williamson, 30 Sept. 1861, John C. Williamson Papers, OHS; Wright, "David Tod," 101–25; Smith, *No Party Now*, 41–42.

60. Trester, "Tod," 127–28; Abbott, *Ohio's War Governors*, 22–27; Wright, "Tod," 101–25.

61. Morton to Lincoln, 10 Sept. 1861, LP, LC, see also letters of 8, 10, 20, 22, 25 Sept. 1861; *InDJ*, 4 Sept. 1861.

62. Lincoln to Morton, 29 Sept. 1861, LP, LC; Harbison, "Lincoln and Indiana Republicans," 287.

63. Morton to Lincoln, 7 Oct. 1861, LP, LC; French, *Morton*, 318–21; *InDJ*, 17, 23 Oct., 8, 18 Nov. 1861.

64. Beale, *The Diary of Edward Bates, 1859–1866*, 194.

65. Gurowski, *Diary*, 1:100.
66. Hancock, "Political History of Delaware during the Civil War, Part III," 7:367; James R. Latimer to John P. Gillis, 5 Oct. 1861, John P. Gillis Papers, DHS; *Del*, 5 Oct. 1861.
67. Simpson and Berlin, *Sherman's Civil War*, 156–57; *OR*, series 1, 4:296–97; Marszalek, *Sherman*, 148–61; *NYTi*, 16 Oct. 1861; Johnson and Buel, *Battles and Leaders*, 1:373–93; James F. Noble to Dennison, 30 Sept. 1861, series 147, OHS; Dennison to Chase, 30 Sept., Dennison to Cameron, 1, 10 Oct. 1861, Telegraphic Dispatches, series 144, OhSA.
68. Bradley, *Cameron*, 191–93; Sherman, *Memoirs*, 1:228–32; *OR*, series 1, 4:308–9; McClure, *Lincoln and Men of War-Times*, 231–32; Johnson and Buel, *Battles and Leaders*, 1:373–93; William B. Britton to Messrs. Editors, 15 Oct. 1861, William B. Britton Papers, WRHS; Laas, *Wartime Washington*, 88.
69. *OR*, series 1, 4:299–300, 307; Johnson and Buel, *Battles and Leaders*, 1:373–93; Morton to Cameron, 11 Oct. 1861, Cameron Papers, LC.
70. *OR*, series 3, 1:575–76, 579, 588–91; Basler, *CW*, 5:13–14; Hunt, *Washburn*, 83–84, 103–4; *WDNI*, 17 Oct. 1861; *BDWC*, 26 Oct., 27 Dec. 1861, 24 Jan. 1862; *DFP*, 20, 23 Oct. 1861; *HW*, 9 Nov. 1861.
71. Burlingame, *Stoddard*, 40; Beale, *Diary of Bates*, 197, 22 Oct. 1861; Meneely, *War Department*, 217–18; Hesseltine, *Lincoln and the War Governors*, 186–90; Pearson, *Andrew*, 1:284–85; Morse, *Memoir of Lee*, 74–75; James J. Mooney to Morgan, 4 Nov. 1861, Morgan Papers, NYSL; Henry Lee to Andrew, 31 Oct., 2 Nov. 1861, Andrew Papers, MHS; *HW*, 9 Nov. 1861.
72. Schouler, *Massachusetts in the Civil War*, 1:234–35; Sprague to Gen. William Barry, 1 Nov. 1861, William Barry Papers, Buffalo and Erie County Historical Society, Buffalo, New York (BECHS).
73. *WDNI*, 27 Jul., 13 Aug. 1861; *StPDPi*, 17 Aug. 1861; *BDA*, 5 Sept. 1861; *LDJ*, 13 Oct. 1861; *StLDMR*, 3 May 1862; *SDU*, 11 Jun. 1862; Woodbury, *Second Rhode Island*, 65–66; Sinisi, *Sacred Debts*, 15–21; Hesseltine, *Lincoln and the War Governors*, 231–32; Davis, *Lincoln's Men*, 33–58.

Chapter Six

1. Shutes, *Lincoln and California*, 31–90, 144–45; *SFDAC*, 25 Oct. 1861; *OS*, 2 Nov. 1861; Bancroft, *Pacific States*, 2:457–58; *WES*, 21, 26, 28 Oct. 1861; *HW*, 23 Nov. 1861; *WDNI*, 31 Oct. 1861; Braden, "The Public Career of Edward Dickinson Baker," 252–75; Baker to Lincoln, 2 Oct. 1860, Francis G. Young to Lincoln, 21 Oct, Frank F. Fargo to Lincoln, 26 Oct. 1861, LP, LC; Matthews, *The Golden State*, 84–128.
2. Shutes, *Lincoln and California*, 87; *SDU*, 5 Sept. 1861; *LAS*, 15, 22 Jun., 7 Sept. 1861; Melendy and Gilbert, *Governors of California*, 101–13, 115, 127; *ChiTri*, 11, 22, 30 Oct. 1861; *WES*, 21, 26, 28 Oct. 1861; *SFDAC*, 20 Oct. 1861; Matthews, *The Golden State*, 84–128.
3. Shutes, *Lincoln and California*, 15, 26, 38, 60–61, 64; Stanley, "Republican Party," 123–29; Melendy and Gilbert, *Governors of California*, 115–27; *HW*, 23 Jan. 1864; Hesseltine, *Lincoln and the War Governors*, 77; *LAS*, 15 Jun., 13 Jul. 1861; *SDU*, 14, 29 Aug., 6, 7 Sept. 1861; *ChiTri*, 11, 22, 30 Oct. 1861.
4. As quoted from a dispatch from San Francisco to New York, *NDM*, 24 Sept. 1861; *SDU*, 15 Mar. 1861; Shutes, *Lincoln and California*, 150–53; Stanley, "Republican Party," 126–31; Melendy and Gilbert, *Governors of California*, 123–25; *ChiTri* 11 Oct. 1861.
5. Downey to George H. Woodman, 14 Dec., Capt. Alonzo Ridley to Downey, 9 Mar. 1861, Maj. James H. Carleton to Downey, 18 Jun. 1861, Governors' Letter Books (John

Downey, Leland Stanford, and Frederick Low), CaSA, cited hereafter as Governors' Letter Books; Edwards, "The Department of the Pacific in the Civil War Years," 58–55, 90, 95; Roland, *Johnston*, 245–50; *OR*, 1, 50:433, 456, 493, 497, 572, 594, 613; *SDU*, 15 Aug., 8, 21 Oct. 1861; *SFDEB*, 11 Aug., 16, 20 Sept. 1861; *SFDAC*, 26 Apr., 14 May, 18 Dec., 1861; Scammell, "Military Units in Southern California, 1853–1862," 229–49; Bancroft, *Pacific States*, 2:49–493; Josephy, Jr., *American Civil War in the American West*, 235–42; Melendy and Gilbert, *Governors of California*, 105–13; Gilbert, "The Confederate Minority in California," 154–70; *LAS*, 4, 11, 18 May, 15, 22 Jun. 1861; Kennedy, *Contest for California*, 217–18; Matthews, *The Golden State*, 84–128; Etulain, *Lincoln and Oregon Country Politics in the Civil War Era*, 85–87, 110–12; Prezelski, *Californio Lancers*, 19–25.

6. Lalande, "'Dixie' of the Pacific Northwest: Southern Oregon's Civil War," 35–43; Bancroft, *Pacific States*, 2:456–57; Dell, *War Democrats*, 125; *OS*, 10, 17 Jun. 1861; Journal of John A. Whiteaker, 12, John A. Whiteaker Papers, UOL; John Whiteaker Scrapbooks, UOL; *OSent*, 21 Sept. 1861; Etulain, *Lincoln and Oregon Country Politics*, 110–12.

7. Journal of Whiteaker, 12, 17, 18, and Whiteaker Scrapbooks, UOL; *OS*, 10, 17 Jun. 1861; "Oregon: Capital, Salem," 323; *MF*, 16 Jun. 1859; *NYH*, 28 Apr., 11 Dec. 1860.

8. *OS*, 10, 17 Jun. 1861; Journal of Whiteaker, 12, 17, 18, UOL; Dell, *War Democrats*, 125, 189; Jewell, "'Doing Nothing with Vengeance,' The Diary of David Hobart Taylor," 598–622; McArthur, *The Enemy Never Came*, 27–29.

9. Edwards, "Six Oregon Leaders," 11–14; *OA*, 8 Jun., Sept. 13, 1862; *OS*, 8 May 1858, 10, 17 Jun. 1861, 10 Nov. 1862; Johannsen, "Whiteaker," 68–71; Dell, *War Democrats*, 125n30, 189n45, Whiteaker Scrapbooks, UOL; McArthur, *The Enemy Never Came*, 27–29; Johannsen, *Frontier Politics and the Sectional Conflict*, 206; *SFDEB*, 13 Oct. 1862.

10. Edwards, "Six Leaders," 18; *OS*, 10, Jun., 22 Jul., 24 Oct., 9 Dec. 1861, 21 Apr. 1862; Johannsen, "Whiteaker," 69–71; Edwards, "Department of the Pacific," 58–59, 70–73; Whiteaker Scrapbooks, UOL; McArthur, *The Enemy Never Came*, 28–29.

11. *OS*, 10, 14, 15 Jun., 22 Jul. (quote), 21 Oct., 11, 16 Nov. 1861; Lalande, "'Dixie' of the Pacific," 48–50; *Or*, 25 Jun., 3 Aug., 11, 25 Sept. 1861; Johannsen, "Whiteaker," 63–87; Edwards, "Six Leaders," 11–14; *OR*, series 1, 50:599, 618, 674.

12. Basler, *CW*, 5:9–10, 15–17; *OR*, series 1, 8:456; J. B. Henderson to Gamble, 21 Oct., Bates to Gamble, 27 Sept., 3 Oct. 1861, Gamble Papers, MoHS; Boman, *Gamble*, 132–43; Niven, *Chase Papers*, 3, 107–11; Rosin, "Gamble," 250–55; Chandler to Wife, "confidential," 12 Oct. 1861, Chandler Papers, LC; *StLDMR*, 13 Nov. 1861; *PhiIn*, 7 Nov. 1861; *InDJ*, 19 Nov. 1861; Beale, *Diary of Bates*, 199, 1 Nov. 1861; Morgan to Lincoln, 6 Nov. 1861, LP, LC.

13. *ChiTri*, 27 Oct. 1862; Engle, *Don Carlos Buell*, 64–97; Engle, *Struggle for the Heartland*, 12–26; Johnson and Buel, *Battles and Leaders*, 1:373–93; Basler, *CW*, 5:15–17; Boman, *Gamble*, 132–43; Bates to Gamble, 27 Sept., 3 Oct. 1861, Gamble Papers, MoHS; Marszalek, *Halleck*, 109; Boman, *Lincoln and Citizens' Rights in Missouri*, 63–92; Sears, *Papers of McClellan*, 144–45; *StLDMR*, 13 Nov. 1861; *OR*, series 1, 3:561–65, series 3, 1:623; Beale, *Diary of Bates*, 201, 219; Hunter to Cameron, 19 Dec. 1861, "private and confidential," Cameron Papers, LC; *ChiTri*, 27 Nov. 1861.

14. *OR*, series 1, 4:342; Sears, *Papers of McClellan*, 125–26.

15. Simeon Nash to Dennison, 18 Nov. 1861, series 147, OHS.

16. *WES*, 2 Nov. 1861; *OR*, series 3, 1:600–25; *NHPSG*, 9 Oct., 27 Nov. 1861; Rawley, *Morgan*, 155; *ISJ*, 14 Oct. 1861; Richards, "The Fifth New Hampshire (Light Infantry)," 241–61; *ISJ*, 14 Oct. 1861; Seward to Morgan, 14 Oct. 1861, LP, LC; Curtin to Seward, 2 Nov., Ellwood Harvey to Curtin, 18 Nov. 1861, Executive Correspondence, PSA; *Baltimore Sun*, 17 Oct. 1861; *BDA*, 17 Oct. 1861; Preston King to Morgan, 27 Aug., 21 Oct. 1861,

Morgan Papers, NYSL; Morgan to Marsena R. Patrick, 20 Nov. 1861, Morgan Papers and Letter Books, NYHS.

17. *OR*, series 3, 1:600–607; New Jersey Attorney General Frederick T. Frelinghuysen to Salmon P. Chase, 17, 26 Oct. 1861; Olden Family Papers, HSP; Charles Olden to Morgan, 2 Nov. 1861, Morgan Papers, NYSL.

18. Frelinghuysen to Chase, 17, 26, 28 Oct. 1861, Olden Family Papers, HSP.

19. *NDM*, 5 Oct. 1861; *TDSGR*, 18 Nov. 1861; Olden to Marcus Ward, 21 Oct., 9 Dec. 1861, Marcus Ward Papers, NJHS; Chase to Morgan, 25 Nov. 1861, Morgan Papers, NYSL; Olden to R. B. Bradford, 18 Sept. 1861, New Jersey Letters, RUL.

20. Wilson, *The Business of Civil War*, 7–33; Weeden, *War Government*, 155–66; Whalon, "Washburn and the War Department," 79–81; Washburn to Oliver O. Howard, 23 Aug. 1861, Howard Papers, BCL.

21. Guentzel, "Ramsey," 380–90; Ramsey to Ignatius Donnelly, 3 Oct. 1861, Governor's Papers, MnHS; *ChiTri*, 10, 28 Sept. 1861; William Windom to Clark Thompson, 29 Jul. 1861, Clark W. Thompson Papers, MnHS; *WSJ*, 7 Sept. 1861; Folwell, *Minnesota*, 2:100; *StPDPi*, 8, 10 Sept., 13, 15, 16, 17 Nov. 1861; Current, *Wisconsin*, 302–10; *WDNI*, 3 Oct. 1861; Sobel and Raimo, *Directory of Governors*, 2:774; Quiner Scrapbook, 53–222; Collins, "Absentee Voting in Civil War Law and Politics," 5–30.

22. Quiner, *Wisconsin*, 122–23; Thwaites, *Messages*, 89–91.

23. *OR*, series 2, 1:609; Dell, *War Democrats*, 117–18; *WDNI*, 6, 7, 8 Nov. 1861; Benton, *Voting in the Field*, 225–49; *NDM*, 9 Nov. 1861; *TDSGR*, 11 Nov. 1861; Baker, *Politics of Continuity*, 70–73.

24. *LDJ*, 15 Nov. 1861; Clark, "Politics in Maryland during the Civil War," 37:378–89, 394–95; *OR*, series 2, 2:99, 116–18; Radcliffe, *Hicks*, 116–18; Seward to Hicks, 14 Oct. 1861, Governors' Letter Books, MdSA; *BA*, 5 Nov. 1861; Mitchell, *Maryland Voices*, 161–62; Benton, *Voting in the Field*, 225–49; Meyers, "Governor Bradford's Private List of Union Men in 1861," 83–90; Baker, *Politics of Continuity*, 72–75.

25. *BC*, 17 Aug. 1861; *NYTi*, 2 Mar. 1881; Clark, "Maryland during the Civil War," 37:384–85; Wagandt, *The Mighty Revolution: Negro Emancipation in Maryland, 1862–1864*, 30–31; Dell, *War Democrats*, 117–18; *NDM*, 9 Nov. 1861; Baker, *Politics of Continuity*, 72–75.

26. Mitchell, *Maryland Voices*, 188–90; Radcliffe, *Hicks*, 118; *NYTi*, 12 Nov. 1861, 2 Mar. 1881; Hicks to James L. Dorsey, 24 May 1863, James L. Dorsey Papers, MdHS; Hicks to Blair, 29 Dec. 1864, Blair Family Papers, LC; *OR*, series 2, 1:704, 711.

27. *OR*, series 3, 1:661; Ambler, *Pierpont*, 117–42; *WDNI*, 8 Nov., 7 Dec. 1861; Langford, "Constitutional Issues," 12–31; Moore, "Slavery as a Factor," 5–89; Ham, "Mind of a Copperhead," 87–105; Shaffer, "Lincoln and West Virginia," 86–100; Curry, *A House Divided*, 175; Winston, "Statehood for West Virginia: An Illegal Act?" 530–34; Pierpont to Col. B. F. Larned, 7 Nov., Pierpont to Rosecrans, 13 Nov. 1861, Executive Letter Books, VSAL; *BDA*, 23 Nov., 16 Dec. 1861; *NYTi*, 25 Oct. 1861.

28. *OR*, series 1, 8:378, 382, 389–90, 455–56; Boman, *Gamble*, 142–46; Marszalek, *Halleck*, 109–14; Canan, "The Missouri Paw Paw Militia, 1863–1864," 431–38; Rosin, "Gamble," 255–70; Boman, *Lincoln and Citizens' Rights in Missouri*, 63–92.

29. David Davis to Cameron, 13 Oct. 1861, "confidential," Cameron Papers, LC; *ISJ*, 1 Oct. 1861; *ChiTri*, 10 Dec. 1861.

30. Calvin Burbank to Cousin Sarah, 11 Nov. 1861, Calvin Burbank Papers, DC.

31. Reed, "Lincoln's Compensated Emancipation Plan," 30; Monty Blair to Lincoln, 21 Nov. 1861, LP, LC; Hancock, *Delaware during the War*, 106–9; Randall, *Lincoln*, 2:143–45;

Nicolay and Hay, *Complete Works of Lincoln*, 7:21–23; Scharf, *Delaware*, 1:331–56; Bevan, *History of Delaware*, 2:641–42; Nevins, *War Becomes Revolution*, 6–9; Munroe, *Delaware*, 140–41, 135–43; *WDNI*, 7 Feb. 1862; Harris, *Lincoln and the Border States*, 159–63; Burlingame, *Lincoln*, 2:229–32; Basler, *CW*, 5:29–31; Cowden, "Heaven Will Frown," 67–93; *DR*, 28 Nov. 1861, 9, 16, 23 Jan. 1862; Henry Lockwood to Burton, 25 Oct. 1861, Burton-Wooten Papers, DPA.

32. Basler, *CW*, 5:34–35; Boman, *Lincoln and Citizens' Rights in Missouri*, 63–92.

33. Gurowski to Andrew, 24 Oct., C. R. Chauncy, 21 Oct., Horace Sargent to Andrew, 22 Oct., [Henry Smith] to Andrew, 26 Oct., Henry Lee to Andrew, 31 Oct., 2 Nov. 2, 1861, Andrew Papers, MHS; Gurowski, *Diary*, 1:42; Benjamin Hutchinson to Mary Hutchinson, 20 Nov. 1861, Hutchinson Papers, UVAL.

34. Gurowski to Andrew, 24 Oct. 1861, Andrew Papers, MHS.

35. Andrew to [], 27 Oct., 3 Nov. 1861, Andrew Papers, MHS, written from the National Hotel, to perhaps Blair or Sumner, or Gurowski. Stout, *Upon the Altar of the Nation*, 115; Pearson, *Andrew*, 1:269–70; *NYTi*, 19 Oct. 1861.

36. Donald, *Lincoln*, 320.

37. Burlingame, *Stoddard*, 44–45; Donald, *Lincoln*, 320; *ChiTri*, 2, 3 Dec. 1861.

38. Basler, *CW*, 5:35–53; Donald, *Lincoln*, 320.

39. *InDJ*, 11 Dec. 1861.

40. *LDT*, 22 Dec. 1861; *LDJ*, 22 Dec. 1861.

41. Tap, *Over Lincoln's Shoulder*, 34; Nevins, *The Improvised War*, 303–4; Harris, *Chandler*, 58–59.

42. Ben Wade to Chandler, "confidential," 8 Oct. 1861, Chandler Papers, LC; Harris, *Chandler*, 57–60; Tap, *Over Lincoln's Shoulder*, 34–39.

43. "Dalton Letters, 1861–1865," 389; [G. M. Laundu] to Cameron, 24 Nov. 1861, "confidential," Joseph Medill to Cameron, 6 Dec. 1861, "private," Cameron Papers, LC; Kelley, "Fossildom, Old Fogyism, and Red Tape," 93–113; *ChiTri*, 18 Nov. 1861; *NYI*, 12 Dec. 1861; *PhiIn*, 4, 7, Nov., 5 Dec. 1861; Burlingame, *Lincoln*, 2:238–42; Marvel, *Lincoln's Autocrat*, 148–49.

44. Gamble to Edward Bates, 3 Dec. 1861, LP, LC; Thomas and Hyman, *Stanton*, 133–35; Bradley, *Cameron*, 202–3; "Reminiscences of Washington 1861," Cameron Papers, William Pitt Fessenden to Cameron, "confidential," 28 Aug. 1861, and Cameron's reply, 30 Aug. 1861, Cameron to Frémont, 30 Aug. 1861, Cameron Papers, LC; R. M. Blatchford to Cameron, "private and confidential," 6 Sept. 1861, Cameron Papers, LC; Nevins, *The Improvised War*, 400–401; Nicolay, *Lincoln: A History*, 5:125–26; Perret, *Lincoln's War*, 105–9; Kelley, "Fossildom," 93–113; Burlingame, *With Lincoln in the White House*, 63.

45. Tap, *Over Lincoln's Shoulder*, 21–28; Harris, "Blair," 121–25; Fennimore, "Blair," 49:207–8; Blair to Chandler, "confidential," 28 Nov. 1861, Chandler Papers, LC; [Persy] Willis to Blair, 8 Oct. 1861, Blair Papers, DPL.

46. *OR*, series 3, 1:765–66; Richard Delafield to Morgan, 5 Sept., Seward to Morgan, 20 Dec. 1861, Morgan Papers, NYSL; Basler, *CW*, 5:74; Quiner, *Wisconsin*, 99–100; *BDWC*, 27 Dec., 24 Jan. 1861; Cameron to Washburn, 16, 18 Nov., Washburn to Lot Morrill, 17 Nov. 1861, Exec. Correspondence, MeSA; Washburn to Fessenden, 19, 24, 27 Dec. 1861, Fessenden Papers, WRHS; *NDM*, 2 Dec. 1861.

47. Marszalek, *Halleck*, 111, 13; Boman, *Gamble*, 150–51; Boman, *Lincoln and Citizens' Rights in Missouri*, 63–92; *OR*, series 2, 1:230–33; series 1, 8:373–90; *ChiTri*, 27 Nov. 1861.

48. *OR*, series 1, 8:448–50; Basler, *CW*, 5:71, 80; *ChiTri*, 31 Oct., 27 Nov. 1861; *NHPSG*, 13, 27 Nov. 1861.

49. *OR*, series 1, 3:468–69, 8:448–49; Robinson to Lincoln, 10 Oct. 1861, LP, LC; Willard P. Hall to Lincoln, 18 Oct. 1861, LP, LC; Blackmar, *Robinson*, 277–78; *LDT*, 13 Oct., 11 Dec. 1861; Rosin, "Gamble," 255–70; *StLDMR*, 12 Jan. 1862; *ChiTri*, 31 Oct., 27 Nov. 1861; *NHPSG*, 13, 27 Nov. 1861.

50. Robinson to Sara, 22 Dec., Robinson to Samuel N. Wood, 19 Oct., 13 Nov., Robinson to Sara, 4, 10 Nov. 1861, 12 Jan. 1862, Robinson Papers, KSHS; Robinson to Lincoln, 10 Oct. 1861, LP, LC; *LDJ*, 16 Nov. 1861; *OR*, series 1, 3:529–30; *ChiTri*, 22, 31 Oct., 27 Nov. 1861; Benedict, *Lane*, 114–17; Smith, *Ewing*, 149–51; *LDT*, 13, 15, Oct. 1861; *NHPSG*, 13, 27 Nov. 1861.

51. Elihu B. Washburne to Lincoln, 17 Oct. 1861, LP, LC; Gamble to John Moore, 30 Nov. 1861, Gamble Papers, MoHS; *OR*, series 1, 17: pt. 2, 92; *LDT*, 10 Dec. 1861; Mark Delahay to Lincoln, 30 Nov. 1861, Robinson Papers, KSHS; *ChiTri*, 31 Oct., 27 Nov. 1861; *NHPSG*, 13, 27 Nov. 1861.

52. Elihu B. Washburne to Lincoln, 17 Oct. 1861, LP, LC.

53. Castel, *Civil War Kansas*, 69–70; Smith, *Ewing*, 150–51; *LDT*, 8 Jan. 1862; Robinson to Samuel N. Wood, 19 Oct. 1861, Robinson to Sara, 8, 22 Dec. 1861, Robinson Papers, KSHS; *ChiTri*, 31 Oct., 27 Nov. 1861; *NHPSG*, 13, 27 Nov. 1861.

54. *OR*, series 1, 7:443–44, 8:448–49; Engle, *Buell*, 94–96; Minor, "Lane and Lincoln," 188–98.

55. *OR*, series 1, 7:482; Engle, *Buell*, 115–16; Alexander Varian to sister, 25 Oct., to father, 30 Oct., 1 Dec. 1861, Alexander Varian Papers, WRHS.

56. *OR*, series 1, 7:511–12; Engle, *Buell*, 96–16; Dennison to Trumbull, 16 Dec. 1861, Trumbull Papers, LC.

57. *OR*, series 2, 1:784–85; Beatie, *Army of the Potomac*, 2:125–27; Andrew to Lincoln, 25 Nov. 1861, LP, LC; Catton, *Mr. Lincoln's Army*, 72–76; Abbott, *Cotton and Capital*, 77; Pearson, *Andrew*, 2:4; Schouler, *Massachusetts in the Civil War*, 1:238–39; Hamrogue, "Andrew," 137–43; Howe, "Note on the Battle Hymn of the Republic," 4; Sumner to Andrew, 19 Dec. 1861, Sumner Papers, HoL.

58. *OR*, series 2, 1:786–88; Beatie, *Army of the Potomac*, 125–27; Catton, *Mr. Lincoln's Army*, 72–76; Schouler, *Massachusetts in the Civil War*, 1:238–40; Hamrogue, "Andrew," 138–42; Sears, *Papers of McClellan*, 146; Milano, "The Copperhead Regiment," 31–63.

59. Sears, *Papers of McClellan*, 146.

60. Beatie, *Army of the Potomac*, 2:127–28; Donald, *Charles Sumner and the Rights of Man*, 48–49; Schouler, *Massachusetts in the Civil War*, 1:238–39; Hamrogue, "Andrew," 138–43; Sumner to Andrew, 9 Jul., Andrew to McClellan, 30 Dec. 1861, Andrew Papers and Letter Books, MHS.

61. Gamble to David Pitman, 14 Dec., Gamble to Halleck, 24 Dec. 1861, Gamble Papers, MoHS.

62. *OR*, series 3, 1:756, 763; Basler, *CW*, 5:81.

63. Washburn to Fessenden, 10 Dec. 1861, Fessenden Papers, WRHS; *OR*, series 3, 1:699–708; Nathaniel P. Banks. Andrew to Fox, 27 Nov. 1861, James Speed to Lincoln, 23 Jan. 1862, LP, LC; Benedict, *Lane*, 184; Abbott, *Cotton and Capital*, 77–80; *OR*, series 1, 15:412–13; Pearson, *Andrew*, 1:124–25.

64. *NYH*, 8, 11 Dec. 1861; Hoffman, *Vermont Cavalryman in War and Love*, 46–47; Marshall, *War of the People*, 54; *NYTi*, 8 Dec. 1861; *PDJ*, 30 Oct. 1861; *OR*, series 3, 1:675–78, 698, 740, 755–57; Curtin to Cameron, 17 Dec. 1861, Cameron Papers, LC; Curtin to Lincoln, 16 Dec. 1861, Executive Correspondence, PSA.

65. Marshall, *War of the People*, 48; Link, "Potomac Fever," 69–88; Message of Holbrook, 10 Oct. 1862, *Journal of the Senate of the State of Vermont, 1862*, 28; Moore, "Holbrook," 65–78; Knight, *No Braver Deeds*, 107–8; Howe to Andrew, 16 Dec. 1861, Andrew Papers, MHS.

66. *OR*, series 3, 1:699–704.

67. James Speed to Lincoln, 22 Dec. 1861, LP, LC; *NDM*, 18 Dec. 1861, "out in the cold"; Reed, "Lincoln's Plan," 30; Avery and Shoemaker, *Messages*, 3:430–50; *LDJ*, 12 Sept. 1861; Harris, *Lincoln and the Border States*, 192–207; *OR*, series 3, 1:699–708.

68. *Congressional Globe*, 2nd Session, 37th Congress, 130, 18 Dec. 1861; Pierce, *Memoirs and Letters of Sumner*, 4:42–64; Hoar, *Charles Sumner*, 8:3–11.

69. Hoar, *Charles Sumner*, 8:14.

70. Burlingame, *Stoddard*, 36; *OR*, series 3, 1:699–708; Meneely, *War Department*, 231–33; Tap, *Over Lincoln's Shoulder*, 38–100; Donald, *Lincoln*, 320; Donald, *Sumner*, 48–50; Beatie, *Army of the Potomac*, 2:127–28; *Congressional Globe*, 2nd session, 37th Congress, 130, 18 Dec. 1861; *HW*, 14 Dec. 1861; Angevine, *The Railroad and the State*, 130–64.

71. *NYH*, 11 Dec. 1861.

72. Burlingame, *Stoddard*, 47; Basler, *CW*, 5:84; *OR*, series 1, 7:524, 526; Perret, *Lincoln's War*, 111; Rothschild, *Lincoln, Master of Men*, 340–41; Dennison to Trumbull, 16 Dec. 1861, Trumbull Papers, LC.

Chapter Seven

1. Clark, *Kirkwood*, 153–54, 297; Lathrop, *Kirkwood*, 285; Kirkwood to Grimes, 20 May 1862, Kirkwood Papers, SHSI.

2. *Inaugural Address Delivered to the Ninth General Assembly of the State of Iowa by Governor Samuel J. Kirkwood, Jan. 15, 1862*, 8–9; Clark, *Kirkwood*, 220–27, 153–54; *EDHE*, 15, 16 Jan., 5 Feb. 1862; *IDSR*, 15 Jan. 1862.

3. As quoted in Clark, *Kirkwood*, 220–27; this letter is also in the Kirkwood Papers, George B. Corkhill to Kirkwood, 29 Jan. 1862, Kirkwood Papers, SHSI; *NYTi*, 7 Jul. 1886; Lathrop, *Kirkwood*, 178–80, 182–201; *BDHE*, 15, 16, 17 Jan. 1862.

4. Fuller, *Messages*, 446–53; Harris, "Blair," 91, 124–29; Moore, *History of Michigan*, 412–13; Fennimore, "Blair," 49:207–11; Henry Crapo to William Crapo, 19 Jan. 1862, Crapo Papers, BHL; May, *Michigan and the Civil War*, 19; Nevins, *The Improvised War*, 171; *DFP*, 15 Jan. 1862; *ChiTri*, 4 Jan. 1862; *BS*, 6 Jan. 1862; Mitchell, "Organizational Performance," 124–26.

5. As quoted in Fennimore, "Blair," 49:208–11; Harris, "Blair," 126.

6. Harris, *Chandler*, 30–33; Fuller, *Messages*, 417–19; *NYTi*, 7 Aug. 1894; Hesseltine, *Lincoln and the War Governors*, 48.

7. Harris, *Chandler*, 33–35.

8. Clark, "Politics in Maryland," 38:226–40; "Bradford's Inaugural Address Delivered in the Senate, January 8, 1862," *Maryland Senate Journal*; *BS*, 2, 3, 9, 10 Jan. 1862; *BA*, 9, 10 Jan. 1862; Wagandt, *Mighty Revolution*, 34–40; *BS*, 10 Jan. 1862; Bradford to Curtin, 11 Jan., Brig. Gen. James Cooper to Bradford, 15 Jan., 26 Feb., Bradford to Cooper, 24 Jan., 1 Mar., Bradford to Lincoln, 5 Mar. 1862, Governor's Letter Books, MdSA; *PhiIn*, 2 Jan. 1862; *Maryland House Journal*, 1862, 164, 173; *OR*, series 3, 1:931–33.

9. *ChiTri*, 4 Jan. 1862; Mitchell, "Organizational Performance," 125–26; Fennimore, "Blair," 49:211–12.

10. Basler, *CW*, 5:86–87; Burlingame, *Lincoln's Journalist*, 187.

11. *OR*, series 1, 8:532–33; Basler, *CW*, 5:91–92.
12. *OR*, series 1, 7:532–35; Meneely, *War Department*, 358–59; *BDHE*, 10 Jan. 1862.
13. Basler, *CW*, 5:92; Niven, *Chase*, 321–23; Burlingame, *Lincoln*, 2:216–21.
14. Beale, *Diary of Bates*, 223–24; Burlingame, *Lincoln*, 2:219–23.
15. John T. Booth Diary, 6 Jan. 1862, John T. Booth Papers, OHS.
16. Meigs, "General M. C. Meigs on the Conduct of the Civil War." 290–93; Meneely, *War Department*, 353–60; Burlingame, *Lincoln*, 2:220.
17. Yates to Trumbull, 25 Jan., 14 Feb. 1862, Trumbull Papers, LC; Trumbull to Yates, 6 Feb. 1862, Reavis Papers, CHM; Nortrup, "Yates," 242–43; *ISJ*, 12 Dec. 1861, 1, 13 Jan. 1862; *ChiTri*, 30 Jan. 1862.
18. Horace Binney Sargent to Andrew, 4, 14 Jan. 1862, Andrew Papers, MHS, first quote, and 14 Jan. 1862, second quote; Randall, *Lincoln*, 2:205–6; Hesseltine, *Lincoln and the War Governors*, 233; *ChiTri*, 4 Jan. 1862.
19. Meneely, *War Department*, 251, 365–67; Niven, *Chase Papers*, 1:324–26; Lincoln to Cameron, 11 Jan. 1862, "private," Cameron to Lincoln, 11 Jan. 1862, Cameron Papers, LC; Donald, *Inside Lincoln's Cabinet*, 60–62; Bradley, *Cameron*, 204–8; McClure, *Lincoln and Men of War-Times*, 150–51; White, *The Life of Lyman Trumbull*, 185–89; Burlingame, *Lincoln's Journalist*, 196; *WDNI*, 21 Jan. 1862; Beale, *Diary of Gideon Welles*, 1:55–59; Marvel, *Lincoln's Autocrat*, 152–55.
20. Morton to Cameron, 13 Jan. 1862, Cameron Papers, LC; *BDHE*, 15 Jan. 1862.
21. Burlingame, *Lincoln Observed*, 46–47; *BDA*, 23 Jan. 1862; *WDNI*, 21 Jan. 1862.
22. *ChiTri*, 15, 22 Jan. 1862.
23. McClure, *Lincoln and Men of War-Times*, 171; *BDA*, 23 Jan. 1862; *NHS*, 8 Feb. 1862; *NDM*, 14 Jan. 1862; *ISJ*, 17 Jan. 1862.
24. Medill to Stanton, 21 Jan. 1862, "private," and Alexander Stewart to Stanton, 20 Jan., John Dix to Stanton, 14 Jan. 1862, "private," Stanton Papers, LC; Burlingame, *Lincoln's Journalist*, 196–97; Burlingame, *Lincoln Observed*, 46–47; Thomas and Hyman, *Stanton*, 33–39, 165–67; Marvel, *Lincoln's Autocrat*, 123–56; Meneely, *War Department*, 355–77; Beale, *Diary of Welles*, 1:55–59; *PhiIn*, 14, 28 Jan. 1862; *NDM*, 14 Jan. 1862; *ISJ*, 17 Jan. 1862.
25. Andrew to Stanton, 14 Jan. 1862, Stanton Papers, LC; Andrew to [?], 16 Jan. 1862, Andrew Papers, MHS; Keller, *Affairs of State*, 15–16.
26. *OR*, series 1, 8:826–27; Boman, *Gamble*, 150–51; *OR*, series 3, 1:875; Rosin, "Gamble," 260–70; Thomas T. Gannt to Montgomery Blair, 18 Jan. 1862, LP, LC; Executive Order, 7 Apr. 1862, Governor's Papers, Letters Sent and Received, RISA; Tod to Stanton, 13 Feb. 1862, Telegraphic Dispatches, series 144, Stanton to Tod, 14 Feb. 1862, Telegraphic Dispatches, series 145, OhSA.
27. *OR*, series 1, 50: pt. 1, 796–97; *SFDEB*, 7, 10 Jan. 1862; Leland Stanford Diary, 22–24 Jan. 1862, Governor's Daily Journals and Diaries, CaSA; *BDA*, 21 Jan. 1862; *ChiTri*, 20 Feb. 1862; *SDU*, 18 Mar. 1862; *NYTi*, 21 Jan., 18 Feb. 1862.
28. *OR*, series 1, 50: pt. 1, 805–6, 893, 962, 1008–9; Edwards, "Department of Pacific," 95–101; Edwards, "Oregon Regiments in the Civil War Years," 29–31; Melendy and Gilbert, *Governors of California*, 115–27; Gilbert, "San Francisco Harbor Defense during the Civil War," 229–40; *SDU*, 10, 11, 25 Jan., 15 Feb. 1862; *Inaugural Address of Leland Stanford, January 10, 1862*; Stanford Diary, 10 Jan. 1862, Governor's Journals and Diaries, CaSA.
29. *OR*, series 3, 1:851–69; Pearson, *Andrew*, 1:301; Schouler, *Massachusetts in the Civil War*, 1:274–91; Trefousse, *Butler*, 92–94; Butler, *Butler's Book*, 300–318; *BDA*, 25 Jan. 1862;

Weeden, *War Government*, 205–6; Hunt, *Washburn*, 104; Hannibal Hamlin to Washburn, 1 Feb., Washburn to Hamlin, 28 Feb. 1862, Washburn Papers, LC.

30. *OR*, series 3, 1:864–65; Tap, *Over Lincoln's Shoulder*, 63; Andrew to Lincoln, 11, 13 Jan. 1862, LP, LC; Pearson, *Andrew*, 1:301–9; Palmer, *Letters of Sumner*, 103; Weeden, *War Government*, 205–6; Schouler, *Massachusetts in the Civil War*, 1:274–91; BDA, 25 Jan. 1862.

31. Pearson, *Andrew*, 1:302–5.

32. Trefousse, *Butler*, 96–97; Butler, *Butler's Book*, 323–34; Hamlin to Washburn, 2 Mar. 1862, Executive Correspondence, MeSA; *OR*, series 1, 6:677–78, 53:507, series 3, 1:896–97; Butler, *Correspondence*, 1:330–34; Pearson, *Andrew*, 1:304–6; Weeden, *War Government*, 205–7; Hunt, *Washburn*, 104; P. H. Watson to 12 Washburn, Feb., Washburn to Morrill, 8 Feb. 1862, Executive Correspondence, MeSA; BDA, 22, 23 Jan. 1862.

33. Pearson, *Andrew*, 1:306; Howe to Andrew, 21 Jan. 1862, Andrew Papers, MHS; Peter H. Watson to Washburn, 12 Feb 1862, Executive Correspondence, MeSA.

34. Pearson, *Andrew*, 1:306–7; Howe to Andrew, 21 Jan. 1862, Andrew Papers, MHS.

35. Sears, *Papers of McClellan*, 156–57; *ChiTri*, 18 Jan. 1862.

36. Moore, *Michigan*, 1:421–22; Robertson, *Michigan in the War*, 20–22; Lathrop, *Kirkwood*, 180–200; Byers, *Iowa in War Times*, 90; Quiner, *Wisconsin*, 122–23; Reid, *Ohio in the War*, 1:62–65; Washburn to Morrill, 17 Dec. 1861, Washburn to Fessenden, 2 Jan. 1862, Executive Correspondence, MeSA; Parish, *The North and the Nation*, 154–55.

37. Basler, *CW*, 5:99–100; *OR*, series 1, 8:826–27, series 3, 1:895; Louis Harvey to Halleck, 17 Feb. 1862, Wisconsin Governor's General Correspondence, Letter Books, SHSW; Engle, "Raised Consciousness," 1–18; Engle, *Yankee Dutchman: The Life of Franz Sigel*, 80–100; Mahin, *The Blessed Place of Freedom: Europeans in Civil War America*, 9–15; Burton, *Melting Pot Soldiers*.

38. Burlingame, *Lincoln's Journalist*, 211–12; Castel, *Civil War Kansas*, 65–80; *OR*, series 1, 8:482, 551, 642; *ToTri*, 8 Feb., 5 Apr. 1862; *ChiTri*, 14, 16, 28 Jan. 1862; Hunter to Trumbull, 21 Feb. 1862, Trumbull Papers, LC; Sears, *Papers of McClellan*, 157–58; Wilson, *Robinson*, 83–84; Blackmar, *Robinson*, 276–88; Robinson to Sara, 12 Jan., 2 Feb., 2 Mar. 1862, Robinson Papers, KSHS; *Senate Journal of the Legislative Assembly of the State of Kansas, 1861–1865*, chap. 8; Smith, *Ewing*, 146–49; *LDT*, 26 Jan., 7, 15, 20 Feb. 1862; Spurgeon, *Soldiers in the Army of Freedom*, 38–59.

39. *OR*, series 1, 8:828, 507; Nevins, *War Becomes Revolution*, 293; Burlingame, *Lincoln's Journalist*, 213.

40. *OR*, series 1, 8:518–23, 530–34.

41. *OR*, series 1, 8:509.

42. *OR*, series 1, 8:512–13.

43. *OR*, series 1, 7:572, 581, 8:508–34; Engle, *Struggle for the Heartland*, 17–39; Marszalek, *Halleck*, 115–17.

44. Tod to Stanton, 28 Jan., Curtin to Stanton, 30 Jan. 1862, Stanton Papers, LC; Dexter Hawkins to Washburn, 7 Mar., Frank Howe to Washburn, 24 May, Washburn to Frank Howe, 24 May 1862, Executive Correspondence, MeSA; Wilson, *Business of Civil War*, 30–33, 68–71; *OR*, series 3, 2:188–95. Critics, such as John Fahnestock, attacked Morton for his patronage abuse. Fahnestock Hand-bill, 1 Jan. 1862, Fahnestock Papers, FHS; Thornbrough, Riker, and Corpuz, *Diary of Fletcher*, 7:97, 266, 304–6; Morton to Cameron, 13 Jan. 1862, Cameron Papers, LC; Hesseltine, *Lincoln and the War Governors*, 240.

45. Basler, *CW*, 5:115; Stanton to Benjamin Wade, Jan. 27, 1862, "*most confidential*," Stanton Papers, LC.

46. Roland, *Johnston*, 279–90; Thomas and Hyman, *Stanton*, 172–73; Engle, *Buell*, 140–59; Engle, *Struggle for the Heartland*, 53–84; *OR*, series 3, 1:875–79; Scott to Stanton, 1, 3 Feb. 1862, Stanton Papers, LC.

47. Roland, *Johnston*, 290–97; Engle, *Buell*, 161–74; Chase to Kirkwood, 19 Feb. 1862, Chase Papers, CGS; Thornbrough, "Morton: The Great War Governor," 72–73; *OR*, series 1, 7:590–95; Marszalek, *Halleck*, 117–18; Cooling, *Forts Henry and Donelson*; Scott to Morton, 5 Feb., Scott to Stanton, 6, 7 Feb. 1862, Stanton Papers, LC. Scott to Stanton, 1, 2, 4, 6, 7 Feb. 1862, "private and confidential," 7 Feb. 1862, Stanton Papers, LC; Thomas and Hyman, *Stanton*, 172–73; Kamm, "The Civil War Career of Thomas A. Scott," 93; *Journal of the Minnesota House and Senate, March 6, 1862*, 448–49.

48. *BDHE*, 25 Feb. 1862; *OR*, 7:588–89, 620–33; Cooling, *Forts Henry and Donelson*; Engle, *Buell*, 161–74.

49. *OR*, series 1, 7:635; Clark, *Kirkwood*, 227–40; Lathrop, *Kirkwood*, 205–11; *IDSR*, 11, 12 Mar. 1862.

50. Hyman and Thomas, *Stanton*, 172–74; *ISJ*, 8 Apr. 1862; *OR*, series 3, 1:889–91; Scott to Stanton, 9, 14, 16 Feb., Stanton to Scott, 21 Feb. 1862, "private and confidential," Stanton Papers, LC.

51. *ISJ*, 8 Apr. 1862; Kirkwood to Washburn, 3 Apr. 1862, Yates Papers, ALPL.

52. Lathrop, *Kirkwood*, 180–81; Kirkwood to Washburn, 3 Apr. 1862, Military Letter Books, Kirkwood Papers, SHSI; *ISJ*, 8 Apr. 1862; Kirkwood to Washburn, 3 Apr. 1862, Yates Papers, ALPL; *OR*, series 3, 1:889–91; Scott to Stanton, 9, 14, 16 Feb., Stanton to Scott, 21 Feb. 1862, "private and confidential," Stanton Papers, LC.

53. Stanton to Dana, 19 Feb. 1862, Stanton Papers, LC; Thomas and Hyman, *Stanton*, 174–75; Stanton to Dana, 23 Feb. 1862, Charles Dana Papers, LC; *NYTri*, 19 Feb. 1862, and Stanton's response, 20 Feb. 1862; *TDSGR*, 22 Feb. 1862; *DR*, 24 Feb. 1862; Burlingame, *Lincoln's Journalist*, 226–27, 240.

54. Stanton to Dana, 19 Feb. 1862, Stanton Papers, LC; second quote from Thomas and Hyman, *Stanton*, 146.

55. Stanton to Scott, 21 Feb. 1862, Stanton Papers, LC, these quotes are taken from two separate letters, both dated 21 Feb.; *OR*, series 1, 7:628, 8:547.

56. Scott to Stanton, 3 Mar. 1862, Stanton Papers, LC; Catton, *Terrible Swift Sword*, 169; Marszalek, *Halleck*, 118–19; *OR*, series 1, 7:636.

57. Stanton to Johnson, 3, 4 Mar. 1862, Stanton Papers, LC; Trefousse, *Andrew Johnson: A Biography*, 155.

58. Nortrup, "Yates," 318, 321; Krenkel, *Yates*, 187–90; *ISJ*, 25, 28 Jan., 1 Feb. 1862; Scott to Stanton, 6 Mar. 1862, Stanton Papers, LC; Clark, *Kirkwood*, 227–30; Lathrop, *Kirkwood*, 207–8; *IDSR*, 4 Mar. 1862; Throne, "The Civil War Diary of John Mackley," 165.

59. Nortrup, "Yates," 318; Krenkel, *Yates*, 187–91; Yates, "Richard Yates: War Governor of Illinois," 175.

60. *ISJ*, 13 Feb. 1862.

61. Krenkel, *Yates*, 190–91; Nortrup, "Yates," 320–21; *ISJ*, 10, 11, 18, 19, 27 Feb. 1862; Yates, "Yates, War Governor," 175; *BDHE*, 18, 20 Feb., 5 Mar. 1862; *InDJ*, 25 Feb. 1862; *NYTi*, 7 Mar. 1862; Catton, *Grant Moves South*, 179; Daniel, *Shiloh: The Battle That Changed the Civil War*, 38; *ChiTri*, 17, 18, 20 Feb., 3 Mar. 1862.

62. *InDJ*, 18, 25 Feb. 1862; *StLDMR*, 18 Feb. 1862; *LDT*, 20 Feb. 1862.

63. Foulke, *Morton*, 1:162–68; Thornbrough, Riker, and Corpuz, *Diary of Fletcher*, 7:346–48, 357; *InDJ*, 18, 21, 25 Feb., 3 Mar. 1862; *BDHE*, 20 Feb. 1862; Stampp, *Indiana Politics during the Civil War*, 98–99; Winslow and Moore, *Camp Morton, 1861–1865: Indianapolis Prison Camp*, 19–25; French, *Morton*, 244–49; Tap, *Over Lincoln's Shoulder*, 123; Sanders, *While in the Hands of the Enemy*, 89; Nation and Towne, *Indiana's War*, 55; Seigel, "She Went to War: Indiana Women Nurses in the Civil War," 2–16; Rodgers, "Hoosier Women and the Civil War Home Front," 108–15.

64. Seward to Morgan, 11 Mar. 1862, George Dawson to Morgan, 6, 7 Mar. 1862, Morgan Papers, NYSL; Rawley, *Morgan*, 168; *NYTi*, 18 Feb. 1883; Henry J. Raymond to James Wadsworth, 9 Feb. 1862, James L. Wadsworth Papers, LC; *OR*, series 3, 1:898; Stanton to Andrew, 14 Mar. 1862, Andrew Papers, MHS; *OR*, series 1, 8:633–34; Halleck to Ramsey, 8 Jan. 1862, Governor's Papers, MnHS.

65. *OR*, series 1, 8:563–64, 557, 587; Boman, *Lincoln and Citizens' Rights in Missouri*, 83–114.

66. *OR*, series 1, 8:570–71.

67. *OR*, series 1, 8:547–48, 551–55, 576, 617, 631; Blackmar, *Robinson*, 276–86.

68. Engle, *Buell*, 205; Villard, *Memoirs*, 1: 232–34; Trefousse, *Johnson*, 155; Basler, *CW*, 5:155; *OR*, series 1, 8:605–6.

69. Beale, *Diary of Bates*, 239; *OR*, series 1, 7:679–80, 8:596; Scott to Stanton, 1, 2, 4, 6, 7 Feb. and 1, 2, 3, 4, 7, 9 Mar., 1862, Stanton Papers, LC.

70. Burlingame, *Stoddard*, 61; Basler, *CW*, 5:144–46; Beale, *Diary of Bates*, 239; Sears, *Papers of McClellan*, 12, 14 Mar. 1862, 207; Basler, *CW*, 5:144–46, 160–61; McClellan to Lincoln, 12 Mar. 1862, LP, LC; *WDNI*, 27 Mar. 1862; Lincoln to James A. McDougal, 14 Mar. 1862, Seward Papers, UR; Palmer, *Letters of Sumner*, 2:103.

71. Horace Binney Sargent to Andrew, 3 Mar. 1862, Andrew Papers, MHS; Randall, *Lincoln*, 2:206.

72. John Wood to Andrew, 18 Feb. 1862, [William Pitt Fessenden] to Andrew, 9 Mar. 1862, Andrew Papers, MHS.

73. Joseph W. Keifer to Wife, 7 Mar. 1862, Joseph W. Keifer Papers, LC; Engle, *Buell*, 208; Eicher, *The Longest Night*, 150–208; Engle, *Struggle for the Heartland*, 92–121.

74. Basler, *CW*, 5:166; Ambler, *Pierpont*, 142–47; Capt. Isaiah Hill to Pierpont, 12 Feb., Pierpont to Morgan, 1 Feb. 1862, Pierpont-Samuels Papers, WvDCH; *WH*, 14 Feb. 1862; Pierpont to Stanton, 14 Feb. 1862, Governor's Letter Books, VSAL; *BS*, 21 Feb. 1862; *WDI*, 24 Feb. 1862; *NYTi*, 2 Mar. 1862; Eicher, *The Longest Night*, 150–215; *OR*, series 1, 6:677–78; Sears, *Papers of McClellan*, 187–89; Marszalek, *Halleck*, 120; Scott to Stanton, 6 Mar., and Halleck to Stanton, 15 Mar. 1862, Stanton Papers, LC; Engle, *Struggle for the Heartland*, 92–121; Mahood, *General Wadsworth*, 75–90.

75. Yates to Trumbull, 25 Jan., 14 Feb. 1862, Trumbull Papers, LC; Nortrup, "The Prorogued Legislature," 5–19; Nortrup, "Yates," 235–51; *ISR*, 3, 11 Feb., 4 Mar. 1862; *Journal of the Constitutional Convention of the State of Illinois, January 7, 1862*, 10, 50–58, 114, 132–34, 156–67, 207–9, 268–69, 937–38; *ChiTri*, 11 Feb., 20 Mar. 1862; Martin Campbell to Yates, 4 Feb., Thomas McGrath to Yates, 21 Apr. 1862, Yates Papers, ALPL; Lusk, *Politics and Politicians*, 142–44; Wilson, *Business of the Civil War*, 22; *ChiTri*, 13 Feb., 14 Mar. 1862; Basler, *CW*, 5:172; *OR*, series 3, 1:919–20; Richard F. Adams to Yates, 6 Feb., Francis A. Hoffman to Yates, 6 Feb., Yates to McClernand, 26 Mar., Yates to Rupel Ward, 24 Mar., E. A. Paine to Yates, 26 Feb., and E. A. Carr to Yates, 18 Mar. 1862, Yates Papers, ALPL.

76. Yates to Trumbull, 25 Jan., 14 Feb. 1862, Trumbull Papers, LC; Nortrup, "The Prorogued Legislature," 16–17; E. A. Paine to Yates, 26 Feb., Martin [Campbell] to Yates, 4 Feb., Richard Adams to Yates, 6 Feb., E. Y. Bridges to Yates, 24 Feb., Col. E. A. Carr to Yates, 18 Mar. 1862, Yates Papers, ALPL.

77. Nortrup, "The Prorogued Legislature," 17, cites B. F. Ford to Yates, 15 Aug. 1862, Yates Papers, ALPL.

78. Trumbull to Yates, 6 Feb. 1862, Reavis Papers, CHM; also cited in Burlingame, *Lincoln*, 2:285–86.

79. *OR*, series 3, 1:923, 935–48; Andrew to Lincoln, 13 Feb. 1862, LP, LC; Basler, *CW*, 6:93; Burlingame, *Stoddard*, 63–64; Rawley, *Morgan*, 169; Brig. Gen. A. L. Pleasanton to Curtin, 18 Feb. 1862, Charles Olden to Curtin, 5 Mar. 1862, Executive Correspondence, PSA; "Resolutions Relative to the Defenses of the Delaware River and Bay," 27 Feb., Brig. Gen. John Newton to Olden, 18 Feb., P. H. Watson, Assistant Secretary of War to Olden, 31 Mar. 1862, Olden Family Papers, HSP; *NDM*, 18 Mar. 1862; *TDSGR*, 19 Mar. 1862; Washburn to Stanton, 11 Mar., Washburn to Fessenden, 2 Jan., Washburn to Gen. Ripley, 11, 13 Jan., Washburn to Seward, 13 Jan. 1862, Executive Correspondence, MeSA, relative to Maine's defenses; Washburn to Fessenden, 11 Jan. 1862, Fessenden Papers, WRHS; Miller, *States at War*, 4:111.

80. Thornbrough, *Indiana*, 170–75; *InDJ*, 22 Mar. 1862; *OR*, series 3, 1:953; Hamilton, *Reminiscences*, 516.

81. *OR*, series 3, 2:2–3; Perret, *Lincoln's War*, 287; Thomas and Hyman, *Stanton*, 200–202; *PDJ*, 22, 23 Jul. 1862; Burlingame, *Stoddard*, 63–66; Tod to Stanton, 13 Feb., Tod to Chase, 13 Feb. 1862, Telegraphic Dispatches, series 144, OhSA; Marvel, *Lincoln's Autocrat*, 178–80.

82. Stanton to Charles Dana, 24 Jan., 1 Feb. 1862, Dana Papers, LC; *OR*, series 3, 2:2–3; Nevins, *War Becomes Revolution*, 63–64; Thomas and Hyman, *Stanton*, 201–2; Scott to Stanton, 6 Mar. 1862, Stanton Papers, LC; Shannon, *Organization of the Union Army*, 1:265–66; Perret, *Lincoln's War*, 201.

83. *OR*, series 3, 2:29; Thomas and Hyman, *Stanton*, 201–2; Shannon, *Organization of the Union Army*, 1:259–92; Nevins, *War Becomes Revolution*, 63–64; *PDJ*, 5 Apr., 23 Jul. 1862; *DFP*, 6 Mar. 1862; *TDSGR*, 26 Jul. 1862; Scott to Stanton, Feb and March 1862, correspondence, Stanton Papers, LC; Marvel, *Lincoln's Autocrat*, 179–82.

84. Burlingame, *Stoddard*, 59; *PDJ*, 5 Apr., 23 Jul. 1862; *TDSGR*, 26 Jul. 1862.

85. *NDM*, 14 Mar. 1862; Jackson, *New Jerseyans in the Civil War*, 50; *TDSGR*, 15 Mar. 1862; *Message of Buckingham, May 7, 1862*; *HEP*, 17 Jan. 1862; Reverend [Toule] to Buckingham, 2 Jan., H. L. Heall to Buckingham, 4 Jan., Reverend Woodruff to Buckingham, 9 Jan. 1862, Governor's Correspondence, CtSA.

86. Shannon, *Organization of the Union Army*, 1:262–92; Clark, *Kirkwood*, 220; Niven, *Connecticut for the Union*, 72–73; Rawley, *Morgan*, 172; Lincoln, *Messages*, 393–408; *OR*, series 3, 2:28, 29, 109; Hesseltine, *Lincoln and the War Governors*, 240; *Message of Buckingham, May 7, 1862*; *HEP*, 17 Jan. 1862; *BDHE*, 14 Mar. 1862.

87. As quoted in Renda, "New Hampshire State Politics," 29–40; *WDNI*, 10, 15 Mar. 1861; Renda, *Running on the Record*, 104–9; *A Memorial. Nathaniel Springer of Bristol, New Hampshire*, 7–43; *NHPSG*, 5 Sept., 9, 30 Oct., 13, 27 Nov., 4 Dec. 1861, 19 Feb. 1862; *NHS*, 8, 19 Feb., 1, 8, 13, 15 Mar. 1862; *DFP*, 20 Mar. 1862; *NDM*, 21 Mar. 1862; White, *The Civil War Diary of Wyman S. White*, 37–38, 70, 134–35.

88. Berry to George G. Fogg, 28 Feb. 1862, George Fogg Papers, NHHS.

Chapter Eight

1. Burlingame, *Stoddard*, 67–68; Basler, *CW*, 5:175–79; Beale, *Diary of Bates*, 244–46; Burlingame, *Lincoln*, 2:304–5; Sears, *To the Gates of Richmond*, 32–33; *OR*, series 1, 12:7; Sears, *Papers of McClellan*, 220–21; Gallagher, *The Richmond Campaign of 1862*.

2. Weeden, *War Government*, 175; *DR*, 23 Jan., 6, 13, 20 Feb., 6, 10 Mar., 9 Jun. 1862; *InDJ*, 22 Mar., 4, 14 Apr. 1862; *BS*, 29 Apr., 21 May 1862; James H. Bayard to Thomas F. Bayard, 26 Mar. 1862, Thomas Bayard Papers, LC; Siddali, *Missouri's War*, 190–93; Gienapp, "Abraham Lincoln and Border States," 13–46; Masur, *An Example for All the Land: Emancipation and the Struggle for Equality in Washington, D.C.*, 17–30; Williams, *Slavery and Freedom in Delaware*, 170–76. Lincoln to Curtin, Curtin to Lincoln, 3 Apr., Hicks to Lincoln, 18 Mar. 1862, LP, LC; Cowden, "*Heaven Will Frown*," 67–93; Wagandt, *Mighty Revolution*, 116–19; W. W. Caulley to Fessenden, 5 Jul. 1862, Fessenden Papers, WRHS; Bradford to Washburn, 30 May 1862, Governor's Letter Books, MdSA; Bradford to Ramsey, 20 May 1862, Governor's Papers, MnHS; Bradford to Buckingham, 20 May 1862, Governor's Correspondence, CtSA; Clark, "Politics in Maryland," 40:299–304; Bradford to Bowie, 19 May 1862, Executive Letter Books, 293, MdSA; Bradford's Journal, 14, 15, 16, 17 May 1862, MdHS; Hicks to Lincoln, 18 Mar. 1862, LP, LC.

3. *HEP*, 4, 5, 8 Apr. 1862; *NDM*, 8 Apr. 1861; *TDSGR*, 7 Apr. 1862; *ChiTri*, 12 Apr. 1862; *BS*, 14 Apr. 1862; *IDSR*, 17 Apr. 1862; Buckingham to Gideon Welles, 11 Apr. 1862, Gideon Welles Papers, CtHS; *NYTi*, 8 Apr. 1862; Lane, *A Political History of Connecticut during the Civil War*, 185; Smith, *No Party Now*, 58, 90.

4. *TDSGR*, 7 Apr. 1862; Buckingham to Andrew, 15 Apr. 1862, Massachusetts Governor's Papers, Executive Department Letters, 1862, MSA; *NYTi*, 8 Apr. 1862.

5. *InDJ*, 10 Apr. 1862; *StLDMR*, 12 Apr. 1862; *LDT*, 15 Apr. 1862; Niven, *Chase Papers*, 3:167–70; Daniel, *Shiloh*, 304–17; Thornbrough, Riker, and Corpuz, *Diary of Fletcher*, 7:392–93; Andrew to Stanton, 9 Apr. 1862, Stanton Papers, LC; Engle, *Buell*, 209–39; Simpson, *Grant*, 127–35; Marszalek, *Sherman*, 174–78; Ambrose, *From Shiloh to Savannah*, 38; Cassius Fairchild to Sarah, 21 Mar. 1862, Fairchild Papers, SHSW; Smith, *Shiloh: Conquer or Perish*, 77–412.

6. *LDJ*, 16 Apr. 1862; *OR*, series 1, 8:661, 675–77, 10, pt. 2:98; Schutz and Trenerry, *Pope*, 76–84; Marszalek, *Halleck*, 121–23; Schenker, Jr., "Ulysses in His Tent: Halleck, Grant, Sherman, and the 'Turning Point of the War,'" 175–221; Alphonso Barto to Father, Sister and Friends, 5 May 1862, Alphonso Barto Papers, ALPL.

7. Alexander Varian to Mary, 18 Apr., Varian to Father, 21 Apr. 1862, Alexander Varian Papers, WRHS; Burlingame, *Stoddard*, 71–72; Perret, *Lincoln's War*, 170–73.

8. William R. Stimson to Wife and Children, 10 Apr. 1862, William R. Stimson Papers, LC.

9. Carr, *The Illini: A Story of the Prairies*, 406–8; *ISJ*, 19, 24, Apr., 15 May 1862; *ChiTri*, 16, 17, 21 Apr. 1862; James M. Sligh to Wife, 19 Apr. 1862, Sligh Family Papers, BHL; Allen to Trumbull, 25 Apr. 1862, Trumbull Papers, LC; Krenkel, *Yates*, 159–70, 179; Eddy, *Patriotism of Illinois*, 1:253; Allen C. Fuller to Yates, 11 Apr. 1862, Yates Papers, ALPL; Daniel, *Shiloh*, 76, 299; Newberry, *The U. S. Sanitary Commission in the Valley of Mississippi during the War of the Rebellion, 1861–1866*, 33–43; Karamanski, *Rally 'Round the Flag*, 97–98; Frank and Reaves, "*Seeing the Elephant*," 154, 160–61; Kiper, *McClernand*, 115; Nortrup, "Yates," 319–21; *ISJ*, 10, 11, 19, 24, 28 Apr., 15 May 1862; Kimball, "Yates," 44–46; *IDSR*, 17 Apr. 1862; Jordan and Thomas, "Reminiscences of an Ohio Volunteer," 309.

10. Carr, *The Illini*, 409; Kimball, "Yates," 44–46; *ISJ*, 24 Apr., 15, 16, 22 May 1862; Nortrup, "Yates," 319; Martin Cassell to Yates, 4 Feb., George W. Stipps to Yates, 15 Jan. 1862, Yates Papers, and Yates to McClernand, 26 Mar. 1862, John McClernand Papers, ALPL; Kiper, *McClernand*, 115; Hicken, *Illinois*, 84; *ISJ*, 28 May, 2 Jun. 1862; *ChiTri*, 15, 17 May 1862.

11. Foulke, *Morton*, 1:162–67; Thornbrough, Riker, and Corpuz, *Diary of Fletcher*, 7:394, 399–400, 408; on the "divine service" see Nation and Towne, *Indiana's War*, 70–71; James M. Sligh to Wife, 19 Apr. 1862, Sligh Family Papers, BHL; James C. Vanderbilt to Mother, 16 Apr. 1862, James C. Vanderbilt Papers, ISL; *OR*, series 3, 2:24; *InDJ*, 10, 11 Apr., 10, 12, 13 May 1862; *StPDPi*, 16 Apr. 1862; Timothy Day to Tod, 21 Apr. 1862, "private," Stanton Papers, LC; Lewis, *Sherman: Fighting Prophet*, 234; Tod to Stanton, 10 Apr., Timothy Day to Stanton, 21 Apr. 1862, Stanton Papers, LC; Abbott, *Ohio's War Governors*, 21–23; Daniel, *Shiloh*, 305; Trester, "Tod," 130–32; Porter, *Ohio Politics*, 92–100.

12. *WSJ*, 19, 24 Apr., 19 May 1862, 29 May 1921; Quiner, *Wisconsin*, 117–18, 211–13; Thwaites, *Messages*, 118–21; *StLDMR*, 14 Apr. 1862.

13. Quiner, *Wisconsin*, 119–26, 166–67; Thwaites, *Messages*, 114–15; *WSJ*, 5 May, 6 Jun. 1862; *DFP*, 24 May 1862; Current, *History of Wisconsin*, 310–11; *WDNI*, 22 Apr. 1862; *ChiTri*, 22 Apr., 8 May 1862; *PhiIn*, 22 Apr. 1862; *DFP*, 7, 24 May 1862; Quiner Scrapbook, 4:72.

14. Basler, *CW*, 5:186–87; Butler and Yates to Lincoln, 9, 18 Apr. 1862, LP, LC.

15. Basler, *CW*, 5:186–87; Lincoln to Yates, 10 Apr. 1862, LP, LC.

16. Davis to Brother, 21 Apr. 1862, Davis Papers, Civil War Times Illustrated Collection, USAMHI; Engle, *Struggle for the Heartland*, 150–80; Eicher, *Longest Night*, 237–42; Hearn, *The Capture of New Orleans*, 1862.

17. Scott to Stanton, 22 Apr. 1862, Stanton Papers, LC; Marszalek, *Halleck*, 122–23; Sears, *Papers of McClellan*, 232, 252; Palmer, *Letters of Sumner*, 2:109–10; Simpson, *Grant*, 135–41.

18. Lucius Fairchild to Father, 24 Apr. 1862, Fairchild Papers, SHSW.

19. Washburn to Fessenden, 21 Apr. 1862, Fessenden Papers, WRHS; Donald, *Lincoln*, 350–63; Basler, *CW*, 5:222–24; Eicher, *Longest Night*, 233–34; Harris, *Lincoln and the Border States*, 174–75.

20. McClure to Slifer, 25 May 1862, "private," Slifer-Dill Papers, DCL; McClellan, *McClellan's Own Story*, 345–46; Burlingame, *With Lincoln in the White House*, 78–79; Thomas and Hyman, *Stanton*, 195; Eicher, *Longest Night*, 241–42, 259–73; *TDSGR*, 28 May 1862; Robertson, *Stonewall Jackson*, 400–415; Basler, *CW*, 5:203, 210; Halleck to Stanton, 6, 7 May, Scott to Stanton, 6, 10 May 1862, Stanton Papers, LC; Burlingame, *Lincoln*, 2:310–15; Taylor, *Orlando M. Poe*, 69; Poe to Austin Blair, 7 May 1862, Second Regimental Service Records, 1861–1865, MiSA; Dubbs, *Defend This Old Town*, 77, 83, 132–38, 147, 153; *TDSGR*, 4 Apr. 1862; *DFP*, 4 Apr., 31 May 1862; Washburn to Fessenden, 9 May 1862, Fessenden Papers, WRHS.

21. *OR*, series 3, 2:44, 70; *WDNI*, 27, 28 May 1862; *TDSGR*, 17, 28 May 1862; *PhiIn*, 17 May, 3 Jun. 1862; Stanton to Sprague, 25, 28 May 1862, Executive Letters Received, RISA; Charles Sedgwick to Dora, 27 May 1862, Sedgwick Papers, SUL; Thomas and Hyman, *Stanton*, 196; Burlingame, *Lincoln*, 2:316–17; *HDT*, 31 May 1862; *DFP*, 3 Jun. 1862; Marvel, *Lincoln's Autocrat*, 196–99.

22. *OR*, series 3, 2:44, 72; Pearson, *Andrew*, 2:12–13; Hamrogue, "Andrew," 147–48; Andrew to Stanton, 23 May 1862, Stanton Papers, LC; *WDNI*, 26, 27, 28 May, 16, 21 Jul., 2 Aug. 1862; *BDA*, 25, 26, 27, 30, 31 May 1862; *BDFP*, 27, 30 May 1862; *BS*, 27 May 1862; *DFP*, 28 May 1862; Niven, *Connecticut for the Union*, 77.

23. *OR*, series 3, 2:45, 68–70, 85–114; Thomas and Hyman, *Stanton*, 200; Hooper to Andrew, 28 May, Horace Binney Sargent to Andrew, 13 Apr., Seward to Andrew, 23 May 1862, Andrew Papers, MHS; Pearson, *Andrew*, 2:17–22; Schouler, *Massachusetts in the Civil War*, 1:333; *OR*, series 3, 2:45; Paludan, *Presidency of Lincoln*, 130–31; *BDFP*, 30 May 1862; Hamrogue, "Andrew," 147–48; *BDA*, 30 May, 4 Jun. 1862; *PDJ*, 26 May 1862; *PhiIn*, 27 May 1862; *BS*, 27 May 1862.

24. Wightman to Lincoln, 23 May 1862, LP, LC; Weeden, *War Government*, 168, 326; Schouler, *Massachusetts in the Civil War*, 1:333; Hamrogue, "Andrew," 147–48; *WDNI*, 27, 28 May 1862; *BDFP*, 27, 30, 31 May 1862; G. Thorne to Andrew, 26 May, O. W. Albee to Andrew, 24 May, N. H. Whiting to Andrew, 15 Jun. 1862, Andrew Papers, MHS.

25. Collier and Collier, *Yours for the Union*, 104, 111.

26. Washburn to Andrew, 24 May 1862, Andrew Papers, MHS; Washburn to Hamlin, 23 May 1862, Washburn Papers, LC.

27. Washburn to Hamlin, 23 May 1862, Washburn Papers, LC; Whalon, "Maine Republicans," 106–7.

28. Pearson, *Andrew*, 2:14–22; *OR*, series 3, 2:44–45; Hamrogue, "Andrew," 147–48; *WDNI*, 26, 27, 28 May 1862; *PDJ*, 26 May 1862; Hunt, *Washburn*, 104–5; Elihu B. Washburn to Bro [Israel], 26 Apr. 1862, Washburn Papers, LC.

29. *OR*, series 3, 2:45–46; Ambler, *Pierpont*, 177–78; Senator Waitman T. Willey presented a petition requesting separate statehood for West Virginia 29 May 1862. Whaley, Willey, and Brown to Pierpont, 2 May 1862, LP, LC; James A. [Jarbon] to Pierpont, 18 Jun., S. Ferguson Beach to Pierpont, 13 May, D. R. King to Pierpont, 29 May, and William Kennady to Pierpont, 14 Apr. 1862, Pierpont-Samuels Papers, WvDCH; Langford, "Constitutional Issues," 14–29; Moore, "Slavery as a Factor," 68–89; Curry, "Ideology and Perception: Democratic and Republican Attitudes on Civil War Politics and the Statehood Movement in West Virginia," 135–54; Shaffer, "Lincoln and West Virginia," 86–100; Pierpont to Lincoln, 20 May 1862, Governor's Executive Letter books, VSAL; *StLDMR*, 30 May 1862; *NDM*, 30 Apr., 27 May, 2 Jun. 1862; *PhiIn*, 23 Apr. 1862; *OR*, series 3, 2:62; Preston King to Morgan, 17 Jan., 15 Apr. 1862, Morgan Papers, NYSL.

30. Hancock, "Diaries of Ferris," 237; Hancock, "Political History of Delaware, Part III," 7:359; Scharf, *Delaware*, 1:367–72; *PDJ*, 8, 9 Jul. 1862; *BDFP*, 4 Apr. 1862; *OR*, series 3, 2:47, 6–62, 80–81; Wickman, *We Are Coming Father Abra'am*, 21–23; Ward, *Army Life in Virginia*, 1–3, 16–17; *BDFP*, 4 Apr. 1862; *PhiIn*, 23 Apr. 1862; Moore, "Holbrook," 65–78; *StPDPi*, 16 Apr. 1862; *ISJ*, 6 Jun. 1862; *Journal of the Senate and the House of New Hampshire*, June Session, 1863, 21–30; *NHS*, 12 Apr., 2, 7 Jun., 19 Jul. 1862; *NHPSG*, 19 Apr., 7 May 1862.

31. *OR*, series 3, 2:60–83; Thomas and Hyman, *Stanton*, 196–97; Basler, *CW*, 5:230–34; Burlingame, *Lincoln*, 2:315–19.

32. *HDT*, 31 May 1862; *OR*, series 3, 2:45–47, 75–87; *BDFP*, 26 May 1862; *StLDMR*, 31 May 1862; *PDJ*, 26 May 1862; Eicher, *Longest Night*, 256–67; Thomas and Hyman, *Stanton*, 196–97; Williams, *Lincoln Finds a General*, 1:206–7.

33. Basler, *CW*, 5:234–36.

34. Morton to Lincoln, 22 May 1862, LP, LC; Basler, *CW*, 5:231; Nortrup, "Yates," 323; Kiper, *McClernand*, 119; *OR*, series 3, 2:43–45; Woodford, *Father Abraham's Children*, 55–56; *ISJ*, 23, 27 May, 12 Jun. 1862; James M. Sligh to Mother, 23 May 1862, Sligh Family Papers, BHL; *StLDMR*, 20 May 1862; *BDHE*, 22 May 1862; *IDSR*, 25 May 1862; Montagne Ferry to Jeanette, 25, 31 May 1862, Ferry Papers, BHL; Henry R. Strong Diary, May–June, 1862, IHS; *ChiTri*, 15, 17 May 1862.

35. James C. Vanderbilt to Mother, 22 May 1862, Vanderbilt Papers, ISL.
36. *OR*, series 1, 10, pt. 1:344–47; Simpson and Berlin, *Sherman's Civil War*, 224–25; Tredway, *Democratic Opposition to the Lincoln Administration in Indiana*, 43; Burrage, *Brown University in the Civil War, a Memoriam*, 109–15; Kamphoefner and Helbich, *Germans in the Civil War*, 254; Foulke, *Morton*, 1:165–67; *InDJ*, 4 Jun. 1862.
37. Basler, *CW*, 5:231; Perret, *Lincoln's War*, 186–87.
38. Hancock, "Diaries of Ferris," 237–38; *OR*, series 3, 2:85; *OR*, series 3, 2:85; Basler, *CW*, 5:239; Eicher, *Longest Night*, 259–67; Morgan to Lincoln, 3 Mar. 1862, LP, LC.
39. *PDJ*, 27 May 1862.
40. Pearson, *Andrew*, 2:17–22; *OR*, series 3, 2:85–86, 93–94; Thomas and Hyman, *Stanton*, 199–200; Hooper to Andrew, 28 May 1862, Andrew Papers, MHS; *PhiIn*, 27 May 1862.
41. *OR*, series 3, 2:93–94.
42. Sumner to Andrew, 28 May 1862, "private," Gurowski to Andrew, 29, 30 May 1862, Andrew Papers, MHS; Palmer, *Letters of Sumner*, 2:114–16; *CDE*, 31 May 1862.
43. Kirkwood to Lt. Col. Addison H. Saunders, 21 May 1862, Kirkwood Papers, IaSA; Fullbrook, "Relief Work in Iowa," 205–7; *OR*, series 3, 2:84–95, 98–99; *ISJ*, 27 May 1862; Thomas and Hyman, *Stanton*, 200.
44. *BDFP*, 24 Jun. 1862; *OR*, series 3, 2:104–5; *BDHE*, 2 Jun. 1862; *HDT*, 30 May 1862; *LDJ*, 4 Jun. 1862; Geary, *We Need Men*, 16–17; Abbott, *Cobbler in Congress*, 128–29; Mitchell, "Organizational Performance," 115–62; Millett and Maslowski, *For the Common Defense*, 199; Sumner to Andrew, 21 Jun. 1862, "private," Andrew Papers, MHS.
45. Marszalek, *Halleck*, 126; *BDFP*, 17 May 1862; *LDT*, 22 Jun. 1862; *BDFP*, 17 May 1862; *NHS*, 24 May 1862.
46. *OR*, series 3, 2:109–15, 142–43.
47. Palmer, *Letters of Sumner*, 2:118–19; OR series 3, 2:110–15, 142–49; Foulke, *Morton*, 1:166–68.
48. *OR*, series 3, 2:163; Thomas and Hyman, *Stanton*, 202–6; *ISJ*, 5 Jun. 1862; Marszalek, *Halleck*, 124–26; Engle, *Struggle for the Heartland*, 187–205.
49. *OR*, series 3, 2:163, 164–68; Niven, *Connecticut for the Union*, 77; Eicher, *Longest Night*, 260–97; Thomas and Hyman, *Stanton*, 202–3; Washburn to Col. Daniel Elliott, 6 Jun. 1862, Executive Correspondence, MeSA.
50. Niven, *Connecticut for the Union*, 71–73; *OR*, series 3, 1:978.
51. *OR*, series 3, 2:176–77; Morton to Lincoln, 25 Jun. 1862, LP, LC; Towne, *A Fierce Wild Joy*, 37–38; Nation and Towne, *Indiana's War*, 177–79; Sylvester, "Morton," 145–50.
52. Gamble to Lincoln, 19 May 1862, LP, LC; [no author] to Brother [Gamble], 1 Jun. 1862, Gamble Papers, MoHS; Boman, *Gamble*, 161–64; Rosin, "Gamble," 260–75, 285–315; Avery and Shoemaker, *Messages*, 3:418–29, 481–84; *LDT*, 2 May 1862; *StLDMR*, 1, 6, 13 May, 3, 16, 18, 23 Jun., 3, 8 Jul. 1862; *OR*, series 3, 2:171, series 1, 13:8; O. M. Hatch, Jesse Dubois, and William Butler to Lincoln, 12 Jun. 1862, Yates Papers, ALPL; *ISJ*, 13, 14 Jun. 1862; William M. McPherson to Montgomery Blair, 23 May 1862, LP, LC; Boman, *Lincoln and Citizens' Rights in Missouri*, 115–23; Schofield, *Forty-six Years in the Army*, 54–56.
53. Gamble to Lincoln, 19 May 1862, LP, LC; *OR*, series 1, 13:414, 438; Anders, "Civil Warfare in North Missouri," 264–86; *StLDMR*, 6 May, 3, 8 Jul. 1862.
54. *StLDMR*, 6 May, 16 Jun. 1862.
55. *LDT*, 8 May, 29 Jul. 1862; Robinson to Sara, 14 Apr. 1862, Robinson Papers, KSHS; Wilson, *Robinson*, 86–93; *StLDMR*, 6, 20 May, 16, 23 Jun. 1862; Castel, *Civil War Kansas*, 71–85; *ChiTri*, 25 Feb. 1862; *OR*, series 1, 8:368–70, 647–48, 661, 832–33, series 3, 2:83–84; Blunt, "General Blunt's Account of His Civil War Experience," 211–65.

56. Wilson, *Robinson*, 86–96; Robinson to Sara, 27, 29 April, 4, 5, 8 May 1862, Robinson Papers, KSHS; Castel, *Civil War Kansas*, 80–85; *OR*, series 1, 8:368–70, 661, 647–48, 832–33, series 3, 2:169–70; *Proceedings in the Cases of the Impeachment of Charles Robinson, Governor, John W. Robinson, Secretary of State, and George S. Hillyer, Auditor of the State of Kansas, Lawrence, Kansas State Journal, 1862*; John J. Ingalls to his Father, 23 Feb. 1862, John J. Ingalls Papers, KSHS; *LDT*, 29, 31 Jul. 1862.

57. *OR*, series 3, 2:171; Thomas and Hyman, *Stanton*, 200–201; Mitchell, "Organizational Performance," 115–62; Parish, *The North and the Nation*, 149–57.

58. F. J. Baum & Co. to Gibbs, 24 April, S. F. Chadwick to Gibbs, 25 Mar. 1862, James Wilson to Gibbs, 16 Apr. 1862, [?] Rogers to Gibbs, 1 Aug. 1860, Addison Crandall Gibbs Papers, OrHS; Edwards, "Six Oregon Leaders," 19–22; Dell, *War Democrats*, 168–69; *WDNI*, 26 Jun. 1862; *OS*, 21 Apr., 5 May 1862; Journal of Whiteaker, 13, UOL; *SR*, 27 Sept. 1862.

59. Edwards, "Six Oregon Leaders," 19–22; Clark, *Pharisee among Philistines: The Diary of Judge Matthew P. Deady, 1871–1892*, 1:xxi; Dell, *War Democrats*, 168–69; *OS*, 16 May 1864.

60. Sears, *Papers of McClellan*, 319, 322–23; Sears, *To the Gates of Richmond*, 347–56; Engle, *Buell*, 240–85; Marszalek, *Halleck*, 126–27; Sears, *McClellan: The Young Napoleon*, 205–20; *OR*, series 1, 11:264–65; Basler, *CW*, 5:286–87.

61. Pierpont to Lincoln, 20 Jun. 1862, LP, LC; Shannon, *Organization of the Union Army*, 1:269.

62. Seward, *Seward at Washington*, 3:100–103; Weeden, *War Government*, 212–13; Taylor, *Seward*, 201; Shannon, *Organization of the Union Army*, 1:269–74; Perret, *Lincoln's War*, 178–79; Stahr, *Seward*, 332–34; Hesseltine, *Lincoln and the War Governors*, 198–203; Pierpont to Lincoln, 20 Jun. 1862, LP, LC; Nicolay and Hay, *Lincoln*, 6:125, 462.

63. *HDT*, 24 Jun. 1862; *ISJ*, 25 Mar. 1862; *DFP*, 31 May 1862.

64. *TDSGR*, 20 Jun. 1862; Nicolay and Hay, *Lincoln*, 6:115–17; Williams, *Lincoln Finds a General*, 1:243–47; Crockett, *Vermont*, 3:542–43; Moore, "Holbrook," 65–78; Basler, *CW*, 5:291.

65. Basler, *CW*, 5:291–92; Shannon, *Organization of the Union Army*, 1:270–72; Hesseltine, *Lincoln and the War Governors*, 198–201; Marvel, *Lincoln's Autocrat*, 211–14.

66. Basler, *CW*, 5:291–92.

67. Sumner to Andrew, 21 Jun. 1862, "private," Andrew Papers, MHS.

68. Ibid.

69. *HEP*, 16 Jun. 1862.

70. Shoemaker, *The Last of the War Governors*, 40–41, 59; Staudenraus, *Mr. Lincoln's Washington*, 175; Weeden, *War Government*, 212; Curtin to Stanton, 19 Jun. 1862, Executive Correspondence, PSA; Seward, *Seward at Washington*, 3:100–103; Shannon, *Organization of the Union Army*, 1:270–72; Sheldon, "Measures for a 'Speedy Conclusion': A Reexamination of Conscription and Civil War Federalism," 478–79; Hesseltine, *Lincoln and the War Governors*, 197–201; *NDM*, 30 Jun., 1 Jul. 1862; Albright, "Curtin," 48:168–70, 48:20–21; Egle, *Curtin*, 304–10; Kate Curtin to Slifer, n.d., 1862, Slifer-Dill Papers, DCL; Nicolay and Hay, *Lincoln*, 6:115–23; Stahr, *Seward*, 332–34.

71. Pearson, *Andrew*, 2:28–29; Morgan to Andrew, 30 Jun. 1862, Massachusetts Governors Papers, Executive Department Letters, 1862, MSA; Rawley, *Morgan*, 175; *NYTi*, 4 Jul., 4 Aug. 1862; Hesseltine, *Lincoln and the War Governors*, 197–201; Hamrogue, "Andrew," 150–51; Harris, "Blair," 134; Albright, "Curtin," 48:20–21; Egle, *Curtin*, 305–10; Shoemaker, *The Last of the War Governors*, 40–41; Stahr, *Seward*, 332–34.

72. Pearson, *Andrew*, 2:30; Weeden, *War Government*, 326–27; Egle, *Curtin*, 309; Albright, "Curtin," 48:20–21; Shoemaker, *The Last of the War Governors*, 20–23; Andrew to Seward, 1 Jul., Andrew to Stanton, 2 Jul., Albert G. Browne to Charles Amory, 3 Jul., Browne to Andrew, 3 Jul., Andrew to Lincoln, 3 Jul. 1862, Massachusetts Governors, Letters Official, 1862, MSA.

73. *OR*, series 3, 2:180–81; 206–7; McClure, *Lincoln and Men of War-Times*, 270–71; Basler, *CW*, 5:291–303; Thomas and Hyman, *Stanton*, 206–7; Hesseltine, *Lincoln and the War Governors*, 198–200; Nicolay and Hay, *Lincoln*, 6:117–20; Seward, *Seward at Washington*, 100–112; Paludan, *Presidency of Lincoln*, 142; Shannon, *Organization of the Union Army*, 1:270–73; Shoemaker, *The Last of the War Governors*, 20–23; Williams, *Lincoln Finds a General*, 1:243–46; Stahr, *Seward*, 332–34.

74. *OR*, series 3, 2:186–87, 205; *BDHE*, 11, 14 Jul. 1862; *NYTi*, 9 Jul. 1862; *PhiBu*, 5 Jul. 1862; Albright, "Curtin," 48:20–21; Seward to Lincoln, 1 Jul. 1862, Seward Papers, UR; *WES*, 2 Jul. 1862; *BDA*, 2, 3 Jul. 1862; William [Howe] to Andrew, 2 Jul. 1862, "confidential," Andrew Papers, MHS; Burlingame, *Lincoln*, 2:324–26; Seward to Lincoln, 1 Jul. 1862, Seward Papers, UR; *Annual Report of the Adjutant General of the State of New York, 1862*, 9–11; Stahr, *Seward*, 332–34; Miller, *States at War*, 4:115–18.

75. Paludan, *Presidency of Lincoln*, 142; *OR*, series 3, 2:180–87; *HDT*, 6 Jul. 1862; Hesseltine, *Lincoln and the War Governors*, 198–200; Rawley, *Morgan*, 174–75; *BDFP*, 2, 3 Jul. 1862; *WES*, 2 Jul. 1862; *WDNI*, 2 Jul. 1862; *BDA*, 2, 3 Jul. 1862; *BS*, 2 Jul. 1862; *NHPSG*, 9 Jul. 1862; Tod to Stanton, 1 Jul. 1862, "private," Telegraphic Dispatches, series 144, OhSA; Burlingame, *Lincoln*, 2:324–26; *PhiIn*, 2 Jul. 1862.

76. Seward, *Seward at Washington*, 110; Harris, "Blair," 134–35; *OR*, series 3, 2:198–205; Weeden, *War Government*, 212–13; Tod to Stanton, 1 Jul. 1862, "private," Telegraphic Dispatches, series 144, OhSA; *LDJ*, 9 Jul. 1862; *ChiTri*, 9 Jul. 1862; *NYTi*, 2, 4 Jul. 1862.

77. Pearson, *Andrew*, 2:34–35; Hamrogue, "Andrew," 150–51; Andrew to Francis P. Blair, Sr., 5 Jul., William [Howe] to Andrew, 2 Jul. 1862, "confidential," Frank Howe to Andrew, 3 Jul. 1862, Andrew Papers and Letter Books, MHS; Hesseltine and Wolf, "New England Governors vs. Lincoln: The Providence Conference,"105–13; Hesseltine and Wolf, "The Altoona Conference and the Emancipation Proclamation," 195–205; McClure, *Lincoln and Men of War-Times*, 270; Albright, "Curtin," 48:20–21; *HDT*, 2 Jul. 1862.

78. Hamrogue, "Andrew," 151; Andrew to Blair, 5 Jul. 1862, Andrew Letter Books, MHS; *HDT*, 2 Jul. 1862; *NYTi*, 2, 4 Jul. 1862.

79. Gurowski, *Diary*, 1:234; Gurowski to Andrew, 30 May, Sumner to Andrew 5, 21 Jun. 1862, Andrew Papers, MHS; Gurowski to Andrew, 10 Sept., 24 Oct. 1861, 8 Jan., 21 Apr., 7, 29, 30 May, 20 Jun. 1862, and Andrew to Gurowski, 9 Feb., 18 Apr., 30 Aug. 1862, Andrew Letter Books, MHS; Hamrogue, "Andrew," 152; Pearson, *Andrew*, 2:25; Fischer, *Lincoln's Gadfly: Adam Gurowski*, 89.

80. *OR*, series 3, 2:199–201; Basler, *CW*, 5:296–97; Hesseltine, *Lincoln and the War Governors*, 198–99; White, *Emancipation, the Union Army, and the Reelection of Lincoln*, 168.

81. *OR*, series 3, 2:199–201; Basler, *CW*, 5:304; Hesseltine, *Lincoln and the War Governors*, 200–202; Marvel, *Lincoln's Autocrat*, 212–13.

82. *OR*, series 1, 11:71; Buckingham, *Life of Buckingham*, 247; Thomas and Hyman, *Stanton*, 200–210; Kirkwood to Lincoln, 8 Jul. 1862, LP, LC; Clark, *Kirkwood*, 230–31; Lathrop, *Kirkwood*, 215–16; *OR*, series 3, 2:198; Fullbrook, "Relief Work in Iowa," 210–11; Briggs, "Enlistment of Iowa Troops," 348–55; *BDHE*, 11, 14 Jul. 1862; *IDSR*, 13 Jul. 1862.

83. *HEP*, 17 Jun., 5 Jul. 1862; Buckingham, *Life of Buckingham*, 249; Niven, *Connecticut for the Union*, 78; *BDFP*, 3 Jul. 1862. *PDJ*, 8 Jul. 1862, reprint of Bradford's address; *HEP*, 5 Jul. 1862; Buckingham, *Life of Buckingham*, 249.

84. Buckingham, *Life of Buckingham*, 300–301; Niven, *Connecticut for the Union*, 72–73, 77–78; *HEP*, 18, 27, 28 Mar. 1862.

85. Buckingham, *Life of Buckingham*, 301, 305–6; *HEP*, 4, 5 Apr. 1862.

Chapter Nine

1. Basler, *CW*, 5:298; Thomas and Hyman, *Stanton*, 206–7; Donald, *Lincoln*, 354–65.

2. [JDA] to Andrew, 3 Jul. 1862, Andrew Papers, MHS; *ChiTri*, 10 Jul. 1862; Burlingame, *With Lincoln in the White House*, 83; Murdock, *Patriotism Limited*, 5–15.

3. Charles Gibson to Gamble, 2 Jul. 1862, "private and confidential," Gamble Papers, MoHS; Kiper, *McClernand*, 124–27.

4. Gurowski to Andrew, 3, 4 Jul. 1862, "private," and [Henry] Ingersoll to Andrew, 7 Jul. 1862, Andrew Papers, MHS.

5. Gurowski to Andrew, 3, 4 Jul. 1862, "private and confidential," Andrew Papers, MHS.

6. Olden to Lincoln, 14 Aug. 1862, LP, LC; *OR*, series 3, 2:202–3, 229; Jackson, *New Jerseymen*, 70; *PhiIn*, 11 Jul. 1862; *NDM*, 14 Jul. 1862.

7. Sprague to Lincoln, 5, 6 Jul., Halleck to Lincoln, 10 Jul. 1862, LP, LC; Marszalek, *Halleck*, 127–28; *OR*, series 1, 16, pt. 2:95, series 1, 17, pt. 2:76, 88; Basler, *CW*, 5:308; Spicer, *History of the Ninth and Tenth*, 284–85.

8. Sprague to Lincoln, 5 Jul. 1862, LP, LC; *StLDMR*, 17 Jul. 1862; Gurowski, *Diary*, 1:235; Thomas and Hyman, *Stanton*, 206–12; Gurowski to Andrew, 12 Jul. 1862, Andrew Papers, MHS.

9. *OR*, series 1, 16, pt. 2:95; Basler, *CW*, 5:305.

10. William Caldwell to Father, 15 Jul. 1862, William Caldwell Papers, BHL; Dennison to Lincoln, 7 Jul. 1862, LP, LC.

11. Niven, *Connecticut for the Union*, 78–79; Croffut and Morris, *Connecticut during the War*, 224–27; *HDT*, 19 Jul. 1862; *HEP*, 24 Jul. 1862; *OR*, series 2, 4:307, series 3, 2:211, series 2, 4:295, 594, 586, 620, 638–39, 749; Gordon, *A Broken Regiment*, 20–23; Weeden, *War Government*, 214; Buckingham to Lincoln, 3 Jul. 1862, LP, LC; McClellan to Morgan, 15 Jul. 1862, Morgan Papers, NYSL; McClellan to Ramsey, 15 Jul. 1862, Governor's Papers, MnHS; Sanders, *While in the Hands of the Enemy*, 141–43; *IDSR*, 13 Jul. 1862; *EDA*, 1 Aug. 1862; Morton to Schyler Colfax, 10 Jul. 1862, Morton Letter Books, ISA.

12. Washburn to Fessenden, 9 Jul. 1862, Fessenden Papers, WRHS; Seward to Washburn, 9 Jul. 1862, Washburn Papers, LC.

13. Washburn to Seward, 2 Jul. 1862, Stanton Papers, LC.

14. *NDM*, 7 Jul. 1862; Nicolay to Chase, 9 Jul. 1862, Chase Papers, LC; Curtin to Nicolay, 10 Jul. 1862, LP, LC; Engle, *Buell*, 257–85; Grimsley, *Hard Hand of War*, 79–100.

15. *OR*, series 3, 2:212–13; Morton, et al. to Lincoln, 10 Jul. 1862, LP, LC.

16. *OR*, series 3, 2:223; Morgan to Lincoln, 14 Jul. 1862, LP, LC.

17. Krenkel, *Yates*, 161–75; Edward Prince to Yates, 7 Apr. 1862, Yates Papers, ALPL; Nortrup, "Yates: A Personal Glimpse," 121–29; *ISJ*, 10 Jul. 1862; William K. Strong to Yates, 10 Jul. 1862, Yates Papers, ALPL.

18. Yates to Lincoln, 11 Jul. 1862, Yates Papers, ALPL; Krenkel, *Yates*, 174–75; Yates to Lincoln, 11 Jul. 1862, LP, LC; *OR*, series 3, 2:218–19; Kimball, "Yates," 24–25; *ISJ*, 12 Jul.

1862; *ChiTri*, 12 Jul. 1862; *IDSR*, 16 Jul. 1862; *WSJ*, 12 Jul. 1862; Yates to Trumbull, 11 Jul. 1862, Trumbull Papers, LC.

19. Buckingham, *Life of Buckingham*, 170; Frank, *With Ballot and Bayonet*, 177.

20. *ISJ*, 17 Jul. 1862; Nortrup, "Yates," 261; Krenkel, *Yates*, 174–79; Joseph Medill to Yates, 19 Jul. 1862, Yates Papers, ALPL; *ChiTri*, 12, 13, 14 Jul. 1862; *NYTi*, 4 Aug. 1862; Engle, *Buell*, 256–85; Keifer to Wife, Eliza, 4, 12, 14 Jul. 1862, Keifer Papers, LC; Dennison to Lincoln, 7 Jul. 1862, LP, LC; *HEP*, 18 Jul. 1862.

21. *ChiTri*, 12, 13, 14 Jul. 1862; *ISJ*, 17, 21 Jul. 1862; *StLDMR*, 13, 16 Jul. 1862; *NYTi*, 20 Jul. 1862; Levi North to Yates, 14 Jul., William K. Strong to Yates, 4 Aug. 1862, Yates Papers, ALPL.

22. As quoted in Curry, *Blueprint for Modern America*, 62; Zachariah Chandler to Wife, 5 Jul. 1862, Chandler Papers, LC; *NHPSG*, 30 Jul. 1862; Paludan, *Presidency of Lincoln*, 144; Beale, *Diary of Bates*, 260; Miller, *The Black Soldiers of Illinois*, 5–6; Reuben Rutherford to Yates, 22 Apr., Charles Boyd to Yates, 17 Jun. 1862, Yates Papers, ALPL.

23. Tod to Stanton, 11 Jul. 1862, "private," Tod to McClellan, 11 Jul. 1862, "private," Telegraphic Dispatches, series 144, OhSA; *OR*, series 3, 2:219; Basler, *CW*, 5:309–12; Donald, *Lincoln*, 358–62; Sears, *McClellan*, 232; Abbott, *Ohio's War Governors*, 26; Witt, *Lincoln's Code*, 210–12.

24. James M. Scovel to Lincoln, 23 Nov. 1863, LP, LC; Nevins, *War Becomes Revolution*, 146–47; *NYTri*, 30 Oct. 1863; *LDJ*, 17 Nov. 1863; Krenkel, *Yates*, 175; Burlingame, *Lincoln Observed*, 72.

25. Beale, *Diary of Welles*, 1:70–71; Welles to M. J. W., 13 Jul., Welles to E. T. W., 13 Jul. 1862, Welles Papers, LC; Pease and Randall, *Diary of Browning*, 1:555; Donald, *Lincoln*, 362–63; Gienapp and Gienapp, *Civil War Diary of Gideon Welles*, 3–4; Krenkel, *Yates*, 176–79; Stahr, *Seward*, 339–40.

26. *OR*, series 3, 2:221, series 1, 17, pt. 2:90; Paludan, *Presidency of Lincoln*, 135, 142–43; *ISJ*, 22 Jul. 1862; Basler, *CW*, 5:312–13; Lincoln to Stanton, 11 Jul. 1862, Stanton Papers, LC; Marszalek, *Halleck*, 128; *ChiTri*, 21 Jul. 1862; *PhiIn*, 21 Jul. 1862; Kimball, "Yates," 48–49; Soldier to Yates, 14 Jul., [T. S. Herod] to Yates, 24 Jul. 1862, Yates Papers, ALPL; *ChiTri*, 25 Aug. 1862.

27. Krenkel, *Yates*, 174–77; Kimball, "Yates," 25–26; *ISJ* 17, 23 Jul. 1862; *ChiTri*, 12 Jul., 6 Aug. 1862; Beale, *Diary of Welles*, 1:70–71; Donald, *Lincoln*, 360–63; Yates to Lincoln, 11 Jul. 1862, LP, LC.

28. Hancock, *Delaware during the War*, 108–10; Delaware General Assembly, *Journal of House of the State of Delaware*, 18 Apr., 22 Jul. 1862; *DR*, 9, 16, 23 Jan.; 6, 13, 20 Feb., 21 Jul., 4 Aug. 1862; Hancock, "Political History of Delaware, Part III," 7:362–64; Burton to Lincoln, 2 Aug. 1862, LP, LC; Clark, "Politics in Maryland," 40:305–7; Reed, "Lincoln's Compensated Emancipation Plan," 50–55; *BS*, 19 Jul. 1862; *PhiIn*, 30 Aug. 1862; John V. Harrington to James Vickers, 12 Jul. 1862, John V. Harrington Papers, DPA; Samuel Townsend to Gideon B. Waples, 21 Jul. 1862, Townsend Family Papers and Waples Family Papers, Special Collections, UDL; Bendler, "The Old Democrat Principles," 23–48; Basler, *CW*, 5:317–19; Paludan, *Presidency of Lincoln*, 133–35.

29. Robert M. Cameron to Ramsey, 22, 27 Jul. 1862, Governor's Papers, MnHS.

30. Eli Southworth to Mother, 7 Jul. 1862, Southworth Newton Family Papers, MnHS; Ramsey Diary, (Executive Journals), between 20 Jun. and 23 Aug. 1862, Stephen Miller to Ramsey, 8, 17 May, 4 Jun., Greeley to Ramsey, 22 Jul. 1862, Ramsey Papers, MnHS; Jeremiah Donahower Journal, 14 Jul. 1862, Stephen Miller to Ramsey, 23 Jul., Ramsey to Ignatius Donnelly, 28 Jun., 7, 13, 14 Jul. 1862, Governor's Papers, MnHS; Kimball, "Yates,"

46–49; Miller, *Black Soldiers of Illinois*, 5–10; *ChiTri*, 17 Jul. 1862; Haugland, "Ramsey and the Republican Party" 125–40; Guentzel, "Ramsey," 400–410; *StPDPi*, 26 Sept. 1862; *ChiTri*, 17 Jul. 1862; Henry Rice to Wife, 17 Oct. 1862, Henry Rice Papers, MnHS.

31. Sprague to Lincoln, 16 Jul. 1862, LP, LC; Browne, Andrew, 68–102.

32. Sprague to Lincoln, 29 Jul. 1862, LP, LC; Donald, *Lincoln*, 364; *PDJ*, 19, 24, 28 Jul. 1862; Marvel, *Burnside*, 102–3; Shoemaker, *The Last of the War Governors*, 15–17 Perhaps it was during this visit to Washington that Sprague and Lincoln conferred over the prospect of Lincoln asking Curtin to call a conference of the governors to ratify the Emancipation Proclamation he was contemplating issuing. Burlingame, *Lincoln*, 2:412–14; *CR*, series 3, 2:225–26; McClellan to Morgan, 15 Jul. 1862, Morgan Papers, NYSL.

33. *OR*, series 3, 2:213, 227; Wickman, *We are Coming Father Abra'am*, 75–94; *BDFR*, 9 Jul. 1862; *BDWC*, 10 Jul. 1862; Buckingham to Lincoln, 10 Jul. 1862, LP, LC; James Dixon to Lincoln, 14 Jul. 1862, LP, LC.

34. Wickman, *We are Coming Father Abra'am*, 98–103; Zeller, *The Ninth Vermont Infantry*, 19–20; *ChiTri*, 17 Jul. 1862; *BDFR*, 9, 12, 18 Jul. 1862; *HDT*, 16 Jul. 1862; *NYTi*, 17 Aug. 1862.

35. *ISJ*, 12 Jul. 1862; Thomas and Hyman, *Stanton*, 206–8; *OR*, series 3, 2:232–40; Pease and Randall, *Diary of Browning*, 1:555; Donald, *Lincoln*, 364; Beale, *Diary of Welles*, 1:70–71; Furgurson, *Freedom Rising*, 194–95.

36. Basler, *CW*, 5:328–31; Paludan, *Presidency of Lincoln*, 145–49; Murdock, *Patriotism Limited*, 5–15; Shannon, *Organization of the Union Army*, 1:276–85, 2:56–57; Donald, *Lincoln*, 364–65; Geary, *We Need Men*, 22–33; Mitchell, "Organizational Performance," 124–25; Harris, *Lincoln and the Border States*, 180–87.

37. Perret, *Lincoln's War*, 202.

38. *ChiTri*, 22 Jul., 13 Sept. 1862; *ISJ*, 19, 23 Jul. 1862; *StLDMR*, 24 Jul. 1862; *NDM*, 24 Jul. 1862; *BDWC*, 31 Jul. 1862; Kimball, "Yates," 18; Paludan, *Presidency of Lincoln*, 145–49; Klingaman, *Abraham Lincoln and the Road to Emancipation, 1861–1865*, 130–78; Hesseltine, *Lincoln and the War Governors*, 264; M. Bradley to Yates and reply, 31 Jul. 1862, Yates Papers, ALPL; *WDNI*, 19 Sept. 1861; *ISJ*, 12 Sept. 1861.

39. *HEP*, 6, 7, 9, 11 Aug. 1862; Donald, *Lincoln*, 364–65; Thomas and Hyman, *Stanton*, 207–8; Burlingame, *Lincoln*, 2:356–60.

40. William B. Britton to Messrs, Editors, 29 Jul. 1862, William B. Britton Papers, WRHS.

41. Henry Ingersoll Bowditch to Andrew, 20 Jul., Gurowski to Andrew, 24, 26 Jul., J.D. Andrews to Andrew, 11 Jul. 1861, Andrew Papers, MHS.

42. Basler, *CW*, 5:336–37; Donald, *Lincoln*, 364–65; Paludan, *Presidency of Lincoln*, 145–49; Niven, *Chase Papers*, 1:348–52; Welles to M. J. W., 30 Jul. 1862, Welles Papers, LC; Burlingame, *Lincoln*, 362–64.

43. Burlingame, *Dispatches from Lincoln's White House*, 88–89.

44. Diary of Almon Graham, 27 Jul. 1862, Almon Graham Papers, BECHS; Dennett, *Diaries of John Hay*, 45; Donald, *Lincoln*, 365–67; Thomas and Hyman, *Stanton*, 215; *HW*, 9 Aug. 1862; Marszalek, *Halleck*, 132–35.

45. Mitchell, *Maryland Voices*, 206–8; John Payne to Bradford, 11 Jul., Bradford to John Payne, 14 Jul. 1862, Governor's Papers and Executive Letter Book, MdSA; *WDNI*, 10 Sept. 1862; Bradford's Journals, 11–15 Jul. 1862, MdHS; *NDM*, 11 Jul. 1862; Gallman, *The North Fights the Civil War*, 188.

46. Mitchell, *Maryland Voices*, 210–11; Bradford to Stanton, 5 Aug., Bradford to Blair, 29 Jul. 1862, Blair Family Papers, LC.

47. John H. Bayne to Bradford, 11 Jul., and Bradford to Bayne, 14 Jul. 1862, Executive Letter book, MdSA; Clark, "Politics in Maryland," 40:304; Bradford to Lincoln, 29 Jul. 1862, LP, LC; Thomas Hicks to Montgomery Blair, 18 Sept. 1862, Blair Family Papers, LC; PhiIn, 9 Sept. 1862.

48. Bradford to Blair, 24, 27 Jul. 1862, Blair Family Papers, LC.

49. OR, series 3, 2:252, 283–85; Tod to Stanton, 19, 30 Jul., 7 Aug. 1862, Telegraphic Dispatches, series 144, OhSA; Nicolay to Peter H. Watson, Asst., 4 Oct. 1862, Letters Received by the Secretary of War, RG 107, LC; Weeden, *War Government*, 220; C. H. Spillman to James Robinson, 18 Aug., Bennet Spears to D. C. Downing, 18 Aug. 1862, Kentucky Governor's Papers and Executive Journals, (James F. Robinson Papers), KDLA; Executive Journal, 31 Aug. 1862, Kentucky Governor's Papers, KDLA; Joshua H. Bates to Yates, 7 Aug. 1862, Yates Papers, ALPL.

50. OR, series 3, 2:251, 252, 287–90; Morgan to Lincoln, 28 Jul., Olden to Lincoln 29 Jul. 1862, LP, LC; Rawley, *Morgan*, 177; *PhiIn*, 18 Jul. 1862; Stanton to Olden, 27 Aug., Joseph Smith, Acting Surgeon General for New Jersey to Olden, 31 Jul. 1862, and C. P. Buckingham to Olden, 16 Jul. 1862; Olden Family Papers, HSP; *NDM*, 19 Jul., 5 Aug. 1862; *TDSGR*, 9, 13 Aug. 1862.

51. Henry Waldron to Blair, 19 Jul., B. A. Carrier to Blair, 21 Jul. 1862, Blair Papers, DPL; OR, series 3, 2:251, 252, 283–84, 287–90; Blair to Lincoln, 29 Jul. 1862, LP, LC; Basler, *CW*, 5:347; Mitchell, "Organizational Performance," 130–35; Moore, "Days of Fife and Drum," 442–43.

52. Boman, *Gamble*, 175–77; Boman, *Lincoln and Citizens' Rights in Missouri*, 125–43; OR, series 1, 13:515, 557–58; Canan, "The Missouri Paw Paw Militia," 431–48; Rosin, "Gamble," 362–73; *ISJ*, 24 Jul. 1862; *StLDMR*, 10, 12, 13 Jul. 1862; Gamble to Chase, 17 Sept., Andrew Brownlow to Gamble, 1 Aug., Gibson to Gamble, 14 Aug. 1862, Gamble Papers, MoHS; Basler, *CW*, 5:347; *ISJ*, 24 Jul. 1862.

53. HEP, 26 Jul. 1862.

54. Basler, *CW*, 5:356–57; OR, series 3, 2:291–92; *NYTri*, 7 Aug. 1862; Catton, *Terrible Swift Sword*, 384; Morton to Lincoln, 30 Jul. 1862, LP, LC; Geary, *We Need Men*, 22–44; HEP, 14 Aug. 1862; Burlingame, *Lincoln*, 2:326–27.

55. HW, 16 Aug. 1862.

56. Barrett and Miller, "Words for the Hour," 92; *NYTi*, 9 Nov. 1915.

57. *Atlantic Monthly* 9 (February 1862):1, 10; Sizer and Cullen, eds., *The Civil War Era: An Anthology of Sources*, 321.

58. Henry Crapo to William Crapo, 18 Jul. 1862, Crapo Papers, BHL.

59. A Widow & Mother to Yates, 4 Aug. 1862, Yates Papers, ALPL.

60. Rawley, *Morgan*, 178–80; Geary, *We Need Men*, 34–39; Timothy Dwight to Buckingham, 5 Aug., Theodore Woosley to Buckingham, 5 Aug., Hr. R. Bigelow to Buckingham, 6 Aug. 1862, Eli Whitney to Buckingham, 8 Aug., A. H. Byington to Buckingham, 6 Aug., James Butler to Buckingham, 7 Aug., Francis C. Sternberg to Buckingham, 10 Aug., William Platt to Buckingham, 11 Aug., Eli Johnson to Buckingham, 11 Aug. 1862, Governor's Correspondence, CtSA; Sheldon, "A Reexamination of Conscription," 482–85.

61. BDFP, 5 Jul. 1862; OR, series 3, 2:291; Geary, *We Need Men*, 32–34; Shannon, *Organization of the Union Army*, 1:276–84; Paludan, *Presidency of Lincoln*, 145–49; Henry Crapo to William Crapo, 23 Jul. 1862, Crapo Papers, BHL.

62. Sears, *Mr. Dunn Browne's Experiences in the Army*, 1–2.

63. HW, 6 Sept. 1862.

64. Hamilton, *Reminiscences*, 498, 525–26; Hamilton to Lincoln, 11 Aug. 1861, LP, LC; Sheldon, "Reexamination of Conscription," 484–89.

65. Daniel Horn to Wife, 9 Aug. 1862, Daniel Horn Papers, HL.

66. Basler, *CW*, 5:367; Samuel L. Casey to Lincoln, 4, 12 Aug., Richard W. Thompson to Lincoln, 18 Aug. 1862, LP, LC; Yates to Morton, 16 Jul. 1862, Morton Telegraph Books, Indiana State Archives, digitized by the Indiana University-Purdue University Indianapolis; *DR*, 18 Aug. 1862; Hancock, "Political History of Delaware," 7:359–60; *OR*, series 3, 2:205, 359, 403; Burton to Lincoln, 2 Aug. 1862, LP, LC; *HEP*, 5, 6 Aug. 1862; *PhiIn*, 30 Aug. 1862; Burton to C. P. Buckingham, 11 Sept. 1862, Executive Papers, DPA; Wickman, "We Are Coming Father Abraham," 183–207; *BDFR*, 5 Aug. 1862.

67. *OR*, series 3, 2:291, 293; *BDWC*, 11, 16, 24 Jul., 4 Aug. 1862; Clark, *Kirkwood*, 230–32.

68. *OR*, series 3, 2:294–95; Castel, "Civil War Kansas and the Negro," 125–38; *StLDMR*, 11, 20 Oct. 1862; James Montgomery to Robinson, 3 Aug., George Hoyt to Robinson, 13 Aug., Charles R. Jennison to Robinson, 22 Aug. 1862, Robinson Papers, KSHS.

69. Berlin, Reidy, and Rowland, *Freedom's Soldiers: The Black Military Experience in the Civil War*, 87–88; Jimerson, *The Private Civil War*, 93; *OR*, series 3, 2:310–12; Lull, *James M. Williams*, 41–51; *OR*, series 3, 2:314; Wubben, "The Uncertain Trumpet: Iowa Republicans and Black Suffrage, 1860–1868," 413–16.

70. Lincoln to George Fisher, 16 Aug., Fisher to Lincoln, 14 Aug. 1862, LP, LC; Hancock, "Political History of Delaware, Part III," 7:368–72; Basler, *CW*, 5:314.

71. Trester, "Tod," 136–37; Reid, *Ohio in the War*, 1:70–74; Pearson, *Andrew*, 2:38–39; Porter, *Ohio Politics*, 100–107; Basler, *CW*, 5:368; Blair, "We Are Coming," 190–92; Egle, *Curtin*, 133–34; Orr, "Cities at War," 321–22.

72. Trester, "Tod," 139–40; *Ohio House Journal*, 1863, 59:7; Hesseltine, *Lincoln and the War Governors*, 263–64; *LDJ*, 16, 21 Jul. 1862; Rawley, *Morgan*, 177; W. Evarts to Morgan, 19 Jul., and W. Bogart to E. D. Morgan, 26 Jul. 1862, Morgan Papers, NYSL.

73. *OR*, series 3, 2:327, 353, 363; Andrew to Lincoln, 28 Jul., 20 Aug., 1862, LP, LC; Abbott, *Cotton and Capital*, 113–16; Hughes, *Letters of Forbes*, 2:47, 59; Blair, "We Are Coming," 190–92; Hamrogue, "Andrew," 183–84; Pearson, *Andrew*, 2:39–40; *BDA*, 25 Aug. 1862; *NYTi*, 3 Sept. 1862.

74. Gurowski to Andrew, 2, 5, 8, 10 Aug. 1862, "confidential," Andrew Papers, MHS; Hamrogue, "Andrew," 155.

75. Pearson, *Andrew*, 2:45–46; Stone, "Sketch of John Albion Andrew," 21–22; Voegeli, "A Rejected Alternative: Union Policy and the Relocation of Southern 'Contrabands' at the Dawn of Emancipation," 776–77; *ChiTri*, 20 Aug. 1862; *StLDMR*, 25 Aug. 1862; Mary Sherburn to Andrew, 4 Aug. 1862, Andrew Papers, MHS.

76. *Lbr*, 22 Aug. 1862.

77. Pearson, *Andrew*, 2:46–47.

78. *OR*, series 3, 2:316, 357–61, 383, series 3, 1:321–23, 332, 345, 354; Washburn to Stanton, 5, 7, 11 Aug. 1862, Executive Correspondence, Washburn to Morrill, 9 Aug. 1862, Governor's Telegram Books, MeSA; C. P. Buckingham to Washburn, 2, 5, 9, 15, 18, 26 Aug. 1862, Executive Correspondence, Washburn to Blaine, 12 Aug, Washburn to Hamlin, 12 Aug. 1862, Governor's Telegram Books, MeSA; *ISJ*, 1, 28 Aug. 1862; *ChiTri*, 4, 5, 25 Aug. 1862.

79. *PhiIn*, 10, 18, 19, 22 Jul., 15, 29 Aug., 5, 6 Sept. 1862; *OR*, series 3, 2:366–67; Burlingame, *Lincoln Observed*, 85; *LDT*, 26 Jul. 1862.

80. Holbrook to Lincoln, 29 Jul. 1862, LP, LC; *OR*, series 3, 2:368; *BDFR*, 5, 12 Aug. 1862.

81. *NYTi*, 27 Aug. 1862; *OR*, series 3, 2:393; Morgan to McClellan, 16 Aug. 1862, Morgan Letter Books, NYSL; *OR*, Series 3, 2:321, 330–32, 343, 345, 354, 375, 387, 446, 450, 459, 1:421;

Egle, *Curtin*, 133–35; Fisher, "Groping toward Victory," 33–334; Porter, *Ohio Politics*, 100–106; William Bradford to Stanton, 5 Aug. 1862, Governor's Letter Books, MdSA; Blair, "We Are Coming," 192–94; *TDSGR*, 16 Sept. 1862; *PhiIn*, 22 Jul. 1862; *SEP*, 16 Aug. 1862; John H. James [Diary], 7 Aug. 1862, John H. James Papers, ALPL.

82. Joab Powell to Yates, 14 Aug. 1862, Yates Papers, ALPL.

83. Wilson, *Robinson*, 97; *OR*, series 3, 2:294, 311–12, 393, 417, 431, 444–45, 479; Castel, *Civil War Kansas*, 86–93; Blunt, "Blunt's Civil War Experience," 211–65; Castel, "Civil War Kansas and the Negro," 125–38; *LDT*, 31 Jul., 1, 3, 5 Aug. 1862; Eldridge to Robinson, 28 Aug., Stanton to Robinson, 28 Aug., James Montgomery to Robinson, 3 Aug., George Hoyt to Robinson, 13 Aug., "private," Charles R. Jennison to Robinson, 22 Aug., Stanton to Lane, 23 Aug. 1862, Robinson Papers, KSHS; Robinson to Stanton, 20 Aug. 1862, Charles Robinson Papers, KCPL; Wilson, *Robinson*, 95–97; Mark Delahay to Lincoln [n.d.] Jul. 1862, LP, LC; *LDT*, 1, 3 Aug. 1862.

84. Robert D. Murray to Robinson, 7 Sept., William H. Wadsworth to Robinson, 16 Sept., A. V Townes to Robinson, 20 Aug. 1862, Robinson Papers, KDLA; *OR*, series 3, 2:401; Kleber, ed., *The Kentucky Encyclopedia*, 777; *NYTi*, 2 Nov. 1882; *LDJ*, 10 Jul. 1861, 21, 22, 24 Jul., 16, 18, 20, 21 Aug. 1862; Dues, "Magoffin," 23–27; Coulter, *Civil War and Re-Adjustment in Kentucky*, 142–45; *Journal of the House of Representatives of the Commonwealth of Kentucky*, 927–35.

85. Robinson to Lincoln, 18 Aug. 1862, LP, LC; Robinson to Yates, 19 Aug. 1862, Yates Papers, FHS; *OR*, series 3, 2:417, series 3, 2:401; Burlingame, *Lincoln's Journalist*, 294; C. H. Spillman [?] to Robinson, 18 Aug., M. C. Johnson to Robinson, 21 Aug., Dr. Samuel McGuire to Robinson, 21 Aug., Governor's Correspondence, Charles Robinson Papers, KSA; *PhiIn*, 3 Sept. 1862.

86. *OR*, series 3, 2:394–413, 417, 429–39, 441, 453, series 1, 13:634; *BDHE*, 5, 12, 13 Aug. 1862; *BDWC*, 1 Aug. 1862; *PhiIn* 15 Aug. 1862; Clark, *Kirkwood*, 230–33; Berlin, *Freedom: A Documentary History of Emancipation*, 1:433–34; Briggs, "Enlistment of the Iowa Troops," 355–60; *IDSR*, 13, 23 Aug. 1862; Robert D. Murray to Robinson, 7 Sept. 1862, Robinson Papers, KDLA; *PhiIn*, 19 Jul., 15, 29 Aug. 1862; Yates to Lincoln, 23, 27 Aug. and Olden to Lincoln, 14 Aug. 1862, LP, LC; Basler, *CW*, 5:391–92; *ChiTri*, 4, 5, 22 Aug. 1862; Nortrup, "Yates," 263–65; Krenkel, *Yates*, 194; Marshall, *A War of the People*, 99–100.

87. *OR*, series 3, 2:455, 461, 471; Niven, *Connecticut for the Union*, 83–84; Buckingham to Lincoln, 28 Jul. 1862, LP, LC; Washburn to Stanton, 28 Aug. 1862; Executive Correspondence, Washburn to Stanton, 23 Aug. 1862, Governor's Telegram Book, MeSA; Mitchell, "Organizational Performance," 130–35; *DFP*, 19, 24 Aug. 1862; James M. Sligh to Wife, 1 Aug. 1862, Sligh Family Papers, BHL.

88. Andrew to Gurowski, 30 Aug., Gurowski to Andrew, 28 Aug. 1862; Andrew Letter Books, MHS; Hamrogue, "Andrew," 155; Clark, *Kirkwood*, 234–35; Shambaugh, *Messages*, 2:502, 504, 311–18; Lathrop, *Kirkwood*, 220–25; Benton, *Voting in the Field*, 47–50; *BDHE*, 23, 29 Aug. 1862; *IDSR*, 2, 4 Sept. 1862; *OR*, series 3, 2:509, 480, 524, 538, 480; Marshall, *A War of the People*, 109–10; *BDFR*, 23 Aug. 1862; *PhiIn*, 9 Sept. 1862; *BDA*, 10 Sept. 1862; Charles H. Keener to Lincoln, 30 Oct. 1862, LP, LC; Andrew to Washburn, 27 Aug., Washburn and Andrew to Lincoln, 27 Aug., Washburn, Berry, Andrew, Buckingham, Sprague to Lincoln, 29 Aug. 1862, Massachusetts Governors, Letters Official, 1862, MSA.

89. *OR*, series 3, 2:297, 314, 506–7, series 1, 19, pt. 2:304; *WSJ*, 29, 30 Jul. 1862; Noyes, "Negro in Wisconsin's War Effort," 73–74; J. B. Soule to Andrew, 6 Aug. 1862, Andrew Papers, MHS; William Bradford to Stanton, 2, 15 Sept. 1862, Governor's Letter Books,

MdSA; *PhiIn*, 9, 10 Sept. 1862; *BDA*, Sept. 8, 1862; Thomas and Hyman, *Stanton*, 241; Castel, "Civil War Kansas and the Negro," 125–38.

90. *WDNI*, 27 Aug. 1862; Niven, *Connecticut for the Union*, 87–89.

91. Ramsey's Message to Legislature, *Minnesota Executive Documents*, 1862, 5, 10–11; Nichols, "The Other Civil War," 2–15; *OR*, series 1, 13:590–99, series 3, 2: 446, 449; Folwell, *Minnesota*, 2:106–70, 212–59, 104–5, 165–75; Guentzel, "Ramsey," 384–98; Haugland, "Ramsey and Republicans," 133–38; "Extracts from Sibley's Letters to His Wife, 1862," Sibley Papers, MnHS; *StPDPi*, 27, 28 Sept. 1862; *BDHE*, 1 Sept. 1862; Josephy, *War in the American West*, 95–130; Ramsey to Yates, 6 Sept. 1862, Yates Papers, ALPL; Tolzmann, *The Sioux Uprising in Minnesota, 1862*; Berg, *38 Nooses*, 5–39, 45–95.

92. *OR*, series 3, 2:508–9, 515, 518, 523; Josephy, *War in the American West*, 98–130; Quiner, *Wisconsin*, 235; Benton, *Voting in the Field*, 53–66.

93. *OR*, series 1, 13:620; Nichols, "The Other War," 7; Josephy, *War in the American West*, 98–130.

Chapter Ten

1. Montgomery Stevens to Stanton, 28 Aug. 1862, Letters Received by the Secretary of War, RG 107, NARA.

2. Andrew to Stanton, 30 Aug. 1862, Massachusetts Governors, Letters Official, 1862, MSA; Schouler, *Massachusetts in the Civil War*, 1:365–66; John W. Emery to Andrew, 23 Aug. 1862, Andrew Papers, MHS.

3. Sprague to Andrew, 19 Aug. 1861, Andrew Papers, MHS; Andrew to Sprague, 30 Aug., 2 Sept. 1862, Massachusetts Governors, Letters Official, 1862, MSA.

4. *BDWC*, 15 Aug. 1862; *ISJ*, 10 Sept. 1862; Sprague to Andrew, 18 Sept. 1862, Massachusetts Governors Papers, Executive Department Letters, 1862, MSA.

5. Washburn to Andrew, 1 Sept., Gurowski to Andrew, 2 Sept., and JDA to Andrew, 2 Sept. 1862 Andrew Papers, MHS; Washburn to Andrew, 1, 2 Sept. 1862, Governor's Telegram Book, MeSA; Whalon, "Washburn and the War Department," 83–84; Stanton, Chase, Smith, and Bates to Lincoln, 2 Sept. 1862, LP, LC.

6. Schouler, *Massachusetts in the Civil War*, 1:366; Hamrogue, "Andrew," 156; Andrew to Sprague, 30 Aug. 1862, Andrew's Letter book, MHS; Andrew to President Rev. Barnas Sears, 29 Aug., Andrew to Stanton, 30 Aug., Andrew to Sprague, 30 Aug., Andrew to Washburn, Berry, Holbrook, Buckingham, 30 Aug. 1862, Massachusetts Governors, Letters Official, 1862, MSA; Sprague to Andrew, 19 Aug. 1862, Andrew Papers, MHS; Burrage, *Brown University in the Civil War*, 27–30; *In Memoriam: Israel Washburn, Jr.*, 133–35; *PDJ*, 4 Sept. 1862; *BS*, 6 Sept. 1862; *BDWC*, 8 Sept. 1862; *BDA*, 4, 5 Sept., 2 Oct. 1862; *CDE*, 17 Oct. 1862; *NHPSG*, 10, 24 Sept 1862; George Randolph to Sprague, 2 Aug., Samuel Arnold to Sprague, 7 Aug., John Norris to Sprague, 6 Aug. 1862, Executive Letters Received, RISA.

7. *PDJ*, 4 Sept. 1862; *NYTi*, 4 Sept. 1862; Whalon, "Maine Republicans," 114–16; Alonzo Gracelon to Israel Washburn Jr., 27 Aug., Washburn to Lincoln, 28 Aug. 1862, LP, LC; Hesseltine, *Lincoln and the War Governors*, 252–53; *BDFP*, 3 Sept. 1862; Hesseltine and Wolf, "New England Governors vs. Lincoln," 105–13; Hamrogue, "Andrew," 156–57; *PhiIn*, 4 Sept. 1862; Charles Gould to Andrew, 6 Sept. 1862, Andrew Papers, MHS; *PDJ*, 5, 8 Sept. 1862; Buckingham to Morgan, 9 Sept. 1862, Morgan Papers, NYSL.

8. Washburn to Lincoln, 28 Aug. 1862, LP, LC.

9. *BDWC*, 8 Sept. 1862; *BDA*, 2 Oct. 1862; *NHPSG*, 10, 24 Sept. 1862; Frank Howe to Andrew, 3, 4 Jul., Frémont to Andrew, 5 Jul. 1862, Andrew Papers, MHS; Hesseltine and

Wolf, "New England Governors vs. Lincoln," 105–12; *NYJC*, 5, 6, 23 Sept. 1862; Hesseltine, *Lincoln and the War Governors*, 252–53; Hamrogue, "Andrew," 156–57; *PDJ*, 5, 8 Sept. 1862.

10. Hesseltine and Wolf, "The Altoona Conference," 195–205; Hesseltine and Wolf, "New England Governors vs. Lincoln, 105–13; Hesseltine, *Lincoln and the War Governors*, 252–54; Andrew to Stanton, 1 Sept. 1862, Massachusetts Governors, Letters Official, 1862, MSA; Hamrogue, "Andrew," 156–60; Andrew to Washburn, 27 Aug. 1862, Andrew's Letter Book, MHS; *OR*, series 3, vol. 2:496; *Addresses By His Excellency Governor John A. Andrew, Hon. Edward Everett, Hon. B. F. Thomas, and Hon. Robert C. Winthrop, August 27, 1862*, 3–7.

11. Hamilton, *Reminiscences*, 524–33; Hesseltine, *Lincoln and the War Governors*, 252–54; Hesseltine and Wolf, "The Altoona Conference," 195–205; *PDJ*, 4 Sept. 1862; Hesseltine, "Lincoln's War Governors,"153–200; Morgan to Stanton, 25 Aug., Stanton to Morgan, 1 Sept. 1862, Morgan Papers, NYSL.

12. Hamilton, *Reminiscences*, 524–33; Niven, *Chase Papers*, 1:378; Stahr, *Seward*, 354–55; Niven, *Chase*, 308–13; Hesseltine and Wolf, "The Altoona Conference," 195–205; Hesseltine and Wolf, "New England Governors vs. Lincoln," 105–13; *PDJ*, 4 Sept. 1862; Hesseltine, "Lincoln's War Governors," 197–98; Hesseltine, *Lincoln and the War Governors*, 252–53.

13. Gurowski to Andrew, [6] Sept. 1862, Andrew Papers, MHS; *StPDG*, 17 Jun. 1894.

14. Andrew to Gurowski, 6 Sept. 1862, Andrew Letter Books, MHS; Andrew to Curtin, 6, 15 Sept. 1862, Massachusetts Governors, Letters Official, 1862, MSA; Pearson, *Andrew*, 2:48; Hamrogue, "Andrew," 155; Washburn to Andrew, 8 Sept. 1862, Governor's Telegram Book, MeSA; Hesseltine, *Lincoln and the War Governors*, 253–54; *BDWC*, 8 Sept. 1862; *NYTi*, 2 Nov. 1862; Yates to Morton, 12, 13 Sept. Curtin to Morton, 6 Sept. 1862, Morton Telegraph Books, IUPUI.

15. Charles Gould to Andrew, 6 Sept., "private," William Dver to Andrew, 7 Sept., JDA to Andrew, [7] Sept. 1862, Andrew Papers, MHS; *ChiTri*, 12 Sept. 1862.

16. *ChiTri*, 8 Sept. 1862.

17. Berry to Lincoln, 30 Jul. 1862, LP, LC; Pearson, *Andrew*, 2:48 Weeden, *War Government*, 229–30; Marvel, "The Deadly Campaign," 107–8; *NHS*, 16 Aug. 1862.

18. Berry to Lincoln, 30 Jul. 1862, LP, LC; Pearson, *Andrew*, 2:48–49; n.a., "Proceedings of the Maine Historical Society," 87–105; Harris, "Blair," 131; *DDA*, 7 Aug. 1862; Fennimore, "Blair," 49:212–13, 219–23; Paludan, *A People's Contest*, 99–100; *OR*, series 3, 2:543–44; Klingaman, *Lincoln*, 178; Hesseltine, *Lincoln and the War Governors*, 250–55; Hesseltine and Wolf, "New England Governors vs. Lincoln," 105–13; Clark, *Kirkwood*, 248–51; Donald, *Lincoln*, 373–74.

19. Washburn to Sedgwick, 11 Sept. 1862, Sedgwick Papers, SUL.

20. Washburn to Fessenden, 12 Sept. 1862, Fessenden Papers, WRHS.

21. Robinson to Sara, 7 Sept. 1862, Robinson Papers, KSHS; Salomon to Yates, 11 Sept. 1862, Yates Papers, ALPL; Donald, *Lincoln*, 370–71; Sears, *McClellan*, 258–60; Marszalek, *Halleck*, 143–46, 145–48; *OR*, series 1, 12, pt. 2:82–83; Beale, *Diary of Welles*, 1:100–122; Donald, *Lincoln*, 370–71; Hennessy, *Return to Bull Run: The Campaign and Battle of Second Manassas*; *NYTi*, 31 Aug., 3, 5 Sept. 1862; *HW*, 20 Sept. 1862.

22. Chandler to Trumbull, 10 Sept. 1862, "confidential," Trumbull Papers, LC; *OR*, series 3, 2:506–7, 537–38; *BS*, 9 Sept. 1862; *PhiIn*, 10 Sept. 1862; Bradford to Blair, 28 Aug., Bradford to Stanton, 28 Aug., Bradford to Blair, 30 Aug., Bradford to Stanton, 2 Sept. 1862, Blair Family Papers, LC.

23. Sears, *Papers of McClellan*, 439; Catton, *Mr. Lincoln's Army*, 163; *OR*, series 1, 19, pt. 2:229, 231, 267; Sears, *Landscape Turned Red: The Battle of Antietam*, 100–109.

24. Welles to M. J. W., 14 Sept. 1862, Welles Papers, LC; Sears, *Papers of McClellan*, 446–47; *OR*, series 1, 19, pt. 2:248, 268–69; Fishel, *The Secret War for the Union*, 214–43; Niven, *Chase Diary*, 1:379–81.

25. *OR*, series 1, 13:597, 616–17; Nichols, "The Other Civil War," 2–15; Guentzel, "Ramsey," 384–98; *PhiIn*, 5 Sept. 1862; Josephy, *War in the American West*, 96–136.

26. *OR*, series 1, 13:599–600; Tolzmann, *Jacob Nix*; Nichols, "The Other Civil War," 2–15; Burlingame, *With Lincoln in the White House*, 88.

27. Basler, *CW*, 5:396–97; *OR*, series 1, 13:597–99.

28. *OR*, series 1, 13:658; Schutz and Trenerry, *Pope*, 175–76; Folwell, *Minnesota*, 2:170; *IDSR*, 10 Sept. 1862; Nichols, "The Other Civil War," 2–15; "Extracts, Sibley," and Sibley to Wife, 11, 17 Sept., 1862, Sibley Papers, MnHS; Josephy, *War in the American West*, 132.

29. *OR*, series 1, 16, pt. 2:421, 440–459, 504; Engle, *Buell*, 283–87; Foulke, *Morton*, 1:184–88; *InDJ*, 6, 13, 22 Sept. 1862; Tod to "The Loyal People of the River Counties," 2 Sept. 1862, Telegraphic Dispatches, series 144, OhSA; Wadsworth to Robinson, 16 Sept. 1862, Robinson Papers, KDLA; Villard, *Memoirs*, 1:304; Treaster, "Tod," 144–48; Reid, *Ohio in the War*, 1:91; *CC*, 5 Sept. 1862; Tod to George B. Wright, 9 Sept. 1862, David Tod Papers, LC; *LDJ*, 30 Sept. 1862; Basler, *CW*, 5:419; Hess, *Banners to the Breeze*; Noe, *Perryville: The Grand Havoc of Battle*, 82–91.

30. Portia Gage to Addison Gibbs, Governor of Oregon, (u.d. 1862), Addison Crandall Gibbs Papers, OrHS; Basler, *CW*, 5:388–89; Lt. Col. C.C. Andrews to Ramsey, 27 Jan. 1863, Governor's Papers, MnHS; Montague to Jeanette, 25 May 1862, Ferry Collection, BHL; J. B. White to Blair, 1 Aug. 1861, RG 44, Records of the Executive Office, 1810–1910, MiSA; Niven, *Connecticut for the Union*, 72.

31. *InDJ*, 13 Sept. 1862; *BDHE*, 16 Sept. 1862; *LDJ*, 10 July, 22 Sept. 1862; *CDE*, 30 Oct. 1862; Coulter, *William G. Brownlow: Fighting Parson of the Southern Highlands*, 224–40.

32. *InDJ*, 13 Sept. 1862.

33. Chandler to Lincoln, 8 Aug. 1862, LP, LC; Harris, "Blair," 131; Fennimore, "Blair," 49:212–13, 219–23.

34. *NYTi*, 26, 27 Sept, 4 Oct. 4 1862.

35. Fennimore, "Blair," 49:212–13, 219–23; Harris, "Blair," 131; *DDA*, 7 Aug. 1862; *ChiTri*, 29 Aug. 1862; Donald, *Lincoln*, 373–74; Blair to William Stevens, 29 Mar. 1862, William Stevens Papers, BHL; Welles to M. J. W., 10 Sept. 1862, Welles Papers, LC.

36. Henshaw and Lafantasie, "Letters Home: Sergeant Charles E. Perkins in Virginia 1862," 124; Sprague to Lincoln, 9 Sept. 1862, LP, LC; John Norris to Sprague, 6 Aug., Thomas Garribrance, 19 Aug., A. W. Chantry, Jr. to Sprague, 18 Aug., Cyrus Francis to Sprague, 15 Aug., William Ellis to Edward Maurau, Rhode Island Adjutant General, 13 Aug. 1862, Executive Letters Received, RISA; *BDA*, 6 Aug. 1862; *NDM*, 8 Aug. 1862; *BDWC*, 16 Aug. 1862.

37. *NYTi*, 26, 27 Sept., 4 Oct. 1862; McClure, *Lincoln and Men of War-Times*, 268–72; Curtin to Andrew, 6 Sept. 1862, Andrew Papers, MHS; Nevins, *War Becomes Revolution*, 239–40; Rawley, *Morgan*, 181; Shoemaker, *The Last of the War Governors*, 9–18; Hesseltine and Wolf, "New England Governors vs. Lincoln," 107; *NYTi*, 22, 26 Sept. 1862; Hesseltine and Wolf, "Altoona Conference," 200–202; Weeden, *War Government*, 228–29; Egle, *Curtin*, 308–9; Albright, "Curtin," 48:19–31; Hamrogue, "Andrew," 161; *WES*, 26 Sept. 1862; *PhiIn*, 25, 26 Sept. 1862; Curtin to Tod, 9 Sept. 1862, Executive Letter Books, PSA; Kashatus, "Pennsylvania's War Governor," 22–31.

38. Schaeffer to Yates, 8 Sept. 1862, Yates Papers, ALPL; Hesseltine, *Lincoln and the War Governors*, 253–54; *WDNI*, 23 Sept. 1862; Morgan to Curtin, 16 Sept., Gamble to Curtin, 8 Sept., Pierpont to Curtin, 18 Sept. 1862, Slifer-Walls Collection, Special Collections/University Archives, Ellen Clarke Bertran Library, BUL.

39. Grinnell, *Men and Events of Forty Years*, 150; McClellan to Lincoln, 13 Sept. 1862, Seward Papers, UR; Sears, *McClellan*, 270–80.

40. Morgan to Curtin, 16 Sept. 1862, Slifer-Walls Collection, BUL; Hiram Barney to Thurlow Weed, 21 Sept. 1862, Thurlow Weed Papers, LC; Curtin to Morgan, 6 Sept. 1862, Morgan Papers, NYSL; Morgan to Solon Humphreys, 23, 27 Sept. 1862, "personal," Morgan Letter Books, NYSL; Albright, "Curtin," 48:22–24.

41. Morgan to Curtin, 30 Sept. 1862, Morgan Papers, NYSL.

42. Curtin to Morgan, 23 Sept. 1862, Morgan Papers, NYSL; Morgan to Solon Humphreys, 23 Sept., Morgan to Curtis Noyes, 23 Sept. 1862, Morgan Letter Books, NYSL; Rawley, *Morgan*, 181–83; Weeden, *War Government*, 232–33; *WES*, 29 Sept. 1862; *NDM*, 23 Sept. 1862.

43. Siddali, *Missouri's War*, 196; Boman, *Gamble*, 180–81; Rosin, "Gamble," 362–67; Bates to Gamble, 19, 21 Sept. 1862; Bates Papers, MoHS; Andrew to Gamble, 29 Sept., James Birch to Gamble, 7 Sept., 1862, Gamble Papers, MoHS; *OR*, series 3, 2:474–75, 579, 591–92; *WDNI*, 27 Sept. 1862; *TDSGR*, 29 Sept. 1862; Gamble to Lincoln, 9 Sept. 1862, LP, LC; Canan, "Missouri Militia," 431–48.

44. *LDJ*, 22 Sept. 1862.

45. Reavis to Yates, 19 Sept. 1862, Reavis Papers, CHM; Nortrup, "Yates," 269; *ISJ*, 7 Oct. 1862; Krenkel, *Yates*, 179; *StLDMR*, 25, 26 Sept. 1862; *ChiTri*, 23 Sept., 2 Oct. 1862; *WDNI*, 23 Sept. 1862; *BDFP*, 6 Oct. 1862.

46. Pope to Yates, 21 Sept. 1862, Yates Papers, ALPL.

47. Blair's Report of the Altoona Conference, 1862, Blair Papers, BHL.

48. W. M. Tracy Cutler to Yates, 18 Sept. 1862, Yates Papers, ALPL; *HDT*, 30 Sept. 1862; *NDM*, 23 Sept. 1862

49. *OR*, series 3, 2:543–44, 583; Austin Blair's Report of the Altoona Conference, 6–24 Sept. 1862, Blair Papers, BHL; Hesseltine and Wolf, "Altoona Conference," 195–205; Clark, *Kirkwood*, 248–51; Buckingham, *Life of Buckingham*, 168–70; *PDJ*, 12, 13 Sept. 1862; *SEP*, 1 Nov. 1862; Burlingame, *Stoddard*, 108; Klingaman, *Lincoln*, 196; Abbott, *Ohio's War Governors*, 25–26; Kimball, "Yates," 21; *WDNI*, 23 Sept. 1862; *WES*, 25, 26 Sept. 1862; Curtin to Tod, 9 Sept. 1862, Executive Correspondence, PSA; Harris, *Lincoln and the Border States*, 200–203.

50. As quoted in Nevins, *War Becomes Revolution*, 239–40; Blair's Report of Altoona Conference, 1862, Blair Papers, BHL; Hesseltine, *Lincoln and the War Governors*, 254–62; Buckingham, *Life of Buckingham*, 261–62; Nivens, *Connecticut for the Union*, 281–82; Burlingame, *Lincoln*, 2:399, 412–14.

51. Buckingham, *Life of Buckingham*, 168–70; *OR*, series 3, 2:582–84, 543–44; *PhiIn*, 3 Oct. 1862; Hesseltine, *Lincoln and the War Governors*, 254–62; McClure, *Lincoln and Men of War-Times*, 270–71; *NYH*, 25 Sept. 1862; Clark, *Kirkwood*, 248–51; Blair's Report of Altoona Conference, 1862, Blair Papers, BHL; Carwardine, *Lincoln: A Life of Purpose and Power*, 192–95; Boman, *Gamble*, 180–81; Ambler, *Pierpont*, 155–59; *OS*, 15 Sept., 6 Oct. 1862; Andrew to Robinson, 29 Sept., Sara to [Mother], 19 Oct. 1862, Robinson Papers, KSHS.

52. Basler, *CW*, 5:427; Hesseltine, *Lincoln and the War Governors*, 254–62.

53. Basler, *CW*, 5:427; *OR*, series 1, 19, pt. 2:310; Curtin to Lincoln, 14, 16 Sept. 1862, LP, LC; *BDA*, 13, 18 Sept. 1862.
54. Basler, *CW*, 5:427–28.
55. Sears, *McClellan*, 324; Sears, *Papers of McClellan*, 473; Sears, *Landscape Turned Red*.
56. Sears, *Mr. Dunn Browne's Experiences*, 10–11.
57. *BDFP*, 1 Oct. 1863; Orr, "Cities at War," 368–69; Smith, *History of the 118th Pennsylvania Volunteers, Corn Exchange Regiment*, 7, 71; Curtin to Lincoln, 17 Sept., Yates to Lincoln, 15 Sept. 1862, LP, LC.
58. *HEP*, 23 Sept. 1862; Bradford's Journal, 21 Sept. 1862, MdHS; Donald, *Lincoln*, 374–76; Masur, *Lincoln's One Hundred Days: The Emancipation Proclamation and the War for the Union*, 2–11, 91–115.
59. Browne, *Andrew*, 74–75; Browne, "Governor Andrew," 249–76; Pearson, *Andrew*, 2:50–51; Weeden, *War Government*, 231; Hamrogue, "Andrew," 161–62; Burlingame, *Lincoln*, 2:411; *BDA*, 22 Sept. 1862; Andrew to Howe, 19 Sept., Andrew to Sprague, 20 Sept. 1862, Massachusetts Governors, Letters Official, 1862, MSA; Hesseltine, *Lincoln and the War Governors*, 256–57.
60. *StLDMR*, 26 Sept. 1862; Hesseltine, *Lincoln and the War Governors*, 256–57.
61. Basler, *CW*, 5:419–25; Nicolay and Hay, *Lincoln: A History*, 6:156–58; Guelzo, *Abraham Lincoln: Redeemer President*, 341; *StLDMR*, 26 Sept. 1862; *ChiTri*, 23 Sept. 1862; *WDNI*, 24 Jul. 1862; *LDJ*, 5 Jan. 1863; Harris, *Lincoln and the Border States*, 186–88.
62. *PhiIn*, 20 Oct. 1862; *StLDMR*, 26 Sept. 1862, *ChiTri*, 23 Sept. 1862.
63. *NYH*, 29 Sept. 1862.
64. *BS*, 25 Sept. 1862; Kiper, *McClernand*, 135; Yates to Lincoln, 26 Sept. 1862, LP, LC; Hamrogue, "Andrew," 163–64; *WES*, 25, 26 Sept. 1862; Kamm, "Scott," 145–46; *PhiIn*, 25 Sept. 1862; *PDJ*, 24, 25 Sept. 1862.
65. Abbott, *Ohio's War Governors*, 25–26; Krenkel, *Yates*, 179; Bradford's Journal, 21 Sept. 1862, MdHS; *NHPSG*, 1, 8 Oct. 1862; *PhiIn*, 25 Sept. 1862; Shoemaker, *Last of the War Governors*, 18–31; *ChiTri*, 23 Sept., 3 Oct. 1862; Pearson, *Andrew*, 2:51–58; *BS*, 26 Sept. 1862; *BDA*, 30 Sept. 1862; *ISJ*, 26 Sept., 7 Oct. 1862; Yates to Morton, 23 Sept. 1862, Morton Telegraph Books, IUPUI; *WES*, 25, 26 Sept. 1862; *NYTi*, 27 Sept. 1862; Davis, *History of Blair County Pennsylvania*, 1:98; Pope to Yates, 21 Sept. 1862, Yates Papers, FHS; Hesseltine, *Lincoln and the War Governors*, 257–59; Hamrogue, "Andrew," 161–67; *WDNI*, 23, 29 Sept. 1862; *NYH*, 29 Sept. 1862.
66. Shoemaker, *Last of the War Governors*, 49–50; *WES*, 25, 26 Sept. 1862; *PhiIn*, 25, 26 Sept. 1862.
67. Hamrogue, "Andrew," 165; *NYH*, 27, 28, 29 Sept. 1862; *NHPSG*, 8 Oct. 1862; *PhiIn*, 25, 26 Sept. 1862; *LDJ*, 25, 27 Sept. 1862; *WES*, 25, 26 Sept. 1862; *PhiIn*, 25, 26 Sept. 1862; *HEP*, 2 Oct. 1862; *BDWC*, 3 Oct. 1862; *ISJ*, 24 Sept. 1862; Andrew to Holbrook, 29 Sept. 1862, Massachusetts Governors, Letters Official, 1862, MSA; Holbrook to Andrew, 2 Oct., Buckingham to Andrew, 2 Oct. 1862, Massachusetts Governors Papers, Executive Department Papers, 1862, MSA; *ChiTri*, 2 Oct. 1862; Hesseltine and Wolf, "The Altoona Conference," 202; McClure, *Lincoln and Men of War-Times*, 269–72; *NYH*, 25, 26, 27, 28, 29 Sept. 1862; *NYTri*, 25 Sept. 1862; Pearson, *Andrew*, 2:51–58; Hesseltine, *Lincoln and the War Governors*, 257–59; Burlingame, *Stoddard*, 108; *WDNI*, 26, 27 Sept. 1862.
68. Bradford to Blair, 17 Oct. 1862, Blair Family Papers, LC; Bradford to Curtin, 16 Sept. 1862; Slifer-Walls Collection, BUL; Beale, *Diary of Welles*, 1:156; Burton to Andrew, 3 Oct. 1861, Massachusetts Governors Papers, Executive Department Letters, 1862, MSA; *PhiIn*, 26 Sept. 1862; Shoemaker, *The Last of the War Governors*, 18–20; Nevins, *War Becomes*

Revolution, 240; *BS*, 27 Sept. 1862; Clark, "Politics in Maryland," 40:307–8; Harris, "Blair," 137–41; *DDA*, 24 Sept. 1862; *DFP*, 25 Sept. 1862; Ridderbusch, "The Lincoln *Reminiscence* Manuscript," 79–80; Davis, *History of Blair County*, 1:87–98; *HEP*, 25 Sept. 1862; Hesseltine, *Lincoln and the War Governors*, 257–60, 267; *WDNI*, 3, 6, 8 Oct. 1862; Hamrogue, "Andrew," 163–69; *WES*, 25, 26 Sept. 1862; *NYTi*, 27 Sept. 1862; Bradford to Hicks, 29 Dec. 1862, Bradford's Papers, MdHS; Baker, *Politics of Continuity*, 81–83.

69. *OR*, series 3, 2:582–84, 543–44; Blair's Report of Altoona Conference, 1862, Blair Papers, BHL; Randall, *Lincoln*, 229–30; Hesseltine and Wolf, "The Altoona Conference," 202–5; Sears, *McClellan*, 324; Sears, *Papers of McClellan*, 473–74; Clark, "Politics in Maryland," 40:307–8; *Maryland Union*, 2 Oct. 1862; *NYH*, 26, 29 Sept. 1862; *NYTi*, 22, 26 Sept. 1912; Ridderbusch, "Lincoln Manuscript," 79–80; Lathrop, *Kirkwood*, 226–33; Davis, *History of Blair County*, 1:87–98; Hesseltine, *Lincoln and the War Governors*, 257–60; *BS*, 26, 27 Sept. 1862; *WES*, 25, 26 Sept. 1862; *PDJ*, 25 Sept. 1862; H. B. Anthony to Gustavus Fox, 29 Sept. 1862, Gustavus Fox Papers, NYHS.

70. Shoemaker, *Last of the War Governors*, 55–56; Morgan to Solon Humphreys, 27 Sept., Morgan to Andrew, 2 Oct. 1862, Morgan Letter Books, NYSL.

71. Holland, *Holland's Life of Lincoln*, 328; Donald, *Lincoln*, 374; Pearson, *Andrew*, 2:51–58; Blaine, *Twenty Years of Congress*, 1:438–39; Hesseltine, *Lincoln and the War Governors*, 262. McClure, Lincoln and Men of War-Times, 268–75; Albright "Curtin," 4:24–26; Hamrogue, "Andrew," 160, argues that, in a letter dated 1892, Curtin described that he consulted Lincoln on the meeting, and it was Lincoln who knew about the meeting and approved of it and advised Curtin, Tod, and Andrew on his imminent Emancipation Proclamation (McClure, *Lincoln and Men of War-Times*, 268–75). Hamrogue also notes that Curtin had written a letter in 1889 to John Andrew's son, John Forrester Andrew (see Curtin to John F. Andrew, 4 Feb. 1889, John F. Andrew Papers, MHS), in which Curtin states that the time had come to set the record straight on the conference and the fact that Lincoln knew about. "It is time now that the history of that importance [sic] conference should be known, and expecially [sic] the fact that Mr. Lincoln knew the conference was to be called, approved of it, and it was your father and myself who settled the questions that the proclamation should come first from the President and the Governors of the Loyal States approve it."

72. *StPDG*, 17 June 1894.

73. Donald, *Lincoln*, 374; *StPDG*, 17 Jun. 1894.

74. *WDNI*, 12 Jul. 1864; *Congressional Globe*, 38 Congress, 1st Session, 1864, 3272–79; Egle, *Curtin*, 310–30, *FCab*, 9 Oct. 1862; Blair's Report of Altoona Conference, 1862, Blair Papers, BHL; Hesseltine and Wolf, "The Altoona Conference," 195–205; Blaine, *Twenty Years*, 1:438–39; Warrington, *A Conspiracy to Defame John A. Andrew*, 1–16.

75. *WDNI*, 12 Jul. 1864; *Congressional Globe*, 38 Congress, 1st Session, 1864, 3272–79; Hesseltine and Wolf, "The Altoona Conference," 195–205; Basler, *CW*, 5:419–425; Segal, *Conversations with Lincoln*, 197–200; Richard Yates to Reverend William W. Patton and Reverend Jno Dempster, 2 Jul. 1864, William Weston Patton Papers, CHM.

76. Pearson, *Andrew*, 2:51–58; Randall, *Lincoln*, 229–31; Albright, "Curtin," 48:26–28; McClure, *Colonel Alexander K. McClure's Recollections of a Half Century*, 360–61; Williams, *Lincoln and the Radicals*, 185–86; *HEP*, 30 Sept., 2, 25 Oct. 1862; *PDJ*, 25, 26, 27 Sept. 1862; *New York Post*, 26, 29 Sept. 1862; Arnold, *Life of Abraham Lincoln*, 266; Nevins, *War Becomes Revolution*, 239–40; Boutwell, *Speeches and Papers Relating to the Rebellion and the Overthrow of Slavery*, 334–36; Holland, *Holland's Life of Lincoln*, 394–95; Niven, *Chase Papers*, 1:403; Blaine, *Twenty Years of Congress*, 1:438–39; Nicolay and Hay, *Lincoln: A*

History, 6:164–67; Hesseltine, *Lincoln and the War Governors*, 262; *NYTi*, 2 Nov. 1862, 8 Feb. 1884, 22, 26 Sept. 1912; Davis, *History of Blair County*, 1:87–98; Hamrogue, "Andrew," 163–68; Egle, *Curtin*, 325–30.

77. *NHPSG*, 1 Oct. 1862; *TDSGR*, 29 Sept. 1862; *BDFP*, 6 Oct. 1862; *ChiTri*, 2 Oct. 1862; *PDJ*, 25 Sept. 1862; *StPDPi*, 3 Oct. 1862; *NDM*, 27 Sept. 1862; *DFP*, 26 Sept. 1862; *BDWC*, 25, 27, 29 Sept. 1862; *SEP*, 1 Nov. 1862.

78. *ChiTri*, 2 Oct. 1862; *PDJ*, 25 Sept. 1862; *BDHE*, 3, 5 Oct. 1862; *HEP*, 26 Sept. 1862; *BDWC*, 25, 27, 29 Sept. 1862; *DFP*, 26 Sept. 1862; *BDA*, 4 Oct. 1862; *StPDPi*, 2 Oct. 1862; *NHPSG*, 1 Oct. 1862; *NDM*, 27 Sept. 1862.

79. *WWP*, 4, 11 Oct. 1862.

80. *BDA*, 2 Oct. 1862.

81. *PhiIn*, 30 Sept. 1862; *ChiTri*, 30 Sept. 1862; *NYTi*, 30 Sept. 1862.

82. *BS*, 26, 27 Sept. 1862; *ISJ*, 27 Sept., 11 Oct. 1862; *NYTi*, 26 Sept. 1862; Egle, *Curtin*, 310–30; Hesseltine and Wolf, "Altoona Conference," 203–5; Lathrop, *Kirkwood*, 226–33; *HW*, 11 Oct. 1862; *WES*, 26 Sept. 1862; Albright, "Curtin," 48:26; *PhiIn*, 26 Sept. 1862; *ChiTri*, 27 Sept. 1862; Grant, *North over South*, 153–72; Robinson, *Conspiracy to Defame John A. Andrew*, 1–16.

83. Ridderbusch, "Lincoln Manuscript," 80–82; *BDHE*, 27 Sept. 1862; *PhiIn*, 26 Sept. 1862; Egle, *Curtin*, 310–30; *PDJ*, 27 Sept. 1862; Holland, *Holland's Life of Lincoln*, 328.

84. Clark, *Kirkwood*, 250–52; Lathrop, *Kirkwood*, 226–33; Blair's Report of Altoona Conference, 1862, Blair Papers, BHL; *LDJ*, 10 Oct. 1862; Hesseltine and Wolf, "The Altoona Conference," 202–5; Hesseltine, *Lincoln and the War Governors*, 260–61; *BDHE*, 18, 27 Sept. 1862; *NHS*, 4, 11 Oct. 1862; Egle, *Curtin*, 320–30.

85. Clark, *Kirkwood*, 252; Lathrop, *Kirkwood*, 226–33; Blair's Report of Altoona Conference, 1862, Blair Papers, BHL; Egle, *Curtin*, 320–30; Burlingame, *Lincoln*, 2:414.

86. Clark, *Kirkwood*, 252; Blair's Report of Altoona Conference, 1862, Blair Papers, BHL; *NYTi*, 14 July 1883; Egle, *Curtin*, 320–30; Burlingame, *Lincoln*, 2:414.

87. Blair's Report of Altoona Conference, 1862, Blair Papers, BHL; *NYTi*, 14 Jul. 1883, 22, 26 Sept. 1912; Egle, *Curtin*, 320–30; *WES*, 26 Sept. 1862; *WDNI*, 27 Sept. 1862.

88. Basler, *CW*, 5:441; *NYTi*, 14 Jul. 1883, 22, 26 Sept. 1912; *WES*, 26 Sept. 1862; *NYTri*, 29 Sept. 1862; *WDNI*, 27 Sept. 1862; Lathrop, *Kirkwood*, 226–33; Donald, *Lincoln*, 378; Nicolay and Hay, *Lincoln: A History*, 6:164–67; *OR*, series 3, vol. 2:582–84; Ridderbusch, "Lincoln Manuscript," 80–82; Byers, *Iowa*, 176; Beale, *Diary of Welles*, 1:153; *NHS*, 4, 11 Oct. 1862; Burlingame, *Stoddard*, 108; *ChiTri*, 2 Oct. 1862; *HEP*, 25 Sept. 1862.

89. Buckingham to Lincoln, 26 Sept. 1862, LP, LC; Buckingham, *Life of Buckingham*, 262–63; Niven, *Connecticut for the Union*, 282; Donald, *Lincoln*, 375–76; *NYTi*, 22, 26 Sept. 1912; Blair's Report of the Altoona Conference, 1862, Blair Papers, BHL.

90. Weeden, *War Government*, 228; Egle, *Curtin*, 329; Blair's Report of Altoona Conference, 1862, Blair Papers, BHL; Shoemaker, *The Last of the War Governors*, 20.

91. Foulke, *Morton*, 1:207; Rawley, *Morgan*, 181.

92. Weeden, *War Government*, 228–30, 326–28; Schouler, *Massachusetts in the Civil War*, 1:372–75; Beale, *Diary of Welles*, 1:153.

93. *NYTri* 29 Sept. 1862; Weeden, *War Government*, 228–30, 326–28; Schouler, *Massachusetts in the Civil War*, 1:326–34; Sheldon, "Reexamination of Conscription," 490–91; *PDJ*, 27 Sept. 1862; *NYTi*, 22, 23 Sept., 1912, 12 Sept. 1915.

94. Ridderbusch, "Lincoln Manuscript," 80–81; Ambler, *Pierpont*, 155–61; *NDM*, 27, 29 Sept. 1862; *WH*, 3 Oct. 1862; Langford, "Constitutional Issues," 14–29; Moore, "Slavery as a Factor," 68–89.

95. Ridderbusch, "Lincoln Manuscript," 80–81; Ambler, *Pierpont*, 155–61.
96. Kiper, *McClernand*, 135–39; Niven, *Chase Papers*, 1:403; Krenkel, *Yates*, 196–97; Donald, *Inside Lincoln's Cabinet*, 161–62.
97. Kiper, *McClernand*, 135–39; Krenkel, *Yates*, 196–97; Beale, *Diary of Welles*, 1:153; NHS, 4 Oct., 15 Nov. 1862.
98. Krenkel, *Yates*, 197.
99. Krenkel, *Yates*, 186–97; Niven, *Chase Papers*, 1:403–5; NYH, 25 Sept. 1862; Donald, *Inside Lincoln's Cabinet*, 161; OR, series 3, 2:579–80; WDNI, 2 Oct. 1862.
100. Sprague to Lincoln, 26 Sept., 16 Oct. 1862, LP, LC; Basler, *CW*, 5:431; PDJ, 5 Aug. 1862.
101. Sprague to Lincoln, 26 Sept. 1862, LP, LC.
102. BDFP, 5, 6, 12 Sept. 1862; NYTi, 4 Sept. 1862; Williams, *Life of Abner Coburn*, 2–36; Dell, *War Democrats*, 170–71; WDNI, 15 Sept. 1861; BDWC, 1 May, 13 Jun., 14 Aug., 10, 11 Sept. 1862; Sobel and Raimo, *Directory of Governors*, 2:612–13; Hamlin, *The Life and Times of Hannibal Hamlin*, 439–40.
103. Stanford to Lincoln, 7, 29 Sep. 1862, LP, LC; Shutes, *Lincoln and California*, 87; Stanley, "Republican Party in California," 132–36, OS, 15 Sept. 1862; SFDAC, 2 Nov. 1862; Melendy and Gilbert, *Governors of California*, 115–27; WDNI, 5, 6, 7, 8 Nov. 1862.
104. Kibby, "Union Loyalty," 318; David, *Lincoln*, 373–74; Niven, *Chase Papers*, 1:402–3; Klingaman, *Lincoln*, 196.
105. Bradford to Curtin, 16 Sept. 1862, Slifer-Walls Collection, BUL; Nevins, *War Becomes Revolution*, 240; Beale, *Diary of Welles*, 1:156: BDHE, 27, 30 Sept, 1862; Klement, "Copperheads and Copperheadism in Wisconsin: Democratic Opposition to the Lincoln Administration," 182–92; Klement, *Lincoln's Critics*, 3–24, 109–18; Gamble to Montgomery Blair, 24 Sept. 1862, LP, LC; Abzug, "The Copperheads: Historical Approaches to Civil War Dissent in the Midwest," 40–55; Donald, *Liberty and Union*, 155; Weber, *Copperheads*, 93; Weeden, *War Government*, 224–47; Niven, *Chase Papers*, 1:400; Donald, *Inside Lincoln's Cabinet*, 158; Boman, *Gamble*, 177.
106. James F. Robinson to Lincoln, 29 Sept., Joshua Speed to Lincoln, 17 Sept. 1862, LP, LC; Engle, *Buell*, 296–97; Foulke, *Morton*, 1:193–96; BDHE, 30 Sept. 1862; Weeden, *War Government*, 234–35; Jonathan Herrold Diary, 30 Sept. 1862, Jonathan Herrold Papers, FHS; Johnson W. Culp Diary, 23 Sept. 1862, Johnson W. Culp Papers, FHS; Foulke, *Morton*, 1:194–95; Hughes and Whitney, *Jefferson Davis in Blue*, 103–26; Clark, *The Notorious "Bull" Nelson*, 137–60; CDE, 7, 8 Oct. 1862; Niven, *Chase Papers*, 1:406–7; NYTi, 7 Oct. 1862; ChiTri, 15 Oct. 1862; Paludan, *Presidency of Lincoln*, 156–57.
107. LDJ, 7 Oct. 1862.

Chapter Eleven

1. BDWC, 14 Oct. 1862; Basler, *CW*, 5:448, 450, 452, 460–62; OR, series 1, vol. 19, 349–50; NT, 18 Feb. 1892; Burlingame, *Lincoln*, 2:410–19.
2. McClellan to Washburn, 4 Oct., Washburn to Gen. Smith, 15 Oct. 1862, Executive Correspondence, MeSA; Sears, *Papers of McClellan*, 489; BDWC, 14 Oct. 1862; Washburn to Hamlin, 8 Oct. 1862, Washburn Papers, LC, two letters of the same date; Whalon, "Washburn and the War Department," 83–84; Basler, *CW*, 5:448, 450, 452, 460–62; Teillard, *Recollections of Abraham Lincoln, 1847–1865*, 147–48; OR, series 1, 19, p. 2:10; Marszalek, *Halleck*, 151; Sears, *McClellan*, 270–335.
3. H. Winslow Abbetts to Robinson, 3 Oct. 1862, Robinson Papers, KDLA; Lathrop, *Kirkwood*, 233–34; Eicher, *Longest Night*, 374–78; Basler, *CW*, 5:453.

4. *WES*, 7 Oct. 1862; Morton to Lincoln, 7 Oct. 1862, LP, LC; Morton to Stanton, 7 Oct. 1862, Stanton Papers, LC; *InDJ*, 10, 11 Oct. 1862; *PhiIn*, 7, 8 Oct. 1862; Basler, *CW*, 5:457–59; *ISJ*, 6 Oct. 1862; *OR*, series, 3, 2:499; Grimsley, *Hard Hand of War*, 84–95; Morton to Yates, 13 Nov. 1862, Reavis Papers, CHM.

5. Thomas Allen to Yates, 13 Oct. 1862, Yates Papers, FHS.

6. Stager to Stanton, 10 Oct. 1862, LP, LC; Niven, *Chase Papers*, 1:418; Noe, *Perryville*, passim; Engle, *Buell*, 286–320; Grimsley, *Hard Hand of War*, 78–79; [n. a.] to Robinson, 13 Oct., John Newman to Robinson, 10 Oct., Joshua Speed to Robinson, 14 Oct. 1862, Robinson Papers, KDLA; Niven, *Chase Papers*, 1:419, 421; Sears, *McClellan*, 330–35; Guroswki, *Diary*, 1:297.

7. *HDT*, 26 Oct. 1862; *HEP*, 8 Nov. 1862; L. D. Ballou to Blair, 3 Oct. 1862, Blair Papers, BHL; *ISJ*, 8 Dec. 1862, *BDHE*, 8 Dec. 1862; Burlingame, *Stoddard*, 112; Donald, *Lincoln*, 381.

8. *NYTi*, 3 Nov. 1862.

9. Robert Smith to Yates, 13 Oct., Yates to Nicolay, 17 Oct., David Davis to Lincoln, 14 Oct. 1862, LP, LC; Voegeli, *Free But Not Equal: The Midwest and the Negro during the Civil War*, 58–62; Smith, *No Party Now*, 55–56; Donald, *Lincoln*, 381–83; *ISJ*, 13 Nov. 1862; John B. McKee to Yates, 23 Sept. 1862, Yates Papers, ALPL.

10. *NYTi*, 7 Nov. 1862; *BP*, 4, 5 Nov. 1862; *LDT*, 9 Nov. 1862; *ISJ*, 6 Dec. 1862; *ChiTri*, 2 Jul. 1862; *WDNI*, 8 Nov. 1862; Escott, *What Shall We Do With the Negro*, 68; John Dix to Edwards Pierrepont, 3 Nov. 1862, "private," John Dix Papers, SUL; Voegeli, 'Union Policy,' 765–90; Voegeli, *Free But Not Equal*, 58–59; *OR*, series 1, 18:391, 395; Pearson, *Andrew*, 2:12–48, 67–68; Gerteis, *From Contraband to Freedom*, 23–24; Hamrogue, "Andrew," 173–80; Beale, *Diary of Welles*, 1:162; Andrew to Bolles, 16 Oct. 1862, Letters Received by the Secretary of War, Record Group 107, NARA; Andrew Letter Books, Dix to Andrew, 23 Sept., Bolles to Andrew, 30 Sept., Bolles to Andrew, 6 Oct. 1862, Andrew Papers, MHS; Hughes, *Letters of Forbes*, 2:16.

11. Daniel Hammond to sons Stephen and Jabez, [14] Nov., Jabez Hammond to Father, Mother, Brother, and Sister, 17 Nov. 1862, Hammond Family Papers, VHS.

12. Nevins, *War Becomes Revolution*, 299–300; Weber, *Copperheads*, 82–125; Grimsley, *Hard Hand of War*, 78–95, 130–38; Morton to Yates, 13 Nov. 1862, Reavis Papers, CHM; Collins, "Absentee Soldier Voting in Civil War Law and Politics," 3–250, 296–300.

13. Thornbrough, Riker, and Corpuz, *Diary of Fletcher*, 7, 553; Foulke, *Morton*, 1, 118, 203–5; Sylvester, "Morton," 120–38, 148–54; Stampp, *Indiana*, 180–223; Paludan, *Presidency of Lincoln*, 157–58; Weber, *Copperheads*, 82–125; Abbott, *Ohio's War Governors*, 26; Reid, *Ohio in the War*, 1:82; *CDE*, 29 Oct., 1 Nov. 1862; George F. Chittenden to Amanda, 15 Oct. 1862, George F. Chittenden Papers, ISL; John S. Davis to Henry Lane, 26 Oct. 1862, Henry S. Lane Papers, IHS; Blair, *With Malice toward Some*, 166–74.

14. *OR*, series 1, 16, pt. 2:619, 634, 13:802–3; *BDHE*, 15 Oct. 1862; Engle, *Buell*, 312–14; Foulke, *Morton*, 1:195–99; Robinson to Lincoln, 6 Oct., Horatio G. Wright to Lincoln, 8 Oct., Samuel Shellabarger to Lincoln, 22 Oct. 1862, LP, LC; Robinson to Sara, 18 Oct. 1862, Robinson Papers, KSHS; Charles Draper and Others to Blair, 6 Sept. 1862, Blair Papers, DPL; *CDE*, 3 Dec. 1862; David Davis to Swett, 26 Nov. 1862, David Davis Papers, ALPL; Marszalek, *Halleck*, 152; Burlingame, *With Lincoln in the White House*, 89; Noe, *Perryville*, 340–42.

15. *OR*, series 3, 2:651, 679; Morton to Lincoln, 7 Oct., Morton and Yates to Lincoln, 25 Oct. 1862, LP, LC; Foulke, *Morton*, 1:195–99; *InDJ*, 10, 11 Oct. 1862; Yates to Morton, 21, 22 Oct. 1862, Morton Telegraph Books, IUPUI.

16. Tod to Stanton, 3 Oct. 1862, Telegraphic Dispatches, series 144, OhSA; *OR*, series 1, 16, pt. 2:652; Alexander Varian to Sister, 5 Oct., Varian to Nettie, 8 Nov. 1862, Varian Papers, WRHS; *HEP*, 27 Oct. 1862.

17. *OR*, series 1, 16, pt. 2:642, 652; Niven, *Chase Papers*, 3:294–95; Joseph Mansfield to Stanton, 28 Aug. 1862, "private," Letters Received by the Secretary of War, RG 107, NARA.

18. White to Lincoln, 22 Oct. 1862, LP, LC; David Davis to Swett, 26 Nov. 1862, David Davis Papers, ALPL; Holloway to Nicolay, 24 Oct. 1862; Morton Letter Books, ISA; Nation and Towne, *Indiana's War*, 132–33; Morton to Yates, 13 Nov. 1862, Reavis Papers, CHM.

19. Basler, *CW*, 5:481; Sears, *McClellan*, 330–38; *NADL*, 28 Oct. 1862; *ChiTri*, 25, 29 Oct. 1862. Holt to Lincoln, 28 Oct., Morton and Yates to Lincoln, 25 Oct. 1862, LP, LC; George Allen to Yates, 3 Nov. 1862, Yates Papers, FHS; Niven, *Chase Papers*, 3:304–5; *NYTi*, 2 Nov. 1862; *OR*, series 1, 16, pt. 2:642; Thornbrough, Riker, and Corpuz, *Diary of Fletcher*, 7:558; Sears, *Papers of McClellan*, 503; Bradford to McClellan, 29 Sept. 1862, Bradford Papers, MdHS; *BDHE*, 29 Oct. 1862; *NDM*, 1 Oct. 1862; *BDA*, 1 Oct. 1862; Gurowski to Andrew, 25, 28 Oct. 1862, Andrew Papers, MHS.

20. Darby Babcock to Yates, 4 Nov., James Loomis to Yates, 30 Oct., John R. Woods to Yates, 3 Nov., M. Bradley to Yates, and reply, 31 Jul., Elder J. Hartley to Yates, 30 Aug., Yates to Hartley, 10 Sept. 1862, Yates Papers, ALPL; Trumbull to Chandler, 9 Nov. 1862, Chandler Papers, LC; Nortrup, "Yates," 272–79; Nevins, *War Becomes Revolution*, 320; Hesseltine, *Lincoln and the War Governors*, 264.

21. Basler, *CW*, 5:496–97; Boman, *Gamble*, 184–86; Boman, *Lincoln and Citizens' Rights in Missouri*, 146–63; Parrish, *Turbulent Partnership: Missouri and the Union*, 135–39; Rosin, *Gamble*, 265–65; *StLDMR*, 25 May, 16 Jun., 11 Aug., 9, 14, 18 Oct., 9, 10 Nov. 1862; Sabina Shroyer to Gamble, 5 Oct. 1862, Gamble Papers, MoHS; Yates to Lincoln, 19 Oct. 1862 LP, LC.

22. Fisher to Seward, 24 Sept., Fisher to Weed, 25 Sept. 1862, Seward Papers and Weed Papers, UR; Hancock, "Political History of Delaware, Part III," 7:370–72; *OR*, series 3, 2:658; Samuel Townsend to Gideon Waples, 21 Jul. 1862, Waples Family Papers, and also Townsend's proclamation to the "Douglas Democracy of Delaware," 20 Oct. 1862, Townsend Family Papers, UDL; Bendler, "The Old Democrat Principles," 37–39; *CDE*, 11 Nov. 1862.

23. *DR*, 1 May, 18, 25 Aug., 10, 13 Nov. 1862; Hancock, "Political History of Delaware, Part III," 7:368–75; Munroe, *History of Delaware*, 130–44; Scharf, *History of Delaware*, 1:348–55; *Del*, 18, 25 Aug., 25 Sept., 8, 10, 13 Nov. 1862; *WDNI*, 5, 6, 7 Nov. 1862; *TDSGR*, 14 Nov. 1862; *CDE*, 11 Nov. 1862; Smith, *No Party Now*, 58; Blair, *With Malice toward Some*, 171–72.

24. *EN*, 15 Nov. 1862; Wilson, *Robinson*, 97–99; Castel, *Civil War Kansas*, 94–96; *LDC*, 15, 25 Nov. 1862; Blackmar, *Kansas: A Cyclopedia of State History*, 1:289–90; *CDE*, 23 Oct. 1862; *LDT*, 1, 3, 10 Aug. 1862.

25. *LDT*, 10, 28 Aug., 2, 5, 6, 11, 13 Sept., 6 Nov. 1862; Blackmar, *Kansas*, 289–90; *NYTi*, 29 Jul. 1888.

26. *LDT*, 6, 11, 13 Sept., 6 Nov., 5 Dec. 1862; Blackmar, *Kansas*, 289–90; Castel, *Civil War Kansas*, 94–109, 89–110.

27. Preston King to Morgan, 20 Oct., Morgan to Thurlow Weed, 27 Jan., 9 Feb., Morgan to Solon Humphreys, 23, 27 Sept. 1862, Morgan Papers and Letter Books, NYSL; *NYTi*, 5, 10, 14 Nov. 1862; *NYTri*, 1, 2, 3, 4 Nov. 1862; James Wadsworth to David Dudley Field, Horace Greely, et al., 14 Sept., Henry J. Raymond to Wadsworth, 4 Oct., 1862,

James Wadsworth Papers, LC; *BS*, 4 Nov. 1862; *ISR*, 5 Nov. 1862; *PhiIn*, 5 Nov. 1862; Beale, *Diary of Welles*, 1:162; Brummer, *Political History of New York*, 220–26; Rawley, *Morgan*, 182; Mitchell, *Seymour*, 245–55; *BDWC*, 2 Oct. 1862; Dix to Edwards Pierrepont, 24 Nov. 1862, Dix Papers, with an enclosure of 15 Sept. 1862, marked "Private," to Dix and his 17 Sept. 1862 response, SUL; *HW*, 11, 25 Oct., 8 Nov. 1862; Mahood, *General Wadsworth*, 114–17; *WDNI*, 7 Oct. 1862; *WES*, 29 Sept. 1862; *DFP*, 30 Sept., 2, 3 Oct. 1862.

28. *NYTi*, 10 Nov. 1862.

29. Robert Livingston to William Seward, 4 Oct, 1862, "confidential," Seward Papers, UR; Donald, *Lincoln*, 382; Paludan, *Presidency of Lincoln*, 156–57; Rawley, *Morgan*, 182–83; *NYTri*, 13 Feb. 1886; Mitchell, *Seymour*, 245–55; Richard Busteed to Morgan, 22 Nov. 1862, Morgan Papers, NYSL; *HW*, 11, 25 Oct., 8 Nov. 1862; *WDNI*, 5, 6, 7, 8 Nov. 1862; *BS*, 6 Nov. 1862; *NYTi*, 5, 6, 9 Nov. 1862; *NDM*, 5 Nov. 1862; David Croly, *Seymour and Blair*, 83–88; "Speech of Horatio Seymour before the Democratic State Convention, 10 Sept. 1862," NYHS; Smith, *No Party Now*, 59–63; Cook and Knox, *Public Record of Horatio Seymour*, 45–58; Bryant to Lincoln, 22 Oct. 1862, LP, LC; Brummer, *Political History of New York*, 228–29; Charles B. Sedgwick to Washburn, 11 Nov. 1862, Washburn Papers, LC.

30. Charles Sumner to Lincoln, 8 Nov. 1862, LP, LC.

31. Hammond, *Diary of a Union Lady, 1861–1865*, 194–96.

32. Heslin, "A Yankee Soldier in a New York Regiment," 131; Howard Malcom Smith Diary, 4, 6, 13 Nov. 1862, Howard Malcolm Smith Papers, LC.

33. Brummer, *Political History of New York*, 226–64; *HW*, 22 Nov. 1862; *NYTi*, 13 Feb. 1886; *NYTri*, 23 Jan. 1863; Mitchell, *Seymour*, 244–55; Tap, *Over Lincoln's Shoulder*, 141; Weed to Seward, 5 Nov. 1862, Seward Papers, UR; Weed, *Autobiography*, 2:431; *WDNI*, 5, 6 Nov. 1862; *CDE*, 13 Nov. 1862; Nevins, *War Becomes Revolution*, 302–3; Speech of Henry J. Raymond, "Governor Seymour and the War," 16 Oct. 1863, NYHS; Beale, *Diary of Welles*, 1:152–54; Weeden, *War Government*, 303–5; Brooks, *Washington in Lincoln's Times*, 183–84.

34. As quoted in Gillette, *Jersey Blue*, 188–203; *NDM*, 29 Sept., 4, 25 Oct., 5 Nov. 1862; Jackson, *New Jerseyans*, 108; Dell, *War Democrats*, 180–81; *WDNI*, 23 Aug. 1861; Tandler, "The Political Front in Civil War New Jersey," 223–33; Nevins, *War Becomes Revolution*, 317–22; *TDSGR*, 1, 14 Oct., 3, 7, 8 Nov. 1862; *PhiIn*, 5 Nov. 1862; *BS*, 6 Nov. 1862; Parker to Rodman M. Price, 8 Sept. 1862, Rodman M. Price Papers, RUL.

35. Yard, *Memorial of Parker*, 1–37, 58–59, 117–22; Stellhorn and Birker, *Governors of New Jersey*, 132–34; Jackson, *New Jerseyans*, 108–9; Gillette, *Jersey Blue*, 188–202; *TDSGR*, 1, 14 Oct., 3 Nov. 1862; Dell, *War Democrats*, 180–81; Tandler, "Political Front," 223–27.

36. Henry Crapo to William Crapo, 10 Nov. 1862, Crapo Papers, BHL; Hesseltine, *Lincoln and the War Governors*, 268; Sobel and Raimo, *Directory of Governors*, 2:748; *DFP*, 2 Oct. 1862; *NYH*, 28, 1862; Moore, *History of Michigan*, 1:423–24; *CCR*, 6 Nov. 1862.

37. Andrew to Daniel Henshaw, 22 Oct. 1862, Andrew Papers, MHS; *NYTri*, 7 Nov. 1862; *HEP*, 25 Oct. 1862; *PDJ*, 25 Oct. 1862; *NDM*, 27 Oct. 1862; Pearson, *Andrew*, 2:53–60; Nevins, *War Becomes Revolution*, 305–7; Paludan, *Presidency of Lincoln*, 156–57; Voegeli, "Union Policy," 780–81; Fennimore, "Blair," 49:223–27; *DFP*, 7, 15 Nov. 1862; Haugland, "Ramsey," 130–45; Smith, *No Party Now*, 62; *BDA*, 8, 9, 10, 12 Oct., 6, 7, 10 Nov. 1862; Hesseltine, *Lincoln and the War Governors*, 265–67.

38. Robinson to Sara, 18 Oct. 1862, Robinson Papers, KSHS; *NYTri*, 7 Nov. 1862; Pearson, *Andrew*, 2:53–60; Nevins, *War Becomes Revolution*, 305–7; Orr, "Cities at War," 343.

39. Sears, *Dunn Browne's Experiences*, 41–42; Gillette, *Jersey Blue*, 204–5; *CDE*, 21 Nov. 1862; Folwell, *Minnesota*, 2:333–35; Morton S. Wilkinson to Lincoln, 7 Oct., Ramsey to Lincoln, 7 Oct. 1862, LP, LC; Guenztel, "Ramsey," 384–99; Downs, "The Soldier Vote and Minnesota Politics, 1862–1865," 187–210.

40. William B. Britton to Messrs. Gazette, 15 Nov. 1862, Britton Papers, WRHS.

41. *OR*, series 3, 2:640–51, 326, 418, 595, 646, 679, 691, 696–97, 735, 739–40, 743; Curtin to Stanton, 7 Oct. 1862, Executive Correspondence, PSA; *PhiIn*, 3, 6, 18, 28 Oct. 1862; Hesseltine, *Lincoln and the War Governors*, 278–79; McClure, *Lincoln and Men of War-Times*, 80–84; Kashatus, "Pennsylvania's War Governor," 28.

42. Quiner, *Wisconsin*, 148–49; Salomon to Lincoln, 1 Dec. 1862, LP, LC; Thwaites, *Messages*, 147–51; *ChiTri*, 29 Nov. 1862; *OR*, series 2, 5:174, series 3, 2:704, 743–46, 760–61, 765, 786; Folwell, *Minnesota*, 2:102–90; Oliver, "Draft Riots in Wisconsin during the Civil War," 334–37; Hesseltine, "Lincoln's Problems in Wisconsin," 194–95; Morton to Yates, 13 Nov. 1862, Reavis Papers, CHM; Hesseltine, *Lincoln and the War Governors*, 280–81.

43. *OR*, series 3, 2:653–56; Burlingame, *Lincoln*, 2:433–34.

44. Morton to Lincoln, 27 Oct., Stanton to McClernand, 29 Oct. 1862, "confidential," 1862, Stanton Papers, LC; Foulke, *Morton*, 1:208–12; *OR*, series 1, 17, pt. 2:332–35; Smith, "Broadsides for Freedom: Civil War Propaganda in New England," 295–96.

45. *OR*, series 3, 2:658, 670, 685, 690, 691–92, series 1, 17:467, 469; 705; Foulke, *Morton*, 1:211–12; Stanton to McClernand, 29 Oct. 1862, "confidential," Stanton Papers, LC; Hollandsworth, *Pretense of Glory*, 83–88; Fullbrook, "Relief Work in Iowa," 211–12; *IDSR*, 25, 26 Nov. 1862; Basler, *CW*, 5:468–69; Kiper, *McClernand*, 140–41; McClernand to Kirkwood, 27 Oct. 1862, McClernand Papers, ALPL.

46. Basler, *CW*, 5:485–86; Marszalek, *Halleck*, 153; Thomas and Hyman, *Stanton*, 250–58; Paludan, *Presidency of Lincoln*, 158–60; Sears, *Papers of McClellan*, 520–25; Sears, *McClellan*, 340–43; Burlingame, *Lincoln*, 2:423–33; Marvel, *Burnside*, 159–63; Gurowski to Andrew, 9 Nov. 1862, Andrew Papers, MHS; *BS*, 7 Nov. 1862; *PhiIn*, 24, 27, 28 Oct., 7 Nov. 1862; Burlingame, *With Lincoln in the White House*, 89–91; *NYTi*, 9, 12 Nov. 1862; *WDNI*, 12, 13 Nov. 1862; Preston King to Morgan, 4 Dec, Morgan to Stanton, 28 Oct., Horatio Seymour to Morgan, 10 Dec. 1862, Morgan Papers, NYSL; Albright, "Curtin," 48:157, 169–71; Curtin to Stanton, 21 Nov., Curtin to James Reynolds, 25 Nov. 1862, Curtin Letter Books, PSA.

47. Sprague to Lincoln, 11 Nov. 1862, LP, LC; Nevins, *War Becomes Revolution*, 330–37; Paludan, *Presidency of Lincoln*, 157–60; Marszalek, *Halleck*, 153–57; *OR*, series 3, 2:703–4; Burlingame, *Stoddard*, 119; Browne to Sprague, 6 Nov., James Elroy to Sprague, 22 Oct. 1862, Executive Letters Received, RISA; *LDJ*, 14, 20 Nov. 1862.

48. *OR*, series 1, 3:703–4, 735–36, 22:801–2, 827, series 3, 2:579, 591–93, 646–47, 658–62, 703–4, 735–36, 882; Gibson to Stanton, 3 Oct., Gibson to Gamble, 3 Oct., Gamble to Halleck, 10 Oct. 1862, Gamble Papers, MoHS; *CDE*, 15 Nov. 1862; Morton to Yates, 13 Nov. 1862, Reavis Papers, CHM; Boman, *Gamble*, 177–84; Gamble to Lincoln, 17 Nov., Gamble to Halleck, [n.d.] Oct., Gamble to Lincoln, 17 Nov., Benjamin Gratz Brown to John G. Nicolay, 25 Nov. 1862, LP, LC; Basler, *CW*, 5:5–17, 515–16, 538, 6:23; Nicolay and Hay, *Complete Works of Lincoln*, 8:90–92; Sutherland, *Savage Conflict*, 121–22.

49. Stone, *Rhode Island*, 178–80; Rable, *Fredericksburg!*, 50–62; Marvel, *Burnside*, 166–74.

50. Clark, *Kirkwood*, 293–94; Rable, *Fredericksburg!*, 50–62; Marvel, *Burnside*, 166–74.

51. PDT, 12 Sept. 1862, LP, LC, enclosed with Gibbs to Lincoln; Dell, *War Democrats*, 168–69; E. M. Banning to [Judge], 18 Aug., J. D. West to Gibbs, 13 Oct., James S. Nesmith

562 Notes to Chapter 11

to Gibbs, 28 Aug. 1862, Gibbs Papers, OrHS; Gibbs to Gen. E. L. Applegate, 28 Nov. 1862, Addison Gibbs Papers, Special Collections, UOL; *OS*, 13 Oct. 1862; McArthur, *The Enemy Never Came*, 40–41.

52. Gibbs to Lincoln, 12 Sept. 1862, LP, LC; Edwards, "Pacific," 136–43; Nesmith to Gibbs, 28 Aug. 1862, Gibbs Papers, OHS; *Senate and House Journal of the State of Oregon*, 3–11.

53. *OR*, series 1, 50, pt. 2:166; Edwards, "Pacific," 136–43; Edwards, "Six Oregon Leaders," 22; Edwards, "Oregon Regiments," 60–70; Anson G. Henry to Lincoln, 17 Oct. 1862, LP, LC.

54. Ramsey to Lincoln, 6 Sept. 1862, LP, LC; Lincoln to Ramsey, 25, 27 Aug., Ramsey to Lincoln, 6 Sept., 14, 22 Oct., John Nicolay to Ramsey, 20 Oct. 1862, Governor's Papers, Executive Journals, MnHS; Ramsey to Lincoln, 28 Nov. 1862, Robert Todd Collection, MnHS; Ramsey to Chase, 12 Jun. 1863, Governor's Papers, MnHS; Babcock, "Minnesota's Frontier," 274–86; Folwell, *Minnesota*, 2:106–211; *OR*, series 1, 13:616–17; Haugland, "Ramsey's Rise to Power," 329–33; Guentzel, "Ramsey," 384–99; Josephy, *War in the American West*, 130–54.

55. *OR*, series 1, 13:685–86; Schutz and Trenerry, *Pope*, 175–77; George A. S. Crooker to Lincoln, 7 Oct. 1862, LP, LC; Nichols, "The Other Civil War," 2–15; "Extracts, Sibley," Sibley Papers, MnHS; *StPDPi*, 22, 23 Oct. 1862; Berg, *38 Nooses*, 37–221; Josephy, *War in the American West*, 130–54.

56. Ramsey to Lincoln, 10 Nov., Nicolay to Hay, 8 Sept., Smith to Lincoln, 10 Nov. 1862, LP, LC; Basler, *CW*, 5:493; *OR*, series 1, 13:787; Folwell, *Minnesota*, 2:187–211; Berg, *38 Nooses*, 37–221; Josephy, *War in the American West*, 130–54; Donald, *Lincoln*, 394.

57. Ramsey to Lincoln, 28 Nov., George A. S. Crooker to Lincoln, 7 Oct. 1862, LP, LC; Ramsey to Stanton, 14 Oct., Nicolay to Ramsey, 23 Oct. 1862, Letters Received by the Secretary of War, RG 107, NARA; Folwell, *Minnesota*, 2:207–12, 187–211; Nichols, "The Other War," 2–15; Guentzel, "Ramsey," 384–99; "Extracts, Sibley," Sibley Papers, MnHS; *StPDPi*, 23 Oct., 8, 12, 27 Nov. 1862; Berg, *38 Nooses*, 37–221; Ramsey to Salomon, 31 Oct. 1862, Executive Correspondence, SHSW; Basler, *CW*, 5:493; *OR*, series 1, 13:787; Nicolay to Ramsey, 20 Oct., Ramsey to Lincoln, 22 Oct. 1862, Governor's Papers, Executive Journals, MnHS; Geary, *We Need Men*, 35.

58. Pope to Lincoln, 8 Nov. 1862, LP, LC; Basler, *CW*, 5:503–4, 512–14, 542–43, 6:6–7; *StPDPi*, 27 Nov. 1862; Donald, *Lincoln*, 394–95; George Robertson to Lincoln, 19 Nov., Utley to Lincoln, 17 Nov., Utley to Randall, 17 Nov. 1862, LP, LC. Only thirty-eight Indians were executed, one was pardoned at the last minute.

59. *OR*, series 3, 2:862, 865; Marvel, *Burnside*, 168–69; Burlingame, *Lincoln*, 2:443–45; John M. Schofield to James S. Thomas, 5 Dec., Curtis to Lincoln, 12 Dec. 1862, LP, LC.

60. Franklin J. Candee to Horace Fenn, 30 Nov. 1862, Horace Fenn Papers, CtHS; Paludan, *Presidency of Lincoln*, 160; Basler, *CW*, 5:511, 514–15; Rable, *Fredericksburg!*, 116–17, 132–33; Marvel, *Burnside*, 169–76; *HEP*, 17 Dec. 1862; *Lbr*, 21 Dec. 1855; Pearson, *Andrew*, 2:63, 68–69; Sargent to Andrew, 11 Nov. 1862, Andrew Papers, MHS; Hesseltine, *Lincoln and the War Governors*, 20–23; Stearns, *Cambridge Sketches*, 263; Robboy and Robboy, "Lewis Hayden: From Fugitive Slave to Statesman," 591–613; Quarles, *The Negro in the Civil War*, 101; *BG*, 20 Nov. 2012.

61. Burlingame, *Stoddard*, 124–25.

62. Basler, *CW*, 5:518–37, 537–38, 542–43; Donald, *Lincoln*, 396–98, 395–96; Burlingame, *Lincoln*, 2:440; Pearson, *Andrew*, 2:68–69; *WES*, 19 Dec. 1862; Beale, *Diary of Welles*, 1:186; Nichols, "The Other Civil War," 2–15; Lincoln to Sibley, 16 Dec., Sibley to Lincoln, 27 Dec. 1862, Sibley Papers, MnHS.

63. *OR*, series 3, 2:902–4; Nicolay and Hay, *Complete Works of Lincoln*, 8:93–131; Hesseltine, *Lincoln and the War Governors*, 277–78; Andrew to Sprague, 6 Nov. 1862, Executive Letters Received, RISA; Marshall, *War of the People*, 99–100; Robinson to Lincoln, 21 Dec. 1862, LP, LC; *LDJ*, 13 Dec. 1862; Peeples and Ridgway to Yates, 20 Nov. 1862, Yates Papers, ALPL.

64. Basler, *CW*, 6:10–11, 21; G. W. McClung to Gamble, 9 Dec. 1862, Gamble Papers, MoHS; Boman, *Lincoln and Citizens' Rights in Missouri*, 146–56.

65. Thornbrough, Riker, and Corpuz, *Diary of Fletcher*, 7, 589–90; Marvel, *Burnside*, 169–76.

66. *BDWC*, 25, 27 Dec. 1862; Dimeglio, "Civil War Bangor," 64; Rable, *Fredericksburg!*, 190–322; Marvel, *Burnside*, 175–200; Paludan, *Presidency of Lincoln*, 167; Eicher, *Longest Night*, 395–405; *InDJ*, 17, 20 Dec. 1862; *NDM*, 17 Dec. 1862; *ChiTri*, 17 Dec. 1862; Journal of Samuel P. Heintzelman, 15–17, Dec. 1862, Samuel P. Heintzelman Papers, LC; Samuel Thompson, *Heintzelman*, 271–72; Horatio Nelson Taft Diary, 1, 2, 4 Jan. 1863, Horatio Taft Papers, LC; *ChiTri*, 17 Dec. 1862; *InDJ*, 20 Dec. 1862.

67. Jackson, *New Jerseyans*, 113–15; Rable, *Fredericksburg!*, 271–322; Marvel, *Burnside*, 202–8.

68. *ChiTri*, 20 Dec. 1862.

69. Col. Aaron Stevens to Nathaniel Berry, 22 Dec. 1862, Aaron Stevens Papers, NHHS.

70. Israel Washburn to Hannibal Hamlin, 17 Dec., Stanton to Washburn, 9 Nov., Washburn to Hamlin, 21 Nov. 1862, Washburn Papers, LC; *WDNI*, 29 Dec. 1862; *BDWC*, 13, 19 Nov., 27 Dec. 1862; Peter H. Watson to Washburn, 30 Oct. 1862, Executive Correspondence, MeSA; Washburn to Oliver O. Howard, 2 Nov. 1862, Howard Papers, BCL; see also Charles Tilden to Washburn, 23 Dec. 1862, Charles W. Tilden Papers, MeSA.

71. Washburn to Hamlin, 17, [20], 24 Dec. 1862, 16 Jan. 1863, Washburn Papers, LC; Whalon, "Maine Republicans," 119–23.

72. Varian to Nettie, 23 Dec. 1862, Varian Papers, WRHS.

73. Mowry, "Reminiscences of Lincoln: Told by the Late Ex-Governor Curtin of Pennsylvania," 4; Perret, *Lincoln's War*, 230; Rice, *Reminiscences of Abraham Lincoln by Distinguished Men of His Time*, 9–10; Burlingame, *Lincoln*, 2:446; *OR*, series 1, 21:860; *WES*, 22 Dec. 1862; *PhiIn*, 11 Dec. 1862; Egle, *Curtin*, 390–91.

74. Whipple, *The Story-Life of Lincoln*, 489–90; Rice, *Reminiscences of Lincoln*, 9–10; Burlingame, *Lincoln*, 2:446.

75. Staudenraus, *Mr. Lincoln's Washington*, 45.

76. *HEP*, 8, 9, 10, 17 Dec. 1862; Niven, *Connecticut for the Union*, 94–95, 104–5; *HC*, 16 Dec. 1862; Gordon, *A Broken Regiment*, 54–59.

77. James H. Bayard to Thomas F. Bayard, 21 Dec. 1862, Thomas Bayard Papers, LC; Sears, *Dunn Browne's Experiences*, 49–51; Niven, *Connecticut for the Union*, 94–95, 104–5; *HEP*, 8, 9, 10, 15, 17 Dec. 1862, 2 Jan. 1863; *HC*, 16 Dec. 1862; *WDNI*, 1 Jan. 1862; Message of Buckingham, 9 Dec. 1862, 9–15; Message of 6 May 1863, 14–15; Van Buren Kinney Reminiscences, Dec. 1862, Van Buren Kinney Papers, CtHS; Pastor George Wood to Buckingham, 24 Oct., M. Lillie to Buckingham, 27 Oct. 1862, Governor's Correspondence, CtSA.

78. As quoted in Paludan, *Presidency of Lincoln*, 172; Randall, *Lincoln*, 2:242–43; Hughes, *Letters of Forbes*, 1:343; Beale, *Diary of Bates*, 269–70; Segal, *Conversations with Lincoln*, 220–32; Perret, *Lincoln's War*, 232–34; Burlingame, *Lincoln*, 2:447–53; James H. Bayard to Thomas F. Bayard, 21 Dec. 21, 1862, Bayard Papers, LC; Stahr, *Seward*, 356–59; Fessenden, *Life and Public Services of William Pitt Fessenden*, 1:230–52; *PhiIn*, 20 Dec. 1862; *HEP*, 22 Dec. 1862; *NDM*, 22 Dec. 1862.

79. Burlingame, *Stoddard*, 108, 127; Thomas and Hyman, *Stanton*, 253; Beale, *Diary of Bates*, 269–70; Segal, *Conversations with Lincoln*, 220–32; Burlingame, *Lincoln*, 2:450–54; Jacob Collamer to Lincoln, 18 Dec. 1862, LP, LC; Perret, *Lincoln's War*, 232–34; Beale, *Diary of Welles*, 1:196–206; *ChiTri*, 20 Dec. 1862; *HEP*, 22 Dec. 1862; *NDM*, 22 Dec. 1862; Stahr, *Seward*, 357–59; Paludan, *Presidency of Lincoln*, 172; Cook, *Civil War Senator: Fessenden*, 153–56.

80. *ChiTri*, 25 Dec. 1862; Beale, *Diary of Bates*, 269–70; Paludan, *Presidency of Lincoln*, 167–75; Burlingame, *Lincoln*, 2:450–54; Donald, *Lincoln*, 400–406; Basler, *CW*, 6:12–13; Beale, *Diary of Welles*, 1:196–206; Thomas and Hyman, *Stanton*, 253–55; Burlingame, *Stoddard*, 127–29; Nivens, *Chase Papers*, 3:340–43; Stahr, *Seward*, 357–59; Niven, *Chase*, 308–13; Perret, *Lincoln's War*, 232–34; *WDNI*, 20 Dec. 1862; Cook, *Civil War Senator*, 153–56.

81. Eicher, *The Longest Night*, 400–433; Gamble to Blair, 24 Sept., Gamble to Lincoln, 5, 18 Dec., Gamble to Curtis, 1 Dec., Lincoln to Gamble, 30 Dec., Gamble to Lincoln, 31 Dec. 1862, Lincoln to Curtis, 5 Jan. 1863, LP, LC; Blair to Gamble, 27 Sept. 1862, Gamble Papers, MoHS; Basler, *CW*, 6:8–11, 13, 21; Boman, *Lincoln and Citizens' Rights in Missouri*, 146–60.

82. Bradford to Blair, 17 Oct., 26 Nov., Thomas Hicks to Blair, 25 Oct., 30 Nov. 1862, Blair Family Papers, LC; A. C. Gibbs to Bradford, 16 Dec. 1862, Governor's Letter Books, MdSA; Clark, "Politics in Maryland," 40:308; Bradford's Journal, 29 Dec. 1862, MdHS; Wagandt, *Mighty Revolution*, 88–89; 94, 116–21; *PhiIn*, 31 Dec. 1862; Baker, *Politics of Continuity*, 81–83.

83. As quoted in Thornbrough, *Indiana*, 174; Thornburgh, "Morton," 81–82; *NYTri*, 18 Dec. 1862; *WDNI*, 20 Dec. 1862; *ISJ*, 17 Dec. 1862.

84. Holbrook's Message to the Legislature, 10 Oct. 1862, *Journal of the Senate of the State of Vermont, 1862*, 23–33; Wickman, *We Are Coming Father Abra'am*, 161–78.

85. Ambler, *Pierpont*, 186–89; Ridderbusch, "Lincoln Manuscript," 82–83; [John] Pierpont to Brother Francis, 28 Sept. 1862, West Virginia Adjutant Generals Collection, Pierpont-Samuels Papers, WvDCH; *LDJ*, 25 Nov. 1862.

86. Ridderbusch, "Lincoln Manuscript," 82–83; Ambler, *Pierpont*, 186–89; Roberts, "Federal Government and Confederate Cotton," 262–75; Abbott, *Cotton and Capital*, 72–80; *ChiTri*, 30 Dec. 1862.

87. Basler, *CW*, 6:22–23.

88. As quoted in Marszalek, *Halleck*, 159; Johnson and Buel, *Battles and Leaders*, 6:470. In December, Halleck and Stanton invited German-American political philosopher Francis Lieber to come to Washington and serve on a board to establish a "code of regulations" for the conduct of troops during war. Published in 1863 under the title *Code for the Government of Armies in the Field*, Lieber's code became the basis for Lincoln's understanding of the laws of war. Witt, *Lincoln's Code*, 229–49.

89. Pearson, *Andrew*, 2:64–65; Sumner to Andrew, 28 Dec. 1862, Andrew Papers, MHS, unable to locate Andrew to Sumner, 25 Dec. 1862, Andrew Letter Books, MHS; Andrew to Icabod Berry, 23 Dec. 1862, John Andrew Papers, NHHS; Andrew Scrapbook, BCL, contains copy of letter from Andrew to Francis W. Bird, 13 Jan. 1863.

90. Thornbrough, Riker, and Corpuz, *Diary of Fletcher*, 7:600–601.

91. Pearson, *Andrew*, 2:64–65.

92. *HEP*, 16 Dec. 1862.

93. Pierpont to Lincoln, 18, 30 Dec., Pierpont to J. G. Blair, 20 Dec., Archibald Campbell to Lincoln, 31 Dec. 1862, LP, LC; Basler, *CW*, 6:17; Burlingame, *Stoddard*, 125–26; *PhiIn*, 10 Dec. 1862; *HEP*, 16 Dec. 1862; Niven, *Chase Papers*, 3:345–49; Ambler, *Pierpont*,

177–85; Paludan, *Presidency of Lincoln*, 178–79; *WDNI*, 11 Dec. 1862; Langford, "Constitutional Issues," 14–31; Moore, "Slavery as a Factor," 68–89; Shaffer, "Lincoln and West Virginia," 86–100; Stealey, *West Virginia's Civil War–Era Constitution*, 105–6; Burlingame, *Lincoln*, 2:460–62; Zimring, "'Secession in Favor of the Constitution,'" 23–51; Sutherland, *Savage Conflict*, 161–63; *WDI*, 6 Dec. 1862.

94. *OR*, series 3, 2:956; *InDJ*, 10, 15, 29 Nov. 1862; Ambler, *Pierpont*, 416–18, Langford, "Constitutional Issues," 14–31; *PhiIn*, 10, 24 Dec. 1862; *NDM*, 11, 24 Dec. 1862; *HEP*, 16 Dec. 1862; Zimring, "'Secession in Favor of the Constitution,'" 23–51.

95. Lincoln's Memorandum, 31 Dec., Stanton to Lincoln, 26 Dec., Blair to Lincoln, 26 Dec., Seward to Lincoln, 26 Dec., Chase to Lincoln, 29 Dec., Bates to Lincoln, 27 Dec., Welles to Lincoln, 29 Dec. 1862, LP, LC; Basler, *CW*, 8:392; Ambler, *Pierpont*, 184–86; Beale, *Diary of Welles*, 1:206–7; Langford, "Constitutional Issues," 14–31; Shaffer, "Lincoln and West Virginia," 86–100; Burlingame, *Lincoln*, 2:460–62; *NDM*, 24 Dec. 1862; *PhiIn*, 24 Dec. 1862.

96. Hicks to Blair, 25 Oct. 1862, Blair Family Papers, LC; Lincoln's Memorandum, 31 Dec. 1862, LC; Langford, "Constitutional Issues," 14–31; Moore, "Slavery as a Factor," 69–89; Shaffer, "Lincoln and West Virginia," 86–100; Zimring, "'Secession in Favor of the Constitution,'" 23–51.

Chapter Twelve

1. Diary of Almon Graham, 1 Jan. 1863, Graham Papers, BECHS.

2. G. A. [Swasy] to Andrew, 2 Jan. 1863, Andrew Papers, MHS; Hervey L. Howe to Brother, 22 Jan. 1863, Hervey L. Howe Papers, SUL.

3. Basler, *CW*, 6:46–48; *OR*, series 1, 21:944–45, 953–54; Marvel, *Burnside*, 208–12; Donald, *Lincoln*, 409–11; Marszalek, *Halleck*, 162–65; Thomas and Hyman, *Stanton*, 251–53; Burlingame, *Stoddard*, 132–34; Horatio Nelson Taft Diary, 1, 2, 4 Jan. 1863, LC; *WDNI*, 1, 3 Jan. 1863.

4. Williams, *Life of Coburn*, 42–75; *BDWC*, 5, 6, 7, 9 Jan. 1863; *HEP*, 8, 9 Jan. 1863; Whalon, "Maine Republicans," 153–55; Stanton to Coburn, 16 [Jan.] 1863, Executive Correspondence, MeSA; Donald, *Lincoln*, 407; Hancock, *Delaware during the Civil War*, 122–23; Cannon to Stanton, 29 Jan. 1863, Stanton Papers, LC; Bowen, *Massachusetts in the War*, 1:52; Staudenraus, *Mr. Lincoln's Washington*, 57–60; Schouler, *Massachusetts in the Civil War*, 1:391–97; *WDNI*, 3 Jan. 1863; *BDA*, 2, 3 Jan. 1863.

5. *Annual Message of Governor Ramsey to the Legislature of Minnesota, Jan. 7, 1863*; *StPDPi*, 9 Jan. 1863; Segal, *Conversations with Lincoln*, 234–35.

6. *BDFP*, 2 Jan. 1863.

7. *OS*, 6 Oct. 1862.

8. As quoted in Sylvester, "Morton," 138–39; Thornbrough, Riker, and Corpuz, *Diary of Fletcher*, 8:6–7; Thornbrough, *Indiana*, 196; *Journal of the Senate of the State of Indiana, 1863*, 697–98; Foulke, *Morton*, 1:213–17; *ChiTri*, 14, 21 Jan. 1863; *CDE*, 21 Jan. 1863; J. L. Beach to Charles Wetherhill, 10 Jan. 1863, Charles Wetherhill Papers, ISA; Tatum, "Please Send Stamps," 201–12; David P. Craig to Wife, 25 Jan. 1863, David P. Craig Papers, ISL; Basler, *CW*, 6:28–31, 52–53; *OR*, series 3, 3:2–3; Donald, *Lincoln*, 407–8; Paludan, *Presidency of Lincoln*, 186–90.

9. *Report of the Adjutant General of the State of Indiana*, 2:589, 591; White, *Emancipation, the Union Army, and the Reelection of Lincoln*, 45.

10. Varian to Sister, 5 Oct. 1862, Varian Papers, WRHS.

11. Aetna Pettis to Wife Julia, 17 Jan. 1863, Aetna Pettis Papers, FHS; James Sligh to Mother, 9 Feb. 1863, Sligh Family Papers, BHL; G. H. Kilborn to McArthur, 23 Dec., 16 Jan. 1863, Reuben McArthur Papers, BHL; Thomas Read to Parents, 7 Jan. 1863, Thomas Read Papers, BHL.

12. George A. Mitchell to Parents, 4 Jan. 1863, George A. Mitchel Papers, NYHS.

13. As quoted in Sylvester, "Morton," 164; A. A. Terrell to Yates, 25 Dec. 1862, Yates Papers, ALPL.

14. *ISJ*, 19 Jan. 1863.

15. *ChiTri*, 15 Jan. 1863; Nortrup, "Yates: Civil War Governor," 279–82; Governor's Message to the General Assembly, 5 Jan. 1863, *Illinois Senate Journal*, 1863, 3–64; Eddy, *Patriotism of Illinois*, 518–19; Guelzo, "Defending Emancipation," 319–20; Lusk, *Politics and Politicians*, 149–61; *ISR*, 3 Jan. 1863; Gillette, *Jersey Blue*, 206–7; Reavis, *Yates*, 26–27; Miller, *Black Civil War Soldiers of Illinois*, 5–10; Grimsley, *Hard Hand of War*, 120–30; *ISJ*, 7 Jan. 1863; L. [Nouland] to Yates, 12 Jan., "private & confidential," John Humphrey to Yates, 6 Jan., William K. Strong to Yates, 8 Jan. 1863, Yates Papers, ALPL.

16. William W. Orme to David Davis, 30 Jan. 1863, David Davis Papers, ALFL.

17. Fuller, *Messages*, 469–75; Fennimore, "Blair," 49:344–54; Harris, "Blair," 143–52; *DFP*, 9 Jan. 1863; *ChiTri*, 16 Jan. 1863; May, *Michigan and the Civil War Years*, 40–41.

18. Fuller, *Messages*, 469–75; [Michigan soldier] to Blair, 7 Mar. 1863, Blair Papers, DPL; Clark, *Kirkwood*, 238–43; Niven, *Connecticut for the Union*, 100–105; *OR* series 2, 4:131–33, 295–99, 474, 598, 638–39, 649–50.

19. Mrs. Samuel Crane, Mrs. Francis Pierpont, and Mrs. L. A. Hagans to Lincoln, 1 Jan. 1863, LP, LC; Langford, "Constitutional Issues," 21–31; Shaffer, "Lincoln and West Virginia," 86–100; *LDJ*, 7 Jan. 1863.

20. Basler, *CW*, 6:39, 424–25; Donald, *Lincoln*, 408; Eicher, *Longest Night*, 419–28; Cozzens, *No Better Place to Die*; McPherson, *Tried By War*, 156; Burlingame, *With Lincoln in the White House*, 102.

21. W. R. Holloway to John G. Nicolay, 2 Jan. 1863, LP, LC; Sylvester, "Morton," 179; Morton to Stanton, 2 Jan. 1863, Morton Letter Books, ISA; *ChiTri*, 14 Jan. 1863; William H. Terrell to John Wilder, 24 Jan. 1863, John T. Wilder Papers, and James C. Vanderbilt to Mother, 24 Jan. 1863, James C. Vanderbilt Papers, ISL; Nation and Towne, *Indiana's War*, 135–38; Sylvester, "Morton," 157–67; *OR*, series 1, 2, pt. 2:297; *InDJ*, 8, 10, 15, 16, 19, 28 Jan. 1863; *DFP*, 11 Feb. 1863; *ChiTri*, 14 Jan. 1863; John L. Ketchman to Jane Ketchman, 18 Jan. 1863, John L. Ketchman Papers, and Ezra Bowlus to Wife and to Samuel Williar, 22 Jan., Feb. 1863, Ezra Bowlus Papers, HIS; *CDE*, 16 Jan. 1863.

22. Foulke, *Morton*, 1:214–15; Thornbrough, *Indiana*, 180–89; Klement, *Copperheads of the Middle West*, 25; Klement, *Dark Lanterns*, 47, 48–49; Nation and Towne, *Indiana's War*, 134–37; French, *Morton*, 253, 313–17; Stampp, *Indiana Politics*, 168–73; Terrell, *Indiana in the War*, 331–33; Dell, *War Democrats*, 151, 200–201; Sylvester, "Morton," 184–87; *InDJ*, 20, 21 Jan. 1863; *ChiTri*, 14 Jan. 1863; George O'Brien to Kirkwood, 7 Apr. 1863, Kirkwood Papers, ISA; Lathrop, *Kirkwood*, 238–42.

23. *OR*, series 3, 3:4; Thornbrough, *Indiana*, 120–30, 184; Foulke, *Morton*, 1:213–17, 231–35; Thornbrough, Riker, and Corpuz, *Diary of Fletcher*, 8:4–7; Pierce, *Memoir and Letters of Charles Sumner*, 4:114; Tredway, *Democratic Opposition*, 170–75; William A. Lawrence Account, William H. Newlin Papers, LC; Weeden, *War Government*, 235–37, 337; *InDJ*, 8, 10, 15, 16, 17, 19, 20 Jan. 1863; *BDWC*, 18 Feb. 1863.

24. Yates to Morton, 19 Jan. 1863, Yates Papers, ALPL; Nortrup, "Yates: Civil War Governor," 282–85; *Illinois Senate Journal*, 1863, 585–86; Yates to Morton, 19 Jan. 1863, John

Brayton Papers, ISL; Nortrup, "Yates, the Prorogued Legislature," 9–34; *ISJ*, 24 Jan. 1863; Sylvester, "Morton," 167–73; *InDJ*, 8, 10, 15, 16, 17, 19, 20, 21 Jan. 1863.

25. Nortrup, "Yates: Civil War Governor," 282–85; *Illinois Senate Journal*, 1863, 585–86; Nortrup, "Yates, the Prorogued Legislature," 9–34; Carr to Yates, 15 Feb., Horatio Wright to Yates, 18 Feb. 1863, "confidential," [T. A.] Eastman to Yates, 18 Feb., Yates to Gen. Wright, 27 Feb. 1863, Yates Papers, ALPL; Tap, *Over Lincoln's Shoulder*, 155, Yates to Chase, 2 Feb. 1863, Chase Papers, CGS.

26. Kiper, *McClernand*, 156–79; *WDNI*, 21 Jan. 1863; Message of the Governor of Ohio to the Fifty-Fifth General Assembly, 5 Jan. 1863, *Ohio House Journal*; Trester, "Tod," 156–58; *Ohio Executive Documents*, 1862, 1:8; Porter, *Ohio Politics*, 114–17; *CDE*, 7, 8 Jan. 1863.

27. *ChiTri*, 21 Jan. 1863; Stanton to Lincoln, [n.d.], 1863, LP, LC; Gillette, *Jersey Blue*, 213–23; Inaugural Address of Joel Parker, *New Jersey Legislative Documents*; Jackson, *New Jerseyans*, 118–19, 122–25; Yard, *Memorial of Parker*, 13–17; *ChiTri*, 21 Jan. 1863; Platt, *Charles Perrin Smith*, 130–31; Dell, *War Democrats*, 202–4; *WDNI*, 21 Jan. 1863; Green, "The Emancipation Proclamation in New Jersey and the Paranoid Style," 112–20; Hatch, "David Naar of Trenton," 82–85; *TDSGR*, 8, 15, 20, 24 Jan., 17 Feb., 2 Mar. 1863.

28. Lincoln to Curtis, 5 Jan. 1863, Gamble to Lincoln, 31 Dec. 1862, Charles Gibson to Lincoln, 23 Feb., William H. Hall to Lincoln, 7 Jan., Charles D. Drake to Lincoln, 22 Jan., Gilchrist Porter to John B. Henderson, 11 Feb., Henderson to Lincoln, Jan, [n.d.] 1863, LP, LC; Burlingame, *Lincoln*, 2:535–37; *OR*, series 1, 22:888, pt. 2:16–18, 78–82; Basler, *CW*, 6:36–38, 52–53; Boman, *Gamble*, 199–203; Andrew Brownlow to Gamble, 1 Aug., Peruque Bridge to Gamble, 9, 12 Sept. 1862, Gibson to Gamble, 4, 6 Jan., Barton Bates to Gamble, 21 Jan. 1863, "private," Gamble Papers, MoHS; Sutherland, *Savage Conflict*, 128–30; Rosin, "Gamble," 285–315; *StLDMR*, 2 Mar. 1863; Boman, *Lincoln and Citizens' Rights in Missouri*, 146–63; Harris, *Lincoln and the Border States*, 308–20; Blackmar, *Robinson*, 290–91; Sobel and Raimo, *Directory of Governors*, 2:460–61; Wilson, *Robinson*, 99–100.

29. Basler, *CW*, 6:36–38; *OR*, series 1, 22, pt. 2:16–18; Boman, *Gamble*, 199–203; Harris, *Lincoln and the Border States*, 308–20; Barton Bates to Gamble, 21 Jan. 1863, "private," Gamble Papers, MoHS.

30. Basler, *CW*, 6:37–38, 65; *OR*, series 1, 22, pt. 2:42–43, series 3, 3:52; Boman, *Gamble*, 200–206; Samuel T. Glover to Ed Bates, 15 May 1863, LP, LC; Gibson to Gamble, 6 Jan., "private," Barton Bates to Gamble, 21 Jan., "private," Gamble to Curtis, 9 Feb. 1863, Gamble Papers, MoHS; Harris, *Lincoln and the Border States*, 308–20.

31. Hervey L. Howe to Brother, 5 Feb., 24 Mar. 1863, Hervey L. Howe Papers, SUL (Hervey was in the 89th New York); Diary of Almon Graham, 4, 5, 6 Feb. 1863, Graham Papers, BECHS; Randall, *Lincoln*, 2:185; Berlin, Reidy, and Rowland, *Freedom's Soldiers*, 11–13; Burlingame, *Stoddard*, 135.

32. Edwin O. Wentworth to Brother John, 13 Feb. 1863, Edwin O. Wentworth Papers, LC.

33. Buckingham to Lincoln, 2 Jan., Lincoln to Buckingham, 12 Jan. 1863, LP, LC; Basler, *CW*, 5, 54; Miller, "Brahmin Janissaries," 227; Berlin, Reidy, and Rowland, *Freedom's Soldiers*, 11–13; Randall, *Lincoln*, 2:185–86; Bowen, *Massachusetts in the War*, 1:52–55; Higginson, *Army Life in a Black Regiment*, 15; Pearson, *Andrew*, 2:144–45; Cornish, *The Sable Arm*, 69; Jimerson, *Private Civil War*, 96–101; Belz, *Abraham Lincoln, Constitutionalism, and Equal Rights in the Civil War Era*, 120–23; *DFP*, 31 Jan. 1863; *TDSGR*, 7 Feb. 1863; Duncan, *Blue-Eyed Child of Fortune*, 20–25; Whalon, "Maine Republicans," 123–26; Luke and Smith, *Soldiering for Freedom*, 17–19; Lincoln to Buckingham, 12 Jan. 1863, LP, LC; Cimbala and Miller, *Union Soldiers and the Northern Home Front*, 334.

34. Foulke, *Morton*, 1:237–41; Thornbrough, *Indiana*, 183–87, 185–89; Thornbrough, Riker, and Corpuz, *Diary of Fletcher*, 8:154; Weeden, *War Government*, 337–38; Nation and Towne, *Indiana's War*, 137–39; Benton, *Voting in the Field*, 281–85; Sylvester, "Morton," 150–203; Nevins, *War Becomes Revolution*, 391–94; *WDNI*, 11 Apr. 1863.

35. As quoted in Frank, *With Ballot and Bayonet*, 104; James S. Thomas to sister [Laura], 9 Feb. 1863, James S. Thomas Papers, IHS; Dell, *War Democrats*, 200–202; Foulke, *Morton*, 1:220–23, 230; Nortrup, "Yates: Civil War Governor," 280–83; Weeden, *War Government*, 337; Benton, *Voting in the Field*, 250–65; Porter, *Ohio Politics*, 114–17.

36. As quoted in Hancock, *Delaware during the War*, 123–30; Hancock, "The Political History of Delaware during the Civil War, Part IV," 8:82–86; Scharf, *History of Delaware*, 1:348–50; *HEP*, 17 Mar. 1863; Cannon to Stanton, 29 Jan. 1863, Stanton Papers, LC; *BS*, 29 Jan. 1863; *ISJ*, 5 Feb. 1863; *NYTi*, 22 March 1863.

37. *PhiIn*, 3 Jan., 16 Mar. 1863; *BDHE*, 20 Mar. 1863; *WDNI*, 18 Mar. 1863; *BDA*, 17 Mar. 1863.

38. White, *Trumbull*, 203–4; Klement, *The Limits of Dissent: Clement L. Vallandigham and the Civil War*, 116–90; Staudenraus, *Mr. Lincoln's Washington*, 25, 69–71; Porter, *Ohio Politics*, 140–50; *PhiIn*, 17 Feb. 1863; *HW*, 28 Feb. 1864.

39. White, *Trumbull*, 203–4.

40. Sears, *Dunn Browne's Experiences*, 58–59, 65–67; Frank, *With Ballot and Bayonet*; Cowden, "Politics of Dissent," 538–54; *BDHE*, 1 Apr. 1863; *ChiTri*, 19 Feb. 1863.

41. Brandt, *Mr. Tubbs' Civil War*, 115; Ambrose, *From Shiloh to Savannah*, 97–99; Gillette, *Jersey Blue*, 232–33; *InDJ*, 20 Feb. 1863.

42. Ambrose, *From Shiloh to Savannah*, 97–99; Frank, *With Ballot and Bayonet*, 138–40; *ISJ*, 20 Feb. 1863; *StLDMR*, 21 Feb. 1863; Kimball, "Yates," 73–81; Lusk, *Politics and Politicians*, 142–62; *ISJ*, 20, 27 Feb. 1862, 29 Jan., 7 Feb. 1863.

43. Foulke, *Morton*, 1:230–34; Stampp, *Indiana Politics during the Civil War*, 173–74; Thornbrough, Riker, and Corpuz, *Diary of Fletcher*, 8:39–50; *ISJ*, 27 Jan. 1863; *InDJ*, 28 Mar. 1863; White, *Emancipation, the Union Army, and the Reelection of Lincoln*, 94–96.

44. Marvel, *Burnside*, 211–15; Donald, *Lincoln*, 409–11; Basler, *CW*, 6:54; Benedict, *Vermont*, 1:347.

45. Schouler, *Massachusetts in the Civil War*, 1:404–5; Basler, *CW*, 6:76–77; Dayton E. Flint Diary, 27 Jan. 1863, Civil War Miscellaneous Collection, USAMHI; *BDWC*, 28 Jan., 5, 12, 14 Feb. 1863; Eicher, *Longest Night*, 388–429.

46. Bowen, *Massachusetts in the War*, 1:52–53, 60–63; Burlingame, *Stoddard*, 135; Burlingame, *Lincoln*, 2: 478–79; Pearson, *Andrew*, 2:71–74, 126–28; Jimerson, *Private Civil War*, 96–101; Belz, *Lincoln*, 120–23; Abbott, *Cotton and Capital*, 119–20; Emilio, *History of the Fifty-fourth Regiment Massachusetts Volunteer Infantry*, 3–29; John Forbes to John Andrew, 2 Feb. 1863, Andrew Papers, MHS; Abbott, "Massachusetts and the Recruitment of Southern Negroes, 1863–1865," 197–202; Berlin, *Freedom's Soldiers*, 11–13; Duncan, *Blue-Eyed Child of Fortune*, 20–25; Hamrogue, "Andrew," 183–87; *BDFP*, 7 Jan. 1863; *DFP*, 31 Jan. 1863; *WDNI*, 20 Mar. 1863; Gold, "Frustrated Glory," 174–204; Ira H. Stoughton to Horace Fenn, 19 Feb., Franklin J. Candee to Horace Fenn, 27 Oct. 1863, Horace Fenn Papers, CtHS; *OR*, series 3, 3:19–20, series 2, 5:108, 363–67; Towne, "Killing the Serpent Speedily," 45–48; Klement, *Dark Lanterns*, 97–134; Sylvester, "Morton," 180–84; Tredway, *Democratic Opposition*, 211–23; Salomon to Stanton, 13, 18, 27 Mar. 1863, Governor's Letter Books, SHSW.

47. Thomas and Hyman, *Stanton*, 262–63; Pearson, *Andrew*, 2:71–73, 96–97; Belz, *Lincoln*, 120–23; Abbott, *Cotton and Capital*, 119–20; Duncan, *Blue-Eyed Child of Fortune*, 20–

25; Luke and Smith, *Soldiering for Freedom*, 28–31; *WDNI*, 5, 20 Mar., 8 Apr. 1863; Andrew to Stearns, 6 Feb. 1863, Governor's Letter Books, MHS; Andrew Sinclair to Andrew, 5 Jan. 1863, Massachusetts Governors, Letters Official, 1863, MSA; Hamrogue, "Andrew," 184–90; Abbott, "Recruitment of Southern Negroes," 197–202; Berlin, *Freedom's Soldiers*, 11–14; Seraile, "Black Regiments in New York," 220–22.

48. Andrew to Francis Shaw, 20, 30 Jan. 1863, Andrew Papers, MHS; Pearson, *Andrew*, 2:71–79; Duncan, *Where Death and Glory Meet: Colonel Robert Gould Shaw and the 54th Massachusetts Infantry*, 52–59; Duncan, *Blue-Eyed Child of Fortune*, 20–25; Abbott, *Cotton and Capital*, 119–20; Schouler, *Massachusetts in the Civil War*, 1:408–9; Emilio, *A Brave Black Regiment*, 3–29.

49. Andrew to Francis Shaw, 30 Jan. 1863, Andrew Papers, MHS; Thomas and Hyman, *Stanton*, 263; Abbott, "Recruitment of Southern Negroes," 197–202; Berlin, *Freedom's Soldiers*, 11–14; Duncan, *Where Death and Glory Meet*, 52–59; Duncan, *Blue-Eyed Child of Fortune*, 20–25; Pearson, *Andrew*, 2:71–73; Hesseltine, *Lincoln and the War Governors*, 287–90, 297–304; Öfele, *German-Speaking Officers*, 80–115; Belz, *Lincoln*, 120–23; Abbott, "Recruitment of Southern Negroes," 197–202; Smith, "Broadsides for Freedom," 297, 303; *BS*, 10 Feb. 1863.

50. As quoted in Jimerson, *Private Civil War*, 96, 100–101; Bowen, *Massachusetts in the War*, 1:52–54; *OR*, series 3, 3:16, 20, 38–39, 46–47; Berlin, *Freedom's Soldiers*, 11–14; Öfele, *German-Speaking Officers*, 80–115; Barbour Lewis to Yates, 30 Mar. 1863, Yates Papers, ALPL.

51. John Beatty to Laura, 15 Mar. 1863, John Beatty Papers, MnHS.

52. Kirkwood to Halleck, 5 Aug., Nathan H. Brainerd to Alexander Clark, 8 Aug. 1862, Kirkwood Papers, SHSI; Jimerson, *Private Civil War*, 93; Berlin, *Freedom's Soldiers*, 87–88; Clark, *Kirkwood*, 294–95; Voegeli, *Free But Not Equal*, 102; Seraile, "Black Regiments in New York," 220–25.

53. Briggs, "Enlistment of Iowa Troops," 362–63; Kirkwood to [Mallon] Kellog, 28 Mar., Kirkwood to Brother [William Kirkwood], 25 Mar. 1863, Military Letter Books, Kirkwood Papers, SHSI.

54. As quoted in Mitchell, *Maryland Voices*, 380–87, 400; F. C. F. Burgess, James W. Neale, George P. Jenkins, and Peregine Davis to Bradford, 4 Feb. 1863, Bradford to Ed Bates, 9 May, Bradford to William Bowie, 19 May, Bradford to A. C. Gibbs, 17 Dec. 1862, G. Fred Maddox to Bradford, 9 Jan., Bradford to Maddox, 15 Jan. 1863 Executive Letter book, MdSA; Berlin, *Freedom: Destruction of Slavery*, 1:366; *PhiIn*, 12 Jan. 1863; Manakee, *Maryland*, 58.

55. Bradford to Maddox, 13 Jan., Bradford to J. Thompson Yates, 14, 17 Mar., J. Thompson Yates to Bradford, 10 Mar. 1863, Executive Letter Books, MdSA, Mitchell, *Maryland Voices*, 387.

56. *BDWC*, 30 Jan. 1863; Clark, "Politics in Maryland," 38:239; Bradford to Maddox, 13 Jan. 1863, Executive Letter Books, MdSA; Mitchell, *Maryland Voices*, 174; "Speech of Bradford at the banquet welcoming Schenck," [n.d.] Jan. 1863, MdHS; Warner, *Generals in Blue*, 422–23.

57. Burlingame, *Stoddard*, 134–35.

58. John B. Burrud to Wife, 2 Feb. 1863, John B. Burrud Papers, HL (Burrud was in the 160th New York); Donald, *Lincoln*, 416–22.

59. Morton to Lincoln, 15, 31 Jan., 9 Feb. 1863, LP, LC; Morton to Stanton, 9 Feb. 1863, Stanton Papers, LC; Donald, *Lincoln*, 419; Foulke, *Morton*, 1:217–18; Nation and Towne, *Indiana's War*, 181–83; Basler, *CW*, 6:87–88; *OR*, series 3, 3:23; Donald, *Lincoln*, 418–19.

60. Basler, *CW*, 6:90, 97; *OR*, series 3, 3:109; Nortrup, "Yates, the Prorogued Legislature," 9–34; Palmer to Yates, 9 Feb., Butler, Hatch, and Dubois to Lincoln, 1 Mar. 1863, John P. Boise to Yates, 6 Mar., Flavino Henderson to Yates, 17 Mar., Dr. E. Engle to Yates, 12 Mar., Henry W. Williams to Yates, 6 Mar., Warren H. Kneeland to Yates, 9 Mar. 1863, Yates Papers, ALPL; Yates to Chase, 2 Feb. 1863, Stanton Papers, LC; Yates to Chase, 2 Feb. 1863, Chase Papers, CGS; Nevins, *War Becomes Revolution*, 390; Klingaman, *Lincoln*, 246–47; *ChiTri*, 26 Feb. 1863; Schenck to Bradford, 30 Mar., Bradford to Schenck, 1 Apr., Gen. Henry Lockwood to Bradford, 27 Mar., John Buck and citizens of Baltimore to Bradford, 2 Apr., Bradford to John Buck, 9 Apr., Bradford to Samuel Dorsett, 25 Mar. 1863, Executive Letter Books, MdSA; Hesseltine, *Lincoln and the War Governors*, 317–18.

61. Palmer, *Personal Recollections*, 152–53; Hesseltine, *Lincoln and the War Governors*, 317–18; Hess, *A German in the Yankee Fatherland*, 69; *ChiTri*, 26 Feb. 1863.

62. *BDHE*, 14 Jan. 1863; Executive Journal, 7 Jan. 1863, Kentucky Governor's Papers, KDLA.

63. Basler, *CW*, 6:42; *OR*, series 1, 20, pt., 2:282; James Speed to Joshua Speed, 19 Jan. 1863, LP, LC; *BDHE*, 14 Jan. 1863; *BS*, 16 Jan. 1863; Green Adams to Lincoln, 31 Dec. 1862, Hamilton Gray to Lincoln, 7 Jan., Green Adams [Memorandum on Kentucky] to Lincoln, Feb. 1863, LC; *LDJ*, 10, 14 Jan. 1863; *BS*, 16 Jan. 1863.

64. Basler, *CW*, 6:42; William C. Goodloe to Green Adams, 25 Jan., George M. Adams to Green Adams, 12 Feb. 1863, LP, LC; *OR*, series 3, 3:39; *BS*, 16 Jan. 1863; Boman, *Lincoln and Citizens' Rights in Missouri*, 163–92.

65. *OR*, series 3, 3:54; Boman, *Gamble*, 200–206; Rosin, "Gamble," 285–315, 375–87; Gamble to Lincoln, 4 Feb. 1863, LP, LC; Barton Bates to Gamble, 21 Jan. 1863, "private," Charles Gibson to Gamble, 4, 6 Jan., Schofield to Gamble, 2 Feb., James Broadhead to Gamble, 18 Feb., William McPherson to Gamble, 23 Feb., J. B. Henderson to Gamble, 30 Mar. 1863, Gamble Papers, MoHS; Boman, *Lincoln and Citizens' Rights in Missouri*, 163–216; Harris, *Lincoln and the Border States*, 308–20; *StLDMR*, 2, 17, 19, 31 Mar. 1863.

66. Gamble to Lincoln, 23 Feb., Hamilton Gamble to Father, 6 Mar., J. B. Henderson to Gamble, 30 Mar. 1863, Gamble Papers, MoHS; Harris, *Lincoln and the Border States*, 308–20.

67. *OR*, series 3, 3:35–36, 45; Geary, *We Need Men*, 54–64; Eicher, *Longest Night*, 438–47, 457–73.

68. *OR*, series 3, 3:37–38.

69. Rosecrans to Ramsey, 21 Feb. 1863, Letters Received, Minnesota, Governor's Papers, Ramsey, MnHS; Geary, *We Need Men*, 56–64; Nevins, *The Organized War, 1863–1864*, 31; Bowen, *History of the 37th Massachusetts Volunteers*, 92–93; Parker, *Henry Wilson's Regiment*, 179.

70. Jimerson, *Private Civil War*, 98–104; Geary, *We Need Men*, 65–77; *Congressional Globe*, Third Session of the Thirty-Seventh Congress, Part II, Washington, 1863, 970–90; *BDFP*, 18 Feb. 1863; Shannon, *Organization of the Union Army*, 1:195–323, 2:11–255; Murdock, *Patriotism Limited*; Bensel, *Yankee Leviathan*, 137–39; Basler, *CW*, 6:115–16; *OR*, series 3, 3:9–10, series 1, 22, pt. 2:180–81, 194–96; Ambler, *Pierpont*, 186–89; Langford, "Constitutional Issues," 17–31; Shaffer, "Lincoln and West Virginia," 86–100; Beale, *Diary of Bates*, 278–85; Boman, *Gamble*, 200–206; William R. Strachan to Lincoln, 10 Mar., relative to claims about Gamble's rebel sympathies, Samuel R. Curtis to Lincoln, 23 Mar., Henry T. Blow to Lincoln, 22 Mar. 1863, LP, LC; Rosin, "Gamble," 385–87; Boman, *Lincoln and Citizens' Rights in Missouri*, 163–92; Harris, *Lincoln and the Border States*, 308–20.

71. Wentworth to Wife, 1 Mar. 1863, Wentworth Papers, LC.

72. Quoted in *BDA*, 9, 26 Mar. 1863; Burlingame, *Stoddard*, 137–41; Geary, *We Need Men*, 56–93.

73. Basler, *CW*, 6:120; Mitchell, *Seymour*, 257, 275, 312–413; *OR*, series 3, 3:166–67; Cook and Knox, *Public Record of Seymour*, 88–164; Paludan, *Presidency of Lincoln*, 193–96; Burlingame, *Stoddard*, 136–37; Weeden, *War Government*, 238–39; Geary, *We Need Men*, 56–93; *BDHE*, 19 Feb. 1863; Mitchell, "Organizational Performance," 138–45.

74. *OR*, series 3, 3:60–61; Basler, *CW*, 6:131; Ephraim Holloway to Father (actually father-in-law), 17 Mar. 1863, Ephraim Holloway Papers, OHS.

75. Morton to Lincoln, 6 Mar., Robinson to Lincoln, 9 Mar., Stanton to Lincoln, 29 Mar. 1863, LP, LC; Morton to Stanton, 6 Mar. 1863, Stanton Papers, LC; *OR*, series 3, 3:62–63, series 1, 23, pt. 2:96–97, 104–5; Lathrop, *Kirkwood*, 238–42; Kirkwood to Stanton, 10 Mar. 1863, Military Letter Books, Kirkwood Papers, SHSI; Briggs, "Enlistment of Iowa Troops," 348–67; Basler, *CW*, 6:141; *LDJ*, 21 Mar. 1863.

76. Rogers to Cozzens, 16 Mar. 1863, Executive Letters Received, RISA; Sobel and Raimo, *Directory of Governors*, 1:1349–50; Raber, "The Formation and Early Development of the Republican Party in Rhode Island, 1850–1865," 141–43; Lamphier, *Kate Chase and William Sprague*, 45–52; Marvel, *Burnside*, 220; *WDNI*, 5 Mar. 1863; *BDA*, 1 Apr. 1863; *NYH*, 3 Mar. 1863; *StLDMR*, 17 Mar. 1863; Shoemaker, *The Last of the War Governors*, 9–11; *PDJ*, 5, 26 Mar. 1863.

77. *NHS*, 6 Mar. 1863.

78. Baron Stow to Gilmore, 1 Jan. 1863, Gilmore Papers, NHHS; *NHPSG*, 11 Sept. 1861, 17 Dec. 1862; *TDSGR*, 13 Jan. 1863; *BDA*, 2 Jan., 9 Mar. 1863; *BDFR*, 18 Mar. 1863; Renda, *Running on the Record*, 112–21.

79. Gilmore received 29,035 votes, Eastman 32,833, and Harriman 4,372. Shafer, *Men of Granite*, 134–35; Waite, *New Hampshire in the Great Rebellion*, 581; Renda, *Running on the Record*, 112–21; Dell, *War Democrats*, 232–34; Benton, *Voting in the Field*, 204–22; *HEP*, 12 Mar. 1863; *DFP*, 6 Mar. 1863; *NHS*, 6, 13 Mar. 1863; Baron Stow to Gilmore, 1 Jan., George Marston to Gilmore, 4 Jan., George Porter to Gilmore, 12 Jan. Joseph Gilmore to Larkin Mason, 29 Mar., William H. Gove to Gilmore, 12 Jan., John Garfield to Gilmore, [n.d.] Jan., James Eastman to Gilmore, 26 Jan., William E. Chandler to Gilmore, 19 Jan., 1863, Gilmore Papers, NHHS; Joseph Gilmore to William E. Chandler, 2 Mar. 1863, William E. Chandler Papers, NHHS; 1863; Marvel, *Lincoln's Autocrat*, 280–81.

80. Basler, *CW*, 6:54; Niven, *Connecticut for the Union*, 305–6; Croffut and Morris, *Connecticut during the War*, 322–28; *WDNI*, 7 Apr. 1863; Cowden, "Politics of Dissent," 538–54; *HEP*, 13 Mar. 1863; Gordon, *A Broken Regiment*, 73–79.

81. *HEP*, 26 Mar. 1863; Niven, *Connecticut for the Union*, 305–8; Croffut and Morris, *Connecticut during the War*, 322–28; *HW*, 11 Apr. 1863; White, *Emancipation, the Union Army and the Reelection of Lincoln*, 24–25; Basler, *CW*, 6:112–13; Thurlow Weed to Lincoln, 8 Mar. 1863, LP, LC; Cowden, "Heaven Will Frown," 25–65; Cowden, "Politics of Dissent," 538–54; *WDNI*, 7 Apr. 1863; *HEP*, 13, 14, 17, 19, 20 Mar. 1863; R. Russell to Buckingham, 2 Jan., Silas Mead to Buckingham, 12 Jan., Atwood Tinsley to Buckingham, 1 Feb., Horace Thurston to Buckingham, 2 Feb. 1863, Governor's Correspondence, CtSA; Mark Howard to Welles, 29 Jan. 1863, Welles Papers, LC; Marvel, *Lincoln's Autocrat*, 281–82.

82. Zon, *The Good Fight That Didn't End: Henry P. Goddard's Accounts of Civil War and Peace*, 133–34.

83. Folwell, *Minnesota*, 2:245–66, 334–36; *StPDPi*, 9, 13, 14 Jan., 18 Apr. 1863; Sobel and Raimo, *Directory of Governors*, 2:775–76; *WDNI*, 11 Apr. 1863; *ChiTri*, 1 Jul. 1863; Guentzel,

"Ramsey," 41014; Haugland, "Ramsey's Rise to Power," 330-33; Haugland, "Ramsey and the Republican Party," 142-45; *BDHE*, 5 Feb. 1863.

84. Folwell, *Minnesota*, 2:333-35; *StPDPi*, 13, 14 Jan., 12, 14 Mar. 1863; Baker, *Lives of the Governors of Minnesota*, 111-27; Sobel and Raimo, *Directory of Governors*, 2:775-76; Ramsey to Lincoln, 6 Mar. 1863, LP, LC; C. C. Andrews to Ramsey, 27 Jan. 1863, Governor's Papers, Ramsey to Stanton, 13 Feb. 1863, Governor's Papers, Executive Journals, MnHS.

85. Basler, *CW*, 6:142; *OR*, series 1, 24, pt. 3:147, series 3, 3:63, 75; Hollandsworth, *Banks*, 99-164; Thomas and Hyman, *Stanton*, 264-66; Nevins, *War Becomes Revolution*, 403; Schouler, *Massachusetts in the Civil War*, 1:411-14. There are numerous letters between Charles Dana and Stanton, Feb. 1863, Stanton Papers, LC.

86. *OR*, series 1, 23, pt. 2:147; Towne, "Killing the Serpent," 45-48; Abbott, *Ohio's War Governors*, 32-34; Trester, "Tod," 174-76; Marvel, *Burnside*, 222-25; Porter, *Ohio Politics*, 120-57; *ODS*, 15 Aug., 28 Dec. 1862, 4 Apr. 1863; *CC*, 13 Aug. 1862; *NYTi*, 12 Aug. 1862; *ChiTri*, 3 Jun. 1863; *PhiIn*, 17 Feb. 1863; *StLDMR*, 28 Mar. 1863.

87. *OR*, series 3, 3:66-68; Clark, *Kirkwood*, 264-68; Kirkwood to Grimes, 25 Nov. 1862, Governor's Letter book, Kirkwood Papers, SHSI; Lathrop, *Kirkwood*, 238-42; Briggs, "Enlistment of Iowa Troops," 355-68; G. A. Bronson to Kirkwood, 13 Mar. 1863, AGO, General Correspondence, IaSA.

88. *OR*, series 3, 3:66-74; Clark, *Kirkwood*, 256-57; Lathrop, *Kirkwood*, 238-42.

89. Clark, *Kirkwood*, 280-81, 294-96; Kirkwood to Harriett N. Kellogg, 28 Mar. 1863, Military Letter Books, Kirkwood Papers, SHSI; *OR*, series 3, 3: 75-76, 82-85, 100-105; Geary, *We Need Men*, 68-93; Miller, *Black Soldiers*, 5-10; Kirkwood to W. C. Kirkwood, 23 Mar. Kirkwood to Crocker, 7 Apr., Kirkwood to Seward, 20 Mar., Kirkwood to L. B. Fleak, 9 Mar. 1863, Military Letter Books, Kirkwood Papers, SHSI; Lathrop, *Kirkwood*, 276-79; Klement, *Dark Lanterns*, 97-134; *InDJ*, 21 Mar. 1863; Wish, "Civil War Letters," 65-66.

90. Weed, *Memoir*, 2:428-29; Weeden, *War Government*, 303; *OR*, series 3, 3:3, 14, 46, 73, 82, 100, 118-24, 215-16, 418-20. Shannon, *Organization of the Union Armies*, 2:162-64; Nicolay and Hay, *Lincoln: A History*, 7:12-13; Thomas and Hyman, *Stanton*, 259; Donald, *Lincoln*, 423; Brummer, *Political History of New York*, 238-57; Mitchell, *Seymour*, 273-75.

91. Weeden, *War Government*, 285-86; Lincoln, *Messages*, 445-85; Cook and Knox, *Public Record of Seymour*, 88-105; *SFDEB*, 3 Feb. 1863; Rundell, "Despotism of Traitors," 349-60; Mitchell, *Seymour*, 260-77; *NYTi*, 3 Jan. 1863; *NYH*, 3 Jan. 1863; *BS*, 5 Jan. 1863; *ISJ*, 5 Jan. 1863; *BDFR*, 8 Jan. 1863; *PDJ*, 8 Jan. 1863; *HEP*, 8 Jan. 1863; *ChiTri*, 9 Jan. 1863; *CDE*, 6 Jan. 1863; *BDWC*, 22 Jan. 1863; Caton, *Miscellanies*, 17-31; John A. Trimble to Seymour, 7, 17 Mar. 1863, John A. Trimble Family Papers, OHS.

92. Beale, *Diary of Welles*, 1:219.

93. Barnes and Barnes, *The American Civil War through British Eyes: Dispatches from British Diplomats*, 2:292-93; Lincoln, *Messages*, 445-83; Brummer, *Political History of New York*, 152-54; Weeden, *War Government*, 238-41.

94. James H. Bayard to Thomas F. Bayard, 9 Jan. 1863, LP, LC; Weeden, *War Government*, 303; Cook and Knox, *Public Record of Seymour*, 88-105; Paludan, *Presidency of Lincoln*, 190-91; Neely, *Fate of Liberty*, 192-95; Foulke, *Morton*, 1:217-18; *WDNI*, 13 Mar. 1863.

95. Morris E. Fitch to Brother, 1 Feb. 186[3], this letter is misdated, A. D. to Cousin Morris E. Fitch, 14 Feb. 1863, Morris E. Fitch Papers, BHL; Mitchell, *Seymour*, 263-67.

96. *AEJ*, 2 Jan. 1863; *PDJ*, 7 Jan. 1863; *BDA*, 2 Jan., 4 Feb. 1863; *PhiIn*, 13 Jan. 1363; Rawley uses this same quote, *Morgan*, 182-87, but in slightly different form. Morgan to Seymour, 28 Jan. 1863, Morgan Letter Books, NYSL; Weeds, *Memoir*, 2:430-32; Lincoln to Weed, 29

Jan. 1863, LP, LC; Brummer, *Political History of New York*, 255–75; Mitchell, *Seymour*, 282–83; *WDNI*, 30 Jan., 7 Feb. 1863; Seymour to Morgan, 26 Jan., 26, 28 Mar. 1863, Morgan Papers, NYSL.

97. As quoted in Rawley, *Morgan*, 182–87; Weed, *Memoir*, 2:430–32; *AEJ*, 2 Jan. 1863; Brummer, *Political History of New York*, 255–74; Preston King to Morgan, 14 Feb. 1863, Morgan Papers, NYSL.

98. Weed, *Memoir*, 2:433; Lincoln to Weed, 29 Jan. 1863, LP, LC; Brummer, *Political History of New York*, 255–75.

99. Brummer, *Political History of New York*, 255; *NYTri*, 23 Jan. 1863; Weed, *Memoir*, 2:433.

100. Basler, *CW*, 6:145–46; Donald, *Lincoln*, 422–23; Paludan, *Presidency of Lincoln*, 190–91; Neely, *Fate of Liberty*, 192–95; Weed, *Memoir*, 2:428–29; Brummer, *Political History of New York*, 255–57; Donald, *Lincoln*, 422–23.

101. As quoted in Mitchell, *Seymour*, 274–81; Robinson to Lincoln, 9 Mar., Seymour to Lincoln, 14 Apr. 1863, LP, LC.

102. Mitchell, *Seymour*, 274–77; Basler, *CW*, 6:147; Joshua Speed and James Guthrie to Lincoln, 22 Mar., Stanton to Lincoln, 29 Mar. 1863, LP, LC.

103. *OR*, series 3, 3:109; Nortrup, "Yates: Civil War Governor," 285–86; Butler, Hatch, and Dubois to Lincoln, 1 Mar. 1863, Yates Papers, ALPL; Lawson, *Patriot Fires*, 73–75.

104. Gillette, *Jersey Blue*, 232–33; Jackson, *New Jerseyans*, 126–27; Miers, *New Jersey and the Civil War*, 101–6; Moore, *The Rebellion Record*, 12:679–83; Green, "Emancipation Proclamation in New Jersey," 108–24; *PhiIn*, 26 Mar. 1863; *WDNI*, 27 Mar., 11 Apr. 1863; Langford, "Constitutional Issues," 15–31; Shaffer, "Lincoln and West Virginia," 86–100; Ham, "Mind of a Copperhead," 93–109.

105. Gillette, *Jersey Blue*, 233–34; *WDNI*, 21, 26 Mar. 1863.

106. Robert Kirkwood to Mother, 27 Mar. 1863, Kirkwood Family Papers, MdHS; Pearson, *Andrew*, 2:81–86; Jackson, *New Jerseyans*, 125–26; Lawson, *Patriot Fires*, 88–97; Klement, *Dark Lanterns*, 45–47; *PhiIn*, 12 Mar. 1863; Collier and Collier, *Yours for the Union*, 215; Freidel, "The Loyal Publication Society," 359–76; Smith, *No Party Now*, 68–73.

107. Stanley, "Republican Party in California," 138–41; *SDU*, 8 Jan. 1863; *SFDEB*, 8, 14, 15 Jan. 1863; *LAS*, 9 May 1863; *Annual Message of Leland Stanford, Jan. 1863*, 4–29; *SDU*, 8 Jan. 1863; Melendy and Gilbert, *Governors of California*, 115–27.

108. *OR*, series 1, 50, pt. 2:305–6, 328–29, 359–60; Edwards, "Department of the Pacific," 146–79; *SFDAC*, 18 Apr. 1863; *SFDEB*, 6 Apr. 1863; *BDWC*, 9 Jan. 1863; Edwards, "Oregon Regiments," 73–75; Melendy and Gilbert, *Governors of California*, 115–27; Abbott, *Cotton and Capital*, 114–17. The Californians serving in Massachusetts would be mustered into two units and called the "California Hundred" and the "California Battalion." McLean, *California Sabers*; *LAS*, 28 Mar., 11, 18 Apr., 6 Jun., 4 Jul. 4,1863; Gibbs to Gen. E. L. Applegate, 14 Apr., 10 May 1862, Gibbs Papers, OrHS.

Chapter Thirteen

1. As quoted in Niven, *Connecticut for the Union*, 308; Welles to Buckingham, 7 Apr. 1863, Buckingham Papers, CtHS; Croffut and Morris, *Connecticut during the War*, 323–26; Thurlow Weed to Lincoln, 8 Mar. 1863, LP, LC; Cowden, "Heaven Will Frown," 25–65; *PhiIn*, 7 Apr. 1863; Buckingham Message, 6 May 1863, 19–20; Dell, *War Democrats*, 163–64; Cowden, "Politics of Dissent," 538–54; *NYI*, 19 March 1863; *HEP*, 8 Apr. 1863; *NYTri*, 7 Apr. 1863; *BDHE*, 1 Apr. 1863; *PDJ*, 7, 13 Apr. 1863; Buckingham to Welles, 10 Apr. 1863,

Welles Papers, CtHS; William B. Barnard to Buckingham, 31 Mar. 1863, Governor's Correspondence, CtSA; Beale, *Diary of Welles*, 1:262–306.

2. Buckingham to Stanton, 8 Apr. 1863, Stanton Papers, LC.

3. *PDJ*, 7, 10 Apr. 1863.

4. *NYTi*, 22 Mar. 1863; Carroll, *Rhode Island*, 2:608–10; *PDJ*, 26, 27 Mar., 1, 2 Apr. 1863; *HEP*, 4 Apr. 1863; *BDA*, 4 Apr. 1863; Smith, *No Party Now*, 90.

5. *NYTi*, 22 Mar. 1863.

6. *ChiTri*, 10 Apr. 1863; Smith, *Genealogical History*, 179–83; *PDJ*, 1, 2 Apr. 1863; Bicknell, *History of Rhode Island*, 3:1155; *NYTi*, 22 Mar. 1863; *NYTri*, 2 Apr. 1863.

7. *OR*, series 3, 3:109–10; Schouler, *Massachusetts in the Civil War*, 1:418–23; Hamrogue, "Andrew," 186–89; William L. Garrison to Andrew, 6 Apr. 1863 Andrew Papers MHS; Andrew to William L. Garrison, 3 Apr. 1863, Anti-Slavery Collection, William L. Garrison Papers, BPL; Luke and Smith, *Soldiering for Freedom*, 29–31.

8. *OR*, series 3, 3:110; Miller, *Hunter*, 142–43; *BDA*, 15 May 1863; *OR*, series 3, 3:118–22, 177–78; Schouler, *Massachusetts in the Civil War*, 1:418–23; *BDA*, 15 May 1863; Hamrogue, "Andrew," 187–90; William Schouler to Andrew, 25 Mar., Stearns to Andrew, 3, 24 Apr. 1863, Andrew Papers, MHS; Hesseltine, *Lincoln and the War Governors*, 288–89; Luke and Smith, *Soldering for Freedom*, 30–31.

9. *NYTi*, 3, 10 Apr. 1863; Foulke, *Morton*, 1:245–46; French, *Morton*, 356–63; Brummer, *Political History of New York*, 298–99; *NYH*, 12 Apr. 1863; *PhiIn*, 7 Apr. 1863; Foulke, *Morton*, 1:245–46; French, *Morton*, 356–63; *WDNI*, 13 Apr. 1863; *InDJ*, 16 Apr. 1863; *ChiTri*, 1 Apr. 1863; *NYH*, 26 May 1863; Wasson, "Civil War Letters of Darwin Cody," 375; Blair, *With Malice toward Some*, 160–81.

10. *OR*, series 3, 3:75, 109, 116; *PDJ*, 13 Apr. 1863; Marvel, *Burnside*, 228–32; Dana to Stanton, 20 Apr. 1863, LP, LC; Jones, *"For My Country": The Richardson Letters, 1861–1865*, 94–95; Clark, *Kirkwood*, 280–82; *OR*, series 3, 3:114–15, 124–25; Frank, *With Ballot and Bayonet*, 104–5; *BDHE*, 1, 13 Apr. 1863; Kirkwood to Gen. [Wilson], 25 Jul., Kirkwood to Grimes, 22 Apr., Kirkwood to Seward, 18 Apr., Kirkwood to Doctor [Nadell], 22 Apr. 1863, Military Letter Books, Kirkwood Papers, SHSI.

11. Lincoln to Curtin, 13 Apr., Curtin to Lincoln, 14 Apr. 1863, LP, LC; Albright, "Curtin," 48:32–36; *PhiIn*, 25, 26 Mar. 1863; Egle, *Curtin*, 144–45.

12. Thornbrough, Riker, and Corpuz, *Diary of Fletcher*, 8:116–18; Marvel, *Burnside*, 231–34; Klement, *Limits of Dissent*, 149–50; Klement, *Dark Lanterns*, 97–134; Towne, "Killing the Serpent," 45–48; *OR*, series 2, 5:573, series 1, 23, pt. 2:147, 237, pt. 1:398–728; Nation and Towne, *Indiana's War*, 138–41, 168–72; *BDHE*, 24 Apr. 1863; *PhiIn*, 21 Apr. 1863; *CDE*, 14, 15 Apr. 1863; Terrell, *Indiana in the War*, 1:463, 465; James M. Butts to Lincoln, 26 Jul. 1863, LP, LC; *InDJ*, 25 Apr. 1863; Zollinger, "I Take My Pen in Hand," 159–60.

13. Ballard, *Vicksburg*, 198–207; Grant, *Memoirs*, 1:530–45; Eicher, *Longest Night*, 440–56; Beale, *Diary of Bates*, 288; *OR*, series 3, 3:124, series 1, 25, pt. 2:246–60; Basler, *CW*, 6:181; Donald, *Lincoln*, 432–33; Burlingame, *Lincoln*, 2:491–92, 496–97; Stealey, *West Virginia's Civil War-Era Constitution*, 100–108; *WDNI*, 20 Apr. 1863; Moore, "Slavery as a Factor," 68–89; Shaffer, "Lincoln and West Virginia," 86–100; Ambler, *Pierpont*, 204–9, 429; Brown, "A History of the Sixth West Virginia Infantry Volunteers," 330–37; *PhiIn*, 2 May 1863.

14. Racine, *"Unspoiled Heart,"* 7; *OR*, series 3, 3:124, 166–67, 170–71; Geary, *We Need Men*, 111–12.

15. As quoted in Racine, *"Unspoiled Heart,"* 297; [Haley], *The Rebel Yell & the Yankee Hurrah*, 76; Jordan, *Red Diamond Regiment*, 48; Burlingame, *Lincoln Observed*, 35–43;

Staudenraus, *Mr. Lincoln's Washington*, 147–64; Furgurson, *Chancellorsville, 1863: The Souls of the Brave*, 60–63.

16. As quoted in Robertson, *The Civil War Letters of General Robert McAllister*, 289–91; Jackson, *New Jerseyans*, 127; Basler, *CW*, 6:165–66; *BDWC*, 4, 7, 22, 30 May, 1, 9 Jun. 1863; *WDNI*, 11 Apr. 1863; *TDSGR*, 24 Apr. 1863; Sears, *Chancellorsville*, 144; Burlingame, *Lincoln Observed*, 35–43; Staudenraus, *Mr. Lincoln's Washington*, 147–54, 161–64; Furgurson, *Chancellorsville*, 60–63; Stone to Cozzens, 5 May 1863, Executive Letters Received, RISA.

17. As quoted in Pula, *The Sigel Regiment, 1862–1865*, 109–10; Keller, *Chancellorsville and the Germans*, 48–49; *BDWC*, 27 Mar. 1863; *InDJ*, 9, 11 Apr. 1863; *PDJ*, 18 Apr. 1863; *PhiIn*, 25, 26, 27 Mar., 7, 9 May 1863.

18. McClernand to Yates, 15 Mar. 1863, Reavis Papers, CHM; Hicken, *Illinois*, 164–65; Thomas and Hyman, *Stanton*, 267–68; Paludan, *Presidency of Lincoln*, 207–9; Eicher, *Longest Night*, 438–73; Kiper, *McClernand*, 205; Eddy, *Patriotism of Illinois*, 450–51; Basler, *CW*, 6:189, 193; *OR*, series 1, 25, pt. 2:372; *PhiIn*, 4, 7 May 1863; Curtin to Lincoln, 1, 2 May 1863, LP, LC.

19. McClernand to Yates, 15 Mar. 1863, Reavis Papers, CHS; Hicken, *Illinois*, 164–65; Thomas and Hyman, *Stanton*, 267–68; Paludan, *Presidency of Lincoln*, 207–9; Kiper, *McClernand*, 205; Eddy, *Patriotism of Illinois*, 450–51.

20. Schultz, *Army Life*, 131; *OR*, series 1, 24:80–81; *ISJ*, 13, 14 May 1863; *ChiTri*, 9 Apr., 13 May 1863; William E. Carpenter Diary, 4 May 1863, Carpenter Papers, HL; Erickson, "With Grant at Vicksburg," 441–503; Thomas, *Three Years with Grant*, 66, 71; Hicken, *Illinois*, 164–65; Ballard, *Vicksburg*, 221–318; Charles Dana to Stanton, 27 Apr. 1863, Stanton Papers, LC; Kiper, *McClernand*, 215–16; Nortrup, "Yates," 326; *ISJ*, 13, 15, 19 May 1863; Simpson, *Grant*, 185–86; Carter, *The Final Fortress*, 191.

21. Simpson, *Grant*, 191; *ISJ*, 15, 19 May 1863; *ChiTri*, 13, 18 May 1863; *PhiIn*, 11 May 1863; *StLDMR*, 18 May 1863; Eicher, *Longest Night*, 459–61. Nortrup, "Yates," 327; Wilson, *Under the Old Flag*, 1:175–76; *NYTi*, 15 May 1863; *ISJ*, 15 May 1863; *HW*, 30 May 1863.

22. *ISJ*, 4, 15, 16, 18, 19 May 1863; William Hoyt to Yates, 2 May, Yates to Lincoln, 15 Jun., Yates to Lincoln, 15 Jun. 1863, Yates Papers, ALPL; *PhiIn*, 11 May 1863; *NYTi*, 15 May 1863; *BDHE*, 18 May 1863; *ChiTri*, 15, 18 May 1863; Nortrup, "Yates," 326; Ballard, *Vicksburg*, 237.

23. Staudenraus, *Mr. Lincoln's Washington*, 179–84; Burlingame, *Lincoln Observed*, 50; Burlingame, *Lincoln*, 2:498; Basler, *CW*, 6:198–201; Thomas and Hyman, *Stanton*, 270–71; Furgurson, *Chancellorsville*, 144; Eicher, *Longest Night*, 474–89.

24. Segal, *Conversations with Lincoln*, 261–62; Donald, *Lincoln*, 435–36; Furgurson, *Chancellorsville*, 318–19; Eicher, *Longest Night*, 474–89.

25. Segal, *Conversations with Lincoln*, 261–62; Thomas and Hyman, *Stanton*, 270–71; Donald, *Lincoln*, 435–36; Furgurson, *Chancellorsville*, 318–19; Morgan to Lincoln, 6 May 1863, LP, LC; Staudenraus, *Mr. Lincoln's Washington*, 179–84; Burlingame, *Lincoln Observed*, 50; Burlingame, *Lincoln*, 2:498.

26. Burlingame, *Inside the White House in War Times*, 112–13; Thomas and Hyman, *Stanton*, 270–71; Schouler, *Massachusetts in the Civil War*, 1:442–43; Basler, *CW*, 6:198–99; Burlingame, *Lincoln*, 2: 498–99.

27. Morton to Lincoln, 6 May 1863, LP, LC; Eicher, *Longest Night*, 486–89; Basler, *CW*, 6:215–16; *OR*, series 2, 5:657; Tap, *Over Lincoln's Shoulder*, 180; Epstein, *Lincoln and Whitman*, 144–46.

28. *OR*, series 1, 25, pt. 2:451–52; Schouler, *Massachusetts in the Civil War*, 1:443.

29. *OR*, series 1, 25, pt. 2:437–38; Schouler, *Massachusetts in the Civil War*, 1:443; *BDA*, 9 May 1863.

30. *OR*, series 1, 25, pt. 2:438.

31. Cimbala and Miller, *Union Soldiers and the Northern Home Front*, 16, 21–22; Curtin to Thompson Westcott, 7, 8 May, 15 Jun. 1863, Executive Correspondence, PSA; *ISJ*, 1 Jun. 1863; *BDHE*, 1 Jun. 1863; Taafe, *Commanding the Army of the Potomac*, 103; Meade to Curtin, 15 May 1863, LP, LC; *WDNI*, 12, 21 May 1861; Harris, "Blair," 160–61; *DFP*, 29 May 1863; *PhiIn*, 7, 8, 14 May 1863; Hebert, *Fighting Joe Hooker*, 227–29; Bertera and Crawford, *The 4th Michigan*, 148; Curtis, *History of the Twenty-Fourth Michigan Iron Brigade*, 142.

32. Ephraim Holloway to Dearest [wife], 12 May 1863, Holloway Papers, OHS; Delos Van Deusen to Wife, 30 May, 19 Jun. 1863, Delos Van Deusen Papers, HL; *OR*, series 2, 5:633–46; Klement, *Limits of Dissent*, 209–11; Donald, *Lincoln*, 441–42; Paludan, *Presidency of Lincoln*, 199; Nevins, *War Becomes Revolution*, 396; Marvel, *Burnside*, 234–37; Neely, *Fate of Liberty*, 65–68; *DFP*, 26 May 1863; *DOS*, 7 May 1863; *BDA*, 15 May 1863; *InDJ*, 6 May 1863; Geary, "Clement L. Vallandigham Writes to John H. George, April 27, 1863," 13–20; *NYH*, 19 May 1863; Mitchell, *Seymour*, 290–93; Becker, "Newspapers in Battle," 42–50; Porter, *Ohio Politics*, 140–65; John Trimble to Samuel Medary, 7 May 1863, John Trimble Papers, OHS; Blair, *With Malice toward Some*, 174–81.

33. Basler, *CW*, 6, 203–4; *OR*, series 3, 3:185–86, 196–221; Wright, "New Jersey's Military Role in the Civil War Reconsidered," 197–210; Blair, *With Malice toward Some*, 174–81.

34. *OR*, series 3, 3:193, 196–97, 199; Briggs, "Enlistment of Iowa Troops," 355–58; Moore, "Holbrook," 65–78; *BDFP*, 28, 29 May 1863; Buckingham to Col. H. H. Abbott, 28 May 1863, Governor's Correspondence, CtSA.

35. *OR*, series 3, 3:190–92, 209; *BDA*, 15 May 1863; Pearson, *Andrew*, 2:128–31; Andrew to Welles, 2 May, Andrew to Lincoln, 27 Apr., Andrew to Sumner, 28 Apr. 1863, LP, LC; Miller, *Hunter*, 142–46; *BDHE*, 21 May 1863; Emilio, *A Brave Black Regiment*, 29; Frémont to Charles Sumner, 9 Jun. 1863, LP, LC; *BDWC*, 2 Jun. 1863; [Stanton] to Lee, 16 May 1863, Lee Family Papers, MHS.

36. Basler, *CW*, 6:298, 416, 418; Smith, "The Recruitment of Negro Soldiers in Kentucky, 1863–1865," 366–31, 416; Luke and Smith, *Soldiering for Freedom*, 47; Segal, *Conversations with Lincoln*, 262–63; Samito, *Becoming American*, 40–42; Seraile, "Black Regiments in New York," 222–23; Glatthaar, *Forged in Battle*, 38; *OR*, series 3, 3:215–16, 372; Shannon, *Organization of the Union Army*, 2:162–64; Hamrogue, "Andrew," 189–92; Stearns to Andrew, 26 May 1863, Andrew Papers, MHS; *BDWC*, 2 Jun. 1863; Marvel, *Burnside*, 253–54.

37. Lathrop, *Kirkwood*, 264; Clark, *Kirkwood*, 238–39, 241–45; *BDHE*, 29 May, 17, 19, 30 Jun. 1863; *ChiTri*, 15 May, 16 Jun. 1863; *ISJ*, 2 Jun. 1863; Cassius Fairchild to Mother, 1 Jun. 1863, Fairchild Papers, SHSW.

38. *BDHE*, 19, 30 Jun. 1863; Clark, *Kirkwood*, 238–39, 241–45; *OR*, series 1, 27, pt. 3:141; Quiner, *Wisconsin*, 223–25; Boutwell, *Reminiscences of Sixty Years*, 2:307; Hollandsworth, *Banks*, 100–121.

39. Basler, *CW*, 6:218; *OR*, series 1, 22, pt. 2:281, 293, 546–61; Charles D. Drake to Lincoln, 29 Apr., Blow to Lincoln, 5 May, Gamble to Lincoln, 2 May, Joseph W. McClurg to Lincoln, 22 May 1863, LP, LC; Boman, *Gamble*, 201–6, 206–10; Castel, *Civil War Kansas*, 110; Rosin, "Gamble," 389; Beale, *Diary of Bates*, 290; Harris, *Lincoln and the Border States*, 320–27; Geiger, "Indebtedness and the Origins of Guerrilla Violence in Civil War Missouri," 49–82; Boman, *Lincoln and Citizens' Rights in Missouri*, 163–216; *StLDMR*, 5, 6, 9, 13, 20 May, 1, 2, 3, 5, 7, 9, 12 Jun. 1863; Berlin, *Freedom: Destruction of Slavery*, 1:405–6; Siddali, *Missouri's War*, 192–93; *WDNI*, 25 Apr. 1863; Carney to Seward, 5 Jun. 1863, Thomas Carney Papers, Kansas Collections, UKL; H. W. Farnsworth to Carney, 18 May, Rever-

end O. C. Beach and W. H. M. Fishback to Carney, 18 May, Col. J. R. Parr to Carney, 17 May 1863, Carney Papers, KSHS.

40. Basler, *CW*, 6:218; *OR*, series 1, 22, pt. 2:291, 293; Blow to Lincoln, 5 May 1863, LP, LC; Boman, *Gamble*, 201–6; Castel, *Civil War Kansas*, 110; Rosin, "Gamble," 389; Beale, *Diary of Bates*, 290; Harris, *Lincoln and the Border States*, 230–37.

41. *OR*, series 1, 22, pt. 2:293; Basler, *CW*, 6:234; Boman, *Gamble*, 201–6; Rosin, "Gamble," 310–39.

42. Nevins, *War Becomes Revolution*, 394; Seymour to Lincoln, 14 Apr. 1863, LP; LC; Mitchell, *Seymour*, 313, 515–16; Croly, *Seymour and Blair*, 94–100; Cook and Knox, *Public Record of Seymour*, 110–11.

43. *OR*, series 3, 3:210, 214; Lincoln to Seymour, 12 May, Seymour to Lincoln, 13 May, Morgan to Stanton, 5 May 1863, LP, LC; Basler, *CW*, 6:211.

44. Seymour to George Pendleton, 14 May 1863, Seymour Papers, NYSL; Mitchell, *Seymour*, 293.

45. *BS*, 19 May 1863; *PhiIn*, 25 May 1863; *DFP*, 28 May 1863; Mitchell, *Seymour*, 290–95; Brummer, *Political History of New York*, 308–9; *NYH*, 19 May 1863; Basler, *CW*, 6:215–16; *OR*, series 2, 5:657; Epstein, *Lincoln and Whitman*, 144; Donald, *Lincoln*, 441–42; Paludan, *Presidency of Lincoln*, 199–202; *StPDPi*, 23 May 1863.

46. Brummer, *Political History of New York*, 312–13; *NYH*, 19 May, 15 Jun. 1863, *NYTri*, 30 May 1863; Paludan, *Presidency of Lincoln*, 199–202; Mitchell, *Seymour*, 295–99.

47. *OR*, series 3, 3:218; Brummer, *Political History of New York*, 320–21; Mitchell, *Seymour*, 314–15; *BDFP*, 9 Jun. 1863; *BDWC*, 10 Jun. 1863; Samito, *Becoming American*, 40–42.

48. Morgan to Lincoln, 15 Jun., Lincoln to Corning, [June] 1863, LP, LC; Donald, *Lincoln*, 442–43; Paludan, *Presidency of Lincoln*, 199–202; Burlingame, *Lincoln*, 2:507–10.

49. Pearson, *Andrew*, 2:86; Andrew to Sumner, 18 Jun. 1863, LP, LC; Hamrogue, "Andrew," 192–95; George Boutwell to Andrew, 30 Jun. 1863, Andrew Papers, MHS; Samito, *Becoming American*, 48–49; Duncan, *Where Death and Glory Meet*, 79–80; *NYI*, 28 May, 1863; *Lbr*, 22 May, 5 Jun. 1863; Emilio, *A Brave Black Regiment*, 27; Glatthaar, *Forged in Battle*, 136.

50. Hamrogue, "Andrew," 192–95; Emilio, *A Brave Black Regiment*, 24–30; *BDA*, 25 Jun. 1863; Samito, *Becoming American*, 48–49.

51. *OR*, series 3, 3:219, 224; Moore, "Holbrook," 65–78; Crockett, *Vermont*, 3:557; Moore, "Holbrook," 65–78; Mrs. Abram Holmes to Holbrook, 27 Feb. 1863, Roswell Holbrook Papers, (Frederick Holbrook), VHS.

52. *OR*, series 3, 3:238, 247–48.

53. Basler, *CW*, 6:238–39; *OR*, series 1, 25, pt. 2:503, 567, 27:47–48, pt. 2:567, pt. 3:76–77, 97, series 3, 3:241, 244–45, 321–22, 324, 325, 341; Thomas and Hyman, *Stanton*, 272; Albright, "Curtin," 48:166–67, 48:36–37; *PhiIn*, 28 May 1863; Egle, *Curtin*, 145–47; Robert Schenck to Curtin, 18 May 1863, Curtin Letter Books, PSA.

54. As quoted in Woodward, "Arthur Ingram Boreman," 53–54; Langford, "Constitutional Issues," 15–31; Moore, "Slavery as a Factor," 69–89; Shaffer, "Lincoln and West Virginia," 86–100; *LDJ*, 18 May 1863; *StLDMR*, 21 Jun. 1863; *BDA*, 22 Jun. 1863; *ChiTri*, 1 Jul. 1863.

55. As quoted in Woodward, "Boreman," 56–57; Boreman Inaugural Address, 20 Jun. 1863, Boreman Papers, WvDCH; *ChiTri*, 1 Jul. 1863; Ambler, *Pierpont*, 210–12; *WDI*, 28 May, 4, 13, 22 Jun. 1863; *OR*, series 1, 27, pt. 3:67, 133.

56. *ChiTri*, 1 Jul. 1863; Boreman Inaugural Address, 20 Jun. 1863, Boreman Papers, WvDCH.

57. *WDI*, 28 May, 12, 22 Jun. 1863; Sutherland, *Savage Conflict*, 235–36; Woodward, "Boreman," 57–69; Johnson and Geiger, "West Virginia's Militia and Home Guards in the Civil War," 68–77; Langford, "Constitutional Issues," 15–31; Moore, "Slavery as a Factor," 69–89; Shaffer, "Lincoln and West Virginia," 86–100; *ChiTri*, 1 Jul. 1863; Ambler, *Pierpont*, 211.

58. Morton to Lincoln, 30 May, Isaac N. Arnold to Lincoln, 9 Jun. 1863, LP, LC; Basler, *CW*, 6:237, 248, 251–52; *OR*, series 3, 3:196, 252, 339–40, 347, 354–55; Tredway, *Democratic Opposition*, 35–36; Towne, "Killing the Serpent," 55–65; Marvel, *Burnside*, 244–46; Klement, *Dark Lanterns*, 97–134; Sylvester, "Morton," 223–24; McClernand to Blair, 5 Jun. 1863, Blair Papers, DPL; Thornbrough, Riker, and Corpuz, *Diary of Fletcher*, 8:138–39:153; Terrell, *Indiana in the War*, 1:463; Nation and Towne, *Indiana's War*, 142–44; Foulke, *Morton*, 1:236–39, 253–72; Morton to Lucian Barbour, 8 Jun. 1863, "confidential," Lucian Barbour Papers, LC.

59. Abbott, *Ohio's War Governors*, 34; Trester, "Tod," 167–71; Reid, *Ohio in the War*, 1:125–29; *Ohio Executive Documents*, 1863, 1:297; Shannon, *Organization of the Union Army*, 2:227–28; Marvel, *Burnside*, 248–55; Salomon to Lincoln, 25 Feb., 18 Jun., Salomon to Stanton, 22 Jun., Salomon to Halleck, 22 Apr., 2 May 1863, Governor's Letter Books, SHSW; James Patrick to Salomon, 24 Mar., C. F. A. Hilbert to Salomon, 4 Mar., J. Nelson Parker to Salomon, 9 Mar., L. D. Fullmer to Salomon, 20 Mar. 1863, Executive Department, Military Correspondence, SHSW; *OR*, series 1, 27, pt. 3:222–23; Towne, *Surveillance and Spies*, 50–60.

60. Cook and Knox, *Public Record of Seymour*, 111–17; *OR*, series 1, 27, pt. 3: 79–80, 111–13, 130–33, 143–417, series 3, vol. 3:349–50, 356; Sears, *Gettysburg*, 23–26; *PhiIn*, 12, 13, 16, 17 Jun. 1863; Abbott, *Ohio's War Governors*, 27–34; Trester, "Tod," 164; *Ohio Executive Documents*, 1863, 1:191; Warner, *Generals in Blue*, 95–96; Fisher, "Groping toward Victory," 30–35; Egle, *Curtin*, 145–47; *BS*, 17 Jun. 1863; Basler, *CW*, 6:200; Robinson to Lincoln, 11 Jun. 1863, LP, LC.

61. *OR*, series 1, 27, pt. 3:112–13, 169–70, 190–91, pt. 2:542; Sutherland, *Savage Conflict*, 166–67; *WDNI*, 17 Jun. 1863; *PhiIn*, 15, 16, 17, 18, 19, 20 Jun. 1863; Parker to Curtin, 22 Jun., Curtin to Parker, 24 Jun. 1863, Curtin Letter Books, PSA; Yard, *Memorial of Parker*, 127, 129; *BS*, 30 Jun. 1863; Egle, *Curtin*, 145–47; Basler, *CW*, 6:257–58; Donald, *Lincoln*, 439; Hollandsworth, *Banks*, 120–30; Abbott, *Cotton and Capital*, 72–80; Alexander J. Hamilton to Major William L. [Burt] 29 Jul. 1863, Andrew Papers, MHS; Thornbrough, Riker, and Corpuz, *Diary of Fletcher*, 8:155.

62. *OR*, series 1, 27, pt. 2:211–15, 270–74, pt. 3:135–39, series 3, 3:417; *PhiIn*, 16, 17, 18, 20 Jun. 1863; Cook and Knox, *Public Record of Seymour*, 111–17; Sears, *Papers of McClellan*, 550; Sears, *McClellan*, 354; Basler, *CW*, 6:282–83; Langford, "Constitutional Issues," 15–31; Moore, "Slavery as a Factor," 69–89; Shaffer, "Lincoln and West Virginia," 86–100; *BS*, 17, 18 Jun. 1863; Sears, *Gettysburg*, 90–105; Trudeau, *Gettysburg: A Testing of Courage*, 34; Basler, *CW*, 6, 277–78; Thomas and Hyman, *Stanton*, 272; Dell, *War Democrats*, 256–57; *NDM*, 19 May 1863; *TDSGR*, 20, 22 May, 3 Jun. 1863; Gillette, *Jersey Blue*, 237–38; Jackson, *New Jerseyans*, 132–33; Yard, *Memorial of Parker*, 127–30; *WDNI*, 6 Jun. 1863.

63. Bradford to Lincoln, 23 Jun., Frank H. Stockett to Lincoln, 22 Jun. 1863, LP, LC; Bradford to Lincoln, 23 Jun., Bradford to Peter G. Grimes, 23 Jun. 1863, Executive Letter Books, MdSA; Mitchell, *Maryland Voices*, 388–89; Clark, "Politics in Maryland during the Civil War," 41:135–36; Dell, *War Democrats*, 256–57; *NDM*, 19 May 1863; *TDSGR*, 20, 22 May, 3 Jun. 1863; Gillette, *Jersey Blue*, 237–38; *OR*, series 3, 3:417; Jackson, *New Jerseyans*, 132–33; Yard, *Memorial of Parker*, 127–30; *WDNI*, 6 Jun. 1863.

64. Tod to Lincoln, 14 Jun., Matthew Birchard et al. to Lincoln, 26 Jun., Lincoln to Birchard et. al., 29 Jun. 1863, LP, LC; Donald, *Lincoln*, 444; *OR*, series 3, 3:364–65; Basler, *CW*, 6:300–306; James M. Ashley to Lincoln, 23 Jun. 1863, LP, LC; Klement, *Limits of Dissent*, 138–256; Paludan, *Presidency of Lincoln*, 199–202; Blair, "A Source of Amusement," 319–38.

65. Lucius Wood to Addie, 23 May 1863, E. G. Wood Family Papers, WRHS.

66. Burlingame, *Lincoln*, 2:558–59.

67. *OR*, series 3, 3:380; Basler, *CW*, 6:287; Abbott, *Ohio's War Governors*, 31–37; Klement, *Limits of Dissent*, 200–42; *WDNI*, 19 Jun. 1863; Speech of John Brough, 10 Jun. 1863, Brough Papers, WRHS; *StLDMR*, 16 Jun. 1863; *ChiTri*, 17 Jun., 2 Jul. 1863; *HEP*, 18 Jun. 1863.

68. Tod to Stanton, 26, 27 Jun. 1863, LP, LC; Abbott, *Ohio's War Governors*, 1:27–37; Fisher, "Groping toward Victory," 35; *OR*, series 3, 3:372, 383, 402, 419, 420; *CDE*, 20 May 1863; Washington, *Eagles on Their Buttons: A Black Infantry Regiment in the Civil War*, 2–20; Dennison to Lincoln, 18 Jun. 1863, LP, LC; Basler, *CW*, 6:287; Reid, *Ohio in the War*, 1:95–98; *ChiTri*, 17 Jun., 2 Jul. 1863.

69. As quoted in Washington, *Eagles on Their Buttons*, 18.

70. *OR*, series 1, 27, pt. 3:140, 241, 296.

71. *OR*, series 3, 3:70–71, 375, 383–85, 391, series 1, 27, pt. 3:141–45, 164; Gallman, *The North Fights the Civil War*, 62–63; Moore, "Holbrook," 65–78; Harris, "Blair," 158–60; *BDFP*, 19 Jun. 1863; Halleck to Blair, 8 Aug. 1863, Blair Papers, DPL; Marvel, *Burnside*, 249–55.

72. Foulke, *Morton*, 1:254–61; *OR*, series 3, 3:423; Holloway to Morton, 25 Mar., Morton to Holloway, 26 Mar., Terrell Entry, 28, 30 Mar. 1863, Morton Telegraph Books, ISA; *InDJ*, 27 Jun. 1863; Nation and Towne, *Indiana's War*, 141–43.

73. Foulke, *Morton*, 1:259–61; Terrell Entry, 28, 30, 31 Mar. 1863, Morton Telegraph Books, ISA.

74. Foulke, *Morton*, 1:260–61; Sylvester, "Morton," 204–11.

75. Foulke, *Morton*, 1:261; Sylvester, "Morton," 204–11.

76. Hunter, *For Duty and Destiny*, 221; Foulke, *Morton*, 1:260–66; Sylvester, "Morton," 208–11; *InDJ*, 29 Jun., 6 Jul. 1863; Terrell Entry, 28, 30, 31 Mar., Holloway to Morton, 1 Apr., 1863, Morton Telegraph Books, ISA.

77. *Illinois Senate Journal*, 23, 381; Nortrup, "Yates, the Prorogued Legislature," 5–34; Guelzo, "Defending Emancipation," 321–23; Yates to Stanton, 15 Jun. 1863, Yates Papers, ALPL; H. B. McCollom to Yates, 9 May, T. D. Clarke to Yates, 24 Jun. 1863, Jacob Ammen Papers, ALPL; Nortrup, "Yates," 286–90; *ISJ*, 17 Apr., 9, 11, 13, 15, 16, 20 Jun. 1863, 17 May 1864; Lusk, *Politics and Politicians*, 160–62; Reavis, *Yates*, 26–28; Dell, *War Democrats*, 207–9; Hesseltine, *Lincoln and the War Governors*, 318; Benton, *Voting in the Field*, 250–65.

78. As quoted in Guelzo, "Defending Emancipation," 321–23; *BP*, as quoted in *ChiTi*, 30 Oct. 1863 (also makes reference to Cromwell, as do other papers); *ISJ*, 9, 11, 13, 15, 16, 20 Jun. 1863, 17 May 1864; Benton, *Voting in the Field*, 260–61; Yates, "Yates," 192–93; *NYTri*, 12 Jun. 1863; *NYTi*, 14 Jun. 1863; Nortrup, "Yates," 286–88; Kimball, "Yates," 55–60; Reavis, *Yates*, 26–28; Nortrup, "Yates, the Prorogued Legislature," 5–34; Hesseltine, *Lincoln and the War Governors*, 318; W. H. Stennett to Yates, 11 Jun. 1863, "private," Ellsworth Lewis to Yates, 10 Jun., Friend Lucas to Yates, 17 Jun., F. A. McNeil to Yates, 27 Jun., Amos Miller to Yates, 11 Jun. 1863, Yates Papers, ALPL.

79. Yates, "Yates," 193; Klement, *Dark Lanterns*, 56–57; Bahde, "'Our Cause Is a Common One,'" 70–98; William P. Cook and E. C. Cook to Yates, 23 Jun. 1863, Yates Papers, ALPL.

80. Yates, "Yates," 193; Klement, *Dark Lanterns*, 56–57.
81. Guelzo, "Defending Emancipation," 320–23; *ISR*, 18 Jun. 1863; Nortrup, "Yates, the Prorogued Legislature," 5–34; Kimball, "Yates," 55–60; Klement, *Dark Lanterns*, 56–57; Dell, *War Democrats*, 207–9; *ISJ*, 9, 11, 13, 15, 16, 20 Jun. 1863; *CDE*, 14 Jun. 1863.
82. Alfred Churchill to Yates, 11 Jun. 1863, Yates Papers, ALPL.
83. *BDHE*, 12 Jun. 1863.
84. Kimball, "Yates," 58–66; Nortrup, "Yates," 296.
85. Avery and Shoemaker, *Messages*, 3:451–64; *Missouri Senate Journal*, Jun. 1863; Basler, *CW*, 6:291; Boman, *Gamble*, 210–12; *StLDMR*, 17, 20, 24 Jun. 1863; Berlin, *Freedom: Destruction of Slavery*, 1:406–7; *WDNI*, 25 Jun. 1863; Rosin, "Gamble," 310–39; *PhiIn*, 24 Jun. 1863; *BDWC*, 19 Jun. 1863.
86. Boman, *Gamble*, 211–15; Avery and Shoemaker, *Messages*, 3:451–64; Rosin, "Gamble," 310–93; Harris, *Lincoln and the Border States*, 320–27.
87. Boman, *Gamble*, 212–15; *Missouri Senate Journal*, Jun. 1863; Avery and Shoemaker, *Messages*, 3:502–4; *StLDMR*, 3 Jul., 1 Aug. 1863; Harris, *Lincoln and the Border States*, 230–37.
88. Boman, *Gamble*, 212–21; Philips, "Gamble and the Provisional Government," 13; *WDNI*, 3 Jul. 1863; Avery and Shoemaker, *Messages*, 3:502–4; *StLDMR*, 25 Jun. 1863; Harris, *Lincoln and the Border States*, 230–37.
89. *OR*, series 1, 24:167–68; Simpson, *Grant*, 190–215; Thomas and Hyman, *Stanton*, 268–69; Kiper, *McClernand*, 272–75.
90. Kiper, *McClernand*, 274; Simpson, *Grant*, 190–215; Nortrup, "Yates," 327; *OR*, series 3, 3:420; Marvel, *Burnside*, 254–58.
91. E. J. More to Wife, 19 Jun. 1863, E. J. More Papers, LC; *BS*, 29 Jun. 1863; Fishel, *Secret War for the Union*, 489–90; *OR*, series 1, 27, pt. 2:211–17; Eicher, *Longest Night*, 490–508; Welles to Curtin, 30 Jun., Curtin to Welles, 2 Jul. 1863, Curtin Letter Books, PSA; *NYTi*, 17 Jun. 1863.
92. Gurowski, *Diary*, 2:241–42.
93. Basler, *CW*, 6:217–18, 311–12; Parker to Lincoln, 29 Jun., Joseph P. Bradley and Marcus L. Ward to Lincoln, 2 Jul., Curtin to Lincoln, 28 Jun. 1863, LP, LC; Marszalek, *Halleck*, 171–76; Thomas and Hyman, *Stanton*, 171–76, 271–73; Paludan, *Presidency of Lincoln*, 204–5; Sears, *Gettysburg*, 121–25; Staudenraus, *Mr. Lincoln's Washington*, 210; Gurowski, *Diary*, 2:238–40, 254; *TDSGR*, 17 Jun. 1863; Gillette, *Jersey Blue*, 238; *WDNI*, 27 Jun. 1863; Jackson, *New Jerseyans*, 136; Donald, *Lincoln*, 444–45.
94. Basler, *CW*, 6:311–12; Randall, *Lincoln*, 2:276–77; Parker to Lincoln, 29 Jun. 1863, LP, LC; Gillette, *Jersey Blue*, 238; Jackson, *New Jerseyans*, 136; Donald, *Lincoln*, 445; Miers, *New Jersey and the Civil War*, 71–73; *WDNI*, 27 Jun. 1863.
95. Gillette, *Jersey Blue*, 238; *NDM*, 17–30 Jun. 1863; *TDSGR*, 17, 18, 20, 23, 24 Jun. 1863; Parker to Curtin, 22 Jun., Curtin to Parker, 24 Jun. 1863, Curtin Letter Books, PSA; Parker to Curtin, 22 Jun., Curtin to Parker, 24 Jun. 1863, Stanton Papers, LC; Jackson, *New Jerseyans*, 136; Yard, *Memorial of Parker*, 127–30; *WDNI*, 24, 25, 27 Jun. 1863; *NYTi*, 26 Jun. 1863. On 29 Jun. Lincoln's call for men went out over the wires to governors. Gibbs and Stanford were excluded. It was all they could do to keep the peace in their respective states, as they were constantly bedeviled by internal affairs, in particular the construction and protection of the Pacific Railroad and the New Almaden Mine. Four months before, Stanford, the railroad's president, ceremoniously turned the first dirt of the western terminus of the road, and, ironically, the very thing that had brought in the war was now being constructed, having wrestled with gauge disputes. It was considered a little irregular that

the governor and the railroad president had both gotten the railroad bill passed through the legislature. Frederick F. Low, a California congressman, recalled that, at the time, Stanford went upon the Senate floor and "cajoled and bullyragged" to get the bill passed. Low commented to Stanford at the time "very frankly" that he did not think "that thing would stand at all," that the treasury had no money, that it was constitutionally questionable, but then the governor "went to work and whipped it around, pulled very strongly on everybody, and everybody was then very strongly in favor of the Pacific Railroad." Becker, *Some Recollections of an Early California Governor Contained in a Short Dictated Memoir by Frederick F. Low*, 36–38. Low told Stanford that he would not sign any bill that asked the state to guarantee $500,000 absolutely, or pay interest on $2,500,000 bonds of the railroad company that he was president of. Low told Stanford that he would only agree to support the measure if the legislature chose to pass a bill guaranteeing to pay twenty years interest on $1,500,00 bonds, but not the principal, which would give them a good deal use of the money. *SFDEB*, 29 Apr., 1, 9, 23 May, 9 Jun. 1863. During the war, it was paramount to keep the productive New Almaden Mine near San Jose, among the nation's largest quicksilver (mercury) mines in operation, for military purposes. Lincoln signed a writ calling on the federal marshal in California, with military assistance, to seize the mine. He appointed Illinois colleague Leonard Swett as government agent for the mine. Meanwhile, Gibbs assisted the military in the construction of forts and in the suppression of the Snake Indians. *OR*, series 3, 3:424–25; Shutes, *Lincoln and California*, 128–30, 139, 158–60; Marszalek, *Halleck*, 188–89; Edwards, "Department of the Pacific," 188–91; Silver, *Lincoln's Supreme Court*, 157–62; Ascher, "Lincoln's Administration of the New Almaden Mine Scandal," 38–51.

96. Julia L. Leeds to "My dear friend," [Samuel Duncan], 11 Mar. 1863, Samuel Duncan Letters, DC; *OR*, series 1, 27, pt. 3:206; Shafer, *Men of Granite*, 134–35; Renda, "Credit and Culpability: New Hampshire Politics," 40–57; Gilmore's address to the Legislature 4 Jun. 1863, *Journals of the Honorable Senate and House of Representatives of New Hampshire*, June Session, 1863, 30–41; Lorenzo Thomas to Gilmore, 9 May, Albert Wallace to Gilmore, 11 May 1863, Gilmore Papers, NHHS; Waite, *New Hampshire*, 581–82; Renda, *Running on the Record*, 114–25; *BS*, 6 Jun. 1863; Benton, *Voting in the Field*, 204–22; Sobel and Raimo, *Directory of Governors*, 3:964; Marvel, "New Hampshire and the Draft, 1863," 60–61; *NHS*, 5, 19 Jun. 1863; *NYTi*, 11 March 1863; Hesseltine, *Lincoln and the War Governors*, 318–19.

Chapter Fourteen

1. Thornbrough, Riker, and Corpuz, *Diary of Fletcher*, 8:164–65.
2. *InDJ*, 4 Jul. 1863.
3. Niven, *Chase Papers*, 1:426; Bates, *Lincoln in the Telegraph Office*, 155; Beale, *Diary of Welles*, 1:358; *OR*, series 3, 3:462–67; Furguson, *Freedom Rising*, 252–54; McClure, *Lincoln and Men of War-Times*, 409–10; *BDFP*, 22, 28 Jul. 1863.
4. Beale, *Diary of Welles*, 1:358; Sears, *Gettysburg*, 154–225; Eicher, *Longest Night*, 509–19; George L. Stearns to Andrew, 2 Jul. 1863, Andrew Papers, MHS; Morgan to Lincoln, 1 Jul. 1863, LP, LC; Seymour to Morgan, [n.d.] Jul. 1863, Morgan Papers, NYSL; Sears, *Papers of McClellan*, 550; Sears, *McClellan*, 354.
5. *WDNI*, 7 Jul. 1863; Sears, *Gettysburg*, 226–492; Eicher, *Longest Night*, 520–50.
6. Sears, *Gettysburg*, 493–51; Eicher, *Longest Night*, 540–50.
7. Basler, *CW*, 6:314; Bates, *Telegraph Office*, 155; Sears, *Gettysburg*, 493–514; Furguson, *Freedom Rising*, 252–57.

8. Charles Merrick to Wife, 13 Jul. 1863, WRHS; Sears, *Gettysburg*, 493–514; Furguson, *Freedom Rising*, 252–57; Boritt, *Gettysburg Gospel*, 36–40.

9. Bates, *Telegraph Office*, 156; Basler, *CW*, 6:319; Kashatus, "Pennsylvania's War Governor," 22–31; David Wills to Curtin, 24 Jul. 1863, Executive Correspondence, PSA; Eicher, *Longest Night*, 555–56; Ballard, *Vicksburg*, 398–404; Hess, *Civil War in the West*, 134–59; Niven, *Connecticut for the Union*, 104–5; Boritt, *Gettysburg Gospel*, 37–49; Wills, *Lincoln at Gettysburg*, 21–23; Egle, *Curtin*, 368–69; *BDA*, 7 Jul. 1863; Maust, *Grappling with Death*, 633–34; Beale, *Diary of Welles*, 1:358–71; Sears, *Gettysburg*, 493–514; Staudenraus, *Mr. Lincoln's Washington*, 200.

10. Staudenraus, *Mr. Lincoln's Washington*, 194; Burlingame, *Stoddard*, 161–62; *WDNI*, 4 Jul. 1863; *BS*, 8 Jul. 1863.

11. Scharf, *History of Delaware*, 1:351–52; Mitchell, *Maryland Voices*, 185–87; Gillette, *Jersey Blue*, 238–39; *BDA*, 6 Jul. 1863; Hancock, *Delaware during the War*, 134–41; *DR*, 17, 20 Aug., 3 Sept. 1863; Hancock, "Political History of Delaware during the War, Part IV," 8:88–89; *Delaware House Journal*, 1864, 184–90, 212–18; *NYTi*, 29 May 1863.

12. Eicher, *Longest Night*, 560–63; *OR*, series 3, 3:481, 483, 486, 487–88, 494, series 1, 23:716–816; Foulke, *Morton*, 1:278–85; Trester, "Tod," 165, 176–77; *BDA*, 10 Jul. 1863; Abbott, *Ohio's War Governors*, 29; Thornbrough, Riker, and Corpuz, *Diary of Fletcher*, 8:172–78; Thomas, *John Hunt Morgan and His Raiders*, 77–85; Foster, "'For the Good of the Cause and Protection of the Border,'" 31–55; Sutherland, *Savage Conflict*, 168–69; Henry Beebee Carrington to Morton, 17 Jul. 1863, Henry B. Carrington Papers, FHS; Nation and Towne, *Indiana's War*, 148–52; Sylvester, "Morton," 225–30; Lucius Wood to Parents and Sister, 16 Jul. 1863, Wood Family Papers, WRHS; Wish, "Civil War Letters," 66–67; Wilson, "Thunderbolt of the Confederacy, or King of Horse Thieves," 126; F. M. [Chundunan] to George S. Cottman, 10 Jul. 1863, George S. Cottman Papers, ISL.

13. *ISJ*, 13, 14, 16 Jul. 1863; *ChiTri*, 6 Jul. 1863; *OR*, series 3, 3:499, 513–14, 526, 537–38, 808–9; Thomas and Hyman, *Stanton*, 280–83; Nevins, *The Organized War*, 120–21; Shannon, *Organization of Union Army*, 2:52–119; Henry O. Kent to Gilmore, 18 Jul. 1863, Gilmore Papers, NHHS; *WDNI*, 21 Jul. 1863; *PDJ*, 10, 13, 17 Jul. 1863; *Conscription in New Hampshire*, 1–23, WRHS; Shafer, *Men of Granite*, 176–77; Marvel, "New Hampshire and the Draft Riot of 1863," 60–72; Frank E. Howe to Gilmore, 14, 22 Jul. 1863, Executive Correspondence, NHDRMA.

14. *NYH*, 7 Jul. 1863; Mitchell, *Seymour*, 304–5; Cook and Knox, *Public Record of Seymour*, 118–24; *OR*, series 1, 27, pt. 3:552–53; Schecter, *The Devil's Own Work*, 26–27; *NYTri*, 6 Jul. 1863; *CDE*, 8 Jul. 1863.

15. As quoted in Mitchell, *Seymour*, 300–301; Cook and Knox, *Public Record of Seymour*, 118; *NYTri*, 6 Jul. 1863; *OR*, series 1, 27, pt. 3:552–53.

16. Mitchell, *Seymour*, 320–39; Cook and Knox, *Public Record of Seymour*, 126–27; Sears, *McClellan*, 354–56; *NYTi*, 15 Jul. 1863; *NYTri*, 15 Jul. 1863; *BDA*, 15 Jul. 1863; Schecter, *The Devil's Own Work*, 184–89.

17. *NYTri*, 13, 15 Jul. 1862; *PhiIn*, 15 Jul. 1863; *BDA*, 15 Jul. 1863; *BS*, 16 Jul. 1863; *HEP*, 16 Jul. 1863; Mitchell, *Seymour*, 320–28, 581–84; Cook and Knox, *Public Record of Seymour*, 126–35; Brummer, *Political History of New York*, 320–25; Schecter, *The Devil's Own Work*, 120–40; *NYTri*, 15 Jul. 1863; *NYH*, 15 Jul. 1863; "Diary of Sidney George Fisher, 1863," 474.

18. Brummer, *Political History of New York*, 320–25; Mitchell, *Seymour*, 299–315, 320–25; Cook and Knox, *Public Record of Seymour*, 126–27; Buckingham, *Life of Buckingham*, 278–81; Niven, *Chase Papers*, 4:84–85; James R. Gilmore to Lincoln, 17, 24 Jul. 1863, LP, LC; Holzer, *State of the Union*, 18–33; Shannon, *Organization of Union Army*, 2:206–16; Dell,

War Democrats, 218–19; Murdock, *Patriotism Limited*, 1–17, 63–77; *OR*, series 1, 27, pt. 2:925–26; *WDNI*, 15, 16, 18 Jul. 1863; Croly, *Seymour and Blair*, 107–13; Howe to Gilmore, 14, 22 Jul. 1863, Executive Papers, NHDRMA; John H. Almy to Buckingham, 16 Jul. 1863, Governor's Correspondence, CtSA.

19. Beale, *Diary of Welles*, 1:372.

20. *OR*, series 3, 3:482, 485, 486, 492, 530–31, series 1, 27, pt. 2:875; Thomas and Hyman, *Stanton*, 281–83; Donald, *Lincoln*, 448–51; *NYTi*, 13, 15 Jul. 1863; *NYH*, 13, 16, 24, 28 Jul. 1863; *NYTri*, 15, 18, 24 Jul. 1863; *WDNI*, 15, 16, 18 Jul. 1863; Nevins, *The Organized War*, 122–23; Brummer, *Political History of New York*, 320–30; James R. Gilmore to Lincoln, 17 Jul. 1863, LP, LC; *InDJ*, 29 Jul. 1863; *ISJ*, 5 Aug. 1863; Geary, *We Need Men*, 108–9; Murdock, *Patriotism Limited*, 63–80; Croly, *Seymour and Blair*, 107–17.

21. Robert A. Maxwell to Lincoln, 15 Jul. 1863, LP, LC; *HW*, 8, 22, 29 Aug. 1863; Bernstein, *New York City Draft Riots*.

22. John Jay to Stanton, 16 Jul., [Amico] to Stanton, 11 Aug. 1863, Stanton Papers, LC.

23. *OR*, series 3, 3:546, 552–53; Bigelow, *Letters and Literary Memorials of Samuel J. Tilden*, 1:184; Mitchell, *Seymour*, 320–30; Brummer, *Political History of New York*, 323–30; Seymour to Lincoln, 19 Jul. 1863, LP, LC; Murdock, *Patriotism Limited*, 63–80; Seymour to Morgan, [n.d.] Jul. 1863, Morgan Papers, NYSL.

24. As quoted in Gorham, *Life and Public Services of Edwin M. Stanton*, 2:109–12; Thomas and Hyman, *Stanton*, 283; Keller, *Affairs of State*, 20.

25. As quoted in Marszalek, *Halleck*, 183; *OR*, series 1, 27, pt. 2; Thomas and Hyman, *Stanton*, 282–83; Burlingame, *Lincoln Observed*, 75–76; Murdock, *Patriotism Limited*, 63–80.

26. *HW*, 8, 22 Aug. 1863.

27. Towne, *Letters of Wood*, 118–19.

28. As quoted in Kimball, "Yates," 17; Shannon, *Organization of the Union Army*, 2:52–119; Murdock, *Patriotism Limited*, 63–80.

29. James Drish to Wife, 10 Jul. 1863, James Drish Papers, ALPL; *ISJ*, 10 Jul. 1863; *WDNI*, 4 Jul. 1863; *ChiTri*, 5 Jul. 1863; Henry Rice to Yates, 3 Jul. 1863, Yates Papers, ALPL; *BDA*, 3 Jul. 1863.

30. Pearson, *Andrew*, 2:131–35; *WDNI*, 15, 16, 18, 23 Jul. 1863; *BDA*, 16 Jul. 1863; Bowen, *Massachusetts in the War*, 66; *NHS*, 17 Jul. 1863; *OR*, series 1, 27, pt. 2:885; *TDSGR*, 16 Jul. 1863; Gillette, *Jersey Blue*, 240–41; Andrew to Stanton, 22 Jul. 1863, LP, LC; Shannon, *Organization of the Union Army*, 2:216–22; Schouler, *Massachusetts in the Civil War*, 1:476–80; Dell, *War Democrats*, 220–30; Murdock, *Patriotism Limited*, 63–80; Beale, *Diary of Welles*, 1:374, 380.

31. *OR*, series 3, 3:494, 515–20; Clark, *Kirkwood*, 276–78; J. M. Hiatt to Kirkwood, 11 Apr., J. G. Detwiler to Kirkwood, 6 Jul. 1863, Kirkwood Papers, Kirkwood to "Dear Doctor," 7 Jul. 1863, Military Letter Books, Kirkwood Papers, ISHS; Lathrop, *Kirkwood*, 249–51.

32. *OR*, series 3, 3:485–88.

33. Basler, *CW*, 6:337–38; Lincoln to Parker, 20, 24, 25 Jul., Parker to Lincoln, 15, 16, 21 Jul. 1863, LP, LC; Gillette, *Jersey Blue*, 242–43; *TDSGR*, 29, 30 Jul., 1, 3 Aug. 1863; *OR*, series 3, 3:485–89, 496, 499, 555–56, series 1, 27, pt. 2:939; Dell, *War Democrats*, 230; *BS*, 17 Jul. 1863; *PhiIn*, 18 Jul. 1863; *PDJ*, 18 Jul. 1863; Henry Burns to Stanton, 29 Jul. 1863, RG 107, Letters Received, "irregular series," NARA; Geary, *We Need Men*, 76; Harris, "Blair," 162–65; *LDJ*, 6 Jul. 1863; Nevins, *The Organized War*, 126; Niven, *Connecticut for the Union*, 88; Croffut and Morris, *Connecticut during the War*, 457–58; Buckingham, *Life of Buckingham*, 279–83.

34. *OR*, series 3, 3:520–21, 534–35, 544–45.

35. *OR*, series 3, 3:548–49, 622.

36. Henry T. Young to Delia, 23, 30 Aug. 1863, Henry T. Young Papers, SHSW.

37. *OR*, series 3, 3:482–83, 525, 528–29, 555–56, 578, 584–85; Geary, *We Need Men*, 108–9; *Annual Report of the Adjutant General of the State of Maine, 1863* (Augusta, 1864), Appendix E, 25, 35, 40, 59, 103; Gold, "Constitutional Problems in Maine during the Civil War," 146–49; Davis Pearson to Curtin, 13 Aug. 1863, Executive Correspondence, PSA; Marvel, "New Hampshire and the Draft," 60–71; Rundell, "Despotism of Traitors," 356–57; Miller, *Black Soldiers*, 6–17; Bowen, *Massachusetts in the War*, 66–67; Pearson, *Andrew*, 2:136–37.

38. *OR*, series 1, 50, pt. 2:570–71, 289, 308–10, 449, 464–65; 473, 545, 570–71; Josephy, *Civil War in the American West*, 260–88; Bancroft, *History of the Pacific States, Oregon*, 2:492–95; Edwards, "Department of Pacific," 156–58, 197–99; *SFDAC*, 5 Apr. 1863; Edwards, "Oregon Regiments," 74–92; Edwards, "Six Oregon Leaders," 24; Etulain, "Lincoln and Oregon Country Politics," 112–13.

39. Basler, *CW*, 6:322; Low to Lincoln, 10 Jul. 1863, LP, LC; *OR*, series 1, 50, pt. 2:513; Shutes, *Lincoln and California*, 128–43; *SFDEB*, 21 Aug. 1863; Silver, *Lincoln's Supreme Court*, 158–62; *NYTi*, 11 Mar. 1863; Thomas and Hyman, *Stanton*, 293–94; Ascher, "Lincoln's Administration and New Almaden Mine," 38–51; Shutes, "Abraham Lincoln and the New Almaden Mine," 3–20; Melendy and Gilbert, *Governors of California*, 115–27; *SDU*, 18 Jun. 1863; *LAS*, 1, 15 Aug. 1863; Beale, *Diary of Welles*, 1:397–98; Marszalek, *Halleck*, 188–90; Marvel, *Lincoln's Autocrat*, 295–97.

40. Basler, *CW*, 6:322, 333–34; *OR*, series 1, 50, pt. 2:522–23, 572; Shutes, *Lincoln and California*, 128–43; Edwards, "Department of Pacific," 163–76; Stanley, "Republican Party in California," 142; *SDU*, 8, 10, 31 Jul. 1863; *LAS*, 11 Jul., 1 Aug. 1863; Beale, *Diary of Welles*, 1:397–98; Shutes, "Lincoln and New Almaden," 3–20; Marszalek, *Halleck*, 188–90; Matthews, *The Golden State*, 176–78.

41. Gamble to Lincoln, 13 Jul., Lincoln to Schofield, 27 May 1863, LP, LC; Basler, *CW*, 6:326–27, 344–45; Boman, *Gamble*, 213–17; *Proceedings of Missouri State Convention, June, 1863*, 10; *OR*, series 1, 22, pt. 2:293; Rosin, "Gamble," 390–400; Burlingame, *Lincoln*, 2:538–39; Berlin, *Freedom: Destruction of Slavery*, 1:406–9; Parrish, *Turbulent Partnership*, 223–24; Boman, *Lincoln and Citizens' Rights in Missouri*, 163–216.

42. John B. Gray to Gamble, 10 Aug., 9 Sept., Gamble to Willard P. Hall, 15 Aug., Bates to Gamble, 3 Aug. 1863, Gamble Papers, MoHS; Gamble to Bates, 10 Aug. 1863, Bates Papers, MoHS; Basler, *CW*, 6:326–27, 344–45; Boman, *Gamble*, 217–26; Rosin, "Gamble," 395–99; Burlingame, *Lincoln*, 2:538–39; Boman, *Lincoln and Citizens' Rights in Missouri*, 163–216; Harris, *Lincoln and the Border States*, 327–50; Boman, *Gamble*, 223–26.

43. Carney to Lincoln, 25 Jun., 19 Jul., Lincoln to Stanton, 17 Jul., Lane to Lincoln, 17 Jul., Lincoln to Lane, 17 Jul., Carney to Lincoln, 19 Jul. 1863, LP, LC; Lincoln to Stanton, 17 Jul. 1863, Stanton Papers, LC; Basler, *CW*, 6:335, 339–40; Castel, *Civil War Kansas*, 116–18; Carney to McDowell, 15, 16 Jun. 1863, McDowell Papers, KSHS; *OR*, series 3, 3:322; Carney to Stanton, 9 May, Stanton to Carney, 11 May 1863, Thomas C. Stevens Papers, KSHS; Lane to Lincoln, 17 Jul. 1863, LP, LC; Smith, *Ewing*, 190–91; *LDT*, 14, 15 Jul. 1863; Carney to James L. McDowell, 9, 15, 16, 26 Jun. 1863, Carney Papers, KSHS.

44. Basler, *CW*, 6:339, 395–97; Lincoln to Carney, 21, Blunt to Lincoln, 31 Jul., Lincoln to Blunt, 18 Aug. 1863, LP, LC; Castel, *Civil War Kansas*, 119–20; *ToTri*, 22 Aug. 1863.

45. Foulke, *Morton*, 1:265–68, 282–85; Basler, *CW*, 6:346–47; Eicher, *Longest Night*, 560–63; *LDJ*, 21 Jan. 1864; Thornbrough, Riker, and Corpuz, *Diary of Fletcher*, 8:172–78, 184; Thomas, *Morgan*, 77–85; Trester, "Tod," 176–80; Abbott, *Ohio's War Governors*, 31–

32; Reid, *Ohio in the War*, 1:145–47; Sutherland, *Savage Conflict*, 168–70; Schouler, *Massachusetts in the Civil War*, 1:489; Henry Beebee Carrington to Morton, 17 Jul. 1863, Carrington Papers, FHS; *InDJ*, 13 Jul. 1863.

46. Buckingham to Ebenezer D. Bassett, 21 Aug. 1863, printed in the *HEP*, 2 Sept. 1863; Eicher, *Longest Night*, 564–68; *BDA*, 30 Jul. 1863; Duncan, *Where Death and Glory Meet*, 106–17; Donald, *Lincoln*, 446–47; Basler, *CW*, 6:327–28; Sears, *Gettysburg*, 493–514; Furgurson, *Freedom Rising*, 257; Bates, *Telegraph Office*, 157; Niven, *Chase Papers*, 4:81–83; Beale, *Diary of Welles*, 1:370–71; Dennett, *Diaries and Letters of Hay*, 69–67; Segal, *Conversations with Lincoln*, 274–75.

47. Seraile, "Black Regiment in New York," 220–26; Basler, *CW*, 6:355; Waite, *New Hampshire*, 288; *OR*, series 3, 3:594; Shafer, *Men of Granite*, 177–78; *NHPSG*, 24 Feb. 1864; *Conscription in New Hampshire*, 1–23, WRHS.

48. *OR*, series 3, 3:599–605; Hess, *Civil War in the West*, 312–15.

49. William Curry to Mattie, 11 Aug. 1863, William Curry Papers, Schoff Civil War Collection, WLCL.

50. *OR*, series 3, 3:608–9, 612–19, 607; Brummer, *Political History of New York*, 330–33, 329–30; Mitchell, *Seymour*, 340–48; *PDJ*, 11 Aug. 1863; *BDFP*, 11 Aug. 1863; Seymour to Lincoln, 3, 7 Aug., Seymour to Fry, 1 Aug. 1863, LP, LC; Murdock, *Patriotism Limited*, 63–80; Donald, *Lincoln*, 447–51; Bigelow, *Letters of Tilden*, 1:184; James B. Fry, *New York and the Conscription of 1863*, 13–17, 32, 40, 51, 55.

51. *OR*, series 3, 3:608–9; Sears, *Papers of McClellan*, 554–55; Brummer, *Political History of New York*, 330–31.

52. Bigelow, *Letters of Tilden*, 1:184–85; Brummer, *Political History of New York*, 329–30; Mitchell, *Seymour*, 340–45; Donald, *Lincoln*, 450–51; Weeden, *War Government*, 293–97; Beale, *Diary of Welles*, 1:395; Murdock, *Patriotism Limited*, 63–80; Hesseltine, *Lincoln and the War Governors*, 300–302.

53. *OR*, series 3, 3:635–36; Basler, *CW*, 6:361–62, 369–70; Beale, *Diary of Welles*, 1:395; Weeden, *War Government*, 296–97; Murdock, *Patriotism Limited*, 63–80.

54. Weeden, *War Government*, 297–306; Lincoln to Stanton, 26 Aug., Lincoln to Seymour, 11, 27 Aug., Seymour to Lincoln, 22 Aug., Seymour to Fry, 15 Aug. 1863, LP, LC; *OR*, series 3, 3:635–36, 639–40, 666–67, 681, 692–94, 699; Basler, *CW*, 6:361–62, 369–70, 381–82, 391–92; Cook and Knox, *Public Record of Seymour*, 141–59; Murdock, *Patriotism Limited*, 63–80; Dix to Stanton, 16 Aug. 1863, Stanton Papers, LC; Brummer, *Political History of New York*, 335–36; *NYH*, 29 Aug. 1863; Beale, *Diary of Welles*, 1:395–97; *BDWC*, 4 Jul. 1863; *BDA*, 4 Jul. 1863.

55. *ISJ*, 22 Aug. 1863.

56. Gilmore to Lincoln, 4 Aug. 1863, LP, LC; Gilmore to Senator John P. Hale, 19 Aug., Rev. H. W. Bellows, 18 Aug., Gilmore to Congressman Edward H. Rollins, 19 Aug., Gilmore to Congressman James W. Patterson, 19 Aug., Gilmore to Senator Daniel Clark, 19 Aug., Gilmore to Nehemiah G. Ordway, 23, 24 Jul., Gilmore to Stanton, 23 Jul. 1863, Gilmore Papers, NHHS; *NHPSG*, 15 Jun. 1864; *Conscription in New Hampshire*, 1–23, WRHS; *NHPSG*, 15 Jun. 1864.

57. Basler, *CW*, 6:368; Staudenraus, *Mr. Lincoln's Washington*, 620–21, 624–25, 222–23, 227, 621–25. Lincoln sent his wife and son to the White Mountains.

58. *OR*, series 1, 22:576–79, series 3, 3:685; Carney to Schofield, 24 Aug. 1863, Thomas Carney Papers, Kansas Collection in the Special Collections, UKL; Ponce, *Kansas's War*, 68–69; Castel, *Civil War Kansas*, 124–43; *ToTri*, 22 Aug. 1863; *LDT*, 22, 23 Aug. 1863; Carney's Message to the Legislature, *Journal of the Senate of the Legislative Assembly of the State*

of Kansas, 1864, 30–31; Joseph D. Greer to Cousin, 23 Aug. 1863, John C. Williamson Papers, OHS; W. F. Wells to Yates, 2 Aug. 1863, Yates Papers, ALPL; Kimball, "Yates," 65–71; Yates to D. B. James, 23 Sept., John Hendricks to Yates, 31 Aug. 1863, Yates Papers, ALPL; Basler, *CW,* 6:383–84; Yates et al to Lincoln, 6 Aug. 1863, LP, LC; Nathan Holt et al. to Arthur I. Boreman, 13 Sept. 1863, Boreman Papers, WvDCH; Woodward, "Boreman," 59–63.

59. Castel, *Civil War Kansas,* 124–53; Schofield, *Forty-six Years,* 81–83; *OR,* series 1, 22:576–93, pt. 2:460–61, 473, 482–88, 491–92, 505–6, 530; Basler, *CW,* 6:415–16, 418, 423; Witt, *Lincoln's Code,* 274–75; Burlingame, *Lincoln,* 2:539–41; Sutherland, *Savage Conflict,* 193–96; Smith, *Ewing,* 194–212; Hesseltine, *Lincoln and the War Governors,* 355; *ToTri,* 22, 23 Aug., 1 Sept. 1863; *LDT,* 22, 23 Aug., 4, 5, 9, 12, 16 Sept. 1863; Zornow, "Missouri Radicals and the Election of 1864," 356–57; *ChiTri,* 9, 10, 18 Sept. 1863; Schofield to Carney, 29 Aug., 3 Sept. 1863, "private," and Carney to Schofield, 11 Sept. 1863, Carney Papers, UKL; Henry Newman to Carney, 25 Aug. 1863, Carney Papers, KSHS.

60. Nevins, *The Organized War,* 162–72; Donald, *Lincoln,* 454–55; Paludan, *Presidency of Lincoln,* 221–23.

61. Nevins, *The Organized War,* 167–72; Bowen, *Massachusetts in the War,* 69–70; Sobel and Raimo, *Directory of Governors,* 1:1581; *BDWC,* 24 Jun., 22 Jul., 31 Aug. 1863; Crockett, *Vermont,* 3:569–70; *NYTi,* 2 Sept. 1863; Dell, *War Democrats,* 240–41; *WDNI,* 29 Jul. 1863; *HEP,* 2 Sept. 1863; Moore, "Holbrook," 65–78; Dowden, "John Gregory Smith," 79–97; *BDFP,* 27, 28, 29 May, 8, 11 Jul. 1863; *PDJ,* 16 Sept. 1863; *ISJ,* 5 Sept. 1863.

62. As quoted in Smith, "Recruitment of Negro Soldiers," 371–72; *LDJ,* 14, 17 Jul., 4, 13 Aug. 1863; *FC,* 8 Jul. 1863; Donald, *Lincoln,* 454–55; Paludan, *Presidency of Lincoln,* 221–23; Nevins, *The Organized War,* 162–72; Sobel and Raimo, *Directory of Governors,* 2:524–25; Marvel, *Burnside,* 264–67; *WDNI,* 8 Aug., 3, 12 Sept. 1863; *BDA,* 3, 6 Aug. 1863; *BS,* 5 Aug., 3 Sept. 1863; *InDJ,* 3 Sept. 1863; *CDE,* 8 Jul. 1863; Burlingame, *Lincoln's Journalist,* 335–37; *LDJ,* 14, 17 Jul. 1863.

63. Berlin, *Freedom: Destruction of Slavery,* 1:508–10, 585–86; *OR,* series 3, 3:855–56, series 1, 30, pt. 2:92–93; Marvel, *Burnside,* 264–67; *LDJ,* 14, 17 Jul., 4, 13 Aug., 3 Sept. 1863; *BDFP,* 17 Aug. 1863; Bramlette to Adams, 22 Mar. 1863, LP, LC; Sinisi, "Modernization and the Federal System: The Example of Kentucky and Its War Claims Against the United States Government," in Cimbala and Miller, *An Uncommon Time: The Civil War and the Northern Homefront,* 326–44; *WDNI,* 8 Aug., 3 Sept. 1863; Smith, *No Party Now,* 99.

64. McClure to Slifer, 9 Jun., 24 Aug. 1863, Slifer-Dill Papers, DCL; Albright, "Curtin," 48:37; Albright, "Curtin," 48:33–42; Gallagher and Shelden, *A Political Nation: New Directions in Mid-Nineteenth-Century American Political History,* 148–54.

65. As quoted in Albright, "Curtin," 48:34–35, 170–72; *OR,* series 3, 3:550; Curtin to Lincoln, 4 Sept. 1863, LP, LC; Donald, *Lincoln,* 454–55; Burlingame, *Lincoln,* 2:565; Paludan, *Presidency of Lincoln,* 226–27; Egle, *Curtin,* 144–45, 160–66, 358–60, 366–67; Nevins, *The Organized War,* 170–72, 178; Shankman, *Pennsylvania Anti-war Movement,* 125–39; Thompson, *Heintzelman,* 282–83; *InDJ,* 6 Aug. 1862; *PhiIn,* 1 Aug. 1863; Brown to Curtin, 27 Aug. 1863, Slifer-Dill, DCL; *NYTi,* 8 Aug. 1863; "Governor Curtin: Phrenological Character Biography," 112–13; McClure, *The Life and Services of Andrew G. Curtin,* 17–20; Kashatus, "Pennsylvania's War Governor," 28–29; "Diary of Fisher, 1863," 88:476; Egle, *Curtin,* 144–45; White, *Emancipation, the Union Army, and the Reelection of Lincoln,* 29–35.

66. Abbott, *Ohio's War Governors,* 39; Dell, *War Democrats,* 244–45; Samuel Galloway to Lincoln, 14 Aug. 1863, LP, LC; *ChiTri,* 17 Jun. 1863; *CDE,* 13, 14 Jun. 1863; Engs and

Brooks, *Their Patriotic Duty: The Civil War Letters of the Evans Family of Brown County, Ohio*, 162, 165; Hesseltine, *Lincoln and the War Governors*, 330–34; *StLDMR*, 13 Oct. 1863; Speech of John Brough, 10 Jun. 1863, WRHS.

67. Clemens L. Clendenen to Family, 16 Sept. 1863, Clemens L. Clendenen Papers, HL.

68. Segal, *Conversations with Lincoln*, 287–89; Beale, *Diary of Welles*, 1:470; Paludan, *Presidency of Lincoln*, 223–25; Nevins, *The Organized War*, 168–71; Trester, "Tod," 184–89; Hesseltine, *Lincoln and the War Governors*, 331–34; Klement, *Limits of Dissent*, 243–45; Abbott, *Ohio's War Governors*, 36–40; Waugh, *Re-electing Lincoln: The Battle for the 1864 Presidency*, 14–17; Dell, *War Democrats*, 244–45; Tod to Stanton, 14 Sept. 1862, Telegraphic Dispatches, series 144, OhSA; *ChiTri*, 17 Jun. 1863.

69. Clark, *Kirkwood*, 300; Kirkwood to William Thomson, 21 Aug., Kirkwood to Gen. [Wilson], 25 Jul. 1863, Military Letter Books, Kirkwood Papers, SHSI; Sobel and Raimo, *Directory of Governors*, 1:433; Lathrop, *Kirkwood*, 252–53; Kiper, *Dear Catherine, Dear Taylor*, 108; *BDHE*, 22 Jun., 11, 13 Jul., 1 Oct. 1863; *ChiTri*, 20 Jun. 1863; *StLDMR*, 4 Aug. 1863; Clark, *Kirkwood*, 270–77; *NYTi*, 3 Sept. 1894; Kelly and Kelly, *Dream's End*, 89–91; Lendt, "Iowa and the Copperhead Movement," 416–18; Union Historical Company, *History of Washington County Iowa*, 525–27; Eichelberger, "Governor Kirkwood and the Skunk River War," 142–45.

70. Lathrop, *Kirkwood*, 265; Jones, *"For My Country,"* 128.

71. Lathrop, *Kirkwood*, 252–66.

72. Timothy Howe to [Reuben], 12 May 1863, Timothy Howe Papers, SHSW; Current, *Wisconsin*, 325–27; *OR*, series 3, 3:592–93, 611, 782–83, 850–51; Sobel and Raimo, *Directory of Governors*, 2:1726–27; *ChiTri*, 1 Sept. 1863; Salomon to Stanton, 8, 15 Aug., 10 Sept. 1863, Governor's Letter Books, SHSW; Byrne, *Uncommon Soldiers*, 92–93; Folwell, *Minnesota*, 2:335–37; Baker, *Governors of Minnesota*, 134–36; *StPDPi*, 20 Aug. 1863; Haugland, "Ramsey," 135–55; Guentzel, "Ramsey," 400–415.

73. As quoted in Mitchell, *Seymour*, 348–50; *BDWC*, 31 Aug. 1863; *HW*, 29 Aug., 26, Sept., 24 Oct. 1863; Basler, *CW*, 6:412–13, 417–18, 435; *OR*, series 3, 3:703, 720–21; Brummer, *Political History of New York*, 338–45; *NYH*, 10, 11 Sept. 1863; *WDNI*, 7, 12 Sept. 1863; Seymour to Morgan, 17 Sept. 1863, Morgan Papers, NYSL.

74. Washburn to Lincoln, 15 Sept. 1863, LP, LC; McPherson, *"We Cannot Escape History,"* 93; *NHS*, 18, 25 Sept. 1863; *BDA*, 15, 16 Sept. 1863, 7 Feb. 1865; *DR*, 17 Sept. 1863; Whalon, "Maine Republicans," 153–58; Abner Coburn to Stanton, 16 Sept. 1863, LP, LC; *BDWC*, 24, 30 Jun., 14, 15, 16, 18, 21 Sept. 1863; Dell, *War Democrats*, 240–43; *NHS*, 18 Sept. 1863; Chase, *Representative Men of Maine*, xlvii–viii; *ISJ*, 5 Sept. 1863; Sobel and Raimo, *Directory of Governors*, 1:107, 3:1581; Becker, *Reflections by Low*, 3–14, 15–65; Stanley, "Republican Party in California," 165–66; Melendy and Gilbert, *Governors of California*, 129–39; *SDU*, 18 Jun. 1863; *ChiTri*, 5 Sept. 1863; *BDWC*, 16 Sept. 1863; Crockett, *Vermont*, 3:569–70; Dowden, "Smith," 79–97; *NYTi*, 2 Sept. 1863; *SFDEB*, 3, 9 Sept. 1863; *HEP*, 2 Sept. 1863; *LAS*, 5 Sept. 1863; Smith, *No Party Now*, 90–91.

75. *InDJ*, 16 Sept. 1863; *BDWC*, 18 Sept. 1863; Chase, *Men of Maine*, xlvii; *BDA*, 15, 16 Sept. 1863; *NHS*, 18 Sept. 1863.

76. *OR*, series 3, 3:787–88, 782–83; *BDA*, 29 Sept. 1863; Burlingame, *Stoddard*, 168; Clark, "Politics in Maryland," 41:132–40; *BS*, 11 Sept. 1863; Wagandt, *Mighty Revolution*, 124–29; *WDNI*, 18, 21 Aug., 22 Sept. 1863; Bradford to Francis Thomas, 9 Sept., Edwin Webster to Bradford, 13 Sept., Bradford to Lincoln, 24 Aug., William Thomas et al. to Bradford, 11 Aug., Bradford to Thomas, 24 Aug., John Sappington to Bradford, 17 Jul., Bradford to Sappington, 30 Jul., George Vickers to Bradford, 14 Sept. 1863, Governor's

Letter Books, MdSA; [Montgomery Blair] to Bradford, 26 Sept., Bradford to Blair, 7 Nov., Thomas Hicks to Blair, 9 Apr. 1863, Blair Family Papers, LC; Berlin, *Freedom: Destruction of Slavery*, 1:338, 372–77; Harris, *Lincoln and the Border States*, 269–75.

77. Clark, "Politics in Maryland," 38:243; Clark, "Politics in Maryland," 41:132–48; *OR*, series 3, 3:470–71; Harris, *Lincoln and the Border States*, 269–75.

78. *OR*, series 3, 3:787–89; Clark, "Politics in Maryland," 38:243–45; Wagandt, *Mighty Revolution*, 124–31; Blassingame, "The Recruitment of Negro Troops in Maryland," 22–24; Bradford to Lincoln, 28 Sept. 1863, LP, LC; Bradford to Stanton, 3 Oct., Bradford to Fry, 10 Oct. 1863, Governor's Letter Books, MdSA; Harris, *Lincoln and the Border States*, 267–75.

79. B. Gratz Brown to Lincoln, 9 Sept., Lincoln to Charles D. Drake et al., 5 Oct., Drake to Lincoln, 31 Jul. 1863, LP, LC; Dell, *War Democrats*, 254–55; Boman, *Lincoln and Citizens' Rights in Missouri*, 163–216; *OR*, series 1, 22, pt. 2:484–91; *WDNI*, 31 Jul. 1863; *ChiTri*, 18 Sept. 1863; *StLDMR*, 26 Aug. 1863; Zornow, "Missouri Radicals," 358–60; Rosin, "Gamble," 400–411; Hamilton Gamble to Father (Gov. Gamble), 26 Aug., Archibald Hamilton to brother, 29 Sept. 1863, Gamble, MoHS.

80. Berlin, *Freedom: Destruction of Slavery*, 1:409–10, 457–58, 460–66; *OR*, series 3, 3:860–61; 1009–10, 1034–36; Boman, *Lincoln and Citizens' Rights in Missouri*, 183–216; James O. Broadhead to Edward Bates, 22 Sept. 1863, LP, LC; [Hamilton?] son to Father [Gov. Gamble], 6 Sept. 1863, Gamble Papers, MoHS; Boman, *Gamble*, 225–28; Rosin, "Gamble," 400–411.

81. Gurowski, *Diary*, 2:321–22, 326; Pearson, *Andrew*, 2:95–100; Thomas and Hyman, *Stanton*, 280–89; Belz, *Lincoln*, 120–24; Glatthaar, *Forged in Battle*, 170–73; Niven, *Chase Papers*, 1:441; *InDJ*, 23 Jul. 1863; Schouler, *Massachusetts in the Civil War*, 1:482–91.

82. Basler, *CW*, 6:474–75, 480–81; Eicher, *Longest Night*, 576–95; Hess, *Civil War in the West*, 189–92; Marvel, *Burnside*, 278–82; Thomas and Hyman, *Stanton*, 287–89; *OR*, series 1, 29:146–47, 149–53, 161–62, 167–69; *ISJ*, 3 Oct. 1863; Cleaves, *The Rock of Chickamauga*, 149–76; Burlingame, *Inside Lincoln's White House*, 98–99; Niven, *Chase Papers*, 1:450–55; Dennett, *Diaries of Hay*, 106; Donald, *Lincoln*, 457–58; Nicolay and Hay, "Abraham Lincoln: A History," 546–69.

83. Curtin to Lincoln, 18 Sept. 1863, LP, LC; Niven, *Chase Papers*, 1:429–30; *WDNI*, 8 Aug., 8, 10 Oct. 1863; Shankman, *Pennsylvania Anti-war Movement*, 126–39; Albright, "Curtin," 48:169–71; Basler, *CW*, 6:444–49, 451–52; *OR*, series 3, 3:817–18, 829, 832, 794–95, 798–99, 822, 838–39, 845–47; Foulke, *Morton*, 1:287; Thomas and Hyman, *Stanton*, 293; *NHS*, 23 Sept., 9 Oct. 1862; Shafer, *Men of Granite*, 177–85; *Conscription in New Hampshire*, 1–23, WRHS; Basler, *CW*, 6:477–78; Curtin to Lincoln, 17 Sept. 1863, LP, LC; Hesseltine, *Lincoln and the War Governors*, 334–35.

84. Burlingame, *At Lincoln's Side*, 57; Burlingame, *Lincoln Observed*, 64; Donald, *Lincoln*, 453; Boman, *Gamble*, 213, 228–29; Segal, *Conversations with Lincoln*, 282–86; Beale, *Diary of Bates*, 308; Niven, *Chase Papers*, 1:457; Charles D. Drake to Lincoln, 3 Oct. 1863, Emil Preetorius to Lincoln, 19 Sept. 1863, LP, LC; Zornow, "Missouri Radicals," 358–61; *StLDMR*, 2, 5 Oct. 1863; *ChiTri*, 10, 18 Sept. 1863; Boman, *Lincoln and Citizens' Rights in Missouri*, 163–216.

85. Burlingame, *At Lincoln's Side*, 57–64, 238; Gamble to Lincoln, 30 Sept., 1 Oct., Carney to Lincoln, 22 Sept., Schofield to Lincoln, 3 Oct., Smith O. Scofield to Stanton, [n.d.] Oct., Lincoln to Drake, 5 Oct., Bates to Lincoln, 22 Oct. 1863, LP, LC; *OR*, series 1, 22, pt. 2:567, 591, 1143; Boman, *Gamble*, 217–19, 229–32; Donald, *Lincoln*, 453–54; Rosin,

"Gamble," 410–15; Beale, *Diary of Bates*, 308–9; Tarbell, "Lincoln's Great Victory in 1864," 268–78; Sutherland, *Savage Conflict*, 195–96.

Chapter Fifteen

1. Basler, *CW*, 6:499–504; Joseph Medill to Lincoln, 3 Oct., Charles D. Drake to Lincoln, 3 Oct., Schofield to Lincoln, 2 Oct., James S. Rollins to Lincoln, 8 Oct. 1863, LP, LC; Sutherland, *Savage Conflict*, 196–97, 204–5; Boman, *Lincoln and Citizens' Rights in Missouri*, 193–240; Burlingame, *Stoddard*, 177; Basler, *CW*, 6:492–93, 499–504; Boman, *Gamble*, 229–31; Beale, *Diary of Bates*, 310; *WDNI*, 27 Oct. 1863; Beale, *Diary of Welles*, 1:471; Zornow, "Missouri Radicals," 360–62.

2. Basler, *CW*, 6:499–504, 526–28; Gamble to Lincoln, 1 Oct., Lincoln to Gamble, 19 Oct., Bates to Lincoln, 22 Oct. "private" 1863, LP, LC; Gibson to Gamble, 13 Oct. 1863, Gamble Papers, MoHS; Boman, *Lincoln and Citizens' Rights in Missouri*, 193–240; Tap, *Over Lincoln's Shoulder*, 176; *ChiTri*, 14 Oct. 1863.

3. Basler, *CW*, 6:491; *OR*, series 3, 3:855–56; *OR*, series 3, 3:881–82; *WDNI*, 28, 31 Oct. 1863; Bradford to Stanton, 3, 8 Oct., Stanton to Bradford, 10 Oct. 1863, Governor's Letter Books, MdSA; Bradford to Lincoln, 1 Oct. 1863, LP, LC; *HEP*, 2 Nov. 1863; Clark, "Politics in Maryland," 41:143–45; Berlin, *Freedom: Destruction of Slavery*, 1:338–39, 510; Wagandt, *Mighty Revolution*, 124–31; Harris, *Lincoln and the Border States*, 273–87.

4. *OR*, series 3, 3:862–63; Bradford to Stanton, 3 Oct. 1863, Governor's Letter Books, MdSA; Clark, "Politics in Maryland," 41:143–46; John W. Crisfield to Lincoln, 17 Sept. 1863, LP, LC; Wagandt, *Mighty Revolution*, 126–32; Blassingame, "Recruitment of Negro Soldiers," 22–23; Woodward and Drum, *Negro in the Military Service of the United States*, 3:1644, 1652–53, 1683; *WDNI*, 3 Nov. 1863; Harris, *Lincoln and the Border States*, 273–87.

5. Bradford to Lincoln, 1 Oct. 1863, LP, LC; Basler, *CW*, 6:495; *OR*, series 3, 3:862–63, 874–75; Clark, "Politics in Maryland," 41:145; Calhoun, *The Marylanders*, 34–50; Wagandt, *Mighty Revolution*, 126–32; Blassingame, "Recruitment of Negro Soldiers," 22–25; *WDNI*, 22, 23 Oct. 1863; Henry Clagett et al. to Bradford, 22 Oct., Bradford to Clagett, 26 Oct., Bradford to Stanton, 3 Oct. 1863, Governor's Letter Books, MdSA; Harris, *Lincoln and the Border States*, 273–87.

6. Reverend J. A. Hawley to Salomon, 19 Oct. 1863, Orin T. Maxon to Salomon, 29 Jul. 1863, Executive Department, Military Correspondence, SHSW.

7. *OR*, series 3, 3:863–66, 878, 888–89, 1090; Coburn to Gen. George Stoneman, 25 Dec. 1863, Executive Correspondence, MeSA; *PDJ*, 18 Dec. 1863; Crockett, *Vermont*, 3:571–73; Wickman, *Letters to Vermont*, 2:110–11; Wickman, *We Are Coming Father Abra'am*, 246–47; Zeller, *Ninth Vermont*, 111–12; Benton, *Voting in the Field*, 80–89; Dowden, "Smith," 85–88; *BDFP*, 10, 12, 21 Oct. 1863; Krenkel, *Yates*, 195–96; *NHPSG*, 7 Oct. 1863; Yates to Stanton, 11 Oct. 1863, Yates Papers ALPL; *ISJ*, 7 Oct. 1863.

8. Gibbs to Lincoln, 24 Sept. 1863, LP, LC; *ISJ*, 19 Oct. 1863; Gibbs to Yates, 24 Sept. 1863, Yates Papers, WC, ALPL; McArthur, *The Enemy Never Came*, 81–82.

9. Thornbrough, Riker, and Corpuz, *Diary of Fletcher*, 8:229–30.

10. Basler, *CW*, 6:515; Grimes to Lincoln, 14 Oct. 1863, LP, LC.

11. Basler, *CW*, 6:515; Tod to Lincoln, 14 Oct. 1863, LP, LC.

12. James M. Scovel to Lincoln, 11 Oct. 1863, LP, LC; *NYTi*, 16, 25 Oct. 1863.

13. *NHPSG*, 4 Nov. 1863; Albright, "Curtin," 48:37; *CP*, 23 Oct. 1863; *ET*, 20 Oct. 1863; White, *Emancipation, the Union Army, and the Reelection of Lincoln*, 28–35; Basler, *CW*, 6:513; Curtin to Edwin Morgan, 1 Oct. 1863, Morgan Papers, NYSL; Eicher, *Longest Night*,

597–600; *BDWC*, 5 Oct. 1863; Nevins, *The Organized War*, 178; *NYTri*, 17 Oct. 1863; *NYTi*, 16 Oct. 1863; Shankman, *Pennsylvania Anti-war Movement*, 126–39; *TDSGR*, 13, 16, 22 Oct. 1863; Egle, *Curtin*, 164–66; *BDA*, 14, 16 Oct. 1863; *DPU*, 2, 18 Sept., 10 Oct. 1863.

14. Basler, *CW*, 6:515; Morton to Lincoln, 14 Oct. 1863, LP, LC; Thornbrough, Riker, and Corpuz, *Diary of Fletcher*, 8:230; Beale, *Diary of Bates*, 310–11; *InDJ*, 14 Oct. 1863.

15. *NYTi*, 15 Nov. 1863; *InDJ*, 16 Nov. 1863; *LDJ*, 20 Nov. 1863; Thornbrough, Riker, and Corpuz, *Diary of Fletcher*, 8:249–50; Basler, *CW*, 6:515; Donald, *Lincoln*, 458–59; Paludan, *Presidency of Lincoln*, 226–28.

16. Kiper, *Dear Catherine*, 108; Sobel and Raimo, *Directory of Governors*, 2:433; *BDHE*, 22 Jun., 6, 7 Oct., 28 Nov. 1863; Gue, *History of Iowa*, 2:93–110; Miller, "A Punishment on the Nation," 96, 102; Schroder, "William M. Stone," 107–18.

17. Stuart, *Iowa Colonels and Regiments: Being a History of Iowa Regiments in the War of the Rebellion*, 15; *BDHE*, 22 Jun., 11 Dec. 1863; Sobel and Raimo, *Directory of Governors*, 2:433; Schroder, "William M. Stone," 107–18.

18. Lucius Wood to Parents and Sister, 11 Oct. 1863, E. G. Wood Family Papers, WRHS; James McClintock Diary, 13 Oct. 1863, HL; Burlingame, *At Lincoln's Side*, 65; Dennison to Lincoln, 4 Oct. 1863, LP, LC; Shankman, "Soldier Votes and Clement L. Vallandigham in the 1863 Ohio Gubernatorial Election," 88–104.

19. Tod to Lincoln, 13 Oct. 1863, LP, LC.

20. Basler, *CW*, 6:513; *NYTri*, 17, 19, Oct. 1863; Black, "Civil War Letters of George M. Wise," 68; Engs and Brooks, *Their Patriotic Duty*, 205; Nevins, *The Organized War*, 177; Abbott, *Ohio's War Governors*, 36–40; Trester, "Tod," 196–202; Waugh, *Re-electing Lincoln*, 14–15; *HW*, 31 Oct., 24 Nov. 1863; *CDE*, 13 Oct. 1863; Shankman, "Soldier Votes," 88–104; Porter, *Ohio Politics*, 180–87; Burlingame, *Lincoln*, 2:564; William Wylie Blair to Margaret, 14 Oct. 1863, William Wylie Blair Papers, HIS; White, *Emancipation, the Union Army, and the Reelection of Lincoln*, 26; Yates, "Yates," 173; Krenkel, *Yates*, 188.

21. *ChiTri*, 17 Jun. 1863; Sobel and Raimo, *Directory of Governors*, 3:1210; Abbott, *Ohio's War Governors*, 35–40; Hooper, "John Brough," 40–50; *HW*, 21 Dec. 1861, 24 Nov., 26 Dec. 1863, 9 Sept. 1865; Shankman, "Soldier Votes," 88–104; Beale, *Diary of Welles*, 1:470–71; Hesseltine, *Lincoln and the War Governors*, 351; Donald, *Lincoln*, 458.

22. Burlingame, *At Lincoln's Side*, 67; *OR*, series 1, 30, pt. 4:404; Thomas and Hyman, *Stanton*, 290; Eicher, *Longest Night*, 592–96; Marvel, *Burnside*, 295–98, Charles Dana to Stanton, 12, 15, 17 Oct. 1863, Stanton Papers, LC.

23. Shannon, *Organization of the Union Army*, 2:127–29; *BDWC*, 30, 31 Oct., 13 Nov. 1863; Basler, *CW*, 6:523–24, 543–45; *OR*, series 3, 3:892; Burlingame, *Stoddard*, 182; A. Burwell to Lincoln, 10 Oct. 1863, A. Jackson et al. to Lincoln, 3 Oct., Charles Gibson and James S. Rollins to Lincoln, 11 Oct. 1863, LP, LC; Boman, *Gamble*, 234; *WDNI*, 19 Oct. 1863; Boman, *Lincoln and Citizens' Rights in Missouri*, 193–240; Hesseltine, *Lincoln and the War Governors*, 306–7.

24. As quoted in Abbott, "Massachusetts and the Recruitment of Southern Negroes," 197–201; Forbes to Andrew, 18, 21, 24, 25, 29 Nov. 1863, Andrew Papers, MHS; Bowen, *Massachusetts in the War*, 1:69–71; Pearson, *Andrew*, 2:137; Shannon, *Organization of the Union Army*, 2:127; *HW*, 28 Nov. 1863; *OR*, series 3, 3:911–13, 933; *TDSGR*, 23 Oct., 2 Nov. 1863; *BS*, 26 Oct. 1863; Geary, *We Need Men*, 111; *WDNI*, 22 Oct. 1863; *NYTi*, 21 Oct. 1863; Speech of Henry J. Raymond, "Governor Seymour and the War," 16 Oct. 1863, NYHS.

25. *CDE*, 1 Oct. 1863; Bramlette to Lincoln, 19 Oct. 1863, LP, LC; Smith, "Recruitment of Negro Soldiers," 374.

26. Basler, *CW*, 6:530–32; Bradford to Lincoln, 31 Oct. 1863, LP, LC; Bradford to Fry, 10 Oct., Bradford to Stanton, 13 Oct. 1863, Governor's Letter Books, MdSA; Mitchell, *Maryland Voices*, 216–17; Wagandt, *Mighty Revolution*, 126–32; *PhiIn*, 5 Nov. 1863; *WDNI*, 5, 7 Nov. 1863; Burlingame, *Lincoln*, 2:566–68; Seraile, "Black Regiments in New York," 226; Speech of Henry J. Raymond, "Governor Seymour and the War," 16 Oct. 1863, NYHS; *OR*, series 3, 3:940; *NHPSG*, 7, 28, 29, 31 Oct. 1863; Cook and Knox, *Public Record of Seymour*, 160–97; *StLDMR*, 4 Nov. 1863.

27. Basler, *CW*, 6:546–47, 549, 550, 552–53; Lincoln to Chandler, 30 Oct. 1863, Chandler Papers, LC; Chandler to Lincoln, 13 Nov., James R. Hood to Lincoln, 22 Oct., John R. Biggs, Jr., to Lincoln, 24 Oct., Lincoln to Frederick Low, 7 Nov., Grimes to Lincoln, 3 Nov., James Dixon to Lincoln, 14 Nov. 1863, LP, LC; Burlingame, *Lincoln*, 2:591–93.

28. *OR*, series 3, 3:968; Bradford to Lincoln, 31 Oct., Montgomery Blair to Lincoln, 1 Nov., Schenck to Lincoln, 2 Nov., Buckingham to Lincoln, 18 Nov. 1863, LP, LC; Bradford to George Vickers, 27 Oct., Bradford to Lincoln, 3 Nov. 1863, Governor's Letter Books, MdSA; Mitchell, *Maryland Voices*, 188–89; *PhiIn*, 4, 5 Nov. 1863; Clark, "Politics in Maryland," 38:245–49; Wagandt, *Mighty Revolution*, 155–65; Benton, *Voting in the Field*, 225–49; *BS*, 4 Nov. 1863; *BDA*, 6 Nov. 1863; Harris, *Lincoln and the Border States*, 273–87; *WDNI*, 3, 4, 5, 7 Nov. 1863; Blair, *With Malice toward Some*, 183–86.

29. Basler, *CW*, 6:556–58.

30. Bradford to Lincoln, 3 Nov., Nicholas Brewer to Lincoln, 13 Nov., Brewer to Lincoln, 31 Oct. 1863, LP, LC; Clark, "Politics in Maryland," 38:250–54; Wagandt, *Mighty Revolution*, 155–75; *WDNI*, 3, 4, 5, 6 Nov. 1863; Benton, *Voting in the Field*, 225–49; *BS*, 4 Nov. 1863; Harris, *Lincoln and the Border States*, 273–87.

31. Gillette, *Jersey Blue*, 243–51; Burlingame, *Stoddard*, 188; Jackson, *New Jerseyans*, 152–54; *WDNI*, 26 Oct., 3, 4, 5 Nov. 1863; *TDSGR*, 3, 12 Nov., 5, 14 Dec. 1863; *InDJ*, 20 Oct. 1863; *BS*, 26 Oct., 5 Nov. 1863; Hancock, *Delaware during the War*, 138; *Del*, 10 Oct., 21, 24 Nov. 1863; Scharf, *History of Delaware*, 1:353–54; Thomas G. Pratt et al. to Bradford, 21 Nov., Bradford to Thos. G. Pratt, Jos. Nicholson, and Wm Tell Claude, 22 Nov. 1863, Governor's Letter Books, MdSA; Pratt to Stanton, 28 Nov. 1863, LP, LC; Mitchell, *Maryland Voices*, 191, 260; *OR*, series 1, 29, pt. 2:394–95, 470, series 2, 6:607, 626; Wagandt, *Mighty Revolution*, 165–90; Clark, "Politics in Maryland," 41:146, 38:254–59; *NHPSG*, 25 Nov., 2 Dec. 1863; *BDA*, 19 Nov. 1863; Benton, *Voting in the Field*, 225–49.

32. Brummer, *Political History of New York*, 346.

33. Burlingame, *Stoddard*, 187; Mitchell, *Seymour*, 350–53.

34. Edwin D. Morgan et al. to John W. Forney, 9 Oct. 1863, John W. Forney Papers, LC; Kimball, "Yates," 69; *NYH*, 30 Oct. 1863; *ChiTri*, 30 Oct. 1863; *NYTi*, 5 Nov. 1863; *ISJ*, 3 Nov. 1863; *HW*, 14 Nov. 1863.

35. *NYTi*, 5 Nov. 1863; Brummer, *Political History of New York*, 345–54; Mitchell, *Seymour*, 350–58; *NYH*, 23, 24 Oct., 1 Nov. 1863; *AEJ*, 9 Oct. 1863; *HW*, 14 Nov. 1863.

36. Bowen, *Massachusetts in the War*, 1:69–71; *NYTi*, 4 Sept. 1863; Paludan, *Presidency of Lincoln*, 226–28; *HEP*, 4 Nov. 1863; *BDA*, 9 Oct., 4 Nov. 1863; *NYTri*, 5 Nov. 1863; Schouler, *Massachusetts in the Civil War*, 1:497–502.

37. Sobel and Raimo, *Directory of Governors*, 1:775–76, 3:1727; Thwaites, *Messages*, 199; Quiner, *Wisconsin*, 193; Current, *Wisconsin*, 327, 407–8; *WSJ*, 28 Nov. 1863; *NYTi*, 3, 8 Nov. 1863; Warner, *Generals in Blue*, 325; Folwell, *Minnesota*, 2:334–37; Baker, *Governors of Minnesota*, 134–36; *StCD*, 5, 10 Nov. 1863.

38. Parker to Lincoln, 4 Nov. 1863, LP, LC; *InDJ*, 20 Oct. 1863.

39. Sears, *Mr. Dunn Browne's Experiences*, 185–87; Burlingame, *Lincoln Observed*, 66–67; *InDJ*, 20 Oct. 1863; Quiner, *Wisconsin*, 162, 993–95; Noyes, "Negro in Wisconsin's War Effort," 74–75; *HEP*, 3 Nov. 1863; Henry Gilmore to Father (Joseph), 3 Nov. 1863, Gilmore Papers, NHHS; *DFP*, 20 Nov. 1863; *OR*, series 3, 3:993.

40. *OR*, series 3, 3:1092–95, 97–98, 1163–64; Curtin to Lincoln, 9 Dec., Delahay to Lincoln, 23 Oct. 1863, LP, LC; Weeden, *War Government*, 289; Hesseltine, *Lincoln and the War Governors*, 306–7; "War Letters of Bowditch," 453, 457, 459; Carney to Stanton, 16 Nov. 1863, Carney Papers, UKL.

41. *OR*, series 3, 3:1013–33, 1091–92, 1099–1100, series 1, 29, pt. 2:458; *BDA*, 23 Nov. 1863; Eicher, *Longest Night*, 597–606; *HW*, 28 Nov. 1863; *NYH*, 15 Nov. 1863; *NYTi*, 17, 19 Nov., 26 Dec. 1863; Beale, *Diary of Bates*, 314–15; Barnes and Barnes, *Civil War through British Eyes*, 3:114–15; Marvel, *Burnside*, 299–320; Towne, *Surveillance and Spies*, 132–36.

42. Mitchell, *Seymour*, 302–3; *BDA*, 20 Nov. 1863; *PhiIn*, 20 Nov. 1863; *InDJ*, 21 Nov. 1863; *ChiTri*, 21 Nov. 1863; Hesseltine, *Lincoln and the War Governors*, 344–45; Boritt, *The Gettysburg Gospel*, 40–44.

43. *InDJ*, 16, 21 Nov. 1863; *PhiIn*, 20 Nov. 1863; *ChiTri*, 21 Nov. 1863; Boritt, *The Gettysburg Gospel*, 60–66.

44. *HW*, 5 Dec. 1863; Carpenter, *Six Months at the White House with Abraham Lincoln*, 242; Perret, *Lincoln's War*, 307–11; Wills, *Lincoln at Gettysburg*, 21–33; Thornbrough, Riker, and Corpuz, *Diary of Fletcher*, 8:251; Burlingame, *Lincoln*, 2:568–77; Cozzens, *Battles and Leaders*, 5:373–77; Thomas, *Lincoln*, 400–403; *WDNI*, 17, 20 Nov. 1863; *InDJ*, 6 Aug., 21 Nov. 1863; *ChiTri*, 21 Nov. 1863; *NYTi*, 20 Nov. 1863.

45. Wright, "Tod," 121; Remensnyder, "Lincoln at Gettysburg," 40–42; *PhiIn*, 20 Nov. 1863; *InDJ*, 21 Nov. 1863; *ChiTri*, 21 Nov. 1863; *NYTi*, 20 Nov. 1863; Gallagher, *Union War*, 76–89; Boritt, *Gettysburg Gospel*, 138–45; Wills, *Lincoln at Gettysburg*, 21–33; Mowry, "Reminiscences of Lincoln," 2542–43; *NYOC*, 15 Jul. 1897; Burlingame, *Lincoln*, 2:568–77.

46. *HW*, 5 Dec. 1863.

47. *CA*, 4 Aug. 1898.

48. *BDWC*, 16, 18 Nov. 1863; *InDJ*, 21 Nov. 1863; *ChiTri*, 21 Nov. 1863; *NYOC*, 15 Jul. 1897; Coburn to Curtin, 15 Nov. 1863, Slifer-Dill Papers, DCL; Gallagher, *The Union War*, 76–89; Boritt, *The Gettysburg Gospel*, 138–45.

49. *LDJ*, 27 Nov. 1863; *InDJ*, 21 Nov. 1863; *ChiTri*, 21 Nov. 1863; *ISJ*, 23 Nov. 1863; *HW*, 5 Dec. 1863; *NYTi*, 20 Nov. 1863.

50. Johnson and Buel, *Battles and Leaders*, 3:679–711, 725; Eicher, *Longest Night*, 605–17; McPherson, *Battle Cry of Freedom*, 679–80; Marvel, *Burnside*, 322–26; Basler, *CW*, 7:16–27; John W. Crisfield to Montgomery Blair, 14 Nov. 1863, LP, LC; Rhodes, *Somerset County Maryland: A Brief History*, 59–60; *CC*, 23 Nov. 1863; Cook and Knox, *Public Record of Seymour*, 370; Nevins, *The Organized War*, 447–50; *ChiTri*, 8 Dec. 1863; Burlingame, *Lincoln*, 2:578; McPherson, *The Political History of the United States of American during the Great Rebellion*, 308–11; *BDA*, 20 Nov. 1863; *WDNI*, 20 Nov. 1863; Donald, *Lincoln*, 460–67; Mitchell, *Seymour*, 302–4; Burlingame, *Lincoln Observed*, 89; Paludan, *Presidency of Lincoln*, 228–29; Randall, *Lincoln the President*, 2:303–12; Perret, *Lincoln's War*, 307–11; Wills, *Lincoln at Gettysburg*; Cozzens, *Battles and Leaders*, 5:373–77.

51. Basler, *CW*, 7:30–31; *OR*, series 1, 31, pt. 2:24; Burlingame, *Stoddard*, 179; Eicher, *Longest Night*, 605–17.

52. Burlingame, *Stoddard*, 193; *WDNI*, 1, 3 Dec. 1863.

53. Burlingame, *Stoddard*, 193.

54. *NYTi*, 5 Nov. 1863.
55. *NHS*, 1 Jan. 1864; *BDWC*, 14 Jan. 1864; Hesseltine, *Lincoln and the War Governors*, 340.
56. *Lbr*, 1 Jan. 1864; *NHPSG*, 6 Jan. 1864.
57. Dennison to Lincoln, 10 Dec. 1863, LP, LC.
58. Basler, *CW*, 7:23–24, 36–56; Chandler to Lincoln, 15 Nov. 1863, Chandler Papers, LC; Paludan, *Presidency of Lincoln*, 250–55; Burlingame, *Lincoln*, 2:593–94.
59. *HW*, 26 Dec. 1863.
60. Burlingame, *Lincoln Observed*, 94.
61. As quoted in Egle, *Curtin*, 284–304, 360–62, 386–87; *HW*, 20 Oct. 1894; McPherson, *Battle Cry of Freedom*, 698–702; Nevins, *Organized War*, 212–70; *ISJ*, 2 Dec. 1863; Ballard, *Vicksburg*, 396–430; Hesseltine, *Lincoln and the War Governors*, 345–46; McClure, *Lincoln and Men of War-Times*, 266–67; Sargent to Andrew, 5 Dec. 1862, "private," Andrew Papers, MHS; Thornbrough, Riker, and Corpuz, *Diary of Fletcher*, 8:267–69; Terrell, *Indiana in the War*, 3:382–83; Thornbrough, *The Negro in Indiana: A Study of a Minority*, 197–203.
62. Dicey, *Six Months in the Federal States*, 1:297; McPherson, *Battle Cry of Freedom*, 698–702; Nevins, *The Organized War*, 212–70.
63. *HW*, 12, 19 Dec. 1863.
64. Lincoln to Stanton, 18 Dec. 1863, LP, LC; Basler, *CW*, 7:57–58; *OR*, series 3, 3:1163–64; Furgurson, *Freedom Rising*, 274–75.
65. Seraile, "Black Regiments in New York," 225–30; *OR*, series 3, 3:1081–82, 1092, 1117–18; George Bliss, Jr., Union League Club Report of the Committee on Volunteering Presented, 13 Oct. 1864, 3–64, MHS.
66. Hervey L. Howe to Brother, 1 Nov. 1863, Howe Papers, SUL; Seraile, "Black Regiments in New York," 228–29.
67. *OR*, series 3, 3:1128–39; Nevins, *The Organized War*, 260–70; Edwards, "Department of the Pacific," 214–15; Melendy and Gilbert, *Governors of California*, 129–39; *LAS*, 26 Dec. 1863; *Second Annual Message of Leland Stanford, December 9, 1863*; *Inaugural Address of Frederick Low*; Woodward, "Issues of War," 24–25; Gibbs to Gen. E. L. Applegate, 26 Oct. 1863, Gibbs Papers, UOL.
68. *OR*, series 3, 3:1167–70, 1174–75, 1186–89; Smith, "Recruitment of Negro Soldiers," 374–75; *PhiIn*, 24 Nov. 1863; *BDA*, 24 Nov., 9 Dec. 1863; Harris, *Lincoln and the Border States*, 223–38; Bramlette's Message, *Journal of the Kentucky House of Representatives*, 7 Dec. 1863, 8–28; Henry Gilmore to Father (Joseph), 3 Nov. 1863, Gilmore Papers, NHHS; *NHPSG*, 7 Oct. 1863, 15 Jun. 1864; William E. Chandler to Gilmore, 10 Dec., Gilmore to Chandler, 14 Dec. 1863, Chandler Papers, NHHS.
69. *OR*, series 3, 3:1196.
70. Nation and Towne, *Indiana's War*, 97.
71. Yates to Sarah Mason, 28 Dec., Mary Newcomb to Yates, 26 Dec., Mary J. Hoover to Yates, 5 Dec., Nancy McKeg to Yates, 3 Nov., 1863, Yates Papers, ALPL; Niven, *Connecticut for the Union*, 97–99; Croffut and Morris, *Connecticut during the War*, 466–70; *BDA*, 28 Dec. 1863.
72. Beale, *Diary of Bates*, 321; Boman, *Gamble*, 236–37; Rosin, "Gamble," 423; Barnes and Barnes, *Civil War through British Eyes*, 3:115–16; *BDA*, 25 Dec. 1863.
73. Sobel and Raimo, *Directory of Governors*, 2:848, Avery, *Messages*, 4:3–7; Hesseltine, *Lincoln and the War Governors*, 374; Boman, *Gamble*, 236–37.

Chapter Sixteen

1. Burlingame, *Stoddard*, 198; Burlingame, *Lincoln Observed*, 99.
2. Burlingame, *Stoddard*, 198; Burlingame, *Lincoln Observed*, 99; NHS, 1 Jan. 1864.
3. *HW*, 9 Jan. 1864.
4. *InDJ*, 2, 4, 5 Jan. 1864; *PhiIn*, 1 Jan. 1864; *ChiTri*, 1, 7, 8, 9 Jan. 1864; Thornbrough, Riker, and Corpuz, *Diary of Fletcher*, 8:303, 308; *ISJ*, 4 Jan. 1864; *LDJ*, 8 Jan. 1864; *WDNI*, 2, 12 21 Jan. 1864; *BDA*, 2 Jan. 1864; *BDFP*, 7 Jan. 1864; *HW*, 23 Jan. 1864; Col. [Frank] Jordan to Curtin, 13 Jan. 1864, Executive Correspondence, PSA; *BDHE*, 15 Jan. 1864; *BDWC*, 9 Jan. 1864.
5. *BDWC*, 4 Jan. 1864.
6. *HW*, 16 Jan. 1864.
7. Ibid., 27 Feb. 1864.
8. Egle, *Curtin*, 169–70; Hancock, "Diaries of Ferris," 248; *WDNI*, 2 Jan. 1864; Burlingame, *Lincoln*, 2: 595–608.
9. *BDA*, 1, 7 Jan. 1864; Donald, *Lincoln*, 477; Paludan, *Presidency of Lincoln*, 260–69; Col. C. C. Andrews [3rd Minn.] to Stanton, 17 Jan. 1864, Stanton Papers, LC.
10. Abbott, *Ohio's War Governors*, 40; *Ohio Executive Documents*, 1863, pt. 1:305–12; *CDE*, 12, 14 Jan. 1864; Mitchell, *Maryland Voices*, 193, 220; Bradford's Message, 7 Jan. 1864; Clark, "Politics in Maryland," 38:256–60, 41:146–49; Wagandt, *Mighty Revolution*, 190–205; *BS*, 8 Jan. 1864; *BDA*, 8 Jan. 1864.
11. Fuller, *Messages of the Governors of Michigan*, 479–90; Benton, *Voting in the Field*, 92–104; Harris, "Blair," 165–70; Fennimore, "Blair," 49:356–57; *DFP*, 20 Jan. 1864.
12. [Soldier] to Blair, 10 Dec. 1863, Blair Papers, DPL.
13. Abbott, *Ohio's War Governors*, 40–41; *Ohio Executive Documents*, 1863, pt. 1:305–12; Shannon, *Organization of the Union Army*, 2:125; Thompson, *Heintzelman*, 286–93; Fisher, "Groping toward Victory," 36–37; *PDJ*, 2 Feb. 1864; *BDA*, 3 Feb. 1864; Towne, *Surveillance and Spies*, 149–63.
14. *Annual Report of the Secretary of War*, 1862, 10–12; *Annual Report of the Secretary of War*, 1863, 2–5; *OR*, series 3, 4:5–21, 180; *NYTi*, 10 Dec. 1863; Eicher, *Longest Night*, 624; White, *Emancipation, the Union Army, and the Reelection of Lincoln*, 168; Reid, *Ohio in the War*, 1:205–7; Hesseltine, *Lincoln and the War Governors*, 349–50.
15. *OR*, series 3, 4:2–8; Basler, *CW*, 7:107–8.
16. *OR*, series 3, 4:9–10; Gurowski, *Diary, 1863–64–65*, 89–90.
17. *OR*, series 3, 4:15, 27; *BDFP*, 7, 28 Jan., 3, 9 Feb. 1864.
18. *OR*, series 3, 4:28–29, 34; *BDFP*, 3, 9, 10 Feb. 1864.
19. Bramlette to Lincoln, 5, 8 Jan. 1864, LP, LC; Basler, *CW*, 7:109, 134; *OR*, series 3, 4:2; *LDJ*, 8, 12, 13 Jan. 1864
20. Basler, *CW*, 7:134.
21. *LDJ*, 8, 12, 13, 19, 20 Jan. 1864; *NYTi*, 25, 26 Feb. 1864; *OR*, 3, 3:1174–75; *BS*, 7 Jan. 1864; Harris, *Lincoln and the Border States*, 230–49.
22. Morton to Lincoln, 18 Jan. 1864, Stanton Papers, LC; *OR*, series 3, 4:38–39, 4:32, 33–34, 36–37, 41, 42–43, 55; Thornbrough, *Indiana*, 209; *NYTi*, 24 Jan. 1864; Bowden, "The Problem of Conscription in Maine during the Civil War," 44–47; *BDWC*, 8 Dec. 1863, 4, 9, 19 Jan. 1864; Cony to Gen. George Stoneman, 25 Dec. 1863, Executive Correspondence, MeSA.
23. Beale, *Diary of Bates*, 331, 336–37; Basler, *CW*, 7:114–16; Vorenberg, *Final Freedom*, 52–53; *Congressional Globe*, 38th Congress, 1st Session (Feb. 8, 1864), 521–22; *Journal of the Senate of the United States*, 38th Congress, 1st Session (Jan. 11, 1864), 67.

24. Brummer, *Political History of New York*, 355–59; Lincoln, *State of New York: Messages*, 520–61; Mitchell, *Seymour*, 354–55; Cook and Knox, *Public Record of Seymour*, 198–212; *WDNI*, 7 Jan. 1864; *BDA*, 7, Jan. 1864; *PhiIn*, 20 Jan. 1864; Egle, *Curtin*, 170–73; *BDHE*, 6 Jan. 1864; *BS*, 7 Jan. 1864; "The Messages of Governors Seymour and Parker," *The Old Guard* (Feb. 1864): 37; *DFP*, 7, 8 Jan. 1864; *HW*, 16, 23 Jan. 1864; Hesseltine, *Lincoln and the War Governors*, 350–53; Belz, *Reconstructing the Union*, 155–66, 169–73.

25. *NYTi*, 10 Jan. 1864.

26. *NYTi*, 10 Jan. 1864; *BDFP*, 8, 20 Jan. 1864; Donald, *Lincoln*, 483–88; *BDA*, 7 Jan. 1864, 20 Feb. 1864; Lincoln, *Messages*, 520–61; Mitchel, *Seymour*, 354–58; Brummer, *Political History of New York*, 356–61; Croly, *Seymour and Blair*, 124–29; *HW*, 16, 23 Jan., 12 Mar. 1864.

27. As quoted in Gillette, *Jersey Blue*, 253; Yard, *Memorial of Parker*, 21–33; *WDNI*, 16 Jan. 1864; *TDSGR*, 16 Jan. 1864; *BDWC*, 18 Jan. 1864; *DFP*, 21 Jan. 1864; "The Messages of Governors Seymour and Parker," 37.

28. Jackson, *New Jerseyans*, 208, 255–57, 161, 207–8; Yard, *Memorial of Parker*, 19–31; Benton, *Voting in the Field*, 269–80; Wright, "New Jersey's Military Role," 197–210; Tandler, "Political Front in New Jersey," 231–31; *NYTi*, 26 Mar. 1864; Trask, "Charles Sumner and the New Jersey Railroad Monopoly during the Civil War," 259–75.

29. Beale, *Diary of Bates*, 328–29; Ebenezer N. O. Clough to Lincoln, 27 Jan. 1864, LP, LC; Boman, *Gamble*, 236–38; Shoemaker, *Messages*, 3:511, 4:27–28; *WDNI*, 5 Feb. 1864; Rosin, "Gamble," 421–42; *StLDMR*, 26, 29, 31 Jan., 2, 3, 4 Feb. 1864, 12 Mar. 1865; *BDHE*, 3 Feb. 1864; *LDT*, 4 Feb. 1863; Boman, *Lincoln and Citizens' Rights in Missouri*, 241–62; Lizzie Brannock to Edwin H. White, 13 Jan. 1864, Edwin H. White Papers, MoHS; *OR*, series 1:34, pt. 2, 28,150.

30. John Dent to Lincoln, 16 Feb. 1864, LP, LC; Blassingame, "Recruitment of Negro Troops," 23–29; *WDNI*, 7, 9 Jan. 1864; *BDFP*, 15 Jan. 1864; *OR*, series 3, 4:46, 790; *BS*, 2, 18, 21 Jan. 1864; Clark, "Politics in Maryland," 41:146–48.

31. Niven, *Connecticut for the Union*, 90–91, 412–13; Basler, *CW*, 7:164; *OR*, series 3, 4:59; *Message of Buckingham, May 3, 1865*, 12–15; *PDJ*, 18 Mar. 1864; *ChiTri*, 26 Mar. 1864; *HW*, 20 Feb. 1864; Hancock, "Political History of Delaware, Part IV," 8:92–93; *Journal of the House of the State of Delaware, 1864*, 20–23; Scharf, *History of Delaware*, 1:355–56; Shannon, *Organization of the Union Army*, 2:130–35; *DR*, 4, 22 Feb. 1864.

32. Pearson, *Andrew*, 2:136–38; J. George Hubbard to Andrew, 19 Jan. 1863, Andrew Letter Books, MHS; Geary, *We Need Men*, 160–62; Abbott, "Massachusetts and the Recruitment of Southern Negroes," 197–210; *WDNI*, 21 Jan. 1864; Frank, *With Ballot and Bayonet*, 132–33.

33. Bramlette to Lincoln, 1 Feb. 1864, LP, LC; Smith, "Recruitment of Negro Soldiers," 374–81; *PhiIn*, 23 Feb. 1864; *OR*, series 3, 4:59–60; Shannon, *Organization of the Union Army*, 2:164; *StLDMR*, 9 Feb. 1864; *LDJ*, 1 Feb. 1864; Luke and Smith, *Soldiering for Freedom*, 42–44; Harris, *Lincoln and the Border States*, 230–49; Lee, "Unionism, Emancipation, and the Origins of Kentucky's Confederate Identity," 213–18.

34. Bramlette to Lincoln, 1 Feb. 1864, LP, LC; Smith, "Recruitment of Negro Soldiers," 376–81; *PhiIn*, 23 Feb. 1864; Harris, *Lincoln and the Border States*, 230–49.

35. Bramlette to Lincoln, 1 Feb., Stanton to Lincoln, 8 Feb., Lincoln to Stanton, 28 Mar. 1864, LP, LC; Smith, "Recruitment of Negro Soldiers," 376–81; Quarles, *Lincoln and the Negro*, 164; *OR*, series 3, 4:176–77, 436–38; Harris, *Lincoln and the Border States*, 230–49.

36. *OR*, series 3, 4:72; Briggs, "Enlistment of Iowa Troops," 366–68; *BDHE*, 18 Jan., 11 Feb. 1864; *IDSR*, 3 Feb. 1864; Gue, *History of Iowa*, 2:93–110; Stone to Lincoln, 26 Feb. 1864, Governors Papers, IaSA.

37. *OR*, series 3, 4:72; Kiper, *Dear Catherine*, 183–84; Briggs, "Enlistment of Iowa Troops," 366–68; *IDSR*, 3 Feb. 1864.

38. Yates to Lincoln, 28 Jan. 1864, LP, LC; A. J. Mathewson to Yates, 29 Jan. 1864, Yates Papers, ALPL; Basler, *CW*, 7:167; *StLDMR*, 16 Feb. 1864; Nortrup, "Yates," 328–29; Nortrup, "Yates: A Personal Glimpse," 134–38; *ISJ*, 19, 24 Jan. 1862; John R. Woods to Yates, 26 Apr. 1864, Yates Papers, WC, ALPL; Gilmore to Stanton, 14 Dec. 1863, Gilmore Papers, NHHS; *BDHE*, 9 Feb. 1864.

39. Stanton, "Charles Dubois Memoir," 321–23; Special Collections, Baily/Howe Library, UVL; Haynes, *A History of the Tenth Vt. Volunteers*, 60; Dowden, "Smith," 90–91; Benedict, *Vermont*, 195; Knight, *No Braver Deeds*, 229; Croffut and Morris, *Connecticut during the War*, 521–22.

40. Nortrup, "Yates, A Personal Glimpse," 135–37; *ISJ*, 24 Jan, 1862; U. S. Nichols et al. to Yates, 16 Mar. 1864, Yates Papers, WC, ALPL.

41. Clark, *Thirty-ninth Illinois*, 166–68; Nortrup, "Yates, A Personal Glimpse," 135–38; Yates to Lincoln, 28 Jan. 1864, LP, LC; Basler, *CW*, 7:167; Nortrup, "Yates," 328–32; *Illinois State Register*, 21, 22 Jan. 1864; Kimball, "Yates," 27–28; *ISJ*, 24 Jan., 3, 7, 16 Feb., 12, 21 Mar. 1864; *DFP*, 24 Mar. 1864; *StLDMR*, 22 May, 22 Jun. 1864.

42. *OR*, series 3, 4:77–101; *InDJ*, 5 Jan. 1864; Terrell, *Indiana in the War*, 2:352–53; Thornbrough, Riker, and Corpuz, *Diary of Fletcher*, 8:306–7; Marszalek, *Sherman*, 248–51; "War Letters of Charles P. Bowditch," 466; *BDWC*, 18, 24 Feb. 1864; *NHPSG*, 3, 10, 17 Feb. 1864.

43. *OR*, series 3, 4:95.

44. Andrew to Lincoln, 12 Feb. 1864, LP, LC; Basler, *CW*, 7:190; Hamrogue, "Andrew," 181–82.

45. Lincoln to Andrew, 18 Feb. 1864, LP, LC; Basler, *CW*, 7:191; Hamrogue, "Andrew," 181–82.

46. Basler, *CW*, 7:204; Schouler, *Massachusetts in the Civil War*, 1:509.

47. Shutes, *Lincoln and California*, 163–65; Burlingame, *Stoddard*, 203–4; Low to Lincoln, 17 Feb. 1864, and Elihu Washburne to Lincoln, 12 Oct. 1863, LP, LC; Donald, *Lincoln*, 480–82; Gillette, *Jersey Blue*, 265–66; Stanley, "Republican Party in California," 151–53; James G. Blaine to Lincoln, 3 Mar. 1864, LP, LC; *WDNI*, 26 Jan., 20, 25 Feb. 1864; *SDU*, 19 Feb. 1864; *LAS*, 13 Feb., 12 Mar. 1864; *WES*, 19 Feb. 1864.

48. Thornbrough, Riker, and Corpuz, *Diary of Fletcher*, 8:337; Zornow, "Indiana and the Election of 1864," 13–38; Thornbrough, *Indiana*, 209–10; Stampp, *Indiana Politics*, 217–24; Donald, *Lincoln*, 483–504.

49. Thornbrough, Riker, and Corpuz, *Diary of Fletcher*, 8:332, 337–38; *InDJ*, 15, 24 Feb. 1864; Richard W. Thompson to John P. Usher, 23 Feb. 1864, LP, LC; Thornbrough, *Indiana*, 344; Stampp, *Indiana Politics*, 217–24; Zornow, "Indiana and the Election of 1864," 19; Foulke, *Morton*, 1:291–94; Sylvester, "Morton," 230–34; *InDJ*, 5, 23, 30 Jan. 1864; Robert Winn to Sister, 25 Feb., 12 Mar. 1864, Winn-Cook Papers, FHS; Harbison, "Indiana Republicans and the Re-election of President Lincoln," 54–56.

50. Basler, *CW*, 7:200, 201; 212–13, 222–23; Donald, *Lincoln*, 480–83; Paludan, *Presidency of Lincoln*, 260–69; Zornow, "Kansas Senators and the Re-election of Lincoln," 133–44; Burlingame, *Stoddard*, 214; *BS*, 23 Feb. 1864; Segal, *Conversations with Lincoln*, 310–16; Ne-

hemiah D. Sperry to Montgomery Blair, 6 Feb., Augustin Chester to Lincoln, 3 Mar., Nehemiah D. Sperry to John G. Nicolay, 10 Feb., W. W. H. Lawrence to Abel C. Wilder and James H. Lane, 15 Feb. 1864, LP, LC; *WDNI*, 23 Feb., 11 Mar. 1864; Welles to E. T. W., 17 Jan., Mark Howard to Welles, 19 Jan., Welles to George Morgan, 18 Mar. 1864, Welles Papers, LC; *HW*, 12, 26 Mar. 1864; Burlingame, *With Lincoln in the White House*, 128.

51. Basler, *CW*, 7:201–2; Ozias M. Hatch to Lincoln, 16 Feb. 1864, LP, LC; *OR*, series 3, 4:135, 137–39, 142–43, 146–47, 150, 151; *Congressional Globe*, 38th Congress, 1st Session, 737–976; *HW*, 27 Feb. 1864; *PhiIn*, 3, 7 Mar. 1864; Donald, *Lincoln*, 484–500; *LDT*, 12 Apr. 1864.

52. Foulke, *Morton*, 2:387–417; Abbott, *Ohio's War Governors*, 42–43; Sylvester, "Morton," 235–44; Towne, *Surveillance and Spies*, 195–205; *OR*, series 3, 4:148–49, 161–63, 221–22; Thompson, *Heintzelman*, 291–97; Thornbrough, Riker, and Corpuz, *Diary of Fletcher*, 8:365; Yates to Stanton, 2 Mar., Nicolay to Stanton, 2 Mar. 1864, LP, LC; *WDNI*, 1, 5 Apr. 1864.

53. Krenkel, *Yates*, 206–7; *OR*, series 3, 4:149–50; Paludan, *Presidency of Lincoln*, 259–63; Donald, *Lincoln*, 490–92; Marszalek, *Halleck*, 194–96; Burlingame, *Stoddard*, 206, 216; Thomas and Hyman, *Stanton*, 297; Marszalek, *Sherman*, 248–56; Perret, *Lincoln's War*, 355–58; Simpson, *Grant*, 257–61; *DFP*, 8 Jan. 1864; *WDNI*, 22 Mar. 1864.

54. Dennison to Lincoln, 12 Mar. 1864, LP, LC; *OR*, series 3, 4:149–50, also series 1, 32, pt. 3:13; Paludan, *Presidency of Lincoln*, 259–62; Donald, *Lincoln*, 490–92; Marszalek, *Halleck*, 194–96; Thomas and Hyman, *Stanton*, 297; Simpson, *Grant*, 257–61; *WDNI*, 22 Mar. 1864.

55. Lincoln to John A. J. Creswell, 7, 17 Mar. 1864, LP, LC; Clark, "Politics in Maryland," 41:148; Nicolay and Hay, *Complete Works of Lincoln*, 8:465; Burlingame, *Stoddard*, 217; Burlingame, *Lincoln Observed*, 104; Perret, *Lincoln's War*, 355–60; Simpson, *Grant*, 257–61; *PhiIn*, 9, 10 Mar. 1864; *WDNI*, 22 Mar. 1864; Burlingame, *With Lincoln in the White House*, 129–30.

56. Grant, *Personal Memoirs*, 2:114–16; Furgurson, *Freedom Rising*, 285; Basler, *CW*, 7:234–35, 236; *OR*, series 3, 4:160–61; Donald, *Lincoln*, 490–92; Paludan, *Presidency of Lincoln*, 259–62; Marszalek, *Halleck*, 195–97; Burlingame, *Stoddard*, 217; Thomas and Hyman, *Stanton*, 297; Nevins, *The Organized War to Victory*, 6–13; Perret, *Lincoln's War*, 355–60; Simpson, *Grant*, 257–61; *PhiIn*, 9, 10 Mar. 1864; *WDNI*, 10, 22 Mar. 1864; Burlingame, *With Lincoln in the White House*, 129–30.

57. Basler, *CW*, 7:244; Donald, *Lincoln*, 490–92; Perret, *Lincoln's War*, 361, 386; Simpson, *Grant*, 257–91; Cameron to Lincoln, 9 Mar. 1864, "private," LP, LC; Burlingame, *Stoddard*, 219; Donald, *Lincoln*, 490–95; Paludan, *Presidency of Lincoln*, 259–65; Engle, *Yankee Dutchman*, 167–73.

58. Burlingame, *Stoddard*, 217; Grant, *Personal Memoirs*, 2:118; Basler, *CW*, 7:199; Nevins, *The Organized War to Victory*, 8–12; Simpson, *Grant*, 261–91; *PhiIn*, 12 Mar. 1864.

59. Burlingame, *Lincoln Observed*, 75–76; Burlingame, *Stoddard*, 217; Shute, *Lincoln and California*, 103–4.

60. Basler, *CW*, 7:239–40; Marszalek, *Halleck*, 195–99; Marzsalek, *Sherman*, 255–56.

61. Seward to Lincoln, 2 Mar. 1864, LP, LC; Castel, *Civil War Kansas*, 94–96, 168–75; *Senate Journal of the Legislative Assembly of Kansas, 1864*, 3–4, 200–202; *OR*, series 3, 3:1156–58; *LDT*, 17 Nov. 1863, 26 Jan., 9, 17, 19 Feb., 12 Apr., 7 May 1864; [Ingersoll] to Andrew, 23 Feb. 1864, Andrew Papers, MHS; *BS*, 13 Feb. 1864; *StLDMR*, 14 Feb. 1864; *InDJ*, 19 Feb. 1864.

62. Bramlette to Lincoln, 8 Mar. 1864, LP, LC; *OR*, series 3, 4:146; Coulter, *Civil War in Kentucky*, 198–200; Smith, "Recruitment of Negro Soldiers," 37–81; *InDJ*, 14, 24 Mar. 1864; *PDJ*, 14 Mar. 1864; *ISJ*, 25 Mar. 1864; Harris, *Lincoln and the Border States*, 230–49.

63. Bramlette to William Goodlo[e], 12 Mar., Wolford to Lincoln, 30 Jul. 1864, LP, LC; *LDJ*, 16 Mar. 1864; Robert Winn to Sister, 17 Mar. 1864, Winn-Cook Papers, FHS; *OR*, series 3, 4:174–75; [F. C.] Cook to Chase, 11 Mar. 1864, RG 107, Letters Received, "irregular series," NARA; Gillman, "Robert J. Breckinridge: Kentucky Unionist," 362–85; Coulter, *Civil War in Kentucky*, 198–200; *InDJ*, 24 Mar. 1864; Lucas, "Freedom Is Better Than Slavery: Black Families and Soldiers in Civil War Kentucky," in *Sister States Enemy States: The Civil War in Kentucky and Tennessee*, edited by Dollar, et. al., 188–216; Bramlette to Burbridge, 14 Mar. 1864, Burbridge Papers, FHS; Lewis, *For Slavery and Union*, 126–27; Gillman, "Breckinridge," 379; Smith, "Recruitment of Nego Soldiers," 378–83; *BDA*, 17 Mar. 1864; *DFP*, 17 Mar. 1864; *ISJ*, 25 Mar. 1864; Howard, "Lincoln Slave Policy in Kentucky," 302–3; Harris, *Lincoln and the Border States*, 232–49.

64. Bramlette to Burbridge, 14 Mar. 1864, Burbridge Papers, FHS; *LDJ*, 14, 16 Mar. 1864.

65. *OR*, series 3, 4:175–76, 201–2; Lincoln, Parole for Frank Wolford, 7 Jul. 1864, Lincoln to Wolford, 17 Jul., William C. Goodloe to Green Clay Smith, 29 May 1864, LP, LC; Gillman, "Breckinridge," 379; Berlin, *Freedom: Destruction of Slavery*, 1:595–96; Wolford to Lincoln, 30 Jul. 1864, LP, LC; *InDJ*, 24 Mar. 1864; Harris, *Lincoln and the Border States*, 230–49.

66. As taken from *LDJ*, 16 Mar. 1864.

67. Griffin, *History of Keen County, New Hampshire*, 508–9; Donald, *Lincoln*, 480; *BDWC*, 10 Mar. 1864; Edward H. Rollins to Lincoln, 8 Feb., Gilmore to Lincoln, 16 Feb. 1864, LP, LC; Joseph A. Gilmore to Lincoln, 12 Feb., Edward H. Rollins to Lincoln, 8 Feb. 1864, LP, LC; Rollins to Gilmore, 9 Feb., Fred Laurence to Gilmore, 6 Feb. 1864, Gilmore Papers, NHHS; *BDA*, 8 Jan., 9 Mar. 1864; Renda, "New Hampshire Politics," 58–75; *NHS*, 8 Jan. 1862; Natt [Cead] to Gilmore, 7 Apr., Gilmore to Edward H. Rollins, 24 Mar., William E. Chandler to Gilmore, 25 Feb., J. W. Patterson to Gilmore, 5 Feb. 1864, Gilmore Papers, NHHS; *ChiTri*, 15 Feb. 1864; *PhiIn*, 27 Feb., 9 Mar. 1864.

68. *OR*, series 3, 4:101, 160; William E. Chandler to Gilmore, 14 Dec. 1863, J. W. Patterson to Gilmore, 5 Feb. 1864, Gilmore Papers, NHHS; *ChiTri*, 15 Feb. 1864; Marvel, *Lincoln's Autocrat*, 321–22.

69. *NHPSG*, 10, 17, 24 Feb., 2 Mar. 1864; *WDNI*, 12 Mar. 1864; Benton, *Voting in the Field*, 204–22; Renda, "New Hampshire Politics," 55–68; Renda, *Running on the Record*, 122–24; *NHS*, 8, 29 Jan., 11 Mar. 1864; *BDA*, 9 Mar. 1864; *PhiIn*, 9 Mar. 1864; *BDWC*, 10 Mar. 1864; *HEP*, 23 Mar. 1864; *DFP*, 4, 8 Mar. 1864; Nehemiah G. Ordway to Lincoln, 10 Mar. 1864, LP, LC; Allen Tenney to Gilmore, 8 Mar., Amos Tuck to Gilmore, 12 Mar., Henry Poor to Gilmore, 14 Mar. 1864, Gilmore Papers, NHHS.

70. William E. Chandler and Edward H. Rollins to Lincoln, 8 Mar. 1864, LP, LC; Sobel and Raimo, *Directory of Governors*, 1:965; Dell, *War Democrats*, 290–91; *WDNI*, 8, 12 Mar. 1864; Renda, "New Hampshire Politics," 55–68; Renda, *Running on the Record*, 123–25; *NHPSG*, 24 Feb. 1864; *BDWC*, 10 Mar. 1864; Hesseltine, *Lincoln and the War Governors*, 357–56; Marvel, *Lincoln's Autocrat*, 321–22.

71. *OR*, series 3, 4:160; William E. Chandler to Gilmore, 24 Feb. 1864, Gilmore Papers, NHHS; Gilmore to Lincoln, 9 Mar. 1864, LP, LC; *ISJ*, 3 Mar. 1864; *ChiTri*, 6 Mar. 1864.

72. Blaine to Lincoln, 3 Mar., Blaine to Isaac N. Arnold, 3 Mar. 1864, LP, LC; *BDWC*, 10 Mar. 1864.

73. Julian R. Cambell to Lincoln, 10 Mar., Smith to Lincoln, 12 Mar. 1864, LP, LC; Basler, *CW*, 7:241; Raber, "Republican Party in Rhode Island," 145–49; *PDJ*, 17 Feb., 22, 23, 25, 28, 29 Mar., 7 Apr. 1864; *NYTi*, 16 Mar., 7, 16, 17 Apr. 1864; Dell, *War Democrats*, 290–92; Benton, *Voting in the Field*, 182–88; *ISJ*, 8 Apr. 1864.

74. "Pennsylvania Volunteer" to Curtin, 15 Mar., "A Soldier in Camp" to Curtin, 14, 15 Mar., Edward Townsend to Brig. Gen. Darius Couch to Curtin, 19 Mar. 1864, Executive Correspondence, PSA; Curtin to Lincoln, 14 Mar. 1864, LP, LC; Wayne McVeagh to Eli Slifer, 28 Dec. 1862, Slifer-Dill Papers, DCL; McClure, *Curtin*, 20–21; Basler, *CW*, 7:245; *OR*, series 3, 4:181; Beale, *Diary of Welles*, 1:533–45; Gustavus Fox to Lincoln, 26 Mar., Welles to Lincoln, 25 Mar. Fox to Welles, 7 Apr. 1864, LP, LC; Beale, Hoogenboom, *Gustavus Vasa Fox of the Union Navy*, 220–21.

75. *OR*, series 3, 4:187–88; Bramlette to Burbridge, 14 Mar., Robert J. Breckinridge to Burbridge, 26 Mar. 1864, Burbridge Papers, FHS; Howard, "Lincoln Slave Policy in Kentucky," 302–3; Smith, "Recruitment of Negro Soldiers," 381–83; *FC*, 16 Mar. 1864; *LDJ*, 17, 18 Mar., 3, 16, 27 Apr. 1864; *WDNI*, 17, 18, Feb., 17 Mar. 1864; Basler, *CW*, 7:226–27, 251.

76. Beale, *Diary of Bates*, 352; Basler, *CW*, 7:272; *OR*, series 3, 4:206; Smith, "Recruitment of Negro Soldiers," 383–85; *StLDMR*, 1 Apr. 1864; *WDNI*, 29 Mar. 1864; Mortimer M. Benton to Salmon Chase, 16 Mar. 1864, LP, LC; Vorenberg, *Final Freedom*, 168–69; George D. Blakely to James Speed, 16 Mar. 1864, Speed Family Papers, FHS; Jonathan Bailey to Burbridge, 21 Jan. 1864, Burbridge Papers, FHS; *LDJ*, 14, 16, 21 Mar., 3, 14, 16, 27 Apr. 1864.

77. *BDA*, 29 Mar. 1864; Bramlette to Lincoln, 30 Mar. 1864, LP, LC.

78. Mitchell, *Maryland Voices*, 419; Wallace to Lincoln, 1 Apr. 1864, LP, LC; Bradford to Wallace, 30, 31 Mar. 1864, LP, LC; Wagandt, *Mighty Revolution*, 200–220; *WDNI*, 22 Mar., 4 Apr. 1864; *BS*, 2 Apr. 1864; *BDA*, 2 Apr. 1864.

79. Mitchell, *Maryland Voices*, 418–19; Berlin, *Freedom's Soldiers*, 216–17; Basler, *CW* 7:276–77; Clark, "Politics in Maryland," 39:325–28; Wagandt, *Mighty Revolution*, 200–220.

80. Gibbs to Lincoln, 5 Mar. 1864, LP, LC; *OR*, series 1, 50, pt. 2:780; Stanley, "Republican Party in California," 151–56; Davis, *History of Political Conventions in California, 1849–1852*, 206–7. The California Legislature passed a bill in this session that brought the state into line by having congressional elections in even-numbered years. *Journal of the Assembly of California*, 1863–64, 591; *Journal of the Senate of California*, 1863–64, 450; *SFDEB*, 4, 26 Mar. 1864.

81. Gilmore to Lincoln, 31 Mar. 1864, LP, LC. Gilmore also sent a jug to Andrew and closed his letter with an enduring question: "When will this cruel war be ended?" Andrew to Gilmore, 2 Apr. 1864, Gilmore Papers, NHHS; Gilmore to Andrew, 31 Mar. 1864, Andrew Papers, MHS.

82. Nortrup, "Yates," 309–12; D. B. Crane to Zach Chandler, 29 Mar. 1864, LP, LC; Tap, *Over Lincoln's Shoulder*, 228–30, 297; E. P. Perry to Yates, 3 Mar., A. C. Weed to Yates, 25 Jun. 1863, Yates Papers, ALPL; Kimball, "Yates," 68–71; *StLDMR*, 31 Mar., 1 Apr. 1864; *ISJ*, 31 Mar., 8 Apr. 1864; *PhiIn*, 1, 7 Apr. 1864; Williams, *Lincoln and the Radicals*, 340; Nevins, *The Organized War to Victory*, 10–11.

Chapter Seventeen

1. Burlingame, *Stoddard*, 219–20.
2. Eicher, *Longest Night*, 641–58.
3. Buckingham to Lincoln, 4, 5 Apr., Nehemiah D. Sperry to James Dixon, 4 Apr. 1864, LP, LC; *OR*, series 3, 4:215; Croffut and Morris, *Connecticut during the War*, 629–30;

Eicher, *Longest Night*, 641–58; Buckingham, *Life of Buckingham*, 360–61; Nevins, *The Organized War*, 115; *PDJ*, 10 Mar. 1864; *PhiIn*, 5, 6 Apr. 1864; *WDNI*, 5, 28 Apr. 1864.

4. Buckingham to Lincoln, 4, 5 Apr., James F. Babcock to Lincoln, 22 Feb. 1864, LP, LC; *OR*, series 3, 4:215–17; Beale, *Diary of Welles*, 2:5–6; *PhiIn*, 5 Apr. 1864; *NHPSG*, 13 Apr. 1864; *Buckingham to Gideon Welles*, 5 Apr. 1864, Gideon Welles Papers, CtHS.

5. *OR*, series 3, 4:215–17; Buckingham to Lincoln, 4, 5 Apr. 1864; *BDWC*, 7 Apr. 1864; Beale, *Diary of Welles*, 2:5–6.

6. *ChiTri*, 27 Mar. 1864; *ISJ*, 6 Apr. 1864; *NYTi*, 5, 6, 7 Mar. 1864; Nevins, *The Organized War*, 115; Waugh, *Re-electing Lincoln*, 103; Beale, *Diary of Welles*, 2:5–6; *PDJ*, 10 Mar. 1864; *PhiIn*, 5 Apr. 1864; *BDWC*, 7 Apr. 1864; *BDHE*, 8 Apr. 1864; *NHPSG*, 13 Apr. 1864; *HW*, 12 Mar. 1864; *Journal of the Senate of Wisconsin*, 1864, 81–83.

7. Basler, *CW*, 7:281–83; *ISJ*, 28 Apr. 1864; *BDA*, 29 Apr. 1864; *PhiIn*, 29 Apr. 1864; *BS*, 29 Apr. 1864; *MD*, 3, 12 Feb. 1864; *BDWC*, 7 Apr. 1864; *BDHE*, 8 Apr. 1864; Hesseltine, *Lincoln and the War Governors*, 356–57; Blair, *With Malice toward Some*, 191–233; White, *Emancipation, the Union Army and the Reelection of Abraham Lincoln*, 98–105.

8. Basler, *CW*, 7:281–83.

9. Ibid.

10. Ibid.

11. Buckingham to Lincoln, 25 May 1860, Hodges to Lincoln, 22 Apr. 1864, LP, LC; Basler, *CW*, 7:308–9; Weeden, *War Government*, 250; Nicolay and Hay, *Complete Works of Lincoln*, 2:509; *LDJ*, 27 Apr. 1864; Burlingame, *Lincoln*, 2:709–10.

12. *NHS*, 1 Jan. 1864.

13. Hancock, "Diaries of Ferris," 250–51; Vorenberg, *Final Freedom*, 53–107.

14. *OR*, series 1, 33:827–29.

15. Dennett, *Diaries and Letters of Hay*, 178–79, Nicolay and Hay, *Lincoln: A History*, 8:348; Grant, *Personal Memoirs*, 2:132; Burlingame and Ettlinger, *Inside Lincoln's White House*, 194; Donald, *Lincoln*, 499.

16. Eicher, *Longest Night*, 660–65; *OR*, series 1, 32, pt. 3:246, 46:11; Nolan, *Butler*, 265–78; Thomas and Hyman, *Stanton*, 298; Marszalek, *Sherman*, 259–65; Simpson, *Grant*, 261–91; *BDWC*, 5 Apr., 19, 20 May 1864; Cony to Hodsdon, 8, 11 Apr., 19, 20 May 1864, Executive Correspondence, MeSA; *BDA*, 27 Apr. 1864; *BDHE*, 28 Apr. 1864; Sherman to Carney, 6 Apr. 1864, Carney Papers, UKL.

17. *OR*, series 3, 4:229.

18. *OR*, series 3, 4:232–36; Gilmore to Edward Rollins, 24 Mar., 26, 27 May, 4 Jun., Natt Head to Gilmore, 7 Apr., Gilmore to William E. Chandler, 14 Dec., Gilmore to Stanton, 27 Oct., 14 Dec. 1863, Gilmore Papers, NHHS; Renda, "New Hampshire Politics," 55–68; *NHPSG*, 15 Jun. 1864; *HW*, 19 Mar. 1864.

19. Basler, *CW*, 7:301–3; William J. Albert to Lincoln, 13 Apr. 1863, LP, LC; Mitchell, *Maryland Voices*, 196; *WES*, 16 Apr. 1864; *BDA*, 19 Apr. 1864; *BS*, 19 Apr. 1864; *FLIM*, 14 May 1864; Schoeberlein, "A Fair to Remember: Maryland Women in Aid of the Union," 466–88.

20. Thompson, *Heintzelman*, 298–300; Speer, *Portals to Hell: Military Prisons of the Civil War*, 75–77, 197–98; *ISJ*, 18, 22 Apr., 6 May 1864; *BDHE*, 25, 28 Apr. 1864; *InDJ*, 16 Apr. 1864; *PhiIn*, 18 Apr. 1864.

21. *OR*, series 3, 4:237–39, 244, 247, 248, 251, 252, 256, 257–61, 268; Basler, *CW*, 7:312–13; Reid, *Ohio in the War*, 1:209; Donald, *Lincoln*, 498–99; Quiner, *Wisconsin*, 178; Abbott, *Ohio's War Governors*, 41; Kimball, "Yates," 36–38; *WDNI*, 22, 23 Apr. 1864; *ISJ*, 26 Apr., 14 May 1864; Briggs, "Enlistment of Iowa Troops," 366–68; *BDHE*, 25, 26, 30 Apr., 7, 9 May

1864; *IDSR*, 7, 29 Apr. 1864; *StLDMR*, 27 Apr., 11 May 1864; *BDA*, 22, 23 Apr. 1864; Letter from Midwestern Governors to Lincoln, 21 Apr. 1864, John Lewis Papers, SHSW; Leeke, *A Hundred Days to Richmond*, 26–48; Hesseltine, *Lincoln and the War Governors*, 350; *LDJ*, 1 Jul. 1864; *BS*, 26 Apr. 1864.

22. Burlingame, *Stoddard*, 223; Eicher, *Longest Night*, 659–73; *PhiIn*, 5, 6, 7 May 1864; Bernard Mullen to Hugh Gallagher, 29 Apr. 1864, Hugh D. Gallagher Papers, IHS; Abbott, *Ohio's War Governors*, 41–43; *ChiTri*, 14 May 1864.

23. Quiner, *Wisconsin*, 229–31; Autobiographical Journal, 25 Apr. 1864, Lewis Papers, SHSW; Basler, *CW*, 7:326; *OR*, series 3, 4:251, 280; *PhiIn*, 17 Jun. 1864; Eicher, *Longest Night*, 659–73.

24. Croffut and Morris, *Connecticut during the War*, 630–31; Buckingham, *Life of Buckingham*, 361; *OR*, series 3, 4:268–69; Eicher, *Longest Night*, 662–79; Benedict, *Vermont*, 418.

25. Jackson, *New Jerseyans*, 163, 168–69; Wright, "New Jersey's Role in the Civil War," 197–210; *TDSGR*, 30 Apr., 23 May 1864.

26. E. J. More to Wife, 8 May 1864, More Papers, LC; Bates, *Telegraph Office*, 246; Donald, *Lincoln*, 500; Thomas and Hyman, *Stanton*, 300–301; Rhea, *The Battle of the Wilderness*, 435–36.

27. Nevins, *The Organized War*, 23; Eicher, *Longest Night*, 679–82; Donald, *Lincoln*, 500.

28. *OR*, series 3, 4:262–64; *BDFP*, 7 May 1864.

29. Schouler, *Massachusetts in the Civil War*, 1:549; Hamrogue, "Andrew," 195–208; *DFP*, 6 Apr. 1864; John M. Forbes to Charles Sedgwick, 3 Jun. 1864, Sedgwick Papers, SUL; Armstrong, *For Courageous Fighting and Confident Dying*, 11; Andrew to Stanton, 14 Mar. 1864, Massachusetts Governors, Letters Official, 1864, MSA.

30. William L. Mead to Louisa, 5 May 1864, George Cornwell Papers, MdHS.

31. Andrew to Lincoln, 24 Mar., 27 May 1864, LP, LC; *OR*, series 3, 4:262–64, 270–77; Andrew to Gen. Dix, 28 Apr. 1864, RG 107, Letters Received, "irregular series," NARA; Belz, *Lincoln*, 122–25, 130–34; John M. Forbes to Charles Sedgwick, 3 Jun. 1864, Sedgwick Papers, SUL; Armstrong, *For Courageous Fighting and Confident Dying*, 11.

32. As quoted in Glatthaar, *Forged in Battle*, 172; Belz, *Lincoln*, 130–34; Pearson, *Andrew*, 2:211; Basler, *CW*, 7:404–5; *OR*, series 3, 4:271–73; Hamrogue, "Andrew," 200–208.

33. As quoted in Hamrogue, "Andrew," 200–208, 212; [a. a. Lehaffer] to Andrew, 11 Mar., [?] to Andrew, 15 Mar., J. M. Forbes to Andrew, 7 Apr., Sumner to Andrew, 31 Mar., 4, 20 Apr. 1864, Andrew Papers, MHS; Andrew to Sumner, 11 Apr., Andrew to Samuel Harrison, 29 Apr., Andrew to Thaddeus Stevens, 4 Jun., Andrew to Hale, 31 May 1864, Andrew Letter Book, MHS; Andrew to Sumner, 21 Jun. 1864, Sumner Papers, HoL; *OR*, series 3, 4:564–65; John M. Forbes to Charles Sedgwick, 3 Jun. 1864, Sedgwick Papers, SUL.

34. Forbes to Sedgwick, 3 Jun. 1864, Sedgwick Papers, SUL.

35. As cited in Hamrogue, "Andrew," 212. I was unable to locate the letter from Lenox to Andrew, 16 Jun. 1864, in the Andrew Papers, MHS; Forbes to Charles Sedgwick, 3 Jun., Sedgwick to Forbes, 10 Jun. 1864, Sedgwick Papers, SUL; Berlin, *Freedom: A Documentary History of Emancipation, 1861–1867*, 2:362–405.

36. Hamrogue, "Andrew," 213; Browne, *Andrew*, 141.

37. Eicher, *Longest Night*, 671–704; Beale, *Diary of Welles*, 2:23–35; Nolan, *Butler*, 265–78; Marszalek, *Halleck*, 203; Engle, *Yankee Dutchman*, 167–96; Thomas and Hyman, *Stanton*, 301–5; Marszalek, *Sherman*, 263–68; Simpson, *Grant*, 292–301; *StLDMR*, 23 May 1864.

38. Burlingame, *Stoddard*, 226; Simpson, *Grant*, 291–315; *OR*, series 3, 4:280–81, 288; Thomas and Hyman, *Stanton*, 300–302.

39. *OR*, series 3, 4:279–80; Mitchell, *Maryland Voices*, 220–21, 425–27; Thomas K. Carroll Jr. to Bradford, 9 May 1864, Governor's Letter Books, MdSA; Clark, "Politics in Maryland," 41:148–49, 38:259–60; Myers, *The Maryland Constitution of 1864*; Bradford to Montgomery Blair, 12 May 1864, LP, LC; *BS*, 28 Apr. 1864; Bradford's Journal, 27 Apr. 1864, MdHS; Cony to John L. Hodsdon, 19, 29 May 1864, Executive Correspondence, MdSA; *BDWC*, 23 May 1864.

40. Cameron to Lincoln, 7 Apr. 1864, LP, LC; *ISJ*, 24 May 1864; *PhiIn*, 25 May 1864, 8 Jul. 1864; *SDU*, 27 May 1864; *ChiTri*, 29 May, 6 Jul. 1864; *OR*, series 3, 4:282–84, 288, 4:386–400; Abbott, "Massachusetts and the Recruitment of Southern Negroes," 200–205; Kiper, *Dear Catherine*, 183; Briggs, "Enlistment of Iowa Troops," 366–72; *BDHE*, 26, 30 Apr., 2, 7 May 1864; Stone to F. C. Bissell, 11 May 1864, AGO, General Correspondence, IaSA; Carpenter, *Six Months*, 82–84; Segal, *Conversations with Lincoln*, 316–17; Burlingame, *Lincoln Observed*, 107; Marvel, *Burnside*, 341–47; *NYTi*, 9 May 1864; Donald, *Lincoln*, 501–2; Basler, *CW*, 7:344, 347–51; Thomas and Hyman, *Stanton*, 301–2.

41. Albert M. Cook to Brother Fred, 28 Apr. 1864, Albert M. Cook Papers, SUL; Brummer, *Political History of New York*, 376–83; *StLDMR*, 22 May 1864; *NYH*, 27 Apr. 1864; Donald, *Lincoln*, 502; Stanley, "Republican Party in California," 155–56; Nortrup, "Yates," 309; Yates to Lincoln, 18 May, Dennison to Lincoln, 25 May, [?] Jun. 1864, LP, LC; Yates to Trumbull, 10 May 1864, Trumbull Papers, LC; *ISJ*, 6 May 1864; Nevins, *The Organized War*, 115; *NYTi*, 16 Jun. 1864; *Lbr*, 24 Jun. 1864.

42. Willard P. Hall to Lincoln, 12 May, Smith O. Scofield to Lincoln, [n.d.], Jun. 1864, LP, LC.

43. *ChiTri*, 1 May 1864; Hall to Lincoln, 12 May, Scofield to Lincoln, [n.d.] Jun. 1864, LP, LC; Basler, *CW*, 7:338; Castel, *Civil War Kansas*, 175–77.

44. Basler, *CW*, 7:338; Castel, *Civil War Kansas*, 175–77.

45. Basler, *CW*, 7:340–41; W. W. H. Lawrence to Abel C. Wilder and James H. Lane, 15 Feb., Carney to Lincoln, 13 May 1864, LP, LC; Castel, *Civil War Kansas*, 174–77; *LDT*, 7 May, 9 Jun., 7, 19 Jul., 8 Aug. 1864.

46. Carney to Lincoln, 16 May 1864, LP, LC; Basler, *CW*, 7:341; *LDT*, 7 May, 9 Jun., 7 Jul. 1864; Castel, *Civil War Kansas*, 175–80.

47. *OR*, series 3, 4:383–85.

48. Basler, *CW*, 7:355–56; Lewis to Lincoln, 24 May 1864, LP, LC; *ChiTri*, 18 May 1864.

49. *OR*, series 3, 4:401; Basler, *CW*, 7:355–56; McPherson, *Battle Cry of Freedom*, 719.

50. Brough to Stanton, 24 May 1864, Telegraphic Dispatches, series 144, OhSA; *OR*, series 1, 36, pt. 3:113–14, series 3, 4:405; Basler, *CW*, 7:359.

51. *OR*, series 3:406, 411–13; Yates to Trumbull, 5 Jun., "confidential," 1864, Yates Papers, WC, ALPL.

52. Engs and Brooks, *Their Patriotic Duty*, 251–52.

53. Benedict, *Vermont*, 456–57; Crockett, *Vermont*, 3:582; Simpson, *Grant*, 291–315; Dowden, "Smith," 90–93; Haynes, *History of the Tenth Regiment*, 69–70; *BDFP*, 18, 23 May 1864.

54. *BDFP*, 18, 23 May 1864.

55. *OR*, series 3, 4:415–17; Eicher, *Longest Night*, 682–92; Simpson, *Grant*, 301–20; Rhea, *Cold Harbor: Grant and Lee, May 26–June 3, 1864*, 386–92; Rhea, "The Overland Campaign of 1864," 17–35. Fewer than 10,000 veterans mustered out during the Overland Campaign. Grant put Hunter in command of West Virginia and reassigned Sigel.

56. Holland, *Holland's Life of Lincoln*, 469–72; Zornow, *Lincoln and the Party Divided*, 72–86; Paludan, *Presidency of Lincoln*, 270–71; Donald, *Lincoln*, 502–3; Burlingame, *Lin-*

coln, 2:627–40; Segal, *Conversations with Lincoln*, 321–22; *WDNI*, 2, 3, 4 Jun. 1864; StLDMR, 28 Jun. 1864; *PhiIn*, 1 Jun. 1864; *ISJ*, 2 Jun. 1864; *HW*, 2 Apr. 1864.

57. Meade, *Life and Letters of George Gordon Meade*, 2:201; Nevins, *The Organized War to Victory*, 39–45; Thomas and Hyman, *Stanton*, 303–4; Simpson, *Grant*, 301–31; *WDNI*, 9, 11 Jun. 1864; Eicher, *Longest Night*, 683–85; Rhea, *Cold Harbor*, 386–92.

58. *NHS*, 11 Mar. 3 Jun. 1864; *WDNI*, 4 Jun. 1864; Eicher, *Longest Night*, 683–85.

59. Governor's Messages, *Journals of the Honorable Senate and House of Representatives of New Hampshire*, June Session, Jun. 1864, 41; *NHS*, 3 Jun. 1864; *NHPSG*, 11 Jun. 1861, 8 Jun. 1864; *BDA*, 3 Jun. 1864; *ChiTri*, 3 Jun. 1864; *WDNI*, 4 Jun. 1864.

60. As quoted in Shafer, *Men of Granite*, 234; *BDA*, 3 Jun. 1864.

61. Shafer, *Men of Granite*, 234; Eicher, *Longest Night*, 683–85; *BDA*, 31 May, 3 Jun. 1864; Cony to John L. Hodsdon, 19, 20 May 1864, Executive Correspondence, MeSA; Gilmore to Edward H. Rollins, 26, 27 May 1864, Gilmore Papers, NHHS; *NHPSG*, 27 Jul. 1864; *ChiTri*, 3 Jun. 1864; *PhiIn*, 6 Jun. 1864.

62. *DR*, 9 Jun. 1864; *PhiIn*, 25 May, 17 Jun. 1864; *ChiTri*, 21 Jun. 1864; *NYTi*, 8, 19 Jun. 1864.

63. *BDWC*, 16 Jun. 1864.

64. Ibid; *NHPSG*, 20 Jun. 1864; Cony to Washburn, 1 May 1864, Washburn Papers, LC; Whalon, "Maine Republicans," 156–58.

65. *HW*, 11 Jun. 1864; Eicher, *Longest Night*, 683–89; Burlingame, *Stoddard*, 232; Thomas and Hyman, *Stanton*, 303–5.

66. *OR*, series 3, 4:425–26; Brummer, *Political History of New York*, 375–91; Segal, *Conversations with Lincoln*, 322–25; Shutes, *Lincoln and California*, 165–66; Burlingame, *Lincoln Observed*, 110–12; Burlingame, *Lincoln*, 2:641–45; Nivens, *The Organized War to Victory*, 74–80; Speiser, "The Ticket's Other Half," 42–69; Sutherland, *Savage Conflict*, 220–26; *WDNI*, 10 Jun. 1864; *OS*, 6, 13 Jun. 1864; *PhiIn*, 10 Jun. 1864; *ChiTri*, 2 Jul. 1864; *LDT*, 7 Jul. 1864; Hamlin, *The Life and Times of Hannibal Hamlin*, 456–73; Blaine, *Twenty Years of Congress*, 1:517; *HW*, 11, 25 Jun. 1864; Burlingame, *With Lincoln in the White House*, 145–46; Whalon, "Maine Republicans," 163–68; Hesseltine, *Lincoln and the War Governors*, 358–59.

67. *PDJ*, 22 Jun. 1864; Sutherland, *Savage Conflict*, 220–26; *OR*, series 3, 4:425–26; Eicher, *Longest Night*, 695; *NYTi*, 3 Jul. 1864; *ChiTri*, 2 Jul. 1864; Towne, *Surveillance and Spies*, 209–12.

68. Eicher, *Longest Night*, 687–704; Lamon to Lincoln, 7 Jun. 1864, LP, LC; *WES*, 9 Jun. 1864; *HW*, 2 Jul. 1864; Basler, *CW*, 7:380–83; Randall and Current, *Lincoln the President*, 13–34; Zornow, *Lincoln and the Party Divided*, 99–103; Paludan, *Presidency of Lincoln*, 270–74; Donald, *Lincoln*, 503–7; Sears, *Papers of McClellan*, 577–79; Sears, *McClellan*, 368–69; Simpson, *Grant*, 315–31; Mitchell, *Seymour*, 360–65.

69. Shutes, *Lincoln and California*, 167; *SFDAC*, 10 Jun. 1864; *LAS*, 6 Aug. 1864.

70. Basler, *CW*, 7:380–83; Donald, *Lincoln*, 506–7; Holland, *Holland's Life of Lincoln*, 392; *PhiIn*, 10 Jun. 1864; *BS*, 10 Jun. 1864; *HW*, 9 Jul. 1864.

71. Basler, *CW*, 7:383–84; Donald, *Lincoln*, 506–7; Segal, *Conversations with Lincoln*, 322–27.

72. *LDJ*, 6 Aug. 1864.

73. Thompson, *Heintzelman*, 299–302; Klement, *Limits of Dissent*, 275–76; Klement, *Dark Lanterns*, 136–43; Lincoln to Heintzelman and Brough, 20 Jun. 1864, LP, LC, says "not sent"; Stanton to Brough, 16 Jun. 1864, Telegraphic Dispatches, series 145, OhSA; Towne, *Surveillance and Spies*, 212–18.

74. OR, series 3, 4:233–34, 436–38, 439–45 451, 468–69; LDJ, 1 Jul. 1864; Howard, "Lincoln Slave Policy in Kentucky," 302–4; Berlin, *Freedom: Destruction of Slavery*, 1:598–600; Sutherland, *Savage Conflict*, 222–26; Vorenberg, *Final Freedom*, 68–69; Cooling, *To the Battles of Franklin and Nashville and Beyond*, 161–63; Burbridge to Bramlette, 16 Jun. 1864, Burbridge Papers, FHS; Smith, "Recruitment of Negro Soldiers," 384–85; *TDSGR*, 25 May 1864; Harris, *Lincoln and the Border States*, 240–53; E. W. Hawkins et al. to Lincoln, 5 Jun., Marcus L. McPherson to Lincoln, 2 Jun., Albert G. Hodges to Lincoln, 19 Jul., William C. Goodloe to Green Clay Smith, 29 May 1864, LP, LC; *StLDMR*, 15 Jul. 1864; *LDJ*, 26 May, 15 Jul. 1864; Towne, *Surveillance and Spies*, 235–45.

75. Segal *Conversations with Lincoln*, 330–31; Basler, *CW*, 7:411–14, Randall and Current, *Lincoln the President*, 183; Donald, *Lincoln*, 508; Thomas and Hyman, *Stanton*, 312–13; Beale, *Diary of Bates*, 381; *WDNI*, 1 Jul. 1864; Beale, *Diary of Welles*, 2:62–63; Burlingame, *Lincoln*, 2:623–25; *BDA*, 1, 2 Jul. 1864; *PhiIn*, 1, 2 Jul. 1864.

76. Segal, *Conversations with Lincoln*, 331.

77. Niven, *Chase Papers*, 4:384–85.

78. Segal, *Conversations with Lincoln*, 330–31.

79. As quoted in Thomas and Hyman, *Stanton*, 313–14; *BDA*, 1, 2 Jul. 1864; *PhiIn*, 1, 2 Jul. 1864.

80. Thomas and Hyman, *Stanton*, 313–14; *WDNI*, 1 Jul. 1864; *BDA*, 1, 2 Jul. 1864; *PhiIn*, 1, 2 Jul. 1864.

81. Thomas and Hyman, *Stanton*, 313–14.

82. Thomas and Hyman, *Stanton*, 314; Basler, *CW*, 7:420; Tod to Lincoln, 30 Jun. 1864, LP, LC; *BDA*, 1, 2 Jul. 1864; *PhiIn*, 1, 2 Jul. 1864.

83. Thomas and Hyman, *Stanton*, 314.

84. Basler, *CW*, 7:419–20, 23; Niven, *Chase Papers*, 1:470–72, 4:379; *BDA*, 7 Jul. 1864; Segal, *Conversations with Lincoln*, 332–33; Donald, *Lincoln*, 508–9; Burlingame, *Lincoln Observed*, 117–20; Thomas and Hyman, *Stanton*, 314–15; Fessenden, *William Pitt Fessenden*, 1:315–18; Beale, *Diary of Welles*, 2:62–65; Cook, *Fessenden*, 169–72; James W. Grimes to William P. Fessenden, 3 Jul. 1864, William Pitt Fessenden Collection, BCL; Abbott, *Ohio's War Governors*, 45; Porter, *Ohio Politics*, 205; Reid, *Ohio in the War*, 1:229–30.

85. Buckingham, *Life of Buckingham*, 489, 360–62.

86. Niven, *Chase Papers*, 1:461; Paludan, *Presidency of Lincoln*, 280–83; Eicher, *Longest Night*, 670–80.

87. Towne, *Letters of Wood*, 177.

88. Thornbrough, Riker, and Corpuz, *Diary of Fletcher*, 8:419–20; Wertheim, "The Indianapolis Treason Trials, the Election of 1864, and the Power of the Partisan Press," 244–50; Klement, *Dark Lanterns*, 132; Towne, *Surveillance and Spies*, 150–66.

Chapter Eighteen

1. Beale, *Diary of Bates*, 382; Duncan, "Maryland's Reaction to Early's Raid in 1864," 248–79; *BS*, 13 Jul. 1864; Egle, *Curtin*, 174–76; Bradford's Journal, 7 Jul. 1864, MdHS; *PhiIn*, 8 Jul. 1864; *WDNI*, 4 Apr., 16 Jul. 1864; Engle, *Yankee Dutchman*, 200–208; Weston, Massachusetts Soldiers Home to Lincoln, 4 Jul. 1864, LP, LC; Foulke, *Morton*, 1:290–302; Eicher, *Longest Night*, 715–17; Marszalek, *Halleck*, 207–8; Thomas and Hyman, *Stanton*, 319; Burlingame, *Stoddard*, 239–40; Burlingame, *Lincoln Observed*, 121–24; Donald, *Lincoln*, 510–11.

2. *OR*, series 1, 37, pt. 2:91, 151–52, series 3, 4:471–72; *WDNI*, 6, 11, 12, 16 Jul. 1864; Hancock, *Delaware during the War*, 143; *DR*, 4 Jul. 1864; Hancock, "Diaries of Ferris," 250–52; Brummer, *Political History of New York*, 410–11; Thomas and Hyman, *Stanton*, 318–19; Abbott, *Ohio's War Governors*, 42; Schouler, *Massachusetts in the Civil War*, 1:566–69; *BDA*, 21 Jul. 1864; *PhiIn*, 6, 11 Jul. 1864; Niven, *Chase Papers*, 1:475–76; Beale, *Diary of Bates*, 384; *InDJ*, 6 Jul. 1864; *BDHE*, 11 Jul. 1864; Charles Sedgwick to Forbes, 3 Jul. 1864, Charles Sedgwick Papers, SUL.

3. Thomas and Hyman, *Stanton*, 319; Brummer, *Political History of New York*, 412–13; *OR*, series 1, 37, pt. 2:16–18, 37, 70, 91, 94; *WDNI*, 4 Jul. 1864; Curtin to Brig. Gen. Couch, 8 Jul. 1864, Executive Correspondence, PSA.

4. *OR*, series 3, 4:470–71, 487, series 1, 37, pt. 2:74, 78; Basler, *CW*, 7:423–24; Eicher, *Longest Night*, 715–18; Furgurson, *Freedom Rising*, 308–12; Marszalek, *Halleck*, 207–9; Burlingame, *Lincoln Observed*, 126; Thomas and Hyman, *Stanton*, 319–20; Donald, *Lincoln*, 517–19; *NYTi*, 6 Jul. 1864; Sutherland, *Savage Conflict*, 222–23; Howard, "Lincoln Slave Policy in Kentucky," 302–5; Joseph Holt to Stanton, 29 Jul. 1864, Stanton Papers, LC; Edward Davis Townsend to Holt, 12 Jul. 1864, Joseph Holt Papers, HL.

5. *OR*, series 3, 4:488–89, series 1, 37, pt. 2:325; *BDWC*, 12 Jul. 1864; *PhiIn*, 14 Jul. 1864 Thomas and Hyman, *Stanton*, 319; *TDSGR*, 14 Jul. 1864.

6. Basler, *CW*, 7:437; Carpenter, *Six Months*, 301; Eicher, *Longest Night*, 715–19; Thomas and Hyman, *Stanton*, 319; Bowden, "Conscription in Maine," 44–50; *OR*, series 3, 4:488–89; *BDWC*, 12 Jul. 1864; *BDA*, 1 Aug. 1864.

7. Cony to Lincoln, 22 Jul., John Hay to Cony, 29, 1864, LP, LC; Furgurson, *Freedom Rising*, 314; Thomas and Hyman, *Stanton*, 320; Donald, *Lincoln*, 518–20; Stanton to Cony, 11 Aug. 1864, Executive Correspondence, MdSA.

8. David Newsom to Yates, 12 Oct. 1864, Yates Papers, ALPL; Edwards, "Department of the Pacific," 257–62; *OR*, series 1, 50, pt. 2:682, 745; *SFDAC*, 1, 28 Sept. 1864; Gibbs Message to the Legislature, 15 Sept. 1864, *Senate and House Journal of the State of Oregon*, Appendix, 1–15; *OS*, 19 Sept. 1864; McArthur, *The Enemy Never Came*, 125–29, 159–61.

9. Beale, *Diary of Welles*, 2:73; Basler, *CW*, 7:440–44, 457–58, 460; Curtin to Lincoln, 16, 18 Jul., John M. Read to Lincoln, 8 Sept. Hunter to Lincoln, 19 Jul. 1864, LP, LC; Bradford's Journals, 11 Jul. 1864, MdHS; Randall and Current, *Lincoln the President*, 195–204; Scharf, *History of Baltimore City and County*, 138; Duncan, "Maryland's Reaction," 248–79; Blondo, "Samuel Green," 25–38, 63–64; *OR*, series 3, 4:497–98, 503, 512–13; Eicher, *Longest Night*, 705–50; Marszalek, *Sherman*, 272–80; Thomas and Hyman, *Stanton*, 320; Donald, *Lincoln*, 518, 520; Burlingame, *Lincoln*, 2:653–56; Castel, *Decision in the West*, 327–440; *DR*, 14, 28 Jul. 1864; *PhiIn*, 12, 13 Jul. 1864; *BDA*, 13 Jul. 1864; *ChiTri*, 15 Jul. 1864.

10. Burlingame, *Lincoln Observed*, 127; *OR*, series 3, 4:494; Eicher, *Longest Night*, 691–715; Millett and Maslowski, *For the Common Defense*, 198–202; Burlingame, *Lincoln*, 2:652–59; Smith, *The Enemy Within: Fears of Corruption in the Civil War North*, 127–53; Andrew to Lincoln, 18 Jul., James Y. Smith to Lincoln, 19 Jul. 1864, LP, LC; Schouler, *Massachusetts in the Civil War*, 1:569; *BDA*, 24 Aug. 1864; Basler, *CW*, 7:448–49; Thomas and Hyman, *Stanton*, 327; Donald, *Lincoln*, 528; *HW*, 6, 13 Aug. 1864; *ChiTri*, 14 Jul. 1864; Alex W. Raffen to Yates, 19 Jul. 1864, Yates Papers, ALPL.

11. Folwell, *Minnesota*, 2:338; Thomas and Hyman, *Stanton*, 328; Sherman to Stephen A. Miller, 1 Aug., Miller to Stanton, 6 Aug., Miller to John Gillman, 29 Jul., Charles Dana to Miller, 1 Aug. 1864, Governor's Papers, Executive Journals, MnHS; Marszalek, *Sherman*, 280; Folwell, *Minnesota*, 2:338.

12. Thomas F. Bayard to James M. Williams, 26 Jul. 1864, Bayard Papers, LC; Hancock, *Delaware during the War*, 135, 139–40; Hancock, "Political History of Delaware, Part IV," 8:92–93; Scharf, *History of Delaware*, 1:356; *DR*, 25 Jul. 1864; *PhiIn*, 23 Jul. 1864; *BS*, 20 Aug. 1864; Cannon to Assembly, 28 Jul., 9 Aug. 1864, Executive Papers, DPA.

13. Bayard to Williams, 26 Jul. 1864, Bayard Papers, LC; *DR*, 11, 15 Aug. 1864; Hancock, "Political History of Delaware," 8:92–93.

14. Bayard to Williams, 26 Jul. 1864, Bayard Papers, LC.

15. Hancock, "Political History of Delaware," 8:93–94; Hancock, *Delaware during the War*, 140–41; *Journal of the House of the State of Delaware, 1864*, 212–18; *DR*, 11, 14, 21, 25 Jul., 11, 15 Aug., 29 Sept. 1864; Miller, *States at War*, 4:174–77.

16. Hancock, "Political History of Delaware," 8:94; Scharf, *History of Delaware*, 1:356–57; Miller, *States at War*, 4:177.

17. *OR*, series 3, 4:544–45, 515–16, 531–34, 538, 550–51, 566, 608–9, series 1, 38, pt. 5:136, 137, 210, vol. 37, pt. 2:384, 43, 751–59; Basler, *CW*, 7:449–50; Gideon Welles to Cony, 29 Jul., 26 Aug. 1864, Executive Correspondence, MeSA; *BDA*, 19 Jul. 1864; *PDJ*, 20 Jul. 1864; *BDA*, 6, 16 Aug. 1864; Bradford to Curtin, 19 Jul. 1864, Executive Correspondence, PSA; Eicher, *Longest Night*, 705–50; Beale, *Diary of Welles*, 2:89; Thomas and Hyman, *Stanton*, 322.

18. Eicher, *Longest Night*, 718–19; Furgurson, *Freedom Rising*, 320–21; Egle, *Curtin*, 174–77; *PhiIn*, 2, 9 Aug. 1864.

19. Thornbrough, *Indiana*, 215–22; Rosecrans to Lincoln, 2, 8 Jun., Yates to Lincoln, 9 Jun., Lincoln to Rosecrans, 10 Jun. 1864, LP, LC; Klement, *Copperheads*, 163–65; Klement, *Dark Lanterns*, 91–147, 151–86; Fesler, "Secret Political Societies in the North during the Civil War," 243–62; Stampp, *Indiana Politics*, 166, 232–33, 244–47; Kimball, "Yates," 69–72; *ISJ*, 2, 4, 8 Nov. 1864; *ChiTri*, 8, 9 Nov. 1864; Van der Linden, *The Dark Intrigue*, 217–25; *OR*, series 1, 39, pt. 2:236–38; Nation and Towne, *Indiana's War*, 183–88; Wertheim, "Indianapolis Treason Trials," 236–50; Rodgers, "Liberty, Will, and Violence," 133–40; Croffut and Morris, *Connecticut during the War*, 633; Beale, *Diary of Bates*, 392; Burlingame, *Lincoln*, 2:668–76.

20. Foulke, *Morton*, 1:399–409; Thornbrough, *Indiana*, 215–22; Klement, *Dark Lanterns*, 165–86; Towne, *Surveillance and Spies*, 219–20, 239–45.

21. Edward Prince to Richard Yates, 15 Jul., Francis Mary Hutchinson to Yates, 26 Aug., James Montgomery to Yates, 27 Aug., W. C. Flagg, 24 Aug., Peeples & Ridgeway to Yates, 16 Aug. 1864, Yates Papers, ALPL (the Prince letter is also cited in Frank, *With Ballot and Bayonet*, 80); Yates to Stanton, 29 Jul. 1864, Stanton Papers, LC; *OR*, series 3, 4:556–59; Klement, *Dark Lanterns*, 134–50, 165–86, 187–217; *ChiTri*, 3 Aug. 1864; Yates to J. Berdan, Nat. Stacey, J. B. Turner, Dr. Cafsel, David O. Smith, and J. O. King, 12 Aug. 1864, Reavis Papers, CHM; Paludan, *Presidency of Lincoln*, 285.

22. Klement, *Dark Lanterns*, 134–45; *InDJ*, 4 Aug. 1864; Towne, *Surveillance and Spies*, 242–45.

23. Forbes to Andrew, 6, 7 Jul. 1864, Hughes, *Letters of Forbes*, 2:277; Abbott, *Cotton and Capital*, 133–35; Abbott, "Massachusetts and the Recruitment of Southern Negroes," 197–210.

24. Simpson, *Sherman's Civil War*, 677–78; *OR*, series 1, 38, pt. 5:303–5; Abbott, *Cotton and Capital*, 134–35; Abbott, "Recruitment of Southern Negroes," 197–210; Geary, *We Need Men*, 159–62.

25. Albert G. Browne to Andrew, 1 Oct. 1864, Andrew Papers, MHS; *OR*, series 3, 4:559–60, 644–45, 648; Abbott, *Cotton and Capital*, 134–35; Abbott, "Recruitment of Southern Negroes," 197–210; Geary, *We Need Men*, 159–62; Briggs, "Enlistment of Iowa

Troops," 366–72; *BDHE*, 27 Jul. 1864; Stone to Gen. Baker, 9 Jul. 1864, AGO, General Correspondence, ISA.

26. Browne to Andrew, 1 Oct. 1864, Andrew Papers, MHS; Nation and Towne, *Indiana's War*, 121; Abbott, *Cotton and Capital*, 134–37; Abbott, "Recruitment and Southern Negroes," 197–210; Geary, *We Need Men*, 159–62.

27. Simon, *Papers of Grant*, 11:361–64; Eicher, *Longest Night*, 720–23; Simpson, *Grant*, 366; Levin, *Remembering the Battle of the Crater*.

28. As quoted in Frank, *With Ballot and Bayonet*, 174; "Not a Nager" to Andrew, 2 Aug. 1864, Governor's Letter Books, MHS; *OR*, series 3, 4:564–65; Eicher, *The Longest Night*, 720–23.

29. Durkin, *"This War Is an Awful Thing,"* 177.

30. As quoted in Shafer, *Men of Granite*, 257–58; *WDNI*, 15 Aug. 1864; *BDA*, 22 Aug. 1864.

31. Burlingame, *Lincoln Observed*, 129.

32. *OR*, series 3, 4:569; Beale, *Diary of Welles*, 2:92.

33. *IDSR*, 25, 28 Aug. 1864; Abbott, *Ohio's War Governors*, 42; *OR*, series 3, 4:263, 265, 266, 405, 471, 569–70.

34. *OR*, series 3, 4:571–72, 575–76, 600–605, 611; Yates to Stanton, 4 Aug., Stanton to Yates, 4 Aug. 1864, Stanton Papers, LC; Brummer, *Political History of New York*, 412–15; *DFP*, 6, 8, 15 Aug. 1864.

35. *OR*, series 3, 4:577–79; Peter L. Foy to Montgomery Blair, 18 Jul., Egbert B. Brown to Oliver D. Greene, 20 Jul. 1864, LP, LC.

36. *OR*, series 3, 4:581; Peeples and Ridgeway, 16 Aug., W. A. Trousdale to Yates, 17 Aug., S. L. Shink to Yates, 24 Aug., J. W. Watt et al. to Yates, 23 Aug., W. C. Flagg to Yates, 22 Aug. 1864, Yates Papers, ALPL.

37. Yates to Lincoln, 21 Aug. 1864, LP, LC; Nortrup, "Yates," 310–11; Sarah Henshaw to Yates, 30 Jul. 1864, Yates Papers, ALPL; *OR*, series 3, 4:585, 598–99; Abbott, *Ohio's War Governors*, 43; Reid, *Ohio in the War*, 1:202.

38. Morton to Lincoln, 9 Aug. 1864, LP, LC; Foulke, *Morton*, 1:303–53; French, *Morton*, 436–47; Klement, *Dark Lanterns*, 150–53; Sylvester, "Morton," 240–60; Morton to Stanton, 19 Aug. 1864, Governor's Telegraph Book, ISA; Wertheim, "Indianapolis Treason Trials," 236–50; *InDJ*, 15, 18, 20 Aug., 23, 26 Sept. 1864; *ChiTri*, 11, 13 Aug., 11 Sept. 1864; *BDWC*, 30 Aug. 1864; *NYI*, 18 Aug. 1864.

39. Turnley to Lincoln, 28 Sept. 1864, LP, LC; French, *Morton*, 436–77; Klement, *Dark Lanterns*, 151–53; Sylvester, "Gone for a Soldier," 215–16; Willard Mendell to Wife, 22 Sept. 1864, Willard Mendell Papers, IHS.

40. Donald, *Lincoln*, 523–25; Paludan, *Presidency of Lincoln*, 280–82; Eicher, *Longest Night*, 719–221; Burligame, *Lincoln*, 2:659–65.

41. Basler, *CW*, 7:474, 506–8; Morgan to Lincoln, 1 Aug., Weed to Seward, 22 Aug. 1864, LP, LC; Segal, *Conversations with Lincoln*, 338–39; Donald, *Lincoln*, 523–25; Paludan, *Presidency of Lincoln*, 280–82; Basler, *CW*, 7:474, 532–33; Eicher, *Longest Night*, 719–21, 726–30; Beale, *Diary of Welles*, 2:93–94; Burlingame, *Lincoln*, 2:659–65.

42. *OR*, series 1, 42, pt. 2:111–12, 193–94; Marszalek, *Halleck*, 212–13; Thomas and Hyman, *Stanton*, 318–19.

43. *OR*, series 1, 42, pt. 2:111–12, 193–94; Basler, *CW*, 7:499; Marszalek, *Halleck*, 212–13; Beale, *Diary of Bates*, 385; Simpson, *Grant*, 367–75.

44. As quoted in Borchard, *Abraham Lincoln and Horace Greeley*, 84–86; Gillette, *Jersey Blue*, 274–75; Rice, *Reminiscences of Lincoln*, 68–70; Brummer, *Political History of New York*, 395–401; Mitchell, *Seymour*, 360–70; Burlingame, *Lincoln*, 2:704–5; Miller, *Lincoln*,

497; Fehrenbacher and Fehrenbacher, *Recollected Words of Abraham Lincoln*, 155; *PhiIn*, 9 Sept. 1864; *BDA*, 9 Sept. 1864; *NHS*, 16 Sept. 1864.

45. Raymond to Lincoln, 24 Aug. 1864, LP, LC; Basler, *CW*, 7:514–15, 517–18; Randall and Current, *Lincoln*, 215; Donald, *Lincoln*, 529; Paludan, *Presidency of Lincoln*, 283; McPherson, *Tried by War*, 240–42.

46. *OR*, series 3, 4:683–84.

47. *OR*, series 3, 4:684; O. Thompson to Lewis, 8 Nov. 1864, Executive Department, Military Correspondence, SHSW.

48. Pearson, *Andrew*, 2:159; Dennison to Lincoln, 2 Sept., James Conkling to Lincoln, 5 Sept., Weed to Seward, 10 Sept. 1864, LP, LC; Smith, *No Party Now*, 116–17; Burlingame, *Lincoln*, 2:667–68.

49. Pearson, *Andrew*, 2:154–58; Weed to Seward, 10 Sept., W. C. Philips to Lincoln, 20 Aug., 1864, LP, LC; Green, *Freedom, Union, and Power*, 278–79; Tarbell, "Lincoln's Great Victory in 1864," 277–78; *NYTi*, 29 Apr. 1872; Schouler, *Massachusetts in the Civil War*, 1:571–73; Thomas, *Lincoln*, 441–43; Castel, *Decision in the West*, 476–78; Hamrogue, "Andrew," 220–22.

50. As quoted in Sears, *McClellan*, 372; Sears, *Papers of McClellan*, 587, 594; *PDJ*, 31 Aug. 1864; *NYTi*, 29 Apr. 1872.

51. Sears, *McClellan*, 372, 374; Mitchell, *Seymour*, 370–82; Burlingame, *Lincoln Observed*, 132–34, 136; Brummer, *Political History of New York*, 414–20; Gillette, *Jersey Blue*, 268–75; Sears, *McClellan*, 369–74; Niven, *Chase Papers*, 4:420–22; Mitchell, *Seymour*, 360–75; Sears, *Papers of McClellan*, 590–96; *NYW*, 29, 30, 31 Aug. 1864; *WDNI*, 1 Sept. 1864; *PDJ*, 31 Aug. 1864; *PhiIn*, 1 Sept. 1864.

52. Palmer, *Letters of Charles Sumner*, 2:251; Mitchell, *Antislavery Politics in Antebellum and Civil War America*, 228–29; McDonough and Noe, *Politics and Culture of the Civil War Era*, 297–303.

53. Cannon to Greely, Godwin, Tilton, 12 Sep. 1864, Theodore Tilton Papers, NYHS; Seymour to Morgan, 12 Aug. 1864, Morgan Papers, NYSL; Brummer, *Political History of New York*, 420; Pearson, *Andrew*, 2:154–60; Nicolay and Hay, *Lincoln: A History*, 9:366; Donald, *Lincoln*, 525, 531; Weed to Seward, 10 Sept., Conkling to Lincoln, 5, 6 Sept. 1864, LP, LC; Nevins, *The Organized War to Victory*, 90–96; Green, *Freedom, Union, and Power*, 278–79; Thomas, *Lincoln*, 441–43; Burlingame, *Lincoln*, 2:665–80.

54. Cannon to Horace Greeley, Parke Godwin, and Theodore Tilton, 12 Sept. 1864, Tilton Papers, NYHS; Hancock, *Delaware during the War*, 147–48; Hancock, "Political History of Delaware," 8:100–101.

55. Hancock, *Delaware during the War*, 148.

56. Gilmore to Tilton, 5 Sept. 1864, Tilton Papers, NYHS; Tilton to Gilmore, 6 Sept. 1864, Gilmore to Larkin D. Mason, 5 Sept., "confidential," Frank Howe to Gilmore, 6 Sept. 1864, "personal," Mason to Gilmore, 7 Sept. 1864, Gilmore Papers, NHHS; Niven, *Chase Papers*, 1:496–97; William E. Chandler to John G. Nicolay, 16 Sept., Nicolay to Chandler, 28 Sept., "private," Chandler to Lincoln, 28 Sept. 1864, LP, LC; Benton, *Voting in the Field*, 204–22; *NHPSG*, 3 Aug. 1864; *BDA*, 11 Aug. 1864; Renda, "New Hampshire Politics," 65–75; *New Hampshire House Journal*, August 1864; *BDA*, 24 Aug., 3 Sept. 1864.

57. Blair to Greeley, Godwin, Tilton, 11 Sept. 1864, Tilton Papers, NYHS; Harris, "Blair," 172; *DFP*, 14 Aug. 1864.

58. Blair to Chandler, 15 Sept., Ben Wade to Chandler, 2 Oct. 1864, Chandler Papers, LC; Josephine Griffing to Lincoln, 24 Sept. 1864, LP, LC.

59. Curtin to Slifer, 28 Jul. 1864, Slifer-Dill Papers, DCL; Curtin to Greeley, Godwin, and Tilton, 8 Sept. 1864, Tilton Papers, NHYS.
60. Cony to Greeley, Godwin, and Tilton, 5 Sept. 1864, Tilton Papers, NYHS; Green, *Freedom, Union, and Power*, 278–79.
61. Smith to Greeley, Godwin, and Tilton, 3 Sept. 1864, Tilton Papers, NYHS.
62. Brough to Tilton, 5 Sept. 1864, Tilton Papers, NYHS.
63. Andrew to Greeley, Godwin, and Tilton, 3 Sept. 1864, Tilton Papers, NYHS; Andrew to Sumner, "private and confidential," 24 Aug. 1864, Sumner Papers, HoL; Hamrogue, "Andrew," 220–22; Burlingame, *Lincoln*, 2: 665–67; Pearson, *Andrew*, 2:162–63; Donald, *Lincoln*, 531; J. Henry Puleston to John G. Nicolay, 5 Sept. 1864, LP, LC; Green, *Freedom, Union, and Power*, 278–79.
64. Lewis to Greeley, Tilton, and Godwin, 7 Sept. 1864, LP, LC; Donald, *Lincoln*, 531.
65. Stone to Greeley and others, 9 Sept. 1864, Tilton Papers, NYHS; Stone to Stanton, 17 Aug. 1864, Governor's Letter Books, IaSA; *IDSR*, 29 July, 13, 17, 23, 24 Aug., 13 Sept. 1864.
66. Boreman to Greely, Godwin, and Tilton, 8 Sept. 1864, Tilton Papers, NYHS.
67. Miller to Greeley, Godwin, and Tilton, 9 Sept. 1864, NYHS.
68. Buckingham to Greeley, Godwin, and Tilton, 3 Sept. 1864, Tilton Papers, NYHS.
69. *LDJ*, 30 Jul., 10 Aug. 1864; *BS*, 29 Sept. 1864.
70. Schouler, *Massachusetts in the Civil War*, 1:575–76; Weeden, *War Government*, 255.
71. Andrew to Howe, 6 Sept. 1864, Andrew Papers and Letter Books, MHS; Hamrogue, "Andrew," 221; Ford, *A Cycle of Adams Letters*, 2:194–96; Morgan to Stanton, 15 Sept. 1864, Stanton Papers, LC; Schouler, *Massachusetts in the Civil War*, 1:575–76.
72. Nortrup, "Yates," 312–13; Yates to editors of *ChiTri*, 4, 8, 17 Sept. 1863.
73. Krenkel, *Yates*, 185; Nortrup, "Yates," 312–14; Yates to Greeley, Godwin, and Tilton, 6 Sept. 1864, Yates Papers, ALPL, and Tilton Papers, NYHS; James C. Conkling to Lincoln, 6 Sept. 1864, LP, LC.
74. Yates to Greeley, Godwin, and Tilton, 6 Sept. 1864, Tilton Papers, NHYS; Krenkel, *Yates*, 185; James C. Conkling to Lincoln, 6 Sept. 1864, LP, LC.
75. Carney to Greeley, Godwin, and Tilton, 12 Sept. 1864, Tilton Papers, NYHS; *LDT*, 18 Jul. 1864; H. E. Lowman to Carney, 18 Aug. 1864, Carney Papers, UKL.
76. Tilton to Nicolay, 6 Sept., Nicolay to Tilton, 6 Sept. 1864, LP, LC; Goodwin, *Team of Rivals: The Political Genius of Abraham Lincoln*, 656–57.
77. Burlingame, *With Lincoln in the White House*, 158.
78. Kiper, *Dear Catherine, Dear Taylor*, 267–69.
79. Nevins, *The Organized War to Victory*, 60–72; Pearson, *Andrew*, 2:160–62; Dennison to Lincoln, 2 Sept. 1864, LP, LC; Thomas, *Lincoln*, 441–43.
80. Pearson, *Andrew*, 2:164; Eicher, *Longest Night*, 710–15; *ISJ*, 8 Sept. 1864; Marszalek, *Sherman*, 284–87; Donald, *Lincoln*, 531; Paludan, *Presidency of Lincoln*, 284–85; Castel, *Decision in the West*, 548–60; *PhiIn*, 3 Sept. 1864; *ChiTri*, 4 Sept. 1864.
81. Charles Sedgwick to Forbes, 5 Sept. 1864, Sedgwick Papers, SUL.
82. Pearson, *Andrew*, 2:164–67; unable to locate letter from Andrew to Forbes, 4 Sept. 1864, in the Andrew Papers, MHS.
83. Pearson, *Andrew*, 2:166–67; Boutwell, *Reminiscences of Sixty Years*, 1:20–21; *WDNI*, 13 Sept. 1864.
84. Pearson, *Andrew*, 2:168–69; Andrew to Yates, 7 Sept. 1864, Yates Papers, ALPL; Dennison to Lincoln, 2 Sept. 1864, LP, LC.
85. Andrew to Howe, 8 Sept. 1864, Andrew Papers, MHS; Pearson, *Andrew*, 2:169–70.

86. John Andrew, *An Address Delivered before the New England Agricultural Society on Hampden Park, Springfield, Massachusetts, September 9, 1864*, in possession of MHS, 1–22; also in *BDA*, 10 Sept. 1864.

87. *OR*, series 3, 4:688, 695, 720–21; Castel, *Decision in the West*, 548–60; Dowden, "Smith," 90–95.

88. *OR*, series 3, 4:688–93, series 1, 39, pt. 2:240–41; Bramlette to Burbridge, 15 Sept. 1864, Burbridge Papers, FHS; Howard, "Lincoln Slave Policy in Kentucky," 302–5; Joseph Holt to Stanton, 29 Jul. 1864, Stanton Papers, LC.

89. Mitchell, *Maryland Voices*, 437–40; Thomas Hicks to Montgomery Blair, 19 Aug. 1864, Blair Family Papers, LC; Sears, *Papers of McClellan*, 590–92, 595–96; Clark, "Politics in Maryland," 41:148–49; Myers, *The Self-Reconstruction of Maryland*, 9–14; Dell, *War Democrats*, 307–8; WDNI, 30 Sept., 7 Oct. 1864; Benton, *Voting in the Field*, 225–49; Baker, *Politics of Continuity*, 107–9.

90. *OR*, series 3, 4:706, 709–10; Thomas and Hyman, *Stanton*, 327–29; Simpson, *Grant*, 370–88.

91. *BDFP*, 7, 14 Sept. 1864; *TDSGR*, 14 Sept. 1864; Sobel and Raimo, *Directory of Governors*, 2:1581; *PhiIn*, 1, 15 Sept. 1864; *InDJ*, 9 Sept. 1864; *BDA*, 9, 13 Sept. 1864; *ChiTri*, 11 Sept. 1864.

92. *BDFP*, 14 Sept. 1864; *ChiTri*, 11 Sept. 1864; *BDA*, 9, 13 Sept. 1864; *PhiIn*, 5 Sept. 1864.

93. *OR*, series 3, 4:714; Dell, *War Democrats*, 296–99; *BDWC*, 3, 15, 16 Sept. 1864; *HW*, 24 Sept. 1864; *WDNI*, 13, 19 Sept. 1864; Benton, *Voting in the Field*, 118–27; Beale, *Diary of Welles*, 2:141; *BDFP*, 7, 14 Sept. 1864; Sobel and Raimo, *Directory of Governors*, 1:613–14; *PDJ*, 14 Sept. 1864; *BDA*, 2, 9, 13 Sept. 1864; *PhiIn*, 13, 14 Sept. 1864.

94. *OR*, series 3, 4:714; Dell, *War Democrats*, 296–99; *BDWC*, 3, 15, 16 Sept. 1864; *HW*, 24 Sept. 1864; Lothrop Lewis Diary, 31 Oct. 1864, Lothrop Lewis Papers, LC; Dell, *War Democrats*, 296–99; *BDA*, 2, 9, 13 Sept. 1864; *PhiIn*, 13, 14 Sept. 1864.

95. *BDWC*, 16 Sept. 1864; *PhiIn*, 13 Sept. 1864.

96. *OR*, series 3, 4:742–43.

97. *OR*, series 3, 4:515, 688, 725–27, 731, series 3, 5:735; Yates to Lincoln, 2 Sept., Yates to Lincoln, Stanton, and Fry, 16 Sept., Smith to Lincoln, 15 Sept. 1864, LP, LC; Nortrup, "Yates," 309; Basler, *CW*, 7:448–49; *BDWC*, 26 Sept. 1864.

98. Nortrup, "Yates," 309; *OR*, series 3, 4:729–32; [Morton] to Stanton, 12 Sept. 1864, Stanton Papers, LC.

99. [Morton] to Stanton, 12 Sept. 1864, Stanton Papers, LC; Thornbrough, *Indiana*, vol. 3, 220–22; Thomas and Hyman, *Stanton*, 327–29; Foulke, *Morton*, 1:228–68; Zornow, *Lincoln and the Party Divided*, 191; Benton, *Voting in the Field*, 290–92; Stampp, *Indiana Politics*, 250–52; Zornow, "Indiana and the Election of 1864," 26–38; Basler, *CW*, 8:8–9; Beale, *Diary of Bates*, 404; *StLDMR*, 8 Sept. 1864; Eicher, *Longest Night*, 743–46; Sears, *Papers of McClellan*, 605–6; Nevins, *The Organized War to Victory*, 92; Mitchell, *Seymour*, 370–82.

100. Kelley to Lincoln, 30 Sept., J. Henry Puleston to John G. Nicolay, 5 Sept., John M. Read to Lincoln, 8 Sept., Thomas Fitzgerald to John G. Nicolay, 29 Sept., Richard M. Blatchford to Seward, 1 Oct., Curtin to Lincoln, 6 Oct., 1864, LP, LC; *WDNI*, 1 Oct. 1864; *BDA*, 7 Sept. 1864; Williams, *Lincoln and the Radicals*, 329; Basler, *CW*, 8:18–19; 20; Donald, *Lincoln*, 532–35; Paludan, *Presidency of Lincoln*, 288–89; Nevins, *The Organized War to Victory*, 105–8.

Chapter Nineteen

1. *OR*, series 1, 41:303–97, 467–69, pt. 3:342, 488, series 3, 4:762, and 778–79, series 1, 41:303–97; Nevins, *The Organized War to Victory*, 125; *ISJ*, 4 Oct. 1864; *PhiIn*, 13 Oct. 1864; Boman, *Lincoln and Citizens' Rights in Missouri*, 241–62; Dennett, *Diaries of John Hay*, 187–94; Dee, *Ohio's War: The Civil War in Documents*, 386–87; Basler, *CW*, 7:385–87; Eicher, *Longest Night*, 755–57; Ayer, *The Great North-Western Confederacy*, 25–64; White, *Emancipation*, 103–27.

2. Basler, *CW*, 8:33–34; Quiner, *Wisconsin*, 857; *IDSR*, 1, 7 Oct. 1864; *ISJ*, 4 Oct. 1864.

3. Sutherland, *Savage Conflict*, 235–45; *BS*, 5 Oct. 1864; *PhiIn*, 29 Oct. 1864.

4. Nicolay to Lincoln, 10 Oct. 1864, LP, LC; Morton to Stanton, 12 Sept., 12 Oct. 1864, Stanton Papers, LC; Winslow Ayer to Yates, 2 Dec. 1864, Yates Papers, ALPL; *BDHE*, 4 Nov. 1862; Eicher, *Longest Night*, 735–39; *ISJ*, 8 Nov. 1864; *InDJ*, 5, 7, 8, 26 Oct. 1864; *PhiIn*, 8 Oct. 1864; Basler, *CW*, 8:57; *OR*, series 1, 41, pt. 4:158, 163, series 3, 4:757–60; Nevins, *The Organized War to Victory*, 132; Foulke, *Morton*, 1:419–22; Thornbrough, Riker, and Corpuz, *Diary of Fletcher*, 8:442; Marszalek, *Sherman*, 294–308; Beale, *Diary of Bates*, 417; Nortrup, "Yates," 314–17; Sylvester, "Morton," 260–82; Ayer, *North-Western Confederacy*, 42–54.

5. Lincoln to Hoffman, 10 Oct. 1864, LP, LC; Basler, *CW*, 8:41–42; Clark, "Politics in Maryland," 41:148–49; *OR*, series 3, 4:756, 762, 781, 786–87.

6. Foulke, *Morton*, 1:366; Bates, *Telegraph Office*, 276; Randall and Current, *Lincoln*, 4:235; Furgurson, *Freedom Rising*, 333–37; Brooks, *Mr. Lincoln's Washington*, 382–83; Thomas and Hyman, *Stanton*, 329–31; Donald, *Lincoln*, 540, 543; Basler, *CW*, 7:506; Segal, *Conversations with Lincoln*, 338; Abbott, *Ohio's War Governors*, 44–45; Waugh, *Re-electing Lincoln*, 338–43; Beale, *Diary of Welles*, 2:175–76; James S. Thomas Diary, 18 Apr. 1864, James S. Thomas Papers, IHS; Harris, *Lincoln and the War Governors*, 120–21.

7. Joseph Shaw to Lincoln, 11 Oct. 1864, LP, LC; Thornbrough, Riker, and Corpuz, *Diary of Fletcher*, 8:447; Basler, *CW*, 8:45–47; Morton to Lincoln, 12, 13 Oct., Morton to Lincoln and Stanton, 13 Oct. 1864, LP, LC; Morton to Stanton, 12 Oct. 1864, Stanton Papers, LC; Donald, *Lincoln*, 539; Benton, *Voting in the Field*, 290–92; Sylvester, "Morton," 264–66; Nation and Towne, *Indiana's War*, 123–24.

8. As quoted in *PhiIn*, 20 Oct. 1864; Foulke, *Morton*, 1:365; Weeden, *War Government*, 342; *WDNI*, 12, 17, 18, 20 Oct. 1864; Elias Kemper to Mother, 24 Oct. 1864, Elias Kemper Papers, FHS.

9. Robertson, *Letters of McAllister*, 518; Thornbrough, Riker, and Corpuz, *Diary of Fletcher*, 8:448–50; Thornbrough, *Indiana*, 222–23; Thomas and Hyman, *Stanton*, 331; Furgurson, *Freedom Rising*, 335; Gillette, *Jersey Blue*, 289–90; Donald, *Lincoln*, 543–45; Dennison to Lincoln, 11 Nov. 1864, LP, LC.

10. *BA*, 26 Oct., 1 Nov. 1864; Clark, "Politics in Maryland," 39:152–53; *BS*, 20, 28 Oct. 1864; Myers, *Self-Reconstruction of Maryland*, 12–16; Fulton to Lincoln, 29 Oct. 1864, LP, LC; Wagandt, *Mighty Revolution*, 221–46; Dell, *War Democrats*, 307–8; *WDNI*, 7, 11, 31 Oct. 1864; *PhiIn*, 31 Oct. 1864; *HW*, 29 Oct. 1864; Benton, *Voting in the Field*, 225–49; Bradford's Journal, 28, 29 Oct. 1864, Greeley to Bradford, 21 Sept. 1864, Bradford Papers, MdHS; Baker, *Politics of Continuity*, 107–10; Basler, *CW*, 8:46–47; Waugh, *Re-electing Lincoln*, 338–53.

11. Burlingame, *Lincoln Observed*, 138; Clark, "Politics of Maryland," 41:149–53; *BA*, 31 Oct. 1864; *PhiIn*, 31 Oct. 1864; *HW*, 29 Oct. 1864; Thomas and Hyman, *Stanton*, 331; Donald, *Lincoln*, 539–45; Wagandt, *Mighty Revolution*, 221–68; Fuke, *Imperfect Equality*, 1–3.

12. Burlingame, *Lincoln Observed*, 138.

13. *ISJ*, 19 Oct. 1864.

14. Mitchell, *Maryland Voices*, 438–39, 452–53; Basler, *CW*, 8:48; Clark, "Politics in Maryland," 41:153–55; *OR*, series 1, 53, pt. 2:587–88; Myers, *Self-Reconstruction of Maryland*, 12–23; Wagandt, *Mighty Revolution*, 221–68; Fuke, *Imperfect Equality*, 3–63; *WDNI*, 7, 11, 22 Oct. 1864; Hoffman to Lincoln, 15 Oct., John S. Berry to Lincoln, 29 Oct., William Price to Lincoln, 24 Oct. 1864, LP, LC; Nevins, *The Organized War to Victory*, 116, 136–37; Buckingham to Lincoln, 14 Oct. 1864, LP, LC; Benton, *Voting in the Field*, 225–49; *BS*, 18, 21, 24 Nov. 1864; Harris, *Lincoln and the Border States*, 295–301.

15. Curtin to Lincoln, 17, 26 Oct. 1864, Stanton Papers, LC; *OR*, series 1, 43, pt. 2:392–93, 434, 451; Basler, *CW*, 8:50.

16. Eicher, *Longest Night*, 744–53; Basler, *CW*, 8:50, 73–74.

17. Marshall, *A War of the People*, 13, 262, 269–70, 277–78; Crockett, *Vermont*, 599–604; *OR*, series 3, 4:918–19; J. Gregory Smith to Stanton, 26 Oct. 1864, Stanton Papers, LC; Eicher, *Longest Night*, 757; *WDNI*, 22 Oct. 1864; *NHPSG*, 26 Oct. 1864; Dowden, "Smith," 93–95; *BDFP*, 20, 21, 25 Oct. 1864; *InDJ*, 21 Oct. 1864; *PhiIn*, 24 Oct. 1864; *ChiTri*, 15 Dec. 1864; Ayer, *Great North-Western Conspiracy*, 70–72; Harris, *Lincoln's Last Months*, 156–60.

18. Smith to Stanton, 26 Oct. 1864, Stanton Papers, LC; Crockett, *Vermont*, 599–604; *OR*, series 3, 4:918–19; *NYTi*, 3 Jan. 1894; Harris, *Lincoln's Last Months*, 156–60; Harris, "Blair," 171; K. C. Banker to Blair, 2 Dec. 1864, Executive Papers, MiSA; *BDFP*, 20, 21, 25 Oct. 1864; *BDWC*, 8 Nov. 1864; *InDJ*, 8 Nov. 1864.

19. Hall to Lincoln, 5 Nov., Nicolay to Lincoln, 10 Oct., Rosecrans to Lincoln, 4 Oct. 1864, LP, LC; Eicher, *Longest Night*, 754–57; *OR*, series 1, see volume 41 for reports; Avery and Shoemaker, *Messages*, 4:8–25; Nicolay to Lincoln, 19 Oct. 1864 Nicolay Papers, LC; Boman, *Lincoln and Citizens' Rights in Missouri*, 241–62; Nevins, *The Organized War to Victory*, 115.

20. John Gibbons to son, Robert, 20 Aug., 7, 27 Sept. 1864, John Gibbons Papers, SHSW; Norman Eastman to Lewis, 15, 25 Oct., Horace James to Lewis, 8 Nov. 1864, Executive Department, Military Correspondence, SHSW; Jeptha S. Dillon to 15 Oct. 1864, Jeptha S. Dillon Papers, HL.

21. Hancock, "Diaries of Ferris," 256; Richardson, "Selections from Frank Dickerson's Civil War Letters," 48–49.

22. Collins, "Absentee Soldier Voting in Civil War Law and Politics," 296–402.

23. *NYTi*, 18 Oct. 1864; *InDJ*, 11, 18, 21, 24 Oct., 1 Nov. 1864; Pearson, *Andrew*, 2:173–74; Hamrogue, "Andrew," 220–22; *PDJ*, 27 Oct. 1864.

24. Sears, *Papers of McClellan*, 616.

25. *StLDMR*, 4 Nov. 1864; *BDWC*, 8 Nov. 1864; White, *Emancipation, the Union Army, and the Reelection of Abraham Lincoln*, 102–28.

26. Brummer, *Political History of New York*, 424–45; *NYH*, 28, 29 Oct., 3, 10, 12, 16, 21 Nov. 1864; *AEJ*, 29 Oct. 1864; Butler, *Butler's Book*, 754, 757; Thomas and Hyman, *Stanton*, 333–34; Mitchell, *Seymour*, 360–82; Longacre, "The Union Army Occupation of New York City, November 1864," 133–58; *NYTi*, 6–18 Nov. 1864; Trefousse, *Butler*, 162–65; Pearson, *Andrew*, 2:173; Dix to Lincoln, 12 Nov., Weed to Lincoln, 6 Nov. 1864, LP, LC; Basler, *CW*, 8:91–92; *OR*, series 1, 43, pt. 2:519–25; Jones, "The Union League Club and New York's First Black Regiment in the Civil War," 318–19; Croly, *Seymour and Blair*, 131–38; Benton, *Voting in the Field*, 132–70; *BDHE*, 7 Nov. 1864; *PhiIn*, 28 Oct. 1864; *BDA*, 7 Nov. 1864; Henry I. Coyler to Sister, 1 Nov. 1864, Henry I. Coyler Papers, HL.

27. *WDNI*, 22 Oct., 7 Nov. 1864; Croly, *Seymour and Blair*, 127–30; Benton, *Voting in the Field*, 132–70; Longacre, "Union Occupation of New York City," 133–58; Mitchell, *Seymour*, 360–82; Trefousse, *Butler*, 162–65; Soldiers of the 90th New York to Seymour, 25 Oct. 1864, Seymour Papers, NYHS; *DFP*, 17 Oct. 1864; *ISJ*, 8, 9 Nov. 1864.

28. Brooks, "Lincoln's Reelection: The Beginning of Lincoln's Second Term," 865–72.

29. *WDNI*, 8 Nov. 1864; Segal, *Conversations with Lincoln*, 355–60; Furgurson, *Freedom Rising*, 338; Burlingame, *Lincoln Observed*, 142–44; Thomas and Hyman, *Stanton*, 333; Donald, *Lincoln*, 544–46; Waugh, *Re-electing Lincoln*, 338–59; Brooks, "Lincoln's Reelection," 865–72.

30. *OR*, series 3, 4:871–72; Brooks, "Lincoln's Reelection," 865–72; *InDJ*, 1, 3 Nov. 1864; Thornbrough, Riker, and Corpuz, *Diary of Fletcher*, 8:460; Furgurson, *Freedom Rising*, 338; Donald, *Lincoln*, 544–45; *WDNI*, 8, 9 Nov. 1864; Thomas and Hyman, *Stanton*, 334; Paludan, *Presidency of Lincoln*, 288–90; Waugh, *Re-electing Lincoln*, 332–59; Benton, *Voting in the Field*, 174–81, 190–204; McSeveney, "Re-electing Lincoln," 139–57.

31. William L. Mead to Louisa, 8 Nov. 1864, Cornwell Correspondence, MdHS; John Tilford, 5, 8 Nov. 1864, John Tilford Diary, FHS; White, *Emancipation, the Union Army, and the Reelection of Abraham Lincoln*, 102–28.

32. Burlingame, *Lincoln Observed*, 143.

33. Andrew to Frank Howe, 8 Nov. 1864, Andrew Letter Books, MHS; Pearson, *Andrew*, 2:176–77; Hamrogue, "Andrew," 221–22; *ChiTri*, 9 Nov. 1864; *BDA*, 9, 10, 12, 14 Nov. 1864.

34. Andrew to Francis Blair, 13 Nov. 1864, Andrew Letter Books, MHS; Pearson, *Andrew*, 2:176–77; Niven, *Chase Papers*, 1:518; Green, *Freedom, Union, and Power*, 126–27; Hamrogue, "Andrew," 222–24.

35. Hamrogue, "Andrew," 221–24.

36. Beale, *Diary of Bates*, 438; Bowen, *Massachusetts in the War*, 1:79; Segal, *Conversations with Lincoln*, 355–60; Shutes, *Lincoln and California*, 168; Stanley, "Republican Party in California," 160–70; *SDU*, 11, 19 Oct., 4, 9 Nov. 1864; Furgurson, *Freedom Rising*, 338–39; *PhiIn*, 9, 10 November 1864.

37. Thornbrough, Riker, and Corpuz, *Diary of Fletcher*, 8:469; Brummer, *Political History of New York*, 438–39; Waugh, *Re-electing Lincoln*, 338–56; *BDA*, 9 Nov. 1864; *ChiTri*, 9 Nov. 1864.

38. James H. Purdy to Cousin Lizzie, [n.d.] Nov. 1864, J. H. Purdy Papers, NYHS.

39. *BDA*, 9 Nov. 1864; *ChiTri*, 9, 10, 12 Nov. 1864; Nevins, *The Organized War to Victory*, 138–39; Burlingame, *Lincoln Observed*, 144; Basler, *CW*, 8:98–99; Bramlette to Lincoln, 9 Nov., Stephen G. Burbridge to Lincoln, 11 Nov. 1864, LP, LC; Waugh, *Re-electing Lincoln*, 338–61.

40. As quoted in Marsazlek, *Halleck*, 214; Crockett, *Vermont*, 614–17; Dowden, "Smith," 90–96; Edward S. Sanford to Lincoln, 8 Nov., Daniel Clark to Lincoln, 9 Nov. 1864, LP, LC; *NHPSG*, 9 Nov. 1864; *BDFP*, 7 Sept. 1864; *BDA*, 9, 10 Nov. 1864.

41. Bramlette to Lincoln, 14, 16, 22 Nov., Lincoln to Wolford, 17 Jul., Wolford to Lincoln, 30 July, E. Smith Lincoln, 7 Dec. 1864, LP, LC; Howard, "Lincoln Slave Policy in Kentucky," 303–6; *LDJ*, 1, 3 Oct., 16 Nov., 10, 11, 12 Jan. 1865; Basler, *CW*, 7:182, 198, 250, 8:120; *OR*, series 1, 45:1010; Nevins, *The Organized War to Victory*, 136–38; Burlingame, *Lincoln Observed*, 144; Harris, *Lincoln and the Border States*, 245–60; Bush, *Butcher Burbridge*, 168–79.

42. *OR*, series 1, 45, pt. 2:93–94; *BDHE*, 28 Nov. 1864; Albert G. Hodges to Lincoln, 1 Dec., Bramlette to Lincoln, 14 Nov., William C. Goodloe and Charles Eginton to Lincoln, 23 Nov., Robert J. Breckinridge to Lincoln, 16 Nov., Hodges to Lincoln, 12 Nov., Theodore S.

Bell et al. to Joseph Holt, 22 Nov., George D. Blakey to Lincoln, 25 Nov., George W. Lewis to Lincoln, 30 Nov. 1864, LP, LC; Sutherland, *Savage Conflict*, 222–24; Beale, *Diary of Bates*, 428; Harris, *Lincoln and the Border States*, 245–60; Towne, *Surveillance and Spies*, 247–63.

43. Van S. Bennett, Diary, 7 [8] Nov. 1864, Van S. Bennett Diary, SHSW.

44. Paludan, *Presidency of Lincoln*, 288–89; Zornow, *Lincoln and the Party Divided*, 198–202; Hesseltine, *Lincoln and the War Governors*, 367–69; Waugh, *Re-electing Lincoln*, 338–53.

45. Henry Crapo to William Crapo, 8, 30 Sept., 9, 22 Oct. 1864, Crapo Papers, BHL; Fennimore, "Blair," 49:359–62; Lewis, *Lumberman from Flint: The Michigan Career of Henry A. Crapo, 1855–1869*, 143–64; *NYTi*, 25 Jul. 1869; *HW*, 10, 24 Sept., 22, 29 Oct. 1864; White, *Emancipation, the Union Army, and the Reelection of Abraham Lincoln*, 110–16; Hesseltine, *Lincoln and the War Governors*, 367–69.

46. Sobel and Raimo, *Directory of Governors*, 2:748–49; Lewis, *Crapo*, 143–64; Hesseltine, *Lincoln and the War Governors*, 367–69; Fennimore, "Blair," 49:360–62; Crapo to Charles, 16 May 1864, May Papers, BHL; Lewis, *Crapo*, 143–66; *NYTi*, 25 Jul. 1869.

47. David Newsom to Yates, 12 Oct. 1864, Yates Papers, ALPL; *StLDMR*, 14 Jun. 1864; Yates to John Palmer, 8 Dec., William Thomas to Yates, 22 Jul., Edward Small to Yates, 14 Jul., George S. Bangs to Yates, 13 Nov. 1864, Yates Papers, ALPL.

48. As quoted in Nortrup, "Yates," 316–17, 333–35; Lusk, *Politics and Politicians*, 162–64; Joseph Gillespie to Lincoln, 29 Dec. 1863, LP, LC; *ISJ*, 14, 16, 22 Nov. 1864; Joseph Peters to Yates, 12 Oct., G. P. Smith to Yates, 14 Oct., Lewis Ellsworth to Yates, 19 Dec. 1864, Yates Papers, ALPL.

49. *LDT*, 1, 7, 12 Oct., 3, 10 Nov. 1864; Plummer, *Frontier Governor: Samuel J. Crawford of Kansas*, 13, 36–42; Castel, *Civil War Kansas*, 169–82, 194, 199–200; Mark Delahay to Lincoln, 14 Nov. 1864, LP, LC, about Carney's defeat; Sobel and Raimo, *Directory of Governors*, 2:460–61; *LDT*, 9 Jun., 7, 19 Jul., 26 Aug., 16, 23, 30 Sept., 1, 7, 12 Oct., 3 Nov. 1864.

50. *BDHE*, 17 Oct. 1864; Sobel and Raimo, *Directory of Governors*, 2:849; Avery and Shoemaker, *Messages*, 4:43–49; *NYTi*, 26 Mar. 1899.

51. Clark, "Politics in Maryland," 39:156–57; Sobel and Raimo, *Directory of Governors*, 2:669; *HW*, 9 Jun. 1866; *BA*, 7, 8, 29 Nov. 1864; Myers, *Self-Reconstruction of Maryland*, 14–16; Wagandt, *Mighty Revolution*, 221–68; *PhiIn*, 20, 25 Oct. 1864; Harris, *Lincoln and the Border States*, 295–301.

52. As quoted in Mitchell, *Seymour*, 382; Dennett, *Diaries and Letters of Hay*, 237–38; Basler, *CW*, 7:514; Nevins, *The Organized War to Victory*, 200–201; Segal, *Conversations with Lincoln*, 358–59; *HW*, 19 Nov. 1864.

53. As quoted in the *NYTi*, 8 Nov. 1864.

54. William C. Brown to Col. Lockwood Doty, 17 Nov. 1864, Maryland Manuscripts, MDMS, 2801, Special Collections, UML; *NYTi*, 8 Nov., 20 Dec. 1864, 27 Dec. 1867.

55. "Our New Governor," *American Phrenological Journal*, 41 (Mar. 1865): 1–2; *NYTi*, 19 Sept., 8, 20 Nov. 1864, 26 Aug. 1885; Lincoln, *Messages*, 583; *PhiIn*, 9 Jan. 1865; Burlingame, *Lincoln Observed*, 152; Donald, *Lincoln*, 547–49.

56. Cannon to Stanton, 27 Oct. 1864, Stanton Papers, LC; *OR*, series 1, 53, pt. 2:485; Hancock, "Political History of Delaware," 8:102–3; *PhiIn*, 7 Nov. 1864; Munroe, *Delaware*, 142; Waugh, *Re-electing Lincoln*; *PhiIn*, 7 Nov. 1864; *Del*, 29 October 1864; *ChiTri*, 11, 16 Nov. 1864; *StLDMR*, 15 Nov. 1864; Miller to Lincoln, 16, 21 Nov., Weed to Lincoln, 6 Oct., Buckingham to Lincoln, 17 Nov., Seymour to Lincoln, 15, 16 Nov. 1864, LP, LC; Basler, *CW*, 8:108–9; Seymour to [?] 24 Nov. 1864, Seymour Papers, NYHS; Arthur I.

Boreman to Lincoln, 16 Nov., James T. Lewis to Lincoln, 23 Nov., Gilmore to Lincoln, 1 Dec., Joel Parker to Lincoln, 17 Nov., Andrew to Lincoln, 16 Nov., Curtin to Lincoln, 30 Nov., Carney to Lincoln, 1 Dec., Bramlette to Lincoln, 18, 24 Nov., Willard P. Hall to Lincoln, 30 Nov. 1864, LP, LC; Benton, *Voting in the Field*, 174–81.

57. Hancock, "Diaries of Ferris," 257; Basler, *CW*, 8:108–10; Brummer, *Political History of New York*, 438–39; *NYTri*, 9 Nov. 1864; Paludan, *Presidency of Lincoln*, 288–90; Hancock, "Political History of Delaware," 8:103–5; Gilmore to Lincoln, 17 Nov. 1864, LP, LC.

58. Beale, *Diary of Bates*, 438; Gillette, *Jersey Blue*, 284–85, 292–93; Jackson, *New Jerseyans*, 205–6; *TDSGR*, 17 Nov. 1864; Pearson, *Andrew*, 2:174–75; Waugh, *Re-electing Lincoln*, 338–61; *PhiIn*, 10, 12 Oct. 1864; *BDA*, 9 Nov. 1864; *ChiTri*, 9 Nov. 1864.

59. *NHS*, 11 Nov. 1864.

60. Oglesby to Lincoln, 20 Nov. 1864, LP, LC; Harris, *Lincoln's Last Months*, 41.

61. Oglesby to Lincoln, 20 Nov. 1864, LP, LC.

62. *HW*, 19 Nov. 1864; portions also cited in Nevins, *The Organized War to Victory*, 197; Burlingame, *Lincoln Observed*, 149–51, 155; Josephine S. Griffing to Lincoln, 24 Sept. 1864, LP, LC.

63. Burlingame, *Lincoln Observed*, 155; *HW*, 19 Nov. 1864; Green, *Freedom, Union, and Power*; Greeley, "Greeley's Estimate of Lincoln," 382.

64. Larkin Mason to Gilmore, 27 Nov. 1864, "confidential," Gilmore Papers, NHHS.

65. As quoted in Holliday, "Relief for Soldiers' Families in Ohio during the Civil War," 107–10.

66. Eicher, *Longest Night*, 760–80; Marszalek, *Sherman*, 294–308; *ChiTri*, 8 Dec. 1864.

67. Basler, *CW*, 8:136–53; Donald, *Lincoln*, 554–55; Burlingame, *Lincoln Observed*, 149; Donald, *Lincoln*, 552–53; Harris, *Lincoln's Last Months*, 94–101.

68. Basler, *CW*, 8:148–49; Myers, *Self-Reconstruction of Maryland*, 9–17.

69. Burlingame, *Lincoln Observed*, 149–51, 155; Harris, *Lincoln's Last Months*, 96–105.

70. *OR*, series 1, 45, pt. 2:194–95; Eicher, *Longest Night*, 775–80; Basler, *CW*, 8:169; Marszalek, *Halleck*, 215–17.

71. *OR*, series 1, 45, pt. 2:227.

72. Basler, *CW*, 8:171–72; Murdock, *Patriotism Limited*, 81–228; *OR*, series 3, 4:927, 928, 5:486–87; Nevins, *The Organized War to Victory*, 145–47.

73. Reuben Farnum to Family, 19 Dec. 1864, Reuben Farnum Family Papers, MnHS; Basler, *CW*, 8:181–82; Thomas and Hyman, *Stanton*, 342–43; Marszalek, *Sherman*, 294–313; Eicher, *Longest Night*, 779–84; Trudeau, *Southern Storm: Sherman's March to the Sea*, 45–508.

74. Basler, *CW*, 8:181–82.

75. Smith to Lincoln, 27 Dec., Sherman to Lincoln, 22 Dec. 1864, LP, LC.

76. As quoted in Cimbala and Miller, *Union Soldiers and the Northern Home Front*, 350.

77. Gilmore to Lincoln, 30 Dec., Ordway to Lincoln, 23, 24 Jul. 1863, Ordway to Lincoln, 10 Mar., 7 May, Timothy David to Lincoln, 31 Dec., Nathaniel Berry to Lincoln, 27 Dec. 1864, LP, LC; Gilmore to James B. Fry, 3 Dec. 1864, "confidential," Gilmore Papers, NHHS; Hesseltine, *Lincoln and the War Governors*, 364–89; Renda, *Running on the Record: Civil War-Era Politics in New Hampshire*, 91; Corning, *Amos Tuck*, 84.

78. Nortrup, "Yates," 334; Yates to S. S. Phelps, 10 Dec. 1864, Yates Papers, ALPL.

79. Nortrup, "Yates," 334–36; *ISJ*, 22 Dec. 1864, 4, 5 Jan. 1865; Krenkel, *Yates*, 231–33; *BDHE*, 3 Dec. 1864; *InDJ*, 8 Dec. 1864; William Sheppard to Yates, [n.d.] Dec. 1864, Yates Papers, ALPL; William Pope to Yates, 1 Dec., E. P. Sloan to Yates, 26 Dec., George Bergen to Yates, 10 Dec., R. S. Wilson to Yates, 29 Dec., "private," R. B. Hatch to Yates, 25 Dec.,

George Bangs to Yates, 14 Dec., Porter Sheldon to Yates, 5 Dec., J. Callaway to Yates, 9 Dec., Lewis Ellsworth to Yates, 19 Dec. 1864, Yates Papers, WC, ALPL.

80. *OR*, series 3, 4:1013–14, 1020–21; *InDJ*, 13 Dec. 1862; Thomas and Hyman, *Stanton*, 360–75.

Chapter Twenty

1. *HW*, 7 Jan. 1865.
2. *Annual Message of the Governor of the State of New York to the Legislature, January 3, 1865*; *HW*, 14 Jan. 1865; *NYTi*, 4 Jan. 1865; *OR*, series 3, 4:1039; Fenton to Lincoln, 27 Jan. 1865, LP, LC; Hesseltine, *Lincoln and the War Governors*, 389.
3. Avery and Shoemaker, *Messages of Governors*, 4:53–64; Vorenberg, *Final Freedom*, 188–89; *PhiIn*, 6 Jan. 1865; *ChiTri*, 4, 5, 6, 7, 8 Jan. 1865; *InDJ*, 6, 9 Jan. 1865.
4. Leander Harris to Wife, 8 Jan. 1865, Leander Harris Papers, DC; Paludan, *Presidency of Lincoln*, 3–20.
5. Simpson and Berlin, *Sherman's War*, 788–801; Niven, *Chase Papers*, 1:514; Furgurson, *Freedom Rising*, 347–48; Thomas and Hyman, *Stanton*, 343–46; Marszalek, *Sherman*, 309–16; Harris, *Lincoln's Last Months*, 57–58; *HW*, 7, 28 Jan. 1865; Marvel, *Lincoln's Autocrat*, 358–60.
6. Foulke, *Morton*, 1:433–35; Thornbrough, Riker, and Corpuz, *Diary of Fletcher*, 9:4–7; Thornbrough, *Indiana*, 227; French, *Morton*, 474–83; Sylvester, *Morton*, 284–87; *InDJ*, 9 Jan. 1865.
7. *ISJ*, 6, 14 Jan. 1865; *Message of Richard Yates to the Illinois General Assembly*, 2 Jan. 1865, 3–67; Vorenberg, *Final Freedom*, 188; *ChiTri*, 5, 6 Jan. 1865; Nortrup, "Yates," 334–45; McPherson, *The Negro's Civil War*, 256–58; Jones, *The Black Laws of Illinois*; Litwack, *North of Slavery*, 71; *HW*, 22 Apr. 1865; Krenkel, *Yates*, 231–35, 238; *BDHE*, 3 Dec. 1864; R. B. Hatch to Yates, 3 Jan., Charles Newcomer to Yates, 5 Jan., Amos Tuck to Yates, 28 Feb., J. G. Wilson to Yates, 5 Jan. 1865, Yates Papers, ALPL; Nortrup, "Yates," 336–38; *WDNI*, 7 Jan. 1865.
8. *ISJ*, 26 May 1864; Plummer, *Lincoln's Rail-Splitter: Governor Richard Oglesby*, 2–43, 82–88, 94–98, 109; *NYTi*, 25 Apr. 1899.
9. Fuller, *Messages*, 419–20, 498–512; *DFP*, 5, 7 Jan. 1865; Fennimore, "Blair," 49:356–69; Green, *Freedom, Union, and Power*, 188; Harris, "Blair," 172–78; Lewis, *Crapo*, 143–64; *NYTi*, 25 Jul. 1869.
10. *OR*, series 3, 4:1081–84; *Message of James Y. Smith, Governor of Rhode Island to the General Assembly*, 9 Jan. 1865, 10.
11. Oglesby to Lincoln, 25 Jan. 1865, Oglesby Papers, ALPL; *OR*, series 1, 45, pt. 2:475; Plummer, *Oglesby*, 126–27.
12. *OR*, series 3, 4:1035, 1038; 1039–40, 1134–42; *OR*, series 1, 45, pt. 2:475; Hesseltine, *Lincoln and the War Governors*, 388–89.
13. *OR*, series 3, 4:1035, 1038–40, 1056–57.
14. Miller to Ramsey, 2 Feb. 1865, Governor's Papers, Executive Journals, MnHS.
15. Miller to Stanton, 24 Feb. 1865, Governor's Papers, Executive Journals, MnHS.
16. Andrew to Weed, 6 Feb. 1865, Andrew Letter Books, MHS; Pearson, *Andrew*, 2:182–92; *OR*, series 3, 4:1055; Burlingame, *Lincoln Observed*, 159; Morgan to Lincoln, 18 Feb. 1865, LP, LC; John Murray Forbes to William P. Fessenden, 31 Jan. 1865, Fessenden Papers, BCL; Donald, *Sumner*, 210–12; Harris, *Lincoln's Last Months*, 84, 88; Rawley, *Morgan*, 201–2; Weed, *Autobiography*, 1:620–23; Hamrogue, "Andrew," 220–25; *NHPSG*, 1 Feb. 1865.

17. Donald, *Sumner*, 210–12; Hamrogue, "Andrew," 220–25; Andrew to Howe, 6, 8 Feb., Andrew to Weed, 6 Feb. 1865, Andrew Letter Books, Forbes to Andrew, 7 Feb. 1865, Andrew Papers, MHS; *OR*, series 3, 4:1059–60, 1038; *BDA*, 13 Jan. 1865.

18. *OR*, series 1, 48:520; Beale, *Diary of Bates*, 439–41; Avery and Shoemaker, *Messages*, 4:53–64; *StLDMR*, 2 Jan. 1865; Clark, "Politics in Maryland," 41:156–58; Clark, "Politics in Maryland," 39:159–60; Myers, *Self-Reconstruction of Maryland*, 15–17; *PhiIn*, 6 Jan. 1865.

19. *InDJ*, 12 Jan. 1865; Fletcher to Lincoln, 11 Jan. 1865, LP, LC; *BDA*, 13, 23 Jan., 2 Feb. 1865; *PDJ*, 13 Jan. 1865; *BDWC*, 13 Jan. 1865.

20. *OR*, series 1, 48:535; Basler, *CW*, 8:217; *PhiIn*, 6 Jan. 1865; Siddali, *Missouri's War*, 216–18; Avery and Shoemaker, *Messages*, 4:53–64; *ChiTri*, 4 Jan. 1865.

21. *OR*, series 1, 48:535, 547, 678, 1010, 1115; Siddali, *Missouri's War*, 216–19.

22. *OR*, series 1, 45, pt. 2:42–43, 167–68, 573, 576–77; Harris, "Blair," 171; *LDJ*, 15 Jan. 1865.

23. *OR*, series 1, 45, pt. 2:42–43, series 3, 4:1230; *LDJ*, 15 Jan. 1865.

24. Eicher, *Longest Night*, 794–96; Marszalek, *Sherman*, 318–25; Thomas and Hyman, *Stanton*, 343–47.

25. Basler, *CW*, 8:231–32, 250–51, 257, 262, 264–65; Mitchell, *Seymour*, 317–19; Fenton to Lincoln, 26 Jan. 1865, LP, LC; *OR*, series 3, 4:1063–64, 1073–75, 1105–20,1134–35, 1149–51, 1166–71, 5:737; Mitchell, *Seymour*, 317–19; *PhiIn*, 4 Jan. 1865; Shannon, *Organization of Union Army*, 2:73; Geary, *We Need Men*, 70–77.

26. *BDA*, 4 Feb. 1865; Remini, *The House*, 186–88; Donald, *Lincoln*, 553–57; Vorenberg, *Final Freedom*, 177–210; Basler, *CW*, 8:250–51, 275–79; Burlingame, *Lincoln Observed*, 159–61; Simpson, *Grant*, 405–25; *NHPSG*, 1 Feb. 1865.

27. *BDA*, 4 Feb. 1865; Remini, *The House*, 186–88; Donald, *Lincoln*, 553–57; Vorenberg, *Final Freedom*, 177–210.

28. Carl Schurz to Wife, 1 Feb. 1865, Carl Schurz Papers, SHSW; also partially cited in Nevins, *The Organized War to Victory*, 214.

29. Henry Boyd to Dear Madam, 25 Feb. 1865, Irvin W. Spooner Papers, VHS; Remini, *The House*, 186–88; Donald, *Lincoln*, 553–57; Gallagher, *The Union War*, 75–119.

30. Andrew to Lincoln, 1 Feb. 1865, LP, LC; Schouler, *Massachusetts in the Civil War*, 1:616–17; Harris, *Lincoln's Last Months*, 132–33; *BDA*, 2 Feb. 1865; Vorenberg, *Final Freedom*, 177–210.

31. *HW*, 11 Feb. 1865; *New Times*, 26 Jan. 1865; Oglesby to Lincoln, 1 Feb. 1865, LP, LC; Basler, *CW*, 8:255; Plummer, *Oglesby*, 127; Vorenberg, *Final Freedom*, 188–89; Harris, *Lincoln's Last Months*, 132; *Congressional Globe*, 38th Congress, 2nd session, 31 Jan. 1865, 189; Basler, *CW*, 8:253–54; Furguson, *Freedom Rising*, 350–51; Donald, *Lincoln*, 563–64.

32. Donald, *Lincoln*, 553–61; Stahr, *Seward*, 420–28; Eicher, *Longest Night*, 793–803.

33. As quoted in Hancock, "Political History of Delaware," 8:160–61; *DR*, 2 Mar. 1865; Cannon's Proclamation to the Delaware General Assembly, 7 Feb., 1865, Cony to Lincoln, 7 Feb., Andrew to Lincoln, 3 Feb., James Y. Smith (RI) to Lincoln, 3 Feb., Morton to Lincoln, 13 Feb. 1865, LP, LC; Essah, *A House Divided*; Dell, *War Democrats*, 320–21; *BS*, 7 Jan. 1865; Harris, *Lincoln's Last Months*, 115–22; Beale, *Diary of Welles*, 2:235; Whalon, "Maine Republicans," 133–35; Vorenberg, *Final Freedom*, 177–210.

34. Hancock, "Political History of Delaware," 8:160–61; *Laws of the State of Delaware, 1865*, 550–55; Munroe, *Delaware*, 142; *NYTi*, 2 Mar. 1865; *PhiIn*, 10 Mar. 1865.

35. G. B. Cochran to James Speed, Speed Family Papers, FHS; Howard, "Lincoln Slave Policy in Kentucky," 304–7; *LDJ*, 10, 11, 12 Jan., 11 Feb. 1865; Bush, *Butcher Burbridge*, 180–92; Bohrnstedt, *While Father Is Away*, 217; *LDJ*, 7, 12 Jan., 9, 22 Feb., 3 Mar. 1865; *StLDMR*,

9 Jan. 1865; *BS*, 11 Jan., 11 Feb. 1865; *ISJ*, 12 Jan. 1865; Harris, *Lincoln and the Border States*, 250–67; Vorenberg, *Final Freedom*, 177–230.

36. Bramlette to Lincoln, 20 Feb., Thomas M. Green to Bramlette, 16 Jan. 1865; Bramlette to Kentucky Legislature, 1 Mar., Albert G. Hodges to Lincoln, 1 Mar., George W. Sulser to Harrison Taylor, 16 Jan., Samuel Haycraft to Charles D. Poston, 13 Feb. 1865, LP, LC; Bush, *Butcher Burbridge*, 180–92; Vorenberg, *Final Freedom*, 216–17; Howard, "Lincoln Slave Policy in Kentucky," 305–7; *LDJ*, 10, 11, 12 Jan., 9 Feb., 3 Mar. 1865; Harris, *Lincoln and the Border States*, 250–67.

37. *TDSGR*, 12, 13, 17 Jan. 1865; *Second Annual Message of Joel Parker*, 11 Jan. 1865, 28; Gillette, *Jersey Blue*, 297–304; Thomas and Hyman, *Stanton*, 347–48; Jackson, *New Jerseyans*, 215; Vorenberg, *Final Freedom*, 156; Basler, *CW*, 8:266, 268–84; Foulke, *Morton*, 1:436; Thornbrough, Riker, and Corpuz, *Diary of Fletcher*, 9:30–31; *InDJ*, 14 Feb. 1865; Donald, *Lincoln*, 557–61; Grant, *Personal Memoirs*, 2:422; Randall and Current, *Lincoln*, 4:333; Hancock, "Political History of Delaware," 8:160–84.

38. Sylvester, "Morton," 286–87; *InDJ*, 7, 12 Feb. 1865.

39. Julian, *Political Recollections, 1840–1872*, 269–72. Julian was referring to Hermann Von Holst's *The Constitutional and Political History of the United States*, which contained a chapter entitled "The Reign of Andrew Jackson." Sylvester, "Morton," 293.

40. Smith to Lincoln, 9, 10 Feb., Lincoln to Smith, 8 Feb., Fenton to Lincoln, 26 Jan., Henry Anthony to Lincoln, 3 Feb. 1865, LP, LC; Bailey, *Communication from His Excellency James Y. Smith to the General Assembly*, 1–8; Basler, *CW*, 8:271–72; *OR*, series 3, 4:1134–42; *TDSGR*, 28, 31 Jan., 18 Feb. 1865; Eicher, *Longest Night*, 798–801; Marszalek, *Sherman*, 320–25.

41. Radcliffe, *Hicks*, 127–28; Burlingame, *Lincoln Observed*, 164; *WDNI*, 13, 14 Feb., 14 Mar., 25 May 1864; *BS*, 16, 17 Feb. 1865; Hicks to Lincoln, 20 Jun., Hicks to Lincoln, 30 May 1864, LP, LC; Harris, *Lincoln's Last Months*, 79–81; *InDJ*, 18, 20 Feb. 1865.

42. Basler, *CW*, 8:308; *StLDMR*, 30 Mar. 1865.

43. Fletcher to Lincoln, 27 Feb. 1865, LP, LC; Basler, *CW*, 8:319–20; *OR*, series 1, 48:997, 1115; *StLDMR*, 25 Feb., 10 Mar., 3 Apr. 1865.

44. *OR*, series 1, 48:769, 816, 1133–36; Plummer, *Crawford*, 43–51; *NYTi*, 22 Oct. 1913.

45. As quoted in Edwards, "Department of Pacific," 270–89; *OS*, 9, 16 Jan. 1865; *SFDAC*, 9 Jan. 1865; *OR*, series 1, 50, pt. 2:1083, 1118, 1166, 1167, 1237; Melendy and Gilbert, *Governors of California*, 129–39; Gilbert, "Confederate Minority in California," 158; Gibbs to Capt. Ivan D. Applegate, 27 Jan. 1865, Gibbs Papers, UOL.

46. Simon, *Papers of Grant*, 14:91; Simpson, *Grant*, 411; Basler, *CW*, 8:326–27, 330–31; *HW*, 18 Mar. 1865; Thomas and Hyman, *Stanton*, 347–49; Furgurson, *Freedom Rising*, 355; *InDJ*, 20 Feb., 1, 2 Mar. 1865; *LDJ*, 5 Mar. 1865; *BS*, 7 Mar. 1865; Thornbrough, Riker, and Corpuz, *Diary of Fletcher*, 9:45.

47. Burlingame, *Lincoln Observed*, 165; Epstein, *Lincoln and Whitman*, 250–57; Harris, *Lincoln's Last Months*, 136–43; *LDJ*, 4, 5 Mar. 1865.

48. Thomas Taylor to Wife, 9 Mar. 1865, Thomas Taylor Papers, OHS.

49. *HW*, 18 Mar. 1865; Basler, *CW*, 8:332–33; Nevins, The Organized War to Victory, 218; Furgurson, *Freedom Rising*, 356–58; Donald, *Lincoln*, 565–66; Paludan, *Presidency of Lincoln*, 304–5; Epstein, *Lincoln and Whitman*, 250–57; Beale, *Diary of Welles*, 2:252; Thomas Taylor to Wife, 9 Mar. 1865, Taylor Papers, OHS.

50. Burlingame, *Lincoln Observed*, 168–70; *WES*, 5, 6 Mar. 1865; Donald, *Lincoln*, 567–68; Epstein, *Lincoln and Whitman*, 257–60.

51. Basler, *CW*, 8:320, 348; *OR*, series 1, 48:1115; *StLDMR*, 15, 19 Mar. 1865; Epstein, *Lincoln and Whitman*, 260–61.

52. Epstein, *Lincoln and Whitman*, 261–66; *WES*, 18 Mar. 1865; Basler, *CW*, 8:360–62; *NYTri*, 18 Mar. 1865; *NYH*, 18 March 1865; Marszalek, *Sherman*, 325–33; Thomas and Hyman, *Stanton*, 349.

53. Basler, *CW*, 8:360–62; *WES*, 18 Mar. 1865; *NYTri*, 18 Mar. 1865; *NYH*, 18 Mar. 1865; Marszalek, *Sherman*, 325–33; Thomas and Hyman, *Stanton*, 349; Epstein, *Lincoln and Whitman*, 261–66.

54. Epstein, *Lincoln and Whitman*, 261–66; *NYTi*, 18 Mar. 1865; Basler, *CW*, 8:360–62; Thomas and Hyman, *Stanton*, 349.

55. *OR*, series 3:4, 1222–30, 149–52.

56. Weitzel to Stanton, 3 Apr. 1865, Telegrams Received by the Secretary of War, RG 107, NARA; Basler, *CW*, 8:372–81; *OR*, series 1, 46, pt. 3:96, 332, 392, 393; Donald, *Lincoln*, 571–80; *WES*, 23 Mar. 1865; Eicher, *Longest Night*, 804–6; Porter, *Campaigning with Grant*, 401–16; Marszalek, *Halleck*, 221; Marszalek, *Sherman*, 335–37; Simpson, *Grant*, 414–20; Harris, *Lincoln's Last Months*, 192–205; Thomas, *Three Years with Grant*, 281–85, 299–302; Grant, *Personal Memoirs*, 583–85; Marvel, *Lee's Last Retreat: The Fighting to Appomattox*.

57. Johnson and Buel, *Battles and Leaders*, 4:728; Segal, *Conversations with Lincoln*, 388–90; Donald, *Lincoln*, 576–78; Harris, *Lincoln's Last Months*, 200–208.

58. Andrew to Stanton, 3 Apr. 1865, Telegrams Received by the Secretary of War, RG 107, NARA; Bowen, *Massachusetts in the War*, 1:80; Schouler, *Massachusetts in the Civil War*, 1:623; Stanton to Morton, 3 Apr. 1865, Morton Telegraph Books, IUPUI.

59. Andrew to Stanton, 3 Apr. 1865, Telegrams Received by the Secretary of War, RG 107, NARA; Bowen, *Massachusetts in the War*, 1:80.

60. Andrew, *An Address Delivered before the New England Agricultural Society on Hampden Park*, 1864; Green, *Freedom, Union, and Power*, 203–4.

61. *Lbr*, 20 Jan. 1865.

62. Hancock, "Diaries of Ferris," 258.

63. *NYTi*, 15 Mar. 1865; Renda, *Running on the Record*, 130–31.

64. Renda, "New Hampshire Politics," 78–81; Sobel and Raimo, *Directory of Governors*, 1:965; Renda, *Running on the Record*, 130–32; *NHPSG*, 15, 22 Mar. 1865; *NYTi*, 15, 26 Mar. 1865; William E. Chandler to Gilmore, 7 Apr. (Letter book), Gilmore to Chandler, 27, 30 Mar., 12 Apr. 1865, (correspondence), Chandler Papers, NHHS; *BDA*, 10 Feb. 1865; *NHPSG*, 15 Feb. 1865; William E. Chandler to Welles, 25 Feb. 1865, Welles Papers, LC. I am grateful to William Marvel for sharing his notes on the Gilmore-Chandler correspondence.

65. Nation and Towne, *Indiana's War*, 192–93; Buckingham to Stanton, 4 Apr. 1865, Telegrams Received by the Secretary of War, RG 107, NARA; Buckingham, *Life of Buckingham*, 430–31; Croffut and Morris, *Connecticut during the War*, 798–99; Niven, *Connecticut for the Union*, 315; *NYTi*, 4, 5, 7 Apr. 1865; *BDA*, 11 Apr. 1865; Joseph Hawley to Charles Dudley Warner, 7 Jan. 1865, Joseph Hawley Papers, CtHS.

66. *NYTi*, 4, 5, 7 Apr. 1865; *BDA*, 11 Apr. 1865; Sperry to Stanton, 3 Apr. 1865, Telegrams Received by the Secretary of War, RG 107, NARA.

67. *NYTi*, 6 Apr. 1865.

68. Dana to Stanton, 9, 10 Apr., Gen. Godfrey Weitzel to Stanton, 10 Apr. 1865, Stanton Papers, LC.

69. Charles Francis Adams Jr. to John Andrew, 3 Apr. 1865, Executive Papers, MSA.

70. Basler, *CW*, 8:388, 393–94; Donald, *Lincoln*, 579–82; *WDNI*, 11, 13 Apr. 1865; *OR*, series 1, 46, pt. 3:574–75; Burlingame, *Lincoln Observed*, 181–83; Harris, *Lincoln's Last Months*, 212–17; *BDA*, 11, 12 Apr. 1865; Thomas and Hyman, *Stanton*, 351–53.

71. *WDNI*, 14 Apr. 1865.

72. Byers, *With Fire and Sword*, 199–201; *WDNI*, 11, 13 Apr. 1865.

73. Cony to Stanton, 10 Apr., Miller to Stanton, 12 Apr., Smith to Stanton, 3 Apr., Curtin to Stanton, 3 Apr., Brough to Stanton, 10 Apr., Bradford to Stanton, 3 Apr., Oglesby to Stanton, 10 Apr. 1865, Telegrams Received by the Secretary of War, RG 107, NARA; *NYTi*, 18 Apr. 1865.

74. *LDJ*, 9 Apr. 1865; Fenton to Lincoln, 11 Apr. 1865, LP, LC; *OR*, series 3, 4:1263; Thomas and Hyman, *Stanton*, 351–55; *PhiIn*, 14 Apr. 1865; *BDA*, 2 Mar., 10, 11 Apr. 1865; Curtin to Stanton, 8 Mar. 1865, Stanton Papers, LC.

75. Haynie, "At the Death Bed of Lincoln," 954; Basler, *CW*, 8:369, 411; Donald, *Lincoln*, 592–93; Yates, "Yates," 196–98; Plummer, *Oglesby*, 105–12; Goodwin, *Team of Rivals*, 733–34; Harris, *Lincoln's Last Months*, 218–25; Burlingame, *Lincoln*, 2:809; *BDA*, 14 Apr. 1865; *PhiIn*, 14, 15, 17 Apr. 1865; *ISJ*, 17 Apr. 1865; Niven, *Chase Papers*, 1:525–26.

76. Hancock, "Diaries of Ferris," 260; *WES*, 14 Apr. 1865; Furgurson, *Freedom Rising*, 376–77; Plummer, *Oglesby*, 108–9.

77. Foulke, *Morton*, 1:438–39.

78. *BDA*, 15 Apr. 1865.

79. Yates, "Yates," 197–98.

80. Haynie, "Death Bed of Lincoln," 954–55; Nicolay and Hay, "Abraham Lincoln. 1: A History, The Fourteenth of April—The Fate of the Assassins—The Mourning Pageant," 428–42; Thomas and Hyman, *Stanton*, 398–99; Nicolay and Hay, *Lincoln: A History*, 10:302; Niven, *Chase Papers*, 1:529; Marszalek, *Sherman*, 325–40; *PhiIn*, 14, 15, 17 Apr. 1865; Raymond and Carpenter, *Lincoln*, 2:785–86; Yates, "Yates," 198; *ISJ*, 17 Apr. 1865; Taft, "Letter 14–Abraham Lincoln's Last Hours," 634–36; *BDA*, 14, 15 Apr. 1865; Furgurson, *Freedom Rising*, 376–85; *ISJ*, 14, 15 Apr. 1865; Foulke, *Morton*, 1:438–39; Donald, *Lincoln*, 594–95; Schroder, "William M. Stone," 116–17.

81. Burlingame, *Lincoln Observed*, 216; Nicolay and Hay, "Abraham Lincoln," 436.

82. *BDA*, 15 Apr. 1865.

83. Burlingame, *Lincoln Observed*, 187; Niven, *Chase Papers*, 1:532; Thomas Taylor to Wife, 17 Apr. 1865, Taylor Papers, OHS; Furgurson, *Freedom Rising*, 385–90; Harris, *Lincoln's Last Months*, 230–46; *WDNI*, 15, 16 Apr. 1865; Edward Rollins to Gilmore, 15 Apr. 1865, Gilmore Papers, NHHS; Gilmore to Edward Rollins, 23 Apr. 1865, Edward Henry Rollins Papers, DC; *PhiIn*, 17 Apr. 1865; Chase to William Sprague, 14 Apr. 1865, Chase Papers, CGS; Foulke, *Morton*, 1:438–39; Furgurson, *Freedom Rising*, 376–85; Donald, *Lincoln*, 594–99; Plummer, *Oglesby*, 108–9; Haynie, "Death Bed of Lincoln," 954–55; Taft, "Lincoln's Last Hours," 634–36; Beale, *Diary of Welles*, 2:286–90; *BDA*, 14, 15 Apr. 1865; *PhiIn*, 14, 15, 17 Apr. 1865; *ISJ*, 17 Apr. 1865; Taft, "Letter 14–Abraham Lincoln's Last Hours," 634–36.

84. Epstein, *Lincoln and Whitman*, 275; Niven, *Chase Papers*, 1:532; Mitchell, *Maryland Voices*, 463; Furgurson, *Freedom Rising*, 385–90; Burlingame, *Lincoln Observed*, 191–94; Hancock, "Diaries of Ferris," 260–61; Harris, *Lincoln's Last Months*, 230–46; Thomas Taylor to Wife, 17 Apr. 1865, Taylor Papers, OHS; *InDJ*, 16 Apr. 1865; *BDA*, 15, 17 Apr. 1865.

85. Shutes, *Lincoln and California*, 184–85; Plummer, *Oglesby*, 109; *InDJ*, 16 Apr. 1865; *PhiIn*, 17 Apr. 1865; *ISJ*, 17 Apr. 1865.

86. Foulke, *Morton*, 1:439; Thornbrough, *Indiana*, 226–27; Thornbrough, Riker, and Corpuz, *Diary of Fletcher*, 9:69; Weeden, *War Government*, 344–45; *InDJ*, 16 Apr. 1865.

87. *InDJ*, 16 Apr. 1865; Foulke, *Morton*, 1:439; Thornbrough, Riker, and Corpuz, *Diary of Fletcher*, 9:69.

88. Holland, *Lincoln*, 432–33; Beale, *Diary of Welles*, 2:287–93; *WDNI*, 19, 21, 22 Apr. 1865; *PhiIn*, 20, 21 Apr. 1865; *BDA*, 17, 20, 21, 22 Apr. 1865; *BS*, 17, 20, 21 Apr. 1865; *TDSGR*, 21 Apr. 1865; Nicolay and Hay, "Abraham Lincoln," 439–40; Weeden, *War Government*, 344–45; Shutes, *Lincoln and California*, 191–92; Harris, *Lincoln's Last Months*, 230–46.

89. Nicolay and Hay, "Abraham Lincoln," 439–44; Plummer, *Oglesby*, 108–13; Harris, *Lincoln's Last Months*, 230–36; *PhiIn*, 17 Apr. 1865; *BDA*, 19, 22 Apr. 1865; *TDSGR*, 19, 20, 22 Apr. 1865; *InDJ*, 30 Apr. 1865.

90. Boman, *Gamble*, 239; Holland, *Lincoln*, 432–39; Harris, *Lincoln's Last Months*, 230–37; *ChiTri*, 2 May 1865; *InDJ*, 4 May 1865; Thornbrough, Riker, and Corpuz, *Diary of Fletcher*, 9:80–82; Miers, *New Jersey and the Civil War*, 130–32; *PhiIn*, 19, 20, 21, 22, 24, 25 Apr. 1865; *BDA*, 22, 24, 25 Apr. 1865; Hancock, "Diaries of Ferris," 261–62; *BS*, 19, 20 Apr. 1865; Nicolay and Hay, "Abraham Lincoln," 439–43.

91. *HW*, 6 May 1865.

92. Emerson, *Representative Men and Miscellanies*, 327–38; Cooke, *Ralph Waldo Emerson, His Life, Writings, and Philosophy*, 152–55; Harris, *Lincoln and the War Governors*, 124–25; *ISJ*, 22 Sept. 1863; Harris, *Lincoln's Last Months*, 236–46.

Epilogue

1. Yates, "Yates," 176–77; Downs, *After Appomattox*, 5–20.

2. Egle, *Curtin*, 190–91.

3. Benedict, *Vermont*, 1:612–13; Crockett, *Vermont*, 3:622–23; Haynes, *History of the Tenth Vermont*, 153; Zeller, *Ninth Vermont*, 216; Gallman, *The North Fights the Civil War*, 180–97; Keller, *Affairs of State*, 12–45; Bensel, *Yankee Leviathan*, 2–17; Sribnick, *A Legacy of Innovation*, 7–13.

4. Benedict, *Vermont*, 1:614–15.

5. As quoted in Baker, *Politics of Continuity*, 139.

6. Andrew Young to Susan, 20 Apr. 1865, Andrew Hale Young Papers, DC; Grant, *North over South*, 160–61.

7. *LDT*, 21 Apr. 1865.

8. Buckingham, *Life of Buckingham*, 431; Niven, *Connecticut for the Union*, 429–48; Croffut and Morris, *Connecticut during the War*, 799–830; Bowen, *Massachusetts in the War*, 82–83.

9. *Message of Buckingham*, 3 May 1865, 14–15.

10. *NYTi*, 2 Nov. 1877.

11. "Not Alarmed By His Yell: A Short Story Illustrating Lincoln's Unerring Judgment," *Michigan Farmer* (13 Feb. 1904):155.

12. Harris, "Blair," 174; Fennimore, "Blair," 49:365–69.

13. Chandler, *Memoir of Andrew*, 244–45; Buckingham, *Life of Buckingham*, 431–38.

14. Weeden, *War Government*, 378–79.

15. *NYTi*, 18 Apr. 1865.

16. *NYTi*, 19 Feb. 1888, 20 Aug. 1894, 25 Jan. 1911, 26 Sept. 1912, 12 Sept. 1915; *NYS*, 28 Aug. 1893; *NLT*, 17 Jun. 1882; Keller, *Affairs of State*, 50–196; Balogh, *A Government Out of Sight*, 277–307. On 25 September 1912, President William H. Taft paid tribute to the governors on the semicentennial observance of the Altoona Conference, 25 Sept. 1912. William Sprague, the last of the "War Governors," died 11 September 1915.

17. *NYTi*, 20 Aug. 1894, 25 Jan. 1911, 26 Sept. 1915.

Bibliography

Manuscripts
Abraham Lincoln Presidential Library, Springfield, Illinois
   William A. Allen
   Jacob Ammen
   Andrews Family
   Harry P. Andrews
   Alphonso Barto
   D. P. Bunn
   George Childress
   William H. Clark
   Coggeshall
   Crum Family
   David Davis
   James Drish
   Jesse K. Dubois
   Charles H. Floyd
   Ozias M. Hatch
   Hopeman
   John W. James
   William J. Kennedy
   Lease Family
   John McClernand
   Orlin Miner
   Mr. Morris
   Richard Oglesby
   Edwin Payne
   John Palmer
   Daniel R. Smith
   Leonard Swett
   F. W. Tupper
   Lyman Trumbull
   John Wilcox
   Richard Yates
   John Ziegler
Bancroft Library, University of California—Berkeley, Berkeley, California
   John G. Downey
   Stanford Leland
   Frederick Low
Bentley Historical Library, University of Michigan, Ann Arbor
   Franklin Bailey

Kinsley Scott Bingham
Austin Blair
William Boston
William Caldwell
William Calkins
William J. Carroll
Zachariah Chandler
Thomas Cooley
Salmon Crane
Henry Crapo
Ferry Collection
Charles Gorham
Morris Stuart Hall
George D. Hill
Rosanna Covey Hulbert
John B. Kay
Ezra Keeler
Frederick Lehman
John W. Longyear
Edwin J. March
Reuben McArthur
Henry G. Noble
Randall Packard
Charles Van Riper
Sligh Family
Luther S. Trowbridge
John Weissert
Wellington White
Marion Wittum

Boston Public Library, Boston, Massachusetts
- Anti-Slavery Collection
    - William Lloyd Garrison

Bowdoin College Library, George J. Mitchell Department of Special Collections & Archives, Brunswick, Maine
- Alumni Biographical Files, John Andrew
- John Andrew Scrapbook
- Oliver Otis Howard

Bucknell University Ellen Clarke Bertran Library, Special Collections, Lewisburg, Pennsylvania
- Slifer-Walls, online
- Edna M. Sheary Project, online

Buffalo and Erie County Historical Society, Buffalo, New York
- William Barry
- Almon Graham

California State Archives, Sacramento, California
- Governor's Office, Letter Books (John Downey, Leland Stanford, Frederick L. Low)

Chicago History Museum, Archives and Manuscripts Division, Chicago, Illinois
- William Weston Patton

    Logan Uriah Reavis
    Lyman Trumbull
Claremont Graduate School, Claremont, California
    Salmon P. Chase Papers (Microfilm Edition)
Connecticut Historical Society, Hartford Connecticut
    Timothy Allyn
    Henry Birge
    William Buckingham
    Civil War Correspondence
    Horace Fenn
    Loren Goodrich
    Joseph Hawley
    Hoadly Collection
    Alexander Holly
    James Howard
    Mark Howard
    Van Buren Kinney
    Alfred Loveland
    Miscellaneous Letters B
    John Norton
    Oliver Henry Perry
    A. P. Plant
    Willis Pomeroy
    George Ripley
    Griffin Stedman
    James Trumbull
    Gideon Welles
Connecticut State Archives and Library, Hartford, Connecticut
    Governor's Incoming Correspondence (William Buckingham)
    Governor's Outgoing Correspondence (William Buckingham)
Dartmouth College, Rauner Special Collections Library, Hanover, New Hampshire
    Ira Barton
    Calvin Burbank
    Joseph M. Clough
    Samuel A. Duncan
    Leander Harris
    David Leigh
    George Morgan
    Edward H. Rollins
    Vel Spencer
    John Wentworth
    Andrew Hale Young
Delaware Historical Society, Wilmington, Delaware
    John P. Gillis
Delaware Public Archives, Dover, Delaware
    Burton-Wooten
    Executive Correspondence (William Burton, William Cannon)
    John V. Harrington

Detroit Public Library, Burton Historical Collection, Detroit, Michigan
    Austin Blair
    E. W. Barber
Dickinson College Library, Archives and Special Collections Department, Carlisle, Pennsylvania
    Eli Slifer-Dill
The Filson Historical Society, Louisville, Kentucky
    Stephen Burbridge
    Henry BeeBee Carrington
    Johnson W. Culp
    John Fahnestock
    Robert Galbraith
    Jonathan Herrold
    Elias Kemper
    N. G. Markum
    Aetna Pettis
    Speed Family
    John Tilford
    Winn-Cook
    Richard Yates
Florida Atlantic University, The Marvin and Sybil Weiner, Spirit of America Collection, Boca Raton, Florida
    Andrew J. Clough
Historical Society of Iowa, Des Moines and Iowa City, Iowa
    Abraham Lincoln
    Governor's Correspondence (Samuel Kirkwood, William Stone)
Historical Society of Princeton
    Olden Family
The Houghton Library, Harvard University, Cambridge, Massachusetts
    Charles Sumner
The Huntington Library and Botanical Gardens, San Marino, California
    Henry G. Ankeny
    Obadiah Baker
    James A. Bates
    Alfred C. Brundage
    John B. Burrurd
    Leonard J. Caplinger
    William Carpenter
    Lewis H. Chamberlain
    Clemens L. Clendenen
    Corneilius Cole
    Joseph Collingwood
    Sheldon Colton
    Henry I. Coyler
    Jeptha Dillon
    Benjamin Dowell
    Delos Van Deusen
    R. Curtis Edgerton

Edmund English
James H. George
Gilmore Family
Hiram Farrand
James Forbes
Stiles Forsha
William F. Gable
Goff-Williams
Levi Grabill [Graybill]
Lemuel Hazzard
Holbrook
Joseph Holt
Daniel Horn
Nelson Huson
Thomas J. Kendall
Jonathan Labrant
Delos Lake
Ward Lamon
Abraham Lincoln
George Lowe
Theophilus Magaw
George McCall
James McClintock
George Mellish
James Nowland
George Patton
Samuel Roper
Edwin M. Stanton
Daniel Sylvester
Edward Townsend
Gideon Welles
Indiana Historical Society, Indianapolis, Indiana
  Conrad Baker
  William Blair
  Ezra Bowlus
  Helim Hatch Dunn
  William English
  Charles Eves
  James Frank Fee
  Calvin Fletcher
  Hugh D. Gallagher
  Alva C. Griest
  William R. Holloway
  John L. Ketchman
  Henry S. Lane
  Andrew J. McGarrah
  Willard Mendell
  Charles Gottlieb Michael

Estelle Morrow
Oliver P. Morton
James L. Orr
William A. Peele
Jacob and Julius Power
Robert J. Price
Thomas Prickett
Alfred Shields
Thomas Small
William Steele
Archibald Stimson
Henry Strong
William Stucky
James S. Thomas
Aurelius Voorhis
Lew Wallace
Williamson D. Ward
David A. Whiteborn
John A. Wilkins

Indiana State Library and State Archives, Indianapolis, Indiana
Flavius Bellamy
John Brayton
George Chittenden
Schyler Colfax
George S. Cottman
David P. Craig
Richard Lew Dawson
Lucius Embree
Allen Hamilton
John H. Holliday
William Holman
David Hutchinson
George Julian
Joanna Lane
William R. Lowes
Pierce-Krull
Oliver P. Morton
Godlove Orth
Albert G. Porter
Luther Short
Richard W. Thompson
James C. Vanderbilt
Charles Wetherhill
John T. Wilder
Anna W. Wright

Indiana University-Purdue University Indianapolis, Indianapolis, Indiana
Governor Morton Telegraph Books

Iowa State Archives, Des Moines and Iowa City, Iowa
    Governor's Letter Books (Samuel Kirkwood, William Stone)
    Adjutant General's Office, General Correspondence and Letter Books
    Governor's Correspondence (Samuel Kirkwood, William Stone)
Kansas City Public Library, Kansas City, Missouri
    Charles Robinson
Kansas State Archives, Topeka, Kansas
    Governor's Correspondence (Charles Robinson, Thomas Carney, Samuel Crawford)
    Adjutant General's Correspondence
Kansas State Historical Society, Topeka, Kansas
    Thomas Carney
    John J. Ingalls
    Charles and Sara T. Robinson
Kentucky Department of Libraries and Archives, Frankfort, Kentucky
    Governor's Papers, Executive Journals (James F. Robinson, Thomas Bramlette)
    Governor's Papers, Correspondence (James F. Robinson and Thomas Bramlette)
Kentucky Historical Society, Frankfort, Kentucky
    George W. Robinson
Library of Congress, Washington, D.C.
    Lucian Barbour
    Thomas Bayard
    Blair Family
    Simon Cameron
    Zachariah Chandler
    Salmon P. Chase
    Charles Dana
    Samuel P. Heintzelman
    Robert E. Jameson
    Joseph W. Keifer
    Lothrop Lewis
    Abraham Lincoln
    Beriah Magoffin
    George B. McClellan
    E. J. More
    William H. Newlin
    Joseph Schnell
    William T. Sherman
    Howard Malcolm Smith
    Edwin M. Stanton
    William R. Stimson
    Horatio Nelson Taft
    Lyman Trumbull
    James Wadsworth
    John Ward
    Israel Washburn
    Gideon Welles
    Frederick H. Wight

Maine State Archives, Augusta, Maine
   Governor's Correspondence (Israel Washburn, Abner Coburn, Samuel Cony)
   Washburn Family
Maryland Historical Society, Baltimore, Maryland
   Augustus Bradford
   George Cornwell
   James L. Dorsey
   Thomas Hicks
   Kirkwood Family
   Levin Richardson
   George Whitmarsh
Maryland State Archives, Baltimore, Maryland
   Governor's Letter Books, 1854–65 (Thomas Hicks, Augustus Bradford)
Massachusetts Historical Society, Boston Massachusetts
   John Andrew
   Richard Cary
   Norwood P. Hallowell
   Lee Family
   Ware Family
   Charles F. Winslow
   Horatio Woodman
Massachusetts State Archives, Boston, Massachusetts
   Massachusetts Governors, Executive Department
   Massachusetts Governors, Letters Official
Michigan State Archives, Lansing, Michigan
   Newton Ainslie
   Frank Button
   Cook Family
   Edwin F. Holmes
   Lyman Family
   James Lyman Diary
   Military Correspondence
   George Myers
   John L. Rolison
   Leonard Smith
Michigan State University Archives, Lansing, Michigan
   Samuel Abbott
   Arnold Family
   Israel Atkins
   Bagley Family
   Bamber Family
   Albert Barker
   James Brandish
   Campbell Family
   Charles Cathcart
   Chamberlain Family
   Horace Jewell
   Newton Kirk

    Lyman Family
    Irenus McGown
    John C. McLain
    Edwin R. Osband
    Earl Tooker
    Warden Family
Minnesota Historical Society/State Archives, St. Paul, Minnesota
    Governor's Papers (Alexander Ramsey, Henry Swift, Stephen Miller)
    Governor's Records, Executive Journals (Alexander Ramsey, Henry Swift, Stephen Miller)
    Governor's Records (Alexander Ramsey, Henry Swift, Stephen Miller)
    Lyman Warren Ayer
    George Adams
    John Reed Beatty
    Joseph Cortiz Dickey
    Jeremiah Donahower
    Ignatius Donnelly
    Reuben Farnum
    John Gillis
    Albion Otis Gross
    Philip Rice Hamlin
    Emil Munch
    James Ramsey
    Edmunch Rice
    Henry M. Rice
    Charles Shedd
    Newton Southworth and Family
    Henry A. Swift
    Charles W. Thompson
    Charles Watson
    Abraham E. Welch
Missouri Historical Society, St. Louis, Missouri
    Edward Bates Family
    Frank Blair
    Hagaman Family
    Hamilton Gamble
    Henry Halleck
    Osiah A. Moser
    Edwain H. White
New Hampshire Division of Records Management and Archives, Concord, New Hampshire
    Executive Correspondence
New Hampshire Historical Society, Tuck Library, Concord, New Hampshire
    John Andrew
    Nathaniel S. Berry
    William E. Chandler
    Joseph Gilmore
    Ichabod Goodwin
    Aaron F. Stevens
    George Towle

New Jersey Historical Society, Newark, New Jersey
   Albert Cheney
   Franklin Jones
   Daniel Larned
   Marcus Ward
   John C. Westerverlt
New York Historical Society, New York, New York
   Commission for the Harbor and Frontier Defense
   Charles Evans
   Gustavus Fox
   Preston King
   Miscellaneous, Theodore Tilton
   George A. Mitchell
   Edwin D. Morgan
   James B. Nelson
   J.H. Purdy
   Horatio Seymour
   War Letters, 1861–1965
   Henry Wise
New York State Library, Albany, New York
   Edwin Morgan
Ohio Historical Society, Columbus, Ohio
   Adjutant General's Office, Correspondence (online)
   Adjutant General's Office, Selected Governor's Papers (William Dennison,
      David Tod, John Brough)
   Adjutant General's Office, Telegraphic Dispatches to Governors
   Adjutant General's Office, Telegraphic Dispatches from Commander-in-Chief
   John T. Booth
   William Dennison's Letterbook
   Hugh B. Ewing
   Governor's Correspondence (online) (William Dennison, David Tod,
      John Brough)
   John Russell
   Thomas Thomson Taylor
   John A. Trimble
   George B. Turner
   John C. Williamson
Ohio State Archives, Columbus, Ohio
   Telegraphic Dispatches, Series 144, 145
Oregon Historical Society, Eugene, Oregon
   John Whiteaker
   Addison Crandall Gibbs
Pennsylvania State Archives, Harrisburg, Pennsylvania
   Executive Correspondence, 1861–65 (Andrew Curtin)
   Andrew Curtin Letter Books, 1861–65
Rhode Island State Archives, Providence, Rhode Island
   Governor's Records, Incoming Letters Received, 1861–65 (William Sprague,
      William Cozzens, James Smith)

Governor's Records, Letters Sent, 1861–65 (William Sprague, William Cozzens,
    James Smith)
Rutgers University Libraries, Special Collections and University Archives,
    New Brunswick, New Jersey
  New Jersey Letters
  Rodman M. Price
State Historical Society of Iowa, Iowa City
  Military Letter Books, Samuel J. Kirkwood
  Samuel J. Kirkwood
State Historical Society of Wisconsin, Madison, Wisconsin
  Wisconsin Executive Department, Military Correspondence (Alexander Randall,
    Louis Harvey, Edward Salomon, James Lewis)
  Wisconsin Governor's General Correspondence, Letter Books (Alexander Randall,
    Louis Harvey, Edward Salomon, James Lewis)
  Joseph Bailey
  Van S. Bennett
  Edwin Brown
  Allen Church
  Henry Clemons
  Alva Cleveland
  Amasa Cobb
  Henry T. Drake
  Fairchild Family
  James Fowler
  John Gibbons
  Timothy Howe
  James T. Lewis
  William De Loss Love
  Samuel Nasmith
  Josiah Noonan
  James M. Perry
  Matthew R. Perry
  Oscar F. Pinney
  Alexander Randall
  Israel Roberts
  Edward Salomon
  George T. Spaulding
  Horace Tenney
  Henry T. Young
Syracuse University Bird Library, Special Collections Research Center,
    Syracuse, New York
  Albert M. Cook
  John Dix
  Hervey L. Howe
  Charles Sedgwick
United States Army Military History Institute, Carlisle Barracks, Pennsylvania
  Civil War Miscellaneous
    Dayton E. Flint

    Civil War Times Illustrated
        Davis Family
    Schoff Civil War
        Alpin Family
        John Pierson
    United States National Archives and Records Administration, Washington, D.C.
        Record Group 107, Records of the Secretary of War, Letters Received
        Record Group 107, Records of the Secretary of War, Letters Received, "Irregular Series"
        Record Group 107, Records of the Secretary of War, Letters Sent
University of Delaware Library, Special Collections, Newark, Delaware
    Townsend Family and Waples Family
University of Kansas, Kansas Collections, Lawrence, Kansas
    Kansas Collection
        Thomas Carney
University of Maine, Raymond H. Fogler Library, Orono, Maine
    Hannibal Hamlin
University of Maryland, Hornbake Library, Special Collections, College Park, Maryland
    Maryland Manuscripts
University of Oregon Library, Special Collections, Eugene, Oregon
    Oliver C. Applegate
    John Whiteaker
University of Rochester Library, Rochester, New York
    William Seward
University of Vermont, Special Collections, Vermont
    Charles Dubois Memoir, transcribed and edited by Michael N. Stanton
University of Virginia, Albert and Shirley Small Special Collections Library, Charlottesville, Virginia
    Hutchinson Family
Vermont Historical Society, Barre, Vermont
    Peter Abbott
    Avery B. Cain
    Erastus Fairbanks
    Hammond Family
    Letter to *Burlington Free Press*
    Roswell Holbrook
    Thomas P. Murphy
    Redfield Proctor
    Joseph Spafford
    Irvin W. Spooner
Vermont State Archives, Montpelier, Vermont
    Erastus Fairbanks
Virginia State Archives and Libraries, Richmond, Virginia
    Virginia Governor's Executive Letter Books
West Virginia Division of Culture and History, Archives and History, Charleston, West Virginia
    Pierpont-Samuels

Western Reserve Historical Society, Cleveland, Ohio
  George Barmann
  William B. Britton
  John Brough
  William Buckingham
  Conscription in New Hampshire
  William P. Fessenden
  Albert G. Hart
  Benjamin T. Jones
  James McMahon
  Francis Pierpont
  Benjamin T. Sells
  James Y. Smith
  Alexander Varian
  George Washburn
  E. G. Wood
  George Wright
William L. Clements Library, University of Michigan, Ann Arbor, Michigan
  John Corliss
  William Curry
  John Hunt
  John Schroeder
  James Alexander Sprowl

Government Documents

Acts of the Legislature of the State of Michigan, 1861–65.
Annual Message of Governor Ramsey to the Legislature of Minnesota, January 7, 1863.
Annual Message of the Governor of the State of New York to the Legislature, January 3, 1865.
Annual Message of Leland Stanford: Governor of the State of California, at the Fourteenth Session of the Legislature, January, 1863.
Annual Report of the Adjutant General of the Commonwealth of Massachusetts, 1861–65.
Annual Report of the Adjutant General of the Commonwealth of Pennsylvania, 1861–65.
Annual Report of the Adjutant General of the State of Connecticut, 1861–65.
Annual Report of the Adjutant General of the State of New Jersey, 1861–65.
Annual Report of the Adjutant General of the State of New York, 1861–65.
Annual Report of Adjutant General of the State of Wisconsin, 1860–64.
Annual Report of the Secretary of War, 1861–65.
Arts and Resolves, Special Session of the Rhode Island Legislature, April 1861.
Avery, Grace G., and Floyd C. Shoemaker, eds. *The Messages and Proclamations of the Governors of the State of Missouri.* 20 vols. Columbia: State Historical Society of Missouri, 1924.
Communication from His Excellency James Y. Smith to the General Assembly, January 9, 1865.
Congressional Globe. Speech in House of Representatives, May 10, 1854, 33rd Congress, 1st Session, appendix, 714–15.
Fuller, George N. *Messages of the Governors of Michigan.* 4 vols. Lansing: Michigan Historical Commission, 1926.

636 Bibliography

General Assembly of the Commonwealth of Kentucky, House and Senate Journals, 1861–65.
House Journal of the Legislative Assembly of the State of Kansas, 1861–65.
Illinois Senate Journal, 1861–65.
Inaugural Address of Frederick Low, 1863.
Inaugural Address Delivered to the Ninth General Assembly of the State of Iowa by Governor Samuel J. Kirkwood, January 15, 1862.
Inaugural Address of Richard Yates, Governor of Illinois to the General Assembly, January 14, 1861.
Journal of the Assembly of California, 1861–65.
Journal of the Constitutional Convention of the State of Illinois, January 7, 1862.
Journal of the House of the State of Delaware, 1861–65.
Journal of the House of the State of Indiana, 1861–65.
Journal of the House of the State of Michigan, 1861–65.
Journal of the House of the State of Vermont, 1861–65.
Journal of Minnesota House and Senate, 1861–65.
Journal of the Proceedings of the House of New Hampshire, 1861–65.
Journal of the Proceedings of the House of the Legislative Assembly of Oregon, 1861–65.
Journal of the Proceedings of the Senate of New Hampshire, 1861–65.
Journal of the Proceedings of the Senate of the Legislative Assembly of Oregon, 1861–65.
Journal of the Senate of California, 1861–65.
Journal of the Senate of the Commonwealth of Pennsylvania, 1861–65.
Journal of the Senate of the State of Connecticut, 1861–65.
Journal of the Senate of the State of Delaware, 1861–65.
Journal of the Senate of the State of Indiana, 1861–65.
Journal of the Senate of the State of Michigan, 1861–65.
Journal of the Missouri State Convention, July 1861.
Journal of the Senate of the State of Vermont, 1861–65.
Kansas Senate Journal, 1861–1865.
Lincoln, Charles Z., ed. *State of New York: Messages of the Governors*. Albany, N.Y.: J. B. Lyon Co., 1909.
Maryland House Journal, 1861–65.
Maryland Senate Journal, 1861–65.
Message of His Excellency, William A. Buckingham Governor of Connecticut, to the Legislature of the State, May 1, 1861.
Message of His Excellency, William A. Buckingham Governor of Connecticut, to the Legislature of the State, May 7, 1862.
Message of His Excellency, William A. Buckingham Governor of Connecticut, to the Legislature of the State, December 9, 1862.
Message of His Excellency, William A. Buckingham Governor of Connecticut, to the Legislature of the State, May 6, 1863.
Message of His Excellency, William A. Buckingham Governor of Connecticut, to the Legislature of the State, May 3, 1865.
Message of James Y. Smith, Governor of Rhode Island to the General Assembly, January 9, 1865.
Message of Richard Yates to the Illinois General Assembly, January 2, 1865.
Michigan House Journal, 1861–65.
Michigan Senate Journal, 1861–65.
Michigan House and Senate Bills, 1861–65.
Minnesota Executive Documents, 1861–65.

Minnesota House Journal, 1861–65.
Minnesota Senate Journal, 1861–65.
Moore, Frank, ed. *Rebellion Record: A Diary of American Events with Documents, Narratives, Illustrations, Incidents, Poetry.* 12 vols. New York: G. P. Putnam's, 1861–68.
New Jersey General Assembly General, 1861–65.
New Jersey War Documents, 1861–65.
Ohio Executive Documents, 1861–65.
Ohio House Journal, 1861–65.
Proceedings in the Cases of the Impeachment of Charles Robinson, Governor, John W. Robinson, Sec'y of State, George S. Hillyer, Auditor of the State of Kansas. Topeka: J.F. Cummings, 1862.
Report of the Adjutant & Inspector General of the State of Vermont, 1861–65.
Report of the Adjutant General of the State of Illinois, 1861–65.
Report of the Adjutant General of the State of Indiana, 1869.
Report of the Adjutant General of the State of Kansas, 1861–65.
Report of the Adjutant General of the State of Maine, 1861–65.
Report of the Adjutant General of the State of New Hampshire, 1861–65.
Reports Made to the General Assembly of the State of Illinois, 1861–65.
Rhode Island General Assembly, 1861–65.
Second Annual Message of Joel Parker, January 11, 1865.
Second Annual Message of Leland Stanford: Governor of the State of California, at the Fifteenth Session of the Legislature, 1863.
Senate Journal of the Legislative Assembly of the State of Kansas, 1861–65.
Shambaugh, Benjamin F., ed. *The Messages and Proclamations of the Governors of Iowa.* 8 vols. Iowa City: State Historical Society of Iowa, 1903.
Speeches and Governor's Messages, 1851–1872.
Thwaites, Reuben G., ed. *Civil War Messages and Proclamations of Wisconsin War Governors.* Madison: Wisconsin History Commission, 1912.
U.S. War Department. *War of Rebellion: A Compilation of the Official Records of the Union and Confederate Armies.* 128 vols. Washington, D.C.: Government Printing Office, 1880–1901.
U.S. Navy Department. *Official Records of the Union and Confederate Navies in the War of the Rebellion.* 30 vols. Washington, D.C.: Government Printing Office, 1894–1927.
Washington Congressional Globe Office, 1851–1872.
West Virginia House Journal, 1861–65.
West Virginia Senate Journal, 1861–65.
Wisconsin Senate Journal, 1861–65.
Wisconsin Assembly Journal, 1861–65.

Newspapers

Albany Argus (New York)
Albany Evening Journal (New York)
American Standard (Jersey City)
The Atlantic Monthly (Boston)
Baltimore American
Baltimore Clipper
Baltimore Daily Gazette
Baltimore Sun
Bangor Daily Whig and Courier (Maine)
Boston Daily Advertiser
Boston Daily Journal
Boston Post
The Broad Axe (St. Paul, Minnesota)
Burlington Daily Free Press (Vermont)

Burlington Daily Hawk-eye (Iowa)
Burlington Weekly Hawk-eye (Iowa)
Central Press (Bellefonte, Pennsylvania)
Chicago Times
Chicago Tribune
Christian Advocate (New York)
Cincinnati Commercial
Cincinnati Daily Enquirer
Cincinnati Daily Gazette
Daily Ohio Statesman (Columbus)
Daily Patriot and Union (Harrisburg, Pennsylvania)
Delawarean (Dover)
Delaware Republican (Wilmington)
Democratic Gazette (Wilmington)
Detroit Daily Advertiser
Detroit Free Press
Emporia News (Kansas)
Evening Telegraph (Harrisburg, PA)
Farmer's Cabinet (Amherst, NH)
Frankfort Commonwealth (Kentucky)
Frank Leslie's Illustrated Magazine (New York, N.Y.)
Harper's Weekly (New York, N.Y.)
Hartford Courant
Hartford Daily Times
Hartford Evening Press
Illinois State Journal (Springfield)
Illinois State Register (Springfield)
Iowa Daily State Register (Des Moines)
Indianapolis Daily Journal
Indianapolis Daily State Sentinel
Kennebec Journal (Maine)
Lancaster Intelligencer (Pennsylvania)
Lawrence Republican (Kansas)
Leavenworth Daily Conservative (Kansas)
Leavenworth Daily Times (Kansas)
Liberator (Boston)
Los Angeles Star
Louisville Daily Journal
Maine Farmer (Augusta)
Milwaukee Sentinel
National Tribune (Washington, D.C.)
New Albany Daily Ledger (Indiana)
Newark Daily Mercury (New Jersey)
New Hampshire Patriot and State Gazette (Concord)
New-Hampshire Statesman (Concord)
New Haven Palladium (Connecticut)
New London Telegram (Connecticut)
New York Evangelist
New York Herald
New York Independent
New York Journal of Commerce
New York Observer and Chronicle
New York Sun
New York Times
New York Tribune
New York World
North American (Philadelphia)
Ohio Daily Statesman
Ohio State Journal (Columbus)
Oregon Argus (Oregon City)
Oregonian (Portland)
Oregon Sentinel (Jacksonville)
Oregon Statesman (Oregon City)
Philadelphia Inquirer
Portland Daily Times (Oregon)
Providence Daily Journal (Rhode Island)
Sacramento Daily Union
San Francisco Daily Alta California
San Francisco Daily Evening Bulletin
Saturday Evening Post (Philadelphia)
State Republican (Eugene, Oregon)
St. Albans Messenger (Vermont)
St. Cloud Democrat (Minnesota)
St. Louis Daily Missouri Republican
St. Louis Missouri Democrat
St. Paul Daily Globe (Minnesota)
St. Paul Daily Pioneer (Minnesota)
St. Paul Daily Press (Minnesota)
Topeka Tribune
Trenton Daily State Gazette and Republican
Trenton Daily True American
Vermont Watchman and State Journal (Montpelier, Vermont)
Washington Daily National Intelligencer (Washington, D.C.)
Washington Evening Star (Washington, D.C.)
Weekly Wisconsin Patriot (Madison)
Wellsburg Herald (West Virginia)
Wheeling Daily Intelligencer (West Virginia)
Wisconsin State Journal (Madison)

Published Sources

A Memorial. Nathaniel Springer Berry of Bristol, New Hampshire. Printed for Private Distribution, 1900.

Abbott, Richard H. *Cobbler in Congress: The Life of Henry Wilson, 1812–1875.* Lexington: University Press of Kentucky, 1972.

———. *Cotton and Capital: Boston Businessmen and Anti-slavery Reform, 1854–1868.* Amherst: University of Massachusetts Press, 1991.

———. "Massachusetts and the Recruitment of Southern Negroes, 1863–1865." *Civil War History* 14 (September 1968): 197–210.

———. *Ohio's War Governors.* Columbus: Ohio State University Press, 1962.

Abbott, Stephen G. *The First Regiment New Hampshire Volunteers in the Great Rebellion.* Keene, Me.: Sentinel Printing Co., 1890.

Abzug, Robert. "The Copperheads: Historical Approaches to Civil War Dissent in the Midwest." *Indiana Magazine of History* 66 (March 1970): 40–55.

Adams, Charles Francis Jr. *Charles Francis Adams, 1835–1915: An Autobiography.* Boston: Houghton Mifflin, 1916.

Adams, David M. "Illinois Soldiers and the Emancipation Proclamation." *Journal of the Illinois State Historical Society* 67 (September 1974): 406–21.

Adams, George Rollie. *General William S. Harney: Prince of Dragoons.* Lincoln: University of Nebraska Press, 2001.

Adams, Virginia M. *On the Altar of Freedom: A Black Soldier's Civil War Letters from the Front.* Amherst: University of Massachusetts Press, 1991.

Albrecht, Robert C. "The Theological Response of the Transcendentalists to the Civil War." *New England Quarterly* 38 (March 1965): 21–34.

Albright, Rebecca G. "The Civil War Career of Andrew Gregg Curtin Governor of Pennsylvania." *Western Pennsylvania Historical Magazine* 47 (October 1964): 323–42.

———. "The Civil War Career of Andrew Gregg Curtin Governor of Pennsylvania." *Western Pennsylvania Historical Magazine* 48 (January 1965): 19–42.

———. "The Civil War Career of Andrew Gregg Curtin Governor of Pennsylvania." *Western Pennsylvania Historical Magazine* 48 (April 1965): 151–74.

Alexander, De Alva Stanwood. *A Political History of the State of New York.* 4 vols. New York: Henry Holt and Co., 1909.

Allison, Hildreth A. "New Hampshire's Contribution to Berdan's Volunteer Sharpshooters." *Historical New Hampshire* 38 (Summer/Fall): 174–83.

Allison, Young E. "Sue Mundy: An Account of the Terrible Kentucky Guerrilla of Civil War Times." *Register of the Kentucky Historical Society* 57 (October 1959): 295–316.

Amar, Akhil Reed. "The David C. Baum Lecture: Abraham Lincoln and the American Union." *University of Illinois Law Review* (2001): 1109–33.

Ambler, Charles H. "The Formation of West Virginia: Debates and Proceedings." *West Virginia History* 2 (April 1941): 171–79.

———. *Francis H. Pierpont Union War Governor of Virginia and Father of West Virginia.* Chapel Hill: University of North Carolina Press, 1937.

Ambrose, Daniel Leib. *From Shiloh to Savannah: The Seventh Illinois Infantry in the Civil War.* Introduction and notes by Dan Sutherland. DeKalb: Northern Illinois University Press, 2002.

Anders, Leslie, ed. "Civil Warfare in North Missouri: The Letters of Alexander C. Walker." *Missouri Historical Review* 95 (April 2001): 264–86.

Anderson, J. L. "The Vacant Chair on the Farm: Soldiers, Husbands, Farm Wives, and the Iowa Home Front, 1861–1865." *The Annuals of Iowa* 66 (Summer/Fall 2007): 241–92.

Anderson, Mary Ann, ed. *The Civil War Diary of Allen Morgan Geer*. Bloomington, Ill.: McClean Count Historical Society, 1977.

Andrew, John A. *An Address Delivered before the New England Agricultural Society on Hampden Park, Springfield, Massachusetts, September 9, 1864*. Boston: Wright and Potter, 1864.

———. *Correspondence between Gov. Andrew and Maj. Gen. Butler*. Boston: J. J. Dyer, 1862.

Andrews, J. Cutler. "The Pennsylvania Press during the Civil War." *Pennsylvania History* 9 (January 1942): 22–36.

Andrews, Matthew Page. *History of Maryland: Province and State*. Garden City, N.J.: Doubleday, 1929.

Angevine, Robert G. *The Railroad and the State: War, Politics, and Technology in Nineteenth-Century America*. Stanford, Calif.: Stanford University Press, 2004.

"April 1861: Minnesota Goes to War." *Publications of the Minnesota Historical Society* 37 (March 1961): 212–13.

Armstrong, William B. *For Courageous Fighting and Confident Dying: Union Chaplains in the Civil War*. Lawrence: University Press of Kansas, 1998.

Arnold, Issac. *The Life of Abraham Lincoln*. Chicago: Jansen, McClung and Co., 1885. Reprint, University of Nebraska Press, 1994.

Ascher, Leonard. "Lincoln's Administration and the New Almaden Mine Scandal." *Pacific Historical Review* 5 (March 1936): 38–51.

Astles, John B. "Reverend W. A. Scott, 'A Southern Sympathizer.'" *California Historical Society Quarterly* 27 (June 1948): 149–56.

Astor, Aaron. *Rebels on the Border: Civil War, Emancipation, and the Reconstruction of Kentucky and Missouri*. Baton Rouge: Louisiana State University Press, 2012.

Ayer, I. Winslow. *The Great North-Western Conspiracy in All Its Startling Details*. Chicago: Rounds & James, Book and Job Printers, 1865.

Babcock, Willoughby M. "Minnesota's Frontier: A Neglected Sector of the Civil War." *Minnesota History* 38 (June 1963): 274–86.

Bahde, Thomas. "'Our Cause Is a Common One': Home Guards, Union Leagues, and Republican Citizenship in Illinois, 1861–1863." *Civil War History* 56 (March 2010): 66–78.

Bailes, Clarice L. "Jacob Dolson Cox in West Virginia." *West Virginia History* 6 (October 1944): 5–58.

Bailey, Louis J. "Caleb Blood Smith." *Indiana Magazine of History* 29 (1933): 213–39.

Baker, James H. *Lives of the Governors of Minnesota*. Vol. 13. St. Paul: Minnesota Historical Society, 1908.

Baker, Jean H. *The Politics of Continuity: Maryland Political Parties from 1858 to 1870*. Baltimore: Johns Hopkins University Press, 1973.

The Ballad of the Abolition Blunder-buss. Boston: n.p., 1861.

Ballard, Michael B. *Vicksburg: The Campaign That Opened the Mississippi*. Chapel Hill: University of North Carolina Press, 2004.

Balogh, Brian. *A Government Out of Sight: The Mystery of National Authority in Nineteenth-Century America*. Cambridge: Cambridge University Press, 2009.

Bancroft, Hubert Howe. *History of the Pacific States of North America.* Vol. 2. San Francisco: A. L. Bancroft and Co., 1882.

Baringer, William E. *A House Dividing: Lincoln as President Elect.* Springfield, Ill.: Abraham Lincoln Association, 1945.

Barnes, James J., and Patience P. Barnes. *The American Civil War through British Eyes: Dispatches from British Diplomats.* Kent, Ohio: Kent State University Press, 2003.

Barney, William L. *The Passage of the Republic: An Interdisciplinary History of Nineteenth-Century America.* Lexington, Mass.: D. C. Heath, 1987.

Barrett, Eugene A. "The Civil War Service of John F. Hartranft." *Pennsylvania History* 32 (April 1965): 166–86.

Barrett, Faith, and Cristanne Miller, eds. *"Words for the Hour:" A New Anthology of American Civil War Poetry.* Boston: University of Massachusetts Press, 2005.

Barrows, Chester L. *William M. Evarts: Lawyer, Diplomat, Statesman.* Chapel Hill: University of North Carolina Press, 1941.

Barth, Gunter, ed. *All Quiet on the Yanhill: The Civil War in Oregon.* Eugene: University of Oregon Books, 1959.

Basler, Roy P., ed. *The Collected Works of Abraham Lincoln.* 8 vols. New Brunswick, N.J.: Rutgers University Press, 1953.

———. *Short History of the American Civil War.* New York: Basic Books, 1967.

Bates, David H. *Lincoln in the Telegraph Office: Recollections of the United States Military Telegraph Corps during the Civil War.* Introduction by James A. Rawley. Lincoln: University of Nebraska Press, 1995.

Beale, Howard K., ed. *The Diary of Edward Bates 1859–1866.* Washington, D.C.: Government Printing Office, 1933.

———, ed. *The Diary of Gideon Welles, Secretary of the Navy under Lincoln and Johnson.* 3 vols. New York: W. W. Norton, 1960.

Beatie, Russel H. *Army of the Potomac.* Vol. 1: Birth of Command, November 1860–September 1861. Cambridge, Mass.: Da Capo Press, 2002.

———. *Army of the Potomac.* Vol. 2: McClellan Takes Command, September 1861–February 1862. Cambridge, Mass.: Da Capo Press, 2004.

Becker, Carl M. "Newspapers in Battle: The Dayton *Empire* and the Dayton *Journal* during the Civil War." *Ohio History* 99 (Winter 1990): 29–50.

———. "Picture of a Young Copperhead." *Ohio History* 71 (January 1962): 3–23.

Becker, Robert H. *Some Reflections of an Early California Governor Contained in a Short Dictated Memoir by Frederick F. Low, Ninth Governor of California, and Notes from an Interview Between Governor Low and Hubert Howe Bancroft in 1883.* Sacramento, Calif.: Sacramento Book Collectors, 1959.

Beitzinger, A. J. "The Father of Copperheadism in Wisconsin." *Wisconsin Magazine of History* 39 (Autumn 1955): 17–29.

Belknap, William W. *History of the Fifteenth Iowa Volunteers.* Keokuk: R. B. Ogeden and Son, 1887.

Belz, Herman. *Abraham Lincoln, Constitutionalism, and Equal Rights in the Civil War Era.* New York: Fordham University Press, 1998.

———. "Henry Winter Davis and the Origins of Congressional Reconstruction." *Maryland Historical Magazine* 67 (Summer 1972): 129–43.

———. *Reconstructing the Union: Theory and Policy during the Civil War.* Ithaca, N.Y.: Cornell University Press, 1969.

Bendler, Bruce. "'The Old Democrat Principles': Samuel Townsend and the Delaware Democratic Party, 1836–1881." *Delaware History* (Spring/Summer 2010): 23–47.
Benedict, Bryce. *Jayhawkers: The Civil War Brigade of James Henry Lane*. Norman: University of Oklahoma Press, 2009.
Benedict, George G. *Vermont in the Civil War: A History of the Part Taken by the Vermont Soldiers and Sailors in the War for the Union, 1861–1865*. 2 vols. Burlington, Vt.: Free Press Association, 1886.
Benedict, Michael Les. "Abraham Lincoln and Federalism." *Journal of the Abraham Lincoln Association* 10 (January 1988): 1–45.
Bennett, Pamela, ed. "Curtis R. Burke's Civil War Journal." *Indiana Magazine of History* 65 (December 1969): 283–327.
———, ed. "Curtis R. Burke's Civil War Journal." *Indiana Magazine of History* 66 (June 1970): 111–72.
Bensel, Richard F. *Yankee Leviathan: The Origins of Central State Authority, 1859–1877*. London: Cambridge University Press, 1990.
Bentley, James R., ed. "The Civil War Memoirs of Captain Thomas Speed." *Filson Club History Quarterly* 44 (July 1970): 235–72.
Benton, Josiah Henry. *Voting in the Field: A Forgotten Chapter of the Civil War*. Boston: Privately Printed, 1915.
Berg, Scott. *38 Nooses: Lincoln, Little Crow, and the Beginning of the Frontier's End*. New York: Pantheon Books, 2012.
Berlin, Ira, et al., *The Destruction of Slavery*. New York: Cambridge University Press, 1985.
Berlin, Ira, Steven Hahn, and René Hayden, eds. *Freedom: A Documentary History of Emancipation, 1861–1867*. 2 vols. New York: Cambridge University Press, 1982.
Berlin, Ira, Joseph Reidy, and Leslie Rowland, eds. *Freedom's Soldiers: The Black Military Experience of the Civil War*. New York: Cambridge University Press, 1998.
Bernstein, Iver. *The New York City Draft Riots: Their Significance for American Society and Politics in the Age of the Civil War*. New York: Oxford University Press, 1990.
Bertera, Martin N., and Kim Crawford. *The 4th Michigan Infantry in the Civil War*. East Lansing: Michigan State University Press, 2010.
Bevan, Wilson Lloyd, ed. *History of Delaware: Past and Present*. 4 vols. New York: Lewis Historical Publishing Company, 1929.
Bicknell, Thomas W. *The History of the State of Rhode Island and Providence Plantations*. 6 vols. New York: The American Historical Society, Inc., 1920.
Bigelow, John, ed. *Letters and Literary Memorials of Samuel J. Tilden*. 2 vols. New York: Harper & Brothers Publishers, 1908.
———. *Retrospections of an Active Life*. 3 vols. New York: Baker and Taylor Co., 1909.
———. *The Life of Samuel J. Tilden*. 2 vols. New York: Harper & Brothers Publishers, 1895.
Bigelow, Martha M. "The Political Service of William Alanson Howard." *Michigan History Magazine* 42 (March 1958): 1–25.
Bilby, Joseph. *Remember You Are New Jerseymen!: A Military History of New Jersey's Troops in the Civil War*. Hightstown, N.J.: Longstreet House, 1998.
Bird, Margaret M., and Daniel W. Crofts. "Soldier Voting in 1864: The David McKelvy Diary." *Pennsylvania Magazine of History and Biography* 115 (July 1991): 371–414.
Black, Wilfred W., ed. "Civil War Letters of George M. Wise." *Ohio Historical Quarterly* 65 (January 1956): 53–81.
———. "Orson Brainard: A Soldier in the Ranks." *Ohio History* 76 (Spring 1967): 54–72.

Blackburn, George M., ed. "The Negro as Viewed By a Michigan Civil War Soldier." *Michigan History Magazine* 47 (March 1963): 75–84.

Blackmar, Frank W., ed. *Kansas: A Cyclopedia of State History, Embracing Events, Institutions, Industries, Counties, Cities, Towns, Prominent Persons, etc.* 2 vols. Chicago: Standard Publishing Company, 1912.

———. *The Life of Charles Robinson: The First State Governors of Kansas.* Reprint, Freeport, N.Y.: Books for Libraries Press, 1971. First published in 1902 by Crane and Company Printers.

Blaine, James G. *Twenty Years of Congress: From Lincoln to Garfield.* 2 vols. Norwich, Conn.: Henry Bill Publishing, 1886.

Blair, William Alan. "'A Source of Amusement': Pennsylvania versus Lee, 1863." *The Pennsylvania Magazine of History and Biography* 115 (July 1991): 319–38.

———. *With Malice toward Some: Treason and Loyalty in the Civil War Era.* Chapel Hill: University of North Carolina Press, 2014.

Blassingame, John W. "The Recruitment of Negro Troops in Maryland." *Maryland Historical Magazine* 58 (March 1963): 20–29.

———. "The Recruitment of Negro Troops in Missouri During the Civil War." *Missouri Historical Review* 58 (April 1964): 326–37.

Bloom, Robert L. "'We Never Expected Battle': The Civilians at Gettysburg, 1863." *Pennsylvania History* 55 (October 1988): 161–200.

Blue, Frederick J. "Friends of Freedom: Lincoln, Chase, and Wartime Racial Policy." *Ohio History* 102 (Summer 1993): 85–97.

Blunt, James G. "General Blunt's Account of His Civil War Experience." *Kansas Historical Quarterly* 1 (May 1932): 211–65.

Bogardus, Frank S. "Daniel W. Voorhees." *Indiana Magazine of History* 27 (1931): 91–103.

Bohn, Roger E. "Richard Yates: An Appraisal of his Value as the Civil War Governor of Illinois." *Journal of the Illinois State Historical Society* 104 (Spring/Summer 2011): 17–37.

Bohrnstedt, Jennifer C., ed. *While Father Is Away: The Civil War Letters of William H. Bradbury.* Lexington: University Press of Kentucky, 2003.

Boman, Dennis K. *Lincoln and Citizens' Rights in Civil War Missouri: Balancing Freedom and Security.* Baton Rouge: Louisiana State University Press, 2010.

———. *Lincoln's Resolute Unionist: Hamilton Gamble, Dred Scott Dissenter and Missouri's Civil War Governor.* Baton Rouge: Louisiana State University Press, 2006.

Bony, F. N. "Turn About and Fair Play: A Connecticut General Befriends a Confederate Governor." *Connecticut Historical Society Bulletin* 31 (April 1966): 33–39.

Boone, Nancy, and Michael Sherman. "Designed to Cure: Civil War Hospitals in Vermont." *Vermont History* 69 (Winter/Spring 2001): 171–200.

Borchard, Gregory A. *Abraham Lincoln and Horace Greeley.* Carbondale: Southern Illinois University Press, 2011.

Boritt, Gabor. *The Gettysburg Gospel: The Lincoln Speech That Nobody Knows.* New York: Simon & Schuster, 2006.

Bosbyshell, Oliver C. *The Forty-eighth in the War.* Philadelphia: Anvil Publishing Co., 1895.

Boutwell, George S. *Reminiscences of Sixty Years in Public Affairs.* 2 vols. New York: McClure, Phillips and Co., 1902.

Bowden, Murray. "The Problem of Conscription in Maine during the Civil War." M.A. thesis, University of Maine, 1943.

Bowen, James L. *History of the 37th Regiment Massachusetts Volunteers in the Civil War of 1861–1865*. Holyoke, Mass.: Clark W. Bryan & Company, Publishers, 1884.

———. *Massachusetts in the War, 1861–1865*. 2 vols. Springfield, Mass.: Clark W. and Bryan and Co., 1889.

Bowman, Shearer Davis. *At the Precipice: Americans North and South during the Secession Crisis*. Chapel Hill: University of North Carolina Press, 2010.

Braden, Gayle A. "The Public Career of Edward Dickinson Baker." Ph.D. diss., Vanderbilt University, 1960.

Bradley, Erwin Stanley. *Simon Cameron, Lincoln's Secretary of War, A Political Biography*. Philadelphia: University of Pennsylvania Press, 1966.

Brandt, Nat, ed. *Mr. Tubbs' Civil War*. Syracuse, N.Y.: Syracuse University Press, 1996.

Briggs, John E. "The Enlistment of Iowa Troops during the Civil War." *Iowa Journal of History and Politics* 15 (July 1917): 323–92.

Brigham, Loriman S., ed. "The Civil War Journal of William B. Fletcher." *Indiana Magazine of History* 57 (March 1961): 43–76.

Bright, Charles, and Susan Harding. *Statemaking and Social Movements*. Ann Arbor: University of Michigan Press, 1984.

Brinks, Herbert. "The Effect of the Civil War in 1861 on Michigan Lumbering and Mining Industries." *Michigan History Magazine* 44 (March 1960): 101–7.

Brooks, Clayton M., ed. *A Legacy of Leadership: Governors and American History*. Philadelphia: University of Pennsylvania Press, 2008.

Brooks, Noah. "Lincoln's Reelection: The Beginning of Lincoln's Second Term–The President's Shrewdness at Hampton's Roads–Lincoln's Second Inauguration." *Century Illustrated Magazine* 49 (April 1965): 865–72.

———. *Washington in Lincoln's Times: A Memoir of the Civil War Era by the Newspaperman Who Knew Lincoln Best*. New York: The Century Co., 1895.

Brown, D. Alexander. *Grierson's Raid*. Urbana: University of Illinois Press, 1954.

Brown, Genevieve G. "A History of the Sixth Regiment West Virginia Infantry Volunteers." *West Virginia History* 9 (July 1948): 315–68.

Browne, Albert G. *Sketch of the Official Life of John A. Andrew as Governor of Massachusetts*. New York: Hurd and Houghton, 1868.

Browne, Robert H. *Abraham Lincoln and the Men of His Times*. 2 vols. Chicago: Blakely-Oswald, 1907.

Brummer, Sidney David. *Political History of New York State during the Period of the Civil War*. New York: Columbia University and Longman's Green and Agents, 1911.

Bryan, George B. "The Public Platform and Patriotism in Vermont during the Civil War." *Vermont History* 51 (Spring 1983): 107–16.

Buchholz, Heinrich E. *Governors of Maryland from the Revolution to the Year 1908*. Baltimore: Williams and Wilkens, 1908.

Buck, Stephen J. "'A contest in which blood must flow like water': DuPage County and the Civil War." *Illinois Historical Journal* 87 (Spring 1994): 2–20.

Bucke, Richard M., Thomas B. Harned, and Horace L. Traubel, eds. *The Complete Writings of Walt Whitman*. Grosse Pointe, Mich.: Scholarly Press, 1968.

Buckingham, Samuel G. *The Life of William A. Buckingham: The War Governor of Connecticut*. Springfield, Mass.: W. F. Adam and Co., 1894.

Buell, Walter. "Zachariah Chandler." *Magazine of Western History* 4 (1886): 271–78, 338–52, 432–44.

Bulla, David W. "Milo Hascall and the Suppression of Democratic Newspapers in Civil War Indiana." Ph.D. diss., University of Florida, 2004.

Bullard, F. Lauriston. "When Lincoln Ruled Alone." *Proceedings of the Massachusetts Historical Society* 68 (1944–47): 301–47.

Burlingame, Michael. *Abraham Lincoln: A Life*. 2 vols. Baltimore: Johns Hopkins University Press, 2008.

———, ed. *Dispatches from Lincoln's White House: The Anonymous Civil War Journalism of Presidential Secretary William O. Stoddard*. Lincoln: University of Nebraska Press, 2002.

———, *The Inner World of Abraham Lincoln*. Urbana: University of Illinois Press, 1994.

———, ed. *Inside the White House in War Times: Memoirs and Reporting Lincoln's Secretary*. Written by William O. Stoddard. Lincoln: University of Nebraska Press, 2000.

———, ed. *Lincoln Observed: Civil War Dispatches of Noah Brooks*. Baltimore: Johns Hopkins University Press, 1998.

———, ed. *Lincoln's Journalist: John Hay's Anonymous Writings for the Press, 1860–1864*. Carbondale: Southern Illinois University Press, 1998.

———, ed. *At Lincoln's Side: John Hay's Civil War Correspondence and Selected Writings*. Carbondale: Southern Illinois University Press, 2000.

———, ed. *An Oral History of Abraham Lincoln: John G. Nicolay's Interviews and Essays*. Carbondale: Southern Illinois University Press, 1996.

———, ed. *With Lincoln in the White House: Letters, Memoranda, and Other Writings of John G. Nicolay, 1860–1865*. Carbondale: Southern Illinois University Press, 2000.

Burlingame, Michael, and John R. Turner Ettlinger, eds. *Inside Lincoln's White House: The Complete Civil War Diary of John Hay*. Carbondale: Southern Illinois University Press, 1997.

Burrage, Henry S. *Brown University in the Civil War: A Memorial*. Providence: Providence Press, Co., 1868.

Burton, Orville Vernon. *The Age of Lincoln*. New York: Hill and Wang, 2007.

Burton, William L. *Melting Pot Soldiers: The Union's Ethnic Regiments*. New York: Fordham University Press, 1998.

Busbey, Hamilton. "Recollections of Abraham Lincoln and the Civil War," *Forum* (March 1911): 282.

Bush, Bryan S. *Butcher Burbridge: Union General Stephen Burbridge and His Reign of Terror over Kentucky*. Morley, Mo: Acclaim Press, 2008.

Butler, Benjamin F. *Autobiography and Personal Reminiscences of Major-General Benjamin F. Butler's Book*. Boston: A. M. Thayer, 1892.

———. *Private and Official Correspondence*. 5 vols. Norwood, Mass.: The Pumton Press, 1917.

Byers, Samuel H. M. *Iowa in War Times*. Des Moines, Iowa: W. D. Condit and Co., 1888.

———. *With Fire and Sword*. New York: The Neale Publishing Company, 1911.

Byrne, Frank L., ed. *Uncommon Soldiers: Harvey Reid and the 22nd Wisconsin March with Sherman*. Knoxville: University of Tennessee Press, 2001.

Cain, Marvin. "Edward Bates and Hamilton R. Gamble: A Wartime Partnership." *Missouri Historical Review* 56 (January 1962): 146–55.

Cain, Marvin, and John Bradbury Jr. "Union Troops and the Civil War in Southwestern Missouri and Northwestern Arkansas." *Missouri Historical Review* 68 (October 1993): 29–47.

Calhoun, Stephen D. *The Marylanders: Without a Shelter or a Crumb.* Bowie, Md.: Heritage Books, Inc., 1993.
Canan, Howard. "The Missouri Paw Paw Militia, 1863–1864." *Missouri Historical Review* 62 (July 1968): 431–48.
Cannon, Jessica Ann. "Lincoln's Divided Backyard: Maryland in the Civil War Era." Ph.D. diss., Rice University, 2010.
Capaldo, Charles F. "Bergen County's Copperhead." *Proceedings of the New Jersey Historical Society* 69 (April 1951): 136–42.
Cardinal, Eric J. "The Ohio Democracy and the Crisis of Disunion, 1860–1861." *Ohio History* 86 (Winter 1977): 19–40.
Carleton, Hiram. *Genealogical and Family History of the State of Vermont.* 2 vols. New York: Lewis Publishing Company, 1903.
Carley, Kenneth. "The Second Minnesota in the West." *Minnesota History* 38 (June 1963): 258–73.
Carman, Henry J., and Reinhard H. Luthin. *Lincoln and the Patronage.* New York: Columbia University Press, 1943.
Carmony, Donald, E., ed. "Jacob W. Bartmess Civil War Letters." *Indiana Magazine of History* 51 (March 1955): 49–74.
———. "Jacob W. Bartmess Civil War Letters." *Indiana Magazine of History* 52 (June 1956): 157–86.
Carnegie, Andrew. *Autobiography of Andrew Carnegie.* Boston: Houghton Mifflin and Co., 1920.
Carpenter, C. C., and George W. Crossley. "Seventh Iowa Volunteers in the Civil War Gave Valiant Service." *Annals of Iowa* 34 (October 1957): 100–11.
Carpenter, Francis B. *Six Months at the White House with Abraham Lincoln.* New York: Hurd and Houghton, 1867.
Carpenter, John. "The New York International Relief Committee: A Chapter in the Diplomatic History of the Civil War." *New York Historical Society Quarterly Bulletin* 56 (July 1972): 239–52.
Carr, Clark E. *The Illini: A Story of the Prairies.* Chicago: A. C. McClurg and Co., 1904.
Carroll, Charles. *Rhode Island: Three Centuries of Democracy.* 2 vols. New York: Lewis Historical Publishing, 1932.
Carter, John D. "Abraham Lincoln and the California Patronage." *American Historical Review* 48 (April 1943): 495–506.
Carter, Samuel. *The Final Fortress: The Campaign for Vicksburg, 1862–1863.* New York: St. Martin's Press, 1980.
Carwardine, Richard J. *Lincoln: A Life of Purpose and Power.* New York: Alfred Knopf, 2003.
———. *Lincoln: Profiles in Power.* London: Pearson Education Limited, 2003.
Cashin, Joan, ed. *The War Was You and Me: Civilians in the American Civil War.* Princeton: Princeton University Press, 2002.
Castel, Albert. "Civil War Kansas and the Negro." *Journal of Negro History* 51 (April 1966): 125–38.
———. *Civil War Kansas: Reaping the Whirlwind.* Lawrence: University Press of Kansas, 1997.
———. *Decision in the West: The Atlanta Campaign of 1864.* Lawrence: University Press of Kansas, 1992.
———. *A Frontier State at War, Kansas, 1861–1865.* Ottawa: Kansas Heritage Press, 1958.

Caton, John Dean. *Miscellanies*. Boston: Houghton, Osgood, 1879.
Catton, Bruce. *The Coming Fury*. Garden City, N.Y.: Doubleday, 1961.
———. *Glory Road: The Army of the Potomac*. Garden City, N.Y.: Doubleday, 1952.
———. *Grant Moves South*. Boston: Little, Brown, and Co. 1960.
———. *Mr. Lincoln's Army*. Garden City, N.Y.: Doubleday, 1962.
———. *Terrible Swift Sword*. Garden City, N.Y.: Doubleday, 1963.
Chandler, Peleg W. *Memoir of Governor Andrew*. Boston: Roberts Brothers, 1880.
Chandler, Robert J. "California's 1863 Loyalty Oaths: Another Look." *Arizona and the West* 21 (1979): 215–34.
———. "Friends in Time of Need: Republicans and Black Civil Rights in California during the Civil War Era." *Arizona and the West* 24 (1982): 319–40.
Chaplin, Jeremiah, and J. D. Chaplin. *Life of Charles Sumner*. Boston: B.B. Russell, 1874.
Chase, Henry. *Early Governors from Representative Men of Maine*. Portland, Me.: Lakeside Press, 1893.
Cheatham, Gary L. "Desperate Characters: The Development and Impact of the Confederate Guerrillas in Kansas." *Kansas History* 14 (Autumn 1991): 144–61.
———. "Divided Loyalties in Civil War Kansas." *Kansas History* 11 (Summer 1988): 93–107.
Chipman, Donald. "An Essex County Soldier in the Civil War: The Diary of Cyrille Fountain." *New York History* 66 (July 1985): 281–317.
Church, Charles A. *A History of the Republican Party in Illinois, 1854–1912*. Rockford, Ill.: Wilson and Brothers and Co., 1912.
Churella, Albert J. *The Pennsylvania Railroad: Building an Empire, 1846–1917*. Philadelphia: University of Pennsylvania Press, 2012.
Cimbala, Paul A., and Randall M. Miller, eds. *An Uncommon Time: The Civil War and the Northern Home Front*. New York: Fordham University Press, 2002.
———, eds. *Union Soldiers and the Northern Home Front: Wartime Experiences, Postwar Adjustment*. New York: Fordham University Press, 2002.
"The Civil War Diary of General Isaac Ridgeway Trimble." *Maryland Historical Magazine* 17 (March 1922): 1–19.
"Civil War Letters of William T. and Joseph L. McClure." *Register of the Kentucky Historical Society* 60 (July 1962): 209–32.
Clark, Charles B. "Politics in Maryland during the Civil War." *Maryland Historical Magazine* 36 (September 1941): 239–62.
———. "Politics in Maryland during the Civil War." *Maryland Historical Magazine* 37 (June 1942): 171–92.
———. "Politics in Maryland during the Civil War." *Maryland Historical Magazine* 37 (December 1942): 378–99.
———. "Politics in Maryland during the Civil War." *Maryland Historical Magazine* 38 (September 1943): 230–60.
———. "Politics in Maryland during the Civil War." *Maryland Historical Magazine* 39 (June 1944): 149–61.
———. "Politics in Maryland during the Civil War." *Maryland Historical Magazine* 40 (September 1945): 233–41.
———. "Politics in Maryland during the Civil War." *Maryland Historical Magazine* 40 (December 1945): 295–311.
———. "Politics in Maryland during the Civil War." *Maryland Historical Magazine* 41 (June 1946): 132–58.

Clark, Charles M. *The History of the Thirty-ninth Regiment Illinois Volunteer Veteran Infantry (Yates Phalanx) in the War of the Rebellion, 1861–1865*. Chicago: Veteran Association of the Regiment, 1889.

Clark, Dan E. *Samuel Jordan Kirkwood*. Iowa City: State Historical Society of Iowa, 1917.

Clark, Donald A. *The Notorious "Bull" Nelson: Murdered Civil War General*. Carbondale: Southern Illinois University Press, 2011.

Clark, George T. *Leland Stanford: War Governor of California, Railroad Builder and Founder of Stanford University*. Stanford: Stanford University Press, 1943.

Clark, Malcolm, ed. *Pharisee among Philistines: The Diary of Judge Matthew P. Deady, 1871–1892*. Portland: Oregon Historical Society, 1975.

Clark, Thomas D. *A History of Kentucky*. New York: Prentice Hall, 1937.

Clarke, James Freeman. *Memorial and Biographical Sketches*. Boston: Houghton, Osgood, and Company, 1878.

Cleaveland, Nehemiah, and Alpheus S. Packard. *History of Bowdoin College*. Boston: James Ripley Osgood & Company, 1882.

Cleaves, Freeman. *Rock of Chickamauga: The Life of General George H. Thomas*. Westport, Conn.: Greenwood Press, 1948.

Clendenen, Clarence. "Dan Showalter: California Secessionist." *California Historical Society Quarterly* 40 (December 1961): 309–25.

Cleveland, Edmund J., Jr. "Early Campaigns in North Carolina." *Proceedings of the New Jersey Historical Society* 70 (December 1952): 61–71.

———. "Early Campaigns in North Carolina." *Proceedings of the New Jersey Historical Society* 73 (January 1953): 62–64.

———. "Early Campaigns in North Carolina." *Proceedings of the New Jersey Historical Society* 73 (April 1953): 136–41.

———. "Early Campaigns in North Carolina." *Proceedings of the New Jersey Historical Society* 73 (July 1953): 204–9.

———. "The Seige of Petersburg." *Proceedings of the New Jersey Historical Society* 66 (April 1948): 25–37.

Coddington, Edwin B. "Pennsylvanians Prepare for Invasion, 1863." *Pennsylvania History* 31 (April 1964): 157–75.

Coffin, Howard. *Full Duty: Vermonters in the Civil War*. Woodstock, Vt.: Countryman Press, 1993.

Cole, Edgar B. "Editorial Sentiment in Pennsylvania in the Campaign of 1860." *Pennsylvania History* 4 (October 1937): 219–34.

Collier, John S., and Bonnie B. Collier, eds. *Yours for the Union: The Civil War Letters of John W. Chase*. New York: Fordham University Press, 2004.

Collins, Cary C. "Grey Eagle: Major General Robert Hudson Milroy and the Civil War." *Indiana Magazine of History* 90 (March 1994): 48–72.

Collins, David A. "Absentee Voting in Civil War Law and Politics," Ph.D. diss., Wayne State University, 2014.

Cook, Robert J. *Civil War Senator: William Pitt Fessenden and the Fight to Save the American Republic*. Baton Rouge: Louisiana State University Press, 2010.

Cook, Thomas M., and Thomas Knox, eds. *Public Record of Horatio Seymour*. New York: I. W. England, 1868.

Cooke, George Willis. *Ralph Waldo Emerson: His Life, Writings, and Philosophy*. Boston: J. R. Osgood and Co., 1881.

Cooling, Benjamin F. *Forts Henry and Donelson: The Key to the Confederate Heartland.* Knoxville: University of Tennessee Press, 1987.

———. *To the Battles of Franklin and Nashville and Beyond: Stabilization and Reconstruction in Tennessee and Kentucky, 1864.* Knoxville: University of Tennessee Press, 2011.

Cooney, Percival J. "Southern California in Civil War Days." *Annual Publications of the Historical Society of Southern California* 13 (1924): 54–68.

Cooper, Leigh G. "The Michigan Politics in the Civil War." Ph.D. diss., University of Michigan, 1917.

Cooper, William J. *We Have the War Upon Us: The Onset of the Civil War, November 1860–April 1861.* New York: Alfred A. Knopf, 2012.

Conrad, Henry C. *History of the State of Delaware.* 3 vols. Wilmington, Del.: Privately Published, 1908.

"Copperhead and Unionist: An Ex-Vermonter Tells His Father Why He Opposes the Civil War." *Vermont History* 41 (Winter 1973): 1–6.

Corning, Charles R. *Amos Tuck.* Exeter, N.H.: News-Letter Press, 1902.

Cornish, Dudley T. "Kansas Negro Regiments in the Civil War." *Kansas Historical Quarterly* 20 (May 1953): 417–29.

———. *The Sable Arm: Negro Troops in the Union Army, 1861–1865.* New York: W. W. Norton and Co., 1966.

Costello, Bartley III. "Vermont in the Civil War." *Vermont History* 29 (October 1961): 220–26.

Cottman, George. "Lincoln in Indianapolis." *Indiana Magazine of History* 24 (March 1928): 2–11.

Coulter, E. Merton. *The Civil War and Re-adjustment in Kentucky.* Chapel Hill: University of North Carolina Press, 1926.

———. *William G. Brownlow: Fighting Parson of the Southern Highlands.* Chapel Hill: University of North Carolina Press, 1937.

Cowden, Joanna D. *"Heaven Will Frown on Such a Cause as This": Six Democrats Who Opposed Lincoln's War.* New York: University Press of America, 2001.

———. "The Politics of Dissent: Civil War Democrats in Connecticut." *New England Quarterly* 56 (1983): 538–54.

Cozzens, Peter. *Battles and Leaders of the Civil War.* Vols. 5 and 6. Champaign: University of Illinois Press, 2004.

———. *No Better Place to Die: The Battle of Stones River.* Urbana-Champaign: University of Illinois Press, 1990.

Cozzens, Peter, and Robert J. Girardi. *The Military Memoirs of General John Pope.* Chapel Hill: University of North Carolina Press, 1998.

Craig, Berry F. "Northern Conquerors and Southern Deliverers: The Civil War Comes to the Jackson Purchase." *Register of the Kentucky Historical Society* 73 (January 1975): 17–30.

Crawford, Robert F., ed. "The Civil War Letters of S. Rodman and Linton Smith." *Delaware History* 21 (Fall–Winter 1984): 86–116.

Cripe, Nicholas M. "The Enigmatic Civil War Career of Hoosier James H. Kinley." *Indiana Magazine of History* 87 (September 1991): 261–78.

Crocker, Helen B. "A War Divides Green River Country." *Register of the Kentucky Historical Society* 70 (October 1972): 295–311.

Crockett, Walter Hill. *Vermont: The Green Mountain State.* 5 vols. New York: The Century History Co., 1921.

Croffut, William A., and John M. Morris. *The Military and Civil History of Connecticut during the War of 1861–65*. New York: Leyard Bill, 1868.
Crofts, Daniel W. *Reluctant Confederates: Upper South Unionists in the Secession Crisis*. Chapel Hill: University of North Carolina Press, 1989.
———. "Secession Winter: William Henry Seward and the Decision for War." *New York History* 65 (July 1984): 229–56.
Croly, David. *Seymour and Blair, Their Lives and Services*. New York: Robinson and Co., 1868.
Cross, Jasper W. "The Civil War Comes to Egypt." *Journal of the Illinois State Historical Society* 44 (Summer 1951): 160–69.
Current, Richard N. *The History of Wisconsin. Volume II: The Civil War Era, 1848–1873*. Madison: State Historical Society of Wisconsin, 1976.
Curry, Leonard P. *Blueprint for Modern America: Non-Military Legislation of the First Civil War Congress*. Nashville: Vanderbilt University Press, 1968.
Curry, Richard O. *A House Divided: A Study of Statehood Politics and the Copperhead Movement in West Virginia*. Pittsburgh: University of Pittsburgh Press, 1964.
———. "Ideology and Perception: Democratic and Republican Attitudes on Civil War Politics and the Statehood Movement in West Virginia." *West Virginia History* 44 (Winter 1983): 135–54.
Curry, Watson. "The Newspaper Press and the Civil War in West Virginia." *West Virginia History* 6 (April 1945): 225–64.
Curtis, O. B. *History of the Twenty-Fourth Michigan Iron Brigade*. Detroit: Winn C. Hammond, 1891.
Dana, Charles A. *Recollections of the Civil War With the Leaders at Washington and in the Field in the Sixties*. New York: Appleton, 1902.
Daniel, Larry J. *Shiloh: The Battle that Changed the Civil War*. New York: Simon and Schuster, 1997.
Davis, Stanton L. *Pennsylvania Politics, 1860–1863*. Cleveland, Ohio: Western Reserve University, 1935.
Davis, Tarring S., ed. *A History of Blair County Pennsylvania*. 2 vols. Harrisburg, Penn.: National Historical Association, 1931.
Davis, William C. *Battle at Bull Run: A History of the First Major Campaign of the Civil War*. Garden City, N.Y.: Doubleday & Company, 1977.
———. *First Blood: Fort Sumter to Bull Run*. Alexandria, Va.: Time-Life Books, 1983.
———. *Lincoln's Men: How President Lincoln Became Father to an Army and a Nation*. New York: Free Press, 1999.
Davis, Winfield J. *History of Political Conventions in California, 1849–1852*. Sacramento: California State Library, 1893.
Dayton, Arctas A. "The Raising of Union Forces in Illinois During the Civil War." *Journal of the Illinois State Historical Society* 34 (December 1941): 401–38.
Dedication of the Statue of Governor Buckingham, Addresses, etc. June 18, 1884. Hartford: Case, Lockwood, and Brainard Co., 1884.
Dee, Christine, ed. *Ohio's War: The Civil War in Documents*. Athens: Ohio University Press, 2006.
Dell, Christopher. *Lincoln and the War Democrats*. Rutherford, N.J.: Fairleigh Dickinson University Press, 1975.
Dennett, Tyler. *Lincoln and the Civil War Diaries and Letters of John Hay*. New York: Dodd, Mead and Co., 1939.

Detzer, David. *Dissonance: The Turbulent Days between Fort Sumter and Bull Run*. New York: Harcourt, Inc., 2006.
"Diary of Charles Ross, 1861." *Vermont History* 29 (April 1961): 65–78.
"Diary of Charles Ross, 1862." *Vermont History* 30 (April 1962): 85–148.
"Diary of Charles Ross, 1863." *Vermont History* 31 (January 1963): 5–64.
"The Diary of Josephine Forney Roedel." *Pennsylvania Magazine of History and Biography* 67 (October 1943): 390–411.
"The Diary of Sidney George Fisher." *Pennsylvania Magazine of History and Biography* 88 (January 1964): 70–93.
Dicey, Edward. *Six Months in the Federal States*. Cambridge: MacMillan and Co., 1863.
———. *Spectator of America*. Edited with an introduction by Herbert Mitgang. Chicago: Quadrangle Books, 1971.
Dimeglio, John E. "Civil War Bangor." M.A. thesis, University of Maine, 1967.
Disbrow, Donald W. "Lincoln's Policies as Seen By a Michigan Soldier." *Michigan History Magazine* 45 (December 1961): 360–64.
"Documents: Letters to John G. Davis." *Indiana Magazine of History* 24 (1928): 203–13.
Dollar, Kent T., W. Calvin Dickinson, and Larry Howard Whiteaker, eds. *Sister States, Enemy States: The Civil War in Kentucky and Tennessee*. Lexington: University Press of Kentucky, 2009.
Donald, David. *Charles Summer and the Rights of Man*. New York: Knopf, 1970.
———, ed. *Inside Lincoln's Cabinet: The Civil War Diaries of Salmon P. Chase*. New York: Longmans, Green, and Co., 1954.
———. *Liberty and Union*. Lexington, Mass.: D. C. Heath, 1978.
———. *Lincoln*. London: Random House, 1995.
Donaldson, Gary. "'Into Africa': Kirby Smith and Braxton Bragg's Invasion of Kentucky." *Filson Club History Quarterly* 61 (October 1987): 444–65.
Dowden, Albert R. "John Gregory Smith." *Vermont History* 32 (April 1964): 79–97.
Downing, Alexander G. *Downing's Civil War Diary*. Des Moines: Historical Department of Iowa, 1916.
Downs, Gregory P. *After Appomattox: Military Occupation and the Ends of War*. Cambridge, Mass.: Harvard University Press, 2015.
Downs, Lynwood G. "The Soldier Vote and Minnesota Politics, 1862–1865." *Minnesota History* 42 (Summer 1970): 187–210.
Dubbs, Carol K. *Defend This Old Town: Williamsburg during the Civil War*. Baton Rouge: Louisiana State University Press, 2002.
Dues, Michael T. "Governor Beriah Magoffin of Kentucky: Sincere Neutral or Secessionist?." *Filson Club History Quarterly* 40 (June 1966): 22–28.
Duke, Frederick. "The Second Confiscation Act: A Chapter in Civil War Politics." Ph.D. diss., University of Chicago, 1966.
Duncan, Richard R. "The Impact of the Civil War on Education in Maryland." *Maryland Historical Magazine* 61 (March 1966): 37–52.
———. "Maryland's Reaction to Early's Raid in 1864: A Summer of Bitterness." *Maryland Historical Magazine* 64 (Fall 1969): 248–79.
Duncan, Russell, ed. *Blue-Eyed Child of Fortune: The Civil War Letters of Colonel Robert Gould Shaw*. Athens: University of Georgia Press, 1999.
———. *Where Death and Glory Meet: Colonel Robert Gould Shaw and the 54th Massachusetts Infantry*. Athens: University of Georgia Press, 1999.

Durkin, James, ed. *This War is an Awful Thing: Civil War Letters of the National Guards the 19th and 20th Pennsylvania Volunteers*. Glenside, Penn.: J. Michael Santarelli Publishing, 1994.

Dustin, Charles M. "The Knights of the Golden Circle." *Pacific Monthly* 26 (November 1911): 495–504.

Dwinell, Harold A. "Vermonter in Gray: The Story of Melvin Dwinell." *Vermont History* 30 (July 1962): 220–37.

Earle, John D. "The Sentiment of the People of California with Respect to the Civil War." *American Historical Association Annual Report* (1907): 125–35.

Easley, Virginia, ed. "Journal of the Civil War in Missouri, 1861: Henry Martin Cheavens." *Missouri Historical Review* 56 (October 1961): 12–25.

Eaton, Clement. "Henry A. Wise: A Study in Virginia Leadership, 1850–1861." *West Virginia History* 3 (April 1942): 187–204.

Eddy, Thomas M. *The Patriotism of Illinois*. 2 vols. Chicago: Clarke, 1865.

Edison, William G. "Louisville, Kentucky, during the First Year of the Civil War." *Filson Club History Quarterly* 38 (July 1964): 224–38.

Edwards, Glenn Thomas. "Benjamin Stark, the U.S. Senate, and 1862 Membership Issues." *Oregon Historical Quarterly* 73 (March 1972): 31–59.

———. "The Department of the Pacific in the Civil War Years." Ph.D. diss., University of Oregon, 1963.

———. "Oregon Regiments in the Civil War Years: Duty on the Indian Frontier." M.A., thesis, University of Oregon, 1960.

———. "Six Oregon Leaders and the Far-Reaching Impact of America's Civil War." *Oregon Historical Quarterly* 100 (1999): 4–31.

Egle, William H. *Andrew Gregg Curtin, His Life and Services*. Philadelphia: Avil Printing, 1895.

Eichelberger, Frank W. "Governor Kirkwood and the Skunk River War." *The Annals of Iowa* 9 (April 1909–10): 142–45.

Eicher, David J. *The Longest Night: A Military History of the Civil War*. New York: Simon & Schuster, 2001.

Eidson, William G., and Vincent Akers, eds. "Democratic Attitudes in Johnson County during the Civil War Era." *Indiana Magazine of History* 70 (March 1974): 44–69.

Elazar, Daniel Judah. *The American Partnership; Intergovernmental Co-Operation in the Nineteenth-Century United States*. 2 vols. Chicago: University of Chicago Press, 1962.

———. "Civil War and the Preservation of Federalism," *Publius* 1 (1971): 39–58.

———. *Cooperation and Conflict: Readings in American Federalism*. Itasca, Ill.: F. E. Peacock Publishers, 1969.

Elbert, E. Duane. "Southern Indiana in the Election of 1860: The Leadership and the Electorate." *Indiana Magazine of History* 70 (March 1974): 1–23.

Ellis, Richard N., ed. "The Civil War Letters of an Iowa Family." *Annals of Iowa* 39 (Spring 1969): 561–85.

———. "Political Pressure and Army Policies on the Northern Plains, 1862–1865." *Minnesota History* 42 (Summer 1970): 43–53.

Emerson, Ralph Waldo. *Representative Men and Miscellanies*. Boston: Houghton Mifflin, 1875.

Emilio, Luis F. *A Brave Black Regiment; History of the Fifty-Fourth Regiment of Massachusetts Volunteer Infantry, 1863–1865*. New York: Arno Press, 1969.

Engle, Stephen D. *Don Carlos Buell: Most Promising of All*. Chapel Hill: University of North Carolina Press, 1999.

———. "A Raised Consciousness: Franz Sigel and German Ethnic Identity in the Civil War." *Yearbook of German-American Studies* 34 (1999): 1–18.

———. *Struggle for the Heartland: The Campaigns from Fort Henry to Corinth*. Lincoln: University of Nebraska Press, 2001.

———. *Yankee Dutchman: The Life of Franz Sigel*. Fayetteville: University of Arkansas Press, 1993.

Engs, Robert, Corey M. Brooks, and Joseph S. Evans, eds. *Their Patriotic Duty: The Civil War Letters of the Evans Family of Brown County, Ohio*. New York: Fordham University Press, 2007.

Epstein, Daniel Mark. *Lincoln and Whitman: Parallel Lives in Civil War Washington*. New York: Ballantine Books, 2004.

Erickson, Edgar, ed. "With Grant at Vicksburg: From the Civil War Diary of Captain Charles E. Wilcox." *Journal of the Illinois State Historical Society* 30 (January 1938): 441–503.

Ericson, Christina, and Barbara Austen. "On the 'Front Lines' of the Civil War Home Front: The Morehouse Family Experiences the New York City Draft Riots, July 1863." *Connecticut History* 39 (2000): 150–65.

Escott, Paul D. *"What Shall We Do With the Negro?": Lincoln, White Racism, and Civil War America*. Charlottesville: University of Virginia Press, 2009.

Etulain, Richard W. *Lincoln and Oregon Country Politics in the Civil War Era*. Corvalis: Oregon State University Press, 2013.

Fairchild, Lucius. "Our Third Class Companions." *Military Order of the Loyal Legion of the United States, Wisconsin Commandery*, 1:433–43.

Fairlie, John A. "The State Governor: I." *Michigan Law Review* 10 (March 1912): 370–83.

———. "The State Governor: Administrative Powers." *Michigan Law Review* 10 (March 1912): 458–75.

Farlow, Joyce, and Louise Barry, eds. "Vincent B. Osborne's Civil War Experience." *Kansas Historical Quarterly* 20 (May 1952): 108–33.

———, eds. "Vincent B. Osborne's Civil War Experience, Part II." *Kansas Historical Quarterly* 20 (August 1952): 187–223.

Fehrenbacher, Don E. and Virginia Fehrenbacher, eds. *Recollected Words of Abraham Lincoln*. Stanford: Stanford University Press, 1996.

Fellman, Michael. "Emancipation in Missouri." *Missouri Historical Review* 88 (October 1988): 36–56.

———. *Inside War: The Guerrilla Conflict in Missouri During the American Civil War*. New York: Oxford University Press, 1990.

Fennimore, Jean Jay. "Austin Blair: Pioneer Lawyer, 1818–1844." *Michigan History Magazine* 48 (March 1964): 1–17.

———. "Austin Blair: Political Idealist, 1845–1860." *Michigan History Magazine* 48 (June 1964): 130–66.

———. "Austin Blair: Civil War Governor, 1861–1862." *Michigan History Magazine* 49 (September 1965): 193–227.

———. "Austin Blair: Civil War Governor, 1863–1864." *Michigan History Magazine* 49 (December 1965): 344–69.

Ferguson, Cynthia C. "The Providence Marine Corps of Artillery in the Civil War." *Rhode Island History* 60 (2002): 54–64.

Fesler, Mayo. "Secret Political Societies in the North during the Civil War." *Indiana Magazine of History* 14 (September 1918): 183–286.
Fessenden, Francis. *Life and Public Services of William Pitt Fessenden*. 2 vols. Boston: Houghton Mifflin, 1907.
Field, Edward, ed. *State of Rhode Island and Providence Plantations at the End of the Century*. 3 vols. Providence, R.I.: Mason Publishing and Printing Co., 1902.
Field, Henry M. *Life of David Dudley Field*. New York: Charles Scribner's Sons, 1898.
Fischer, LeRoy H. *Lincoln's Gadfly: Adam Gurowski*. Norman: University of Oklahoma Press, 1964.
Fish, Carl R. "The Raising of the Wisconsin Volunteers, 1861." *The Military Historian and Economist* 1 (1916): 258–73.
Fishel, Edwin C. *The Secret War for the Union: The Untold Story of Military Intelligence in the Civil War*. New York: Houghton Mifflin Company, 1996.
Fisher, Noel. "Groping toward Victory: Ohio's Administration of the Civil War." *Ohio History* 105 (Winter 1996): 25–45.
Fliss, William M. "Wisconsin's 'Abolitionist Regiment': The Twenty-second Volunteer Infantry in Kentucky, 1862–1863." *Wisconsin Magazine of History* 86 (Winter 2002–03): 2–17.
Folsom, William R. "Vermont at Bull Run." *Vermont Historical Society Proceedings* 19 (January 1951): 5–21.
———. "Vermont at Gettysburg." *Vermont Historical Society Proceedings* 20 (July 1952): 161–79.
Folwell, William W. *A History of Minnesota*. 4 vols. St. Paul: Minnesota Historical Society, 1924.
Ford, Andrew. *The Story of the 15th Regiment Massachusetts Volunteer Infantry*. Clinton, Mass.: Press of W. J. Coulter, 1898.
Ford, Worthington C., ed. *A Cycle of Adams Letters, 1861–1865*. Boston: Houghton Mifflin Company, 1920.
———, ed. "Sumner's Letters to Governor Andrew, 1861." *Proceedings of the Massachusetts Historical Society* 60 (April 1927): 223–33.
Fordney, Ben Fuller. "George Stoneman: Civil War Soldier and Governor of California." *Southern California Quarterly* 84 (Summer 2002): 115–34.
Foster, John M., Jr. " 'For the Good of the Cause and the Protection of the Border': The Service of the Indiana Legion in the Civil War, 1861–1865." *Civil War History* 55 (March 2009): 31–55.
Foster, John Y. *New Jersey and the Rebellion: A History of the Services of the Troops and People of New Jersey in Aid of the Union Cause*. Newark: Martin R. Dennis and Co., 1868.
Foulke, William D. *Life of Oliver P. Morton*. 2 vols. Indianapolis: AMS Press, 1899.
Fowles, Lloyd W. "No Backward Step: The Connecticut Gubernatorial Elections of 1861 and 1862." *Connecticut Historical Society Bulletin* 27 (January 1962): 1–7.
Frank, Joseph A. *With Ballot and Bayonet: The Political Socialization of American Civil War Soldiers*. Athens: University of Georgia Press, 1998.
Frank, Joseph A., and George K. Reaves. *"Seeing the Elephant": Raw Recruits at the Battle of Shiloh*. New York: Greenwood Press, 1989.
Franklin, John Hope. "James T. Ayers: Civil War Recruiter." *Journal of the Illinois State Historical Society* 40 (September 1947): 267–97.

Frazier, Margaret, and James Goodrich, eds. "'Life Is Uncertain . . .' Willard Mendenhall's Civil War Diary, Part II." *Missouri Historical Review* 79 (October 1984): 65–88.
Freidel, Frank. "The Loyal Publication Society: A Pro-Union Propaganda Agency." *The Mississippi Valley Review* 26 (December 1939): 359–76.
French, William M. *Life, Speeches, State Papers and Public Services of Governor Oliver P. Morton.* Cincinnati: Moore, Wilstach, and Baldwin, 1864.
Fry, James B. *New York and the Conscription of 1863: A Chapter in the History of the Civil War.* New York: G. P. Putnam's Sons, 1864.
Fuke, Richard P. *Imperfect Equality: African-Americans and the Confines of White Racial Attitudes in Post-Emancipation Maryland.* New York: Fordham University Press, 1999.
Fullbrook, Earl S. "Relief Work in Iowa during the Civil War." *Iowa Journal of History and Politics* 16 (April 1918): 155–276.
Furgurson, Ernest B. *Chancellorsville, 1863: The Souls of the Brave.* New York: Alfred A. Knopf, 1992.
———. *Freedom Rising: Washington in the Civil War.* New York: Alfred A. Knopf, 2004.
———. *Not War But Murder: Cold Harbor, 1864.* New York: Alfred A. Knopf, 2000.
Gallagher, Gary W., ed., *The Richmond Campaign of 1862: The Peninsula and the Seven Days.* Chapel Hill: University of North Carolina, 2000.
———. *The Union War.* Cambridge, Mass.: Harvard University Press, 2011.
Gallagher, Gary W., and Rachel A. Shelden, eds. *A Political Nation: New Directions in Mid-Nineteenth-Century American Political History.* Charlottesville: University of Virginia Press, 2012.
Gallagher, Patrick. "Through Battle, Prison, and Disease: The Civil War Diaries of George Richardson Crosby." *Vermont History* 76 (Winter/Spring 2008): 19–45.
Gallman, J. Matthew. *Mastering Wartime: A Social History of Philadelphia during the Civil War.* New York. Cambridge University Press, 1990.
———. *The North Fights the Civil War: The Home Front.* Chicago: I. R. Dee, 1994.
———. "Preserving the Peace: Order and Disorder in Civil War Philadelphia." *Pennsylvania History* 55 (October 1988): 201–15.
Gambone, Joseph G. "Samuel C. Pomeroy and the Senatorial Election of 1861." *Kansas Historical Quarterly* 37 (Spring 1971): 15–32.
Gara, Larry. "Slavery and the Slave Power: A Crucial Distinction." *Civil War History* 15 (March 1969): 5–18.
Gardner, Washington. "Civil War Letters." *Michigan History Magazine* 1 (October 1917): 3–18.
Gates, Arnold. *The Rough Side of War: The Civil War Journal of Chelsey A. Mormon, 1st Lieutenant, Company D. 59th Illinois Volunteer Infantry Regiment.* Garden City, Ill.: Basin Publishing, 1987.
Geary, James W. "Clement L. Vallandigham Writes to John H. George, April 27, 1863: His Last Existing Letter before His Notorious Arrest." *Historical New Hampshire* 30 (Spring 1975): 13–20.
———. *We Need Men: The Union Draft in the Civil War.* Dekalb: Northern Illinois University, 1991.
Geiger, Mark W. *Financial Fraud and Guerrilla Violence in Missouri's Civil War, 1861–1865.* New Haven, Conn.: Yale University Press, 2010.

———. "Indebtedness and the Origins of Guerrilla Violence in Civil War Missouri." *Journal of Southern History* 75 (February 2009): 49–82.
George, Joseph Jr. "Philadelphians Greet Their President-Elect, 1861." *Pennsylvania History* 29 (October 1962): 381–90.
———. "Charles J. Stillé, 'Angel of Consolation.'" *Pennsylvania Magazine of History and Biography* 85 (July 1961): 303–15.
Gerteis, Louis S. *Civil War St. Louis*. Lawrence: University Press of Kansas, 2004.
———. *From Contraband to Freedom: Federal Policy toward Southern Blacks, 1861–1865*. New York: Greenwood, 1973.
Gibney, Abbott M. "Your Affectionate Son: The Civil War Letters of Frank E. Lansing." *Michigan History Magazine* 58 (Spring 1974): 25–53.
Gienapp, William E. "Abraham Lincoln and the Border States." *Journal of the Abraham Lincoln Association* 13 (1992): 13–46.
———. "Salmon P. Chase, Nativism, and the Formation of the Republican Party in Ohio." *Ohio History* 93 (Winter 1984): 5–39.
Gienapp, William E., and Erica L., Gienapp, eds. *The Civil War Diary of Gideon Welles: Lincoln's Secretary of the Navy*. Champaign-Urbana: University of Illinois Press, 2014.
Gilbert, Benjamin F. "California and the Civil War: A Bibliographical Essay." *California Historical Society Quarterly* 40 (December 1961): 289–307.
———. "The Confederate Minority in California." *California Historical Society Quarterly* 20 (June 1941): 154–70.
———. "San Francisco Harbor Defense during the Civil War." *California Historical Society Quarterly* 33 (September 1954): 229–40.
Gillette, William. *Jersey Blue: Civilian Politics in New Jersey, 1854–1865*. New Brunswick, N.J.: Rutgers University Press, 1994.
Gillman, Will D., Jr. "Robert J. Breckinridge: Kentucky Unionist." *Register of the Kentucky Historical Society* 69 (October 1971): 362–85.
Gilmore, Donald L. *Civil War on the Missouri-Kansas Border*. Gretna, La.: Pelican Publishing, 2006.
Glashan, Roy R. *American Governors and Gubernatorial Elections, 1775–1978*. Westport, Conn.: Meckler Books, 1979.
Glatthaar, Joseph T. *Forged in Battle: The Civil War Alliance of Black Soldiers and White Officers*. New York: Free Press, 1990.
Glazer, Walter S. "Wisconsin Goes to War." *Wisconsin Magazine of History* 50 (Winter 1967): 147–65.
Goebel, Robert W. "Casualty of War: The Governorship of Beriah Magoffin, 1859–1862." M.A. thesis, University of Louisville, 2005.
Gold, David M. "Constitutional Problems in Maine during the Civil War." *Maine Historical Society Quarterly* 22 (Winter 1983): 127–58.
———. "Frustrated Glory: John Francis Appleton and Black Soldiers in the Civil War." *Maine Historical Society Quarterly* 31 (Summer 1991): 174–204.
———. "Testimonials to Hon. Israel Washburn." *Collections and Proceedings of the Maine Historical Society* 2 (May 1891): 86–105.
Goldman, Henry H. "Southern Sympathy in Southern California, 1860–1865." *Journal of the West* 4 (October 1965): 577–86.
Goodrich, Dewitt C., and Charles R. Tuttle. *An Illustrated History of the State of Indiana*. Indianapolis: Richard S. Pearle, and Co., 1879.

Goodrich, Thomas. *War to the Knife: Bleeding Kansas, 1854–1861.* Mechanicsburg, Penn.: Stackpole Books, 1998.
Goodwin, Doris Kearns. *Team of Rivals: The Political Genius of Abraham Lincoln.* New York: Simon & Schuster, 2005.
Gordon, Lesley J. *A Broken Regiment: The 16th Connecticut's Civil War.* Baton Rouge: Louisiana State University Press, 2015.
Gorham, George C. *Life and Public Services of Edwin M. Stanton.* 2 vols. New York: Houghton, Mifflin and Company, 1899.
Gorley, Hugh A. "The Loyal Californians of 1861." *Military Order of the Loyal Legion of the United States War Papers* (1893), No. 12.
The Governor: The Office and Its Power. Lexington, Ky.: The Council of State Governments, 1972.
"Governor Curtin: Phrenological Character Biography." *American Phrenological Journal* 38 (October 1863): 112–13.
Grant, Susan-Mary. *North over South: Northern Nationalism and American Identity in the Antebellum Era.* Lawrence: University Press of Kansas, 2000.
Grant, Ulysses S. *Personal Memoirs of U. S. Grant.* 2 vols. New York: Charles L. Webster & Company, 1886.
Gray, Wood. *The Hidden Civil War: The Story of the Copperheads.* New York: Viking Press, 1942.
Graystone, Florence L. "Lamdin P. Milligan: A Knight of the Golden Circle." *Indiana Magazine of History* 43 (1947): 379–92.
Green, Larry A. "The Emancipation Proclamation in New Jersey and the Paranoid Style." *Proceedings of the New Jersey Historical Society* 91 (Summer 1973): 108–24.
Green, Michael S. *Freedom, Union, and Power: Lincoln and His Party during the Civil War.* New York: Fordham University Press, 2004.
Greenberg, Irwin F. "Charles Ingersoll: The Aristocrat as Copperhead." *Pennsylvania Magazine of History and Biography* 93 (April 1969): 190–217.
Grenier, Judson. "Colonel Jack Watson: Copperhead Assemblyman in Civil war California." *The Californian* 12 (1995): 14–35.
Griffin, Simon G. *The History of Keene, New Hampshire.* Keene, N.H.: Sentinel Print Co., 1904.
Grimsley, Mark. *The Hard Hand of War: Union Military Policy toward Southern Civilians, 1861–1865.* New York: Cambridge University Press, 1995.
Grinnell, Josiah Bushnell. *Men and Events of Forty Years: Autobiographical Reminiscences of an Active Career from 1850 to 1890, by the Late Josiah Bushnell Grinnell.* Boston: D. Lathrop Co., 1891.
Gue, Benjamin F. *History of Iowa from the Earliest Times to the Beginning of the Twentieth Century.* 4 vols. New York: Century History Co., 1903.
Guelzo, Allen C. *Abraham Lincoln: Redeemer President.* Grand Rapids: W. B. Eerdmans, 1999.
———. "Defending Emancipation: Abraham Lincoln and the Conkling Letter, 1863." *Civil War History* 48 (December 2002): 313–37.
Guentzel, Richard D. "Alexander Ramsey: First Territorial and Second State Governor of Minnesota." Ph.D. diss., Lincoln: University of Nebraska, 1976.
Gunderson, Robert. *Old Gentleman's Convention: The Washington Peace Conference of 1861.* Madison: University of Wisconsin Press, 1961.

———. "The Washington Peach Conference of 1861: Selection of Delegates." *Journal of Southern History* 24 (August 1958): 347–59.
Gurowski, Adam. *Diary from November 12, 1862, to October 18, 1863.* New York: Carleton, 1864.
———. *Diary, 1863–'64 –'65.* Washington, D.C.: W. H. and O. H. Morrison, 1866.
Haffner, Gerald O., ed. "Civil War Letters of George W. Clark." *Register of the Kentucky Historical Society* 62 (October 1964): 307–17.
Hagerty, Edward J. *Collis' Zouaves: The 114th Pennsylvania Volunteers in the Civil War.* Baton Rouge: Louisiana State University, 1998.
Hake, Herbert. "The Political Firecracker: Samuel J. Kirkwood." *The Palimpsest* 56 (January 1975): 2–14.
Haley, John West, ed. *The Rebel Yell and the Yankee Hurrah: The Civil War Journal of a Maine Volunteer.* Camden, Me.: Down East Books, 1985.
Hall, Florence Howe. *The Story of the Battle Hymn of the Republic.* New York: Harper and Brothers, 1916.
Ham, Gerald. "The Mind of a Copperhead: Letters of John J. Davis on the Secession Crisis and Statehood Politics in Western Virginia, 1860–1862." *West Virginia History* 24 (January 1963): 93–109.
Hamilton, James A. *Reminiscences of James A. Hamilton.* New York: Charles Scribner and Co., 1869.
Hamlin, Charles Eugene. *The Life and Times of Hannibal Hamlin.* Cambridge, Mass.: Riverside Press, 1899.
Hammond, Harold E., ed. *Diary of a Union Lady, 1861–1865 by Maria Lydig Daly.* New York: Funk and Wagnalls, 1962.
Hammond, Mary A., ed. "'Dear Mollie': Letters of Captain Edward A. Acton to His Wife, 1862." *Pennsylvania Magazine of History and Biography* 89 (January 1965): 3–51.
Hampel, Robert L., and Charles W. Ormsby. "Crime and Punishment on the Civil War Home Front." *Pennsylvania Magazine of History and Biography* 106 (April 1982): 223–44.
Hamrogue, John. "John A. Andrew, Abolitionist Governor, 1861–1865." Ph.D. diss., Fordham University, 1974.
Hanchett, William, ed. "An Illinois Physician and the Civil War Draft, 1864–1865: Letters of Dr. Joshua Nichols Speed." *Journal of the Illinois State Historical Society* 59 (Summer 1966): 143–60.
Hancock, Harold Bell. *Delaware during the Civil War, a Political History.* Wilmington: Historical Society of Delaware, 1961.
———. "The Political History of Delaware during the Civil War." Ph.D. diss., Ohio State University, 1955.
———. "The Political History of Delaware during the Civil War, Part I: The Campaign and Elections of 1860." *Delaware History* 7 (September 1956): 105–41.
———. "The Political History of Delaware during the Civil War, Part II: The Coming of the War." *Delaware History* 7 (March 1957): 217–61.
———. "The Political History of Delaware during the Civil War, Part III: A House Divided." *Delaware History* 7 (September 1957): 337–75.
———. "The Political History of Delaware during the Civil War, Part IV: Two Years of Tension." *Delaware History* 8 (March 1958): 75–106.

———. "The Political History of Delaware during the Civil War, Part V: The End of the War." *Delaware History* 8 (September 1958): 159–84.
———, ed. "Alexander B. Cooper's Civil War Memories in Camden." *Delaware History* 20 (Spring–Summer 1982): 50–72.
———, ed. "The Civil War Diaries of Anna M. Ferris." *Delaware History* 9 (April 1961): 221–64.
Harbison, Winfred A. "Indiana Republicans and the Re-election of President Lincoln." *Indiana Magazine of History* 38 (1938): 42–64.
———. "Lincoln and Indiana Republicans, 1861–1862." *Indiana Magazine of History* 33 (1937): 277–303.
———, ed. "Zachariah Chandler's Part in the Re-election of Abraham Lincoln." *Mississippi Valley Historical Review* 22 (September 1935): 267–76.
Hardin, Lennette M. "A Study of the Public Speaking of Arthur I. Boreman." M.A. thesis, West Virginia University, 1962.
Harmon, George D. "The Pennsylvania Clergy and the Civil War." *Pennsylvania History* 6 (April 1939): 86–102.
Harris, Robert C. "Austin Blair of Michigan: A Political Biography." Ph.D. diss., Michigan State University, 1960.
Harris, William C. *Lincoln and the Border States: Preserving the Union*. Lawrence: University Press of Kansas, 2011.
———. *Lincoln and the Union Governors*. Carbondale: Southern Illinois University Press, 2013.
———. *Lincoln's Last Months*. Cambridge, Mass.: Harvard University Press, 2004.
———. *Lincoln's Rise to the Presidency*. Lawrence: University Press of Kansas, 2007.
Harris, Wilmer C. *Public Life of Zachariah Chandler, 1851–1875*. Lansing: Michigan Historical Commission, 1917.
Harrison, Lowell H. "The Civil War in Kentucky: Some Persistent Questions." *Register of the Kentucky Historical Society* 76 (January 1978): 1–21.
———. "Governor Magoffin and the Secession Crisis." *Register of the Kentucky Historical Society* 72 (April 1974): 91–110.
———. "John C. Breckinridge: Nationalist, Confederate Kentuckian." *Filson Club History Quarterly* 47 (April 1973): 125–44.
Harvey, Cordelia A. P. "A Wisconsin Woman's Picture of President Lincoln." *Wisconsin Magazine of History* 1 (1918): 233–55.
Hatch, Carl E. "David Naar of Trenton: Profile of the Anti-Negro Mind." *New Jersey History* 85 (Summer 1968): 72–87.
Hatcher, Richard W., III, and William G. Piston. "Kansans Go to War: The Wilson's Creek Campaign, Reported by the Leavenworth *Daily Times*." *Kansas History* 16 (Autumn 1993–94): 180–99.
Haugland, John C. "Alexander Ramsey and the Birth of Party Politics in Minnesota." *Minnesota History* 39 (Summer 1964): 37–48.
———. "Alexander Ramsey and the Republican Party, 1855–1875: A Study in Personal Politics." Ph.D. diss., University of Minnesota, 1961.
———. "Politics, Patronage, and Ramsey's Rise to Power, 1861–1863." *Minnesota History* 37 (December 1961): 324–33.
Havran, Martin J. "Windsor and Detroit Relations During the Civil War." *Michigan History Magazine* 38 (December 1954): 371–89.

Haynes, E. M. *A History of the Tenth Regiment Vt. Volunteers.* Rutland, Vt.: Tuttle Company Printers, 1894.

Haynes, John D., and Doris D. MaGuire. "Charles Graham Halpine: Life and Adventures of Miles O'Reilly." *New York Historical Society Quarterly Bulletin* 51 (October 1967): 326–44.

Haynie, Edwin C. "At the Death Bed of Lincoln." *Century Magazine* 51 (April 1896): 954–55.

Headly, P. C. *Massachusetts in the Rebellion.* Boston: Walker, Fuller and Co., 1866.

Hearn, Chester G. *The Capture of New Orleans, 1862.* Baton Rouge: Louisiana State University Press, 1995.

Heath, Gary E. "The St. Albans Raid: Vermont Viewpoint." *Vermont History* 33 (January 1965): 250–54.

Hebert, Walter H. *Fighting Joe Hooker.* Indianapolis: Bobbs-Merrill, 1944. Reprint, University of Nebraska Press, 1999.

Heilbron, Bertha L. "Manifest Destiny in Minnesota's Republican Campaign of 1860." *Minnesota History* 37 (June 1960): 52–57.

Helmreich, Paul C. "The Diary of Charles G. Lee in the Andersonville and Florence Prison Camps, 1864." *Connecticut Historical Society Bulletin* 41 (January 1976): 12–28.

Hemphill, Anne E., ed. "The 1864 Diary of Cpl. Seth Kelly." *Kansas History* 1 (Autumn 1978): 189–210.

Hendrick, Burton. *Lincoln's War Cabinet.* Boston: Little, Brown, and Co., 1946.

Hennessy, John J. *Return to Bull Run: The Campaign and Battle of Second Manassas.* New York: Simon and Schuster, 1993.

Henshaw, Ray, and Glenn W. Lafantasie, eds. "Letters Home: Sergeant Charles E. Perkins in Virginia 1862." *Rhode Island History* 39 (November 1980): 106–31.

Herriott, F. I. "Iowa and the First Nomination of Abraham Lincoln." *Annals of Iowa* 8 (April 1907): 81–115; 8 (October 1907): 186–220; 8 (July 1908): 444–66; 9 (April 1909): 45–64; 9 (October 1909): 186–228.

Heslin, James J. "The Diary of a Union Soldier in Confederate Prisons." *New York Historical Society Quarterly Bulletin* 41 (July 1957): 233–78.

———. "From the Wilderness to Petersburg: The Diary of Surgeon Frank Ridgeway." *New York Historical Society Quarterly Bulletin* 45 (April 1961): 113–40.

———. "Peaceful Compromise in New York City, 1860–61." *New York Historical Society Quarterly Bulletin* 44 (October 1960): 349–62.

———. "A Yankee Soldier in a New York Regiment." *New York Historical Society Quarterly Bulletin* 50 (April 1966): 109–50.

Hess, Earl J. *Banners to the Breeze: The Kentucky Campaign, Corinth and Stones River.* Lincoln, Nebraska: University of Nebraska Press, 2000.

———. *The Civil War in the West: Victory and Defeat from the Appalachians to the Mississippi.* Chapel Hill: University of North Carolina Press, 2012.

———, ed. *A German in the Yankee Fatherland: The Civil War Letters of Henry A. Kircher.* Kent, Ohio: Kent State University Press, 1983.

———. *Liberty, Virtue, and Progress: Northerners and their War for the Union.* New York: Fordham University Press, 1997.

Hesseltine, William B. "Abraham Lincoln and the Politicians." *Civil War History* 6 (March 1960): 43–54.

———. "Lincoln, the Governors and States' Rights." *Social Studies* 39 (December 1948): 350–55.

———. *Lincoln and the War Governors*. New York: Alfred Knopf, 1948. Reprint Gloucester, Mass.: Peter Smith, 1972.

———. "Lincoln's Problems in Wisconsin." *Wisconsin Magazine of History* 48 (Spring 1965): 187–95.

———. "Lincoln's War Governors." *Abraham Lincoln Association Quarterly* 4 (1946): 153–200.

———, ed. *The Tragic Conflict: The Civil War and Reconstruction*. New York: George Braziller, 1962.

Hesseltine, William B., and Hazel C. Wolf. "The Altoona Conference and the Emancipation Proclamation." *Pennsylvania Magazine of History and Biography* 71 (1947): 195–205.

———. "The Cleveland Conference of 1861." *Ohio Archeological and Historical Quarterly* 56 (1947): 258–65.

———. "New England Governors vs. Lincoln: The Providence Conference." *Rhode Island History* 5 (1946): 105–13.

Hicken, Victor. *Illinois in the Civil War*. Urbana: University of Illinois Press, 1966.

Higginson, Thomas W. *Army Life in a Black Regiment*. Boston: Fields, Osgood, and Co., 1870.

Hinckley, Ted. "Davenport in the Civil War." *Annals of Iowa* 34 (October 1958): 401–19.

Hines, Richard K. "Settlement, Race Politics, and the Civil War: The Political Transformation of Illinois." Ph.D. diss., Washington State University, 2001.

History of the Nineteenth Regiment Massachusetts Volunteer Infantry. Salem, Mass.: The Salem Press, 1906.

Hittel, Theodore H. *History of California*. 4 vols. San Francisco: N. J. Stone & Company, 1898.

Hoar, George F. *Charles Sumner: His Complete Works*. 30 vols. Boston: Lee and Shepard, 1900.

Hofer, J. M. "Development of the Peace Movement in Illinois during the Civil War." *Journal of the Illinois State Historical Society* 24 (April 1931): 110–28.

Hoffman, Elliott W., ed. *A Vermont Cavalryman in War and Love: The Civil War Letters of Brevet Major General William Wells and Anna Richardson*. Lynchburg, Va.: Schroeder Publications, 2007.

Holcombe, John W. and Hubert M. Skinner. *Life and Public Services of Thomas A. Hendricks*. Indianapolis: Carlan Hollenbeck, 1886.

Holden, Walter. "The Bridge that Saved the Army." *Historical New Hampshire* 35 (Winter 1980): 391–416.

Holland, James G. *Holland's Life of Abraham Lincoln*. Springfield, Mass.: Gurdonbill, 1866. Reprint, University of Nebraska, 1998.

Hollandsworth, James G., Jr. *Pretense of Glory: The Life of General Nathaniel P. Banks*. Baton Rouge: Louisiana State University Press, 1998.

Holliday, Joseph E. "Relief for Soldiers' Families in Ohio during the Civil War." *Ohio History* 71 (July 1962): 97–112.

Holt, Robert. "The Political Career of William A. Richardson." *Journal of the Illinois State Historical Society* 26 (October 1933): 226–69.

Holzer, Harold. *Lincoln at Cooper Union: The Speech That Made Abraham Lincoln President*. New York: Simon & Schuster, 2006.

———. *Lincoln: President-Elect: Abraham Lincoln and the Great Secession Winter, 1860–1861*. New York: Simon & Schuster, 2008.

———, ed. *The State of the Union: New York and the Civil War*. New York: Fordham University Press, 2002.
Holzman, Robert S. "Ben Butler in the Civil War." *New England Quarterly* 30 (September 1957): 330–45.
Hood, James L. "For the Union: Kentucky's Unconditional Unionist Congressman and the Development of the Republican Party in Kentucky, 1863–1865." *Register of the Kentucky Historical Society* 76 (July 1978): 197–215.
Hoogenboom, Ari Arthur. *Gustavus Vasa Fox of the Union Navy: A Biography*. Baltimore: John Hopkins University Press, 2008.
Hooper, Osman Castle. "John Brough." *Ohio Archaeological and Historical Quarterly* 13 (1904): 40–70.
Horner, Harlan H. "Lincoln Rebukes a Senator." *Journal of the Illinois State Historical Society* 44 (Summer 1951): 103–19.
———. "Lincoln Scolds a General." *Wisconsin Magazine of History* 36 (Winter 1952–53): 90–96.
Houghton, Henry. "The Ordeal of Civil War: A Recollection." *Vermont History* 41 (Winter 1973): 31–49.
Howard, Oliver Otis. *Autobiography of Oliver Otis Howard*. 2 vols. New York: Baker and Taylor Company, 1907.
Howard, Victor B. "Lincoln Slave Policy in Kentucky: A Study of Pragmatic Strategy." *Register of the Kentucky Historical Society* 80 (Summer 1982): 281–308.
Howe, Julia Ward. "Note on the Battle Hymn of the Republic." *Century Illustrated Magazine* 34 (August 1887): 4.
Howland, Glenn C. "Organize! Organize! The Lincoln Wide-Awakes in Vermont." *Vermont History* 48 (Winter 1980): 28–32.
Hubbell, John T., ed. "Stand by the Colors: The Civil War Letters of Leander Stem." *Register of the Kentucky Historical Society* 73 (April 1975): 171–94; (July 1975): 291–313; (October 1975): 396–415.
Hubbs, Ronald M. "The Civil War and Alexander Wilkin." *Minnesota History* 39 (Spring 1965): 173–90.
Huch, Ronald K., ed. "The Civil War Letters of Herbert Saunders." *Register of the Kentucky Historical Society* 69 (January 1971): 17–29.
Huggins, Dorothy H. "Women in War-Time San Francisco, 1864: The Ladies' Christian Commission Fair." *California Historical Society Quarterly* 24 (September 1945): 261–70.
Hughes, Nathaniel Cheairs, Jr., and Gordon D. Whitney. *Jefferson Davis in Blue: The Life of Sherman's Relentless Warrior*. Baton Rouge: Louisiana State University, 2002.
Hughes, Sarah Forbes, ed. *Letters and Recollections of John Murray Forbes*. 3 vols. Boston: Houghton Mifflin, 1899.
Hunt, Aurora. *The Army of the Pacific*. Glendale, Calif.: Clark, 1951.
Hunt, Gaillard. *Israel, Elihu and Cadwallader Washburn: A Chapter in American Biography*. New York: The MacMillan Company, 1925.
Hunt, William. *The Book of Governors*. Los Angeles: Washington Topographers, 1935.
Hunter, Lloyd Arthur, ed. *For Duty and Destiny: The Life and Civil War Diary of William Taylor Scott, Hoosier Soldier and Educator*. Indianapolis: Indiana Historical Society Press, 2010.
Hunter, William A., ed. "The Civil War Diaries of Leonard C. Ferguson." *Pennsylvania History* 14 (July 1947): 196–224.

———. "The Civil War Diaries of Leonard C. Ferguson." *Pennsylvania History* 14 (October 1947): 289–313.
Hurn, Ethel. *Wisconsin Women in the War between the States*. Madison: Wisconsin Historical Commission, 1911.
Hyatt, Hudson. "Captain Hyatt: Being the Letters Written during the Years 1863–1864." *Ohio Archeological and Historical Quarterly* 53 (1944): 166–250.
Hyman, Harold. "Lincoln and Congress: Why Not Congress and Lincoln." *Journal of the Illinois State Historical Society* 68 (February 1975): 57–73.
———. "Oroville's Reputation Redeemed: A Loyalty Investigation in California, 1862." *Pacific Historical Review* 26 (May 1956): 173–78.
In Memoriam: Israel Washburn Jr. Portland, Maine: Stephen Berry, 1884.
Jackson, W. Sherman. "The Collapse of the Peculiar Institution through Military and Legal Action." *Ohio History* 83 (Summer 1974): 183–91.
Jackson, William. *New Jerseyans in the Civil War: For Union and Liberty*. New Brunswick, N.J.: Rutgers University Press, 2000.
Jeffreys-Jones, Rhodri, and Bruce Collins. *The Growth of Federal Power in American History*. DeKalb: Northern Illinois University Press, 1983.
Jewell, James R. "'Doing Nothing with Vengeance,' The Diary of David Hobart Taylor, First Oregon Cavalry, January 1 through May 31, 1862." *Oregon Historical Quarterly* 110 (Winter 2009): 598–622.
Jimerson, Randall C. *The Private Civil War: Popular Thought during the Sectional Conflict*. Baton Rouge: Louisiana State University, 1998.
Johannsen, Robert W., ed. "A Breckinridge Democrat on the Secession Crisis: Letters of Isaac I. Stevens, 1860–1861." *Oregon Historical Society Quarterly* 55 (December 1954): 283–310.
———. *Frontier Politics and the Sectional Conflict: The Pacific Northwest on the Eve of the Civil War*. Seattle: University of Washington Press, 1955.
———. "John Whiteaker, Governor of Oregon, 1858–1862." *Reed College Bulletin* 26 (January 1948): 63–87.
Johnson, Mary E. and Joe Gieger, Jr. "West Virginia's Militia and Home Guard in the Civil War." *West Virginia History* 58 (March 1999): 68–167.
Johnson, Richard. *A Soldier's Reminiscences in Peace and War*. Philadelphia: Lippincott, 1886.
Johnson, Robert U., and Clarence C. Buel, eds. *Battles and Leaders of the Civil War*. 4 vols. New York: Century, 1887.
Jones, Gordon C., ed. *"For My Country": The Richardson Letters, 1861–1865*. Wendell, N.C.: Broadfoot Pub. Co., 1984.
Jones, Jacqueline. "Men and Women in Northern New England during the Era of the Civil War." *Maine Historical Society Quarterly* 33 (Fall 1993): 70–87.
Jones, John. *The Black Laws of Illinois: And a Few Reasons Why They Should be Repealed*. Chicago: Tribune Book and Job Office, 1864.
Jones, Thomas L. "The Union League Club and New York's First Black Regiment in the Civil War." *New York History* 87 (Summer 2006): 313–43.
Jordan, Holman D., Sr. "The Eighth Regiment of Vermont Volunteers in the Laforche Country, 1862–1863." *Vermont History* 31 (April 1963): 106–16.
Jordan, Philip D., and Charles M. Thomas. "Reminiscences of an Ohio Volunteer." *Ohio Archeological and Historical Quarterly* 48 (1939): 304–23.
Jordan, William B. Jr., ed. *The Civil War Journals of John Mead Gould, 1861–1866*. Baltimore: Butternut and Blue, 1997.

———, ed. *Red Diamond Regiment: The 17th Maine Infantry, 1862–1865*. Shippensburg, Pa.: White Mane Publishers, 1996.
Jorstad, Erling. "Minnesota's Role in the Democratic Rift of 1860." *Minnesota History* 37 (June 1960): 45–51.
Josephy, Alvin, Jr. *The American Civil War in the American West*. New York: Alfred A. Knopf, 1992.
Julian, George W. *Political Recollections, 1840–1872*. Chicago: Jansen, McClurg and Company, 1884.
Kaiser, Leo, ed., "Letters from the Front." *Illinois State Historical Journal* 56 (Summer 1963): 150–64.
Kamm, Samuel R. "The Civil War Career of Thomas A. Scott." Ph.D. Diss., University of Pennsylvania, 1940.
Kamphoefner, Walter, and Wolfgang Helbich, eds. *Germans in the Civil War: The Letters They Wrote Home*. Translated by Susan Carter Vogel. Chapel Hill: University of North Carolina Press, 2006.
Karamanski, Theodore. *Rally 'Round the Flag: Chicago and the Civil War*. Lanham, Md.: Rowman & Littlefield, 2006.
Kashatus, William C. "Pennsylvania's War Governor." *Pennsylvania Heritage* 36 (Winter 2010): 22–31.
Keller, Christian B. *Chancellorsville and the Germans: Nativism, Ethnicity, and the Civil War Memory*. New York: Fordham University Press, 2007.
Keller, Morton. *Affairs of State: Public Life in Late Nineteenth Century America*. Cambridge, Mass.: Belknap Press of Harvard University Press, 1977.
Kelley, Brooks M. "Fossildom, Old Fogyism, and Red Tape." *Pennsylvania Magazine of History and Biography* 90 (January 1966): 93–114.
Kelly, Jack. "John J. Crittenden and the Constitutional Union Party." *Filson Club History Quarterly* 48 (July 1974): 265–76.
Kelly, Orr and Mary Davies Kelly, eds. *Dream's End: Two Iowa Brothers in the Civil War*. New York: Kodansha International, 1998.
Kelsey, Kerck. *Israel Washburn Jr., Maine's Little-Known Giant of the Civil War*. Rockport, Maine: Picton Press, 2004.
———. "Maine's War Governor: Israel Washburn Jr. and the Race to Save the Union," *Maine History* 42 (2006): 235–57.
Keneally, Thomas. *American Scoundrel: The Life of the Notorious Civil War General Dan Sickles*. New York: Doubleday, 2002.
Kennedy, Elijah R. *The Contest for California in 1861: How Colonel E.D. Baker Saved the Pacific States to the Union*. New York: Houghton Mifflin Co., 1912.
Kibby, Leo. "California Soldiers in the Civil War." *California Historical Society Quarterly* 40 (December 1961): 343–49.
———. "Some Aspects of California's Military Problems during the Civil War." *Civil War History* 5 (September 1959): 251–62.
———. "Union Loyalty of California's Civil War Governors." *California Historical Society Quarterly* 44 (December 1965): 311–22.
Kimball, Emery L. "Richard Yates: His Record as Civil War Governor of Illinois." *Journal of the Illinois State Historical Society* 23 (April 1930): 1–83.
Kiper, Richard L., ed. *Dear Catharine, Dear Taylor: The Civil War Letters of a Union Soldier and His Wife*. Lawrence: University Press of Kansas, 2002.

———. *Major General John Alexander McClernand: Politician in Uniform*. Kent, Ohio: Kent State University Press, 1999.
Kirkpatrick, Arthur R. "The Admission of Missouri to the Confederacy." *Missouri Historical Review* 55 (July 1961): 366–86.
———. "Missouri's Secessionist Government, 1861–1865." *Missouri Historical Review* 45 (January 1951): 124–37.
Kleber, John E. ed. *The Kentucky Encyclopedia*. Lexington: University Press of Kentucky, 1992.
Klement, Frank. "'Brick' Pomeroy: Copperhead and Curmudgeon." *Wisconsin Magazine of History* 25 (Winter 1951): 106–13.
———. "Copperheads and Copperheadism in Wisconsin: Democratic Opposition to the Lincoln Administration." *Wisconsin Magazine of History* 42 (Spring 1959): 182–92.
———. *The Copperheads of the Middle West*. Chicago: University of Chicago Press, 1960.
———. *Dark Lanterns: Secret Political Societies, Conspiracies, and Treason Trials in the Civil War*. Baton Rouge: Louisiana State University Press, 1984.
———. "The Hopkins Hoax and the Golden Circle Rumors in Michigan, 1861–1862." *Michigan History Magazine* 47 (March 1963): 1–14.
———. *The Limits of Dissent: Clement L. Vallandigham and the Civil War*. Lexington: University of Kentucky Press, 1970.
———. *Lincoln's Critics: The Copperheads of the North*. Edited by Steven K. Rogstand. Shippensburg, Penn.: White Mane Books, 1999.
———. "Milwaukee Women and the Civil War." *Historical Messenger of the Milwaukee County Historical Society* 21 (March 1965): 9–14.
———. "Rumors of Golden Circle Activity in Iowa during the Civil War." *Annals of Iowa* 37 (Winter 1965): 523–36.
———. "The Soldier in Wisconsin during the Civil War." *Wisconsin Magazine of History* 28 (September 1944): 37–47.
———. "Wisconsin and the Re-election of Lincoln in 1864." *Historical Messenger of the Milwaukee Historical Society* 22 (March 1966): 20–42.
Klingaman, William. *Abraham Lincoln and the Road to Emancipation, 1861–1865*. New York: Viking, 2001.
Knapp, Charles M. *New Jersey Politics during the Period of the Civil War and Reconstruction*. Geneva, N.J.: W. F. Humphrey, 1924.
Knight, Brian L. *No Braver Deeds: The Story of the Equinox Guards*. Manchester, Vt.: Friends of Hildene, Inc., 2004.
Koerting, Gayla. "For Law and Order: Joseph Holt, the Civil War, and the Judge Advocate General's Department." *Register of the Kentucky Historical Society* 97 (Winter 1999): 1–26.
Kornweibel, Theodore, Jr. "The Occupation of Santa Catalina Island during the Civil War." *California Historical Society Quarterly* 46 (December 1967): 345–57.
Krenkel, John H., ed. *Richard Yates, Civil War Governor. By Richard Yates and Catherine Yates Pickering*. Danville, Ill.: Interstate Printers and Publishers, 1966.
Laas, Virginia. *Wartime Washington: The Civil War Letters of Elizabeth Blair Lee*. Urbana: Illinois University Press, 1991.
Lalande, Jeff. "'Dixie' of the Pacific Northwest: Southern Oregon's Civil War." *Oregon Historical Quarterly* 100 (1999): 35–43.

Lamphier, Peg A. *Kate Chase and William Sprague: Politics and Gender in a Civil War Marriage*. Lincoln: University of Nebraska Press, 2003.
Lane, J. Robert. *A Political History of Connecticut during the Civil War*. Washington, D.C.: Catholic University Press, 1941.
Lang, Theodore F. *Loyal West Virginia*. Baltimore: Deutsch Publishing, Co., 1895.
Langford, Victor. "Constitutional Issues Raised by West Virginia's Admission into the Union." *West Virginia History* 2 (October 1940): 12–35.
Lathrop, Charles. *A History of the First Regiment of Iowa Cavalry*. Lyons, Iowa: Beers and Eaton Printers, 1890.
Lathrop, Henry W. *The Life and Times of Samuel J. Kirkwood*. Iowa City, Iowa: Lathrop, 1893.
Lawson, Melinda. *Patriot Fires: Forging a New American Nationalism in the Civil War North*. Lawrence: University Press of Kansas, 2002.
Leach, Margaret. *Reveille in Washington, 1860–1865*. New York: Harper, 1941.
Lee, Bill R. "Missouri's Fight Over Emancipation in 1863." *Missouri Historical Review* 45 (April 1951): 256–74.
Lee, Jacob F. "Unionism, Emancipation, and the Origins of Kentucky's Confederate Identity." *Register of the Kentucky Historical Society* 111 (Spring 2013): 199–223.
Lee, R. Alton. "The Corwin Amendment in the Secession Crisis." *The Ohio Historical Quarterly* 70 (January 1961): 1–26.
Leeke, Jim, ed. *A Hundred Days to Richmond*. Bloomington: Indiana University Press, 1999.
Leonard, Elizabeth D. *Lincoln's Forgotten Ally: Judge Advocate General Joseph Holt of Kentucky*. Chapel Hill: University of North Carolina Press, 2011.
Lendt, David L. "Iowa and the Copperhead Movement." *Annals of Iowa* 40 (Fall 1970): 412–62.
———. "Iowa's Civil War Marshall: A Lesson in Expedience." *Annals of Iowa* 43 (Fall 1975): 132–39.
Lerch, Kathryn W. "The 8th New York Heavy Artillery in Baltimore, 1862–1864." *Maryland Historical Magazine* 92 (Spring 1997): 93–118.
"The Letters of Samuel James Reader, 1861–1863: Pioneer of Soldier Township, Shawnee County." *Kansas Historical Quarterly* 9 (February 1940): 26–57.
"Letters of a War Governor." *The Iowa Historical Record* 2 (July 1886): 321–28, 372–78.
"Letters of a War Governor." *The Iowa Historical Record* 7 (January 1891): 39–41.
Levene, Byron H. "Lincoln and McCormick: Two American Emancipators." *Wisconsin Magazine of History* 42 (Winter 1958–59): 97–101.
Levin, Kevin M. *Remembering the Battle of the Crater: War as Murder*. Lexington: University Press of Kentucky, 2012.
Levine, Peter. "Draft Evasion in the North during the Civil War, 1863–1865." *Journal of American History* 67 (March 1981): 816–34.
Lewellen, Fred B. "Political Ideas of James W. Grimes." *Iowa Journal of History and Politics* 42 (October 1944): 339–404.
Lewis, Lloyd. *Captain Sam Grant*. Boston, Mass.: Little Brown and Co., 1950.
———. *Sherman: Fighting Prophet*. New York: Harcourt, Brace and Company, 1932.
Lewis, Martin D. *Lumberman from Flint: The Michigan Career of Henry A. Crapo, 1855–1869*. Detroit: Wayne State University Press, 1958.
Lewis, Patrick A. *For Slavery and Union: Benjamin Buckner and Kentucky Loyalties in the Civil War*. Lexington: University Press of Kentucky, 2015.

Lewis, Virgil A. *How West Virginia Was Made, Proceedings of the First Convention of the People of Northwestern Virginia at Wheeling, May 13–15, 1861, and the Journal of the Second Convention of the People of Northwestern Virginia.* Charleston, W.Va.: News-Mail Company Public Printers, 1909.

Lindenbusch, John H., ed. "The Military History of Daniel Eldredge, Written by Himself." *Historical New Hampshire* 19 (Winter 1964): 3–49.

Link, Kenneth. "Potomac Fever: The Hazards of Camp Life." *Vermont History* 51 (Spring 1983): 69–88.

Lipson, Leslie. *The American Governor from Figurehead to Leader.* Chicago: University of Illinois Press, 1939.

Litwack, Leon. *North of Slavery: The Negro in the Free States, 1790–1860.* Chicago: University of Chicago Press, 1961.

Lockwood, John and Charles Lockwood. *The Siege of Washington: The Untold Story of the Twelve Days that Shook the Union.* New York: Oxford University Press, 2011.

Longacre, Edward G. "The Union Army Occupation of New York City, November 1864." *New York History* 65 (April 1984): 133–58.

———, ed. "Chaos Still Reigns in this Camp—Letters of Lieutenant George N. Bliss, 1st New England Cavalry, March–September, 1862." *Rhode Island History* 36 (1997): 15–24.

Lore, Charles B. "The Life and Character of George P. Fisher." *Papers of the Historical Society of Delaware* (1902): 3–16.

Losson, Chris. "Jacob Dolson Cox: A Military Biography." Ph.D. diss., University of Mississippi, 1993.

Love, William. *Wisconsin in the War of Rebellion.* Chicago: Church and Goldman, 1866.

Loving, Jerome M., ed. *Civil War Letters of George Washington Whitman.* Durham, N.C.: Duke University Press, 1975.

Lowden, Lucy. "The Only Fit and Proper Nomination: New Hampshire at Chicago—1860." *Historical New Hampshire* 29 (Spring 1974): 20–41.

Lowe, Donald. "Army Memoirs of Lucius W. Barber." *Journal of the Illinois State Historical Society* 56 (Summer 1963): 298–315.

Lowry, Thomas P., ed. *Swamp Doctor: The Diary of a Union Surgeon in the Virginia and North Carolina Marshes.* Mechanicsburg, Penn.: Stackpole Books, 2001.

Luke, Bob, and John David Smith. *Soldiering for Freedom: How the Union Army Recruited, Trained, and Deployed the U.S. Colored Troops.* Baltimore: Johns Hopkins University Press, 2014.

Lull, Robert W. *Civil War General and Indian Fighter James M. Williams: Leader of the 1st Kansas Colored Volunteer Infantry and the 8th U.S. Cavalry.* Denton: University of North Texas Press, 2013.

Lusk, David. *Politics and Politicians: A Succinct History of the Politics of Illinois From 1856 to 1884.* Springfield, Ill.: H. W. Rokker, 1884.

Luthin, Reinhard H. "A Discordant Chapter in Lincoln's Administration: The Davis-Blair Controversy." *Maryland Historical Magazine* 39 (March 1944): 25–48.

———. "Indiana and Lincoln's Rise to the Presidency." *Indiana Magazine of History* 38 (1942): 385–406.

Lyford, James O. *Life of Edward H. Rollins.* Boston: Dana Estes and Co., 1906.

Mackay, Winnifred K. "Philadelphia during the Civil War, 1861–1865." *Pennsylvania Magazine of History and Biography* 70 (January 1946): 3–51.

Macleod, Julia H. "John G. Downey as One of the Kings." *California Historical Society Quarterly* 36 (December 1957): 327–31.

Macnamara, Daniel G. *The History of the Ninth Regiment Massachusetts Volunteer Infantry June, 1861–June, 1864*. Boston: E. B. Stillings, 1899. Reprint by Christian G. Samito, New York: Fordham University Press, 2000.

MacVicar, Barbara M. "Southern and Northern Methodism in Civil War California." *California Historical Society Quarterly* 40 (December 1961): 327–42.

Mahin, Dean B. *The Blessed Place of Freedom: Europeans in Civil War America*. Dulles, Va.: Brassey's, Inc., 2002.

Mahon, John K., ed. "The Civil War Letters of Samuel Mahon, Seventh Iowa Infantry." *Iowa Journal of History* 51 (July 1953): 233–66.

Mahood, Wayne. *General Wadsworth: The Life and Times of Brevet Major General James S. Wadsworth*. Cambridge, Mass.: Da Capo Books, 2003.

Manakee, Harold R. *Maryland in the Civil War*. Baltimore: Maryland Historical Society, 1961.

Mannis, Jedediah, and Galen R. Wilson, eds. *Bound to Be a Soldier: The Letters of Private James T. Miller, 111th Pennsylvania Infantry, 1861–1864*. Knoxville: University of Tennessee Press, 2001.

Mansch, Larry D. *Abraham Lincoln, President-Elect: The Four Critical Months from Election to Inauguration*. Jefferson, N.C.: McFarland and Co. Inc., 2005.

Marshall, Jeffrey D., ed. *A War of the People: Vermont Civil War Letters*. Hanover, N.H.: University Press of New England, 1999.

Marszalek, John F. *Commander of All Armies: The Life of Henry W. Halleck*. Cambridge, Mass.: Harvard University Press, 2004.

———. *Sherman: A Soldier's Order for Passion*. New York: Free Press, 1993.

Martin, N. B. "Letters of a Union Officer: L. F. Hubbard and the Civil War." *Minnesota History* 35 (September 1957): 313–19.

Marvel, William. "Answering Lincoln's Call: The First New Hampshire Volunteers." *Historical New Hampshire* 39 (Fall/Winter 1984): 138–50.

———. "Back From the Gates of Hell: The Deadly Campaign of the Drafted Militia." *Historical New Hampshire* 44 (Fall 1989): 105–19.

———. *Burnside*. Chapel Hill: University of North Carolina Press, 1991.

———. *Lincoln's Autocrat: The Life of Edwin Stanton*. Chapel Hill: University of North Carolina Press, 2015.

———. *Lee's Last Retreat: The Fight to Appomattox*. Chapel Hill: University of North Carolina Press, 2002.

———. *Mr. Lincoln Goes to War*. Boston: Houghton Mifflin Company, 2006.

———. "New Hampshire Confederates." *Historical New Hampshire* 38 (Winter 1983): 251–57.

———. "New Hampshire and the Draft, 1863." *Historical New Hampshire* 36 (Spring 1981): 58–72.

———. "A Poor Man's Fight: Civil War Enlistment Patterns in Conway, New Hampshire." *Historical New Hampshire* 43 (Spring 1988): 29–40.

Masur, Kate. *An Example for All the Land: Emancipation and the Struggle Over Equality in Washington, D.C.* Chapel Hill: University of North Carolina Press, 2010.

Masur, Louis P. *Lincoln's Hundred Days: The Emancipation Proclamation and the War for the Union*. Cambridge: Belknap Press of Harvard University Press, 2012.

Matthews, Glenna. *The Golden State in the Civil War: Thomas Starr King, the Republican Party, and the Birth of Modern California*. New York: Cambridge University Press, 2012.

Maust, Roland R. *Grappling with Death: The Union Second Corps Hospital at Gettysburg.* Dayton, OH: Morningside, 2001.
May, George S. *Michigan and the Civil War Years, 1860–1866: A Wartime Chronicle.* Lansing: Michigan Civil War Centennial Observance Commission, 1964.
———. "Politics in Ann Arbor during the Civil War." *Michigan History Magazine* 37 (March 1953): 53–73.
Mayberry, Virginia, and Dawn E. Bakken. "The Civil War Homefront: The Diary of a Young Girl, 1862–1863." *Indiana Magazine of History* 87 (March 1991): 24–78.
McAfee, Ward M. "California: House Divided." *Civil War History* 33 (June 1987): 115–30.
McArthur, Scott. *The Enemy Never Came: The Civil War in the Pacific Northwest.* Caldwell, Idaho: Caxton Press, 2012.
McCandless, Perry, ed. "The Civil War Journal of Stephen Keyes Fletcher." *Indiana Magazine of History* 54 (June 1958): 141–90.
McClellan, George B. *McClellan's Own Story: The War for the Union, the Soldiers Who Fought It, the Civilians Who Directed It, and His relation to It and Them.* New York: Webster, 1886.
McClintock, Russell. *Lincoln and the Decision for War: The Northern Response to Secession.* Chapel Hill: University of North Carolina Press, 2008.
McClure, Alexander K. *Abraham Lincoln and Men of War-Times.* Philadelphia: Times Publishing Co., 1892.
———. *Colonel Alexander K. McClure's Recollections of Half a Century.* Salem, Mass.: Salem Press, Co., 1902.
———. *The Life and Services of Andrew Curtin.* Harrisburg: C. M. Busch, State Printer of Pennsylvania, 1895.
McDonald, Forrest. *States' Rights and the Union.* Lawrence: University of Kansas Press, 2002.
McDonough, Daniel, and Kenneth W. Noe, eds. *Politics and Culture of the Civil War Era: Essays in Honor of Robert W. Johannsen.* Cranberry, N.J.: Associated University Press, 2006.
McDonough, James L. *Shiloh: In Hell before Night.* Knoxville: University of Tennessee Press, 1977.
McLachlan, James, ed. "The Civil War Diary of Joseph H. Coit." *Maryland Historical Magazine* 60 (September 1965): 245–60.
McLaughlin, Florence, ed. "'Dear Sister Jennie—Dear Brother Jacob': The Correspondence Between a Northern Soldier and His Sister in Mechanicsburg, Pennsylvania, 1861–1864." *Western Pennsylvania Historical Magazine* 60 (April 1977): 109–44.
McLean, James. *California Sabers: The 2nd Massachusetts Cavalry in the Civil War.* Bloomington: Indiana University Press, 2001.
McPherson, Edward. *The Political History of the United States during the Great Rebellion.* Washington, D.C.: Philip and Solomons, 1865.
McPherson, James M. *Battle Cry of Freedom: The Civil War Era.* New York: Oxford University Press, 1988.
———. *The Negro's Civil War. How American Negroes Felt and Acted during the War for the Union.* New York: Pantheon Books, 1965.
———. *Tried By War: Abraham Lincoln as Commander in Chief.* New York: Penguin Press, 2008.
———, ed. *"We Cannot Escape History": Lincoln and the Last Best Hope of Earth.* Urbana-Champaign: University of Illinois Press, 1995.

McPherson, James M., and William J. Cooper. *Writing the Civil War: The Quest to Understand.* Columbia: University of South Carolina Press, 1998.

McSeveney, Samuel T. "Re-electing Lincoln: The Union Party Campaign and the Military Vote in Connecticut." *Civil War History* 32 (June 1986): 139–58.

Meade, George. *Life and Letters of George Gordon Meade.* 2 vols. New York: Charles Scribner's Sons, 1913.

Meigs, Montgomery C. "General M. C. Meigs on the Conduct of the Civil War." *American Historical Review.* 26 (January 1921): 285–303.

Melendy, H. Brett, and Benjamin F. Gilbert. *The Governors of California.* Georgetown, Calif.: Talisman Press, 1965.

Mellon, Knox, Jr., ed. "Letters of James Greenalch." *Michigan History* 44 (June 1960): 188–240.

Melton, John L., ed. "The Diary of a Drummer." *Michigan History Magazine* 43 (September 1959): 315–48.

Meneely, A. Howard. *The War Department, 1861: A Study in Mobilization and Administration.* New York: Columbia University Press, 1928.

Merk, Frederick. *Economic History of Wisconsin during the Civil War Decade.* Madison: State Historical Society of Wisconsin, 1916.

Merriam, George S. *Life and Times of Samuel Bowles.* 2 vols. New York: The Century Co., 1885.

"The Messages of Governors Seymour and Parker." *The Old Guard* 2 (February 1864): 37.

Messent, Peter, and Steve Courtney, eds. *The Civil War Letters of Joseph Hopkins Twichell: A Chaplain's Story.* Athens: University of Georgia Press, 2006.

Messmer, Charles. "Louisville and the Confederate Invasion of 1862." *Register of the Kentucky Historical Society* 55 (October 1957): 299–324.

———. "Louisville on the Eve of the Civil War." *Filson Club History Quarterly* 50 (July 1976): 249–89.

———. "Louisville during the Civil War." *Filson Club History Quarterly* 52 (April 1978): 206–33.

Meyers, William Starr. "Governor Bradford's Private List of Union Men in 1861." *Maryland Historical Magazine* 7 (March 1912): 83–90.

Miers, Earl S., ed. *New Jersey and the Civil War.* Princeton, N. J.: D. Van Nostrand, 1964.

Milano, Anthony J. "The Copperhead Regiment: The 20th Massachusetts Infantry." *Civil War Regiments* 3 (1993): 31–63.

Miller, Brian Craig, ed. *"A Punishment on the Nation": An Iowa Soldier Endures the Civil War.* Kent: Kent State University Press, 2012.

Miller, Edward A., Jr. *The Black Civil War Soldiers of Illinois: The Story of the Twenty-Ninth U.S. Colored Infantry.* Columbia: University of South Carolina, 1998.

———. *Lincoln's Abolitionist General: The Biography of David Hunter.* Columbia: University of South Carolina Press, 1997.

Miller, Richard F. "Brahmin Janissaries: John A. Andrew Mobilizes Massachusetts' Upper Class for the Civil War." *New England Quarterly* 75 (June 2002): 204–34.

———. "For His Wife, His Widow, and His Orphan: Massachusetts and Family Aid During the Civil War." *The Massachusetts Historical Review* 6 (2004): 71–106.

———, ed. *States at War.* 5 vols. Lebanon, N.H.: University Press of New England, 2013–15.

Miller, William Lee. *President Lincoln: The Duty of a Statesman.* New York: Knopf Publishing Group, 2008.

Millett, Alan R., and Peter Maslowski. *For the Common Defense: A Military History of the United States of America*. New York: Free Press, 1984.
Millsap, Kenneth. "The Election of 1860 in Iowa." *Iowa Journal of History* 48 (April 1950): 97–120.
Minick, Rachel. "New York Ferry Boats in the Union Navy." *New York Historical Society Quarterly Bulletin* 49 (January 1965): 53–87.
Minor, Craig. "Lane and Lincoln." *Kansas History* 24 (Autumn 2000): 186–99.
Mitchell, Charles W., ed. *Maryland Voices of the Civil War*. Baltimore, Md.: John Hopkins University Press, 2007.
———. "The Whirlwind Now Gathering: Baltimore's Pratt Street Riot and the End of Maryland Secession." *Maryland Historical Magazine* 97 (March 2002): 202–32.
Mitchell, Reid. *The Vacant Chair: The Northern Soldier Leaves Home*. New York: Oxford University Press, 1993.
Mitchell, Robert E. "The Organizational Performance of Michigan's Adjutant General and the Federal Provost Marshal General in Recruiting Michigan's Boys in Blue." *Michigan Historical Review* 28 (Fall 2002): 115–62.
Mitchell, Stewart. *Horatio Seymour of New York*. Cambridge: Harvard University Press, 1938.
Mitchell, Thomas G. *Anti-Slavery Politics in Antebellum and Civil War America*. Westport, Conn.: Praeger Publishers, 2007.
Mitgang, Herbert, ed. *Abraham Lincoln: A Press Portrait*. Chicago: Quadrangle Books, 1971.
Moe, Richard. *The Last Full Measure: The Life and Death of the First Minnesota Volunteers*. St. Paul: Minnesota Historical Society, 1993.
Montgomery, Horace. "A Union Officer's Recollections of the Negro as a Soldier." *Pennsylvania History* 28 (April 1961): 156–86.
Moody, William P. "The Civil War and Reconstruction in California Politics." Ph.D. diss., University of California Los Angeles, 1951.
Mooney, Chase C. "A Union Chaplain's Diary." *Proceedings of the New Jersey Historical Society* 75 (January 1957): 2–16.
Moore, Charles. "The Days of Fife and Drum." *Historical Collections* 28 (1897–98): 437–53.
———. *History of Michigan*. 4 vols. Chicago: Lewis Publishing Co., 1915.
Moore, Frank, ed. *The Rebellion Record: A Diary of American Events*. 12 vols. New York: G. P. Putnam, D. Van Nostrand, 1861–1863, 1864–1868.
Moore, George E. "Slavery as a Factor in the Formation of West Virginia." *West Virginia History* 18 (October 1956): 5–89.
Moore, Kenneth A. "Frederick Holbrook." *Vermont History* 32 (April 1964): 65–78.
Morgan, H. Wayne. "A Civil War Diary of William McKinley." *Ohio Historical Quarterly* 69 (July 1960): 272–90.
Morris, Roy Jr. *Sheridan: The Life and Wars of General Phil Sheridan*. New York: Crown Publishers, 1992.
Morse, John T., ed. *Memoir of Colonel Henry Lee*. Boston: Little, Brown and Co., 1905.
Morton, Louis. "Vermonters at Cedar Creek." *Vermont History* 33 (April 1965): 326–40.
Moses, John. *Illinois, Historical and Statistical*. 2 vols. Chicago: Fergus Printing Company, 1892.
Mowry, Duane. "A Statesman's Letters of the Civil War Period." *Journal of the Illinois State Historical Society* 2 (July 1909): 43–50.

Mowry, William A. "Reminiscences of Lincoln: Told By the Late Ex-Governor Curtin, of Pennsylvania." *The Independent* 49 (August 1897): 4.

"Mrs. Cooke's Civil War Diary, 1863–1864." *Vermont Historical Society Proceedings* 25 (January 1957): 56–65.

Mulligan, Thomas C. "Lest the Rebels Come to Power: The Life of William Dennison, 1815–1882: Early Ohio Republican." Ph.D. diss., Ohio State University, 1994.

Munroe, John A. *History of Delaware*. Newark: University of Delaware Press, 1979.

Murdock, Eugene. *Patriotism Limited, 1862–1865: The Civil War Draft and the Bounty System*. Kent, Ohio: Kent State University Press, 1967.

Myers, William S. *The Maryland Constitution of 1864*. Baltimore: Johns Hopkins University Press, 1901.

———. *The Self-Reconstruction of Maryland, 1864–1867*. Baltimore: Johns Hopkins University Press, 1909.

Nash, Eugene A. *A History of the Forty-fourth Regiment New York Volunteer Infantry*. Chicago: R. B. Donnelly and Sons, 1911.

Nation, Richard A., and Stephen E. Towne, eds. *Indiana's War: The Civil War in Documents*. Athens: Ohio University Press, 2009.

Neely, Mark E. *The Fate of Liberty: Abraham Lincoln and Civil Liberties*. New York: Oxford University Press, 1991.

———. *Lincoln and the Triumph of the Nation: Constitutional Conflict in the American Civil War*. Chapel Hill: University of North Carolina Press, 2011.

Nelson, Jacquelyn S. "The Military Response of the Society of Friends in Indiana to the Civil War." *Indiana Magazine of History* 81 (June 1985): 101–30.

Nelson, James G. "My Dear Son: Letters to a Civil War Soldier." *Filson Club History Quarterly* 56 (April 1982): 151–69.

Nesenhoener, Stefan. "Maintaining the Center: John Pendleton Kennedy, the Border States, and the Secession Crisis." *Maryland Historical Magazine* 89 (Winter 1994): 413–26.

Nevins, Allan. *The Emergence of Lincoln*. New York: Charles Scribner's Sons, 1950.

———. *Fremont: Pathfinder of the West*. Lincoln: University of Nebraska Press, 1992.

———. *The War for the Union: The Improvised War, 1861–1862*. New York: Charles Scribner's Sons, 1959.

———. *The War for the Union: The Organized War, 1863–1864*. New York: Charles Scribner's Sons, 1971.

———. *The War for the Union: The Organized War to Victory, 1864–1865*. New York: Charles Scribner's Sons, 1971.

———. *The War for the Union: War Becomes Revolution*. New York: Charles Scribner's Sons, 1960.

Newberry, J. S. *The U. S. Sanitary Commission in the Valley of Mississippi during the War of the Rebellion, 1861–1866*. Cleveland: Fairbanks, Benedict, & Co., 1871.

Newell, Graham S. "Erastus Fairbanks." *Vermont History* 32 (April 1964): 59–64.

Nichols, David A. "The Other Civil War: Lincoln and the Indians." *Minnesota History* 44 (Spring 1974): 2–15.

Nicklason, Fred. "The Secession Winter and the Committee of Five." *Pennsylvania History* 38 (October 1971): 372–88.

Nicolay, John G., and John Hay. *Abraham Lincoln: A History*. 10 vols. New York: Century Co., 1890.

———. "Abraham Lincoln: A History. 1: The Fourteenth of April–The Fate of the Assassins–The Mourning Pageant." *Century Illustrated Magazine* 39 (January 1890): 428–42.
———. *Complete Works of Abraham Lincoln*. 12 vols. New York: Francis D. Tandy Co., 1905.
Niven, John. *Connecticut for the Union*. New Haven, Conn.: Yale University Press, 1965.
———. *Salmon P. Chase: A Biography*. New York: Oxford University Press, 1995.
———, ed. *The Salmon P. Chase Papers*. 5 vols. Kent, Ohio: Kent State University Press, 1994.
Noe, Kenneth W. "The Conservative: A Civil War Soldier's Musical Condemnation of Illinois Copperheads." *Illinois Historical Journal* 84 (Winter 1991): 268–72.
———. *Perryville: The Grand Havoc of Battle*. Lexington: University Press of Kentucky, 2001.
Nolan, Dick. *Benjamin Franklin Butler: The Damnedest Yankee*. Novato, Calif.: Presidio Press, 1991.
Nolin, Kelly A., ed. "The Civil War Letters of S. E. and S. M. Pingree, 1862–1864." *Vermont History* 63 (Spring 1995): 80–94.
———. "The Civil War Letters of SGT. J. O. Cross, 29th Connecticut Volunteer Infantry (Colored)." *Connecticut Historical Society Bulletin* 60 (Summer/Fall 1995): 211–35.
Norris, James, ed. "A Northern Businessman Opposes the Civil War: Excerpts from the Letters of R. G. Dun." *Ohio History* 71 (July 1962): 138–47.
Norton, Frederick C. *The Governors of Connecticut*. Hartford: Connecticut Magazine Co., 1905.
Nortrup, Jack J. "Richard Yates: Civil War Governor of Illinois." Ph.D. diss., University of Illinois, 1960.
———. "Richard Yates: A Personal Glimpse of the Illinois Soldier's Friend." *Journal of the Illinois State Historical Society* 56 (Summer 1963): 121–38.
———. "Yates, the Prorogued Legislature, and the Constitutional Convention." *Journal of the Illinois State Historical Society* 62 (Spring 1969): 5–34.
"Not Alarmed By His Yell: A Short Story Illustrating Lincoln's Unerring Judgment." *Michigan Farmer* (February 13, 1904): 155.
Noyes, Edward. "The Negro in Wisconsin's War Effort." *The Lincoln Herald* 69 (Summer 1967): 70–82.
O'Brien, Lillian, and John D. Haynes. "The Battle of Port Royal Ferry, South Carolina with the Liberty for New Year's Eve and Day, 1862 from the Journal of John Stanford Barnes." *New York Historical Society Quarterly Bulletin* 47 (April 1963): 109–36.
Öfele, Martin W. *German-Speaking Officers in the U.S. Colored Troops, 1863–1867*. Gainesville: University Press of Florida, 2004.
O'Leary, Jenny, and Harvey H. Jackson, eds. "The Civil War Letters of Captain Daniel O'Leary, U.S.A." *Register of the Kentucky Historical Society* 77 (Summer 1979): 157–85.
Oliver, David L. "The Contribution of Kentucky to Lincoln's Fourth of July Session of Congress, 1861." *Register of the Kentucky Historical Society* 60 (April 1962): 134–42.
Oliver, John W. "Draft Riots in Wisconsin during the Civil War." *Wisconsin Magazine of History* 2 (1919): 334–37.
"Oregon: Capital, Salem," *The American Almanac and Repository of Useful Knowledge* 25 (1860): 323.
Orme, William Ward. "Civil War Letters of Brigadier General William Ward Orme, 1862–66." *Journal of the Illinois State Historical Society* 23 (July 1930): 246–315.

Orr, Timothy J. "Cities at War: Union Army Mobilization in the Urban Northeast, 1861–1865." Ph.D. diss., Penn State University, 2010.

"Our New Governor." *American Phrenological Journal* 41 (March 1865): 1–2.

Oyos, Matthew. "The Mobilization of the Ohio Militia in the Civil War." *Ohio History* 98 (Summer 1989): 147–74.

Palmer, Beverly W. *The Selected Letters of Charles Sumner*. Boston: Northeastern University Press, 1990.

Palmer, John M. *Personal Recollections*. Cincinnati: Robert Clarke Co., 1901.

Paludan, Phillip Shaw. *A People's Contest: The Union and the Civil War, 1861–1865*. New York: Harper & Row, 1988.

———. "Federalism in the Civil War Era." *Halcyon* 10 (1988): 27–39.

———. *The Presidency of Abraham Lincoln*. Lawrence: University Press of Kansas, 1994.

Parker, John L. *History of the Twenty-Second Massachusetts Infantry, the Second Company Sharpshooters, and the Third Light Battery, in the War of the Rebellion*. Boston: Regimental Association, 1887.

Parish, Peter J. *The North and the Nation in the Era of the Civil War*. Edited by Adam I. P. Smith, and Susan-Mary Grant. New York: Fordham University Press, 2003.

———. "A Talent for Survival: American Federalism in the Era of the Civil War." *Historical Research* 62 (1989): 178–92.

Parker, John Lord. *Henry Wilson's Regiment. History of the Twenty-second Massachusetts Infantry, the Second Company Sharpshooters, and the Third Light Battery, in the War of the Rebellion*. Boston: Press of Rand Avery Co., 1887.

Parker, Theodore R. "Western Pennsylvania and the Naval War on the Inland Rivers, 1861–1863." *Pennsylvania History* 16 (July 1949): 221–29.

Parks, George E. "One Story of the 109th Illinois Volunteer Infantry Regiment." *Journal of the Illinois State Historical Society* 56 (Summer 1963): 282–97.

Parrish, William E. *Frank Blair: Lincoln's Conservative*. Columbus: University of Missouri Press, 1998.

———. *Turbulent Partnership: Missouri and the Union*. Columbus: University of Missouri Press, 1963.

Parsons, Joseph. "Indiana and the Call for Volunteers, April 1861." *Indiana Magazine of History* 54 (March 1958): 1–23.

Patrick, Jeffrey L. and Robert J. Willey, eds. *Fighting for Liberty and Right: The Civil War Diary of William Bluffton Miller, First Sergeant, Company K, Seventy-fifth Indiana Volunteer Infantry*. Knoxville: University of Tennessee Press, 2005.

Patton, John. *Austin Blair, War Governor: An Address*. 1898.

Pearson, Henry G. *The Life of John A. Andrew*. 2 vols. Boston: Houghton Mifflin, 1904.

Pease, T. C., and James G. Randall, eds. *The Diary of Orville Hickman Browning*. 2 vols. Springfield: Illinois State Historical Library, 1925–33.

Perret, Geoffrey. *Lincoln's War: The Untold Story of America's Greatest President as Commander in Chief*. New York: Random House, 2004.

"Personal Narratives of the Civil War in the Collection of the Vermont Historical Society." *Vermont History* 31 (April 1963): 117–21.

Peskin, Allan. "The Hero of the Sandy Valley: James A. Garfield's Kentucky Campaign of 1861–1862." *Ohio History* 72 (January 1963): 3–24; 72 (April 1963): 129–39.

"Peter Wilson in the Civil War." *Iowa Journal of History and Politics* 40 (April 1942): 153–203; (July 1942): 261–320; (October 1942): 339–414.

Peterson, John M., ed. "Letters of Edward and Sarah Fitch, Lawrence, Kansas, 1855–1863, Part II." *Kansas History* 12 (Summer 1989): 78–100.

Peterson, Richard H. "The United States Sanitary Commission and Thomas Starr King in California, 1861–1864." *California History* 72 (Winter 1993–94): 324–37.

Peterson, William S. "A History of Camp Butler, 1861–1866." *Illinois Historical Journal* 82 (Summer 1989): 74–92.

Philips. John F. "Hamilton Rowan Gamble and the Provisional Government of Missouri." *Missouri Historical Review* 5 (October 1910): 1–14.

Phillips, Christopher. *Damned Yankee: The Life of General Nathaniel Lyon.* Columbia: University of Missouri Press, 1990.

———. *Missouri's Confederate Governor: Claiborne Fox Jackson and the Creation of Southern Identity with the Border West.* Columbia: University of Missouri Press, 2000.

Phisterer, Frederick, ed. *New York in the War of the Rebellion, 1861 to 1865.* Albany, N.Y.: J. B. Lyon Company, State Printers, 1912.

Pierce, Edward L. *Memoir and Letters of Charles Summer.* 4 vols. Boston: Richard Brothers, 1877–93.

Pierpont, Francis H. *Letter of Governor Pierpont to His Excellency the President and the Honorable Congress of the United States.* Washington, D.C.: McGill and Witherow, Printers, 1864.

Pillsbury, Hobart. *New Hampshire: Resources, Attractions, and Its People, A History.* 5 vols. New York: The Lewis Historical Publishing Co., 1927.

Piston, William Garrett. "The 1st Iowa Volunteers: Honor and Community in the Ninety-Day Regiment." *Civil War History* 44 (March 1998): 5–23.

Piston, William Garrett, and Richard W. Hatcher III. *Wilson's Creek: The Second Battle of the Civil War and the Men Who Fought It.* Chapel Hill: University of North Carolina Press, 2006.

Platt, Hermann K., ed. *Charles Perrin Smith: New Jersey Political Reminiscences, 1828–1882.* New Brunswick, N.J.: Rutgers University Press, 1965.

Plummer, Mark A. *Frontier Governor: Samuel J. Crawford of Kansas.* Lawrence: University Press of Kansas, 1971.

———. *Lincoln's Rail-Splitter: Governor Richard Oglesby.* Urbana-Champaign: University of Illinois Press, 2001.

Pohl, James. "From Davenport to Vicksburg: The Odyssey of a Soldier in the Civil War." *Annals of Iowa* 40 (Winter 1971): 494–517.

Pollock, Ivan L. "The Iowa War Loan of 1861." *Iowa Journal of History and Politics* 15 (October 1917): 467–502.

———. "State Finances in Iowa during the Civil War." *Iowa Journal of History and Politics* 16 (January 1918): 53–107.

Ponce, Pearl T., ed. *Kansas's War: The Civil War in Documents.* Athens: Ohio University Press, 2011.

Porter, George. *Ohio Politics during the Civil War Period.* New York: Columbia University Press, 1911.

Porter, Horace. *Campaigning with Grant.* New York: Century Company, 1897. Reprint, edited by Brooks Simpson, University of Nebraska Press, 2000.

Porter, Noah. "Memoir of the Hon. William A. Buckingham, LL.D." *New England Historical and Genealogical Register* 30 (January 1876): 2–9.

Potter, Marguerite. "Hamilton R. Gamble: Missouri's War Governor." *Missouri Historical Review* 34 (October 1940): 25–71.

Povenmire, H. M., ed. "Diary of Jacob Adams." *Ohio State Archeological and Historical Quarterly* 38 (1929): 627–721.

Powell, Walter. "'Heaven Alone Can Soothe the Heart': A New Haven Family's Search for Its Missing Son, Major Edward F. Blake." *Connecticut Historical Bulletin* (1983): 53–71.

Powell, Walter A. *A History of Delaware*. Boston: Christopher Publishing House, 1928.

Pratt, Harry E. "The Repudiation of Lincoln's War Policy, 1862: Stuart-Swett Congressional Campaign." *Journal of the Illinois State Historical Society* 24 (April 1931): 129–40.

Prezelski, Tom. *Californio Lancers: The 1st Battalion of Native Cavalry in the Far West, 1863–1866*. Norman: University of Oklahoma Press, 2015.

Pritchett, John P., Frances Katzman, and Howard Dellon. "The Union Defense Committee of the City of New York during the Civil War." *New York Historical Society Quarterly Bulletin* 30 (July 1946): 142–60.

Pula, James S. *The Sigel Regiment: A History of the 26th Wisconsin Volunteer Infantry, 1862–1865*. Campbell, Calif.: Savas Publishing Co., 1998.

Pullen, John. *The Twentieth Maine*. Philadelphia: J. B. Lippincott, 1957.

Purdy, Mary. "The Governorship of John Gately Downey of California, 1860–1862." M.A. thesis, Stanford University, 1933.

Quarles, Benjamin. *Lincoln and the Negro*. New York: Oxford University Press, 1962.

———. *The Negro in the Civil War*. Boston: Little, Brown, and Co., 1953.

Quiner, Edwin Bentley. *The Military History of Wisconsin: A Record of the Civil and Military Patriotism of the State in the War for the Union*. Chicago: Clarke and Co., 1866.

Raber, Laurence B. "The Formation and Early Development of the Republican Party in Rhode Island, 1850–1865." M.A. thesis, University of Rhode Island, 1965.

Rable, George C. *Fredericksburg! Fredericksburg!* Chapel Hill: University of North Carolina, 2002.

Racine, Philip N., ed. Unspoiled Heart: The Journal of Charles Mattocks of the 17th Maine. Knoxville: University of Tennessee Press, 1994.

Radcliffe, George L. *Governor Thomas H. Hicks of Maryland and the Civil War*. Baltimore: Johns Hopkins University Press, 1901.

Ramsey, Alexander. "Minnesota and the War" in *Glimpses of the Nation's Struggle, Minnesota Commandery*, edited by Edward D. Neill. 3 vols. St. Paul: St. Paul Book and Stationary Company, 1890.2:227–31.

Ramsey, Richard David. "The Marsh-Carrington Letters: Part One." *Connecticut Historical Bulletin* 42 (1977): 114–28.

Randall, James G. "Civil and Military Relationships under Lincoln." *Pennsylvania Magazine of History and Biography* 69 (July 1945): 199–206.

———. *Lincoln the President*. 4 vols. New York: Dodd, Mead & Company, 1945. Revised edition, with new introduction by Richard Current. New York: Da Capo Press, 1997.

Raney, William F. *Wisconsin: A Story of Progress*. New York: Prentice Hall, 1940.

Ranney, Joseph A. "Suffering the Agonies of Righteousness." *Wisconsin Magazine of History* 75 (Winter 1992): 83–116.

Rawley, James A. *Edwin D. Morgan, 1811–1883: Merchant in Politics*. New York: Columbia University Press, 1955.

———. "Lincoln and Governor Morgan." *Abraham Lincoln Quarterly* 6 (March 1951): 272–300.

———. *The Politics of Union: Northern Politics during the Civil War*. Lincoln: University of Nebraska Press, 1974.
Raymond, Henry J. and Frank B. Carpenter, *The Life and Public Services of Abraham Lincoln*. 2 vols. New York: Derby and Miller, 1865.
Reavis, Logan U. *The Life and Public Services of Richard Yates: The War Governor of Illinois*. St. Louis: J. H. Chambers & Co., 1881.
Reed, H. Clay. "Lincoln's Compensated Emancipation Plan and its Relation to Delaware." *Delaware Notes* (1931): 27–78.
Reed, Thomas. *Tibbits' Boys: A History of the Twenty-first New York Cavalry*. Lanham, Md.: University Press of America, 1997.
Reid, Whitelaw. *Ohio in the War*. 2 vols. Cincinnati: Moore, Wilstach and Baldwin, 1868.
Reinsburg, Mark, ed. "A Bucktail's Voice: Civil War Correspondence of Pvt. Cordello Collins." *Western Pennsylvania Historical Magazine* 48 (July 1965): 235–48.
Remensnyder, Junius Benjamin. "With Lincoln at Gettysburg." *McClure's* 54 (March 1922): 40–46.
Remini, Robert V. *The House: The History of the House of Representatives*. New York: Smithsonian Books in Association with Harpers Collins, 2006.
Renda, Lex. "Credit and Culpability: New Hampshire State Politics during the Civil War." *Historical New Hampshire* 48 (Spring 1993): 3–84.
———. *Running on the Record: Civil War-Era Politics in New Hampshire*. Charlottesville: University Press of Virginia, 1997.
Rhea, Gordon. *The Battle of the Wilderness, May 5–6, 1864*. Baton Rouge: Louisiana State University Press, 2004.
———. *Cold Harbor: Grant and Lee, May 26–June 3, 1864*. Baton Rouge: Louisiana State University Press, 2007.
Rhodes, Jason. *Somerset County, Maryland: A Brief History*. Charleston, S.C.: History Press, 2007.
———. "The Overland Campaign of 1864." *Hallowed Ground* 15 (Spring 2014): 17–35.
Rice, Allen T., ed. *Reminiscences of Abraham Lincoln by Distinguished Men of His Time*. New York: Harper and Brothers Publishers, 1909.
Richards, Donald H. "The Fifth New Hampshire Volunteers (Light Infantry)." *Historical New Hampshire* 28 (Winter 1973): 241–61.
Richardson, Lucy, ed. "Selections from Frank Dickerson's Civil War Letters." *Maine Historical Society Quarterly* 28 (Summer 1988): 36–53.
Ridderbusch, Michael R., ed. "The Lincoln Reminiscence Manuscript in the Francis Harrison Pierpont Papers." *West Virginia History* 1 (Spring 2007): 75–92.
Rissle, Albert G. *Recollections of War Times*. New York: G.P. Putnam's Sons, 1895.
Roark, James. "George W. Julian: Radical Land Reformer." *Indiana Magazine of History* 64 (March 1968): 25–36.
Robboy, Stanley J., and Anita W. Robby. "Lewis Hayden: From Fugitive-Slave to Statesman." *New England Quarterly* 46 (December 1973): 591–613.
Roberts, Sellew A. "The Federal Government and Confederate Cotton." *American Historical Review* 32 (January 1927): 262–75.
Robertson, James I., Jr., ed. *The Civil War Letters of General Robert McAllister*. New Brunswick, N.J.: Rutgers University Press, 1965.
———. *Stonewall Jackson: The Man, the Soldier, the Legend*. New York: Macmillan, 1997.
———, ed. "Such Is War: The Letters of an Orderly in the Seventh Iowa Infantry." *Iowa Journal of History* 58 (October 1960): 321–56.

Robertson, John. *Michigan in the War*. Lansing, Mich.: W. S. George and Co., 1880.
Robinson, Elwyn B. "The Press: President Lincoln's Philadelphia Organ." *Pennsylvania Magazine of History and Biography* 65 (April 1941): 157–70.
Robinson, John W. "A California Copperhead: Henry Hamilton and the Los Angeles *Star*." *Arizona and the West* 23 (1981): 213–30.
———. "Colonel Edward J. C. Kewen: Los Angeles' Fire-Eating Orator of the Civil War Era." *Dogtown Territorial Quarterly* 38 (1999): 46–59.
———. *Los Angeles in Civil War Days, 1860–1865*. Los Angeles: Dawson's Book Shop, 1977.
Robinson, William S. *A Conspiracy to Defame John A. Andrew*. Boston: Wright & Potter, 1862.
Rodgers, Thomas E. "Hoosier Women and the Civil War Home Front." *Indiana Magazine of History* 97 (June 2001): 105–28.
———. "Liberty, Will, and Violence: The Political Ideology of the Democrats of West-Central Indiana during the Civil War." *Indiana Magazine of History* 92 (June 1996): 133–59.
———. "Republicans and Drifters: Political Affiliations and Union Army Volunteers in West Central Indiana." *Indiana Magazine of History* 92 (December 1996): 321–45.
Roe, Alfred S. *The Tenth Regiment Massachusetts Volunteer Infantry*. Springfield, Mass.: Tenth Regimental Veteran Association, 1898.
Roe, Alfred S., and Charles Nutt. *History of the First Regiment of Heavy Artillery*. Worcester, Mass.: The Regimental Association, 1917.
Roland, Charles P. *Albert Sidney Johnston: Soldier of the Republics*. Austin: University of Texas Press, 1964.
Rosenberg, Morton M. "The Election of 1859 in Iowa." *Iowa Journal of History* 57 (January 1959): 1–22.
———. "The People of Iowa on the Eve of the Civil War." *Annals of Iowa* 39 (Fall 1967): 105–33.
Rosentreter, Roger L. "Michigan My Michigan." *Michigan History Magazine* 82 (September 1998): 22–27.
Rosin, Wilbert. "Hamilton Rowan Gamble." Ph.D. diss., University of Missouri, 1960.
Ross, Earle D. "Northern Sectionalism in the Civil War Era." *Iowa Journal of History and Politics* 30 (October 1932): 455–512.
Ross, Russell M. "The Powers of the Governor of Iowa." *Iowa Journal of History* 52 (April 1954): 129–40.
Rothschild, Alonzo. *Lincoln, Master of Men: A Study in Character*. Boston: Houghton Mifflin, 1924.
Roy, Charles. "Richard W. Thompson: A Political Conservative in the Fifties." *Indiana Magazine of History* 27 (September 1931): 183–206.
Rugh, Susan. "Awful Calamities Now Upon Us: The Civil War in Fountain Green, Illinois." *Journal of the Illinois State Historical Society* 93 (Spring 2000): 9–40.
Rundell, Walter, Jr. "Despotism of Traitors: The Rebellious South through New York Eyes." *New York History* 45 (October 1964): 331–67.
Russ, William A., Jr. "Franklin Weirick: 'Copperhead' of Central Pennsylvania." *Pennsylvania History* 5 (October 1938): 245–56.
Russell, William. "A Biography of Alexander K. McClure." Ph.D. diss., University of Wisconsin, 1953.

———. "A. K. McClure and the People's Party in the Campaign of 1860." *Pennsylvania History* 28 (October 1961): 335–45.
Rutland, Robert. "The Copperheads of Iowa: A Re-examination." *Iowa Journal of History* 52 (January 1954): 1–30.
Sage, Leland. "William B. Allison's First Term in Congress, 1863–1865." *Iowa Journal of History* 50 (October 1952): 315–44.
Salter, William. *The Life of James W. Grimes: Governor of Iowa, 1854–1858*. New York: D. Appleton and Company, 1876.
Samito, Christian G. *Becoming American under Fire: Irish Americans, African Americans, and the Politics of Citizenship during the Civil War Era*. Ithaca, N.Y.: Cornell University Press, 2009.
Sampson, Robert D. "'Pretty Damned Warm Times': The 1864 Charleston Riot and the 'inalienable right of revolution.'" *Illinois Historical Journal* 89 (Summer 1996): 99–116.
"Samuel Kirkwood's First Meeting with Lincoln." *The Iowa Historical Record* 7 (January 1891): 34–38.
Sanderlin, Walter S. "A House Divided: The Conflict of Loyalties on the Chesapeake and Ohio Canal, 1861–1865." *Maryland Historical Magazine* 42 (September 1947): 206–13.
Sanders, Charles W. *While in the Hands of the Enemy: Military Prisons of the Civil War*. Baton Rouge: Louisiana State University Press, 2005.
Scammell, J. M. "Military Units in Southern California, 1853–1862." *California Historical Society Quarterly* 29 (September 1950): 229–49.
Schaefer, James A. "Governor William Dennison and Military Preparations in Ohio, 1861." *Lincoln Herald* 78 (June 1976): 52–61.
Scharf, John T. *History of Baltimore City and County, from the Earliest Period to the Present Day*. Philadelphia: Louis H. Everts, 1881.
———. *History of Delaware, 1609–1888*. 2 vols. Philadelphia: C. J. Richards and Co., 1888.
———. *History of Maryland from the Earliest Period to the Present Day*. 3 vols. Baltimore: John B. Piet, 1879.
Schecter, Barnet. *The Devil's Own Work: The Civil War Draft Riots and the Fight to Reconstruct America*. New York: Walker & Co., 2005.
Schenker, Jr., Carl R. "Ulysses in His Tent: Halleck, Grant, Sherman, and 'The Turning Point of the War.'" *Civil War History* 56 (June 2010): 175–221.
Scheuer, Jeffrey. "Blue Ghost: The Civil War Letters of Alvah Kirk." *New York History* 73 (April 1992): 169–92.
Schlesinger, Arthur M., ed. "A Blue Jacket's Letters Home, 1863–1864." *New England Quarterly* 1 (October 1928): 554–603.
Schmidt, Hubert G. "Jediah Alexander: Civil War Editor." *Journal of the Illinois State Historical Society* 40 (June 1947): 135–53.
Schmidt, Marcus P. "The Dependence of the Lincoln Administration on the Northwestern Governors," M.A. thesis, University of Wisconsin, 1936.
Schneider, John C. "Detroit and the Problem of Disorder." *Michigan History Magazine* 58 (Spring 1974): 4–24.
Schoeberlein, Robert W. "A Fair to Remember: Maryland Women in Aid of the Union." *Maryland Historical Magazine* 90 (Winter 1995): 466–88.
Schofield, John M. *Forty-six Years in the Army*. Norman: University of Oklahoma Press, 1998.
Schouler, William. *A History of Massachusetts in the Civil War*. 2 vols. Boston: E. P. Dutton and Co., 1868.

Schroder, Alan M. "William M. Stone: Iowa's Other Civil War Governor." *Palimpsest* 63 (1982): 107–118.

Schroeder, Glenna R., ed. "The Civil War Diary of Chaplain Stephen C. Bowers." *Indiana Magazine of History* 79 (June 1983): 167–85.

Schultz, Robert G., ed. *Army Life: From a Soldier's Journal: By Albert O. Marshall.* Fayetteville: University of Arkansas Press, 2009.

Schutz, Wallace J., and Walter N. Trenerry. *Abandoned by Lincoln: A Military Biography of General John Pope.* Urbana: University of Illinois Press, 1990.

Scott, Kenneth. "Press Opposition to Lincoln in New Hampshire," *New England Quarterly* 21 (September 1948): 326–41.

Scott, Kim Allen. "The Preacher, the Lawyer, and the Spoils of War." *Kansas History* 13 (Winter 1993): 206–17.

Scott, Robert G. *Fallen Leaves.* Kent, Ohio: Kent State University Press, 1991.

Seabrook, William L. *Maryland's Great Part in Saving the Union.* Westminster, Md.: AM Sentinel Company, 1868.

Sears, Stephen W. *Chancellorsville.* Boston: Houghton Mifflin, Co., 1996.

———, ed. *The Civil War Papers of George B. McClellan: Selected Correspondence 1860–1865.* New York: Da Capo Press, 1992.

———, ed. *Controversies and Commanders: Dispatches from the Army of the Potomac.* Boston: Houghton Mifflin, 1999.

———. *George B. McClellan: The Young Napoleon.* New York: Ticknor and Fields. 1998.

———. *Gettysburg.* Boston: Houghton Mifflin, 2003.

———. *Landscape Turned Red: The Battle of Antietam.* New Haven: Ticknor and Fields, 1983.

———, ed. *Mr. Dunn Browne's Experiences in the Army: The Civil War Letters of Samuel W. Fiske.* New York: Fordham University Press, 1998.

———. *To the Gates of Richmond: The Peninsula Campaign.* Boston: Houghton Mifflin Harcourt, 2001.

Segal, Charles M., ed. *Conversations with Lincoln.* New York: G. P. Putnam and Sons, 1961.

Seigel, Peggy B. "She Went to War: Indiana Women Nurses in the Civil War." *Indiana Magazine of History* 86 (March 1990): 1–27.

Sennott, George. *Sennott on Andrew and Butler.* Boston: Redding and Co., 1862.

Seraile, William. "The Struggle to Raise Black Regiments in New York State, 1861–1864." *New York Historical Society Quarterly Bulletin* 58 (July 1974): 215–33.

Seward, Frederick W. *Seward at Washington as Senator and Secretary of State: A Memoir of His Life, 1846–1861.* New York: Derby and Miller, 1891.

Sewell, Richard H. "Michigan Farmers and the Civil War." *Michigan History Magazine* 44 (December 1960): 353–74.

Shafer, Duane E. *Men of Granite: New Hampshire's Soldiers in the Civil War.* Columbia: University of South Carolina Press, 2008.

Shaffer, Dallas. "Lincoln and the 'Vast Question' of West Virginia." *West Virginia History* 32 (January 1971): 86–100.

Shankman, Arnold. "Draft Resistance in Civil War Pennsylvania." *Pennsylvania Magazine of History and Biography* 101 (April 1977): 190–204.

———. "Freedom of the Press during the Civil War: The Case of Albert D. Boileau." *Pennsylvania History* 42 (October 1975): 305–15.

———. *The Pennsylvania Anti-war Movement, 1861–1865*. Rutherford, N.J.: Farleigh Dickinson University Press, 1980.

———. "Soldier Votes and Clement L. Vallandigham in the 1863 Ohio Gubernatorial Election." *Ohio History* 82 (Winter 1973): 88–104.

———. "William B. Reed and the Civil War." *Pennsylvania History* 39 (October 1972): 455–68.

Shannon, Fred A. *The Organization and Administration of the Union Army, 1861–1865*. 2 vols. Cleveland, Ohio: Arthur H. Clark, 1928.

———. "States' Rights and the Union Army." *Mississippi Valley Historical Review* 12 (June 1925): 51–71.

Sheldon, Rachel A. "Measures for a 'Speedy Conclusion': A Reexamination of Conscription and Civil War Federalism." *Civil War History* 45 (December 2009): 469–98.

Sherman, Caroline B., ed. "A New England Boy in the Civil War." *New England Quarterly* 5 (April 1932): 310–43.

Sherman, Rachel. "St. Johnsbury Puts the Civil War to Rest." *Vermont History* 76 (Winter/Spring 2008): 63–66.

Sherman, William T. *Memoirs of General William T. Sherman*. New York: D. Appleton, 1875.

Shoemaker, Henry W. *The Last of the War Governors*. Altoona, Penn.: Altoona Tribune Publishing Co., 1916.

Shoemaker, Michael. "The Michigan Thirteenth." *Pioneer Collections* 4 (1881): 133–68.

Shutes, Milton H. "Abraham Lincoln and the New Almaden Mine." *California Historical Society Quarterly* 15 (March 1936): 2–20.

———. *Lincoln and California*. Stanford, Calif.: Stanford University Press, 1943.

Siddali, Silvana R., ed. *Missouri's War: The Civil War in Documents*. Athens: Ohio University Press, 2009.

Siegel, Alan. *For the Glory of the Union: Myth, Reality and the Media in Civil War New Jersey*. Rutherford, N.J.: Farleigh Dickinson University Press, 1964.

Silver, David M. *Lincoln's Supreme Court*. Urbana-Champaign: University of Illinois Press, 1998.

Simon, Donald J. "The Third Minnesota Regiment in Arkansas, 1863–1865." *Minnesota History* 40 (Summer 1967): 281–92.

Simon, John Y., et al., eds. *Papers of Ulysses S. Grant*. 24 vols. Carbondale: Southern Illinois University Press, 1967.

Simpson, Brooks. *Ulysses S. Grant: Triumph Over Adversity, 1822–1865*. New York: Houghton Mifflin, 2000.

Simpson, Brooks, and Jean V. Berlin, eds. *Sherman's Civil War: Selected Correspondence of William T. Sherman 1860–1865*. Chapel Hill: University of North Carolina Press, 1999.

Sinisi, Kyle S. *Sacred Debts: State Civil War Claims, 1861–1880*. New York: Fordham University Press, 2003.

Sizer, Lyde C. and Jim Cullen, eds. *The Civil War Era: An Anthology of Sources*. Malden, Mass.: Blackwell Publishers, 2005.

Slap, Andrew L., and Michael Thomas Smith, eds. *This Distracted and Anarchical People: New Answers for Old Questions About the Civil War-Era North*. New York: Fordham University Press, 2013.

Smith, Adam I. P. *No Party Now: Politics in the Civil War North*. New York: Oxford, 2006.

Smith, Bradford. "Vermont's Godfather of the Republican Party." *Vermont Historical Society Proceedings* 22 (July 1954): 189–93.
Smith, David M., ed. "The Civil War Diary of Colonel John Henry Smith." *Iowa Journal of History* 47 (April 1949): 140–70.
Smith, George W. "Broadsides for Freedom: Civil War Propaganda in New England." *New England Quarterly* 21 (September 1948): 291–312.
———. "Generative Forces of Union Propaganda: A Study in Civil War Pressure Groups." Ph.D. diss., University of Wisconsin, 1939.
Smith, H. Allen. *A Genealogical History of the Descendants of the Rev. Nehemiah Smith of New London County, Conn., With Mention of His Brother John and Nephew Edward: 1638–1888*. Albany, N.Y.: Joel Munsell's Sons, Publishers, 1889.
Smith, John David. *Lincoln and the U.S. Colored Troops*. Carbondale: Southern Illinois University Press, 2013.
———. "The Health of Vermont's Civil War Recruits." *Vermont History* 43 (Summer 1975): 185–92.
———. "The Recruitment of Negro Soldiers in Kentucky, 1863–1865." *Register of the Kentucky Historical Society* 72 (October 1974): 364–90.
Smith, John L. *History of the 118th Pennsylvania Volunteers Corn Exchange Regiment, From Their First Engagement at Antietam to Appomattox*. Philadelphia: J. L. Smith, 1905.
Smith, Michael Thomas. *The Enemy Within: Fears of Corruption in the Civil War North*. Charlottesville: University of Virginia Press, 2011.
Smith, Ron, ed. *The Civil War Diaries of Mifflin Jennings 11th Iowa Infantry*. Topeka, KS: Ron Smith, 1999.
Smith, Ronald D. *Thomas Ewing Jr.: Frontier Lawyer and Civil War General*. Columbia: University of Missouri Press, 2008.
Smith, Thomas H. "Crawford County 'Ez Trooly Dimecratic' A Study of Midwestern Copperheadism." *Ohio History* 76 (Spring 1967): 33–53.
Smith, Timothy B. *Shiloh: Conquer or Perish*. Lawrence: University Press of Kansas, 2014.
Smith, Wayne. "Pennsylvania and the American Civil War: Recent Trends and Interpretations." *Pennsylvania History* 51 (July 1984): 206–31.
Smith, William E. *The Francis Preston Blair Family in Politics*. 2 vols. New York: MacMillan, 1933.
Snead, Thomas L. *The Fight for Missouri*. New York: Charles Scribner's Sons, 1888.
Snyder, Charles M. "They Lay Where They Fell: The Everests, Father and Son." *Vermont History* 32 (July 1964): 154–62.
Snyder, Timothy R. "'Making No Child's Play of the Matter': Governor Hicks and the Secession Crisis Reconsidered." *Maryland Historical Magazine* 101 (2006): 304–31.
Sobel, Robert, and John Raimo, eds. *Biographical Directory of the Governors of the United States, 1789–1978*. 4 vols. Westport, Conn.: Meckler Books, 1974.
Soule, Allen. "Vermont in 1861." *Vermont History* 30 (April 1962): 149–61.
Sowle, Patrick. "Cassius Clay and the Crisis of the Union, 1860–1861." *Register of the Kentucky Historical Society* 65 (April 1967): 144–49.
Spaulding, Imogene. "The Attitude of California to the Civil War." *Annual Publications of the Historical Society of California* 9 (1912): 104–31.
Speed, Thomas. *The Union Cause in Kentucky, 1860–1865*. New York: G. P. Putnam's Sons, 1907.
Speer, Lonnie R. *Portals to Hell: Military Prisons of the Civil War*. Mechanicsburg, Penn.: Stackpole, 1997.

Speiser, Matt. "The Ticket's Other Half: How and Why Andrew Johnson Received the 1864 Vice Presidential Nomination." *Tennessee Historical Quarterly* 65 (March 2006): 42–69.
Spicer, William A. *History of the Ninth and Tenth Regiments, Rhode Island Volunteers and the Tenth Rhode Island Battery in the Union Army in 1862*. Providence, R.I.: Snow & Farnham Printers, 1892.
Spruance, John. *Delaware Stays in the Union: The Civil War Period, 1860–1865*. Newark: University of Delaware Press, 1955.
Spurgeon, Ian Michael. *Soldiers in the Army of Freedom: The 1st Kansas Colored, the Civil War's First African American Combat Unit*. Norman: University of Oklahoma Press, 2014.
Sribnick, Ethan G., ed. *A Legacy of Innovation: Governors and Public Policy*. Philadelphia: University of Pennsylvania Press, 2008.
Stackpole, Everett S. *History of New Hampshire*. New York: American Historical Society, 1917.
Stahr, Walter. *Seward: Lincoln's Indispensable Man*. New York: Simon & Schuster, 2012.
Stampp, Kenneth M. "The Impact of the Civil War upon Hoosier Society." *Indiana Magazine of History* 38 (March 1942): 1–16.
———. *Indiana Politics during the Civil War*. Bloomington: Indiana University Press, 1948.
———. "Kentucky's Influence upon Indiana in the Crisis of 1861." *Indiana Magazine of History* 29 (1943): 263–76.
———, ed. "Letters from the Washington Peace Conference of 1861." *Journal of Southern History* 9 (August 1943): 394–403.
Stanley, Gerald. "Civil War Politics in California." *Southern California Quarterly* 64 (Summer 1982): 115–32.
———. "The Republican Party in California, 1856–1868." Ph.D. diss., University of Arizona, 1973.
Stanley, R., and George O. Hall. *Eastern Maine and the Rebellion*. Bangor, Me.: R. H. Stanley and Co., 1887.
Stanly, Edward. *A Military Governor among Abolitionists*. New York: n.p., 1865.
Stanton, Michael "The Civil War Memoir of Charles Dubois." *Vermont History* 76 (Winter/Spring 2008): 47–61.
Stanyan, John W. *A History of the Eighth Regiment New Hampshire Volunteers*. Concord, N.H.: Iva Evans, 1892.
Starr, Stephen Z. "The Inner Life of the First Vermont Volunteer Cavalry." *Vermont History* 46 (Summer 1978): 157–74.
———. "The Second Michigan Volunteer Cavalry: Another View." *Michigan History Magazine* 60 (Summer 1976): 161–82.
———. "The Third Ohio Cavalry: A View from the Inside." *Ohio History* 85 (Autumn 1976): 306–18.
Stashower, Daniel. *The Hour of Peril: The Secret Plot to Murder Lincoln before the Civil War*. New York: St. Martin's Press, 2013.
Staudenraus, P. J., ed. *Mr. Lincoln's Washington: Selections from the Writings of Noah Brooks, Civil War Correspondent*. South Brunswick, N.J.: Yoseloff, 1967.
Stealey III, John E. *West Virginia's Civil War-Era Constitution: Loyal Revolution, Confederate Counter-Revolution, and the Convention of 1872*. Kent, Ohio: Kent State University Press, 2013.

———. "West Virginia's Constitutional Critique of Virginia: The Revolution of 1861–1863." *Civil War History* 57 (March 2011): 9–47.
Stearns, Frank Preston. *Cambridge Sketches*. Philadelphia: J. B. Lippincott Company, 1905.
Steinmetz, Samuel, Jr. "New Jersey, State of Conflict, 1861–1865." *Proceedings of the New Jersey Historical Society* 80 (October 1962): 236–44.
Stellhorn, Paul A., and Michael J. Birker, eds. *The Governors of New Jersey, 1664–1974*. Trenton, N.J.: New Jersey Historical Commission, 1982.
Stephenson, Isaac. *Recollections of a Long Life, 1829–1915*. Chicago: Donnelley and Sons, 1915.
Stephenson, Wendell H. *The Political Career of General James H. Lane*. Topeka: Kansas State Historical Society, 1930.
Sterling, Bob. "Discouragement, Weariness, and War Politics: Desertions from Illinois Regiments during the Civil War." *Illinois Historical Journal* 82 (Winter 1989): 239–62.
Sterling, Robert E. "Civil War Draft Resistance in the Middle West." Ph.D. diss., Northern Illinois University, 1974.
Stevens, John A. *Union Defense Committee of City of New York Minutes, Reports and Correspondence, with Historical Introduction*. New York: Union Defense Committee, 1885.
Stoler, Mildred C. "The Democratic Element in the New Republican Party in Indiana." *Indiana Magazine of History* 36 (September 1940): 185–207.
Stone, Charles M. "A Vermonter Describes the Mood at Lincoln's First Inaugural." *Vermont History* 36 (Spring 1968): 61–63.
Stone, Eben F. "Sketch of John Albion Andrew." *Essex Institute Historical Collections* 27 (1890): 1–30.
Stone, Edwin W. *Rhode Island in the Rebellion*. Providence, R.I.: George W. Whitney, 1864.
Stone, Geoffrey R. "Abraham Lincoln's First Amendment." *New York University Law Review* 78 (April 2003): 1–29.
Stout, Harry S. *Upon the Altar of the Nation: A Moral History of the Civil War*. New York: Viking, 2006.
Stowell, Daniel W. "We Will Fight for Our Flag: The Civil War Letters of Thomas Barnett, Ninth Illinois Volunteer Infantry." *Journal of Illinois History* 3 (Autumn 2000): 201–22.
Sutherland, Daniel E. *A Savage Conflict: The Decisive Role of Guerrillas in the American Civil War*. Chapel Hill: University of North Carolina Press, 2009.
Stuart, Addison A. *Iowa Colonels and Regiments: Being a History of Iowa Regiments in the War of the Rebellion: And Containing a Description of the Battles in Which They Fought*. Des Moines: Mills and Co., 1865.
Stutler, Boyd. *West Virginia in the Civil War*. Charleston, W.Va.: Educational Foundation, 1963.
Sulgrove, B. R. *History of Indianapolis and Marion County, Indiana*. Philadelphia: C. H. Events and Co., 1884.
Swisher, Jacob, and Carl H. Erbe. *Iowa History as Told in Biography*. Cedar Falls, Iowa: Holst Printing, 1932.
Sylvester, Lorna L., ed. "Gone for a Soldier: The Civil War Letters of Charles Harding Cox." *Indiana Magazine of History* 68 (March 1972): 181–239.

———. "Oliver P. Morton and Hoosier Politics during the Civil War." Ph.D. diss., Indiana University, 1968.
Taafe, Stephen R. *Commanding the Army of the Potomac*. Lawrence: University Press of Kansas, 2006.
Taft, Charles Sabin. "Letter 14–Abraham Lincoln's Last Hours." *Century Illustrated Magazine* 45 (February 1893): 634–36.
Talmadge, John E. "A Peace Movement in Civil War Connecticut." *New England Quarterly* 37 (September 1964): 306–21.
Tandler, Maurice. "The Political Front in Civil War New Jersey." *Proceedings of the New Jersey Historical Society* 83 (October 1965): 223–33.
Tap, Bruce. *Over Lincoln's Shoulder: The Committee on the Conduct of the War*. Lawrence: University Press of Kansas, 1998.
Tapp, Hamilton. "The Assassination of General William Nelson September 29, 1862, and Its Ramifications." *Filson Club History Quarterly.* 19 (October 1945): 195–207.
———. "Robert J. Breckinridge during the Civil War." *Filson Club HistoryQuarterly* 11 (April 1937): 120–44.
Tarbell, M. Ida, "Lincoln Gathering an Army." *McClure's Magazine* 12 (February 1899): 323–30.
———. "Lincoln's Great Victory in 1864." *McClure's Magazine* 13 (July 1899): 268–78.
Tatum, Margaret B., ed. "Please Send Stamps: The Civil War Letters of William A. Clark." *Indiana Magazine of History* 91 (June 1995): 197–225.
Taylor, John M. *William Henry Seward: Lincoln's Right Hand*. New York: HarperCollins, 1991.
Taylor, Lenette S. *"The Supply for Tomorrow Must Not Fail": The Civil War of Captain Simon Perkins, Jr., a Union Quartermaster*. Kent, Ohio: Kent State University Press, 2004.
Taylor, Paul. *Orlando M. Poe: Civil War General and Great Lakes Engineer*. Kent, Ohio: Kent State University Press, 2009.
Taylor, Robert M. *The State of Indiana History 2000: Papers Presented at the Indiana Historical Society Grand Opening*. Indianapolis: Indiana Historical Commission, 2001.
Teillard, Dorothy Lamon. *Recollections of Abraham Lincoln, 1847–1865*. Chicago: A.C. McClurg and Company, 1895.
Terrell, William H. H. *Indiana in the War of the Rebellion*. Indianapolis: Douglas and Conner, 1869.
Thayer, William R. *The Life Letters of John Hay*. 2 vols. Boston: Houghton Mifflin, 1915.
Thomas, Benjamin P. *Abraham Lincoln: A Biography*. New York: Alfred Knopf, 1952.
———, ed. *Three Years with Grant: As Recalled by War Correspondent Sylvanus Cadwallader*. New York: Alfred A. Knopf, 1955. Reprint, University of Nebraska Press, 1996.
Thomas, Benjamin P., and Harold M. Hyman. *Stanton: The Life and Times of Lincoln's Secretary of War*. New York: Alfred A. Knopf, 1962.
Thomas, Edward H. *John Hunt Morgan and His Raiders*. Lexington: University Press of Kentucky, 1985.
Thomas, Joseph W. "Campaigns of Generals McClellan and Rosecrans in Western Virginia, 1861–1862." *West Virginia History* 5 (July 1944): 245–308.

Thompson, D. G., ed. "From Chancellorsville to Gettysburg: A Doctor's Diary." *Pennsylvania Magazine of History* 89 (July 1965): 292–315.

Thompson, Jerry. *Civil War to the Bloody End: The Life and Times of Major Samuel P. Heintzelman*. College Station: Texas A & M University Press, 2006.

Thornbrough, Emma Lou. *Indiana in the Civil War Era: 1850–1880*. Vol. 3. Indianapolis: Indiana Historical Society, 1965.

———. "Judge Perkins and the Indiana Supreme Court and the Civil War." *Indiana Magazine of History* 60 (1960): 79–96.

———. *The Negro in Indiana: A Study of a Minority*. Indianapolis: Indiana Historical Bureau 1957.

———. "The Race Issue in Indiana Politics during the Civil War." *Indiana Magazine of History* 47 (1951): 165–88.

Thornbrough, Gayle, Dorothy L. Riker, and Paula Corpuz, eds. *The Diary of Calvin Fletcher*. 9 vols. Indianapolis: Indiana Historical Society, 1980.

Thornburgh, John. "Oliver P. Morton: The Great War Governor." In *Glimpses of the Nation's Struggle*. Edited by Edward D. Neill by the *Military Order of the Loyal Legion of the United States, Minnesota Commandery*. New York: D. D. Merrill Company, 1893. 4:66–92.

Thornton, Harrison J. "The State University of Iowa and the Civil War." *Annals of Iowa* 30 (January 1950): 198–209.

Thornton, Harry. "Recollections of the War By a Confederate Officer from California." *Southern California Quarterly* 45 (September 1963): 195–218.

Throne, Mildred, ed. "The Civil War Diary of John Mackley." *Iowa Journal of History* 48 (April 1950): 141–68.

———, ed. "Civil War Letters of Abner Dunham." *Iowa Journal of History* 53 (October 1955): 341–66.

———, ed. "Erastus B. Soper's History of Company D., Twelfth Iowa Infantry, 1861–1866." *Iowa Journal of History* 56 (April 1958): 153–87.

———, ed. "Reminiscences of Jacob C. Switzer of the Twenty-second Iowa." *Iowa Journal of History* 56 (January 1958): 37–76.

Thurner, Arthur W., ed. "A Young Soldier in the Army of the Potomac: Diary of Howard Helman, 1862." *Pennsylvania Magazine of History and Biography* 87 (April 1963): 139–55.

Tolzmann, Don Heirich, ed. *The Sioux Uprising in Minnesota, 1862: Jacob Nix's Eyewitness History*. Indianapolis: Max Kade German American Center and Indiana Heritage Society, 1994.

Towers, Frank. "Strange Bedfellows: The Union Party and the Federal Government in Civil War Baltimore." *Maryland Historical Magazine* 106 (Spring 2011): 7–35.

Towne, Stephen E., ed. *A Fierce, Wild Joy: The Civil War Letters of Colonel Edward J. Wood, 48th Indiana Volunteer Infantry*. Knoxville: University of Tennessee Press. 2007.

———. "Killing the Serpent Speedily: Governor Morton, General Hascall, and the Suppression of the Democratic Press in Indiana, 1863." *Civil War History* 52 (March 2006): 41–65.

———. *Surveillance and Spies in the Civil War: Exposing Confederate Conspiracies in America's Heartland*. Athens: Ohio University Press, 2015.

Trask, David F. "Charles Sumner and the New Jersey Railroad Monopoly during the Civil War." *Proceedings of the New Jersey Historical Society* 75 (October 1957): 260–75.

Tredway, Gilbert R. *Democratic Opposition to the Lincoln Administration in Indiana.* Indianapolis: Indiana Historical Bureau, 1973.

Trefousse, Hans L. *Andrew Johnson: A Biography.* New York: W. W. Norton, 1989.

———. *Ben Butler: The South Called Him Beast.* New York: Twayne, 1957.

———. "Ben Wade and the Negro." *Ohio Historical Quarterly* 68 (April 1959): 161–76.

———. *Thaddeus Stevens: Nineteenth-Century Egalitarian.* Chapel Hill: University of North Carolina Press, 1997.

Treichel, James A. "Lew Wallace at Fort Donelson." *Indiana Magazine of History* 59 (1963): 3–18.

Trenerry, Walter N. "The Minnesota Rebellion Act of 1862: A Legal Dilemma in the Civil War." *Minnesota History* 35 (March 1956): 1–10.

———. "When the Boys Came Home." *Minnesota History* 38 (June 1963): 287–97.

Trester, Delmer J. "The Political Career of David Tod." Ph.D. diss., Ohio State University, 1951.

Trudeau, Noah Andre. *Gettysburg: A Testing of Courage.* New York: HarperCollins, 2002.

———. *Southern Storm: Sherman's March to the Sea.* New York: Harper, 2008.

True, Marshall. "A Reluctant Warrior Advises the President: Ethan Allen Hitchcock, Abraham Lincoln, and the Union Army, Spring 1862." *Vermont History* 50 (Summer 1982): 143–50.

Tunnell, Ted. "With Banner, Gun, and Sword: Marshall Harvey Twitchell and the 4th Vermont Go to War." *Vermont History* 59 (Spring 1991): 69–84.

Turkoly-Joczik, Robert L. "Fremont and the Western Department." *Missouri Historical Review* 82 (July 1988): 363–85.

Turner, Wallace B. "The Secession Movement in Kentucky." *Register of the Kentucky Historical Society* 66 (July 1968): 259–78.

Tusken, Roger. "In the Bastile of the Rebels." *Journal of the Illinois State Historical Society* 56 (Summer 1963): 316–39.

Tyson, Raymond W. "Henry Winter Davis: Orator for the Union." *Maryland Historical Magazine* 58 (March 1963): 1–19.

Union Historical Company. *The History of Washington County, Iowa.* Des Moines: Union Historical Company, 1880.

Upham, Cyril B. "Arms and Equipment for the Iowa Troops in the Civil War." *Iowa Journal of History and Politics* 16 (January 1918): 3–52.

Upton, Emory. *The Military Policy of the United States.* Washington: Government Printing Office, 1904.

Ural, Susannah J., ed. *Civil War Citizens: Race, Ethnicity, and Identity in America's Bloodiest Conflict.* New York: New York University Press, 2010.

Vaill, Amber. "The Civil War Draft in Palmer: Reaction in a Small Town." *Historical Journal of Massachusetts* 33 (Summer 2005): 92–108.

Van der Linden, Frank. *The Dark Intrigue: The True Story of a Civil War Conspiracy.* Golden, Colo.: Fulcrum Publishing, 2007.

Villard, Harold G., and Oswald Garrison Villard. *Lincoln on the Eve of 1861: A Journalist's Story by Henry Villard.* New York: Alfred A. Knopf, 1941.

Villard, Henry. *Memoirs of Henry Villard: Journalist and Financier, 1835–1900.* 2 vols. Boston: Houghton Mifflin and Company, 1904.

Voegeli, V. Jacque. *Free But Not Equal: The Midwest and the Negro during the Civil War.* Chicago: University of Chicago Press, 1967.

———. "A Rejected Alternative: Union Policy and the Relocation of Southern 'Contrabands' at the Dawn of Emancipation." *Journal of Southern History* 69 (November 2003): 765–90.

Vorenberg, Michael. *Final Freedom: The Civil War, the Abolition of Slavery, and the Thirteenth Amendment.* New York: Cambridge University Press, 2004.

Wagandt, Charles L. *The Mighty Revolution: Negro Emancipation in Maryland, 1862–1864.* Baltimore: Maryland Historical Society, 2004.

Wainwright, Nicholas. "The Loyal Opposition in Civil War Philadelphia." *Pennsylvania Magazine of History and Biography* 88 (July 1964): 294–315.

———, ed., *Philadelphia Perspective: The Diary of Sidney George Fisher Covering the Years, 1834–1871.* Philadelphia: Historical Society of Pennsylvania, 1967.

Waite, Otis Frederick. *New Hampshire in the Great Rebellion.* Whitefish, Mont.: Kessinger Publishing Company, 2007.

Walbridge, Hiram, *Correspondence between His Excellency and President Abraham Lincoln, the Hon. Simon Cameron, Secretary of War.* New York: J. F. Trow, Printer, 1865.

Walcott, Charles. *History of the Twenty-first Regiment Massachusetts Volunteers.* New York: Houghton Mifflin, 1882.

Wallace, Lew. *Lew Wallace: An Autobiography.* New York: Harper Brothers, 1907.

Walsh, Justin E. "Radically and Thoroughly Democratic. Wilbur F. Storey and the Detroit Free Press, 1853–1861." *Michigan History Magazine* 47 (September 1963): 193–225.

"War Letters of Charles P. Bowditch." *Proceedings of the Massachusetts Historical Society* 57 (October 1923–June 1924): 414–95.

Ward, Eric, ed. *Army Life in Virginia: The Civil War Letters of George G. Benedict.* Mechanicsburg, Penn.: Stackpole Books, 2002.

Warner, Ezra. *Generals in Blue.* Baton Rouge: Louisiana State University Press, 1964.

Warrington. *A Conspiracy to Defame John A. Andrew.* Boston: Wright and Potter Printers, 1862.

Warshauer, Matthew. *Connecticut in the American Civil War: Slavery, Sacrifice, and Survival.* Middletown, Conn.: Wesleyan University Press, 2011.

Washington, Versalle F. *Eagles on Their Buttons: A Black Infantry Regiment in the Civil War.* Columbia: University of Missouri Press, 1999.

Wasson, Stanley P., ed. "Civil War Letters of Darwin Cody." *Ohio Historical Quarterly* 68 (October 1959): 371–407.

Waugh, John C. *Re-electing Lincoln: The Battle for the 1864 Presidency.* New York: Crown Publishers, 1997.

Weber, Jennifer L. *Copperheads: The Rise and Fall of Lincoln's Opponents in the North.* New York: Oxford University Press, 2008.

Weed, Thurlow. *Life of Thurlow Weed, Including His Autobiography and a Memoir.* 2 vols. Boston: AMS Press, 1884.

Weeden, William B. *War Government: Federal and State, 1861–1865.* Boston: Houghton Mifflin and Co., 1906.

Wells, Jonathan. "The Transformation of John Pendleton Kennedy: Maryland, the Republican Party, and the Civil War." *Maryland Historical Magazine* 95 (Fall 2000): 291–308.

Welty, Raymond L. "The Policing of the Frontier by the Army, 1860–1870." *Kansas Historical Quarterly* 7 (August 1938): 246–57.

Wertheim, Lewis J. "The Indianapolis Treason Trials, the Election of 1864, and the Power of the Partisan Press." *Indiana Magazine of History* 85 (September 1989): 236–50.
Wetmore, Ruth. "The Life of Louis Powell Harvey." M.A. thesis, University of Wisconsin, 1918.
Whalon, Michael W. "Israel Washburn and the War Department." *Journal of Social Science* 46 (April 1971): 79–85.
———. "Maine Republicans, 1854–1866: A Study in Growth and Political Power." Ph.D. diss., University of Nebraska, 1968.
Whipple, Wayne. *The Story-Life of Lincoln: A Biography Composed of Five Hundred True Stories*. Philadelphia: The John C. Winston, Company, 1908.
White, Horace. *The Life of Lyman Trumbull*. Boston: Houghton Mifflin, 1913.
White, Jonathan W. *Emancipation, the Union Army, and the Reelection of Abraham Lincoln*. Baton Rouge: Louisiana State University Press, 2014.
———, ed. *A Philadelphia Perspective: The Civil War Diary of Sidney George Fisher*. New York: Fordham University Press, 2007.
White, Russell C., ed. *The Civil War Diary of Wyman S. White: First Sergeant of Company F. 2nd United States Sharpshooter Regiment, 1861–1865*. Baltimore: Butternut and Blue, 1992.
Wickman, Donald H., ed. *Letters to Vermont: From Civil War Soldier Correspondent to the Home Press*. 2 vols. Bennington, Vt.: Images from the Past, Inc., 1998.
———. *We are Coming Father Abra'am: The History of the 9th Vermont Volunteer Infantry*. Lynchburg, Va.: Schroeder Publications, 2005.
Wilkinson, Norman, B. "The Brandywine Home Front during the Civil War, Part I: 1861." *Delaware History* 9 (April 1961): 265–81.
———. "The Brandywine Home Front during the Civil War, Part II: 1862." *Delaware History* 10 (April 1963): 197–234.
———. "The Brandywine Home Front during the Civil War, Part III: 1863." *Delaware History* 11 (October 1964): 111–48.
———. "The Brandywine Home Front during the Civil War, Part IV: 1864–1865." *Delaware History* 11 (October 1965): 301–29.
Wilkinson, Warren. *'Mother May You Never See the Sights I Have Seen': The Fifty-seventh Massachusetts Veteran Volunteers in the Army of the Potomac, 1864–1865*. New York: Harper Collins, 1990.
Willey, W. P. *An Inside View of the Formation of the State of West Virginia*. Wheeling, W.Va.: The News Publishing Company, 1901.
Williams, Charles E. *The Life of Abner Coburn*. Bangor, Me.: Press of Thomas W. Burr, 1885.
Williams, Frederick D., ed. "The Civil War Diary of David Allen Richards." *Michigan History Magazine* 39 (June 1955): 183–220.
———. "The Civil War Recollections of Cornelia C. Hampton." *Michigan History Magazine* 40 (June 1956): 167–89.
———. "Michigan Soldiers in the Civil War." *Michigan History Magazine* 44 (March 1960): 1–35.
———, ed. *The Wild Life of the Army: Civil War Letters of James A. Garfield*. East Lansing: Michigan State University Press, 1964.
Williams, Kenneth P. *Lincoln Finds a General*. 5 vols. New York: Macmillan, 1949–57.

Williams, T. Harry. "Badger Colonels and the Civil War Officer." *Wisconsin Magazine of History* 47 (Autumn 1963): 35–46.
———. "Benjamin F. Wade and the Atrocity Propaganda of the Civil War." *Ohio Archeological and Historical Quarterly* 48 (January 1939): 33–43.
———. *Lincoln and the Radicals*. Madison: University of Wisconsin Press, 1941.
Williams, William H. *Slavery and Freedom in Delaware, 1639–1865*. Wilmington, Del.: SR Books, 1996.
Wills, Garry. *Lincoln at Gettysburg: The Words That Remade America*. New York: Simon & Schuster, 1992.
Wilson, Don W. *Governor Charles Robinson of Kansas*. Lawrence: University Press of Kansas, 1975.
Wilson, James H. *Under the Old Flag: Recollections of Military Operations in the War for the Union*. 2 vols. New York: Appleton, 1912.
Wilson, Mark R. *The Business of Civil War: Military Mobilization and the State, 1861–1865*. Baltimore, Md.: Johns Hopkins University Press, 2006.
Wilson, William B. *A Few Facts and Actors in the Tragedy of the Civil War in the United States*. Philadelphia: Published by the Author, 1892.
Wilson, William E. "Thunderbolt of the Confederacy, or King of Horse Thieves." *Indiana Magazine of History* 54 (1958): 119–30.
Winslow, Hattie L., and Joseph R. H. Moore. *Camp Morton, 1861–1865: Indianapolis Prison Camp*. Indianapolis: Indiana Historical Society, 1995.
Winston, Sheldon. "Statehood for West Virginia: An Illegal Act?" *West Virginia History* 30 (April 1969): 530–34.
Wish, Harvey, ed. "Civil War Letters and Dispatches." *Indiana Magazine of History* 33 (1937): 62–74.
Wister, Fanny K. "Sarah Butler Wister's Civil War Diary." *Pennsylvania Magazine of History and Biography* 102 (July 1978): 271–327.
Witt, John Fabian. *Lincoln's Code: The Laws of War in American History*. New York: Free Press, 2012.
Woodburn, James. "Party Politics in Indiana during the Civil War." *Annual Report of the American Historical Association* (1902): 223–51.
Woodbury, Augustus. *The Second Rhode Island Regiment: A Narrative of Military Operations*. Providence, R.I.: Valpey, Angell, and Co., 1875.
Woodford, Frank B. *Father Abraham's Children: Michigan Episodes in the Civil War*. Detroit: Wayne State University Press, 1961.
Woodward, Daniel H. "The Civil War of a Pennsylvania Trooper." *Pennsylvania Magazine of History and Biography* 87 (January 1963): 39–62.
Woodward, Elon A., and Richard C. Drum, eds. *The Negro in Military Service of the United States, 1939–1886: A Compilation of Official Records, State Papers, Historical Extracts, etc., Relating to His Military Status and Service from the Date of His Introduction into the British North American Colonies*. 7 vols. Washington, D.C.: Government Printing Office, 1888.
Woodward, Isaiah A. "Arthur Ingram Boreman: A Biography." Ph.D. diss., West Virginia University, 1970.
———. "Opinions of President Lincoln and His Cabinet on Statehood for Western Virginia, 1862–1863." *West Virginia History* 21 (April 1960): 158–85.
Woodward, Walter C. "The Rise and Early History of Political Parties in Oregon." *Oregon Historical Society Quarterly* 12 (December 1911): 301–60.

———. "The Rise and Early History of Political Parties in Oregon." *Oregon Historical Society Quarterly* 13 (March 1912): 16–70.
Woolard, Annette. "Camp Life of Delaware Troops in the Union Army." *Delaware History* 21 (Spring-Summer 1984): 1–21.
Woolsey, Ronald C. "Disunion or Dissent? A New Look at an old Problem in Southern California Attitudes toward the Civil War." *Southern California Quarterly* 66 (Fall 1984): 185–206.
———. "The Politics of a Lost Cause: 'Seceshers' and Democrats in Southern California during the Civil War." *California History* 69 (1990–91): 372–83.
Wright, Edward N. *Conscientious Objectors in the Civil War*. Philadelphia: University of Pennsylvania Press, 1931.
Wright, George B. "Honorable David Tod: Biography and Personal Recollections." *Ohio Archaeological and Historical Quarterly* 8 (1900): 125.
Wright, William C. "New Jersey's Military Role in the Civil War Reconsidered." *New Jersey History* 92 (Winter 1974): 197–210.
Wubben, Hubert H. *Civil War Iowa and the Copperhead Movement*. Ames: Iowa State University Press, 1980.
———. "The Uncertain Trumpet: Iowa Republicans and Black Suffrage, 1860–1868." *Annals of Iowa* 47 (Summer 1984): 409–29.
Wurthman, Leonard Jr. "Frank Blair: Lincoln's Congressional Spokesman." *Missouri Historical Review* 64 (April 1970): 263–88.
Yard, James S., Jr. *Memorial of Joel Parker*. Freehold, N.J.: Monmouth Democrat Print, 1889. Reprint, Kessinger Publishing Company, 2007.
Yates, Richard. *Speeches and Governor's Messages, 1851–72*.
Yates, Richard, Jr. "Richard Yates: War Governor of Illinois." *Transactions of the Illinois State Historical Society* (1923): 171–205.
Young, F. G. "Indebtedness Due to the Needs of Public Defense." *Oregon Historical Society Quarterly* 11 (December 1910): 403–17.
Young, John Edward. "An Illinois Farmer during the Civil War." *Journal of the Illinois State Historical Society*. 26 (April–July 1933): 70–135.
Young, Robin. *For Love and Liberty: The Untold Civil War Story of Major Sullivan Ballou and His Famous Love Letter*. New York: Thunder's Mouth Press, 2006.
Zacharias, Donald W. "John J. Crittenden Crusades for the Union and Neutrality in Kentucky." *Filson Club History Quarterly* 38 (July 1964): 193–205.
Zeller, Paul G. *The Ninth Vermont Infantry: A History and Roster*. Jefferson, N.C.: McFarland and Co., 2008.
Zeilinger, Elna, and Larry Schweikart, eds. "They Also Serve . . . The Diary of Benjamin Franklin Hackett, 12th Vermont Volunteers." *Vermont History* 51 (Spring 1983): 98–106.
Zimring, David R. " 'Secession in Favor of the Constitution': How West Virginia Justified Separate Statehood during the Civil War." *West Virginia History* 3 (Fall 2009): 23–51.
Zink, Steven D., ed. "If I was thare I could tel you a good bit more: The Civil War Letters of Private Jackson Davis." *Indiana Magazine of History* 78 (March 1982): 38–58.
Zollinger, Vivian. "I Take My Pen in Hand." *Indiana Magazine of History* 93 (June 1997): 111–96.
Zon, Calvin Goddard, ed. *The Good Fight That Didn't End: Henry P. Goddard's Accounts of Civil War and Peace*. Columbia: University of South Carolina Press, 2008.

Zornow, William F. "Indiana and the Election of 1864." *Indiana Magazine of History* 45 (1949): 13–38.
———. "The Kansas Senators and the Re-election of Lincoln." *Kansas Historical Quarterly* 19 (May 1951): 133–44.
———. *Lincoln and the Party Divided*. Norman: University of Oklahoma Press, 1954.
———. "The Missouri Radicals and the Election of 1864." *Missouri Historical Review* 45 (July 1951): 354–70.

Index

A&P Coburn Surveyors, 237. *See also* Eleazar Coburn & Sons
Adams, Charles Francis Jr., 418, 469
Adams, Charles Francis Sr., 27, 28, 33
Aiken, William A., 57
Alabama, 185, 403
Albany, N.Y., 13, 247, 284, 299, 300, 325, 416, 438, 470; State Military Board, 76
Albany Evening Journal, 14, 285
Alexandria, Va., 80, 138, 183, 188, 201
Allen, Thomas, 240
Allison, William B., 114, 251
Almy, John, 257
Altoona, 185, 217, 223–25, 227, 229–33, 235, 239, 242, 246, 248; conference, 224, 232, 235, 237
Alvord, Benjamin, 406, 463, 464
American Confederate Union, 59
American Party, 64, 442
Anderson, John W., 252
Anderson, Robert, 32, 35, 36, 39, 78, 110, 116
Andrew, John, Altoona, 223–25, 227–31, 235–36, 241–42, 248, 249, 253–54, 260–61, 263; Andrew-Butler controversy, 148, 150, 157, 159, 162; Astor House, 184–87, 189–90, 192–95, 197, 199; Baltimore riot, 58–60, 62; Battle of Bull Run, 95–97, 101–2; biography, 30; black troops, 269, 272–73, 286, 290, 295, 297, 300–301; and Butler, 105–6, 108; conscription, 319, 334, 341–42, 344; election of 1861, 113; election of 1863, 345, 355; election of 1864, 410–12, 416–17, 419–23, 435, 437–38, 456, 459; emancipation, 207–9; fugitive slaves, 136, 137, 139, 140, 144, 145, 147; Gurowski, 131; letter to Lincoln, 31, 33, 35; in New York, 26–28; mobilization, 44–48, 55; Peace Conference, 21–22; politics of conscription, 360, 362, 366, 368–70, 373, 382, 387–91, 395, 398, 404–5; Providence meeting, 215, 217, 219; Stanton's call for men, 171–73, 176–78; 211–12, 214
Annapolis, Md., 47, 145, 178, 438, 448; Bradford, 313, 336, 360; occupation of, 58, 60, 78
Anthony, Henry B., 37
Antietam Creek, 226, 236, 239, 241, 422, 437; Battle of, 226, 231, 233
Appalachian Mountains, 48, 68, 110, 116, 141, 147, 152, 154, 158, 438; economics west of, 28, 69; secessionists west of, 80, 115
Appomattox Courthouse, 469, 475
Arkansas, 157, 158, 180, 202, 222, 239, 246, 255, 381, 428; River, 267
Arnold, Samuel G., 280
Association for Promoting Colored Volunteers, 297
Association of Free Colored Citizens of Massachusetts, 468
Astor House, 183, 185, 187
Atlanta, Ga., 309, 392, 421–25, 429, 446, 447
Augusta, Me., 84, 163, 263, 418, 448, 470

Baker, Edward D., 119, 123
Baltimore, Md., 54, 128, 201, 219, 385, 430, 472; black soldiers, 385; civilian hostility, 16, 45–47; railroad, 18, 80, 87; Republican convention, 395, 397, 418, 436; riot, 57–58
Baltimore American, 79, 431
Bancroft, John, 295
Bangor Daily Whig and Courier, 71, 216, 256
Banks, Nathaniel P., 173–76, 251, 260, 282, 297, 381, 384, 389; defeat of, 170–71, 173–74; siege of Port Hudson, 304, 315

Barnum, Phineas T., 101
Bassett, Ebenezer D., 325
Bates, Edward, 9, 82–83, 145, 158, 242, 363, 388; and Gamble, 80, 97–98, 110, 365
Battle of Ball's Bluff, 117, 119
Battle of Chancellorsville, 294–95, 301, 314
Battle of Iuka, 243
Battle of Kernstown, 160, 409
Battle of Mine Creek, 440–41
Battle of New Market, 389, 392, 404
Battle of Rich Mountain, 93
Battle of the Crater, 411
Battle of Westport, 434
Baxter, Algernon S., 151
Baxter, Henry H., 75
Bayard, James A., 63, 75, 130, 196, 270
Bayard, James H., 257
Bayard, Thomas F., 407–8
Bayne, John H., 201
Beatty, John, 273
Beauregard, Pierre Gustav Toutant, 37, 178–79, 239
Beecher, Henry Ward, 480
Bell, John C., 19
Bell, Theodore S., 378
Benedict, George G., 53
Benjamin, Judah Phillip, 318
Bennett, James Gordon, 316
Berry, Nathaniel "Nat" Springer, 125, 174, 217, 228–29, 232, 235, 256, 351, 395, 480; nomination, 27; election of 1860, 36–37; reelection, 164
Biddle, Edward C., 42
Bigelow, John, 70
Birney, William, 333
Black codes, 432, 453, 459
Black soldiers, 280–90, 346, 349, 351, 378–79, 399, 408, 435–41; 54th Massachusetts regiment, 273, 290, 300, 324, 334, 388; black regiments, 283, 290, 297, 311, 333, 342, 354, 363, 366, 388, 411, 435, 469–70; conscription, 198, 206, 209–10, 216, 299, 370; debate about, 199, 242, 268–69; equal pay, 355, 388, 411; opposition to, 273–74, 382; support for, 194, 212, 273–75, 278, 306, 324–25
Blaine, James G., 84, 376, 425

Blair, Austin, biography, 28, 29, 70; troops in Washington, 91, 94, 99, 102; inaugural address; radicalism, 143, 144, 178; meeting at Cleveland, 186, 190, 194; Altoona, 219, 221, 222, 224, 229, 231, 234, 235, 295; message to legislature, 360, 361, 398, 418, 421, 454, 457, 479, 480, 481
Blair, Francis P. Jr., 75, 78–79, 111, 208, 244
Blair, Francis P. Sr., 187, 438
Blair, Montgomery, 111, 201, 230, 259, 262, 333, 433, 439, 440; relationship with Abraham Lincoln, 79, 427; as Postmaster General, 66–67, 133
Blenker, Louis, 165
Blind Memorandum, 415
Bliss, George, 354
Blunt, James G., 180, 323, 434
Booth, John Wilkes, 471
Boreman, Arthur I., 87, 292, 302, 305, 326, 370, 419, 429
Boston, Mass., 44, 84, 111, 117, 171–172, 214, 376, 423, 468; Common, 173, 176, 263, 459; conscription, 249, 319; Educational Commission for Freedmen, 241; Faneuil Hall, 422; and military suppliers, 52, 73–74; recruitment of soldiers, 106, 288; Union Club of, 286, volunteers, 46, 176, 204
Boston Daily Advertiser, 458, 471
Boston Daily Journal, 117
Boutwell, George, 48, 55, 66, 92, 231
Bowditch, Charles W., 92
Bowditch, Henry Ingersoll, 199
Bowles, William A., 409, 429
Boyd, Henry, 459
Boyle, Jeremiah T., 42, 220, 329
Bradbury, Bion, 237, 328
Bradford, Augustus Williamson, Altoona, 219, 228–30, 235; black enlistment, 365, 378, 379, 385, 390, 404, 406, 424, 431, 432; election, 128; Emancipation Proclamation, 259, 274; Gettysburg Campaign, 304, 305, 313; message to legislature, 360; election of 1863, 441, 442; runaway slaves, 201; slave enlistment, 333, 336, 342, 343
Bradford, Elizabeth, 385
Brady, James T., 318

Bragg, Braxton, 205, 210, 214, 220, 238–40, 259, 266, 274, 311, 334, 395
Bramlette, Thomas E., election of, 328–29, 333; recruiting, 355, 362–63, 366–67, 374–75, 378; and Morgan's raid, 398–400, 405, 424, 438, 439, 461, 477
Breckinridge, Robert J., 375, 378; and Democrats, 58
Bright, Jesse D., 243
Britton, William B., 199, 249
Brodhead, Edward. H., 167
Brohead, Edward N., 416
Brooks, Noah, 146, 257, 315, 412, 464; and Abraham Lincoln, 294, 352, 370, 407, 436–37, 447, 472
Brough, John, 306; election of, 330–31, 339–40, 348, 360–61, 371; meeting in Indianapolis, 385, 386, 392, 393, 398–401, 404, 413, 417, election of 1864, 419, 420, 422, 429, 430, 445, 450, 457, 471–73
Brown, B. Gratz, 333
Brown, George W., 45, 52
Brown, John, 51, 144, 253, 327, 408
Brown, William C., 432, 443
Browne, Albert G. Jr., 411
Browne, Dunn, 226
Browning, Orville H., 10, 112
Brownlow, William Gannaway, 221
Bryant, William Cullen, 297
Buchanan, James, 146
Buckingham, Catharinus P., 186–88
Buckingham, William, 27, 96, 179, 191, 196–97, 225, 251, 257, 398, 402; Altoona, 185, 229–30; arrest of dissidents, 100–101; battlefield conditions, 448; black soldiers, 212, 216, 272, 325, 366; Buckingham Day, 478; Connecticut Assembly, 269; Connecticut Chaplain's Aid Association, 163; Connecticut regiments, 150, 271, 304; conscription, 205, 297; desertion, 277; election of 1858, 34, 37; election of 1864, 419; emancipation, 215, 234; Lincoln's funeral, 473; military support, 38, 57; popularity of, 59; reelection, 166, 289, 299, 381–83, 469; renomination, 281; secession, 82; supplies, 337, 356, 387
Buckner, Simon Bolivar, 155

Buell, Don Carlos, 149, 152, 192, 194–96, 206, 210, 220, 225, 229; battle at Doctor's Creek, 240; and Halleck, 141, 151, 153; and McClellan, 124–25; invasion of Tennessee, 145, 155, 157, 178, 205; reinstatement, 238; relations with governors, 129, 136–37, 239, 242–43; Shiloh, 166
Buffalo, N.Y., 13, 181, 347
Buford, John, 313
Bull Run, 90–91, 101, 104, 115, 121, 241; Battle of, 92–95, 97; Congress, 99; Second Battle of, 218
Burbank, Calvin, 130
Burbridge, Stephen, 375, 378, 398–99, 405, 438–39, 461
Bureau of Colored Troops, 273, 297
Bureau of Finance, U.S., 307
Burlington, Vt., 52, 138, 367
Burlington Daily Free Press, 59, 205, 264, 394, 425
Burlington Daily Hawk-eye, 25, 310
Burnside, Ambrose, 94, 253–56, 259, 282, 291, 315, 328, 340, 346, 381; 1st Rhode Island Volunteers, 48, 91; appointment to Army of the Potomac, 250–51; arrest of Vallandigham, 295–96, 302–3; Fredericksburg, 255–56; and Lincoln, 258, 260, 263; Mud March, 271–72
Burrud, John B., 275
Burton, William, 40, 92, 130, 162, 174, 186, 196, 206–7; abolition, 149, 165; Altoona manifesto, 230; election, 63–64
Butler, Benjamin F., 60–61, 78–79; dispute with Andrew, 105–6, 117, 147–48, 251, 384, 392, 436
Butler, Cornelius, 212
Byers, Samuel Hawkins, 470

Cadwallader, George, 79
Cairo, Ill., 49, 69, 109–10, 151, 156, 241
Caldwell, William, 191
California, 22, 29, 51, 85, 113, 119–23, 181, 208; election of 1862, 237, 242, 287, 288; problems of recruitment, 321, 322, 329, 331, 332, 338; renomination of Lincoln, 369; Emancipation Proclamation, 379, 399, 406, 435, 438, 454, 462, 463, 472; gold rush, 122, 332

Cameron, James, 91
Cameron, Robert, 196
Cameron, Simon, 48–51, 90, 95–97, 99, 101–6, 108–13, 115–17, 129, 138–39, 146–48; call for troops, 41–42, 54; Charleston Harbor, 32; Cleveland conference, 70–71; Confederate plan of attack on Washington, 100; and Curtin, 39; fugitive slaves, 136; Hicks' petition for troops, 45–46; Indianapolis conference, 81; Maryland remaining in the Union, 58; Militia Act, 34; national volunteer army, 85–86; and Ramsey, 39–40; relations with Randall, 127; volunteer regiments, 61–63, 65, 67–68, 72–73; War Committee, 133; War Department, 80, 82–83; Western Department, 87; Whiteaker's governorship, 122; and Yates, 49
Campbell, Archibald W., 80, 261
Campbell, John A., 460
Camp Curtin, 45, 476
Camp Jackson, 78, 98
Canada, 55, 267, 347–48, 385, 409, 433, 457
Candee, Franklin J., 254
Cannon, Le Grand B., 354
Cannon, William, 270, 315, 344, 396, 404, 407–8, 417, 443–44, 460–62; Delaware legislature, 366; gubernatorial election, 244–45; inaugural speech, 263
Capitol Building, 403, 473
Capitol Hill, 137, 198–99, 275, 285–86, 376, 379–80, 440, 449, 458, 463; Lincoln's address at, 254; military encampments at, 66, 88
Carlisle, John S., 80, 88
Carney, Thomas, 245–46, 268, 325, 327, 340, 370, 373, 421, 428, 440; and Lincoln, 323, 326, 335, 374, 391–92
Carpentier, Horace, 119
Carrington, Henry B., 49, 403
Causey, Peter F., 64
Central Pacific Railroad, 120
Chambers, Ezekiel F., 442
Chambersburg, Penn., 170, 301, 409, 412
Chandler, Peleg, 84
Chandler, William E., 280–81, 376

Chandler, Zachariah, 75, 194, 222, 242, 244, 272, 352, 418, 439; and Blair, 89, 194, 219, 221, election of 1857, 29; Radicals, 22, 89, 219, 222, 248, 374; War Committee, 132–33
Charleston, S.C., 70, 87
Charleston Harbor, 32, 36–37, 324
Chase, John W., 172
Chase, Salmon P., 69, 125, 145, 184, 257, 322, 372, 402, 418, 449; affirmation of Congress's approval of the Electoral College returns, 12; allowance of regiments to carry state flags, 59; appointment of Low as collector for the Port of San Francisco, 332; approval of Altoona address, 233; Battle of Gettysburg, 313; Yates' letter regarding Copperheads, 276; election of 1861, 51; emancipation, 177; gubernatorial visit to Washington, 235–36; Kansas impeachment crisis, 180–81; Lincoln's swearing in ceremony, 465; New York War Committee meeting in Providence, 216; preparations for Fort Sumter, 36; resignation as Treasury Secretary, 400–401; Sprague's senatorial aspirations, 279–80; Unionists and Lincoln's renomination, 369–70; Washburn's faith in, 218
Chattanooga, Tenn., 184, 324, 334, 340, 342, 346, 347, 349, 350, 368; and Buell, 194, 205, 210, railroad, 266
Chicago, Ill., 204, 227, 231, 241, 260, 409, 449, 453; Democratic Convention, 416–17; Lincoln's funeral procession, 473; military suppliers, 74; and Yates, 209, 244, 316, 368
Chicago Times, 194, 306
Chicago Tribune, 147, 198, 217, 232, 256, 258, 290, 336, 391; Copperheads, 265; on Lincoln, 113, 268; on Morton, 11; on "Old John Brown," 144; on Stanton, 146; on Yates, 194, 449
Chickamauga Creek, 334, 342, 347, 349
Churchill, Alfred, 309
Cincinnati, Ohio, 10–11, 74, 78, 107, 109–10, 220, 339, 409, 445; defense of, 49, 68; conference at Spencer

House, 70, 72, 80; Northern Department, 433
Cincinnati Advertiser, 340
Cincinnati Daily Enquirer, 341
Cincinnati Gazette, 79
Clark, John G., 168
Clarke, Sidney, 180
Clay, Cassius M., 146
Clay, Henry, 87, 253
Clendenen, Clemens, 330
Cleveland, Ohio, 70, 72, 80, 186, 330, 394, 457
Clough, Andrew J., 24
Coburn, Abner, 237, 263, 271–72, 292, 332, 351
Cochran, John B., 461
Coggeshall, William, 12, 66, 115
Colfax, Schuyler, 459
Columbus, Ohio, 306, 371
Compromise of 1850, 56
Concord, N.H., 125, 163, 312, 379, 385, 395, 412, 438, 474
Confiscation Act, 205
Congress, United States, 194–95, 248, 277–79, 283, 450–51, 469, 481; 28th, 40; 29th, 40; 37th, 132, 254; 38th, 350, 403, 446; abolition, 235; and Andrew, 95, 341–42; army recruitment, 94, 163; black soldiers, 137, 334, 366, 388; bounties, 361; California, 332; and Cameron, 90; compensation to slave owners, 370; compromise within, 20–21; Copperheadism, 270, 286; the draft, 192, 222; emancipation, 182, 191, 196; Federal Bureau of Emancipation, 352; Fenton, 443; funding the war, 38, 72, 87, 89, 99, 102, 139, 149, 181; and Hall, Willard Preble, 357; House of Representatives, 45, 58, 88, 231, 338, 342, 449, 458, 459; Joint Committee on the Conduct of the War, 132; and Kansas, 122; and Lincoln, 103, 131, 134, 184, 196, 257, 359, 371; Militia Act, 202; and Morgan, Edwin D., 88, 192; Senate, 52, 89, 139, 208, 287, 344, 364, 373, 413, 439, 441, 443, 449, 453, 458, 463, 581 (n.95); Senate Finance Committee, 402; Senate Military Committee, 162, 185, 276; secession, 24; slavery, 15, 35; and Stanton, Edwin, 253; state powers, 83; Union Party, 431, 442, volunteers, 201
Conkling, Roscoe, 246, 391
Connecticut, 59, 226, 242, 297, 325, 346, 387, 402, 417, 448; 13th Amendment, 460; Assembly, 269; black soldiers, 212, 269; Buckingham, 27, 34, 82, 281, 289–90, 366, 478; Chaplains' Aid Association, 163; conscription, 205; election of 1858, 34; election of 1861, 36–37; election of 1862, 166; election of 1864, 381–82, 469; Hazard Powder Company, 38; and McClellan, 419–20; pledges military support for war, 57; Radicals, 179; recruitment, 191; Republicans, 328; soldier enfranchisement, 435; Sons of, 257; suspension of civil rights, 100–101
Conscription Act, 318, 410
Constitution, U.S., 52, 99, 121, 128, 157, 242, 341, 363; 13th Amendment, 383, 456, 458–62, 464; abolition, 363; constitutional authority, 85–86; constitutional rights, 100; black enfranchisement, 241; emancipation, 310, 345; Emancipation Proclamation, 264; equal rights, 451–52; federal authority, 454; gubernatorial powers, 59, 68, 85; and Lincoln, 240, 267–68, 270, 417; martial law, 284; preservation of, 94; slavery, 20, 27, 97, 107, 144, 230; state militias, 33, 130; states' rights, 12, 40, 83, 350; suspension of the writ of habeas corpus, 247; unconstitutional laws, 26; war powers, 83, 160–61; western Virginia, 79–80, 86
Constitutional Union Party, 302
Cony, Samuel, 328, 331–32, 358–59, 389, 396, 405–6, 408, 418, 425, 470
Cook, Burton C., 397
Cook, Ike, 309
Cooper, Abram Nash, 412
Copperheads, 289, 310, 341, 362, 364–65, 405–6, 412–13, 421, 440, 456; and Canada, 385; conscription, 326; Copperheadism, 286, 312, 381; defeat of, 438; the draft, 393, 428, 430; efforts to suppress, 322, 339, 386, 404, 430; legislature, 265, 367; press, 461;

Copperheads (cont.)
opposition to war, 207, 460; resistance to federal expansion, 299, 307, 321, 331–32, 371, 380, 382, 409; Sons of Liberty, 371; support for, 327; suspension of habeas corpus, 334; and Vallandigham, 270, 305–6, 399; and Yates, 276, 316
Corinth, Miss., 158, 166, 170, 175, 178, 190, 239, 243, 340, 454
Corkhill, George B., 143
Corning, Erastus, 299–300
Corson, Robert R., 448
Corwine, Richard M., 84
Couch, Darius Nash, 304
Couch, Samuel Kirkwood, 142
Covode, John, 132
Cozzens, William Cole, 280, 289, 351
Crapo, Henry Howland, 204, 248, 439–40, 454
Crapo, William, 204, 248
Crawford, George A., 135
Crawford, Samuel J., 440–41, 463
Crawford v. Robinson, 135
Creswell, John A., 372, 463, 471
Crittenden, John J., 20
Crittenden, Thomas P., 70
Crocker, Charles, 120
Crook, George, 409
Cumberland River, 124, 151, 153; Army of, 446; Department of, 340
Curry, William, 325
Curtin, Andrew, 218, 256–57, 286, 291–93, 295, 352, 390, 396, 412, 438; 13th amendment, 456, 470; Altoona Conference, 217, 229–32, 222–25, 228; and Andrew, 360, 422–23; Antietam, 226; bounties, 211; and Burton, 186; call for militia defense against Lee's Confederates, 304–5, 312; and Cameron, 42; Camp Curtin, 476; Cleveland conference, 70; defense of Washington, 44–46; deployment to Pennsylvania-Maryland border, 408–9; draft, 207, 347, 354; Early's raid of Pennsylvania, 432; election of 1863, 329–30; fear of attack on Washington, 404; gubernatorial elections, 329; gubernatorial response to Lee's Maryland Campaign, 219–20; Halleck's appointment as chief of staff, 373; Harper's Ferry, 171; Harrisburg, 311, 348; and Hicks, 19; Hoffman House gubernatorial reunion, 480; Jersey Blues, 314; Joint Committee, 133–34; Lincoln's failure to pay expenses of Pennsylvania campaign, 335; and McClellan, 154; and McClure, 170; meeting with Lincoln on state militias and emancipation, 165; meeting with Lincoln, 16; New York City conference, 26–27, 184–85; objections sent to Lincoln over War Department directives, 479; Ohio River, 80; order for defense of port cities, 161–66; Peace Conference, 21; Pennsylvania, 338; proposal to raise militia for national guard, 386; quotas, 63; recruitment, 362; Republican Party, 39; response to Early's crossing of the Potomac River, 404; Saratoga Springs, 418; soldier conditions, 67, 377, 480; and Stanton, 301; trip to Washington regarding Fort Sumter, 37; trip to Washington to deliver regimental colors with Lincoln, 11; Unionist election efforts in New York, 344–45; Virginia, 470, 476, 479; visit to Lincoln and the Army of the Potomac, 329; volunteers, 55, 209; War Department, 103, 249; Washington visit, 250, 427; wire to Lincoln regarding border states, 71–72
Curtis, George, 444–45
Curtis, Samuel R., 158, 268, 276, 298, 310, 374, 428, 441, 447; correspondence with Lincoln, 255, 278; Department of the Missouri, 246; victory at Westport, 434

Dalton, John Call Jr., 133
Dana, Charles, 155, 163, 282, 293, 469
Danforth, John, 419
Davidson, Catharine E., 226
Davis, David, 107, 265
Davis, Henry Winter, 379, 414
Davis, Jefferson, 3, 16, 102, 122–23, 238, 311, 318, 409, 467–68
Dayton, William, 15

Deitzler, George W., 21, 50
Delaney, Mark W., 180
Delaware, 21, 74–75, 257, 417, 435, 443; 13th amendment, 460–62; bounties, 366, 407–8; and Burton, 6, 92; and Cannon, 263, 270; defense of, 315; emancipation, 383, 451; General Assembly, 245, 270; gubernatorial elections, 242, 244–46, 343–45; influence in Washington, 159–60; political conflict over loyalty to Union, 63–65; quotas, 337; railroad, 245; recruitment of troops, 40, 102, 186, 196; River, 134, 162; slavery, 2, 130; Sons of Liberty, 371

Delaware Republican, 460

Democratic Party, 166, 247, 283, 303, 331, 340, 410, 435, 443, 461; convention, 115, 416–17; convention of the Northwest, 308

Dennison, William, 30, 37, 62, 68–69, 91, 114–16, 136, 191, 372, 397; appeasement of Magoffin, 42–43; call for educated troops, 95–97; Cincinnati delegation, 11–12; Cleveland conference, 70–71; control over the Mississippi and Ohio Rivers, 116; defense of Ohio River and Cincinnati, 49; German population, 74; Indianapolis conference, 80–81; Joint Committee on the Conduct of the War [War Committee], 133–34; Kentucky loyalists, 28; letter to Lincoln on Brough's nomination, 306; Lincoln's reliance on governors regarding Kentucky, 98, 105, 109; McClelland, 9; military review board, 95; New York City conference, 26–27; Peace Conference, 20–21; poor conditions at soldier camps, 84; Proclamation of Amnesty and Reconstruction, 351; recruitment of troops, 41, 103, 125; replacement of Blair as postmaster general, 427; Whigs, 13

Department of New England, 106
Department of the Gulf, 148, 251
Department of the Pacific, 406
Department of the South, 158
Department of the West, 81, 87, 124
Des Moines, Iowa, 142, 367, 419

Detroit, Mich., 202, 222, 319, 457; River, 433
Devens, Charles, 248
Dicey, Edward, 8, 353
Dickinson, Daniel S., 418
Diven, Alexander S., 300, 318
Dix, John A., 73, 85, 128, 241, 326, 343, 347, 386, 418, 436
Dixon, Archibald, 378
Dodd, Harrison H., 409, 429
Dodge, Grenville, 457
Dole, William P., 51
Donnelly, Ignatius L., 281
Dorsey, James L., 46
Doty, Lockwood, 432
Douglas, Stephen A., 88, 112, 115, 244, 246; and Democrats, 182, 190, 247, 338
Dover, Del., 130, 443
Downey, John W., 22, 29, 85, 120–21, 147, 322, 331
Drake, Charles D., 244
Dred Scott v. Sandford, 98, 310
Dubois, Charles, 367
Du Pont, Henry, 63, 206; and DuPont Company, 64

Early, Jubal, 311, 404–5, 426, 432
Eastman, Ira, 280, 312
Eckel, Henry, 64
Edmunds, George, 367
Educational Commission for Freedmen, 241
Eleazar Coburn & Sons, 237. *See also* A&P Coburn Surveyors
Ellet, Charles Jr., 277
Emancipation, 299, 308, 310, 316, 342, 344, 345, 354; Committee on, 310
Emancipation Proclamation, 165, 230, 235–40, 248, 254, 263–64, 270, 351, 451, 453; announcement of, 185, 200, 225; criticism of, 261, 272, 284; defense of, 228–29; issuance of, 226; effect on war, 231–32, 259; Missouri exemption, 244
Emerson, Levi, 56
Emerson, Ralph Waldo, 286, 444, 447, 474
Emigrant Aid Company, 272
Emporia News [KS], 245

Enrolled Militia, 336
Enrollment Act, 278
Etheridge, Emerson, 342
Europe, 55, 208; and Europeans, 117, 176; immigrants, 366
Evans, Andrew, 393
Evans, Jesse, 50
Evans, Sam, 393
Everett, Edward, 92, 348
Ewing, Thomas Jr., 52, 135, 327

Fairbanks, Erastus, 26–27, 34, 52–53, 58, 75, 92–93, 96, 113, 230
Falmouth, Va., 169, 269, 278, 292
Faneuil Hall, 92, 390, 422
Farmer's Cabinet, 231
Farnum, Reuben, 448
Farragut, David, 414, 423
Fayetteville, Ark., 158, 255
Federal Bureau of Emancipation, 352
Fenton, Reuben, 415
Fenton, William, 435, 439, 442, 443, 451, 457, 466, 470, 473
Ferguson, Benjamin, 127
Ferrero, Edwin, 411
Ferris, Anna M., 65, 174, 176, 383, 434, 443, 471
Fessenden, William Pitt, 20, 75, 138, 170, 192, 218, 397–98, 401
Field, David Dudley, 417
Fishback, William H. M., 323
Fisher, George P., 130, 196, 207
Fisher, Sidney George, 244–45
Fiske, Samuel, 205, 226, 248
Fitch, Morris E., 284
Fletcher, Calvin, 10, 243, 255, 261, 266, 313, 338, 370, 403, 438
Fletcher, Thomas Clement, 441, 451, 456–57, 463, 465–66, 473, 480
Florida, 56, 170, 364, 368, 381; Department of, 158
Fogg, George G., 164
Foote, Andrew, 153, 337
Forbes, John Murray, 44–45, 84, 272, 286, 341, 388, 410, 422
Ford's Theatre, 471
Forney, John W., 88, 344
Forster, Robert H., 295

Fort Donelson, 153–56, 158, 159, 162, 164, 167, 210
Fort Henry, 153, 155, 158, 159, 164
Fort Leavenworth, 50, 81, 108, 124, 151, 206, 245, 327
Fort Monroe, 79, 165
Fort Popham, 406
Fort Sumter, 47, 66, 138, 140, 142, 182, 184, 259, 480; defeat, 38, 49; supplies, 32, 35–37
Fort Wagner, 324, 334
Foster, Charles, 297
Foster, Henry D., 39
Fowler, Henry, 351, 383
Fox, Gustavus, 148, 377
Frankfort, Ky., 110, 202, 398
Frankfort Commonwealth, 378, 398, 438–39
Frederick, Md., 60, 219, 405, 432
Fredericksburg, Va., 248, 251, 253–56, 263–65, 269, 280, 292, 314, 386–87, 393–94
Frémont, John, 110, 133, 158, 165, 174, 228, 240, 394, 397, 418; 1861 declaration of martial law in Missouri, 104, 106–8, 116–17, 382; fear of Lane's brigade in Kansas and Missouri, 135; Grant's proclamation to Paducah Kentuckians, 109; gubernatorial push to remove McClellan from army command, 149; Lane's appointment to brigadier general, 111–12; Lincoln's retraction of proclamation of martial law, 118, 139; military review board, 95; occupation of border states, 97–98; response to recruitment of Confederate troops in border states, 102–3; Unionists and Lincoln's renomination, 369–70; Whigs, 13
Frost, Daniel, 78
Fry, James B., 279, 300, 320, 347, 413, 447, 457–58; draft, 296, 316, 318, 325, 360, 429; quotas, 337, 390, 426, 455; West Point, 279
Fugitive Slave Law, 201
Fulton, Charles C., 431
Funk, Isaac, 310

Gage, Portia, 221
Gamble, Hamilton, 102, 237, 251, 255, 268, 276, 283, 298, 310–11, 461; Altoona

Conference, 229–32; attempts to maintain peace in Missouri, 104; Battle of Wilson's Creek, 102; biography, 98; death of, 365; Emancipation Proclamation, 244; and Frémont, 107–8; invasions west of the Mississippi River, 180, 202; Kansas-Missouri War, 150–51; and Lincoln, 123, 180, 322, 325, 335; Lincoln's casket, 473; Lincoln's reliance on governors regarding Kentucky, 98; and McClellan, 123–24; Missouri state militia, 123–24; Missouri, 97–98, 103, 110–12, 180, 224, 356; occupation of border states, 97–98; Pennsylvania, 333–34; Radicals, 354, 357; response to recruitment of Confederate troops in border states, 102–3; Shelby's Confederate cavalry invasion, 336; state militia, 123, 202; Virginia, 80
General Assembly, 52
General Order No. 18, 157
General Order No. 38, 281
Georgetown, 88
Georgetown Pike, 398
Georgia, 368, 384, 389, 392–94, 396, 405, 407, 415, 457; emancipation, 170; secession, 64; Sherman's March to the Sea, 447–48, 452; Sherman's victory in Atlanta, 421–24
Germans, 158, 165, 168, 292–93, 301, 373, 389, 394; regiments, 74, 103, 150
Gettysburg, Penn., 311, 313–15, 322, 339, 347–49, 381, 422
Gettysburg Address, 349
Gibbons, James S., 203–4
Gibbons, John, 434
Gibbs, Addison Crandall, 182, 266, 287–88, 321, 350, 406, 464, 580–81 (n.95); abolition, 379; as Douglas Democrat, 338; Indians, 251–52, 463; Union Party, 181
Gibson, Charles, 189, 276
Gilmore, Joseph, 384, 395, 418, 445, 469; bounties, 362; gubernatorial elections, 312, 314, 405–6; and Lincoln, 326, 375–76, 379, 449; quotas, 337, 368; recruitment, 355, 412; and son Henry Gilmore, 47–58
Goddard, Henry Perkins, 281

Godwin, Parke, 416
Gooch, Daniel, 132
Goodloe, William C., 374–75
Goodwin, Ichabod, 27, 395
Gould, Charles, 215, 217
Graham, Almon, 200, 263
Grant, Ulysses S., 301, 379–82, 387–88, 391–98, 447, 454, 457–58, 464, 469; appointment to highest command, 371–73; Battle of Shiloh, 166–69; Butler sent to New York City as military mediator, 436; Department of the Cumberland, 340; Department of the Ohio, 340; Department of the Tennessee, 340; discussion with Sherman and Lincoln on strategy on the Potomac River, 467; draft, 365, 414–15; Fort Donelson, 153–55; Fort Gaines, 414; Frémont's declaration of martial law in Missouri, 104, 106–8; Illinois, 250; joins Army of the Potomac on the field, 384; Kentucky telegram, 362–63; and Lee, 402, 460; Lincoln's expedition to Vicksburg, 250; Military Division of the Mississippi, 340; proclamation to Paducah Kentuckians, 109; proposal to raise militia for national guard, 386; removal and restoration of command, 158, 160; request to wire governors for troops, 424–25; Rosecrans' action against Bragg's Confederates at Tullahoma, 311; seizure of Paducah, 110; Sherman partnership, 389, 402, 404, 411, 415; Siege of Vicksburg, 297–98, 304, 267, 274, 276–77, 282, 291–93; strategy east of the Mississippi River, 151–52; Tennessee offensive, 347, 349–50; transport of army across the Mississippi River, 293; volunteers, 405; and Yates, 76, 275–76, 294
Greeley, Horace, 91, 221, 233, 297, 391, 409, 415–17, 420–21
Green, Samuel, 406
Grimes, James, 35, 75, 272, 282, 338
Grinnell, Josiah Bushnell, 35, 223
Gurowski, Adam, 71, 116, 131, 189–90, 208, 212, 217, 311

Habeas corpus, writ of, 130, 238, 269, 302, 327, 351; constitutionality of suspension, 247; Copperheads, 334; justification for suspension, 300; legality of suspension, 250; opposition to suspension, 142, 240, 248, 254, 283, 287, 424; support for suspension, 269, 351

Hale, George S., 388

Haley, John, 292

Hall, Willard P., 323, 357, 391, 413, 428, 434

Hall, William A., 357

Halleck, Henry, 153–55, 170, 175, 182–83, 190–91, 194–97, 226, 260, 438; Army of Mississippi, 177–78; Army of the Potomac, 130–31, 158; Battle of Shiloh, 166–69; Battle of the Crater, 411–12; black troops, 273–74; bounties, 220; Burnside, 263; California militia, 85; call for volunteers, 174; conduct by Union commanders, 134–35; Conscription Act riots, 318–19; Copperhead incident in Paris, Ill., 371; Corinth, 239; defense of Harper's Ferry, 404; denunciation by Sumner, 137; Department of Missouri, 124; Department of the Mississippi appointment, 158–60; Department of the Ohio, 124; Donelson campaign, 162; draft, 414–15; East Tennessee, 145; Emancipation Proclamation, 200, 276; establishment of ambulance corps, 229; and Gamble, 251; Grant's removal and restoration of command, 158, 160; gubernatorial push to remove McClellan from army command, 149; and Hooker, 312; Indians, 253; invasions west of the Mississippi River, 18; Kansas-Missouri War, 150–51; Lane's brigade in Kansas and Missouri, 135; and McClellan, 141; militia for national guard, 386; Missouri militia, 202–3; Mobile & Ohio railroad lines, 158; opposition to Lane's recruitment tactics, 206; Pittsburg Landing, 179–80; poor relations with Buell, 136; and Ramsey, 213; runaway slaves, 134; Sigel's appointment to Department of West Virginia, 372–73; and Stanton, 157; supply shortages in St. Louis, 97, 129; suspension of the writ of habeas corpus, 130; War Department, 307

Halpine, Charles G., 278

Hamblin, Edward O., 127

Hamilton, J. Alexander, 205, 216

Hamlin, Hannibal, 61, 89, 173, 218, 237, 397, 402

Hampton Roads, 161, 170, 460

Hanna, Amos, 440

Harding, Benjamin F., 122, 464

Harney, William, 78, 81

Harper's Ferry, 18, 171, 173–75, 260, 287, 324, 389, 404

Harper's Weekly, Congress, 353; conscription, 205; Edward VII's visit, 14; election of 1864, 444; Grant, 397; Illinois' repeal of black laws, 459–60; Lincoln, 74, 348, 352, 464–65, 473–74; Lincoln's reelection, 445; New Year's 1864, 358; New Year's 1865, 451; New York riots, 319; partisan politics, 359; Seymour, 247; Stanton's decree and threat of draft, 203

Harriman, Walter, 280

Harrington, Edward W., 376, 469

Harris, Ira, 471

Harris, Leander, 88

Harris, William C., 2

Harrisburg, Penn., 163, 275; Camp Curtin, 476; and Curtin, 16, 219, 291, 293, 295, 305, 311, 313, 330, 348; enlistment, 311

Harrison, Samuel, 388

Hartford, Conn., 104, 163, 234, 251, 319, 382, 448, 469

Hartford Daily Times, 175

Hartford Evening Press, 59, 66, 166, 199, 203, 226, 257, 261

Harvey, Louis P., 127, 128, 149, 167, 168, 331

Hatch, George, 68

Hathaway, John W., 272

Hawkins, Dexter, 152

Hawley, John A., 337

Hay, John, 9, 17, 23, 55–56, 65–66, 95, 146, 150, 437, 473

Hayden, Lewis, 253–54, 468

Haynie, Isham N., 471

Hecker, Frederick, 74

Heffren, Horace, 429

Heintzelman, Samuel, 361, 371, 385, 399
Hendricks, Thomas A., 472
Henry, Anson, 294
Herman, Henry M., 297
Hesseltine, William B., 1–2
Hicks, Thomas, 13, 41, 58, 79, 128, 139, 144, 259, 262, 461–63; Baltimore Affair, 45–47; invasion of Maryland, 60–61; Loyalists, 19–20; loyalty to Union, 18; murder plot, 16; Peace Conference, 23
Higginson, Thomas Wentworth, 269
Hilton Head, S.C., 164, 297, 411
Hincks, Edward W., 376
Hodges, Albert G., 378, 382, 438
Hoffman, Henry W., 430
Hogg, Harvey, 41
Holbrook, Frederick, 138, 174, 198, 260, 351; biography, 114; Savage's Station, 183; the draft, 210, 296–97, 307; election, 237; support for Emancipation Proclamation, 229
Holland, Josiah G., 230
Holloway, Ephraim, 296
Holt, Joseph, 253, 410, 413
Hood, James R., 342
Hood, John B., 446–47
Hood, Thomas, 71
Hooker, Joseph, 272, 292, 294–96, 311, 312, 433, 457
Hooper, Samuel, 176
Hopkins, Mark, 120
Horn, Daniel, 206
Horsey, Stephen, 429
How, John, 372
Howard, Joseph, 425
Howard, Oliver Otis, 84–85
Howe, Frank, 138, 148, 152, 420, 422–23, 438
Howe, Hervey L., 269, 354
Howe, Julia Ward, 203
Howe, Samuel Gridley, 58
Howe, Timothy, 75
Howland, John D., 63
Humphreys, Andrew, 409, 429
Hunter, David, 111, 149, 170–71, 180, 208, 278, 290, 297, 382, 404; Department of Kansas, 124, 150, 153; Jayhawkers, 150, 158
Hunter, Robert, 460
Huntington, Collis P., 120

Illinois, 156, 196, 224–25, 271, 348, 358, 462; 13th amendment, 459–61; Burnside, 291; conscription, 210, 326, 426; Copperheads, 306, 367, 380; defense of, 76, 105; economic connection to Ohio River, 69; election of 1862, 243–44; election of 1863, 364; election of 1864, 424; electoral procedure, 5; enfranchisement of soldiers, 434–35, 437; Fort Donelson, 154–55; Frémont, 111; Gage, Portia, 221; Indians, 49–50; legislation forbidding black immigration, 241, 265; legislature, 41, 161, 270, 303; Lincoln's assassination at Ford's Theatre, 471–73; Lincoln's expedition to Vicksburg, 250; McClernand, 235; national conscription efforts, 337–39; National Union Committee, 397–98; Northern Department, 361, 433; Oglesby, 454; one-hundred-day men, 429; Pittsburg Landing, 167; Pope, 84, 168; potential attack by Missouri, 48, 50; proposal to raise militia for national guard, 386; recruitment, 61, 276; repeal of black laws, 453, 459–60; Republican Party State Central Committee, 243; Republicans, 267; results of Democratic Convention of the Northwest, 308–9; Shelby's Confederate cavalry invasion, 336; Sons of Liberty, 371; Supreme Court, 309; Trumbull, 51, 75, 219; uprising, 409–10, 413; Western Department, 87; wounded soldiers, 294; Yates, 37, 86, 236, 406
Illinois State Journal, 43, 194, 432, 449
Illinois State Register, 194, 413
Indiana, 62–63, 105, 308, 384, 398, 424, 426, 430–31, 469, 472–73; 13th amendment, 460–61; and Brooks, 437; and Cameron, 41; Camp Jackson violence, 78; Copperheads, 403, 413–14; defense of, 116; Department of the Ohio, 124; and Dole, William P., 51; draft, 192; economic connection to Ohio River, 69; election of 1862, 242–43; election of 1863, 364; electoral procedure, 5; Emancipation Proclamation, 451; Joint Committee on the Conduct of the War

Indiana (cont.)
[War Committee], 132–34; Julian's cooperation with congressmen, 74–75; Kentucky, 178; Lee's invasion of Pennsylvania, 313; legislature, 270, 284, 303, 370, 462; and Lincoln, 109, 179, 466; and Morgan, John Hunt, 315; and Morton, Oliver P., 10, 96, 175, 179, 271, 275, 404, 453, 466; Northern Department, 361, 433; one-hundred-day men, 429; proposal to raise militia for national guard, 386; quotas, 296; recruitment, 362; Republicans, 267; Sanitary Commission, 156–57; secession, 266; and Sherman, 175; soldier voting laws, 434–35; Sons of Liberty, 371, 409; "Tod's Elephant" controversy, 323–24; United States House of Representatives, 338; War Department, 109, 307; war supplies, 103, 162; Whiteaker's governorship, 122

Indianapolis, Ind., 255, 270, 385, 404, 409, 437, 450–51, 473; 12th Indiana's supply shortage, 103–4; Copperhead incident in Paris, Ill., 371; gubernatorial conference in, 80–81; defense of Ohio River, 62; Lincoln's expedition to Vicksburg, 250; Lincoln's request for recruitment reports, 202; Lincoln's visit to, 10; and Morton, 11, 220, 295; "Tod's Elephant" controversy, 323–24; volunteer troops, 41

Indianapolis Daily Journal, 156, 166, 332

Indians, 35, 50, 82, 123, 147, 220, 251–54, 330, 455, 463; conscription during conflicts with, 320; Dakota, 231, 252; Nez Perce, 252; protection from, 49, 121, 213, 287, 321; Sioux, 212–14, 219, 252–53, 281, 331, 345; Snake, 321, 581 (n.95); territories, 111, 246; treatment of, 438; Yankton, 213

Iowa, 42, 75, 251, 337–39, 358, 419, 429, 438, 462, 470; black troops, 273–74; Davis' approval of raising Confederate troops, 102; defense of, 61; the draft, 320–21, 326, 367; election of 1861, 113–14; enfranchisement of soldiers, 434–35; Fort Donelson, 154–55; General Assembly, 212; gubernatorial elections, 329; Indians, 49–50, 213; and Kirkwood, 35, 102, 142–43, 330; Knights of the Golden Circle, 283; and McClellan, 233–35; Military Department of the Northwest, 220; military strength, 43, 104, 211; National Union Committee, 397–98; proposal to raise militia for national guard, 386; Peace Conference, 21–22; Shelby's Confederate cavalry invasion, 336; Western Sanitary Commission, 297–98

Irish, 74–75, 150, 301, 307, 368
Iron Brigade, 387
Island No. 10, 166

Jackson, Alfred Eugene "Mudwall", 429
Jackson, Claiborne, 41–42, 68, 78, 87, 98
Jackson, Miss., 104, 292–93, 297
Jackson, Stonewall, 160, 170, 174–75, 178–79, 183, 219; valley campaign, 170
Jacksonian Democracy, 338, 340
Jacobs, John A., 375
James River, 191, 398, 467
Jay, John, 318
Jayhawkers, 150–51, 158, 179, 327, 440, 463
Jefferson, Samuel, 245
Jennison, Charles R., 108, 145, 150, 327
Jersey Blues, 67, 163, 292, 312, 387
Johnson, Andrew, 132, 155, 397
Johnson, Bradley, 406, 418, 431
Johnson, George V., 139
Johnston, Albert Sidney, 29, 152–53, 169, 297, 324, 404
Jones, John, 453
Jordan, J. Henry, 57–58
Judd, Norman B., 14, 16, 30
Julian, George, 75, 132, 462

Kansas, 87, 153, 157–59, 179–81, 206, 210–11, 335, 370, 428–29, 440–41; 13th amendment, 460–61; conduct of Union commanders, 134–35; Confederate raid on Lawrence, 327; the draft, 463; electoral procedure, 5; enfranchisement of soldiers, 434–35; Federal troops at Fort Leavenworth, 81; Frontier Guard's defense of the White House, 66; illegal election of Carney, 373–74; Indians, 49–50; Kansas-Missouri War, 150–51;

Kansas-Nebraska Act, 35, 56, 89, 443;
 decline in Lincoln's popularity, 421;
 McClellan's creation of Department of,
 124; military discord in, 391–92;
 potential attack by Missouri, 50; politics
 of Frémont's command, 108, 111–12;
 Republican Party emergence, 55–56;
 Robinson's biography, 51–52; Robinson-
 Lane rivalry, 150; statehood, 122; "Tod's
 Elephant" controversy, 323–24
Kansas-Nebraska Act, 35, 51, 56, 89, 443
Kansas State Journal, 52
Keifer, Joseph Warren, 160
Kellogg, William Pitt, 471
Kelly, Benjamin F., 80
Kennedy, John Pendleton, 19
Kentucky, 121, 155, 167, 291, 313, 382, 429,
 454, 457, 463; 13th amendment, 460–61;
 abolition, 451–52; Altoona, 230; black
 soldiers, 328–29, 366–67, 374–75,
 377–78, 398–400, 410; as border state,
 10, 28; and Bragg, 238–40; and
 Bramlette, 438–39; Confederate
 invasion of, 202, 214, 220–22, 315, 398;
 and Davis, 102; defense of, 210–11;
 Department of, 150, 153; Department of
 Missouri, 124; elections, 275, 424;
 election of 1864, 443–45; emancipation,
 107, 276, 333; enfranchisement of
 soldiers, 434–35; General Assembly, 71,
 105; influence in Washington, 159–60;
 legislature, 42; and Lincoln, 42–43, 112,
 405; loyalists, 139; and Magoffin, 12, 62;
 Military Board of, 186; military
 operations in, 98, 108, 149, 178, 196, 261;
 Mill Springs, 152, 164; and Morton, 206;
 neutrality of, 79, 82, 104; public
 opinion, 63–64, 69; Proclamation of
 Neutrality, 78; recruitment, 362–64;
 secessionist movements in, 41, 48, 70,
 115–16; Sons of Liberty, 371; Union
 forces in, 81, 110, 134, 185; Unionists, 109
King, Preston, 246, 284
Kinsley, Edward, 209
Kirkham, Robert, 276
Kirkwood, Samuel, 44, 61, 68, 114, 149, 153,
 177, 186, 293–96, 351; address to Iowa
 legislature, 142–43; Altoona Conference,
 229–32; Battle of Wilson's Creek, 102;
 biography, 35; black troops, 273–74;
 concern over Indian conflicts, 28, 213;
 Copperhead resistance to the draft, 326;
 dismissal by Stanton at War Department,
 236; draft enforcement, 319; election of
 1861, 51–52; election of 1863, 330;
 encouragement of desertions by Knights
 of the Golden Circle, 282–83; enrollment
 of troops, 211–12; fear of potential attack
 by Missouri, 50; Fort Donelson, 154–55;
 Hoffman House gubernatorial reunion,
 480; Kansas-Missouri War, 150–51;
 Knights of the Golden Circle, 283;
 Lincoln's call for regiments, 306–7;
 McClellan, 233–35; national conscription
 efforts, 337–39; request to Iowa General
 Assembly to provide funds for civilian
 defense, 212; response to Burnside's
 appointment, 251; response to Frémont's
 declaration of martial law, 104; response
 to Halleck's call for volunteers, 174;
 Shelby's Confederate cavalry invasion,
 336, Western Sanitary Commission,
 297–98
Knight, Nehemiah, 215–16
Knights of the Golden Circle, 161, 276, 283,
 287, 361, 408, 429
Knoxville, Tenn., 339, 346, 350, 362

Lake, Jed, 330
Lake Erie, 347, 385
Lamon, Ward Hill, 16, 347
Lane, James H., 66, 75, 87, 136, 145, 158, 180,
 245–46, 323, 440–41; 1st Kansas Colored
 Volunteers, 269; appointment to
 brigadier general, 111–12; brigade in
 Kansas and Missouri, 135; conduct of
 Union commanders, 134–35; Confederate
 raid on Lawrence, Kansas, 327; election of
 1861, 51–52; illegal election of Carney,
 373–77; Kansas-Missouri War, 150–55;
 military discord in Kansas and Missouri,
 391–92; Missouri's "Jacobin Delegation,"
 335; politics of Frémont's command, 108;
 recruitment tactics, 206, 210–12
Lanier, James F.D., 308
Lansing, Mich., 143, 163, 360–61, 438

Latham, Milton S., 29
Latimer, James R., 116
Lawrence, Kans., 51, 159, 327
Lawrence Republican, 51
League, Joshua, 76
Leavenworth Daily Times, 246
Lee, Henry, 30
Lee, Robert E., 226, 238, 307, 324, 346, 381, 384, 393–97, 396, 404; Army of the Potomac, 301; Battle of Gettysburg, 313–14; Chancellorsville, 294; and Grant, 402, 460; gubernatorial call for militia defense against, 304–5; gubernatorial response to Maryland Campaign, 219–20; and Hooker, 292, 294; invasion of Delaware, 315; invasion of Maryland and Kentucky, 214, 224–25, 236; invasion of Pennsylvania, 311, 313; New York City draft riots, 344; Petersburg, 411; Richmond, 182, 251; Second Battle of Bull Run, 218; Sharpsburg, 223; Sherman's discussion with Grant and Lincoln on ending conflict on Potomac River, 467; surrender at Appomattox Courthouse, 469–70; Virginia, 389, 391, 409, 457, 466
Leesburg, Va., 117, 219, 405
Lenox, Charles W., 389
Letcher, John, 61, 407
Lewis, James T., 331, 345, 385–88, 392, 416, 419, 455, 480
Liberator, 209
Lincoln, Abraham, 8, 11, 13–14, 21, 30; Altoona address, 233; Antietam, 226; appointment of Fighting Joe Hooker, 272; arming slaves, 133; arrives in Washington, D.C., 17; assassination, 471–73, 480, 580–81 (n.95); Baltimore, 45–47; Battle of Gettysburg, 313; Berry's reassurance to Lincoln of support for the Union, 217; black enrollment in border states, 367; call for regiments, 306–7; call for volunteers in Maryland and Delaware, 40–41, 43; Charleston Harbor, 32; Chase's letter regarding war preparations, 36; Chase's resignation as Treasury Secretary, 400; Cleveland conference, 70–71; conduct of Union commanders, 134–35; Congress's approval of the Electoral College returns, 12; conscription, 3, 198–99, 208, 250, 277–79, 365; Conscription Act riots, 318–19; correspondence with Morgan, 32–33; correspondence with Seward on military situation, 184; Curtin meeting, 16; Curtin's visit to Lincoln and the Army of the Potomac, 329; delivery of Pennsylvania regimental colors in Washington, 113; Department of the Ohio, 124; dismissal of Schofield, 354; early relationship with Yates, 9–10; Early's crossing of the Potomac River, 404–5; Early's raid of Pennsylvania, 432; East Tennessee, 145; election of 1863, 329, 364; election of 1864, 381, 391, 438; Emancipation Proclamation, 185, 200, 225–26, 230, 263–64; establishment of ambulance corps, 229; expedition to Vicksburg, 250; failure to pay expenses of Curtin's Pennsylvania campaign, 335; fear of Lane's brigade in Kansas and Missouri, 135; Frémont's command over Mountain Department, 158; Frémont's declaration of martial law in Missouri, 104, 106–8; Frontier Guard's defense of the White House, 66; Grant's appointment to highest command, 371–73; gubernatorial meeting on Sumter, 37; gubernatorial response to Lee's Maryland Campaign, 219–20; gubernatorial visit to Washington, 235–36; guerilla warfare in Missouri and Midwest, 413–14; Halleck's suspension of the writ of habeas corpus, 130; Hicks' petition for troops, 45–46; inauguration, 23–25, 119–20; Indianapolis conference, 81; Indianapolis visit, 10; Joint Committee on the Conduct of the War [War Committee], 132–34, 335; Kirkwood's 1861 visit to Springfield, 35–36; Maryland's secession concern, 64; military retaliation against Dakota Indians in Minnesota, 252; military supervision of polls, 343; New Jersey visit, 15–16, 37; order for defense of port cities and

coasts, 134, 161–62; Pennsylvanian resistance to draft, 249; Proclamation of Amnesty and Reconstruction, 351–52; recruitment of slaves in Maryland, 336–37; replacement of Blair as postmaster general, 427; replacement of Buell with Rosecrans, 243; retraction of Frémont's proclamation of martial law, 118, 139, 382; Robinson-Lane feud, 245; seizure of St. Louis arsenal, 42, 48–49, 65, 78–79; Senate ratification of the 13th amendment, 458; Seward meeting at Willard's Hotel, 17; Seward's call for men, 183–86; Seymour's denunciation of Lincoln, 283–85; Seymour's opposition to black soldiers, 273–74; Seymour's petition to postpone the draft, 316–17; Shelby's Confederate cavalry invasion, 336; Sherman and Grant on strategy on the Potomac River, 467; Sigel's appointment to Department of West Virginia, 372–73; Stanton, 244–45, 259, 293, 308, 316, 361, 476, 478; suspension of draft in New York City, 317–18; suspension of writ of habeas corpus, 117, 130, 238, 240, 247, 250, 254, 269, 302, 327, 334, 351, 424; volunteer regiments, 61–63, 72–73; Wade-Davis bill, 414
Longfellow, Henry Wadsworth, 30
Los Angeles Star, 121
Louisiana, 57, 260, 275, 277, 297, 311, 373
Louisville, Ky., 62, 81, 110, 115–16, 153, 154, 156, 220, 238, 329, 378, 392, 454, 477
Louisville Daily Journal, 42, 70, 128, 166, 224, 375, 399
Low, Frederick, 322, 331–32, 340, 369, 379, 399, 463–64, 581 (n.95)
Lucas, Josiah M., 19
Ludington, Elisha H., 439
Lyon, Nathaniel, 78, 81, 87
Lyons, Lord Richard, 284, 347

Maddox, G. Fred, 274
Madison, Wis., 168, 293, 419, 434, 438, 448; Courthouse, 367
Madison & Indiana Railroad, 340
Magoffin, Beriah, 12, 41–42, 62, 68, 70, 78, 104–6, 110, 139, 211

Maine, 84, 152, 173, 192, 216, 239, 338, 389, 396, 412; 13th amendment, 460–61; Coburn's address on Augusta, 263; and Cony, 358, 405–6, 408, 418; election of 1861, 113–14; election of 1863, 328–32; election of 1864, 425; enfranchisement of soldiers, 434–35; fall election of 1862, 242–43; and Fessenden, 75, 397–98, 401–2; field conditions, 271–72, 292; Fort Donelson, 154–55; and Hamlin, 61; railroad, 237; recruitment, 206; renomination of Lincoln, 376; Stanton's replacement of Hunter with abolitionist Blunt, 180; Union Leagues, 369; volunteers, 82; War Department, 162; and Washburn, 34, 56, 138, 256; writ of habeas corpus, 117
Mallory, Robert, 231
Manassas, Va., 91, 152, 173, 182, 381
Marcy, William L., 190, 247, 285
Markley, John, 229
Marsh, Isaac, 273
Marshall, Albert O., 293
Martha's Vineyard, 208
Martindale, John H., 66
Maryland, 109, 240, 348–49, 360, 424, 430–32, 441, 446, 462–63; 13th amendment, 460–61; abolition, 19, 372, 379, 451–52; Antietam, 226; Baltimore riot, 57–58; Baltimore, 45–47, 79; border state, 61–62, 365; Bradford's refusal to sign Altoona address, 237; call for militia defense against Lee's Confederates, 304–5; campaign, 219; communications with Washington lost, 54–55; Confederate raids in, 414; Confederates burn down Bradford's Baltimore home, 406–7; deployment to Pennsylvania-Maryland border, 408–9; draft, 342, 390; Early's crossing of the Potomac River, 404–5; election of 1861, 113–14, 127–28; electoral procedure, 5; Emancipation Proclamation, 237–38, 259, 276; enfranchisement of soldiers, 434–35; establishment of ambulance corps, 229; federal influence in, 345; and Fletcher, Calvin, 313; Fugitive Slave Law, 201; and Gamble, 104; gubernatorial push to remove McClellan from army command, 149; gubernatorial

Maryland (cont.)
response to Lee's Campaign, 219–20; Hicks murder plot, 13–16; influence in Washington, 159–60; invasion of, 214, 222, 224–25, 236; Jefferson Davis' approval of raising Confederate troops, 102; Lee's departure from, 238, 315; Lincoln and black enrollment in border states, 367; and Lincoln, 23, 471; Loyalists, 19–20; martial law in, 78, 82, 107; military supervision of polls, 343; quotas, 63, 201; reconstruction, 333; recruitment of slaves, 274, 336–37, 375; response to recruitment of Confederate troops in border states, 102–3; runaway slaves, 134; secession, 58, 64, 78; slavery, 18, 130, 144, 276; Sons of Liberty, 371; and Stanton, 249; state constitution, 442, 477; state fair, 385; suspension of writ of habeas corpus, 238; Unionists, 139; volunteers, 40–41, 43

Mason, Larkin, 445

Mason-Dixon Line, 106

Massachusetts, 137, 139–40, 148, 263, 369, 376, 388–91, 459; 13th amendment, 460–61; 54th Massachusetts all-black regiment, 300–301, 324, 334; appointment of Fighting Joe Hooker, 272; Association of Free Colored Citizens of, 468; black soldiers, 173, 290, 469–70; Boston, 46, 173; and Boutwell, George, 55, 92; and Butler, Benjamin F., 58; Cleveland meeting, 70–71; Copperheads, 438; and Crapo, Henry Howland, 439–40; draft, 207, 278, 297; election of 1861, 113–14; election of 1862, 242–43; election of 1863, 328–32, 345, 364; election of 1864, 419; emancipation, 208–9; and Forbes, John Murray, 44–45, 341–42; Fort Sumter, 35; fugitive slaves, 136, 269; influence in Washington, 159–60; Joint Committee on the Conduct of the War [War Committee], 132–34; legislature, 479; military review board, 95; national conscription efforts, 337–39; New England Emigrant Aid Company, 51; Peace Conference, 21–22; People's Party, 248; Radicalism, 248; recruitment, 102, 176, 187, 288, 360–63; refusal to enact soldier voting laws, 434–35; repeal of personal liberty laws, 27; response to Early's crossing of the Potomac River, 404; and Robinson, 51–52; Senate Military Committee, 185; soldier conditions, 84, 97; soldiers stationed in Washington after Baltimore Affair, 47–48, 66, 88; Statehouse, 253; Sumner's cooperation with congressmen, 74–75

Mattocks, Charles, 292

Maxwell, Robert A., 318

May, Charles, 143

McAllister, Robert, 292, 431

McCausland, John, 409

McClellan, George B., 203, 215, 255, 311, 381, 398, 420–21, 435, 443; Altoona, 217; and Andrew, 228; Buell's poor relations with Midwestern governors, 136, 444; call for troops, 185, 187–88; casualty reports, 154; Chandler-Wade-Sumner Radical cabal, 242; Cleveland conference, 70–71; command of the Army of the Potomac, 104, 130–31, 158; criticism of, 243; Democrats, 394–95; denunciation by Sumner, 137; Department of Kansas, 124; Department of Missouri, 124; Department of the Gulf, 148; Department of the Ohio, 78, 124; East Tennessee, 145; effect on war, 192, 195–200; election of 1864, 416–17, 426; Fort Donelson, 154–55; Fort Monroe, 165; and Gamble, 123–24; gubernatorial response to Lee's Maryland Campaign, 219–20; Indianapolis conference, 80–81; James River, 191; Joint Committee on the Conduct of the War [War Committee], 132–34; and Kirkwood, 233–34; Lincoln and Radical's shared war aims, 196; and Lincoln, 163, 169, 172, 174–75, 203, 255, 426; Manassas, 381; Militia Act, 203; Missouri state militia, 123–24; New Jersey, 312, 444; New York War Committee meeting in Providence, 216–17; New York, 157; Pennsylvania, 225–26; relief of duty, 149, 158–60, 169, 229, 250–51; replacement by Rosecrans,

94; replacement of McDowell, 93; Robinson-Lane rivalry, 150; Seven Day's Battle, 182, 189–90; Sharpsburg, 223, 226; and Stanton, 179; supply shortages, 97, 129, 194; typhoid, 140–41, 144; Virginia Peninsula, 162, 166, 169, 183; War Department, 154, 159, 174; and Washburn, 170, 218, 239; Washington D.C., 116, 157, 160, 177, 203, 255; western activity of army, 152–53
McClernand, John A., 153, 235–36, 250, 267, 293, 311
McClure, Alexander, 16, 146, 170, 232, 249
McDonald, Joseph E., 414
McDowell, Irvin, 78, 80, 91, 93, 174, 406, 464
McFarland, Andrew, 86
McPherson, James B., 372–73
Mead, William L., 388, 437
Meade, George Gordon, 311–12, 314, 324, 346, 373, 380, 381, 384, 386, 389, 395
Medill, Joseph, 147, 336
Meigs, Montgomery C., 112, 145, 152, 325
Memphis, Tenn., 98, 156, 178–79, 294
Memphis & Charleston Railroad, 158
Merrick, Charles, 314
Metropolitan Hotel, 240, 462
Mexican War, 42, 357, 445
Michigan, 70, 75, 94, 99, 124, 137, 264, 295, 418; 13th amendment, 460–61; black enfranchisement, 241; Blair's address to state legislators, 143–44, 360–61; Blair's popularity with Radicals, 248; Blair's recommendations for defending the coast, 28; Chandler's criticism of Lincoln's approach to war, 89; election of 1862, 242–43; election of 1864, 439–40, 454; electoral procedure, 5; enfranchisement of soldiers, 434–35; gubernatorial response to Maryland Campaign, 219–20; guerilla warfare, 457; Joint Committee on the Conduct of the War [War Committee], 132–34; Northern Department, 433, 460; Senate, 440; volunteer recruitment, 178; weather hindrances to war effort, 112, 358
Middle Department, 379
Military Academy, U.S., 84
Military Department of the Northwest, 220
Militia Act, 38, 72, 198, 202–3; bill, 204
Miller, Stephen, 330, 345, 407, 419, 455, 470
Milligan, Lambdin P., 409, 429
Mill Springs, Ky., 152, 159, 164
Milroy, Robert, 304
Milwaukee, Wis., 167–68, 232, 250, 290, 297, 301, 320
Minneapolis, Minn., 331
Minnesota, 75, 127, 137, 196, 214, 358, 407, 419, 456; 13th amendment, 460–61; defense against Indians, 252, 455, 463; District of, 345; the draft, 320–21, 416; election of 1861, 113–14; election of 1863, 329–30; electoral procedure, 5; enfranchisement of soldiers, 434–35; Fort Donelson, 154–55; gubernatorial elections, 329; lack of enlistments during Lee's Maryland Campaign, 219–20; Military Department of the Northwest, 220; Peace Conference, 22; Ramsey's address to state legislature, 264; Ramsey's election to United States Senate, 281; River, 213; Sherman's scorched earth policy, 448; statehood, 282; volunteer regiments, 39–40, 174; weather hindrances to war effort, 112
Mississippi, 222, 239, 249, 281, 311, 315, 321, 368, 428; Army of, 177–78, 267; Mobile & Ohio railroad lines, 158; Pierpont, 87; Siege of Vicksburg, 292, 297–98, 304
Mississippi River, 222, 239, 249, 253, 255, 267, 275, 294, 330, 441; arming civilians in St. Louis, 76; conscription, 296; control over, 116, 179; Copperhead resistance to the draft, 326; Department of the West, 81, 87; Department of, 158; Grant's strategy east of, 151–52; Grant's transport of army westward, 293; gubernatorial visit to Washington, 235–36; Indians, 49–50, 219–20; Lincoln's correspondence with Seward on military situation near, 184; Lincoln's view of war west of, 251, 463; military affairs near, 180, 202, 391–92; Military Division, 340; occupation of border states, 97–98; Price's raid, 433–34; reliance on as major economic highway, 28, 291; weather hindrances to war effort, 112, 134

Missouri, 121, 128, 130, 185, 222–23, 357, 457, 459, 465–66; 13th amendment, 456, 460–61; abolition, 451–52; Battle of Wilson's Creek, 102; black soldiers, 367; Camp Jackson, 98; Confederate raid on Lawrence, Kansas, 327; constitutional convention on abolition, 456; Constitutional Convention, 310; counterrevolutionary plot, 409–10; defense against Indians, 463; Department of the Mississippi, 158; Department of, 124, 246; East Tennessee, 145; election of 1863, 345, 364; election of 1864, 441; electoral procedure, 5; Emancipation Proclamation, 237, 244, 276; enfranchisement of soldiers, 434–35; fear of invasion by Lane's brigade, 135; Federal occupation of, 87, 97–98; Federal troops at Fort Leavenworth, 81; federalism, 43; Frank Blair's cooperation with congressmen, 74–75; and Frémont, 104, 106–8, 133; and Gamble, 97–98, 103, 110–12, 180, 224, 255, 268, 298, 356; gubernatorial push to remove McClellan from army command, 149; guerilla warfare, 413; and Halleck, 162, 200; influence in Washington, 159–60; Jefferson Davis' approval of raising Confederate troops, 102; Kansas-Missouri War, 150–51; Knights of the Golden Circle, 282–83; Lane's "Jacobin Delegation," 335; Lane's appointment to brigadier general, 111–12; Lee's invasion of Pennsylvania, 313; legislation on state militia, 123–24; Lincoln's dismissal of Schofield, 354; and McClellan, 116; military discord in, 391–92; New Madrid, 162, 168; Nicolay's survey in St. Louis, 428, 433–34; occupation of, 157; politics of Frémont's command in Kansas, 108; public opinion on slavery, 109, 121; Radicals, 343, 365; recruitment, 97; response to recruitment of Confederate troops in border states, 102–3; retaliation against Jayhawkers, 179; River, 81, 150; runaway slaves, 134, 334; secessionists, 41–42, 48–51, 82, 115; seizure of St. Louis arsenal, 42, 48–49, 65, 78–79; Shelby's Confederate cavalry invasion, 336; slavery, 322, 333–34, 424; Sons of Liberty, 371; State Convention, 97; state militia, 48, 202–3; supply shortages in St. Louis, 97; Supreme Court, 98; "Tod's Elephant" controversy, 323–24; Unionists, 139; writ of habeas corpus, 130

Mitchell, George A., 264
Mobile & Ohio Railroad, 158
Montpelier, Vt., 52, 163, 433, 448
Monument Square, 46, 201
Morgan, Edwin D., 73, 76–77, 96, 184–87, 195, 223–24, 284–85, 390, 420; Altoona Conference, 229–32; biography, 15; and Cameron, 54–55, 101; Camp Morgan, 60; Cleveland conference, 70; Congress, 88; correspondence with Lincoln, 32–33; defense of Washington, 44–46; election of 1863, 344–45; German regiments, 150; Joint Committee, 133–34; Lincoln's suspension of the writ of habeas corpus, 300; Lincoln's visit to New York, 13–15; military review board, 95; National Union Committee, 397–98; national volunteer army, 85–86; New York City conference, 26–27; New York, 202, 204–05, 436; order for defense of port cities, 161–62; Peace Conference, 20; recruitment of troops, 34, 103, 105, 125, 210–11; Republican Party, 246; and Stanton, 354; visit to New York regiments near the Potomac River, 138; volunteer recruitment, 173–74, 176, 178; war resources, 65, 112, 157; welfare of troops, 90
Morgan, George D., 55
Morgan, John Hunt, 196, 298, 315, 323–24, 329
Morgantown, W. Va., 87, 293
Morton, Oliver P., 293, 370, 384–85, 388, 392, 398–99, 429–31, 461, 471–73; 12th Indiana's supply shortage, 103–04; 13th amendment, 462; abolition, 149; Altoona, 229, 239; appeasement of Magoffin, 42–43; bounties, 211, 220; and Buell, 136, 206, 238, 243; and Cameron, 41, 146; *Chicago Tribune*, 11; Cleveland conference, 70; Copperheads, 371,

413–14; and Crapo, 454; defense of Ohio River, 62; Democratic Party, 410; Democrats, 49, 270; draft, 192, 212, 279, 296–97; election of 1863, 338–40; election of 1864, 437; and Fletcher, 255, 261, 266, 403; Fort Donelson, 156, 162; Fort Henry, 153; German population, 74, 150; gubernatorial establishment of organizational framework, 68–69; guerilla warfare in Kentucky, 457; Halleck's appointment as chief of staff, 373; Indiana, 10, 96, 116, 175, 179, 271, 275, 404, 453, 466; Indianapolis conference, 80–81; Joint Committee on the Conduct of the War [War Committee], 133–34; lack of funds, 33, 315; and Lincoln, 78, 165, 295, 302–3, 437; Lincoln's expedition to Vicksburg, 250; Lincoln's reliance on governors regarding Kentucky, 98, 105, 109; Lincoln's request for recruitment reports, 202; Loyalists, 112; *New York Times*, 339, 435; New York, 34, 308, 324; Peace Conference, 20–21; quotas, 63, 368; Radicals, 421–22; recruitment, 183–86, 356, 362–63; reliance on the Mississippi River as major economic highway, 291; request to postpone draft, 424–25; resignation, 403; response to Early's crossing of the Potomac River, 404; secessionist plots uncovered by, 115; soldier welfare, 167, 260, 426; speech at Maison Dorée Hotel, 290; and Stanton, 146, 212, 368, 450; Sumter, 37; Union Party, 330; Vallandigham's plot and arrest, 347–48; volunteer recruitment, 178; War Department, 96, 126, 307; Washington, D.C., 239–40, 290, 420, 437; and Yates, 78, 107, 267
Mosby, John Singleton, 324
Moses, John, 192–93, 236
Mountain Department, 158, 165
Mullaly, John, 299
Murfreesboro, Tenn., 259, 266, 446
Murray, Robert D., 211

Nash, Simeon, 125
Nashville, Tenn., 153, 155–56, 158–60, 164, 260, 266, 373, 422, 446, 447

National Conscription Act, 278–79
National Hotel, 91, 235, 466, 471
National Union Party, 397, 399
Nebraska, 51, 89, 443
Negro Exclusion Law, 241
Nelson, William, 62, 105, 110
Nesmith, J. W., 75, 464
New Almaden Quicksilver Mine, 321–22, 332, 580–81 (n.95)
Newark Daily Mercury, 63, 163, 192, 247
Newberry, John S., 319
New England Agricultural Society, 423, 468
New England Emigrant Aid Company, 51
New Hampshire, 47, 320, 362, 368, 375, 379, 385, 449, 452, 477; 11th New Hampshire of the 9th Corps, 396; 13th amendment, 460–61; Berry's reassurance to Lincoln of support for the Union, 217; election of 1862, 242–43, 280–81, 312; election of 1863, 328–32; election of 1864, 381, 391, 395, 438; election of Berry, 36; election of Smyth, 468–69; enfranchisement of soldiers, 434–35; First Congressional District, 355; Gilmore's support for soldiers, 314, 418, 445; repeal of personal liberty laws, 27; repeal of personal liberty laws, 27; Siege of Petersburg, 412; Statehouse, 395; Supreme Court, 376
New Hampshire Patriot and State Gazette, 87, 232
New-Hampshire Statesman, 280, 444
New Haven, Conn., 101, 387; Soldier's Aid Society, 356
New Jersey, 202, 228, 237, 247, 286, 314, 324, 346, 364, 419; 13th amendment, 461–62; and Olden, 96, 190; black soldiers, 387; call for militia defense, 304–5, 312, 341; defense of, 61; Democratic minorities, 74; election of 1862, 242–43; election of 1864, 443–45; electoral procedure, 5; Lincoln's inaugural visit, 15–16, 37; McClellan's victory, 444; Parker's inaugural message, 267–68; Peace Conference, 21–22; public sentiment, 67; quotas, 320; resource procurement, 125–26, 173; Seymour's visit, 316–17; soldier voting laws, 431, 434–35; Unionists, 344

New Madrid, Mo., 158–59, 162, 168
New Orleans, La., 57, 148, 169, 246, 251, 260, 282, 422; Port of, 471
Newport, R.I., 81, 251, 280
Newsom, David, 406, 440
New York, 120, 132–33, 200, 241, 280, 293, 426, 437–38, 442–43; 13th amendment, 460; abolition, 203; black soldiers, 269, 273–74, 278, 300; Bureau of Military Statistics, 432; Cleveland assemblage, 70; Congressional Republicans delegation, 183; and Curtin, 222; Democratic minorities, 74; disenfranchisement of New York soldiers, 436; draft, 318, 320–21, 325–26, 390–91, 413; election of 1862, 242–43; election of 1863, 344–45, 364; election of 1864, 415–16, 420; electoral procedure, 5; Emancipation Proclamation, 264; enfranchisement of soldiers, 434–35; federal influence in, 345; Fenton's trip to Washington regarding excessive quota, 451; Fort Lafayette, 282; and Gibbs, 181–82; and Gilmore, 469; influence in Washington, 159–60; and Lincoln, 54, 202, 351, 383, 415–16, 420, 471; Lincoln's loss of popularity, 421; and McClellan, 157; military resources, 65, 173; Militia Bill, 204; and Morgan, 54, 202; Morgan's visit to New York regiments near the Potomac River, 138; and Morton, 308, 324, 348; National Union Committee, 397–98; national volunteer army, 85–86; National War Committee, 205, 215–16; New York journalists' meeting, 417; New York State Colored Volunteers, 297; Pennsylvania state treasury, 219; proposal to raise militia for national guard, 386; quotas, 457–58, 466; and Randall, 93; recruitment, 40, 105, 125, 279; regiments deployed to protect Washington, 66; Republican Convention, 227; response to Early's crossing of the Potomac River, 404–05; riots, 319; and Seymour, 339; and Seymour, Origen S., 381; Seymour's denunciation of Lincoln, 283–85; Seymour's election as Constitutional Democrat, 246–47; Seymour's order for troops to move into Pennsylvania, 305; Seymour's petition to postpone the draft, 316–17; soldier welfare and morale, 90, 257, 275, 393–94; Sons of Liberty, 371; and Stanton, 297, 324, 390; and Stevens, Montgomery, 214; and Stone, Charles P., 137; Union Defense Committee, 73, 76–77, 185; Union League, 354, 43; Unionist election efforts, 344; Vallandigham's arrest, 299–300; and Washburn, 152; Washington D.C., 308
New York City, 82, 101, 138, 176, 184–85, 193, 246, 286, 390, 466; arrival of 9th Vermont, 198; as Union's supply depot, 55, 73–74, 152; Butler sent as military mediator, 436; Central Park, 92; City Hall, 395; the draft, 319, 331, 344; Erie Canal, 13; Hoffman House gubernatorial reunion, 480; Morgan's invitation to governors, 26; Morton's speech at the Maison Doreé Hotel, 290; New York journalists' meeting, 417; state of emergency, 317; suspension of draft, 318; Union Central Committee, 413; Union Defense Committee, 73; volunteers, 204; Wood's advocacy of secession, 14
New York Herald, 23, 37, 140, 228
New York Times, 63, 92, 199, 289, 350, 364, 382, 431, 435; conscription, 210; election of Frederick Smyth, 468; federal sovereignty, 223; Lincoln's meeting with Seward, 17; and Morton, 339; popular sentiment, 222; Republican victory in New England, 469; and Seymour, 345; suspension of draft in New York City, 318; war governors, 478, 481
New York Tribune, 91, 155, 221, 235, 248, 260, 282, 300, 415
New York World, 232, 417
Nicolay, John G., 111, 202, 220, 252, 254, 266, 421, 428, 433–34, 473
North, Levi, 196
North Carolina, 290, 296, 452, 457, 466

Northern Department, 361, 433
Northwest Virginia Railroad, 80
Norton, Henry B., 304
Norwich, Conn., 38, 57, 304
Nugent, Robert, 299, 317
Nutt, Henry C., 151

Odell, Moses Fowler, 132
Oglesby, Richard, 440, 444, 454, 455, 459, 471–73
Ohio, 60, 192, 249, 256, 306–7, 325, 399–400, 419, 450, 464–65; 13th amendment, 460–61; Army of, 315; behavior of troops, 91–92; Brough, 360, 393; Canal, 339; Chase, 59; Chase's allowance of regiments to carry state flags, 59; Cincinnati delegation, 11–12; Cleveland conference, 70–71; Copperheads, 207, 306, 409; Davidson, Catharine E., 226; defense of, 105; Democratic and ethnic minorities, 74; Dennison, 37, 136; Dennison's opposition to Peace Conference, 20–21; Dennison's replacement of Blair as postmaster general, 427; Department of Susquehanna, 304; Department of the Ohio, 124; Department of, 78, 124, 220, 291, 340; draft, 249, 424–25; economic connection to Ohio River, 69; election of 1861, 113–14; election of 1862, 242–43, 245; election of 1864, 430–31; electoral procedure, 5; enfranchisement of soldiers, 434–35; gubernatorial elections, 329; Halleck, 307; Indiana-Ohio state line, 473; influence in Washington, 159–60; Joint Committee on the Conduct of the War [War Committee], 132–34; legislature, 270, 391; Lincoln, 125, 145; military review board, 95; National Union Committee, 397–98; New York conference, 26–27; Northern Department, 361, 433; Peace Conference delegates, 21; poor conditions in Ohio regiments, 67, 84; proposal to raise militia for national guard, 386; Radicals, 354; railroad, 80, 87, 158; recruitment, 40, 103; Republican Party, 49; River, 10, 28, 49, 62, 69, 71, 80, 110, 151, 302; Senate, 115, 340; soldier pay, 445; Sons of Liberty, 371; Swift, 281–82; Tod, 277, 323–24, 330; Tod's replacement of Chase as Treasury Secretary, 401; United States House of Representatives, 338; Vallandigham, 295–96, 299–300, 305, 348; volunteer troops, 41; Wade's cooperation with congressmen, 74–75; Whigs in the 1859 election, 13
Ohio River, 28, 69, 80, 110, 116, 151, 302; Army of, 315; Department of, 78, 124, 220, 291, 340; canal, 339
Ohio State Journal, 324
Ohio Statesman, 123, 264
Olden, Charles S., 20, 22, 61, 96, 134, 162, 190, 202, 228, 247; Altoona, 230; enlisting troops, 173, 184–85; fundraising, 125–26; invitation to Lincoln, 15–16; Jersey Blues, 67, 163
Old National Hotel, 471–72
Olds, Edson B., 207, 282
Olmsted, Frederick Law, 92
Opdyke, George, 290, 297, 317, 415–16
Order of the American Knights, 385, 428
Ordway, Nehemiah G., 449
Oregon, 75, 119, 242, 287, 321, 435, 462–64; and Gibbs, 181–82, 251, 266, 297; House of Representatives, 122; Indians, 123, 147; Loyal Leagues, 406; Pacific Republic, 131, 379; Senate, 123; statehood, 122; Trail, 182, 252, 321, 406; and Whiteaker, 6, 22, 121–22
Orme, William Ward, 265
Overland Mail Route, 121
Overland Telegraph Company, 119

Parker, Joel, 314, 320, 346–47, 364, 387, 396, 419–20, 461, 473; call for militia defense, 304–5, 312, 341; election of 1862, 247; election of 1863, 344; fear of attack on Washington, 404; McClellan's victory in New Jersey, 444; review of Jersey Blues, 292; volunteers, 355
Pennsylvania, 170, 257, 287, 319, 359, 377, 425, 430–31, 438, 447; 13th amendment, 456, 460–61; Altoona, 231; Baltimore affair en route to Washington, 45–46;

714 Index

Pennsylvania (cont.)
  Battle of Gettysburg, 313; and Boreman, Arthur, 302; Camp Curtin, 476; Cleveland conference, 70; Confederate raids in, 414; and Curtin, 39, 42, 103, 352–53, 479; Curtin's speech in Harrisburg, 311; defense against Lee's Confederates, 304–5, 324; defense of Washington, 88; democrats, 275; Department of Susquehanna, 304; deployment to Pennsylvania-Maryland border, 408–9; Early's raid, 404, 432; election of 1862, 242–44; election of 1863, 329, 364; electoral procedure, 5; enfranchisement of soldiers, 127, 434–35; and Fenton, Reuben, 415; fugitive slaves, 136–37; and Gamble, 98, 333–34; and Grant, 347; gubernatorial elections, 329; gubernatorial meeting with Lincoln in Washington, 37; influence in Washington, 159–60; invasion of, 293, 311–13; Joint Committee on the Conduct of the War [War Committee], 132–34; Lee's Maryland Campaign, 219–20; legislature, 391, 456, 460, 476, 479; Lincoln's delivery of state regimental colors in Washington, 113; Lincoln's failure to pay expenses of Curtin's campaign, 335; and McClellan, 225–26, 228; national conscription efforts, 337–39; New York City draft riots, 344; Northwestern Virginia Railroad, 80; Peace Conference, 21; Railroad, 227; and Ramsey, 40; recruitment and enrollment, 55, 63, 209; resistance to draft, 249, 291, 301; Saratoga Springs, 418; Seymour's order for New York troops to move into, 305; soldier conditions in Washington, 67, 295; Sons of Liberty, 371; and Stevens, Thaddeus, 75; U.S. House of Representatives, 338; Wilderness Woods, 387
Petersburg, Va., 398, 411, 412, 414, 423, 425, 443, 457, 459, 467
Philadelphia, Pa., 16, 64, 67, 185, 193, 235, 305, 322, 396, 405; and Curtin, 219, 226, 286–87, 377; Delaware River, 134, 162; speech to the Sanitary Commission at Great Central Fair, 395; volunteers, 204, 304
Pierpont, Francis S., 80, 129, 173, 228, 260, 292; at Altoona, 229, 235; appointment as provisional governor, 86–87; correspondence with Lincoln, 160, 182; West Virginian statehood, 261, 302
Pittsburgh, Pa., 210, 323, 338; Landing, 160, 166–68, 180
Pomeroy, Samuel C., 52, 323, 370, 373, 374, 391
Pope, John, 104, 107, 151, 182, 195, 200, 218, 224, 240, 320; Army of Virginia, 203, 205; Indians, 252; victory at Island No. 10, 166; Lincoln's inauguration, 14, 84; Military Department of the Northwest, 220; siege of New Madrid, 158, 168
Portland, Ore., 182, 379
Potomac River, 127, 159, 171, 175–76, 219, 243, 315, 324, 437; arming slaves, 133; Army of, 94, 104, 130, 144, 152, 158, 165, 195, 250–51, 255, 258, 271, 301, 313, 329, 345, 384, 389, 404, 406, 409, 445, 467, 476; army's return to Washington, 195; Ball's Bluff, 117; Curtin's visit, 329; defense of Washington, 94; Department of, 158; Early's crossing of, 404–5, 409; Fort Monroe, 165; Fredericksburg, 255; Grant joins army on the field, 384; Halleck's appointment as commander of army, 158; McClellan, 130–31, 223; McClellan's appointment as commander of army, 104; McDowell's troops occupy Alexandria, 80; Morgan's visit to New York regiments near, 138; Mud March, 271; Northern volunteers, 58; President's Special War Order No. 1, 152; Sharpsburg, 226; strategy for ending conflict with Lee's army, 467
Price, Sterling, 102, 239, 428, 429, 433, 434, 441
Providence, R.I., 48, 197, 215–17, 289, 290

Quantrill, William Clarke, 327, 331

Radicals, 214, 227, 253, 291, 370–71, 380, 394, 399, 421–22; 13th amendment, 462; abolition, 149, 363; black enfranchisement, 241; and Blair, Austin, 22; Blair's address to Michigan state legislators, 143–44; Blair's popularity with Michigan Radicals, 248; and Buckingham, 179; and Chandler, 22; demands for resignations, 333; Department of the Gulf, 148; election of 1862, 242–43; Frémont's command over Mountain Department, 158; Frémont's declaration of martial law in Missouri, 104, 106–8; and Gamble, 354, 357; and Gibbs, 182; gubernatorial response to Maryland Campaign, 219–20; Joint Committee on the Conduct of the War [War Committee], 133–34; Lane and Radical Kansans, 327; Lincoln's war aims, 196, 345, 383; Missouri Constitutional Convention, 310; Missouri Radicals, 365; Missouri Unionists, 343; National Union Committee, 397–98; opposition to slavery, 350; and Padelford, Seth, 14; quarrels with conservatives, 336, 343; Radical Republicans, 235–37, 308, 416, 459; Radical Unionists, 451; Reconstruction, 412–14; Second Confiscation Act, 199; and Seymour, 317; Seymour's public condemnation of Lincoln, 300; Wade-Davis bill, 414; war aims and policy, 139–40, 145, 169–70

Ramsey, Alexander, 73, 127, 134, 196–97, 213, 230, 277, 330, 348, 455; address to Minnesota state legislature, 264; biography, 40; election to United States Senate, 281; gubernatorial response to Lee's Maryland Campaign, 219–20; military retaliation against Dakota Indians, 252; Minnesota volunteer regiments, 39–40; Peace Conference, 22; response to Halleck's call for volunteers, 174; concern over Indian conflicts, 28; winter closure of Mississippi River, 112

Randall, Alexander, 22, 73, 84, 90, 93, 135, 138, 168, 414; Cleveland Conference, 70–71; criticism of, 127; German regiment, 103; Indians, 28

Randall, James G., 231
Randall, James Ryder, 57
Rapidan River, 346, 386–87

Rappahannock River, 251, 254–55, 266, 271, 292, 294–95, 346
Rathbone, Henry R., 471
Raymond, Henry J., 199, 420
Reavis, Logan Uriah, 224
Reconstruction, 412, 414, 420, 422, 438, 446, 461
Redfield, Timothy P., 328, 425
Red River, 373, 381
Republican Party, 257, 339, 345, 418, 441, 454, 458, 477; and Curtin, 39; and Fenton, 415; and Gilmore, 312; and Lane, 135; and Morgan, 246; and Ramsey, 40; and Salomon, 168; and Washburn, 34; convention, 370, 395, 417, 420; election of 1862, 242–43; election of 1863, 328–32; election of 1864, 375–77, 439–40; endorsement of military rule, 308; formation of, 11, 55–56, 65, 89; Joint Committee on the Conduct of the War [War Committee], 134; in Ohio, 49; Republican Party State Central Committee, 243; Robinson-Lane feud, 245; slavery, 43, 468; support for Lincoln's renomination, 369–70
Rhode Island, 48, 56, 65–66, 73, 89, 289–90, 376–77, 418, 455, 469; 13th amendment, 460–61; the draft, 320–21; election of 1862, 242–43; election of 1863, 328–32; enfranchisement of soldiers, 434–35; repeal of personal liberty laws, 27; Sprague's election, 14; Sprague's reelection, 37; Sprague's senatorial aspirations, 279–80
Rice, Henry, 75, 281
Richmond, Va., 175, 182–84, 251, 368, 384, 392, 395, 469; advance on, 89, 91–92, 151, 189–91, 194; and Lincoln, 260, 324; and McClellan, 175, 182, 200; Union victory at, 467–68
Robinson, Charles [KS], 50, 87, 111–12, 136, 153, 158, 179–81, 268, 351; Altoona Conference, 229–30; appointment of delegates to Peace Conference, 21; conduct of Union commanders, 134–35; election of 1861, 51–52; election of 1863, 328–32; Federal troops at Fort Leavenworth, 8; feud with Lane, 24;

Robinson, Charles [KS] (cont.)
Frémont's declaration of martial law in Missouri, 104, 106–8; Kansas-Missouri War, 150–51; Lane's brigade in Kansas and Missouri, 135; opposition to Lane's recruitment tactics, 206, 210–11; politics of Frémont's command, 108
Robinson, James Carroll [IL], 453
Robinson, James F. [KY], 211, 219–20, 230, 238–39, 276, 328, 351, 374
Rollins, Edward H., 375–76
Rosecrans, William S., 239, 274, 277, 281, 315, 334, 340, 354, 434, 441; action against Bragg's Confederates at Tullahoma, 311; military activity at Stones River in Murfreesboro, 259, 266; replacement of Buell, 243; replacement of McClellan, 94; rumor of sabotage of Lincoln's reelection, 428–29
Russell, Charles, 332
Russell, Earl, 284

Sacramento, Calif., 119, 121, 237
Salomon, Edward, 209, 212–13, 218–19, 228, 290, 297, 301, 331, 351; Altoona Conference, 229–32; the draft, 249–50, 320–21; black soldiers, 194; German troops, 292–93; gubernatorial visit to Washington, 235–36; Hoffman House gubernatorial reunion, 480; and Lincoln, 186; national conscription efforts, 337–39; Republican Party, 168; volunteer recruitment, 178
San Francisco, Calif., 85, 120, 121, 321, 322, 332, 438
San Francisco Daily Alta California, 472
Sanitary Commission, 92, 356, 396; and Christian Commission, 406
Saratoga Springs, 418, 427
Sargent, Horace Binney, 145, 159
Saulsbury, Gove, 460
Saulsbury, Willard, 130, 196, 270
Saunders, Addison H., 177
Savannah, Ga., 168, 429, 441, 446, 447, 448, 452, 457
Saxton, Rufus, 174
Schaeffer, Anton B., 223

Schenck, Robert C., 274, 333, 337, 342–44, 349
Schnabel, Ellis B., 101
Schnell, Joseph, 88
Schofield, John, 180, 202, 322, 327, 333, 335–36, 446; appointment as commander, 298; attempts at raising troops, 311, 334, 455; dismissal as commander, 354, 357
Schouler, William, 45
Schurz, Carl, 373, 458
Scott, Thomas, 99
Scott, Winfield, 13, 39, 57, 70, 79–81, 109, 124, 147, 152–55, 169; Fort Sumter, 35; invasion of Kentucky, 109; and McClellan, 123, 131; seizure of Baltimore, 79; resignation, 123
Scovel, James M., 338
Scudder, George Pratt, 271
Sears, Barnas, 215
Sedgwick, Charles, 21, 218, 388, 422
Seven Days' Battle, 182, 189
Seward, William, 51, 65, 70, 190, 199, 208, 242, 244, 257–58, 460; Altoona address, 233; correspondence with Morgan, 13; correspondence with Tod on public opposition to war, 207; and Curtin, 222; emancipation, 195; and Gurowski, 131; Jayhawkers, 151; Lincoln's correspondence on military situation near the Mississippi River, 184; Lincoln's reelection, 397; meeting with Lincoln at Willard's Hotel, 17; and Meigs, 325; New York War Committee meeting in Providence, 216–17; possibility of Europeans entering war, 117; recruitment, 183–86; Washburn, 192
Seymour, Horatio, 268, 289, 297, 309, 325–26, 349, 391, 398, 405; biography, 247; Conscription Act, 279, 318–19; denunciation of War Department, abuse of civil liberties, and Lincoln, 283–85; disenfranchisement of New York soldiers, 436; election as Constitutional Democrat, 246–47; election of 1864, 415–17, 426, 438, 442–43; homefront dissension, 275; Lincoln's suspension of the writ of habeas corpus, 300; New Brunswick visit,

316–17; *New York Times*, 345, 435; New York under leadership of, 339; opposition to black soldiers, 273–74, 341, 354; order for New York troops to move into Pennsylvania, 305; politics of conscription, 299–301, 316–17; proposal to raise militia for national guard, 386; public condemnation of Lincoln, 300; public response to New York City draft, 344, 390, 413; Radicalism, 317, 364; response to Early's crossing of the Potomac River, 404; Seymourites, 261; Soldier's Voting Bill, 344; suspension of draft in New York City, 318; Vallandigham's plot and arrest, 347–48; volunteers, 304, 355
Seymour, Origen S., 381, 469
Seymour, Thomas H., 281, 417
Shannon, Wilson, 181
Sharpsburg, Md., 223, 226
Shaw, Joseph, 431
Shaw, Robert Gould, 273, 334
Shelby, Jo, 336, 357, 434
Shenandoah Valley, 173, 324, 384, 389, 423; battles at Winchester, 304, 426; and Early, 405, 432; and Sheridan, 414, 426, 429; and Stonewall Jackson, 160, 170
Sheridan, Philip H., 392, 414, 428, 429, 432, 433
Sherman, John, 346, 374
Sherman, Thomas W., 105–6
Sherman, William T., 340, 368, 371–73, 421–24, 426, 428–31, 446–48, 469–70, 472; black soldiers, 452; Conscription Act, 410; control over the Mississippi and Ohio Rivers, 116; Corinth, 175; discussion with Lincoln and Grant on strategy on the Potomac River, 467; dispute with Miller, 407; Frémont's declaration of martial law in Missouri, 116–17; Georgia campaign, 384, 392–93, 441; Grant partnership, 389, 402, 404, 411, 415; Memphis, 178; Northern Department, 433; Pittsburg Landing, 160; raid of Kentucky by John Hunt Morgan, 398; replacement by Buell, 124; South Carolina campaign, 457, 460, 462; Vicksburg, 301
Shiloh, 166, 167, 169, 170, 173, 175, 226, 339, 422
Shurtleff, Giles Waldo, 306
Sibley, Henry H., 213, 252
Sidell, William H., 374
Sigel, Franz, 158, 373, 384, 389, 392, 394, 404, 426
Simmons, James F., 280
Slavery, 45, 109, 115, 122, 137, 143–44, 189, 197, 271, 390; and Andrew, 212, 215; abolition of, 28, 30, 64, 96, 150, 242, 269, 364–65, 379, 451; arming of slaves, 133–34; civil unrest, 190, 275–76; compensation, 159, 336, 370; Congressional action, 15, 20, 24, 196, 443; constitutionality of, 107; constitutional amendments, 97, 461; Copperheadism, 286; defense of, 88; Democrats, 25, 123; emancipation, 140, 174, 179, 186–87, 194–95, 208–9, 216, 259, 287; emancipation movements, 221; Emancipation Proclamation, 226–27, 230–32, 248, 264; expansion of, 55–56; Florida, 170; Georgia, 170; South Carolina, 170; fugitive slaves, 165, 194, 201, 206, 212, 274, 305, 334, 340, 448; Kansas, 50–51; and Lincoln, 129–30, 214; Maryland, 57, 372; Missouri, 103, 111, 180; New Hampshire, 280; opposition to abolition, 12, 206, 276, 340, 366; popular sentiment, 222, 250; preservation of the Union, 172; Radicalism, 182, 241, 244, 350; rebel slaves, 221, 243; Republicans, 11, 120–21; states' rights, 5, 16, 49; support for abolition, 378, 383, 424, 430–31, 459; war, 117, 171, 177, 199, 265, 267, 384, 452; Whigs, 87, 128
Slidell, John, 318
Slifer, Eli, 329, 418
Sloan, Samuel, 318
Smalley, Benjamin, 237
Smith, Andrew J., 373
Smith, Charles F., 110, 158
Smith, Green C., 375
Smith, James Y., 289–90, 293, 321, 376–77, 455, 469, 480
Smith, John Gregory, 337, 340, 362, 367, 393–94, 418, 425, 433, 448, 476; biography, 331–32; nomination of, 328; and state militia, 423

Smith, Kirby, 210–11
Smith, Robert, 241
Smith, Worthington C., 433
Smyth, Frederick, 468
Snethen, Worthington, 13, 16
Soldier's Home, 184, 326, 367, 405
Soldier's Voting Act, 344, 436
Sons of Liberty, 361, 371, 409, 429
South Carolina, 133, 170, 269, 278, 290, 324, 354, 388, 411, 437, 440, 452, 457, 460, 462
Southworth, Eli, 197
Speed, James, 461
Speed, Joshua, 105, 107
Sperry, Nehemiah D., 469
Spooner, John A., 410–11
Sprague, William, 60, 66, 94, 183, 186, 197, 239, 241, 272, 377; Altoona Conference, 229–32; Andrew, 34, 215, 228; biography, 14; black soldiers, 194, 222; calls legislature into session, 48; Camp Sprague, 89; election of 1861, 37, 166; gubernatorial visit to Washington, 235–36; Halleck, 190; Harper's Ferry, 171; Hoffman House gubernatorial reunion, 480; New York War Committee meeting in Providence, 216–17; offer to lead volunteers, 73; personal liberty laws, 27; senatorial aspirations, 279–80; Seymour's petition to postpone the draft, 316–17
Springfield, Ill., 38, 69, 192, 196, 265, 276, 294, 409, 423, 472–73; 13th amendment, 459; arrival of Grant, 76; assignment of Pope as brigadier general, 84; California Republican delegations, 119; local press' support for Yates, 449; McClernand's arrival, 250; results of Democratic Convention of the Northwest, 308–9; Shelby's Confederate cavalry invasion, 336; Soldier's Home, 367; Yate's early relationship with Lincoln, 9–10
Springfield Republican, 226, 248
Stager, Anson, 186
St. Albans, Vt., 331, 433, 438, 470
Stanford, Leland, 119–20, 123, 147, 237, 287–88, 321–22, 351, 580–81 (n.95)
Stanton, Edwin M., 207, 225–26, 375–76, 378, 381, 384–85, 387, 399, 447, 469–70; and Andrew, 187, 360; appointment in 1862, 449; black soldiers, 133, 272–73, 290, 333–34, 341, 346, 354–55, 435; bounties, 202, 361; and Bramlette, 439; and Buckingham, 191; and Buell, 243; call for militia defense against Lee's Confederates, 304–5; Cape Fear River visit, 457; casualty reports, 294–95; Chase's resignation as Treasury Secretary, 400–401; commutation, 365–66; Confederate invasions of border states, 315; Confederate raid on Lawrence, Kansas, 327; constitutional convention on abolition in Missouri, 456; and Cony, 406, 408; Copperheads, 289, 326; and Curtin, 427; dismissal of Kirkwood at War Department, 236; draft, 203, 211, 255, 259, 277, 296, 319–21, 326, 455; Early's crossing of the Potomac River, 404–5; election of 1861, 51–52; election of 1862, 281; election of 1864, 443; election of 1863, 329; encouragement of desertions by Knights of the Golden Circle, 282–83, 299; federal influence in border states, 345; Fort Donelson, 154–55, 162; General Orders No. 104, 209; General Orders No. 18, 157; General Orders No. 94, 203; Gettysburg, 311; and Grant, 293, 340, 350, 415; gubernatorial response to Lee's Maryland Campaign, 219–20; gubernatorial visit to Washington, 235–36; guerilla warfare in Missouri and Midwest, 413–14; Harrison's Landing Letter, 195, 479; Indians, 214, 251–53; and Jay, John, 318; Joint Committee on the Conduct of the War [War Committee], 133; Knights of the Golden Circle, 283; legislators' resolution to acknowledge Confederacy, 266–67; Lincoln and Radical's shared war aims, 196; and Lincoln, 244–45, 259, 293, 308, 316, 361, 476, 478; Lincoln's death, 476; Lincoln's expedition to Vicksburg, 250; martial law, 240–41, 307; Maryland, 249; and McClellan, 179, 182; military discord in Kansas and Missouri, 391–92; and Morton, 146, 212, 264, 368, 450; national conscription efforts, 337–39; New York, 297, 324, 390; Northern

Department, 433; opposition to Lane's recruitment tactics, 206; Pennsylvanian resistance to draft, 249; postponement of draft, 458; proposal to raise militia for national guard, 386; protection of New York soldiers at the polls, 436; public hostility in response to the draft in Kansas, 463; quotas, 198, 204, 320, 210; Radical quarrels with conservatives, 336; and Ramsey, 213; recruitment of slaves in Maryland, 336–37; recruitment, 163, 169, 171, 185, 362, 367; replacement of Hunter with abolitionist Blunt, 180; request to wire governors for troops, 424–25; response to Early's crossing of the Potomac River, 404; Richmond, 467; Rosecrans' request to end the draft, 428; secession, 28; Senate Military Committee, 162; and Seymour, 316; and Sherman, 301; soldier welfare, 298; Soldier's Voting Bill, 344; Stanton's call, 173–78; and Stoddard, 159; "Tod's Elephant" controversy, 323–24; and Tod, 152; treatment of free blacks, 452; Vallandigham's plot and arrest, 347–48; Vermont state militia, 423; Virginia, 295, 387, 393; volunteers, 149, 164, 178, 186, 254; War Department, 146–48, 450, 479; Washburn's faith in, 218; Washington, D.C., 159, 184, 251, 329; and Yates, 286, 291, 306, 388, 410, 426
Stanton, Frederick, 52
Stark, Benjamin, 75, 123
Starne, Alexander, 270
Stearns, George Luther, 272
Stearns, William A., 360
Stephens, Alexander H., 232, 460
Stevens, Aaron F., 256, 412
Stevens, Henry, 53
Stevens, John Austin Jr., 216
Stevens, John G., 67
Stevens, Montgomery, 214
Stevens, Thaddeus, 75, 447
Stewart, John W., 433
Stimson, William R., 167
St. Louis, Mo., 82, 95, 98, 109–11, 135, 179, 200, 297, 372, 441; constitutional convention on abolition in Missouri, 456; Department of Missouri, 124; Frémont's declaration of martial law in Missouri, 104, 106–08; Halleck's departure to Pittsburg Landing, 179–80; Missouri state militia, 123–24; Nicolay's survey of Missouri, 428, 433–34; seizure of arsenal, 42, 48–49, 65, 78–79; supply shortages, 97, 129; Western Department, 87
St. Louis Daily Missouri Republican, 123, 194, 227, 435
St. Louis Missouri Democrat, 322
Stoddard, William O., 117, 141, 159, 254, 275, 288, 344, 358, 373, 386; and Lincoln, 66, 200; and McClellan, 94, 381
Stone, Charles P., 136–37
Stone, William M., 330, 339, 340, 367, 385, 388, 392, 397, 398
Stott, William Taylor, 308
Stout, Byron G., 248
Stow, Baron, 280
Stowe, Harriet Beecher, 6
St. Paul, Minn., 163, 220, 470
Stranahan, F. Stewart, 433
Sturgis, Russell, 332
Sturgis, Samuel, 111
Sumner, Charles, 31, 81, 97, 148, 178, 184, 209, 397, 456; black soldiers, 388; correspondence with Andrew, 27–28, 137, 417; enlistment of slaves, 178; fall election of 1862, 242–43; fugitive slaves, 139; gubernatorial cooperation with congressmen, 74–75; military review board, 95; Senatorial criticism of approach to war, 89
Sumner, Edwin, 29, 121
Sumner, George, 31, 242, 246, 253, 260, 272
Supreme Court, U.S., 146, 265, 322, 465
Susquehanna River, 312, 315; Department of, 304
Swan, Joseph, 71
Swann, Thomas, 441, 463, 471
Swayne, Noah H., 71
Swett, Leonard, 322, 581 (n.95)
Swift, Henry A., 281, 320, 330–31, 351

Taft, Horatio N., 89
Taney, Roger B., 21

720 *Index*

Taylor, Thomas, 464–65
Taylor, Zachary, 40, 87
Temple, John B., 186
Temple, William, 245
Ten Eyck, John, 461
Tennessee, 132, 166, 185, 202, 221–22, 266, 313, 315, 452; Army of, 446–47; Department of Missouri, 124; eastern, 98, 145, 184, 191; furlough, 335; and Grant, 347, 395; occupation of, 153, 155, 157–59; Reconstruction, 397; recruitment, 355, 410; Republican congressional plot, 342; Shiloh, 166–68; support for Confederacy, 43, 78; Tullahoma, 311; Union control over, 350
Tennessee River, 110, 151, 153, 158, 160, 166, 168, 346, 349, 447; Department of, 340
Terrell, William H., 307
Texas, 150, 180
Thacher, Solon O., 441
Thayer, John C., 92–93
Thomas, George H., 110, 383
Thomas, James, 270, 340, 446–47
Thompson, J. Edgar, 227
Tilden, Samuel J., 318, 326
Tillapaugh, James M., 301
Tilton, Theodore, 416, 421–22
Tod, David, 176, 185–86, 195, 243, 249, 270, 277, 282, 347–48, 351; abolition, 149; Altoona Conference, 225, 228–32; biography, 114–15; Chase's replacement as Treasury Secretary, 401; civilian resistance to draft, 303, 305; correspondence with Seward on public opposition to war, 207; election of 1863, 338; German regiments, 150; gubernatorial visit to Washington, 235–36; Lincoln's request for recruitment reports, 202; meeting with Lincoln on state militias and emancipation, 165; popularity in Ohio, 330, 401; and Stanton, 152; "Tod's Elephant" controversy, 323–24; and Vallandigham, 306, 339–40; volunteer recruitment, 178
Topeka, Kans., 108, 181, 268, 323, 374, 463
Tower, N.B., 469
Townsend, Frederick, 325
Tracy, Andrew, 114

Treasury Department, U.S., 66, 118, 125, 411
Trenton, N.J., 267, 286, 387
Trenton Daily State Gazette and Republican, 461
Trumbull, Jonathan, 59
Trumbull, Lyman, 26, 51, 75, 89, 145, 161, 219, 244, 270–71
Tuck, Amos, 449
Tucker, John, 67
Turnley, Hiram S., 414
Tuttle, James M., 330, 339

Underground Railroad, 253
Union Convention, 391, 398–99
Union League, 286, 357, 369
Union Party, 115, 166, 181, 244, 415, 464; coalition with War Democrats, 330–31, 359; convention, 245, 306; election of 1864, 397, 419–20, 431, 436–37, 442
Usher, John P., 252

Vallandigham, Clement Laird, 49, 281, 305, 330, 339, 340, 348, 399, 409; arrest of, 295–96, 299–300, 302, 308, 316; Copperheadism, 270, 306, 371
Van Buren, John Dash, 285, 316
Vanderbilt, James C., 175
Vandever, William, 44
Van Dorn, Earl, 239
Van Rensselaer, Alex, 354
Varian, Alexander, 166, 256, 264
Vermont, 183, 198, 271, 307, 312, 362, 367, 459, 470, 476; 13th amendment, 460–61; brigade, 477; Central Railroad, 331; Confederate raid of, 433; the draft, 210, 412; election of 1861, 113–14; election of 1862, 242–43; election of 1863, 328–32; election of 1864, 425; enfranchisement of soldiers, 434–35, 337; establishment of state militia, 423; and Fairbanks, 26, 52; Holbrook's devotion to soldiers, 260; and Howe, Frank, 138; Irish troops, 75; New York City conference, 26–27; reelection of Lincoln, 418, 438; soldier casualties, 393–94; State Agricultural Society, 114; state flag, 58–59; and Thayer, John C., 92; University of, 53, 331; war preparations, 125

Vickers, George, 128
Vicksburg, Miss., 258, 274, 282, 291–92, 295, 297, 306, 319, 368, 371; Ellet's entrance into the Mississippi Gibraltar, 277; expedition to, 250; Grant's siege and capture of, 304, 311, 314–16, 339; Mississippi River, 179, 267; Morton's order to stop supply boat, 69; Sherman's wire to Stanton, 301; soldier relief after battle, 322
Villard, Henry, 23
Virginia, 65, 129, 144, 148, 153, 243, 265, 405, 415, 476; 12th Indiana's supply shortage, 103–04; Army of, 182, 203, 219, 457; black soldiers, 369; and Buckingham, 257, 387; Bull Run (Manassas), 90–92, 96; burning down of Letcher's home, 406–07; Cleveland conference, 70; and Curtin, 470; and Dennison, 68; Department of Northeast, 78; development of West Virginia, 79–80, 82, 86–88, 109, 259, 302; economic connection to Ohio River, 69; election of 1864, 424; and Gamble, 80, 98; Green Mountain Men, 210; and Hooker, 292; invasion of border states, 60–62, 222; and Lee, 182, 251, 324, 389, 391, 409, 457, 466; Lee's return from Maryland, 315; Lee's surrender to Grant at Appomattox, 469; and Lincoln, 183–84, 260, 395–98; Loyalists, 139; martial law in border states, 107; Mud March, 271; national army, 67; National Conscription Act, 278; Northwestern Virginia Railroad, 80; oversubscribed regiments, 394; peninsula, 160–62, 165–66, 169, 173, 183, 195, 384; and Pope, 205; Rappahannock River, 254; response to Lee's Maryland Campaign, 219–20; Richmond, 324; runaway slaves, 134; secession, 40, 41–42, 44; secessionist plots uncovered by Morton, 115; Seven Day's Battle, 189–90; and Sheridan, 433; and Sherman, 452; Siege of Petersburg, 412; Sigel's appointment to Department of West Virginia, 372–73; slavery, 468; and Smith, 367; soldier enfranchisement, 335; and Stanton, 295, 387, 393; and Swann, Thomas, 441; Third Battle of Winchester, 426; and Washburn, 256; Yates' refusal to attend Peace Conference, 20
Von Matzdorff, Alwin, 292

Wade, Benjamin, 75, 89, 132, 133, 144, 145, 158, 242, 374
Wade, Richard, 414
Wade-Davis Bill, 414, 420
Wadsworth, Edward R., 167
Wadsworth, James S., 85, 160, 246
Wagstaff, William R., 245
Walbridge, Hiram, 82
Waldron, Henry, 202
Walker, John C., 308
Wallace, Lew, 41, 379, 432, 443
War Committee, 133, 134, 136, 144
Ward, John, 59
Ward, Marcus L., 247
Ward, Samuel Gray, 286
War Democrats, 247, 330, 331, 338, 344, 346, 350, 359, 381, 397
War Department, 56, 176, 259, 291, 378, 390, 423, 430, 437; 13th amendment, 458; acceptance of 1st Kansas Colored Volunteers, 269; and Aiken, William A., 57; allowance of regiments to carry state flags, 59; and Andrew, 97, 195; and Bates, 82–83; Battle of Wilson's Creek, 102; black soldiers, 133, 268–69, 333; bounties, 407; Bureau of Colored Troops, 273; and Butler, 106; and Cameron, 68, 80, 90; casualty reports, 314, 334; Chase's resignation as Treasury Secretary, 400–401; conduct of Union commanders, 134–35; confidence in, 176; conscription, 207, 209–11, 277–79, 296–97, 320–21, 365–66, 416, 456; and Curtin, 249, 479; Curtin's demand to end state recruiting by, 103; defense of Delaware River, 162; Department of the West, 81; establishment of bureau to pay freed slave Union workers, 253; Fenton's trip to Washington regarding New York quota, 451; Indiana, 109, 307; Joint Committee on

War Department (cont.)
the Conduct of the War [War Committee], 132–34; and Lincoln, 91, 153, 174, 255, 326, 366; Lincoln's dismissal of Schofield, 354; and McClellan, 154, 159; military review board, 95; Missouri militia, 202–3; and Morton, 96; officer assignments, 150; Pennsylvanian resistance to draft, 249; and Pomeroy, 323; proposal to raise militia for national guard, 386; public perception of war's progress, 171; quotas, 116, 204, 368, 451; recruitment, 179, 181; response to recruitment of Confederate troops in border states, 102–3; Scott's command of telegraph and railroad operations, 99; Seymour's denunciation of, 283–85; soldier enfranchisement, 127; and Stanton, 146–48, 450, 479; Stanton's dismissal of Kirkwood, 236; supplies and transport from Washington, 82, 84; transfer of power from governors to military quartermaster, 126; volunteers, 85–86, 136; Washburn's request for supplies, 82; and Yates, 48

War Office of the Government, 200, 236

Washburn, Israel, 84–85, 170, 173–74, 192, 228, 256, 293–94, 332; abolition, 149; Altoona Conference, 229–32; concern over troops, 138, 239; correspondence with Andrew, 215; election of 1861, 113–14; election of 1863, 328; Fort Donelson, 154–55; Kansas-Nebraska bill, 56; and McClellan, 218; meeting with Lincoln on state militias and emancipation, 165; military review board, 95; New York City conference, 26–27; New York War Committee meeting in Providence, 216; opposition to Peace Conference, 20; order for defense of port cities, 134, 161–62; recruitment tactics, 206; Republican Party, 34, 237; request for supplies from War Department, 82; supply shortages, 152; travel to Washington regarding Fort Sumter, 37; volunteer regiments, 61–63; War Department's transfer of power to military quartermaster, 126; Yates' visit to Stanton, 236

Washburn, Peter T., 433, 476
Washburne, Elihu, 16–17, 135, 449
Washington, D.C., 214, 407, 413, 417, 423, 426, 449, 462, 464–66; 13th amendment, 456–58; 38th Congress, 350, 403; abolition, 383; Altoona, 217; Anderson, 110; Andrew, 131, 187, 208, 212, 341; arrival of troops, 65–68; Battle of Gettysburg, 313; Berry, 125; black soldiers, 334; Blair, 94; border states, 78–82; Boutwell, George, 55, 92; Bradford, 305, 333; Bramlette, 399; Brooks, Noah, 315; building an army, 73–77; Butler, 148; cabinet meeting on emancipation and arming blacks, 200; California Republican delegations, 119; Cameron, 109; Carney, 323, 373–74, 391; casualties, 295, 402; Chandler, 222; Cleveland conference, 71–72; communication technical issues, 54–55, 62–63; Confederate plan of attack, 100; Confiscation Act, 205; Connecticut's support for, 57; Cony, 389; Corkhill, George B., 143; Curtin visits troops, 256–58; Curtin, 113, 250, 311, 427, 479; defense of, 44–46, 50, 173–78; Department of the Ohio, 124; draft, 318, 430; Early's crossing of the Potomac River, 404–5; East Tennessee, 145; election of 1864, 436–445; Emancipation Proclamation, 229–30; Fenton's trip regarding New York quota, 451; Fisher, 244–45; free blacks, 369; Frémont's declaration of martial law in Missouri, 104, 106–08; Frontier Guard, 66; fugitive slaves, 136; Gamble, 123, 224, 298, 322, 357; Gamble's visit to address occupation of border states, 97–98; Governors go to Washington, 232–38, 348; Grant's Army of the Potomac, 372–80, 384; Grant's Tennessee offensive, 347; gubernatorial fear of attack, 404; gubernatorial visits to soldiers, 112–113; gubernatorial visits, 37, 165, 235–36, 385–88; Halleck, 200, 373; Hathaway, John W., 272; Indianapolis conference, 81; Indians, 253; Jackson, Stonewall, 178–79; Jackson's Valley Campaign, 170; Kansas impeachment crisis, 180–81; Kinsley, Edward, 209;

Kirkwood at Battle of Wilson's Creek, 102; Lee's surrender, 469–70; Lincoln and Radical's shared war aims, 196; Lincoln returns from Falmouth, 292; Lincoln's death, 472–73; Lincoln's delivery of Pennsylvania regimental colors, 113; Maryland volunteers, 45–47; McClellan, 116, 157, 160, 169, 177, 203, 255; Minnesota volunteer regiments, 39–40; Morgan's visit to New York regiments near the Potomac River, 138; Morton, 239–40, 290, 307, 420, 437; New Year's Day 1863, 263; New Year's Day 1864, 358–59; New York, 308; order for defense of port cities, 161–62; Peace Conference, 17–23; Pennsylvanian soldier conditions, 67; Pierpont's visit, 260; proposal to raise militia for national guard, 386; Providence sentiments, 216; public hostility in response to the draft in Kansas, 463; Ramsey, 127; Republican convention, 395; Republican National Committee, 370; Sanitary Commission, 156–57; Scott, 152–53; secessionist plots uncovered by border state governors, 115–16; Second Confiscation Act, 199; Seven Day's Battle, 189–90; slavery, 130, 133; soldier encampments, 88–93; Soldier's Home, 326; soldiers' arrival in Washington after Baltimore Affair, 45–48; Sprague, 186, 279–80; Stanton, 159, 184, 251, 329; states' influence on, 159–60; Stoddard, 254; suspension of the writ of habeas corpus, 117; telegraph miscommunication, 362; Tidewater slaves, 432; transformation of, 132; transport of troops to, 58–59; Van Buren, John Dash, 316; Vermont, 433; volunteers, 43; Washburn, 34, 82, 138; *Washington Daily National Intelligencer*, 89, 231, 404, 437, 470; Weed, Thurlow, 283–85; Welles, 104; West Virginia, 129; wounded soldiers, 396–97; Yates, 84, 86, 192, 420

Washington Daily National Intelligencer, 89, 231, 404, 437, 470

Webb, James W., 14

Weed, Thurlow, 14, 24, 208, 244–45, 247, 391, 415, 456; and Lincoln, 26, 283; and Morgan, 24, 184, 210, 284–85, 390, retirement, 285; at Willard's Hotel, 91; and William Babcock, 33

Weekly Wisconsin Patriot, 232

Weer, William, 180

Weitzel, Godfrey, 467

Welles, Gideon, 3–4, 34, 101, 104, 195, 219, 246, 284, 289, 412

Wells, Henry, 331, 345

Wells, William, 138

Wentworth, Edwin O., 269, 278

Wentworth, John, 69

Western Sanitary Commission, 297–98

West Point, and Robert Anderson, 32; and John W. Phelps, 58; and Henry Du Pont, 63; and John H. Martindale, 66; and Irvin McDowell, 78; and John Pope, 84, 151; and William T. Sherman, 124; and John Schofield, 180; and Charles Olden, 190; and Joseph Hooker, 272; and James B. Fry, 279; dedication ceremony at, 398

West Virginia, 174, 259, 266, 292, 305, 313, 326, 419, 429, 435; Department of, 373; statehood, 235, 261–62, 302; ratification of the 13th Amendment, 460–61

Wetmore, Prosper, 215

Wheeling, Va., 79, 86, 93, 129, 265

Whig Party, 39–40, 87, 292, 340; and Whigs, 98, 128, 143, 211, 237, 302, 312

Whitaker, Walter C., 175

White, Horace, 107, 243

Whiteaker, John, 22, 121–23, 147, 230, 252

White House, 57, 196, 209, 294, 336, 375, 378, 401, 436, 471; cabinet, 258; and Curtin, 39, 256; Frontier Guard, 66, 87; Lincoln's illness, 349; Maryland loyalists, 432; reaction to Lee's surrender, 470; telegraph, 434

Whitely, William G., 63

Whitman, Walt, 14, 60, 466, 472

Whitmarsh, George, 32

Wickliffe, Charles A., 328

Wightman, 171–72

Wilcox, William L., 19

Wilder, Carter A., 245

Wilderness Woods, 294, 386–87

Wilkinson, Morton, 39

Willard's Hotel, 23, 84, 91, 94, 131, 235, 256, 372, 387, 472
Willey, Waitman T., 80
Williams, James M., 408
Williams, John E., 216
Williams, Joseph, 237
Wills, David, 314, 347
Wilmington, Del., 63, 65, 174, 176, 270, 383, 434
Wilmot, David, 40
Wilson, Henry, 84, 95, 185, 195, 276, 278, 387
Wilson, Reuben, 168
Wilson, Rufus, 230
Winchester, Va., 160, 404, 409, 426, 432; Battle of, 174, 304
Windom, William, 127
Wisconsin, 127–28, 167–69, 249–50, 293, 345, 358, 361, 364, 393; 13th amendment, 460–61; black soldiers, 212; conscription, 320–21, 416, 455; Constitutional Convention and State Assembly, 346; election of 1861, 113–14; election of 1863, 329; election of 1864, 419; electoral procedure, 5; enfranchisement of soldiers, 434–35; Fort Donelson, 154–55; gubernatorial elections, 329; Howe, Timothy, 75; Indian uprising, 213; loss of soldier morale, 93; Military Department of the Northwest, 220; national conscription efforts, 337–39; one-hundred-day men, 429; proposal to raise militia for national guard, 386; Randall, 90; Republican Party (state), 458; response to recruitment of Confederate troops in border states, 102–03; Salomon, 209, 290, 331; Soldier's Aid Society, 387; volunteer recruitment, 178; weather hindrances to war effort, 112
Wisconsin State Journal, 56
Wolcott, Erastus B., 167, 387, 416
Wolford, Frank, 374–75
Wood, Edward J., 319
Wood, Fernando, 14
Wood, Lucius, 306, 339
Woodbridge, Frederick E., 367
Woodward, George W., 329

Wool, John E., 55, 65, 76, 326
Worthington, Thomas, 91
Wright, Francis, 56, 282
Wright, George, 121, 122, 147, 220, 252, 287, 321, 322
Wright, Joseph, 243

Yale University, 204, 331
Yates, Richard, 219, 223, 271, 310, 356, 406, 429–30, 471–72, 476; abolition, 149; alcoholism, 368; Altoona Conference, 224–25, 228–32; and Andrew, 420; appeasement of Magoffin, 42–43; arming civilians in St. Louis, 76; Battle at Doctor's Creek, 240; bounties, 250; and Buell, 136, 243; and Cameron, 49; citizen morale, 192; Cleveland conference, 70; concern over Indian conflicts, 28; Copperheads, 306, 316, 326, 367, 371–72, 380, 385; and Crapo, 454; Democratic Convention of the Northwest, 308–09; Democrats, 286; dismissal of Kirkwood at War Department, 236; draft, 195, 199, 210; early relationship with Lincoln, 9–10; election of 1862, 244; election of 1863, 338–40; election of 1864, 440; emancipation, 194, 196, 265; Fort Donelson, 154–55; German population, 74, 150; and Grant, 76, 275–76, 294; gubernatorial establishment of organizational framework, 68–69; gubernatorial visits to Washington, 37, 235–36; guerilla warfare in Missouri and Midwest, 413–14; and Halleck, 129, 373; Illinois legislature, 270; Indianapolis conference, 80–81; and Lincoln, 161, 168–69, 286, 326, 422, 437; Lincoln's reliance on governors regarding Kentucky, 98, 105; local press' support for, 449; martial law, 209; and McClernand, 293; military review board, 95; and Morton, 78, 107, 267; and Moses, John, 192–93; national conscription efforts, 337–39; National Union Committee, 397–98; New Madrid, 168; New York riots, 319; Ohio River, 80; opposition to black enfranchisement,

241; Peace Conference, 20–21; Pittsburg Landing, 167; and Pope, 84; quotas, 426; Radicals, 370; recruitment of Confederate troops in border states, 102–03; Rosecrans' action against Bragg's Confederates at Tullahoma, 311; secessionism, 145; secessionist plots uncovered by, 115; seizure of St. Louis arsenal, 42, 48–49, 65; Senatorial aspirations, 453; Shelby's Confederate cavalry invasion, 336; Sherman's army, 392; soldier enfranchisement, 437; soldier welfare and morale, 156; Springfield visit, 10; and Stanton, 286, 291, 306, 388, 410, 426; and Tod, 330; travel to Washington regarding Fort Sumter, 37; Unionist election efforts in New York, 344–45; and Vallandigham, 399; volunteers, 41, 61–62, 211; War Department, 48, 126; Washington, D.C., 84, 86, 192, 420

Yeatman, James E., 79
Yorktown, Va., 173, 177, 337
Young, Andrew Hale, 477
Young, Henry T., 320
Young, John Russell, 235